The Cambridge Handbook of Workplace Affect

Are you struggling to improve a hostile or uncomfortable environment at work, or interested in how such tension can arise? Experts in organizational psychology, management science, social psychology, and communication science show you how to implement interventions and programs to manage workplace emotion. The connection between workplace affect and relevant challenges in our society, such as diversity and technological changes, is undeniable; thus learning to harness that knowledge can revolutionize your performance in tackling workday issues. Applying major theoretical perspectives and research methodologies, this book outlines important concepts such as display rules, emotional intelligence, emotional labor, work motivation, well-being, and discrete emotions. Understanding these ideas will show you how affect can promote team effectiveness, leadership, and conflict resolution. If you require a foundation for understanding workplace affect or a springboard into deeper, more interdisciplinary research, this book presents an integrative approach that is indispensable.

LIU-QIN YANG is an associate professor of psychology at Portland State University, USA. Her work has been funded by the National Institute for Occupational Safety and Health, Centers for Disease Control and Prevention, and National Institute for Transportation and Communities.

RUSSELL CROPANZANO is a professor of organizational behavior at the University of Colorado Boulder, USA, and a fellow of both the Academy of Management and the Association for Psychological Science.

CATHERINE S. DAUS is a professor of psychology at Southern Illinois University Edwardsville, USA, with a Ph.D. from Purdue University, USA.

VICENTE MARTÍNEZ-TUR is a professor of organizational psychology at the University of Valencia, Spain. He coordinates research projects, funded by the Spanish government, about the impact of work and organizational processes on service users.

T0371620

The Cambridge Handbook of Workplace Affect

Edited by

Liu-Qin Yang
Portland State University

Russell Cropanzano
University of Colorado Boulder

Catherine S. Daus
Southern Illinois University Edwardsville

Vicente Martínez-Tur
University of Valencia

CAMBRIDGE
UNIVERSITY PRESS

CAMBRIDGE
UNIVERSITY PRESS

University Printing House, Cambridge CB2 8BS, United Kingdom

One Liberty Plaza, 20th Floor, New York, NY 10006, USA

477 Williamstown Road, Port Melbourne, VIC 3207, Australia

314–321, 3rd Floor, Plot 3, Splendor Forum, Jasola District Centre,
New Delhi – 110025, India

79 Anson Road, #06–04/06, Singapore 079906

Cambridge University Press is part of the University of Cambridge.

It furthers the University's mission by disseminating knowledge in the pursuit of education, learning, and research at the highest international levels of excellence.

www.cambridge.org
Information on this title: www.cambridge.org/9781108494038
DOI: 10.1017/9781108573887

First published 2020

Printed in the United Kingdom by TJ International Ltd, Padstow, Cornwall

A catalogue record for this publication is available from the British Library.

Library of Congress Cataloging-in-Publication Data
Names: Yang, Liu-Qin, 1979– editor.
Title: The Cambridge handbook of workplace affect / edited by Liu-Qin Yang, Portland State University, Russell Cropanzano, University of Colorado at Boulder, Catherine Daus, Southern Illinois University, Edwardsville, Vincente Martinez-Tur, University of Valencia.
Description: Cambridge, United Kingdom ; New York, NY : Cambridge University Press, 2020. | Series: Cambridge handbooks in psychology | Includes bibliographical references and index.
Identifiers: LCCN 2019050324 (print) | LCCN 2019050325 (ebook) | ISBN 9781108494038 (hardback) | ISBN 9781108573887 (ebook)
Subjects: LCSH: Organizational behavior. | Organizational sociology. | Affect (Psychology) | Psychology, Organizational.
Classification: LCC HD58.7 .C3434 2020 (print) | LCC HD58.7 (ebook) | DDC 302.3/5–dc23
LC record available at https://lccn.loc.gov/2019050324
LC ebook record available at https://lccn.loc.gov/2019050325

ISBN 978-1-108-49403-8 Hardback
ISBN 978-1-108-46378-2 Paperback

Contents

Figures

Tables

Contributors

NEAL M. ASHKANASY, School of Business, University of Queensland

LARISSA K. BARBER, Department of Psychology, San Diego State University

TALYA N. BAUER, School of Business Administration, Portland State University

EMORIE D. BECK, Department of Psychology, Washington University in St. Louis

LIANA BERNARD, Department of Psychology, Portland State University

AGATA BIALKOWSKI, School of Business, University of Queensland

LOUIS BOEMERMAN, Psychology Department, Pennsylvania State University

SHANIQUE G. BROWN, Department of Psychology, Wayne State University

ABRAHAM P. BUUNK, Department of Psychology, University of Groningen, and Netherlands Interdisciplinary Demographic Institute

ANNE CASPER, Department of Psychology, University of Mannheim

RUSSELL CROPANZANO, Leeds School of Business at the University of Colorado Boulder

JOCELYN ALISA DANA-LÊ, Department of Management, Michigan State University

CATHERINE S. DAUS, Department of Psychology, Southern Illinois University Edwardsville

JAMES M. DIEFENDORFF, Department of Psychology, University of Akron

PIETERNEL DIJKSTRA, Institute for Social Psychology: Research, Education and Coaching, Groningen

ALLISON M. ELLIS, Orfalea College of Business, California Polytechnic State University

KATELYN E. ENGLAND, Psychology Department, Pennsylvania State University

CYNTHIA D. FISHER, Bond Business School, Bond University

KEATON A. FLETCHER, School of Psychology, Georgia Institute of Technology

CATALINA FLORES, Department of Psychology, University of Akron

ROBERT FOLGER, Department of Management, University of Central Florida

NURIA GAMERO, Department of Social Psychology, University of Seville

M. ESTHER GARCÍA-BUADES, Department of Psychology, University of the Balearic Islands

DONALD E. GIBSON, O'Malley School of Business, Manhattan College

REBECCA GODARD, Department of Psychology, University of British Columbia

PILAR GONZÁLEZ-NAVARRO, Research Institute of Personnel Psychology, Organizational Development, and Quality of Working Life, University of Valencia

VICENTE GONZÁLEZ-ROMÁ, Research Institute of Personnel Psychology, Organizational Development, and Quality of Working Life, University of Valencia

ALICIA A. GRANDEY, Psychology Department, Pennsylvania State University

CHARMINE E. J. HÄRTEL, School of Business, University of Queensland

MIKKI HEBL, Department of Psychological Sciences, Rice University

M. SANDY HERSHCOVIS, Haskayne School of Business, University of Calgary

ANNEKATRIN HOPPE, Department of Psychology, Humboldt University of Berlin

XINYU HU, Department of Psychology, Northern Illinois University

UTE R. HÜLSHEGER, Department of Work and Social Psychology, Maastricht University

RONALD H. HUMPHREY, Department of Entrepreneurship and Strategy, Lancaster University

MAIKE HUNDELING, Institute of Psychology, University of Kassel

STEFANIE K. JOHNSON, Leeds School of Business at the University of Colorado Boulder

PETER J. JORDAN, Department of Employment Relations and Human Resources, Griffith University

RUTH KANFER, School of Psychology, Georgia Institute of Technology

BRITTANY K. LAMBERT, Leeds School of Business at the University of Colorado Boulder

PAUL E. LEVY, Department of Psychology, University of Akron

WENDONG LI, Department of Management, Chinese University of Hong Kong

LAUREN R. LOCKLEAR, Department of Management, University of Central Florida

MARY SUE LOVE, Department of Management and Marketing, Southern Illinois University Edwardsville

ZHANNA LYUBYKH, Haskayne School of Business, University of Calgary

DOUGLAS MAGILL, Department of Psychology, University of Akron

LARRY R. MARTINEZ, Department of Psychology, Portland State University

VICENTE MARTÍNEZ-TUR, Research Institute of Personnel Psychology, Organizational Development, and Quality of Working Life, University of Valencia

KARLIJN MASSAR, Department of Work and Social Psychology, Maastricht University

SEBASTIANO MASSARO, Surrey Business School, University of Surrey

THEODORE C. MASTERS-WAAGE, Lee Kong Chian School of Business, Singapore Management University

KATHARINE MCMAHON, Department of Psychology, Portland State University

ALEXANDRA MICHEL, Federal Institute for Occupational Safety and Health, Dortmund

KARA NG, Alliance Manchester Business School, University of Manchester

DIEP NGUYEN, School of Business and Law, Edith Cowan University

MARA OLEKALNS, Melbourne Business School, University of Melbourne

SILVIA ORTIZ-BONNIN, Department of Psychology, University of the Balearic Islands

CASSANDRA N. PHETMISY, Department of Psychological Sciences, Rice University

ANAT RAFAELI, Faculty of Industrial Engineering and Management, Technion – Israel Institute of Technology

JOCHEN REB, Lee Kong Chian School of Business, Singapore Management University

LAURA REES, Smith School of Business, Queen's University

ARIEL ROBERTS, Department of Psychology, University of Akron

KATHRIN ROSING, Institute of Psychology, University of Kassel

REBECCA L. SCHAUMBERG, The Wharton School, University of Pennsylvania

ANTJE SCHMITT, Department of Psychology, University of Groningen

BRENT A. SCOTT, Department of Management, Michigan State University

MEGAN SNOEYINK, Department of Psychology, Portland State University

KETAKI SODHI, Department of Psychology, University of Akron

ZHAOLI SONG, Department of Management and Organization, National University of Singapore

SABINE SONNENTAG, Department of Psychology, University of Mannheim

PAUL E. SPECTOR, Department of Psychology, University of South Florida

ALICE F. STUHLMACHER, Department of Psychology, DePaul University

COREY TATEL, School of Psychology, Georgia Institute of Technology

LOUIS TAY, Department of Psychology, Purdue University

STUTI THAPA, Department of Psychology, Purdue University

AMANDA L. THAYER, Department of Psychology, University of Akron

GINA THOEBES, Department of Psychology, University of Akron

JESSICA L. TRACY, Department of Psychology, University of British Columbia

RAYMOND N. C. TRAU, Macquarie Business School, Macquarie University

ASHLEA C. TROTH, Department of Employment Relations and Human Resources, Griffith University

NICK TURNER, Haskayne School of Business, University of Calgary

LAURA VENZ, Institute for Management and Organisation, Leuphana University Lüneburg

YATING WANG, Department of Management and Organization, National University of Singapore

PETER WARR, Institute of Work Psychology, University of Sheffield

LIU-QIN YANG, Department of Psychology, Portland State University

DIETER ZAPF, Department of Psychology, Goethe University Frankfurt

XIN ZHANG, Department of Management, Chinese University of Hong Kong

JESSIE (FENGMIN) ZHEN, Department of Psychology, Portland State University

ROSARIO ZURRIAGA, Research Institute of Personnel Psychology, Organizational Development, and Quality of Working Life, University of Valencia

Foreword

I recently heard a fascinating talk by an astronomer about the roller-coaster, decade-long journey to get a new telescope into orbit. I was struck by the amount of emotion imbuing the description of an exact scientist's work. Telescopes were described as "awesome" (positive emotion?). The importance of teamwork and perseverance in overcoming constant challenges was highlighted. The work was labeled as achievable only by people thriving under stress. Work performance was sometimes hampered by frustrations. Teamwork and perseverance were key to overcoming challenges. And on it went. Many of the elements of emotion described in this volume were echoed in the astronomer's description of a highly technical pursuit. This should not be surprising. Emotion is integral in any type of work, which is why the research on emotion at work discussed in the different chapters of this book is so important.

My astronomer heroine didn't mention anything about customer service, emotional labor, emotional intelligence, decision-making, organizational justice. She also did not mention gender, though she may be more attuned to emotion as a woman. An astronomer building telescopes doesn't need to be explicit about the emotions in the work. But does this mean they are not there? Of course not. Indeed, it would be very difficult for anyone living and working in the twenty-first century to escape service interactions, decision-making, justice or gender issues, or emotion. This underscores the importance of the stream of research investigating emotion at work, which is celebrated in this volume.

Our job, as researchers of affect in organizations, is to highlight the presence of emotion; to unravel how, when, and why emotion emerges; and to identify the implications of emotions. I am not sure that the study of emotions is now center stage in organizational scholarship, as some chapter authors suggest. But we have made major progress in the awareness of and knowledge about emotion in organizations. When research on the topic started, thirty-five years ago, we had to defend the mere legitimacy of talking about emotion. Today, we have thirty-eight chapters, reviewing hundreds of articles, that dissect the emotion in different aspects of people and work in organizations. Such wonderful progress!

I occasionally find myself pondering . . . What do people think of when someone says that they research emotion in organizations? Do their thoughts have anything to do with the content of the chapters in this book? Probably not. Does that mean we are in trouble? I don't think so. When people think of astronomy, they don't think of the frustrations of building telescopes. The issue of emotion in organizations is simultaneously ubiquitous and subdued. We all feel it, but most people don't have a vocabulary for talking about it. The simple question of where affect resides in organizations is complex, as is fabulously illustrated in the chapters of this book. The emotion equation in organizations includes multiple components: actors (i.e. people who emote), receivers (i.e. subordinates, managers, coworkers, customers), observers (people not directly involved in an emotional event), and organizations (where the work occurs). All are tinted by emotion.

So, there is emotion experienced by individuals, as suggested in the chapters on neuroscience, personality, genetics, motivation, and health, as well as in chapters on specific emotions and on self-conscious emotions. There is also emotion integral to social interactions, as shown in the chapters on gender effects, customer service, justice, and especially other-focused emotion. Organizational-level norms or rules, and the aggregate of organizational climate and culture, add complexity. The organizational complexities underlay my original flirtation with emotion in organizations as expressed in the idea of emotional labor. Affective climate, workplace diversity, and technology (also discussed in the chapters of this book) further formulate emotion as an organization-wide construct.

The chapters in this volume review a lot of useful knowledge that has been accumulated about what, why, where, when, and how emotion emerges and influences people and organizations. As with the building of telescopes, however, we still have a long way to go. I hope the chapter on looking into the future inspires further research. I particularly urge students and scholars to seek new sources of data, and to study and embrace new tools. The Big Data revolution currently offers lots of new opportunities, with large archives of people's behaviors and expressions (e.g. Twitter, Facebook, Quora, Reddit). There are also new tools for obtaining this data (e.g. scraping data, application programming interfaces) and for analyzing emotions in them (currently used primarily by computer scientists in the processes known as sentiment analysis). Research utilizing such data and tools should build on the excellent foundations laid by the chapters of this book. They will help us emotion researchers reach the stars.

Anat Rafaeli
Technion – Israel Institute of Technology

Part I

Theoretical and Methodological Foundations

1 Emotion at Work

From the "Leaner Years" to the "Affective Revolution"

Catherine S. Daus, Russell Cropanzano, Vicente Martínez-Tur, and Liu-Qin Yang*

In 2017, the Onassis Cultural Center in New York hosted an exhibition called "A World of Emotions" (Levere, 2017). This exhibition was publicized as "Bringing to vivid life the emotions of the people of ancient Greece, and prompting questions about how we express, control, and manipulate feelings in our own society" (Onassis USA, 2017). The historical epoch covered was from 700 BC to AD 200, very roughly from a time near the end of the classical period to the middle of the Hellenistic period. One commentary on this exhibition suggested: "These objects provide a timely opportunity to think about the role of feelings in our personal, social and political lives and help advance the relatively new field of the history of emotions" (Levere, 2017).

While this exhibition focused on the ancient Greeks, it is important to understand that they were hardly the first people to think and write about affect – consider that the Epic of Gilgamesh and the biblical book of Exodus, among others, predated classical Greek writings. In the prologue of the Epic of Gilgamesh – which many believe to be the first surviving great work of literature – the author, Sîn-lēqi-unninni, referring to his hero, writes: "He had seen everything, experienced all emotions" (Mitchell, 2004, p. 8). Clearly emotions were perceived as critically relevant to life. In Exodus, we see the Israelites *groaning* to God to release them from their misery (Exodus 2:23–25; 3:7). The Greek contribution to the characterization of emotion, shared by Chinese thinkers (Virág, 2017), was that they were willing to consider "hot" affect rationally. That is, they applied the lens of reason to human feelings. To be sure, their analysis was pre-scientific; the institutions of science would not be invented for another few centuries. However, through introspection, careful thought, and dialogue, these ancient thinkers were able to arrive at ideas that were surprisingly modern or, at least, surprisingly recognizable to a contemporary audience. Plato, for example, divided the soul into three parts: reason, spirit, and appetite (for a review, see Annas, 2003). In the healthy mind, reason, which was the smallest of the three, would mediate between the other two (Dixon, 2003), which roughly translate to anger/temper (spirit) and love, hunger, thirst (appetite). The Epicureans grounded their goal of a flourishing life in terms of affect. Like modern Utilitarians, they saw the best life as one that cultivated pleasure and avoided pain (Cooper, 2012). However, concerning emotion, perhaps the most sophisticated ancient thinkers were the Stoics. Stoic philosophers viewed negative emotion (*pathē*) as occurring when we give irrational "assent" to bodily feelings (Graver, 2007). In other words, the *pathē* are a consequence of dysfunctional judgments (cognitions), and people can improve their well-being by controlling their thinking

* This research was partly supported by the by the Grant # T03OH008435 awarded to Portland State University, funded by the Centers for Disease Control and Prevention, National Institute for Occupational Safety and Health. Its contents are solely the responsibility of the authors and do not necessarily represent the official views of NIOSH, CDC or HHS.

(Sellers, 2006). If the reader finds this familiar, it is likely more than a serendipitous resemblance. Stoic philosophical thought influenced the development of modern cognitive behavioral therapy (Robertson, 2017).

With so auspicious a history, one would think that emotion would have become a major topic in organizational psychology and organizational behavior (OB) as the disciplines developed after World War II. Sadly, this was not to be, despite a promising start in the 1930s. During that decade, researchers experimented with a diversity of ideas and methodologies. For example, in his 1932 book *Workers' Emotions in Shop and Home*, Rexford Hersey tracked railroad employees' daily moods over a period of months. He mapped mood cycle and found that negative mood (when compared to positive and neutral moods) was related to lower job performance. Reports of the Hawthorne Studies, so named because they were conducted at Western Electric's Hawthorne Manufacturing facility, began in the 1920s and would continue into the 1950s (e.g. Baritz, 1960; Mayo, 1930). These studies examined, among other things, the variability of emotion over time, mutual sentiments with teams, and hostility. Of course, these older studies had a number of problems that have been identified by modern scholars (Muldoon, 2017). Still, the Hawthorne studies used a number of methodologies, such as observations and test-room interventions, that showed promise (Mayo, 1933; 1945).

Despite this promising research, post-war researchers attended mostly to other concerns (Grandey, 2008). It was this unwelcoming conceptual landscape that led Mowday and Sutton (1993, p. 197) to lament that employees were depicted as "cognitive stick figures whose behavior is unaffected by emotion." About the same time, Pekrun and Frese (1992, p. 152) famously mused, "We should not have consented to write an article on work and emotion" because "in order to do a review, one needs literature that can be reviewed." Brief and Weiss (2002) describe this period as "the Leaner Years" (p. 279), though eventually it gave way to the "Hot 1990s" or what Barsade, Brief, and Spataro (2003, p. 3) would call "affective revolution." How organizational psychology and organizational behavior got past the leaner years and into the affective revolution is a story of overcoming two challenges – the first of which was the cognitive revolution, and the second of which was a lack of a shared language.

Beginning in the 1950s, the so-called "cognitive revolution" dominated scientific psychology (Miller, 2003). Among other things, this intellectual movement emphasized such concepts as "*information, computation, and feedback*" (Pinker, 2002, p. 31, italics in original). Whatever its merits, the cognitive revolution had a deleterious effect on affect research (Ashforth & Humphrey, 1995). It is widely believed that the cognitive models simply displaced interest in affect, and this is somewhat true. However, it is more precise to say that during the leaner years, affect was understood in terms of cognitive processing and, therefore, the former was subordinate to the latter. For example, affect was described as contained within cognitive schemas (Sujan & Bettman, 1989), tagged to a schema (Fiske, Neuberg, Beattie, & Milberg, 1987), or resulting from a discrepancy between a real-world event and a schema (Purcell, 1986). In each case, the cognitive schema is the focal concept; affect is a component, an appendage, or an outcome, respectively.

The second challenge was the lack of a shared language for discussing affect. Without a common language, affect researchers were in no position to meet the trials posed by the cognitive revolution. This state of affairs existed because basic concepts – affect, attitude, mood, and emotion – had yet to be distinguished from one another. For example, "attitudes" were viewed as a type of affect. On this thinking, job satisfaction studies, of which there were many, became affect research. In an influential series of papers, Weiss and his colleagues (Brief & Weiss, 2002; Weiss, 2001; Weiss & Brief, 2001; Weiss & Cropanzano, 1996) hammered out a solution to this problem. "Affect" is understood to be a general term that refers to people's feelings about objects or events. A "mood" is free-floating affect, unattached to a stimulus. When compared to emotions, moods tend to be of longer duration and less intense. "Attitudes" are multi-faceted constructs, which contain affect but also include characteristic cognitions and behavioral predispositions. Emotions are generally of shorter duration and greater intensity than moods, and are directed at a target, as when you feel "angry" with a coworker or "happy" with a performance review.

Eventually, this better conceptualizing of our topic would allow affect researchers to provide strong alternatives to cognitively oriented theories of work behavior. Addressing these two challenges greatly increased the volume of affect research (Grandey, 2008). Having lived through this period, one gets the feeling of watching a reservoir, filled well past capacity, just as the dam breaks. When it broke there was a flood, as the number of published articles on mood or emotion more than doubled between 1972 and 2001 (Grandey, 2008). These articles approached affect from a number of perspectives. Below, we consider the history of some of the major research traditions that provided structure and impetus for subsequent explorations on affect and emotions. We have chosen the areas of emotional labor, affectivity and discrete emotions (focusing on positive and negative affectivity and affective events theory), and emotional intelligence, as these areas particularly have had frequent, long-term, consistent, and far-reaching academic and applied impact.

The Sociology of Workplace Emotion: Display Rules and Emotional Labor

Perhaps because of the influence of the cognitive revolution, the revival of the study of affect first came not from psychologically oriented researchers, but from sociology. In the 1983 publication of *The managed heart: Commercialization of human feeling,* Hochschild (1983) introduced the concepts of display rules and emotional labor to a management audience. This book was based on her earlier work, published a few years previously (Hochschild, 1979). Reflecting her sociological background, Hochschild employed both observational methods and intensive interviewing.[1] She profiled the often extreme pressure felt by employees due to the perceived necessity of managing their own emotions. Flight attendants and bill collectors repeatedly reported frequent circumstances of having to "put on a show" to navigate the emotional landscape during interactions on the job. There followed a series of articles that underscored the centrality of emotional displays at work (Rafaeli, 1989; Rafaeli & Sutton, 1987, 1990; Sutton, 1991; Sutton & Rafaeli, 1988).

Apart from research on display rules, Hochschild (1979; 1983) further paved the way for future investigations of emotion regulation and emotional labor. This work highlighted two broad processes that employees could use to manage emotions: *surface acting* (managing the expression of, but not the felt, emotion) and *deep acting* (managing or modulating the felt emotion). By the late 1990s and early 2000s, emotional labor had become a major area of study (e.g. Ashforth & Humphrey, 1993; Brotheridge, 1999; Grandey, 2000, 2003; Morris & Feldman, 1996), and this continues to the present. In this volume, we devote four full chapters to the topic – Chapter 11 on display rules and emotional regulation, Chapter 21 on service encounters, Chapter 22 on emotion management, and Chapter 23 on emotional labor. But here we

[1] This book provides several chapters that cover the diverse array of research methods used to study affect and emotion in organizations. Specifically, Chapters 6 on quantitative methods, 7 on qualitative methods, and 2 on neuroscience collectively cover a plethora of approaches.

are getting ahead of our story, for by the 1990s, researchers were beginning to stir.

The Psychology of Workplace Emotion: Affectivity and Discrete Emotions

While Hochschild (1979; 1983) may have originally taken a sociological perspective on workplace emotion, her contributions go well beyond any single discipline. An analysis that emphasizes emotional displays, which Hochschild provided, demands a broader look at the causes and consequences of workplace emotion for the workers themselves and for others around them. We mention several works that bridged the passageway from emotional labor primarily being "housed" in sociology, to psychologists recognizing the critical explanatory and applied power of emotional labor concepts in the work setting, emphasizing the very personal nature and outcomes of emotional labor. For example, in 1993 the book *Emotion in organizations*, edited by Fineman, demonstrated this bridge. While the book contained chapters dedicated to emotional labor (James, 1993; Putnam & Mumby, 1993), and a preface by Hochschild (1993), there was much beyond this. There were chapters on discrete emotions, including fear (Flam, 1993) and nostalgia (Gabriel, 1993). In like fashion, Ashforth and Humphrey (1995) also considered research on display rules in the workplace, which by that time was beginning to mature, but these authors added a more general analysis and critique (for a similar but more current view, see Elfenbein, 2007). Also deserving mention is the book *Emotions in the workplace*, edited by Lord, Klimoski, and Kanfer (2002). Its publisher claimed it to be "the first to bring together recent findings in one place and present a solid industrial/organizational research perspective on this complex area of inquiry." Works such as these brought the study of emotions in the workplace to the forefront of inquiry and challenged the "all things cognitive" consensus and paradigm that had primarily prevailed since the cognitive revolution.

Positive and Negative Affectivity

During the 1980s, a number of social–personality psychologists began to take a hard look at the concept of moods. When research participants rated themselves or others on words pertaining to affect, the resulting factor solution produced two dimensions. When this solution was then rotated 45°, the dimensions pertained to two hedonic types of affect – positive affect and negative affect (Tellegen, 1985; Watson & Clark, 1992). In other words, positive and negative feelings were independent of one another (Burke, Brief, George, Roberson, & Webster, 1989). An individual could be high on both, low on both, or high on one and low on the other (Larsen & McGraw, 2011; Larsen, McGraw, & Cacioppo, 2001). From the vantage point of more than three decades later, we have learned to become comfortable with the positive affect/negative affect factor structure. However, at the time it was a counterintuitive breakthrough, providing a conceptual and measurement model for research in organizational psychology and organizational behavior. According to Watson and Clark (1984), positive affect and negative affect were characteristic of both states (temporary fluctuations in mood) and traits (long-term predispositions to feel good or bad)–positive affectivity (PA) and negative affectivity (NA). With some justification, Watson and Tellegen (1985, p. 219) were able to proclaim that "psychology has re-discovered affect."

It is worth noting that the affective circumplex model (Russell, 1980) complicated positive affect and negative affect research. As noted above, the separation of positive from negative affect came from a 45° rotation of affect ratings. However, if these findings were not rotated, then a different solution appeared. There were again two factors. The strong first factor was "hedonic tone" or "pleasantness" (Larsen & Diner, 1992; Weiss & Cropanzano, 1996). It ranged from highly negative, through neutral, to highly positive. The weaker second factor was "intensity" or "activation." It ranged from low intensity to high (Judge & Larsen, 2001). Following from earlier work, organizational scholars have integrated these two solutions – positive affect/negative affect and hedonic tone/intensity – into the affective circumplex, suggesting that mood can be represented by either set of axes (Cropanzano, Weiss, Hale, & Reb, 2003; Grandey, 2008).

With these structural issues addressed, research on workplace affect began to build quickly. For example, Staw, Bell, and Clausen (1986) found evidence for the relationship of trait affect and job satisfaction by doing a retrospective reanalysis of archival data. Using data collected over a near fifty-year timespan, they showed a small but significant relationship between affective dispositions and job satisfaction at several later points in time. Likewise, Cropanzano, James, and Konovsky (1993) found that NA and PA predicted work attitudes, including job satisfaction and organizational commitment. This work has withstood the test of time. In one of the first meta-analyses examining affectivity and job satisfaction, Connolly and Viswesvaran (2000) reported fairly strong relationships between PA and job satisfaction (.49) and NA and job satisfaction (−.33). Later meta-analyses would further document this relationship (Bowling, Hendricks, & Wanger, 2008; Bruk-Lee, Khoury, Nixon, Goh, & Spector, 2009), as well as extending it to other work attitudes (Thoresen, Kaplan, Barsky, Warren, & de Chermont, 2003).

These examples, though well known, only scratch the surface. A large body of research has examined the relations between employee affect and employee performance, in a variety of forms, such as creative performance, task performance, organizational citizenship behavior, and counterproductive work behavior. Isen and Baron (1991; see also Isen 1999) maintained that positive affect predicts creative work behavior, an interesting finding that was later amended. George and Zhou (2002) found that positive moods boosted creative performance among people who were high in clarity of feelings, and who also worked in environments that rewarded and recognized creativity. When employees were low in clarity of feelings, while working in environments that did not reward and recognize creativity, then positive mood was negatively related to creative performance.

Likewise, attention was devoted to the relationship between affect, especially positive, and negotiator behavior. Carnevale and Isen (1986) reported that PA boosted integrative solutions while bargaining. Baron (1990) found that positive moods encouraged bargainers to be more cooperative and less contentious. Furthermore, George (1995) and Barsade (2002) found that positive leader mood promotes leader effectiveness, a finding that is supported by contemporary research (Joseph, Dhanani, Shen, McHugh, & McCord, 2015). There was also a flurry of interest in mood and OCB: some studies found that affectivity was a reliable predictor (George, 1991; George & Brief, 1992; Lee & Allen, 2002), while others were less supportive (Organ & Konovsky, 1989; Williams & Anderson, 1991). Clarifying these matters, a meta-analysis by Kaplan, Bradley, Luchman, and Haynes (2009) found that PA was positively related to job performance ratings and organizational citizenship behaviors, whereas NA was negatively related to these criteria. NA also predicted counterproductive work behavior (for similar findings, see Dalal, 2005). Here we mention a few chapters in our volume specifically relevant to the discussion of affect and performance: Chapter 9 (on emotion and various forms of job performance); Chapter 10 (on affect, creativity and innovation); Chapter 13 (on affect and workplace judgment and decision-making); and Chapter 25 (Performance management and workplace affect).

By the 1990s, research on PA and NA was an important driver of the affective revival. This scholarly interest in affect is reflected throughout the present volume; see Chapters 3 (on personality and affect); 4 (workplace affect and motivation); 25 (performance management and workplace affect); 27 (gender and workplace affect); and 32 (happiness in its many forms). However, there was a dark lining to this silver cloud. In a manner of speaking, the two-factor model of affect had become too successful. Research on affect had indeed returned, but research on discrete emotions, specifically, continued to lag (Gooty, Gavin, & Ashkanasy, 2009; Lazarus & Cohen-Charash, 2001; Weiss & Brief, 2001).

Affective Events Theory

Affective events theory (AET) is a general theory of workplace emotion that seeks to describe within-person changes in affective states (Weiss, 2002; Weiss & Cropanzano, 1996). According to AET, these fluctuations are stochastic. There are regular changes in affect, which oscillate according to describable laws (Weiss & Beal, 2005). They are predictable, though not perfectly so. Individual difference traits are important to AET in that they shape the distribution of affective states, which are experienced by individual workers (Cropanzano, Dasborough, & Weiss, 2017). At a basic level, AET posits a conceptual mismatch within many theories of workplace emotion, in that other theories use a putatively stable feature of the work environment, such as climate or support, to account for an unstable emotional state. As a result, these theories are trying to use a rough constant to account for a predictable change (Weiss & Beal, 2005). A more plausible approach, at least according to AET, is to consider changing workplace stimuli (events) as precursors of affective states. Initial research into the theory was supportive (Weiss, Nicolas, & Daus, 1999; Weiss, Suckow, & Cropanzano, 1999), and various reviews have noted the importance of AET in inspiring investigations of workplace affect, especially discrete emotions (e.g. Ashton-James & Ashkanasy, 2002; Fisher & Ashkanasy, 2000). This focus on discrete emotions, mentioned in the above section as well as here, represents both a lament (on the lack of empirical attention) and an invitation (for future investigations), which we also discuss in our closing chapter.

Given its influence, it is easy to forget that AET was originally developed to better understand job satisfaction (the 1996 article was entitled "An affective events approach to job satisfaction"), placing it squarely within the 1990s research tradition. However, its generality was recognized early on and its applications rapidly expanded to such domains as performance (Beal, Weiss, Barros, & MacDermid, 2005), work stress (Trougakos, Beal, Green, & Weiss, 2008), and leadership (Cropanzano et al., 2017).

There is another aspect of AET that bears mention. Affective events theory places a great deal of emphasis on phenomenal structure. Within the organizational research literature, the distinctions among "affect," "mood," and "discrete emotion," which were discussed earlier, were articulated within the context of AET (e.g. by Weiss, 2002) and extended to levels beyond the individual, as in the study of group affect (e.g. Ilies, Wagner, & Morgeson, 2007), team mood (e.g. Totterdell, 2000), and emotional climate (e.g. Härtel, Gough, & Härtel, 2006).[2] Notably, AET even provided a list of basic emotions, including such states as anger, fear, joy, and the like (Weiss & Cropanzano, 1996). This helped create interest in discrete emotions, which is evident in the present volume (see especially Chapters 29–35). Additionally, AET emphasized the distinction between "states" and "traits," though this was apparent in other work as well (such as that of Watson & Clark, 1984). In these ways, AET was more than (just) a theory. Rather, the work of Weiss and his colleagues (e.g. Brief & Weiss, 2002; Weiss, 2001; Weiss & Beal, 2005; Weiss

[2] This book also covers levels beyond the individual; see especially Chapters 18 and 28.

& Brief, 2001) helped provide the conceptual infrastructure upon which later workplace emotion research rested.

Emotional Intelligence: Science vs. Practice

A final tradition involves the tortuous history of the study of emotional intelligence (EI). This work is thoroughly reviewed in Chapter 12. For now, we consider its historic emergence over the past few decades. The construct of EI can be defined as an "ability to monitor one's own and others' feelings and emotions, to discriminate among them, and to use this information to guide one's thinking and actions" (Salovey & Mayer, 1990, p. 189). Though particular models varied, academic research originally understood EI as a set of related abilities pertaining to emotions (for an illustration of early work that helped pave the way for future EI, see Beldoch, 1964; for early construct and definitional clarification, see Mayer, Caruso, & Salovey, 1999; Mayer & Salovey, 1997; Salovey & Mayer, 1990). To date, the most commonly utilized model is the "four branch model," which proposes that emotional intelligence is comprised of four related but distinguishable skills: perceiving emotions, using emotions, understanding emotions, and managing emotions (Salovey & Grewal, 2005, pp. 281–282).

This early research, though relevant to work organizations, was not widely known to organizational scholars until the publication of Goleman's book *Emotional intelligence: Why it can matter more than IQ* (1995). This volume and his later publications (e.g. Goleman, 1998; Goleman, Boyatzis, & McKee, 2002) were written in an accessible and popular style, leading to the commercialization of EI (Landy, 2005). Additionally, Goleman (1998, p. 318) reconceptualized EI, expanding it to include five broad competencies: self-awareness, self-regulation, motivation, empathy, and social skills. Despite the name, this new concept of "emotional" intelligence is about more than emotion. For instance, it includes cognition (self-awareness), behavioral regulation (motivation), and interpersonal skills (social skills). In later work, Goleman et al. (2002, pp. 253–256) adjusted this list somewhat to encompass self-awareness, self-management, social awareness, and relationship management. They then added three to six facets for each competency, creating a full eighteen dimensions. These dimensions were broad and eclectic, including such diverse things as "service," "initiative," "accurate self-assessment," and "change catalyst."

It is important to recognize that Goleman (1995, 1998) did not simply establish a different model. Rather, this work went so far beyond the original *emotional* focus that Goleman had created a different type of EI, which was substantially broader than the original construct. Consequently, this new family of theories was conceptually distinct from the original EI research. This and related "mixed models" of EI (Daus & Ashkanasy, 2005, p. 455) combined skills, competencies, and personality traits into an ad hoc mix. This approach, the mixed model, has been criticized by researchers (e.g. Ciarrochi, Chan, & Caputi, 2000; Mayer, Roberts, & Barsade, 2008; Murphy, 2006), who are more likely to favor an ability model (Daus & Ashkanasy, 2005; Mayer, Caruso, & Salovey, 2016). However, the mixed models remain popular (cf. Goleman et al., 2002). Despite the concerns with Goleman's (1995, 1998) approach to EI, it does suggest an interesting historical possibility. As we have seen, organizational research was initially slow, almost unwilling, to fully incorporate affect into models of workplace behavior (e.g. Weiss & Brief, 2001). Practitioners filled this lacuna. Being closer to actual workplaces, they appear to have more deeply felt the incompleteness of academic thinking. EI research may not have been perfect, but it appealed to practitioners, especially, and helped fill the theoretical void we have discussed regarding emotions in organizational life.

Regardless of its conceptual travails, emotional intelligence remains an important construct. People high in emotional intelligence have better physical health (Martins, Ramalho, & Morin, 2010; Schutte, Malouff, Thorsteinsson, Bhullar, & Rooke, 2007) and report higher well-being (Sánchez-Álvarez, Extremera, & Fernández-Berrocal, 2016). They also appear to be more effective workers, though this depends on how EI is measured. A meta-analysis by O'Boyle, Humphrey, Pollack, Hawver, and Story (2011) found that all types of EI (ability, self-report, mixed models) predicted job performance beyond the effects of cognitive ability and personality.

Conclusion

Reflecting upon our history and with knowledge of the chapters in our volume, we can thus say with some assurance that the study of affect in work organizations has finally arrived. The history and theoretical paradigms we have reviewed here are simply the tip of the iceberg regarding current scholarship on emotions in organizational life. What follows is a series of more detailed and thorough reviews. We conclude simply with an invitation to dive into our offerings and feel confident that you will find much to stimulate your research and applied imaginings.

References

Annas, J. (2003). *Plato: A brief insight*. New York, NY: Sterling.

Ashforth, B. E., & Humphrey, R. H. (1993). Emotional labor in service roles: The influence of identity. *Academy of Management Review, 18*, 88–115.

Ashforth, B. E., & Humphrey, R. H. (1995). Emotion in the workplace: A reappraisal. *Human Relations, 48*, 97–125.

Ashton-James, C. E., & Ashkanasy, N. M. (2005). What lies beneath? A process analysis of affective events theory. In N. M. Ashkanasy, W. J. Zerbe, and C. E. J. Härtel (Eds.), *The effect of affect in organizational settings* (pp. 23–46). Bingley, UK: Emerald.

Baitz, L. (1960). *The servants of power: A history of the use of social science in American industry.* Middletown, CT: Wesleyan University Press.

Baron, R. A. (1990). Environmentally induced positive affect: Its impact on self-efficacy, task performance, negotiation, and conflict. *Journal of Applied Social Psychology, 20*, 368–384.

Barsade, S. G. (2002). The ripple effect: Emotional contagion and its influence on group behavior. *Administrative Science Quarterly, 47*, 644–675.

Barsade, S. G., Brief, A. P., & Spataro, S. E. (2003). The affective revolution in organizational behavior: The emergence of a paradigm. In J. Greenberg (Ed.), *Organizational behavior: The state of the science* (pp. 3–52). Mahwah, NJ: Erlbaum.

Beal, D. J., Weiss, H. M., Barros, E., & MacDermid, S. J. (2005). An episodic process model of affective influences on performance. *Journal of Applied Psychology, 90*, 1054–1068.

Beldoch, M. (1964). Sensitivy to expression of emotional meaning in three modes of communication. In J. R. Davitz & M. Beldoch (Eds.), *The communication of emotional meaning* (pp. 31–42). New York, NY: McGraw-Hill.

Bowling, N. A., Hendricks, E. A., & Wagner, S. H. (2008). Positive and negative affectivity and facet satisfaction: A meta-analysis. *Journal of Business and Psychology, 23*, 115–125.

Brief, A. P., & Weiss, H. M. (2002). Organizational behavior: Affect in the workplace. *Annual Review of Psychology, 53*, 279–307.

Brotheridge, C. M. (1999). Unwrapping the black box: A test of why emotional labour may lead to emotional exhaustion. In D. Miller (Ed.), *Proceedings of the Administrative Sciences Association of Canada, Organizational Behaviour Division* (pp. 11–20). Saint John, New Brunswick.

Bruk-Lee, V., Khoury, H. A., Nixon, A. E., Goh, A., & Spector, P. E. (2009). Replicating and extending past personality/job satisfaction meta-analyses. *Human Performance, 22*, 156–189.

Burke, M. J., Brief, A. P., George, J. M., Roberson, L., & Webster, J. (1989). Measuring affect at work:

confirmatory analyses of competing mood structures with conceptual linkage to cortical regulatory systems. *Journal of personality and social psychology, 57*, 1091–1102.

Carnevale, P. J., & Isen, A. M. (1986). The influence of positive affect and visual access on the discovery of integrative solutions in bilateral negotiation. *Organizational Behavior and Human Decision Processes, 37*, 1–13.

Ciarrochi, J. V., Chan, A. Y. C., & Caputi, P. (2000). A critical evaluation of the emotional intelligence construct. *Personality and Individual Differences, 28*, 539–561.

Connolly, J. J., & Viswesvaran, C. (2000). The role of affectivity in job satisfaction: A meta-analysis. *Personality and Individual Differences, 29*, 265–281.

Cooper, J. M. (2012). *Pursuits of wisdom: Six ways of life in ancient philosophy: From Socrates to Plotinus*. Princeton, NJ: Princeton University Press.

Cropanzano, R., Dasborough, M., & Weiss, H. M. (2017). Affective events and the development of leader-member exchange. *Academy of Management Review, 42*, 233–258.

Cropanzano, R., James, K., & Konovsky, M. A. (1993). Dispositional affectivity as a predictor of work attitudes and job performance. *Journal of Organizational Behavior, 14*, 595–606.

Cropanzano, R., Weiss, H. M., Hale, J. M. S., & Reb, J. (2003). The structure of affect: Reconsidering the relationship between negative and positive affectivity. *Journal of Management, 29*, 831–857.

Dalal, R. S. (2005). A meta-analysis of the relationship between organizational citizenship behavior and counterproductive work behavior. *Journal of Applied Psychology, 90*, 1241–1255.

Daus, C. S., & Ashkanasy, N. M. (2005). The case for the ability-based model of emotional intelligence in organizational behavior. *Journal of Organizational Behavior, 26*, 453–466.

Dixon, T. (2003). *From passions to emotions: The creation of a secular psychological category*. Cambridge, UK: Cambridge University Press.

Elfenbein, H. A. (2007). Emotion in organizations. In J. P. Walsh & A. P. Brief (Eds.), *Academy of Management Annals* (Volume 1, pp. 315–86). New York, NY: Routledge.

Fineman, S. (1993). *Emotion in organizations*. London, UK: Sage.

Fisher, C. D., & Ashkanasy, N. M. (2000). The emerging role of emotions in work life: An introduction. *Journal of Organizational Behavior, 21*, 123–129.

Fiske, S. T., Neuberg, S. L., Beattie, A. E., & Milberg, S. J. (1987). Category-based and attribute-based reactions to others: Some informational conditions of stereotyping and individuating others. *Journal of Experimental Social Psychology, 23*, 299–427.

Flam, H. (1993). Fear, loyalty and greedy organizations. In S. Fineman (Ed.), *Emotion in organizations* (pp. 58–75) London, UK: Sage.

Gabriel, Y. (1993). Organizational nostalgia – Reflections on "the golden age." In S. Fineman (Ed.), *Emotion in organizations* (pp. 118–141) London, UK: Sage.

George, J. M. (1991). State or trait: Effects of positive mood on prosocial behaviors at work. *Journal of Applied Psychology, 76*, 299–307.

George, J. M. (1995). Leader positive mood and group performance: The case of customer service. *Journal of Applied Social Psychology, 25*, 778–794.

George, J. M., & Brief, A. P. (1992). Feeling good doing good: A conceptual analysis of the mood at work organizational spontaneity relationship. *Psychological Bulletin, 112*, 310–329.

George, J. M., & Zhou, J. (2002). Understanding when bad moods foster creativity and good ones don't: The role of context and clarity of feelings. *Journal of Applied Psychology, 87*, 687–697.

Goleman, D. (1995). *Emotional intelligence: Why it can matter more than IQ*. New York, NY: Bantam Books.

Goleman, D. (1998). *Work with emotional intelligence*. New York, NY: Bantam Books.

Goleman, D., Boyatzis, R., & McKee, A. (2002). *Primal leadership: Realizing the power of emotional intelligence*. Cambridge, MA: Harvard University Press.

Gooty, J., Gavin, M., & Ashkanasy, N. M. (2009). Emotions research in OB: The challenges that lie ahead. *Journal of Organizational Behavior, 30*, 833–838.

Grandey, A. A. (2000). Emotion regulation in the workplace: A new way to conceptualize emotional labor. *Journal of Occupational Health Psychology*, *5*, 95–110.

Grandey, A. A. (2003). When "the show must go on": Surface acting and deep acting as determinants of emotional exhaustion and peer-rated service delivery. *Academy of Management Journal*, *46*, 86–96.

Grandey, A. A. (2008). Emotions at work: A review and research agenda. In Barling, J., & Cooper, C. L. (Eds.) *SAGE handbook of organizational behavior, Volume 1: Micro approaches* (pp. 234–261). Thousand Oaks, CA: Sage Publications.

Graver, S. R. (2007). *Stoicism and emotion*. Chicago, IL: University of Chicago Press.

Härtel, C. E. J., Gough, H., & Härtel, G. F. (2006). Service providers' use of emotional competencies and perceived workgroup emotional climate to predict customer and provider satisfaction with service encounters. *International Journal of Work Organization and Emotion*, *1*, 232–254.

Hersey, R.B. (1932). *Worker's emotions in shop and home: A study of individual workers from the psychological and physiological standpoint*. Philadelphia: University of Pennsylvania Press.

Hochschild, A. R. (1979). Emotion work, feeling rules and social structure. *American Journal of Sociology*, *85*, 551–575.

Hochschild, A. R. (1983). *The managed heart*. Berkeley: University of California Press.

Hochschild, A. R. (1993). Preface. In S. Fineman (Ed.), *Emotion in organizations* (pp. ix–xiii). London, UK: Sage.

Ilies, R., Wagner, D. T., & Morgeson, F. P. (2007). Explaining affective linkages in teams: Individual differences in susceptibility to contagion and individualism-collectivism. *Journal of Applied Psychology*, *92*, 1140–1148.

Isen, A. M. (1999). On the relationship between affect and creative problem solving. In S. W. Russ (Ed.), *Affect, creative experience, and psychological adjustment* (pp. 3–17). Philadelphia, PA: Taylor & Francis.

Isen, A. M., & Baron, R. A. (1991). Positive affect as a factor in organizational behavior. In L. L. Cummings & B. M. Staw (Eds.), *Research in organizational behavior* (Volume 13, pp. 1–53). Greenwich, CT: JAI.

James, N. (1993). Divisions of emotional labour: Disclosure and cancer. In S. Fineman (Ed.), *Emotion in organizations* (pp. 94–117). London, UK: Sage.

Joseph, D. L., Dhanani, L. Y., Shen, W., McHugh, B. C., & McCord, M. A. (2015). Is a happy leader a good leader? A meta-analytic investigation of leader trait affect and leadership. *Leadership Quarterly*, *26*, 558–577.

Judge, T. A., & Larsen, R. J. (2001). Dispositional affect and job satisfaction: A review and theoretical extension. *Organizational Behavior and Human Decision Processes*, *86*, 67–98.

Kaplan, S., Bradley, J. C., Luchman, J. N., & Haynes, D. (2009). On the role of positive and negative affectivity in job performance: A meta-analytic investigation. *Journal of Applied Psychology*, *94*, 162–176

Landy, F. J. (2005). Some historical and scientific issues related to research on emotional intelligence. *Journal of Organizational Behavior*, *26*, 411–424.

Larsen, J. T., & McGraw, A. P. (2011). Further evidence for mixed emotions. *Journal of Personality and Social Psychology*, *100*, 1095–1110.

Larsen, J. T., McGraw, A. P., & Cacioppo, J. T. (2001). Can people feel happy and sad at the same time? *Journal of Personality and Social Psychology*, *81*, 684–696.

Larsen, R. J., & Diener, E. (1992). Promises and problems with the circumplex model of emotion. In M. S. Clark (Ed.), *Review of personality and social psychology: Emotion* (Volume 13, 25–59). Newbury Park, CA: Sage.

Lazarus, R. S., & Cohen-Charash, Y. (2001). Discrete emotions in everyday life. In R. Payne & C. Cooper (Eds.), *Emotions at work* (pp. 47–81). New York, NY: John Wiley & Sons.

Lee, K., & Allen, N. J. (2002). Organizational citizenship behavior and workplace deviance: The role of affect and cognition. *Journal of Applied Psychology*, *87*, 131–142.

Levere, J. (2017, April). What can the emotions of Ancient Greeks teach us about the role of feelings in society today? *Forbes* (30 April), www.forbes.com/sites/janelevere/2017/04/30/what-can-the-emotions-of-ancient-greeks-teach-us-about-the-role-of-feelings-in-society-today/#3db10d9f1263

Lord, R. G., Klimoski, R. J., & Kanfer, R. (Eds.) (2002). *Emotions in the workplace: Understanding the structure and role of emotions in organizational behavior* (Volume 7). San Francisco, CA: Jossey-Bass.

Martins, A., Ramalho, N., & Morin, E. (2010). A comprehensive meta-analysis of the relationship between emotional intelligence and health. *Personality and Individual Differences*, *49*, 554–564.

Mayer, J. D., Caruso, D., & Salovey, P. (1999). Emotional intelligence meets traditional standards for an intelligence. *Intelligence*, *27*, 267–298.

Mayer, J. D., Caruso, D. R., & Salovey, P. (2016). The ability model of emotional intelligence: Principles and updates. *Emotion Review*, *8*, 290–300.

Mayer, J. D., Roberts, R. D., Barasade, S. G. (2008). Human abilities: Emotional intelligence. *Annual Review of Psychology*, *50*, 507–536.

Mayer, J. D., & Salovey, P. (1997). What is emotional intelligence? In P. Salovey & D. Sluyter (Eds.), *Emotional development and emotional intelligence: Educational implications* (pp. 3–31). New York, NY: Basic Books.

Mayo, E. (1930). The Western Electric Company experiment. *Human Factor*, *6*(1), 1–2.

Mayo, E. (1933). *The human problems of an industrial civilization*. New York, NY: Macmillan.

Mayo, E. (1945). *The social problems of an industrial civilization*. Boston, MA: Harvard University Press.

Miller, G. A. (2003). The cognitive revolution: A historical perspective. *Trends in Cognitive Science*, 7, 141–144.

Mitchell, S. (2004). *Gilgamesh: A new English version*. London, UK: Simon and Schuster.

Morris, J. A., & Feldman, D. C. (1996). The dimensions, antecedents, and consequences of emotional labor. *Academy of Management Journal*, *21*, 996–1010.

Mowday, R. T., & Sutton, R. I. (1993). Organizational behavior: Linking individuals and groups to organizational contexts. *Annual Review of Psychology*, *44*, 195–229.

Muldoon, J. (2017). The Hawthorne studies: An analysis of critical perspectives, 1932–1958. *Journal of Management History*, *21*, 1751–1348.

Murphy, K. R. (Ed.) (2006). *A critique of emotional intelligence: What are the problems and how can they be fixed?* New York, NY: Routledge.

O'Boyle, E. H., Jr., Humphrey, R. H., Pollack, J. M., Hawver, T., & Story, P. A. (2011). The relation between emotional intelligence and job performance: A meta-analysis. *Journal of Organizational Behavior*, *32*, 788–818.

Onassis USA (2017). *A World of Emotions: Ancient Greece, 700 BC – 200 AD* (exhibition web pages), https://onassisusa.org/exhibitions/a-world-of-emotions

Organ, D. W., & Konovsky, M. A. (1989). Cognitive versus affective determinants of organizational citizenship behavior. *Journal of Applied Psychology*, *74*, 157–164.

Pekrun, R., & Frese, M. (1992). Emotions in work and achievement. *International Review of Industrial and Organizational Psychology*, 7, 153–200.

Pinker, S. (2002). *The blank slate: The modern denial of human nature*. New York, NY: Viking Press.

Purcell, A. T. (1986). Environmental perception and affect: A schema discrepancy model. *Environment and Behavior*, *18*, 3–30.

Putnam, L. L., & Mumby, D. K. (1993). Organizations, emotion and the myth of rationality. In S. Fineman (Ed.), *Emotion in organizations* (pp. 36–57). London, UK: Sage.

Rafaeli, A. (1989). When clerks meet customers: A test of variables related to emotional expressions on the job. *Journal of Applied Psychology*, *74*, 385–393.

Rafaeli, A., & Sutton, R. I. (1987). Expression of emotion as part of the work role. *Academy of Management Review*, *12*, 23–37.

Rafaeli, A., & Sutton, R. I. (1990). Busy stores and demanding customers: How do they affect the display of positive emotions? *Academy of Management Journal*, *33*, 623–637.

Robertson, D. (2017). *How to think like a Roman emperor: The stoic philosophy of Marcus Aurelius*. New York, NY: St. Martin's.

Russell, J. A. (1980). A circumplex model of affect. *Journal of Personality and Social Psychology*, *39*, 1161–1178.

Salovey, P., & Grewal, D. (2005). The science of emotional intelligence. *Psychological Science*, *6*, 281–285.

Salovey, P., & Mayer, J. (1990). Emotional intelligence. *Imagination, Cognition and Personality, 9*, 185–211.

Sánchez-Álvarez, N. Extremera, N., & Fernández-Berrocal, P. (2016). The relation between emotional intelligence and subjective well-being: A meta-analytic investigation. *Journal of Positive Psychology, 11*, 276–285.

Schutte, N. S., Malouff, J. M., Thorsteinsson, E. B., Bhullar, N., & Rooke, S. E. (2007). A meta-analytic investigation of the relationship between emotional intelligence and health. *Personality and Individual Differences, 42*, 921–933.

Sellers, J. (2006). *Stoicism*. Chesham, UK: Acumen.

Staw, B. M., Bell, N. E., & Clausen, J. A. (1986). The dispositional approach to job attitudes: A lifetime longitudinal test. *Administrative Science Quarterly*, 56–77.

Sujan, M., & Bettman, J. R. (1989). The effects of brand positioning strategies on consumers' brand and category perceptions: Some insights from schema research. *Journal of Marketing Research, 26*, 451–467.

Sutton, R. I. (1991). Maintaining norms about expressed emotions: The case of bill collectors. *Administrative Science Quarterly, 36*, 245–268.

Sutton, R. I., & Rafaeli, A. (1988). Untangling the relationship between displayed emotions and organizational sales: The case of convenience stores. *Academy of Management Journal, 31*, 461–487.

Tellegen, A. (1985). Structures of mood and personality and their relevance to assessing anxiety, with an emphasis on self-report. In A. H. Tuma & J. D. Maser (Eds.), *Anxiety and the anxiety disorders* (pp. 681–706). Hillsdale, NJ: Erlbaum.

Thoresen, C. J., Kaplan, S. A., Barsky, A. P., Warren, C. R., & de Chermont, K. (2003). The affective underpinnings of job perceptions and attitudes: A meta-analytic review and integration. *Journal of Applied Psychology, 129*, 914–925.

Totterdell, P. (2000). Catching moods and hitting runs: Mood linkage and subjective performance in professional sport teams. *Journal of Applied Psychology, 85*, 848–859.

Trougakos, J. P., Beal, D. J., Green, S. G., & Weiss, H. M. (2008). Making the break count: An episodic examination of recovery activities, emotional experiences, and positive affective displays. *Academy of Management Journal, 51*, 131–146.

Virág, C. (2017). *The emotions in early Chinese philosophy*. Oxford, UK: Oxford University Press.

Watson, D., & Clark, L. A. (1984). Negative affectivity: The disposition to experience negative emotional states. *Psychological Bulletin, 96*, 465–490.

Watson, D., & Clark, L. A. (1992). On traits and temperaments: General and specific factors of emotional experience and their relation to the five-factor model. *Journal of Personality, 60*, 441–476.

Watson, D., & Tellegen, A. (1985). Towards a consensual structure of mood. *Psychological Bulletin, 98*, 127–144.

Weiss, H. M. (2002). Conceptual and empirical foundations for the study of affect at work. In R. G. Lord, R. J. Klimoski, & R. Kanfer (Eds.), *Emotions in the workplace* (pp. 20–63). San Francisco, CA: Jossey-Bass.

Weiss, H. M., & Beal, D. J. (2005). Reflections on affective events theory. *Research on Emotions in Organizations, 1*, 1–21.

Weiss, H. M., & Brief, A. P. (2001). Affect at work: A historical perspective. In R. L. Payne & C. L. Cooper (Eds.), *Emotions at work: Theory, research, and application in management* (pp. 133–172). Chichester, UK: John Wiley & Sons.

Weiss, H. M., & Cropanzano, R. (1996). An affective events approach to job satisfaction. In B. M. Staw & L. L. Cummings (Eds.), *Research in organizational behavior* (Volume 18, pp. 1–74). Greenwich, CT: JAI.

Weiss, H. M., Nicholas, J. P., & Daus, C. S. (1999). An examination of the job effects of affective experiences and job beliefs on job satisfaction and variations in affective experiences over time. *Organizational Behavior and Human Decision Processes, 79*, 1–24.

Weiss, H. M., Suckow, K., & Cropanzano, R. (1999). Effects of justice conditions on discrete emotions. *Journal of Applied Psychology, 84*, 786–794.

Williams, L. J., & Anderson, S. E. (1991). Job satisfaction and organizational commitment as predictors of organizational citizenship and in-role behaviors. *Journal of Management, 17*, 601–617.

2 The Organizational Neuroscience of Emotions

Sebastiano Massaro

The study of emotions has taken center stage in several areas of organizational scholarship over the past few decades. The mid-1990s saw the emergence of the seminal affective events theory (AET; Weiss & Cropanzano, 1996), which proposes that discrete workplace "affective events" elicit "affective responses" that then influence attitudinal and behavioral outcomes. Since then, research has experienced an affective revolution (Barsade, Brief, & Spataro, 2003). Work on emotional contagion (e.g. Barsade, 2002), discrete emotions (e.g. Lazarus & Cohen-Charash, 2001), and multi-level integrations (e.g. Ashkanasy, 2003a; Elfenbein, 2007), among other topics, has rapidly advanced both theory and practice, becoming integral to the lexicon of organizational scholars (Brief & Weiss, 2002).

More recently, Becker and Cropanzano (2010), building on information deriving from increasingly sophisticated methods of investigating human neurophysiology and cognition, proposed organizational neuroscience (ON). ON is an informative perspective incorporating knowledge about the neural substrates supporting individuals' cognitive machinery into organizational theory (Becker, Cropanzano, & Sanfey, 2011). Although the field is still nascent, interest in using neuroscience as an opportunity to advance explanations of administrative behavior has rapidly spread to other domains of managerial research, including strategic management (Powell, 2011) and entrepreneurship (Day, Boardman, & Krueger, 2017; Drover, Massaro, Cerf, & Busenitz, 2017). Moreover, journals have dedicated special issues to neuroscience (e.g. *Organizational Research Methods*, *Journal of Business Ethics*, *Organizational Behavior and Human Decision Processes*), and at several scholarly meetings (e.g. Academy of Management, Society for Industrial and Organizational Psychology, American Psychological Association) the number of sessions devoted to the topic has steadily increased. Yet as is typical of an emerging field, the development of ON has been characterized by both hype and hope (see Ashkanasy, Becker, & Waldman, 2014). In addition, scholars have pursued a variety of theoretical perspectives (cf. Lee, Senior & Butler, 2012), resulting in a fragmented research program thus far. This chapter, while arguing for a more unified development of ON, purposely aims at infusing workplace affect research with neuroscience knowledge to show why and in what ways ON can offer a productive platform for the advancement of organizational studies on emotions.

First, some caveats. Investigating the intersection of emotion and neuroscience is certainly not new. From Hippocrates (460–370 BC), who in *De morbo sacro* ("The sacred disease," 400 BC; Hippocrates, trans. 1923) argued that the brain gives rise to emotions and judgments, to Descartes (1596–1650) contending that human "passions" cannot be localized in the body (Descartes, 1649); from William James's (1842–1910) peripheralist theory, which holds that emotions are stimuli-driven automatic perceptions of specific bodily changes (James, 1884), to the debate on the relations between emotions and cognition (Lazarus, 1982; Zajonc, 1984), people have long been fascinated by the association between emotions and the brain. Here I focus on the most recent research in affective neuroscience as inaugurated by neuroimaging techniques. These powerful methods have greatly advanced our understanding of how the brain encodes, accumulates, and retrieves knowledge about emotions; how emotional states regulate and shape cognitive processes, such as decision-making; and how emotions influence behavior (e.g. Damasio, 1996; Davidson & Irwin, 1999; Lane & Nadel, 1999; LeDoux, 1998; Panksepp, 1998; Rolls, 2000).

Second, ON is not (and should not be) merely a narrow investigation of activated or deactivated brain areas. Neuroscience, and by extension affective and organizational neuroscience, investigates the entire nervous system and its relationship to behavior (Massaro & Pecchia, 2019). The nervous system is a complex structure comprising central and peripheral autonomic parts, the latter discernible in the sympathetic and parasympathetic systems (i.e. the systems responsible for the "fight-or-flight" and the "rest-and-digest" responses, respectively). Moreover, neuroscience is concerned with multi-level interconnections from the submolecular to the cellular, anatomical, behavioral, and social levels of analysis (Cacioppo, Berntson, Sheridan, & McClintock, 2000; Ochsner & Lieberman, 2001). Within the ON perspective, for example, an angry employee could be characterized by the combination of low serotonin, high dopamine, and high noradrenaline in the body (Lövheim, 2012), or an altered responsiveness of the brain circuitry amygdala-hypothalamus-periaqueductal gray (Blair, 2012), or increased heart rate mapped onto behavioral processes occurring in certain social interactions (Denson, Grisham, & Moulds, 2011), or all these features together. As a consequence, many methods, and functional neuroimaging in particular, can be used to capture these points.

Finally, readers should be aware that the terminology of affective science has been used inconsistently in both organizational literature (see Barsade & Gibson, 2007, for an exhaustive thesaurus) and neuroscience literature. Emotions are complex phenomena involving different interpretations, theories, and focuses of inquiry. Importantly, such a multifaceted body of knowledge offers a valuable point of entry to explore ON initiatives in workplace affect research. As Panksepp (1998) notes, only with concurrent neuroscience analyses can affective concepts be used non-circularly in the scientific discourse.

Thus, I begin by explaining why and in what ways the ON perspective and its core methods matter for emotion research in the workplace. I also draw theoretical parallels to AET, arguably one of the most acknowledged frameworks supporting the scholarship in workplace affect. I then review recent neuroscience evidence on topics relevant to organizational research in emotion, considering both the intra-individual and interpersonal dimensions. I conclude by presenting some questions for future research that ON might address in furthering our understanding of the "emotional workplace."

The Methodological Rationale

The methodological advancements recently put forward by neuroimaging represent the most logical entry point to substantiate the usefulness of neuroscience in management research (Massaro, 2015). In particular, in affective research, scholars have suggested the existence of a "misalignment of theory and methods" due to the use of self-reported and observational data (Briner & Kiefer, 2005; Gooty, Gavin, & Ashkanasy, 2009). Thus, methods capturing the neural and physiological correlates of affect can provide novel and reliable measures that promise to mitigate this imbalance (Becker & Menges, 2013; Massaro, 2014).

Several peripheral physiological reactions, those automatic responses of the nervous system that generally occur beyond one's awareness, may now be monitored to investigate emotional arousal and valence. These responses include respiration rates and heart rate variability (HRV; Massaro & Pecchia, 2019), electromyography (EMG) tracing of facial cues (Hazlett & Hazlett, 1999), and changes in skin conductance response (Christopoulos, Uy, & Yap, 2019). Organizational researchers can also assess neural changes through functional imaging, which more precisely shows "what," "where," and "when" affective events occur in the brain. In particular, electrophysiological methods based on assessing brain electrical activities (e.g. electroencephalography, EEG) or their tomographic quantification (qEEG; Teplan, 2002), or magnetic activity (magnetoelectroencephalography, MEG; Ahlfors & Mody, 2019) capture cortical events underlying affective states in almost real time (milliseconds). Moreover, functional magnetic resonance imaging (fMRI), which typically assesses the increase in the oxygenated blood flow accompanying cerebral activity (Aine, 1995), allows mapping activation of deeper areas in the brain, including the so-called limbic system (MacLean, 1952), a cluster of regions strongly involved in our emotional life (Figure 2.1).

Finally, metabolic imaging, including positron emission tomography (PET), is less common due to the use of dangerous ionizing radiations. Despite low spatial and temporal resolutions (30s–minutes), this technique yields high specificity (Cabeza & Nyberg, 2000).

Given the variety of methods available, Massaro (2018) has recently illustrated a methodological framework to guide ON research (Table 2.1). Accordingly, when investigating affective states as functions of the measurement of neural activity, researchers can best understand and apply these methods by considering their correlational, causational, or manipulating properties.

Importantly, all these approaches generate objective measures, improving the examination of emotional experiences in the workplace beyond what could be achieved with observations or subjective data. Moreover, neuroscience tools can often provide real-time information about someone's emotional state, overcoming demand effects that often sway self-reported data (Thorson, West, & Mendes, 2017). Added to this, due to their unobtrusiveness, many neuroscience instruments allow researchers to assess affective processes without disrupting their dynamics, including those that occur during interpersonal interactions or in real-world organizations.

Finally, thanks to the growing availability of wearable and portable technologies (e.g.

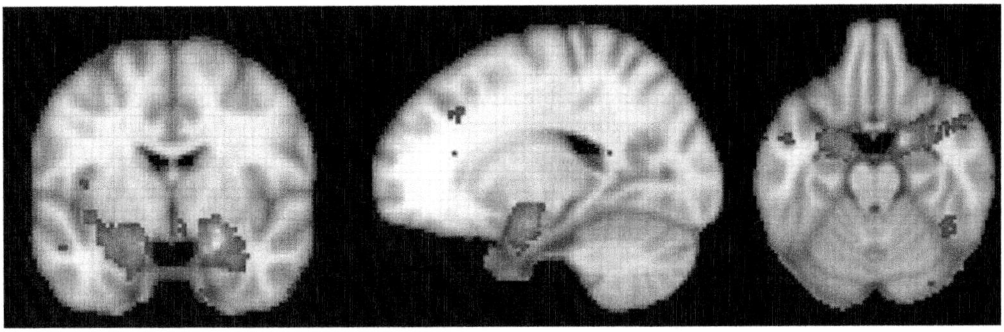

Figure 2.1 Activations peaks (darkened in image) of brain structures conventionally associated with the limbic circuit; images were obtained by performing a meta-analysis (based on a framework developed by Yarkoni, Poldrack, Nichols, Van Essen, & Wager, 2011) of over 400 fMRI activation studies, published between 1992 and 2018, that reported "emotion(s)" as a keyword

Table 2.1 Classification of organizational neuroscience methods based on their testing rationale (adapted from Massaro, 2018)

Type of test	Definition	Method linking regional neural activity to mental function
Association	Experimental methods that involve a manipulation of a psychological state or behavior, the simultaneous measurements of the neural activity, and the subsequent analysis of the correlation between the two	fMRI PET EEG MEG Physiological (HRV; skin conductance)
Necessity	Experimental methods that involve a disruption of the neural activity and aim to show how this event impairs a specific behavior or psychological function	Lesion studies TMS
Sufficiency	Experimental methods that involve enhancing a neural activity and seeking to establish that this process results in a specific behavior or psychological state	TMS (anodal)

smartwatches, portable EEG caps), parallel measurements of different individuals might advance our knowledge of such interpersonal affective dynamics as occur in emphatic processes within organizations. This feature is also particularly promising in upholding the requirement of ecological validity necessary for ON investigations to thrive (Massaro, 2018).

The Theoretical Rationale

Methodological advantages have been the driving force behind the ON approach thus far. Yet inquiries into workplace affect offer another valuable prospect for appreciating the informative power of ON. Herein lies the opportunity to integrate and advance management theory with insights from neuroscience theory concerning the functioning mechanisms of the brain. Specifically, affective research recognizes that emotions are complex states and highly mutable phenomena (e.g. Beal, Weiss, Barros, & MacDermid, 2005); a better knowledge of their mechanisms and dynamics might thus substantially improve existing theory (e.g. Askanasy & Humprey, 2011; Brief & Wiess, 2002) and illuminate how affective mechanisms develop within and between organizational actors (Ashkanasy, 2003a; 2003b).

Consider the possible parallel between AET and neuroscience theory on the information-processing of emotions (Figure 2.2; see also Elfenbein, 2007, for a comparison between AET and emotions as stimuli-driven processes, yet lacking the neuroscience perspective).

AET is an acknowledged organizational research framework that examines the structure, causes, and consequences of affective experiences at work (Weiss & Cropanzano, 1996). It starts from the concept that work events are proximal causes of affective reactions: what happens at work can be seen as discrete and cumulative events that trigger employees' internal influences – "affective reactions" – that then, along with affective disposition, shape organizational behavioral outputs (Weiss & Cropanzano, 1996; Weiss & Beal, 2005).

ON can be of particular help in disentangling what occurs in the black box of individual

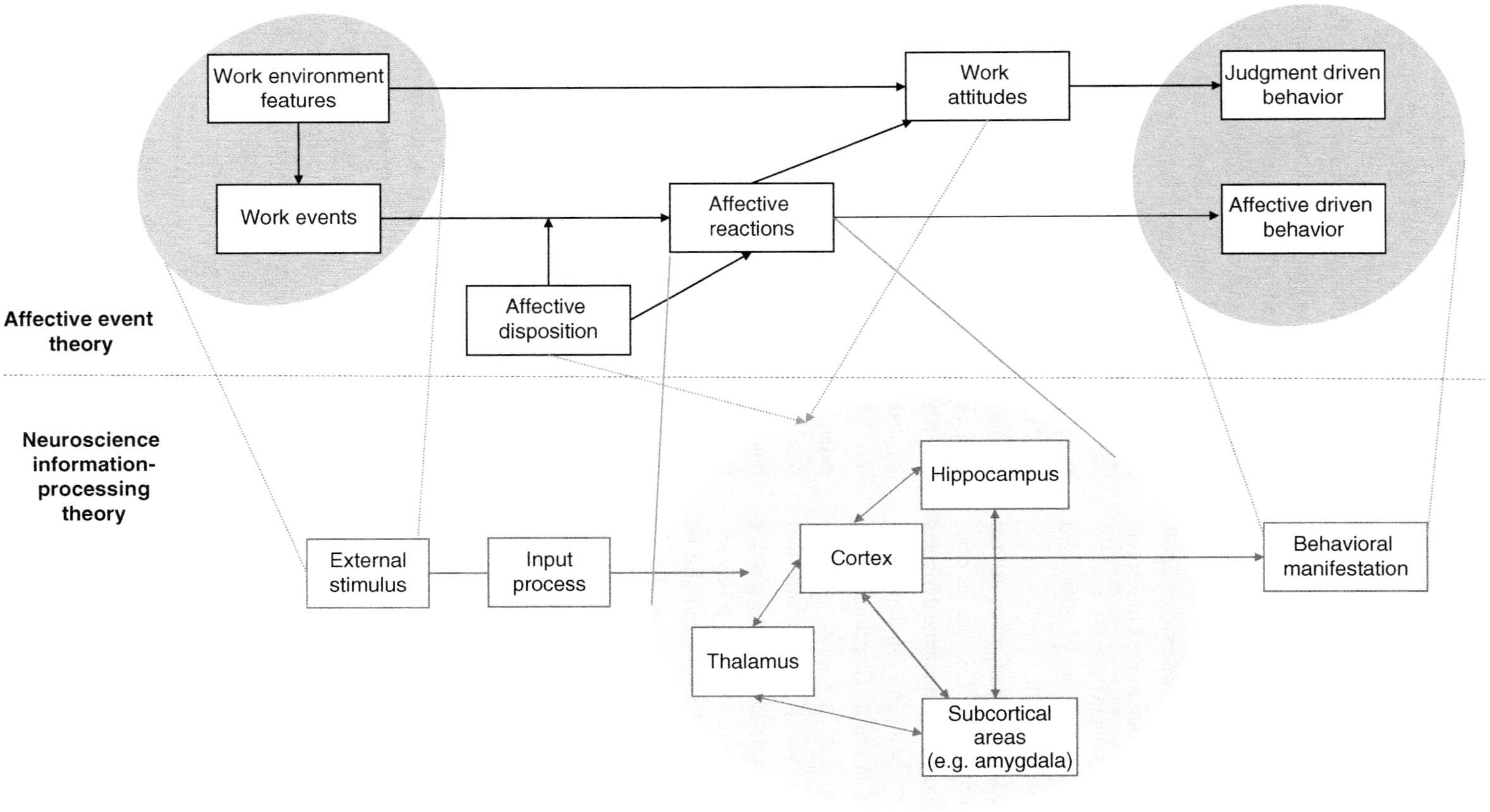

Figure 2.2 Integration of affective event theory (Weiss & Cropanzano, 1996) with an organizational neuroscience perspective to disentangle the core brain structures and mechanisms involved in "affective reactions"

affective reactions. Indeed, contemporary neuroscience research contends that affective responses are mental representations that prepare the organism for certain behaviors, usually associated with survival value (Lane & Nadel, 1999). This concept follows the evidence, generalizable beyond research on emotions, that the brain works as an information processing system for external stimuli through a series of complex anatomic and physiological interconnections. These circuits are genetically predetermined to respond to external stimuli, and connections are reciprocal; they rely on both feedback and feedforward patterns (Tau & Peterson, 2010).

At its simplest, the starting point, much like the focus on affective events in AET, is that an emotionally salient stimulus in the environment triggers an input process for the brain. We can think about a discrete event, say an unjust happening in the workplace (Barsky & Kaplan, 2007), a recollection of that occasion, or even a cognition of something emotionally weighted taking place in the organization. Affective mental processes, including perceptions and judgments, can also be subconsciously activated (Chartrand & Bargh, 2002; Higgins, 1996) as responses to biologically significant triggers (e.g. threats, primary needs, associational cues) through our sensorial or cognitive pathways (e.g. attention, memory, perception). This insight is already significant for ON research because it provides neurobiological support for the analysis of both conscious emotions (i.e. the subjective feeling of the evaluation and appraisal of an affective event) and implicit or unconscious emotions (i.e. the detection of a potential stimulus) (Barsade, Ramarajan, & Westen, 2009). Moreover, it supports the idea that emotional climates in organizations (e.g. stressful administrations, toxic workplaces) can implicitly influence employees' affective reactions and ultimately their organizational behaviors by acting at the subconscious level (Carr, Schmidt, Ford, & DeShon, 2003; Chartrand & Bargh, 2002).

In the brain, information is carried through the sensory cortex and then routed into the thalamus for processing and, simultaneously, to other specialized cortical structures for further processing (e.g. occipital and temporal lobes). The thalamus is an integrative structure of the brain that plays a major role in regulating arousal, circadian rhythm, and, through the thalamo-cortico-thalamic circuit, human consciousness (Jones, 2012).

The information is also routed to other subcortical areas. Pioneering work by Papez (1937) and MacLean (1952) suggests that emotions are located in a group of subcortical structures called the "limbic system" (MacLean, 1952).[1] In particular, within these limbic areas, information reaching the amygdalae promotes the release of hormonal responses through the pituitary system, leads to autonomic activations through the brain stem, and, through the basal forebrain, supports mechanisms of arousal (LeDoux, 2000, who also gives a fuller account of emotion circuits in the brain). These relays are essential because they promote adaptive bodily (i.e. hormonal, autonomic, and neuromodulatory) and behavioral reactions preparing the organism to respond to the stimulus (Phelps, 2009).

Processed information is thus sent to the hippocampus, entering into the memory system to be organized, disseminated, and associated with the cortical areas related to long-term retention. Together with one's unique background, this information shapes affective traits and attitudes (Ekman & Davidson, 1994). This state of neuroscience knowledge may help refine organizational theory on affect by suggesting a neurobiological mechanism of interaction between the processing of new information from the environment and existing internal information stored in the memory. Moreover, this knowledge

[1] Current affective neuroscience has allowed research to move from a global view on emotions to recognizing distinctive aspects of each emotion, each forming a part of its own circuit and a different part of the traditional limbic circuit (Ward, 2010).

can support further investigations on the interplay between one's affective reactions, dispositions, and attitudes in the workplace (e.g. Thoresen, Kaplan, Barsky, Warren, & de Chermont, 2003).

Finally, following evaluation of the significance of the affective stimulus, modulation of the automatic behavior, cognitive appraisal, and associated decision processes, the brain produces a final response: actual decision, normally involving the prefrontal cortex, as well as parallel and associated motor responses involving the motor cortex (Adolphs & Damasio, 2001). Once again, this process proves relevant to workplace research because it suggests that emotions and higher-level cognition are highly interrelated processes requiring overlapping neural systems. Thus changes in cognitive abilities necessarily relate to changes in emotion, and vice versa. Organizational research should then investigate them in conjunction.

Neuroscience research has proposed several integrative theories of emotions (e.g. LeDoux, 2000), including the "somatic marker hypothesis" (Damasio, 1996), a theory evolutionarily grounded and generalizable across emotional events. This theory holds that when a person is confronted with emotional stimuli, both the brain and the body change. Somatic markers are thus internal bodily states connected to external events that influence cognitive processing. This insight is important to guide ON research because it supports predictions that variations in the intensity of bodily reactions to a stimulus are markers of the intensity of emotions. Put in other terms, by appreciating neural and physiological responses, organizational researchers can open a window to observe and assess the affective reactions of professionals.

Between Affective Neuroscience and Workplace Affect Research

Having explained the processing mechanism of affective events in the brain, I now review neuroscience knowledge relevant to workplace affect research. In line with the most recent accounts of emotions in ON (Haley, Hodgkinson, & Massaro, 2018), I organize this evidence in the areas of intra- and inter-individual emotions. Specifically, I present evidence related to basic emotions, complex intra-individual affective processes, and inter-individual social emotions. As often occurs in neuroscience and ON, this is not a fixed categorization, but rather a pragmatic device to organize current knowledge.

Basic Emotions

A widely accepted understanding of emotions is that they are affective states focused on a specific target or cause, are short-lived and intense, and entail a range of synchronized features and neurophysiological responses (Ekman, 1992; Phelps, 2009). The so-called basic emotions (also known as primary) represent the most common categorization in both neuroscience (e.g. Ortony & Turner, 1990) and organizational scholarship (e.g. Elfenbein, 2007). Despite debates about the actual number of basic emotions (e.g. Plutchik, 1980), Ekman's original research (Ekman, Friesen, & Ellsworth, 1971) acknowledges six cross-cultural emotions (see also Ekman, 1994), that can be encoded through facial expressions. These emotions are anger, disgust, fear, sadness, happiness, and surprise. As we shall now see, each presents characteristic neural circuitry and correlates (Lindquist, Wager, Kober, Bliss-Moreau, & Barrett, 2012, who also provide a meta-analysis). Understanding their neural correlates and mechanisms is particularly important for workplace research because it would answer calls for higher specificity in empirical research on emotions when investigating affective states that are generalizable across organizations and their actors (e.g. Barsade et al., 2003).

Anger

Organizational research has increasingly explored anger as a key emotion to explain workplace phenomena (e.g. Geddes & Callister, 2007). Intriguingly, research has reported both negative outcomes from anger expression – such as reduced productivity and job satisfaction, increased job stress, and mutual comebacks (Friedman, Anderson, Brett, et al., 2004; Glomb, 2002) – and positive ones. For instance, anger has been found to drive problem solving, promote mutual understanding, fuel work motivation, and improve attitudes, and it may offer competitive advantage by fostering an adaptive drive for competition and learning (Gibson & Callister, 2010; Fitness, 2000; Kiefer, 2002). Given this imbalance and the ongoing discussion about the theorizing of anger in the workplace (Geddes & Callister, 2007), researchers have supported the use of neuroscience methods as "essential to begin to capture more objectively how anger is experienced and expressed" (Gibson & Callister, 2010, p. 19; also provides a review).

Identifying the neural foundations of anger has, however, proven difficult: meta-analytical evidence shows that the medial and ventromedial and lateral prefrontal cortex (PFC), the anterior and posterior cingulate cortex, and the thalamus all play critical roles in the neural circuitry (Murphy, Nimmo-Smith, & Lawrence, 2003; Phan, Wager, Taylor, & Liberzon, 2002).

More recently, Denson, Pedersen, Ronquillo, and Nandy (2009) have investigated the neural correlates of anger in an experiment in which they elicited anger by addressing participants in an insulting manner; this induction was then followed by an fMRI session. The researchers found that self-reported feelings of anger, but of no other emotion, positively correlated with activation in the left dorsal anterior cingulate cortex. Moreover, general aggression was associated with increased activity in the left dorsal anterior cingulate cortex, but displaced aggression was not; instead, displaced aggression was significantly associated with increased activity in the medial prefrontal cortex. Extending these results, Blair (2012) investigated reactive aggression to suggest that the prefrontal cortex moderates such circuits in the presence of anger.

Moving beyond brain imaging, electromyography (EMG) has been used to measure facial markers of anger. Dynamic expressions induce EMG activity interpretable as facial mimicry more evidently than in cases of static expressions (Sato, Fujimura, & Suzuki, 2008). Moreover, HRV has been proposed as a key correlate of adaptive emotion regulation in response to anger (Denson, Grisham, & Moulds, 2011). A recent ON study uses the Prisoner's Dilemma framework to show that elicited anger in research participants reduces their cooperation, their individual monetary gains, and their global aggregated performance relative to control conditions (Castagnetti, Massaro, & Proto, 2018). This evidence can be explained through a mechanism of anger-induced emotional regulation, which is accurately traceable through depression of HRV high-frequency bands.

Disgust

Disgust is a response of refusal toward something or someone potentially harmful, nasty, or unpleasant. It has been theorized as a withdrawal emotion (Rozin & Fallon, 1987), and is also often presented as one of our "hardwired" emotions; disgust would have evolved as a response to unpleasant foods that could be a potential source of harm (Wicker, Keysers, Plailly, et al., 2003). Perhaps because disgust is habitually associated with taste and other such primary senses, it has rarely been investigated in organizational research.

One notable exception is Pelzer (2002), who argues that disgust is the most severe reaction to negative perceptions occurring in organizational life. Specifically, such an effect is morally salient as constituting "a revolt of the body against a perception of something unacceptable, harmful, damaging, poisoning" (p. 841). Further supporting this concept, research shows that people tend to react to certain moral violations with a sense of disgust (e.g. Skarlicki, Hoegg, Aquino, & Nadisic, 2013).

By providing a direct example of the usefulness of ON, Cropanzano, Massaro, and Becker (2017) present disgust as an emotion involved in deontic justice, a key driver of workplace fairness (Cropanzano, Goldman, & Folger, 2003), suggesting that the insula – a small region of the cortex hidden behind the temporal lobes – is a core site for the existence of "justice rules." This evidence resonates with mainstream neuroscience research: Mataix-Cols, An, Lawrence, et al. (2008) show that the anterior part of the insula is activated in response to facial expressions of disgust. Moreover, Moll, de Oliveira-Souza, Moll, et al. (2005) reveal that the experience of disgust, when dissociated into "pure disgust" as opposed to "moral indignation," recruits both the frontal and temporal lobes. This evidence supports the role of the prefrontal cortex in moral judgment and may be helpful to integrate the most recent scholarship on justice arguing that disgust sensitivity is a strong predictor of extreme deontic judgment (Robinson, Xu, & Plax, 2018).

The key involvement of the insula in disgust has been confirmed by several other methodological perspectives. For instance, Calder, Keane, Manes, Antoun, and Young (2000) show that lesions on the anterior insula indicate deficits in the experience of disgust, and electrical stimulation of the anterior insula during neurosurgery triggered nausea – a strong marker of disgust (Jones, Ward, & Critchley, 2010). Moreover, the insula is thought to be a core site for interoception, one's perception of the body's internal state, which is a construct strongly associated with the cognitive processing of emotional awareness (Barrett & Simmons, 2015).

While the insula is center stage in the neural circuit for disgust, it is also worth mentioning that Phan et al. (2002) conducted a meta-analysis of PET and fMRI activation studies, showing that disgust can be associated with the subcallosal basal ganglia, a region of the brain generally involved in motor functional coordination. Sprengelmeyer, Rausch, Eysel, and Przuntek (1998) argue that the activations seen in the basal ganglia in response to disgust may represent a state of preparedness triggered by a warning stimulus to process emotionally salient information. Thus in organizational settings, the basal ganglia may play a key role for workers in arranging appropriate "affective responses" toward emotional events (Panksepp, 1998). Future researchers in ON might find it valuable to consider these regions, probably in conjunction with the insula, as candidate areas to explain violations of organizational values such as fairness, trust, and justice (Massaro & Becker, 2015).

Fear

Fear is probably the most investigated emotion in neuroscience. Its core neural circuit develops around the amygdala (LeDoux, 2003). Phan et al. (2002) show that nearly 60 percent of fear induction studies report activation in the amygdala. The amygdala has been implicated in the recognition of fearful facial expressions (Adolphs, Tranel, Damasio, & Damasio, 1995), in fear conditioning (Bechara, Tranel, Damasio, et al., 1995; LaBar, LeDoux, Spencer, & Phelps, 1995), and in the evocation of fearful emotional responses from direct stimulation (Halgren, Walter, Cherlow, & Crandall, 1978). The amygdala also appears to be crucial in the detection and coordination of appropriate responses to threat and danger (Amaral, 2002).

Yet one major cross-disciplinary challenge in affective research is the ability to reliably distinguish fear and anger (Stemmler, Heldmann, Pauls, & Scherer, 2001). To tackle this issue, Whalen, Shin, McInerney, et al. (2001) compared neural activation of fearful, angry, and neutral faces, to find that the ventral amygdala shows higher activity when facing a condition with a negative valence (i.e. fearful or angry) in comparison to the control condition; yet when the fearful and angry face conditions were equated, the dorsal amygdala was activated only in the former.

Moving to analyses of the wider nervous system, studies on fear have also identified an extensive pattern of sympathetic activations (Kreibig, 2010). Fear-associated responses show unique cardiac sympatho-vagal activation and withdrawal dynamics (Rainville, Bechara, Naqvi, & Damasio, 2006), indicating that these features can be used as autonomic biomarkers for this basic emotion. The increasing specificity of these findings suggests that in organizational research, anger, which is often difficult to dissociate from other negative emotions following induction procedures (i.e. video or picture stimuli, or memory recollections; see also Phelps, 2009), can be discerned by a concomitant assessment of subjects' neurophysiological correlates. This opportunity is of particular relevance for ON, given the increasing availability of portable tools that assess peripheral measures readily applicable to organizational investigations.

Sadness

Sadness is another relevant emotion for the workplace. It is associated with absenteeism (Porath & Pearson, 2012), but also with increased organizational citizenship behavior and workplace deviance (Lee & Allen, 2002). In leadership, Lewis (2000) reveals that followers facing a "sad leader" felt less enthusiasm and more fatigue compared to those observing a leader expressing anger or no emotion.

In neuroscience, sadness induction studies generally report activation in the cingulate cortex (e.g. Barrett, Pike, & Paus, 2004). Specifically, Liotti, Mayberg, Brannan, et al. (2000) show that sadness induces activity in the anterior cingulate cortex. In recent years, this brain region has become an important topic of research because it involves specific processing modules for both cognitive and emotional information and integrates input representations from cognitive and emotional networks (Bush, Luu, & Posner, 2000). Anatomical and brain-mapping studies support the distinction between a cognitive–affective division of the cingulate. The presence of a dorsal-cognitive and rostral-ventral-affective division may thus promote research seeking to further understand the interactions between cognition and emotion associated with sadness (Lane, Reiman, Axelrod, et al., 1998). Research shows that the dorsal division signals the occurrence of conflicts in information processing, thereby triggering compensatory adjustments in cognitive control; this signaling regulates cognitive control to prevent further conflicting appraisals (see Bush et al., 2000).

Finally, of particular impact for organizational behavior research on the role of rewards in motivating employees (e.g. Wiersma, 1992), Gehring and Willoughby (2002) find that the cingulate engages when research participants were told the outcomes of their decisions in a gambling task, indicating that this region is susceptible to aversive results related to external reward. This function could thus work following a cost–benefit evaluation that integrates information about outcomes of past actions and present environmental requests (Rushworth & Behrens, 2008).

Happiness

The neuroscience of positive emotions has only recently received scientific attention (Burgdorf & Panksepp, 2006). Biological theories suggest that there may be several distinct forms of positive emotions, but all are closely related to subneocortical brain regions: happiness seems to engage a widely distributed neural network (Ward, 2015). In one of the early functional imaging studies of happiness, George, Ketter, Parekh, et al. (1995) investigated the brain activity of healthy women during transient sadness and happiness using PET. The participants were required to recall life events that they found happy, sad, and neutral; they were also presented happy, sad, or neutral human faces. Happiness was associated with significant and widespread reductions in cortical cerebrovascular flow, especially in the right prefrontal and bilateral temporal-parietal regions. Adding to this body of knowledge, Sato, Kochiyama, Uono, et al. (2015) investigated the structural neural substrate of happiness and found a positive relationship between a score of subjective happiness and gray matter volume in the right precuneus, suggesting that this area mediates subjective happiness by integrating its emotional and cognitive components.

Over the years, neuroimaging research has consistently shown that the ventral striatum and putamen respond to presentation of happy faces (e.g. Whalen, Rauch, Etcoff, et al., 1998), pleasant pictures (e.g. Davidson & Irwin, 1999), and competitive and sexual arousal (Rauch, Shin, Dougherty, et al., 1999). These areas are characterized by rich innervations of dopaminergic neurons, which respond to incentive reward and motivation toward reaching planned goals (Telzer, 2016). This convergence represents a useful insight for the growing body of organizational research exploring the causal links between happiness, employees' rewards, and organizational behavior outputs (e.g. Lyubomirsky, King, & Diener, 2005; Ryan & Deci, 2001).

Surprise

There is growing evidence suggesting that dopaminergic systems in the brain are recruited in anticipatory positive affective states. Moreover, research has shown that the amygdala's central nucleus, the cholinergic neurons of the nucleus basalis, and their innervation of the posterior parietal cortex are critical to surprise enhancements in associative learning (Wessel, Danielmeier, Morton, & Ullsperger, 2012). Wessel et al. have investigated the neural sites of surprise by administering an error-monitoring/novelty-oddball task in which the frequency of new surprising trials was matched to the frequency of errors. Combining electroencephalographic recordings and event-related functional magnetic resonance imaging (fMRI), they compared neural responses to errors with neural responses to novel events, revealing increased activity in the posterior medial frontal cortex and anterior midcingulate.

This evidence suggests strong associations between awareness of surprising events and associative learning, as processes mediated by shared neural systems. Thus these findings could further knowledge in organizational research on the way in which surprising situations, such as a newcomer's entry experience (Louis, 1980) or a person-environment fit (Caplan, 1987), influence employees' learning. In the future, on the practical side, this knowledge could also allow for the formulating of surprise-eliciting "nudges" as possible interventions to improve organizational learning.

Intra-individual Emotional Processes

While studies on basic emotions have been one of the most visible backers of affective neuroscience, research has also focused on bettering our understanding of the complexity surrounding individuals' emotional experiences (Panksepp, 1998). While it is not possible to provide a full account of this emerging research stream, I mention here three areas worthy of attention for research in the workplace.

Emotional intensity and valence

The individual propensity to respond, more or less intensively, to affect-related events is an important area of workplace affect research. For example, den Bos, Maas, Waldring, and Semin (2003) show that people high in affect intensity display robust affective responses after experiencing outcome and procedural fairness. However, when affect intensity is low there are marginal fairness effects. This evidence suggests that affect intensity may play a fundamental role in the psychology of affective reactions to unfair events, offering generalization to several contextual and organizational circumstances (den Bos et al., 2003). Thus, advancing knowledge on why and in what ways people differently weigh their emotions is a compelling and timely ambition.

Neuroscience has provided important insights into how strongly people feel their emotions (e.g. Cooper & Knutson, 2008). For example, Ewbank, Barnard, Croucher, Ramponi, and Calder (2009) suggest that the amygdala's response to emotional stimuli is not a function of valence alone, but also a function of the stimuli's significance. In an fMRI experiment, these authors find that the left amygdala has a significantly larger response to high-impact stimuli than to neutral and low-impact ones. This finding is significant because it shows the discriminatory potential of neuroimaging in assessing salience of affective states, and might thus be useful for enriching organizational research looking at unraveling this aspect (e.g. Rafaeli & Sutton, 1989).

Adding to this knowledge, Cunningham, Van Bavel, and Johnsen (2008) provide fMRI evidence that the relation between affective valence and the amygdala's activity can be modulated by evaluative goals. When research participants were asked to provide affective evaluations on facial stimuli, the amygdala's modulation was more pronounced for positive than for negative information. Altogether, this evidence supports the view that our brain systems process both intensity and valence of emotional information in a flexible manner.

Complex emotions

Affective neuroimaging research has produced a growing number of studies on self-conscious emotions, those emotions that are evoked when a person reflects on their self or evaluates their self in relation to the environment (Lewis, 1993). These processes can occur implicitly or explicitly and require the capacity for introspection and self-knowledge leading to complex emotions such as regret, guilt, shame, embarrassment, and pride (Müller-Pinzler, Krach, Krämer, & Paulus, 2016). Importantly for ON, these emotions can drive immediate punishment or reinforcement of behavioral outcomes, and therefore can motivate social behavior, which in turn helps to retain social structures (Tangney, Stuewig, & Mashek, 2007). Within this domain, research on regret has offered a landmark example to investigate the involvement of the orbitofrontal cortex and of the amygdala during choice, when the brain is anticipating possible future consequences (i.e. anticipated regret; Coricelli, Dolan, & Sirigu, 2007).

Emotional regulation

A growing stream of research in affective neuroscience concerns the mechanisms of emotional regulation, which are widely acknowledged constructs related to emotional labor (Grandey, 2000). Neuroscience research has recently shown that emotional regulation includes a series of complex processes such as reappraisal, selective attention, and emotional extinction, each featuring distinct neural correlates (see for review Dunsmoor, Niv, Daw, & Phelps, 2015; Ochsner & Gross, 2005).

Braunstein, Gross, and Oschner (2017) cluster these mechanisms into four categories: explicit-controlled; implicit-controlled; explicit-automatic; and implicit-automatic regulation strategies. These clusters are based on a neuroscience-driven analysis of the orthogonal dimensions explicit–implicit, which accounts for the regulation targets, and controlled–automatic, which instead covers the nature of the emotional process at stake. Thus, a placebo mechanism is an explicit-automatic process that recruits both the ventromedial and dorsolateral prefrontal cortex (Wager & Atlas, 2015), whereas emotional extinction is an implicit-automatic process recruiting the ventromedial prefrontal cortex alone (Phelps, Delgado, Nearing, & LeDoux, 2004). Comparatively, reappraisal, selective attention, and distraction belong to the explicit-controlled cluster and involve the prefrontal cortex, inferior parietal gyrus, and dorsal anterior cingulate cortex (Ochsner, Bunge, Gross, & Gabrieli, 2002; Van Dillen, Heslenfeld, & Koole, 2009). Finally, implicit-controlled regulation strategies, such as affective labeling, automatic goal pursuit, and reversal learning, involve ventromedial and postero-medial prefrontal cortex and the dorsal anterior cingulate cortex (Buhle, Silvers, Wager, et al., 2014; Lieberman, 2007).

This framework suggests the possibility of recognizing emotional regulation mechanisms on the basis of different activations in the neural systems involved. Moreover, it provides the opportunity to form hypotheses and predictions about the influence of situational and workplace factors on emotional regulation strategies. For instance, stress can impair explicit-controlled regulation by impairing optimal prefrontal functioning (Arnsten, 2009). Thus, as Braunstein et al. (2017) argue, it is also possible to deduce that implicit-automatic emotional regulation strategies would not be as impacted by stress because stress reinforces non-prefrontal dependent responses.

Interpersonal and Social Emotions

Affective neuroscience research is often accompanied by investigations in the social domain. Charles Darwin (1896) suggested that emotional expressions evolved both as a means of social communication and to determine others' intentions. Indeed, recognizing the emotional states of others is a critical component of social interactions, because we use our emotional responses to regulate our behavior toward others. An interpersonal ON perspective on emotions is thus useful when moving from investigations of individual actors to those on dyads, teams, or groups, where workers can experience emotions related to and interconnected with those around them.

Emotional contagion, affective empathy, and theory of mind

The way in which individuals represent the emotional states of others has been a major area of interest for both organizational scholars (e.g. Barsade, 2002; Kellett, Humphrey, & Sleeth, 2002; Hareli, & Rafaeli, 2008) and neuroscience scholars (e.g. Ruby & Decety, 2004). Neuroscience research has proposed that three main systems, supported by partially separable neural circuits, are involved in our capacity to understand other people's emotions (Singer, 2009).

Emotional contagion The first system concerns our ability to understand others' motor intentions and action goals. This system is often associated to mirror neurons (see Gallese & Goldman, 1998). Mirror neurons represent a cluster of premotor cortex neurons observed in monkeys to "fire" when they either perform goal-related movements or watch others, including humans, doing the same (Rizzolatti & Craighero, 2004). Correspondingly, research has shown evidence for the possible existence of mirror neurons in humans. While there has been intense debate on the topic (Keysers, 2009), research has shown that in humans the inferior frontal cortex and the anterior cingulate respond when a person sees another one experiencing an emotion, leading to the idea that those areas could be the neural sites for emotional contagion (Keysers & Gazzola, 2006).

Affective empathy According to Kanske, Böckler, Trautwein, and Singer (2015), there are two further neural systems that can help individuals to understand the emotions of others. One route, known as the affective route or simulation theory, involves the direct ability to imitate and thus understand others' emotions and results in empathy. This route generally involves the anterior insula and middle anterior cingulate cortex. Neuroscience research suggests that empathy represents the first step of a succession that begins with affect sharing, a subsequent imitation of another person's feelings, which may then motivate other-related concerns, including engagement in helping behavior (Singer, 2009). Moreover, observation of this process enables us to detach affective empathy from the closely linked process of emotional contagion, the phenomenon of having one person's emotions and related behavior directly trigger similar patterns in other people (Barsade, 2002). Differently from empathy, in the latter casea person would not realize that the other's emotions were the trigger: emotional contagion would not be an empathic response as such.

Neuroscience research has also converged around the idea that there is an underlying mechanism of shared brain networks which give humans the ability to empathize (Decety, 2010). Intriguingly, when investigating the neural substrates of empathy neuroscientists tend to use paradigms in which both the participant and a confederate received painful stimulations: Singer, Seymour, O'Doherty, et al. (2004) found an overlap between the receiving and observing conditions in various brain areas, including the bilateral anterior insulae and middle anterior cingulate cortex.

Theory of mind The third mechanism requires people representing and reasoning about others' beliefs and thoughts, a process referred to as mentalizing or theory of mind (ToM). This path involves the ventral temporoparietal junction, along with anterior and posterior midline regions (Dodell-Feder, Koster-Hale, Bedny, & Saxe, 2011). A meta-analysis by Bzdok, Schilbach, Vogeley, et al. (2012), which investigated the neural networks activated during ToM, supports these findings. Moreover, Schurz, Radua, Aichhorn, Richlan, and Perner (2014) find that the temporoparietal junction and medial prefrontal cortex are consistently activated in ToM. Importantly, however, while these networks form the basis of ToM, differentiated patterns within the overall network are engaged during different tasks. For example, there are specific activation clusters for false-belief tasks, wherein the temporo-parietal junction is activated (Aichhorn, Perner, Weiss, et al., 2009), and for rational action judgment tasks, wherein the paracingulate cortex is activated (Walter, Adenzato, Ciaramidaro, et al., 2004).

This point is particularly germane for ON, given that one frequent criticism of the ON perspective is that experimental neuroscience paradigms often rely on situations fixed a priori and not based on the real world. Indirectly tackling this concern, Wolf, Dziobek, and Heekeren (2010) investigated ToM in close to real-life conditions by using a paradigm that involves the video-based "Movie for the Assessment of Social Cognition" (Dziobek, Fleck, Kalbe, et al., 2006). In this study, the authors show that brain areas such as the superior temporal sulcus, temporoparietal junction, medial prefrontal cortex, temporal poles, and precuneus are activated depending on the task's components. Thus, face processing and recognition activate the occipito-parietotemporal cortices; language comprehension activates the temporal lobes, lateral prefrontal cortex, and precuneus; and self-awareness activates the dorsomedial prefrontal cortex and the precuneus.

Emotional intelligence and leadership

Emotional intelligence (EI) represents a consistent focal point for research in the workplace (e.g. Law, Wong, & Song 2004). Although the neural substrates of EI are still largely unknown, it is recognized that the prefrontal cortex may play a crucial role. For instance, Kruger, Barbey, McCabe, et al. (2009) studied a unique sample of combat veterans in order to examine strategic and experiential EI. They find that these capabilities depend on distinct neural correlates. Ventromedial PFC damage diminishes strategic EI and thus obstructs the understanding of emotional information; dorsolateral PFC damage diminishes experiential EI, impairing the perception and integration of emotional information. These findings are relevant for ON research because they suggest that EI should be investigated under its individual components and in conjunction with cognitive intelligence.

Finally, the most developed area in ON, which has also shown implications for emotional research, concerns leadership (e.g. Antonakis, Ashkanasy, & Dasborough, 2009). Largely concentrated in the work by Waldman and colleagues, and in the use of qEEG (Waldman, Balthazard, & Peterson, 2011), a rich body of research in neuroleadership has bloomed over the last few years. Of relevance for this work's purpose, these researchers have suggested that qEEG coherence measurements can be an optimal means of examining those leadership behaviors that are likely to require an interface between the brain's emotional and cognitive systems (Cacioppo, Berntson, & Nusbaum, 2008). Specifically, they report that the presence of high coherence in the right hemisphere of leaders' brains could imply greater emotional balance and ToM (Thatcher, North, & Biver, 2007).

Closing Thoughts and Future Research

In this chapter I undertook an ON approach to investigate the thriving and multifaceted domain of workplace affect, arguing that neuroscience can provide a substantial step toward furthering research on emotions in organizational studies. Notwithstanding the multitude of organizational and neuroscience research on affect, which could only be summarized here, and the important headway that neuroscience has made in the past two decades, many questions at the interface between these two fields remain unanswered. For instance, how can organizational research on cognition further integrate the evidence coming from affective neuroscience? What kinds of employees are most susceptible to grasping others' emotions, and can this capacity be "mapped" neurophysiologically? Are dual-system accounts of behavior in management adequate to fully capture the complexity of affectivity in the workplace? Can neurofeedback help workers learn to be more in tune with others' emotions, helping to create improved organizational climates? These are just some of the intriguing questions that are likely to populate future ON research on emotions.

References

Adolphs, R., & Damasio, A. R. (2001). The interaction of affect and cognition: A neurobiological perspective. In J. P. Forgas (Ed.), *Handbook of affect and social cognition* (pp. 27–49). Mahwah, NJ: Lawrence Erlbaum.

Adolphs, R., Tranel, D., Damasio, H., & Damasio, A. R. (1995). Fear and the human amygdala. *Journal of Neuroscience, 15*, 5879–5891.

Ahlfors, S. P., & Mody, M. (2019). Overview of MEG. *Organizational Research Methods, 22*, 95–115.

Aichhorn, M., Perner, J., Weiss, B., Kronbichler, M., Staffen, W., & Ladurner, G. (2009). Temporo–parietal junction activity in theory–of–mind tasks: Falseness, beliefs, or attention. *Journal of Cognitive Neuroscience, 21*, 1179–1192.

Aine, C. J. (1995). A conceptual overview and critique of functional neuroimaging techniques in humans: I. MRI/FMRI and PET. *Critical Reviews in Neurobiology, 9*, 229–309.

Amaral, D. G. (2002). The primate amygdala and the neurobiology of social behavior: Implications for understanding social anxiety. *Biological Psychiatry, 51*, 11–17.

Antonakis, J., Ashkanasy, N. M., & Dasborough, M. T. (2009). Does leadership need emotional intelligence? *Leadership Quarterly, 20*, 247–261.

Arnsten, A. F. (2009). Stress signalling pathways that impair prefrontal cortex structure and function. *Nature Reviews Neuroscience, 10*, 410–422.

Ashkanasy, N. M. (2003a). Emotions in organizations: A multilevel perspective. In F. Dansereau & F. J. Yammarino (Eds.), *Research in multi–level issues* (pp. 9–54). Oxford, UK: Elsevier/JAI.

Ashkanasy, N. M. (2003b). Emotions at multiple levels: An integration. In F. Dansereau & F. J. Yammarino (Eds.), *Research in multi–level issues* (pp.71–81). Oxford, UK: Elsevier/JAI.

Ashkanasy, N. M., & Humphrey, R. H. (2011). Current emotion research in organizational behavior. *Emotion Review, 3*, 214–224.

Ashkanasy, N. M., Becker, W. J., & Waldman, D. A. (2014). Neuroscience and organizational behavior: Avoiding both neuro-euphoria and neuro-phobia. *Journal of Organizational Behavior, 35*, 909–919.

Barrett, J., Pike, G. B., & Paus, T. (2004). The role of the anterior cingulate cortex in pitch variation during sad affect. *European Journal of Neuroscience, 19*, 458–464.

Barrett, L. F., & Simmons, W. K. (2015). Interoceptive predictions in the brain. *Nature Reviews Neuroscience*, *16*, 419–429.

Barsade, S. G. (2002). The ripple effect: Emotional contagion and its influence on group behavior. *Administrative Science Quarterly*, *47*, 644–675.

Barsade, S. G., & Gibson, D. E. (2007). Why does affect matter in organizations? *Academy of Management Perspectives*, *21*, 36–59.

Barsade, S. G., Brief, A. P., & Spataro, S. E. (2003). The affective revolution in organizational behavior: The emergence of a paradigm. In J. Greenberg (Ed.), *Organizational behavior: The state of the science* (pp. 3–52). Hillsdale, NJ: Erlbaum.

Barsade, S. G., Ramarajan, L., & Westen, D. (2009). Implicit affect in organizations. *Research in Organizational Behavior*, *29*, 135–162.

Barsky, A., & Kaplan, S. A. (2007). If you feel bad, it's unfair: A quantitative synthesis of affect and organizational justice perceptions. *Journal of Applied Psychology*, *92*, 286–295.

Beal, D., Weiss, H., Barros, E., & MacDermid, S. (2005). An episodic process model of affective influences on performance. *Journal of Applied Psychology*, *90*, 1054–1068.

Bechara, A., Tranel, D., Damasio, H., Adolphs, R., Rockland, C., & Damasio, A. R. (1995). Double dissociation of conditioning and declarative knowledge relative to the amygdala and hippocampus in humans. *Science*, *269*, 1115–1118.

Becker, W. J., & Cropanzano, R. (2010). Organizational neuroscience: The promise and prospects of an emerging discipline. *Journal of Organizational Behavior*, *31*, 1055–1059.

Becker, W. J., Cropanzano, R., & Sanfey, A. G. (2011). Organizational neuroscience: Taking organizational theory inside the neural black box. *Journal of Management*, *37*, 933–961.

Becker, W. J., & Menges, J. I. (2013). Biological implicit measures in HRM and OB: A question of how not if. *Human Resource Management Review*, *23*, 219–228.

Blair, R. J. R. (2012). Considering anger from a cognitive neuroscience perspective. *Wiley Interdisciplinary Reviews: Cognitive Science*, *3*, 65–74.

Braunstein, L. M., Gross, J. J., & Ochsner, K. N. (2017). Explicit and implicit emotion regulation: a multi–level framework. *Social Cognitive and Affective Neuroscience*, *12*, 1545–1557.

Brief, A. P., & Weiss, H. M. (2002). Organizational behavior: Affect in the workplace. *Annual Review of Psychology*, *53*, 279–307.

Briner, R. B., & Kiefer, T. (2005). Psychological research into the experience of emotion at work: Definitely older, but are we any wiser? In N. M. Ashkanasy, C. E. J. Hartel, & W. J. Zerbe (Eds.), *The effects of affect in organizational settings* (pp. 281–307). Bingley, UK: Emerald.

Buhle, J. T., Silvers, J. A., Wager, T. D., Lopez, R., Onyemekwu, C., Kober, H., . . . & Ochsner, K. N. (2014). Cognitive reappraisal of emotion: A meta-analysis of human neuroimaging studies. *Cerebral Cortex*, *24*, 2981–2990.

Burgdorf, J., & Panksepp, J. (2006). The neurobiology of positive emotions. *Neuroscience & Biobehavioral Reviews*, *30*, 173–187.

Bush, G., Luu, P., & Posner, M. I. (2000). Cognitive and emotional influences in anterior cingulate cortex. *Trends in Cognitive Sciences*, *4*, 215–222.

Bzdok, D., Schilbach, L., Vogeley, K., Schneider, K., Laird, A. R., Langner, R., & Eickhoff, S. B. (2012). Parsing the neural correlates of moral cognition: ALE meta–analysis on morality, theory of mind, and empathy. *Brain Structure and Function*, *217*, 783–796.

Cabeza, R., & Nyberg, L. (2000). Imaging cognition II: An empirical review of 275 PET and fMRI studies. *Journal of Cognitive Neuroscience*, *12*, 1–47.

Cacioppo, J. T., Berntson, G. G., & Nusbaum, H. C. (2008). Neuroimaging as a new tool in the toolbox of psychological science. *Current Directions in Psychological Science*, *17*, 62–67.

Cacioppo, J. T., Berntson, G. G., Sheridan, J. F., & McClintock, M. K. (2000). Multilevel integrative analyses of human behavior: Social neuroscience and the complementing nature of social and biological approaches. *Psychological Bulletin*, *126*, 829–843.

Calder, A. J., Keane, J., Manes, F., Antoun, N., & Young, A. W. (2000). Impaired recognition and experience of disgust following brain injury. *Nature Neuroscience*, *3*, 1077–1078.

Caplan, R. D. (1987). Person–environment fit theory and organizations: Commensurate dimensions, time perspectives, and mechanisms. *Journal of Vocational Behavior, 31*, 248–267.

Carr, J. Z., Schmidt, A. M., Ford, J. K., & DeShon, R. P. (2003). Climate perceptions matter: A meta–analytic path analysis relating molar climate, cognitive and affective states, and individual level work outcomes. *Journal of Applied Psychology, 88*, 605–619.

Castagnetti, S. A., Massaro, S., & Proto, E. (2018). The influence of anger on strategic cooperative interactions. *Academy of Management Proceedings* (p. 14162). Briarcliff Manor, NY: Academy of Management.

Chartrand, T. L., & Bargh, J. A. (2002). Nonconscious motivations: Their activation, operation, and consequences. In A. Tesser, D. A. Stapel, & J. V. Wood (Eds.), *Self and motivation: emerging psychological perspectives* (pp. 13–41). Washington, DC: American Psychological Association.

Christopoulos, G. I., Uy, M. A., & Yap, W. J. (2019). The body and the brain: Measuring skin conductance responses to understand the emotional experience. *Organizational Research Methods, 22*, 394–420.

Cooper, J. C., & Knutson, B. (2008). Valence and salience contribute to nucleus accumbens activation. *NeuroImage, 39*, 538–547.

Coricelli, G., Dolan, R. J., & Sirigu, A. (2007). Brain, emotion and decision making: The paradigmatic example of regret. *Trends in Cognitive Sciences, 11*, 258–265.

Cropanzano, R., Goldman, B., & Folger, R. (2003). Deontic justice: The role of moral principles in workplace fairness. *Journal of Organizational Behavior, 24*, 1019–1024.

Cropanzano, R. S., Massaro, S., & Becker, W. J. (2017). Deontic justice and organizational neuroscience. *Journal of Business Ethics, 144*, 733–754.

Cunningham, W. A., Van Bavel, J. J., & Johnsen, I. R. (2008). Affective flexibility: evaluative processing goals shape amygdala activity. *Psychological Science, 19*, 152–160.

Damasio, A. R. (1996). The somatic marker hypothesis and the possible functions of the prefrontal cortex. *Philosophical Transactions of the Royal Society B: Biological Sciences, 351*, 1413–1420.

Darwin, C. R. (1896). *The expression of emotions in man and animals*. New York, NY: Philosophical Library.

Davidson, R. J., & Irwin, W. (1999). The functional neuroanatomy of emotion and affective style. *Trends in Cognitive Sciences, 3*, 11–21.

Day, M., Boardman, M. C., & Krueger, N. F. (Eds.). (2017). *Handbook of research methodologies and design in neuroentrepreneurship*. Cheltenham, UK: Edward Elgar.

Decety, J. (2010). The neurodevelopment of empathy in humans. *Developmental Neuroscience, 32*, 257–267.

Denson, T. F., Grisham, J. R., & Moulds, M. L. (2011). Cognitive reappraisal increases heart rate variability in response to an anger provocation. *Motivation and Emotion, 35*, 14–22.

Denson, T. F., Pedersen, W. C., Ronquillo, J., & Nandy, A. S. (2009). The angry brain: Neural correlates of anger, angry rumination, and aggressive personality. *Journal of Cognitive Neuroscience, 21*, 734–744.

Descartes, R. (1989). *The passions of the soul* (trans. S. H. Voss). Indianapolis, IN: Hackett.

Dodell-Feder, D., Koster-Hale, J., Bedny, M., & Saxe, R. (2011). fMRI item analysis in a theory of mind task. *NeuroImage, 55*, 705–712.

Drover, W., Massaro, S., Cerf, M., & Busenitz, L. (2017). Neuro-entrepreneurship. *Academy of Management Proceedings*, 2017(1), https://doi.org/10.5465/AMBPP.2017.13893abstract

Dunsmoor, J. E., Niv, Y., Daw, N., & Phelps, E. A. (2015). Rethinking extinction. *Neuron, 88*(1), 47–63.

Dziobek, I., Fleck, S., Kalbe, E., Rogers, K., Hassenstab, J., Brand, M., . . . & Convit, A. (2006). Introducing MASC: A movie for the assessment of social cognition. *Journal of Autism and Developmental Disorders, 36*, 623–636.

Ekman, P. (1992). An argument for basic emotions. *Cognition and Emotion, 6*, 169–200.

Ekman, P. (1994). Strong evidence for universals in facial expressions: a reply to Russell's mistaken critique. *Psychological Bulletin, 115*, 268–287.

Ekman, P. E., & Davidson, R. J. (1994). *The nature of emotion: Fundamental questions*. New York, NY: Oxford University Press.

Ekman, P., Friesen, W. V., & Ellsworth, P. (1972). *Emotion in the human face*. New York, NY: Pergamon.

Elfenbein, H. A. (2007). Emotion in organizations: A review and theoretical integration. *Academy of Management Annals, 1*, 315–386.

Ewbank, M. P., Barnard, P. J., Croucher, C. J., Ramponi, C., & Calder, A. J. (2009). The expressions of fear versus anger. *Emotion, 1*, 70–83.

Fitness, J. (2000). Anger in the workplace: An emotion script approach to anger episodes between workers and their superiors, co-workers and subordinates. *Journal of Organizational Behavior, 21*, 147–162.

Friedman, R., Anderson, C., Brett, J., Olekalns, M., Goates, N., & Lisco, C. C. (2004). The positive and negative effects of anger on dispute resolution: Evidence from electronically mediated disputes. *Journal of Applied Psychology, 89*, 369–376.

Gallese, V., & Goldman, A. (1998). Mirror neurons and the simulation theory of mind-reading. *Trends in Cognitive Sciences, 2*, 493–501.

Geddes, D., & Callister, R. R. (2007). Crossing the line(s): A dual threshold model of anger in organizations. *Academy of Management Review, 32*, 721–746.

Gehring, W. J., & Willoughby, A. R. (2002). The medial frontal cortex and the rapid processing of monetary gains and losses. *Science, 295*, 2279–2282.

George, M. S., Ketter, T. A., Parekh, P. I., Horwitz, B., Herscovitch, P., & Post, R. M. (1995). Brain activity during transient sadness and happiness in healthy women. *American Journal of Psychiatry, 152*, 341–351.

Gibson, D. E., & Callister, R. R. (2010). Anger in organizations: Review and integration. *Journal of Management, 36*, 66–93.

Glomb, T. M. (2002). Workplace anger and aggression: Informing conceptual models with data from specific encounters. *Journal of Occupational Health Psychology, 7*, 20–36.

Gooty, J., Gavin, M., & Ashkanasy, N. M. (2009). Emotions research in OB: The challenges that lie ahead. *Journal of Organizational Behavior, 30*, 833–838.

Grandey, A. A. (2000). Emotional regulation in the workplace: A new way to conceptualize emotional labor. *Journal of Occupational Health Psychology, 5*(1), 95–110.

Halgren, E., Walter, R. D., Cherlow, D. G., & Crandall, P. H. (1978). Mental phenomena evoked by electrical stimulation of the human hippocampal formation and amygdala. *Brain: A Journal of Neurology, 101*, 83–115.

Hareli, S., & Rafaeli, A. (2008). Emotion cycles: On the social influence of emotion in organizations. *Research in Organizational Behavior, 28*, 35–59.

Hazlett, R. L., & Hazlett, S. Y. (1999). Emotional response to television commercials: Facial EMG vs. self–report. *Journal of Advertising Research, 39*, 7–23.

Healey, M. P., Hodgkinson, G. P., & Massaro, S. (2018). Can brains manage? The brain, emotion, and cognition in organizations. In L. Petitta, C. E. J. Härtel, N. M. Ashkanasy, & W. Zerbe (Eds.), *Individual, relational, and contextual dynamics of emotions* (Research on Emotion in Organizations, Volume 14) (pp. 27–58). Bingley, UK: Emerald.

Higgins, E. T. (1996). Knowledge activation: Accessibility, and salience. In E. T. Higgins & A. W. Kruglanski (Eds.), *Social psychology: Handbook of basic principles* (pp. 133–168). New York, NY: Guilford.

Hippocrates (1923). The sacred disease. In *Loeb Classical Library: Hippocrates* (Volume 2, trans. W. H. S. Jones, pp. 129–183). Cambridge, MA: Harvard University Press.

James, W. (1884). What is an emotion? *Mind, 9*, 188–205.

Jones, C. L., Ward, J., & Critchley, H. D. (2010). The neuropsychological impact of insular cortex lesions. *Journal of Neurology, Neurosurgery & Psychiatry, 81*, 611–618.

Jones, E. G. (2012). *The thalamus*. New York, NY: Plenum Press.

Kanske, P., Böckler, A., Trautwein, F. M., & Singer, T. (2015). Dissecting the social brain: Introducing the EmpaToM to reveal distinct neural networks and brain–behavior relations for empathy and theory of mind. *NeuroImage, 122*, 6–19.

Kellett, J. B., Humphrey, R. H., & Sleeth, R. G. (2002). Empathy and complex task performance: Two routes to leadership. *Leadership Quarterly, 13*, 523–544.

Keysers, C. (2009). Mirror neurons. *Current Biology, 19*, 971–973.

Keysers, C., & Gazzola, V. (2006). Towards a unifying neural theory of social cognition. *Progress in Brain Research, 156*, 379–401.

Kiefer, T. (2002). Analyzing emotions for a better understanding of organizational change: Fear, joy, and anger during a merger. In N. Ashkanasy, C. Härtel, & W. Zerbe (Eds.), *Managing emotions in the workplace*. Armonk, NY: M. E. Sharpe.

Kreibig, S. D. (2010). Autonomic nervous system activity in emotion: A review. *Biological Psychology, 84*, 394–421.

Krueger, F., Barbey, A. K., McCabe, K., Strenziok, M., Zamboni, G., Solomon, J., . . . & Grafman, J. (2009). The neural bases of key competencies of emotional intelligence. *Proceedings of the National Academy of Sciences, 106*, 22486–22491.

LaBar, K. S., LeDoux, J. E., Spencer, D. D., & Phelps, E. A. (1995). Impaired fear conditioning following unilateral temporal lobectomy in humans. *Journal of Neuroscience, 15*, 6846–6855.

Lane, R. D., & Nadel, L. (Eds.). (1999). *Cognitive neuroscience of emotion*. New York, NY: Oxford University Press.

Lane, R. D., Reiman, E. M., Axelrod, B., Yun, L. S., Holmes, A., & Schwartz, G. E. (1998). Neural correlates of levels of emotional awareness: Evidence of an interaction between emotion and attention in the anterior cingulate cortex. *Journal of Cognitive Neuroscience, 10*, 525–535.

Law, K. S., Wong, C. S., & Song, L. J. (2004). The construct and criterion validity of emotional intelligence and its potential utility for management studies. *Journal of Applied Psychology, 89*(3), 483–496.

Lazarus, R. S. (1982). Thoughts on the relations between emotion and cognition. *American Psychologist, 37*(9), 1019–1024.

Lazarus, R. S., & Cohen–Charash, Y. (2001). Discrete emotions in organizational life. In R. Payne and C. L. Cooper (Eds.), *Emotions in organizations* (pp. 48–81). Chichester, UK: Wiley.

LeDoux, J. (1998). *The emotional brain: The mysterious underpinnings of emotional life*. New York, NY: Simon and Schuster.

LeDoux, J. (2003). The emotional brain, fear, and the amygdala. *Cellular and Molecular Neurobiology, 23*, 727–738.

LeDoux, J. E. (2000). Emotion circuits in the brain. *Annual Review of Neuroscience, 23*, 155–184.

Lee, K., & Allen, N. J. (2002). Organizational citizenship behavior and workplace deviance: The role of affect and cognitions. *Journal of Applied Psychology, 87*, 131–142.

Lee, N., Senior, C., & Butler, M. J. (2012). The domain of organizational cognitive neuroscience: Theoretical and empirical challenges. *Journal of Management, 38*, 921–931.

Lewis, K. M. (2000). When leaders display emotion: How followers respond to negative emotional expression of male and female leaders. *Journal of Organizational Behavior, 21*, 221–234.

Lewis, M. (1993). Self-conscious emotions: Embarrassment, pride, shame, and guilt. In M. Lewis & J. M. Haviland (Eds.), *Handbook of emotions* (pp. 563–573). New York, NY: Guilford.

Lieberman, M. D. (2007). Social cognitive neuroscience: A review of core processes. *Annual Review of Psychology, 58*, 259–289.

Lindquist, K. A., Wager, T. D., Kober, H., Bliss–Moreau, E., & Barrett, L. F. (2012). The brain basis of emotion: A meta–analytic review. *Behavioral and Brain Sciences, 35*, 121–143.

Liotti, M., Mayberg, H. S., Brannan, S. K., McGinnis, S., Jerabek, P., & Fox, P. T. (2000). Differential limbic–cortical correlates of sadness and anxiety in healthy subjects: Implications for affective disorders. *Biological Psychiatry, 48*, 30–42.

Louis, M. R. (1980). Surprise and sense making: What newcomers experience in entering unfamiliar organizational settings. *Administrative Science Quarterly, 25*, 226–251.

Lövheim, H. (2012). A new three–dimensional model for emotions and monoamine neurotransmitters. *Medical Hypotheses, 78*, 341–348.

Lyubomirsky, S., King, L., & Diener, E. (2005). The benefits of frequent positive affect: Does happiness lead to success? *Psychological Bulletin*, *131*, 803–855.

MacLean, P. D. (1952). Some psychiatric implications of physiological studies on frontotemporal portion of limbic system (visceral brain). *Clinical Neurophysiology*, *4*, 407–418.

Massaro, S. (2014). Neuroscience: Promising tools to advance organizational research on affect. *Academy of Management Proceedings*, *2014*(1), https://doi.org/10.5465/ambpp.2014.12260abstract

Massaro, S. (2015). Neuroscientific methods applications in strategic management. In G. Dagnino & C. Cinci (Eds.), *Strategic management: A research method handbook* (pp. 253–282). New York, NY: Routledge.

Massaro, S. (2018). Neuroscience methods: A framework for managerial and organizational cognition. In R. J. Galavan, K. J. Sund, & G. P. Hodgkinson (Eds.), *Methodological challenges and advances in managerial and organizational cognition* (pp. 241–278). Bingley, UK: Emerald.

Massaro, S., & Becker, W. J. (2015). Organizational justice through the window of neuroscience. In D. Waldman & P. Baltazhard (Eds.), *Organizational neuroscience* (pp. 257–276). Bingley, UK: Emerald.

Massaro, S., & Pecchia, L. (2019). Heart rate variability (HRV) analysis: A methodology for organizational neuroscience. *Organizational Research Methods*, *22*, 354–393.

Mataix-Cols, D., An, S. K., Lawrence, N. S., Caseras, X., Speckens, A., Giampietro, V., . . . & Phillips, M. L. (2008). Individual differences in disgust sensitivity modulate neural responses to aversive/disgusting stimuli. *European Journal of Neuroscience*, *27*, 3050–3058.

Moll, J., de Oliveira–Souza, R., Moll, F. T., Ignácio, F. A., Bramati, I. E., Caparelli–Dáquer, E. M., & Eslinger, P. J. (2005). The moral affiliations of disgust: A functional MRI study. *Cognitive and Behavioral Neurology*, *18*, 68–78.

Müller-Pinzler, L., Krach, S., Krämer, U. M., & Paulus, F. M. (2016). The social neuroscience of interpersonal emotions. In M. Wöhr and S. Krach (Eds.), *Social behavior from rodents to humans* (pp. 241–256). New York, NY: Springer.

Murphy, F. C., Nimmo–Smith, I. A. N., & Lawrence, A. D. (2003). Functional neuroanatomy of emotions: A meta–analysis. *Cognitive, Affective, & Behavioral Neuroscience*, *3*, 207–233.

Ochsner, K. N., Bunge, S. A., Gross, J. J., & Gabrieli, J. D. (2002). Rethinking feelings: An fMRI study of the cognitive regulation of emotion. *Journal of Cognitive Neuroscience*, *14*, 1215–1229.

Ochsner, K. N., & Gross, J. J. (2005). The cognitive control of emotion. *Trends in Cognitive Sciences*, *9*, 242–249.

Ochsner, K. N., & Lieberman, M. D. (2001). The emergence of social cognitive neuroscience. *American Psychologist*, *56*, 717–734.

Ortony, A., & Turner, T. J. (1990). What's basic about basic emotions? *Psychological Review*, *97*(3), 315–331.

Panksepp, J. (1998). *Affective neuroscience: The foundations of human and animal emotions*. New York, NY: Oxford University Press.

Papez, J. W. (1937). A proposed mechanism of emotion. *Archives of Neurology & Psychiatry*, *38*, 725–743.

Pelzer, P. (2002). Disgust and organization. *Human Relations*, *55*, 841–860.

Phan, K. L., Wager, T., Taylor, S. F., & Liberzon, I. (2002). Functional neuroanatomy of emotion: A meta–analysis of emotion activation studies in PET and fMRI. *NeuroImage*, *16*, 331–348.

Phelps, E. A. (2009). The study of emotion in neuroeconomics. In P. W. Glimcher, C. F. Camerer, E. Fehr, and R. A. Poldrack (Eds.), *Neuroeconomics: Decision making and the brain* (pp. 233–250). London, UK: Academic.

Phelps, E. A., Delgado, M. R., Nearing, K. I., & LeDoux, J. E. (2004). Extinction learning in humans: Role of the amygdala and vmPFC. *Neuron*, *43*, 897–905.

Plutchik, R. (1980). *Emotion: A psychoevolutionary synthesis*. New York, NY: Harper & Row.

Porath, C. L., & Pearson, C. M. (2012). Emotional and behavioral responses to workplace incivility and the impact of hierarchical status. *Journal of Applied Social Psychology*, *42*, 326–357.

Powell, T. C. (2011). Neurostrategy. *Strategic Management Journal*, *32*, 1484–1499.

Rafaeli, A., & Sutton, R. I. (1989). The expression of emotion in organizational life. *Research in Organizational Behavior*, *11*, 1–42.

Rainville, P., Bechara, A., Naqvi, N., & Damasio, A. R. (2006). Basic emotions are associated with distinct patterns of cardiorespiratory activity. *International Journal of Psychophysiology*, *61*, 5–18.

Rauch, S. L., Shin, L. M., Dougherty, D. D., Alpert, N. M., Orr, S. P., Lasko, M., . . . & Pitman, R. K. (1999). Neural activation during sexual and competitive arousal in healthy men. *Psychiatry Research: Neuroimaging*, *91*, 1–10.

Rizzolatti, G., & Craighero, L. (2004). The mirror–neuron system. *Annual Review of Neuroscience*, *27*, 169–192.

Rolls, E. T. (2000). On the brain and emotion. *Behavioral and Brain Sciences*, *23*, 219–228.

Rozin, P., & Fallon, A. E. (1987). A perspective on disgust. *Psychological Review*, *94*, 23–41.

Ruby, P., & Decety, J. (2004). How would you feel versus how do you think she would feel? A neuroimaging study of perspective-taking with social emotions. *Journal of Cognitive Neuroscience*, *16*, 988–999.

Rushworth, M. F., & Behrens, T. E. (2008). Choice, uncertainty and value in prefrontal and cingulate cortex. *Nature Neuroscience*, *11*, 389–397.

Ryan, R. M., & Deci, E. L. (2001). On happiness and human potentials: A review of research on hedonic and eudaimonic well–being. *Annual Review of Psychology*, *52*, 141–166.

Sato, W., Fujimura, T., & Suzuki, N. (2008). Enhanced facial EMG activity in response to dynamic facial expressions. *International Journal of Psychophysiology*, *70*, 70–74.

Sato, W., Kochiyama, T., Uono, S., Kubota, Y., Sawada, R., Yoshimura, S., & Toichi, M. (2015). The structural neural substrate of subjective happiness. *Scientific Reports*, *5*(16891), www.nature.com/articles/srep16891

Schurz, M., Radua, J., Aichhorn, M., Richlan, F., & Perner, J. (2014). Fractionating theory of mind: A meta–analysis of functional brain imaging studies. *Neuroscience & Biobehavioral Reviews*, *42*, 9–34.

Singer, T. (2009). Understanding others: Brain mechanisms of theory of mind and empathy. In P. W. Glimcher, C. F. Camerer, E. Fehr, and R. A. Poldrack (Eds.), *Neuroeconomics: Decision making and the brain* (pp. 249–266). London, UK: Academic.

Singer, T., Seymour, B., O'Doherty, J., Kaube, H., Dolan, R. J., & Frith, C. D. (2004). Empathy for pain involves the affective but not sensory components of pain. *Science*, *303*, 1157–1162.

Skarlicki, D. P., Hoegg, J., Aquino, K., & Nadisic, T. (2013). Does injustice affect your sense of taste and smell? The mediating role of moral disgust. *Journal of Experimental Social Psychology*, *49*, 852–859.

Sprengelmeyer, R., Rausch, M., Eysel, U. T., & Przuntek, H. (1998). Neural structures associated with recognition of facial expressions of basic emotions. *Proceedings of the Royal Society B: Biological Sciences*, *265*, 1927–1931.

Stemmler, G., Heldmann, M., Pauls, C. A., & Scherer, T. (2001). Constraints for emotion specificity in fear and anger: The context counts. *Psychophysiology*, *38*, 275–291.

Tangney, J. P., Stuewig, J., & Mashek, D. J. (2007). What's moral about the self-conscious emotions? In J. L. Tracy, R. W. Robins, & J. P. Tangney (Eds.), *The self-conscious emotions: Theory and research* (pp. 21–37). New York, NY: Guilford.

Tau, G. Z., & Peterson, B. S. (2010). Normal development of brain circuits. *Neuropsychopharmacology*, *35*, 147–168.

Telzer, E. H. (2016). Dopaminergic reward sensitivity can promote adolescent health: A new perspective on the mechanism of ventral striatum activation. *Developmental Cognitive Neuroscience*, *17*, 57–67.

Teplan, M. (2002). Fundamentals of EEG measurement. *Measurement Science Review*, *2*, 1–11.

Thatcher, R. W., North, D., & Biver, C. (2007). Intelligence and EEG current density using low-resolution electromagnetic tomography (LORETA). *Human Brain Mapping*, *28*, 118–133.

Thoresen, C. J., Kaplan, S. A., Barsky, A. P., Warren, C. R., & de Chermont, K. (2003). The affective underpinnings of job perceptions and attitudes: A meta–analytic review and integration. *Psychological Bulletin*, *129*, 914–945.

Thorson, K. R., West, T. V., & Mendes, W. B. (2018). Measuring physiological influence in dyads:

A guide to designing, implementing, and analyzing dyadic physiological studies. *Psychological Methods*, *23*(4), 595–616.

Van den Bos, K., Maas, M., Waldring, I. E., & Semin, G. R. (2003). Toward understanding the psychology of reactions to perceived fairness: The role of affect intensity. *Social Justice Research*, *16*, 151–168.

Van Dillen, L. F., Heslenfeld, D. J., & Koole, S. L. (2009). Tuning down the emotional brain: An fMRI study of the effects of cognitive load on the processing of affective images. *NeuroImage*, *45*, 1212–1219.

Wager, T. D., & Atlas, L. Y. (2015). The neuroscience of placebo effects: Connecting context, learning and health. *Nature Reviews Neuroscience*, *16*, 403–418.

Waldman, D. A., Balthazard, P. A., & Peterson, S. J. (2011). Leadership and neuroscience: Can we revolutionize the way that inspirational leaders are identified and developed?. *Academy of Management Perspectives*, *25*, 60–74.

Walter, H., Adenzato, M., Ciaramidaro, A., Enrici, I., Pia, L., & Bara, B. G. (2004). Understanding intentions in social interaction: The role of the anterior paracingulate cortex. *Journal of Cognitive Neuroscience*, *16*, 1854–1863.

Ward, J. (2015). *The student's guide to cognitive neuroscience*. New York, NY: Psychology.

Weiss, H. M., & Beal, D. (2005). Reflections on affective events theory. In N. M. Ashkanasy, C. E. J. Härtel, & W. J. Zerbe (Eds.), *The effects of affect in organizational settings* (pp. 1–21). San Diego, CA: Elsevier.

Weiss, H. M., & Cropanzano, R. (1996). Affective events theory: A theoretical discussion of the structure, causes and consequences of affective experiences at work. *Research in Organizational Behavior*, *18*, 1–74.

Wessel, J. R., Danielmeier, C., Morton, J. B., & Ullsperger, M. (2012). Surprise and error: common neuronal architecture for the processing of errors and novelty. *Journal of Neuroscience*, *32*, 7528–7537.

Whalen, P. J., Rauch, S. L., Etcoff, N. L., McInerney, S. C., Lee, M. B., & Jenike, M. A. (1998). Masked presentations of emotional facial expressions modulate amygdala activity without explicit knowledge. *Journal of Neuroscience*, *18*, 411–418.

Whalen, P. J., Shin, L. M., McInerney, S. C., Fischer, H., Wright, C. I., & Rauch, S. L. (2001). A functional MRI study of human amygdala responses to facial expressions of fear versus anger. *Emotion*, *1*, 70–83.

Wicker, B., Keysers, C., Plailly, J., Royet, J. P., Gallese, V., & Rizzolatti, G. (2003). Both of us disgusted in *my* insula: The common neural basis of seeing and feeling disgust. *Neuron*, *40*, 655–664.

Wiersma, U. J. (1992). The effects of extrinsic rewards in intrinsic motivation: A meta-analysis. *Journal of Occupational and Organizational Psychology*, *65*, 101–114.

Wolf, I., Dziobek, I., & Heekeren, H. R. (2010). Neural correlates of social cognition in naturalistic settings: A model-free analysis approach. *NeuroImage*, *49*, 894–904.

Yarkoni, T., Poldrack, R. A., Nichols, T. E., Van Essen, D. C., & Wager, T. D. (2011). Large-scale automated synthesis of human functional neuroimaging data. *Nature Methods*, *8*, 665–670.

Zajonc, R. B. (1984). On the primacy of affect. *American Psychologist*, *39*, 117–123.

3 Personality Affect Construal Theory

A Model of Personality and Affect in the Workplace

Stuti Thapa, Emorie D. Beck, and Louis Tay

Even decades after the affective revolution (Ashkanasy & Dorris, 2017), affect remains an integral part of organizational psychology. The two primary perspectives in affective research center on affect as a dispositional construct (i.e. a trait) or a momentary construct (i.e. a state) (Brief & Weiss, 2002). Dispositional perspectives of affect refer to a general tendency to experience certain types and levels of affective state. This can reflect personality traits and affective dispositions (Watson & Clark, 1984; Watson & Tellegen, 2002). Momentary affect refers to emotions experienced in the moment, including both the valence of feelings (i.e. positive, negative) and discrete emotions (e.g. guilt, awe). Integrating person, situation, and emotional construal perspectives, this chapter seeks to incorporate decades of work on affective dispositions, momentary affect, and personality to present a conceptual model that specifies how these come together to produce in-the-moment emotions embedded in specific situations. In doing so, we provide theoretical specificity connecting these dispositional and momentary perspectives, answering the call for more multi-level and systems-based theories: for example, how does personality unfold to impact state-level emotions (Ilies, Schwind, & Heller, 2007)?

Within organizational research, earlier studies on affect often examined the relationship between dispositional affect and work outcomes, where high average levels of positive affectivity and low average levels of negative affectivity have been tied to better performance, including task performance (Kaplan, Bradley, Luchman, & Haynes, 2009), lower counterproductive work and higher organizational citizenship behavior (Dalal, 2005), more positive job attitudes (Thoresen, Kaplan, Barsky, Warren, & De Chermont, 2003), turnover intentions (Bouckenooghe, Raja, & Butt, 2013), and more. A critical assumption of each of these studies is that these affective dispositions are *causal* – that is, the disposition activates specific affective states resulting in the enactment of specific behaviors and attitudes at a given time within a workplace.

However, a major issue with trait-level, dispositional constructs is that they predict only a small proportion of the variance in actual behavior. Moreover, they do not make a strong case as to why affective states and experiences vary within a person over time. Conceptual and empirical work on affect has thus increasingly turned to using in-the-moment relationships between state-level affect and work behaviors to understand how and why work behaviors manifest in different ways. Past work has made theoretical links between state-level affect and behavior (Weiss & Cropanzano, 1996), and experimental studies have shown effects of emotional induction on work behavior (e.g. George, 1991). The development of experience-sampling methods (ESM) (Gabriel et al., 2018) has given researchers the means of examining momentary affect *in situ*, where the focus is more on naturalistic consequences of state-level affect. Daily affect has been linked to performance (Shockley, Ispas, Rossi, & Levine, 2012), creativity (Binnewies & Wörnlein, 2011; Waugh, Thompson, & Gotlib, 2011), daily work engagement (Ouweneel, Le

Blanc, Schaufeli, & van Wijhe, 2012), and more. This relatively new methodological tool has allowed researchers to test and theorize relationships between affect and work behavior in a more dynamic fashion than before, and within a multi-level framework, without defaulting to trait-level focus.

Despite the connection between dispositional affect and work outcomes and that between state-level affect and work outcomes, there is less conceptual work in organizational psychology on the relation between dispositional affect and state-level affect. However, decades of research in personality suggest that momentary and dispositional constructs, including affect, can be linked by considering traits to be average levels of states (Buss & Craik, 1983; Fleeson, 2001; Watson & Tellegen, 2002; Zuckerman, 1979). A growing number of perspectives conceptualize traits as density distributions of states in which parameters of the density distribution can be beyond the mean (e.g. intra-individual standard deviation, minima, maxima, etc.) (Fleeson & Jayawickreme, 2015). However, they recognize that such observation of variability is not an explanation of it (Jayawickreme, Zachry, & Fleeson, 2019). In other words, there is little attempt in organizational psychology to explain how different components of dispositions fundamentally lead to specific instantiations of affect within situations.

Moreover, when applied to much of the work on workplace affect, these techniques account only for positive and negative affective variability, which omits examining the way that individuals experience a variety of discrete emotions in the workplace (e.g. pride, gratitude, awe, anger, envy). Recently, there has been increased interest in the role of discrete emotion in organizations, both theoretically (Fehr, Fulmer, Awtrey, & Miller, 2017; Lindebaum & Geddes, 2016) and in empirical terms (Yeung & Shen, 2019). There has been some theoretical grounding for understanding how longer-term and state-level affect are linked to workplace behaviors while accounting for situational events (e.g. uplifts and hassles) through affective events theory (Weiss & Cropanzano, 1996). Affective events theory presents work events as causal entities, while trait- and state-level affect moderate our behavioral reactions to said events. In a similar vein, we seek here to provide a model that integrates person, situation, and emotion construal perspectives and includes developments in social and personality psychology. We refer readers to past work reviewing empirical associations between personality and affect (Eid & Diener, 1999; Williams, 1989; Wilt, Bleidorn, & Revelle, 2017), and we aim to go beyond these works to explicate the process through which personality traits lead to emotional experiences, particularly the experience of discrete emotions, while embracing the contextual complexities involved.

Overview: Personality Affect Construal Theory (PACT)

As shown in Figure 3.1, we introduce our model, personality affect construal theory (PACT), that has several critical components, the overarching goal of which is to explain how emotions are instantiated in the workplace. Our model includes the person perspective, which is grounded in the affect (A), behavior (B), cognition (C), and desire (D) components of personality (Wilt & Revelle, 2015). These provide the functional components underlying different personality trait taxonomies: for example, the "big five" (Barrick & Mount, 1991; Costa & McCrae, 1992; Goldberg, 1990) and HEXACO (Lee & Ashton, 2004). Specifically, we draw on theories of personality that see dispositions as emergent from patterns of relationships among psychological precursors rather than as causal units in and of themselves (Mischel & Shoda, 1995; Wilt & Revelle, 2015). Moreover, to understand how relationships among these psychological precursors give rise to emotion, we draw on psychological constructivist perspectives of emotions (e.g.

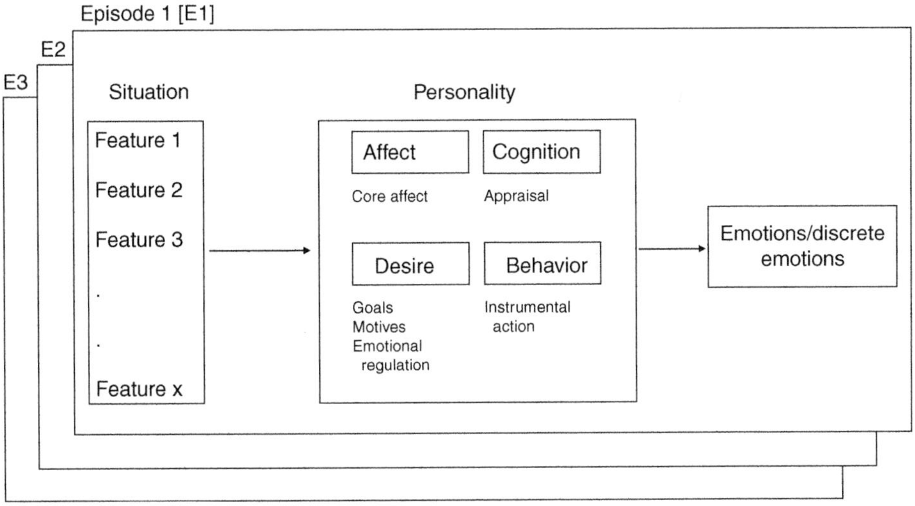

Figure 3.1 Integrative model of personality, emotion, and situation; each slice (E1–E3) represents an emotion episode containing individual interactions of personality components and situation

Russell, 2003, 2009) and discuss how different basic components of personality can lead to discrete emotion states. In addition, our model integrates workplace situations as a contextual moderator that interact with personality components to foster, trigger, or press emotions and/or emotional reactions in the moment.

In the following sections, we will highlight the missing components of personality explanations when discussing affective experience, clarify our model assumptions, and then discuss each component of PACT in context of the workplace. We will then provide conceptual, methodological, and practical implications of this model in organizations and organization research.

Missing Components of Personality in Relation to Affective Experience

First and foremost, we define personality as any stable individual difference. In organizational psychology, there has been substantial work devoted to understanding how personality is linked to the tendency to experience different emotions (e.g. Watson & Clark, 1984; Watson & Tellegen, 2002) to different degrees (e.g. Fisher, 2002) in different contexts (e.g. Oerlemans & Bakker, 2014). These dispositional tendencies have been closely aligned to "big five" traits – typically neuroticism and extraversion. Neuroticism explicitly includes negative-affect-type facets such as hostility, depression, anxiety, and emotional volatility that – not surprisingly – have been empirically linked to experiences of negative emotions (McNiel & Fleeson, 2006). Similarly, extraversion has facets such as warmth, gregariousness, and positive affectivity that are also associated with positive emotion experiences (Howell, Ksendzova, Nestingen, Yerahian, & Iyer, 2017). Correspondingly, positive and negative affectivity are trait manifestations of a tendency to experience positive or negative emotion respectively. Other research has investigated discrete emotion-specific personality traits such as guilt-proneness (Grandey, Tam, & Brauburger, 2002).

Studies in personality have also taken a methodological approach in which dispositions predict *dynamics* of affective states. Trait levels are associated with affect *frequency*, where individuals of more positive dispositions report more occurrences of happy moments (Fisher, 2002); *variability*, where neuroticism predicts increased variability in negative and positive affect (Murray, Allen, & Trinder, 2002) and extraversion predicts positive affect variability (e.g. Kuppens, Van Mechelen, Nezlek, Dossche, & Timmermans, 2007); and *peaks* (i.e. maxima), where the excitement-seeking facet of extraversion is associated with greater peak experiences of positivity (Williams, 1989). In the above cases, affective states serve as descriptions of personality (Wilt & Revelle, 2015) that manifest in a number of ways.

Yet observations of links between states and traits or among different affective and personality states are descriptive, rather than causal explanations of how personality "produces" affective states. We seek to propose psychological and situational mechanisms to further explicate the link between personality and affective states, specifically emotions. In the following section, we define underlying personality components and how they interact with situations to produce emotional experiences.

ABCD Personality Components as Intervening Units from Personality to Emotional Experiences

Before introducing each of the components of our model – affect, behavior, cognition, and desire – it is important to outline what they are. Herein, these components are units of human psychology that broadly classify the observable indicators of trait levels.[1] They are also important elements that interact with each other or with the situation to influence the perception of emotional experience. This conceptualization is largely inspired by Mischel & Shoda's (1995) Cognitive–Affective Personality System (CAPS) model, where the interactions among cognitive–affective units (encodings, expectancies and beliefs, affects, competencies, and self-regulatory plans and goals) mediate the relationship between psychological features of situations and behavior. For more information on the CAPS model we refer readers to the original paper (Mischel & Shoda, 1995) as well as recent reviews on the topic (Beck & Jackson, 2019a, 2019b). We theorize that the resulting construction of emotion is a result of interaction between these units and we further describe where our understanding of emotion is derived from.

While the schools of thought on the conceptualizations of emotion are varied (e.g. Barrett, 2006; Ekman, 1992; Frijda, 1988), we draw here primarily on the psychological constructivist view of emotions – where emotions are results of subjective perceptions of individuals – as it is in line with our views on how the interplay of personality, affect, and context produce emotion. In this view, emotions are constructed by individuals as they make sense of a situation and may eventually be labeled in the forms of discrete emotions. This constructed emotion state or episode is distinct from the core affect – namely the primitive feeling state (Russell, 2003) described as one of the components of this model.

In the next sections we describe each ABCD unit of personality independently and examine how each relates to emotional experience.

Affect

Wilt and Revelle (2015) define affect as "internal and evaluative, valenced states, including patterns of feelings, emotions, and feeling-like states" (p. 482). Affect in terms of valence has been arguably the most studied state-level affective construct in organizational psychology

[1] The precise mechanisms through which personality can be classified as interrelations among ABCD indicators that produce behavior, and the methods used to test the proposition, are beyond the scope of this chapter. However, we refer readers to recent empirical (Beck & Jackson, 2019a; Wright et al., 2019) and theoretical work (Beck & Jackson, 2019b, 2019c) on the topic.

(Barsade & Gibson, 2007; Brief & Weiss, 2002). In the present chapter, we adopt Russell's (2003, 2009) definition of affect as "core" affect: "pre-conceptual primitive process, which is more of a pre-conceptual state." This conceptualization is broadly adopted in organizational psychology and undergirds the dimensional structure of affect (Cropanzano, Weiss, Hale, & Reb, 2003) as well as dimensional and hierarchical framework of affect (positive affect [PA] and negative affect [NA]) (Tellegen, Watson, & Clark, 1999). In other words, it is a non-reflecting feeling of good or bad, lethargic or energized. Therefore, rather than a broad definition of affect that also encompasses complex emotional states, core affect operates as a circumplex of valence (pleasure–displeasure) and arousal (activation–deactivation; Russell, 1980; Yik, Russell, & Steiger, 2011). Thus, core affect is one of the foundational components of emotion (Russell, 2009), though insufficient in itself to fully construct emotional experience.

Behavior

Behaviors are defined as overt and directly observable actions, including both active (e.g. bike-riding) and passive (e.g. watching television) behaviors. There are two ways in which behavior functions in this model to produce emotion – (1) as an input variable that influences predisposition to experience certain emotions, and (2) as an output variable of an emotional experience. As an input, different behaviors are associated with different traits and some situations are predisposed to induce such behavior in association with personality. For example, extraverted individuals are likely to engage in active and social actions and, therefore, receive positive emotional experience from such actions (Wilt, Noftle, Fleeson, & Spain, 2012). For the output side, different emotions have different action tendencies. In other words, different emotions may have the same valence but induce different actions. In Russell's model of emotion, the parallel for behavior is instrumental action. Instrumental action is an additional means for distinguishing emotions, beyond just valence. An example of different instrumental action for different emotion is how people freeze when they are scared, as compared to lashing out when they are angry, even though fear and anger are both negative emotions.

Cognition

The study of personality and emotion devote considerable attention to observable (and/or reportable) patterns of thoughts and their relationship to observable manifestations and self-reports of personality and emotion. According to Russell (2003) and others (Barrett, 2009; Moors, Ellsworth, Scherer, & Frijda, 2013), cognitions are necessary for *emotion experience* because it is through these cognitive processes and core affect that emotions are construed. In Wilt and Revelle's ABCD model, cognition is "how we think" and encompasses mental contents and processes including appraisals, attention, memory, problem solving, and interpretations. In Russell's model, these cognitive processes include appraisals and emotional meta-experience (second-order experience where one perceives oneself as having an emotion).

Appraisals, in particular, have gained considerable attention in emotion literature and have been incorporated in multiple theories of emotion, including Russell's (2003) model of core affect, Ekman's (1992) theory of basic emotion, and Weiss & Cropanzano's (1996) affective events theory. Appraisal is defined as evaluation of the significance of an event. Broadly, there are two categories of appraisals – primary and secondary (Russell, 2003). Primary appraisals are the most basic form and occur when individuals evaluate whether a triggering event is relevant to their well-being. If the event is (preconsciously) relevant, secondary appraisal occurs. There is considerable debate on the number and types of appraisals, but most theorists agree that goal congruence, goal relevance, certainty, coping potential, and agency have been consistently demonstrated to be critical for emotional experience (Moors et al., 2013).

Evidence suggests that appraisals of situational experiences are critically tied to emotion experience. In one study, Kuppens et al. (2007) tested individual differences in which situations predicted appraisals associated with anger and how those associations, in turn, were associated with the experience of anger. They found that across contexts and people, frustration was the only necessary but not sufficient appraisal of the experience of anger. However, across people, the situations linked with different appraisals and the appraisals linked with the experience of anger showed clear individual differences, highlighting the importance of looking beyond aggregate patterns within a population. Similarly, appraisal of importance of events and situations can affect duration of emotions, where high-importance events trigger persistent emotions (Verduyn & Lavrijsen, 2015).

In sum, a growing body of literature in the psychologies of cognition, emotion, and more suggests that there are important cognitive underpinnings in models of emotion when looking at both personality and situational influences.

Desire

In Wilt and Revelle's ABCD model, desires are defined as "goals, wants, strivings, and motivations." Motivation is integral to different phenomena in organizational science and closely tied to valued outcomes such as employee performance and success (Amabile, Hill, Hennessey, & Tighe, 1994; Grant, 2008). In Russell's (2003) model, he defines emotion regulation as a desire and attempt for self-control in order to adjust our arousal levels to match our self-characterization, which makes it a psychological construct related to desire in the ABCD model (Russell, 2009). Emotion regulation is an important construct in the context of the workplace since it is relevant for different emotion relevant work behaviors such as surface acting (presenting an emotion they are required to present at a job), or deep acting (feeling the emotion you are required to present at the job) (Grandey, 2003; Gross, 1998).

There is growing evidence suggesting a connection between goals/desires and affect through velocity, such that rate at which a person is progressing toward their goals can affect emotional states (Wilt et al., 2017). If perceived velocity matches or surpasses the reference point of their rate of progress, positive emotions are produced. If velocity is lower, negative emotions are produced. Imagine, for example, you are writing a chapter for a handbook. When you are making final edits and rapidly progressing toward finishing the goal, you are probably experiencing positive affect. However, if you feel like you have hit a dead end and are no longer making progress toward completing it, you are likely to experience negative affect. In other words, in this case, goals are the link between personality and emotional states. In one study, for example, the state of extraversion was associated with higher velocity (movement toward a goal), while the state of neuroticism was associated with lower velocity. Velocity, in turn, mediated the relationship between states of extraversion and neuroticism and positive and negative emotion. The desire component of personality is therefore a valuable connection particularly in consideration of emotion and state-level personality.

Situations

Situations are critical for understanding within-person variability. Lewin (1951), for example, argued that behavior is a function of both the person and the situation, or B = *f* (P,S). There have been some efforts to conceptualize and operationalize situational influences in organizational research. Meyer, Dalal, & Hermida (2010) reviewed the importance of situational strength in organizational science, conceptualized as external cues that hint at desirability of certain behaviors resulting in psychological pressure to partake in or avoid specific actions that then reduce trait–behavior relationships. Other efforts include establishing a taxonomy of situations, using Q-sort data from the Riverside Situational Q-sort (Funder, Furr, & Colvin, 2000); the DIAMONDS taxonomy (Rauthmann et al., 2014); and a lexical technique based on characteristics of situations, CAPTION (Parrigon, Woo, Tay, Wang, & Wang, 2016). The importance of considering personality–situation integration in organizational research has been highlighted in personnel selection work where assessment methods such as situational judgment tests and assessment centers could be used to obtain personality characteristics in specific job-relevant situations (Lievens, 2017).

Specifically, in an organizational context, it is also important to consider work events as well as the social context of the worker when conceptualizing situational influence on emotions. Affective events theory (AET) also emphasizes the need for evaluating emotion-generating events (or affective events) as a major proximal cause of emotion in the workplace. This is particularly important for practical implications of our model. Qualitative studies have found specific work situations to cause discrete emotional reactions. For instance, interpersonal mistreatment, such as mistreatment by customers (Grandey et al., 2002), unjust treatment, disrespect, and public humiliation (Basch & Fisher, 2000; Fitness, 2000) cause anger. On the other hand, situations such as recognition from supervisors for work performance can instill pride (Grandey et al., 2002); and changes in motivating job characteristics such as job autonomy, which can be understood as a combination of desire/motivation and situation, relate to employee happiness during daily work activities (Oerlemans & Bakker, 2018).

In much of the study of how situations influence emotion experience and manifestations of personality, people are asked how they generally respond to situations of a specific kind, where situations are measured as binary (in a situation or not). In such stimulus-response style inventories (Endler & Hunt, 1968), the relationships between situations and person-level variables (behavior, emotion, affect, etc.) can be conceptualized as *if . . . then* contingent relationships, where there is thought to be a conditional probabilistic relationship between experiencing a binary context/situation variable and an affective or behavioral state (Wright & Mischel, 1987). The profile of these *if . . . then* contingencies are, in this view, personality. Mischel & Shoda (1995) further extended this argument such that the interactions among mediating units defined the probabilistic relationships between person and context (cf. Beck & Jackson, 2019a, 2019b, for a full discussion). In Figure 3.1, this is represented by the layers in the middle panel, showing how ABCD units combine differently across different contexts to produce different discrete emotion experiences.

Outcomes of the System: State-Level Emotions

In recent years, the study of emotion has shifted from the topic of evolutionarily distinct basic emotions (e.g. Ekman, 1992) to examining the underlying sociocognitive features of emotion (Barrett, 2009; Russell, 2003). Different discrete emotions may be driven by different psychological processes and mechanisms and, subsequently, predict different organizational outcomes and behaviors (for reviews, see Gooty, Connelly, Griffith, & Gupta, 2010; Gooty, Gavin, & Ashkanasy, 2009; Lindebaum & Jordan, 2012). In his model of emotion construal, Russell (2003, 2009) argues that components such as core affect, perception of affective quality, attribution to object, appraisals, action, emotional meta-experience, and emotional regulation interact to produce the emotional experience we label as prototypical emotion.

As mentioned before, we conceptualize core affect as the affective unit of ABCD model of personality; perception of affective quality, attribution to object, and appraisals as the cognitive unit; emotional regulation as the desire unit; and instrumental action as behavior. Russell also describes antecedent event as one of the components of emotional experience, which is captured in layers of situation in our model. Taking this understanding of emotion, our model attempts to explain how discrete emotions occur in the workplace. Instead of using traits as predictive variables of emotion, we unpack personality into components that then construct perception of emotion in the workplace. Figure 3.1 illustrates how situation and personality components interact to construct emotion in the workplace.

An important contribution of this model is that we take a look at emotion through the interactive lens of situation and personality components. Since emotions are object-specific, different situations can induce different emotions. However, there is also individual difference in ways of qualitatively experiencing the same emotion, which can be understood as a result of the combination of different components of personality. Therefore, the same emotion can look qualitatively different as a combination of person × situation factors.

We provide an example of such interaction in Figure 3.2, where we have four different experiences underlying the same emotion: anger. Anger is a negative emotion that can be induced by different situations or persons and can have multiple appraisals proceeding it (frustration, threat to self-esteem, and other-blame), and different action tendencies (Kuppens & Van Mechelen, 2007; Kuppens, et al., 2007). Here, we show how different situations (mistreatment by customer vs. failing at a task) can result in the same level of anger and have qualitative differences in the type of appraisals, desires, and behaviors in individual experience. In situation 1, we highlight how two employees mistreated by a customer can experience negative affect and evaluate the situation to be of high importance. However, employee A then appraises the event as threatening to their self-esteem, which is a precursor for anger and aggression, but feels motivated to regulate emotion to protect their job and therefore engages in surface acting behaviors where they present a pleasant exterior that they do not feel. Employee B, on the other hand, has a different secondary appraisal where they find it to be the customer's fault and are not motivated to regulate their emotion. They therefore lash out at the customer. Both experience the same level of anger and same situational cause but have qualitative difference in individual experience that construes the anger. Similarly, in situation 2, the situation itself may look same on the surface but have different features for the individual: for example, in situation 2a, employee C may fail at a task that is goal-relevant but non-typical for them. They therefore experience negative affect, appraise the situation to be frustrating, but have high motivation to fulfill their original goal. Therefore, they work harder. However, employee D with the same experience, but with a task that is non-goal-relevant but typical to them, may appraise the situation to be threatening to self-esteem and have low motivation to fulfill their original goal and, therefore, give up.

Using different combinations of personality components and situation, we distill the same emotion into qualitatively different experiences. Our model looks at employee emotional experience as a work outcome and puts a spotlight on the interactivity of situational and individual components in construing emotion.

Discussion

Our integrative model of personality, situation, and emotion aims toward an integrative account of how these constructs interact to produce emotional experience. Using ABCD components of personality, we provide a framework for

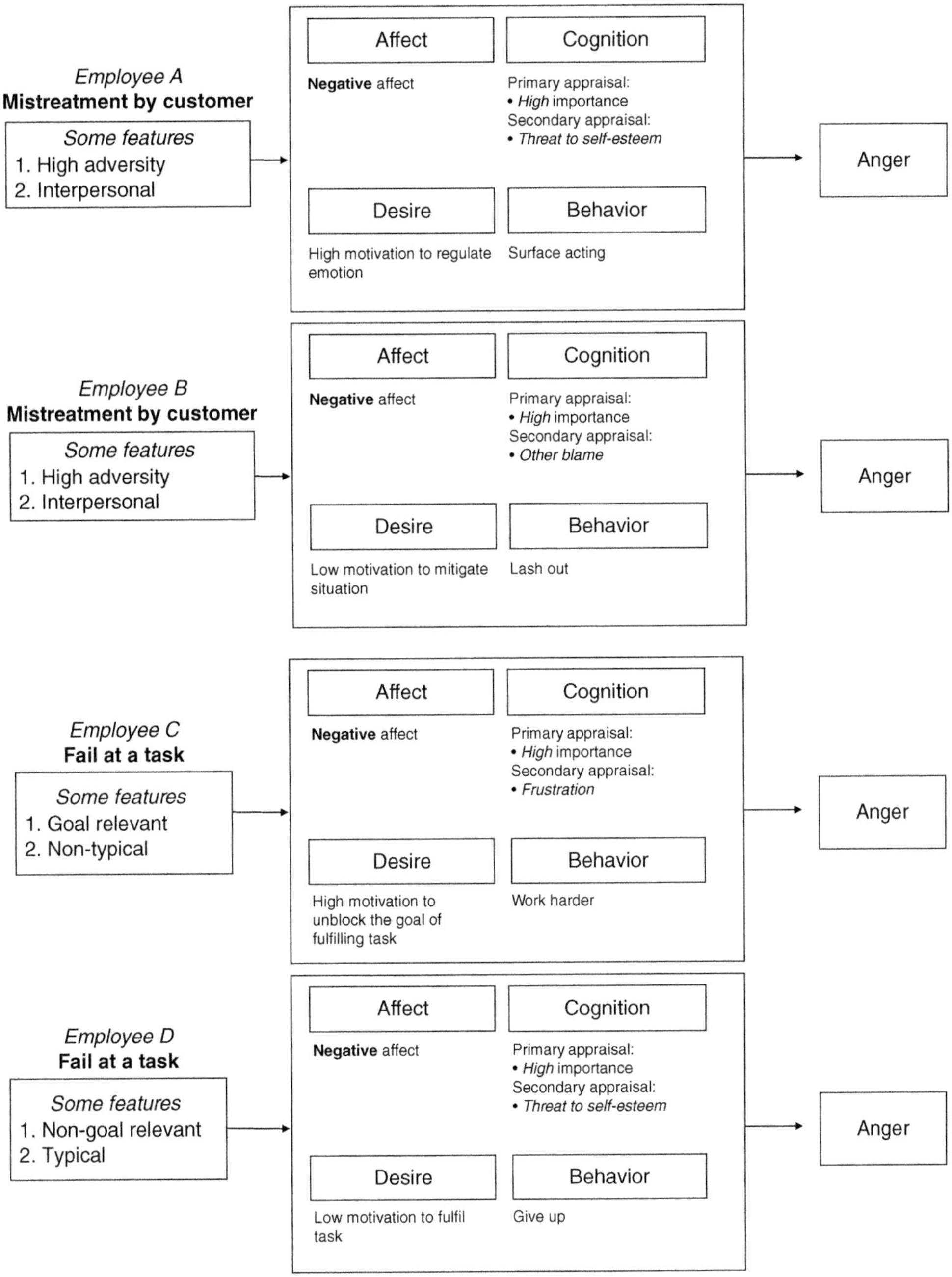

Figure 3.2 Interaction of situation and personality components where the same emotion, anger, is experienced by different individuals in different situations

understanding how traits can lead to construction of specific emotions through interaction with situations. Using this model, we can deconstruct our understanding of affect-relevant traits beyond average levels of specific affect or trajectories of affect over time.

The proposed model can inform organizational research in several ways. First and foremost, we present a person-centric understanding of personality and emotion in the workplace. In the PACT model, different components (ABCD) of personality interacting with different features of situations can lead to the same discrete emotion. These interactions can highlight qualitative differences in emotional experience of individuals, which on surface level may be quantitatively similar. These qualitative differences can be unpacked more systematically using the proposed conceptual model to enhance our understanding of employee experiences. Indeed, Weiss & Rupp (2011) highlighted the lack of and need for theoretical and empirical study of employee-centric emotional experience in organizational science.

In addition, this model disentangles the relationship between personality and emotion beyond just predictor–outcome formulation. Personality can be conceived of as a combination of ABCD components that interact with situations to create emotion. Therefore, future theoretical explanations of workplace emotion can consider a componential version of personality in which the components can act as explanatory variables. Understanding how different combinations of affect, behavior, cognition, and desire can lead to the same discrete emotions, we can unpack workplace experience as an interactive sphere within the individual.

Further, we bring emotion to the forefront as an organizational outcome that is of interest in itself. The importance of studying employee affective states has been largely presented as a predictor of organizational outcomes and well-being. We propose that it is necessary to further understand the emotional experiences of employees instantiated on a momentary level. Understanding the role of personality in construing these emotions (through interaction with situations) can enable a richer understanding of emotional experience and the construal of discrete emotions, which researchers have called for in organizational science (e.g. Gooty et al., 2009; Lindebaum & Jordan, 2012).

Implications and Future Directions

The PACT model makes several additional methodological and practical contributions to the literature. Methodologically, the PACT model highlights the importance of studying the abovementioned constructs *in situ*. Each slice of the model is an episode that can be empirically studied. While affect itself has been looked at extensively in experience-sampling studies, personality has largely been measured in more general, trait-level context in organizational science. Measuring personality components with items corresponding to the ABCD components along with situational information would allow researchers to have richer understanding of how they interact to produce in-the-moment emotional experience. Furthermore, this model draws a distinction between core affect and discrete emotions themselves and provides a framework for further investigation of discrete emotions in the workplace.

Despite the promises, a number of challenges remain. In order to test propositions of this model, novel methods are called for. Real-time investigations of interactions between situation and ABCD components, along with in-the-moment emotions, require novel research designs and analytical tools. Although there have been some recent attempts at creating better ambulatory scales (Wright & Zimmermann, 2019), modeling ESM data as networks (Beck & Jackson, 2019a; Wright et al., 2019), and proposing new models for understanding such data (e.g. Beck & Jackson, 2019b), there is still a critical need for more work in this area.

There are several practical implications of this model. Traditional personnel selection and assessment methods rarely address the dynamic nature of personality: rather, it is used as a stable construct that predicts performance and other job-relevant outcomes. However, from the inception of this field of enquiry, personality scientists have meant to capture the dynamic components of personality just as much as, if not more than, the stable components (Allport, 1937; Cattell, 1957; cf. Beck & Jackson, 2019c, for a review). We underscore the need for more dynamic and within-person-based study of personality and situations in the workplace to understand how they contribute to work outcomes. Recent works have proposed revised situational judgment tests to understand within-person variability in personality within specific job-relevant situations (Lievens, 2017). Further investigation into the area can provide rich context for understanding employee life for both selection and developmental purposes. Another implication concerns employee well-being: experienced emotions are a crucial part of worker subjective well-being (Tenney, Poole, & Diener, 2016). This model provides a framework for practitioners to develop individualized employee well-being programs focused on job-relevant situations, state-level personality components, and emotional experience, and to measure dynamic changes. We call for further empirical work in both theoretical and practical areas.

References

Amabile, T. M., Hill, K. G., Hennessey, B. A., & Tighe, E. M. (1994). The work preference inventory: Assessing intrinsic and extrinsic motivational orientations. *Journal of Personality and Social Psychology*, *66*(5), 950–967.

Ashkanasy, N. M., & Dorris, A. (2017). Emotions in the workplace. *Annual Review of Organizational Psychology and Organizational Behavior*, *4*, 67–90. https://doi.org/10.1146/annurev-orgpsych-032516–113231

Barrett, L. F. (2006). Are emotions natural kinds? *Perspectives on Psychological Science*, *1*(1), 28–58, https://doi.org/10.1111/j.1745–6916.2006.00003.x

Barrett, L. F. (2009). Variety is the spice of life: A psychological construction approach to understanding variability in emotion. *Cognition and Emotion*, *23*(7), 1284–1306, https://doi.org/10.1080/02699930902985894

Barrick, M. R., & Mount, M. K. (1991). The big five personality dimensions and job performance: A meta-analysis. *Personnel Psychology*, *44*(1), 1–26, https://doi.org/10.1111/j.1744–6570.1991.tb00688.x

Barsade, S. G., & Gibson, D. E. (2007). Why does affect matter in organizations? *Academy of Management Perspectives*, *21*(1), 36–59.

Basch, J., & Fisher, C. D. (2000). Affective job events–emotions matrix: A classification of job related events and emotions experienced in the workplace. In N. M. Ashkanasy, C. E. J. Härtel, & W. J. Zerbe (Eds.), *Emotions in the workplace: Research, theory, and practice* (pp. 36–48). Westport, CT: Quorum.

Beck, E. D., & Jackson, J. J. (2019a). Consistency and change in idiographic personality: A longitudinal ESM network study. *Journal of Personality and Social Psychology*, 23 May, https://doi.org/10.1037/pspp0000249

Beck, E. D., & Jackson, J. J. (2019b). Network approaches to representation and understanding personality dynamics, https://doi.org/10.31234/osf.io/8qws9

Beck, E. D., & Jackson, J. J. (2019c). Within-person variability, https://doi.org/10.31234/osf.io/kavbp

Binnewies, C., & Wörnlein, S. C. (2011). What makes a creative day? A diary study on the interplay between affect, job stressors, and job control. *Journal of Organizational Behavior*, *32*(4), 589–607, https://doi.org/10.1002/job.731

Bouckenooghe, D., Raja, U., & Butt, A. N. (2013). Combined effects of positive and negative affectivity and job satisfaction on job performance and turnover intentions. *Journal of Psychology*, *147*(2), 105–123, https://doi.org/10.1080/00223980.2012.678411

Brief, A. P., & Weiss, H. M. (2002). Organizational behavior: Affect in the workplace. *Annual Review of Psychology*, *53*(1), 279–307, https://doi.org/10.1146/annurev.psych.53.100901.135156

Buss, D. M., & Craik, K. H. (1983). The act frequency approach to personality. *Psychological Review*, *90*(2), 105–126.

Costa, P. T., & McCrae, R. R. (1992). Normal personality assessment in clinical practice: The NEO Personality Inventory. *Psychological Assessment*, *4*(1), 5.

Cropanzano, R., Weiss, H. M., Hale, J. M. S., & Reb, J. (2003). The structure of affect: Reconsidering the relationship between negative and positive affectivity. *Journal of Management*, *29*(6), 831–857, https://doi.org/10.1016/S0149-2063(03)00081–3

Dalal, R. S. (2005). A meta-analysis of the relationship between organizational citizenship behavior and counterproductive work behavior. *Journal of Applied Psychology*, *90*(6), 1241–1255, https://doi.org/10.1037/0021–9010.90.6.1241

Eid, M., & Diener, E. (1999). Intraindividual variability in affect: Reliability, validity, and personality correlates. *Journal of Personality and Social Psychology*, *76*(4), 662–676, https://doi.org/10.1037/0022–3514.76.4.662

Ekman, P. (1992). Are there basic emotions? *Psychological Review*, *99*(3), 550–553, https://doi.org/10.1037/0033-295X.99.3.550

Endler, N. S., & Hunt, J. M. (1968). S-R inventories of hostility and comparisons of the proportions of variance from persons, responses, and situations for hostility and anxiousness. *Journal of Personality and Social Psychology*, *9*(4), 309–315.

Fehr, R., Fulmer, A., Awtrey, E., & Miller, J. A. (2017). The grateful workplace: A multilevel model of gratitude in organizations. *Academy of Management Review*, *42*(2), 361–381, https://doi.org/10.5465/amr.2014.0374

Fisher, C. D. (2002). Antecedents and consequences of real-time affective reactions at work. *Motivation and Emotion*, *26*(1), 28.

Fitness, J. (2000). Anger in the workplace: An emotion script approach to anger episodes between workers and their superiors, co-workers and subordinates. *Journal of Organizational Behavior*, *21*, 147–162.

Fleeson, W. (2001). Toward a structure- and process-integrated view of personality: Traits as density distribution of states. *Journal of Personality and Social Psychology*, *80*(6), 1011–1027, https://doi.org/10.1037/a0035325

Fleeson, W., & Jayawickreme, E. (2015). Whole trait theory. *Journal of Research in Personality*, *56*, 82–92, https://doi.org/10.1016/j.jrp.2014.10.009

Frijda, N. H. (1988). The laws of emotion. *American Psychologist*, *43*, 349–358, https://doi.org/10.1037/0003-066X.43.5.349

Funder, D. C., Furr, R. M., & Colvin, C. R. (2000). The Riverside Behavioral Q-sort: A tool for the description of social behavior. *Journal of Personality*, *68*(3), 451–489.

Gabriel, A. S., Podsakoff, N. P., Beal, D. J., Scott, B. A., Sonnentag, S., Trougakos, J. P., & Butts, M. M. (2018). Experience sampling methods. *Organizational Research Methods*, 22, https://doi.org/10.1177/1094428118802626

George, J. M. (1991). State or trait: Effects of positive mood on prosocial behaviors at work. *Journal of Applied Psychology*, *76*, 299–307.

Goldberg, L. R. (1990). An alternative "description of personality": The big-five factor structure. *Journal of Personality and Social Psychology*, *59*(6), 1216–1229.

Gooty, J., Connelly, S., Griffith, J., & Gupta, A. (2010). Leadership, affect and emotions: A state of the science review. *Leadership Quarterly*, *21*(6), 979–1004, https://doi.org/10.1016/j.leaqua.2010.10.005

Gooty, J., Gavin, M., & Ashkanasy, N. M. (2009). Emotions research in OB: The challenges that lie ahead. *Journal of Organizational Behavior*, *30*(6), 833–838. https://doi.org/10.1002/job.619

Grandey, A. A. (2003). When "the show must go on": Surface acting and deep acting as determinants of emotional exhaustion and peer-rated service delivery. *Academy of Management Journal*, *46*(1), 86–96.

Grandey, A. A., Tam, A. P., & Brauburger, A. L. (2002). Affective states and traits in the workplace: Diary and survey data from young workers. *Motivation and Emotion*, *26*(1), 33–55.

Grant, A. M. (2008). Does intrinsic motivation fuel the prosocial fire? Motivational synergy in predicting persistence, performance, and productivity. *Journal of Applied Psychology*, *93*(1), 48–58, https://doi.org/10.1037/0021–9010.93.1.48

Gross, J. J. (1998). The emerging field of emotion regulation. *Review of General Psychology*, *2*(3), 271, https://doi.org/http://dx.doi.org/10.1037/1089–2680.2.3.271

Howell, R. T., Ksendzova, M., Nestingen, E., Yerahian, C., & Iyer, R. (2017). Your personality on a good day: How trait and state personality predict daily well-being. *Journal of Research in Personality*, *69*, 250–263, https://doi.org/10.1016/j.jrp.2016.08.001

Ilies, R., Schwind, K. M., & Heller, D. (2007). Employee well-being: A multilevel model linking work and nonwork domains. *European Journal of Work and Organizational Psychology*, *16*(3), 326–341, https://doi.org/10.1080/13594320701363712

Jayawickreme, E., Zachry, C. E., & Fleeson, W. (2019). Whole trait theory: An integrative approach to examining personality structure and process. *Personality and Individual Differences*, *136*, 2–11, https://doi.org/10.1016/J.PAID.2018.06.045

Kaplan, S., Bradley, J. C., Luchman, J. N., & Haynes, D. (2009). On the role of positive and negative affectivity in job performance: A meta-analytic investigation. *Journal of Applied Psychology*, *94*(1), 162.

Kuppens, P., & Van Mechelen, I. (2007). Interactional appraisal models for the anger appraisals of threatened self-esteem, other-blame, and frustration. *Cognition and Emotion*, *21*(1), 56–77, https://doi.org/10.1080/02699930600562193

Kuppens, P., Van Mechelen, I., Nezlek, J. B., Dossche, D., & Timmermans, T. (2007). Individual differences in core affect variability and their relationship to personality and psychological adjustment. *Emotion*, *7*(2), 262–274, https://doi.org/10.1037/1528-3542.7.2.262

Kuppens, P., Van Mechelen, I., Smits, D. J. M., De Boeck, P., & Ceulemans, E. (2007). Individual differences in patterns of appraisal and anger experience Individual differences in patterns of appraisal and anger experience. *Cognition and Emotion*, *21*(4), 689–713, https://doi.org/10.1080/02699930600859219

Lee, K., & Ashton, M. C. (2004). Psychometric properties of the HEXACO Personality Inventory. *Multivariate Behavioral Research*, *39*(2), 329–358, https://doi.org/10.1207/s15327906mbr3902_8

Lievens, F. (2017). Assessing personality–situation interplay in personnel selection: Toward more integration into personality research. *European Journal of Personality*, *31*, 424–440, https://doi.org/10.1002/per.2111

Lindebaum, D., & Geddes, D. (2016). The place and role of (moral) anger in organizational behavior studies. *Journal of Organizational Behavior*, *37*, 738–757, https://doi.org/10.1002/job

Lindebaum, D., & Jordan, P. J. (2012). Positive emotions, negative emotions, or utility of discrete emotions? *Journal of Organizational Behavior*, *33* (7), 1027–1030, https://doi.org/10.1002/job.605

McNiel, J. M., & Fleeson, W. (2006). The causal effects of extraversion on positive affect and neuroticism on negative affect: Manipulating state extraversion and state neuroticism in an experimental approach. *Journal of Research in Personality*, *40*(5), 529–550, https://doi.org/10.1016/j.jrp.2005.05.003

Meyer, R. D., Dalal, R. S., & Hermida, R. (2010). A review and synthesis of situational strength in the organizational sciences. *Journal of Management*, *36*(1), 121–140, https://doi.org/10.1177/0149206309349309

Mischel, W., & Shoda, Y. (1995). A cognitive–affective system theory of personality: Reconceptualizing situations, dispositions, dynamics, and invariance in personality structure. *Psychological Review*, *102* (2), 246–268.

Moors, A., Ellsworth, P. C., Scherer, K. R., & Frijda, N. H. (2013). Appraisal theories of emotion: State of the art and future development. *Emotion Review*, *5*(2), 119–124, https://doi.org/10.1177/1754073912468165

Murray, G., Allen, N. B., & Trinder, J. (2002). Longitudinal investigation of mood variability and the FFM: Neuroticism predicts variability in extended states of positive and negative affect. *Personality and Individual Differences*, *33*, 1217–1228.

Oerlemans, W. G. M., & Bakker, A. B. (2014). Why extraverts are happier: A day reconstruction study. *Journal of Research in Personality*, *50*, 11–22, https://doi.org/10.1016/j.jrp.2014.02.001

Oerlemans, W. G. M., & Bakker, A. B. (2018). Motivating job characteristics and happiness at work: A multilevel perspective. *Journal of Applied Psychology*, *103*, 1230–1241, https://doi.org/10.1037/apl0000318

Ouweneel, E., Le Blanc, P. M., Schaufeli, W. B., & van Wijhe, C. I. (2012). Good morning, good day: A diary study on positive emotions, hope, and work engagement. *Human Relations*, *65*(9), 1129–1154, https://doi.org/10.1177/0018726711429382

Parrigon, S., Woo, S. E., Tay, L., Wang, T., & Wang, T. (2016). CAPTION-ing the situation : A lexically-derived taxonomy of psychological situation characteristics. *Journal of Personality and Social Psychology*, *112*(4), 642–681.

Rauthmann, J. F., Gallardo-Pujol, D., Guillaume, E. M., Todd, E., Nave, C. S., Sherman, R. A., . . . & Funder, D. C. (2014). The situational eight DIAMONDS: A taxonomy of major dimensions of situation characteristics. *Personality Processes and Individual Differences*, *107*(4), 677–718.

Russell, J. A. (1980). A circumplex model of affect. *Journal of Personality and Social Psychology*, *39* (6), 1161–1178, https://doi.org/10.1037/h0077714

Russell, J. A. (2003). Core affect and the psychological construction of emotion. *Psychological Review*, *110* (1), 145–172, https://doi.org/10.1037/0033-295X .110.1.145

Russell, J. A. (2009). Emotion, core affect, and psychological construction. *Cognition and Emotion*, *23*(7), 1259–1283, https://doi.org/10 .1080/02699930902809375

Shockley, K. M., Ispas, D., Rossi, M. E., & Levine, E. L. (2012). A Meta-analytic investigation of the relationship between state affect, discrete emotions, and job performance. *Human Performance*, *25*(5), 377–411, https://doi.org/10 .1080/08959285.2012.721832

Tellegen, A., Watson, D., & Clark, L. A. (1999). On the dimensional and hierarchical structure of affect. *Psychological Science*, *10*(4), 297–303, https://doi .org/10.1111/1467–9280.00157

Tenney, E. R., Poole, J. M., & Diener, E. (2016). Does positivity enhance work performance? Why, when, and what we don't know. *Research in Organizational Behavior*, *36*, 27–46, https://doi.org /10.1016/j.riob.2016.11.002

Thoresen, C. J., Kaplan, S. A., Barsky, A. P., Warren, C. R., & De Chermont, K. (2003). The affective underpinnings of job perceptions and attitudes: a meta-analytic review and integration. *Psychological Bulletin*, *129*(6), 914–945, https:// doi.org/10.1037/0033–2909.129.6.914

Verduyn, P., & Lavrijsen, S. (2015). Which emotions last longest and why: The role of event importance and rumination. *Motivation and Emotion*, *39*(1), 119–127, https://doi.org/10.1007 /s11031-014–9445-y

Watson, D., & Clark, L. A. (1984). Negative affectivity: The disposition to experience aversive emotional states. *Psychological Bulletin*, *96*(3), 465–490, https://doi.org/10.1037/0033–2909.96.3.465

Watson, D., & Tellegen, A. (2002). Aggregation, acquiescence, and the assessment of trait affectivity. *Journal of Research in Personality*, *36*, 589–597.

Waugh, C. E., Thompson, R. J., & Gotlib, I. H. (2011). Flexible emotional responsiveness in trait resilience. *Emotion*, *11*(5), 1059–1067, https://doi .org/10.1037/a0021786

Weiss, H. M., & Cropanzano, R. (1996). Affective events theory: A theoretical discussion of the structure, causes and consequences of affective experiences at work. In B. M. Staw & L. L. Cummings (Eds.), *Research in organizational behavior: An annual series of analytical essays and critical reviews*, Volume 18 (pp. 1–74). Elsevier Science/JAI.

Weiss, H. M., & Rupp, D. E. (2011). Experiencing work: An essay on a person-centric work psychology. *Industrial and Organizational Psychology*, *4*(1), 83–97, https://doi.org/10.1111/j .1754–9434.2010.01302.x

Williams, D. G. (1989). Neuroticism and extraversion in different factors of the affect intensity measure. *Personality and Individual Differences*, *10*(10), 1095–1100.

Wilt, J., Bleidorn, W., & Revelle, W. (2017). Velocity explains the links between personality states and affect. *Journal of Research in Personality*, *69*, 86–95, https://doi.org/10.1016/j.jrp.2016.06.008

Wilt, J., Noftle, E. E., Fleeson, W., & Spain, J. S. (2012). The dynamic role of personality states in mediating the relationship between extraversion and positive affect. *Journal of Personality*, *80*(5), 1205–1236, https://doi.org/10.1111/j.1467–6494 .2011.00756.x

Wilt, J., & Revelle, W. (2015). Affect, behaviour, cognition and desire in the Big Five: An analysis of item content and structure: ABCD scales. *European Journal of Personality, 29*(4), 478–497, https://doi.org/10.1002/per.2002

Wright, A., Gates, K. M., Arizmendi, C., Lane, S. T., Woods, W. C., & Edershile, E. A. (2019). Focusing personality assessment on the person: Modeling general, shared, and person specific processes in personality and psychopathology. *Psychological Assessment, 31*(4), 502.

Wright, A., & Zimmermann, J. (2019). Applied ambulatory assessment: Integrating idiographic and nomothetic principles of measurement. *Psychological Assessment*, 21 March, https://doi.org/10.1037/pas0000685

Wright, J. C., & Mischel, W. (1987). A conditional approach to dispositional constructs: The local predictability of social behavior. *Journal of Personality and Social Psychology, 53*(6), 1159–1177.

Yeung, E., & Shen, W. (2019). Can pride be a vice and virtue at work? Associations between authentic and hubristic pride and leadership behaviors. *Journal of Organizational Behavior, 40*, 605–624, https://doi.org/10.1002/job.2352

Yik, M., Russell, J. A., & Steiger, J. H. (2011). A 12-point circumplex structure of core affect. *Emotion, 11*(4), 705–731, https://doi.org/10.1037/a0023980

Zuckerman, M. (1979). Traits, states, situations, and uncertainty. *Journal of Behavioral Assessment, 1* (1), 33–54.

4 Workplace Emotions and Motivation

Toward a Unified Approach

Keaton A. Fletcher, Ruth Kanfer, and Corey Tatel

Affect and emotions play a key role in motivational processes, working together to make sense of one's experience and to guide behavior. Until recently, however, research on motivation in the workplace has advanced largely independently from research exploring the role of emotions and affect at work. To better understand the human experience of work, we must explore the connections between these aspects as they influence thoughts, feelings, and behaviors related to work. In this chapter we describe theory and research that supports the ultimate development of a unified perspective; namely, an approach that takes into account how emotional experiences affect and interact with motivational forces to influence work behavior and its outcomes.

Our chapter is organized into three sections. We begin by briefly defining key constructs: motivation, goals, affect, mood, and emotions. Next, we compare and contrast how affect and emotions are conceptualized in different work motivation perspectives. In the final section we summarize progress, identify abiding challenges, and suggest potentially fruitful research directions and implications for practice.

Defining and Distinguishing Key Concepts

At the broadest level, "work motivation" can, as an umbrella term, denote the person and environmental determinants, psychological processes, and outcomes associated with the individual's choice and pursuit of meaningful goals and valued outcomes. Included in this definition are more narrow concepts that help to explain observable changes in the initiation, direction, intensity, and persistence of voluntary action (Kanfer, Frese, & Johnson, 2018; Pinder, 1984). Over the past century many work motivation theories have been proposed (see Kanfer, 2012). Most, but not all, of these theories focus on determinants, mechanisms, and consequences of consciously-mediated goals, such as task accomplishment, job and team performance, and career success. Through most of the mid- to late twentieth century, work motivation researchers focused on what may be called non-emotional goals: goals that arise from reflection rather than reflexive or otherwise affectively-driven impulses and feelings. Setting a quarterly sales target, for example, is an achievement-type goal that develops based more on a conscious deliberation on conditions and resources, rather than on emotional feeling states. Integral to these perspectives is the idea of goals, which can be defined as future valued outcomes (Locke & Latham, 2006) that have both cognitive and affective components, but that have been generally studied (until recently) as a deliberative, conscious process.

The conceptualization of motivation as a goal-oriented process is consistent with the notion of work motivation as a malleable psychological state that explains how/why an individual performs "a particular behavior on a particular occasion" (Baumeister, 2016, p. 2). At the same time, other motivation researchers have conceptualized motivation in terms of general, trait-like motivational patterns and drives that explain constellations of outcome preferences and associated behaviors directed toward fulfillment of broad needs or desires (e.g. achievement, relatedness, etc.). Although this perspective is not the emphasis of this chapter, keeping this understanding of motivation paradigms in mind is helpful for researchers concerned with disentangling the myriad links between affect and motivation.

"Affect" is another broad umbrella term that captures an individual's feeling state or dispositional experience, typically encompassing both emotions and moods. Much of this chapter focuses on the link between motivation and emotions in the workplace, but we do briefly touch on other affective states (e.g. mood). Moods are affective states that are typically not tied to specific stimuli and are not particularly intense (Brief & Weiss, 2002). Emotions, on the other hand, are often conceptualized as complex reactions to specific stimuli that have three major components: a subjective thought/feeling quality (e.g. anger or joy), a physiological quality, and a behavioral quality (a motivational or action readiness; Roseman, 2008). Although there is growing recognition that emotions can motivate specific action (Eder, 2017; Ridderinkhof, 2017), accounts of how these multi-form events have their behavioral effects vary. Several general approaches and work motivation theories (e.g. affective events theory; Weiss & Cropanzano, 1996) focus on the role of cognitive appraisal as a mediator of the action process, supporting the idea proposed by Buck (1999) that emotions represent personally meaningful readouts of events and stimuli that have motivational implications. Some researchers (e.g. Baumeister, 2016) even argue that emotion exists in order to serve and facilitate motivation.

Similar to motivational theories, affect can be viewed as either a feeling state (e.g. emotion or mood) that is relatively malleable and tied to more discrete behaviors in specific situations, or as a general disposition that describes a pattern of thoughts, behaviors, and action tendencies. Again, although this trait perspective is not the main emphasis of the present chapter, keeping it in mind may be helpful for researchers working on the ties between affect, motivation, and behavior in the workplace.

Distinguishing Motivation, Mood, and Emotion

Motivation and affect are inexorably related. Although a broad examination of motivation and affect is beyond the scope of our chapter, the distinction between momentary motivations, mood, and emotion may hold implications for the broader constructs (Table 4.1). Mood is clearly distinct from motivation and more discrete emotions. Mood tends to be slow to change and long-lasting, predisposes an individual to a broad range of cognitions and behaviors, and cannot be clearly linked to any one specific stimulus (Beedie, Terry, & Lane, 2005). Motivation, on the other hand, can be thought of hierarchically, unfolding over a range of time frames, depending on the nature of the motivating stimuli (e.g. writing a report, cognitively recovering during lunch). As such, motivation can be short-term or long-term, but typically occurs in response to a specific internally accepted goal that predisposes the individual to a specific pattern of behaviors and cognitions. For example, many sales agents receive an annual bonus based on dollar sales for the year. The affective evaluation of the bonus as a positive-valence outcome can encourage the adoption of a more difficult sales goal, which in turn demands momentarily higher levels of attention and effort. Emotions, and also aspects of motivation, tend to be viewed as quite ephemeral, occurring in response to a range of external stimuli, predisposing the individual to a narrow (in comparison to mood) range of behavioral and cognitive processes (Beedie et al., 2005). For example, isolation or insults can elicit feelings of sadness, and sadness elicits tendencies to withdraw from social contact. Given these unique aspects, one may argue that emotions

Table 4.1 Distinguishing features of motivation, emotion, and mood

Feature of state	Motivation	Emotion	Mood
Duration	**Momentary to long-lasting** seconds to months	**Momentary** seconds to hours	**Long-lasting** hours to months
Origin	**Internal** e.g. goals and drives	**External** e.g. environmental stimuli	**Internal** unidentified internal patterns
Specificity of eliciting stimuli	**Specific** stimuli are tied to their specific motivational response	**Varied** varied stimuli can elicit an emotion	–
Specificity of behavioral outcome	**Specific** behavior maps directly onto goal	**Narrow** behavior follows general pattern for emotion	**Broad** behavior predispositions are influenced by mood

are an inherently motivational affective state. Motivation and emotion, then, work together to influence individual behavior.

Yet, as many researchers have noted, the interplay between motivation and emotion is nuanced. When emotion and motivation are aligned, outcomes can be amplified. In other words, if internally set goals (e.g. competitive mastery) align with external emotional stimuli (e.g. winning an award for best painting), then the behavioral outcomes should be clearer. A positive interaction with one's leader, for example, may elicit happiness or excitement that amplifies one's longer-standing motivation to perform citizenship behaviors. There are situations, however, where emotions may misalign with motivation and work against the goal-directed process. Take, for example, anger toward one's supervisor. In this case, anger may elicit counterproductive behaviors (e.g. theft, gossip, violence) that do not align with the individual's goals (e.g. job stability, pay). Yet motivation devoid of emotion may be undesirable as well. Many argue that motivation capitalizes upon emotion to promote goal-directed behavior (e.g. Perugini & Bagozzi, 2001). Emotions, in some sense, act as feedback from the environment that goal-directed behaviors are successful and that the goal is situationally valued. Without this feedback, motivation may wane over time, or may fail to recalibrate. Ordóñez and colleagues (2009) described scenarios in which goal setting, unchecked by emotions, led to unethical behavior (e.g. fraud). Take the 2016 Wells Fargo fraud case, in which over 5,600 Wells Fargo employees engaged in a range of fraudulent behavior (e.g. creation of fake accounts, opening of credit cards, or changing mortgages without client knowledge) that cost the organization over $1.1 billion dollars, due to unrealistically high sales goals (Wattles, Geier, Egan, & Wiener-Bronner, 2018). In this example, if there had been environmental stimuli that elicited emotional reactions such as guilt, fear, or shame, these might have aided in modulating individual motivations. Keeping these relationships in mind, we argue that motivation and emotion typically act symbiotically to keep individuals engaged in productive, desirable, and socially acceptable behavior.

Emotions in the Context of Work Motivation Theories

Most motivational theories accord affect a role in the prediction of behavior, but theories differ in how they define and incorporate affect. Hedonic expectancy-value theories (e.g. Vroom, 1964), for example, typically incorporate affect in terms of the anticipated pleasure or pain associated with projected outcomes of action. Other theories increasingly popular during the past decade, such as self-determination theory (SDT; Deci & Ryan, 1985), emphasize the positive affect and well-being brought about by engaging in actions that satisfy intrinsic motives (e.g. autonomy, competence, relatedness). Yet other theories (e.g. regulatory focus theory; Brockner & Higgins, 2001) propose that individual differences in motivational traits and states interact in their influence on goal choice and behavior. Below, we briefly review four major motivational theories of work and the role of emotions: SDT, equity theory, expectancy theory, and regulatory focus theory. We also highlight two affect-oriented theories (core affect and affective events theory) that explicitly include motivation in order to expand our understanding of the interplay between motivation and affect.

Self-Determination Theory

Deci and Ryan (1985) outline three universal motives or psychological needs that inform individual behavior: autonomy, competence, and relatedness. According to SDT, individuals seek work experiences that allow them to feel they have some control over their environment and behaviors, that give them the opportunity to demonstrate task competence/mastery, and that allow for the prospect of developing meaningful interpersonal relationships. SDT further posits that environmental stimuli that become associated with these motives can facilitate the internalization and integration of extrinsic motivation (Gagné & Deci, 2005). Although emotions and mood are not explicitly delineated in SDT formulations, they are implicitly recognized as potential points of environmental feedback. If, for example, an employee's autonomy is being challenged by an overbearing boss, the employee may feel anger, which in turn might help to calibrate motivation to pursue and adopt goal assignments from the boss and/or to engage in job search behavior. Similarly, employee joy experienced when mastering a new task is expected to function as a reward that stimulates further task effort. In the same manner, sadness and anger in response to performance-goal-based failure is expected to motivate withdrawal or avoidance behavior with respect to the task. Although Ryan and Deci (2008) propose that emotions "provide people with valuable cues about when they are or are not getting what they need" (p. 190) and that "central to emotions such as anger and sadness are experiences of need thwarting" (p. 190), little empirical work has actually been done on the role of explicit emotions as points of information that regulate need pursuit within the context of SDT.

Bartholomew, Ntourmanis, Ryan, Bosch, and Thøgersen-Ntoumani (2011) explored the mediating role of need satisfaction and need thwarting in the relationship of autonomy and control with positive affect, negative affect, and burnout among teenage athletes. Their findings show that need satisfaction experiences over the prior month positively predicted subsequent positive affect, while negatively predicting negative affect and burnout. On the other hand, experiences that thwarted satisfaction of autonomy, competence, and relatedness needs significantly and positively predicted subsequent negative affect and burnout (but not positive affect). At the episodic level, the authors found a similar pattern of results: need satisfaction, but not need thwarting, predicted positive affect, while need thwarting, but not need satisfaction, predicted negative affect. Together, these findings lend some support to the supposition that emotions and affect serve as a potential internal gauge, both in the moment and across longer periods of time, of the alignment between one's internal goals/needs and external environmental stimuli. Future studies may more explicitly link specific emotions (beyond positive/negative affect) with momentary perceptions of goal/need achievement/thwarting. Further, by exploring, in real time, the relationship between perceptions of goal achievement/thwarting, emotions, and subsequent adjustments to goals/needs or behaviors, we can more clearly understand the role emotions play in SDT.

Equity Theory

Adams (1965) proposed that individuals are motivated to maintain a perceived equity in the ratio of inputs to outcomes between themselves and other parties (e.g. their employer). Emotions are given an explicit role in equity theory, such that when an inequity is perceived, an individual experiences negative emotions. Specifically, if the individual feels as if they are putting in more effort for less reward compared to others, they feel anger and are motivated to decrease this discrepancy by either increasing their outcomes or decreasing their input. On the other hand, if individuals feel as if they are receiving more for less effort in comparison to others, they will feel guilt and will be motivated to decrease this discrepancy by putting in more effort or decreasing their rewards. Adams (1965) argued that the threshold for experiencing guilt in response to inequity may be higher than the threshold for experiencing anger. In this model, emotions act as a feedback mechanism by which environmental stimuli (i.e. discrepancies in effort/reward ratios) influence motivated behavior. Although equity theory has fallen out of vogue in recent years, we argue that by better integrating the role of emotions, and examining behavior and motivation on an episodic level, equity theory may yet yield meaningful insight into the experience of work.

Although explicit tests and applications of equity theory have recently been relatively limited to marriage psychology (e.g. Lively, Steelman, & Powell, 2010), equity theory is often invoked when researches explore the role of distributive justice perceptions and their link to outcomes. For example, one study (Krischer, Penney, & Hunter, 2010) found that perceptions of distributive justice negatively predicted emotional exhaustion (measured with items from the Job-Related Affective Well-being Scale (Van Katwyk, Fox, Spector, & Kelloway, 2000) such as *I feel depressed*, *I feel frustrated*), but that this relationship was weakest when individuals engaged in high levels of counterproductive work behaviors (CWBs). These results suggest that individuals who engage in CWBs may be balancing out the perceived inequity associated with low levels of distributive justice, thereby reducing their felt negative affect. Again, these findings are based on general perceptions, leaving room for a more momentary examination to explore the nature of these relationships.

Expectancy Theory

Many theories of motivated behavior share a basis in instrumentality theory (Vroom, 1964), which proposes that motivation is the outcome of the interaction between an individual's perceived valence of an outcome ("Do I want this outcome?"), perceived instrumentality ("Can I do the behavior?"), and perceived expectancy ("If I do the behavior, I will get the outcome"). Here, again, we see emotion playing a significant, albeit somewhat implicit, role in the form of the valence component of this formula. The felt emotional experience can be seen as the outcome itself, or as an evaluation of the outcome. In other words, if the individual is considering whether to take on a new project at work, the expected emotional experience associated with taking on this new project may be the outcome by which the individual judges valence. Or, the individual may be considering the increased attention the project will bring, and the emotional experience of that attention (positive or negative) is the information by which the outcome is judged. Regardless, the explicit role of emotion in expectancy theories can and should be further explored. Specifically, an examination of the role emotion plays in informing the valence component of the model may be particularly fruitful.

Although direct tests of expectancy theory are increasingly uncommon in recent years, one study (Erez & Isen, 2002) explored the effects of a mood induction on different components of the expectancy system. Results suggest that positive affect increased expected performance, valence of outcomes, and, less consistently, expected reward. This effect increased in strength as the difficulty and attractiveness of the task increased. Here, unlike in previous examinations, state affect is proposed to be influencing how individuals are evaluating the task and themselves. So, rather than directly acting as environmental feedback, affect is indirectly providing feedback into the system, boosting confidence and expectancy, in the case of positive affect. This relationship may, however, be dynamic, such that as performance is pursued, emotional experiences may emerge, altering the affective state, and more directly influencing expected performance and valence. This dynamic nature of the relationship, along with how expectancy theory generally fails to directly capture the nature of time, is explicitly highlighted by George and Jones (2000). Specifically, in their general review of the treatment of time in organizational theory, George and Jones (2000) argue that all motivational theories, expectancy theory, in particular, fail to adequately integrate the role of the past (e.g. self-efficacy, trait motivation, previous affective state) with the role of the present and future (e.g. expected outcomes, changing performance information).

Regulatory Focus Theory

Higgins (1997) proposed an extension of traditional hedonic theories of motivation, arguing that individuals regulate their behavior in two ways: promotion focus and prevention focus. A promotion focus captures an individual's desire to achieve new positive outcomes, aligning more closely with an ideal self. A prevention focus, on the other hand, captures an individual's desire to minimize negative outcomes. Brockner and Higgins (2001) proposed an explicit link between goal-progress, promotion or prevention focus, and felt emotions. Specifically, they argued that a promotion focus is aligned with a cheerful–dejected dimension of emotion, such that goal progress is associated with cheerfulness and goal hindrance is closely linked with dejection. A prevention focus, they argued, is aligned with a quiescent–agitated dimension of felt emotion, such that goal progress links with quiescence and goal hindrance links with agitation. As with other theories, emotions act as an experienced form of environmental feedback, informing individuals whether they are moving toward or away from their goals. Of note, however, is that this theory suggests that one's motivational state (prevention or promotion) may alter the emotional experience, thereby indicating a more nuanced relationship between motivation and emotion than other theories previously described.

Empirical examinations of regulatory focus theory have treated promotion and prevention focus as dispositional constructs (e.g. Amodio, Shah, Sigelman, Brazy, & Harmon-Jones, 2004; Koopmann, Johnson, Wang, Lanaj, Wang, & Shi, 2018) or as malleable, state-like constructs (e.g. Leone, Perugini, & Bagozzi, 2010). The relationship between promotion/prevention focus and emotions may alter depending on which lens one chooses to look through. Results suggest that at a neurological level, individuals who are higher in trait promotion focus show more resting activation (captured by an electroencephalogram) in the left frontal cortex (a region associated with anger and approach-oriented behavior; Harmon-Jones & Allen, 1998), while those who are higher in trait prevention focus show more activation in the right frontal cortex (a region typically associated with withdrawal-related emotions such as fear or anxiety; Davidson, 2004). Moving past a physiological correlation between the experience of emotion and regulatory focus, evidence suggests that a tendency to consciously reappraise one's emotions can weaken the relationship between dispositional prevention focus (but not promotion focus) and chronic emotional exhaustion (Koopmann et al., 2018). Although this provides some potential insight into the complex relationship between regulatory focus and affect, these findings cannot speak to momentary reciprocal relationships between these constructs. Leone and colleagues (2010), on the other hand, showed that the pattern of relationships between regulatory focus and emotion found at the dispositional level also held at the momentary, episodic level. Specifically, they found that if people expected to be dejected if they failed a task, they were more likely to want to do the task if they were high in either state or trait promotion focus. Similarly, if participants expected high levels of agitation in response to failing the task, they were more likely to want to do it if they were high in trait or state prevention focus. Together, these studies suggest that our understanding of regulatory focus can span multiple levels: neurological, momentary, and dispositional. However, theory may need to be further developed to capture the reciprocal and dynamic nature of experienced performance and emotion and anticipated performance and emotion.

Core Affect and Work Motivation

Seo, Feldman Barnett, and Bartunek (2004) proposed a model based on the concept of core affect that describes how emotions affect motivational processing. As delineated by Russell and Feldman-Barrett (1999), core affect refers to emotional experiences that can be characterized in terms of both valence and activation. In the Seo et al. (2004) model, core affect is argued to influence motivation processing directly and indirectly through the cognitive appraisal process. A distinct advantage of the core affect model is the integration of two distinct streams of literature: research that views affect as information for motivation (e.g. Schwarz, 1990) and research that views the role of affect as indirect, through its influence on how information is perceived or interpreted (e.g. Vroom, 1964). In other words, affect may influence behavior through a hedonic principle or by altering how information is perceived and processed. For example, individuals in better moods expect better outcomes from their behavior and thus focus more on these potential outcomes (e.g. Erez & Isen, 2002). Seo and colleagues (2004) further propose that the valence dimension of core affect influences motivation and persistence through beliefs about the attractiveness of behavior outcomes and perceptions of goal progress, respectively. In contrast, the arousal dimension of the affective state is posited to be associated with motivational *effort* toward a goal. Consistent with this formulation, organizational findings show that affect influences cognitive processes during the goal setting process and also influences the judgments people make about progress (Seo et al., 2004).

To date, few studies have empirically tested the Seo et al. (2004) model. Seo and colleagues (2010) provide initial empirical support for the model in findings based on experience-sampling of students engaged in an investment simulation. The researchers found that on days when participants reported higher positive affect, they also reported higher expectancy judgments, spent more time researching their decisions, and made more favorable evaluations of goal progress. These results support the notion that affective states impact motivational outcomes primarily through their effects on cognitive processing, although the conceptualization of core affect along two dimensions suggests that arousal might also exert a direct link between affective state and the amount of effort one puts into a task.

Affective Events Theory

According to affective events theory (AET; Weiss & Cropanzano, 1996), work events that trigger affective reactions exert their influence on motivated behavior in two ways: through (largely) non-conscious behavioral reactions, and through cognitively-mediated work attitudes and behaviors. AET addresses an abiding issue in the organizational literature: why do individuals who generally hold a positive attitude toward their job sometimes (and often unexpectedly) behave in a counterproductive manner at work? According to the theory, affective reactions to events may produce both affect-driven behaviors (e.g. anger, organizational citizenship behaviors) as well as judgment-driven behaviors (e.g. continuance commitment, turnover). As in the core affect (Seo et al., 2004) model, affect is assumed to play two roles: providing information upon which affect-driven behaviors are instigated, and the adoption of a perceptive lens through which job attitudes are formed and used to guide longer-term-motivated behaviors. AET has been applied to the study of motivated behavior in the context of downsizing (Paterson & Cary 2002), bullying at work (Ayoko, Callan, & Hartel, 2003), organizational injustice (Wisenfeld, Brockner, & Martin, 1999; Schaubroeck & Lam, 2004), interpersonal conflict with customers (Grandey, Tam, & Brauberger, 2002), and breaches in psychological contracts (Conway & Briner, 2002). One important feature of most research investigating AET is the use of experience-sampling methodologies that allow researchers to evaluate momentary changes in the relationships between event characteristics, affective states, attitudes, and the direction, intensity, or persistency of behavior. AET and experience-sampling methodologies provide promising avenues for better understanding how affective work events contribute to the demonstration of less frequent but important work behaviors such as micro-aggressions and courage in the workplace.

Summary, Abiding Issues, and Future Research Directions

As we note above, the role that emotions and state affect are accorded in motivational theories ranges from implied to explicit, but their role is generally viewed as a method of incorporating responses to environmental feedback into ongoing motivational processes. In comparison, more affect-centric theories (e.g. core affect and AET) afford motivation a secondary role in the experience of work. We argue that although researchers can place motivation or affect at the center of their focus, to truly understand how individuals maintain goal pursuit and adjust to environmental input, we need to continue exploring the nuanced, dynamic interface of motivation and emotion.

Moving forward, we suggest that examining how affect and motivation change together over time may help address lingering questions regarding their nuanced relationship. Many studies collect data on affect and motivation at the beginning or end of the work day. However, there is likely a decaying effect of state affect over time. For example, if one experiences an affective episode early in the morning, the strength of the emotion along with its subsequent impact on motivation may not be reported accurately at the end of the day. Others may measure affect and motivation at a single point in time, failing to capture the dynamic interplay between the two, or assuming state-level relationships when what was really captured is more akin to dispositional relationships. Affective events theory's emphasis on the dynamic nature of affect has spurred some work on temporal issues (Zohar, Tzischinski, & Epstein, 2003; Fuller et al., 2003; Judge & Ilies, 2004); however, more studies are needed to understand longitudinal and episodic experiences at work. Clearly there are many ways in which affect and motivation are linked in a dynamic process. Below we present some potentially fruitful avenues for future research (see Table 4.2 for

Table 4.2 Summary of possible avenues for research on motivation–affect relations

Topic area	Possible research avenues	Potential methodologies
Affect as a predictor of motivation	Neurological associations between affect and motivational processes (e.g. goal setting, decision-making)	Lab-based decision-making studies using fMRI
	Temporal stability of the influence of affect on motivation	Experience-sampling throughout the work day
	Nature of the motivational targets of affect (e.g. outcomes, behaviors, decisions)	Qualitative exploration of goal setting or decision-making processes
Affect and motivation as co-occurring constructs	Affective and motivational components of emergent states in teams	Group affect inductions to influence group constructs Content analysis of group interactions to explore affect and motivational contagion
	Nature of individual-level mixed affective/motivational states	Measurement design and validation of mixed emotional/motivational states
	Affect and motivational processes and outcomes in response to stress	Measurement of psychophysiological indicators of stress in response to affectively laden decision-making processes
Affect as an outcome of motivation	Motivational processes of emotion regulation	Experience-sampling throughout the work day
	Motivational processes of emotion influence	Daily-diary reflections on episodes of emotion influence

a summary) that address both the nature of the relationship and the implications of that relationship in the context of working.

Three features of the research suggestions presented in Table 4.2 warrant note. First, and most critically, we recommend that researchers in this area adopt a more dynamic perspective that allows for more precise evaluation of how affective states and motivation inform and act on each other over time and give rise to differences in the direction and intensity of action and in the personal states of health and well-being. Specifically, we argue for theory development and evaluation that follows the suggestions of George and Jones (2000), acknowledging the interplay of past and future states, how (and how rapidly) emotional or motivational states may change, whether change is incremental (as may be the case with the relationship between mood and goal-pursuit) or discontinuous (as may be the case if a new emotion hijacks motivation), and whether the relationships between motivation and emotion can be represented as feedback loops or cycles that gain or lose intensity. This may require further exploration at the neurological level, examining temporal fluctuations in activity in areas of the brain associated with emotion and motivation. Or, it may necessitate intensive experience-sampling methodologies or lab-based studies that can better tease apart the reciprocal relationships between these constructs.

Further, to better understand the relationship between affect and motivation over time and across individuals, we need to better understand our measures. By clarifying what exactly we are capturing (i.e. motivation, goals, mood, emotions, traits, etc.) we can better facilitate research and practice in these areas, thereby improving the health and performance of the modern workforce. Researchers must also become vigilant about capturing affect and motivation at the temporal level of investigation. Specifically, in order to speak to momentary relationships and processes, researchers should be measuring momentary states, rather than dispositions or aggregations. Researchers also need to move past simply looking at positive and negative affect, instead intentionally theorizing about, and measuring, specific emotional experiences. Computational modeling techniques may be of use in these endeavors, forcing researchers to be more specific about the nature of the relationships among variables in their theories.

Lastly, although it was beyond the scope of this particular review, we argue that it is critical to explore the nature of the relationship between affect and motivation at multiple levels. This chapter focuses primarily on the momentary/episodic level; however, one could explore the interactions between trait affect and trait motivation (though the bulk of research that occupies this intersection has been at this level), or perhaps even explore the interaction between affect and motivation at the group level. There exists some work on these topics, but, especially at the group level, little is truly known about the nature of the relationship between these two constructs.

Overall, when it comes to how motivation and state affect are linked, we see that one's perspective may shift as to whether emotions serve motivation or motivation is a byproduct of emotions. Emotions are either implicitly or explicitly included in all of the major motivation theories, and so must be better explored. We see, however, that across all of these theories, emotions can be viewed as a form (either directly or indirectly) of translating environmental feedback into meaningful internal information that aids in (re)adjusting goals and motivational states. But perhaps most importantly, we see that there is quite a bit of opportunity for future research when examining, and theorizing about this relationship on a momentary basis. We advise researchers to address this gap so as to advance both the science and the practice.

References

Adams, J. S. (1965). Inequity in social exchange. In L. Berkowitz (Ed.), *Advances in experimental social psychology* (Volume 2, pp. 267–299). New York, NY: Academic.

Amodio, D. M., Shah, J. Y., Sigelman, J., Brazy, P. C., & Harmon-Jones, E. (2004). Implicit regulatory focus associated with asymmetrical frontal cortical activity. *Journal of Experimental Social Psychology*, *40*(2), 225–232.

Ayoko, O. B., Callan, V. J., & Härtel, C. E. (2003). Workplace conflict, bullying, and counterproductive behaviors. *International Journal of Organizational Analysis*, *11*(4), 283–301.

Bartholomew, K. J., Ntoumanis, N., Ryan, R. M., Bosch, J. A., & Thøgersen-Ntoumani, C. (2011). Self-determination theory and diminished functioning: The role of interpersonal control and psychological need thwarting. *Personality and Social Psychology Bulletin*, *37*(11), 1459–1473.

Baumeister, R. F. (2016). Toward a general theory of motivation: Problems, challenges, opportunities, and the big picture. *Motivation and Emotion*, *40*(1), 1–10.

Beedie, C., Terry, P., & Lane, A. (2005). Distinctions between emotion and mood. *Cognition and Emotion*, *19*(6), 847–878.

Brief, A. P., & Weiss, H. M. (2002). Organizational behavior: Affect in the workplace. *Annual Review of Psychology*, *53*(1), 279–307.

Brockner, J., & Higgins, E. T. (2001). Regulatory focus theory: Implications for the study of emotions at work. *Organizational Behavior and Human Decision Processes*, *86*(1), 35–66.

Buck, R. (1999). The biological affects: A typology. *Psychological Review*, *106*(2), 301–336.

Conway, N., & Briner, R. B. (2002). A daily diary study of affective responses to psychological contract breach and exceeded promises. *Journal of Organizational Behavior*, *23*(3), 287–302.

Davidson, R. J. (2004). What does the prefrontal cortex "do" in affect? Perspectives on frontal EEG asymmetry research. *Biological Psychology*, *67* (1–2), 219–234.

Deci, E., & Ryan, R. M. (1985). *Intrinsic motivation and self-determination in human behavior.* New York, NY: Springer Science & Business Media.

Eder, A. B. (2017). From boxology to scientific theories: On the emerging field of emotional action sciences. *Emotion Review*, *9*, 343–355.

Edmans, A., Garcia, D., & Norli, Ø. (2007). Sports sentiment and stock returns. *Journal of Finance*, *62* (4), 1967–1998.

Erez, A., & Isen, A. M. (2002). The influence of positive affect on the components of expectancy motivation. *Journal of Applied Psychology*, *87*(6), 1055–1067.

Fuller, J. A., Stanton, J. M., Fisher, G. G., Spitzmüller, C., Russell, S. S., & Smith, P. C. (2003). A lengthy look at the daily grind: Time series analysis of events, mood, stress, and satisfaction. *Journal of Applied Psychology*, *88*(6), 1019–1033.

Gagné, M., & Deci, E. L. (2005). Self-determination theory and work motivation. *Journal of Organizational Behavior*, *26*(4), 331–362.

George, J. M., & Jones, G. R. (2000). The role of time in theory and theory building. *Journal of Management*, *26*(4), 657–684.

Grandey, A. A., Tam, A. P., & Brauburger, A. L. (2002). Affective states and traits in the workplace: Diary and survey data from young workers. *Motivation and Emotion*, *26*(1), 31–55.

Harmon-Jones, E., & Allen, J. J. (1998). Anger and frontal brain activity: EEG asymmetry consistent with approach motivation despite negative affective valence. *Journal of Personality and Social Psychology*, *74*(5), 1310–1316.

Higgins, E. T. (1997). Beyond pleasure and pain. *American Psychologist*, *52*(12), 1280–1300.

Judge, T. A., & Ilies, R. (2004). Affect and job satisfaction: A study of their relationship at work and at home. *Journal of Applied Psychology*, *89*(4), 661–673.

Kanfer, R., Frese, M., & Johnson, R. E. (2017). Motivation related to work: A century of progress. *Journal of Applied Psychology*, *102*(3), 338–355.

Koopmann, J., Johnson, R. E., Wang, M., Lanaj, K., Wang, G., & Shi, J. (2018). A self-regulation perspective on how and when regulatory focus differentially relates to citizenship behaviors. *Journal of Applied Psychology*, *104*, 629–641

Krischer, M. M., Penney, L. M., & Hunter, E. M. (2010). Can counterproductive work behaviors be productive? CWB as emotion-focused coping. *Journal of Occupational Health Psychology*, *15*(2), 154–166.

Leone, L., Perugini, M., & Bagozzi, R. (2005). Emotions and decision making: Regulatory focus moderates the influence of anticipated emotions on action evaluations. *Cognition & Emotion*, *19*(8), 1175–1198.

Lively, K. J., Steelman, L. C., & Powell, B. (2010). Equity, emotion, and household division of labor response. *Social Psychology Quarterly*, *73*(4), 358–379.

Locke, E. A., & Latham, G. P. (2006). New directions in goal-setting theory. *Current Directions in Psychological Science*, *15*(5), 265–268.

Ordóñez, L. D., Schweitzer, M. E., Galinsky, A. D., & Bazerman, M. H. (2009). Goals gone wild: The systematic side effects of overprescribing goal setting. *Academy of Management Perspectives*, *23* (1), 6–16.

Paterson, J. M., & Cary, J. (2002). Organizational justice, change anxiety, and acceptance of downsizing: Preliminary tests of an AET-based model. *Motivation and Emotion*, *26* (1), 83–103.

Perugini, M., & Bagozzi, R. P. (2001). The role of desires and anticipated emotions in goal-directed behaviours: Broadening and deepening the theory of planned behaviour. *British Journal of Social Psychology*, *40*(1), 79–98.

Pinder, C. C. 1984. *Work motivation: Theory, issues, and applications*. Glenview, IL: Scott, Foresman.

Ridderinkhof, K. R. (2017). Emotion in action: A predictive processing perspective and theoretical synthesis. *Emotion Review*, *9*, 319–325.

Roseman, I. J. (2008). Motivations and emotivations: Approach, avoidance, and other tendencies in motivated and emotional behavior. In A. J. Elliot (Ed.), *Handbook of approach and avoidance motivation* (pp. 343–366). New York, NY: Psychology.

Russell, J. A., & Barrett, L. F. (1999). Core affect, prototypical emotional episodes, and other things called emotion: Dissecting the elephant. *Journal of Personality and Social Psychology*, *76*(5), 805–819.

Ryan, R. M., & Deci, E. L. (2008). A self-determination theory approach to psychotherapy: The motivational basis for effective change. *Canadian Psychology/Psychologie Canadienne*, *49*(3), 186–193.

Schaubroeck, J., & Lam, S. S. (2004). Comparing lots before and after: Promotion rejectees' invidious reactions to promotees. *Organizational Behavior and Human Decision Processes*, *94*(1), 33–47.

Schwarz, N. (1990). Feelings as information: Informational and motivational functions of affective states. In E. T. Higgins & R. M. Sorrentino (Eds.), *Handbook of motivation and cognition: Foundations of social behavior* (Volume 2, pp. 527–561). New York, NY: Guilford.

Seo, M. G., Bartunek, J. M., & Feldman Barrett, L. (2010). The role of affective experience in work motivation: Test of a conceptual model. *Journal of Organizational Behavior*, *31*(7), 951–968.

Seo, M. G., Feldman Barrett, L., & Bartunek, J. M. (2004). The role of affective experience in work motivation. *Academy of Management Review*, *29* (3), 423–439.

Van Katwyk, P. T., Fox, S., Spector, P. E., & Kelloway, E. K. (2000). Using the Job-Related Affective Well-Being Scale (JAWS) to investigate affective responses to work stressors. *Journal of Occupational Health Psychology*, *5*(2), 219–230.

Vroom, V. (1964). *The motivation to work*. New York, NY: Wiley.

Wattles, J., Geier, B., Egan,M., & Wiener-Bronner, D. (2018). Wells Fargo's 20-month nightmare. *CNN Business*, 24 April, https://money.cnn.com/2018/04/24/news/companies/wells-fargo-timeline-shareholders/index.html

Weiss, H., & Cropanzano, R. (1996). Affective events theory: A theoretical discussion of the structure, causes, and consequences of affective experiences at work. *Research in Organizational Behavior*, *18*, 1–74.

Wiesenfeld, B. M., Brockner, J., & Martin, C. (1999). A self-affirmation analysis of survivors' reactions to unfair organizational downsizings. *Journal of Experimental Social Psychology*, *35* (5), 441–460.

Zohar, D., Tzischinski, O., & Epstein, R. (2003). Effects of energy availability on immediate and delayed emotional reactions to work events. *Journal of Applied Psychology*, *88*(6), 1082–1093.

5 Behavioral Genetics and Affect at Work

A Review and Directions for Future Research

Wen-Dong Li, Xin Zhang, Zhaoli Song, and Yating Wang

Recent years have witnessed a surge of management research on biology and affect (see Chapter 2 on the organizational neuroscience of emotions). An important reason is perhaps that management researchers have gradually realized the prominence of biological factors, including brain functions, hormones, and genetic factors, in modulating our attitudes and behaviors (e.g. Arvey, Li, & Wang, 2016; Arvey, Wang, Song, Li, & Day, 2014; Ashkanasy, Becker, & Waldman, 2014; Becker, Cropanzano, & Sanfey, 2011; Li, Stanek, Zhang, Ones, & McGue, 2016; Senior, Lee, & Butler, 2011; Waldman, Balthazard, & Peterson, 2011; Ward, Volk, & Becker, 2015). In this chapter, we will concentrate on the role of behavioral genetics and how this approach contributes to workplace affect. First, we will discuss the importance of behavioral genetics in fostering a more nuanced understanding of workplace affect. Second, we will review previous research, including both twin studies and molecular genetics research, on the influences of genetic factors on affect in the workplace, and we will selectively survey research on affect in general. Third, building upon recent research on behavioral genetics (Arvey & Bouchard, 1994; Arvey et al., 2016; Ilies, Arvey, & Bouchard, 2006; Li, Ilies, & Wang, 2017; Zyphur, Zhang, Barsky, & Li, 2013), affective events theory (AET) (Weiss & Beal, 2005; Weiss & Cropanzano, 1996), and personality development (Wrzus & Roberts, 2017), we will discuss an integral theoretical framework of workplace affect including influences from both genetic factors and environmental factors. We also offer some possible directions for future research.

Before touching upon the importance of taking a perspective from behavioral genetics in understanding workplace affect, it is important to define genetic influences and delineate what research represents behavioral genetics research. Genetic influences refer to influences on behaviors or attitudes caused by inherited variations in genetic materials (e.g. DNA sequences) (Plomin & Simpson, 2013). In behavioral genetics, genetic influences are often indicated with the term "heritability," estimated statistically as "the percentage of the total phenotypic variance accounted for by genetic variance" (Arvey & Bouchard, 1994, p. 60). The remainder of the total variance is often characterized as influences of environmental variables (including measurement error). It is important to note that high heritability estimates, or large genetic influences, do not address issues of malleability or changeability. In other words, having a high heritability (an interindividual difference) does not necessarily mean that one variable is not likely to change (an intraindividual difference). In fact, genetic influences have been shown to vary across different groups of people; even for the same group of people, genetic influences may change over time (Arvey et al., 2016).

Why It Is Important to Take a Behavioral Genetics Approach in Organizational Research

In principle, behavioral genetics research has manifested itself in two lines of research: classical twin studies and DNA-based molecular genetics research. Classical twin studies are a useful approach for organizational research because they shed light on the relative importance of nature versus nurture in shaping important work outcome, such as leadership (Arvey, Zhang, Avolio, & Krueger, 2007), entrepreneurship (Nicolaou, Shane, Cherkas, Hunkin, & Spector, 2008), work characteristics (Li, Zhang, Song, & Arvey, 2016), personality traits (Judge, Ilies, & Zhang, 2012; Li, 2011), and job satisfaction (Arvey, Bouchard, Segal, & Abraham, 1989), to name a few. Genes cannot magically affect behaviors or attitudes. Their influences are often channeled through individual difference variables such as intelligence, personality, and physical characteristics. The mechanisms through which genes may shape work variables are often called selection, either self-selection or organizational selection (Arvey, Li, & Wang, 2016). That is, people with certain genes may select themselves into certain careers, organizations, or work environments: "self-selection." At the same time, people may also be selected by organizations because of specific individual characteristics attributable to genetic endowments: "organizational selection." Thus behavioral genetics research may address the question of to what extent one work variable (e.g. affect) is shaped by selection or environmental causation.

Twin studies provide a useful approach to examine influences from the whole person (e.g. intelligence, personality traits, physical characteristics, etc.) versus the environment. There may be many individual difference variables that have effects on one work variable (and most of them are affected by both nature and nurture) and thus examining influences from the person may necessitate dozens of studies focusing on each one of such individual characteristics. Classical twin studies provide a more efficient approach that enables researchers to examine influences from all possible individual difference variables (Li, Stanek et al., 2016). Thus, this approach has been widely used in the history of organizational research. Even such variables as work characteristics that have been traditionally conceived as mostly environmental are in fact found to be prone to influences from genetic factors (Li, Zhang et al., 2016). These phenomena are called "gene–environment correlations," highlighting the notion that the exposure to certain situations depends upon a person's genotype. Recently, twin studies have been further extended to examine a) gene–environment interactions (e.g. genetic influences may be contingent on environmental factors) (Zhang, Ilies, & Arvey, 2009); b) change of genetic influences over time (e.g. genetic influences may over time increase or decrease as people age) (Li, Stanek et al., 2016); and c) to what extent one relationship of interest is caused by selection or environmental variables (e.g. the degree to which one relationship is driven by self-selection and/or organization selection or by environmental causation) (Judge, Ilies, & Zhang, 2012).

Classical twin studies often take advantage of the quasi-natural experimental nature of twin studies by comparing the similarities between identical twins and fraternal twins. Because this methodology has been described elsewhere (e.g. Arvey et al., 2016), we provide only a brief description of this paradigm. Identical twins are assumed to share 100 percent of their genes while fraternal twins share, on average, 50 percent. By comparing the similarities, researchers are able to estimate influences from genetic factors as well as from environmental factors (Arvey & Bouchard, 1994).

Although useful, classic twin studies typically treat genetic factors as latent variables and thus are silent on pinpointing specific DNA or genetic material responsible for genetic influences as shown by heritability estimates. This is where molecular genetics research makes a contribution. Molecular genetics research focus on influences from specific DNA polymorphisms or variations (Arvey et al., 2016; Song, Li, & Wang, 2015). Thus molecular genetics research is informative in providing more precision in theoretical explanation by specifying how particular genes are involved in overall genetic influences. Molecular genetics research may also enhance our understanding of the specific pathways through which genes may influences work variables (Li et al., 2015; Song, Li, & Arvey, 2011) and potential moderating factors (Chi, Li, Wang, & Song, 2016). Theoretical developments in molecular genetics research, such as theory on genetic trade-offs, also enable researchers to uncover novel pathways and gene–environment interactions. Genetic trade-offs occur when the same genes have both beneficial or detrimental influences on variables associated with evolutionary fitness. For example, the same genes contributing to high intelligence may also enhance the probability of autism. Early molecular genetics research adopted a theory-driven approach, the candidate gene approach. Recently, researchers have started to conduct genome-wide association studies and have even used genetic information based on whole-genome sequencing in their research (Savage et al., 2018).

Previous Research on the Relationships between Genetic Factors and Workplace Affect

In this section, we will provide a selective review of prior research on the relationships between genetic factors and workplace affect. We will cover both twin studies and molecular genetics research. Considering the dearth of research on this issue, when necessary, we will also selectively survey research on genetic influences on affect in general.

Twin Studies on Job Satisfaction

Although job satisfaction per se does not squarely represent affect, we will use research on genetic influences on job satisfaction as a starting point because of the limited research attention to the relationships between behavioral genetics and workplace affect. Arvey et al. (1989) conducted the landmark behavioral genetics study in organizational research with a method studying identical twins reared apart. They estimated that genes may account for approximately 30 percent of the variance in job satisfaction, which was confirmed later (Arvey, McCall, Bouchard, & Taubman, 1994).

Research on genetic influences on job satisfaction is rooted in the dispositional approach to organizational behavior. Weiss and Cropanzano (1996) offered a summary of research adopting a dispositional perspective on job satisfaction (for more recent reviews, see Arvey et al., 2016; Judge & Kammeyer-Mueller, 2012). Here, we focus on recent research. This line of research has become influential, probably starting with the research by Staw and Ross (1985). In the early stage, the dispositional approach to the study of job satisfaction hinged on a (premature) assumption that stability in job satisfaction reflects influences of dispositions (Staw & Ross, 1985; Weiss & Cropanzano, 1996). The logic is that, if job satisfaction remains stable over time across various situations (i.e. when environmental factors change), this may be a good indication that stable (i.e. non-changeable) dispositions may play a role in shaping job satisfaction, independent of environmental influences. This assumption is premature, on reflection, for the following reasons. First, stability in job satisfaction may also reflect similar environmental influences over time. Second, stability does not elucidate any explanation of how dispositional influences may play out in shaping job satisfaction. As later research has shown, one important mechanism is through selecting compatible work environments (Judge, Bono, & Locke, 2000). Third, and perhaps most important, the fact that dispositional variables affect job satisfaction does not necessarily suggest stability in mean levels of rank-order consistency among job satisfaction measures over time, nor stability in the magnitude of influences from dispositional variables. One example is recent research by Li et al. (2016) with a three-wave longitudinal twin study conducted in Minnesota. They found that over time, genetic influences changed as people aged. In the early stage of an individual's career, genetic factors explained about 30 percent of all the variance in job satisfaction, but later the proportion changed to approximately 20 percent. One explanation of such findings is that over time as people accumulate more work experiences, the influences from genetic factors may become diluted.

Personality traits may represent important pathways for genetic influences on job satisfaction. Judge et al. (2012) revealed that core self-evaluations may be one such mediating personality factor, a finding that was also extended to financial well-being (Zyphur, Li, Zhang, Arvey, & Barsky, 2015) and general well-being (Li, Zhang et al., 2016). Positive and negative affectivity was reported to also mediate genetic influences on job satisfaction (Li, Zhang et al., 2016).

Recent twin studies also uncovered the extent to which the relationships between job satisfaction and other variables are driven by the person (e.g. through selection) or the environment. Judge et al. (2012) found that while the relationship between core self-evaluations and job satisfaction was influenced by both genetic and environmental factors, the relationship between job satisfaction and health problems was primarily explained by genetic factors. Li et al. (2016b) reported that the relationship between job demands and subjective well-being was predominantly driven by genetic influences, and so was the relationship between job control and physical well-being. The relationships of work social support with the two well-being variables were mostly explained by environmental factors. Such findings challenged the assumption in the area of job design research that a) job characteristics are mostly influenced by environmental factors and thus b) the relationships between job characteristics and work outcome variables are also predominantly environmental.

Twin Studies on Affectivity

Positive and negative affectivity, two personality traits representing two tendencies of experiencing positive and negative affect in general, are found to be affected by genetic factors. For instance, Tellegen et al. (1988) found that genetic factors accounted for 40 percent and 55 percent of the variance in positive and negative emotionality (similar to positive and negative affectivity) respectively. This finding is consistent with the bulk of behavioral genetics research on personality traits, which shows that genetic factors generally explain 40 to 60 percent of the variance (Bouchard, 2004). Recent research has looked into the change of genetic influences on personality traits (Turkheimer, Pettersson, & Horn, 2014). Meta-analyses of longitudinal twin studies have shown that genetic influences on extraversion (similar to positive affectivity) increased until people reach their early forties and then declined over time. On the other hand, genetic influences on neuroticism (similar to negative affectivity) seemed to decrease after people reach adulthood (Kandler, 2012).

Twin Studies on State Affect

Behavioral genetics research on state positive and negative affect was spurred by the two-factor theory of affect (Diener & Larsen, 1984). This theory proposes first that positive and negative affect are two distinct factors. It further proposes, based on empirical findings, that state positive affect is primarily driven by environmental factors while state negative affect is more shaped by genetic factors. Evidence from behavioral genetics research seems to support this prediction. Baker, Cesa, Gatz, and Mellins (1992) asked twin participants to report their affect in the past few weeks in a one-time cross-sectional study. They found significant genetic influences on negative affect (34 percent), but not on positive affect. Riemann, Angleitner, Borkenau, and Eid (1998) collected data on state mood across five situations in one day. They reported that genetic influences on state negative mood ranged from 6 to 32 percent across the five situations, with an average of 24 percent. By contrast, genetic influences on state positive mood varied from 0 to 21 percent, with a mean effect of 18 percent. Such findings, thought a bit different from the Baker et al. (1992) study, seem also consistent with the two-factor theory in general.

Behavioral genetics research has also adopted formal experience-sampling methods (Beal, 2015). In their study of female twins with momentary affect data collected ten times per day across five consecutive days, Jacobs et al. (2013) observed significant genetic influence (18 percent) on the average level of negative affect. Moreover, they also found that genetic factors accounted for 18 percent and 35 percent, respectively, of the variance in intra-individual variability in positive and negative affect across time. Menne-Lothmann et al. (2012) examined genetic and environmental effects on positive affect assessed ten times per day across five consecutive days. They found small (19 percent) genetic influences on the mean level of positive affect. Neiss and Almeida (2004) conducted a more thorough study looking at how genetic and environmental factors influence negative affect as measured with three methods: monthly recall (i.e. recalling affective experiences in the past month), weekly recall (i.e. recalling affective experiences in the past week) and daily recall (i.e. recalling once per day across eight consecutive days). They found genetic factors accounted for 9, 20, and 14 percent of the variance in monthly, weekly, and daily negative affect respectively. Genetic influence on intra-individual variation in negative affect seems minimal, though. More recently, Zheng, Plomin, and von Stumm (2016) examined genetic and environmental influences on state affect in a more ambitious twin study with data collected once a day across one month. They found that approximately 50 percent of the variance in the mean levels of negative affect and approximately 18 percent of the variance in positive affect were accounted for by genetic factors. In addition, genetic factors also explained about 30 and 50 percent, respectively, of the variance in intra-individual variability of positive and negative affect over time.

In conclusion, the findings seem a bit mixed in terms of whether genetic factors exert significant influences on state positive affect, but the evidence suggests significant genetic influences on negative affect, especially when assessed across time and situations. Moreover, genetic factors also shape intra-individual variabilities of positive and negative affect. Given the dearth of research looking into the influence of individual difference variables on state positive and negative affect, we encourage future research to tackle this issue from a broader theoretical perspective of person–environment interplay. According to this view, the person may shape the type of experiences he or she has, and the person may react differently to the same experiences. A section later in this chapter, "Toward an Extended Theoretical Framework of Affective Events Theory," presents our proposal for a theoretical model reflecting this.

Molecular Genetics Studies on Job Satisfaction, Affectivity, and Affect

So far, we are aware of only one study identifying a linkage between specific genes and job satisfaction. Using data from the National Adolescent Longitudinal Study, Song, Li, and Arvey (2011) found two genetic markers that bore significant relationships with job satisfaction: one dopamine receptor gene, DRD4 VNTR, and one serotonin transporter gene, 5-HTTLPR. Given that serotonin and dopamine are involved in regulation of emotions, this selection of genetic markers related to the two systems makes sense. The researchers further found that pay mediated the relationship between job satisfaction and the DRD4 genetic marker. Though built on previous research and theoretical frameworks, a limitation of this research with a candidate gene approach is that the two genetic markers accounted for only a small amount of variance in job satisfaction. Although this is understandable, considering the many possibilities of dozens or even thousands of genes being involved in genetic modulation of attitudes and behaviors, future research should examine other genetic markers, and perhaps also examine how gene–environment interactions (e.g. with genes and environmental factors interacting with each other in a manner similar to statistical interaction) shape job satisfaction. However, given the scarcity of research attention in this area and the difficulty and cost of collecting genetic data, we believe that the candidate gene approach remains useful for examining the age-old question of the effects of nature and nurture on job satisfaction from a more theory-driven perspective.

Molecular genetics research on personality traits also started with the identification of specific genes using the candidate gene approach (Lesch et al., 1996). In their landmark study published in *Science*, Lesch et al. found that a serotonin gene, 5 HTT, was significantly related to a personality trait closely identified with negative affectivity, neuroticism. Since then, researchers have examined other genetic markers that may account for individual differences in trait affectivity. Such research has been summarized in a meta-analysis of genome-wide association studies with more than 70,000 participants (De Moor et al., 2015). A human genome is the individual's complete set of genetic materials (DNA). It contains all the information that is needed to build a human being. The human genome is made up of 3.2 billion bases of DNA. A single-nucleotide polymorphism is the most common form of variation across the whole human genome. In a genome-wide association study, researchers scan genetic markers across genomes of a large number of people in order to find single-nucleotide polymorphisms that may be related to a variable of interest. A robust finding of this meta-analysis is that one genetic marker assessed by single-nucleotide polymorphisms has been consistently shown to be related to neuroticism. Note that with all the genetic markers measured in that study, they explained 15 percent of the variance in neuroticism. More and more researchers then began to use genome-wide association studies in their search for genetic markers that may be related to personality traits.

Other breakthroughs have been made more recently. For example, in a paper published in *Nature*, Okbay et al. (2016) examined how dozens of genetic markers were related to subjective well-being (measured as both life satisfaction and positive affect), neuroticism, and depressive symptoms in more than 100,000 participants. They found several genetic markers that bore consistent relationships with the three variables. Furthermore, the genetic correlations among the three variables were high, meaning that they are influenced by a lot of the same genetic markers. This may be related to human affect regulatory systems and immune systems. A more recent *Nature* paper identified about 600 new genes that may be related to neuroticism in more than 400,000 individuals (Nagel et al., 2018). Furthermore, polygenic scores – that is, total scores summarizing the influences of all those single genetic markers that may be related to neuroticism – explained about 5 percent of the variance in neuroticism. Although the effect size is not huge, it implies that the polygenic scores had a correlation of around .22 with neuroticism. This is not a necessarily a trivial correlation according to conventional standards. The authors further found that those genes are often expressed in tissues in brain regions including the frontal cortex, the cortex, and the anterior cingulate cortex. They may also be related to several cell types, such as serotonergic neurons, dopaminergic neuroblasts, and medium spiny neurons, which play important roles in human serotonin and dopamine systems in regulating behaviors and affect.

Future research is needed to reveal more genetic markers that may be involved in genetic influences on trait affectivity, which in turn may be used in examining how genes interact with environmental factors in shaping affect (Nagel et al., 2018). Based on developments in basic biological research, organizational researchers may also capitalize on opportunities to examine more interesting interplay between the person and the environment (Arvey et al., 2016). One possible way ahead is to build on exploratory research linking genes and trait affectivity and thus to generate polygenic scores from dozens or hundreds of relevant genes. Then such scores could be used as variables to reflect trait affectivity, which may enable us to examine multiple pathways linking genes to behaviors or attitudes and to examine nuanced gene–environment interactions.

A caveat associated with searching for genes that may have main effects on personality traits or behaviors is that such a "main effect" approach may overlook other important mechanisms whereby genes may be involved in modulating significant outcomes. For instance, Li et al. (2015) found two different pathways linking dopamine transporter gene DAT1 and leadership role occupancy. One pathway is through mild rule breaking and the other through proactive personality. The two pathways may contradict each other, making the overall relationship between this gene and leadership nonsignificant. Such genetic tradeoffs are not rare (Arvey et al., 2016). In addition, the influences of one gene on an outcome may be positive under one condition and become negative in another condition (Chi et al., 2016). For a large sample with individuals from various environments, the main effect of this gene may also be nonsignificant. To uncover pathways of genetic influences, we need to explore possible gene–environment interaction mechanisms such as epigenetic changes of gene expression due to stressful early life experiences or parenting styles (McGowan et al., 2009). Theory-driven research is also needed in order to unravel the nuanced ways through which genes are involved in modulating behaviors and attitudes.

Toward an Extended Theoretical Framework of Affective Events Theory

Although useful, previous theoretical frameworks on workplace affect are not without limitations. So far, a dominant theoretical framework has been affective events theory (Weiss & Beal, 2005; Weiss & Cropanzano, 1996). More recently, researchers developed another theoretical framework to further elucidate how events affect workplace behaviors, affect, and attitudes in general (Morgeson, Mitchell, & Liu, 2015). One possible limitation concerns the role that dispositional factors may play in shaping not only affective experiences but also work events that people may encounter. Such theories have chiefly portrayed dispositional factors as a moderator in the relationship between work events and affective reactions. Such a narrow view has overlooked other possible ways through which dispositions may have influences. As Weiss and Kurek (2003) pointed out:

> Although most emotion theories use these events as the starting point for emotion generation, the events we experience are not entirely externally caused or random. We make decisions that expose us to certain events. Although there are certainly events that are beyond our control, we create our own environments in which we have a greater tendency to experience certain types of events (p. 133).

They further contended that "Personality may actually influence the events we experience, or more precisely, the behavioral manifestations of personality traits may influence the nature of these events" (p. 136). In fact, in their seminal paper, Weiss and Cropanzano (1996) recognized that "individuals are not passive recipients of environmental pressure. Instead, individuals move through their lives both influencing and being influenced by their environments" (p. 39). However, the notion that dispositional variables may affect the occurrence of work events, thus also influencing the ensuing affective reactions and processes, have yet to fully discussed or examined.

We propose a theoretical model (Figure 5.1) as a potential extension of AET, by more seriously taking into account the roles that individual difference variables (e.g. genes) may play in shaping workplace affect and related processes. As the point of departure, we posit that individual difference variables may affect occurrence of work events and that such influences become more salient when work events are aggregated across a longer period of time (Proposition 1). This proposition stems from research on main effects of individual difference variables on occurrence of work events. In addition to the above arguments, Charles and Almeida (2007) found that genetic factors accounted for 37 percent of the variance in aggregated daily stressor occurrence collected once a day across eight consecutive days. Such arguments and evidence clearly demonstrate the importance of selection effect: people with certain characteristics select, or are selected into, compatible environments.

Building on Proposition 1, we further argue that there exist cyclical and reciprocal relationships among work events, affective reactions, and work behaviors and attitudes. Work behaviors and attitudes (and also affective reactions) may also shape the occurrence of work events, leading to a cycle among the relationships in the three core constructs of AET: work events, affective reactions, and work behaviors/attitudes (Proposition 2). Weiss and Cropanzano (1996) pointed out likely influences of affects on occurrence of work events: "being in a positive mood increases the estimated probabilities of the occurrence of positive events and being in a negative mood increases the estimated probabilities of the occurrence of negative events" (p. 64). We extend this argument and propose that, in the long run, work behaviors and attitudes may also shape the

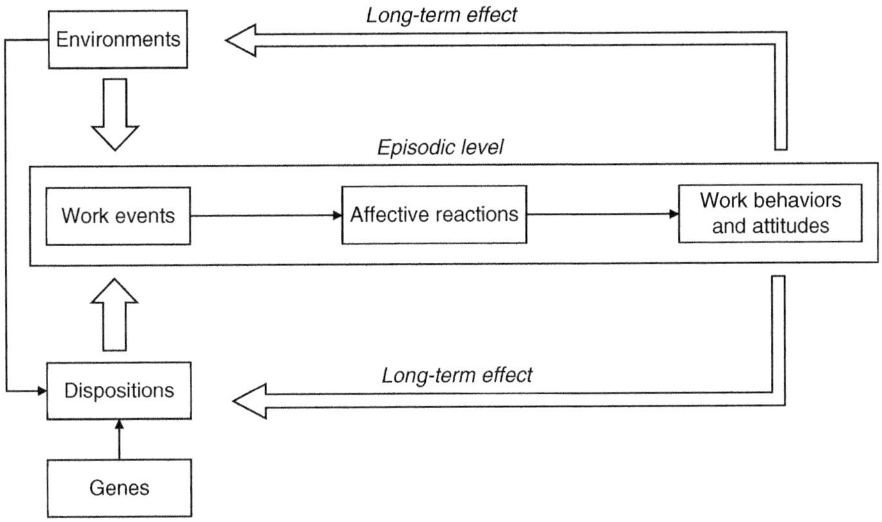

Figure 5.1 An extended model of affective events theory

probability of occurrence of work events – either directly, or indirectly by altering the environment. This proposal draws upon research on proactivity (Frese, Garst, & Fay, 2007; Grant & Ashford, 2008; Li, Fay, Frese, Harms, & Gao, 2014).

Our last proposition focuses on the long-term influences of episode-level processes among work events, affective reactions, and work attitudes and behaviors on the potential change of disposition, such as personality traits. Organizational studies have typically taken a static view on personality and thus assumed that adult personality traits cannot change (Li et al., 2014). However, recent research in personality psychology has shown that adult personality can change and that a major driving force is work experiences (Bleidorn, Hopwood, & Lucas, 2018; Roberts & Mroczek, 2008). By drawing on a recent theory of personality change (Wrzus & Roberts, 2017), we expect that repeated AET processes from work events, affective reactions, and work attitudes and behaviors, over time, may prompt personality development through implicit and explicit mechanisms (Proposition 3). One implicit mechanism may include habit formation and reinforcement learning, and one explicit mechanism may encompass self-reflection.

A Summary of Possible Future Research Directions

Below, we offer some final suggestions for future research taking a dispositional perspective more seriously in examining workplace affect.

1. Twin studies remain useful. They enable us to look at interesting questions (e.g. change of genetic influences, gene–environment interactions) about genetic influences on workplace affect.
2. Molecular genetics research using a candidate gene approach is needed. Researchers could use this approach to examine how a specific gene, identified based on previous research or theory, is involved in modulating workplace affect.
3. Researchers should also conduct explorative molecular genetics research to search for specific novel genes that may be involved in shaping workplace affect.
4. Molecular genetics research using polygenic scores, epigenetics, and neurogenetics, based on basic exploratory genetics research in biology, may also be fruitful. Researchers could examine the pathways that may mediate genetic influences, or environmental factors that may moderate genetic influences on workplace affect.
5. Researchers should also consider using both experience-sampling methods and behavioral genetics approaches to examine interesting cycles and dynamic relationships related to workplace affect over short periods of time.
6. Organizational researchers should also garner funding to conduct longitudinal behavioral genetics research to examine fine-grained relationships between genes and environmental factors and how they jointly shape workplace affect, its change, or dynamic relationships with other variables.

References

Arvey, R. D., & Bouchard, T. J. (1994). Genetics, twins, and organizational behavior. *Research in Organizational Behavior*, *16*, 47–82.

Arvey, R. D., Bouchard, T. J., Segal, N. L., & Abraham, L. M. (1989). Job satisfaction: Environmental and genetic components. *Journal of Applied Psychology*, *74*, 187–192.

Arvey, R. D., Li, W. D., & Wang, N. (2016). Genetics and organizational behavior. *Annual Review of Organizational Psychology and Organizational Behavior*, *3*, 167–190.

Arvey, R. D., McCall, B. P., Bouchard, T. J., & Taubman, P. (1994). Genetic influences on job satisfaction and work value. *Personality and Individual Differences*, *17*, 21–33.

Arvey, R. D., Wang, N., Song, Z., Li, W., & Day, D. (2014). The biology of leadership. In D. Day (Ed.), *Oxford handbook of leadership and organizations* (pp. 75–92). New York, NY: Oxford University Press.

Arvey, R. D., Zhang, Z., Avolio, B. J., & Krueger, R. F. (2007). Developmental and genetic determinants of leadership role occupancy among women. *Journal of Applied Psychology, 92*, 693–706.

Ashkanasy, N. M., Becker, W. J., & Waldman, D. A. (2014). Neuroscience and organizational behavior: Avoiding both neuro-euphoria and neuro-phobia. *Journal of Organizational Behavior, 35*, 909–919.

Baker, L. A., Cesa, I. L., Gatz, M., & Mellins, C. (1992). Genetic and environmental influences on positive and negative affect: Support for a two-factor theory. *Psychology and Aging, 7*, 158–163.

Beal, D. J. (2015). ESM 2.0: State of the art and future potential of experience sampling methods in organizational research. *Annual Review of Organizational Psychology, 2*, 383–407.

Becker, W. J., Cropanzano, R., & Sanfey, A. G. (2011). Organizational neuroscience: Taking organizational theory inside the neural black box. *Journal of Management, 37*, 933–961.

Bleidorn, W., Hopwood, C. J., & Lucas, R. E. (2018). Life events and personality trait change. *Journal of Personality, 86*, 83–96.

Bouchard, T. J. (2004). Genetic influence on human psychological traits. *Current Directions in Psychological Science, 13*, 148–151.

Charles, S. T., & Almeida, D. M. (2007). Genetic and environmental effects on daily life stressors: More evidence for greater variation in later life. *Psychology and Aging, 22*, 331–340.

Chi, W., Li, W. D., Wang, N., & Song, Z. (2016). Can genes play a role in explaining turnover? An examination of gene–environment interaction from human capital theory. *Journal of Applied Psychology, 101*, 1030–1044.

De Moor, M. H., Van Den Berg, S. M., Verweij, K. J., Krueger, R. F., Luciano, M., Vasquez, A. A., . . . & Amin, N. (2015). Meta-analysis of genome-wide association studies for neuroticism, and the polygenic association with major depressive disorder. *JAMA Psychiatry, 72*, 642–650.

Diener, E., & Larsen, R. J. (1984). Temporal stability and cross-situational consistency of affective, behavioral, and cognitive responses. *Journal of Personality and Social Psychology, 47*, 871–883.

Frese, M., Garst, H., & Fay, D. (2007). Making things happen: Reciprocal relationships between work characteristics and personal initiative in a four-wave longitudinal structural equation model. *Journal of Applied Psychology, 92*, 1084–1102.

Grant, A. M., & Ashford, S. J. (2008). The dynamics of proactivity at work. *Research in Organizational Behavior, 28*, 3–34.

Ilies, R., Arvey, R. D., & Bouchard, T. J. (2006). Darwinism, behavioral genetics, and organizational behavior: A review and agenda for future research. *Journal of Organizational Behavior, 27*, 121–141.

Jacobs, N., Menne-Lothmann, C., Derom, C., Thiery, E., Van Os, J., & Wichers, M. (2013). Deconstructing the familiality of variability in momentary negative and positive affect. *Acta Psychiatrica Scandinavica, 127*, 318–327.

Judge, T. A., Bono, J. E., & Locke, E. A. (2000). Personality and job satisfaction: The mediating role of job characteristics. *Journal of Applied Psychology, 85*, 237–249.

Judge, T. A., Ilies, R., & Zhang, Z. (2012). Genetic influences on core self-evaluations, job satisfaction, and work stress: A behavioral genetics mediated model. *Organizational Behavior and Human Decision Processes, 117*, 208–220.

Judge, T. A., & Kammeyer-Mueller, J. D. (2012). Job attitudes. *Annual Review of Psychology, 63*, 341–367.

Kandler, C. (2012). Nature and nurture in personality development: The case of neuroticism and extraversion. *Current Directions in Psychological Science, 21*, 290–296.

Lesch, K. P., Bengel, D., Heils, A., Sabol, S. Z., Greenberg, B. D., Petri, S., . . . & Murphy, D. L. (1996). Association of anxiety-related traits with a polymorphism in the serotonin transporter gene regulatory region. *Science, 274*, 1527–1531.

Li, W. D. (2011). Proactive personality and work success: Disentangling genetic and environmental influences. Paper presented at the 2011 Annual Academy of Management Meeting, San Antonio, Texas.

Li, W. D., Fay, D., Frese, M., Harms, P. D., & Gao, X. (2014). Reciprocal relationships between proactive personality and work characteristics: A latent change score approach. *Journal of Applied Psychology, 99*, 948–965.

Li, W. D., Ilies, R., & Wang, W. (2017). Behavioral genetics and leadership research. In B. Schyns, R. J. Hall, & P. Neves (Eds.), *Handbook of Methods in Leadership Research* (pp. 127–145). Northampton, MA: Elgar.

Li, W. D., Stanek, K., Zhang, Z., Ones, D. S., & McGue, M. (2016). Are genetic and environmental influences on job satisfaction stable over time? A three-wave longitudinal twin study. *Journal of Applied Psychology, 101*, 1598–1619.

Li, W. D., Wang, N., Arvey, R., Soong, R., Saw, S. M., & Song, Z. (2015). A mixed blessing? Dual mediating mechanisms in the relationship between dopamine transporter gene DAT1 and leadership role occupancy. *Leadership Quarterly, 26*, 671–686.

Li, W. D., Zhang, Z., Song, Z., & Arvey, R. (2016). It is also in our nature: Genetic influences on work characteristics and in explaining their relationships with well-being. *Journal of Organizational Behavior, 37*, 868–888.

McGowan, P. O., Sasaki, A., D'Alessio, A. C., Dymov, S., Labonté, B., Szyf, M., . . . & Meaney, M. J. (2009). Epigenetic regulation of the glucocorticoid receptor in human brain associates with childhood abuse. *Nature Neuroscience, 12*, 342–348.

Menne-Lothmann, C., Jacobs, N., Derom, C., Thiery, E., van Os, J., & Wichers, M. (2012). Genetic and environmental causes of individual differences in daily life positive affect and reward experience and its overlap with stress-sensitivity. *Behavior Genetics, 42*, 778–786.

Morgeson, F. P., Mitchell, T. R., & Liu, D. (2015). Event system theory: An event-oriented approach to the organizational sciences. *Academy of Management Review, 40*, 515–537.

Nagel, M., Jansen, P. R., Stringer, S., Watanabe, K., de Leeuw, C. A., Bryois, J., . . . Muñoz-Manchado, A. B. (2018). Meta-analysis of genome-wide association studies for neuroticism in 449,484 individuals identifies novel genetic loci and pathways. *Nature Genetics, 50*, 920–927.

Neiss, M., & Almeida, D. M. (2004). Age differences in the heritability of mean and intraindividual variation of psychological distress. *Gerontology, 50*, 22–27.

Nicolaou, N., Shane, S., Cherkas, L., Hunkin, J., & Spector, T. D. (2008). Is the tendency to engage in entrepreneurship genetic? *Management Science, 54*, 167–179.

Okbay, A., Beauchamp, J. P., Fontana, M. A., Lee, J. J., Pers, T. H., Rietveld, C. A., . . . & Meddens, S. F. W. (2016). Genome-wide association study identifies 74 loci associated with educational attainment. *Nature, 533*, 539–542.

Plomin, R., & Simpson, M. A. (2013). The future of genomics for developmentalists. *Development and Psychopathology, 25*(4pt2), 1263–1278.

Riemann, R., Angleitner, A., Borkenau, P., & Eid, M. (1998). Genetic and environmental sources of consistency and variability in positive and negative mood. *European Journal of Personality, 12*, 345–364.

Roberts, B. W., & Mroczek, D. (2008). Personality trait change in adulthood. *Current Directions in Psychological Science, 17*, 31–35.

Savage, J. E., Jansen, P. R., Stringer, S., Watanabe, K., Bryois, J., de Leeuw, C. A., . . . & Coleman, J. R. (2018). Genome-wide association meta-analysis in 269,867 individuals identifies new genetic and functional links to intelligence. *Nature Genetics, 50*, 912–919.

Senior, C., Lee, N., & Butler, M. J. R. (2011). Organizational cognitive neuroscience. *Organization Science, 22*, 804–815.

Song, Z., Li, W., & Wang, N. (2015). Progress in molecular genetics and its potential implications in organizational behavior research. In S. M. Colarelli & R. D. Arvey (Eds.), *The Biological Foundations of Organizational Behavior* (pp. 23–46). Chicago, IL: University of Chicago Press.

Song, Z., Li, W. D., & Arvey, R. D. (2011). Associations between dopamine and serotonin genes and job satisfaction: Preliminary evidence from the Add Health Study. *Journal of Applied Psychology, 96*, 1223–1233.

Staw, B. M., & Ross, J. (1985). Stability in the midst of change: A dispositional approach to job attitudes. *Journal of Applied Psychology, 70*, 469–480.

Tellegen, A., Lykken, D. T., Bouchard, T. J., Wilcox, K. J., Segal, N. L., & Rich, S. (1988). Personality similarity in twins reared apart and together. *Journal of Personality and Social Psychology, 54*, 1031–1039.

Turkheimer, E., Pettersson, E., & Horn, E. E. (2014). A phenotypic null hypothesis for the genetics of personality. *Annual Review of Psychology, 65*, 515–540.

Waldman, D. A., Balthazard, P. A., & Peterson, S. J. (2011). Leadership and neuroscience: Can we revolutionize the way that inspirational leaders are identified and developed? *Academy of Management Perspectives, 25*, 60–74.

Ward, M. K., Volk, S., & Becker, W. J. (2015). An overview of organizational neuroscience. In D. A. Waldman & P. A. Balthazard (Eds.), *Organizational Neuroscience* (pp. 17–50). Bingley, UK: Emerald.

Weiss, H. M., & Beal, D. J. (2005). Reflections on affective events theory. In N. M. Ashkanasy, W. J. Zerbe, & C. E. J. Härtel (Eds.), *The effect of affect in organizational settings* (pp. 1–21). Bingley, UK: Emerald.

Weiss, H. M., & Cropanzano, R. (1996). Affective events theory: A theoretical discussion of the structure, causes and consequences of affective experiences at work. In B. M. Staw & L. L. Cummings (Eds.), *Research in organization behavior* (Volume 18, pp. 1–74). Greenwich, CT: JAI.

Weiss, H. M., & Kurek, K. E. (2003). Dispositional influences on affective experiences at work. In M. R. Barrick & A. M. Ryan (Eds.), *Personality and work* (pp. 121–149). San Francisco, CA: Jossey-Bass.

Wrzus, C., & Roberts, B. W. (2017). Processes of personality development in adulthood: The TESSERA framework. *Personality and Social Psychology Review, 21*, 253–277.

Zhang, Z., Ilies, R., & Arvey, R. D. (2009). Beyond genetic explanations for leadership: The moderating role of the social environment. *Organizational Behavior and Human Decision Processes, 110*, 118–128.

Zheng, Y., Plomin, R., & von Stumm, S. (2016). Heritability of intraindividual mean and variability of positive and negative affect: Genetic analysis of daily affect ratings over a month. *Psychological Science, 27*, 1611–1619.

Zyphur, M. J., Li, W.-D., Zhang, Z., Arvey, R. D., & Barsky, A. P. (2015). Income, personality, and subjective financial well-being: the role of gender in their genetic and environmental relationships. *Frontiers In Psychology, 6*, 1–16.

Zyphur, M. J., Zhang, Z., Barsky, A. P., & Li, W.-D. (2013). An ACE in the hole: Twin family models for applied behavioral genetics research. *Leadership Quarterly, 24*, 572–594.

6 A Review of Quantitative Methods to Measure Workplace Affect

Liu-Qin Yang, Katharine McMahon, and Jessie (Fengmin) Zhen*

Building on past reviews on affect research (e.g. Akinola, 2010; Ashkanasy & Dorris, 2017; Larsen & Fredrickson, 1999; Mauss & Robinson, 2009; Peterson, Reina, Waldman, & Becker, 2015), in this chapter we review existing quantitative methods to measure workplace affect and affect regulation, and propose directions for future development in quantitative measurement of these processes. We endorse that affect is a multifaceted, dynamic process comprised of psychological and physiological experiences that informs thought and motivates action (Izard, 2009). Affect can be understood as a trait (general tendency to experience positive or negative feelings) or a state (momentary emotions in response to certain events). Consistent with the rest of this handbook, we use "affect" as an umbrella term that encompasses emotion, feeling, and other related terms.

Through this review, we intend to make the following contributions to the literature. First, we offer a toolbox from which readers interested in workplace affect research and applications may select validated, quantitative measurement scales and techniques appropriate for their purposes. Second, by including methods for self-ratings, other-ratings, and objective ratings of both affect and affect regulation strategies, our review complements the recent reviews on this topic by providing a more comprehensive account of workplace affect research. Finally, going beyond the recent reviews on this topic, we suggest some practical and realistic future research directions by highlighting the potential ways to capitalize on the advantages of self-rating methods and specifying ways to investigate multi-method approaches in measuring workplace affect.

We will first review existing measures of affect; we will then review existing measures of affect regulation that are applicable in organizational research; lastly, we will evaluate the current state of the art in affect-related quantitative measurement and propose future directions for method development.

Our review aims to provide examples of available measures of affect that have been previously validated and utilized in organizational research. As there are copious measures in the field, especially for self-rating, we do not intend to include all existing measures. Some measures (e.g. physiological), in particular, have not been used as frequently in organizational settings, and therefore we have also reviewed studies not specific to the workplace context in order to include such measures.

Existing Measures of Affect

Before we review the existing measures of workplace affect, we would like to discuss two distinct meta-theoretical perspectives on affective processes, namely the discrete versus dimensional affect perspectives (Cropanzano, Ambrose &

* This research was partly supported by the by the Grant # T03OH008435 awarded to Portland State University, funded by the Centers for Disease Control and Prevention and the National Institute for Occupational Safety and Health. Its contents are solely the responsibility of the authors and do not necessarily represent the official views of NIOSH, CDC, or HHS.

Van Waggoner, in press). This distinction will then guide our organizing of affect measures. The discrete affect perspective or approach corresponds to a meta-theoretical view that affective experiences derive from individuals making a series of appraisals upon detecting a salient event in the environment. Affect theories such as discrete appraisal theory (Roseman, Spindel, & Jose, 1990) and affect program theory (e.g. Ekman, 1992) support such a perspective on how individuals label their affective experiences as unique discrete emotions. In contrast, the dimensional affect approach corresponds to a meta-theoretical view that affective experiences derive from the activation of pre-existing expectations (associative networks in the brain; Russell, 2003) and the integration of such expectations with environmental cues and physical cues within the individual. Psychological construction theory supports such a perspective on how individuals organize their affective experiences along a few different and continuous axes or dimensions (Mauss & Robinson, 2009; Russell, 2003). Within the dimensional affect approach, two frameworks are most commonly used in the research of workplace affect. The model proposed by Watson and colleagues (Watson, Clark, & Tellegen, 1988) focuses on positive and negative affect as two distinct dimensions; the one proposed by Russell (1980) and Larsen and Diener (1992) focuses on the dimensions of valence (i.e. positive versus negative) and arousal/activation (i.e. high versus low arousal). Some work has suggested the viability of integrating these frameworks into a circumplex model in which the valence and activation taxonomy represents the unrotated factor analysis solution whereas the positive and negative affect taxonomy represents a rotated factor analysis solution (e.g. Cropanzano, Weiss, Hale, & Reb, 2003) (see also Chapter 1). Furthermore, Watson and colleagues (Watson et al., 1988; Watson & Clark, 1999) have made efforts to integrate affect research by proposing an affect hierarchy model where discrete affect types (e.g. joy and anxiety) are related yet distinct experiences that constitute the higher-order constructs of general positive and negative affect.

In the organizational psychology literature, there are quantitative methods to measure experienced affect at work for self-, other-, and objective ratings. Specifically, methods for self-ratings of affect include text-based standardized scales (the scale items being words or sentences) and picture-based scales (using pictures or images); methods for other-ratings include observation- and text-analysis-based affect measures; whereas methods for objective ratings of affect are mainly physiological measures. In the following sections, we will introduce representative measures for self-, other-, and objective ratings. Wherever applicable, we will organize the methods according to the dimensional versus discrete affect approach. For the measures using the dimensional affect approach, wherever applicable we will organize them by Watson and colleagues' (1988) and Russell's (1980) frameworks based on which one they were developed and validated by.

Additionally, it is important to distinguish whether these measures assess explicit versus implicit affect. Explicit affect represents affect experienced or expressed consciously, whereas implicit affect is defined as affective experiences that occur outside of the individual's conscious awareness yet that influence his/her ongoing thought, behavior, and even conscious affective experiences (Barsade, Ramarajan, & Western, 2009). For self-ratings, there are measures for both explicit and implicit affect experienced; for other-ratings, there are mainly measures for explicit affect; for objective ratings, the measures (e.g. brain activities) could capture both explicit and implicit affect, but there are no clear conclusions in terms of mapping specific measures with the construct of explicit or implicit affect (e.g. Mauss & Robinson, 2009; Peterson et al., 2015). Wherever possible, we will separate explicit from implicit measures.

Measurement Methods for Self-Ratings

Measurement methods for self-ratings include text-based measurement scales and picture-based ones. We will organize the measures for self-ratings by the dimensional and discrete affect approaches.

Dimensional Affect Approach

If one were to use the dimensional affect approach as the meta-theoretical perspective, there would be choices of both text-based and picture-based affect scales for self-ratings. The former includes scales that measure both explicit and implicit affect, whereas the latter includes only scales that measure explicit affect.

Text-based measures of explicit general affect. In Watson and colleagues' (1988) framework, the positive affect and negative affect schedule (PANAS) is among the most commonly used measures in organizational research. It uses twenty words/items to measure general positive and negative affect, with ten words/items for each dimension, rated on a Likert scale. These measures of general affect have been validated in samples with different backgrounds (e.g. students, employees), and shown to be reliable in research among employees working in various industries (e.g. Watson & Clark, 1988, 1999). In recent years, PANAS and its shortened versions have been used in many intra-individual analyses of dynamic affective experiences at work (e.g. Yang, Simon, Wang, & Zheng, 2016). More recently, based on Watson and colleagues' framework, Levine and colleagues (2011) used a behaviorally anchored rating scale to develop and validate a ten-item state–trait emotion measure (STEM) in English, Chinese, and Romanian, to measure positive and negative affect at work (five items/sentences each), each composed of five discrete affect dimensions.

Multiple validated measures also draw on Russell's (1980) framework. First of all, Russell and colleagues developed the commonly employed current mood questionnaire (Barrett & Russell, 1999), which assesses general levels of valence and activation. It includes two or three affective adjectives or statements for each dimension (i.e. pleasant, unpleasant, activated, deactivated) that are rated on a Likert scale, and has been found to be reliable and valid among samples with different backgrounds. Second, other research teams developed validated and reliable measures using employee samples with various backgrounds, such as the thirty-item scale and its shortened versions used by Van Katwyk, Fox, Spector, and Kelloway (2000) and the sixteen-item one by Warr, Bindl, Parker, and Inceoglu (2014). Both scales measure four dimensions – high-pleasure and high-activation, high-pleasure and low-activation, low-pleasure and high-activation, low-pleasure and low-activation – with a Likert scale used to rate sentences and affect adjectives, respectively. Lastly, some measures also use a semantic differential approach to measure the general affect dimensions in Russell's (1980) framework, where two adjectives describing polarized affect states occupy two ends of the rating continuum. For example, the pleasure–arousal dominance scale (Mehrabian & Russell, 1974) uses eighteen pairs of adjectives to measure the dimensions of pleasure (vs. displeasure), arousal (vs. nonarousal), and dominance (vs. submissiveness), with six pairs for each dimension (e.g. calm–excited on a Likert scale). It has been shown to be reliable and valid among various populations.

In addition to those measures based on Watson and colleagues' (1988) and Russell and colleagues' (1980) frameworks, organizational researchers have also applied general affect scales from other literatures, such as the six-dimension profile of mood states scale, or its shortened version (with sixty-five and thirty-seven items respectively), which was originally developed and validated in clinical settings (McNair, Droppleman, & Lorr, 1992). Some recent applications of this measure in organizational research indicate that it is reliable and valid across employee samples with various backgrounds.

Text-based measures of implicit general affect. In the literature, few measures are available to measure implicit affect. One example is a twenty-item (word) measure used by Johnson and colleagues that uses the word fragment format to assess implicit, general positive and negative affectivity (Johnson, Tolentino, Rodopman, & Cho, 2010). Another example is the implicit positive and negative affect test, an interpretation-based measure that asks participants to interpret the emotional meaning of six seemingly foreign words and use such interpretations to rate the relevance of six emotional words on a Likert scale (Quirin, Kazén, & Kuhl, 2009). These measures are purported to assess trait and/or state general affect. To date, their application in organizational research has been limited.

Picture-based measures of explicit general affect. We describe two representative nonverbal pictorial measures for self-ratings of affect: the self-assessment manikin (SAM) and the affective slider, both of which are based on Russell's (1980) affect framework and used along with a certain number of pictures chosen from the international affective picture system or IAPS (Betella & Verschure, 2016; Bradley & Lang, 1994; Lang, Bradley, & Cuthbert, 1997). The SAM measure uses a set of graphic characters arranged horizontally and in order, to reflect continuous affective states between low vs. high pleasantness, low vs. high arousal, and low vs. high dominance, available in paper or digital versions. It allows participants to pick a particular character as the rating on a continuum regarding each of the three affect dimensions (a nine-point scale being more common), for each of the twenty-one pictures chosen from IAPS. In contrast, the affective slider is a digital version of pictorial measure that uses slider controls between two pairs of opposing emotion icons, to assess only the pleasantness and arousal dimensions. Although both of these pictorial measures have been widely used in various disciplines, there have been relatively few applications of them in organizational research.

Discrete Affect Approach

If one were to use the discrete affect approach as the meta-theoretical perspective, there would be choices among only text-based affect scales for self-ratings. And, to the best of our knowledge, there are no published measures of implicit discrete affect.

Text-based measures of explicit discrete affect. Among organizational psychologists, a variety of measures have been used to assess single or multiple discrete affects. We describe a few representative multi-dimension and single-dimension measures. Among the most commonly used multi-dimension measures, PANAS-X, the extended version of PANAS, has sixty items in total rated on a Likert scale, with a range of three to eight items (words) to assess each of the eleven discrete affect dimensions (e.g. fear, hostility, joviality, attentiveness; Watson & Clark, 1999). Additionally, Spielberg and Reheiser developed and validated measures to assess multiple discrete affect dimensions (Spielberger & Reheiser, 2004): for example, the state–trait personality inventory (STPI) assesses state and trait anger, anxiety, curiosity, and depression, with ten items (sentences) for each of the eight dimensions. Further, the STEM scale by Levine and colleagues (2011) includes ten items (sentences) to measure ten discrete affect dimensions (e.g. joy, pride, anxiety, sadness), with work-specific BARS and one item for each dimension. These measures have been shown to be reliable and valid across different populations and work settings.

We further describe representative single-dimension measures for two discrete affects: envy and gratitude. For envy, a commonly used measure is the dispositional envy scale by Smith and colleagues (Smith, Parrott, Diener, Hoyle, & Kim, 1999), with eight items (sentences) rated on a Likert scale. For gratitude, a commonly used measure is the six-item dispositional gratitude scale (McCullough, Emmons, & Tsang, 2002), with sentences rated on a Likert scale. These scales are commonly used to measure dispositional affect, and adapted to measure state affect. They have been found to be reliable and valid among various populations and work settings.

Methods for Other-Ratings

For other-ratings, text-analysis-based and observation-based affect measures are viable to use in organizational settings. Conceptually these methods measure expressed, explicit affect as opposed to experienced affect assessed by the self- and objective rating methods.

Dimensional Affect Approach

We first introduce two representative text-analysis-based affect measures, developed under the frameworks proposed by Watson and colleagues (1988) and Russell (1980) respectively. Both methods are equipped to analyze text-based documents (e.g. blogs, responses to open-ended questions) and use computer software to score affect dimensions. Using Watson and colleagues' (1988) framework, Pennebaker and colleagues developed and validated the linguistic inquiry and word count (LIWC) method, which was implemented in compatible computer software (Pennebaker, Chung, Ireland, Gonzales, & Booth, 2007). Specifically, LIWC can be used to rate general positive and negative affect, assessed with 620 and 744 words, respectively. LIWC has gone through multiple versions, the most recent of which (published in 2015) comes with a new design and higher capacity in text analysis. Using Russell's (1980) framework, Whissell and colleagues developed and validated a dictionary of affect in language (DAL), which has 4,500 words in total and can be used to provide ratings of pleasantness and activation on a Likert scale (e.g. Whissell, Fournier, Pelland, Weir, & Makarec, 1986). Both of these methods have been applied among samples of different backgrounds in organizational research.

Additionally, we introduce one representative observation-based method that follows the dimensional affect approach. Krauss, Apple, Morency, Wenzel, and Winton (1981) had others rate target persons' affect by evaluating audiovisual presentations, verbal or written transcripts, audiotrack (e.g. speaking with content filtered out to capture only pitch, loudness, rate, etc.), and visible (silent video) information. The affect ratings were categorized into evaluation/valence factors, activity factors, and potency/activation factor, which is consistent with Russell's (1980) framework.

Discrete Affect Approach

We first introduce one text-analysis-based method for other-ratings of discrete affect. Pennebaker and colleagues' (2007) LIWC assesses discrete affect including anxiety, anger, and sadness, with each discrete affect assessed by 91–499 words. We then introduce two representative observation-based methods that follow the discrete affect approach. First, Barsade and O'Neill (2014) developed and validated a single-item observation scale of unit-level companionate love culture in a long-term care setting, to be rated by outside raters (e.g. research assistants), employees, and patients' family members. Secondly, the facial action coding system (FACS) rubric used by Ekman and colleagues (e.g. Ekman & Friesen, 2003) and the more recent development of it (e.g. FaceReader 5.0) represent a category of observation-based other-rating methods that code facial expressions of the target person into specific discrete affects (e.g. happiness, sadness, anger).

Physiological Indicators for Objective Ratings

Objective ratings of experienced affect incorporate physiological reactions that correspond to general affect and discrete affect. All the methods that we describe here are capable of measuring dimensional and discrete affect. In this section we do not differentiate explicit versus implicit affect because there have been no clear conclusions when it comes to which of these physiological methods measure. A more comprehensive review of these physiological indicators can be found in Peterson and colleagues (2015).

First, we describe measurement techniques corresponding to facial electromyographic (EMG) activity and autonomic responses. The international affective picture system (IAPS) by Lang, Greenwald, Bradley and Hamm (1993) was partially developed by using EMG activity as evidence for the pictures' successful and reliable elicitation of specific emotions. Facial expressions correspond to general affect, especially in relation to valence – Russell's (1980) affect framework – and specific muscle activity correlates to discrete affect, such as the six universal emotions (D'Arcey, 2013). For example, disgust produces a facial grimace, and fear-inducing pictures result in the relaxation of corrugator muscles. Beyond facial reactions, autonomic responses – including cardiovascular and electrodermal (EDA) responses – relate to general and discrete affect. In terms of general affect dimensions, peak heart rate corresponds to affect valence and EDA activity (previously known as skin conductance reactivity) relates to affect arousal with adequate reliability (Lang et al., 1993), which is consistent with Russell's (1980) framework. Identified patterns of reduced or increased heart rate and/or EDA activity provide researchers with indicators of discrete affect (Lang et al., 1993). A more recent study employed wearable devices measuring EDA activity, skin temperature, and heart rate, in response to elicited discrete affect, specifically, sadness, anger, fear, surprise, frustration, and amusement (Lisetti & Nasoz, 2004). Its results showed significant increases in EDA activity corresponding to frustration, increases in heart rate for fear, and decreases for anger.

Additionally, empirical studies have made efforts to apply methods such as electroencephalography (EEG), quantitative electroencephalography (qEEG), and functional magnetic resonance imaging (fMRI) in research on affect (Peterson et al., 2015). Some studies have used fMRI technology (Hsu, Anen, & Quartz, 2008) to examine the correspondence of local brain activity and general negative affect; this corresponds to Watson and colleagues' (1988) framework. Others have examined brain activity, such as event-related potential (ERP) patterns, in the encoding of emotional facial expressions of happiness, sadness, fear, and anger (Brenner, Rumak, Burns, & Kieffaber, 2014). The relationship between affect and neural activity, as shown through the activation of brain regions resulting from emotion-evoking stimuli, allows researchers to consider brain activity as an indicator for experienced affect.

Summary

Among the existing quantitative methods to measure experienced affect, the vast majority are self-rated, use a Likert format, and focus on explicit affect. Among the methods for self-ratings, the vast majority are word- or sentence-based standard measures as opposed to pictorial methods. In general, the internal consistency reliability (e.g. Cronbach's alpha) is somewhat lower for text-analysis-based methods, mainly due to the way that affect is communicated in text as part of a document (e.g. blog post or open-ended response to an interview question). Specifically, words that convey the same affect dimension (e.g. "hate," "kill," or "annoyed" for the dimension of anger; Pennebaker et al., 2007) are not always expected to appear within the same document (corresponding to a situation/scenario) repeatedly or consistently, because the communicator does not always believe such affect-related messages need to be repeated in a particular scenario.

Existing Measures of Affect Regulation

Affect regulation refers to the processes whereby individuals alter and express the affect they experience (Gross, 1998). Gross suggests that affect regulation can either be conscious or unconscious, and therefore individuals may manage their affect either explicitly or implicitly. Implicit affect regulation is defined as unconscious and unintentional affect-regulatory responses (Koole, Webb & Sheeran, 2015). Particularly, we contend that affect expressiveness – the extent to which an individual expresses the experienced affect outwardly – is an important aspect of workplace affect regulation, because the expressed affect carries substantial social information and plays a significant role in our understanding of interpersonal and team processes in the workplace (Barsade, 2002; Van Kleef, 2010).

In organizational research, commonly used measures of affect regulation include scales for general affect regulation and emotional labor. Emotional labor measures will be covered in detail in Chapter 11 of this volume; in this chapter, we will introduce quantitative approaches that measure explicit and implicit forms of general affect regulation strategies. As with the quantitative methods for affect, there are measures for self-, other-, and objective ratings of affect regulation. For self-ratings, there are measures developed and validated for both explicit and implicit affect regulation, whereas for other- and objective ratings there are only measures for explicit affect regulation.

Measures for Self-Ratings of Affect Regulation

Explicit Affect Regulation

A commonly used approach to measure explicit affect regulation is sentence-based measures for self-ratings. We introduce three representative ones. Riggio (1986) developed and validated a 105-item social skills inventory in a Likert format, with fifteen items in each of its seven dimensions. Specifically, the subscales of emotional expressiveness and emotional control can be used to measure different aspects of affect regulation. Additionally, Gratz and Roemer (2004) developed and validated a -item difficulties of emotion regulation scale to assess six dimensions of explicit affect regulation in a Likert format (e.g. impulse control difficulties, lack of emotional awareness). Lastly, specific to the emotional expressiveness, Kring and colleagues' (1994) developed and validated a seventeen-item emotional expressivity scale, using a Likert format. All these measures have been applied in work settings and found to be reliable and valid.

Implicit Affect Regulation

Implicit affect regulation can be assessed by self-rating measures using words or sentences as items, in a Likert format or scored by reaction time in a computerized format. Mauss and colleagues (2006) developed a computerized test, based on reaction time, of emotion regulation and implicit association, measuring affect expression, and found a positive relationship between individuals' implicit evaluation of affect regulation and their actual affect responses. Martinez-Iñigo and colleagues (2007) developed and validated a four-item Likert scale to measure automatic regulation – a regulation strategy that operates on naturally felt emotions and seems to benefit employee stress management among healthcare workers. Another reliable Likert measure of implicit affect regulation is the four-item, self-report behavioral automaticity index subscale of the self-report habit index developed by Gardner and colleagues (2012) to specifically assess implicit reappraisal (i.e. automatic use of reappraisal strategies). All these measures have been applied in work settings and found to be reliable and valid (e.g. Hülsheger, Lang, Schewe, & Zijlstra, 2015).

Methods for Other-Ratings of Explicit Affect Regulation

Other-ratings of affect regulation are generally accomplished using observations by trained others, such as researchers or colleagues of the focal individuals. These rating methods are often advantageous in assessing target individuals' emotional expressiveness or additional affect-expression-related dimensions, with little bias. For example, in applications of FACS and related methods, observers are trained to rate affect expressions of the target individuals based on observations of their facial cues, body movements, and voice pitch. Studies by these scholars found evidence that observations of these physical qualities can reliably differentiate honest and deceptive expressions of pleasure (e.g. Ekman, O'Sullivan, Friesen, & Scherer, 1991). These methods have evolved significantly due to technological advancements by including features such as more efficient automatic coding processes and larger training databases.

Physiological Indicators for Objective Ratings of Explicit Affect Regulation

Some techniques that assess physiological indicators of affect regulation have shown credible results. We describe two techniques to measure brain activity: fMRI and ERP. Ochsner and colleagues (2002) used fMRI to examine individuals' affect regulation, and found correspondence between prefrontal cortex activity and reappraisal of negative scenes (which reduced negative affect). Recently, Kim and colleagues (2015) used fMRI to investigate brain activity in relation to suppression and aggressive behaviors at work. Moser and colleagues (2006) examined how individuals' affect regulation (e.g. suppression) changed their brain's electrophysiological activity, and suggested that ERP could be useful in studying affect regulation.

Summary

In the quantitative measurement of general affect regulation, more measures and methods have been developed and validated for explicit affect regulation than for implicit affect regulation. Specifically, word-/sentence-based measures for self-ratings and methods for other- and objective ratings are available to measure explicit regulation, whereas only word-/sentence-based measures for self-ratings are available to measure implicit regulation. In the application of these measures and methods to organizational research, more work has been done in the area of explicit regulation than that of implicit regulation. Such a state of measurement development and application corresponds to the state of theoretical development in explicit vs. implicit affect regulation. Because the effort toward, and advancement in, implicit regulation has been more recent, not surprisingly, researchers and practitioners are faced with more challenges in terms of reliably and accurately assessing its processes as well as proposing and implementing strategies to influence them (Barsade et al., 2009; Koole et al., 2015).

Quantitative Affect Measurement: State of the Art and Future Directions

State of the Art

In the organizational research literature on affect and affect regulation, we observe four characteristics of quantitative measurement. First of all, more advancement in quantitative measurement has been made for explicit affect and explicit affect regulation than for the corresponding implicit constructs and processes. This difference is twofold, because there is not only a larger number of validated measures and methods, but also a greater variety of approaches (self-, other-, and objective ratings) to quantitatively assess explicit affect and affect regulation. Such a difference partially reflects the difference in theoretical development between explicit and implicit affect-related processes, as well as the difference in organizational constraints inherent in implementing research and interventions focused on explicit vs. implicit affect processes (Barsade, 2009; Koole et al., 2015; Uhlmann et al., 2012-). Second, though cost-effective and convenient self-rating scales remain popular, the measurement errors inherent in self-ratings, which are due to such factors as recall errors and mood-consistency effects (Robinson & Clore, 2002), make it worthwhile for future research to investigate ways to address this limitation. For example, we could explicitly assess such measurement errors (and account for them accordingly), and increase the reliability and validity of measurement through strategies such as applying more than one measure of the same affect construct (e.g. using both self- and other-rating measures).

Third, few measures and methods are designed to assess collective-level (e.g. group-level) affect processes in the work settings. One exception is the measure of compassionate love culture (Barsade & O'Neill, 2014). The authors developed the measure using a referent shift (i.e. referring to "other employees in your unit" in the item), with a purpose of measuring shared affect culture at the group-level. As teamwork becomes increasingly important in the workplace, quantitative measurement of group-level affect processes will carry more significance for future research and managerial practices in managing group dynamics at work (Barsade & Knight, 2015).

Finally, few studies in the literature have applied more than one type of quantitative affect measurement that might complement each other and triangulate the accuracy of the measurements (e.g. using an other-rating method in addition to a self-rating scale). The advantages of measurement methods for other-ratings or objective ratings include (but are not limited to) their capacities to provide ratings less susceptible to subjective reporting biases and to capture affect-related information through perspectives (e.g. neurological and cognitive) that self-ratings can't obtain. Disadvantages of these rating methods are that they can be expensive (e.g. using brain scans or tracking EDA activities) and/or time-consuming (e.g. gathering multiple credible text documents per individual for LIWC). Nevertheless, we believe in the value of employing more than one type of measurement for affect-related processes. For example, in research or an intervention focused on applicants' affect experiences and intention to accept job offers, would applying a PANAS measure of affect for self-ratings and a LIWC analysis of interview scripts (responses to open-ended interview questions) be able to capture applicants' affect experiences more reliably and accurately? There are, of course, considerations on feasibility in applying more than one measure; however, the development of technology-based measurement techniques will probably allow for more future applications that include multiple measures used simultaneously (Rafaeli, Ashtar, & Altman, 2019; Zeng, Pantic, Roisman, & Huang, 2009).

Future Directions

Based on our review of the quantitative measurement literature on affect and affect regulation, we propose the following directions for future research. Please note that these suggestions are presented in no particular order.

More systematic research to examine the viability of multi-method approaches. It has been commonly recognized that using solely self-rating scales to assess affect and other organizational phenomena may bring about potential biases, such as recall errors, as noted in the previous section. Accordingly, there have been many calls for the multi-method approaches to quantitative measurement in affect research and broader organizational research (e.g. Ganster, Crain, & Brossoit, 2018; Larsen & Fredrickson, 1999; Peterson et al., 2015). Yet only limited empirical research has been done to examine the viability of such approaches (with exceptions, e.g. Blascovich,

Mendes, & Seery, 2002; Lisetti & Nasoz, 2004). In the context of affect research, the key question pertinent to this issue is whether a researcher intends to use multiple measures to triangulate the same affect construct or to assess different affect constructs (which sometimes complement each other to help in understanding a broader phenomenon). For example, Lisetti and Nasoz (2004) found that the pattern recognition algorithms based on EDA activity identified the same sets of discrete affect as the self-ratings on a Likert scale by the participants, but with higher accuracy than the self-ratings.

On the other hand, it is equally (if not more) important for affect researchers to use multi-method approaches to examine different yet closely related constructs by selecting methods that are most advantageous in measuring the specific construct(s), so that these methods complement each other. For example, the phenomenon of dynamic affect change (or affective shift) illustrated in Yang and colleagues (2016) could benefit from data simultaneously collected via self-ratings of explicit affect scales and wearable devices capturing heart rate, in research using experience-sampling methods (ESM). In this case, the affect levels measured by heart rate could indicate both explicit and implicit affect. If it were the latter, we might gain insights on how the self-ratings of explicit affect and heart rate data of implicit affect differentially predict different work behaviors or health outcomes, but we might not expect to see a convergence between self-ratings and heart rate measurements, given the distinct processes associated with explicit and implicit affect (e.g. Barsade et al., 2009).

In general, it seems reasonable to suggest including psychological rating scales and physiological measures within the same study as one strategy for the multi-method approach. However, it is important to note that the strength of inference for physiological measures is bounded by factors such as context and sensitivity of physiological indicators and thus it is often challenging to select a specific physiological indicator to represent a psychological construct such as affect (Akinola, 2010; Cacioppo & Tassinary, 1990).

Using repeated measurements of states to assess affect-related individual traits. Consistent with the broader observation by Beal (2015) on innovative approaches to research employing ESM, there is important potential value in expanding on research that uses repeated measurement of state affect to assess affect-related individual traits or characteristics, especially for measures of self-ratings. In assessing affect dispositions, organizational researchers have started to use aggregated, average affect levels across many state measurements of affect (e.g. to report affect-related states once a day) (Huang & Ryan, 2011). Doing so is consistent with tenets of the whole trait theory and with the evidence for the high convergence between aggregated levels of state affect (as estimates of typical states and behaviors with less influence of recall errors) and the traditional one-time assessment of trait affectivity informed by semantic memory (Fleeson & Jayawickreme, 2015).

Affective spin also represents a dispositional indicator of variability in affective state as measured by ESM (Beal, Trougakos, Weiss, & Dalal, 2013). With the support of some nascent empirical work done in organizational research (Beal et al., 2013), we are confident that both these types of affect disposition could predict important outcomes in organizational research, such as employee well-being and creativity, or the moderation of between- or within-person relationships in work environments (e.g. unfair events) and employee outcomes (burnout). With the choice of appropriate and affordable methods, researchers can also use repeated physiological measurement in ESM research and can aggregate the data to assess more stable affect constructs (e.g. implicit trait affectivity). Furthermore, the fluctuations in state affect regulation also enable it to be aggregated to capture dispositional representations of regulation such as emotional control capacity (as average scores of daily measurements) or the proficiency of emotional regulation skills (as standard deviations).

More use of technology-assisted measurement techniques. There are two aspects to this suggestion. First, technological advancements can be used to increase the feasibility and accessibility, and decrease the costs, of applying physiological methods of affect measurement in future organizational research on affect (e.g. Ganster et al., 2018; Peterson et al., 2015). For example, the advantages of qEEG, including temporal resolution that can capture immediate concomitant brain activity, the portability of the device, and participant maneuverability during the data collection, offer a promising avenue for future research (Peterson et al., 2015). Real-time measurement of emotion via physiological signals may also become more viable. For example, one device, the BioCrystal, is designed for various environments and uses physiological data to evaluate the user's affective state in real time, responding with ambient display using color-changing light (Roseway, Lutchyn, Johns, Mynatt, & Czerwinski, 2015). As a last example, the development of wrist bracelets (Burleson, 2011) has made the process of measuring electrodermal activity (EDA) as an indicator of emotions much more affordable and user-friendly.

Second, advancements in technology, including artificial-intelligence-based methods, has encouraged the development of, and improvements in, methods for other-ratings of affect. As an example of observation-based methods for others' ratings, affect recognition measures have improved significantly (Lisetti & Nasoz, 2004; Wolf, 2015) due to technological advancements. Results from Lisetti and Nasoz (2004) promoted the idea of multimodal affective user interface that can be developed in order to recognize its user's affective state, to react to environmental factors, and even to interact with the user. Such advancements could benefit research and applications in the realm of experienced affect and affect regulation (e.g. offering physiological information as feedback to facilitate the user's internal affect regulation).

Conclusions

This chapter has reviewed existing literature on quantitative measurement techniques in the areas of affect and affect regulation. We have evaluated the reliabilities, validities, and applications of methods for self-, other- and objective ratings, particularly in the context of organizational research. Based on such evaluations, we have suggested four directions for future development and application of quantitative measurement in these areas of research, namely a) to conduct more systematic research to examine the viability of multi-method approaches, b) to use repeated within-person state measurements in innovative ways, and c) to embrace technology-assisted measurement techniques.

References

Akinola, M. (2010). Measuring the pulse of an organization: Integrating physiological measures into the organizational scholar's toolbox. *Research in Organizational Behavior, 30*, 203–223.

Ashkanasy, N. M., & Dorris, A. D. (2017). Emotions in the workplace. *Annual Review of Organizational Psychology and Organizational Behavior, 4*, 67–90.

Barrett, L. F., & Russell, J. A. (1999). The structure of current affect: Controversies and emerging consensus. *Current Directions in Psychological Science, 8*, 10–14.

Barsade, S. G. (2002). The ripple effect: Emotional contagion and its influence on group behavior. *Administrative Science Quarterly, 47*, 644–675.

Barsade, S. G., & Knight, A. P. (2015). Group affect. *Annual Review of Organizational Psychology and Organizational Behavior, 2*, 21–46.

Barsade, S. G., & O'Neill, O. A. (2014). What's love got to do with it? A longitudinal study of the culture of companionate love and employee and client outcomes in a long-term care setting. *Administrative Science Quarterly, 59*, 551–598.

Barsade, S. G., Ramarajan, L., & Westen, D. (2009). Implicit affect in organizations. *Research in Organizational Behavior, 29*, 135–162.

Beal, D. J. (2015). ESM 2.0: State of the art and future potential of experience sampling methods in organizational research. *Annual Review of Organizational Psychology and Organizational Behavior, 2*, 383–407.

Beal, D. J., Trougakos, J. P., Weiss, H. M., & Dalal, R. S. (2013). Affect spin and the emotion regulation process at work. *Journal of Applied Psychology, 98*, 593–605.

Betella, A., & Verschure, P. F. M. J. (2016). The affective slider: A digital self-assessment scale for the measurement of human emotions. *PLoS ONE, 11*, e0148037.

Blascovich, J., Mendes, W. B., & Seery, M. D. (2002). Intergroup encounters and threat: A multi-method approach. In D. M. Mackie & E. R. Smith (Eds.), *From prejudice to intergroup emotions: Differentiated reactions to social groups* (pp. 89–109). New York, NY: Psychology.

Bradley, M. M., & Lang, P. J. (1994). Measuring emotion: The self-assessment manikin and the semantic differential. *Journal of Behavior Therapy and Experimental Psychiatry, 25*, 49–59.

Brenner, C. A., Rumak, S. P., Burns, A. M., & Kieffaber, P. D. (2014). The role of encoding and attention in facial emotion memory: An EEG investigation. *International Journal of Psychophysiology, 93*, 398–410.

Burleson, W. (2011). Advancing a multimodal real-time affective sensing research platform. In R. A. Calvo & S. D'Mello (Eds.), *New perspectives on affect and learning technologies* (pp. 97–112). New York, NY: Springer.

Cacioppo, J. T., & Tassinary, L. G. (1990). *Principles of psychophysiology: Physical, social, and inferential elements*. New York, NY: Cambridge University Press.

Cropanzano, R., Ambrose, M. A., & Van Waggoner, H. P. (in press). *Organizational justice and workplace emotion*. In E. A. Lind (Ed.), *Social psychology and justice*. Abingdon, UK: Routledge.

Cropanzano, R., Weiss, H. M., Hale, J. M., & Reb, J. (2003). The structure of affect: Reconsidering the relationship between negative and positive affectivity. *Journal of Management, 29*, 831–857.

D'Arcey, J. T. (2013). *Assessing the validity of FaceReader using facial EMG* (unpublished master's thesis), California State University, Chico, CA.

Ekman, P. (1992). An argument for basic emotions. *Cognition and Emotion, 6*, 169–200.

Ekman, P., & Friesen, W. V. (2003). *Unmasking the face: A guide to recognizing emotions from facial expressions*. Los Altos, CA: Malor.

Ekman, P., O'Sullivan, M., Friesen, W. V., & Scherer, K. R. (1991). Face, voice, and body in detecting deceit. *Journal of Nonverbal Behavior, 15*, 125–135.

Fleeson, W., & Jayawickreme, E. (2015). Whole trait theory. *Journal of Research in Personality, 56*, 82–92.

Ganster, D. C., Crain, T. L., & Brossoit, R. M. (2018). Physiological measurement in the organizational sciences: A review and recommendations for future use. *Annual Review of Organizational Psychology and Organizational Behavior, 5*, 267–293.

Gardner, B., Abraham, C., Lally, P., & de Bruijn, G. J. (2012). Towards parsimony in habit measurement: Testing the convergent and predictive validity of an automaticity subscale of the Self-Report Habit Index. *International Journal of Behavioral Nutrition and Physical Activity, 9*, 102.

Gratz, K. L., & Roemer, L. (2004). Multidimensional assessment of emotion regulation and dysregulation: Development, factor structure, and initial validation of the difficulties in emotion regulation scale. *Journal of Psychopathology and Behavioral Assessment, 26*, 41–54.

Gross, J. J. (1998). The emerging field of emotion regulation: An integrative review. *Review of General Psychology, 2*, 271–299.

Hsu, M., Anen, C., & Quartz, S. R. (2008). The right and the good: Distributive justice and neural encoding of equity and efficiency. *Science, 320*, 1092–1095.

Huang, J. L., & Ryan, A. M. (2011). Beyond personality traits: A study of personality states and situational contingencies in customer service jobs. *Personnel Psychology, 64*, 451–488.

Hülsheger, U. R., Lang, J. W., Schewe, A. F., & Zijlstra, F. R. (2015). When regulating emotions at work pays off: A diary and an intervention study on emotion regulation and customer tips in service jobs. *Journal of Applied Psychology, 100*, 263–277.

Izard, C. E. (2009). Emotion theory and research: Highlights, unanswered questions, and emerging issues. *Annual Review of Psychology, 60*, 1–25.

James, K., Lovato, C., & Khoo, G. (1994). Social identity correlates of minority workers' health. *Academy of Management Journal, 37*, 383–396.

Johnson, R. E., Tolentino, A. L., Rodopman, O. B., & Cho, E. (2010). We (sometimes) know not how we feel: Predicting job performance with an implicit measure of trait affectivity. *Personnel Psychology, 63*, 197–219.

Kim, M. Y., & James, L. R. (2015). Neurological evidence for the relationship between suppression and aggressive behavior: Implications for workplace aggression. *Applied Psychology, 64*, 286–307.

Koole, S. L., Webb, T. L., & Sheeran, P. L. (2015). Implicit emotion regulation: Feeling better without knowing why. *Current Opinion in Psychology, 3*, 6–10.

Krauss, R. M., Apple, W., Morency, N., Wenzel, C., & Winton, W. (1981). Verbal, vocal, and visible factors in judgments of another's affect. *Journal of Personality and Social Psychology, 40*, 312–320.

Kring, A. M., Smith, D. A., & Neale, J. M. (1994). Individual differences in dispositional expressiveness: Development and validation of the Emotional Expressivity Scale. *Journal of Personality and Social Psychology, 66*, 934–949.

Lang, P. J., Bradley, M. M., & Cuthbert, B. N. (1997). *International affective picture system (IAPS): Technical manual and affective ratings*. Gainesville, FL: NIMH Center for the Study of Emotion and Attention.

Lang, P. J., Greenwald, M. K., Bradley, M. M., & Hamm, A. O. (1993). Looking at pictures: Affective, facial, visceral, and behavioral reactions. *Psychophysiology, 30*, 261–273.

Larsen, R. J., & Diener, E. (1992). Promises and problems with the circumplex model of emotion. In M. S. Clark (Ed.), *Review of personality and social psychology, No. 13. Emotion* (pp. 25–59). Thousand Oaks, CA: Sage.

Larsen, R. J., & Fredrickson, B. L. (1999). Measurement issues in emotion research. In D. Kahneman, E. Diener, & N. Schwarz (Eds.), *Well-being: The foundations of hedonic psychology* (pp. 40–60). New York, NY: Russell Sage Foundation.

Levine, E. L., Xu, X., Yang, L. Q., Ispas, D., Pitariu, H. D., Bian, R., . . . & Musat, S. (2011). Cross-national explorations of the impact of affect at work using the State-Trait Emotion Measure: A coordinated series of studies in the United States, China, and Romania. *Human Performance, 24*, 405–442.

Lisetti, C. L., & Nasoz, F. (2004). Using noninvasive wearable computers to recognize human emotions from physiological signals. *EURASIP Journal on Applied Signal Processing, 2004*, 1672–1687.

Martínez-Iñigo, D., Totterdell, P., Alcover, C. M., & Holman, D. (2007). Emotional labour and emotional exhaustion: Interpersonal and intrapersonal mechanisms. *Work and Stress, 21*, 30–47.

Mauss, I. B., Evers, C., Wilhelm, F. H., & Gross, J. J. (2006). How to bite your tongue without blowing your top: Implicit evaluation of emotion regulation predicts affective responding to anger provocation. *Personality and Social Psychology Bulletin, 32*, 589–602.

Mauss, I. B., & Robinson, M. D. (2009). Measures of emotion: A review. *Cognition and Emotion, 23*, 209–237.

McCullough, M. E., Emmons, R. A., & Tsang, J. A. (2002). The grateful disposition: A conceptual and empirical topography. *Journal of Personality and Social Psychology, 82*, 112–127.

McNair, D. M., Droppleman, L. F., & Lorr, M. (1992). *Edits manual for the profile of mood states: POMS*. San Diego, CA: Edits.

Mehrabian, A., & Russell, J. A. (1974). *An approach to environmental psychology*. Cambridge, MA: MIT Press.

Moser, J. S., Hajcak, G., Bukay, E., & Simons, R. F. (2006). Intentional modulation of emotional responding to unpleasant pictures: An ERP study. *Psychophysiology*, *43*, 292–296.

Ochsner, K. N., Bunge, S. A., Gross, J. J., & Gabrieli, J. D. (2002). Rethinking feelings: An FMRI study of the cognitive regulation of emotion. *Journal of Cognitive Neuroscience*, *14*, 1215–1229.

Pennebaker, J. W., Chung, C. K., Ireland, M., Gonzales, A., & Booth, R. J. (2007). *The development and psychometric properties of LIWC2007*. Austin, TX: LIWC.net.

Peterson, S. J., Reina, C. S., Waldman, D. A., & Becker, W. J. (2015). Using physiological methods to study emotions in organizations. In C. E. J Härtel, W. J. Zerbe, and N. M. Ashkanasy (Eds.), *New ways of studying emotions in organizations* (Volume 11, pp. 1–27). Bingley, UK: Emerald.

Quirin, M., Kazén, M., & Kuhl, J. (2009). When nonsense sounds happy or helpless: The implicit positive and negative affect test (IPANAT). *Journal of Personality and Social Psychology*, *97*, 500–516.

Rafaeli, A., Ashtar, S., & Altman, D. (2019). Digital traces: New data, resources and tools for psychological science research. *Current Directions in Psychological Science*, https://doi.org/10.1177/0963721419861410

Riggio, R. E. (1986). Assessment of basic social skills. *Journal of Personality and Social Psychology*, *51*, 649–660.

Robinson, M. D., & Clore, G. L. (2002). Belief and feeling: Evidence for an accessibility model of emotional self-report. *Psychological Bulletin*, *128*, 934–960.

Roseman, I. J., Spindel, M. S., & Jose, P. E. (1990). Appraisal of emotion eliciting events: Testing a theory of discrete emotions. *Journal of Personality and Social Psychology*, *59*, 99–91.

Roseway, A., Lutchyn, Y., Johns, P., Mynatt, E., & Czerwinski, M. (2015). BioCrystal: An ambient tool for emotion and communication. *International Journal of Mobile Human Computer Interaction*, *7*, 20–41.

Russell, J. A. (1980). A circumplex model of affect. *Journal of Personality and Social Psychology*, *39*, 1161–1178.

Russell, J. A. (2003). Core affect and the psychological construction of emotion. *Psychological Review*, *110*, 145–172.

Smith, R. H., Parrott, W. G., Diener, E. F., Hoyle, R. H., & Kim, S. H. (1999). Dispositional envy. *Personality and Social Psychology Bulletin*, *25*, 1007–1020.

Spielberger, C. D., & Reheiser, E. C. (2004). Measuring anxiety, anger, depression, and curiosity as emotional states and personality traits with the STAI, STAXI, and STPI. In M. J. Hersen, D. L. Segal, and M. Hersen (Eds.), *Comprehensive Handbook of Psychological Assessment* (Volume 2, pp. 70–86). Hoboken, NJ: Wiley.

Uhlmann, E. L., Leavitt, K., Menges, J. I., Koopman, J., Howe, M., & Johnson, R. E. (2012). Getting explicit about the implicit: A taxonomy of implicit measures and guide for their use in organizational research. *Organizational Research Methods*, *15*, 553–601.

Van Katwyk, P. T., Fox, S., Spector, P. E., & Kelloway, E. K. (2000). Using the Job-Related Affective Well-Being Scale (JAWS) to investigate affective responses to work stressors. *Journal of Occupational Health Psychology*, *5*, 219–230.

Van Kleef, G. A. (2010). The emerging view of emotion as social information. *Social and Personality Psychology Compass*, *4*, 331–343.

Warr, P., Bindl, U. K., Parker, S. K., & Inceoglu, I. (2014). Four-quadrant investigation of job-related affects and behaviours. *European Journal of Work and Organizational Psychology*, *23*, 342–363.

Watson, D., & Clark, L. A. (1999). *The PANAS-X: Manual for the positive and negative affect schedule-expanded form*. Iowa City: University of Iowa.

Watson, D., Clark, L. A., & Tellegen, A. (1988). Development and validation of brief measures of positive and negative affect: The PANAS scales. *Journal of Personality and Social Psychology*, *54*, 1063–1070.

Whissell, C., Fournier, M., Pelland, R., Weir, D., & Makarec, K. (1986). A dictionary of affect in language: IV. Reliability, validity, and applications. *Perceptual and Motor Skills*, *62*, 875–888.

Wolf, K. (2015). Measuring facial expression of emotion. *Dialogues in Clinical Neuroscience*, *17*, 457–462.

Yang, L. Q., Simon, L. S., Wang, L., & Zheng, X. (2016). To branch out or stay focused? Affective shifts differentially predict organizational citizenship behavior and task performance. *Journal of Applied Psychology*, *101*, 831.

Zeng, Z., Pantic, M., Roisman, G. I., & Huang, T. S. (2009). A survey of affect recognition methods: Audio, visual, and spontaneous expressions. *IEEE Transactions on Pattern Analysis and Machine Learning*, *31*, 39–58.

7 Qualitative Methods to Study Workplace Affect

Capturing Elusive Emotions

Donald E. Gibson

Introduction

Capturing the essence of workplace affect and its impact has always been challenging, because affect is challenging. It comes in many forms, including moods, state emotions, and dispositional traits, and occurs at multiple levels – individual, team, and organizational – that interact and change dynamically. In this chapter, I will outline qualitative approaches to studying affective phenomena. The primary emphasis will be on state discrete emotions and state moods – in the case of emotions, affective responses focused on a specific target or cause and relatively intense and short-lived, and in the case of moods, more diffuse feeling states not directed to a specific cause (see Barsade & Gibson, 2007) – because these phenomena are most difficult to capture with the tools typically available to organizational researchers. Dispositional traits and sentiments, for example, are relatively reliable and stable and may be measured effectively through a combination of self-report and observational measures (e.g. Staw & Barsade, 1993). Emotions are dynamic, often sudden, fleeting, and disruptive; moods may be a chronic, nagging, bubbling brew. Organizational researchers need appropriate methods to capture this complexity.

Defining Qualitative Approaches to Emotion

Why are qualitative approaches appropriate for studying emotions? First, they are particularly well-suited to accounting for and exploring context, thus facilitating a deeper understanding of participants' perspectives. These methods allow us to study organizational phenomena experienced at a moment in time and involve participants who actively engage in the social construction of reality and sensemaking (see Maitlis, 2005; Weick, 1995). That is, qualitative methods seek to measure and assess both observed "objective" and "subjective" realities. As Briner and Kiefer (2005, p. 300) note, "Without some understanding of the specific emotion-provoking event and context, and meaning of that event, we are only assessing emotion in a very partial way." Second, they provide one window into the multiple attributes that comprise emotion: as Larson, Diener, and Lucas (2002, p. 67) put it, emotions are a "multi-attribute process that unfolds over time, with the attributes unfolding at different rates." Emotions and moods manifest in multiple channels (experiential, physiological, expressive, cognitive and behavioral), and the channels themselves are loosely coupled such that measures of different emotion attributes (such as self-report and physiological) may not correlate highly. "In an ideal world," Larson et al. note, "measuring emotion would entail assessment across multiple attributes simultaneously" (2002, p. 67). Given this complexity, it is critical that methods investigating affect be 1) sensitive to context, and 2) able to capture these multiplex, often unpredictable attributes.

Qualitative research has several distinguishing characteristics that help to meet these criteria (see Cassell & Symon, 2004; Lee, 1999). These approaches primarily emphasize *interpretation* rather than quantification, measurement, and analysis of causal relations (though qualitative researchers often use forms of quantification to clarify categorical analyses). There is substantial *flexibility* in research design and process, such that the design may change to adapt to the needs of the individual and/or organizational context or developments that occur *in situ* during the research. This research tends to be focused more on *description* than on causality, and to examine *processes* rather than predicting outcomes, the endpoint being conceptual insights, new understanding of phenomena, and generation of theories. As we shall see, sequences of events, such as episodes or narrative, may comprise the primary sources of qualitative data (see Boje, 2001). Finally, qualitative research tends to be grounded in a local context within which the phenomena of interest occur, and therefore the results are less generalizable than those gathered using quantitative measures; the interest is in contextual depth over sample generalizability.

Despite the appropriateness of qualitative methods for studying emotional phenomena, and the excellent exemplars that exist of groundbreaking research in emotions (e.g. Hochschild, 1983; see also Rynes & Bartunek, 2016), studies using these methods are numerically dwarfed by quantitative studies. Using search terms in psychology databases, for example, reveals that 5 to 10 percent of studies on affect in organizations primarily use qualitative approaches.[1] As we'll see, neither qualitative nor quantitative methods are complete or perfect, but each has relative advantages and disadvantages for providing convincing exploration of these concepts.

I will also emphasize that the line dividing "qualitative" and "quantitative" research is often fuzzy, and much work using qualitative methods tends to be combined with methods commonly associated with quantitative analysis (see Lee, 1999; Sutton & Rafaeli, 1988). This may include studies beginning with qualitative inquiry that leads to quantitative hypothesis-testing. For example, Brown, Westbrook, and Challagalla (2005) conducted exploratory interviews with seven salespeople, and then tested their hypotheses about negative emotions following a major sale through a quantitative national mail survey. Kirrane, O'Shea, Buckley, Grazi, and Prout (2017, p. 358) began with an inductive "visual data-mapping technique" depicting the meaning and personal experience of silence and discrete emotions with 110 full-time employees, then tested the hypotheses generated with a multi-country quasi-experimental vignette study. Studies may have qualitative data analyzed through linguistic and other content analysis techniques that provide summary statistics (e.g. Pennebake, Boyd, Jordan, & Blackburn, 2015). Others use multi-methods; for example, Amabile, Barsade, Mueller, and Staw (2005) combine qualitative narrative diary data on creativity with numerical questionnaire data on a range of emotional responses, to create a multilevel model. More and more, qualitative data are gathered and measured with the application of increasingly sophisticated media and software (Christianson, 2018).

[1] While qualitative methods have been seen as especially appropriate for studying multi-attribute emotions, quantitative data gathering and analysis remains the dominant research approach, as research on emotions has ballooned in recent years (Ashkanasy & Dorris, 2017). For example, as an admittedly crude indicator, a PsycINFO search of *emotion* AND *workplace* reveals 921 academic journal articles (dating back to 1928). Removing terms relating to clinical and health studies ("health personnel attitudes"; "depression") reduces the number to 765. Searching *emotion* AND *workplace* AND *qualitative* with the same restrictions results in 73 study citations (9.5 percent of the total). Using *affect* AND *organization* reveals an even lower proportion of qualitative research (at least as described in the abstract), between 4 and 6 percent. Extending this approach, combining a range of search terms in PsycINFO suggests that qualitative approaches comprise 5 to 10 percent of workplace studies of emotions resulting in academic articles, and many of these are mixed-method studies.

Primary Methodological Approaches: A Caution on Self-Report

As Gephart (2004, p. 455) notes, "qualitative research starts from and returns to words, talk, and texts as meaningful representations of concepts." By far the most common method used to learn about organizational participants' emotional experiences is to ask them. "Self-report is the most common and potentially the best way to measure a person's emotional experiences" (Robinson & Clore, 2012, p. 934). However, there are obvious disadvantages to relying on self-report data, including memory bias, the salience of intense emotional events, and the tendency to recall negative experiences more vividly than positive ones (Baumeister, Bratslavsky, Finkenauer, & Vohs, 2001). Self-reports rely on the honesty of participants, and given that workplaces differ substantially in their acceptance of strong emotion expression (Geddes & Callister, 2007), participants may be reluctant to reflect on their emotional experiences honestly, especially in the case of emotions that may cast them in a negative light, such as anger, envy, anxiety, sadness, and disgust.

While these cautions must be heeded, self-report measures will probably remain the dominant approach to studying emotions: they are easily understood by respondents, are low in cost (compared, for example, to gathering physiological and neurological data), and can be done with relatively large samples using both qualitative and quantitative survey methods. For capturing many types of emotional phenomena, self-report methods may be the only way to gain insight, even while acknowledging the limitations.

Methodologies for Conducting Qualitative Research on Emotions

There is a wide range of qualitative methods used to study workplace affect in general and emotions in particular (Cassell & Symon, 2004). This chapter should be regarded as introductory rather than comprehensive; readers seeking more detail on qualitative techniques and analysis should see further excellent work in this area (e.g. Cassell & Symon, 2012, Elsbach & Kramer, 2016; Eriksson & Kovalainen, 2008). In the descriptions of methods that follow, it should also be noted that some are primarily data collection methods (interviews, participant observation), while others are primarily data analysis methods (e.g. template analysis, script analysis). I will not make a sharp distinction in these approaches, because in qualitative research they are often combined, but will note where it is important to separate the two.

Ethnography: Participant and Non-participant Observation

Ethnography refers to a range of methods or styles of research aimed at studying people in their natural settings carrying out everyday activities. One challenge of studying emotion is that of getting as "close" to the phenomenon as possible, in terms of proximity and time. The concept is for the researcher to get to know the setting (and actual activities) intimately, "in order to collect data in a systematic manner but without meaning being imposed on them externally" (Brewer, 2000, p. 10). Researchers seek to achieve this closeness by directly participating in the event (participant observation), or by observing people in their workplace milieu as events unfold in real time (either as a direct observer or by videotaping or audiotaping interactions and conversations). Participant observation explicitly involves the observer's own experience as an important and legitimate source of data (Waddinton, 2004). The advantage of such study is the generation of rich data encountered as close as possible to real time; the primary disadvantage is the limitation on extrapolating from the data to other contexts.

The philosophical and epistemological approach underlying much of ethnography (and many of the qualitative methods below) is grounded theory, the notion that theory can be generated from the data collected rather than derived beforehand. As a methodology, grounded theory is a style of both gathering and analyzing qualitative data (Glaser & Strauss, 1967). Grounded theory "provides new insights into the understanding of social processes emerging from the context in which they occur, without forcing and adjusting the data to previous theoretical frameworks" (Länsisalmi, Peiró, & Kivimäki, 2004, p. 242). In the selection of data sources, grounded theory emphasizes *triangulation*, the strategy of combining different types of data such as those collected through interviews, participant observation, and document analysis. Thus, in his study of bill collectors' expressed emotions, Sutton (1991) made twenty-five visits to a debt collection agency, observed experienced collectors, interviewed a wide range of managers and trainers, read extensive documentation, and participated as a debt collector himself to derive emotion norms. Hochschild (1983) drew data from a survey of students, interviews with airline flight attendants, managers, and recruiters, and participant observation in training classes. The point is to immerse oneself as much as possible into the life and culture of an organization and its workers, developing new theoretical insights based on this variety of data sources.

As noted, participant observation does not have to be in person, and technology is increasingly being used to foster observations at heightened levels of detail. For example, Liu and Maitlis (2014) investigated how emotion affects strategizing processes by analyzing interactions between top management team members of a computer game company. Audio and video recordings and transcripts of nine meetings over three months allowed the researchers to use "microethnography," the microscopic analysis of recorded activities to analyze displayed emotions, an approach akin to conversation analysis or close textual reading (Samra-Fredericks, 2004). Their close and repeated scrutiny of video recordings of meetings allowed them to code nonverbal cues of often very subtle displayed emotions associated with different types of strategizing. Christianson (2018) notes the increasing use of video observation as data, particularly when examining groups. Toubiana and Zietsma (2017) explored how emotions influence organizations in situations of institutional complexity by analyzing emotionally-laden expressions of shaming and shunning, primarily through Facebook messages (1,849 unique comments were analyzed, along with 11,293 "likes"). Ayoko, Konrad, and Boyle (2012) analyzed online transcripts of eight virtual teams to examine emotions and conflict; Coget, Haag, and Gibson (2011) conducted semi-structured interviews and analyzed video data of film directors making critical decisions on set to determine how anger and fear shaped patterns of decision-making.

Interviews

The goal of a qualitative interview, which typically consists of posing questions to the respondent, is to see the research phenomenon from the interviewee's perspective and to "understand how and why they come to have this particular perspective" (King, 2004, p. 11). Interviews may range along a continuum from highly structured, in which identical questions are asked of all interviewees, to loosely structured ("semi-structured") based on a set of overall guiding questions that may be changed in the interviewing process, to little structure at all, in which the interviewee takes the lead in reflecting on a phenomenon of interest.

King (2004) also offers a typology of interviews based on their epistemological assumptions. At one end of a continuum are *realist* interviews, which assume that participants' accounts have a direct relationship to their lived, actual experiences in the workplace and beyond. Realist researchers look for ways to compare across interviewees and other documented sources (triangulation), and therefore focus on consistency and structure in interview questions, so that comparisons can convincingly be made. *Phenomenological* interviews emphasize the importance of the interviewer "bracketing" his or her presuppositions in constructing and implementing the interview, acknowledging biases so these can be taken explicitly into account in understanding an interviewee's view of the world. These interviews can provide data for interpretative phenomenological analysis (Smith, 1996), which seeks to offer insights into how a given person, in a given context, makes sense of a given phenomenon. *Social* or *radical constructionist* interviews emphasize that all people actively construct their world: that is, there is no "real," objective world that an interviewee can describe; rather, an interviewee is always constructing their world based on their need to achieve goals. As King (2004, p. 13) notes, when someone says they are "feeling sad," for example, the social constructivist would view this statement not as a description of an emotion inside the person, but "as a discursive act within an interaction, aimed at achieving an objective – eliciting sympathy, disclaiming responsibility, etc."

Interviews are fundamental data-gathering techniques for a range of emotion studies, including more specific techniques outlined below, such as critical incidents, script analysis, and narrative analysis. Examples are widespread and, as noted above, it is increasingly common to sequence qualitative interviews followed by quantitative measures to refine the concepts and test relationships. Examples using data solely from interviews include Lindebaum and Fielden's (2010, p. 443) study of anger in construction program management through nineteen semi-structured interviews conducted with a "non-random, purposive sample" of managers at four different UK construction organizations. Hayward and Tuckey (2011) conducted twelve semi-structured interviews with nurses exploring their regulation of emotion through the manipulation of emotional boundaries to create distance from patients and family members. They employed the "cognitive interview format" used in eyewitness testimony (see Fisher, Geiselman, & Armador, 1989), which emphasizes reconstructing a witness's experience at the time of a crime, including the physical aspects of the situation, emotions felt, and relevant thoughts.

Critical Incidents

Critical incident technique (CIT) began from a realist, positivist perspective in the 1950s to focus on managerial and employee performance. In order to gain insight into soft skills, researchers asked employees to recall the most "critical" events they had encountered in their job and describe them in detail (Flanagan, 1954). Later, from the 1990s onward, the use of CIT from a social constructionist or phenomenological perspective became more common (see summary in Chell, 2004). The latter approach, through the process of semi- or unstructured interviews, seeks to "capture the thought processes, the frame of reference and the feelings about an incident or set of incidents, which have meaning for the respondent" (Chell, 2004, p. 47). The basic interview structure is to introduce respondents to the overall theme sought by the researcher (e.g. "Tell me about a time when you felt angry at work."), listen to the respondent's description of the incident, and then probe for details: What happened next? Why did it happen? How did it happen? With whom did it happen? What did the concerned parties feel? What were the consequences – immediately and longer term? The critical incident approach, and other methods used to derive participants' perspectives on emotion episodes, are the basis for a wide range of studies. For example, Ford, Agosta, Huang, and Shannon (2018) used the technique to explore the types of workplace situations eliciting moral emotions of gratitude, anger, admiration, and contempt. Velasco (2017) studied instances of boredom among front-line service employees using CIT followed by a short survey. The qualitative study generated categories on events causing boredom, and then used the survey to test relationships to job characteristics, satisfaction, and creativity. Waddington (2013) combined CIT with a daily diary approach (see below) such that twenty participants over a ten-day period filled out "critical incident reports" at the end of each day documenting their experiences and feelings about workplace gossip. Daus and Brown (2012) studied emotions in police work by conducting semi-structured interviews with twenty officers, focusing on critical incidents such as domestic violence calls. They content-analyzed the data using a grounded theory approach to develop themes and categories, then focused on the emotional content of the language expressed by using linguistic analysis software (LIWC; see Pennebaker, Chung, Ireland, Gonzalez, & Booth, 2007; Pennebaker et al., 2015).

Episodic Script Analysis

This analysis refers to an individual's understanding of "emotion episodes" and especially the prototypical sequence of events characterizing particular emotions, such as anger, fear, pride, and joy, etc. (Gibson, 2008; Shaver, Schwartz, Kirson, & O'Connor, 1987). These approaches emphasize that individuals often organize their emotional experience as prototypical scripts about what causes specific emotions, what feelings are likely to result, whether they are expressed and/or regulated in some way, and what consequences are likely to arise from such feelings and expressions. An emotion episode comprises four primary elements: (a) an antecedent or triggering event; (b) an emotional experience or reaction, and a sense of "feeling" the emotion; (c) expression, determined by the intensity of felt emotion and effort at regulating expression or behavior; and (d) an outcome or consequence, "which may include the individual's own reaction to the episode as well as the response of others" (Gibson, 2010, p. 68).

A central emphasis in emotion scripts is that while emotions all have important biological underpinnings and tendencies, this approach is seeking the "socially-shared, culturally-specific knowledge about emotions" (Fitness, 2000, p. 148; Kent, Jordan, & Troth, 2014) that individuals have, which is dramatically shaped by the workplace context (Gibson, 2008). That is, emotion scripts contain both a *descriptive element* – the knowledge individuals have of how anger or fear works – and a *normative element* of how a specific emotion *should* be expressed or felt in a particular situation.

Studies using this approach in organizations have included Fischer's (1991) study of anger and fear episodes in both "public" (organizational) and "private" spheres based on fifty-six employee interviews; Gibson's (1997) studies of "basic" emotion scripts and their typical elements, drawing on emotional experiences of 143 MBA students; and Fitness's (2000) study of anger scripts based on a sample of 175 employee-generated episodes. All three find that participants generate relatively cohesive scripts for emotions. For example, Fitness (2000) found substantial agreement on prototypical anger-eliciting events (e.g. perceptions of injustice), and connected anger scripts to power, finding that high-power respondents are likely to be angered by different eliciting events, likely to express their anger to a greater degree, and more likely to think that an anger incident had been successfully resolved than lower-power respondents.

Narrative Analysis

Narratives, like scripts, describe "spoken or written text that involves temporal sequences of events and actions" (Maitlis, 2012, p. 492), but the focus is somewhat different. Whereas script approaches seek to generate prototypical sequences that are focused on broad contexts (such as "workplace" scripts versus "home" or "private" scripts), narrative analysis is focused on stories taking place in specific organizational contexts at specific times. They seek to get at how people create meaning through their social construction of feelings, thoughts, and actions (Boje, 2001). Gathering data for organizational narratives often takes an ethnographic approach, and may occur through participant and non-participant observation, document analysis, and video or audio recording. For example, Maitlis and Ozcelik (2004) generated six narratives of toxic decision processes in symphony orchestras based on interviews with a range of participants, observations of meetings and rehearsals, and extensive documentary analysis.

Diaries/Experiential Sampling

While respondent recall of critical events and scripted responses provide valuable perspective on emotional processes over a sequence – feeling, then expression or control, then outcome – they are subject to the memory and salience biases identified above. One route to reduce these biases, particularly for aggregating emotional state data over time, are experience-sampling methods (ESM; see Csikszentmihalyi & Larson, 1987), also called ecological momentary assessments (EMA). These approaches, aimed at getting closer to real-time responses, either record participant responses at various times during the day (time-based, or "interval-contingent" studies), record responses when a particular event occurs ("event-contingent" studies), or, most commonly, prompt responses through a randomly-timed signal ("signal-contingent" studies; see Scollon, Kim-Prieto, & Diener, 2009; Fisher & To, 2012). As with many of the qualitative approaches outlined here, ESM relies on self-reports entered as survey responses or textual data entered in diary form. The difference is the frequency with which the report occurs, and the emphasis on completion by participants in natural settings. Rather than explicitly seeking critical incidents, for example, these methods can assess the regular flow of events and identify the changing nature of emotions over time as close to that actually experienced as possible. These texts can then be content analyzed or subjected to quantitative methods, depending on the research question asked.

There are three main advantages of ESM approaches (Beal & Weiss, 2003). First, respondent states and behaviors may vary meaningfully over time, and this is especially true for moods and emotions. By capturing an emotional state closer to when it actually occurs, researchers get a more accurate view of how emotions may change over time, increasing the ecological validity of the research. Second, examining potential causal relationships between emotional states and organizational outcomes (e.g. positive affect and job satisfaction) may not be well captured by between-person analysis and retrospective aggregation, and ESM, critically, allows within-person analyses. Third, this method helps to overcome memory biases inherent in respondent attempts to recall past emotional experiences by capturing perceptions closer to when they actually occur (see also Scollon et al., 2009).

The challenges to using this method primarily relate to the level of effort required by participants (see Beal & Weiss, 2003; Fisher & To, 2012). Participants must commit to days, or a week, or more of data collection, often at multiple times each day. The commitment required, and the difficulty of obtaining full compliance, tends to lead to smaller sample sizes (though with a larger number of data-points), and a potential selection effect due to who is willing to fully commit to the study. The use of personal digital assistants (e.g. tablets or smartphones) may ameliorate some of these problems, as they increase convenience for respondents and accuracy of timing and completion for researchers.

Several excellent studies of workplace emotions have used ESM methods. Weiss, Nicholas, and Daus (1999) measured moods of twenty-four middle managers via diary entries that participants were asked to complete four times each day. They found that average measures of mood over the sixteen days made an independent contribution to predictions of overall job satisfaction, above and beyond dispositional happiness. Fisher (2000, p. 185) used ESM with 121 employed persons over a two-week period to test whether real-time affect is related to overall satisfaction, but "not identical to satisfaction," confirming her prediction with measures of positive emotion frequency. Grandey, Tam, and Brauburger (2002) explored the paths of affective events theory (Weiss & Cropanzano, 1996) through an event-contingent diary study asking respondents to record any events that "made you feel strongly while at work" immediately following the events. The study had thirty-six participants reporting 169 diary events, and found linkages between negative and positive emotional states and organizational outcomes. Amabile et al. (2005) studied how affective states relate to creativity at work through the use of an electronic event sampling methodology (daily emailed questionnaires during the project phase under review) of 222 employees in seven companies. They found that positive affect did relate positively to creativity of their respondents, and they were able to note that there was an "incubation period" of up to two days between positive affect and creative outputs.

Template Analysis

I have focused, so far, primarily on methods of gathering qualitative data. The ultimate challenge in using these methodologies, however, may lie in the *interpretation* of these data: how should researchers make sense of voluminous, mostly textual data in a structured and methodologically defensible way? Typically, this is done through a *coding* process, where researchers group themes they are focusing on, or have discovered, to gather data under relevant ideas or topics that, in turn, help to conceptualize higher-order discoveries. As one example, *template analysis* begins with a few predefined codes, often derived from the primary interview questions, that provide the "initial template" (King, 2004). A key feature of template analysis is that groups of similar codes are clustered together to produce more general higher-order codes, in a hierarchical organization. An important difference between this approach and grounded theory or interpretative phenomenological analysis is that template analysts use codes defined a priori that are then refined in the analysis process, rather than developing solely as a result of data analysis.

Computer Aided Qualitative Data Analysis

To aid in coding, researchers increasingly turn to Computer Assisted Qualitative Data Analysis Software (CAQDAS), which helps speed the process of organizing and interpreting large qualitative datasets. It should be emphasized, however, that CAQDAS allows researchers to organize and effectively examine data, but does not itself do the interpreting (see Zamawe, 2015). These programs can, however, significantly help researchers by facilitating deeper and more sophisticated analyses of larger datasets that would be very difficult without computational assistance.

Among the best-known programs are NUD*IST, NVivo, ATLAS.ti, MAXDA, and QDA Miner. Although the features offered by the programs differ, they generally enable the researcher to "index segments of text to particular themes, to link research notes to coding, and to carry out complex search and retrieve operations" (King, 2004, p. 263). NUD*IST, one of the earliest programs, was developed for qualitative data management in the 1980s. NVivo is an improved and expanded version of NUD*IST, with more powerful tools to examine relationships among themes, character-based coding, rich text capabilities, and multimedia functions. NVivo has also added features that allow people from different geographical spaces to work on the same data files at the same time (Zamawe, 2015).

Challenges and Future Directions of Qualitative Work in Emotions Research

The preceding outline of methods is a scan of the rich set of extant qualitative research examining emotions. While technology increasingly aids the collection (i.e. videotaping and microethnographic approaches) and limited analysis (through CAQDAS) of data, the basic approach remains the same: in order to understand participant emotional responses in organizations, researchers need to understand as much about context as possible. Qualitative approaches enhance and add to primarily quantitative approaches by adding essential context; abstracting emotional responses such as anger, envy, and fear from their proximal organizational causes and norms can provide us with confirmation of the biological and social scripts people carry in their heads about how emotions operate, but provide precious little data on the actual operation of specific emotions in specific organizational settings. Qualitative methods provide one avenue to these data.

As the topics examined in this handbook demonstrate, the movement in research on affect is toward specificity, as indicated, for example, in the increasing attention to discrete emotions (Barsade & Gibson, 2007). Going forward, qualitative methods will need to mirror this increasing specificity, and are well structured to do so. Applying technology allows for more fine-grained analysis of emotional experiences and behaviors, as the video work of Liu and Maitlis (2014) well exemplifies. More sophisticated use of ESM techniques will provide data that is ever closer to the actual moment-by-moment experience of emotion, aided by the convenience of smartphones and social media. The increasing use of videoconferencing provides a way to examine cross-cultural emotional displays more readily (see Ozcelik & Paprika, 2010); online or artificial-intelligence-generated communications can elicit real emotions on the part of respondents, convincing them, for example, that their negotiation opponent is happy or angry (Van Kleef, De Dreu, & Manstead, 2004). At the same time, the recognition that multi-attribute emotions need to be studied through multi-method means will continue to foster studies that creatively combine qualitative and quantitative methods.

The danger is that by applying increasingly sophisticated technology to increasingly specific emotional phenomena, the inexorable outcome tends to be the use of quantitative models to count the pieces and capture impact. That is, if technology allows increased sample sizes (e.g. through micro-slices of videotaped emotional displays), the temptation will be great to analyze these data through quantitative approaches. This is a logical progression and has followed the development of more refined psychological and sociological tools for studying emotion (e.g. by using the affective circumplex; Larson, Diener, & Lucas, 2002). The key element for qualitative researchers is to retain the essence of the context, the specificity of a particular setting at a particular time and place. This is where the "interesting" research comes from (Rynes & Bartunek, 2016), and it continues to be the source of vital theoretical development and exploration. As we become more sophisticated in our inquiry into emotional responses, let's not forget the power of actually *talking* to people with their real concerns and complex goals, experiencing their emotions in real settings, in real time.

References

Amabile, T. M., Barsade, S. G, Mueller, J. S., & Staw, B. M. (2005). Affect and creativity at work. *Administrative Science Quarterly, 50*, 367–403.

Ashkanasy, N. M., & Dorris, A. D. (2017). Emotions in the workplace. *Annual Review of Organizational Psychology and Organizational Behavior, 4*, 67–90.

Ayoko, O. B., Konrad, A. M., & Boyle, M. V. (2012). Online work: Managing conflict and emotions for performance in virtual teams. *European Management Journal, 30*, 156–174.

Barsade, S. G. & Gibson, D. E. (2007). Why does affect matter in organizations? *Academy of Management Perspectives, 21*(1), 36–59.

Baumeister, R. F., Bratslavsky, E., Finkenauer, C., & Vohs, K. D. (2001). Bad is stronger than good. *Review of General Psychology, 5*, 323–370.

Beal, D. J., & Weiss, H. M. (2003). Methods of ecological momentary assessment in organizational research. *Organization Research Methods, 6*(4), 440–464.

Boje, D. (2001). *Narrative methods for organizational and communication research*. Thousand Oaks, CA: Sage.

Brewer, J. D. (2000). *Ethnography*. Buckingham, UK: Open University Press.

Briner, R. H. & Kiefer, T. (2005). Psychological research into the experience of emotion at work: Definitely older, but are we any wiser? In N. M. Ashkanasy, C. E. J. Härtel, & W. J. Zerbe (Eds.), *Research on emotion in organizations: The effects of affect in organizational settings* (Volume 1, pp. 289–315). Oxford, UK: Elsevier.

Brown, S. P., Westbrook, R. A., & Challagalla, G. (2005). Good cope, bad cope: Adaptive and maladaptive coping strategies following a critical negative work event. *Journal of Applied Psychology, 90*(4), 792–798.

Cassell, C., & Symon, G. (Eds.) (2004). *Essential guide to qualitative methods in organizational research*. London, UK: Sage.

Cassell, C., & Symon, G. (2012). *The practice of qualitative organizational research: Core methods and current challenges*. London, UK: Sage.

Christianson, M. K. (2018). Mapping the terrain: The use of video-based research in top-tier organizational journals. *Organizational Research Methods, 21*(2), 261–287.

Coget, J., Haag, C., & Gibson, D. E. (2011). Anger and fear in decision-making: The case of film directors on set. *European Management Journal, 29*, 476–490.

Csikszentmihalyi, M., & Larson, R. W. (1987). Validity and reliability of the experience-sampling method. *Journal of Nervous and Mental Disease, 175*, 526–536.

Daus, C. S., & Brown, S. (2012). The emotion work of police. In N. M. Ashkanasy, C. E. J. Härtel, & W. J. Zerbe (Eds.), *Research on emotions in organizations: Experiencing and managing emotions in the workplace* (Volume 8, pp. 305–329).

Elsbach, K. D., & Kramer, R. M. (Eds.) (2016). *Handbook of qualitative organizational research: Innovative pathways and methods*. New York, NY: Routledge.

Eriksson, P., & Kovalainen, A. (2008). *Qualitative research in business studies*. London, UK: Sage.

Fisher, C. D. (2000). Mood and emotions while working: Missing pieces of job satisfaction? *Journal of Organizational Behavior, 21*, 185–202.

Fisher, R. P., Geiselman, R. E., & Armador, M. (1989). Field test of the cognitive interview: Enhancing the recollection of the actual victims and witnesses of crimes. *Journal of Applied Psychology, 7*(5): 722–727.

Fisher, C. D., & To, M. I. (2012). Using experience sampling methodology in organizational behavior. *Journal of Organizational Behavior, 33*(7), 865–877.

Fitness, J. (2000). Anger in the workplace: An emotion script approach to anger episodes between workers and their superiors, co-workers and subordinates. *Journal of Organizational Behavior, 21*, 147–162.

Ford, M. T., Agosta, J. P., Huang, J., & Shannon, C. (2018). Moral emotions toward others at work and implications for employee behavior: A qualitative analysis using critical incidents. *Journal of Business Psychology, 33*, 155–180.

Geddes, D. & Callister, R. R. (2007). Crossing the line(s): A dual threshold model of anger in organizations. *Academy of Management Review, 32* (3), 721–746.

Gephart, R. P. (2004). Qualitative research and the *Academy of Management Journal. Academy of Management Journal, 47*(4), 454–462.

Gibson, D. E. (1997). The struggle for reason: The sociology of emotions in organizations. In R. J. Erickson and B. Cuthbertson-Johnson (Eds.), *Social perspectives on emotion* (Volume 4, pp. 211–256). Greenwich, CT: JAI.

Gibson, D. E. (2008). Emotion scripts in organizations: A multi-level model. In N. Ashkanasy and C. Cooper (Eds.), *Research companion to emotion in organizations* (pp. 263–283). London, UK: Edward Elgar Publishers.

Glaser, B. G. & Strauss, A. L. (1967). *The discovery of grounded theory: Strategies for qualitative research*. New York, NY: De Gruyter.

Grandey, A. A., Tam, A. P., & Brauburger, A. L. (2002). Affective states and traits in the workplace: Diary and survey data from young workers. *Motivation and Emotion, 26*(1), 31–55.

Hayward, R. M., & Tuckey, M. R. (2011). Emotions in uniform: How nurses regulate emotion at work via emotional boundaries. *Human Relations, 64*(11), 1501–1523.

Hochschild, A. R. (1983). *The managed heart: Commercialization of human feeling*. Berkeley: University of California Press.

Kent, S., Jordan, P. J., & Troth, A. C. (2014). Institutional theory, normative pressures, emotions, and indirect aggression. *Research on Emotion in Organizations, 10*, 197–218.

King, N. (2004). Using templates in the thematic analysis of text. In C. Cassell & G. Symon (Eds.), *Essential guide to qualitative methods in organizational research* (pp. 256–170). London, UK: Sage.

Kirrane, M., O'Shea, D., Buckley, F., Grazi, A., & Prout, J. (2017). Investigating the role of discrete emotions in silence versus speaking up. *Journal of Occupational and Organizational Psychology, 90* (3), 354–378.

Länsisalmi, H., Peiró, J., & Kivimäki, M. (2004). Grounded theory in organizational research. In C. Cassell & G. Symon (Eds.), *Essential guide to qualitative methods in organizational research* (pp. 242–255). London, UK: Sage.

Larson, R. J., Diener, E., & Lucas, R. E. (2002). Emotion models, measures, and individual differences. In R. G. Lord, R. J. Klimoski, & R. Kanfer (Eds.), *Emotions in the workplace: Understanding the structure and role of emotions in organizational behavior* (pp. 64–106). San Francisco, CA: Jossey-Bass.

Lee, T. W. (1999). *Using qualitative methods in organizational research*. Thousand Oaks, CA: Sage.

Lindebaum, D., & Fielden, S. (2010). 'It's good to be angry': Enacting anger in construction project management to achieve perceived leader effectiveness. *Human Relations, 64*(3), 437–458.

Liu, F., & Maitlis, S. (2014). Emotional dynamics and strategizing processes: A study of strategic conversations in top team meetings. *Journal of Management Studies, 51*(2), 202–234.

Maitlis, S. (2005). The social processes of organizational sensemaking. *Academy of Management Journal, 48*(1), 21–49.

Maitlis, S. (2012). Narrative analysis. In C. Cassell & G. Symon (Eds.), *Qualitative organizational research: Core methods and current challenges* (pp. 492–508). London, UK: Sage.

Maitlis, S. & Ozcelik, H. (2004). Toxic decision processes: A study of emotion and organizational decision making. Organization Science, 15(4), 375–393.

Ozcelik, H., & Paprika, Z. Z. (2010). Developing emotional awareness in cross-cultural communication: A videoconferencing approach. Journal of Management Education, 34(5), 671–699.

Pennebaker, J. W., Boyd, R. L., Jordan, K., & Blackburn, K. (2015). *The development and psychometric properties of LIWC2015*. Austin: University of Texas at Austin.

Pennebaker, J. W., Chung, C. K., Ireland, M., Gonzales, A., & Booth, R. J. (2007). *The development and psychometric properties of LIWC2007*. Austin: University of Texas at Austin and University of Auckland, New Zealand.

Robinson, M. D., & Clore, G. L. (2012). Belief and feeling: Evidence for an accessibility model of emotional self-report. *Psychological Bulletin, 128* (6), 934–960.

Rynes, S. L., & Bartunek, J. M. (2016). Qualitative research: It just keeps getting more interesting! In K. D. Elsbach & R. M. Kramer (Eds.), *Handbook of qualitative organizational research: Innovative pathways and methods* (pp. 9–23). New York, NY: Routledge.

Samra-Fredericks, D. (2004). Talk-in-interaction /conversation analysis. In C. Cassell & G. Symon (Eds.), *Essential guide to qualitative methods in organizational research* (pp. 214–227). London, UK: Sage.

Scollon, C. N., Kim-Prieto, C., & Diener, E. (2009). Experience sampling: Promises and pitfalls, strengths and weaknesses. In E. Diener (Ed.), *Assessing well-being: The collected works of Ed Diener* (pp. 157–180). Berlin, Germany: Springer.

Shaver, P., Schwartz, J., Kirson, D., & O'Connor, C. (1987). Emotion knowledge: Further exploration of a prototype approach. *Journal of Personality and Social Psychology, 52*, 1061–1086.

Smith, J. A. (1996). Beyond the divide between cognition and discourse: Using interpretative phenomenological analysis in health psychology. *Psychology and Health, 11*, 261–271.

Staw, B. M., & Barsade, S. G. (1993). Affect and managerial performance: A test of the sadder-but-wiser vs. happier-and-smarter hypotheses. *Administrative Science Quarterly, 38*, 304–331.

Sutton, R. I. (1991). Maintaining norms about expressed emotions: The case of bill collectors. *Administrative Science Quarterly, 36*, 245–268.

Sutton, R. I., & Rafaeli, A. (1988). Untangling the relationship between displayed emotions and organizational sales: The case of convenience stores. *Academy of Management Journal, 31*(3), 461–487.

Toubiana, M., & Zietsma, C. (2017). The message is on the wall? Emotions, social media and the dynamics of institutional complexity. *Academy of Management Journal, 60*(3), 922–953.

Van Kleef, G. A., De Dreu, C. K. W., & Manstead, A. S. R. (2004). The interpersonal effects of anger and happiness in negotiations. *Journal of Personality and Social Psychology, 86*(1), 57–76.

Velasco, F. (2017). Understanding workplace boredom among service employees: Qualitative insights and employee outcomes. *Journal of Managerial Issues, 29*(3), 278–293.

Waddington, K. (2013). Using qualitative diary research to understand emotion at work. In A. B. Bakker & K. Daniels (Eds.), *A day in the life of a happy worker* (pp. 132–149). New York, NY: Psychology Press.

Weick, K. A. (1995). *Sensemaking in organizations*. Thousand Oaks, CA: Sage.

Weiss, H. M., & Cropanzano, R. (1996). Affective events theory: A theoretical discussion of the structure, causes and consequences of affective experiences at work. In B. M. Staw & L. L. Cummings (Eds.), *Research in organizational behavior* (pp. 1–74). Greenwich, CT: JAI.

Weiss, H. M., Nicholas, J. P., & Daus, C. S. (1999). An examination of the joint effects of affective experiences and job beliefs on job satisfaction and variations in affective experiences over time. *Organizational Behavior and Human Decision Processes, 78*, 124.

Zamawe, F. C. (2015). The implication of using NVivo software in qualitative data analysis: Evidence-based reflections. *Malawi Medical Journal, 27*, 13–15.

Part II

Workplace Affect and Individual Worker Outcomes

8 Affect, Stress, and Health

The Role of Work Characteristics and Work Events

Laura Venz, Anne Casper, and Sabine Sonnentag

Research on organizational behavior and occupational health has undergone an "affective revolution" highlighting the crucial role of affective work-related experiences for individuals and organizations (Ashkanasy & Dorris, 2017). In this chapter, we present a process model of work-related affect, stress, and health (see Figure 8.1). We review and integrate organizational stress and affect research, covering cross-sectional and longitudinal studies (i.e. focusing on chronic processes and between-person differences) as well as experience-sampling studies (i.e. focusing on transient processes and within-person variability). We discuss complex relationship patterns and causal pathways, and offer avenues for future research.

Work-Related Affect, Stress, and Health

Affect, stress, and health are core topics of organizational psychology research. In an attempt to integrate this wide field of literature, we adopt a broad view on affective experiences as an umbrella term subsuming emotion, affect, mood, and feelings of stress and strain. Nevertheless, there are distinctions

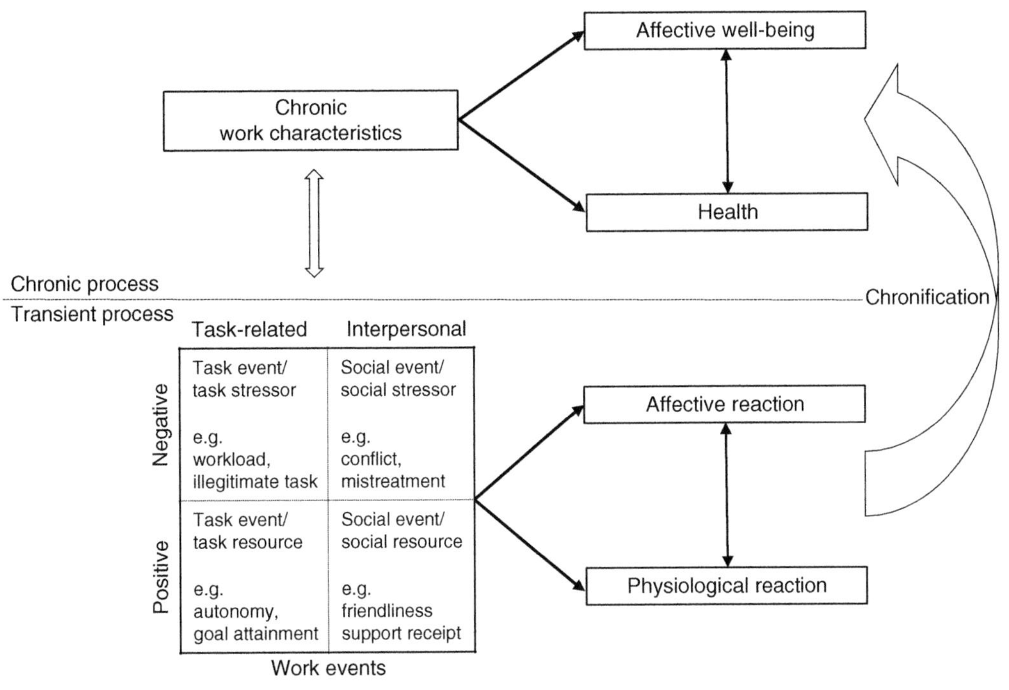

Figure 8.1 A process model of work-related affect, stress, and health

among these terms (Ashkanasy & Dorris, 2017): whereas the terms *affect*, *mood*, and *emotion* describe core affective experiences that differ in activation, intensity, duration, and specificity, stress and strain are affect-laden constructs that cover affective but also cognitive, behavioral, or physiological aspects, specifically as responses to stressors (Sonnentag & Frese, 2012).

A distinction also has to be made regarding time-related aspects of these experiences. Dudenhöffer and Dormann (2013) distinguished immediate, short-term, mid-term, and long-term affective experiences, which are linked over time. Specifically, immediate and short-term psychological experiences (e.g. affect, emotions) and physiological experiences (e.g. blood pressure, hormone release) may result in more long-term or chronic health outcomes such as depression, cardiovascular problems, and other physiological symptoms (Ganster & Rosen, 2013).

Many stress and affect theories – such as the prominent job demands–resources (JD–R) model (Demerouti, Bakker, Nachreiner, & Schaufeli, 2001) and affective events theory (AET; Weiss & Cropanzano, 1996) – propose that any affective experience (e.g. discrete emotions, affect-laden psychological experiences such as burnout, and physiological experiences) arises from environmental stimuli (e.g. Lazarus, 1991). In organizational research, these environmental stimuli have been defined in terms of workplace characteristics, such as job demands and resources, as well as work events.

Like affective experiences, workplace characteristics vary in time, ranging from one-time, single events to a series of events across a certain period of time (e.g. one week) to chronic workplace characteristics (Pindek, Arvan, & Spector, 2019). Single or short-term workplace characteristics activate immediate and short-term affective and physiological reactions – a relationship usually examined using experience-sampling methods. In generating repeated experiences of certain reactions, chronic workplace characteristics – usually examined in cross-sectional or longitudinal studies – also shape employees' affect, stress, and health. As such, affective and physiological reactions are short-term reactions that may develop into mid- to long-term well-being and health. In our conceptual model (Figure 8.1), we take this processual character of affect, stress, and health into consideration and include interrelated transient and chronic processes.

We distinguish between negative (e.g. job stressors, negative events) and positive (e.g. job resources, positive events) workplace characteristics (see, e.g., Basch & Fisher, 2000), which may play differential roles for affect, stress, and health as they may either frustrate or satisfy personal needs and goals (Lazarus, 1991). Specifically, negative stimuli indicate threat to goal achievement and elicit negative reactions via an energy-consuming pathway (Demerouti et al., 2001), while positive stimuli elicit positive reactions via a motivational process of need satisfaction (Wang, Zhu, Song, Dormann, & Bakker, 2018). Moreover, we differentiate between task and interpersonal work characteristics (e.g. Ohly & Schmitt, 2015).

Task and Interpersonal Work Characteristics

Task Characteristics, Affect, Stress, and Health

Task-related work characteristics comprise people's work assignments and relate to the basic human values of agency, competence, and achievement (Ohly & Schmitt, 2015). Task-related work characteristics may be of negative valence (e.g. workload, hindrances) or of positive valence (e.g. autonomy, goal attainment).

Negative Task Characteristics

Fairly consistent empirical evidence suggests that negative task characteristics (e.g. task-related stressors) are related to unfavorable affective experiences such as distress, fatigue, exhaustion, and depressive symptoms (Bowling, Alarcon, Bragg, & Hartmann, 2015; Crawford, LePine, & Rich, 2010). Importantly, meta-analyses based on longitudinal studies suggest that these stressors indeed predict an increase in negative affective experiences over time (Ford et al., 2014; Lesener, Gusy, & Wolter, 2019).

Workload and time pressure. A meta-analysis showed that high workload is linked to physical symptoms (particularly fatigue) cross-sectionally and longitudinally (Nixon, Mazzola, Bauer, Krueger, & Spector, 2011). Also, workload was indirectly associated with increases in psychological ill-being over time via increased burnout (de Beer, Pienaar, & Rothmann, 2016). In a two-wave study, time pressure was related to increases in high- and low-activation unpleasant affect and decreases in low-activation pleasant affect (Stiglbauer, 2018). Pindek et al.'s (2019) meta-analysis further found workload to be positively related to strain between and within persons. In a diary study, Ilies, Dimotakis, and De Pater (2010) found that workload was positively related to affective distress and blood pressure during the workday and to exhaustion and strain in the evening. Moreover, day-specific time pressure was positively related to anxiety (Prem, Kubicek, Diestel, & Korunka, 2016).

Hindrance stressors. Hindrance stressors are factors that threaten task accomplishment (e.g. role ambiguity, role conflict, situational constraints, and hassles; Crawford et al., 2010). Meta-analytically, a composite measure of hindrance stressors was positively related to burnout (Crawford et al., 2010) and strain between and within persons (Pindek et al., 2019). More specific meta-analyses showed that role ambiguity and role conflict were positively related to exhaustion (Alarcon, 2011), depression (Schmidt, Roesler, Kusserow, & Rau, 2014), and physical symptoms (Nixon et al., 2011). At the day level, hindrance stressors were positively related to anxiety and anger (Rodell & Judge, 2009). Further, interruptions from online messages were positively related to negative affect via time pressure (Sonnentag, Reinecke, Mata, & Vorderer, 2018). Moreover, tasks that are unnecessary or that do not match employees' qualifications (i.e. illegitimate tasks) were cross-sectionally related to resentment, irritability, and burnout (Semmer et al., 2015) and to increases in anger and depressive mood at the day level (Eatough et al., 2016). Additionally, goal-disruptive events were positively related to negative affect and fatigue (Zohar, Tzischinski, & Epstein, 2003).

Positive Task Characteristics

Positive task characteristics refer to job resources and, in particular, to the "classic" job characteristics of autonomy, skill variety, task significance, task identity, and feedback from the job (Hackman & Oldham, 1976) as well as to other task-relevant aspects such as goal attainment.

Job resources and job characteristics. Meta-analytically, job resources (including task resources and other resources) were negatively related to burnout both cross-sectionally (Crawford et al., 2010) and longitudinally (Lesener et al., 2019). Likewise, meta-analytic results showed that autonomy, task significance, and task identity were negatively related to exhaustion (Humphrey, Nahrgang, & Morgeson, 2007). Autonomy, task identity, and feedback were negatively associated with "stress" as an outcome (Humphrey et al., 2007). Further, in a cross-sectional study, persons in jobs with higher task significance and autonomy reported more pleasant affect, while persons in jobs with less task identity, less feedback, and more skill variety experienced more unpleasant affect (Saavedra & Kwun, 2000). At the day level, autonomy was associated with high positive emotions (Xanthopoulou, Bakker, Demerouti, & Schaufeli, 2012) and low anxiety (Prem et al., 2016).

Goal attainment. In a qualitative diary study, employees reported feelings of pride after receiving positive performance feedback as well as when they themselves felt that they had performed well (Grandey, Tam, & Brauburger, 2002). Other diary studies showed that task accomplishment satisfaction was linked to increases in positive and decreases in negative affect over the workday (Gabriel, Diefendorff, & Erickson, 2011), and that achievement-related events were associated with positive affect (Wang et al., 2018).

Altogether, empirical research indicates that task characteristics and events shape employee affect, stress, and health. Negative task-related aspects such as high workload and hindrance stressors were consistently related to unfavorable affective outcomes with regard to both short- and long-term consequences. Concerning positive task characteristics, autonomy was the most consistent predictor of affective and health-related outcomes at the between-person level. Within persons, goal attainment consistently predicted short-term positive affective consequences. There is a lack of longitudinal research regarding longer-term consequences of positive task-related aspects.

Interpersonal Characteristics, Affect, Stress, and Health

The social dimension of work characteristics involves a sense of belonging in relation to others (Ohly & Schmitt, 2015). Thus, interpersonal job characteristics are workplace stimuli involving interactions with others, including supervisors, coworkers, and customers (Grandey et al., 2002).

Negative Interpersonal Characteristics and Events

Research indicates that other people at work can be a source of negative affect, social stress, and ill-being. For instance, in their meta-analyses, Spector and Jex (1998), Bowling and Beehr (2006), and Hershcovis (2011) showed several types of social stressors to relate to a broad set of affect, stress, and health outcomes. Further, Nixon et al. (2011) and Stansfeld and Candy (2006) meta-analytically showed social stressors and poor work relationships to relate to physical and mental ill-being longitudinally.

Tuckey and Neall (2014) found bullying to positively relate to emotional exhaustion over a six-month period as well as on a weekly basis. Pindek et al. (2019) reported a positive meta-analytical relationship between mistreatment and strain within and between persons. Diary studies showed social stressors such as incivility (Zhou, Yan, Che, & Meier, 2015) and negative workplace interactions (Dimotakis, Scott, & Koopman, 2011) to relate to negative affective states, psychological symptoms, and physical ill-being (Meier, Semmer, & Gross, 2014). Besides research that looked at interpersonal characteristics and events irrespective of the interaction partner, other studies specifically focused on supervisors, coworkers, and customers.

Negative supervisor-related characteristics. Meta-analyses found negative leader behaviors to relate negatively to employee well-being (Hershcovis, 2011) and general health (Hershcovis & Barling, 2010) and positively to negative affective symptoms, burnout, stress, and health complaints (Montano, Reeske, Franke, & Hüffmeier, 2017). Liang, Hanig, Evans, Brown, and Lian (2018) showed abusive supervision to be negatively related to employee physical health over time. Further, experience-sampling studies found negative supervisor events to relate to negative affective states (Volmer, 2015), anger (Grandey et al., 2002), and low hedonic mood (Miner, Glomb, & Hulin, 2005). In their laboratory study examining email incivility, Giumetti et al. (2013) found participants to report higher negative affect and lower energy, but no differences in cardiac activity, after working with an uncivil supervisor.

Negative coworker-related characteristics. Hershcovis and Barling (2010) meta-analytically showed negative coworker behaviors to relate positively to emotional exhaustion and depression and negatively to physical well-being and general health. Sliter, Pui, Sliter, and Jex (2011) reported coworker conflict predicting burnout, but not physical symptoms, three months later. Pereira and Elfering (2014) found coworker-related stressors to be associated with psychosomatic complaints both cross-sectionally and one year later. Also, experience-sampling studies related negative coworker interactions to low hedonic mood (Miner et al., 2005), high anger (Grandey et al., 2002), and burnout (Taylor, Bedeian, Cole, & Zhang, 2017).

Negative customer-related characteristics. Hershcovis and Barling's (2010) meta-analysis revealed outsider aggression to relate positively to emotional exhaustion and depression and negatively to physical well-being and general health. Sliter et al. (2011) found customer interpersonal conflict to predict burnout, but not physical symptoms, three months later. Dudenhöffer and Dormann (2013) reported mid-term (two weeks) and short-term (daily) relationships between customer-related stressors and negative affect. Similarly, experience-sampling studies showed negative customer interactions to be related to low enthusiasm (Ohly & Schmitt, 2015), high anger (Grandey et al., 2002), negative affect (Liu et al., 2017), and emotional exhaustion (Zhan, Wang, & Shi, 2016). In laboratory studies, Rupp and Spencer (2006) found unfair customer behavior to predict anger, and Wegge, Vogt, and Wecking (2007) showed customer rudeness to predict higher negative mood and tiredness, but not higher cortisol levels.

Positive Interpersonal Characteristics and Events

Fortunately, people encounter not only negative but also positive interpersonal work characteristics, including social support, positive leadership, and friendly customers. Meta-analytically, social support was negatively related to anxiety, stress, and burnout (Humphrey et al., 2007). However, workplace support did not predict changes in emotional exhaustion and physical symptoms longitudinally (De Jonge & Dormann, 2006), and interpersonal work events did not predict changes in positive affect over time (Casper, Tremmel, & Sonnentag, 2019). At the day level, a psychological climate of cooperation and warmth was positively related to positive emotions (Xanthopoulou et al., 2012) and positive workplace interactions were related to state positive affect, but not state negative affect (Dimotakis et al., 2011).

Positive supervisor-related characteristics. Mainly based on cross-sectional studies, Halbesleben's (2006) meta-analysis showed a negative relationship between supervisor support and employee burnout. Likewise, Montano et al. (2017) showed positive leadership to relate positively to well-being and negatively to negative affective symptoms, burnout, stress, and health complaints. In their meta-analysis of baseline-adjusted prospective longitudinal studies, Lang, Ochsmann, Kraus, and Lang (2012) reported increased odds ratios of musculoskeletal symptoms over time for low supervisor support. However, longitudinal evidence on the role of positive leadership is inconclusive, as several studies could not relate positive leader behaviors to employee well-being over time (e.g. van Dierendonck, Haynes, Borrill, & Stride, 2004; K. Nielsen, Randall, Yarker, & Brenner, 2008).

Similarly, evidence for short-term affective consequences of positive supervisor behavior is mixed: S.-H. Lin, Scott, and Matta (2018) found week-specific transformational leadership to be positively related to follower positive affect, but unrelated to emotional exhaustion, whereas Tepper et al. (2018) showed day-specific transformational leadership to relate to both higher positive and lower negative affect. Xanthopoulou et al. (2012) found day-specific supervisory coaching to predict positive emotions, but Miner et al. (2005) could not identify positive supervisor events being related to employee hedonic mood.

Positive coworker-related characteristics. Halbesleben's (2006) meta-analysis showed coworker support to be negatively related to exhaustion. Tse and Dasborough (2008) found positive coworker relationships and team-member exchange to be associated with higher positive but not higher negative emotions. In their meta-analysis of baseline-adjusted prospective longitudinal studies, Lang et al. (2012) found coworker support to be unrelated to the development of musculoskeletal symptoms. Examining short-term affective reactions, Miner et al. (2005) showed positive coworker events to positively relate to hedonic mood.

Positive customer-related characteristics. Empirical research about positive customer events is scarce. Positive customer treatment was related to increases in positive affect (Zhan et al., 2016), and customer positive affective display predicted subsequent employee positive affect (Rothbard &Wilk, 2011). In laboratory studies, fair customer behavior positively predicted happiness (Rupp & Spencer, 2006), and study participants treated in a friendly manner reported more pleasant mood than those rudely treated (Wegge et al., 2007).

Altogether, empirical research indicates that interpersonal work characteristics and events play an important role for employee affect, stress, and health. In particular, negative interpersonal stimuli were consistently related to negative affective experiences and ill-being, both concurrently and over time. Evidence for the role of positive interpersonal characteristics is less conclusive, as they were not consistently related to changes in affective experiences over time.

Complex Relationship Patterns and Causal Pathways

Although our model, which differentiates between task versus interpersonal work characteristics and positive versus negative valence, strives to provide a rather comprehensive picture, the processes occurring on the job might be even more complex. In this section we present interaction effects between various workplace characteristics and discuss issues related to causality.

Interaction of Positive and Negative Workplace Characteristics

Most workplaces are characterized by complex configurations of various work characteristics. This phenomenon has received substantive research attention within research on the job demands–job control model (Karasek, 1979) that suggested that high job control as a positive workplace characteristic buffers the effects of job stressors on affective and health outcomes. Empirical support for this model, however, is relatively weak (Häusser, Mojzisch, Niesel, & Schulz-Hardt, 2010). Day-level studies addressing the interplay of various types of work events revealed complex interaction patterns between positive and negative events (Gross et al., 2011; Zohar et al., 2003). These findings suggest that positive events can offset the impact of negative events and vice versa.

Interactions of Momentary Events and Chronic Work Characteristics

Importantly, it is not only work events present on a specific day that play a role in the affective experiences associated with them. The impact of momentary, acute events may depend on more chronic workplace characteristics. Empirical studies suggest that day-specific job stressors are more strongly related to strain symptoms when organizational support is low (Ilies et al., 2010) and the level of chronic social stressors is high (Gross et al., 2011). It seems that people in an unfavorable social context are more vulnerable to acute negative events. At the same time, they also seem to benefit more from positive events (Gabriel et al., 2011).

Role of Individual Differences

Individual differences play an important role in affective reactions to work characteristics and events. Studies examined Big Five dimensions such as neuroticism and extraversion, but also looked at other individual difference variables. With respect to neuroticism and related constructs (high trait negative affect, low emotional stability), there is rather consistent evidence that people high in these traits react negatively to negative events. For instance, Rodell and Judge (2009) found that persons high in neuroticism experience more anger when facing hindrance stressors. Zhou et al. (2015) reported that incivility is more strongly associated with negative affect when emotional stability is low. Similar patterns between the experience of negative events and increased negative affect were found for other negatively-toned individual differences as well (Meier et al., 2014; Sliter et al., 2011). With respect to extraversion, findings are less consistent (e.g. Rodell & Judge, 2009).

Reverse Causality

In line with affect and stress theories, we focused on research examining chronic workplace characteristics and more acute work events as predictors of affect, stress, and health. In fact, the majority of studies within organizational psychology addressed this causal path from workplace stimuli to affect and health. However, work characteristics might also be linked to affective experiences in another causal pattern. For instance, affect and health might have an impact on the events people experience at work.

Meta-analyses of longitudinal studies found evidence for both the paths from workplace characteristics to strain symptoms and from strain symptoms to workplace characteristics (Ford et al., 2014; Lesener et al., 2019). High job stressors and low job resources predicted an increase in strain symptoms over time, and strain symptoms predicted an increase in job stressors and a decrease in job resources over time. With respect to interpersonal events, a meta-analysis on longitudinal studies showed not only that workplace bullying predicted mental-health problems, but also that mental-health problems predicted subsequent bullying experiences (M. B. Nielsen & Einarsen, 2012).

In their longitudinal study examining task and interpersonal events and their relationship with positive and negative affect, Casper et al. (2019) largely supported the reverse-effect perspective. Positive affect predicted increases in perceived positive task and interpersonal events over two three-month periods, and negative affect predicted increases in perceived negative task and interpersonal events, whereas paths from work events to affect over time were mainly nonsignificant.

Day-level studies examined how affective states may lead to the experience of specific events. For instance, Daniels, Beesley, Wimalasiri, and Cheyne (2013) reported that when design engineers were fatigued they engaged in less problem solving. Further, affective states play a particular role for the instigation of interpersonal events. Specifically, people in a positive mood may engage in more proactive (Bindl & Parker, 2012) and helping behavior (Dalal, Lam, Weiss, Welch, & Hulin, 2009). Similarly, negative affective states may increase the likelihood of engaging in negative social interactions (Dalal et al., 2009).

Even when affective states do not create real work events, being in a certain mood will influence the perception and evaluation of events. People in a positive affective state experience actual events more positively than people in a more negative state. Similarly, people in a negative affective state perceive negative events more negatively. For instance, Rothbard and Wilk (2011) reported that when customer service employees experienced positive mood in the morning they perceived customer affective display more positively.

Taken together, empirical evidence shows not only that workplace characteristics and events predict subsequent affective experiences but also that affective experiences predict subsequent work characteristics, suggesting complex reciprocal relationships.

Discussion

Taxonomy of Work Characteristics

The proposed differentiation of work characteristics into positive versus negative and task versus interpersonal stimuli provides a parsimonious classification with the potential to advance research on affect, stress, and health. As our literature review revealed, studies that include both task and interpersonal characteristics are rare. This scarcity is disadvantageous as it does not allow for a comparison of different stimuli. For instance, whereas some scholars argued that anger is a socially-induced emotion (Gibson & Callister, 2010), as long as interpersonal stimuli are not considered in comparison with task stimuli, we cannot draw this conclusion. Similarly, when adopting an explicit stress perspective focusing on negative stimuli, the unique effects of *positive* work characteristics are under-researched (Wang et al., 2018). We thus advocate future research to include both interpersonal and task as well as positive and negative work characteristics in studying affect, stress, and health.

Notwithstanding its usefulness, our classification cannot fully represent the complexity of stimuli relevant for work-related experiences. First, interpersonal and task characteristics are not completely disconnected as some work characteristics and events (e.g. task conflict, recognition) entail both interpersonal and task aspects. Hence not all work characteristics are clearly classifiable into either one of the categories. Also, some circumstances entail work-related yet not task-related aspects. For instance, job insecurity shows negative associations with psychological and physical health and affective well-being (Jiang & Lavaysse, 2018).

Second, the categorization of work events and characteristics into positive versus negative implies that positive characteristics are beneficial for health and well-being while negative characteristics are detrimental. However, the relationships might be more complex. For instance, exposure to stressors such as high workload may also have positive consequences because it provides the opportunity to develop skills, resilience, and self-efficacy (Ilies, Aw, & Pluut, 2015), which may also contribute to well-being. Similarly, positive work characteristics might also have negative consequences. For instance, receiving social support may result in feelings of deficiency (Beehr, Bowling, & Bennett, 2010). Thus, we suggest that future research should examine negative consequences of workplace characteristics that are typically seen as positive and positive consequences of those that are typically seen as negative.

Lastly, not only do employees experience work events that happen to them, but they also create events themselves – which in turn influences their subsequent affective experiences. For instance, with respect to task events, people might engage in job crafting (Wrzesniewski & Dutton, 2001), which is positively related to positive affective states and mental health by reducing hindrances or increasing challenges (Tims, Bakker, & Derks, 2013). With respect to interpersonal events, helping behavior that shapes the interpersonal environment is both an enriching and depleting experience, being associated with positive states and exhaustion (Glomb, Bhave, Miner, & Wall, 2011; W. Lin, Koopmann, & Wang, 2018).

Processual Character of Affect, Stress, and Health

Overall, the experience-sampling studies reviewed for this chapter suggest that workplace stimuli have an immediate effect on employees' affect and stress. Cross-sectional research supports such concurrent relationships. However, longitudinal studies imply that, over time, this effect could fade (Matthews & Ritter, 2018) – indicating that relationships between work characteristics and affect, stress, and health might unfold differentially over time (Bono, Glomb, Shen, Kim, & Koch, 2013). However, research that examines the dynamics of affect, stress, and health is still rare. This is unfortunate because virtually all affect and stress theories are specified in terms of within-person processes (Gabriel et al., 2018). We suggest that future research should address the role of time in more detail.

A critical issue constraining such research is that most theories – be they affect or stress theories – do not provide guidance as to how workplace characteristics unfold over time (e.g. frequency, trends, cycles) or to the temporal variability and natural fluctuations of affect, stress, and health outcomes (cf. Matthews & Ritter, 2018). Accordingly, as is apparent in the studies reviewed here, the temporal lags used in organizational affect and stress research are rather arbitrary, ranging from minutes to weeks to several years. Yet it remains unclear in which exact timeframes the processes of interest unfold.

Another important question refers to the role of positive workplace stimuli in the chronification process. In line with Baumeister, Bratslavsky, Finkenauer, and Vohs (2001), who stated that "bad" stimuli predict larger, more consistent, and more lasting effects than "good" stimuli, we identified negative work characteristics as related to ill-being over time, but found inconsistent evidence for the long-term effects of positive characteristics. However, due to a lack of longitudinal research in general and research on the long-term consequences of positive work characteristics in particular, conclusions might be premature.

The lack of longitudinal research also restricts knowledge about the mechanisms linking workplace stimuli with poor health outcomes. Indeed, only few of the studies reviewed here examined mediation – and of those that did, few used longitudinal (e.g. Liang et al., 2017), experience-sampling (e.g. Dimotakis et al., 2011; Ilies et al., 2010), or laboratory (e.g. Giumetti et al., 2013) designs. These studies indicate that affective reactions mediate the relationships between work characteristics and health and well-being (Pieper & Brosschot, 2005). Other research has emphasized physiological processes such as that described in the allostatic load model (Ganster & Rosen, 2013), comprising dysregulations of important regulatory systems such as the hypothalamic–pituitary–adrenal axis. Pathways referring to health behavior may also play a role (Siegrist & Rödel, 2006). For instance, research has shown that people tend to consume more unhealthy food (Liu et al., 2017) and exercise less (Stults-Kolehmainen & Sinha, 2014) when facing job stressors, which in turn relates to unfavorable health outcomes (French, Allen, & Henderson, 2018).

To move the field forward, future research should explicitly address the role of time and dynamic processes in affect, stress, and health. As such, there is a need for advanced longitudinal studies that ideally combine experience-sampling approaches with longer time lags, and that take recurring work characteristics, mediation processes, and reversed causality as well as prolonged activation and chronification processes into account, to accurately capture the processual character of affect, stress, and health.

References

Alarcon, G. M. (2011). A meta-analysis of burnout with job demands, resources, and attitudes. *Journal of Vocational Behavior*, *79*, 549–562. http://dx.doi.org/:10.1016/j.jvb.2011.03.007

Ashkanasy, N. M., & Dorris, A. D. (2017). Emotions in the workplace. *Annual Review of Organizational Psychology and Organizational Behavior*, *4*, 67–90.

http://dx.doi.org/:10.1146/annurev-orgpsych-032516-113231

Basch, J., & Fisher, C. D. (2000). Affective events–emotions matrix: A classification of work events and associated emotions. In N. M. Ashkanasy, C. E. Härtel, & W. J. Zerbe (Eds.), *Emotions in the workplace: Research, theory, and practice* (pp. 36–48). Westport, CT: Quorum/Greenwood.

Baumeister, R. F., Bratslavsky, E., Finkenauer, C., & Vohs, K. D. (2001). Bad is stronger than good. *Review of General Psychology*, *5*, 323–370, http://dx.doi.org/:10.1037/1089–2680.5.4.323

Beehr, T. A., Bowling, N. A., & Bennett, M. M. (2010). Occupational stress and failures of social support: When helping hurts. *Journal of Occupational Health Psychology*, *15*, 45–59, http://dx.doi.org/:10.1037/a0018234

Bindl, U. K., & Parker, S. K. (2012). Affect and employee proactivity: A goal-regulatory perspective. In N. M. Ashkanasy, C. E. Härtel, & W. J. Zerbe (Eds.), *Research on emotions in organizations* (Volume 8, pp. 225–254). Bingley, UK: Emerald.

Bono, J. E., Glomb, T. M., Shen, W., Kim, E., & Koch, A. J. (2013). Building positive resources: Effects of positive events and positive reflection on work stress and health. *Academy of Management Journal*, *56*, 1601–1627. http://dx.doi.org/:10.5465/amj.2011.0272

Bowling, N. A., Alarcon, G. M., Bragg, C. B., & Hartman, M. J. (2015). A meta-analytic examination of the potential correlates and consequences of workload. *Work and Stress*, *29*, 95–113, http://dx.doi.org/:10.1080/02678373.2015.1033037

Bowling, N. A., & Beehr, T. A. (2006). Workplace harassment from the victim's perspective: A theoretical model and meta-analysis. *Journal of Applied Psychology*, *91*, 998–1012. http://dx.doi.org/:10.1037/0021–9010.91.5.998

Casper, A., Tremmel, S., & Sonnentag, S. (2019). The power of affect: A three-wave panel study on reciprocal relationships between work events and affect at work. *Journal of Occupational and Organizational Psychology*, http://dx.doi.org/:10.1111/joop.12255

Crawford, E. R., LePine, J. A., & Rich, B. L. (2010). Linking job demands and resources to employee engagement and burnout: A theoretical extension and meta-analytic test. *Journal of Applied Psychology*, *95*, 834–848, http://dx.doi.org/:10.1037/a0019364

Dalal, R. S., Lam, H., Weiss, H. M., Welch, E. R., & Hulin, C. L. (2009). A within-person approach to work behavior and performance: Concurrent and lagged citizenship–counterproductivity associations, and dynamic relationships with affect and overall job performance. *Academy of Management Journal*, *52*, 1051–1066, http://dx.doi.org/:10.5465/AMJ.2009.44636148

Daniels, K., Beesley, N., Wimalasiri, V., & Cheyne, A. (2013). Problem solving and well-being: Exploring the instrumental role of job control and social support. *Journal of Management*, *39*, 1016–1043, http://dx.doi.org/:10.1177/0149206311430262

de Beer, L. T., Pienaar, J., & Rothmann, S. (2016). Work overload, burnout, and psychological ill-health symptoms: A three-wave mediation model of the employee health impairment process. *Anxiety, Stress, and Coping*, *29*, 387–399, http://dx.doi.org/:10.1080/10615806.2015.1061123

De Jonge, J., & Dormann, C. (2006). Stressors, resources, and strain at work: A longitudinal test of the triple-match principle. *Journal of Applied Psychology*, *91*, 1359–1374. http://dx.doi.org/:10.1037/0021–9010.91.5.1359

Demerouti, E., Bakker, A. B., Nachreiner, F., & Schaufeli, W. B. (2001). The job demands–resources model of burnout. *Journal of Applied Psychology*, *86*, 499–512. http://dx.doi.org/:10.1037/0021–9010.86.3.499

Dimotakis, N., Scott, B. A., & Koopman, J. (2011). An experience sampling investigation of workplace interactions, affective states, and employee well-being. *Journal of Organizational Behavior*, *32*, 572–588, http://dx.doi.org/:10.1002/job.722

Dudenhöffer, S., & Dormann, C. (2013). Customer-related social stressors and service providers' affective reactions. *Journal of Organizational Behavior*, *34*, 520–539, http://dx.doi.org/:10.1002/job.1826

Eatough, E. M., Meier, L. L., Igic, I., Elfering, A., Spector, P. E., & Semmer, N. K. (2016). You want me to do what? Two daily diary studies of illegitimate tasks and employee well-being. *Journal of Organizational Behavior*, *37*, 108–127, http://dx.doi.org/:10.1002/job.2032

Ford, M. T., Matthews, R. A., Wooldridge, J. D., Mishra, V., Kakar, U. M., & Strahan, S. R. (2014). How do occupational stressor–strain effects vary with time? A review and meta-analysis of the relevance of time lags in longitudinal studies. *Work and Stress*, *28*, 9–30, http://dx.doi.org/:10.1080/02678373.2013.877096

French, K. A., Allen, T. D., & Henderson, T. G. (2018). Challenge and hindrance stressors and metabolic risk factors. *Journal of Occupational Health Psychology*, http://dx.doi.org/:10.1037/ocp0000138

Gabriel, A. S., Diefendorff, J. M., & Erickson, R. J. (2011). The relations of daily task accomplishment satisfaction with changes in affect: A multilevel study in nurses. *Journal of Applied Psychology*, *96*, 1095–1104, http://dx.doi.org/:10.1037/a0023937

Gabriel, A. S., Podsakoff, N. P., Beal, D. J., Scott, B. A., Sonnentag, S., Trougakos, J. P., & Butts, M. M. (2018). Experience sampling methods: A discussion of critical trends and considerations for scholarly advancement. *Organizational Research Methods*, http://dx.doi.org/:10.1177/1094428118802626

Ganster, D. C., & Rosen, C. C. (2013). Work stress and employee health: A multidisciplinary review. *Journal of Management*, *39*, 1085–1122, http://dx.doi.org/:10.1177/0149206313475815

Gibson, D. E., & Callister, R. R. (2010). Anger in organizations: Review and integration. *Journal of Management*, *36*, 66–93, http://dx.doi.org/:10.1177/0149206309348060

Giumetti, G. W., Hatfield, A. L., Scisco, J. L., Schroeder, A. N., Muth, E. R., & Kowalski, R. M. (2013). What a rude e-mail! Examining the differential effects of incivility versus support on mood, energy, engagement, and performance in an online context. *Journal of Occupational Health Psychology*, *18*, 297–309, http://dx.doi.org/:10.1037/a0032851

Glomb, T. M., Bhave, D. P., Miner, A. G., & Wall, M. (2011). Doing good, feeling good: Examining the role of organizational citizenship behaviors in changing mood. *Personnel Psychology*, *64*, 191–223, http://doi.org/:10.1111/j.1744–6570.2010.01206.x

Grandey, A. A., Tam, A. P., & Brauburger, A. L. (2002). Affective states and traits in the workplace: Diary and survey data from young workers. *Motivation and Emotion*, *26*, 31–55, http://dx.doi.org/:10.1023/a:1015142124306

Gross, S., Semmer, N. K., Meier, L. L., Kälin, W., Jacobshagen, N., & Tschan, F. (2011). The effect of positive events at work on after-work fatigue: They matter most in face of adversity. *Journal of Applied Psychology*, *96*, 654–664, http://dx.doi.org/:10.1037/a0022992

Hackman, J. R., & Oldham, G. R. (1976). Motivation through the design of work: Test of a theory. *Organizational Behavior and Human Performance*, *16*, 250–279. http://dx.doi.org/:10.1016/0030–5073(76)90016–7

Halbesleben, J. R. B. (2006). Sources of social support and burnout: A meta-analytic test of the conservation of resources model. *Journal of Applied Psychology*, *91*, 1134–1145, http://dx.doi.org/:10.1037/0021–9010.91.5.1134

Häusser, J. A., Mojzisch, A., Niesel, M., & Schulz-Hardt, S. (2010). Ten years on: A review of recent research on the Job Demand–Control(–Support) model and psychological well-being. *Work & Stress*, *24*, 1–35, http://dx.doi.org/:10.1080/02678371003683747

Hershcovis, M. S. (2011). "Incivility, social undermining, bullying . . . oh my!" A call to reconcile constructs within workplace aggression research. *Journal of Organizational Behavior*, *32*, 499–519, http://dx.doi.org/:10.1002/job.689

Hershcovis, M. S., & Barling, J. (2010). Comparing victim attributions and outcomes for workplace aggression and sexual harassment. *Journal of Applied Psychology*, *95*, 874–888, http://dx.doi.org/:10.1037/a0020070

Humphrey, S. E., Nahrgang, J. D., & Morgeson, F. P. (2007). Integrating motivational, social, and contextual work design features: A meta-analytic summary and theoretical extension of the work design literature. *Journal of Applied Psychology*, *92*, 1332–1356, http://dx.doi.org/:10.1037/0021–9010.92.5.1332

Ilies, R., Aw, S. S. Y., & Pluut, H. (2015). Intraindividual models of employee well-being: What have we learned and where do we go from here? *European Journal of Work and Organizational Psychology*, *24*, 827–838, http://dx.doi.org/:10.1080/1359432X.2015.1071422

Ilies, R., Dimotakis, N., & De Pater, I. E. (2010). Psychological and physiological reactions to high workloads: Implications for well-being. *Personnel Psychology*, *63*, 407–436, http://dx.doi.org/:10.1111/j.1744–6570.2010.01175.x

Jiang, L., & Lavaysse, L. M. (2018). Cognitive and affective job insecurity: A meta-analysis and a primary study. *Journal of Management*, *44*, 2307–2342, http://dx.doi.org/:10.1177/0149206318773853

Karasek, R. (1979). Job demands, job decision latitude, and mental strain: Implications for job redesign. *Administrative Science Quarterly*, *24*, 285–306, http://dx.doi.org/:10.2307/2392498

Lang, J., Ochsmann, E., Kraus, T., & Lang, J. W. (2012). Psychosocial work stressors as antecedents of musculoskeletal problems: A systematic review and meta-analysis of stability-adjusted longitudinal studies. *Social Science and Medicine*, *75*, 1163–1174, http://dx.doi.org/:10.1016/j.socscimed.2012.04.015

Lazarus, R. S. (1991). Progress on a cognitive–motivational–relational theory of emotion. *American Psychologist*, *46*, 819–834, http://dx.doi.org/:10.1037/0003-066X.46.8.819

Lesener, T., Gusy, B., & Wolter, C. (2019). The job demands–resources model: A meta-analytic review of longitudinal studies. *Work and Stress*, *33*, 76–103, http://dx.doi.org/:10.1080/02678373.2018.1529065

Liang, L. H., Hanig, S., Evans, R., Brown, D. J., & Lian, H. (2018). Why is your boss making you sick? A longitudinal investigation modeling time-lagged relations between abusive supervision and employee physical health. *Journal of Organizational Behavior*, *39*, 1050–1065, http://dx.doi.org/:10.1002/job.2248

Lin, S.-H., Scott, B. A., & Matta, F. K. (2018). The dark side of transformational leader behaviors for leaders themselves: A conservation of resources perspective. *Academy of Management Journal*, http://dx.doi.org/:10.5465/amj.2016.1255

Lin, W., Koopmann, J., & Wang, M. (2018). How does workplace helping behavior step up or slack off? Integrating enrichment-based and depletion-based perspectives. *Journal of Management*, http://dx.doi.org/:10.1077/0149206318795275

Liu, Y., Song, Y., Koopman, J., Wang, M., Chang, C.-H., & Shi, J. (2017). Eating your feelings? Testing a model of employees' work-related stressors, sleep quality, and unhealthy eating. *Journal of Applied Psychology*, *102*, 1237–1258, http://dx.doi.org/:10.1037/apl0000209

Matthews, R. A., & Ritter, K. J. (2018). Applying adaptation theory to understand experienced incivility processes: Testing the repeated exposure hypothesis. *Journal of Occupational Health Psychology*, http://dx.doi.org/:10.1037/ocp0000123

Meier, L. L., Semmer, N. K., & Gross, S. (2014). The effect of conflict at work on well-being: Depressive symptoms as a vulnerability factor. *Work and Stress*, *28*, 31–48, http://dx.doi.org/:10.1080/02678373.2013.876691

Miner, A. G., Glomb, T. M., & Hulin, C. (2005). Experience sampling mood and its correlates at work. *Journal of Occupational and Organizational Psychology*, *78*, 171–193, http://dx.doi.org/:10.1348/096317905X40105

Montano, D., Reeske, A., Franke, F., & Hüffmeier, J. (2017). Leadership, followers' mental health and job performance in organizations: A comprehensive meta-analysis from an occupational health perspective. *Journal of Organizational Behavior*, *38*, 327–350, http://dx.doi.org/:10.1002/job.2124

Nielsen, K., Randall, R., Yarker, J., & Brenner, S. O. (2008). The effects of transformational leadership on followers' perceived work characteristics and psychological well-being: A longitudinal study. *Work and Stress*, *22*, 16–32, http://dx.doi.org/:10.1080/02678370801979430

Nielsen, M. B., & Einarsen, S. (2012). Outcomes of exposure to workplace bullying: A meta-analytic review. *Work and Stress*, *26*, 309–332, http://dx.doi.org/:10.1080/02678373.2012.734709

Nixon, A. E., Mazzola, J. J., Bauer, J., Krueger, J. R., & Spector, P. E. (2011). Can work make you sick? A meta-analysis of the relationships between job stressors and physical symptoms. *Work and Stress*, *25*, 1–22, http://dx.doi.org/:10.1080/02678373.2011.569175

Ohly, S., & Schmitt, A. (2015). What makes us enthusiastic, angry, feeling at rest or worried? Development and validation of an affective work events taxonomy using concept mapping methodology. *Journal of Business and Psychology*, *30*, 15–35, http://dx.doi.org/:10.1007/s10869-013–9328-3

Pereira, D., & Elfering, A. (2014). Social stressors at work, sleep quality and psychosomatic health complaints – a longitudinal ambulatory field study. *Stress and Health*, *30*, 43–52, http://dx.doi.org/:10.1002/smi.2494

Pieper, S., & Brosschot, J. F. (2005). Prolonged stress-related cardiovascular activation: Is there any? *Annals of Behavioral Medicine*, *30*, 91–103, http://dx.doi.org/:10.1207/s15324796abm3002_1

Pindek, S., Arvan, M. L., & Spector, P. E. (2019). The stressor–strain relationship in diary studies: A meta-analysis of the within and between levels. *Work and Stress*, *33*, 1–21, http://dx.doi.org/:10.1080/02678373.2018.1445672

Prem, R., Kubicek, B., Diestel, S., & Korunka, C. (2016). Regulatory job stressors and their within-person relationships with ego depletion: The roles of state anxiety, self-control effort, and job autonomy. *Journal of Vocational Behavior*, *92*, 22–32, http://dx.doi.org/:10.1016/J.JVB.2015.11.004

Rodell, J. B., & Judge, T. A. (2009). Can "good" stressors spark "bad" behaviors? The mediating role of emotions in links of challenge and hindrance stressors with citizenship and counterproductive behaviors. *Journal of Applied Psychology*, *94*, 1438–1451, http://dx.doi.org/:10.1037/a0016752

Rothbard, N. P., & Wilk, S. L. (2011). Waking up on the right or wrong side of the bed: Start-of-workday mood, work events, employee affect, and performance. *Academy of Management Journal*, *54*, 959–980, http://dx.doi.org/:10.5465/amj.2007.0056

Rupp, D. E., & Spencer, S. (2006). When customers lash out: The effects of customer interactional injustice on emotional labor and the mediating role of discrete emotions. *Journal of Applied Psychology*, *91*, 971–978, http://dx.doi.org/:10.1037/0021–9010.91.4.971

Saavedra, R., & Kwun, S. K. (2000). Affective states in job characteristics theory. *Journal of Organizational Behavior*, *21*, 131–146, http://dx.doi.org/:10.1002/(SICI)1099–1379(200003)21:2<31::aid-job39>3.0.CO;2-Q

Schmidt, S., Roesler, U., Kusserow, T., & Rau, R. (2014). Uncertainty in the workplace: Examining role ambiguity and role conflict, and their link to depression – a meta-analysis. *European Journal of Work and Organizational Psychology*, *23*, 91–106, http://dx.doi.org/:10.1080/1359432X.2012.711523

Semmer, N. K., Jacobshagen, N., Meier, L. L., Elfering, A., Beehr, T. A., Kälin, W., & Tschan, F. (2015). Illegitimate tasks as a source of work stress. *Work and Stress*, *29*, 32–56, http://dx.doi.org/:10.1080/02678373.2014.1003996

Siegrist, J., & Rödel, A. (2006). Work stress and health risk behavior. *Scandinavian Journal of Work, Environment and Health*, *32*, 473–481, http://dx.doi.org/:10.5271/sjweh.1052

Sliter, M. T., Pui, S. Y., Sliter, K. A., & Jex, S. M. (2011). The differential effects of interpersonal conflict from customers and coworkers: Trait anger as a moderator. *Journal of Occupational Health Psychology*, *16*, 424–440, http://dx.doi.org/:10.1037/a0023874

Sonnentag, S., & Frese, M. (2012). Stress in organizations. In N. W. Schmitt & S. Highhouse (Eds.), *Handbook of psychology, Volume 12: Industrial and organizational psychology* (2nd ed., pp. 560–592). Hoboken, NJ: Wiley.

Sonnentag, S., Reinecke, L., Mata, J., & Vorderer, P. (2018). Feeling interrupted – being responsive: How online messages relate to affect at work. *Journal of Organizational Behavior*, *39*, 369–383, http://dx.doi.org/:10.1002/job.2239

Spector, P. E., & Jex, S. M. (1998). Development of four self-report measures of job stressors and strain: Interpersonal conflict at work scale, organizational constraints scale, quantitative workload inventory, and physical symptoms inventory. *Journal of Occupational Health Psychology*, *3*, 356–367, http://dx.doi.org/:10.1037/1076–8998.3.4.356

Stansfeld, S., & Candy, B. (2006). Psychosocial work environment and mental health: A meta-analytic review. *Scandinavian Journal of Work, Environment and Health*, *32*, 443–462.

Stiglbauer, B. (2018). Differential challenge and hindrance stressor relations with job-related core affect. *International Journal of Stress Management*, *25*, 62–80, http://dx.doi.org/:10.1037/str0000076

Stults-Kolehmainen, M. A., & Sinha, R. (2014). The effects of stress on physical activity and exercise. *Sports Medicine*, *44*, 81–121, http://dx.doi.org/:10.1007/s40279-013–0090-5

Taylor, S. G., Bedeian, A. G., Cole, M. S., & Zhang, Z. (2017). Developing and testing a dynamic model of workplace incivility change. *Journal of Management*, *43*, 645–670, http://dx.doi.org/:10.1177/0149206314535432

Tepper, B. J., Dimotakis, N., Lambert, L. S., Koopman, J., Matta, F. K., Man Park, H., & Goo, W. (2018). Examining follower responses to transformational leadership from a dynamic, person–environment fit perspective. *Academy of Management Journal*, *61*, 1343–1368, http://dx.doi.org/:10.5465/amj.2014.0163

Tims, M., Bakker, A. B., & Derks, D. (2013). The impact of job crafting on job demands, job resources, and well-being. *Journal of Occupational Health Psychology*, *18*, 230–240, http://dx.doi.org/:10.1037/a0032141

Tse, H. H., & Dasborough, M. T. (2008). A study of exchange and emotions in team member relationships. *Group and Organization Management*, *33*, 194–215, http://dx.doi.org/:10.1177/1059601106293779

Tuckey, M. R., & Neall, A. M. (2014). Workplace bullying erodes job and personal resources: Between- and within-person perspectives. *Journal of Occupational Health Psychology*, *19*, 413–424, http://dx.doi.org/:10.1037/a0037728

Van Dierendonck, D., Haynes, C., Borrill, C., & Stride, C. (2004). Leadership behavior and subordinate well-being. *Journal of Occupational Health Psychology*, *9*, 165–175, http://dx.doi.org/:10.1037/1076–8998.9.2.165

Volmer, J. (2015). Followers' daily reactions to social conflicts with supervisors: The moderating role of core self-evaluations and procedural justice perceptions. *Leadership Quarterly*, *26*, 719–731, http://dx.doi.org/:10.1016/j.leaqua.2015.01.005

Wang, N., Zhu, J., Song, Z., Dormann, C., & Bakker, A. (2018). The daily motivators: Positive work events, psychological needs satisfaction and work engagement. *Applied Psychology*, http://dx.doi.org/:10.1111/apps.12182

Wegge, J., Vogt, J., & Wecking, C. (2007). Customer-induced stress in call centre work: A comparison of audio- and videoconference. *Journal of Occupational and Organizational Psychology*, *80*, 693–712, http://dx.doi.org/:10.1348/096317906X164927

Weiss, H. M., & Cropanzano, R. (1996). Affective events theory: A theoretical discussion of the structure, causes and consequences of affective experiences at work. In B. M. Staw & L. L. Cummings (Eds.), *Research in organizational behavior: An annual series of analytical essays and critical reviews* (Volume 18, pp. 1–74). Greenwich, CT, and London, UK: Elsevier Science/JAI Press.

Wrzesniewski, A., & Dutton, J. E. (2001). Crafting a job: Revisioning employees as active crafters of their work. *Academy of Management Review*, *26*, 179–201, http://dx.doi.org/:10.5465/AMR.2001.4378011

Xanthopoulou, D., Bakker, A. B., Demerouti, E., & Schaufeli, W. B. (2012). A diary study on the happy worker: How job resources relate to positive emotions and personal resources. *European Journal of Work and Organizational Psychology*, *21*, 489–517, http://dx.doi.org/:10.1080/1359432x.2011.584386

Zhan, Y., Wang, M., & Shi, J. (2016). Interpersonal process of emotional labor: The role of negative and positive customer treatment. *Personnel Psychology*, *69*, 525–557, http://dx.doi.org/:10.1111/peps.12114

Zhou, Z. E., Yan, Y., Che, X. X., & Meier, L. L. (2015). Effect of workplace incivility on end-of-work negative affect: Examining individual and organizational moderators in a daily diary study. *Journal of Occupational Health Psychology, 20*, 117–130, http://dx.doi.org/:10.1037/a0038167

Zohar, D., Tzischinski, O., & Epstein, R. (2003). Effects of energy availability on immediate and delayed emotional reactions to work events. *Journal of Applied Psychology, 88*, 1082–1093.

9 Emotion and Various Forms of Job Performance

Paul E. Spector

The employee outcome that has the greatest impact on organizational functioning is job performance in its various forms. Most of the literature directed toward understanding job performance has tended to focus on individual factors, such as ability and personality, as well as environmental conditions that might affect it, such as leadership. Far less attention has been given to the role of emotions in performance, except, perhaps, for emotion as a personality trait. In this chapter I will review the literature on different forms of emotion – that is, emotional traits, emotional states, and emotion regulation (emotional labor) – and how they relate to various aspects of performance, specifically counterproductive work behavior (behaviors that harm organizations and organization stakeholders), organizational citizenship behavior (positive performance behavior that goes beyond assigned tasks), task performance, and safety performance (following safety rules in carrying out the job).

The Nature of Emotion

Emotion can be viewed from a variety of perspectives, and it can be assessed in a number of ways. First, emotion can be considered purely from a perspective of direction, that is, positive versus negative. To that end, a number of scales such as the JAWS (Van Katwyk, Fox, Spector, & Kelloway, 2000) and PANAS (Watson, Clark, & Tellegen, 1988) have been developed in which items reflecting specific emotions (e.g. anger or contentment) are summed into an overall score of positive or negative emotion. Alternately, measures are also available to assess specific emotions separately, such as anger, anxiety, or depression (Caplan, Cobb, French, Van Harrison, & Penneau, 1980). Second, emotion can be considered as a dispositional tendency to experience either positive (positive affectivity) or negative (negative affectivity) emotional states across situations (Watson & Clark, 1984).

Emotion can also be explored from the perspective of emotion regulation. There are two aspects that have been studied. First, organizations, particularly in customer service, can implement emotional display rules that dictate the appropriate emotional states to express toward customers. In North America, for example, it is generally expected that customer service employees appear happy and warm toward customers (Grandey & Melloy, 2017). When employees comply with display rules, they might do so by faking emotions or by self-regulation so that they feel the emotions they are encouraged to display. Faking of emotions results in the potentially stressful state of emotional dissonance in which the emotions displayed are different from the emotions felt (Grandey & Melloy, 2017).

Second, emotion regulation can be considered as an ability that varies among individuals. Emotional intelligence (EI) is defined in part as the ability to regulate emotion in the self and others. This would include the ability to successfully display the emotions demanded by the employer, and the ability to manipulate emotions in others. Thus a successful salesperson would be able to appear friendly and happy toward a customer and make the customer feel positive emotions toward him or her and, perhaps more importantly, toward the product or service in question. This suggests that at least for sales, there should be a direct relationship between EI and performance.

Affective States, Traits, and Performance

As noted by Rotundo and Xie (2008), performance consists of a variety of employee behaviors that can be classified as task performance (completing core tasks that are clearly within the role of the position), organizational citizenship behavior or OCB (behaviors that benefit the organization or people within the organization but are not part of core tasks), and counterproductive work behavior or CWB (behaviors that harm organizations or people within organizations). Both OCB and CWB can be further subdivided into types. The simplest classification is by whether the target of the behavior is the organization or people in the organization, both for OCB (McNeely & Meglino, 1994) and for CWB (Robinson & Bennett, 1995). Further breakdowns have been suggested for both, such as the five CWB facets (Spector et al., 2006) of abuse (mistreating other people), production deviance (purposely doing work incorrectly), sabotage (damaging or defacing property), theft (from others or the organization), and withdrawal (not working when scheduled). Performance can also be considered in relation to particular tasks, as with creative performance or customer service performance.

By far the most research attention linking emotions to performance has been on CWB, where there is a clearly established connection. Although there are models linking emotion to various forms of performance, what is lacking is an overall theoretical framework that connects all forms of performance.

We can consider two aspects of emotion that have relevance to performance. First there is the arousal component that occurs during the active experience of an emotional state. A high level of emotional arousal impacts cognitive processing: this is where a person's attention becomes narrowly focused, and complex processing begins to break down. This is described by the well-known Yerkes-Dodson Law that states there is an inverse U relationship between arousal and performance, moderated by the cognitive complexity of the task involved (Yerkes & Dodson, 2008). For simple tasks the optimal level is rather high, as low levels of arousal are associated with boredom. For complex tasks, the optimal level is rather low, as arousal will interfere with complex cognitive processing. This leads to the supposition that the effects of emotional arousal are dependent on the nature of tasks.

The second pathway is through motivation, as emotional states and traits can impact an individual's goals and intentions. This is perhaps most relevant for CWB, where negative emotions have been clearly linked to this class of behaviors. It can, however, also be relevant for positive forms of performance, as varying emotional states might play a role in an individual's decisions about how efforts are directed.

Emotion and CWB

Of all the forms of performance, CWB is the one that is most connected to emotion: specifically, negative emotional states. In large part this is because the roots of CWB research are in the study of human aggression (Fox & Spector, 1999) and of injustice (Skarlicki & Folger, 1997), two areas that prominently feature a role for emotions. The typical role for emotion is reflected in the stressor–emotion model of CWB, which suggests that stressful job conditions lead to negative emotions and then CWB (Spector & Fox, 2005). This model proposes that emotion serves as a mediator and that CWB is a response rather than a driver of stressful job conditions. Indeed, CWB studies have shown a link from stressors to negative emotion (e.g. Fida, Paciello, Tramontano, Barbaranelli, & Farnese, 2015; Fida, Paciello, Tramontano, Fontaine, et al., 2015), a link from negative emotion to CWB (e.g. Krischer, Penney, & Hunter, 2010; Rupprecht, Kueny, Shoss, & Metzger, 2016), and the temporal precedence from stressor to emotion to CWB (e.g. Banks, Whelpley, Oh, & Shin, 2012; Matta, Erol-Korkmaz, Johnson, & Biçaksiz, 2014; Yang & Diefendorff, 2009).

It should be kept in mind that while there is clear evidence linking emotion to stressors and CWB, the evidence for the mediating role of emotions is not strong. Most of that evidence comes from cross-sectional studies that demonstrate correlation patterns consistent with mediation, but the designs themselves do not rule out other temporal flows. Furthermore, few studies have been designed to specifically rule out the possibility that CWB could affect emotions and/or job stressors. An exception is Meier and Spector (2013), who conducted a five-wave longitudinal study that suggested that CWB might be the driver of stressors. These results were replicated in a two-wave study by Arvan, Shimon, and Kessler (2015).

Although most studies of emotional states used general indices of negative emotion or positive emotion, a handful have explored individual emotional states. Bauer and Spector (2015) explored relationships of eight emotions with five CWB facets. Although all correlations were significant, when they regressed each facet on the emotions they found that the patterns varied by facet. Specifically, abuse was related to anger, jealousy, and shame; production deviance to boredom, sadness, and shame; sabotage and withdrawal to boredom and shame; and theft to anger and shame. It is interesting that shame was significantly related to all five facets. Although the stressor–emotion model might suggest that shame leads to CWB, it seems more likely that individuals who engage in CWB will feel ashamed of their behavior. This suggests the possibility of a far more complex role for emotion as both a driver and a consequence of CWB.

Personality has been the most frequent topic of CWB research (Piotrowski, 2013), and one of the major personality traits studied has been negative affectivity or NA (often operationalized as emotional stability, reverse coded). At least five meta-analyses have clearly shown that the trait of NA relates to overall CWB as well as CWB directed toward organizations and people (Berry, Carpenter, & Barratt, 2012; Berry, Ones, & Sackett, 2007; Dalal, 2005; Hershcovis & Barling, 2010; Kaplan, Bradley, Luchman, & Haynes, 2009). These studies show that individuals who are high in negative affective traits have a tendency to engage in CWB.

Emotion and OCB

The role of emotions in OCB is less clear than for CWB. Spector and Fox (2002) suggested that emotions would relate similarly but oppositely to CWB and OCB. The explanation is that individuals experiencing negative emotion would inhibit their OCB, whereas those experiencing positive emotions would feel good about their employers and want to offer support through helpful behavior. In their meta-analysis, Chang, Johnson, and Yang (2007) combined a variety of measures that reflected psychological strains at work, including negative emotions, and found a small negative relationship with overall OCB (mean $r = -.13$), as well as OCB directed to organizations (−.13) and people (−.17). On the trait side, meta-analyses find modest correlations of OCB with NA of −.10 or less (Chiaburu, Oh, Berry, Li, & Gardner, 2011; Dalal, 2005; Kaplan et al., 2009; Podsakoff, MacKenzie, Paine, & Bachrach, 2000). Mean correlations of OCB with measure of positive affectivity have been in the mid to high .20s (Dalal, 2005; Kaplan et al., 2009).

Unfortunately, it is far from clear the extent to which findings in the literature reflect emotion's relationships with OCB, given the confounding of measures of OCB with those of CWB. Dalal (2005) presented meta-analytic evidence that the inclusion of what he termed antithetical items in OCB scales distorted correlations with CWB. Antithetical items are those that either had overlapping content with CWB scales by reflecting the absence of CWB, or were CWB items that were reverse scored. In other words, OCB was in part operationalized as having not engaged in CWB, even if no helpful behaviors had been performed. Dalal showed that the strong negative relationships between CWB and OCB were almost entirely explained by the inclusion of antithetical items. Fox, Spector, Goh, Bruursema, and Kessler (2012) developed the Organizational Citizenship Behavior Checklist (OCB-C), which controlled for antithetical items. A series of studies using the OCB-C showed how OCB might relate to emotions. Positive emotional states related significantly and positively to OCB in two of three samples; however negative emotional states relate significantly and positively, rather than negatively, to OCB across three samples (Fox et al., 2012; Spector & Che, 2014). Furthermore, the trait of NA did not relate significantly to OCB when CWB content was controlled (Spector & Che, 2014). This line of research suggests that whether or not CWB content was controlled, positive emotions related to OCB. For negative emotions, however, controlling CWB content resulted in an opposite relationship with OCB; individuals experiencing negative emotion are likely to engage in more, not less, OCB.

The connection between OCB and negative emotion is determined by the specific emotion and situation. For example, Bolino and Grant (2016) provide specific examples of emotional states leading to particular kinds of OCB, such as righteous indignation leading someone to defend a coworker. That negative emotions might relate positively to both CWB and OCB can be explained by several mechanisms that suggest that OCB can be forced upon employees either by necessity (having to compensate for a poorly performing colleague) or by supervisors (Vigoda-Gadot, 2006), which can lead employees to engage in the required OCB and then respond with CWB (Spector & Fox, 2010a, 2010b). This suggests that the role of emotions in OCB can be complex, and that it probably matters why an individual engages in the behavior. It also is likely that negative emotion might play a role in an individual's decision to engage or not engage in OCB, but also that engaging in OCB might lead to negative emotion.

Emotion and Task Performance

The relationship of both state and trait emotions with task performance has been generally small. For trait affect, mean correlations in meta-analyses are −.13 for negative affectivity and .16 for positive affectivity or PA (Kaplan et al., 2009; Shockley, Ispas, Rossi, & Levine, 2012). Kaplan et al. (2009) showed that the nature of the performance measure matters in that correlations of both NA and PA with task performance are higher when performance is self-rated than supervisor-rated, although supervisor-rated performance is still significantly related to both affective traits. Objective measures of task performance, however, are not significantly related to NA or PA. On the state side, negative emotions are negatively related and positive emotions are positively related to task performance, with meta-analytic mean correlations less than .20 (Shockley et al., 2012).

One setting in which emotion might be expected to have an impact on task performance is sales, and here we can find studies that use not only performance ratings but also objective measures of sales volume. Although meta-analyses of trait emotion (neuroticism) have failed to find an overall significant relationship with sales performance or sales volume (Barrick & Mount, 1991; Vinchur, Schippmann, Switzer,

& Roth, 1998), results have not been entirely consistent. For example, Erez and Judge (2001) found a significant correlation of −.29 between a measure of neuroticism and sales from company records. The relationship of state emotions with sales has also been inconsistent across studies. For example, Bluen, Barling, and Burns (1990) found a nonsignificant relationship between feelings of depression and sales. However, Kim, Park, and Niu (2017) found in a daily diary study a significant correlation between positive emotion during the day and an objective measure of sales, whereas Yeung and Fung (2012) found in a diary study that daily positive (.37) and negative (−.30) emotion related to daily self-ratings of sales performance. Perhaps more important than general affective states is affect felt specifically toward customers. Sharma and Levy (2003) asked customer service representatives to write descriptions of specific customers and how they felt about them. Their descriptions were rated for affect felt about customers, and those ratings correlated with sales records (.64). Whether the feelings were driving sales or were the result of sales success is not possible to determine from this study, but it does raise the possibility that emotions are most relevant to task performance when they are expressed in relation to individuals that are relevant to that performance, such as customers with sales. I will return to this point in a later section of this chapter, on emotional labor.

It should not be surprising that relationships between emotion and task performance aren't larger. Task performance is complex and can be affected by a variety of contextual variables, including the nature of tasks and the setting in which performance occurs. For example, negative trait affect concerns an individual's ability to handle stressful job conditions. With high-demand jobs that expose individuals to stressful job conditions, we would expect high NA individuals to be more affected by those conditions than low NA individuals. Thus we might expect that the relationship between NA and task performance would be moderated by the stressful nature of a job. With jobs where demands are low, it seems far less likely that being high in NA would affect task performance.

Accidents and Safety

An important aspect of job performance is safety performance: that is, the extent to which individuals follow policies and protocols to safely perform their jobs, such as wearing required safety gear and following safe procedures to accomplish specific tasks. Safety performance can involve all three of the other forms of job performance. Griffin and Neal (2000) have divided safety performance into safety compliance, which is analogous to task performance as it concerns following safety requirements, and safety participation, which is analogous to OCB as it concerns going beyond safety requirements in promoting and supporting safety. When employees purposely break safety rules and intentionally perform in an unsafe manner that risks their own safety and/or that of other employees, they can be said to be engaging in a form of CWB.

Studies of safety have focused attention on both safety performance itself, and accidents/injuries as a potential by-product of poor safety performance. Meta-analyses have explored affective traits, generally in the context of the five-factor personality model (Digman, 1990), finding small and generally nonsignificant correlations with accidents/injuries (Beus, Dhanani, & McCord, 2015; Clarke & Robertson, 2005). Beus et al. (2015) found that trait anger was significantly related to unsafe behavior, suggesting that the absence of emotional stability might be a factor in unsafe behavior, but perhaps not in the outcomes of unsafe behavior.

Negative emotion, operationalized as emotional exhaustion, has been linked to safety performance (Li, Jiang, Yao, & Li, 2013) and negative emotions at the state level in general have been linked to workplace injuries (Salminen, Perttula, Hirvonen, Perkiö-Mäkelä, & Vartia, 2017), although the magnitude of the relationship is quite small. A qualitative study by Catino and Patriotta (2013) provides some insights into how emotions can interfere with safety performance. They interviewed military pilots who pointed out that negative emotions, such as anxiety or fear, decrease attention to the task at hand and can result in errors that can lead to accidents. Interestingly, the pilots suggested that too much positive emotion can led to overconfidence and risky behavior that can also contribute to errors and accidents. This suggests that it is important for employees in high-risk situations, such as piloting an aircraft, to regulate both negative and positive emotions so that they remain calm and relatively relaxed.

Affective Regulation and Job Performance

It should be kept in mind that people's emotions are not automatic responses to the work environment over which individuals have no control. Rather, employees are actively engaged in the regulation of those emotions, and in many circumstances will inhibit the expression as well as feelings of both negative and positive emotions. Such emotion regulation can be an effective means of overcoming potentially detrimental effects of emotional experience on performance. Emotional labor is concerned with how individuals self-regulate emotions at work, either in response to organizational demands or as a means of coping with affective events. Emotional intelligence is an individual difference variable that reflects differences in the ability to regulate emotions.

Emotional Labor

Emotional labor concerns job requirements that employees express desired emotions or suppress the expression of undesired emotions (Grandey & Melloy, 2017). The requirements for emotional labor can be found most often in jobs that require contact with the public: for example, when customer service representatives are expected to express positive feelings toward customers. Two broad types of emotion-regulation approaches have been noted: deep acting, in which the employee engages in emotion regulation processes that result in actually feeling the desired state, and surface acting, in which the employee fakes the expression of emotion, for example smiling when sad.

Emotional labor has been a frequent topic for research, with the majority of studies focused on potential detrimental effects of being forced to express emotions regardless of the employee's initial emotional state. The type of emotional labor seems to matter, as surface acting can be detrimental to an employee's well-being whereas deep acting does not appear to have the same negative effects (Hülsheger & Schewe, 2011). There has been some research linking emotional labor to performance. For task performance, meta-analyses show little relationship for either surface acting or deep acting (Hülsheger & Schewe, 2011; Kammeyer-Mueller et al., 2013). Thus it would seem that engaging in emotional labor makes no difference with task performance. However, it should be noted that one of the main purposes of emotional labor is to enhance the customer experience, so it might not be particularly relevant in jobs that do not involve customers. Where studies have looked at an indicator of customer service performance, that of customer satisfaction, emotional labor would seem to be important. Indeed, in their meta-analysis, Hülsheger and Schewe (2011) showed that customer satisfaction had a mean correlation of .30 with deep acting, but a mean correlation of only −.04 with surface acting. Thus it would seem that deep acting, and not surface acting, can be effective in enhancing task performance for customer service jobs.

There has been less attention paid to the possible role of emotional labor and emotion regulation in the other forms of job performance. One of the few studies to link emotion regulation to CWB looked at the impact of suppressing negative emotion (Baka, 2015). Results suggested that when it comes to emotion suppression, the specific emotion matters. They found that when nurses were exposed to workplace aggression, suppressing anger resulted in an increase in their CWB, whereas suppressing anxiety resulted in a decrease in subsequent CWB. In another health-care study, Yue, Wang, and Groth (2016) found that both deep acting and surface acting significantly related to CWB and OCB. Deep acting related positively to both forms of job performance, whereas surface acting related positively to CWB but negatively to OCB. Taken together these studies suggest that emotional labor has complex relationships with CWB and OCB, but there are too few studies to understand what the mechanisms might be.

Emotional Intelligence

It has been proposed that individuals differ in their emotional intelligence (EI): that is, their ability to regulate their own emotions and the emotions of others (Mayer & Salovey, 1993). In the context of this chapter, the question arises whether this ability would relate to the various forms of job performance. Meta-analyses of ability measures of EI (measures that use ability-type items rather than self-reports) find little relationship with either CWB (Miao, Humphrey, & Qian, 2017) or task performance (Joseph & Newman, 2010). However, there is a small but significant correlation of EI with OCB (mean $r = .13$).

As noted earlier with task performance, the role of emotion in performance depends upon the nature of the job, and it seems likely that EI would be most relevant for jobs that have emotion-display rules: that is, jobs that require emotional labor. Joseph and Newman (2010) tested this possibility in their meta-analysis by classifying samples into those that are in jobs with high versus low emotional labor requirements. They found support for the hypothesis that the amount of emotional labor requirement at the job level moderated the relationship between EI and task performance. When emotional labor requirements were low, EI was nonsignificantly related to performance (mean $r = .01$). When emotional labor requirements were high, however, the mean correlation between EI and task performance was a significant .22. Based on these results, we might expect that EI would be most relevant in sales jobs where employees need to promote positive feelings in customers. In three separate sales samples from the insurance and real estate industries, Kidwell, Hardesty, Murtha, and Sheng (2011) showed that an EI ability measure related to objective measures of sales and customer retention.

Conclusions

The connections between emotions and job performance are complex, making it difficult to draw any simple conclusions. The aspect of performance that is most consistently related to emotion is CWB. There is consistent evidence that environmental factors that elicit negative emotions, such as job stressors, also can be antecedent to CWB. Although it is tempting to conclude that emotion is a mediator of these relationships, there is evidence that at least under some conditions, CWB may be antecedent rather than, or in addition to, being a consequence.

The connection between emotion and OCB is not clear, largely due to measures of OCB in most studies being confounded with measures of CWB. As noted, there is reason to suggest that CWB and OCB can co-occur and might be positively rather than negatively related. Thus it does not seem to be the case that relationships of emotion with OCB are opposite to those with CWB.

In fact, relationships of emotion with OCB scales that control for CWB overlap are quite small.

Finally, correlations of emotion with task performance and safety performance are quite small. Although there is a tendency for individuals high in NA to perform somewhat lower, this tendency is probably affected by a number of contextual factors that are not well understood. At the current time we cannot say unequivocally that individuals high in NA are likely to be poor performers unless the job is high in stress. For accidents, it is likely the proximal emotional state that is relevant rather than more distal emotional traits. Thus an individual who is experiencing strong negative emotions is likely to be distracted, and that distraction can result in an accident. Finally, emotion regulation plays an important role in job performance, and people vary in their emotional intelligence: that is, their ability to regulate emotions in themselves and others. Emotional labor, with specific display rules, exists in many jobs and job settings. Although emotional labor, specifically surface acting, can be detrimental to employee well-being, the role of emotional labor in task performance is more variable, as it is mainly in customer service situations where deep acting can enhance the customer experience. However, emotion regulation outside of the display rules of organizations can be important in safety, given that maintaining control of immediate emotional states when in high-risk situations is important to avoid errors and accidents.

References

Arvan, M. L., Shimon, Y., & Kessler, S. R. (2015). Examining temporal precedence in the relationship between customer mistreatment and customer CWB. Paper presented at the Southern Management Association, St. Petersburg Beach.

Baka, Ł. (2015). How do negative emotions regulate the effects of workplace aggression on counterproductive work behaviours? *Polish Psychological Bulletin*, *46*(3), 326–335.

Banks, G. C., Whelpley, C. E., Oh, I.-S., & Shin, K. (2012). (How) are emotionally exhausted employees harmful? *International Journal of Stress Management*, *19*(3), 198–216, doi:10.1037/a0029249

Barrick, M. R., & Mount, M. K. (1991). The big five personality dimensions and job performance: A meta-analysis. *Personnel Psychology*, *44*(1), 1–26.

Bauer, J. A., & Spector, P. E. (2015). Discrete negative emotions and counterproductive work behavior. *Human Performance*, *28*(4), 307–331, doi:10.1080/08959285.2015.1021040

Berry, C. M., Carpenter, N. C., & Barratt, C. L. (2012). Do other-reports of counterproductive work behavior provide an incremental contribution over self-reports? A meta-analytic comparison. *Journal of Applied Psychology*, *97*(3), 613–636, http://dx.doi.org/10.1037/a0026739

Berry, C. M., Ones, D. S., & Sackett, P. R. (2007). Interpersonal deviance, organizational deviance, and their common correlates: A review and meta-analysis. *Journal of Applied Psychology*, *92*(2), 410–424, http://dx.doi.org/10.1037/0021-9010.92.2.410

Beus, J. M., Dhanani, L. Y., & McCord, M. A. (2015). A meta-analysis of personality and workplace safety: Addressing unanswered questions. *Journal of Applied Psychology*, *100*(2), 481–498, doi:10.1037/a0037916

Bluen, S. D., Barling, J., & Burns, W. (1990). Predicting sales performance, job satisfaction, and depression by using the Achievement Strivings and Impatience–Irritability dimensions of Type A behavior. *Journal of Applied Psychology*, *75*(2), 212–216, doi:10.1037/0021-9010.75.2.212

Bolino, M. C., & Grant, A. M. (2016). The bright side of being prosocial at work, and the dark side, too: A review and agenda for research on other-oriented motives, behavior, and impact in organizations. *Academy of Management Annals*, *10*(1), 599–670, doi:10.1080/19416520.2016.1153260

Caplan, R. D., Cobb, S., French, J. R. P., Van Harrison, R., & Penneau, S. R. (1980). *Job demands and worker health*. Ann Arbor: University of Michigan, Institute for Social Research.

Catino, M., & Patriotta, G. (2013). Learning from errors: Cognition, emotions and safety culture in the Italian Air Force. *Organization Studies*, *34*(4), 437–467, doi:10.1177/0170840612467156

Chang, C.-H., Johnson, R. E., & Yang, L.-Q. (2007). Emotional strain and organizational citizenship behaviours: A meta-analysis and review. *Work & Stress*, *21*(4), 312–332, doi:10.1080/02678370701758124

Chiaburu, D. S., Oh, I.-S., Berry, C. M., Li, N., & Gardner, R. G. (2011). The five-factor model of personality traits and organizational citizenship behaviors: A meta-analysis. *Journal of Applied Psychology*, *96*(6), 1140–1166, doi:10.1037/a0024004

Clarke, S., & Robertson, I. (2005). A meta-analytic review of the Big Five personality factors and accident involvement in occupational and non-occupational settings. *Journal of Occupational and Organizational Psychology*, *78*(3), 355–376, doi:10.1348/096317905X26183

Dalal, R. S. (2005). A meta-analysis of the relationship between organizational citizenship behavior and counterproductive work behavior. *Journal of Applied Psychology*, *90*(6), 1241–1255, http://dx.doi.org/10.1037/0021-9010.90.6.1241

Digman, J. M. (1990). Personality structure: Emergence of the five-factor model. *Annual Review of Psychology*, *41*, 417–440.

Erez, A., & Judge, T. A. (2001). Relationship of core self-evaluations to goal setting, motivation, and performance. *Journal of Applied Psychology*, *86*(6), 1270–1279, doi:10.1037/0021-9010.86.6.1270

Fida, R., Paciello, M., Tramontano, C., Barbaranelli, C., & Farnese, M. L. (2015). "Yes, I Can": the protective role of personal self-efficacy in hindering counterproductive work behavior under stressful conditions. *Anxiety, Stress, & Coping*, *28*(5), 479–499, doi:10.1080/10615806.2014.969718

Fida, R., Paciello, M., Tramontano, C., Fontaine, R. G., Barbaranelli, C., & Farnese, M. L. (2015). An integrative approach to understanding counterproductive work behavior: The roles of stressors, negative emotions, and moral disengagement. *Journal of Business Ethics*, *130*(1), 131–144, doi:10.1007/s10551-014-2209-5

Fox, S., & Spector, P. E. (1999). A model of work frustration–aggression. *Journal of Organizational Behavior*, *20*(6), 915–931, http://dx.doi.org/10.1002/%28SICI%291099-1379%28199911%2920:6%3C915::AID-JOB918%3E3.0.CO;2-6

Fox, S., Spector, P. E., Goh, A., Bruursema, K., & Kessler, S. R. (2012). The deviant citizen: Measuring potential positive relations between counterproductive work behaviour and organizational citizenship behaviour. *Journal of Occupational and Organizational Psychology*, *85* (1), 199–220, http://dx.doi.org/10.1111/j.2044-8325.2011.02032.x

Grandey, A. A., & Melloy, R. C. (2017). The state of the heart: Emotional labor as emotion regulation reviewed and revised. *Journal of Occupational Health Psychology*, *22*(3), 407–422, doi:10.1037/ocp0000067

Griffin, M. A., & Neal, A. (2000). Perceptions of safety at work: A framework for linking safety climate to safety performance, knowledge, and motivation. *Journal of Occupational Health Psychology*, *5*(3), 347–358.

Hershcovis, M. S., & Barling, J. (2010). Towards a multi-foci approach to workplace aggression: A meta-analytic review of outcomes from different perpetrators. *Journal of Organizational Behavior*, *31*(1), 24–44.

Hülsheger, U. R., & Schewe, A. F. (2011). On the costs and benefits of emotional labor: A meta-analysis of three decades of research. *Journal of Occupational Health Psychology*, *16*(3), 361–389, doi:10.1037/a002287610.1037/a0022876.supp (Supplemental)

Joseph, D. L., & Newman, D. A. (2010). Emotional intelligence: An integrative meta-analysis and cascading model. *Journal of Applied Psychology*, *95*(1), 54–78, doi:10.1037/a0017286

Kammeyer-Mueller, J. D., Rubenstein, A. L., Long, D. M., Odio, M. A., Buckman, B. R., Zhang, Y., & Halvorsen-Ganepola, M. D. K. (2013). A meta-analytic structural model of dispositonal affectivity and emotional labor. *Personnel Psychology*, *66*(1), 47–90, doi:10.1111/peps.12009

Kaplan, S., Bradley, J. C., Luchman, J. N., & Haynes, D. (2009). On the role of positive and negative affectivity in job performance: A meta-analytic investigation. *Journal of Applied*

Psychology, 94(1), 162–176, doi:10.1037/a0013115

Kidwell, B., Hardesty, D. M., Murtha, B. R., & Sheng, S. (2011). Emotional intelligence in marketing exchanges. *Journal of Marketing, 75*(1), 78–95.

Kim, S., Park, Y., & Niu, Q. K. (2017). Micro-break activities at work to recover from daily work demands. *Journal of Organizational Behavior, 38* (1), 28–44, doi:10.1002/job.2109

Krischer, M. M., Penney, L. M., & Hunter, E. M. (2010). Can counterproductive work behaviors be productive? CWB as emotion-focused coping. *Journal of Occupational Health Psychology, 15*(2), 154–166, doi:10.1037/a0018349

Li, F., Jiang, L., Yao, X., & Li, Y. (2013). Job demands, job resources and safety outcomes: The roles of emotional exhaustion and safety compliance. *Accident Analysis and Prevention, 51*, 243–251, doi:10.1016/j.aap.2012.11.029

Matta, F. K., Erol-Korkmaz, H. T., Johnson, R. E., & Biçaksiz, P. (2014). Significant work events and counterproductive work behavior: The role of fairness, emotions, and emotion regulation. *Journal of Organizational Behavior, 35*(7), 920–944, doi:10.1002/job.1934

Mayer, J. D., & Salovey, P. (1993). The intelligence of emotional intelligence. *Intelligence, 17*(4), 433–442, https://doi.org/10.1016/0160-2896(93)90010-3

McNeely, B. L., & Meglino, B. M. (1994). The role of dispositional and situational antecedents in prosocial organizational behavior: An examination of the intended beneficiaries of prosocial behavior. *Journal of Applied Psychology, 79*(6), 836–844.

Meier, L. L., & Spector, P. E. (2013). Reciprocal effects of work stressors and counterproductive work behavior: A five-wave longitudinal study. *Journal of Applied Psychology, 98*(3), 529–539, http://dx.doi.org/10.1037/a0031732

Miao, C., Humphrey, R. H., & Qian, S. (2017). Are the emotionally intelligent good citizens or counterproductive? A meta-analysis of emotional intelligence and its relationships with organizational citizenship behavior and counterproductive work behavior. *Personality and Individual Differences, 116*, 144–156, https://doi.org/10.1016/j.paid.2017.04.015

Piotrowski, C. (2013). Counterproductive Work Behavior: Topical domain in emergent research. *Journal of Instructional Psychology, 40*(3), 78–80.

Podsakoff, P. M., MacKenzie, S. B., Paine, J. B., & Bachrach, D. G. (2000). Organizational citizenship behaviors: A critical review of the theroetical and empirical literature and suggestions for future research. *Journal of Management, 26*(3), 513–563, http://dx.doi.org/10.1177/014920630002600307

Robinson, S. L., & Bennett, R. J. (1995). A typology of deviant workplace behaviors: A multidimensional scaling study. *Academy of Management Journal, 38* (2), 555–572, http://dx.doi.org/10.2307/256693

Rotundo, M., & Xie, J. L. (2008). Understanding the domain of counterproductive work behaviour in China. *International Journal of Human Resource Management, 19*(5), 856–877, http://dx.doi.org/10.1080/09585190801991400

Rupprecht, E. A., Kueny, C. R., Shoss, M. K., & Metzger, A. J. (2016). Getting what you want: How fit between desired and received leader sensitivity influences emotion and counterproductive work behavior. *Journal of Occupational Health Psychology, 21*(4), 443–454, doi:10.1037/a0040074

Salminen, S., Perttula, P., Hirvonen, M., Perkiö-Mäkelä, M., & Vartia, M. (2017). Link between haste and occupational injury. *Work: Journal of Prevention, Assessment & Rehabilitation, 56*(1), 119–124, doi:10.3233/WOR-162471

Sharma, A., & Levy, M. (2003). Salespeople's affect toward customers: Why should it be important for retailers? *Journal of Business Research, 56*(7), 523–528, doi:10.1016/S0148-2963(01)00248-X

Shockley, K. M., Ispas, D., Rossi, M. E., & Levine, E. L. (2012). A meta-analytic investigation of the relationship between state affect, discrete emotions, and job performance. *Human Performance, 25*(5), 377–411, doi:10.1080/08959285.2012.721832

Skarlicki, D. P., & Folger, R. (1997). Retaliation in the workplace: The roles of distributive, procedural, and interactional justice. *Journal of Applied Psychology, 82*(3), 434–443, doi:10.1037/0021-9010.82.3.434

Spector, P. E., & Che, X. X. (2014). Re-examining citizenship: How the control of measurement artifacts affects observed relationships of organizational citizenship behavior and organizational variables. *Human Performance*, *27* (2), 165–182, doi:10.1080/08959285.2014.882928

Spector, P. E., & Fox, S. (2002). An emotion-centered model of voluntary work behavior: Some parallels between counterproductive work behavior and organizational citizenship behavior. *Human Resource Management Review*, *12*(2), 269–292, http://dx.doi.org/10.1016/S1053-4822%2802%2900049-9

Spector, P. E., & Fox, S. (2005). The stressor-emotion model of counterproductive work behavior. In S. Fox & P. E. Spector (Eds.), *Counterproductive work behavior: Investigations of actors and targets* (pp. 151–174). Washington, DC: American Psychological Association.

Spector, P. E., & Fox, S. (2010a). Counterproductive work behavior and organisational citizenship behavior: Are they opposite forms of active behavior? *Applied Psychology: An International Review*, *59*(1), 21–39, http://dx.doi.org/10.1111/j.1464-0597.2009.00414.x

Spector, P. E., & Fox, S. (2010b). Theorizing about the deviant citizen: An attributional explanation of the interplay of organizational citizenship and counterproductive work behavior. *Human Resource Management Review*, *20*(2), 132–143, http://dx.doi.org/10.1016/j.hrmr.2009.06.002

Spector, P. E., Fox, S., Penney, L. M., Bruursema, K., Goh, A., & Kessler, S. (2006). The dimensionality of counterproductivity: Are all counterproductive behaviors created equal? *Journal of Vocational Behavior*, *68*(3), 446–460, http://dx.doi.org/10.1016/j.jvb.2005.10.005

Van Katwyk, P. T., Fox, S., Spector, P. E., & Kelloway, E. K. (2000). Using the Job-Related Affective Well-Being Scale (JAWS) to investigate affective responses to work stressors. *Journal of Occupational Health Psychology*, *5*(2), 219–230, http://dx.doi.org/10.1037/1076-8998.5.2.219

Vigoda-Gadot, E. (2006). Compulsory citizenship behavior: Theorizing some dark sides of the good soldier syndrome in organizations. *Journal for the Theory of Social Behaviour*, *36*(1), 77–93, http://dx.doi.org/10.1111/j.1468-5914.2006.00297.x

Vinchur, A. J., Schippmann, J. S., Switzer, F. S., III, & Roth, P. L. (1998). A meta-analytic review of predictors of job performance for salespeople. *Journal of Applied Psychology*, *83* (4), 586–597.

Watson, D., & Clark, L. A. (1984). Negative affectivity: The disposition to experience aversive emotional states. *Psychological Bulletin*, *96*(3), 465–490, http://dx.doi.org/10.1037/0033-2909.96.3.465

Watson, D., Clark, L. A., & Tellegen, A. (1988). Development and validation of brief measures of positive and negative affect: The PANAS scales. *Journal of Personality and Social Psychology*, *54* (6), 1063–1070, http://dx.doi.org/10.1037/0022-3514.54.6.1063

Yang, J., & Diefendorff, J. M. (2009). The relations of daily counterproductive workplace behavior with emotions, situational antecedents, and personality moderators: A diary study in Hong Kong. *Personnel Psychology*, *62*(2), 259–295, doi:10.1111/j.1744-6570.2009.01138.x

Yerkes, R. M., & Dodson, J. D. (2008). The relation of strength of stimulus to rapidity of habit formation. *Journal of Comparative Neurology & Psychology*, *18*, 459–482.

Yeung, D. Y., & Fung, H. H. (2012). Impacts of suppression on emotional responses and performance outcomes: An experience-sampling study in younger and older workers. *Journals of Gerontology: Series B: Psychological Sciences and Social Sciences*, *67*(6), 666–676, doi:10.1093/geronb/gbr159

Yue, Y., Wang, K. L., & Groth, M. (2016). The impact of surface acting on coworker-directed voluntary workplace behaviours. *European Journal of Work and Organizational Psychology*, *25*(3), 447–458, doi:10.1080/1359432X.2015.1111874

10 The Role of Affect and Its Regulation for Creativity and Innovation

Maike Hundeling and Kathrin Rosing

Creativity and innovation play an important role in today's work life as they are key to enhancing organizations' competitiveness (e.g. Amabile, 1988; Anderson, Potočnik, & Zhou, 2014; Bledow, Frese, Anderson, Erez, & Farr, 2009). Creativity may be defined as a facet of innovation that refers to the generation and development of new and useful ideas (Amabile, 1983, 1996). Innovation, in contrast, is "the intentional introduction and application within a role, group or organization of ideas, processes, products or procedures, new to the relevant unit of adoption, designed to significantly benefit the individual, the group, the organization or wider society" (West & Farr, 1990, p. 9). In other words, whereas creativity refers to the generation of ideas, innovation additionally includes the implementation of those ideas.

In creativity and innovation literatures, researchers agree that creativity and innovation often are accompanied by affect and affect-related constructs. Amabile, Barsade, Mueller, and Staw (2005) claim that "[c]reative activity appears to be an affectively charged event, one in which complex cognitive processes are shaped by, co-occur with, and shape emotional experience" (p. 367). For example, the generation and implementation of a new product may cause feelings that are associated with failure or success (e.g. Ivcevic & Brackett, 2015).

There is some variability regarding the terminology used in creativity research to study those feelings. Like many other researchers (e.g. Brief & Weiss, 2002; Gross, 2015; Weiss & Cropanzano, 1996), we summarize them in the generic term "affect," which also comprises frequently used affect-related variables such as emotion (e.g. sadness) and mood (e.g. feeling down). As most of the research reviewed in this chapter is concerned with affective states, we will explicitly mention when we refer to affect as a dispositional trait.

The purpose of this chapter is to review and integrate the research on affect and affect-related variables in relation to creativity and innovation in organizations. The relationship between affect and creativity has been studied in psychology for decades (e.g. Baas, De Dreu, & Nijstad, 2008; Mumford, 2003): A large body of research has demonstrated that positive affect enhances creativity (for an overview see Baas et al., 2008). In contrast, the relationship between negative affect and creativity is commonly assumed to be negative, even though some researchers have demonstrated that negative affect may also increase creativity (e.g. Kaufmann, 2003; Kaufmann & Vosburg, 1997). Thus, as the findings are divergent, the affect–creativity relationship appears to be more complex than one might assume. We will address this issue and examine which further affect-related aspects, beyond the valence of affect, may be crucial for creativity.

Compared to the long tradition of research on the affect–creativity relationship, significantly less research exists about the link between affect and innovation. For that reason we will also review findings from entrepreneurship literature, which is substantially connected with the innovation literature and also provides evidence regarding the affect–innovation relationship.

In this chapter, we will first review research on positive affect and its influence on creativity and innovation. Second, we will move on to negative affect and summarize what is known about negative affect and its impact on creativity and innovation. Third, taking into account that the effects of positive affect and negative affect on creativity and innovation are not independent, we then present several interactive and dynamic perspectives on affect that have been linked to creativity. For example, Fong (2006) argued for an ambivalent perspective: that is, the assumption that the simultaneous experience of positive and negative affect leads to creativity. Another recent line of research has argued for a dynamic perspective, describing an interplay between positive and negative affect over time that fosters creativity (Bledow, Rosing, & Frese, 2011).

While affect itself is relevant for creativity and innovation, its regulation may also have an impact. Thus, fourth, we will examine the role of affect regulation in the context of organizational creativity and innovation. Building on Gross (2015), "affect regulation" refers to the individual's ability to influence affective states when those affective states prevent the realization of specific goals, and comprises coping, emotion regulation, and mood regulation. Research on the role of regulation efforts and creativity and innovation indicates that regulatory behaviors are resources for successfully completing creative tasks (De Stobbeleir, Ashford, & Buyens, 2011).

Finally, we will discuss several research gaps and offer suggestions for future research directions.

Positive Affect and Its Impact on Creativity and Innovation

In creativity research, there is substantive evidence for the assumption that positive affective states are related to enhanced creativity (e.g. Amabile et al., 2005; Baas et al., 2008; Davis, 2009). The overall pattern of findings implies that positive affect leads to broadened attention and cognitive flexibility: that is, an adjustable way of processing and generating information in order to switch between different approaches or perspectives (Nijstad, De Dreu, Rietzschel, & Baas, 2010). Generally, this is in line with the broaden-and-build theory of positive emotions (Fredrickson, 1998, 2001), which maintains that positive affect broadens the individual's scopes of attention and cognition and, therefore, helps them to put forth novel paths of thought and actions.

In their extensive overview on empirical research regarding the relationship between affect and creativity and innovation, Rank and Frese (2008) pointed out that experimental research by Isen and colleagues (e.g. Ashby, Isen, & Turken, 1999; Isen, 1993; Isen, Daubman, & Nowicki, 1987) provides comprehensive empirical support for the link between positive affect and creativity. Research based on field studies further substantiates these findings. For example, Amabile et al. (2005) analyzed within-person fluctuations in creativity with respect to long-time work tasks and found a linear positive relationship between positive affect and creativity. They proposed an organizational affect–creativity cycle drawing on Isen's work and on broaden-and-build theory (Frederickson, 1998, 2001). This cycle implies that positive affect facilitates cognitive variation, thereby initiating an incubation process that yields new associations. As a result, creativity evokes and may in turn provoke (further) affect or reaction from others.

In general, meta-analytic results supported the impact of positive affect on creativity. Baas et al. (2008) meta-analytically examined creativity as a function of specific affective states. Based on 66 reports with a total of 102 independent samples and about 7,000 research participants, their results imply that positive affect relates to higher levels of creativity than shown in affect-neutral controls ($r = .15$). This effect was more pronounced for experimental than for correlational studies. Interestingly, no significant differences between positive and negative affect were found. This result is in line with Davis (2009), whose meta-analysis also revealed that the effect of positive affect appears to be contingent on the referent affective state (neutral affective states, negative affective states). The results are based on 62 experimental and 10 nonexperimental studies and showed that the creativity-enhancing effects of positive affect are noticeably robust in relation to neutral affect ($d = .52$). Compared to negative affective states, however, creativity-enhancing effects of positive affect are smaller ($d = .18$). Additionally, Davis's (2009) results revealed that other factors such as affect intensity or affect attributions appear to moderate the affect–creativity relationship. For example, regarding affect attributions, the effect of positive affect on creativity depends on whether individuals are aware of the source of their affect. The effect is stronger when they are not aware of the affect's source.

Overall, the effect sizes are not as large as could have been expected. One possible explanation might be Baas et al.'s (2008) important observation that in order to predict creativity the activation of affect is at least as important as the valence of affect. Baas et al. (2008) highlighted that affective states can be distinguished with respect to hedonic tone, the level of activation, and their association with regulatory focus[1]. According to the authors, activation of affect refers to the individual's level of arousal. Specifically, moderate levels of arousal help individuals to search and integrate information and take into account various alternatives. The authors indicate that creativity is enhanced most by activating positive affective states that are associated with an approach motivation and promotion focus (e.g. happiness).

On the basis of those findings, within the last ten years, research concentrating on the role of affect activation has expanded tremendously, and new theoretical approaches have been developed. In particular, the dual pathway to creativity model (De Dreu, Baas, & Nijstad, 2008) appears to be seminal within the abovementioned research trend on affect activation. According to this model, creativity can be facilitated in qualitatively different ways: through a cognitive flexibility route, through a persistence route, or through both. The cognitive flexibility route involves surveying *many* conceptual categories, whereas the persistence route involves surveying *fewer* categories in greater depth (Nijstad et al., 2010). In a nutshell, the dual pathway model assumes that the activation of affect determines whether creativity occurs or not, whereas the valence of affect determines the relevant pathway (flexibility vs. persistence) for creativity to occur. For example, positive affect such as happiness increases flexibility while negative affect, such as anger, increases persistence. Thus, affect activation and valence interact to promote creativity. Specifically, the authors argue that activating affective states (e.g. being angry, being happy) foster creative fluency and originality, in contrast with deactivating affective states (e.g. being sad, being relaxed).

Empirical evidence for the dual pathway model's assumptions was found in several studies. For example, De Dreu and colleagues (2008) found that activating affect with a positive tone fosters

[1] Regulatory focus theory (Higgins, 1997) considers the motivational aspects of self-regulation and builds on the assumption that there are "different ways of approaching different types of desired end-states" (p. 1281). Those end-states involve aspects such as advancements and growth on the one hand, and aspects such as obligations and protection on the other hand. Referring to these convergent states, regulatory focus theory distinguishes two perspectives of individual self-regulation, namely promotion focus and prevention focus. According to Higgins (1997), individuals with a chronic promotion focus have a strong need for growth or change, and are strongly guided by their ideals. In contrast, individuals with a chronic prevention focus have a strong need for security and are guided by their obligations. Taken together, each regulatory focus influences distinct processing strategies (Friedman & Förster, 2001).

creative fluency and originality because of greater cognitive flexibility. They conducted a meta-analysis based on twenty studies of their research group and confirmed the assumption that positive activating affect (happiness, elation) enhances creativity via the flexibility pathway.

To, Fisher, Ashkanasy, and Rowe (2012) also built on De Dreu et al.'s (2008) suggestion that affect activation and affect valence interact to promote creativity and found that individuals' creative process engagement was higher during activating positive (e.g. being exited) and activating negative (e.g. being angry) affect in comparison to positive as well as negative deactivating affect (e.g. being relaxed, being discouraged).

Hirt, Devers, and McCrea (2008) also referred to the dual pathway framework to identify mechanisms behind the relationship between positive affect and cognitive flexibility. They conducted three experimental studies in order to examine the possibility that hedonic contingency theory (Hirt, Levine, McDonald, Melton, & Martin, 1997) may be an important mechanism underlying the relationship between positive affect and cognitive flexibility. This theory assumes that positive affect is more prone to be reduced by specific tasks than negative affect and, therefore, happy individuals consider possible (hedonic) consequences of their actions. Thus, the enhanced cognitive flexibility of happy individuals may be due to their strong efforts to maintain or even enhance their happiness. Hirt et al.'s (1997, 2008) research provides support for the assumptions of hedonic contingency theory. One principal finding was that happy study participants being confronted with an affect-threatening task were able to protect their positive affect and transformed the task in a creative way. As a result, they maintained their positive affect as well as their interest in the task.

In sum, creativity research has concentrated on the valence of affect for decades, whereas recent research additionally sheds light on the relevance of affect activation. In general, researchers agree that positive affect fosters creativity (e.g. Baas et al. 2008; Davis, 2009). However, research efforts that have been made especially in the last ten years suggest that particularly activating positive affect leads to increased cognitive flexibility in working on a creative task. This flexibility "represents the possibility of achieving creative insights, problem solutions, or ideas through the use of broad and inclusive cognitive categories, through flexible switching among categories, approaches, and sets, and through the use of remote (rather than close) associations" (Nijstad et al., 2010, p. 43). Thus, when positive affect is activating, specific cognitive processes can unfold, which in turn lead to a high level of creativity.

Considerably less research effort has been made with regard to the relationship between affect and innovation. However, there is no reason why affect should matter only with regard to idea generation, given that idea implementation is also accompanied by affective states. In general, in their review, Rank and Frese (2008) suggest that the implementation of an idea often involves the need to overcome barriers such as change resistance, which gives rise to such affects as anger or anxiety. Moreover, a successful product launch is likely to evoke positive affect sucsh as joy, pride, or relief, whereas a failed product realization may yield frustration. Thus Rank and Frese (2008) argue that positive affect fosters innovation as well as creativity. According to the authors, variables such as control, self-efficacy, and organizational commitment can also be regarded as affect-related predictors of innovation. For example, the affective component of organizational commitment "refers to employees' emotional attachment to, identification with, and involvement in, the organization" (Allen & Meyer, 1990, p. 1). Consequently, organizational commitment includes the positive feeling that it is a pleasure to be part of a specific organization and thus enhances the individual's motivation to be involved and to initiate changes within this organization. Rank and Frese (2008) also reviewed studies with dependent variables related to innovation. For example, they referred to George and Brief (1992), who assumed organizational spontaneity to be fostered by positive affect. Accordingly, organizational spontaneity may be important for innovation, as it includes relevant behaviors such as making constructive suggestions. Moreover, Rank and Frese (2008) highlight the role of positive affect for innovation negotiations: "Individuals in a positive mood are more likely to formulate optimistic expectations, to use more cooperative bargaining strategies and to actually produce more successful negotiation outcomes" (p. 107). Thus, positive affect and affect-related constructs can be assumed to foster specific behaviors relevant to innovation.

As innovation is assumed to be crucial for success in new ventures, the entrepreneurship literature may also provide further evidence regarding the benefits of affect for innovation. Baron and Tang (2011), for example, proposed that entrepreneurs' dispositional positive affect is related to their creativity, which in turn relates to firm-level innovation. These relationships are stronger in dynamic than in stable environments. The researchers' assumptions were supported by the results of a field study among entrepreneurs.

Results provided by Foo, Uy, and Baron (2009) can also be applied to innovation. They assumed and found that positive affect fosters efforts on venture tasks that go beyond what is immediately required. They argued that positive affect influences future-oriented thinking that may lead to extra efforts as it induces proactive behaviors. Such proactive behaviors may play an important role for innovation, as they require anticipating future events or outcomes.

To conclude, previous research reveals that positive affect is beneficial for creativity as well as for innovation or innovation-related behavior. However, compared with creativity, substantially fewer efforts have been made to precisely examine the relationship between positive affect and innovation.

Negative Affect and Its Impact on Creativity and Innovation

As pointed out above, a large body of research supports the view that positive affect facilitates creativity and innovation. However, effects regarding the relationship between negative affect and creativity are less conclusive. Lindebaum and Jordan (2017) have stated that generally, many organizational researchers assume that negative feelings bring on negative results. In line with that, several creativity researchers have postulated that negative affect inhibits creative outcomes (e.g. Isen et al., 1987; Lyubomirsky, King, & Diener, 2005). One of the most common explanations for this argument is that negative affect reduces cognitive flexibility (e.g. Isen, 1999; Isen et al., 1987). Drawing on Beal, Weiss, Barros, and MacDermid (2005), another reason could be that negative affect "redirect[s] the attentional focus from the task to the circumstances" (p. 1059) and thus depletes cognitive resources, which are needed for creative performance. Within this perspective, negative affect is seen as a distraction from the task and, thus, as discouraging and interfering with creativity (To, Fisher, & Ashkanasy, 2015). Meta-analytic results by Baas et al. (2008) tentatively imply that (in correlational studies) negative affect tends to relate to less creativity than affect-neutral controls ($r = -.08$).

Nevertheless, some researchers found exceptions to the proposed general pattern that positive affect enhances creativity and negative affect impedes it, providing evidence that negative affect facilitates creativity under certain circumstances (e.g. George & Zhou, 2002, 2007; Kaufmann & Vosburg, 1997, 2002). Within these studies, negative affect is not seen as a distraction from creativity, but as an important signal that something has gone wrong and must be corrected immediately. This is in line with the feelings-as-information perspective (Schwarz, 1990, 2001) and the mood-as-input model (e.g. Martin, Ward, Achee, & Wyer, 1993), both assuming that affective states provide informational cues: positive affect signals good progress, whereas negative affect signals that more efforts are necessary. Thus, according to this theoretical perspective, individuals use affect to evaluate their level of goal attainment and work harder when they experience negative affect. This may also involve an increased search for creative solutions.

The assumptions of the mood-as-input model are also reflected in the dual pathway model (De Dreu et al., 2008). As highlighted earlier, the model assumes that negative affect results in increased persistence, which in turn leads to creative solutions (persistence pathway). However, De Dreu and colleagues (2008) specify that this is the case only for activating affect. Thus, unlike the flexibility pathway, the persistence pathway describes how creativity is achieved through hard work as well as through systematic and in-depth exploration of only a few categories or possibilities (Nijstad et al., 2010).

Laboratory studies by De Dreu et al. (2008) and Nijstad et al. (2010) supported the notion that creativity is fostered by negative activating affect. De Dreu and colleagues (2008) found that activating affect with a negative tone fosters creative fluency and originality because it evokes greater persistence. Similarly, Nijstad and colleagues (2010) presented evidence that negative activating affect (e.g. anger, fear) enhances creativity via the persistence route, based on a meta-analysis of 20 studies conducted in their research group.

In line with affect activation research, Baas, De Dreu, and Nijstad (2011a) examined experimentally whether anger (negative, activating affect with promotion focus) fosters creativity. Their results implied that compared to sadness (negative, deactivating affect with promotion focus) and affect-neutral states, anger results in more creativity. However, angry individuals experienced a greater decline in creative productivity over time than individuals who are in a sad or affect-neutral state. The authors suggested that this decline is caused by resources depletion, inasmuch as angry individuals use their energy for creative production early on, but they tire faster than sad or affect-neutral individuals, which in turn results in reduced creativity.

Despite the important insight that negative activating affect has the potential to foster creativity, until recently little was known about the conditions under which this relationship occurs. To et al. (2015) addressed this gap and examined possible moderators of the relationship between negative affect and creative process engagement. Their field data show that activating negative affect is positively related to creative process engagement when resources such as trait learning goal orientation and perceived psychological empowerment are both high. To et al. (2015) argue that under these conditions, individuals stay focused, persist, and are encouraged to try out new alternatives.

To conclude, there is still ongoing debate regarding the role of negative affect in creativity and innovation. The question remains whether negative affect fosters or hinders creativity. Generally, there is consensus that the impact of negative affect on creativity is more complex and difficult to predict than the impact of positive affect (Baas et al., 2011a). Research efforts that have been made in the last ten years suggest that in particular, activating negative affect can lead to increased cognitive energy and persistence in working on a task, and to increased creativity as a consequence.

There is only limited research focusing on the relationship between negative affect and innovation. As Rank and Frese (2008) pointed out, study results are inconclusive. On the one hand, there is research indicating that low levels of negative affect are conducive for innovation. For example, Rank and Frese (2008) referred to Howell and Shea (2001), who studied the behavior of innovation champions. Innovation champions are persons who informally promote innovation in organizations. Howell and Shea (2001) found that champion behavior was lower when innovation was framed as response to a threat. As threats are often linked to negative outcomes, a threat may also reflect negative affect.

On the other hand, there is also research indicating that higher levels of negative affect are conducive for innovation. As mentioned earlier, entrepreneurship research conducted by Foo et al. (2009) can also be applied to innovation and gives important insights. Drawing on Carver (2003) and the feelings-as-information perspective (Schwarz, 1990, 2001), Foo et al. argued that negative affect signals an inadequate progress toward goals or a current task, so that increased working efforts are necessary for goal attainment. Foo et al. (2009) assumed and found that negative affect was positively related to effort on venture tasks requiring immediate attention. Unexpectedly, negative affect was also positively related to venture efforts beyond what is immediately required. Hence, the authors suggested that negative affect signals that things are not going well in the venture and entrepreneurs may engage in future-oriented behaviors. Those behaviors may also be relevant for innovation.

In sum, extant research suggests that negative affect may be beneficial for creativity when it is activating. However, with respect to innovation as the outcome variable, there is little research examining whether the results of creativity research are transferrable to innovation outcomes.

Interactive and Dynamic Perspectives on Affect and Creativity

The research discussed in the preceding sections has shown that both positive and negative affect have the potential to enhance creativity and innovation. However, most of the research presented so far has focused on *either* positive *or* negative affect, independently. In contrast, in their comprehensive review on workplace affect and workplace creativity, James, Brodersen, and Eisenberg (2004) assumed that creativity may be fostered when positive and negative affective states occur together. Similarly, Amabile and colleagues (2005) underscored that the effects of positive affect and negative affect on creativity should not be regarded separately. In fact, the authors suggest that "simultaneously experiencing positive and negative emotions may serve to activate a greater number of memory nodes, thereby increasing both cognitive variability and creativity" (p. 372). They refer to this simultaneity of positive and negative affect as "affective ambivalence." However, Amabile et al. (2005) did not find empirical evidence for a relationship between affective ambivalence and creativity.

The effects of affective ambivalence on creativity were further studied by Fong (2006). She found that individuals who felt affectively ambivalent were better at recognizing unusual relationships between concepts, a skill that is considered to be relevant for bringing forth creative ideas. Further, individuals may interpret affective ambivalence as an unusual experience, which in turn enhances their sensitivity to unusual associations between apparently unrelated concepts as well as their creativity.

A concept similar to affective ambivalence is the positivity ratio: that is, the ratio of positive to negative affective states. Rego, Sousa, Marques, and Cunha (2012) argued that high positivity ratios "broaden the individual's momentary thought–action repertoire" (p. 262) and foster creative problem solving, but only up to a point. According to the authors, being too happy increases the risk of becoming complacent and overconfident in approaching problems, which may impede individuals' creative potential. Using field data, they found support for their assumptions: the results revealed an inverted U-shaped pattern for the relationship between positivity ratio and creativity.

In a similar vein, George and Zhou (2007) suggested that workers might experience high levels of both positive and negative affect at the same time. Therefore, they argued for taking positive as well as negative affect into account when studying behavior at work, and they drew on the feelings-as-information framework (Schwarz, 1990, 2001). For example, a negative affective state may signal that further efforts are needed to complete a creative task satisfactorily. George and Zhou (2007) assumed joint interactions between positive and negative affect in the context of creativity and developed a dual tuning perspective. According to this perspective, negative affect may promote opportunity identification and prompt people to work on solutions to change the status quo. Positive affect, on the other hand, fosters such aspects as confidence and divergent thinking. Thus, negative as well as positive affect may contribute to creative output "through their differential tuning effects" (George & Zhou, 2007, p. 607). The field study results provided by George and Zhou (2007) confirm the dual tuning perspective. They found that in a supportive context (e.g. developmental feedback provided by supervisors), positive and negative affect complement each other in contributing to creativity. Specifically, negative affect had the strongest positive relation to creativity when the context was supportive and when positive affect was high.

While the abovementioned studies suggest an interactive perspective on positive and negative affect and creativity, other researchers proposed dynamic approaches. For example, Akbari Chermahini and Hommel (2012) experimentally examined whether different types of cognitive processes (divergent vs. convergent thinking) might influence people's affect. They found that divergent thinking (i.e. generating many target-related responses) is related to a more positive affective state, while convergent thinking (i.e. focusing on one possible response) is related to a more negative affective state. According to the authors, this result underlines that convergent and divergent thinking support two different types of cognitive control: an exclusive control state tends to induce negative affect, whereas a distributed control state tends to induce positive affect. This research suggests that the relationship between affect and creativity is not unidirectional but rather reciprocal. However, we agree with Akbari Chermahini and Hommel (2012) that more research is necessary to understand the reciprocal and thus dynamic relationship between affect and cognition in greater detail.

A combination of interactions as well as temporal dynamics of positive affect, negative affect, and creativity was proposed by Bledow, Rosing, and Frese (2013). They addressed the limitations of the dual tuning model, arguing that it does not take into account the specific dynamics of positive and negative affect, especially the benefits of decreasing negative affect for creativity. They referred to personality systems interactions (PSI) theory (Kuhl, 2000, 2001) and its focus on affect changes, and they assumed a dynamic interplay of positive and negative affect in fostering creativity. They also built on the affective shift model of work engagement (Bledow, Schmitt, Frese, & Kühnel, 2011), which suggests that negative affect is positively related to work engagement, on the condition that negative affect is followed by positive affect. Accordingly, Bledow et al. (2013) proposed an affective shift model of creativity and argued that creativity is higher when negative affect is followed by a down-regulation of negative affect and an increase in positive affect. For example, an author quarreling with his editor about a creative ending to his latest book would do well to take a walk and try to shift attention to more positive things before sitting back down to continue writing. Bledow et al.'s (2013) assumption was supported in an experience-sampling study and in an experimental study. In line with PSI theory, the authors argued that the down-regulation of negative affect is assumed to facilitate new associations needed for idea development.

The conducive integration of positive and negative affect can be located within the dialectic perspective on innovation (Bledow, Frese, Anderson, Erez, & Farr, 2009), which assumes duality as a key psychological determinant of creativity and innovation. To date, creativity and innovation researchers concerned with affect interactions and dynamics have primarily focused on creativity as the outcome variable. The benefits of affect interactions and dynamics for innovation remain largely unexplored.

To sum up, a static perspective on affect appears to be insufficient to explain its impact on creativity and innovation. However, despite initial efforts to examine interactive and dynamic effects of positive and negative affect, this issue is a rather new development in the literature and requires further research.

Regulation of Affect and Its Impact on Creativity and Innovation

In addition to positive and negative affect, the regulation of affect is also relevant for creativity and innovation. Regulation strategies are of great relevance for goal attainment because affective states frequently result in a redirection of the attentional focus away from the task, which in most cases lowers performance (Beal et al., 2005). Accordingly, regulating (i.e. monitoring and influencing) affective states, which are related to creativity, "can make the difference between persisting or giving up on a project" (Ivcevic & Brackett, 2015, p. 480). Further, with respect to the dynamic perspective, regulation of affect is also relevant to maintaining balance between positive and negative affect (Bledow et al., 2013). This balance is of great importance in dealing with the complexity of creativity and innovation. However, despite the relevance of affect regulation, little is known so far about how the strategies that individuals use to actively monitor and influence their affective states are linked to creativity and innovation.

Some researchers have begun to examine possible conditions and mechanisms in the link between affect regulation ability and creativity. For example, Ivcevic and Bracket (2015) assessed the connection between openness to experience and the ability to regulate affect. They highlighted that openness to experience is the personality trait that is linked most consistently to creativity. Following McCrae (1994, 1996), they underlined that openness to experience includes such traits as seeking new experiences, imaginative thinking, or tolerance for ambiguity and is thus seen as a critical personality disposition for creativity. Ivcevic and Bracket (2015) assumed that the relationship between affect regulation ability and creativity is moderated by openness to experience, such that the relationship is stronger for individuals with a relatively high level of openness to experience. They argued that for individuals who do not like working on ideas and who prefer routine tasks (indicators of low openness to experience), creativity will be unlikely regardless of affect regulation ability. Further, they assumed that affect regulation ability helps individuals to maintain their passion for creative achievement and persistence in the task, as those forms of engagement with creative activity are vulnerable to being influenced by social forces such as evaluation and rewards. Thus the authors hypothesized that passion and persistence mediate the relationship between affect regulation ability and creativity for individuals with high openness to experience. Their hypotheses were largely supported within a field study among high school students.

Another approach to explaining how individuals actively monitor and influence their affective states is self-regulation theory, which emphasizes that change in affect may be needed to stay on the right track to reach a goal (Carver &

Scheier, 1990; Kuhl, 2000). Thus insights about how affect regulation may be linked to creativity and innovation can be drawn from the line of work that has linked self-regulation to creativity and innovation. According to Carver and Scheier (2011), the term "self-regulation" refers to cognitive processes applied by individuals to reach a certain purpose. These processes comprise "self-corrective adjustments" (p. 3), which emerge within a single person and which are needed to stay on the right track to reach a goal. This viewpoint builds on the assumption "that behavior is a continual process of moving toward (and sometimes away from) goal representations" (p. 3). Individual self-regulation can also be described as ongoing comparison between an existing state and a target state while a specific problem is being solved (see also the TOTE [test–operate–test–exit] unit; Miller, Galanter, & Pribram, 1960). For example, negative affect may be seen as an indicator for moving away from a specific goal representation, and thus self-regulatory efforts are needed to return to the right track (Carver, 2003).

Carver and Scheier (1981, 2011) argued that one central concept of self-regulation is feedback control. In line with this argument, De Stobbeleir et al. (2011) have examined the role of feedback seeking as a key self-regulation tactic of individuals to enhance their creative performance. The authors define "feedback seeking" as "individuals' proactive search for evaluative information about their performance" (p. 812). They argue that due to the chaotic nature of creative processes it is necessary for individuals to acquire feedback proactively, as managers do not always provide feedback at exactly the time when it is needed. Further, because creativity is seen as a social process, it is important for individuals to interact with others who may stimulate and support their creativity. Studying 456 supervisor–employee dyads from different organizations, De Stobbeleir et al. (2011) essentially found that feedback inquiry about job performance partially mediates the way cognitive style relates to perceived organizational support for creativity and supervisors' ratings of creative performance.

Although researchers have generally highlighted that affect regulation is of great relevance for creative performance, the relationship between affect regulation and creativity has not been studied in detail. Moreover, future research is necessary to examine innovation as the dependent variable. Specific insights about how affect regulation may be linked to creativity and innovation may be drawn from self-regulation research. Further, Gross's (1998) classic work on affect regulation may be a meaningful starting point for studying the influences of distinct types of affect regulation (e.g. modification of the situation, deployment of attention, change of cognitions) on creativity and innovation.

Conclusion and Research Directions

The research presented in this chapter has highlighted that creativity "appears to be an affectively charged event" (Amabile et al., 2005, p. 367). In particular during the last decade, considerable progress has been made in enhancing our understanding of how affect and affect-related variables positively or negatively impact organizational creativity.

Research on the role of positive affect suggests that activating positive affect fosters creativity as it leads to increased cognitive flexibility when working on creative tasks. Likewise, research on the role of negative affect reveals that activating negative affect is also beneficial for creativity as it leads to increased persistence when working on creative tasks. A few researchers have postulated that a focus on either positive or negative affect alone is not sufficient. For example, the "dynamic perspective on affect and creativity" (Bledow et al., 2013, p. 432) integrated both views and proposed a dynamic interplay of positive and negative affect in fostering creativity. Consequently, a static perspective on either positive or negative affect appears to be insufficient to explain the impact of affect on creativity within rapidly changing work environments as it does not take into account possible increases, decreases, and interactions of affect over time. However, such an integrative and interactive perspective offers vast potential for future research, especially because it addresses many limitations of preceding research. For example, it highlights the beneficial role of down-regulation of negative affect for creativity and, thus, the dynamic perspective also provides important insights concerning the role of affect regulation for creativity and innovation.

Another regulatory construct relevant for research on the relationship of affect to creativity and innovation is regulatory focus (Higgins, 1997). As mentioned before, regulatory focus theory distinguishes two self-regulatory foci: a promotion focus (e.g. need for growth and change) and a prevention focus (e.g. need for security). Although a vast body of research has linked regulatory focus theory to creativity and innovation, this line of research hardly receives any attention in affect research (for an exception see Baas et al., 2008). In general, study results indicate that both promotion focus and prevention focus have an effect on creative and innovative activities (e.g. Friedman & Förster, 2001; Herman & Reiter-Palmon, 2011; Lam & Chui, 2002). A promotion focus is associated with activities linked to creativity (e.g. idea generation), while a prevention focus is associated with activities linked to innovation (e.g. idea evaluation or implementation). Compared with prevention-focused individuals, promotion-focused individuals are assumed to have a greater tendency to show for example a risk-taking behavior or think divergently, which are both important strategies for creativity, but not for innovation. Contrarily, prevention-focused individuals are often assumed to have a greater tendency to show a rather careful and thorough behavior, which is essential for idea implementation activities, but not for idea generation activities.

A promising example for linking regulatory focus, affect, and creativity is the study provided by Baas, De Dreu, and Nijstad (2011b). The authors integrated research on the interplay of regulatory focus, affect, and activation with research on cognitive functions underlying creativity. They proposed and found that regulatory closure (whether or not a promotion or prevention goal is fulfilled) is a primary condition for the relationship between regulatory focus and creative performance and that affect activation has a mediating function. Specifically, the authors argue that unfulfilled goals result in enhanced activation as the motivation to fulfill a specific goal is maintained. This is the case for both promotion and prevention focus. However, the closure (i.e. fulfillment) of these goals has different effects for promotion and prevention focus. While promotion success activates and motivates the individual to engage in further goals or tasks, prevention success leads to deactivation, relief, and disengagement. In other words, when prevention goals are successfully regulated, the individual gets deactivated and less creative. By contrast, when prevention goals are unfulfilled, activation and alertness is maintained. Thus, contrary to what is often assumed, prevention focus states and promotion focus states can produce similar creativity levels. Taken together, future research on affect regulation and creativity and innovation may give more weight to insights from research on regulation of behavior (e.g. regulatory focus) because affect and behavior are closely interwoven constructs.

Compared with creativity, substantially fewer efforts have been made to precisely examine the affect–innovation relationship. Interestingly, this research gap mirrors a more general shortcoming within innovation research: there is a lack of knowledge about processes underlying idea implementation, while idea generation has been studied much more extensively. As it remains unclear whether the research results for creativity can be transferred to innovation, further research is needed, even though several studies presented in this chapter suggest that positive as well as negative affect influence innovation or at least innovation-related behavior. We hope that this chapter will assist future researchers to further develop this important field.

References

Akbari Chermahini, S., & Hommel, B. (2012). Creative mood swings: Divergent and convergent thinking affect mood in opposite ways. *Psychological Research*, *76*(5), 634–640. https://doi.org/10.1007/s00426-011–0358-z

Allen, N. J., & Meyer, J. P. (1990). The measurement and antecedents of affective, continuance and normative commitment to the organization. *Journal of Occupational Psychology*, *63*(1), 1–18. https://doi.org/10.1111/j.2044–8325.1990.tb00506.x

Amabile, T. M. (1983). The social psychology of creativity: A componential conceptualization. *Journal of Personality and Social Psychology*, *45* (2), 357–376. https://doi.org/10.1037/0022–3514.45.2.357

Amabile, T. M. (1988). A model of creativity and innovation in organizations. In B. M. Stew & L. L. Cummings (Eds.), *Research in organizational behavior* (Volume 10, pp. 123–167). Greenwich, CT: JAI.

Amabile, T. M. (1996). *Creativity in context: Update to "The social psychology of creativity."* Boulder, CO: Westview.

Amabile, T. M., Barsade, S. G., Mueller, J. S., & Staw, B. M. (2005). Affect and creativity at work. *Administrative Science Quarterly*, *50*(3), 367–403. https://doi.org/10.2189/asqu.2005.50.3.367

Anderson, N., Potočnik, K., & Zhou, J. (2014). Innovation and creativity in organizations: A state-of-the-science review, prospective commentary, and guiding framework. *Journal of Management*, *40*(5), 1297–1333. https://doi.org/10.1177/0149206314527128

Ashby, F. G., Isen, A. M., & Turken, A. U. (1999). A neuropsychological theory of positive affect and its influence on cognition. *Psychological Review*, *106*(3), 529–550. https://doi.org/10.1037/0033-295X.106.3.529

Baas, M., De Dreu, C. K. W., & Nijstad, B. A. (2008). A meta-analysis of 25 years of mood-creativity research: Hedonic tone, activation, or regulatory focus? *Psychological Bulletin*, *134*(6), 779–806. https://doi.org/10.1037/a0012815

Baas, M., De Dreu, C. K., & Nijstad, B. A. (2011a). Creative production by angry people peaks early on, decreases over time, and is relatively unstructured. *Journal of Experimental Social Psychology*, *47*(6), 1107–1115. https://doi.org/10.1016/j.jesp.2011.05.009

Baas, M., De Dreu, C. K., & Nijstad, B. A. (2011b). When prevention promotes creativity: The role of mood, regulatory focus, and regulatory closure. *Journal of Personality and Social Psychology*, *100* (5), 794–809. https://doi.org/10.1037/a0022981

Baron, R. A., & Tang, J. (2011). The role of entrepreneurs in firm-level innovation: Joint effects of positive affect, creativity, and environmental dynamism. *Journal of Business Venturing*, *26*(1), 49–60. https://doi.org/10.1016/j.jbusvent.2009.06.002

Beal, D. J., Weiss, H. M., Barros, E., & MacDermid, S. M. (2005). An episodic process model of affective influences on performance. *Journal of Applied Psychology*, *90*(6), 1054–1068. https://doi.org/10.1037/0021–9010.90.6.1054

Bledow, R., Frese, M., Anderson, N. R., Erez, M., & Farr, J. L. (2009). A dialectic perspective on innovation: Conflicting demands, multiple pathways, and ambidexterity. *Industrial and Organizational Psychology*, *2*(3), 305–337. https://doi.org/10.1111/j.1754–9434.2009.01154.x

Bledow, R., Rosing, K., & Frese, M. (2013). A dynamic perspective on affect and creativity. *Academy of Management Journal*, *56*(2), 432–450. https://doi.org/10.5465/amj.2010.0894

Bledow, R., Schmitt, A., Frese, A., & Kühnel, J. (2011). The affective shift model of work engagement. *Journal of Applied Psychology*, *96*(6), 1246–1257. https://doi.org/10.1037/a0024532

Brief, A. P., & Weiss, H. M. (2002). Organizational behavior: Affect in the workplace. *Annual Review of Psychology*, *53*, 279–307. https://doi.org/10.1146/annurev.psych.53.100901.135156

Carver, C. S. (2003). Pleasure as a sign you can attend to something else: Placing positive feelings within a general model of affect. *Cognition and Emotion*,

17(2), 241–261. https://doi.org/10.1080/02699930302294

Carver, C. S., & Scheier, M. F. (1981). *Attention and self-regulation: A control-theory approach to human behavior*. New York: Springer.

Carver, C. S., & Scheier, M. F. (1990). Origins and functions of positive and negative affect: A control-process view. *Psychological Review, 97*(1), 19–35. https://doi.org/10.1037/0033-295X.97.1.19

Carver, C. S., & Scheier, M. F. (2011). Self-regulation of action and affect. In K. D. Vohs & R. F. Baumeister (Eds.), *Handbook of self-regulation: Research, theory, and applications* (Volume 2, pp. 3–21). New York, NY: Guilford.

Davis, M. A. (2009). Understanding the relationship between mood and creativity: A meta-analysis. *Organizational Behavior and Human Decision Processes*, *108*(1), 25–38. https://doi.org/10.1016/j.obhdp.2008.04.001

De Dreu, C. K., Baas, M., & Nijstad, B. A. (2008). Hedonic tone and activation level in the mood-creativity link: Toward a dual pathway to creativity model. *Journal of Personality and Social Psychology, 94*(5), 739–756. https://doi.org/10.1037/0022–3514.94.5.739

De Stobbeleir, K. E. M., Ashford, S. J., & Buyens, D. (2011). Self-regulation of creativity at work: The role of feedback-seeking behavior in creative performance. *Academy of Management Journal, 54*(4), 811–831. https://doi.org/10.5465/amj.2011.64870144

Fong, C. T. (2006). The effects of emotional ambivalence on creativity. *Academy of Management Journal*, *49*(5), 1016–1030. https://doi.org/10.5465/amj.2006.22798182

Foo, M.-D., Uy, M. A., & Baron, R. A. (2009). How do feelings influence effort? An empirical study of entrepreneurs' affect and venture effort. *Journal of Applied Psychology, 94*(4), 1086–1094. https://doi.org/10.1037/a0015599

Frederickson, B. L. (1998). What good are positive emotions? *Review of General Psychology, 2*(3), 300–319. https://doi.org/10.1037/1089–2680.2.3.300

Frederickson, B. L. (2001). The role of positive emotions in positive psychology. *American Psychologist, 56*(3), 218–226. https://doi.org/10.1037/0003-066X.56.3.218

Friedman, R. S., & Förster, J. (2001). The effects of promotion and prevention cues on creativity. *Journal of Personality and Social Psychology, 81*(6), 1001–1013. https://doi.org/10.1037//0022–3514.81.6.1001

George, J. M., & Brief, A. P. (1992). Feeling good – doing good: A conceptual analysis of the mood at work–organizational spontaneity relationship. *Psychological Bulletin, 112*(2), 310–329. https://doi.org/10.1037/0033–2909.112.2.310

George, J. M. & Zhou, J. (2002). Understanding when bad moods foster creativity and good ones don't: The role of context and clarity of feelings. *Journal of Applied Psychology, 87*(4), 687–697. https://doi.org/10.1037/0021–9010.87.4.687

George, J. M. & Zhou, J. (2007). Dual tuning in a supportive context: Joint contributions of positive mood, negative mood, and supervisory behaviors to employee creativity. *Academy of Management Journal, 50*(3), 605–622. https://doi.org/10.5465/amj.2007.25525934

Gross, J. J. (1998). The emerging field of emotion regulation: An integrative review. *Review of General Psychology, 2*(3), 271–299. https://doi.org/10.1037/1089–2680.2.3.271

Gross, J. J. (2015). Emotion regulation: Current status and future prospects. *Psychological Inquiry, 26*(1), 1–26. https://doi.org/10.1080/1047840X.2014.940781

Herman, A., & Reiter-Palmon, R. (2011). The effect of regulatory focus on idea generation and idea evaluation. *Psychology of Aesthetics, Creativity, and the Arts*, *5*(1), 13–20. https://doi.org/10.1037/a0018587

Higgins, E. T. (1997). Beyond pleasure and pain. *American Psychologist, 52*(12), 1280–1300. https://doi.org/10.1037/0003-066X.52.12.1280

Hirt, E. R., Devers, E. E., & McCrea, S. M. (2008). I want to be creative: Exploring the role of hedonic contingency theory in the positive mood–cognitive flexibility link. *Journal of Personality and Social Psychology, 94*(2), 214–230. https://doi.org/10.1037/0022–3514.94.2.94.2.214

Hirt, E. R., Levine, G., McDonald, H., Melton, R., & Martin, L. L. (1997). The role of mood in quantitative and qualitative aspects of performance: Single or multiple mechanisms? *Journal of Experimental Social Psychology*, *33*(6), 602–629. https://doi.org/10.1006/jesp.1997.1335

Howell, J. M., & Shea, C. M. (2001). Individual differences, environmental scanning, innovation framing, and champion behavior: Key predictors of project performance. *Journal of Product Innovation Management*, *18*(1), 15–27. https://doi.org/10.1111/1540–5885.1810015

Isen, A. M. (1993). Positive affect and decision making. In M. Lewis & J. M. Haviland (Eds.), *Handbook of emotions* (pp. 261–277). New York, NY: Guilford.

Isen, A. M. (1999). Positive affect. In T. Dalgleish & M. J. Power (Eds.), *Handbook of cognition and emotion* (pp. 521–539). New York, NY: Wiley.

Isen, A. M., Daubman, K. A., & Nowicki, G. P. (1987). Positive affect facilitates creative problem solving. *Journal of Personality and Social Psychology*, *52* (6), 1122–1131. https://doi.org/10.1037/0022–3514.52.6.1122

Ivcevic, Z., & Brackett, M. A. (2015). Predicting creativity: Interactive effects of openness to experience and emotion regulation ability. *Psychology of Aesthetics, Creativity, and the Arts*, *9* (4), 480–487. https://doi.org/10.1037/a0039826

James, K., Brodersen, M., & Eisenberg, J. (2004). Workplace affect and workplace creativity: A review and preliminary model. *Human Performance*, *17*(2), 169–194. https://doi.org/10.1207/s15327043hup1702_3

Kaufmann, G. (2003). The effect of mood on creativity in the innovation process. In L. V. Shavinina (Ed.), *The international handbook on innovation* (pp. 191–203). Oxford, UK: Elsevier Science.

Kaufmann, G., & Vosburg, S. K. (1997). "Paradoxical" mood effects on creative problem-solving. *Cognition & Emotion*, *11*(2), 151–170. https://doi.org/10.1080/026999397379971

Kaufmann, G., & Vosburg, S. K. (2002). The effects of mood on early and late idea production. *Creativity Research Journal*, *14*(3–4), 317–330. https://doi.org/10.1207/S15326934CRJ1434_3

Kuhl, J. (2000). A functional-design approach to motivation and self-regulation: The dynamics of personality systems interactions. In M. Boekaerts, P. R. Pintrich, & M. Zeidner (Eds.), *Handbook of self-regulation* (pp. 111–169). San Diego, CA: Academic.

Kuhl, J. (2001). *Motivation und Persönlichkeit: Interaktionen psychischer Systeme* [Motivation and personality: Interactions of psychological systems]. Göttingen, Germany: Hogrefe.

Lam, T. W. H., & Chiu, C. Y. (2002). The motivational function of regulatory focus on creativity. *Journal of Creative Behavior*, *36*(2), 138–150. https://doi.org/10.1002/j.2162–6057.2002.tb01061.x

Lindebaum, D., & Jordan, P. J. (2014). When it can be good to feel bad and bad to feel good: Exploring asymmetries in workplace emotional outcomes. *Human Relations*, *67*(9), 1037–1050. https://doi.org/10.1177/0018726714535824

Lyubomirsky, S., King, L., & Diener, E. (2005). The benefits of frequent positive affect: Does happiness lead to success? *Psychological Bulletin*, *131*(6), 803–855. https://doi.org/10.1037/0033–2909.131.6.803

Martin, L. L., Ward, D. W., Achee, J. W., & Wyer, R. S. (1993). Mood as input: People have to interpret the motivational implications of their moods. *Journal of Personality and Social Psychology*, *64*(3), 317–326. https://doi.org/10.1037/0022–3514.64.3.317

McCrae, R. R. (1994). Openness to experience: Expanding the boundaries of Factor V. *European Journal of Personality*, *8*(4), 251–272. https://doi.org/10.1002/per.2410080404

McCrae, R. R. (1996). Social consequences of experiential openness. *Psychological Bulletin*, *120* (3), 323–337. https://doi.org/10.1037/0033–2909.120.3.323

Miller, G. A., Galanter, E., & Pribram, K. H. (1960). *Plans and the structure of behavior*. New York, NY: Holt, Rinehart & Winston.

Mumford, M. D. (2003). Where have we been, where are we going? Taking stock in creativity research. *Creativity Research Journal*, *15*(2–3), 107–120. https://doi.org/10.1080/10400419.2003.9651403

Nijstad, B. A., De Dreu, C. K. W., Rietzschel, E. F., & Baas, M. (2010). The dual pathway to creativity model: Creative ideation as a function of flexibility and persistence. *European Review of Social Psychology*, *21*(1), 34–77. https://doi.org/10.1080/10463281003765323

Rank, J., & Frese, M. (2008). The impact of emotions, moods and other affect-related variables on creativity, innovation and initiative. In N. Ashkanasy & C. L. Cooper (Eds.), *Research companion to emotion in organizations* (pp. 103–119). Cheltenham, UK: Edward Elgar.

Rego, A., Sousa, F., Marques, C., & Cunha, M. P. E. (2012). Optimism predicting employees' creativity: The mediating role of positive affect and the positivity ratio. *European Journal of Work and Organizational Psychology*, *21*(2), 244–270. https://doi.org/10.1080/1359432X.2010.550679

Schwarz, N. (1990). Feelings-as-information: Informational and motivational functions of affective states. In E. T. Higgins & R. M. Sorrentino (Eds.), *Handbook of motivation and cognition: Foundations of social behavior* (Volume 2, pp. 527–561). New York, NY: Guilford.

Schwarz, N. (2001). Feelings-as-information: Implications for affective influences on information processing. In L. L. Martin & G. L. Clore (Eds.), *Theories of mood and cognition: A user's guidebook* (pp. 159–176). Mahwah, NJ: Lawrence Erlbaum.

To, M. L., Fisher, C. D., & Ashkanasy, N. M. (2015). Unleashing angst: Negative mood, learning goal orientation, psychological empowerment and creative behaviour. *Human Relations*, *68*(10), 1601–1622. https://doi.org/10.1177/0018726714562235

To, M. L., Fisher, C. D., Ashkanasy, N. M., & Rowe, P. A. (2012). Within-person relationships between mood and creativity. *Journal of Applied Psychology*, *97*(3), 599–612. https://doi.org/10.1037/a0026097

Weiss, H., & Cropanzano, R. (1996). Affective events theory: A theoretical discussion of the structure, causes and consequences of affective experiences at work. In B. M. Staw & L. L. Cummings (Eds.), *Research in organizational behavior* (Volume 18, pp. 1–74). Greenwich, CT: JAI.

West, M. A., & Farr, J. L. (1990). Innovation at work. In M. A. West & J. L. Farr (Eds.), *Innovation and creativity at work: Psychological and organizational strategies* (pp. 3–13). Chichester, UK: John Wiley & Sons.

11 Emotional Labor

Display Rules and Emotion Regulation at Work

Alicia A. Grandey, Katelyn E. England, and Louis Boemerman

Emotional labor continues to gain popular media interest (Ben-Achour, 2015; Levy, 2018) and scholarly interest (Grandey, Diefendorff, & Rupp, 2013; Hülsheger & Schewe, 2011). Emotional labor is when employees manage emotions as part of a work role (Hochschild, 1983), such as a service provider's cheery greeting to customers or a therapists' suppression of shock at their client's secrets. Prototypically, emotional labor is performed during interactions with the public, by service employees who are selected for and/or trained in emotional displays with links to financial or professional gains (Grandey, Diefendorff, et al., 2013; Hochschild, 1983), though this conceptualization is broadening to include coworkers and leader–follower interactions. The potential trade-off between the performance goals of the organization and the employees' well-being is central to the study of emotional labor.

In this chapter, we provide a focused summary of the two dominant approaches to emotional labor: *display rules*, or the emotional job expectations that vary by occupation or target, and *emotion regulation*, or the effortful strategies to conform to those expectations that vary by person and events (Brotheridge & Grandey, 2002; Grandey, Diefendorff, et al., 2013). For each of these two approaches, we review the *construct* (i.e. the definition, dimensions and common measures), the *consequences* (i.e. the evidence for how the concept is associated with performance and well-being), and the *context* (i.e. the personal and situational antecedents and moderators of outcomes). Our purpose is to provide a broad overview for new scholars; for detail about theoretical mechanisms and future directions, please see previously published reviews (Grandey & Gabriel, 2015; Grandey & Melloy, 2017; Mallory & Rupp, 2017), books (Grandey, Diefendorff, et al., 2013), and meta-analyses (Hülsheger & Schewe, 2011; Kammeyer-Mueller et al., 2013; Mesmer-Magnus, DeChurch, & Wax, 2012).

Display Rules: Emotional Labor as Work Role Expectations

Display Rules: Construct

Emotional display rules are communicated through formal policies and practices (i.e. recruitment, selection, training, performance monitoring) and informal norms and socialization (i.e. climate, culture) (Gabriel, Cheshin, Moran, & Van Kleef, 2016; Pugh, Diefendorff, & Moran, 2013). Display rules act as goals for work behaviors: if the internal state is discrepant from the display rule, employees are motivated to regulate their expressions (Diefendorff & Gosserand, 2003), especially if there are practices (i.e. rewards and consequences) that make one committed to the goal (Gosserand & Diefendorff, 2005).

Types and Dimensions of Display Rules

There are three main types of display rules studied in the literature: *integrative* display rules for positive emotions (e.g. happiness and compassion, as expected in service, healthcare, and education) (Barsade & O'Neill, 2014; Brotheridge & Grandey, 2002); *differentiating* display rules for negative emotions (e.g. anger and contempt, as expected in bill collectors, the military, and police interrogators) (Rafaeli & Sutton, 1991); and *neutralizing* display rules that convey rationality (e.g. as expected in judges and doctors) (Ashforth & Humphrey, 1995). The vast majority of this research has focused on integrative display rules to "show positive" and "hide negative" (Diefendorff & Richard, 2003; Kammeyer-Mueller et al., 2013). In contrast, organizations may lack display rules and encourage authentic emotional expression (Christoforou & Ashforth, 2015; Goldberg & Grandey, 2007; Grandey, Foo, Groth, & Goodwin, 2012). Parke and Seo (2017) provide a taxonomy of "affective climates," crossing emotional valence (positive to negative) with authenticity (high to low) to produce four main types of display rules across organizations.

An important question for emotional display rules is whether they are unique job requirements (in-role), or voluntary prosocial behaviors such as citizenship behavior (extra-role). In the first study to test this idea, the majority of the working student respondents (> 90 percent) endorsed integrative emotional displays as "in-role" (Diefendorff, Richard, & Croyle, 2006), especially when the job involved interacting with customers or other employees. However, this could be due to the types of jobs held by a student sample. Results of a follow-up study with full-time working adults (Grandey, Diefendorff, Grabarek, & Diamond, 2009) are shown in Table 11.1. Integrative displays with customers were endorsed as in-role by a smaller majority than the prior study

Table 11.1 Comparing in-role requirements for emotional displays and citizenship behaviors by target and occupation

		Customers		Coworkers	
Occupation	*n*	Emotional displays	Service citizenship	Emotional displays	Organizational citizenship
Customer service	64	67.7	76.9	36.1	29.3
Sales/retail	32	65.1	71.2	38.4	36.0
Healthcare	43	70.0	84.1	32.9	32.1
Education	34	54.8	78.2	26.7	10.0
Admin/clerical	46	63.2	78.8	33.1	35.5
Technical/financial	31	54.9	76.9	33.1	30.2
Physical labor	9	42.8	65.6	13.3	19.8
Supervisor/leader	27	49.6	61.8	37.8	30.3
Overall	**286**	**58.51**^{a}	**74.19**^{b}	**31.43**^{c}	**27.90**^{c}

Notes: Values indicate percentage of respondents endorsing the behavior as an in-role requirement (1) instead of extra-role or irrelevant (0). In bottom row, superscript values that are different are significantly different from each other. Sample consisted of working non-student respondents (55.6% female) who worked more than 20 hours a week and had at least some interaction with customers and coworkers (Grandey et al., 2009). **Emotional displays** measured with 6 items: showing enthusiasm/friendliness/concern and hiding stress/disappointment/frustration. **Service citizenship** measured with 5 items: Bettencourt, L. A., Gwinner, K. P., & Meuter, M. L. (2001). A comparison of attitude, personality, and knowledge predictors of service-oriented organizational citizenship behaviors. *Journal of Applied Psychology, 86*(1), 29–41. **Organizational citizenship** measured with 5 items: Williams, L. J., & Anderson, S. E. (1991). Job satisfaction and organizational commitment as predictors of organizational citizenship and in-role behaviors. *Journal of Management, 17*(3), 601–617.

(58.51 percent) and more likely in "people work" occupations than other occupations (e.g. healthcare 70 percent; see Table 11.1). Further, when the target was a coworker, positive displays were less in-role (31.43 percent), similar to citizenship behavior (27.9 percent). This supports the supposition that those in "people work" occupations and interactions with customers uniquely see emotions as part of the job, rather than as voluntary prosocial behavior.

Multiple Levels and Measurement of Display Rules

These display rules emerge from multiple sources and have been studied at different levels of analysis. See Table 11.2 for example measures. The most common approach is *individual perceptions* – the extent employees believe that they are expected to show positive or hide negative at work – which is a function of the employee's personality, relationship to the target, and contextual situation (Kammeyer-Mueller et al., 2013). Display rules can also be assessed at the *job or occupational level*, sometimes by aggregating individual perceptions (see Table 11.1; Brotheridge & Grandey, 2002). To obtain display rules without relying on self-reported perceptions, researchers use the public database O*Net (www.onetonline.org/), which provides incumbent ratings for the emotional demands and activities for specific job titles (Bhave & Glomb, 2016; Glomb, Kammeyer-Mueller, & Rotundo, 2004; Grandey, Chi, & Diamond, 2013; Grandey, Kern, & Frone, 2007).

Display rules have also been manipulated in the lab: participants are instructed to follow positive display rules or negative display rules (Bono & Vey, 2007) or neutral display rules (Trougakos, Jackson, & Beal, 2011), or to display autonomy (Goldberg & Grandey, 2007), and then asked to perform a work simulation. Finally, display rules can occur at the *group or organizational* level. In one early example of this approach, Diefendorff and colleagues (2011) found that hospital nurses had shared perceptions of integrative display rules that differed in strength across departments. Other field studies found that work units shared perceptions of norms for authenticity (Grandey et al., 2012) and the explicitness of display rules (Christoforou & Ashforth, 2015).

Display Rules: Consequences

Job Performance

Positive display rules guide employee behavior toward the desired standard (Diefendorff & Gosserand, 2003) and are linked to effective interpersonal performance (Christoforou & Ashforth, 2015; Goldberg & Grandey, 2007; Trougakos et al., 2011). Negative display rules are more rare, though displays of contempt (Melwani & Barsade, 2011) or anger (van Kleef, De Dreu, & Manstead, 2004) can increase status and influence others. While display rules direct emotional behavior, they can reduce attention to other behaviors. Positive display rules resulted in more errors compared to display autonomy (Goldberg & Grandey, 2007) and neutralizing display rules reduced task persistence compared to positive display rules (Trougakos et al., 2011). In a field study of retail stores, display rules had an inverted-U effect, such that more controlling rules were correlated with less voluntary citizenship behavior and poorer sales performance (Christoforou & Ashforth, 2015).

Strain and Well-Being

In general, perceptions of "hide negative" display rules are linked to negative affect and strain whereas positive display rules have a more mixed result (Diefendorff & Richard, 2003; Kammeyer-Mueller et al., 2013). Positive display rules reduce expressive autonomy and authenticity (Grandey, Rupp, & Brice, 2015) but are positively linked to job satisfaction (Brotheridge & Grandey, 2002; Diefendorff et al., 2011) and vigor (Bhave & Lefter, 2017). In fact, positive display rules improved moods and job satisfaction compared to neutralizing display rules

Table 11.2 Examples of emotional labor measures: emotional display rules and emotion regulation

	Source examples	Item examples
Display rules		
Employee perceptions – integrative display rules	**Emotional work requirements**: Best, Downey & Jones (1997) in Brotheridge & Grandey (2002) Show positive and hide negative display rules: Diefendorff, Croyle, & Gosserand (2005)	My organization expects me to . . . . . . reassure people who are distressed or upset. . . . express feelings of sympathy. . . . hide my disgust over something someone has done.
Employee perceptions – discrete emotions	**Display rule assessment inventory**: Diefendorff & Gregarus (2009), response categories from "suppress emotion" to "amplify emotion"	When I feel <insert emotion>, I . . . . . . express my feelings, but with more intensity than my true feelings. . . . express my feelings with no inhibitions. . . . express my feelings, but with less intensity than my true feelings. . . . remain neutral and express nothing.
Group perceptions	**Explicitness of display rules**: Christoforou & Ashforth (2015) in retail stores Positive display rules: Diefendorff et al. (2011) in hospital units Climate of authenticity: Grandey et al. (2016) in hospital units	Rate agreement with items: I received training regarding how to behave and to express myself with customers. The expectations of my organization with regard to expressing appropriate emotions when interacting with customers were made clear to me.
Manipulated/ experimental	**Show positive vs. display autonomy** (call center simulation): Goldberg & Grandey (2007) Show positive or show neutral (poll-taker simulation): Trougakos et al. (2011) Show positive or show negative (tour guide or bill collector simulation): Bono & Vey (2007)	**Experimental instructions**: Our organization and its customers value . . . . . . employees being very friendly and outgoing. Our motto here is "putting a smile on your face will put the smile in your voice!"(show positive display rules) . . . employees being real and being themselves. Our motto here is "We want you to be you!" (display autonomy)
Other-rated/ observer	**O*Net – Occupational emotional demands**: Diefendorff et al. (2006); Bhave & Glomb (2016); Grandey et al. (2013)	How important are the following to this job? Performing for or working directly with the public Concern for others Cooperation Self-control Stress tolerance

(cont.)

Table 11.2 (cont.)

Emotion regulation		
Employee reported – emotion regulation strategies	**Emotion regulation scale** – all surface acting (SA) and deep acting (DA) items shown in column to the right: Brotheridge & Lee (2003) Faking, perspective-taking, reappraisal, and venting in response to hostile interactions: Grandey, Dickter, & Sin (2004) Faking, suppression, attention deployment, and cognitive change: Diefendorff et al. (2019)	Hide my true feelings about situations (SA) Resist expressing my true feelings (SA) Pretend to have emotions that I don't really have (SA) Try to actually experience the emotions that I must show (DA) Make an effort to actually feel the emotions that I need to display (DA) Really try to feel the emotions I have to show as part of my job (DA)
Employee reported – discrete emotion strategies	**Discrete emotional expression scale**: Glomb & Tews (2004)	How often do you . . . . . . genuinely express <emotion> when you feel that way? (authentic) . . . express feelings of <emotion> when you really don't feel that way? (SA – fake) . . . keep <emotion> to yourself when you really feel that way? (SA – hide)
Group perceptions	**Workgroup deep acting**: Becker & Cropanzano (2015) in hospital nurses, used Grandey et al. (2004) deep acting items (all four shown)	I generally tried to look at the positive side of things to change how I feel. I attempted to focus on happier things. I tried to see things from the other person's point of view. I tried to reinterpret what people said or did so that I don't take their actions personally.
Manipulated/ experimental	**Stimuli for deep acting or none**: Grandey, Houston, & Avery (2019) Stimuli for surface acting or deep acting: Grandey et al. (2005) Trained confederate to perform surface and deep acting: Henning-Thurau et al. (2006) Trained participant for deep acting: Hülsheger et al. (2014)	 (DA)  (none)
Observer-rated surface and deep acting	**Customer-rated:** Groth et al. (2009) (adapted Brotheridge & Lee items) Coworker- or subordinate-rated: Grandey (2003); Fisk & Friesen (2012)	The employee tried to actually experience the emotions s/he had to show to me. (DA) The employee just pretended to have the emotions s/he displayed to me. (SA)

Note: Source examples shown in bold type indicate the source of the items in the "Item examples" column.

(Diefendorff et al., 2006; Trougakos et al., 2011). An experimental role-play found that occupational requirements to show positive versus those to show negative did not differ in terms of reported and physiological stress (Bono & Vey, 2007).

Display Rules: Context

Antecedents

Display rules are not simply a function of the job. They are a function of employee personality: trait positive affectivity is linked to showing positive display rules and trait negative affectivity is linked to hiding negative display rules (Kammeyer-Mueller et al., 2013). They are also a function of the target: display rules are weaker for similar-power and close targets (i.e. close coworkers) than for differential power and less close targets (i.e. supervisors, subordinates, more distant coworkers) (Diefendorff & Greguras, 2009; Diefendorff, Morehart, & Gabriel, 2010). Display rules are also a function of broader cultural norms. Integrative display rules with customers were more strongly endorsed by US service employees than by Chinese employees (Allen, Diefendorff, & Ma, 2014) or French employees (Grandey, Rafaeli, Ravid, Wirtz, & Steiner, 2010).

Moderators

The fit between display rules, the employee, and the context determines outcomes. Positive display rules were less distressing than negative rules for extraverts (Bono & Vey, 2007), but positive display rules induced physiological stress for those who are more neurotic than those who are less so (Hopp, Rohrmann, Zapf, & Hodapp, 2010), consistent with a personality fit perspective. Positive display rules are more stressful when employees are facing unpleasant or hostile customers, which requires more regulatory effort (Goldberg & Grandey, 2007; Hopp et al., 2010). Consistent with an effort–reward imbalance perspective, financial rewards for performance buffer dissatisfaction from display rules (Grandey, Chi, et al., 2013). Jobs with positive display rules along with professional identity and social status, such as those in management, healthcare, or education, seem to see more benefits than entry-level service jobs (Bhave & Glomb, 2016; Grandey & Diamond, 2010; Humphrey, Ashforth, & Diefendorff, 2015).

Emotional Labor as Emotion Regulation Strategies

Emotion Regulation: Construct

In Hochschild's (1983) original work, dramaturgical acting strategies were used to produce emotions (Grandey, 2003). Later, the psychological model of emotion regulation was used to understand emotional labor (Grandey, 2000; Gross, 1998).

Types and Dimensions

Hochschild (1983) observed flight attendants and identified two effortful strategies for managing emotions with the public: surface acting and deep acting. *Surface acting* is changing expressions by hiding felt and/or showing unfelt emotions to match the display rules, whereas *deep acting* is changing inner feelings through cognitive strategies (e.g. reappraisal, refocusing) or physiological strategies (e.g. deep breathing, drinking coffee) such that feelings and expressions match display rules. Both are effortful and tend to be positively correlated at the person level (Grandey, 2003; Mesmer-Magnus et al., 2012) and the event level (Gabriel & Diefendorff, 2015). Scholars have also argued that *showing felt emotions*, or authentic displays, is a third response to display rules (Ashforth & Humphrey, 1993; Diefendorff, Croyle, & Gosserand, 2005; Glomb & Tews, 2004). More recently, scholars have drawn on the broader emotion regulation literature (Gross, 1998) and shown that employees use a wide variety of strategies, including *situation selection*, *situation modification*, and cognitive *distraction* (Diefendorff, Gabriel, Nolan, & Yang, 2019; Diefendorff, Richard, & Yang, 2008).

Multiple Levels and Measurement of Emotion Regulation

As shown in Table 11.2, surface and deep acting are typically measured as self-reported tendencies in the work role (Brotheridge & Lee, 2003) or in response to events (Gabriel & Diefendorff, 2015) and specific emotions (Glomb & Tews, 2004). Emotion regulation styles may emerge at the group level through socialization and role modeling processes (Becker, Cropanzano, & Butts, 2015), though it is more common to assess within-person variations across days (Scott, Barnes, & Wagner, 2012; Wagner, Barnes, & Scott, 2014) and events (Diefendorff et al., 2019; Diefendorff et al., 2008) consistent with the variable and dynamic nature of emotions (Grandey & Melloy, 2017).

Non self-reported approaches to assessing emotion regulation strategies have also been used. Experimentally, scholars have manipulated training for deep acting (Hülsheger, Lang, Schewe, & Zijlstra, 2014), surface or deep acted positive displays with photos and videos (Grandey, Fisk, Mattila, Jansen, & Sideman, 2005; Grandey, Houston, & Avery, 2019; Houston, Grandey, & Sawyer, 2018), and even faked anger compared to genuine anger (Côté, Hideg, & van Kleef, 2013; Hideg & van Kleef, 2017). Finally, surface and deep acting is measured by observers: coworkers (Grandey, 2003), customers (Groth, Hennig-Thurau, & Walsh, 2009) and followers of leaders (Fisk & Friesen, 2012) assess the extent the employee appears to be faking or trying to feel emotional displays.

Emotion Regulation: Consequences

According to meta-analyses and cross-lagged studies, surface acting is strongly negatively related to employee well-being with weak negative associations with performance, and deep acting is moderately positively related to job performance with weak and mixed associations with well-being (Hülsheger & Schewe, 2011; Hülsheger, Lang, & Maier, 2010; Kammeyer-Mueller et al., 2013; Mesmer-Magnus et al., 2012).

Job Performance

Deep acting positively influences evaluations of emotional performance and customer satisfaction via improved trust, exceeded expectations, and perceived service orientation (Cheshin, Amit, & Van Kleef, 2018; Chi & Grandey, 2016; Groth et al., 2009; Houston et al., 2018; Hülsheger & Schewe, 2011). Service employees using deep acting receive more tips (Chi, Grandey, Diamond, & Krimmel, 2011; Hülsheger et al., 2014) and teams that tend to use deep acting have improved team outcomes (Becker et al., 2015). Both strategies are linked to motivational resources such as vigor/exhaustion or regulatory depletion (Xanthopoulou, Bakker, Oerlemans, & Koszucka, 2018): daily deep acting enhances energy, which then improved conflict handling with customers (Huang, Chiarburu, Zhang, Li, & Grandey, 2015) and reduced interpersonal mistreatment (Deng, Walter, Lam, & Zhao, 2017). In contrast, daily surface acting depletes self-control, which means more service sabotage (Chi & Grandey, 2016), less coworker-directed citizenship behavior (Trougakos, Beal, Cheng, Hideg, & Zweig, 2015) and more coworker and subordinate harming (Deng et al., 2017; Yam, Fehr, Keng-Highberger, Klotz, & Reynolds, 2016).

Employee Strain and Well-Being

Surface acting creates dissonance between displays and feelings and also creates inauthenticity, which predicts negative moods, energy depletion, job burnout, and job dissatisfaction, even after controlling for negative states and traits (Hülsheger & Schewe, 2011; Judge, Woolf, & Hurst, 2009; Kammeyer-Mueller et al., 2013; Scott & Barnes, 2011; Xanthopoulou et al., 2018). Surface acting is also linked to absences and turnover due to emotional exhaustion

(Goodwin, Groth, & Frenkel, 2011; Nguyen, Groth, & Johnson, 2016). A recent study suggests that faking *positive* is problematic compared to feeling positive, but faking *negative* improved well-being more than feeling badly, though this may be a function of the managerial sample (Lennard, Scott, & Johnson, 2019). Deep acting has mixed relationships with moods and exhaustion (Hülsheger & Schewe, 2011; Judge et al., 2009), but some find social benefits from appearing authentic (Zhan, Wang, & Shi, 2015), which can be energy-enhancing (Xanthopoulou et al., 2018).

Implications go beyond the work context. Surface acting has negative mood spillover affecting work–family conflict and marital dissatisfaction (Grandey & Krannitz, 2016; Krannitz, Grandey, Liu, & Almeida, 2015; Wagner et al., 2014; Yanchus, Eby, Lance, & Drollinger, 2010), and diminished self-control affecting sleep (e.g. can't turn off television) and heavy alcohol use (e.g. can't stop drinking) (Grandey, Frone, Melloy, & Sayre, 2019; Wagner et al., 2014). Daily use of deep acting enhances self-control, which reduces harming behavior (Deng et al., 2017) and alcohol consumption (Sayre, Grandey, & Chi, 2018).

Emotion Regulation: Context

Antecedents

Display rules predict more effortful emotion regulation strategies (Goldberg & Grandey, 2007; Kammeyer-Mueller et al., 2013). At the person level, employees higher in neuroticism use more surface acting, and those higher in agreeableness use more deep acting (Diefendorff et al., 2005; Diefendorff et al., 2011). Other individual differences also predict surface and deep acting (see Dahling & Johnson, 2013); for example, prosocial work motives predict deep acting whereas preventive or instrumental motives predict surface acting (Maneotis, Grandey, & Krauss, 2014; Von Gilsa, Zapf, Ohly, Trumpold, & Machowski, 2014) and the need to belong to a group (e.g. when one is a minority) predicts using surface acting (Kim, Bhave, & Glomb, 2013; Yagil & Medler-Liraz, 2017).

Situationally, the frequency of mistreatment predicts surface acting but not deep acting (Sliter, Jex, Wolford, & McInnerney, 2010; Wu & Hu, 2013), though *in vivo* lab studies show that both surface and deep acting are used to cope (Gabriel & Diefendorff, 2015; Goldberg & Grandey, 2007). A negative spiral occurs, where employee surface acting evokes negative reactions by the target (Zhan et al., 2015), which increases employee negative mood and reduces self-control (Deng et al., 2017), which in turn evokes more surface acting (Groth & Grandey, 2012). Positive or supportive interactions increase the likelihood of deep acting, suggesting a way to break the spiral (Mesmer-Magnus et al., 2012).

Moderators

Surface acting has mixed effects on service performance, depending on the skill of the actor (Chi et al., 2011) and expectations of the customer (Grandey, Fisk, Mattila, et al., 2005; Grandey, Houston, et al., 2019). When employees are efficacious or skilled in surface acting (e.g. self-monitors, extraverts), it is linked to less strain, reduced absences, and better performance (e.g. as shown by tips) (Chi et al., 2011; Deng et al., 2017; Judge et al., 2009; Nguyen et al., 2016; Pugh, Groth, & Hennig-Thurau, 2011) because less effort is required than for less skilled surface actors.

The job context also moderates outcomes: surface acting is less problematic when work behaviors are autonomous (Grandey, Fisk, & Steiner, 2005; Grandey, Frone, et al., 2019; Johnson & Spector, 2007) and financially rewarded (Grandey, Chi, et al., 2013), and deep acting is more beneficial when the job tasks are intrinsically challenging (Huang et al., 2015). Finally, the social context matters. Surface acting is exhausting and distressing unless employees are also engaging in prosocial helping behavior (Uy, Lin, & Ilies, 2016) and in authentic emotional behavior with their coworkers (Grandey et al., 2012; McCance, Nye, Wang, Jones, & Chiu, 2013), and are receiving social support from the organization (Duke, Goodman, Treadway, & Breland, 2009) or developing rewarding relationships with clients (Grandey, Houston, et al., 2019; Wang & Groth, 2014).

Future Directions and Conclusions

Theorizing and empirical evidence around emotional labor has come a long way since the early qualitative work by Hochschild (1983). Current work demonstrates that employees vary in the expectations for emotional displays and effortful regulation, and that these emotional display rules – and how the employees regulate to conform to them – have implications for performance and for their own health and well-being. Scholars present competing views about whether emotional labor is more beneficial or harmful (Grandey et al., 2015; Humphrey et al., 2015), and whether the benefits and costs are real or simply spurious due to shared variance with affectivity and mood (Semmer, Messerli, & Tschan, 2016). Today's scholars must capture the transient nature of emotions and emotion regulation by using within-personal methodology and should compare distinct theoretical mechanisms to better understand why and when emotional labor is beneficial or harmful.

References

Allen, J. A., Diefendorff, J. M., & Ma, Y. (2014). Differences in emotional labor across cultures: A comparison of Chinese and US service workers. *Journal of Business and Psychology*, *29*, 21–35.

Ashforth, B. E., & Humphrey, R. H. (1993). Emotional labor in service roles: The influence of identity. *Academy of Management Review*, *18*(1), 88–115.

Ashforth, B. E., & Humphrey, R. H. (1995). Emotion in the workplace – a reappraisal. *Human Relations*, *48* (2), 97–125.

Barsade, S., & O'Neill, O. A. (2014). What's love got to do with it? The influence of a culture of companionate love in the long-term care setting. *Administrative Science Quarterly*, *59*(4), 551–598.

Becker, W. J., Cropanzano, R., & Butts, M. (2015). Good acting requires a good cast: A meso-level model of deep acting in work teams. *Journal of Organizational Behavior*, *36*(2), 232–249.

Ben-Achour, S. (2015). Don't worry, be happy! Or else you're fired. *KERA News*, 23 November, www.keranews.org/post/dont-worry-be-happy-or-else-youre-fired

Bhave, D., & Glomb, T. M. (2016). The role of occupational emotional labor requirements on the surface acting–job satisfaction relationship. *Journal of Management*, *42*(3), 722–741.

Bhave, D., & Lefter, A. (2017). The other side: Occupational interactional requirements and work–home enrichment. *Academy of Management Journal*, *61*(1), http://doi.org/10.5465/amj.2016.0369

Bono, J. E., & Vey, M. A. (2007). Personality and emotional performance: Extraversion, neuroticism, and self-monitoring. *Journal of Occupational Health Psychology*, *12*(2), 177–192.

Brotheridge, C., & Grandey, A. (2002). Emotional labor and burnout: Comparing two perspectives of "people work." *Journal of Vocational Behavior*, *60*, 17–39.

Brotheridge, C., & Lee, R. T. (2003). Development and validation of the Emotional Labour Scale. *Journal of Occupational and Organizational Psychology*, *76*, 365–379.

Cheshin, A., Amit, A., & Van Kleef, G. A. (2018). The interpersonal effects of emotion intensity in customer service: Perceived appropriateness and authenticity of attendants' emotional displays shape customer trust and satisfaction. *Organizational Behavior and Human Decision Processes*, *144*, 97–111.

Chi, N.-W., & Grandey, A. (2016). Emotional labor predicts service performance depending on activation and inhibition regulatory fit. *Journal of Management*, *45*(2), 673–700, https://doi.org/10.1177/0149206316672530

Chi, N.-W., Grandey, A., Diamond, J., & Krimmel, K. (2011). Want a tip? Service performance as a function of extraversion and emotion regulation. *Journal of Applied Psychology, 96*(6), 1337–1346.

Christoforou, P. S., & Ashforth, B. (2015). Revisiting the debate on the relationship between display rules and performance: Considering the explicitness of display rules. *Journal of Applied Psychology, 100*, 249–261.

Côté, S., Hideg, I., & van Kleef, G. A. (2013). The consequences of faking anger in negotiations. *Journal of Experimental Social Psychology, 49*(3), 453–463.

Dahling, J. J., & Johnson, H. (2013). Motivation, fit, confidence, and skills: How do individual differences influence emotional labor? In A. A. Grandey, J. M. Diefendorff, & D. E. Rupp (Eds.), *Emotional labor in the 21st century: Diverse perspectives on emotion regulation at work*. New York, NY: Psychology/Routledge.

Deng, H., Walter, F., Lam, C. K., & Zhao, H. H. (2017). Spillover effects of emotional labor in customer service encounters toward coworker harming: A resource depletion perspective. *Personnel Psychology, 70*(2), 469–502, doi:10.1111/peps.12156

Diefendorff, J., Croyle, M., & Gosserand, R. (2005). The dimensionality and antecedents of emotional labor strategies. *Journal of Vocational Behavior, 66* (2), 339–357.

Diefendorff, J., Erickson, R. J., Grandey, A., & Dahling, J. J. (2011). Emotional display rules as work unit norms: A multilevel analysis of emotional labor among nurses. *Journal of Occupational Health Psychology, 16*(2), 170–186.

Diefendorff, J. M., Gabriel, A. S., Nolan, M. T., & Yang, J. (2019). Emotion regulation in the context of customer mistreatment and felt affect: An event-based profile approach. *Journal of Applied Psychology*, 104(7), doi:10.1037/apl0000389

Diefendorff, J. M., & Gosserand, R. H. (2003). Understanding the emotional labor process: A control theory perspective. *Journal of Organizational Behavior, 24*(8), 945–959.

Diefendorff, J. M., & Greguras, G. J. (2009). Contextualizing emotional display rules: Taking a closer look at targets, discrete emotions, and behavior responses. *Journal of Management, 35*(4), 880–898.

Diefendorff, J. M., Morehart, J., & Gabriel, A. S. (2010). The influence of power and solidarity on emotional display rules at work. *Motivation & Emotion, 34*, 120–132.

Diefendorff, J. M., & Richard, E. (2003). Antecedents and consequences of emotional display rule perceptions. *Journal of Applied Psychology, 88*(2), 284–294.

Diefendorff, J. M., Richard, E. M., & Croyle, M. H. (2006). Are emotional display rules formal job requirements? Examination of employee and supervisor perceptions. *Journal of Occupational and Organizational Psychology, 79*(2), 273–298.

Diefendorff, J. M., Richard, E. M., & Yang, J. (2008). Linking emotion regulation strategies to affective events and negative emotions at work. *Journal of Vocational Behavior, 73*(3), 498–508.

Duke, A. B., Goodman, J. M., Treadway, D. C., & Breland, J. W. (2009). Perceived organizational support as a moderator of emotional labor/outcomes relationships. *Journal of Applied Social Psychology, 39*(5), 1013–1034.

Fisk, G. M, & Friesen, J. P. (2012). Perceptions of leader emotion regulation and LMX as predictors of followers' job satisfaction and organizational citizenship behaviors. *Leadership Quarterly, 23*, 1–12.

Gabriel, A. S., Cheshin, A., Moran, C. M., & Van Kleef, G. A. (2016). Enhancing emotional performance and customer service through human resources practices: A systems perspective. *Human Resource Management Review, 26*, 14–24.

Gabriel, A. S., & Diefendorff, J. (2015). Emotional labor dynamics: A momentary approach. *Academy of Management Journal, 58*(6), 1804–1825.

Glomb, T. A., Kammeyer-Mueller, J. D., & Rotundo, M. (2004). Emotional labor demands and compensating wage differentials. *Journal of Applied Psychology, 89*(4), 700–714.

Glomb, T. M., & Tews, M. J. (2004). Emotional labor: A conceptualization and scale development. *Journal of Vocational Behavior, 64*(1), 1–23.

Goldberg, L., & Grandey, A. (2007). Display rules versus display autonomy: Emotion regulation, emotional exhaustion, and task performance in a call center simulation. *Journal of Occupational Health Psychology, 12*(3), 301–318.

Goodwin, R. E., Groth, M., & Frenkel, S. J. (2011). Relationships between emotional labor, job performance, and turnover. *Journal of Vocational Behavior, 79*, 538–548.

Gosserand, R. H., & Diefendorff, J. M. (2005). Emotional display rules and emotional labor: The moderating role of commitment. *Journal of Applied Psychology, 90*(6), 1256–1264.

Grandey, A. (2000). Emotion regulation in the workplace: A new way to conceptualize emotional labor. *Journal of Occupational Health Psychology, 5*(1), 95–110.

Grandey, A. (2003). When "the show must go on": Surface and deep acting as predictors of emotional exhaustion and service delivery. *Academy of Management Journal, 46*(1), 86–96.

Grandey, A., Chi, N.-W., & Diamond, J. (2013). Show me the money! Do financial rewards for performance enhance or undermine the satisfaction from emotional labor? *Personnel Psychology, 66* (3), 569–612.

Grandey, A., & Diamond, J. (2010). Interactions with the public: Bridging job design and emotional labor perspectives. *Journal of Organizational Behavior, 31*, 338–350.

Grandey, A., Diefendorff, J., Grabarek, P., & Diamond, J. (2009). Emotional displays as requirement: Differences across targets and performance effects. Symposium presentation for the 23rd Annual Meeting of the Society of Industrial and Organizational Psychology, New Orleans, LA.

Grandey, A., Diefendorff, J., & Rupp, D. E. (2013). Bringing emotional labor into focus: A review and integration of three research lenses. In A. A. Grandey, J. M. Diefendorff, & D. E. Rupp (Eds.), *Emotional labor in the 21st century: Diverse perspectives on emotion regulation at work*. New York, NY: Psychology/ Routledge.

Grandey, A., Fisk, G., Mattila, A., Jansen, K. J., & Sideman, L. (2005). Is service with a smile enough? Authenticity of positive displays during service encounters. *Organizational Behavior & Human Decision Processes, 96*(1), 38–55.

Grandey, A., Fisk, G. M., & Steiner, D. D. (2005). Must "service with a smile" be stressful? The moderating role of personal control for American and French employees. *Journal of Applied Psychology, 90*(5), 893–904.

Grandey, A., Foo, S. C., Groth, M., & Goodwin, R. E. (2012). Free to be you and me: A climate of authenticity alleviates burnout from emotional labor. *Journal of Occupational Health Psychology, 17*(1), 1–14.

Grandey, A., Frone, M., Melloy, R., & Sayre, G. (2019). When are fakers also drinkers? A self-control view of emotional labor and alcohol consumption among US service workers. *Journal of Occupational Health Psychology*, 24(4), 482–497.

Grandey, A., & Gabriel, A. (2015). Emotional labor at a crossroads: Where do we go from here? *Annual Review of Organizational Psychology and Organizational Behavior, 2*, 323–349.

Grandey, A., Houston, L., & Avery, D. R. (2019). Fake it to make it: Emotional labor reduces the racial disparity in service performance judgments. *Journal of Management, 45*(5), https://doi.org/10.1177/0149206318757019

Grandey, A., Kern, J., & Frone, M. (2007). Verbal abuse from outsiders versus insiders: Comparing frequency, impact on emotional exhaustion, and the role of emotional labor. *Journal of Occupational Health Psychology, 12*(1), 63–79.

Grandey, A., & Krannitz, M. A. (2016). Emotion regulation at work and at home. In T. Allen & L. Eby (Eds.), *The Oxford handbook of work and family* (pp. 81–94). New York, NY: Oxford University Press.

Grandey, A. A., & Melloy, R. C. (2017). The state of the heart: Emotional labor as emotion regulation reviewed and revised. *Journal of Occupational Health Psychology, 22*(3), 407–422, doi:http://dx.doi.org/10.1037/ocp0000067

Grandey, A., Rafaeli, A., Ravid, S., Wirtz, J., & Steiner, D. (2010). Emotion display rules at work in the global service economy: The special case of the customer. *Journal of Service Management, 21*(3), 388–412.

Grandey, A. A., Rupp, D., & Brice, W. N. (2015). Emotional labor threatens decent work: A proposal to eradicate emotional display rules. *Journal of Organizational Behavior*, *36*, 770–785.

Gross, J. J. (1998). Antecedent- and response-focused emotion regulation: Divergent consequences for experience, expression, and physiology. *Journal of Personality and Social Psychology*, *74*(1), 224–237.

Groth, M., & Grandey, A. (2012). From bad to worse : Negative exchange spirals in employee–customer service interactions. *Organizational Psychology Review*, *2*(3), 208–233.

Groth, M., Hennig-Thurau, T., & Walsh, G. (2009). Customer reactions to emotional labor: The roles of employee acting strategies and customer detection accuracy. *Academy of Management Journal*, *52*(5), 958–974.

Hideg, I., & van Kleef, G. A. (2017). When expressions of fake emotions elicit negative reactions: The role of observers' dialectical thinking. *Journal of Organizational Behavior*, *38*(8), 1196–1212.

Hochschild, A. R. (1983). *The managed heart: Commercialization of human feeling*. Berkeley: University of California Press.

Hopp, H., Rohrmann, S., Zapf, D., & Hodapp, V. (2010). Psychophysiological effects of emotional dissonance in a face-to-face service interaction. *Anxiety, Stress and Coping*, *23*(4), 399–414.

Houston, L., Grandey, A., & Sawyer, K. (2018). Who cares if "service with a smile" is authentic? An expectancy-based model of customer race and differential service interactions. *Organizational Behavior and Human Decision Processes*, *144*, 86–96.

Huang, J. L., Chiarburu, D. S., Zhang, X., Li, N., & Grandey, A. (2015). Rising to the challenge: Deep acting is more beneficial when tasks are appraised as challenging. *Journal of Applied Psychology*, *100* (5), 1398–1408.

Hülsheger, U. R., Lang, J. W. B., & Maier, G. W. (2010). Emotional labor, strain, and performance: Testing reciprocal relationships in a longitudinal panel study. *Journal of Occupational Health Psychology*, *15*(4), 505–521.

Hülsheger, U. R., Lang, J. W. B., Schewe, A. F., & Zijlstra, F. R. H. (2014). When regulating emotions at work pays off: A diary and an intervention study on emotion regulation and customer tips in service jobs. *Journal of Applied Psychology*, *100*(2), 263–277, http://dx.doi.org/10.1037/a0038229

Hülsheger, U. R., & Schewe, A. F. (2011). On the costs and benefits of emotional labor: A meta-analysis of three decades of research. *Journal of Occupational Health Psychology*, *16*(3), 361–389.

Humphrey, R. H., Ashforth, B. E., & Diefendorff, J. M. (2015). The bright side of emotional labor. *Journal of Organizational Behavior*, *36*, 749–769.

Johnson, H.-A. M., & Spector, P. E. (2007). Service with a smile: Do emotional intelligence, gender, and autonomy moderate the emotional labor process? *Journal of Occupational Health Psychology*, *12*(4), 319–333.

Judge, T. A., Woolf, E. F., & Hurst, C. (2009). Is emotional labor more difficult for some than for others? A multi-level, experience sampling study. *Personnel Psychology*, *62*, 57–88.

Kammeyer-Mueller, J. D., Rubenstein, A. L., Long, D. M., Odio, M. A., Buckman, B. R., Zhang, Y., & Halvorsen-Ganepola, M. D. K. (2013). A meta-analytic structural model of dispositional affectivity and emotional labor. *Personnel Psychology*, *66*, 47–90.

Kim, E., Bhave, D. P., & Glomb, T. M. (2013). Emotion regulation in workgroups: The roles of demographic diversity and relational work context. *Personnel Psychology*, *66*, 613–614.

Krannitz, M. A., Grandey, A., Liu, S., & Almeida, D. (2015). Workplace surface acting and marital partner discontent: Anxiety and exhaustion spillover mechanisms. *Journal of Occupational Health Psychology*, *20*(3), 314–325.

Lennard, A. C., Scott, B. A., & Johnson, R. E. (2019). Turning frowns (and smiles) upside down: A multilevel examination of surface acting positive and negative emotions on well-being. *Journal of Applied Psychology*, *4*, doi:10.1037/apl0000400

Levy, K. (2018). How faking your feelings at work can be damaging. *BBC Worklife*, 20 June, www.bbc.com/worklife/article/20180619-why-suppressing-anger-at-work-is-bad

Mallory, D., & Rupp, D. E. (2017). Focusing in on the emotion laborer: Emotion regulation at work. In R. Baumeister & K. Vohs (Eds.), *Handbook of self-regulation: research, theory, and applications* (3rd edition, pp. 323–344). New York, NY: Guilford.

Maneotis, S. M., Grandey, A., & Krauss, A. D. (2014). Understanding the "why" as well as the "how": Service performance is a function of prosocial motives and emotional labor. *Human Performance, 27*, 1–18.

McCance, A. S., Nye, C. D., Wang, L., Jones, K. S., & Chiu, C. (2013). Alleviating the burden of emotional labor: The role of social sharing. *Journal of Management, 39*(2), 392–415.

Melwani, S., & Barsade, S. G. (2011). Held in contempt: The psychological, interpersonal, and performance consequences of contempt in a work context. *Journal of Personality and Social Psychology, 101*(3), 503–520.

Mesmer-Magnus, J. R., DeChurch, L. A., & Wax, A. (2012). Moving emotional labor beyond surface and deep acting: A discordance–congruence perspective. *Organizational Psychology Review, 2*(1), 6–53.

Nguyen, H., Groth, M., & Johnson, A. (2016). When the going gets tough, the tough keep working: Impact of emotional labor on absenteeism. *Journal of Management, 42*(3), 615–643.

Parke, M. R., & Seo, M. G. (2017). The role of affect climate in organizational effectiveness. *Academy of Management Review, 42*(2), 334–360.

Pugh, S. D., Diefendorff, J. M., & Moran, C. M. (2013). Emotional labor: Organization-level influences, strategies, and outcomes. In A. A. Grandey, J. M. Diefendorff, & D. E. Rupp (Eds.), *Emotional labor in the 21st century: Diverse perspectives on emotion regulation at work*. New York, NY: Psychology/Routledge.

Pugh, S. D., Groth, M., & Hennig-Thurau, T. (2011). Willing and able to fake emotions: A closer examination of the link between emotional dissonance and employee well-being. *Journal of Applied Psychology, 96*(2), 377–390.

Rafaeli, A., & Sutton, R. I. (1991). Emotional contrast strategies as means of social influence: Lessons from criminal interrogators and bill collectors. *Academy of Management Journal, 34*(4), 749–775.

Sayre, G., Grandey, A., & Chi, N.-W. (2018). Emotional labor and alcohol use: Why and when regulating at work helps or harms regulating after work. Paper presented at the Annual Conference of the Society for Industrial and Organizational Psychology, Chicago, IL.

Scott, B., & Barnes, C. M. (2011). A multilevel field investigation of emotional labor, affect, work withdrawal, and gender. *Academy of Management Journal, 54*, 116–136.

Scott, B. A., Barnes, C. M., & Wagner, D. T. (2012). Chameleonic or consistent? A multilevel investigation of emotional labor variability and self-monitoring. *Academy of Management Journal, 55*(4), 905–926.

Semmer, N. K., Messerli, L., & Tschan, F. (2016). Disentangling the components of surface acting in emotion work: Experiencing emotions may be as important as regulating them. *Journal of Applied Social Psychology, 46*, 46–64.

Sliter, M., Jex, S., Wolford, K., & McInnerney, J. (2010). How rude! Emotional labor as a mediator between customer incivility and employee outcomes. *Journal of Occupational Health Psychology, 15*(4), 468–481.

Trougakos, J. P., Beal, D. J., Cheng, B. H., Hideg, I., & Zweig, D. (2015). Too drained to help: A resource depletion perspective on daily interpersonal citizenship behaviors. *Journal of Applied Psychology, 100*(1), 227–236.

Trougakos, J. P., Jackson, C. L., & Beal, D. J. (2011). Service without a smile: Comparing the consequences of neutral and positive display rules. *Journal of Applied Psychology, 96*(2), 350–362.

Uy, M., Lin, K., & Ilies, R. (2016). Is it better to give or receive? The role of help in buffering the depleting effects of surface acting. *Academy of Management Journal, 60*(4), https://doi.org/10.5465/amj.2015.0611

van Kleef, G. A., De Dreu, C. K. W., & Manstead, A. S. R. (2004). The interpersonal effects of anger and happiness in negotiations. *Journal of Personality and Social Psychology, 86* (1), 57–76.

Von Gilsa, L., Zapf, D., Ohly, S., Trumpold, K., & Machowski, S. (2014). There is more than obeying display rules: Service employees' motives for emotion regulation in customer interactions. *European Journal of Work and Organizational Psychology, 23*(6), 884–896, doi:10.1080/1359432X.2013.839548

Wagner, D. T., Barnes, C. M., & Scott, B. A. (2014). Driving it home: How workplace emotional labor harms employee home life. *Personnel Psychology, 67*(2), 487–516.

Wang, K. L., & Groth, M. (2014). Buffering the negative effects of employee surface acting: The moderating role of employee–customer relationship strength and personalized services. *Journal of Applied Psychology, 99*(2), 341–350.

Wu, T. Y., & Hu, C. (2013). Abusive supervision and subordinate emotional labor: The moderating role of openness personality. *Journal of Applied Social Psychology, 43*(5), 956–970.

Xanthopoulou, D., Bakker, A. B., Oerlemans, W. G., & Koszucka, M. (2018). Need for recovery after emotional labor: Differential effects of daily deep and surface acting. *Journal of Organizational Behavior, 39*(4), 481–494.

Yagil, D., & Medler-Liraz, H. (2017). Personally committed to emotional labor: Surface acting, emotional exhaustion and performance among service employees with a strong need to belong. *Journal of Occupational Health Psychology, 22*(4), 481–491.

Yam, K. C., Fehr, R., Keng-Highberger, F. T., Klotz, A. C., & Reynolds, S. (2016). Out of control: A self-control perspective on the link between surface acting and abusive supervision. *Journal of Applied Psychology, 101*(2), 292–301.

Yanchus, N. J., Eby, L. T., Lance, C. E., & Drollinger, S. (2010). The impact of emotional labor on work–family outcomes. *Journal of Vocational Behavior, 76*(1), 105–117.

Zhan, Y., Wang, M., & Shi, J. (2015). Interpersonal process of emotional labor: The role of negative and positive customer treatment. *Personnel Psychology*, https://doi.org/10.1111/peps.12114

12 Advancing the Field

Reviewing the Status of Emotional Intelligence in the Workplace

Catherine S. Daus and Mary Sue Love

In this chapter, we hope to elucidate the definition of emotional intelligence (EI) and to provide support for homing in on one specific approach to its study. The ability approach, as developed by Mayer, Salovey, and Caruso (Mayer, Caruso, & Salovey, 2016; Mayer, Salovey, & Caruso, 1997; 2002; Mayer & Salovey, 1997; Salovey & Mayer, 1990), is the one that most researchers adhere to (at least in a definitional sense). We review how research using this ability approach has related emotional intelligence to workplace predictors and outcomes; we then point out gaps in current understanding and suggest promising future research directions.

We open the chapter, somewhat unconventionally, with a discussion of the challenges and criticisms that have been lodged against the construct of EI as it has evolved in the last three decades, setting the stage for definitional clarity.

Challenges and Criticisms

Popularization and Commercialization

EI scholars have been in the unfortunate position of fighting for its legitimacy for years. Frank Landy (2005) illustrates the sort of sentiment they have sought to redress: "It appears that emotional intelligence, as a concept related to occupational success, exists outside the typical scientific domain" (Landy, 2005, p. 411). Much of this pushback, we suspect, was partly due to the early popularization of the concept of EI with Goleman's bestselling 1995 book, *Emotional intelligence: Why it can matter more than IQ*, and a *Time Magazine* cover story in the same year (Gibbs, 1995). This popularization carried with it both a blessing and a curse. Goleman and the *Time Magazine* article each made somewhat wild and grandiose claims about the newly proposed construct that were either simply unprovable (as on *Time*'s front cover: "Emotional intelligence may be the best predictor of success in life," Gibbs, 1995), or overstated and beyond empirical evidence available at that point in time. This commercialization and popularization, combined with overstated and unsupported claims, have contributed to EI being late to be accepted within the academic community.

At the time, Mayer and Salovey were not as well known as they have become. While their Mayer-Salovey-Caruso Emotional Intelligence Test (MSCEIT) (formerly the Multi-Factor Emotional Intelligence Test, MEIS) is not the only useful and valid ability measure, their model *has* survived the academic tests of rigor and longevity; at the time of writing, it stands alone in the field as a legitimate construct with proven important outcomes.

Lack of Discriminant Validity from Cognitive Ability and Personality

Early criticism of EI (Davies, Stankov, & Roberts, 1998; Landy, 2005; Locke, 2005) argued that it was simply a form of cognitive ability applied to a specific domain (emotions). Mayer and colleagues (1997; 1999; 2008; 2016; 2018) have consistently and compellingly argued that

EI is distinct as it focuses on a specific area of problem solving, and EI is the ability to reason about emotion, whereas *g* – that is, general intelligence (Sternberg & Wagner, 1993; Wagner & Sternberg, 1985) – involves more abstract reasoning. The empirical evidence supports Mayer and colleagues' early suppositions and later conclusions (Joseph & Newman, 2010, Mayer, Roberts, & Barsade, 2008).

Clearly, there are nuanced relationships between specific branches and specific operationalizations of cognitive ability. Overall, EI ability scores are moderately linked with verbal indices of intelligence; and specifically, of the four branches of EI (discussed in the next section of this chapter), the emotional understanding branch has the strongest individual relationship with cognitive ability, showing a respectable level of discriminant validity. Moreover, meta-analytic studies by Joseph and Newman (2010) and O'Boyle and colleagues (2011) examining EI and workplace performance show incremental validity above and beyond cognitive ability and personality, further solidifying the status of EI as discriminable from cognitive ability. Finally, Fiori and Vesely-Maillefer (2018) have reviewed research showing moderate correlations between measures of intelligence (particularly crystallized intelligence) and tests of EI ability.

The same criticism was lodged early on regarding EI and personality (e.g. Davies et al., 1998), arguing that EI is not distinct enough from personality to justify its conception as a distinct construct. Yet as Daus and Ashkanasy (2005) argued in response, such reviews confused the discussion because they did not distinguish among types of measures (i.e. ability measures were not separated from other measure types). Further, we argue that other measures (mixed model and self-report) often show moderate to fairly large overlaps with personality. For example, Petrides and Furnham (2001) showed that neuroticism and extroversion primarily capture Bar-On's (2000) dimensions, further justifying their use of the term "trait EI." It is our contention, however, that these other non-ability measures' relationships with personality (which are often moderate to strong) confuse the issue of whether EI as an ability is distinct from personality.

In truth, there are individual studies using ability measures that show a substantial overlap between EI and either cognitive ability or personality (e.g. Fiori & Antonakis, 2011). Yet the preponderance of evidence from both quantitative and qualitative reviews of the literature shows little to (at most) moderate overlap between ability EI and either cognitive ability or personality (Fiori & Vesely-Maillefer, 2018; Joseph & Newman, 2010; Mayer et al., 2016; O'Boyle et al., 2011). Fiori and Vesely-Maillefer (2018) have argued that a more fine-grained exploration and understanding of EI is necessary: specifically, they suggest that knowledge of emotions is (and should be) more related to crystallized intelligence, while processing of emotional information is (and should be) more related to fluid intelligence. These researchers (Vesely-Maillefer, Udayar, & Fiori, 2018) have also shown that interactions of ability EI, trait EI, and emotion processing ability predicted performance on an emotionally-laden task. This supports our contention, discussed later in this chapter, that it is incumbent upon researchers for the advancement of the science of EI to explore more complex relationships. Next, we will discuss concerns regarding measuring EI.

Measurement Concerns

The main concern we address with measurement is the widespread use of self-report measures – both those tapping into the ability model and mixed-model measures, which are much broader. While it is not the intent of the present authors to claim that self-report measures in general are inherently flawed or valueless, it is our position (consistent with previous writing: Daus & Ashkanasy, 2005) that self-report measures will never measure ability EI with any level of real accuracy. This strong sentiment is rooted in a very basic supposition: if one truly believes EI to be a set of abilities, asking someone about their perception of their own ability makes no real sense as a valid indicator of that ability. Imagine, as a proxy for the measurement of cognitive ability, asking people to what extent they agree with the statement "In general, I am intelligent in most ways." Indeed, research shows that self-report measures of intelligence are not good proxies for actual intelligence (Paulhas, Lysy, & Yik, 1998). If one supports the basic supposition regarding EI – that it is a form of intelligence – then, a priori, self-report measures lack validity as respondents are reporting their self-concept rather than solving problems[1] (see Miller & Lovler, 2019, for recent explanations and discussions of the latest standards of educational and psychological testing). Empirical evidence also supports this contention of a lack of convergence between self-report EI and an ability measure of EI (Brackett, Rivers, Shiffman, Lernery, & Salovey, 2006; Joseph & Newman, 2010; Mayer et al., 2008).

One intriguing aspect of self-report measurement of EI, however, is why there is a healthy and growing database of empirical work showing that self-report EI does, indeed, predict job performance. Joseph, Jin, Newman, and O'Boyle (2015) tackled this very issue in their meta-analysis of self-report EI and job performance. These researchers re-analyzed their own work and found that after controlling for several covariates, self-reported EI had a much lower relationship with supervisor-rated performance (β = .29) and near-zero relationship with other job performance indicators. The covariates included ability EI, *g* (general intelligence), self-efficacy, and self-rated job performance, as well as three of the Big Five personality traits: conscientiousness, extraversion, and emotional stability (the reverse of neuroticism). Their conclusion is that self-report EI reflects a combination of ability EI, self-perceptions, personality, and cognitive ability. These conclusions are conceptually similar to the known positive relationships between self-esteem and positive self-reporting on the Big Five (Robins, Tracy, Trzesniewski, Potter, & Gosling, 2001), and between positive (and negative, inversely) affect and the Big Five (Ahadi & Rothbart, 1994). Thus, we expect positive relationships underlying self-report EI and other positively valenced constructs. We now move into defining EI, informed by the above criticisms.

Defining Emotional Intelligence

Four Branches – History and Evolution

Just over twenty-five years after introducing the EI construct, Mayer, Caruso, and Salovey (2016) gave a historical overview and an update on their own perspective regarding EI. In 1990, Salovey and Mayer had suggested that some people might be more intelligent about emotions than others, and they focused on problem solving in relation to emotion. They proposed the classic definition of emotional intelligence as "The ability to monitor one's own and others' feelings, to discriminate among them, and to use this information to guide one's thinking and action" (p. 189). Later, they (Mayer & Salovey, 1997) further developed these problem-solving capacities into their classic and currently prevailing four-branch model. The four branches, intended to be roughly hierarchically arranged according to increasing cognitive complexity, are 1) perceiving emotions; 2) facilitating thought using emotions; 3) understanding emotions; and 4) managing emotions (Mayer et al., 2016). We subscribe to this four-branch definition.

[1] Thanks to Jack Mayer, who highlighted this point in a friendly review of our chapter.

Distinguishing Emotional Intelligence from Other Similar Constructs

Due to the plethora of definitions of EI, most of them broader than Mayer, Salovey, and Caruso's suggested model, it is incumbent upon academics and practitioners alike to be crystal clear what EI is, and what it is not. In a recent chapter in a handbook on intelligence, Mayer (2018, p. 274) discusses how several intelligences may fall under a larger umbrella of "people-centered" intelligences. This is to distinguish more traditionally defined cognitive types of intelligences that are "about things" from the set of intelligences that don't fit with the others and that are "about people." We will now highlight the three most relevant types of people intelligence (social, practical, and personal) and discuss their overlap with and distinctiveness from EI. We draw largely from Mayer et al.'s 2016 review (which includes a comparison of emotional, social, and personal intelligences: p. 296) as well as classic sources regarding practical intelligence. These are summarized in Table 12.1.

Table 12.1 Types of intelligence and how they differ from emotional intelligence

Type	Definition	How differs from EI
Social	The ability to understand and get along with others and to manage relationships	Focus is on the individual operating well within the social norms and mores of society, with particular skill sets of understanding power and group dynamics
Practical	"Street smarts"	Focus is on practical problem solving in context for personal well-being and survival
Personal	The ability to reason about one's own and others' personality	Focus is on understanding personality and motives of both self and others

Types of People Intelligence

In their seminal article on EI, Salovey and Mayer (1990) discuss the historical relationship between EI and *social intelligence*, a concept first proposed by Thorndike (1920), which is, loosely, the ability to understand, get along with, and manage relationships with other people.

Practical intelligence involves having implicit knowledge about context and then applying information accurately for that specific context. "It is the ability to adapt to, shape, and select everyday environments" or, more colloquially, "street smarts" (Sternberg et al., 2000, pp. 1 & 32). As such it somewhat intersects with more traditional cognitive intelligences and people intelligences.

More newly conceptualized than social and practical intelligence is *personal intelligence*, introduced by Mayer (2009). As Mayer and colleagues (2016) state rather simply, personal intelligence is "The ability to reason about personality – both our own and others'." (p. 296) Mayer suggests a similar structure for personal intelligence to his four-branch structure for EI but focusing on inner awareness and self-development.

Emotional intelligence overlaps conceptually with personal intelligence in that both emphasize understanding emotions, but they differ in their end goals. For personal intelligence, understanding one's own emotions and motives as they underlie action and interpersonal relationships is key; but for EI, understanding emotions is to serve the purpose of helping facilitate the "desired emotional states and experiences in oneself and others" (Mayer et al., 2016; p. 296). In its function of improving social interactions, personal intelligence shares goals with social intelligence; yet social intelligence has a bit more of a manipulative tone, in that the end goal is to be able to influence and direct a group or a social environment in the way one desires (Mayer et al., 2016). Perhaps the broadest category is practical intelligence, which might be said to include the goals of the three other categories discussed: ultimately to promote the individual's overall well-being and achievement of life goals.

Finally, some argue that *interpersonal accuracy* (IPA, also known as nonverbal sensitivity), "the ability to accurately judge others' emotions, intentions, traits, truthfulness, and other social characteristics" (Schlegel, Boone, & Hall, 2017, p. 104), is another broad umbrella concept encompassing ability measures of EI. Further, in their review, Schmid, Mast, and Hall (2018) suggest that IPA affects social outcomes because those who are more skilled at it show greater ability to change their behavior to match expectations.

Ability EI, Self-Report EI, and the Mixed Model

A review of EI research would be remiss if it didn't attempt, at some level, to disentangle the ability model from other models or approaches also claiming to characterize EI. In an attempt to clarify what EI is, and to distinguish it from other models that have confused both the academic and applied world, Mayer, Salovey, and Caruso (2000) aimed to crystallize how ability EI is distinct from other models and measurement approaches. Mayer and colleagues (2000) label Goleman's (1995) and others' models "mixed models ... because the models mix together many attributes unrelated to emotion, intelligence, or emotional intelligence, in with the emotional intelligence concept" (p. 8). Daus and Ashkanasy have also attempted to clarify distinctions between ability EI and other types of models and measurements (Ashkanasy & Daus, 2005; Daus & Ashkanasy, 2005), as have others subsequently (Conte, 2005; Fiori & Vesely-Maillefer, 2018; Mayer, Roberts, & Barsade, 2008; Mayer et al., 2016). One way of clarifying things that has proven useful is Ashkanasy and Daus's (2005) categorization of three "streams" or approaches to EI. The first stream is the ability-based approach, informed by the four-branch model of Mayer and Salovey (1997). The second stream utilizes the ability model conceptually but measures it with self-report assessments. The third stream primarily uses the "mixed model" approach popularized by Goleman (see also Bar-On, 2000).

Measurement of Emotional Intelligence

In this section, we review the most common ability EI measures. Self-report measures are rooted in the MSC (Mayer, Salovey, & Caruso) Ability Model. Schutte and colleagues (1998) developed one of the earliest and most commonly used self-report measures of EI. A sample item is: "I expect that I will do well on most things I try." Wong and Law (2002) developed a sixteen-item self-report measure and attempted to use it to predict leadership abilities. A sample item is: "I am sensitive to the feelings and emotions of others."

Table 12.2 summarizes the most common ability measures that have been promulgated to measure EI: their developers, rationales, and measurement systems. Multiple studies (Banziger, Scherer, Hall, & Rosenthal, 2011; MacCann & Roberts, 2008; Matsumoto & Ekman, 1989; Matusmoto, LeRoux, Wilson-Cohn, Raroque, Kooken, Ekman et al., 2000; Mayer, Salovey, Caruso, & Sitarenios, 2003; Nowicki & Duke, 1994; Papadogiannis, Logan, & Sitarenios, 2009) attest to the various strong psychometric properties of these measures. See also Schlegel et al. (2017) for a review of IPA measures that includes some of the above, as well as different measures of IPA.

Table 12.3 summarizes the main attributes of the MSCEIT, the most direct measure of the four-branch model. The original idea was to develop

Table 12.2 Ability measures of emotional intelligence

Measure	Authors	Rationale	How measured
Profile of Nonverbal Sensitivity (PONS)	Rosenthal, DePaulo, & Jall, 1979; Rosenthal, Archer, Hall, DiMatteo, & Rogers, 1979	Gauges individual differences in ability to recognize emotions, interpersonal attitude, and communicative intensions	Participants see/hear 220 video and audio clips portraying a young woman in varying emotional situations and choose which phrases best describe each clip
Diagnostic Analysis of Nonverbal Accuracy (DANVA)	Nowicki and Duke, 1994	Addresses issues in the use of the PONS in child populations	Participants attempt to mimic the emotions they are seeing or hearing in a series of slides and audio recordings
Mayer-Salovey-Caruso Emotional Intelligence Test (MSCEIT, formerly MEIS)	Mayer, Salovey, & Caruso, 2002; Mayer, Salovey, & Caruso, 1997	Assesses performance on emotion tasks and problem solving	141 items across eight tasks (two tasks per branch of EI); participants identify emotions in faces and pictures, evaluate how different moods interact with cognitive activities, and assess how emotions change and how to regulate emotion
Japanese and Caucasian Brief Affect Recognition Test (JACBART)	Matusmoto, LeRoux, Wilson-Cohn, Raroque, Kooken, Ekman, et al., 2000	Measures the ability to recognize seven universal emotions (anger, contempt, disgust, fear, happiness, sadness, surprise)	Participants see one-second clips of emotional expressions embedded into a neutral expression recorded by both males and females across two visibly different races
Situational Test of Emotional Understanding and Situational Test of Emotional Management (STEU; STEM)	MacCann & Roberts, 2008	Improves on "rate the extent" issues in MSCEIT	STEU contains 42 items identifying 14 emotions adapted for either no context, personal, or work context; STEM was reduced to 30 items

a performance- or task-based measure that could be scored somewhat "objectively." The developers' approach parallels cognitive ability models in that it assesses one's ability via a test with "right" and "wrong" answers. The tests assess performance on emotion tasks and problem solving. Scoring can be done using either consensus (comparing chosen answers to what others in the sample chose), or expert, (comparing chosen answers to answers supplied by experts).

Table 12.3 Mayer-Salovey-Caruso Emotional Intelligence Test (MSCEIT)

Branch	Assessment criteria	Testing method
Perceiving emotions	Identifying emotions in faces and pictures	Participants choose the degree to which different discrete emotions best match or fit the cognitive activity or sensation presented
Facilitating thought using emotions	Evaluating how different moods interact with specific cognitive activities (such as reasoning and decision-making), and comparing emotions to other sensations such as color, light, and temperature	Same as above
Understanding emotions	Evaluating how emotions change and morph over time within certain contexts, and how emotions combine and interact to form new emotions	Multiple choice; participants choose the best option from among five
Managing emotions	Evaluating courses of action that might be taken to preserve or induce a certain mood or emotion	Situational questions; participants choose the best action option from among five

Predictors of EI

In this section, we briefly review predictors of EI, namely demographics and personality.

Demographics

In their early writing, Mayer and Salovey (1997) argued that EI skills are partly established early in childhood through parenting and education, but that they also can be developed over time. Research has tended to support this view (Marsland & Likavec, 2003; Mayer, Caruso, & Salovey, 1999). Recently, Cabello, Sorrel, Fernández-Pinto, Extremera, and Fernández-Berrocal (2016) found evidence of an inverted-U-shaped curve between EI and age such that EI increases from childhood through adulthood, but then begins to diminish at advanced ages.

When research finds gender differences in EI abilities, it almost always shows that women have higher skills (Brackett, Mayer, & Warner, 2004; Cabello et al., 2016; Mayer et al., 2000). Joseph and Newman (2010) review related evidence regarding gender differences in emotion-related skills and abilities that supports this. Their meta-analysis results further confirmed that women tend to have stronger EI skills – although, interestingly enough, they found no gender differences for self-report ability models. Joseph and Newman (2010), although cautioning against overgeneralizing beyond their meta-analysis results due to small sample sizes of studies reporting race, also found some evidence for EI skills being higher in White versus Black subjects, while Black subjects reported higher scores on self-report ability measures.

Personality Traits

Joseph and Newman (2010) reported in their meta-analysis that the ability model had significant relationships between specific branches of EI and personality; specifically, conscientiousness is positively related to emotion perception, and emotional stability (the reverse of neuroticism) is positively related to emotion regulation. O'Boyle and colleagues (2011) found similar relationships between ability EI and personality: neuroticism was negatively related to EI, and the other four of the Big Five traits were positively related, with agreeableness having the strongest relationship ($r = .22$). In a meta-analytic review of EI and the Dark Triad personality traits of narcissism, Machiavellianism, and psychopathy (Miao, Humphrey, Qian, & Pollack, 2019), the authors found EI to be significantly and negatively related to Machiavellianism and psychopathy, and not related to narcissism.

EI and Workplace Outcomes

We now dive into literature regarding EI and important workplace outcomes. A large percentage of work in this arena has focused on leadership and/or performance.

Leadership

Leadership, particularly transformational leadership, is one of the most commonly studied outcomes of EI. For example, Leban and Zulauf (2004) examined the relationship of 24 leader project manager's MSCEIT scores and found a significant relationship between leaders' overall EI, notably the understanding emotion branch, and the inspiration dimension (as rated by subordinates) of transformational leadership, as well as between leaders' strategic EI (which comprises the branches of understanding and managing emotion) and the transformational leadership branches of idealized influence and individual consideration. Rubin and colleagues (Rubin, Munz, & Bommer, 2005) examined facial recognition (using the Diagnostic Analysis of Nonverbal Accuracy, DANVA) and found significant relationships between this skill and subordinate-rated transformational leadership; this relationship was particularly strong for leaders high on extroversion. Kellett, Humphrey, and Sleeth (2006) found that three peer-rated qualities – empathy, the ability to express emotions, and the ability to read the emotions of others accurately – related to peer ratings of task leadership and relationship leadership, with peer-rated empathy playing a particularly strong role. Similarly, Kerr, Garvin, Heaton, and Boyle (2006) showed that thirty-eight supervisors' MSCEIT scores, particularly the experiential branches of EI, were positively predictive of subordinates' perceptions of leadership effectiveness. Mills (2009) performed a meta-analysis between EI and leadership effectiveness and found a significant relationship across forty-eight studies; however, unfortunately the review collapsed across ability and mixed measures.

In a study where group members rated team leaders on their EI, Hur, van den Berg, and Wilderom (2001) showed that perceptions of leaders' EI skills were positively related to perceptions of leaders' transformational leadership and effectiveness as well as perceptions of service climate. The study further underscores the relationships between (at least) perceptions of another's EI skills and their effectiveness. The research does not always unequivocally support ability EI predicting perceptions of leader effectiveness. For example, Dabke (2016) failed to establish ability EI as a predictor *above and beyond transformational leadership perceptions*, but showed positive associations between ability EI and perceptions of performance. It is fair to conclude that a good percentage of research supports the supposition that ability EI positively predicts subordinate perceptions of leadership effectiveness.

Research (Côté, Lopes, Salovey, & Miners, 2010) has also examined ability EI and its relationship with *leader emergence*. Ability EI (measured pre-task) predicts who is rated as the leader by the group (post task). Particularly predictive of this is the understanding emotions branch of EI.

Performance

Joseph and Newman (2010) found in their meta-analysis that the mixed model actually had better predictive validity for job performance than the ability model. Additionally, these authors imposed standards regarding the operationalization of job performance, including only studies with employed participants (i.e. not student samples), and also excluding studies that used self-ratings of job performance. Furthermore, they examined whether EI added incremental validity over cognitive ability and personality (further distinguishing them from those constructs) and found little evidence that ability measures showed substantial incremental validity over *both* the Big Five and cognitive ability, while mixed models did.

O'Boyle, Humphrey, Pollack, Hawver, and Story (2011) found similar relationships in their meta-analysis, which they argued was more comprehensive than Joseph and Newman's (2010) because it included 65 % more studies. Focusing primarily on results for the ability measures, or Stream 1, these authors showed small incremental validity of the ability model above and beyond personality and cognitive ability, and found that it was substantially less predictive than the mixed or self-report streams.

Future Directions

Distinction of approaches and legitimacy of measures

In conducting this review, it became apparent that, while the state of empirical study regarding EI in the workplace has advanced greatly since the start of the twenty-first century, there are still basic gaps needing more data and support. We call for continued rigor and distinction in which type of EI perspective is being tapped. Hundreds of articles were dismissed from inclusion in this review because the researchers did not use an ability perspective in measuring EI. So first, there must be careful use of terminology and selection of measures and instruments. Moreover, many of those excluded articles *introduced* EI using an ability framework and definition, but then measured or implemented it using another framework. As the field continues to progress, it becomes more vital to clarify these distinctions.

The study of EI in the workplace continues to be in need of fairly simple, applied research regarding, first, ability EI as a set of trainable skills and abilities in a variety of workplace contexts; and second, ability EI as a predictor of a variety of performance outcomes in varying occupational settings. This research need not be overly complex to illustrate some basic utility for implementation of EI skills into the workforce. In a review, Daus and Cage (2008) examined literature supporting the potential for arguing that EI is trainable, and found very little evidence of *ability* EI training interventions in the workplace (see Groves, McEnrue, & Shen, 2008 for a notable exception, although even their intervention was with working students and not in the workplace). Over a decade later, there is still little such evidence and an even greater imperative for this sort of applied, practical illustration of the usefulness of EI in the workplace.

It would also behoove EI researchers to use validated non-ability models of EI in workplace settings. For example, self-report measures of EI might be particularly useful for personal development and/or coaching. The abovementioned training study by Groves and colleagues (2008) used a self-report EI instrument as a first step for participants in training, to establish a sort of baseline self-reflection. We see such interventions as holding extreme promise for development and coaching. Trait-based EI measures might also be explored for use in the facilitation of group communication, processes, and conflict prevention. Once again, however, this of course necessitates scientifically rigorous studies to validate such uses.

Regarding self-development, recent research provides a near-comical view of the links between self-perceptions of EI abilities and subsequent willingness to engage in developmental activity. Sheldon, Dunning, and Ames (2014) gave over 300 students the MSCEIT and had them estimate how accurate and predictive their scores were. Poor performers showed less motivation for participating in self-development opportunities, even though they were the ones who might have benefited from them the most. Overcoming the motivation hurdle is just one of many avenues for this self-development perspective.

Finally, we would be negligent if we didn't highlight that in our review of the literature regarding performance outcomes, much of what we reviewed showed a strong advantage for *non*-ability measures in their predictive capability. We must ponder, then: if, as we have claimed, self-report and mixed-model measures are not truly capturing the essence of EI, *what exactly are they capturing ... and why do they show greater promise than ability measures in predicting performance?* We offer one potential explanation. Ability EI's relatively weak capacity to predict performance parallels the lack of a strong relationship between job satisfaction and job performance, bemoaned as the Holy Grail in decades of job satisfaction research (Weiss, 2002). As Fisher (1980) so eloquently laid out, perhaps it is something of a red herring to expect such relationships – regarding job satisfaction and job performance, the way we tend to pursue such relationships empirically is to take a broad measure of job satisfaction, and expect it to predict in a very specific context. As a parallel suggestion, perhaps we need to refine the contexts in which we are expecting ability EI to predict job performance, *as well as the specific operationalizations of job performance we choose to examine.* As Joseph and Newman's (2010) review found, EI ability measures predicted better in high-emotional-labor jobs. Contexts matter – perhaps especially so for potential predictability.

Disentangling the Nomological Net of EI and Related Constructs

A second key area for further exploration and growth in the field is also related to construct refinement, but at a more conceptual and macro level. Mayer and colleagues do this to some extent in their 2016 review, in which they discuss EI as being positioned among other "hot" intelligences – social and personal intelligence. As we advance in knowledge of these intelligences, we are excited to see nuanced understandings, both theoretical and practical, of how they play out both independently and interactively. Might there emerge, for example, a pattern of profiles of individuals in terms of the different hot intelligences, like that which has distinguished research on organizational commitment (Markovits, Davis, & Van Dick, 2007; Sinclair, Tucker, Cullen, & Wright, 2005)? Both advanced theorizing and methodologically and analytically sophisticated study designs should be on the horizon.

Examining profiles of the different branches or dimensions of EI is a further exciting potential area for future research. For example, is it possible that someone could be very strong on reading emotions, but poor at managing them? And wouldn't this particular situation, as an example, potentially pose unique issues for that person (picture the person delivering a lecture or presentation, knowing they are "flopping" and getting exceedingly anxious because of this knowledge, and only making it all worse). Or is the constant management of emotion required in high-emotional-labor jobs, for example teaching, less stressful for those who don't really understand others' emotions well (thus buffering them, in a sense), such that those with aspects of *lower* EI might be *more* protected?

Similarly, perhaps with some branches, at least in some contexts, there may be a point of diminishing returns on increasing levels of the skill – does the expected utility, then, flatten out? Does it actually diminish, following a curvilinear pattern, much as Baron, Hmieleski, and Henry (2012) demonstrated in their study on positive affect and beneficial effects for entrepreneurs? Both theoretical as well as analytical approaches to curvilinear relationships call for more complexity. As an example of a more complex approach of the kind we'd like to see more of, Cote and Miners (2006) showed how EI acted as a *moderator* between cognitive ability and supervisor-rated job performance and organizational citizenship behaviors, in that EI became more important as cognitive ability was lower. As the study of EI turns thirty, it is just such nuance that the field needs in order to advance the science.

References

Ahadi, S. A., & Rothbart, M. K. (1994). Temperament, development, and the Big Five. In C. F. Halverson, Jr., G. A. Kohnstamm, & R. P. Martin (Eds.), *The developing structure of temperament and personality from infancy to adulthood*. New York, NY: Psychology.

Ashkanasy, N. M., & Daus, C. S. (2005). Rumors of the death of emotional intelligence in organizational behavior are vastly exaggerated. *Journal of Organizational Behavior, 26*, 441–452.

Bänziger, T., Scherer, K. R., Hall, J. A., & Rosenthal, R. (2011). Introducing the MiniPONS: A short multichannel version of the profile of nonverbal sensitivity (PONS). *Journal of Nonverbal Behavior, 35*, 189–204.

Bar-On, R. (2000). Emotional and social intelligence: Insights from the Emotional Quotient Inventory. In R. Bar-On & J. D. A. Parker (Eds.), *The handbook of emotional intelligence: Theory, development, assessment, and application at home, school, and in the workplace* (pp. 363–388). San Francisco, CA: Jossey-Bass.

Baron, R. A., Hmieleski, K. M., & Henry, R. A. (2012). Entrepreneurs' dispositional positive affect: The potential benefits – and potential costs – of being "up." *Journal of Business Venturing, 27*, 310–324.

Brackett, M. A., Mayer, J. D., & Warner, R. M. (2004). Emotional intelligence and its relation to everyday behaviour. *Personality and Individual Differences, 36*, 1387–1402.

Brackett, M. A., Rivers, S. E., Shiffman, S., Lerner, N., & Salovey, P. (2006). Relating emotional abilities to social functioning: A comparison of self-report and performance measures of emotional intelligence. *Journal of Personality and Social Psychology, 91*, 780–795.

Cabello, R., Sorrel, M. A., Fernández-Pinto, I., Extremera, N., & Fernández-Berrocal, P. (2016). Age and gender differences in ability emotional intelligence in adults: A cross-sectional study. *Developmental Psychology, 52*, 1486–1492.

Conte, J. M. (2005). A review and critique of emotional intelligence measures. *Journal of Organizational Behavior, 26*, 433–440.

Côté, S., Lopes, P. N., Salovey, P., & Miners, C. T. (2010). Emotional intelligence and leadership emergence in small groups. *Leadership Quarterly, 21*, 496–508.

Côté, S., & Miners, C. T. (2006). Emotional intelligence, cognitive intelligence, and job performance. *Administrative Science Quarterly, 51*, 1–28.

Dabke, D. (2016). Impact of leaders' emotional intelligence and transformational behavior on perceived leadership effectiveness: A multiple source view. *Business Perspectives and Research, 4*, 27–40.

Daus, C. S., & Ashkanasy, N. M. (2005). The case for the ability-based model of emotional intelligence in organizational behavior. *Journal of Organizational Behavior, 26*, 453–466.

Daus, C. S., & Cage, T. (2008). Learning to face emotional intelligence: Training and workplace applications. In N. M. Ashkanasy & C. L. Cooper (Eds.), *Research Companion to Emotion in Organizations* (pp. 245–260). Cheltenham, UK, and Northampton, MA: Edward Elgar.

Davies, M., Stankov, L., & Roberts, R. D. (1998). Emotional intelligence: In search of an elusive construct. *Journal of Personality and Social Psychology, 75*, 989–1015.

Fiori, M., & Antonakis, J. (2011). The ability model of emotional intelligence: Searching for valid measures. *Personality and Individual Differences, 50*, 329–334.

Fiori, M., & Vesely-Maillefer, A. K. (2018). Emotional intelligence as an ability: Theory, challenges, and new directions. In K. V. Keefer, J. D. A. Parker, & D. H. Saklofske (Eds.), *Emotional intelligence in education* (pp. 23–47). Cham, Switzerland: Springer.

Fisher, C. D. (1980). On the dubious wisdom of expecting job satisfaction to correlate with performance. *Academy of Management Review, 5*, 607–612.

Gibbs, N. (1995). Emotional intelligence: The EQ factor. *Time Magazine, 2* October, 23–32.

Goleman, D. (1995). *Emotional intelligence: Why it can matter more than IQ*. New York, NY: Bantam.

Groves, K. S., Pat McEnrue, M., & Shen, W. (2008). Developing and measuring the emotional intelligence of leaders. *Journal of Management Development, 27*, 225–250.

Hur, Y., van den Berg, P. T., & Wilderom, C. P. (2011). Transformational leadership as a mediator between emotional intelligence and team outcomes. *Leadership Quarterly, 22*, 591–603.

Joseph, D. L., Jin, J., Newman, D. A., & O'Boyle, E. H. (2015). Why does self-reported emotional intelligence predict job performance? A meta-analytic investigation of mixed EI. *Journal of Applied Psychology, 100*, 298–342.

Joseph, D. L., & Newman, D. A. (2010). Emotional intelligence: An integrative meta-analysis and cascading model. *Journal of Applied Psychology, 95*, 54–78.

Kellett, J. B., Humphrey, R. H., & Sleeth, R. G. (2006). Empathy and the emergence of task and relations leaders. *Leadership Quarterly, 17*, 146–162.

Kerr, R., Garvin, J., Heaton, N., & Boyle, E. (2006). Emotional intelligence and leadership effectiveness. *Leadership & Organization Development Journal, 27*, 265–279.

Landy, F. J. (2005). Some historical and scientific issues related to research on emotional intelligence. *Journal of Organizational Behavior, 26*, 411–424.

Leban, W., & Zulauf, C. (2004). Linking emotional intelligence abilities and transformational leadership styles. *Leadership & Organization Development Journal, 25*, 554–564.

Locke, E. A. (2005). Why emotional intelligence is an invalid concept. *Journal of Organizational Behavior, 26*, 425–431.

MacCann, C., & Roberts, R. (2008). New paradigms for assessing emotional intelligence: Theory and data. *Emotion*, 8, 540–551.

Markovits, Y., Davis, A. J., & Van Dick, R. (2007). Organizational commitment profiles and job satisfaction among Greek private and public sector employees. *International Journal of Cross Cultural Management, 7*, 77–99.

Marsland, K. W., & Likavec, S. C. (2003). Maternal emotional intelligence, infant attachment and child socio-emotional competence. Paper presented at the 15th Annual Meeting of the American Psychological Society, Atlanta, GA.

Matsumoto, D., & Ekman, P. (1989). American–Japanese cultural differences in intensity ratings of facial expressions of emotion. *Motivation and Emotion, 13*, 143–157.

Matsumoto, D., LeRoux, J., Wilson-Cohn, C., Raroque, J., Kooken, K., Ekman, P., & Amo, L. (2000). A new test to measure emotion recognition ability: Matsumoto and Ekman's Japanese and Caucasian Brief Affect Recognition Test (JACBART). *Journal of Nonverbal Behavior, 24*, 179–209.

Mayer, J. D. (2009). Personal intelligence expressed: A theoretical analysis. *Review of General Psychology, 13*, 46–58.

Mayer, J. D. (2018). Intelligences about things and intelligences about people. In Sternberg, R. J. (Ed.), *The nature of human intelligence*. Cambridge, UK: Cambridge University Press.

Mayer, J. D., Caruso, D. R., & Salovey, P. (1999). Emotional intelligence meets traditional standards for an intelligence. *Intelligence, 27*, 267–298.

Mayer, J. D., Caruso, D. R., & Salovey, P. (2016). The ability model of emotional intelligence: Principles and updates. *Emotion Review, 8*, 290–300.

Mayer, J. D., Roberts, R. D., & Barsade, S. G. (2008). Human abilities: Emotional intelligence. *Annual Review of Psychology, 59*, 507–536.

Mayer, J. D. & Salovey, P. (1997). What is emotional intelligence? In D. Sluyter (Ed.), *Emotional development and emotional intelligence:*

Educational implications. (pp. 3–34). New York, NY: Basic Books.

Mayer, J. D., Salovey, P., & Caruso, D. R. (1997). *Emotional IQ test* (CD-ROM). Needham, MA: Virtual Knowledge.

Mayer, J. D., Salovey, P., & Caruso, D. R. (2000). Models of emotional intelligence. In R. J. Sternberg (Ed.), *Handbook of intelligence* (pp. 396–420). Cambridge, UK: Cambridge University Press.

Mayer, J. D., Salovey, P., & Caruso, D. R. (2002). Mayer-Salovey-Caruso *Emotional Intelligence Test* (MSCEIT) users' manual. Toronto, ON: Multi-Health Systems.

Mayer, J. D., Salovey, P., & Caruso, D. R. (2008). Emotional intelligence: New ability or eclectic traits?*American Psychologist, 63*, 503–0 517.

Mayer, J. D., Salovey, P., Caruso, D. R., & Sitarenios, G. (2003). Measuring emotional intelligence with the MSCEIT V2.0. *Emotion, 3*, 97–105.

Miao, C., Humphrey, R. H., Qian, S., & Pollack, J. M. (2019). The relationship between emotional intelligence and the dark triad personality traits: A meta-analytic review. *Journal of Research in Personality, 78*, 189–197.

Miller, L. A., & Lovler, R. L. (2019). *Foundations of psychological testing: A practical approach*. Thousand Oaks, CA: Sage.

Mills, L. B. (2009). A meta-analysis of the relationship between emotional intelligence and effective leadership. *Journal of Curriculum and Instruction, 3*, 22–38.

Nowicki, S., & Duke, M. P. (1994). Individual differences in the nonverbal communication of affect: The Diagnostic Analysis of Nonverbal Accuracy Scale. *Journal of Nonverbal Behavior, 18*, 9–35.

O'Boyle, E. H., Jr., Humphrey, R. H., Pollack, J. M., Hawver, T. H., & Story, P. A. (2011). The relation between emotional intelligence and job performance: A meta-analysis. *Journal of Organizational Behavior, 32*, 788–818.

Papadogiannis, P. K., Logan, D., & Sitarenios, G. (2009). An ability model of emotional intelligence: A rationale, description, and application of the Mayer Salovey Caruso Emotional Intelligence Test (MSCEIT). In C. Stough, D. H. Saklofske, & J. D. A. Parker (Eds.), *Assessing emotional intelligence* (pp. 43–65). New York, NY: Springer.

Paulhus, D. L., Lysy, D. C., & Yik, M. S. (1998). Self-report measures of intelligence: Are they useful as proxy IQ tests? *Journal of Personality, 66*, 525–554.

Petrides, K. V., & Furnham, A. (2001). Trait emotional intelligence: Psychometric investigation with reference to established trait taxonomies. *European Journal of Personality, 15*, 425–448.

Robins, R. W., Tracy, J. L., Trzesniewski, K., Potter, J., & Gosling, S. D. (2001). Personality correlates of self-esteem. *Journal of Research in Personality, 35*, 463–482.

Rosenthal, R., Archer, D., Hall, J. A., DiMatteo, M. R., & Rogers, P. L. (1979). *Sensitivity to nonverbal communication: The PONS test*. Baltimore, MD: Johns Hopkins University Press.

Rosenthal, R., DePaulo, B. M., & Jall, J. A. (1979). *The PONS test manual: Profile of nonverbal sensitivity*. Boston, MA: Northeastern University.

Rubin, R. S., Munz, D. C., & Bommer, W. H. (2005). Leading from within: The effects of emotion recognition and personality on transformational leadership behavior. *Academy of Management Journal, 48*, 845–858.

Salovey, P., & Mayer, J. D. (1990). Emotional intelligence. *Imagination, Cognition and Personality, 9*, 185–211.

Schlegel, K., Boone, R. T., & Hall, J. A. (2017). Individual differences in interpersonal accuracy: A multi-level meta-analysis to assess whether judging other people is one skill or many. *Journal of Nonverbal Behavior, 41*, 103–137.

Schmid Mast, M., & Hall, J. A. (2018). The impact of interpersonal accuracy on behavioral outcomes. *Current Directions in Psychological Science, 27*, 309–314.

Schutte, N. S., Malouff, J. M., Hall, L. E., Haggerty, D. J., Cooper, J. T., Golden, C. J., & Dornheim, L. (1998). Development and validation of a measure of emotional intelligence. *Personality and Individual Differences, 25*, 167–177.

Sheldon, O. J., Dunning, D., & Ames, D. R. (2014). Emotionally unskilled, unaware, and uninterested in learning more: Reactions to feedback about deficits in emotional intelligence. *Journal of*

Applied Psychology, *99*, doi:10.5465/AMBPP.2013.11901abstract

Sinclair, R. R., Tucker, J. S., Cullen, J. C., & Wright, C. (2005). Performance differences among four organizational commitment profiles. *Journal of Applied Psychology*, *90*, 1280–1287.

Sternberg, R. J., Forsythe, G. B., Hedlund, J., Wagner, R. K., Williams, W. M., Horvath, J. A., . . . & Grigorenko, E. (2000). *Practical intelligence in everyday life*. Cambridge, UK: Cambridge University Press.

Sternberg, R. J., & Wagner, R. K. (1993). The g-ocentric view of intelligence and job performance is wrong. *Current Directions in Psychological Science*, *2*, 1–4.

Thorndike, E. (1920). A constant error in psychological ratings. *Journal of Applied Psychology*, *4*, 25–29.

Vesely-Maillefer, A., Udayar, S., & Fiori, M. (2018). Enhancing the prediction of emotionally intelligent behavior: The PAT Integrated Framework involving trait EI, ability EI, and emotion information processing. *Frontiers in Psychology*, *9*, doi:10.3389/fpsyg.2018.01078

Wagner, R. K., & Sternberg, R. J. (1985). Practical intelligence in real-world pursuits: The role of tacit knowledge. *Journal of Personality and Social Psychology*, *49*, 436–458.

Weiss, H. M. (2002). Deconstructing job satisfaction: Separating evaluations, beliefs and affective experiences. *Human Resource Management Review*, *12*, 173–194.

Wong, C. S., & Law, K. S. (2002). The effects of leader and follower emotional intelligence on performance and attitude: An exploratory study. *Leadership Quarterly*, *13*, 243–274.

13 Affect and Workplace Judgment and Decision-Making

Shanique G. Brown and Alice F. Stuhlmacher

Judgment and decision-making (JDM) are ubiquitous within organizations. Leaders initiate critical judgments and decisions about organizational strategy and operating procedures. Continuous judgments and decisions are generated relating to the recruitment, selection, performance management, and departure of organizational talent. Every employee makes judgments and decisions on career directions, task acceptance, resource use, and time allocations across both work and non-work tasks. Employees generate frequent high-stakes judgments and decisions in courtrooms, as well as split-second decisions in emergency rooms and cockpits. It is hard to imagine workplace decisions and judgments such as these occurring without affective processes being involved.

While it is clear that workplace judgments and decisions involve cognitively complex processes, they also intersect with affective processes based in moods and discrete emotions. Interestingly, a thorough review of judgment and decision research done thirty years ago (Stevenson, Busemeyer, & Naylor, 1990) did not mention any affective processes. However, much has changed in the last couple of decades, and as we will discuss, much remains to be explored.

Our review summarizes key findings related to the role of affect in JDM within the workplace context. First, we offer a brief overview of the JDM and affect literature to orient readers to the constructs and their theoretical development. Second, we present a summary of key JDM findings related to trait affect, state affect or moods, and discrete emotions and discuss why these are important. Finally, we briefly highlight opportunities for future research and practice relating affect with JDM. Consequently, we suggest that a working knowledge of the influence and impact of affective processes in JDM should inform both research and organizational activities.

Judgment and Decision-Making Frameworks

Judgment and decision-making are tightly coupled processes in organizations. Judgment involves rating or forming an idea, while the decision-making process involves making a choice toward a course of action (Bonner, 1999; Stevenson et al., 1990). Many frameworks have been applied to workplace JDM. Some offer prescriptive approaches geared toward how to make effective and efficient decisions. These approaches are often analytic and highly structured in that they rely on such things as cost–benefit calculations, decision trees, or expert systems (Simon, 1987; Stevenson et al., 1990). In contrast to these highly rational–analytic approaches, descriptive approaches aim to detail the human limitations, biases, irrational processes, and behaviors involved in JDM. From earlier works outlining a simple dichotomy of logical versus emotional frameworks, the field has evolved to explore how these systems are related and connected.

The currently popular frameworks describing the course of decision-making are dual-process models (e.g. Epstein, 1994; Evans, 2008;

Stanovich & West, 2003). Dual-process models propose that the course of decisions can be intuitive or reflective. For simplicity and consistency, this chapter primarily uses the "intuitive" and "reflective" labels for the dual processes, but there are rich streams of literature that use other terminology such as System 1 and System 2 (Stanovich, 1999, 2004), heuristic and systematic (Chaiken, 1980; Chen & Chaiken, 1999), or experiential and rational (Epstein; 1994; Epstein & Pacini, 1999). Reflective processes are seen as requiring deeper information processing and analysis than intuitive processes. Intuitive processes are seen as quicker and more action-oriented than the more effort-based analysis in reflective processing. Relevant to this chapter, moods and emotions have been more strongly linked to intuitive processes than reflective ones.

Affective Models Relating to JDM

Recent reviews of the literature have highlighted several themes in the thirty-five years of research on emotions and decision-making (Lerner, Li, Valdesolo, & Kassam, 2015). It is generally accepted that various types of emotions impact decision-making by influencing the content (i.e. *what* is considered) of the judgment. For example, a supervisor's affect might influence their attention to, memory of, or recall of behaviors (Varma, DeNisi, & Peters, 1996). In addition to the content of decisions, emotions can influence depth of thought (i.e. degree of systematic vs. automatic processing) and goal activation (Lerner & Keltner, 2000). Debate continues as to when affect has a positive influence in the quality of JDM; however, it is clear that emotions can have a negative impact on decision-making quality (see Phillips, Fletcher, Marks, & Hine, 2016).

Integrative theories, such as the affect infusion model (AIM; Forgas, 1995), clarify the potential role of affect during JDM processes. AIM explains the mechanism and the degree to which state affect (e.g. mood) influences (or infuses) social judgments. AIM outlines four judgment-related strategies: direct access, motivated processing, heuristic, and substantive. The direct access and motivated strategies involve less affect infusion as they are very purposeful and structured. By contrast, the heuristic and substantive strategies involve more affect infusion and are generative or creative in nature. The type of judgment strategy will depend on situational characteristics, the judge, and/or the target.

AIM also outlines two mechanisms whereby affect serves as an influence: affect priming and affect-as-information. Affect may influence thinking through a priming mechanism (Forgas, 1995). An example of affect priming could occur in the course of evaluating employee performance: negative affect may generate more critical incidents of poor rather than outstanding performance (Feldman, 1981). Through this mechanism, affect enables access to specific information through selective attention, encoding, and retrieval, which can inform judgments (Bower, 1981). Moreover, the affect infusion mechanism is dependent on the complexity of the processing required, with more unusual and complex situations resulting in increased affect infusion. While AIM can be used to address the role of affect from a broad perspective, the specific impact of affect plus JDM is regarded as contextually dependent.

The influence of affect in decision-making has been examined in three areas: a) affect not directly linked to the decision task (i.e. incidental mood states and discrete emotions) that may serve as an antecedent or mediator; b) affect resulting from the decision task (i.e. integral affect); and c) affect as a by-product of a decision (Anderson, 2007; George & Dane, 2016; Lerner et al., 2015). "Incidental affect" refers to affective states that are irrelevant to the task at hand but that influence judgments and decisions (Schwarz, 2001). An incidental affective state or mood could be carried over from a previous event or experience that is unrelated to the required judgment or decision. For example, a leader's positive mood resulting from taking a pet to work may influence judgments about work-related events such as a tardy employee. Incidental affect, as a mediator, can influence the quality of decisions made by serving as a source of bias.

Unlike incidental affect, "integral affect" refers to "affective influences that result from consideration of the decision or judgmental target itself" (Vastfjall et al., 2016, p. 1). An example would be if a workgroup member decides to put extra effort into a task after feeling pride about the success of the team. Integral emotions may serve either as beneficial guides or as a source of bias when making judgments and decisions (Lerner et al., 2015). Affect can also exist as a side consequence or by-product of JDM processes. For example, given that affect is related to critical outcomes including job performance and satisfaction (Weiss & Cropanzano, 1996), an employee may feel increased job satisfaction after seeing the success of a decision. However, not all affective processes are interchangeable. It is helpful to consider an organizing framework to make sense of the types of impact that such processes can have.

Affective Processes in JDM by Levels of Analysis

Affect can be organized by levels of analysis (Rosenberg, 1998). Higher-level themes, such as traits, have an organizing influence on lower-level enablers such as mood and emotions (Mayer, 1995; Rosenberg, 1998). Each level has a unique influence on JDM processes and outcomes.

First Level: Trait Affect and JDM

Trait affect refers to individual differences that are relatively stable and predispose an individual toward certain affective responses (Watson & Clark, 1984). Dispositional or trait affect can include both negative affectivity (i.e. tendency toward unpleasant arousal) and positive affectivity (i.e. tendency toward pleasant arousal) (Watson & Clark, 1984).

Within the literature on organizational behavior, much attention has been given to the effect of trait affect on job performance (e.g. Kaplan, Bradley, Luchman, & Haynes, 2009), with less specific attention to its effects on judgments and decisions. This pattern might be due to the notion that decision-making has closer ties to state affect rather than trait affect (George, 1991, 1992). While an individual may have a general tendency toward a particular affective tone (i.e. trait affect), factors within the work environment may result in changes to affective experiences (i.e. state affect) and may thereby contribute to direct effects of judgment and decision-making outcomes (Meyer, Dalal, & Hermida, 2010; Mischel, 1973). Nonetheless, this reinforces the notion of traits – the higher-level construct – having an organizing function (Rosenberg, 1998).

Additionally, within the context of work, we see trait affect having some priming effects on judgment and decision-making. As proposed by AIM, the effect of trait affect on JDM appears to be consistent with patterns of affect priming. For example, the depressive realism perspective – or the "sadder-but-wiser" effect – was introduced to explain the observation that individuals with high negative trait affect rely on more realistic information and use less bias when making judgments (Alloy & Abramson, 1979). Trait negative affect signals that a problem exists and directs attention to solving that problem. Consequently, individuals with high neuroticism – or other types of negative trait affect – are more likely to withdraw from organizational decision-making situations when the course of action is failing (Wong, Yik, & Kwong, 2006). In other words, negative trait affectivity is associated with less escalation of commitment. Benefits of negative trait affect are also observed in workgroup decision-making.

When information is distributed in workgroups (i.e. information is known to a single member or subset of members), members engage in more information elaboration when group-level trait negative affectivity is high, resulting in more effective decision-making (Kooij-de Bode, van Knippenberg, & van Ginkel, 2010).

The priming mechanism has also been associated with other affective traits including affective orientation, guilt, and shame. Affective orientation refers to the tendency to be aware of affective cues and utilize these cues during the decision-making process (Booth-Butterfield & Booth-Butterfield, 1990). Individuals who are high in affective orientation are more likely to rely on the use of intuition when making decisions (Sinclair, Ashkanasy, & Chattopadhyay, 2010). Further, individuals with high dispositional guilt are more likely to engage in self-regulative thinking, reducing the likelihood of unethical decision-making (Johnson & Connelly, 2016).

Thus although trait-level affect is at the most distal level from actual decisions, it offers a piece of the puzzle for understanding affective processes in the workplace.

Second Level: State Affect, Mood, and JDM

At the second level, we attend to findings related to mood – a transient affective state that lacks a contextual stimulus (Forgas & George, 2001). In the levels-of-analysis framework, moods share features with both affective traits and emotions and are therefore placed at the intermediate level (Rosenberg, 1998). Moods or state affect *incidentally* inform judgments and decisions at work. Like trait affectivity, state affect also can have positive and negative dimensions. State affect is considered to have more direct influence on JDM than trait affectivity (e.g. George, 1991). Consistent with AIM, moods often affect JDM through a direct route – functioning as information – and are often associated with some misattribution (Forgas, 1995). For example, an employee may misattribute their mood when making a judgment about a colleague – mistakenly applying their positive mood as positive "information" about the target of their judgment.

With this perspective, a body of literature has emerged examining the effect of incidental mood (i.e. unrelated to the target) on judgments and decisions (George & Dane, 2016). Incidental affect or one's mood at a particular moment may affect judgments related to taking risks, having an exogenous effect (Johnson & Tversky, 1983). For example, a CEO experiencing personal challenges that induce a negative mood might be less inclined to make a decision involving high financial risks. Incidental mood states, based on the affect-as-information principle, may serve as heuristics during the process of making judgments (Schwarz, 2012).

The impact of incidental moods on judgments and decisions has been explored extensively in the literature (e.g. Au, Chan, Wang, & Vertinsky, 2003). For example, an interviewer's mood can influence judgments about a job candidate's suitability for hire. When in a positive mood, interviewers tend to rate candidates higher on job-related dimensions and make more lenient hiring decisions than when in a negative mood (Baron, 1987). In workgroups, positive mood may negatively influence decision-making as members engage in less information elaboration (van Knippenberg, Kooij-de Bode, & van Ginkel, 2010). The impact of mood also has been found to influence judgments and decisions during the performance appraisal process (Robbins & DeNisi, 1998; Sinclair, 1988) in that mood affected information processing (such as weighting and recall) as well as rating halo and accuracy.

Third level: Emotions and JDM

Finally, at the third level of the affective levels-of-analysis model, emotions function to inform work-related judgments and decisions. Like mood, emotions are transient affective states, but unlike mood, emotions tend to be short-lived and are generally portrayed as being caused by a specific event (Forgas & George, 2001). Emotions may be influenced by both trait affect tendencies and work events (Weiss & Cropanzano, 1996). While the literature has advanced to consider the direct impact of emotions on JDM, a consequentialist theory of the role of emotions in decision-making initially positioned emotions as being a by-product of the decision-making process (Anderson, 2007). These two trends in the literature are important as they have helped to clarify the role of emotions in decision-making – either integral or incidental.

Integral emotions can serve as internal monitors of JDM processes. For example, anger, a negative emotion, if evoked from a harmful situation, may stimulate fast and adaptive decision-making (Bodenhausen, Sheppard, & Kramer, 1994). From a theoretical point of view, the integral influence of emotions on decision-making can be examined using theories including the dual-process models, cognitive experiential self-theory, and the framing effect (Mikels, Shuster, & Thai, 2015). For example, based on the dual-process model, emotions are linked to the intuitive processing of System 1 – supporting the acquisition of information, especially in novel situations (Epstein, 1994). More specifically, an emotion such as anger may activate adaptive responses in a decision-making context (Bodenhausen et al., 1994), while regret from a previous loss may result in favoring particular items (e.g. losing shares) when making future judgments (Summers & Duxbury, 2012). Thus integral emotions can help to guide both the content and process of JDM (Forgas & George, 2001).

Incidental emotions also contribute to JDM. The appraisal tendency framework can account for the effect of incidental emotions on judgment and decision processes (Mikels et al., 2015). According to the appraisal tendency framework, an individual will appraise a JDM event based on the experience of incidental (i.e. unrelated) emotion (Lerner & Keltner, 2000). For example, incidental fear has been seen to facilitate more ethical decision-making, while incidental anger inhibited ethical decision-making (Kligyte, Connelly, Thiel, & Devenport, 2013). To be precise, using a sensemaking approach to understand the influence of incidental emotions on ethical decision-making, unregulated incidental anger has been associated with more retaliation and less recognition of the circumstances related to an event, when compared to incidental fear. These findings underscore the importance of considering trait affect and other carried-over emotional states that may have motivational properties that play a role in informing JDM (Lerner & Tiedens, 2006). For example, supervisor diary-keeping of employee performance can strengthen the relationship between supervisor affect and performance ratings (Varma et al., 1996). Rather than diary-keeping reducing the effect of liking on ratings, more attention to high-performing employees perhaps actually increased supervisor liking of high-performing employees. In addition to actual integral or incidental emotions, anticipated emotions are involved in JDM processes, serving as by-products of the processes or influencing choice (Anderson, 2007; Ng, Wong, & Fai, 2008). Anticipated regret is one example.

The role of regret is an area of extensive attention in decision-making (George & Dane, 2016). The anticipation of regret may be induced by several factors such as the perception that a preferred alternative is inferior to another alternative, or if the consequences expected from the decision become apparent very soon after the decision is made (Zeelenberg, 1999).

Decision-makers may also experience anticipated regret in situations where they feel a high degree of social responsibility (Anderson, 2005). An example of high social responsibility is the context of police work. Based on responses to work-related decision-making scenarios typical of police work, anticipated regret can play a role in explaining avoidant decisions by police officers (Brown & Daus, 2016). Additionally, decision-makers are more likely to experience anticipated regret when decisions are irreversible (Zeelenberg, Beattie, Van der Pligt, & De Vries, 1996). Thus, in addition to emotions serving as a by-product or consequence of decisions, anticipating emotions is yet another way affect is involved in JDM.

In addition to considering these levels, it also helpful to explore how the levels interact.

Interactions among Levels

The levels-of-analysis framework for organizing affect offers a representation of the relative position of trait affect, state affect or mood, and discrete emotions, as well as a description of how the three levels interact to influence outcomes. Trait affect, with its organizing function, may set thresholds that inform the likelihood of an individual experiencing certain moods or emotions (Rosenberg, 1998). Trait affect may also override the influence of more transient state affective processes. For example, in workgroups, members with higher trait negative affect are less sensitive to positive mood manipulations and, consequently, less likely to engage in reduced information elaboration and poor decision-making (van Knippenberg et al., 2010). This finding, and others exploring the interaction between trait and state affect (Salovey & Mayer, 1990), imply that there would be value in further research attention to the interaction among levels of affect on JDM outcomes at work.

Figure 13.1 summarizes the characteristics of each affective level and its role in JDM processes. The figure suggests that while higher affective levels are more stable and longer-lasting, they are more distal to the JDM process. Higher levels are expected to influence the lower affective levels. The mid- and lower levels are not as stable or long-lasting as trait affect. Consequently, although closer to the JDM process, this lesser stability makes emotions particularly subject to other influences. This, as we discuss next, suggests that it will be especially important to understand the effects of context in considering the relationship between JDM and affect.

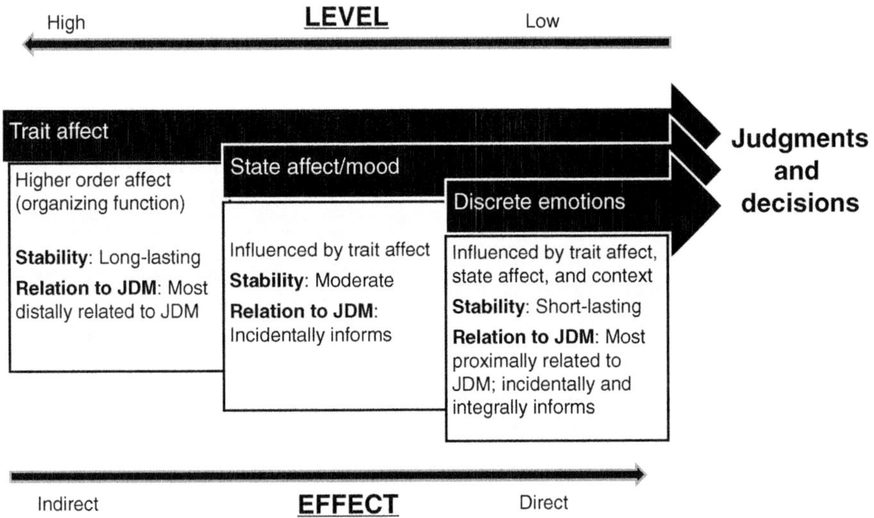

Figure 13.1 Overview of the role of affect by levels of analysis in judgment and decision-making

Future Directions for Research on Affect and Workplace JDM

JDM research has begun to pay close attention to context factors, and we agree that context is critical for understanding the role of affect in JDM. Context can involve a variety of factors including task characteristics, the measurement of decision quality, and decision styles and other individual differences.

A number of important task-related factors are related to decision-making (Hamilton, Shih, & Mohammed, 2017). Factors such as time pressure, the importance of the decision, and task familiarity connect with affective processes. Research on levels of affect suggests that trait affect plays a minor role in each decision, but may have a bigger role when other situational constraints are weak. For example, an employee deciding to place a catering order for a group lunch next week may experience a quite different affective landscape from that experienced when making decisions on a workplace emergency response in the face of an impending tornado. The context sets the stage for affective events as well as for the intuitive or reflective decision processes. A strong affective event involving high stakes and time pressure (such as a tornado) increases the possibility for less reflective and more emotional decisions, with emotions perhaps playing a more direct role in the JDM process. Intriguingly, according to AIM, the infusion of affect in JDM processes increases as the complexity and unfamiliarity with the situation increases (Forgas, 1995).

In considering complexity and unfamiliarity, other contextual factors might provide "guardrails" to emotions' influence in decision-making. Consider a situation where an organization has strong norms, policies, or procedures. These might reduce intuitive decision-making but increase reflective decision-making processes. For example, if an organization has run a number of drills and simulations in preparation for a certain type of event (e.g. customer service interaction, active shooter), this could shift the initial emotional response that someone may experience in encountering an event for the first time. In light of this, we need a better understanding of the organizational context of norms, training, and policies that might shape affective responses.

Likewise, the particular type of task may trigger different decision-making preferences (Hamilton et al., 2017). Human resource decisions about people may prompt different affective processes from decisions about budget and finances. Both kinds of decisions could be driven by intuitive or reflective processing, but some "people" issues may be less rule-based, leading to more intuitive decision-making and a particular sensitivity to mood and emotions. The extent that emotions are involved might relate to organizational culture and norms, as well as the personality of the decision-maker. For instance, a highly conscientious decision-maker may strongly attend to organizational discipline policy, where others may make similar decisions more influenced by emotions. Thus, understanding emotions can offer insights into how to make fairer and less biased decisions. As another illustration, rather than trying to retrain implicit biases, according to decision-making literature, a more fruitful route might be to encourage more reflective processing or structural features that support less emotionally-driven hiring. When hiring decisions are made based on decision rules and conscious processing, this can remove some of the affective processes that are connected to intuitive processing and irrational decisions.

Affective processes in JDM also need to attend to the type of criteria used to benchmark successful decisions. The choice of measures of decision quality is critical. The metrics for a quality decision can be performance-related as well as tied to the psychological experience (Phillips et al., 2016). Performance-related metrics tend to be compared to a "correct" answer, while a separate set of metrics relate to what is experienced (such as decision time, confidence, satisfaction, and ease). A meta-analysis by Phillips et al. (2016) found that reflective decision-making styles were positively related to both performance criteria (r =.11) and psychological experience criteria (r = .14). Intuitive styles were negatively related to performance (r = −.09) and positively related to psychological criteria (r = .06). Given that some of these psychological criteria appear to have some strong affective dimensions (i.e. ratings of satisfaction, ease) it seems a fruitful area for exploring more on how metrics, decision style, and affective antecedents and consequences intersect.

Additionally, the impact of state and trait affect warrants more exploration in the JDM process. Many organizationally important individual differences have both state and trait components (e.g. relational orientation, self-esteem) where affect may be involved. For example, consider that procrastination can be seen as a state or a trait where the decision to procrastinate on tasks can be seen as a way to manage negative moods (Pychyl & Sirois, 2013). Trait affect would intersect with state affect that results from challenging tasks that create particular moods. In short, the context can create weak or strong situations for affective processes to interact, and we encourage further exploration of these nuanced trade-offs.

Conclusion

Within the workplace, judgment and decisions impact all aspects of organizational life including allocating resources, employee selection, affirmative action efforts, negotiation offers, and customer service. We have discussed how affect informs judgments and decisions and may function as antecedent, intervening, and/or consequent variables in JDM processes.

As our environment – including our work environment – continues to become more complex, we expect that research will increasingly need to attend to affective processes to help us understand and improve human decision-making and judgments. Despite the current enthusiasm for artificial intelligence and computer simulations to relieve workers of the burden of routine judgments and decisions, it is unlikely that humans will ever be completely removed from workplace judgments and decisions. If nothing else, decisions about automated systems are made by humans with affective traits who are bombarded by stimuli that impact moods and emotions. As such, it is critical that research continues to advance our understanding of the role of affect in JDM and especially of when and how affect aids or impairs JDM outcomes. With this knowledge, researchers and practitioners will be better positioned to describe these processes and to develop strategies for effective JDM.

References

Alloy, L. B., & Abramson, L. Y. (1979). Judgment of contingency in depressed and nondepressed students: Sadder but wiser? *Journal of Experimental Psychology: General*, *108*, 441–485.

Anderson, C. J. (2007). The functions of emotion in decision making and decision avoidance. In K. D. Vohs, R. F. Baumeister, & G. Loewenstein (Eds.), *Do emotions help or hurt decision making? A hedgefoxian perspective* (pp. 183–201). New York, NY: Russell Sage Foundation.

Au, K., Chan, F., Wang, D., & Vertinsky, I. (2003). Mood in foreign exchange trading: Cognitive processes and performance. *Organizational Behavior and Human Decision Processes*, *91*, 322–338.

Baron, R. A. (1993). Interviewers' moods and evaluations of job applicants: The role of applicant qualifications. *Journal of Applied Social Psychology*, *23*, 253–271.

Bodenhausen, G. V., Sheppard, L. A., & Kramer, G. P. (1994). Negative affect and social judgment: The differential impact of anger and sadness. *European Journal of Social Psychology, 24*, 45–62.

Bonner, S. E. (1999). Judgment and decision-making research in accounting. *Accounting Horizons, 13*, 385–398.

Booth-Butterfield, M., & Booth-Butterfield, S. (1990). Conceptualizing affect as information in communication production. *Human Communication Research, 16*, 451–476.

Bower, G. H. (1981). Mood and memory. *American Psychologist, 36*, 129–148.

Brown, S. G., & Daus, C. S. (2016). Avoidant but not avoiding: The mediational role of anticipated regret in police decision-making. *Journal of Police and Criminal Psychology, 31*, 238–249.

Chaiken, S. (1980). Heuristic versus systematic information processing and the use of source versus message cues in persuasion. *Journal of Personality and Social Psychology, 39*, 752–766.

Chaiken, S., & Trope, Y. (Eds.) (1999). *Dual-process theories in social psychology*. New York, NY: Guilford.

Epstein, S. (1994). Integration of the cognitive and the psychodynamic unconscious. *American Psychologist, 49*, 709–724.

Epstein, S., & Pacini, R. (1999). Some basic issues regarding dual-process theories from the perspective of cognitive–experiential self-theory. In S. Chaiken & Y. Trope (Eds.), *Dual-process theories in social psychology* (pp. 462–482). New York, NY: Guilford.

Evans, J. S. B. T. (2008). Dual-processing accounts of reasoning, judgment, and social cognition. *Annual Review of Psychology, 59*, 255–278.

Feldman, J. (1981). Beyond attribution theory: Cognitive processes in performance appraisal. *Journal of Applied Psychology, 66*, 127–148.

Forgas, J. P. (1995). Mood and judgment: The affect infusion model (AIM). *Psychological Bulletin, 117*, 39–66.

Forgas, J. P., & George, J. M. (2001). Affective influences on judgments and behavior in organizations: An information processing perspective. *Organizational Behavior and Human Decision Processes, 86*, 3–34.

George, J. M. (1991). State or trait: Effects of positive mood on prosocial behaviors at work. *Journal of Applied Psychology, 76*, 299–307.

George, J. M. (1992). The role of personality in organizational life: Issues and evidence. *Journal of Management, 18*, 185–213.

George, J. M., & Dane, E. (2016). Affect, emotion, and decision making. *Organizational Behavior and Human Decision Processes, 136*, 47–55.

Hamilton, K., Shih, S. I., & Mohammed, S. (2017). The predictive validity of the decision styles scale: An evaluation across task types. *Personality and Individual Differences, 119*, 333–340.

Johnson, E., & Tversky, A. (1983). Affect, generalization and the perception of risk. *Journal of Personality and Social Psychology, 45*, 20–31.

Johnson, J. F., & Connelly, S. (2016). Moral disengagement and ethical decision-making: The moderating role of trait guilt and shame. *Journal of Personnel Psychology, 15*, 184–189.

Kaplan, S., Bradley, J. C., Luchman, J. N., & Haynes, D. (2009). On the role of positive and negative affectivity in job performance: A meta-analytic investigation. *Journal of Applied Psychology, 94*, 162–176.

Kligyte, V., Connelly, S., Thiel, C., & Devenport, L. (2013). The influence of anger, fear, and emotion regulation on ethical decision making. *Human Performance, 26*, 297–326.

Kooij-de Bode, H. J., Van Knippenberg, D., & Van Ginkel, W. P. (2010). Good effects of bad feelings: Negative affectivity and group decision-making. *British Journal of Management, 21*, 375–392.

Lerner, J. S., & Keltner, D. (2000). Beyond valence: Toward a model of emotion-specific Influences on judgement and choice. *Cognition & Emotion, 14*, 473–493.

Lerner, J. S., Li, Y., Valdesolo, P., & Kassam, K. S. (2015). Emotion and decision making. *Annual Review of Psychology, 66*, 799–823.

Lerner, J. S., & Tiedens, L. Z. (2006). Portrait of the angry decision maker: How appraisal tendencies shape anger's influence on cognition. *Journal of Behavioral Decision Making, 19*, 115–137.

Mayer, J. D. (1995). The system–topic framework and the structural arrangement of systems within and around personality. *Journal of Personality, 63*, 459–493.

Meyer, R. D., Dalal, R. S., & Hermida, R. (2010). A review and synthesis of situational strength in the organizational sciences. *Journal of Management, 36*, 121–140.

Mikels, J. A., Shuster, M. M., & Thai, S. T. (2015). Aging, emotion, and decision making. In T. M. Hess, J. Strough, & C. E. Löckenhoff (Eds.), *Aging and decision making: Empirical and applied perspectives* (pp. 169–188). San Diego, CA: Elsevier Academic.

Mischel, W. (1973). Toward a cognitive social learning reconceptualization of personality. *Psychological Review, 80*(4), 252–283.

Ng, C. K., Wong, K. F. E., & Fai, E. (2008). Emotion and organizational decision-making: The roles of negative affect and anticipated regret in making decisions under escalation situations. In N. Ashkanasy & C. Copper (Eds.), *Emotions in organizations* (pp. 45–60). Cheltenham, UK: Edward Elgar.

Phillips, W. J., Fletcher, J. M., Marks, A. D., & Hine, D. W. (2016). Thinking styles and decision making: A meta-analysis. *Psychological Bulletin, 142*, 260–290.

Robbins, T. L., & DeNisi, A. S. (1998). Mood vs. interpersonal affect: Identifying process and rating distortions in performance appraisal. *Journal of Business and Psychology, 12*, 313–325.

Rosenberg, E. L. (1998). Levels of analysis and the organization of affect. *Review of General Psychology, 2*(3), 247–270.

Salovey, P., & Mayer, J. D. (1990). Emotional intelligence. *Imagination Cognition and Personality, 9*, 185–211.

Schwarz, N. (2001). Feelings as information: implications for affective influences on information processing. In L. L. Martin & G. L. Clore (Eds.), *Theories of mood and cognition: A user's guidebook* (pp. 159–176). Hillsdale, NJ: Lawrence Erlbaum.

Schwarz, N. (2012). Feelings-as-information theory. In P. Van Lange, A. Kruglanski, & E. T. Higgins (Eds.), *Handbook of theories of social psychology* (Volume 1, pp. 289–308). Los Angeles, CA: Sage.

Simon, H. A. (1987). Making management decisions: The role of intuition and emotion. *Academy of Management Perspectives, 1*, 57–64.

Sinclair, M., Ashkanasy, N. M., & Chattopadhyay, P. (2010). Affective antecedents of intuitive decision-making. *Journal of Management & Organization, 16*, 382–398.

Sinclair, R. C. (1988). Mood, categorization breadth, and performance appraisal: The effects of order of information acquisition and affective state on halo, accuracy, information retrieval, and evaluations. *Organizational Behavior and Human Decision Processes, 42*, 22–46.

Sirois, F., & Pychyl, T. (2013). Procrastination and the priority of short-term mood regulation: Consequences for future self. *Social and Personality Psychology Compass, 7*, 115–127.

Stanovich, K. E. (1999). *Who is rational? Studies of individual differences in reasoning*. Mahwah, NJ: Erlbaum.

Stanovich, K. E. (2004). *The robot's rebellion: Finding meaning in the age of Darwin*. Chicago, IL: Chicago University Press.

Stanovich, K. E., & West, R. F. (2003). The rationality debate as a progressive research program. *Behavioral and Brain Sciences, 26*, 531–533.

Stevenson, M. K., Busemeyer, J. R., & Naylor, J. C. (1990). Judgment and decision-making theory. In M. D. Dunnette & L. M. Hough (Eds.), *Handbook of industrial and organizational psychology* (Volume 1, pp. 283–374). Palo Alto, CA: Consulting Psychologists.

Summers, B., & Duxbury, D. (2012). Decision-dependent emotions and behavioral anomalies. *Organizational Behavior and Human Decision Processes, 118*, 226–238.

van Knippenberg, D., Kooij-de Bode, H. J., & van Ginkel, W. P. (2010). The interactive effects of mood and trait negative affect in group decision making. *Organization Science, 21*, 731–744.

Varma, A., DeNisi, A., & Peters, L. H. (1996). Interpersonal affect and performance appraisal: A field study. *Personnel Psychology, 49*, 341–360.

Västfjäll, D., Slovic, P., Burns, W. J., Erlandsson, A., Koppel, L., Asutay, E., & Tinghög, G. (2016). The arithmetic of emotion: Integration of incidental and

integral affect in judgments and decisions. *Frontiers in Psychology*, *7*, Article 325.
Watson, D., & Clark, L. A. (1984). Negative affectivity: The disposition to experience aversive emotional states. *Psychological Bulletin*, *96*, 465–490.
Weiss, H. M., & Cropanzano, R. (1996). Affective events theory: A theoretical discussion of the structure, causes and consequences of affective experiences at work. In B. M. Staw & L. L. Cummings (Eds.), *Research in organization behavior* (Volume 19, pp. 1–74). Greenwich, CT: JAI.
Wong, K. F. E., Yik, M., & Kwong, J. Y. (2006). Understanding the emotional aspects of escalation of commitment: The role of negative affect. *Journal of Applied Psychology*, *91*, 282–297.
Zeelenberg, M., Beattie, J., Van der Pligt, J., & De Vries, N. K. (1996). Consequences of regret aversion: Effects of expected feedback on risky decision making. *Organizational Behavior and Human Decision Processes*, *65*, 148–158.
Zeelenger, M. (1999). Anticipated regret, expected feedback and behavioral decision making. *Journal of Behavioral Decision Making*, *12*, 93–106.

14 The Mindful Emotion Management Framework

How Mindfulness Helps Employees Manage Emotions through Reactivity, Regulation, and Reappraisal

Jochen Reb and Theodore C. Masters-Waage

Introduction

We may be living in a free-market economy, but that does not mean we are encouraged to express our emotions freely and authentically in organizations. Instead, societal and organizational norms, behavioral expectations (especially in customer service interactions), and even political considerations (e.g. laughing at a boss's boring joke) put employees' emotional resilience to the test. Thus how well employees can regulate, or manage, their emotions has implications for their performance and well-being at work and, given that work tends to occupy a central role in most adults' lives, also for their effectiveness and well-being overall (Weiss & Cropanzano, 1996). In this chapter, we attempt to synthesize recent research on the role of mindfulness in emotion regulation by developing an integrative *mindful emotion management framework.*

Organizations can to some extent help employees regulate their emotions, for example by shaping the work environment so as to induce positive affect (Ashforth & Humphrey, 1995). However, executing such a situational strategy is limited by the constraints that organizations face. For example, jobs in service by their nature expose employees to situations, such as interactions with disgruntled customers, that tend to induce negative affect. Research has therefore examined individual difference variables that may aid emotional regulation, such as emotional intelligence (Zeidner, Matthews, & Roberts, 2004).

At a process level, research has examined a number of different emotion regulation strategies, focusing on emotion suppression and cognitive reappraisal (Gross, 2013). An emergent research area examines the role of mindfulness in emotion regulation. Mindfulness can be defined as a state of awareness in which attention is directed toward moment-to-moment experience (Brown, Ryan, & Creswell, 2007; Kabat-Zinn, 2003) and in which the experiences arising are observed "from a distance," in a process known as meta-awareness or decentering, implying a lower level of identification, mental commentary, and judgmental evaluation (Dahl, Lutz, & Davidson, 2015). In this way, mindfulness helps individuals change their *relation* to moment-to-moment experiences (observing experiences as experiences, without overidentification), rather than trying to change the *content* of experiences (e.g. avoiding, suppressing, or removing unpleasant experiences, such as sadness) (Hofmann & Asmundson, 2008).

Since the 1970s mindfulness research has been gaining traction in the biopsychological and medical literature. A number of meta-analytic studies have shown robust effects of mindfulness on improving well-being (Gu, Strauss, Bond, & Cavanagh, 2015) and reducing stress (Chiesa & Serretti, 2009). Further, using fMRI and other brain imaging techniques, researchers have been able to measure consistent and long-lasting neurological changes in the brains of mindfulness practitioners (Singleton et al., 2014; Tang, Hölzel, & Posner, 2015). Based on such results, mindfulness has seen growing interest from organizational scholars, with beneficial effects shown across a number of domains including burnout, performance, leadership, and decision-making, among others (Good et al., 2016; Reb & Atkins, 2015).

The Mindful Emotion Management Framework

One of the primary domains of mindfulness research has been in emotion. A number of studies have shown that mindfulness can improve emotion regulation in clinical and non-clinical populations (e.g. Guendelman, Medeiros, & Rampes, 2017; Hill & Updegraff, 2012; Hülsheger, Alberts, Feinholdt, & Lang, 2013). Several researchers have proposed models for how mindfulness enhances emotion management (e.g. Cebolla et al., 2018; Creswell & Lindsay, 2014; Garland, Farb, Goldin, & Fredrickson, 2015; Teper & Inzlicht, 2013). These models focus on distinct aspects and stages of the emotion management process and do so using neurological, psychological, and behavioral arguments. In the mindful emotion management framework (MEMF), we attempt to integrate the key features of these models and their underlying research to develop an overarching framework of mindful emotion management. We then apply this framework to a number of common organizational phenomena and activities.

Figure 14.1 outlines the MEMF. The assumed underlying process is that affective events (Weiss & Cropanzano, 1996) give rise to emotions (stage 1), which affect behavior (stage 2); individuals often "hold on" to these affective episodes, leading their resulting emotions to persist over time and have long-term effects (stage 3). For example, a sudden work deadline (event) might evoke anxiety (emotion), which in turn leads to rushing a task (behavior); this affective episode can persist over time if the employee keeps worrying about how well the task was completed or about future sudden deadlines, potentially leading to chronic stress (long-term effects). *Managing emotions* is the overarching term we use to refer to the strategies that individuals can use to manage each of these stages; we will look at each stage now.

First Stage: Emotion Reactivity

The first stage is from an event to an emotion. The more fine-grained account of this process is that an event leads to an affective response in the body, e.g. increased heart rate, which is then in turn interpreted by the brain as an emotion, e.g. anxiety

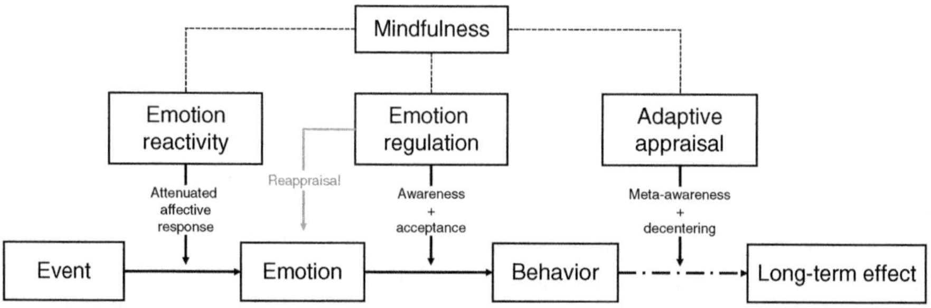

Figure 14.1 The mindful emotion management framework (MEMF)
Notes: the dotted line between the last stages of the model demonstrates the process by which the first two stages lead to long-term effects. The "reappraisal" process at the emotion stage, shown in gray, is a newly proposed mechanism and requires future empirical investigation, as discussed in the final section of this chapter.

(Damasio, 1998). The likelihood that an event will lead to an emotion thus depends on the extent of the affective response, i.e. emotional reactivity (Zelkowitz & Cole, 2016). The MEMF suggests that mindfulness reduces emotional reactivity to affective events (see Figure 14.1), consistent with recent evidence. For example, after just fifteen minutes of practicing mindful breathing participants responded to adverse images with less negative affect and were more willing to view them again if requested (Arch & Craske, 2006). Further, individuals with depression or anxiety disorders who are generally acutely reactive to emotional stimuli show a decrease in emotion reactivity after completing a mindfulness training program (Brown, Weinstein, & Creswell, 2012), even when compared to an active control group (Hoge et al., 2014). Also, mindful individuals show an attenuated physiological response to socially stressful events (Britton, Shahar, Szepsenwol, & Jacobs, 2012).

This shift may be due to the distinct manner in which mindful individuals process affective events in the brain. In particular mindfulness has been shown to alter both the structure and activation of the amygdala, a key brain area involved in emotion, stress, and the "fight or flight" response (Phelps, 2006). Mindfulness is associated with reduced gray matter (i.e. size) and resting reactivity of the amygdala, along with functional connectivity between the amygdala and other brain regions associated with emotion (Frewen et al., 2010; Hölzel et al., 2009; Taren, Creswell, & Gianaros, 2013). Moreover, just eight weeks of mindfulness practice led to changes in the amygdala that are correlated with reduced stress and emotional reactivity (Hölzel et al., 2009). Beyond the amygdala, research has also shown that mindfulness changes neural responses to images invoking sadness (Farb et al., 2010). Overall, mindfulness appears to be related to distinct neurological processing of affective events that leads to reduced emotional reactivity. These neurobiological processes appear to affect the emergence of emotions at an unconscious level without cognitive mediation (in contrast to other antecedent-focused regulation strategies, such as cognitive reappraisal). An implication of these processes is that more mindful individuals experience both less intense negative (e.g. anger at a poorly performing subordinate) and positive (e.g. excitement about an important project) emotions.

Second Stage: Emotion Regulation

The second stage is from emotion to behavior. Emotions, through their action tendencies, motivate behavior; sometimes, these action tendencies motivate behaviors that are unsuitable in the workplace context (e.g. responding aggressively to a rude customer) and therefore employees try to regulate the emotion and its action tendency. Brockman, Ciarrochi, Parker, and Kashdan (2017) compared the effectiveness of three different emotion regulation strategies: emotion suppression, cognitive reappraisal, and mindful emotion regulation. *Emotion suppression* is a response-focused strategy that attempts to inhibit in particular the expressive–behavioral consequences of emotional experiences (e.g. trying not to show frustration on one's face after not receiving a promotion). Whereas many individuals habitually use this approach to suppress the effects of strong emotions, it can, counterproductively, exacerbate an emotion (Gross, 2002). *Cognitive reappraisal* is an antecedent strategy that attempts to regulate emotions by influencing the cognitions that give rise to, sustain, intensify, or reduce emotions (e.g. generating thoughts about the downsides of a promotion such as having to move to a different city, more stress etc.). This strategy is generally thought to be quite effective at regulating emotions, yet with limitations. For example, Brockman et al. (2017) found that cognitive reappraisal led to increased positive affect but did not help to regulate negative affect.

In fact, Brockman et al. (2017) found that *mindful emotion regulation* was the only regulation strategy that significantly led to both increased positive and reduced negative affect. This is consistent with other research showing the efficacy of mindfulness in emotion regulation (e.g. Guendelman et al., 2017; Hill & Updegraff, 2012). Teper, Segal, and Inzlicht (2013) argue that the key mechanisms behind this are 1) a heightened introspective *awareness* of emotions arising in the present moment and 2) the ability to *accept* these feelings. *Awareness*, they argue, makes mindful individuals more adept at conflict monitoring, that is, noticing when their emotional state is incongruent with their goal state; and *acceptance* leads to less resistance when regulating that emotional state. By noticing incongruent emotional states faster and experiencing less resistance, mindful individuals are able to more effectively regulate emotions (Teper & Inzlicht, 2013). This is supported by research showing that mindfulness increases conflict monitoring in other domains (Jha, Krompinger, & Baime, 2007), improves attentional capacity and executive control (Chambers, Lo, & Allen, 2008; Mrazek, Franklin, Phillips, Baird, & Schooler, 2013), and makes individuals more accepting of their emotional states (Hayes & Feldman, 2004; Teper & Inzlicht, 2013).

According to affective events theory (AET; Weiss & Cropanzano, 1996), regulating one's emotional response will have a knock-on effect on behavior, i.e. one's action tendency. In line with this prediction, Arch and Craske (2006) found that after viewing adverse images, mindful individuals were more willing to remain in contact with the image compared to a control group. Similarly, Ortner, Kilner, and Zelazo (2007) found that mindfulness decreased the effect of emotional interference in subjects' performance, compared to an active control, during a reaction time task. Finally, mindful individuals have been shown to be less retaliatory in response to acts of first-party injustice; this relationship was mediated by the individual's emotion response to injustice, which was subdued in the mindfulness condition (Long & Christian, 2015).

Third Stage: Adaptive Appraisal

The third stage focuses on the persistence of emotions beyond the initial episode. Rather than subsiding when an affective event concludes, emotional states have a tendency to continue (Hajcak & Olvet, 2008). A key cause of this persistence is continued appraisal. Unfortunately, negative emotions tend to persist longer, whereas positive emotions rarely stick around as long, possibly due to humans' innate negativity bias (Ito, Larsen, Smith, & Cacioppo, 1998). In particular, individuals often ruminate, prolonging the emotional impact of negative events. In severe cases this can lead to mood disorders such as depression or chronic anxiety (McLaughlin & Nolen-Hoeksema, 2011).

Mindfulness has been shown to reduce habitual negative appraisal and rumination, evidenced by its effectiveness as a treatment for addiction and depression (Brewer, Elwafi, & Davis, 2013; Hofmann, Sawyer, Witt, & Oh, 2010). Garland et al. (2015) propose that the key mechanisms behind this are meta-awareness and decentering. *Meta-awareness* is the ability to become aware of one's own thoughts and *decentering* involves creating a psychological distance between oneself and those thoughts; both are core aspects of mindfulness (Lebois et al., 2015; Papies, Pronk, Keesman, & Barsalou, 2015) and are related to the awareness and acceptance mechanisms discussed earlier. Interestingly, while most research has focused on the regulation of negative emotions, Brockman et al. (2017) also reported that mindfulness led to increased positive affect. The cognitive appraisal process proposed by Garland et al. (2015) is a possible mechanism for this. By creating a psychological distance between themselves and their experiences, mindful individuals have more control over which aspects of their experience they appraise and can thus adaptively select to appraise the positive experiences. Therefore, at the third stage, mindfulness may not only allow individuals to reduce habitual negative appraisal of emotion and rumination, but also to make adaptive positive appraisals, aided by decentering and meta-awareness.

We now describe several workplace applications of the MEMF.

Mindful Emotion Management in the Workplace

Stress and Burnout

Stress and burnout are common experiences in organizational life. Stress in the workplace arises in response to stressors such as an abusive supervisor or customer. Stress entails both physiological and emotional components, which, when prolonged, can lead to burnout, a chronic state of detachment from work characterized by emotional exhaustion and a loss of identity and motivation.

The stress-reducing effect of mindfulness has been extensively studied, with a number of mechanisms being identified (Chin, Slutsky, Raye, & Creswell, 2018; Creswell & Lindsay, 2014; Hölzel et al., 2009; Taren et al., 2013). First of all, mindfulness has been shown to moderate responses to stressors by increasing stress resilience through reducing reactivity (first mechanism in the MEMF); see the mindfulness stress buffer account of Creswell and Lindsay (2013). Second, mindfulness has been shown to moderate how individuals regulate stress and its effect on behaviors (second mechanism), thus reducing its negative consequences (Desrosiers, Vine, Klemanski, & Nolen-Hoeksema, 2013).

Finally, prolonged stress is a key antecedent of job burnout (Bakker & Demerouti, 2007) and workplace mindfulness interventions have been shown to reduce employee burnout (Luken & Sammons, 2013). It is likely that mindful individuals' enhanced emotion resilience and regulation play a key role in reducing emotional exhaustion, a core dimension of burnout. However, burnout is also related to how individuals appraise their work environment, i.e. increased depersonalization and cynicism (Bakker & Demerouti, 2007; Maslach, Schaufeli, & Leiter, 2001). Individuals who develop a negative schema about the workplace are likely to ruminate on the stressful events. We suggest that mindfulness also moderates the relationship through adaptive reappraisal (third mechanism). Specifically, by disengaging from the habitual negative appraisal of stressful work events mindful individuals may be able to adaptively make a positive appraisal (e.g. viewing stressors as challenges). Some preliminary support for this comes from research showing that mindfulness was positively related to how engaging and meaningful employees felt their work was (Malinowski & Lim, 2015; Reb, Narayanan, & Ho, 2013).

Emotional Labor

In some workplace roles individuals are required to manage their emotion expressions to satisfy the emotional requirements of their job, which is referred to as emotional labor. The archetypal example of this is customer service employees displaying an outwardly positive façade irrespective of their true emotional state. When employees display one emotion but feel something different, this is known as surface acting, whereas if individuals are able to match their own internal state with the emotion they express, this is known as deep acting (Grandey, 2003; Wang, Berthon, Pitt, & McCarthy, 2016). A wealth of research shows the negative effects of emotional labor and specifically surface acting on job satisfaction and in particular emotional exhaustion (e.g. Hülsheger & Schewe, 2011). Jeung, Kim, and Chang (2018) argue that this is a result of individuals' regulatory strategy: specifically, employees attempt to suppress

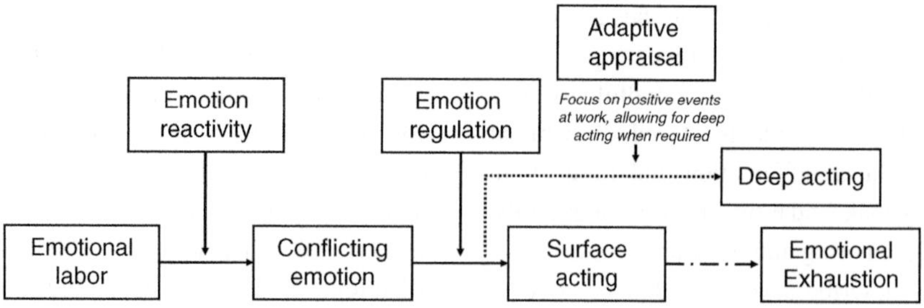

Figure 14.2 The mindful emotion management framework applied to emotional labor

emotions, which over time results in depletion and stress.

Figure 14.2 applies the MEMF to emotional labor. Situations that require emotional labor often lead to conflicting emotions, as when a tired employee is expected to smile for a customer and feels frustrated about this. We suggest that through decreased reactivity (first mechanism), mindfulness will reduce the propensity for such conflicting emotions to arise. In the case that a conflicting emotion has arisen, emotional labor is required to manage this emotional state. This is the point at which Jeung et al. (2018) propose that individuals often engage in emotion suppression. Alternatively, according to the model proposed by Teper et al. (2013), mindful individuals, who are particularly adept at conflict monitoring, may be able to use both awareness and acceptance to manage the conflict state, which has been shown to be a more effective strategy (Brockman et al., 2017). Therefore, through emotion regulation (second mechanism), mindfulness might improve how individuals manage conflicting emotions and thus the extent to which they require surface acting. Further, as the conflicting emotions are effectively managed individuals face less resistance in engaging with the emotion they are required to display, thus increasing the chance of deep acting (Grandey 2003).

Moreover, it is possible that through adaptive reappraisal (third mechanism) mindful individuals can shift how they evaluate their own emotional state by reducing the habitual tendency to focus on negative feelings and instead shift awareness to positive feelings (Wang et al., 2016), further facilitating deep acting. Preliminary support for this proposition comes from field evidence that mindfulness both decreased surface acting and led to increased deep acting in casino workers (Li, Wong, & Kim, 2017).

Consistent with our theoretical framework, a number of studies show employee mindfulness to be related to lower emotional exhaustion, lower burnout, and higher job satisfaction (Grégoire, Lachance, & Taylor, 2015; Reb, Narayanan, Chaturvedi, & Ekkirala, 2017). Further, Hülsheger et al. (2013) found that the mediating process responsible for this was mindfulness moderating surface acting.

Team Conflict

The ability to manage conflict effectively can make or break a team. The emotions activated during conflict play a significant role in whether that conflict is managed productively or unproductively (Todorova, Bear, & Weingart, 2014; Yang & Mossholder, 2004). Specifically, positive emotions have been shown to facilitate cooperative solutions to conflict (Staw, Sutton, & Pelled, 1994), whereas negative emotions often exacerbate team conflict (Rispens & Demerouti, 2016). Moreover, when conflict continues over time the rift becomes larger as task conflict, which can be

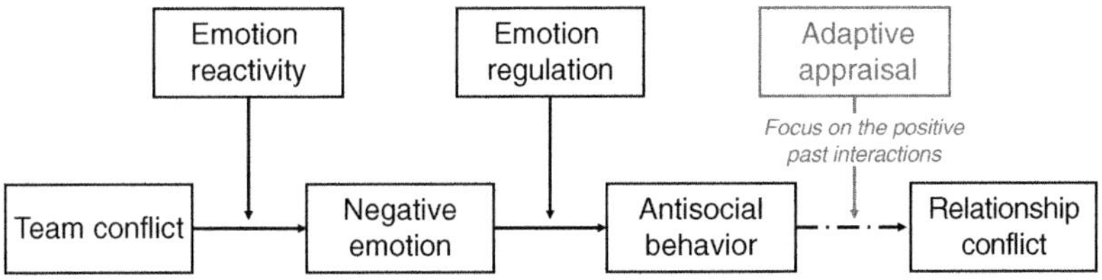

Figure 14.3 The mindful emotion management framework applied to team conflict
Note: the final stage, represented in gray, has not yet been empirically studied.

healthy at controlled levels (Todorova et al., 2014), leads into more detrimental relationship conflict.

Conflict often leads to strong emotional reactions. The MEMF posits that mindfulness will moderate this emotional reaction (first mechanism; see Figure 14.3). Further, enhanced conflict monitoring through increased awareness and acceptance of emotional events (second mechanism) will allow individuals to more effectively manage emotions arising from conflict situations (Teper et al., 2013), thus moderating the effect of negative emotions on retaliatory and antisocial behaviors. Supporting this claim, there is evidence showing that mindfulness leads to increased cooperation in groups. A field study conducted by Kersemaekers et al. (2018) showed that a workplace mindfulness intervention led to improvements in team and organizational climate, with the largest effect seen on team cooperation and collaboration. Beyond promoting individual-level cooperative behaviors, mindfulness may have a broader effect on how a team manages conflict. Yu and Zellmer-Bruhn (2016) recently reported results from a combination of lab and field studies that found team mindfulness was related to reduced team-level relationship conflict, reduced connection between task and relationship conflict, and reduced spillover from team relationship conflict to individual social undermining. The authors proposed that the ability to manage intense negative emotions is a core component in this process. In the third stage, mindfulness may support reappraisal that prevents longer-term damage to interpersonal relations due to conflict episodes and their intense negative emotions.

Decision-Making

Karelaia and Reb (2015) recently explored various benefits of mindfulness in decision-making, with emotion regulation being one area. When Herbert Simon presented his theory of bounded rationality, dispelling the myth of the economically rational decision-maker, he also highlighted that no theory of decision-making would be complete without understanding the role that emotions play (Simon, 1987). Over recent years, a large amount of empirical research has corroborated this assertion (Lerner, Li, Valdesolo, & Kassam, 2015). And while it is the case that emotion can benefit our decisions (e.g. Cassotti et al., 2012), it is also true that emotions can lead to biased and ineffective decisions (Shiv, Loewenstein, & Bechara, 2005). Overall, individuals who are able to manage (not necessarily avoid or suppress) their emotions during decision-making may have an advantage. Past research investigating emotion regulation strategies in decision-making has revealed findings similar to those seen in other areas: 1) that emotion suppression is counterproductive and 2) that cognitive reappraisal is only partly beneficial (Miu & Crişan, 2011; van't Wout, Chang, & Sanfey, 2010). Lerner et al. (2015) distinguished between strategies seeking to minimize emotion response and those seeking to reduce the effect of the emotional state on decision-making. While the majority of these specific techniques proved ineffective, Lerner et al. (2015) did not consider a combination of both strategies. As the MEMF proposes, mindfulness both reduces emotional reactivity and improves regulation of one's emotional state.

In their review, Lerner et al. (2015) distinguish between the effect of incidental emotion, i.e. emotion carrying over from previous events, and the effect of integral emotion, i.e. emotions arising from the decision itself. The case for the effect of mindful emotion management on incidental emotion is largely akin to the arguments presented in earlier sections of this chapter: mindful individuals are able to manage emotions more effectively and thus less likely to have them transfer to other tasks. The relationship between mindfulness and integral emotion is potentially more complex. A decision event can often be innocuous and lead to minimal or no emotional reaction, but at other times decisions can lead to strong emotional states. A defining factor in this is the *context* of the decision in the form of "frames."

A long history of experiments conducted across a number of fields has shown that manipulating the *framing* of a decision can elicit different emotional states and thus lead people to make biased decisions (De Martino, Kumaran, Seymour, & Dolan, 2006). However, one's susceptibility to a frame depends at least partly on the emotional reaction. If mindful individuals react less emotionally (first mechanism) and are more aware of subtle emotional states arising and better able to regulate them (second mechanism), it follows that they may be less susceptible to the integral emotions associated with a frame. A study conducted by Hafenbrack, Kinias, and Barsade (2014) lends initial support to the supposition that these mechanisms are functioning in that way. Their study showed that mindful individuals were less susceptible to the sunk cost bias: the tendency to overweight retrospective costs in our decisions (i.e. framing a decision irrationally because of past costs). Moreover, Hafenbrack et al. (2014) showed that a reduction in negative emotion mediated this relationship.

Overall, mindful emotion management provides an intriguing direction for managing the effect emotions have on decision-making. We have looked specifically at integral emotions arising from decision frames; however, it is likely that mindfulness could apply to other processes. For example, one strategy proposed by Lerner et al. (2015) was the "dual-emotion theory" where individuals counteract the effect of one emotion, e.g. sadness, by inducing another, e.g. gratitude. This mechanism is akin to the adaptive appraisal (third) mechanism in the MEMF, suggesting that mindfulness may facilitate dual emotion management.

Mind the Hype

We have proposed a wide range of salubrious (moderating) effects of mindful emotion management in the workplace, with some empirical evidence supporting the proposed MEMF and its specific applications (although much future research is still waiting to be conducted). Before we conclude, it is important to note that mindfulness is not a panacea for all emotion regulation issues or workplace problems. In this section, we want to highlight some of the challenges and limitations.

First, at the conceptual level, van Dam et al. (2018) point out that no agreed-upon definition of mindfulness yet exists. While the inability of scholars to agree upon a unitary description of a psychological process is not confined to the mindfulness literature but is seen in the discipline of psychology more widely (Davidson & Dahl, 2018), increasing clarity is nonetheless an important goal that researchers should strive toward. Note that while this chapter has not weighed into this debate, the key mechanisms focused on in the

MEMF are attention/awareness and acceptance/decentering. This bi-dimensional perspective of mindfulness is consistent with a number of contemporary views (Cardaciotto et al., 2008; Lindsay & Creswell, 2017).

A further complication in the mindfulness literature is that the term can refer to a dispositional trait, a transitory state, a skill, or even a practice. This is because mindfulness is generally considered to be an underlying construct, i.e. facet of the mind, that both occurs naturally and can be trained (Brown & Ryan, 2003; Tang, Hölzel, & Posner, 2016). However, the variety of methods in which this construct is assessed, e.g. self-report or training programs, makes it challenging to identify the underlying effects (Van Dam et al, 2018). Further, a number of researchers have questioned the validity of widely used self-report measures of mindfulness (Van Dam et al., 2018; Wheeler, Arnkoff, & Glass, 2015). In sum, not unlike other literatures, the mindfulness literature faces the challenge of defining and clarifying the mindfulness construct, and validly operationalizing, measuring, and manipulating it.

Design-wise, the majority of studies have used designs relatively low on internal validity. For example, most intervention studies studying mindfulness have used relatively simple pre–post designs (Creswell, 2017). Such methods are not sufficiently rigorous to provide strong evidence for the effectiveness of mindfulness interventions. Of course, mindfulness research is no exception, with organizational research commonly using correlational survey research. Still, future research should use more rigorous designs, such as randomized controlled trials with active control conditions.

Another methodological challenge for studies investigating mindfulness in the workplace is deciding which of the plethora of mindfulness-based interventions to use. Predominantly, studies have used the Mindfulness Based Stress Reduction (MBSR) program, which is the most popular course used in the clinical literature (Kabat-Zinn, 2003). However, researchers should question whether such a program is applicable in workplace settings. Recently programs have emerged that present more specific training for mindfulness in the workplace (e.g. Young, 2016). While such innovations are an important first step, they also require careful empirical validation. From a more practical perspective, researchers can explore the complementary effects of mindfulness training along with other interventions, e.g. exercise, yoga, or positive psychology (de Bruin, Formsma, Frijstein, & Bögels, 2017; Mrazek, Mooneyham, Mrazek, & Schooler, 2016).

Related, the literature on mindfulness has been largely shaped by the standards and goals of clinical psychology, which are different from those of organizational settings. For example, while clinicians aim to create lasting changes in their patient's trait mindfulness, it may suffice in the workplace arena for people to have only short periods of state mindfulness. This is an idea explored by Hafenbrack (2017), who suggests the use of on-the-spot interventions that lead to momentary increases in mindfulness at opportune moments, e.g. before a team meeting or before engaging in a task requiring emotional labor.

The Future for the Mindful Emotion Management Framework

The MEMF aims to provide a springboard for future research by synthesizing several streams of the mindfulness literature. However, we acknowledge that at this point, the framework is preliminary; it should be updated as scholars obtain a deeper understanding of the mechanisms behind mindful emotion management.

First, future research could clarify the relation between mindfulness and reappraisal. Currently reappraisal is considered only in terms of how individuals manage their thoughts about events and thus indirectly their emotional state (third mechanism). However, there is the potential for a more direct effect of reappraisal on emotions. As outlined in the description of the first stage, emotions are best characterized as interpretations of one's affective state (Damasio, 1998). Expanding on this, according to the Theory of Constructed Emotion (see Barrett, 2007, 2017a) emotions are not genetically determined predispositions to act and feel in a certain way. Instead, emotions are actively constructed by individuals based on how their internal state matches their current external environment. For example, an increased heart rate and sweaty palms (internal state) could be interpreted as a feeling of anxiety, if one is at the hospital (external environment), or as a feeling of excitement, if at a sports game.

Therefore, emotions depend on how one interprets (appraises) the context of one's affective response (Schacter & Singer, 1962). With that in mind, the mechanism discussed in the third stage, where awareness and decentering lead mindful individuals to have more control over the appraisals they make, could take place at an earlier stage in the MEMF: that is, mindful individuals have more control over how they appraise their physiological response to a situation, determining whether they feel stress or excitement. This hypothesis has not been explicitly tested in the mindfulness literature, although Barrett (2017b) alluded to it in a recent discussion of her theory. Therefore, it is included in Figure 14.1 as a speculative suggestion for future research and demonstrates how the framework could evolve in the future.

Second, it is not clear to what extent mindful emotion regulation makes use of conscious as well as unconscious processes. It seems that unconscious processes are more important during the first stage; however, especially with increased practice, mindful emotion management may also become less effortful at later stages in the process.

Third, Chambers, Gullone, and Allen (2009) argue that mindful emotion management works by changing the relation to one's emotions rather than the content of emotions. Mindful individuals are seen as neither avoiding negative emotions nor seeking positive emotions. However, it remains to be seen whether such an approach is feasible in organizational settings, or whether mindfulness can be used flexibly, depending on employees' goals, to change the content, intensity, and duration of emotions, along with one's relation to these experiences.

Fourth, the current framework begins with an affective event. However, some researchers have argued that emotion regulation also includes the selection of situations so as to avoid certain emotions (e.g. by avoiding one's abusive boss) or seek them out. Future research could extent the MEMF to the five "entry points" of emotion regulation proposed by Barrett and Gross (2001): situation selection and modification, attentional deployment, cognitive change, response selection, and response modulation.

Finally, it is worth noting that recent research suggests that emotion regulation strategies are not universally adaptive or maladaptive. Cognitive reappraisal could, for example, lead to experiential avoidance (Chambers et al., 2009), and emotion suppression may be required during certain workplace situations to prevent escalation of conflict. Similarly, reduced emotional reactivity (first mechanism) should theoretically reduce incidences of positive emotion at work, although this effect may be hard to observe as adaptive reappraisal (third mechanism) might be working in the opposite direction. Future research should examine the contextual factors influencing when mindful emotion management is more or less adaptive. Based on such research, the MEMF can be improved and will hopefully grow alongside the evolving field of mindfulness as it moves from infancy into maturity.

References

Arch, J. J., & Craske, M. G. (2006). Mechanisms of mindfulness: Emotion regulation following a focused breathing induction. *Behaviour Research and Therapy, 44*(12), 1849–1858, https://doi.org/10.1016/j.brat.2005.12.007

Ashforth, B. E., & Humphrey, R. H. (1995). Emotion in the workplace: A reappraisal. *Human Relations, 48* (2), 97–125, https://doi.org/10.1177/001872679504800201

Bakker, A. B., & Demerouti, E. (2007). The job demands–resources model: State of the art. *Journal of Managerial Psychology, 22*(3), 309–328, https://doi.org/10.1108/02683940710733115

Barrett, L. F. (2006). Are emotions natural kinds? *Perspectives on Psychological Science, 1*, 28–58.

Barrett, L. F. (2017a). *How emotions are made: The secret life of the brain*. Boston, MA: Houghton Mifflin Harcourt.

Barrett, L. F. (2017b). The theory of constructed emotions: An active inference account of interocepetion and categorization. *Social Cognitive and Affective Neuroscience, 12*, 1–23.

Barrett, L. F., & Gross, J. J. (2001). Emotional intelligence: A process model of emotion representation and regulation. In T. J. Mayne & G. A. Bonanno (Eds.), *Emotions: Current issues and future directions* (pp. 286–310). New York, NY: Guilford.

Brewer, J. A., Elwafi, H. M., & Davis, J. H. (2013). Craving to quit: Psychological models and neurobiological mechanisms of mindfulness training as treatment for addictions. *Psychology of Addictive Behaviors, 27*(2), 366–379. https://doi.org/10.1037/a0028490

Britton, W. B., Shahar, B., Szepsenwol, O., & Jacobs, W. J. (2012). Mindfulness-based cognitive therapy improves emotional reactivity to social stress: Results from a randomized controlled trial. *Behavior Therapy, 43*(2), 365–380, https://doi.org/10.1016/j.beth.2011.08.006

Brockman, R., Ciarrochi, J., Parker, P., & Kashdan, T. (2017). Emotion regulation strategies in daily life: Mindfulness, cognitive reappraisal and emotion suppression. *Cognitive Behaviour Therapy, 46*(2), 91–113, https://doi.org/10.1080/16506073.2016.1218926

Brown, K. W., & Ryan, R. M. (2003). The benefits of being present: Mindfulness and its role in psychological well-being. *Journal of Personality and Social Psychology, 84*(4), 822–848.

Brown, K. W., Ryan, R. M., & Creswell, J. D. (2007). Mindfulness: Theoretical foundations and evidence for its salutary effects. *Psychological Inquiry, 18* (4), 211–237, https://doi.org/10.1080/10478400701598298

Brown, K. W., Weinstein, N., & Creswell, J. D. (2012). Trait mindfulness modulates neuroendocrine and affective responses to social evaluative threat. *Psychoneuroendocrinology, 37*(12), 2037–2041, https://doi.org/10.1016/j.psyneuen.2012.04.003

Cardaciotto, L., Herbert, J. D., Forman, E. M., Moitra, E., & Farrow, V. (2008). The assessment of present-moment awareness and acceptance: The Philadelphia Mindfulness Scale. *Assessment, 15*(2), 204–223.

Cassotti, M., Habib, M., Poirel, N., Aïte, A., Houdé, O., & Moutier, S. (2012). Positive emotional context eliminates the framing effect in decision-making. *Emotion, 12*(5), 926–931, https://doi.org/10.1037/a0026788

Cebolla, A., Galiana, L., Campos, D., Oliver, A., Soler, J., Demarzo, M., . . . & García-Campayo, J. (2018). How does mindfulness work? Exploring a theoretical model using samples of meditators and non-meditators. *Mindfulness, 9*(3), https://doi.org/10.1007/s12671-017–0826-7

Chambers, R., Gullone, E., & Allen, N. B. (2009). Mindful emotion regulation: An integrative review. *Clinical Psychology Review, 29*(6), 560–572.

Chambers, R., Lo, B. C. Y., & Allen, N. B. (2008). The impact of intensive mindfulness training on attentional control, cognitive style, and affect. *Cognitive Therapy and Research, 32*(3), 303–322, https://doi.org/10.1007/s10608-007–9119-0

Chiesa, A., & Serretti, A. (2009). Mindfulness-based stress reduction for stress management in healthy people: A review and meta-analysis. *Journal of Alternative and Complementary Medicine, 15*(5), 593–600, https://doi.org/10.1089/acm.2008.0495

Chin, B., Slutsky, J., Raye, J., & Creswell, J. D. (2018). Mindfulness training reduces stress at work: A randomized controlled trial. *Mindfulness, 10*(4), 1–12, https://doi.org/10.1007/s12671-018–1022-0

Creswell, J. D. (2017). Mindfulness interventions. *Annual Review of Psychology, 68*(1), 491–516, https://doi.org/10.1146/annurev-psych-042716-051139

Creswell, J. D., & Lindsay, E. K. (2014). How does mindfulness training affect health? A mindfulness stress buffering account. *Current Directions in Psychological Science*, *23*(6), 401–407, https://doi.org/10.1177/0963721414547415

Dahl, C. J., Lutz, A., & Davidson, R. J. (2015). Reconstructing and deconstructing the self: Cognitive mechanisms in meditation practice. *Trends in Cognitive Sciences*, *19*(9), 515–523, https://doi.org/10.1016/j.tics.2015.07.001

Damasio, A. R. (1998). Emotion in the perspective of an integrated nervous system. *Brain Research Reviews*, *26*(2–3), 83–86.

Davidson, R. J., & Dahl, C. J. (2018). Outstanding challenges in scientific research on mindfulness and meditation. *Perspectives on Psychological Science*, *13*(1), 62–65, https://doi.org/10.1177/1745691617718358

de Bruin, E. I., Formsma, A. R., Frijstein, G., & Bögels, S. M. (2017). Mindful2Work: Effects of combined physical exercise, yoga, and mindfulness meditations for stress relieve in employees: A proof of concept study. *Mindfulness*, *8*(1), 204–217, https://doi.org/10.1007/s12671-016-0593-x

De Martino, B., Kumaran, D., Seymour, B., & Dolan, R. J. (2006). Frames, biases, and rational decision-making in the human brain. *Science*, *313* (5787), 684–687, https://doi.org/10.1126/science.1128356

Desrosiers, A., Vine, V., Klemanski, D. H., & Nolen-Hoeksema, S. (2013). Mindfulness and emotion regulation in depression and anxiety: Common and distinct mechanisms of action. *Depression and Anxiety*, *30*(7), 654–661, https://doi.org/10.1002/da.22124

Farb, N. A., Anderson, A. K., Mayberg, H., Bean, J., McKeon, D., & Segal, Z. V. (2010). Minding one's emotions: Mindfulness training alters the neural expression of sadness. *Emotion*, *10*(1), 25–33, https://doi.org/10.1037/a0017151

Frewen, P. A., Dozois, D. J. A., Neufeld, R. W. J., Lane, R. D., Densmore, M., Stevens, T. K., & Lanius, R. A. (2010). Individual differences in trait mindfulness predict dorsomedial prefrontal and amygdala response during emotional imagery: An fMRI study. *Personality and Individual Differences*, *49*(5), 479–484, https://doi.org/10.1016/j.paid.2010.05.008

Garland, E. L., Farb, N. A., Goldin, P. R., & Fredrickson, B. L. (2015). The mindfulness-to-meaning theory: Extensions, applications, and challenges at the attention–appraisal–emotion interface. *Psychological Inquiry*, *26*(4), 377–387, https://doi.org/10.1080/1047840X.2015.1092493

Good, D. J., Lyddy, C. J., Glomb, T. M., Bono, J. E., Brown, K. W., Duffy, M. K., . . . & Lazar, S. W. (2016). Contemplating mindfulness at work: An integrative review. *Journal of Management*, *42*(1), 114–142, https://doi.org/10.1177/0149206315617003

Grandey, A. A. (2003). When "the show must go on": Surface acting and deep acting as determinants of emotional exhaustion and peer-rated service delivery. *Academy of Management Journal*, *46*(1), 86–96, https://doi.org/10.2307/30040678

Grégoire, S., Lachance, L., & Taylor, G. (2015). Mindfulness, mental health and emotion regulation among workers. *International Journal of Wellbeing*, *5*(4), 96–119, https://doi.org/10.5502/ijw.v5i4.444

Gross, J. (2002). Emotion regulation: Affective, cognitive, and social consequences. *Psychophysiology*, *39*(3), 281–291, https://doi.org/10.1017/S0048577201393198

Gross, J. (2013). *Handbook of emotion regulation*. New York, NY: Guilford.

Gu, J., Strauss, C., Bond, R., & Cavanagh, K. (2015). How do mindfulness-based cognitive therapy and mindfulness-based stress reduction improve mental health and wellbeing? A systematic review and meta-analysis of mediation studies. *Clinical Psychology Review*, *37*, 1–12, https://doi.org/10.1016/j.cpr.2015.01.006

Guendelman, S., Medeiros, S., & Rampes, H. (2017). Mindfulness and emotion regulation: Insights from neurobiological, psychological, and clinical studies. *Frontiers in Psychology*, *8*, 94–116, https://doi.org/10.3389/fpsyg.2017.00220

Hafenbrack, A. C. (2017). Mindfulness meditation as an on-the-spot workplace intervention. *Journal of Business Research*, *75*, 118–129, https://doi.org/10.1016/j.jbusres.2017.01.017

Hafenbrack, A. C., Kinias, Z., & Barsade, S. G. (2014). Debiasing the mind through meditation: Mindfulness and the sunk-cost bias. *Psychological Science*, *25*(2), 369–376, https://doi.org/10.1177/0956797613503853

Hajcak, G., & Olvet, D. M. (2008). The persistence of attention to emotion: Brain potentials during and after picture presentation. *Emotion*, *8*(2), 250–255, https://doi.org/10.1037/1528-3542.8.2.250

Hayes, A. M., & Feldman, G. (2004). Clarifying the construct of mindfulness in the context of emotion regulation and the process of change in therapy. *Clinical Psychology: Science and Practice*, *11*(3), 255–262, https://doi.org/10.1093/clipsy/bph080

Hill, C. L. M., & Updegraff, J. A. (2012). Mindfulness and its relationship to emotional regulation. *Emotion*, *12*(1), 81–90, https://doi.org/10.1037/a0026355

Hofmann, S. G., & Asmundson, G. J. G. (2008). Acceptance and mindfulness-based therapy: New wave or old hat?. Clinical Psychology Review, *28* (1), 1–16.

Hofmann, S. G., Sawyer, A. T., Witt, A. A., & Oh, D. (2010). The effect of mindfulness-based therapy on anxiety and depression: A meta-analytic review. *Journal of Consulting and Clinical Psychology*, *78*(2), 169–183, https://doi.org/10.1037/a0018555

Hoge, E., Bui, E., Marques, L., Metcalf, C., Morris, L. K., Robinaugh, D. J., . . . & Simon, N. M. (2014). Randomized controlled trial of mindfulness meditation for generalized anxiety disorder: Effects on anxiety and stress reactivity. *Clinical Psychiatry*, *74*(8), 786–792, https://doi.org/10.4088/JCP.12m08083.

Hölzel, B. K., Carmody, J., Evans, K. C., Hoge, E. A., Dusek, J. A., Morgan, L., . . . & Lazar, S. W. (2009). Stress reduction correlates with structural changes in the amygdala. *Social Cognitive and Affective Neuroscience*, *5*(1), 11–17, https://doi.org/10.1093/scan/nsp034

Hülsheger, U. R., Alberts, H. J. E. M., Feinholdt, A., & Lang, J. W. B. (2013). Benefits of mindfulness at work: The role of mindfulness in emotion regulation, emotional exhaustion, and job satisfaction. *Journal of Applied Psychology*, *98*(2), 310–325, https://doi.org/10.1037/a0031313

Hülsheger, U. R., & Schewe, A. F. (2011). On the costs and benefits of emotional labor: A meta-analysis of three decades of research. *Journal of Occupational Health Psychology*, *16*(3), 361–389, https://doi.org/10.1037/a0022876

Ito, T. A., Larsen, J. T., Smith, N. K., & Cacioppo, J. T. (1998). Negative information weighs more heavily on the brain: The negativity bias in evaluative categorizations. *Journal of Personality and Social Psychology*, *75*(4), 887–900, www.ncbi.nlm.nih.gov/pubmed/9825526

Jeung, D. Y., Kim, C., & Chang, S. J. (2018). Emotional labor and burnout: A review of the literature. *Yonsei Medical Journal*, *59*(2), 187–193, https://doi.org/10.3349/ymj.2018.59.2.187

Jha, A. P., Krompinger, J., & Baime, M. J. (2007). Mindfulness training modifies subsystems of attention. *Cognitive, Affective and Behavioral Neuroscience*, *7*(2), 109–119, https://doi.org/10.3758/CABN.7.2.109

Kabat-Zinn, J. (2003). Mindfulness-based interventions in context: Past, present, and future. *Clinical Psychology: Science and Practice*, *10*(2), 144–156, https://doi.org/10.1093/clipsy/bpg016

Karelaia, N., & Reb, J. (2015). Improving decision making through mindfulness. In Reb, J., & Atkins, P. W. B. (Eds.), *Mindfulness in organizations: Foundations, research, and applications* (pp. 163–189). Cambridge, UK: Cambridge University Press.

Kersemaekers, W., Rupprecht, S., Wittmann, M., Tamdjidi, C., Falke, P., Donders, R., . . . & Kohls, N. (2018). A workplace mindfulness intervention may be associated with improved psychological well-being and productivity: A preliminary field study in a company setting. *Frontiers in Psychology*, *9*(195), 1–11, https://doi.org/10.3389/fpsyg.2018.00195

Lebois, L. A. M., Papies, E. K., Gopinath, K., Cabanban, R., Quigley, K. S., Krishnamurthy, V., . . . & Barsalou, L. W. (2015). A shift in perspective: Decentering through mindful attention to imagined stressful events. *Neuropsychologia*, *75*, 505–524, https://doi.org/10.1016/j.neuropsychologia.2015.05.030

Lerner, J. S., Li, Y., Valdesolo, P., & Kassam, K. S. (2015). Emotion and decision making. *Annual*

Review of Psychology, *66*(1), 799–823, https://doi.org/10.1146/annurev-psych-010213–115043

Li, J. J., Wong, I. A., & Kim, W. G. (2017). Does mindfulness reduce emotional exhaustion? A multilevel analysis of emotional labor among casino employees. *International Journal of Hospitality Management*, *64*, 21–30.

Lindsay, E. K., & Creswell, J. D. (2017). Mechanisms of mindfulness training: Monitor and Acceptance Theory (MAT). *Clinical Psychology Review*, *51*, 48–59.

Long, E. C., & Christian, M. S. (2015). Mindfulness buffers retaliatory responses to injustice: A regulatory approach. *Journal of Applied Psychology*, *100*(5), 1409–1422.

Luken, M., & Sammons, A. (2013). Systematic review of mindfulness practice for reducing job burnout. *American Journal of Occupational Therapy*, *70*(2), 1–10, https://doi.org/10.5014/ajot.2016.016956

Malinowski, P., & Lim, H. J. (2015). Mindfulness at work: Positive affect, hope, and optimism mediate the relationship between dispositional mindfulness, work engagement, and well-being. *Mindfulness*, *6* (6), 1250–1262, https://doi.org/10.1007/s12671-015–0388-5

Maslach, C., Schaufeli, W. B., & Leiter, M. P. (2001). Job burnout. *Annual Review of Psychology*, *52*(1), 397–422, https://doi.org/10.1146/annurev.psych.52.1.397

McLaughlin, K. A., & Nolen-Hoeksema, S. (2011). Rumination as a transdiagnostic factor in depression and anxiety. *Behaviour Research and Therapy*, *49*(3), 186–193, https://doi.org/10.1016/J.BRAT.2010.12.006

Miu, A. C., & Crişan, L. G. (2011). Cognitive reappraisal reduces the susceptibility to the framing effect in economic decision making. *Personality and Individual Differences*, *51*(4), 478–482, https://doi.org/10.1016/j.paid.2011.04.020

Mrazek, M. D., Franklin, M. S., Phillips, D. T., Baird, B., & Schooler, J. W. (2013). Mindfulness training improves working memory capacity and GRE performance while reducing mind wandering. *Psychological Science*, *24*(5), 776–781, https://doi.org/10.1177/0956797612459659

Mrazek, M. D., Mooneyham, B. W., Mrazek, K. L., & Schooler, J. W. (2016). Pushing the limits: Cognitive, affective, and neural plasticity revealed by an intensive multifaceted intervention. *Frontiers in Human Neuroscience*, *10*(117), https://doi.org/10.1177/0049124195023003006

Ortner, C. N., Kilner, S. J., & Zelazo, P. D. (2007). Mindfulness meditation and reduced emotional interference on a cognitive task. *Motivation and Emotion*, *31*(4), 271–283.

Papies, E. K., Pronk, T. M., Keesman, M., & Barsalou, L. W. (2015). The benefits of simply observing: Mindful attention modulates the link between motivation and behavior. *Journal of Personality and Social Psychology*, *108*(1), 148–170, https://doi.org/10.1037/a0038032

Phelps, E. A. (2006). Emotion and cognition: insights from studies of the human amygdala. *Annual Review of Psychology*, *57*, 27–53.

Reb, J., & Atkins, P. W. B. (Eds.) (2015). *Mindfulness in organizations: Foundations, research, and applications*. Cambridge, UK: Cambridge University Press.

Reb, J., Narayanan, J., & Chaturvedi, S. (2014). Leading mindfully: Two studies on the influence of supervisor trait mindfulness on employee well-being and performance. *Mindfulness*, *5*(1), 36–45, https://doi.org/10.1007/s12671-012–0144-z

Reb, J., Narayanan, J., Chaturvedi, S., & Ekkirala, S. (2017). The mediating role of emotional exhaustion in the relationship of mindfulness with turnover intentions and job performance. *Mindfulness*, *8*(3), 707–716, https://doi.org/10.1007/s12671-016–0648-z.

Reb, J., Narayanan, J., & Ho, Z. W. (2013). Mindfulness at work: Antecedents and consequences of employee awareness and absent-mindedness. *Mindfulness*, *6*(1), 111–122, https://doi.org/10.1007/s12671-013–0236-4

Rispens, S., & Demerouti, E. (2016). Conflict at work, negative emotions, and performance: A diary study. *Negotiation and Conflict Management Research*, *9* (2), 103–119, https://doi.org/10.1111/ncmr.12069

Schachter, S., & Singer, J. (1962). Cognitive, social, and physiological determinants of emotional state. *Psychological Review*, *69*(5), 379–399.

Shiv, B., Loewenstein, G., & Bechara, A. (2005). The dark side of emotion in decision-making: When individuals with decreased emotional reactions make more advantageous decisions. *Cognitive Brain Research*, *23*(1), 85–92, https://doi.org/10.1016/j.cogbrainres.2005.01.006

Simon, H. A. (1987). Making management decisions: The role of intuition and emotion. *Academy of Management Perspectives*, *1*(1), 57–64, https://doi.org/10.5465/ame.1987.4275905

Singleton, O., Hölzel, B. K., Vangel, M., Brach, N., Carmody, J., & Lazar, S. W. (2014). Change in brainstem gray matter concentration following a mindfulness-based intervention is correlated with improvement in psychological well-being. *Frontiers in Human Neuroscience*, *8*, 33, https://doi.org/10.3389/fnhum.2014.00033

Staw, B. M., Sutton, R. I., & Pelled, L. H. (1994). Employee positive emotion and favorable outcomes at the workplace. *Organization Science*, *5*(1), 51–71, https://doi.org/10.1287/orsc.5.1.51

Tang, Y. Y., Hölzel, B. K., & Posner, M. I. (2015). The neuroscience of mindfulness meditation. *Nature Reviews Neuroscience*, *16*(4), 213–225, https://doi.org/10.1038/nrn3916

Tang, Y. Y., Hölzel, B. K., & Posner, M. I. (2016). Traits and states in mindfulness meditation. *Nature Reviews Neuroscience*, *17*(59), https://doi.org/10.1038/nrn.2015.7

Taren, A. A., Creswell, J. D., & Gianaros, P. J. (2013). Dispositional mindfulness co-varies with smaller amygdala and caudate volumes in community adults. *PLoS ONE*, *8*(5), 1–7, https://doi.org/10.1371/journal.pone.0064574

Teper, R., & Inzlicht, M. (2013). Meditation, mindfulness and executive control: The importance of emotional acceptance and brain-based performance monitoring. *Social Cognitive and Affective Neuroscience*, *8*(1), 85–92, https://doi.org/10.1093/scan/nss045

Teper, R., Segal, Z. V., & Inzlicht, M. (2013). Inside the mindful mind. *Current Directions in Psychological Science*, *22*(6), 449–454, https://doi.org/10.1177/0963721413495869

Todorova, G., Bear, J. B., & Weingart, L. R. (2014). Can conflict be energizing? A study of task conflict, positive emotions, and job satisfaction. *Journal of Applied Psychology*, *99*(3), 451–467, https://doi.org/10.1037/a0035134

Van Dam, N. T., van Vugt, M. K., Vago, D. R., Schmalzl, L., Saron, C. D., Olendzki, A., . . . & Meyer, D. E. (2018). Mind the hype: A critical evaluation and prescriptive agenda for research on mindfulness and meditation. *Perspectives on Psychological Science*, *13*(1), 36–61, https://doi.org/10.1177/1745691617709589

van't Wout, M., Chang, L. J., & Sanfey, A. G. (2010). The influence of emotion regulation on social interactive decision-making. *Emotion*, *10*(6), 815–821, https://doi.org/10.1037/a0020069

Wang, E., Berthon, P., Pitt, L., & McCarthy, I. P. (2016). Service, emotional labor, and mindfulness. *Business Horizons*, *59*(6), 655–661, https://doi.org/10.1016/j.bushor.2016.07.002

Weiss, H. M., & Cropanzano, R. S. (1996). Affective events theory: A theoretical discussion of the structure, causes and consequences of affective experiences at work. *Research in Organizational Behavior*, *18*, 1–74, https://doi.org/1–55938-938–9

Wheeler, M. S., Arnkoff, D. B., & Glass, C. R. (2016). What is being studied as mindfulness meditation? *Nature Reviews Neuroscience*, *17*(59), doi:10.1038/nrn.2015.6

Yang, J., & Mossholder, K. W. (2004). Decoupling task and relationship conflict: The role of intragroup emotional processing. *Journal of Organizational Behavior*, *25*(5), 589–605, https://doi.org/10.1002/job.258

Young, J. H. (2016). *Mindfulness-based strategic awareness training: A complete program for leaders and individuals*. Chichester, UK: John Wiley & Sons.

Yu, L., & Zellmer-Bruhn, M. (2016). Introducing team mindfulness and considering its safeguard role against conflict transformation and social undermining. *Academy of Management Journal*, *61*(1), 324–347, https://doi.org/10.5465/amj.2016.0094

Zeidner, M., Matthews, G., & Roberts, R. D. (2004). Emotional intelligence in the workplace: A critical review. *Applied Psychology*, *53*(3), 371–399, https://doi.org/10.1111/j.1464–0597.2004.00176.x

Zelkowitz, R. L., & Cole, D. A. (2016). Measures of emotion reactivity and emotion regulation: Convergent and discriminant validity. *Personality and Individual Differences*, *102*, 123–132, https://doi.org/10.1016/j.paid.2016.06.045

15 Benefits of Negative Affective States

Antje Schmitt*

Workers can have bad days at work. Frustration, sadness, and fear are naturally occurring emotions in daily work life (Bledow, Schmitt, Frese, & Kühnel, 2011; Weiss & Cropanzano, 1996) and they often depend on the occurrence of events at work such as frustrating interactions with customers, receiving negative feedback, or frequent interruptions (Ohly & Schmitt, 2015; Weiss & Cropanzano, 1996). In general, the affective repertoire of individuals is skewed toward negativity (Baumeister, Bratslavsky, Finkenhauer, & Vohs, 2001): four of the six basic emotions (fear, anger, disgust, sadness) are negative (Ekman, 1992), and workers report a greater variety in their negative emotions than in their positive emotions (e.g. Dasborough, 2006). Even though positive emotions happen more frequently at work, negative ones are more easily recalled and have a stronger effect on overall affective outcomes at work (Miner, Glomb, & Hulin, 2005).

Theory and research suggest that negative affect may have detrimental consequences in the short and long term. Experiencing and dealing with negative affect at work – such as feeling sad, angered, or afraid – takes up the individual's limited regulatory resources; as a result, there are fewer resources available for pursuing work tasks (Beal, Weiss, Barros, & MacDermid, 2005; Ellis & Ashbrook, 1988; Seckler, Funken, & Gielnik, 2017). Accordingly, negative affect at work may have undesirable consequences in the form of job withdrawal, aggression, and poor performance (Barsade & Gibson, 2007; Ellis & Ashbrook, 1988; Rowe & Fitness, 2018). Moreover, some studies that are not specifically related to the work setting report longer-term harmful consequences of negative emotions for individual health and well-being, such as weaker immune functioning, delayed wound-healing, and higher levels of morbidity and mortality (for an overview, see Kiecolt-Glaser, 2009).

Accordingly, given these potential risks and threats that are associated with negative affect, research and practice tend to draw the simplistic inference that experiencing negative affect at work needs to be avoided (Campos, 2003). However, this advice overlooks the fact that negative feelings and emotions are natural states that cannot be fully prevented; their occurrence is often beyond personal control and usually serves a purpose (Campos, 2003; Tamir, 2009). Apart from their detrimental effects, research shows that negative moods and emotions may have functional benefits for individuals at work (for overviews, see Barsade & Gibson, 2007; Lebel, 2017; Seckler et al., 2017).

One central function of negative affect is to inform individuals about their progress in relation to a goal (e.g. one might feel frustrated or sad because one was unable to complete an important project at work on time), which is the first step toward reacting to dissatisfying, threatening, or dangerous situations that need to be addressed (Frijda, 2007; Larsen, 2000). Some research suggests that people occasionally prefer to feel and express unpleasant affective states, especially when they believe these will be useful in attaining relevant goals (e.g. Tamir, 2009). Moreover, negative affective states may have an important social function. For instance, guilt helps people to reconsider previous actions that may have been harmful

* The author thanks Inge Wolsink for her helpful suggestions and comments on an earlier version of this chapter.

to others and it may prevent them from repeating their behavior (Baumeister, Vohs, DeWall, & Zhang, 2007). Sadness motivates people to establish social connections (Forgas, 2017). When sadness is shared with others at work, it can provide an opportunity for openness and intimacy (Lindebaum, Geddes, & Jordan, 2018). In other words, besides the adverse consequences of negative affective states, negative affect serves an evolutionary purpose, and it might be a motivating force for positive outcomes as well.

The key goal of this chapter is to integrate the perspectives on the potential benefits of negative affective states and thereby present a more nuanced approach to their consequences. In general, assumptions about the role of negative affective states on work-related outcomes are complex. Mechanisms and boundary conditions need to be considered to answer questions such as when, how, and for whom negative affect at work may have benefits (Barsade & Gibson, 2007; Lebel, 2017; Rowe & Fitness, 2018). Specifically, the emphasis of this chapter is to review the literature on the role of cognitive, motivational, and social mechanisms that link negative affect with worker outcomes such as creativity, work engagement, proactive work behavior, and helping behavior as well as to highlight the role of affect regulation as a boundary condition. A conceptual model of these links is depicted in Figure 15.1.

Affect: Definition, Structure, and Dimensionality

The term "affect" covers emotions, feelings, and moods, and can be anything from a short-term transient state to a more long-term stable trait (Barsade & Gibson, 2007; Parkinson, Briner, Reynolds, & Totterdell, 1995). This chapter focuses on the potential benefits of negative affective *states*, which vary among workers across different time periods such as work days, weeks, or months (Bledow et al., 2011;

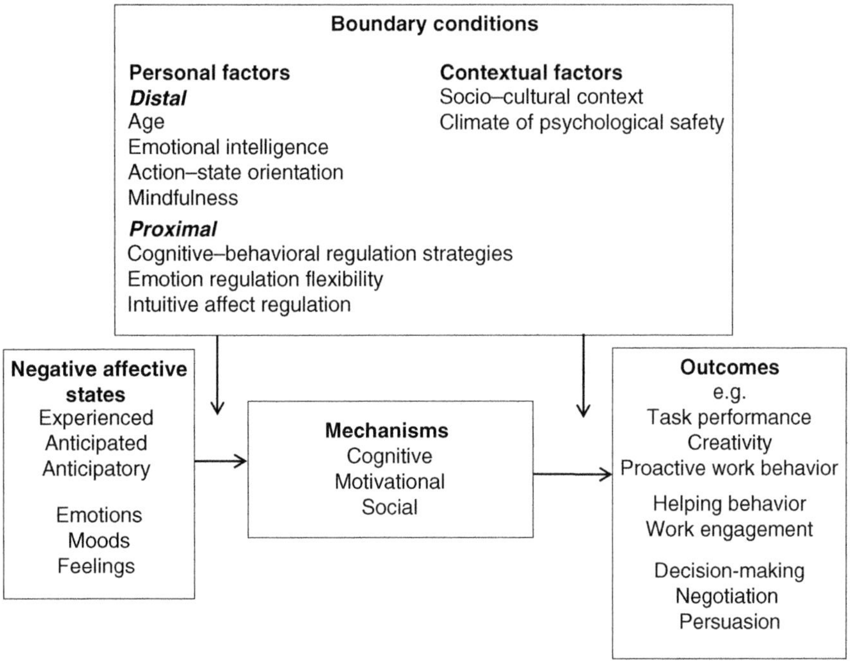

Figure 15.1 Conceptual model: mechanisms and boundary conditions that link negative affect with worker outcomes

Miner et al., 2005; Zacher, Schmitt, Jimmieson, & Rudolph, 2019).

"Negative emotions" are short-lived affective states that are elicited by a particular cause (Frijda, 2007; Weiss & Cropanzano, 1996). For example, frustration or anger occur when a colleague has not done their part of a team task. Negative emotions have traditionally been studied in terms of discrete entities (e.g. sadness, anger, disgust) that, according to some researchers, are linked with unique action tendencies (Ekman, 1992; Frijda, 2007). While present-oriented emotions are usually caused by current events, future-oriented emotions are affective reactions to future events. Specifically, future-oriented anticipatory emotions, such as fear or hope, may be experienced in anticipation of a future event. Future-oriented anticipated emotions, such as anticipated guilt or regret, are emotions that workers expect to experience once a certain positive or negative event has or has not occurred in the future (Baumeister et al., 2007; Baumgartner, Pieters, & Bagozzi, 2008). "Negative moods" are more diffused feelings that tend to last longer and to be less intense than discrete emotions (e.g. being in a sad or bored mood across a work day) (Frijda, 2007).

Benefits of Negative Affect: How, When, and for Whom?

Most research on the consequences of negative affect at work in general, and on its positive consequences in particular, focuses on overall negative affective experiences, a category that encompasses multiple negative emotions (e.g. Bledow et al., 2011; George & Zhou, 2007). In terms of more distinct negative emotions, the activating states of anger, anxiety, and depression have frequently been studied in the field of industrial and organizational (IO) psychology (Lindebaum & Geddes, 2016; Weiss & Cropanzano, 1996). Less is known about the potential benefits of more complex self-conscious negative emotions that are often relevant in social or interpersonal work interactions (e.g. envy, regret, shame, guilt). For instance, some research argues that envy (i.e. the feeling of wanting something that another person has or does, which results from social comparison) may play a functional and positive role in the organizational context due to its motivational potential (Duffy, Shaw, & Schaubroeck, 2008).

Some potential benefits of negative affective states that have been discussed and investigated in the literature are decision-making, learning, negotiation success and persuasion, creativity, work engagement, proactive work behavior (especially problem identification), and helping behavior (Baumeister et al., 2007; Bledow, Rosing, & Frese, 2013; Bledow et al., 2011; De Drue, Baas, & Nijstad, 2008; Forgas, 2017; Lebel, 2017). Importantly, however, the potential benefits of negative affect for work-related outcomes are not direct, but appear to depend on a number of underlying mechanisms and boundary conditions. It is also argued that negative affect should neither be too strong nor too weak; it should be of moderate intensity in order to be functional or to trigger positive consequences (Seckler et al., 2017).

Mechanisms

Cognitive, motivational, and social factors are found or are proposed to account for the beneficial consequences of negative affect. While reviewing the literature, it becomes evident that these underlying mechanisms are frequently discussed in the domain of IO psychology, but are not often empirically tested.

Cognitive Factors

Negative emotions and mood may affect how information is processed in the brain. Specifically, negative affect influences cognitive processes such as attentional focus, memory, information evaluation, judgment, learning, and decision-making. These cognitive processes play a role in a variety of behaviors at work such as creativity, proactivity, and helping (Baumeister et al., 2007; De Drue et al., 2008; Lebel, 2017). Negative affect provides a signal that an individual is in an undesirable or threatening situation, and the individual can process information more accurately and carefully by keeping a focus on the details in the environment in order to respond effectively (De Drue et al., 2008; Loewenstein & Lerner, 2003). Previous research has shown that creativity and problem-solving abilities are facilitated by negative affective states through focused and narrowed attention and systematic rather than more holistic cognitive processing (De Drue et al., 2008; George & Zhou, 2007; Lebel, 2017). This is the case for negative emotions high in motivational orientation, such as disgust or anger, whereas negative emotions low in motivational orientation (e.g. sadness) tend to broaden attentional focus (Gable & Harmon-Jones, 2010). Presumably through enhancing systematic cognition, certain negative emotions relate to more accurate judgments. This is reflected in favorable outcomes such as lower susceptibility to cognitive biases – for example, the fundamental attribution error, halo effects, and stereotypical thinking – and greater accuracy in understanding the essence of performance feedback given at work (Lindebaum et al., 2018; Loewenstein & Lerner, 2003).

Motivational Factors

Negative affect can signal a discrepancy between the desired state and the present state of affairs. This perceived discrepancy implies the need to improve the status quo through stimulating action depending on the specific motivational tendencies of the emotion (Carver, 2006; Forgas, 2017; Gable & Harmon-Jones, 2010; Lebel, 2017). For instance, anger is an emotion with a high motivational tendency or impulse to act that elicits a narrow attentional focus and generates approach-oriented behavior (Gable & Harmon-Jones, 2010), which may in turn be used to act against the anger-eliciting source (e.g. directly approaching a colleague and letting them know that their behavior triggered the anger) (Lebel, 2017). Specifically, effort and persistence, as two of the main characteristics of human motivation (Kanfer, Chen, & Pritchard, 2008), are proposed as mediators in the relationship between negative affect and organizational behavior. For instance, Foo and colleagues (2009) demonstrated in a sample of entrepreneurs that negative affect predicts entrepreneurial efforts on tasks that require immediate attention. In experimental studies, De Dreu and colleagues (2008) found that the induction of negative affect enlarged the number of new ideas that participants generated through increased persistence on the task.

In contrast, the theory of emotion as feedback (Baumeister et al., 2007) argues that it is not the key function of currently experienced emotions to cause behaviors in the present moment; rather, anticipated emotions are the drivers of behavior and decision-making. Individuals may engage in behaviors based on the anticipation of how they would feel if they behaved in that particular way. An anticipated negative emotion (e.g. anger) that is experienced at work may have positive motivational consequences (e.g. increasing effort to resolve a problem that has caused the feeling of anger) given that workers expect to improve their feelings and to avoid or prevent increasing anger in the future (Baumeister et al., 2007; Grant & Ashford, 2008). Hence, learning about potential negative affective outcomes of one's decisions and actions influences individual behavior in the present with the aim of minimizing or avoiding the occurrence of negative emotions and improving one's affective state. Research argues that anticipating negative affective consequences may have beneficial effects, as it may help workers take better decisions and engage in more favorable, socially valued, and desirable behaviors (Baumeister et al., 2007; Grant &

Wrzesniewski, 2010). For instance, Grant and Wrzesniewski (2010) argued that workers who are concerned about the welfare of others are more likely to anticipate guilt when they fail to treat others with kindness and respect and, thus, tend to try to prevent situations that may make them feel guilty. Accordingly, they found that other-oriented workers high in core self-evaluations (i.e. who are confident in and feel positive about their abilities) increased their level of effort and performance at work to avoid feeling guilty and to protect their view of themselves as being responsible and reliable (see Bagger, Reb, & Li, 2014, for another example of the role of negative anticipated emotions at work). Overall, however, more research on the role of anticipated negative affect in the work context and consequences for workers' behavior and decision-making is needed.

Social Factors

Some research reveals that negative affect might have positive consequences on the interpersonal life. However, social mechanisms have mostly been studied in experimental laboratory settings outside of the workplace (Forgas, 2017). For instance, negative affect such as anger has been found to increase attention to issues of injustice and violations of fairness norms; and it can relate to less selfish decisions and actions (Lindebaum et al., 2018; Morris & Keltner, 2000). Furthermore, negative affect such as frustration or sadness may signal to others that social support is needed for building or strengthening social connectedness between interaction partners by verbalizing and sharing emotional experiences (Lindebaum & Geddes, 2016). Consequently, support from colleagues, supervisors, and mentors at work – through listening, advice-giving, or instrumental assistance – may help workers to down-regulate negative affect, develop self-efficacy in their abilities to manage difficult experiences, and increase workers' motivation to engage in constructive responses such as initiating change to improve the work situation (e.g. by speaking up with concerns and suggestions) (Lebel, 2017; Lindebaum et al., 2018).

Boundary Conditions

Personal and contextual boundary conditions determine when and for whom negative affect results in positive consequences (for an overview, see also Barsade & Gibson, 2007; Seckler et al., 2017). This section of the chapter focuses on the personal factors of affect regulation: specifically, regulation strategies and regulation flexibility as proximal or more immediate boundary conditions, as well as distal personal factors (i.e. age, emotional intelligence, action–state orientation, and mindfulness). The role of external factors at the societal and organizational levels, such as the sociocultural context and the organizational climate and culture will also be discussed (see Figure 15.1).

Proximal Moderator: Regulation of Negative Affect

People's sensitivity to negative affective states must be differentiated from their ability to regulate those states (Doerwald, Scheibe, Zacher, & Van Yperen, 2016; Kuhl, Quirin, & Koole, 2015). Research argues that the experience of negative affect can be turned into an advantage when it is paired with affect regulation skills. Being able to successfully regulate one's own negative moods and emotions plays an important role in learning and personal development (Kuhl et al., 2015) and it is especially important at work, where individuals have to meet occupational goals (Barsade & Gibson, 2007; Forgas, 2017). Workers may have various motives for regulating their negative feelings, such as social motives (e.g. adapting to socially appropriate or organizationally relevant norms; influencing others' behaviors at work; not wanting to harm others) or hedonic motives (e.g. aspiring to feel better or to feel the emotion that one yearns for) (Baumeister et al., 2007; Tamir, 2009, 2016). Some research suggests that people do not necessarily want to feel positive, but prefer functional and useful emotions depending on the goal that a person aims to attain in a certain situation (Tamir, 2009, 2016). Negative feelings can be useful and functional, especially in some professions (e.g. police officers or security personnel) or in certain situations at work. For example, expressing the anger or frustration that a person feels may help them to think about and implement solutions to a long-standing problem that caused the emotion.

The question of how individuals regulate their affective states has been examined within different lines of research (Bledow et al., 2013; Grandey, 2000; Gross, 2015; Koole, 2009; Mayer & Salovey, 1995). Much research in IO psychology is based on Gross's (1998) process model of emotion regulation (for an extension, see Gross, 2015). This model describes various cognitive–behavioral strategies, such as seeing a situation in a different light or seeking help from others, which people may use to modify the conditions in which affect occurs, the experience of emotions (including their intensity, frequency, and duration), or the way in which emotions are expressed (Doerwald et al., 2016; Gross, 1998; Naragon-Gainey, McMahon, & Chacko, 2017). Another stream of research is based on the concept of emotional labor, which assumes that emotions are regulated and controlled in line with prescribed display rules of the organization or job (Grandey, 2000; Hülsheger, Lang, Schewe, & Zijlstra, 2015). Individuals may adapt their inner feelings to meet organizational requirements by using "deep acting strategies," whereas they do not modify their true inner emotions but only change their emotional expressions when using "surface acting strategies."

Adaptive and maladaptive cognitive–behavioral regulation strategies. Several studies in IO, social, experimental, and clinical psychology have identified regulation strategies that are more effective or functional in managing negative affect than others. Such strategies might include trying to resolve a problematic situation; acceptance (i.e. acknowledging negative emotions); reappraisal (i.e. cognitive reframing of an unpleasant situation); distracting from the affective state; relaxation; actively forgetting (Gross, 2015; Larsen, 2000; Naragon-Gainey et al., 2017); and social strategies such as interpersonal sharing of negative affect, socializing, and using social feedback for affect regulation (Côté, 2005; Lindebaum et al., 2018). For instance, reappraisal could help workers to channel the energy of an unpleasant situation and the respective emotional state (e.g. anger due to an unfair customer) and turn it into a positive outcome (Grant, 2013). Similarly, deep acting that aims at changing workers' inner feelings has been shown to be more effective in managing negative moods and emotions than surface acting strategies (Grandey, 2000). Also, acceptance was found to buffer the adverse impact of negative work events on indicators of daily well-being. Kuba and Scheibe (2017) showed that in times when workers were able to accept negative emotions, they experienced a lower increase in negative emotions and less reduction in work engagement on days when negative work events happened. Moreover, generating action plans may help workers to guide their behavior and better focus on their work goals instead of ruminating on a situation that caused negative emotions at work (Lebel, 2017; Schmitt, Gielnik, & Seibel, 2019). Cognitive strategies that have commonly been identified as maladaptive are rumination, suppression, and avoidance of thoughts about negative events, negative feelings, or physical sensations (Hülsheger et al., 2015; Naragon-Gainey et al., 2017).

Emotion regulation flexibility. Some recent research shifts away from treating any strategy as generally adaptive or maladaptive and argues that there is not a single strategy that would be consistently effective to regulate negative affective states (the "fallacy of uniform efficacy": Bonanno & Burton, 2013). Instead, some research focuses on the concept of emotion regulation flexibility, which refers to people's ability to adjust or match their regulatory strategy to the environmental requirements. In other words, according to this approach, regulation strategies should be chosen based on situational circumstances (Bonanno & Burton, 2013; Rowe & Fitness, 2018). For instance, in opposition to the overall premise that reappraisal is always adaptive, it is found to be a maladaptive strategy for managing negative emotions in situations involving high emotional intensity (Cheng, Lau, & Chan, 2014). Emotional suppression seems to be a more appropriate strategy for regulating negative emotions of high intensity (Bonanno & Burton, 2013). Emotional suppression can also be functional for regulating negative emotions, such as anxiety, that appear in achievement- or performance-related contexts such as examinations (Rottweiler, Taxer, & Nett, 2018). Also, while previous research has mostly focused on the maladaptive consequences of suppression for *experiencing* negative affect, it has been found that suppressing the *expression* of negative affect can be functional in the workplace (see Bonanno & Burton, 2013). However, there is a lack of systematic research on worker flexibility in connection with emotion regulation strategies and on how flexibility may result in individual benefits.

Intuitive affect regulation. The regulation of affect can be conscious and initiated by deliberate cognitive or behavioral regulation strategies, but it may also occur without self-awareness on an unconscious or even subconscious level (Koole, 2009). Accordingly, some research on the regulation of negative affect does not focus on deliberate cognitive action regulation strategies but claims that affect regulation is an intuitive process that does not necessarily need any conscious action or effort (Gross, 2015; Koole & Jostmann, 2004; Quirin, Bode, & Kuhl, 2011). Bledow and colleagues (2013; 2011) argued that the interplay of negative and positive affect in terms of dynamic shifts (i.e. up-regulation of positive affect and down-regulation of negative affect) is important for effective affect regulation and outcomes such as creativity and work engagement. High creativity was found when workers initially experienced negative affect that provided a basis for developing ideas by triggering high attention to discrepancies and detailed information processing, followed by a decrease in negative affect and the up-regulation of positive affect. While down-regulating negative affect helps to come up with new cognitive associations, the up-regulation of positive affect enables behavioral initiation and engagement in an activity (Bledow et al., 2011; Quirin et al., 2011). Similar results were found for the outcome of organizational citizenship behavior in workers (Yang, Simon, Wang, & Zheng, 2016). Interestingly, however, the study by Yang and colleagues (2016) showed that task-related performance was highest when individuals up-regulated their positive affect across the work day while also up-regulating their negative affect. This implies that different affect regulation patterns have distinct consequences for work-related outcomes (Yang et al., 2016).

Distal Personal Factors as Determinants of Negative Affect Regulation

Research has identified person factors that indicate individual differences in the extent to which people respond to negative emotions and in the way they regulate their affective states.

Age. Research suggests that older workers seem to be as competent as or at times even slightly more effective than younger workers in managing their own affective states. Older workers bring more knowledge and competencies on how to regulate emotions; they also tend to control their emotional reactions better (for an overview, see Doerwald et al., 2016; Scheibe, Yeung, & Doerwald, 2019). Since much of the research on the affect regulation advantages of older individuals is based on general population samples, additional research is needed to examine whether the findings also apply to the more specific group of older people in the workplace (Doerwald et al., 2016; Scheibe et al., 2019).

Emotional intelligence. Individual differences in the regulation of one's own negative affect are an integral part of the emotional intelligence concept (Joseph & Newman, 2010; Mayer & Salovey, 1995). Empirical evidence shows that when confronted with negative experiences, people with high emotional intelligence are more likely to use adaptive regulation strategies to regulate their emotions. People high in emotional intelligence report suppressing affective states to a lesser extent and are more likely to seek for support from close others (MacCann, Fogarty, Zeidner, & Roberts, 2011; Schutte, Manes, & Malouff, 2009). Research on emotional intelligence in IO psychology has increased within the last two decades (Mayer, Roberts, & Barsade, 2008) and the concept has inspired strong interest among practitioners. Yet the concept of emotional intelligence is, in fact, sometimes criticized for its lack of theoretical clarity and scientific rigor (Ashkanasy & Daus, 2005; Joseph & Newman, 2010).

Action–state orientation describes individual differences in implicit or intuitive regulation competencies that affect the way people regulate their negative emotions, thoughts, and behaviors at work (Diefendorff, Hall, Lord, & Strean, 2000; Koole & Jostmann, 2004; Wanberg, Zhu, & Van Hooft, 2010). People high in action orientation tend to stay focused on working toward their goals and to detach from thoughts that interfere with their goals. While action-oriented individuals are more likely to down-regulate negative affect in stressful conditions, state-oriented people tend to ruminate on negative emotional states and past failures, resulting in a lower ability to stay focused on their occupational tasks and activities. Action-oriented people may find negative affect functional for personal development and learning. They have better access to their selves such that they may activate knowledge of favorable personal experiences (e.g. the mastery of challenging situations in the past) which helps them to down-regulate negative affect (Koole & Jostmann, 2004; Kuhl et al., 2015).

Mindfulness is another attribute that determines whether negative affect may have beneficial consequences (Hülsheger, Alberts, Feinholdt, & Lang, 2013). Mindfulness means that individuals are open-minded to ongoing experiences and approaching events in a non-judgmental way. Mindfulness can be conceptualized as a trait as well as a psychological state that fluctuates across time (Glomb, Duffy, Bono, & Yang, 2011). It has been found to affect mental health in workers and their satisfaction and performance outcomes through improved emotion regulation (Glomb et al., 2011; Hülsheger et al., 2013). For instance, Hülsheger and colleagues (2013) showed that for individuals high in trait mindfulness and on days when individuals are in a mindful state, mindfulness was positively related to daily job satisfaction and negatively related to worker exhaustion. These relationships were mediated by surface acting, such that mindfulness helps terminate negative thoughts and reduces people's impulse to counter them which, in turn, improves job satisfaction and reduces emotional exhaustion (Hülsheger et al., 2013).

Contextual Factors: Culture and Organizational Climate

Characteristics of the sociocultural context, such as cultural value differences, determine how individuals appraise and regulate negative affect and whether negative feelings may have beneficial effects (Grandey, Foo, Groth, & Goodwin, 2012; Matsumoto, Yoo, & Nakagawa, 2008; Tamir, 2016). Compared to individuals from collectivistic cultures such as those from Asia, people raised in Western cultures tend to prefer decreasing their negative feelings and maximizing positive feelings. Moreover, while suppression as a single strategy to regulate negative affect is widely considered to be less functional in individualistic cultures, it is seen as a more adaptive strategy in collectivist cultures (Koopmann-Holm & Tsai, 2014).

Research highlights the importance of psychological safety as an organizational- or team-level climate factor for regulating negative feelings such as those resulting from failures at work (Baer & Frese, 2003; Edmondson, 1999). "Psychological safety" refers to individuals' shared evaluation that their team or organization is a safe place, that risks can be taken, and that problems can be shared without being afraid of the negative consequences for the individual. Psychological safety creates an atmosphere of openness, as it enables workers to feel welcome to address their problems openly, to admit errors and failures, and to speak up (Edmondson, 1999). Working in a climate of psychological safety has, therefore, the potential to buffer the detrimental consequences of negative affective states and maladaptive affect regulation for work outcomes. It may also amplify the relationships between negative affect and individual consequences such as voicing concerns and proactively engaging in behavior to change an unfavorable situation.

General Discussion and Implications

Negative affect can have detrimental effects on worker health- and performance-related outcomes as well as on their social lives. Yet the relationships between negative affective states and outcomes are usually more complex. Negative feelings might be beneficial for achieving work-related goals in that such feelings may stimulate analytical thinking processes and increase the individual's persistence in working toward the goal, but negative feelings can also reduce persistence and goal achievement because they require a considerable amount of regulatory resources that may interfere with a person's work tasks (Beal et al., 2005). Moreover, negative feelings may have benefits for some outcomes (e.g. creativity), but they may prove to be disadvantageous for other outcomes (e.g. task accomplishment). Also, whether or not personal consequences arise from negative affect depends on the distinct emotion that is felt in a certain situation at work or in anticipation of future events at work (Baumeister et al., 2007; Baumgartner et al., 2008), and on the level of motivational intensity (Gable & Harmon-Jones, 2010).

Overall, the research reviewed in this chapter reveals that under certain conditions, when it is effectively regulated, negative affect may result in positive outcomes for workers through cognitive, motivational, and social processes. This perspective is in line with previous arguments that negative affective states are not inherently good or bad only because of their valence, but rather that they are more or less functional and valuable under varying conditions (Lindebaum & Jordan, 2014; Tamir, 2009).

Implications for Future Research

Future research should focus on a more systematic examination of distinct negative affective states in relation to different action tendencies when studying the consequences of negative affect (Baumeister et al., 2007; Frijda, 2007). Action tendencies direct and coordinate behavior, prepare a person to take action whenever necessary, and help address problems in social interactions. While there is some research on the consequences of negative activating affect such as anger at work, research on the potential positive outcomes of more complex or social emotions such as guilt, jealousy, or shame is widely lacking. Research in IO psychology is further needed on the consequences of anticipatory emotions (i.e. experienced at present in anticipation of an event that might occur in the future) and anticipated emotions (i.e. expected to be experienced once a certain event has occurred in the future) (Baumeister et al., 2007; Baumgartner et al., 2008).

Some of the processes and boundary conditions discussed in this chapter are based on theory and research in fundamental cognitive and emotional psychology and social, developmental, and clinical psychology. These processes and conditions have not been comprehensively tested in the work context. More research is needed to extend our limited knowledge of the individual differences that may moderate the relationships between negative affect and work outcomes such as mindfulness or action–state orientation in the workplace. Moreover, there are only a few studies on the role of the broader cultural context, sociocultural values, and the organizational and team-related aspects that might determine whether and when workers may benefit from negative feelings at work.

Finally, future research is also needed to disentangle shorter- and longer-term consequences of negative affect and affect regulation strategies at work. For example, consequences differ depending on whether certain emotions (e.g. anger, guilt, or fear) occur rarely or more frequently. Similarly, with regard to the consequences of certain affect regulation strategies, Naragon-Gainey and colleagues (2017) state that any distraction may function as an adaptive regulation strategy in the short term but eventually results in negative health consequences when used more frequently in the longer term.

Practical Implications

Negative emotions and feelings resulting from unfavorable events appear in our daily work life and cannot be completely eliminated (Bledow et al., 2011; Grandey et al., 2012). The current chapter emphasizes the role of boundary conditions such as affect regulation skills and strategies, personal attributes, and contextual factors that need to be considered in practice so that negative affective experiences at work can be turned into positive outcomes such as creativity, work engagement, task engagement, or proactive work behavior.

This review indicates that organizations should offer support, guidance, and assistance so that workers can develop the competencies that are needed to manage and regulate negative affect at work. Individuals should benefit from learning strategies to keep a balance between positive and negative affective states at work; they should be able to down-regulate negative affect at work when it is experienced while up-regulating positive emotions (Bledow et al., 2013). Research on emotion regulation flexibility suggests that it is useful for individual well-being and performance to have a broad repertoire of affect regulation strategies. Strategies such as acceptance of negative emotions, reappraisal, or suppression of the expression of negative emotions at work can then be applied depending on the requirements of the context (Bonanno & Burton, 2013). Results based on existing research further indicate that it is promising to learn skills such as mindfulness. It has been shown that mindfulness can positively affect individual health- and performance-related outcomes through improved emotion regulation (Glomb et al., 2011; Hülsheger et al., 2013). Providing external support (e.g. through training or coaching) should be especially relevant for workers with low intuitive affect regulation skills (i.e. state-oriented individuals) who have problems in down-regulating negative experiences internally.

Furthermore, it is certainly important that organizations create an open and authentic culture of trust, support, and safety where individuals can show the emotions they feel (Edmondson, 1999;

Grandey et al., 2012). Also, a climate where errors that create negative emotions are seen as positive – so that workers learn from them – has been shown to play an important role in enhancing worker performance, proactivity (i.e. self-initiated change and future-oriented work behavior), and innovative behavior at work (Frese & Keith, 2015; Keith & Frese, 2005).

References

Ashkanasy, N. M., & Daus, C. S. (2005). Rumors of the death of emotional intelligence in organizational behavior are vastly exaggerated. *Journal of Organizational Behavior, 26*, 441–452.

Baer, M., & Frese, M. (2003). Innovation is not enough: Climates for initiative and psychological safety, process innovation, and firm performance. *Journal of Organizational Behavior, 24*, 45–68.

Bagger, J., Reb, J., & Li, A. (2014). Anticipated regret in time-based work–family conflict. *Journal of Managerial Psychology, 29*, 304–320.

Barsade, S. G., & Gibson, D. E. (2007). Why does affect matter in organizations? *Academy of Management Perspectives, 21*, 36–59.

Baumeister, R. F., Bratslavsky, E., Finkenhauer, C., & Vohs, K. D. (2001). Bad is stronger than good. *Review of General Psychology, 5*, 323–370.

Baumeister, R. F., Vohs, K. D., DeWall, C. N., & Zhang, L. (2007). How emotion shapes behavior: Feedback, anticipation, and reflection, rather than direct causation. *Personality and Social Psychology Review, 11*, 167–203.

Baumgartner, H., Pieters, R., & Bagozzi, R. P. (2008). Future-oriented emotions: Conceptualization and behavioral effects. *European Journal of Social Psychology, 38*, 685–696.

Beal, D. J., Weiss, H. M., Barros, E., & MacDermid, S. M. (2005). An episodic process model of affective influences on performance. *Journal of Applied Psychology, 90*, 1054–1068.

Bledow, R., Rosing, K., & Frese, M. (2013). A dynamic perspective on affect and creativity. *Academy of Management Journal, 56*, 432–450.

Bledow, R., Schmitt, A., Frese, M., & Kühnel, J. (2011). The affective shift model of work engagement. *Journal of Applied Psychology, 96*, 1246–1257.

Bonanno, G. A., & Burton, C. L. (2013). Regulatory flexibility: An individual differences perspective on coping and emotion regulation. *Perspectives on Psychological Science, 8*, 591–612.

Campos, J. J. (2003). When the negative becomes positive and the reverse: Comments on Lazarus's critique of positive psychology. *Psychological Inquiry, 14*, 110–113.

Carver, C. S. (2006). Approach, avoidance, and the self-regulation of affect and action. *Motivation and Emotion, 30*, 105–110.

Cheng, C., Lau, H.-P., & Chan, M.-P. (2014). Coping flexibility and psychological adjustment to stressful life changes: A meta-analytic review. *Psychological Bulletin, 140*, 1582–1607.

Côté, S. (2005). A social interaction model of the effects of emotion regulation on work strain. *Academy of Management Review, 30*, 509–530.

Dasborough, M. T. (2006). Cognitive asymmetry in employee emotional reactions to leadership behaviors. *Leadership Quarterly, 17*, 163–178.

De Drue, C. K. W., Baas, M., & Nijstad, B. A. (2008). Hedonic tone and activation level in the mood–creativity link: Toward a dual pathway to creativity model. *Journal of Personality and Social Psychology, 94*, 739–756.

Diefendorff, J. M., Hall, R. J., Lord, R. G., & Strean, M. L. (2000). Action–state orientation: Construct validity of a revised measure and its relationship to work-related variables. *Journal of Applied Psychology, 85*, 250–263.

Doerwald, F., Scheibe, S., Zacher, H., & Van Yperen, N. W. (2016). Emotional competencies across adulthood: State of knowledge and implications for the work context. *Work, Aging and Retirement, 2*, 159–216.

Duffy, M. K., Shaw, J. D., & Schaubroeck, J. M. (2008). Envy in organizational life. In R. H. Smith (Ed.), *Envy: Theory and research* (pp. 167–189). New York, NY: Oxford University Press.

Edmondson, A. C. (1999). Psychological safety and learning behavior in work teams. *Administrative Science Quarterly, 44*, 350–383.

Ekman, P. (1992). An argument for basic emotions. *Cognition and Emotion, 6*, 169–200.

Ellis, H. C., & Ashbrook, P. W. (1988). Resource allocation model of the effects of depressed mood states on memory. In K. Fiedler & J. Forgas (Eds.), *Affect, cognition, and social behavior: New evidence and integrative attempts* (pp. 25–43). Toronto, Canada: Hogrefe.

Foo, M. D., Uy, M. A., & Baron, R. A. (2009). How do feelings influence effort? An empirical study of entrepreneurs' affect and venture effort. *Journal of Applied Psychology, 94*, 1086–1094.

Forgas, J. P. (2017). Can sadness be good for you? On the cognitive, motivational, and interpersonal benefits of mild negative affect. *Australian Psychologist, 52*, 3–13.

Frese, M., & Keith, N. (2015). Action errors, error management, and learning in organizations. *Annual Review of Psychology, 66*, 661–687.

Frijda, N. H. (2007). *The laws of emotion*. Mahwah, NJ: Lawrence Erlbaum.

Gable, P., & Harmon-Jones, E. (2010). The blues broaden, but the nasty narrows: Attentional consequences of negative affects low and high in motivational intensity. *Psychological Science, 21*, 211–215.

George, J. M., & Zhou, J. (2007). Dual tuning in a supportive context: Joint contributions of positive mood, negative mood, and supervisory behaviors to employee creativity. *Academy of Management Journal, 50*, 605–622.

Glomb, T. M., Duffy, M. K., Bono, J., & Yang, T. (2011). Mindfulness at work. In J. Martocchio, H. Liao, & A. Joshi (Eds.), *Research in personnel and human resources management* (Volume 30, pp. 115–157). Bingley, UK: Emerald.

Grandey, A. A. (2000). Emotion regulation in the workplace: A new way to conceptualize emotional labor. *Journal of Occupational Health Psychology, 5*, 95–110.

Grandey, A. A., Foo, S. C., Groth, M., & Goodwin, R. E. (2012). Free to be you and me: A climate of authenticity alleviates burnout from emotional labor. *Journal of Occupational Health Psychology, 17*, 1–14.

Grant, A. M. (2013). Rocking the boat but keeping it steady: The role of emotion regulation in employee voice. *Academy of Management Journal, 56*, 1703–1723.

Grant, A. M., & Ashford, S. J. (2008). The dynamics of proactivity at work. *Research in Organizational Behavior, 28*, 3–34.

Grant, A. M., & Wrzesniewski, A. (2010). I won't let you down . . . or will I? Core self-evaluations, other-orientation, anticipated guilt and gratitude, and job performance. *Journal of Applied Psychology, 95*, 108–121.

Gross, J. J. (1998). The emerging field of emotion regulation: An integrative review. *Review of General Psychology, 2*, 271–299.

Gross, J. J. (2015). The extended process model of emotion regulation: Elaborations, applications, and future directions. *Psychological Inquiry, 26*, 130–137.

Hülsheger, U. R., Alberts, H., Feinholdt, A., & Lang, J. W. B. (2013). Benefits of mindfulness at work: The role of mindfulness in emotion regulation, emotional exhaustion, and job satisfaction. *Journal of Applied Psychology, 98*, 310–325.

Hülsheger, U. R., Lang, J. W. B., Schewe, A. F., & Zijlstra, F. R. H. (2015). When regulating emotions at work pays off: A diary and an intervention study on emotion regulation and customer tips in service jobs. *Journal of Applied Psychology, 100*, 263–277.

Joseph, D. L., & Newman, D. A. (2010). Emotional intelligence: An integrative meta-analysis and cascading model. *Journal of Applied Psychology, 95*, 54–78.

Kanfer, R., Chen, G., & Pritchard, R. D. (2008). *Work motivation: Past, present, and future*. New York, NY: Routledge.

Keith, N., & Frese, M. (2005). Self-regulation in error management training: Emotion control and metacognition as mediators of performance effects. *Journal of Applied Psychology, 90*, 677–691.

Kiecolt-Glaser, J. K. (2009). Psychoneuroimmunology: Psychology's gateway to the biomedical future. *Perspectives on Psychological Science, 4*, 367–369.

Koole, S. L. (2009). The psychology of emotion regulation: An integrative review. *Cognition and Emotion, 23*, 4–41.

Koole, S. L., & Jostmann, N. B. (2004). Getting a grip on your feelings: Effects of action orientation and external demands on intuitive affect regulation.

Journal of Personality and Social Psychology, 87, 974–990.

Koopmann-Holm, B., & Tsai, J. L. (2014). Focusing on the negative: Cultural differences in expressions of sympathy. *Journal of Personality and Social Psychology, 107*, 1092–1115.

Kuba, K., & Scheibe, S. (2017). Let it be and keep on going! Acceptance and daily occupational well-being in relation to negative work events. *Journal of Occupational Health Psychology, 22*, 59–70.

Kuhl, J., Quirin, M., & Koole, S. L. (2015). Being someone: The integrated self as a neuropsychological system. *Social and Personality Psychology Compass, 9*, 115–132.

Larsen, R. J. (2000). Toward a science of mood regulation. *Psychological Inquiry, 11*, 129–141.

Lebel, R. D. (2017). Moving beyond fight and flight: A contingent model of how the emotional regulation of anger and fear sparks proactivity. *Academy of Management Review, 42*, 190–206.

Lindebaum, D., & Geddes, D. (2016). The place and role of (moral) anger in organizational behavior studies. *Journal of Organizational Behavior, 37*, 738–757.

Lindebaum, D., Geddes, D., & Jordan, P. J. (2018). Theoretical advances around social functions of emotion and talking about emotion at work. In D. Lindebaum, D. Geddes, & P. J. Jordan (Eds.), *Social functions of emotion and talking about emotion at work* (pp. 1–19). Cheltenham, UK: Edward Elgar.

Lindebaum, D., & Jordan, P. J. (2014). When it can be good to feel bad and bad to feel good: Exploring asymmetries in workplace emotional outcomes. *Human Relations, 67*, 1037–1050.

Loewenstein, G., & Lerner, J. S. (2003). The role of affect in decision making. In R. J. Davidson, H. H. Goldsmith, & K. R. Scherer (Eds.), *Handbook of affective science* (pp. 619–642). Oxford, UK: Oxford University Press.

MacCann, C., Fogarty, G. J., Zeidner, M., & Roberts, R. D. (2011). Coping mediates the relationship between emotional intelligence (EI) and academic achievement. *Contemporary Educational Psychology, 36*, 60–70.

Matsumoto, D., Yoo, S. H., & Nakagawa, S. (2008). Culture, emotion regulation, and adjustment. *Journal of Personality and Social Psychology, 94*, 925–937.

Mayer, J. D., Roberts, R., & Barsade, S. G. (2008). Human abilities: Emotional intelligence. *Annual Review of Psychology, 59*, 507–536.

Mayer, J. D., & Salovey, P. (1995). Emotional intelligence and the construction and regulation of feelings. *Applied & Preventive Psychology, 4*, 197–208.

Miner, A. G., Glomb, T. M., & Hulin, C. (2005). Experience sampling mood and its correlates at work. *Journal of Occupational and Organizational Psychology, 78*, 171–193.

Morris, M. W., & Keltner, D. (2000). How emotions work: The social functions of emotional expression in negotiations. *Research in Organizational Behavior, 22*, 1–50.

Naragon-Gainey, K., McMahon, T. P., & Chacko, T. P. (2017). The structure of common emotion regulation strategies: A meta-analytic examination. *Psychological Bulletin, 143*, 384–427.

Ohly, S., & Schmitt, A. (2015). What makes us enthusiastic, angry, feeling at rest or worried? Development and validation of an affective work events taxonomy using concept mapping methodology. *Journal of Business and Psychology, 30*, 15–35.

Parkinson, B., Briner, R. B., Reynolds, S., & Totterdell, P. (1995). Time frames for mood: Relations between momentary and generalized ratings of affect. *Personality and Social Psychology Bulletin, 21*, 331–339.

Quirin, M., Bode, R. C., & Kuhl, J. (2011). Recovering from negative events by boosting implicit positive affect. *Cognition and Emotion, 25*, 559–570.

Rottweiler, A.-L., Taxer, J. L., & Nett, U. E. (2018). Context matters in the effectiveness of emotion regulation strategies. *AERA Open, 4*, https://doi.org/10.1177/2332858418778849

Rowe, A. D., & Fitness, J. (2018). Understanding the role of negative emotions in adult learning and achievement: A social functional perspective. *Behavioral Sciences, 8*, 27–47.

Scheibe, S., Yeung, D. Y., & Doerwald, F. (2019). Age-related differences in levels and dynamics of workplace affect. *Psychology and Aging*, *34*, 106–123.

Schmitt, A., Gielnik, M. M., & Seibel, S. (2019). When and how does anger during goal pursuit relate to goal achievement? The roles of persistence and action planning. *Motivation and Emotion*, *43*, 205–217.

Schutte, N., Manes, R., & Malouff, J. (2009). Antecedent-focused emotion regulation, response modulation and well-being. *Current Psychology*, *28*, 21–31.

Seckler, C., Funken, R., & Gielnik, M. M. (2017). Learning from entrepreneurial failure: Integrating emotional, motivational, and cognitive factors. In J. E. Ellingson & R. A. Noe (Eds.), *Autonomous learning in the workplace* (pp. 54–77). New York, NY: Routledge.

Tamir, M. (2009). What do people want to feel and why? Pleasure and utility in emotion regulation. *Current Directions in Psychological Science*, *18*, 101–105.

Tamir, M. (2016). Why do people regulate their emotions? A taxonomy of motives in emotion regulation. *Personality and Social Psychology Review*, *20*, 199–222.

Wanberg, C. R., Zhu, J., & Van Hooft, E. A. J. (2010). The job search grind: Perceived progress, self-reactions, and self-regulation of search effort. *Academy of Management Journal*, *53*, 788–807.

Weiss, H. M., & Cropanzano, R. (1996). Affective events theory: A theoretical discussion of the structure, causes and consequences of affective experiences at work. *Research in Organizational Behavior*, *18*, 1–74.

Yang, L.-Q., Simon, L. S., Wang, L., & Zheng, X. (2016). To branch out or stay focused? Affective shifts differentially predict organizational citizenship behavior and task performance. *Journal of Applied Psychology*, *101*, 831–845.

Zacher, H., Schmitt, A., Jimmieson, N. L., & Rudolph, C. (2019). Dynamic effects of personal initiative on engagement and exhaustion: The role of mood, autonomy, and support. *Journal of Organizational Behavior*, *40*, 38–58.

16 Interventions to Improve Employee Well-Being

Ute R. Hülsheger, Annekatrin Hoppe, and Alexandra Michel

Considering that work itself and work characteristics have a considerable impact on individuals' well-being and considering that adults spend more than one-third of their waking hours at work (Burke, 2017), researchers as well as practitioners have sought to identify ways to improve employee well-being through workplace interventions. Well-being is an umbrella concept that has been conceptualized in different ways and encompasses a wide range of dimensions (Burke, 2017). Organizational research has predominantly adopted the hedonic perspective of well-being (Sonnentag, 2015), which focuses on people's emotional/affective and cognitive evaluations of their lives and concerns what laypeople refer to as happiness and satisfaction (Diener, Oishi, & Lucas, 2003). In this tradition, high subjective well-being is indicated by the experience of positive affective states, the absence of negative affective states, and positive cognitive evaluations of being satisfied with one's life as a whole or with specific life domains, such as work (Diener et al., 2003; Sonnentag, 2015). Frequently, intervention research focuses on employee experiences that signal a lack of well-being, such as negative emotions, psychological strain, psychosomatic complaints, work–family conflict, or burnout. Increasingly, however, scholars have also been addressing positive aspects of work-related well-being including positive emotions, job satisfaction, work engagement, thriving, or flow (Sonnentag, 2015). The breadth of the overall concept of employee well-being and its underlying dimensions will be reflected in our review of intervention research, which has also used a wide range of well-being-related outcome variables.

Similar to the variety of well-being outcomes being studied in the literature, there is also a wide range of interventions that target employee well-being. An important distinction concerns the level of the intervention (Burke, 2017; Tetrick & Winslow, 2015). Interventions can reside at the level of the organization, e.g. via the introduction of work–family programs; at the job/task level, e.g. focusing on reducing detrimental job demands by job redesign; or at the individual level, where they would be aimed at promoting well-being by increasing employees' abilities to address and cope with job demands (Burke, 2017).

Another distinction can be made between stress management interventions and positive psychology interventions (Biron, 2014; Burke, 2017). Stress management interventions target the negative and focus primarily on reducing negative experiences and outcomes, while positive psychology interventions focus explicitly on the enhancement of positive outcomes and the strengthening of individual resources (Burke, 2017). Notably, however, this distinction is not always as clear-cut as it may appear. Interventions targeting primarily resources and positive outcomes by enhancing, for example, self-efficacy or positive thinking may not only increase positive psychological states such as engagement but also help to reduce negative outcomes such as strain and burnout. The distinction is therefore predominantly a paradigmatic one, with stress management approaches targeting primarily the reduction of psychosocial risks and stress, and the positive-oriented approaches focusing primarily on human flourishing, satisfaction, and well-being (Biron, 2014). Ultimately, both are important in promoting employee well-being and may be combined in organizational practice.

It is beyond the scope and feasibility of this chapter to address all types of interventions. Traditional organizational- and job-/task-level interventions as well as stress management interventions have been described exhaustively elsewhere (Briner & Reynolds, 1999; LaMontagne, Keegel, Louie, Ostry, & Landsbergis, 2007; Richardson & Rothstein, 2008; Semmer, 2006; Tetrick & Winslow, 2015). The goal of the present chapter is therefore to focus on more recent developments in the intervention literature and to review findings on work-related positive psychology interventions, which are instrumental in strengthening individual resources and promoting employee well-being and human flourishing. In choosing the interventions presented here, we took a bottom-up approach and selected interventions (a) that fit the definition of positive psychology interventions, (b) that are work-related, and (c) for which empirical evidence was available. In the remainder of the chapter we will therefore review evidence on mindfulness-based interventions, recovery interventions, positive thinking interventions, self-efficacy interventions, self- and emotion-regulation interventions, and job-crafting interventions.

Mindfulness-Based Interventions

Mindfulness (also discussed in Chapter 14 of this book) refers to how individuals relate to experiences in their everyday life. In a mindful state of consciousness, attention and awareness are directed to the external environment, i.e. to external events happening in the present moment but also to internal reactions to these external events (e.g. emotions, thoughts) and to internal experiences such as bodily sensations (Good et al., 2016; Shapiro, Carlson, Astin, & Freedman, 2006). Scholars assert that mindfulness may benefit employee well-being because key aspects of mindfulness such as an orientation to the present moment and experiential processing of information promotes adaptive forms of stress appraisal, facilitates self- and emotion regulation and therefore helps employees to deal with work demands and challenging work events (Good et al., 2016; Hülsheger, Alberts, Feinholdt, & Lang, 2013; Weinstein, Brown, & Ryan, 2009). Over the last decade, there has been a surge in interest in mindfulness-based interventions in the world of work. Organizations such as Google, IBM, SAP, AETNA, General Mills, and Intel have started offering mindfulness-based training programs to their workforce in an attempt to increase workplace functioning in general and employee well-being in particular. Mindfulness interventions aim to help individuals cultivate their ability to be mindful. They typically consist of a bundle of meditation practices that develop participants' skills in intentionally relating to external and internal present-moment experiences in an open and receptive way (e.g. the Mindfulness Based Stress Reduction program, Kabat-Zinn, 1990; for an overview see Alberts & Hülsheger, 2015).

There has been a noticeable recent uptick in scholarly interest in mindfulness in the organization sciences and an accumulation of empirical evidence on the effectiveness of mindfulness interventions for organizationally-relevant outcomes (for reviews see Eby et al., 2017; Jamieson & Tuckey, 2017). A study using a randomized waitlist control group design showed that a two-week mindfulness self-training intervention had positive effects on job satisfaction and decreased emotional exhaustion of participants working in emotionally demanding jobs (Hülsheger et al., 2013). Similar results were found in a quasi-experimental study on job satisfaction and life satisfaction (Rexroth, Michel, & Bosch, 2017). Furthermore, participants following a three-week online mindfulness self-training intervention experienced higher satisfaction with work-life balance and less strain-based work–family conflict than participants who were randomly assigned to a waitlist control group (Michel, Bosch, & Rexroth, 2014). Similarly, positive effects on work–family conflict have been documented for a one-hour mindfulness-based workshop followed by two weeks of behavioral self-monitoring (Kiburz, Allen, & French, 2017). Mindfulness interventions have also proven to be effective in improving employees' physical well-being in terms of sleep quality, heart rhythm coherence ratio, and heart rate variability (Hülsheger, Feinholdt, & Nübold, 2015; Querstret, Cropley, & Fife-Schaw, 2016; Wolever et al., 2012). However, no effects were found for blood pressure (Wolever et al., 2012).

Although findings of intervention studies have not always been consistent, taken together, the current body of evidence suggests that mindfulness interventions may benefit employee well-being. This is also supported by the first meta-analysis to focus exclusively on intervention studies conducted in the context of work and using working adults as participants (Virgili, 2015). Effects were medium to large in size, suggesting that mindfulness interventions help to reduce psychological distress in working adults. Notably, however, the meta-analysis was based on a relatively small number of studies (k = 19) and included not only controlled but also uncontrolled intervention studies.

Recovery Interventions

Shifting the focus from long- to more short-term processes, occupational health researchers increasingly acknowledge the role of day-to-day recovery from work stress (Sonnentag & Fritz, 2015). A relatively new type of intervention therefore seeks to improve employee well-being by targeting employee recovery, referring to "the process of reducing or eliminating physical and psychological strain symptoms that have been caused by job demands and stressful events at work" (Sonnentag & Fritz, 2015, p. 72). This is in line with a key proposition of the effort–recovery model (Meijman & Mulder, 1998), which posits that energy and resources that are spent during work need to be recovered after work in order to prevent chronic impairments of employee health and well-being (see also Geurts & Sonnentag, 2006). The key mechanisms driving beneficial effects of recovery activities and processes during leisure time are recovery experiences of psychological detachment, relaxation, mastery, and control (Sonnentag & Fritz, 2007). The recovery experience of psychological detachment has been found to be especially important in reducing fatigue, while control has been found to stimulate vigor (Bennett, Bakker, & Field, 2018). Two research groups therefore developed recovery interventions with a focus on these four recovery experiences and evaluated them using quasi-experimental designs (Hahn, Binnewies, Sonnentag, & Mojza, 2011; Siu, Cooper, & Phillips, 2014). Overall, findings were mixed: while one study found significant effects of the intervention on recovery experiences, on negative affect, and on sleep quality but not on emotional exhaustion (Hahn et al., 2011), effects of the second intervention trended toward the expected direction (higher positive emotions, lower emotional exhaustion, fewer psychosomatic symptoms) but did not reach statistical significance (Siu et al., 2014).

Positive Thinking Interventions

A typical positive psychology intervention that aims at increasing positive affect and well-being is positive thinking. Positive thinking is a cognitive strategy that promotes optimistic thinking and reflection on positive events or experiences (Seligman, Steen, Park, & Peterson, 2005). Reflecting on these positive events or experiences triggers positive emotions (e.g. happiness) which, in turn, build well-being, as suggested by the broaden-and-build theory (Fredrickson, 1998). Within the working context, positive thinking interventions have been adapted for reflection upon positive work events. For example, in an intervention study with caregivers, participants were asked on a daily basis to think about a positive and meaningful event they had experienced on a specific work day which made them feel good or happy and to savor this event (Clauss et al., 2018). Typically, these interventions last only a few minutes and can therefore be easily integrated into breaks during the work day or performed after work hours. The positive psychology literature consists of several studies that reveal positive intervention effects on happiness, life satisfaction, and other well-being outcomes (e.g. Chan, 2011; Seligman et al., 2005). Interestingly, studies conducted in the work setting with a specific focus on the reflection of positive work events reveal a much less consistent picture. Of the four available studies comparing intervention and control group participants with an experimental or quasi-experimental design, two studies reveal positive intervention effects on psychological well-being and happiness (Bono, Glomb, Shen, Kim, & Koch, 2013; Chancellor, Layous, & Lyubomirsky, 2015), one study shows clear null effects (Meier, Cho, & Dumani, 2016), and one study shows effects of the intervention on well-being and optimism primarily for employees with a high need for recovery (Clauss et al., 2018). These mixed findings suggest that positive work reflection interventions should be paired with other intervention components that have obtained more consistent results in evaluation studies, such as mindfulness exercises.

Self-Efficacy Interventions

According to Bandura's social cognitive theory, self-efficacy is the "belief in one's capabilities to organize and execute the course of action required to produce given attainments" (Bandura, 1997, p. 3). Self-efficacy may be developed by, for example, task mastery – watching and modeling relevant others – and by social persuasion, as when respected others such as managers express their confidence that the employee has the ability to do a certain task or when they provide positive process feedback (see Luthans, Avey, & Patera, 2008). Self-efficacy has been argued to benefit not only performance-related outcomes but also affective and attitudinal work outcomes such as job satisfaction (McNatt & Judge, 2008). Specifically, self-efficacy theory maintains that self-efficacy positively influences employee affect by facilitating cognitive and action-oriented responses to anxiety and coping (Bandura, 1997). While individuals with low self-efficacy may view work challenges as unmanageable and ruminate about their own incapacity to address them, individuals high in self-efficacy maintain more positive attitudes in the face of difficulties, have better coping skills, and therefore feel more positive (cf. McNatt & Judge, 2008).

Only a few intervention studies have explicitly aimed to advance self-efficacy. For example, McNatt and Judge (2008) developed an intervention based on self-efficacy theory and tested it in a field experiment with an accounting firm's newcomers. The intervention consisted of an interview and written communications provided by firm management (participants were asked to take on new responsibilities, to be proactive, and to have confidence in themselves). Results showed that intervention group participants increased their self-efficacy and job attitudes after the intervention and showed reduced turnover rates five months later.

Focusing on health and human services professionals exposed to indirect trauma, Cieslak et al. (2016) developed and evaluated a four-week internet-based self-efficacy intervention with a randomized control group design. Results revealed that intervention group participants reduced their secondary traumatic stress and improved their self-efficacy after the intervention. In addition, mediation analyses showed that self-efficacy after the intervention mediated the intervention effect on secondary traumatic stress and secondary post-traumatic growth at follow-up.

Using a control-group design, Linden, Muschalla, Hansmeier, and Sandner (2014) evaluated effects of an occupational healthcare management program that aimed to improve employees' health status, increase their work ability, and reduce their sickness absence time. The program consisted of group sessions with working team members focusing on self-efficacy and self-management of the individual as well as the whole team. Sickness absence rates did indeed significantly decrease as a result of the intervention. Explicitly testing the mediating role of self-efficacy in a stress management coaching intervention, Ebner, Schulte, Soucek, and Kauffeld (2017) showed that the positive relation between self-management skills (promoted in the coaching) and individual coping was mediated by self-efficacy.

Kirk, Schutte, and Hine (2011) pointed to the relevance of individual differences while evaluating intervention effectiveness. The authors evaluated effects of an expressive writing intervention on emotional self-efficacy, emotional intelligence, and affect. Intervention group participants were asked to write about their deepest thoughts and feelings about one aspect of life on four consecutive days. Results showed that intervention group participants with lower pre-test self-efficacy significantly increased their levels of self-efficacy. Moreover, emotional intelligence and positive affect were promoted. In line with this, Lloyd, Bond, and Flaxman (2017) showed that work-related self-efficacy can moderate the impact of a worksite stress management training intervention. Using a randomized control group design with UK government employees, they were able to show that the intervention led to reductions in psychological strain, emotional exhaustion, and depersonalization. However, results also revealed that only employees with low baseline levels of work-related self-efficacy and high baseline levels of intrinsic motivation experienced reductions in emotional exhaustion and depersonalization.

Taking a broader view, Luthans, Avey, and Patera (2008) consider self-efficacy to be one component of psychological capital in addition to hope, optimism, and resiliency. They developed and evaluated a web-based training aiming to promote psychological capital with an experimental randomized control group design. Study participants took part in two forty-five-minute training sessions in two consecutive weeks. The intervention group received two psychological capital sessions whereas the control group received decision-making exercises. For the intervention group, the first session focused on efficacy and resilience and the second session on hope and optimism. Results showed positive training effects on self-efficacy as a part of psychological capital.

Taken together, these findings show that self-efficacy can be trained and promoted. However, it is important to note that only a few studies have focused exclusively on the promotion of self-efficacy. Evidence stems from studies showing that self-efficacy can be improved by a variety of different interventions that ultimately benefit employee health and well-being.

Self-Regulation and Emotion-Regulation Interventions

Self-regulation in general and emotion-regulation in particular are key to maintaining employee well-being and health as these skills foster individuals' ability to appraise and adaptively respond to stressors (John & Gross, 2004). Although self-regulation of action (here referred to as self-regulation) and self-regulation of emotion (emotion-regulation) refer to different regulation processes they are also closely intertwined. Thus self-regulation research may explain how people actively manage their emotional lives, whereas emotion-regulation research could describe how people direct their behaviors in emotion-arousing situations (Koole, Van Dillen, & Sheppes, 2013).

Self-Regulation Interventions

Various self-regulation (often combined with emotion-regulation) interventions have been developed and evaluated. For example, Potter, Deshields, Berger, Clarke, Olsen, and Chen (2013) developed and evaluated a compassion fatigue (i.e. combination of secondary traumatic stress and burnout experienced by healthcare providers) resiliency program for oncology nurses. The five-week program consisted of small group activities aiming to promote resilience through self-regulation, intentionality, self-validation, connection, and self-care exercises. Fourteen nurses took part in the pilot study. Pre-program, post-program, and six-month follow-up comparisons showed that nurses significantly reduced their levels of secondary traumatic stress and felt better prepared to manage intrusive thoughts and feelings. Moreover, Lackey (2014) was able to show that a psychological resilience intervention improved self-awareness and self-regulation in response to a stressor for healthcare leaders. Focusing on the healthcare sector, Foster et al. (2018) evaluated the effects of a resilience program with a single-group pre-test/post-test design including a three-month follow-up measurement. Results revealed that nurses benefited from learning cognitive emotion-regulation strategies and relational skills in terms of improved mental health, well-being, and workplace resilience.

Studies on worksite health promotion interventions focusing on the promotion of physical activities (Hallam & Petosa, 2004; Skaggs, 2015) and regulation of eating behavior preventing/reducing obesity (e.g. worksite weight-loss intervention, Sandon, 2016) have also shown beneficial effects of self-regulation on self-efficacy, physical activity, weight and other health related-outcomes including affective well-being (see Hallam & Petosa, 2004; Sandon, 2016; Skaggs, 2015).

Emotion-regulation Interventions

Emotion-regulation interventions can be clustered into three groups according to their focus: (1) goal-oriented emotion regulation, (2) need-oriented goal orientation and (3) person-oriented self-regulation and emotion-regulation (for an overview see Koole et al., 2013). Applying goal-oriented emotion regulation is either triggered by individuals' beliefs that the utility of another emotional state is higher than utility of the current emotional state or that a specific goal, task or norm might change the significance of emotionally relevant information (e.g. temper control). Need-oriented emotion-regulation (e.g. training of reappraisal or coping styles) helps to shorten the duration of negative emotional states and may help to preserve resources. Person-oriented emotion regulation (e.g. mindfulness meditation trainings; also see this chapter) enables individuals to regulate their actions in harmony with their inner needs, motives and experiences (see for more details Koole et al., 2013).

Among examples of emotion-regulation interventions in the work-context and their effects, McCraty, Atkinson, Lipsenthal, and Arguelles (2009) conducted a randomized-waiting control group study with correctional officers. Intervention group participants took part in a two-day training consisting of five training modules, i.e. (1) identification of risk factors and their relation to health and well-being, (2) learning a positive emotion-refocusing technique improving decision-making in challenging situations, (3) coherent communication, (4) tools promoting inner quality and (5) workplace applications. Study results revealed significant improvements of physiological markers (e.g. heart rate and blood pressure), motivation, goal clarity, social support as well as reductions in psychological distress in comparison to control group participants. Another intervention study showed that workplace aerobic laughter (Beckman, Regier, & Young, 2007) can help increase self-regulation, optimism, positive emotions, and social identification. These effects were sustainable at the 90 days-follow-up measurement. Other studies have shown that training employees to change emotions by reappraising work situations increases feelings of high pleasure (Richard, 2006). Furthermore, applying deep-acting instead of surface-acting emotion-regulation strategies was shown to promote employees' positive mood and cognitive task performance (Feldman, 2008). Overall, intervention studies on self-regulation and emotion-regulation strategies apply a variety of techniques and outcome variables, which make it challenging to compare and contrast content and effectiveness.

Job-Crafting Interventions

Job crafting is a form of proactive work behavior that is actively initiated by employees and involves reducing hindering job demands, increasing challenging job demands, and seeking structural and social resources at work (Tims & Bakker, 2010). Employees who engage in job-crafting behaviors aim to change the characteristics of their job for the better. It is a form of job redesign initiated at the individual level and functions bottom-up. A meta-analysis on job crafting that involved 122 studies and over 35,000 employees has shown a variety of positive outcomes for job crafting (Rudolph, Katz, Lavigne, & Zacher, 2017). Findings of the meta-analysis reveal positive effects of job crafting on job satisfaction and work engagement as well as negative effects on work-related strain. Among these outcomes, the largest proportion of variance is explained for work engagement, a positive work-related state of mind characterized by positive affect and high activation (Schaufeli & Bakker, 2004).

Job-crafting interventions typically build on the three job-crafting strategies mentioned above: employees are trained in reducing hindering job demands (e.g. reducing monotonous tasks), encouraged to increase challenging job demands (e.g. looking for more interesting tasks that involve learning opportunities), and encouraged to seek job resources (e.g. asking for feedback from a colleague) (van den Heuvel, Demerouti, & Peeters, 2015). These aims are pursued with goal-setting strategies and reflection exercises. Typically, interventions consist of two half- to one-day workshops with several weeks between these workshops to apply and reflect on the various job-crafting strategies (e.g. van den Heuvel et al. 2015; Demerouti, Xanthopoulou, Petrou, & Karaghounis, 2017). For example, in a first training session participants learn about the concept of job crafting and reflect on their job demands and resources. They then craft a plan on how to change specific job demands and to seek resources in the following weeks. In a second session they reflect upon their experiences within the group and eventually adapt their strategies (see Sakuraya, Shimazu, Imamura, Namba, & Kawakami, 2016). Some interventions also draw on the concept of cognitive crafting (Wrzesniewski & Dutton, 2001) that aims at changing the way one perceives one's own job or aspects of the job with respect to its meaningfulness (e.g. Sakuraya et al., 2016).

Turning to the effects of job-crafting training, most studies tested intervention effects on work engagement, which has been identified as a core work-related correlate for job crafting in the meta-analysis by Rudolph and colleagues (2017). For example, in an intervention study with healthcare professionals using a quasi-experimental design involving an intervention and a control group, Gordon and colleagues (Gordon, Demerouti, LeBlanc, Bakker, Bipp, & Verhagen, 2017) revealed positive effects on work engagement along with other performance outcomes. Likewise, two quasi-experimental job-crafting intervention studies with teachers (Van Wingerden, Bakker, & Derks, 2017a) and healthcare professionals (Van

Wingerden, Bakker, & Derks, 2016) arrived at increasing work engagement through the intervention. However, a highly comparable study with similar training approaches and intervention design could not reveal effects on work engagement (e.g. Van Wingerden, Bakker, & Derks, 2017b). When focusing on other affective well-being outcomes, two recently published studies have shown pre- and post-intervention effects on negative affect (van den Heuvel et al. 2015) and affective well-being (Demerouti, Xanthopoulou, Petrou, & Karaghounis, 2017). Moreover, several studies have revealed effects of job-crafting interventions on employee strain, such as a reduction in exhaustion (e.g. Gordon et al., 2017) and in psychological distress (Sakuraya et al. 2016). The authors argue that these effects are explained through the reduction of hindering job demands: given that hindrance demands are a major predictor for strain (Podsakoff et al., 2007), a reduction of hindering job demands is likely to reduce strain-related outcomes such as exhaustion and psychological distress.

Although findings of job-crafting intervention studies have not always been consistent, taken together, the current body of research suggests that job-crafting interventions promote work engagement and affective well-being. By contrast, the studies cited above reveal quite a diverse picture on how the interventions affect specific job-crafting behaviors (i.e. reducing hindrance demands, increasing challenge demands, and seeking resources). At the most, there seems to be some evidence that work engagement and positive affect are primarily promoted through the job-crafting strategies of seeking job resources and challenges at work (see Gordon et al., 2017; Van Wingerden, Bakker, & Derks, 2017a; Demerouti, Xanthopoulou, Petrou, & Karaghounis, 2017). Therefore, whereas changes in more distal outcomes show a somewhat comprehensive picture, the more proximal outcomes and mechanisms through which job-crafting interventions unfold need further exploration.

Concluding Comments

Many organizations strive toward developing a satisfied, psychologically and physically healthy, and productive workforce. The present review has provided an overview of a range of positive psychology interventions that have been developed in the last decade to achieve this goal. Our review shows that although important strides have been made in developing and evaluating such interventions, considerably more research is needed to allow reliable, evidence-based recommendations to be made for practice.

For instance, while we have focused on randomized controlled studies whenever available, many studies on workplace well-being interventions are quasi-experimental in nature, based on small sample sizes, or rely on simple pre- and post-intervention comparisons, limiting the ability to draw reliable conclusions about the effectiveness of the investigated interventions. More research using rigorous designs is therefore needed, and this involves not only the random assignment of participants to conditions, but also the inclusion of active control groups in addition to no-intervention or waitlist control groups. Most studies also involve relatively short timespans, providing insights into only the short-term effectiveness of interventions. While this is understandable considering the difficulties in conducting intervention studies, longer time lags in follow-up measurements are urgently needed in order to assess the long-term effectiveness and sustainability of interventions. More research is also needed to identify the key ingredients and mechanisms driving positive intervention effects. This is especially true for interventions involving multiple components, such as job-crafting interventions or emotion-regulation interventions. Furthermore, research studying who benefits from interventions, who does not, and why these differences exist is duly needed. Finally, practical questions such as how to motivate employees to participate in well-being interventions in the first place and how to keep them engaged in intervention practices need more attention.

In conclusion it is worth noting that individual well-being interventions presented here should go hand-in-hand with organizational interventions focusing on improving the work environment by, for example, redesigning jobs to reduce work demands and increase resources, increasing social support at work, or enhancing supportive leadership styles.

References

Alberts, H. J. E. M., & Hülsheger, U. R. (2015). Applying mindfulness in the context of work: Mindfulness interventions. In J. Reb & P. Atkins (Eds.), *Mindfulness in organizatons: Foundations, research, and applications* (pp. 100–132). Cambridge, UK: Cambridge University Press.

Bandura, A. (1997). *Self-efficacy: The exercise of control*. New York, NY: W. H. Freeman.

Beckman, H., Regier, N., & Young, J. (2007). Effect of workplace laughter groups on personal efficacy beliefs. *Journal of Primary Prevention*, *28*(2), 167–182.

Bennett, A. A., Bakker, A. B., & Field, J. G. (2018). Recovery from work-related effort: A meta-analysis. *Journal of Organizational Behavior*, *39*, 262–275, https://doi.org/10.1002/job.2217

Biron, C. (2014). Positive vs. stress interventions: Does it really matter? In C. Biron, R. J. Burke, & C. L. Cooper (Eds.), *Creating healthy workplaces: Stress reduction, improved well-being, and organizational effectiveness* (pp. 321–326). Farnham, UK: Gower.

Bono, J. E., Glomb, T. M., Shen, W., Kim, E., & Koch, A. J. (2013). Building positive resources: Effects of positive events and positive reflection on work stress and health. *Academy of Management Journal*, *56*(6), 1601–1627.

Briner, R. B., & Reynolds, S. (1999). The costs, benefits, and limitations of organizational level stress interventions. *Journal of Organizational Behavior*, *20*, 647–664.

Burke, R. J. (2017). Work and well-being. In R. J. Burke & K. M. Page (Eds.), *Research handbook on work and well-being*. Cheltenham, UK: Edward Elgar.

Chan, D. W. (2011). Burnout and life satisfaction: Does gratitude intervention make a difference among Chinese school teachers in Hong Kong? *Educational Psychology*, *31*(7), 809–823, https://doi.org/10.1080/01443410.2011.608525

Chancellor, J., Layous, K., & Lyubomirsky, S. (2015). Recalling positive events at work makes employees feel happier, move more, but interact less: A 6-week randomized controlled intervention at a Japanese workplace. *Journal of Happiness Studies*, *16*, 871–887, https://doi.org/10.1007/s10902-014-9538-z

Cieslak, R., Benight, C. C., Rogala, A., Smoktunowicz, E., Kowalska, M., Zukowska, K., . . . & Luszczynska, A. (2016). Effects of internet-based self-efficacy intervention on secondary traumatic stress and secondary posttraumatic growth among health and human services professionals exposed to indirect trauma. *Frontiers in Psychology*, *7*(e17), https://doi.org/10.3389/fpsyg.2016.01009

Clauss, E., Hoppe, A., O'Shea, D., González Morales, M. G., Steidle, A., & Michel, A. (2018). Promoting personal resources and reducing exhaustion through positive work reflection among caregivers. *Journal of Occupational Health Psychology*, *23*(1), 127–140, https://doi.org/10.1037/ocp0000063

Demerouti, E., Xanthopoulou, D., Petrou, P., & Karagkounis, C. (2017). Does job crafting assist dealing with organizational changes due to austerity measures? Two studies among Greek employees. *European Journal of Work and Organizational Psychology*, *26*(4), 574–589, https://doi.org/10.1080/1359432X.2017.1325875

Diener, E., Oishi, S., & Lucas, R. E. (2003). Personality, culture, and subjective well-being: Emotional and cognitive evaluations of life. *Annual Review of Psychology*, *54*, 403–425, https://doi.org/10.1146/annurev.psych.54.101601.145056

Ebner, K., Schulte, E., Soucek, R., & Kauffeld, S. (2017). Coaching as stress-management intervention: The mediating role of self-efficacy in a framework of self-management and coping. *International Journal of Stress Management*, *25*, 209–233.

Eby, L. T., Allen, T. D., Conley, K. M., Williamson, R. L., Henderson, T. G., & Mancini, V. S. (2017). Mindfulness-based training interventions for employees: A qualitative review of the literature. *Human Resource Management Review, 29*(2), 156–178, https://doi.org/10.1016/j.hrmr.2017.03.004

Feldman, M. (2008). *Controlling our emotion at work: Implications for interpersonal and cognitive task performance in a customer service simulation* (doctoral dissertation, University of Central Florida).

Foster, K., Shochet, I., Wurfl, A., Roche, M., Maybery, D., Shakespeare-Finch, J., & Furness, T. (2018). On PAR: A feasibility study of the Promoting Adult Resilience programme with mental health nurses. *International Journal of Mental Health Nursing, 27*, 1470–1480.

Fredrickson, B. L. (1998). What good are positive emotions? *Review of General Psychology, 2*, 300–319, http://dx.doi.org/10.1037/1089–2680.2.3.300

Geurts, S. A., & Sonnentag, S. (2006). Recovery as an explanatory mechanism in the relation between acute stress reactions and chronic health impairment. *Scandinavian Journal of Work, Environment & Health, 32*(6), 482–492, https://doi.org/10.5271/sjweh.1053

Good, D. J., Lyddy, C. J., Glomb, T. M., Bono, J. E., Brown, K. W., Duffy, M. K., . . . & Lazar, S. W. (2016). Contemplating mindfulness at work: An integrative review. *Journal of Management, 42*, 114–142, https://doi.org/10.1177/0149206315617003

Gordon, H. J., Demerouti, E., Le Blanc, P. M., Bakker, A. B., Bipp, T., & Verhagen, M. A. (2018). Individual job redesign: Job crafting interventions in healthcare. *Journal of Vocational Behavior, 104*, 98–114, https://doi.org/10.1016/j.jvb.2017.07.002

Hahn, V. C., Binnewies, C., Sonnentag, S., & Mojza, E. J. (2011). Learning how to recover from job stress: Effects of a recovery training program on recovery, recovery-related self-efficacy, and well-being. *Journal of Occupational Health Psychology, 16*(2), 202–216, https://doi.org/10.1037/a0022169

Hallam, J. S., & Petosa, R. (2004). The long-term impact of a four-session work-site intervention on selected social cognitive theory variables linked to adult exercise adherence. *Health Education & Behavior, 31*, 88–100, https://doi.org/10.1177/1090198103259164

Hülsheger, U. R., Alberts, H. J. E. M., Feinholdt, A., & Lang, J. W. B. (2013). Benefits of mindfulness at work: The role of mindfulness in emotion regulation, emotional exhaustion, and job satisfaction. *Journal of Applied Psychology, 98*, 310–325.

Hülsheger, U. R., Feinholdt, A., & Nübold, A. (2015). A low-dose mindfulness intervention and recovery from work: Effects on psychological detachment, sleep quality, and sleep duration. *Journal of Occupational and Organizational Psychology, 88*, 464–489, doi:10.1111/joop.12115

Jamieson, S. D., & Tuckey, M. R. (2017). Mindfulness interventions in the workplace: A critique of the current state of the literature. *Journal of Occupational Health Psychology, 22*, 180–193, https://doi.org/doi.org/10.1037/ocp000004

John, O. P., & Gross, J. J. (2004). Healthy and unhealthy emotion regulation: Personality processes, individual differences, and life span development. *Journal of Personality, 72*(6), 1301–1334.

Kabat-Zinn, J. (1990). *Full catastrophe living: Using the wisdom of your mind to face stress, pain and illness*. New York, NY: Dell.

Kiburz, K. M., Allen, T. D., & French, K. A. (2017). Work-family conflict and mindfulness: Investigating the effectiveness of a brief training intervention. *Journal of Organizational Behavior, 38*, 1016–1037, https://doi.org/10.1002/job.2181

Kirk, B. A., Schutte, N. S., & Hine, D. W. (2011). The effect of an expressive-writing intervention for employees on emotional self-efficacy, emotional intelligence, affect, and workplace incivility. *Journal of Applied Social Psychology, 41*(1), 179–195, https://doi.org/10.1111/j.1559–1816.2010.00708.x

Koole, S. F., Van Dillen, L. F., & Sheppes, G. (2013). The self-regulation of emotion. In K. Vohs & R. F. Baumeister (Eds.), *Handbook of self-*

regulation: Research, theory, and applications (2nd edition, pp. 22–40). New York, NY: Guilford.

Lackey, E. D. (2014). *Self-regulation and heart rate variability coherence: Promoting psychological resilience in healthcare leaders* (doctoral dissertation, Benedictine University, Lisle, IL).

LaMontagne, A. D., Keegel, T., Louie, A. M., Ostry, A., & Landsbergis, P. A. (2007). A systematic review of the job-stress intervention evaluation literature, 1990–2005. *International Journal of Occupational and Environmental Health*, *13*, 268–280, https://doi.org/10.1179/oeh.2007.13.3.268

Linden, M., Muschalla, B., Hansmeier, T., & Sandner, G. (2014). Reduction of sickness absence by an occupational health care management program focusing on self-efficacy and self-management. *Work*, *47*(4), 485–489.

Lloyd, J., Bond, F. W., & Flaxman, P. E. (2017). Work-related self-efficacy as a moderator of the impact of a worksite stress management training intervention: Intrinsic work motivation as a higher order condition of effect. *Journal of Occupational Health Psychology*, *22*, 115–127.

Luthans, F., Avey, J. B., & Patera, J. L. (2008). Experimental analysis of a web-based training intervention to develop positive psychological capital. *Academy of Management Learning & Education*, *7*(2), 209–221.

Meier, L. L., Cho, E., & Dumani, S. (2016). The effect of positive work reflection during leisure time on affective well-being: Results from three diary studies. *Journal of Organizational Behavior*, *37*(2), 255–278, http://dx.doi.org/10.1002/job.2039

McCraty, R., Atkinson, M., Lipsenthal, L., & Arguelles, L. (2009). New hope for correctional officers: An innovative program for reducing stress and health risks. *Applied Psychophysiology and Biofeedback*, *34*(4), 251–272, https://doi.org/10.1007/s10484-009–9087-0

McNatt, D. B., & Judge, T. A. (2008). Self-efficacy intervention, job attitudes, and turnover: A field experiment with employees in role transition. *Human Relations*, *61*(6), 783–810.

Meier, L. L., Cho, E., & Dumani, S. (2016). The effect of positive work reflection during leisure time on affective well-being: Results from three diary studies. *Journal of Organizational Behavior*, *37*(2), 255–278, https://doi.org/10.1002/job.2039

Meijman, T. F., & Mulder, G. (1998). Psychological aspects of workload. In P. J. D. Drenth & H. Thierry (Eds.), *Handbook of work and organizational psychology: Work psychology* (pp. 5–33). Hove, UK: Psychology.

Michel, A., Bosch, C., & Rexroth, M. (2014). Mindfulness as a cognitive–emotional segmentation strategy: An intervention promoting work–life balance. *Journal of Occupational and Organizational Psychology*, *87*, 733–754, https://doi.org/10.1111/joop.12072

Podsakoff, N., LePine, J., & LePine, M. (2007). Differential challenge stressor – hindrance stressor relationships with job attitudes, turnover intentions, turnover, and withdrawal behavior: A meta-analysis. *Journal of Applied Psychology*, *92*, 438–454.

Potter, P., Deshields, T., Berger, J. A., Clarke, M., Olsen, S., & Chen, L. (2013). Evaluation of a compassion fatigue resiliency program for oncology nurses. *Oncology Nursing Forum*, *40*(2), 180–187, https://doi.org/10.1188/13.ONF.180–187

Querstret, D., Cropley, M., & Fife-Schaw, C. (2016). Internet-based instructor-led mindfulness for work-related rumination, fatigue and sleep: Assessing facets of mindfulness as mechanisms of change – A randomised waitlist control trial. *Journal of Occupational Health Psychology*, *22*, 153–169, https://doi.org/http://dx.doi.org/10.1037/ocp0000028

Rexroth, M., Michel, A., & Bosch, C. (2017). Promoting well-being by teaching employees how to segment their life domains. *German Journal of Work and Organizational Psychology*, *61*(4), 197–212, https://doi.org/10.1026/0932–4089/a000253

Richard, E. M. (2006). *Applying appraisal theories of emotion to the concept of emotional labor* (doctoral dissertation, Lousiana State University).

Richardson, K. M., & Rothstein, H. R. (2008). Effects of occupational stress management intervention programs: A meta-analysis. *Journal of Occupational Health Psychology*, *13*(1), 69–93.

Rudolph, C. W., Katz, I. M., Lavigne, K. N., & Zacher, H. (2017). Job crafting: A meta-analysis of relationships with individual differences, job characteristics, and work outcomes. *Journal of Vocational Behavior, 102*, 112–138, https://doi.org/10.1016/j.jvb.2017.05.008

Sandon, L. (2016). *Pilot study: Effect of a worksite weight-loss intervention and social influence on self-efficacy and self-regulation for eating and exercise* (doctoral dissertation, Texas Woman's University).

Sakuraya, A., Shimazu, A., Imamura, K., Namba, K., & Kawakami, N. (2016). Effects of a job crafting intervention program on work engagement among Japanese employees: A pretest-posttest study. *BMC Psychology, 4*(1), 49–57, https://doi.org/10.1186/s40359-016–0157-9

Schaufeli, W. B., & Bakker, A. B. (2004). Job demands, job resources, and their relationship with burnout and engagement: A multi-sample study. *Journal of Organizational Behavior, 25*(3), 293–315, https://doi.org/10.1002/job.248

Seligman, M. E., Steen, T. A., Park, N., & Peterson, C. (2005). Positive psychology progress: Empirical validation of interventions. *American Psychologist, 60*(5), 410–421.

Semmer, N. K. (2006). Job stress interventions and the organization of work. *Scandinavian Journal of Work and Environmental Health, 32*, 515–527.

Shapiro, S. L., Carlson, L. E., Astin, J. A., & Freedman, B. (2006). Mechanisms of mindfulness. *Journal of Clinical Psychology, 62*(3), 373–386.

Siu, O. L., Cooper, C. L., & Phillips, D. R. (2014). Intervention studies on enhancing work well-being, reducing burnout, and improving recovery experiences among Hong Kong health care workers and teachers. *International Journal of Stress Management, 21*, 69–84, https://doi.org/10.1037/a0033291

Skaggs, J. W. (2015). *Evaluation of two educational exercise adherence interventions on rates of exercise and exercise adherence* (doctoral dissertation, Ohio State University).

Sonnentag, S. (2015). Dynamics of well-being. *Annual Review of Organizational Psychology and Organizational Behavior, 2*(1), 261–293, https://doi.org/10.1146/annurev-orgpsych-032414–111347

Sonnentag, S., & Fritz, C. (2007). The recovery experience questionnaire: Development and validation of a measure. *Journal of Occupational Health Psychology, 12*(3), 204–221.

Sonnentag, S., & Fritz, C. (2015). Recovery from job stress: The stressor-detachment model as an integrative framework. *Journal of Organizational Behavior, 36*, S72–S103.

Tetrick, L. E., & Winslow, C. J. (2015). Workplace stress management interventions and health promotion. *Annual Review of Organizational Psychology and Organizational Behavior, 2*(1), 583–603, https://doi.org/10.1146/annurev-orgpsych-032414–111341

Tims, M., & Bakker, A. B. (2010). Job crafting: Towards a new model of individual job redesign. *SA Journal of Industrial Psychology, 36*(2), 1–9, https://doi.org/10.4102/sajip.v36i2.841

van den Heuvel, M., Demerouti, E., & Peeters, M. C. (2015). The job crafting intervention: Effects on job resources, self-efficacy, and affective well-being. *Journal of Occupational and Organizational Psychology, 88*(3), 511–532, https://doi.org/10.1111/joop.12128

Van Wingerden, J., Bakker, A. B., & Derks, D. (2016). A test of a job demands-resources intervention. *Journal of Managerial Psychology, 31*(3), 686–701, http://dx.doi.org/10.1108/JMP-03–2014-0086

Van Wingerden, J., Bakker, A. B., & Derks, D. (2017a). Fostering employee well-being via a job crafting intervention. *Journal of Vocational Behavior, 100*, 164–174, https://doi.org/10.1016/j.jvb.2017.03.008

Van Wingerden, J., Bakker, A. B., & Derks, D. (2017b). The longitudinal impact of a job crafting intervention. *European Journal of Work and Organizational Psychology, 26*(1), 107–119, https://doi.org/10.1080/1359432X.2016.1224233

Virgili, M. (2015). Mindfulness-based interventions reduce psychological distress in working adults: A meta-analysis of intervention studies. *Mindfulness, 6*, https://doi.org/10.1007/s12671-013–0264-0

Weinstein, N., Brown, K. W., & Ryan, R. M. (2009). A multi-method examination of the effects of mindfulness on stress attribution, coping, and emotional well-being. *Journal of Research in Personality, 73*, 374–385.

Wolever, R. Q., Bobinet, K. J., McCabe, K., Mackenzie, E. R., Fekete, E., Kusnick, C. A., & Baime, M. (2012). Effective and viable mind-body stress reduction in the workplace: A randomized controlled trial. *Journal of Occupational Health Psychology, 17*(2), 246–258.

Wrzesniewski, A., & Dutton, J. E. (2001). Crafting a job: Revisioning employees as active crafters of their work. *Academy of Management Review, 26*(2), 179–201, https://doi.org/10.5465/amr.2001.4378011

Part III

Workplace Affect and Interpersonal and Team-Level Processes

17 Leadership, Affect, and Emotion in Work Organizations

Russell Cropanzano, Stefanie K. Johnson, and Brittany K. Lambert

Leader Affect and Emotion

In this chapter, we review the literature on leadership and emotion. Progress in understanding the junction of these two ideas has been steady but slow. To address this concern, at the conclusion of this chapter, we briefly discuss two theoretical obstacles that, in our view, have slowed progress. However, we begin with the larger substance of our chapter, which focuses on leaders' affect at three levels of analysis – the overall climate, the work team, and, finally, the leader himself or herself. We show that leader emotion can be important at all three levels of analysis. At the highest level of analysis, leaders create emotional climate through personnel practices, by rewarding (or punishing) culturally appropriate emotion displays, and by their treatment of individual employees. Moving to teams and dyads, we will see that emotions can influence followers through contagion or emotional correspondence. Finally, looking within the leader, our review underscores how emotional intelligence is crucial for effective leadership.

Level 3: Leadership and Emotional Climates

As Parke and Seo (2017) assert, organizations differ in terms of their emotional climates, just as a given organization might have a strong safety climate, ethical climate, or diversity climate. In early work on this topic, De Rivera (1992, p. 197) defined emotional or affective climate as "an objective group phenomenon that can be palpably sensed – as when one enters a party or a city and feels an attitude of gaiety or depression, openness or fear" (see also Ashkanasy & Hartel, 2014; Barsade & O'Neill, 2014; see also Chapters 18 and 28 in this volume). Leaders can have a strong influence on creating a shared affective climate (Humphrey, 2008; Pescosolido, 2003; Toegel, Kilduff, & Anand, 2013).

Attraction, Selection, and Retention

Though sometimes neglected by management scholars, a fundamental way to shape climate has to do with the persons who are employed within an organization at any one time. Schneider (1987) argued that organizations shape their culture by whom they *attract*, whom they *select*, and whom they *retain* (see also Schneider, Smith, & Goldstein, 2000). While a full review of this area is beyond the scope of this chapter, it is worth mentioning that evidence generally supports this attraction–selection–attrition model (Schneider et al., 2000). To the extent that leaders elect to hire and retain employees based upon their emotional tendencies, then these workers will tend to exhibit similarities simply due to their shared individual differences. Intuitively, it would seem that the norm might be to try to hire people who are high in positive affect. While this may often be true, it is unlikely to be universal. In some organizations, leaders may elect to avoid happy people because they are seen as not being tough enough to survive in a competitive environment (Ely & Meyerson, 2010; Vuori & Huy, 2016).

Leader Responses to Subordinate Affective Displays

Leaders also influence the affective climate in how they respond to affective displays in the workplace (Hochschild, 1983). Leaders may positively reinforce or punish displays of emotion, sending a message about what is acceptable in terms of affective displays. Generally, positive emotional displays are preferred. For example, service organizations often communicate the importance of demonstrating positive affect to customers (Ashkanasy & Daus, 2002; Morris & Feldman, 1996; Rafaeli & Sutton, 1987). There are exceptions, of course. Some organizations seek to hire people who can "cut it." Such competitive organizations tend to communicate those values to employees (Ely & Meyerson, 2006; Vuori & Huy, 2016). Likewise, workers in certain types of jobs, such as bill collectors, may require norms promoting negative emotional expressions (Sutton, 1991).

Even where positive affective climates are otherwise appropriate, there is a risk when organizations aggressively promote such climates. Parke and Seo (2017) suggest that affective climates vary in valence (negative or positive) but also in authenticity (hide or show your feelings). If leaders punish followers for demonstrating negative emotions such as frustration, anger, or fear, for example, it conveys the message that positive emotions are valued over authentic emotions (e.g. Bryant & Cox, 2006). Instead of just punishing negative affective displays, leaders would be better served by supporting followers when they experience negative emotions. Such tactics might include listening, reframing, transforming through positivity, and advising (Toegel et al., 2013) or teaching employees how to manage negative emotions (Kegan, Lahey, Fleming, & Miller, 2014). Negative emotions are validated when leaders support subordinates who are experiencing them. However, there also needs to be a culture norm to confront and improve worker experiences, not simply to allay the expression of negative feelings (Geddes & Callister, 2007; Toegel et al., 2013). In this way, leaders can create a climate where positive emotions are valued, but so is authenticity and taking a proactive approach to improving negative situations. In sum, leaders can serve as an important driver of affective climate whether through the information they communicate to followers or through how they treat followers.

Level 2: Leadership and Emotional Expression in Teams and Dyads

Apart from the manner in which employees are treated, leader mood states also impact work behavior (George, 1995). For example, Barsade (2002) observed that team members reported more positive affect when their leader also displayed positive feelings. When teams experienced these pleasant feelings, they exhibited less interpersonal conflict and superior cooperation. Likewise, Johnson (2008) found that leaders' expression of positive and negative affect influenced the positive affect felt by subordinates. These positive feelings, in turn, positively related to organizational citizenship behaviors. In a later study, Chi, Chung, and Tsai (2011) found that leaders' positive moods boosted the positive affective tone of the group while also increasing perceptions of transformational leadership. In turn, positive affective tone and transformational leadership then impacted team members' goal commitment, satisfaction, helping behavior, and job performance. Certain circumstances appear to increase the magnitude of these effects. Gaddis, Connelly, and Mumford (2004) found that leaders who deliver negative feedback while also displaying negative affect are viewed as less competent and their subordinates showed poorer subsequent performance. If they delivered similar feedback while displaying positive affect, they were viewed as more competent and their subordinates showed higher subsequent performance.

In addition to influencing subordinate cognitions and behaviors, leader mood states can be directly transmitted to their employees. "Emotional contagion" refers to the movement of affective states from one individual to another (Hatfield, Cacioppo, & Rapson, 1992; 1994). While both moods and emotions can exhibit contagion, most of the (leadership) research to date has focused on the former. Historically, contagion was understood to be unconscious (George, 2002), but later authors allowed for conscious contagion (Bakker, Westman, & van Emmerik, 2009). With this in mind, Tee (2015) has argued that there are two types of contagion. Implicit contagion is automatic and unconscious, while explicit contagion is deliberate. Regardless of the particulars, contagion is an important process through which followers "catch" the moods of their leaders, coming to exhibit similar feeling states (e.g. Sy, Côté, & Saavedra, 2005; Johnson, 2009; Volmer, 2012). These "caught" moods, in turn, can influence judgments of leader effectiveness. Leaders who express positive affect are rated as more charismatic (Bono & Ilies, 2006) than are leaders who express negative affect (Johnson, 2008; 2009). These effects appear to travel from leader to follower and vice versa.

Leadership and Discrete Emotions

Historically, most research in the behavioral sciences has emphasized global affective states. However, there is a modest but growing literature on leader discrete emotions, which we will illustrate by considering a few emotions that have been widely studied. Two of these are happiness and sadness. Generally speaking, leaders are viewed more favorably when they express the former and less favorably when they express the latter. For example, Sullivan and Masters (1988) played videotapes of candidate speeches from the 1984 US presidential election campaigns. They found that "happy/reassuring" expressions led to positive emotional responses in viewers. This occurred even when the videos had no accompanying sound. While these happy leaders tended to be more influential, leaders who express sadness are likely to be perceived as less dominant (Knutson, 1996; Tiedens, 2001, Study 4). Likewise, leaders are judged as more effective when they express happiness as opposed to sadness (Visser, van Knippenberg, van Kleef, & Wisse, 2013), and this is true for both men and women (Lewis, 2000). However, this is not always the case. Appropriate sadness is accepted. Following a crisis, leaders who display sadness are viewed more favorably (Madera & Smith, 2009).

Anger is another widely studied emotion that is usually viewed as negative (Gibson & Callister, 2010). In general, managers who display anger tend to evoke reciprocal anger in subordinates (Johnson & Connelly, 2014) and can be rated as less effective than are those who do not display this emotion (Glomb & Hulin, 1997). In two studies, Koning and van Kleef (2015) found that leader expressions of anger tend to reduce citizenship behaviors from subordinates. Despite these findings, anger is not entirely bad for the person experiencing it. It can make people feel optimistic about themselves (Lerner & Tiedens, 2006) and more optimistic when judging risk (Lerner & Keltner, 2001). Expressing anger can also improve how a leader is judged by others. In four studies, Tiedens (2001) found that leaders who expressed anger were rated as having higher status. Knutson (1996) found that leaders who displayed angry expressions were viewed as high in dominance though low in affiliation. Male leaders (but not female: Lewis, 2000) who express anger (as opposed to sadness) are sometimes viewed as more competent leaders (Tiedens, 2001), though this is not always the case (Glomb & Hulin, 1997). Anger can even boost employee performance under certain conditions (Lindebaum & Fielden, 2011; van Kleef,

Homan, Beersma, van Knippenberg, van Knippenberg, & Damen, 2009). Chi and Ho (2014) found that expressing anger tends to boost performance when subordinates are high in conscientiousness or agreeableness, but that otherwise the anger led to diminished performance. Given these sorts of observations, it is not surprising to learn that leaders sometimes display sham anger as a means of influencing others (Fitness, 2000).

A more controversial emotion is guilt, which does not enjoy a particularly good reputation in popular thought. Guilt is a negative judgment of our actions. We feel guilty when we do something that does not live up to our own internal standards (Tangey & Dearing, 2002). In this way, guilt, though painful, can motivate efforts to correct misdeeds (Baumeister, Stillwell, & Heatherton, 1994; Johnson & Connelly, 2014) and make amends with those we have wronged (Tangney, 1995). Guilt may also assist in the socialization process (Ausubel, 1955). Because they are more responsive to others, individuals prone to guilt engage in more leadership behaviors and are rated as more effective leaders (Schaumberg & Flynn, 2012). Of course, like the other emotions on this list, guilt is not universally a good thing. When working in teams, individuals experiencing guilt can be so eager to make amends to their victim that they treat others unfairly (de Hooge, Nelissen, Breugelmans, & Zeelenberg, 2011); they may even engage in unhealthy self-punishment (Nelissen & Zeelenberg, 2009).

Given some potential benefits, why does guilt seem to enjoy such an unhealthy reputation? Part of the answer is that guilt is sometimes confused with shame. When people feel shame, they judge themselves, not just their acts. That is, shame leads you to question yourself as a person (Tangey & Dearing, 2002). Far from promoting leadership skills, people who feel shame tend to protect themselves by withdrawing, denying, and externalizing blame (Tangney, 1995). Externalization, in turn, promotes anger, aggression, and even crime (Stuewig, Tangney, Heigel, Harty, McCloskkey, 2010; Tangney, Stuewig, & Martinez, 2014). Consequently, while guilt may improve leader performance in some circumstances, shame seems to be generally negative.

Level 1: The Emotionally Intelligent Leader

Leadership is a process of social interaction (Humphrey, 2002; Kerr, Garvin, Heaton, & Boyle, 2005; Pirola-Merlo, Hartel, Mann, & Hirst, 2002) and in order to be socially effective, leaders must themselves be *emotionally intelligent* (George, 2000; Kerr et al., 2005; Mayer, Caruso, & Salovey, 2000). An emotionally intelligent leader has "the ability to monitor one's own and others' feelings to discriminate among them, and to use this information to guide one's thinking and action" (Salovey & Mayer, 1990, p. 185). Not surprisingly, there is a growing body of evidence suggesting that being an effective leader and being emotionally intelligent go hand-in-hand (Ashkanasy & Tse, 2000; Boal & Hooijberg, 2000; George, 2000; Goleman, 1998; Kerr et al., 2005; Rosete & Ciarrochi, 2005). Consider a few of the most salient responsibilities of a leader. Leaders will have to manage crises at some point in their careers, and during a crisis the control of emotions is essential (Riggio & Reichard, 2008). Likewise, thriving leader–follower relationships are key to leader effectiveness (Uhl-Bien, 2003) and understanding the emotions of followers is helpful in fostering stronger relationships (Riggio & Reichard, 2008). Furthermore, recent and provocative evidence suggests that emotional intelligence predicts performance beyond cognitive intelligence (Mayer, Roberts, & Barsade, 2008; Elfenbein, 2007).

For all that, the precise definition and measurement of emotional intelligence is highly contested. As a complete review of this literature is beyond the scope of our present comments, we recommend the reader to Chapter 12 in this book. For now, we organize our discussion into three simplified dimensions proposed by Heneman, Judge, and Kammeyer-Mueller (2019) that best illustrates the nexus of the leadership and emotional intelligence literatures. According to Heneman and colleagues, an emotionally intelligent leader is high in awareness of others, self-awareness, and emotional regulation. We will now discuss each of these dimensions in turn, paying special attention to their various facets.

Dimension 1: Awareness of Others

"Awareness of others" refers to the ability to "recognize and understand others' emotions" (Heneman et al., 2019, p. 450). Drawing from Mayer and Salovey's (1997) abilities-focused model of emotional intelligence, leaders would need to *perceive emotions* and *understand emotions* in order to work with followers in an emotionally intelligent way (Mayer, Salovey, & Caruso, 2008). Additionally, in the original discussion on emotional intelligence (Salovey & Mayer, 1990), researchers highlighted *empathy* as being critical to emotional interactions with others. We discuss these three abilities below.

Perceiving Emotions. Perceiving emotions is the ability to recognize emotions accurately, as when seeing anxiety and worry on the faces of subordinates (Mayer et al., 2008; Gardner & Stough, 2002). This skill is important because the more accurately leaders perceive emotions, the more appropriately leaders can respond and express them to others (Salovey & Mayer, 1990). Scholars further add that this ability assists leaders in differentiating between honest and false emotions in others (Caruso, Mayer, & Salovey, 2002; Gardner & Stough, 2002). One study using the Mayer Salovey Caruso Emotional Intelligence Test (MSCEIT; Mayer, Salovey, & Caruso, 2000), showed specifically that a leader's ability to perceive emotions is highly correlated with their performance ratings (Kerr et al., 2005).

Understanding Emotions. "The understanding of emotion reflects the capacity to analyze emotions, appreciate their probable trends over time, and understand their outcomes" (Mayer, Salovey, & Caruso, 2004, p. 199). This ability involves being able to answer: "What sorts of feelings emerge from a situation and how might those feelings change over time?" (Mayer et al., 2008, p. 7). Caruso and colleagues (2002) suggest that this ability is critical to effective leadership because it allows a leader to understand multiple points of view.

Empathy. Scholars define empathy as understanding the feelings and/or the subjective experiences of others and experiencing them personally (George, 2000; Mehrabian & Epstein, 1972; Wispé, 1986). Work by Kellett, Humphrey, and Sleeth (2006) found that high empathy ratings were related to task and relational leadership. Moreover, empathy mediated the effect of other emotional abilities (i.e. identifying and expressing emotions) on task and relational leadership (see also Kellett et al., 2002). Likewise, research has found that empathy is indeed predictive of many other positive leadership outcomes including perceptions of job performance (Sadri, Weber, & Gentry, 2011), actual performance (Tobolski & Kerr, 1952), displays of organizational citizenship behaviors (Joireman, Kamdar, Daniels, & Duell, 2006), and overall effectiveness (Ashkanasy, Hartel, & Daus, 2002; George, 2000).

Dimension 2: Self-Awareness

Self-awareness is the ability to recognize and understand one's own emotions (Heneman et al., 2019). Foundational work illuminates why this skill is so essential – emotions function as a signal to let us and others know about our concerns or preferences (Frijda, 1988). Put differently, emotions' function is to help make sense out of one's experiences in life (Rodriguez, 2013). In the leadership literature, research shows that self-aware leaders are more effective (Atwater, Ostroff,

Yammarino, & Fleenor, 1998). Mayer and Salovey (1997) maintain that, as with awareness of others, leaders high in self-awareness are good at *perceiving* their own emotions and *understanding* them. However, given that leadership is a process of relating to other people, it follows that most of the leadership research focuses on a leaders' ability to perceive and understand the emotions of *others*. Thus, there is limited research on the effects of a leader perceiving and understanding their *own* emotions.

Research in psychology supports claims that the ability to perceive and understand one's own emotions is important to leadership. Psychology refers to this skill as *emotional differentiation*, the ability to distinguish among emotions (e.g. "I feel *sad* that my favorite direct-report is leaving" vs. "I feel something *unpleasant* about my favorite direct-report leaving"). In fact, theorists assert that the more precise with language one can be about what is felt, the higher well-being will be (Kashdan, Barrett, & McKnight, 2015). Precision of emotional language and/or knowledge allows for more effective emotional regulation (Kashdan et al., 2015; Barrett, Gross, Christensen, & Benvenuto, 2001). In fact, some of the most prominent scales of measuring emotional regulation in psychology use self-awareness as one of the key components (Gratz & Roemer, 2004). Thus a leader who can precisely perceive and understand his or her own emotions will theoretically be able to *regulate emotions* with greater skill – the third dimension of an emotionally intelligent leader to be discussed next.

Dimension 3: Emotion Regulation

Emotion regulation refers to the ability to manage and use emotions in an effective fashion (see Chapters 11, 21, and 22 in this volume). Foundational scholarship on emotions alludes to the importance of this dimension. Fridja (1988) observes that emotions have an overriding effect on consideration and consequences when it comes to responding behaviors and thoughts – that is, emotions can take over (a phenomenon known as *control precedence*). Given this, leaders need a way to assist them in being deliberate with corresponding thoughts and behaviors in the face of strong, often negative, emotions. The most commonly employed tool is called *emotional regulation* – "the process by which individuals influence which emotions they have, when they have them, and how they experience and express these emotions" (Gross, 1998, p. 275). Hochschild (1983) conceptualized "emotion regulation for the work role" as *emotional labor* (Grandey, 2000). Ashforth and Humphrey (1993) broadened the definition of emotional labor to make it more useful for leadership scholarship: "the act of displaying the appropriate emotion (conforming with a display rule)" (p. 90).

The appropriate display of emotion can be an integral part of successful leadership performance (Grandey, 2000; Pugh, 2001; Totterdell & Holman, 2003), and much research has been done linking leaders' positive (or negative) display of emotions to subsequent group positive (or negative) outcomes (George & Bettenhausen, 1990; Lewis, 2000; Gaddis, Connelly, & Mumford, 2004). There are three primary emotional labor (i.e. emotional regulation) strategies available to leaders. That is to say, leaders can display emotions experienced in these three ways (Gardner, Fischer, & Hunt, 2009) – *surface acting* (Grandey, 2000; Hochschild, 1983), *deep acting* (Grandey, 2000; Hochschild, 1983), and *genuine emotions* (Ashforth & Humphrey, 1993). We describe them each below.

Surface Acting. Humphrey and Ashforth (1993) maintain that *surface acting* involves simulating emotions that are not actually felt, as when maintaining a smile in the presence of an abusive customer. For leadership purposes, surface acting requires a leader to "choke down unwanted feelings" in order to display a controlled front to their followers (Beal, Trougakos, Weiss, & Green, 2006; Grandey, 2000; Hochschild, 1983). In general, research has shown that surface acting leads to less favorable outcomes on desired follower impressions (Beal et al. 2006) and that leaders are viewed as less authentic when they surface act (Brotheridge & Lee, 2002). However, there are instances where followers are more amenable to surface acting. If leaders employ surface acting only on occasion, leaders' positive emotion displays predict followers' positive performance (Wang & Seibert, 2015). On the other hanbd, the same study showed that if leaders surface act frequently, leaders' displayed emotions have no effect on follower performance because followers have deemed their leaders' emotions as not genuine.

Research has shown that a consistent amount of surface acting (and deep acting – to be discussed in the next section) can lead to exhaustion, disengagement, and burnout (Grandey, 2003). Surface acting is particularly harmful and has been linked to more severe negative outcomes, even physical harm (Gross, 2002). Though breaks and rest can help replenish emotional resources (Trougakos, Beal, Green, & Weiss, 2008), altering emotional expressions to fit a set of norms does not seem to be the best option for leaders in the workplace.

Deep Acting. Instead of merely modifying a response, a leader can employ *deep acting* and change their own actual experience of the emotion (Beal et al., 2006; Grandey, 2000; Hochschild, 1983; Gardner et al., 2009). In leaders, it is more effective than surface acting in achieving desired follower impressions (Beal et al. 2006) and more positively associated with perceptions of authenticity (Brotheridge & Lee, 2002). In a study on emotional labor strategies, leaders' deep acting improved job satisfaction among employees with low-quality relationships, while leaders' surface acting harmed job satisfaction among these individuals (Fisk & Friesen, 2011).

Genuine Emotions. *Genuine emotional displays* or "naturally felt emotions" (Diefendorff, Croyle, & Gosserand, 2005, p. 339) is the third form of emotional labor strategy available to leaders (Ashforth & Humphrey, 1993). Leadership research on genuine display of emotions is modest at best and lacks empirical results. A recent theory asserts that organizations that allow their employees to freely express emotions, as long as they are not too disruptive, are more relational, productive, creative, and reliable (Park & Seo, 2017). Gardner and colleagues (2009) propose that genuine emotional displays improve subordinate evaluations of the leader and build trust in leader authenticity.

Theoretical Obstacles and Future Needs

Despite promising findings, such as those reviewed here, progress in understanding leader feeling states has been mixed. At least two theoretical obstacles are responsible for this state of affairs: definitional imprecision and an overreliance on valance symmetry. We consider these briefly, as doing so will help define the focus of this chapter.

Definitional Needs: Moods and Emotions

For purposes of understanding leadership, it is vital to recognize that emotions are multifaceted experiences, which differ from moods in a number of respects (Elfenbein, 2007; Fulmar & Barry, 2009). The multifaceted experience of emotions, as opposed to the more unitary nature of mood, has important implications for leadership. When we say that a leader and follower are aligned *affectively,* we may mean something straightforward, such as that they both have the same mood, potentially as a result of contagion (e.g. George, 1995). However, emotions are a bit more complicated. Although emotions can also have contagion effects, they can also have correspondence effects – you may react to someone's anger with a corresponding emotion (fear, shame) *or* with anger in return. Because of the inherently cognitive aspect of emotions, we are more likely to see divergence between leaders' and followers' emotions because they do not feel or think similarly about a particular target. For instance, Zoghbi Manrique de Lara (2006) found that both managers and subordinates may be afraid, but they tend to fear different things. Likewise, if emotions were truly shared, then individuals would tend to respond similarly toward that object. Again, this is not always true. For example, it is safer for a supervisor to express his or her anger than it is for a subordinate to do the same (Callister, Geddes, & Gibson, 2017).

Aligned emotions can be a powerful (and potentially dangerous) leadership tool, as they harness a comprehensive set of motivational processes – feeling, thinking, and acting – for the leader's purposes; but this alignment is often absent. Misaligned emotions often have less pervasive motivational effects. A leader who is envious of a subordinate could disrupt their working relationship (Leheta, Dimotakis, & Schatten, 2017). Similarly, angry managers might get their way in the short term, perhaps by engendering fear (Fitness, 2000), but this use of coercion is unlikely to lead to the employee internalizing their leader's wishes.

Our recommendation is that future researchers attend carefully to the distinction between emotions and mood, as these are distinct phenomena (Weiss & Cropanzano, 1996). However, this distinction necessitates different theorizing for each; one cannot simply import theories of mood into a conceptual model of emotion without some revision. For example, a theory of aligned mood cannot be directly changed into a theory of aligned emotion without taking into account the target, supporting cognitions, and behavioral predilections. This creates both opportunities and challenges for future scholars.

Valance Symmetry and Its Discontents

"Valance" refers to the hedonic tone of a mood or emotion, which can be either negative or positive (Fortin, Balder, Wiesenfeld, & Wheeler-Smith, 2015). A theoretical prediction exhibits valance *symmetry* if the antecedent and consequence have the same hedonic tone. This often implies that positive feelings have positive consequences and negative feelings have negative consequences (Leheta et al., 2017). For example, George (1995) found that positive leader moods boosted customer service performance among employees. There are many examples of successful valance-symmetric studies, as we have previously discussed in the course of this chapter. For the moment, we wish to discuss two potential problems with the overreliance on this intuitive approach to model-building. The first has to do with important exceptions to this assumption, and the second with an oversimplification of the concept of emotions.

Leader affect and the borders of valance symmetry. Valance-symmetric predictions tend to associate positive leader affect with positive consequence and negative leader affect with negative consequences. There is good reason for this. Various authors have discussed the virtues of positive feeling states (e.g. Isen, 1999; 2000; Isen & Baron, 1991). Leadership high in trait positive affect are more likely to be seen as transformational and, in turn, are rated as more effective (Joseph, Dhanani, Shen, McHugh, & McCord, 2015). Joseph and colleagues also found that leaders high in trait negative affect were less likely to be seen as transformational and, in turn, were rated as less effective. On balance, valance-symmetric effects are common (van Kleef & Côté, 2014).

However, as Grandey (2008, p. 246) points out, there are "contingences for effectiveness" that create boundary conditions for the valence symmetry hypothesis. To illustrate this complexity, it is useful to consider a few examples. These asymmetries are most pronounced when it comes to discrete emotions but are also evident in relation to mood. For example, when guiding a new venture, maintaining a positive mood is often helpful (Baron, 2008). However, when positive affect gets too high, founders show deficits in their motivation and decision-making (Baron, Hmieleski, & Henry, 2012).

Moving to discrete emotions, disgust may help us make stronger moral judgments, which can prevent acceptance of unethical actions (Skarlicki, Hoegg, Aquino, & Nadisic, 2013). In a similar fashion, contentious anger can force positive changes by leading individuals to confront harm-doers (Barclay, Skarlicki, & Pugh, 2005; Tripp, Bies, & Aquino, 2007), and so on.

Valance symmetry and the nature of emotions. A straightforward distinction between positive and negative affect makes sense when one is describing moods (Larsen & Diener, 1992; Watson & Tellegan, 1985). People often report feeling "good" or "bad" (Judge & Larsen, 2001; Weiss, 2002), or ambivalent (Larsen & McGraw, 2011; Larsen, McGraw, & Cacioppo, 2001), and these positive and negative feeling states can be captured along one or two dimensions (Cropanzano, Weiss, Hale, & Reb, 2003). However, the positive/negative distinction becomes messy when classifying emotions. In an insightful review, Lazarus and Cohen-Charash (2001, p. 50) observe that "We usually forget ... that the distinction between negative and positive depends on whether the criterion for emotional valance is its subjective feel, its social consequences, or the antecedent conditions arousing the emotion." They go on to add that "so-called positively valenced emotions often contain negative features and so-called negatively valanced emotions often have positive features" (p. 54).

To better understand this point, consider nostalgia. Nostalgia involves a longing for the past (Batcho, 1995). It involves "feeling happy and sad at the same time" (Wildschut, Sedikides, Arndt, & Routledge, 2006; Wildschut, Stephan, Sedikides, Routledge, & Arndt, 2008, p. 1). In previous times, nostalgia was viewed as a negative emotion, even as a mental illness, though it is now seen as a positive feeling state (Burton, 2015). Nostalgia does not fit neatly as either a positive or negative emotion. It contains elements of both.

Summary. Unlike mood states, emotional experiences need not be uniformly positive or uniformly negative. When researchers classify emotions into broadly "positive" and "negative" categories, there is a corresponding loss of information. Moreover, positive emotions sometimes have negative consequences, whereas negative emotions sometimes have positive consequences (Lazarus & Cohen-Charash, 2001). Researchers need to consider the valance of the outcomes apart from the valance of the feeling states. Sometimes these will be consistent, but this is not always true.

Conclusions

In this chapter, we have discussed the relationship between leadership and emotions at three levels of analysis – the organization, the dyad/team, and the individual leader. We can think of these matters as an ultimate goal, producing an organization that is both productive and pleasant, and two broad "how?" questions. Organizations can be made more effective through appropriate emotional displays toward individual subordinates and workgroups. Further, leaders are better able to produce these emotional displays when they are high in emotional intelligence and, therefore, better able to manage their own feeling states. Beyond this, we concluded with two broad theoretical obstacles for future researchers to consider. We encouraged scholars to pay closer attention to definitional considerations, especially as regards affect and emotion, and how these differences impact theorizing. We also argued that research needs to move beyond simple valance-symmetric predictions, good-to-good and bad-to-bad, in order to build a richer understanding of emotion in work life.

References

Ashforth, B. E., & Humphrey, R. H. (1993). Emotional labor in service roles: The influence of identity. *Academy of Management Review, 18*, 88–115.

Ashkanasy, N. M., & Daus, C. S. (2002). Emotion in the workplace: The new challenge for managers. *Academy of Management Perspectives, 16*, 76–86.

Ashkanasy, N. M., & Härtel, C. E. (2014). Positive and negative affective climate and culture: The good, the bad, and the ugly. *The Oxford handbook of organizational climate and culture* (pp. 136–152). Oxford, UK: Oxford University Press.

Ashkanasy, N. M., Härtel, C. E., & Daus, C. S. (2002). Diversity and emotion: The new frontiers in organizational behavior research. *Journal of Management, 28*, 307–338.

Ashkanasy, N. M., & Tse, B. (2000). Transformational leadership as management of emotion: A conceptual review. In G. R. Ferris (Ed.), *Research in personnel and human resources management* (Volume 15, pp. 121–174). Amsterdam, Netherlands: Elsevier Science/JAI.

Atwater, L. E., Ostroff, C., Yammarino, F. J., & Fleenor, J. W. (1998). Self-other agreement: Does it really matter? *Personnel Psychology, 51*, 577–598.

Ausubel, D. P. (1955). Relationships between shame and guilt in the socialization process. *Psychological Review, 67*, 378–390.

Bakker, A. B., Westman, M., & van Emmerik, I. J. H. (2009). Advancements in crossover theory. *Journal of Managerial Psychology, 24*, 206–219.

Barclay, L. J., Skarlicki, D. P., & Pugh, S. D. (2005). Exploring the role of emotions in injustice perceptions and retaliation. *Journal of Applied Psychology, 90*, 629–643.

Baron, R. A. (2008). The role of affect in the entrepreneurial process. *Academy of Management Review, 33*, 328–340.

Baron, R. A., Hmieleski, K. M, & Henry, R. A. (2012). Entrepreneurs' dispositional positive affect: The potential benefits – and potential costs – of being "up." *Journal of Business Venturing, 27*, 310–324.

Barrett, L. F., Gross, J., Christensen, T. C., & Benvenuto, M. (2001). Knowing what you're feeling and knowing what to do about it: Mapping the relation between emotion differentiation and emotion regulation. *Cognition and Emotion, 15*, 713–724.

Barsade, S. G. (2002). The ripple effect: Emotional contagion and its influence on group behavior. *Administrative Science Quarterly, 47*, 644–675.

Barsade, S. G., & O'Neill, O. A. (2014). What's love got to do with it? A longitudinal study of the culture of companionate love and employee and client outcomes in a long-term care setting. *Administrative Science Quarterly, 59*, 551–598.

Batcho, K. I. (1995). Nostalgia: A psychological perspective. *Perceptual and Motor Skills, 80*, 131–143.

Baumeister, R. F., Stillwell, A. M., & Heatherton, T. D. (1994). Guilt: An interpersonal approach. *Psychological Bulletin, 115*, 243–267.

Beal, D. J., Trougakos, J. P., Weiss, H. M., & Green, S. G. (2006). Episodic processes in emotional labor: Perceptions of affective delivery and regulation strategies. *Journal of Applied Psychology, 91*, 1053–1065.

Boal, K. B., & Hooijberg, R. (2000). Strategic leadership research: Moving on. *Leadership Quarterly, 11*, 515–549.

Bono, J., & Ilies, R. (2006) Charisma, positive emotions, and mood contagion. *Leadership Quarterly, 17*, 317–334.

Brotheridge, C. M., & Lee, R. T. (2002). Testing a conservation of resources model of the dynamics of emotional labor. *Journal of Occupational Health Psychology, 7*, 57–67.

Bryant, M., & Cox, J. W. (2006). The expression of suppression: Loss and emotional labour in narratives of organisational change. *Journal of Management & Organization, 12*, 116–130.

Burton, N. (2015). *Heaven and hell: The psychology of the emotions*. Sandford-on-Thames UK: Acheron.

Callister, R. R., Geddes, D., & Gibson, D.F. (2017). When is anger helpful or hurtful? Status and role impact on anger expression and outcomes. *Negotiation and Conflict Management Research, 10*, 69–87.

Caruso, D. R., Mayer, J. D., & Salovey, P. (2002). Emotional intelligence and emotional leadership. In R. E. Riggio, S. E. Murphy, & F. J. Pirozzolo (Eds.), *LEA's organization and management series:*

Multiple intelligences and leadership (pp. 55–74). Mahwah, NJ: Erlbaum.

Chi, N.-W., Chung, Y.-Y., & Tsai, W. C. (2011). How do happy leaders enhance team success? The mediating roles of transformational leadership, group affective tone, and team processes. *Journal of Applied Social Psychology, 41*, 1421–1454.

Chi, N-W., & Ho, T. R. (2014). Understanding when leader negative emotional expression enhances follower performance: The moderating roles of follower personality traits and perceived leader power. *Human Relations, 67*, 1051–1072.

Cropanzano, R., Weiss, H., Hale, J., & Reb, J. (2003). The structure of affect: Reconsidering the relationship between negative and positive affectivity. *Journal of Management, 29*, 831–857.

De Hooge, I. E., Nelisen, R. M., Breugelmans, S. M., & Zeelenberg, M. (2011) What is moral about guilt? Acting "prosocially" at the disadvantage of others. *Journal of Personality and Social Psychology, 100*, 462–473.

De Rivera, J. (1992). Emotional climate: Social structure and emotional dynamics. *International Review of Studies of Emotion, 2*, 197–218.

Diefendorff, J. M., Croyle, M. H., & Gosserand, R. H. (2005). The dimensionality and antecedents of emotional labor strategies. *Journal of Vocational Behavior, 66*, 339–357.

Elfenbein, H. A. (2007). Emotion in organizations. In J. P. Walsh & A. P. Brief (Eds.), *Academy of management annals* (Volume 1, pp. 315–386). New York, NY: Routledge.

Ely, R. J., & Meyerson, D. E. (2006). Unmasking manly men: The organizational reconstruction of men's identity. In *Academy of Management Proceedings* (Volume 1, pp. J1–J6). New York, NY: Briarcliff Manor.

Ely, R. J., & Meyerson, D. E. (2010). An organizational approach to undoing gender: The unlikely case of offshore oil platforms. *Research in Organizational Behavior, 30*, 3–34.

Fisk, G. M., & Friesen, J. P. (2012). Perceptions of leader emotion regulation and LMX as predictors of followers' job satisfaction and organizational citizenship behaviors. *Leadership Quarterly, 23*, 1–12.

Fitness, J. (2000). Anger in the workplace: An emotion script approach to anger episodes between workers and their superiors, co-workers, and subordinates. *Journal of Organizational Behavior, 21*, 147–162.

Fortin, M., Blader, S. L., Wiesenfeld, B. M., & Wheeler-Smith, S. L. (2015). Justice and affect: A dimensional approach. In R. Cropanzano & M. A. Ambrose (Eds.), *Oxford handbook of justice in work organizations* (pp. 419–439). Oxford, UK: Oxford University Press.

Frijda, N. H. (1988). The laws of emotion. *American Psychologist, 43*, 349–358.

Fulmer, I. S., & Barry, B. (2009). Managed hearts and wallets: Ethics issues in emotional influence by and within organizations. *Business Ethics Quarterly, 19*, 155–191.

Gaddis, B., Connelly, S., & Mumford, M. D. (2004). Failure feedback as an affective event: Influences of leader affect on subordinate attitudes and performance. *Leadership Quarterly, 15*, 663–686.

Gardner, L., & Stough, C. (2002). Examining the relationship between leadership and emotional intelligence in senior level managers. *Leadership and Organization Development Journal, 23*, 68–78.

Gardner, W. L., Fischer, D., & Hunt, J. G. J. (2009). Emotional labor and leadership: A threat to authenticity? *Leadership Quarterly, 20*, 466–482.

Geddes, D., & Callister, R. R. (2007). Crossing the line(s): A dual threshold model of anger in organizations. *Academy of Management Review, 32*, 721–746.

George, J. M. (1995). Leader positive mood and group performance: The case of customer service. *Journal of Applied Social Psychology, 25*, 778–794.

George, J. M. (2000). Emotions and leadership: The role of emotional intelligence. *Human Relations, 53*, 1027–1055.

George, J. M. (2002). Affect regulation in groups and teams. In R. G. Lord, R. J. Klimoski, & R. Kanfer (Eds.), *Emotions in the workplace: Understanding the structure and role of emotions in organizations* (pp. 183–217). San Francisco, CA: Jossey-Bass.

George, J. M., & Bettenhausen, K. (1990). Understanding prosocial behavior, sales performance, and turnover: A group-level analysis in a service context. *Journal of Applied Psychology, 75*, 698–709.

Gibson, D. E., & Callister, R. R. (2010). Anger in organizations: Review and integration. *Journal of Management, 36*, 66–93.

Glomb, T. M., & Hulin, C. (1997). Anger and gender effects in observed supervisor–subordinate dyadic interactions. *Organizational Behavior and Human Decision Processes, 72*, 281–307.

Goleman, D. (1998). *Working with emotional intelligence*. New York, NY: Bantam.

Grandey, A. A. (2000). Emotional regulation in the workplace: A new way to conceptualize emotional labor. *Journal of Occupational Health Psychology, 5*, 95–110.

Grandey, A. A. (2003). When "the show must go on": Surface acting and deep acting as determinants of emotional exhaustion and peer-rated service delivery. *Academy of Management Journal, 46*, 86–96.

Grandey, A. A. (2008). Emotions at work: A review and research agenda. In Barling, J., & Cooper, C. L. (Eds.) *SAGE handbook of organizational behavior, Volume 1: Micro approaches* (pp. 234–261). Thousand Oaks, CA: Sage.

Gratz, K. L., & Roemer, L. (2004). Multidimensional assessment of emotion regulation and dysregulation: Development, factor structure, and initial validation of the difficulties in emotion regulation scale. *Journal of Psychopathology and Behavioral Assessment, 26*, 41–54.

Gross, J. J. (1998). The emerging field of emotion regulation: An integrative review. *Review of General Psychology, 2*, 271–299.

Gross, J. J. (2002). Emotion regulation: Affective, cognitive, and social consequences. *Psychophysiology, 39*, 281–291.

Hatfield, E., Cacioppo, J., & Rapson, R. L. (1992). *Primitive emotional contagion*. In M. S. Clark (Ed.), *Review of personality and social psychology* (Volume 14, pp. 151–177). Newbury Park, CA: Sage.

Hatfield, E., Cacioppo, J., & Rapson, R. (1994). *Emotional contagion*. New York, NY: Cambridge University Press.

Heneman, H. G., III, Judge, T. A., & Kammeyer-Mueller, J. (2019). *Staffing organizations*. Columbus, OH: Pangloss Industries.

Hochschild, A. R. (1983). *The managed heart: Commercialization of human feeling*. Berkeley: University of California Press.

Humphrey, R. H. (2002). The many faces of emotional leadership. *Leadership Quarterly, 13*, 493–504.

Humphrey, R. H. (Ed.) (2008). *Affect and emotion: New directions in management theory and research*. Charlotte, NC: Information Age.

Isen, A. M. (1999). On the relationship between affect and creative problem solving. In S. W. Russ (Ed.), *Affect, creative experience, and psychological adjustment* (pp. 3–17). Philadelphia, PA: Taylor & Francis.

Isen, A. M. (2000). Positive affect and decision making. In M. Lewis & J. Haviland-Jones (Eds.), *Handbook of emotions* (2nd edn, pp. 417–435). New York, NY: Guilford.

Isen, A. M., & Baron, R. A. (1991). Positive affect as a factor in organizational behavior. *Research in Organizational Behavior, 13*, 1–53.

Johnson, G., & Connelly, S. (2014). Negative emotions in informal feedback: The benefits of disappointment and drawbacks of anger. *Human Relations, 67*, 1265–1290.

Johnson, S. K. (2008). I second that emotion: Effects of emotional contagion and affect at work on leader and follower outcomes. *Leadership Quarterly, 19*, 1–19.

Johnson, S. K. (2009). Do you feel what I feel? Mood contagion and leadership outcomes. *Leadership Quarterly, 20*, 814–824.

Joireman, J., Kamdar, D., Daniels, D., & Duell, B. (2006). Good citizens to the end? It depends: Empathy and concern with future consequences moderate the impact of a short-term time horizon on organizational citizenship behaviors. *Journal of Applied Psychology, 9*, 1307–1320.

Joseph, D. L., Dhanani, L. Y., Shen, W., McHugh, B. C., & McCord, M. A. (2015). Is a happy leader a good leader? A meta-analytic investigation of leader trait affect and leadership. *Leadership Quarterly, 26*, 558–577.

Judge, T. A., & Larsen, R. J. (2001). Dispositional affect and job satisfaction: A review and theoretical extension. *Organizational Behavior and Human Decision Processes, 86*, 67–98.

Kashdan, T. B., Barrett, L. F., & McKnight, P. E. (2015). Unpacking emotion differentiation: Transforming unpleasant experience by perceiving distinctions in negativity. *Current Directions in Psychological Science, 24,* 10–16.

Kegan, R., Lahey, L., Fleming, A., & Miller, M. (2014). Making business personal. *Harvard Business Review, 92,* 44–52.

Kellett, J. B., Humphrey, R. H., & Sleeth, R. G. (2002). Empathy and complex task performance: Two routes to leadership. *Leadership Quarterly, 13,* 523–544.

Kellett, J. B., Humphrey, R. H., & Sleeth, R. G. (2006). Empathy and the emergence of task and relations leaders. *Leadership Quarterly, 17,* 146–162.

Kerr, R., Garvin, J., Heaton, N., & Boyle, E. (2005). Emotional intelligence and leadership effectiveness. *Leadership and Organization Development Journal, 27,* 265–279.

Knutson, B. (1996). Facial expressions of emotion influence interpersonal trait inferences. *Journal of Nonverbal Behavior, 20,* 165–182.

Koning, L. F., & van Kleef, G. A. (2015). How leaders' emotional displays shape followers' organizational citizenship behavior. *Leadership Quarterly, 26,* 489–501.

Larsen, J. T., & McGraw, A. P. (2011). Further evidence for mixed emotions. *Journal of Personality and Social Psychology, 100,* 1095–1110.

Larsen, J. T., McGraw, A. P., & Cacioppo, J. T. (2001). Can people feel happy and sad at the same time? *Journal of Personality and Social Psychology, 81,* 684–696.

Larsen, R. J., & Diener, E. (1992). Promises and problems with the circumplex model of emotion. In M. S. Clark (Ed.), *Review of personality and social psychology: Emotion* (Volume 13, pp. 25–59). Newbury Park, CA: Sage.

Lazarus, R. S., & Cohen-Charash, Y. (2001). Discrete emotions in everyday life. In R. Payne & C. Cooper (Eds.), *Emotions at work* (pp. 47–81). New York, NY: John Wiley & Sons.

Leheta, D., Dimotakis, N., & Schaten, J. (2017). The view over one's shoulder: The causes and consequences of leaders' envy of followers. *Leadership Quarterly, 28,* 451–468.

Lerner, J. S., & Keltner, D. (2001). Fear, anger, and risk. *Journal of Personality and Social Psychology, 81,* 146–156.

Lerner, J. S., & Tiedens, L. Z. (2006). Portrait of the angry decision maker: How appraisal tendencies shape anger's influence on cognition. *Journal of Behavioral Decision Making, 19,* 115–137.

Lewis, K. M. (2000). When leaders display emotion: How followers respond to negative emotional expression of male and female leaders. *Journal of Organizational Behavior, 21,* 221–234.

Lindebaum, D., & Fielden, S. (2011). "It's good to be angry": Enacting anger in construction project management to achieve perceived leader effectiveness. *Human Relations, 64,* 437–458.

Madera, J. M., & Smith, D. B. (2009). The effects of leader negative emotions on evaluations of leadership in a crisis situation: The role of anger and sadness. *Leadership Quarterly, 20,* 103–114.

Mayer, J. D., Caruso, D. R., and Salovey, P. (2000). Emotional intelligence meets traditional standards for an intelligence. *Intelligence, 27*(4), 267–98.

Mayer, J. D., Roberts, R. D., & Barsade, S. G. (2008). Human abilities: Emotional intelligence. *Annual Review of Psychology, 59,* 507–536.

Mayer, J. D., & Salovey, P. (1997). What is emotional intelligence? In P. Salovey & D. Sluyter (Eds.), *Emotional development and emotional intelligence: Educational implications* (pp. 3–31). New York, NY: Basic Books.

Mayer, J. D., Salovey, P., & Caruso, D. R. (2000). Models of emotional intelligence. In R. J. Sternberg (Ed.), *Handbook of intelligence* (pp. 396–420). Cambridge, UK: Cambridge University Press.

Mayer, J. D., Salovey, P., & Caruso, D. R. (2004). Emotional intelligence: Theory, findings, and implications. *Psychological Inquiry, 15,* 197–215.

Mayer, J. D., Salovey, P., & Caruso, D. R. (2008). Emotional intelligence: New ability or eclectic traits? *American Psychologist, 63,* 503–517.

Mehrabian, A., & Epstein, N. (1972). A measure of emotional empathy 1. *Journal of Personality, 40,* 525–543.

Morris, J. A., & Feldman, D. C. (1996). The dimensions, antecedents, and consequences of emo#tional labor. *Academy of Management Review, 21,* 986–1010.

Nelissen, R. M. A., & Zeelenberg, M. (2009). When guilt evokes self-punishment: Evidence for the existence of a dobby effect. *Emotion*, *9*, 118–122.

Parke, M. R., & Seo, M. G. (2017). The role of affect climate in organizational effectiveness. *Academy of Management Review*, *42*, 334–360.

Pescosolido, A. T. (2002). Emergent leaders as managers of group emotion. *Leadership Quarterly*, *13*, 583–599.

Pirola-Merlo, A., Härtel, C., Mann, L., & Hirst, G. (2002). How leaders influence the impact of affective events on team climate and performance in R&D teams. *Leadership Quarterly*, *13*, 561–581.

Pugh, S. D. (2001). Service with a smile: Emotional contagion in the service encounter. *Academy of Management Journal*, *44*, 1018–1027.

Rafaeli, A., & Sutton, R. I. (1987). Expression of emotion as part of the work role. *Academy of Management Review*, *12*, 23–37.

Riggio, R. E., & Reichard, R. J. (2008). The emotional and social intelligences of effective leadership: An emotional and social skill approach. *Journal of Managerial Psychology*, *23*, 169–185.

Rodriguez, T. (2013). Negative emotions are key to well-being. *Scientific American*, *24*(May), 26–27.

Rosete, D., & Ciarrochi, J. (2005). Emotional intelligence and its relationship to workplace performance outcomes of leadership effectiveness. *Leadership and Organization Development Journal*, *26*, 388–399.

Sadri, G., Weber, T. J., & Gentry, W. A. (2011). Empathic emotion and leadership performance: An empirical analysis across 38 countries. *Leadership Quarterly*, *22*, 818–830.

Salovey, P., & Mayer, J. D. (1990). Emotional intelligence. *Imagination, Cognition and Personality*, *9*, 185–211.

Schaumberg, R. L., & Flynn, F. J. (2012). Uneasy lies the head that wears the crown: The link between guilt proneness and leadership. *Journal of Personality and Social Psychology*, *103*, 327–342.

Schneider, B. (1987). The people make the place. *Personnel Psychology*, *40*, 437–453.

Schneider, B., Smith, D. B., & Goldstein, H. W. (2000). Attraction–selection–attrition: Toward a person–environment psychology of organizations. In W. B. Walsh, K. H. Craik, & R. H. Price (Eds.), *Person–environment psychology: New directions and perspectives* (pp. 61–85). Mahwah, NJ: Lawrence Erlbaum.

Skarlicki, D., Hoegg, J., Aquino, K., & Nadisic, T. (2013). Does justice affect your sense of taste and smell? The mediating role of moral disgust. *Journal of Experimental Social Psychology*, *49*, 852–859.

Stuewig, J., Tangney, J. P., Heigel, C., Harty, L., & McCloskey, L. A. (2010). Shaming, blaming, and maiming: Functional links among the moral emotions, externalization of blame, and aggression. *Journal of Research in Personality*, *44*, 91–102.

Sullivan, D. G., & Masters, R. D. (1988). "Happy warriors": Leaders' facial displays, viewers' emotions, and political support. *American Journal of Political Science*, *32*, 345–368.

Sutton, R. I. (1991). Maintaining norms about expressed emotions: The case of bill collectors. *Administrative Science Quarterly*, *36*, 245–268.

Sy, T., Côté, S., & Saavedra, R. (2005). The contagious leader: Impact of the leader's mood on the mood of group members, group affective tone, and group processes. *Journal of Applied Psychology*, *90*, 295–305.

Tangney, J. P. (1995). Shame and guilt in interpersonal relationships. In J. P. Tangney & K. W. Fischer (Eds.), *Self-conscious emotions: The psychology of shame, guilt, embarrassment, and pride* (pp. 114–139). New York, NY: Guilford.

Tangney, J. P., & Dearing, R. (2002). *Shame and guilt*. New York, NY: Guilford.

Tangney, J. P., Stuewig, J., & Martinez, A. G. (2014). Two faces of shame: Understanding shame and guilt in the prediction of jail inmates' recidivism. *Psychological Science*, *25*, 799–805.

Tee, E. Y. J. (2015). The emotional link: Leadership and the role of implicit and explicit emotional contagion processes across multiple organizational levels. *Leadership Quarterly*, *26*, 654–670.

Tiedens, L. Z. (2001). Anger and advancement versus sadness and subjugation: The effect of negative emotion expressions on social status conferral. *Journal of Personality and Social Psychology*, *80*, 86.

Tobolski, F. P., & Kerr, W. A. (1952). Predictive value of the Empathy Test in automobile salesmanship. *Journal of Applied Psychology*, *36*, 310–311.

Toegel, G., Kilduff, M., & Anand, N. (2013). Emotion helping by managers: An emergent understanding of discrepant role expectations and outcomes. *Academy of Management Journal, 56*, 334–357.

Totterdell, P., & Holman, D. (2003). Emotion regulation in customer service roles: Testing a model of emotional labor. *Journal of Occupational Health Psychology, 8*, 55–73.

Tripp, T. M., Bies, R. J., & Aquino, K. (2007). A vigilante model of justice: Revenge, reconciliation, forgiveness, and avoidance. *Social Justice Research, 20*, 10–34.

Trougakos, J. P., Beal, D. J., Green, S. G., & Weiss, H. M. (2008). Making the break count: An episodic examination of recovery activities, emotional experiences, and positive affective displays. *Academy of Management Journal, 51*, 131–146.

Uhl-Bien, M. (2003). Relationship development as a key ingredient for leadership development. In S. E. Murphy & R. E. Riggio (Eds.), *The future of leadership development* (pp. 129–147). Mahwah, NJ: Erlbaum.

van Kleef, G. A., & Côté, S. (2014). On the social influence of negative emotional expressions. In W. G. Parrott (Ed.), *The positive side of negative emotions* (pp. 126–145). New York, NY: Guilford.

van Kleef, G. A., Homan, A. C., Beersma, B., van Knippenberg, D., van Knippenberg, B., & Damen, F. (2009). Searing sentiment or cold calculation? The effects of leader emotional displays on team performance depend on follower epistemic motivation. *Academy of Management Journal, 52*, 562–580.

Visser, V. A., van Knippenberg, D., van Kleef, G. A., & Wisse, B. (2013). How leader displays of happiness and sadness influence follower performance: Emotional contagion and creative versus analytical performance. *Leadership Quarterly, 24*, 172–188.

Volmer, J. (2012). Catching leaders' mood: Contagion effects in teams. *Administrative Sciences, 2*, 203–220.

Vuori, T. O., & Huy, Q. N. (2016). Distributed attention and shared emotions in the innovation process: How Nokia lost the smartphone battle. *Administrative Science Quarterly, 61*, 9–51.

Wang, G., & Seibert, S. E. (2015). The impact of leader emotion display frequency on follower performance: Leader surface acting and mean emotion display as boundary conditions. *Leadership Quarterly, 26*, 577–593.

Watson, D., & Tellegen, A. (1985). Towards a consensual structure of mood. *Psychological Bulletin, 98*, 127–144.

Weiss, H. M. (2002). Conceptual and empirical foundations for the study of affect at work. In R. Lord, R. J. Klimoski, & R. Kanfer (Eds.), *Emotions in the workplace: Understanding the structure and role of emotions in organizational behavior* (pp. 20–63). San Francisco, CA: Jossey-Bass.

Weiss, H. M., & Cropanzano, R. (1996). Affective events theory: A theoretical discussion of the structure, causes and consequences of affective experiences at work. In B. M. Staw & L. L. Cummings (Eds.), *Research in organizational behavior* (Volume 19, pp. 1–74). Greenwich, CT: JAI.

Wildschut, T., Sedikides, C., Arndt, J., & Routledge, C. D. (2006). Nostalgia: Content, triggers, functions. *Journal of Personality and Social Psychology, 91*, 975–993.

Wildschut, T., Stephan, E., Sedikides, C., Routledge, C., & Arndt, J. (2008). Feeling happy and sad at the same time: Nostalgia informs models of affect. Paper presented at the 9th Annual Meeting of the Society for Personality and Social Psychology, Albuquerque, NM, February.

Wispé, L. (1986). The distinction between sympathy and empathy: To call forth a concept, a word is needed. *Journal of Personality and Social Psychology, 50*, 314–321.

Zoghbi Manrique de Lara, P. (2006). Fear in organizations: Does intimidation by formal punishment mediate the relationship between interactional justice and workplace internet deviance? *Journal of Managerial Psychology, 2*, 580–592.

18 Affective Climate in Teams

Nuria Gamero and Vicente González-Romá

In recent years, there has been an increasing focus on the collective affective experiences of work teams. Affective climate (affective experiences shared by team members) has become an important factor in understanding how teams work and the results they produce. Many efforts have been dedicated to identifying the processes through which this collective phenomenon emerges and its antecedents and consequences. In this chapter, we review the literature on affective climate. We begin by addressing what affective climate is, how it is described, and the mechanisms explaining how team members share affect. We follow up by describing emergence processes of affective climate in teams and reviewing its antecedents and consequences. Next, we dedicate a section to examining the dynamic nature of this phenomenon. We conclude by noting some emerging areas of research in the affective climate literature.

Affective Climate as a Team Emergent State

Affect is an indispensable part of team dynamics. Team life is inherently affective. Affective states induced at work are transmitted from one member of a team to another (Barsade & Knight, 2015). Work teams are affective "incubators" in which the affective experiences of team members, such as their affective dispositions, emotions, or feelings, are combined to form a collective affective state that influences team members (Kelly & Barsade, 2001). Generally, affective climate is defined as a shared affective state. If the members of a team experience similar affective states (positive and/or negative) while doing their job, these affective experiences will have consequences at both the individual and team levels, influencing the behavior of the team members and the results of the team. Drawing on Marks, Mathieu, and Zaccaro's (2001) input–processes–states–outputs (IPSO) team model, affective climate is formed as an emergent state of work teams, that is, a construct that "originates in the ... affect ... of individuals, is amplified by their interactions, and manifests as a higher-level, collective phenomenon" (Kozlowski & Klein, 2000, p. 55).

Different terms have been used to refer to this emergent state resulting from shared affective experiences in teams, such as group affective tone (e.g. Collins, Lawrence, Troth, & Jordan, 2013; George, 1996; Sy, Côté, & Saavedra, 2005), group affect (e.g. Barsade & Gibson, 2012; Hentschel, Shemla, Wegge, & Kearney, 2013; Ilies, Wagner, & Morgeson, 2007), team mood (e.g. González-Romá & Gamero, 2012; Totterdell, 2000), and group emotion (e.g. Barsade & Gibson, 1998; Pescosolido, 2002). Recently, the term 'affective climate' began to be widely used to refer to shared affective experiences in a work team (e.g. Ashkanasy & Härtel, 2014; Cropanzano & Dasborough, 2015; Gamero, González-Romá, & Peiró, 2008; Maimone & Sinclair, 2010; Menges, Walter, Vogel, & Bruch, 2011). The climate concept has a long tradition in the organizational literature. Organizational research has usually considered "climate" to describe unit members' shared perceptions (Reicher & Schneider, 1990). Nonetheless, climate can also represent other shared experiences or responses. For example, the term "cognitive climate" was proposed by Kirton and McCarthy (1988) to refer to the cognitive styles that team members use to solve their problems. Similarly, the term "emotional climate" was suggested by De Rivera (1992) to refer to shared emotional responses by a collective. González-Romá, Peiró, Subirats, and Mañas (2000) recommended using the term "affective climate" instead of "emotional climate" because "affect" is a broad term that traditionally includes other concepts, such as mood, emotions, sentiments, and dispositional affect.

As with other kinds of climates, affective climate is usually described according to its content using affective dimensions or facets. All these facets can be located within a more general conceptual framework: the circumplex model of affect (Warr, 1990; Weiss & Copranzano, 1996). This model locates specific affective states in the conceptual space defined by two orthogonal primary dimensions: hedonic tone or valence (pleasure – displeasure) and arousal (low activation – high activation). In the affect literature, different affective facets have been proposed. However, affective facets focused on hedonic tone (e.g. negative and positive affective climate) are the ones most frequently used (Sevastos, Smith, & Cordery, 1992).

Different mechanisms and processes have been proposed to explain how team members share affect in teams. Affective climate is created and sustained through a combination of two kinds of processes, top-down and bottom-up. Top-down processes would explain how the team context has an impact on shaping members' affective experience. Several complementary top-down processes may act as mechanisms that promote affective convergence in teams (George, 1996): Schneider's (1987) attraction–selection–attrition (ASA) framework, socialization processes (Fisher, 1986), and the exposure to common affective events and similarity in group tasks and outcomes for team members.

The bottom-up processes would explain how the affective experiences the team members bring with them to the team are communicated to other team members to shape their team's collective experience of affect. Among the bottom-up processes, the one that has received the most attention and for which there is most evidence of its effects is emotional contagion (Barsade, 2002). Hatfield, Cacioppo, and Rapson (1994) defined this as "the tendency to unintentionally and automatically mimic and synchronize facial expressions, vocalizations, postures, and movements with those of another person and, consequently, to converge emotionally" (p. 157). The impact of emotional contagion would depend on team members' degree of susceptibility to contagion: some would be more susceptible than others, that is, more prone to "being infected" by the affective states of other members with whom they interact. Members who are highly susceptible to contagion are more likely to share affective experiences with their teammates than less susceptible members (Ilies et al., 2007; Sy & Choi, 2013). Some team members' demographic characteristics would determine the extent to which they are influenced by the affective experiences of others on the team. For instance, older team members and women are more susceptible to emotional contagion (Totterdell, 2000; Doherty, Orimoto, Singelis, Hatfield, & Hebb, 1995). There are also other more explicit and voluntary bottom-up processes leading to affective sharedness within teams, such as emotional comparison, behavioral entrainment, and affective interpersonal influence (Kelly & Barsade, 2001). These processes involve deliberate attempts to change affective states.

The action of both implicit and explicit bottom-up processes would depend to a certain extent on social interactions among team members (González-Romá, Peiró, & Tordera, 2002; Kozlowski & Klein, 2000). Regular and continuous interactions within teams create opportunities to both display and detect members' affective state information that can shape team affective climate (Kelly, 2003). Therefore, the greater the frequency of team members' interactions, the greater the affective convergence in a work team over time. Some team characteristics such as team size and tenure or the level of interdependence on team tasks would determinate the frequency with which team members interact and, therefore, the degree of affective convergence. Thus, small teams (e.g. Jackson & Joshi, 2004) where team members are stable in tenure (e.g. Totterdell, Wall, Holman, Diamond, & Epitropaki, 2004) and highly interdependent (e.g. Bartel & Saavedra, 2000; Klep, Wisse, & Van der Flier, 2011) have a greater potential for affective convergence.

Affective Emergence in Teams

Team affective climate is an emergent collective construct that stems from team members' affective experiences. According to Kozlowski and Klein (2000), two general types of emergence can be distinguished: composition and compilation. *Composition* emergence describes how individual-level properties (e.g. individual positive affect) combine "to yield a higher-level property [e.g. team affect] that is essentially the same as its constituent elements" (Kozlowski & Klein, 2000, p. 16). These authors explain how convergence, sharing, and within-unit agreement develop to yield a *shared* unit property (Kozlowski & Klein, 2000). Through processes of emotional contagion, social influence, and social interaction, individual team members come to share their affective experiences (e.g. they experience *similar* levels of a certain individual property such as positive affect at work). This sharedness yields a shared team property that manifests at a higher level (e.g. team positive affect). Therefore, following a composition model, affect can emerge at the team level as a shared team property: *affective team climate*, which is usually operationalized by computing the team's average score on the specific affect dimension involved.

Affect can also emerge at the team level following *compilation* emergence, in which a number of processes promote variability and different patterns of individual-level properties within the team (Kozlowski & Klein, 2000). These processes explain how different types and/or amounts of individual properties combine to form higher-order *configural* properties (Kozlowski & Klein, 2000). For instance, different amounts of social interaction among team members may lead to different degrees of within-team agreement on positive affect. These differences can be represented by a configural team-level property: *affective climate strength* (also called affective homogeneity). In single mode distributions, affective climate strength can be represented by within-team variance in affect.

In other cases, different organizational factors may lead to non-uniform affective patterns (i.e. within-team multiple grouping or multimodal distributions of affective content). For instance, team leaders who maintain relationships of different quality (high vs. low quality) with distinct subgroups of team members may contribute to developing non-uniform affective patterns, with a subgroup scoring high on positive affect (the one with high-quality relationships with the leader) and another subgroup scoring low on positive affect (the one with low-quality relationships with the leader). Distinct patterns of within-team affect can be represented by another configural team-level property: *affective climate uniformity* (Kozlowki & Klein, 2000). The operationalization of this property is more complex than in the previous cases because it is based on the identification of different types of within-team configurations of the specific individual property involved (see González-Romá & Hernández, 2014; Loignon, Woehr, Loughry, & Ohland, 2019).

Researchers have usually assumed that affect emerges at the team level based on a composition model, and they have investigated the antecedents and outcomes of affective climate as a shared property (e.g. Gamero et al., 2008). However, it is important to note that affect can emerge following compilation models (e.g. Barsade, Ward, Turner, & Sonnenfeld, 2000), which expands the possibilities of affect research at higher levels.

Antecedents of Team Affective Climate

There is a growing body of literature focused on analyzing factors that contribute to maintaining or increasing positive affective climate once it has emerged in teams. All these studies have taken on an affective-compositional perspective. Researchers who have examined antecedents of affective climate have followed Marks et al.'s (2001) IPSO model. At the organizational level, the main input variable has been emotional culture, which limits the affective expression within teams. At the team level, empirical research has highlighted the role of the team leader and team composition.

Antecedents at the Organizational Level: Organizational Affective Culture

A key force that drives affective experiences shared by team members is the *organizational affective culture* (Barsade & Gibson, 2012). This significant element of teams' affective context may be broadly defined as the set of behavioral norms, artefacts, and underlying values and assumptions that govern the way organizational members express affect, and the degree of perceived appropriateness of these affective states (Barsade & Knight, 2015). Most empirical evidence to date has focused on one of the subcomponents of such cultures: affective norms (Ekman, 1973). Organizations may develop specific norms to promote suitable affective experiences and their appropriate display. These affective norms may guide organizational members' affective expressions, indicating to them which affective experiences should be expressed and how (Walter & Bruch, 2008). Expressions of positive and negative affective experiences can be shaped by norms about the appropriateness of affective expressions that develop within organizations (Bartel & Saavedra, 2000). These norms can be implicit, explicit, or even institutionalized through training or manuals (Sutton, 1991). In contrast to other unconscious processes, such as emotional contagion, the majority of individuals are aware that norms exist (Walter & Bruch, 2008). Some empirical evidence supports the relationship between affective regulation norms and convergence in members' affective experiences expressed within teams. For instance, Bartel and Saavedra (2000), in a study with seventy teams, concluded that the more mood-regulation norms a group has, the greater the degree of mood convergence within the group. These results were found with both positive and negative moods.

Antecedents at the Team Level: the Team Leader's Affect and Team Composition

Team leaders shape their teams' affective climate through both conscious and unconscious affective displays (Barsade & Gibson, 2012). Leaders transmit their individual affective states to other team members through emotional contagion (Sy et al., 2005), and this process is facilitated by their high visibility in the team (George, 1995). Furthermore, as formal power holders, leaders set patterns of group interactions and have more opportunities to spread their own affective experiences (Gibson & Schroeder, 1999). Leaders' affective expressions can act as signals that inform team members about whether the team goals have been reached. Team members may interpret their leader's positive affect as a sign of the team's progress, experiencing, in turn, positive affective states.

Effective leaders also manage team affective climate "by understanding the collective response of the team to situations and obstacles it faces and by responding emotionally in ways that help the team to cope more effectively" (Barsade & Gibson, 2012, p. 121). There is some empirical evidence supporting the role of leaders' affect in producing affective experiences in their teams. Chi, Chung, and Tsai (2011) found, in a sample of eighty-five sales teams, that individual team members whose leaders feel and express positive affective states tend to have more positive and less negative affective experiences, with the team as a whole having a more positive affective climate. Sy et al. (2005) found that teams with leaders who were in a positive mood had a more positive affective tone than teams with leaders in a negative mood. Seong and Choi (2014), in a study with ninety-six work teams from the defense industry, showed that leader positive affect is a driver of team positive affect.

Team composition is another factor in the development of affective climate. Team demographic composition (the distribution of members' demographic characteristics in a team) contributes to shaping shared affective states. When team members perceive their teams as highly diverse demographically, they tend to feel more shared negative affect. Hentschel et al. (2013) showed that within-team perceived diversity in age, gender, educational level, nationality, or tenure was positively associated with team negative affect. As Phillips and Lount (2007) argued, diversity in teams may indicate a potential for difficult interactions with other (different) team members and, therefore, foster negative team affect. These relationships can be based on the similarity–attraction paradigm (Byrne, 1971), which suggests that people tend to be attracted to those who are similar to them. This preference is based on the reinforcing value of similarity.

Team composition based on skills and traits also has an impact on affective experiences within team. Teams composed of members with high emotional intelligence (i.e. a high individual capacity to identify and manage one's own emotions, as well as the emotions of others) have a greater affective ability to generate and sustain a positive affective climate (Prado, Gamero, & Medina, 2018). Collins, Jordan, Troth, and Lawrence (2014) showed that teams with higher average emotional intelligence were better at managing the team affective environment. Likewise, team composition based on trait affect (i.e. the general tendency to experience a particular affect) has a direct effect on team affective climate (Collins, Jordan, Lawrence, & Troth, 2016). George (1990) found that teams mostly composed of members with positive trait affect developed positive affective climates.

Consequences of Team Affective Climate

At the individual level, empirical evidence supports the key role of affective climate in team members' individual attitudes, behaviors, and well-being. Thus, shared positive affective experiences foster prosocial behavior (George, 1990) and organizational spontaneity (George & Brief, 1992), and they reduce job absenteeism (Barsade & O'Neill, 2014; Mason & Griffin; 2003). Rhee (2007) also found that members who shared positive affect were more satisfied with their teams. Conversely, shared negative affective experiences, such as team envy, have a negative influence on satisfaction with the team (Duffy & Shaw, 2000).

At the team level, the organizational literature has emphasized the role of affective climate in understanding team functioning and team processes. Sy et al. (2005), studying fifty-six project teams, found that team positive affect was associated with greater team coordination over time. Barsade (2002) showed that teams with high positive affect exhibited more cooperation and less conflict than teams with high negative affect. Supporting these findings, West, Patera, and Carsten (2009) found that team optimism improved team processes, such as cooperation and coordination, and reduced within-team conflict. Choi and

Cho (2011), in a longitudinal study, showed that negative group affect increased task conflict over time.

Affective climate also influences essential team outcomes, including team satisfaction, team creativity and decision-making, and team performance. West et al. (2009) found that member's shared positive affect was associated with greater team satisfaction. Chi et al. (2011) reported that positive affective climate positively influenced team satisfaction. The empirical evidence about the influence of affective climate on team creativity and decision-making is scarce and shows inconsistent results (Neal, Ashkanasy, & Fisher, 2017). Some studies found that a positive affective climate leads to greater team creativity and decision-making (e.g. Bramesfeld & Gasper, 2008; Grawitch, Munz, & Kramer, 2003). These studies are based on the assumption that happy team members would benefit from flexible thinking to make the best decisions about problems. They would also make more novel suggestions and be more effective in following and combining each other's ideas. Nonetheless, other researchers argue that positive affective team climate may be detrimental. George and King (2007) pointed out that team members who share positive affective states may experience a pleasant team environment that could discourage them from considering novel ideas and expressing opposing opinions that might endanger this positive environment, thus promoting groupthink. Some studies also show that negative affective climates improve team creativity and decision-making (Jones & Kelly, 2009; Kooij-de Bode, Van Knippenberg, & Van Ginkel, 2010). As these studies suggest, the existence of a negative affective climate in teams indicates dissatisfaction with the object of judgment, leading teams to persist longer and continue to strive for better solutions instead of conforming with an inferior solution. Empirical research has shown some contextual factors that act as moderators and could explain these inconsistent results, such as the degree of persistence on team tasks (Jones & Kelly, 2009), team trust (Tsai, Chi, Grandey, & Fung, 2012), or the type of team task (Kelly & Spoor, 2006).

The relationship between team affective climate and team performance has captured the most researchers' attention in this area (van Kleef & Fischer, 2016). Affective climate would influence team performance through its effect on team members' initial effort on work tasks and their choice of appropriate goals. Thus, as George and Brief (1996) argued, team members with positive affect see greater rewards for their performance, they construct their evaluations and judgments using more positive content recalled from memory, and they attribute successes to internal factors and failures to external factors, which influences their beliefs about the effort–performance relationship. Affective climate would also influence members' persistence and effort on the tasks they perform. Members with positive affect see themselves as more self-efficacious, set a higher reference criterion level, and may judge themselves as making more progress toward a goal than members with negative affect. By contrast, negative affective climate would hamper team performance because it distracts team members' attention from the job itself and reduces the attentional resources they have available to perform their team tasks (George & Brief, 1996). A large amount of evidence shows that positive affective climate is positively related to team performance (e.g. George, 1995; Hmieleski, Cole, & Baron, 2012; Kelly & Spoor, 2006; Mason & Griffin, 2005; Tanghe, Wisse, & Flier, 2010). Although there is less evidence about the impact of negative affective climate, in general it seems to have a detrimental effect on team performance. For instance, Cole, Walter, and Bruch (2008) showed that team members' shared negative affect was negatively related to team performance. Duffy and Shaw (2000) demonstrated, in a longitudinal study of 143 teams, the detrimental influence of group envy on team performance.

Nonetheless, some researchers have indicated that high positive affective climate is not universally helpful to team performance, and that, in certain conditions, it might be unfavorable. Thus the climate of a team comprised of members with high positive affect might contribute to unrealistic euphoria, optimism, and groupthink. In this context, team members may be unproductive because their affective experiences may have to be managed in order for progress to be made, especially on complex tasks that do not have a simple solution and require discussion and creativity (George & King, 2007; Kelly & Spoor, 2006). Among the moderating variables influencing this relationship, researchers have proposed team trust and team emotional skills. Tsai et al. (2012) showed that high team positive affect was detrimental to team performance on complex tasks when team trust was high. In this context, team members were less likely to break team harmony and express differing opinions, and they tended to provide deliberated answers on team tasks. Likewise, Collins et al. (2016) demonstrated that, on complex decision-making and creative idea-generation tasks, high positive affective climate was positively associated with team performance only when teams had greater emotional skills.

Other researchers have also examined the conditions where negative affective climate negatively influences team performance. Knight and Eisenkraft (2015), using meta-analysis, demonstrated that this negative relationship was moderated by two contextual factors, the team's affect source (exogenous vs. endogenous to the group) and the team's life span (one-shot vs. ongoing teams). They found that negative affective climate hindered team performance only when experienced in an ongoing team where shared affect emanated from an endogenous source. Moreover, Cole et al. (2008) found that the relationship between negative affective climate and team performance was moderated by nonverbal expressivity, so that when team members displayed their experienced negative emotions, the aforementioned negative relationship was stronger.

Although the majority of the research on the effects of affective climate on team outcomes has been dominated by the study of shared affect, some theoretical arguments suggest that affective climate strength is an important factor in predicting team performance. According to the similarity–attraction paradigm (Byrne, 1971), affective homogeneity could be positively related to team performance. As indicated earlier, the similarity–attraction paradigm posits that individuals tend to be attracted to and prefer to interact with other individuals or groups who have (or are perceived to have) attitudes, values, or affects similar to their own (Williams & O'Reilly, 1998). Similarity in affective experiences would act as reinforcement that would increase attraction among team members because it allows people to confirm the appropriateness of their affects. By contrast, dissimilarity is seen as frustrating. Therefore, members of affectively homogeneous teams will feel more comfortable with their mutual interactions, which will lead to higher levels of trust and rapport with each other. The communication and coordination within the team will be more fluid, and members will engage in more cooperative behavior, enhancing team performance (Barsade & Gibson, 1998). The scarce empirical results published to date have shown a positive relationship between team affective homogeneity and performance outcomes. Barsade, Ward, Turner, and Sonnenfeld (2000) focused on dispositional positive affect, and they found, in a sample of sixty-two top management teams, that affective homogeneity was positively associated with company financial performance. More recently, Kaplan, Laport, and Waller (2013) found that diversity in trait positive affect hindered team effectiveness in a sample of twenty-one nuclear power plant crews during a crisis simulation.

Temporal Dynamics of Team Affective Climate

Teams are dynamic entities. However, it is difficult to find research that examines them as such (Cronin, 2015). Teams may experience different affective states throughout their life cycle, fluctuating over time for various reasons. Affective climate is a product of bottom-up and top-down forces, and it is sensitive to changes in the (social) environment (e.g. the occurrence of setbacks or successes) (van Keef & Fischer, 2016). Teams' affective states can also vary in the different stages of team task completion (Collins et al., 2013).

Once affective climate emerges, it can exhibit other dynamic properties, such as within-team variability, growth trajectories, and cyclical fluctuations over time (Kozlowski, 2015). First, the emergence of affective climate in a team would not necessarily have to be stable and enduring. Although interaction dynamics would increase the convergence of team members' affective experiences over time, team stressors and conflicts (e.g. an uneven distribution of the workload within the team) may reduce the degree of affective agreement within the team, making members' affective experiences no longer homogeneous. As stressors and conflicts disappear, within-team variability will also decline. Second, team affective climate may exhibit different dynamic trajectories (i.e. linear/non-linear increases/decreases in the level or amount of affective climate over time). For instance, a team that is making progress on a work project would exhibit an ascending trajectory in the level of positive affective climate while the project lasts. By contrast, the level of positive affective climate could decrease monotonically in a team experiencing increasingly demanding working conditions in a given period (such as high temporal pressure or workload, or unsatisfactory results). Finally, team affective climate could fluctuate cyclically depending on periodic events within the team (e.g. weekly work meetings, monthly social activities) and periodic demands (e.g. annual performance reviews).

All these affective dynamics can develop within a team once affective climate has emerged. However, research examining the different ways affective climate unfolds over time, and the consequences of this, is still scarce (e.g. González-Romá, Gamero, Fortes-Ferreira, & Peiró, 2010; Knight, 2011).

Emerging Areas of Research

In this chapter, we have concisely reviewed the current state of the research on affective climate in teams. This literature is still growing, and there are some inconclusive findings that call for more research. We also need a more complete view of the nomological network of team affective climate. Moreover, emerging research gaps should be addressed. First, although studies examining the effects of affective climate strength have shown promising initial results, research is needed about the influence of another configural property of affective climate, affective climate uniformity, on team processes and outcomes. Research on the ways affective climate is configured and differentially influences group development and outcomes over time will offer a more comprehensive view of the consequences of affective climate. Second, examining the impact of other affective team properties on affective climate and its relationship with team outcomes, such as team emotional intelligence (Elfenbein, 2006), is also an emergent area of research. Third, new technologies have introduced changes in teamwork and the way team members share affect virtually. Future research on the way that affective climate emerges in teams who are working through new technologies, and the way it influences their outcomes, could also be fruitful (Barsade & Gibson, 2012). Lastly, the temporal dynamics of affective climate have been studied very little. It is essential for empirical research to pay attention to affective dynamics that develop within a team once affective climate has emerged, and the effect of these dynamics on group processes and outcomes. Addressing these gaps in the research will help to provide a more accurate view of the role played by affective climate in team functioning and outcomes.

References

Ashkanasy, N. M., & Härtel, C. E. (2014). Positive and negative affective climate and culture: The good, the bad, and the ugly. In K. M. Barbera (Ed.), *The Oxford handbook of organizational climate and culture* (pp. 136–152). New York, NY: Oxford University Press.

Barsade, S. G. (2002). The ripple effect: Emotional contagion and its influence on group behavior. *Administrative Science Quarterly, 47*, 644–675.

Barsade, S. G., & Gibson, D. E. (1998). Group emotion: A view from top and bottom. In D. Grenfeld, B. Manmix, & M. Neak (Eds.), *Research on managing groups and teams* (pp. 81–102). Stanford, CT: JAI Press.

Barsade, S. G., & Gibson, D. E. (2012). Group affect: Its influence on individual and group outcomes. *Current Directions in Psychological Science, 21*, 119–123.

Barsade, S. G., & Knight, A. P. (2015). Group affect. *Annual Review of Organizational Psychology and Organizational Behavior, 2*, 21–46.

Barsade, S. G., & O'Neill, O. A. (2014). What's love got to do with it? A longitudinal study of the culture of companionate love and employee and client outcomes in a long-term care setting. *Administrative Science Quarterly, 59*, 551–598.

Barsade, S. G., Ward, A. J., Turner, J. D., & Sonnenfeld, J. A. (2000). To your heart's content: A model of affective diversity in top management teams. *Administrative Science Quarterly, 45*, 802–836.

Bartel, C., & Saavedra, R. (2000). The collective construction of work group moods. *Administrative Science Quarterly, 45*, 197–231.

Bramesfeld, K. D., & Gasper, K. (2008). Happily putting the pieces together: A test of two explanations for the effects of mood on group-level information processing. *British Journal of Social Psychology, 47*, 285–309.

Brown, K. G., & Kozlowski, S. W. (1999). Dispersion theory: Moving beyond a dichotomous conceptualization of emergent organizational phenomena. Klein (discussant) symposium, "New perspectives on higher level phenomena in industrial/organizational psychology," presented at the 14th Annual Meeting of the Society of Industrial and Organizational Psychology, Atlanta, GA.

Byrne, D. (1971). *The attraction paradigm*. New York, NY: Academic.

Chan, D. (1998). Functional relationships among constructs in the same content domain at different levels of analysis: A typology of composition models. *Journal of Applied Psychology, 83*, 234–246.

Chi, N. W., Chung, Y. Y., & Tsai, W. C. (2011). How do happy leaders enhance team success? The mediating roles of transformational leadership, group affective tone, and team processes. *Journal of Applied Social Psychology, 41*, 1421–1454.

Choi, K., & Cho, B. (2011). Competing hypotheses analyses of the associations between group task conflict and group relationship conflict. *Journal of Organizational Behavior, 32*, 1106–1126.

Cole, M., Walter, F., & Bruch, H. (2008). Affective mechanisms linking dysfunctional behavior to performance in work teams: A moderated mediation study. *Journal of Applied Psychology, 93*, 945–958.

Collins, A. L., Jordan, P. J., Lawrence, S. A., & Troth, A. C. (2016). Positive affective tone and team performance: The moderating role of collective emotional skills. *Cognition and Emotion, 30*, 167–182.

Collins, A. L., Jordan, P. J., Troth, A. C., & Lawrence, S. A. (2014). The impact of team emotional intelligence on team affect, conflict and performance: A preliminary analysis. *British Academy of Management Conference Proceedings*. London, UK: British Academy of Management.

Collins, A. L., Lawrence, S. A., Troth, A. C., & Jordan, P. J. (2013). Group affective tone: A review and future research directions. *Journal of Organizational Behavior, 34*, S43–S62.

Cronin, M. A. (2015). Advancing the science of dynamics in groups and teams. *Organizational Psychology Review, 5*, 267–269.

Cropanzano, R., & Dasborough, M. T. (2015). Dynamic models of well-being: Implications of affective events theory for expanding current views on personality and climate. *European Journal of Work and Organizational Psychology, 24*, 844–847.

De Rivera, J. (1992). Emotional climate: Social structures and emotional dynamics. *International Review of Studies on Emotions, 2*, 197–218.

Doherty, R. W., Orimoto, L., Singelis, T. M., Hatfield, E., & Hebb, J. (1995). Emotional contagion: Gender and occupational differences. *Psychology of Women Quarterly, 19*, 355–371.

Duffy, M., & Shaw, J. D. (2000). The Salieri Syndrome: Consequences of envy in groups. *Small Group Research, 31*, 3–23.

Ekman, P. (1973). *Darwin and facial expression: A century of research in review.* New York, NY: Academic.

Elfenbein, H. A. (2006). Team emotional intelligence: What it can mean and how it can impact performance. In V. Druskat, F. Sala, & G. Mount (Eds.), *The link between emotional intelligence and effective performance* (pp. 165–184). Mahwah, NJ: Lawrence Erlbaum.

Fisher, C. D. (1986). Organizational socialization: An integrative review. In K. M. Rowland & G. R. Ferris (Eds.), *Research in personnel and human resources management* (Volume 4, pp. 101–145). Greenwich, CT: JAI.

Gamero, N., González-Romá, V., & Peiró, J. M. (2008). The influence of intra-team conflict on work teams' affective climate: A longitudinal study. *Journal of Occupational and Organizational Psychology, 81*, 47–69.

George, J. M. (1990). Personality, affect, and behavior in groups. *Journal of Applied Psychology, 7 5*, 107–116.

George, J. M. (1995). Leader positive mood and group performance: The case of customer service. *Journal of Applied Social Psychology, 25*, 778–794.

George, J. M. (1996). Group affective tone. In M. A. West (Ed.), *Handbook of work group psychology* (pp. 77–94). Chichester, UK: John Wiley & Sons.

George, J. M., & Brief, A. P. (1992). Feeling good – doing good: A conceptual analysis of the mood at work–organizational spontaneity relationship. *Psychological Bulletin, 112*, 310–329.

George, J. M., & Brief, A. P. (1996). Motivational agendas in the workplace: The effects of feelings on focus of attention and work motivation. In L. L. Cummings & B. M. Staw (Eds.), *Research in organizational behavior* (pp. 75–109). Greenwich, CT: JAI.

George, J. M., & King, E. B. (2007). Potential pitfalls of affect convergence in teams: Functions and dysfunctions of group affective tone. In E. A. Mannix, M. A. Neale, & C. P. Anderson (Eds.), *Research on managing groups and teams: Affect and groups* (Volume 10, pp. 97–123). Greenwich, CT: JAI.

Gibson, D. E., & Schroeder, S. J. (2003). Who ought to be blamed? The effect of organizational roles on blame and credit attributions. *International Journal of Conflict Management, 14*, 95–117.

González-Romá, V., & Gamero, N. (2012). Does positive team mood mediate the relationship between team climate and team performance? *Psicothema, 24*, 94–100.

González-Romá, V., Gamero, N., Fortes-Ferreira, L., & Peiró, J. M. (2010). Enabling formalization, collective mood, and team performance: Testing a dynamic mediated longitudinal relationship. Comunication presented to the 27th International Congress of Applied Psychology, Melbourne, Australia.

González-Romá, V., Peiró, J. M., & Tordera, N. (2002). An examination of the antecedents and moderator influences of climate strength. *Journal of Applied Psychology, 87*, 465–473.

González-Romá, V., Peiró, J. M., Subirats, M., & Mañas, M. A. (2000). The validity of affective workteam climates. In M. Vartiainen, F. Avallone, & N. Anderson (Eds.), *Innovative theories, tools, and practices in work and organizational psychology* (pp. 97–109). Göttingen, Germany: Hogrefe & Huber.

Grawitch, M. J., Munz, D. C., & Kramer, T. J. (2003). Effects of member mood states on creative performance in temporary workgroups. *Group*

Dynamics: Theory, Research, and Practice, *7*, 41–54.

Hareli, S., & Rafaeli, A. (2008). Emotion cycles: on the social influence of emotion in organizations. *Research in Organizational Behavior*, *28*, 35–59.

Hatfield, E., Cacioppo, J., & Rapson, R. L. (1994). *Emotional contagion*. Cambridge, UK: Cambridge University Press.

Hentschel, T., Shemla, M., Wegge, J., & Kearney, E. (2013). Perceived diversity and team functioning: The role of diversity beliefs and affect. *Small Group Research*, *44*, 33–61.

Hmieleski, K. M., Cole, M. S., & Baron, R. A. (2012). Shared authentic leadership and new venture performance. *Journal of Management*, *38*, 1476–1499.

Ilies, R., Wagner, D. T., & Morgeson, F. P. (2007). Explaining affective linkages in teams: individual differences in susceptibility to contagion and individualism–collectivism. *Journal of Applied Psychology*, *92*, 1140–1148.

Jackson, S., & Joshi, A. (2004). Diversity in social context: A multi-attribute, multilevel analysis of team diversity and sales performance. *Journal of Organizational Behavior*, *25*, 675–702.

Jones, E. E., & Kelly, J. R. (2009). No pain, no gains: Negative mood leads to process gains in idea-generation groups. *Group Dynamics*, *13*, 75–88.

Kaplan, S., LaPort, K., & Waller, M. J. (2013). The role of positive affectivity in team effectiveness during crises. *Journal of Organizational Behaviour*, *34*, 473–491.

Kelly, J. R. (2003). Mood and emotion in groups. In M. Hogg & S. Tindale (Eds.) *Blackwell handbook in social psychology*, Volume 3: *Group processes* (pp. 164–181). Malden, MA: Blackwell Publishers.

Kelly, J. R., & Barsade, S. G. (2001). Mood and emotion in small groups and workteams. *Organizational Behavior and Human Decision Processes*, *86*, 99–130.

Kelly, J. R., & Spoor, J. R. (2006). Affective influence in groups. In J. P. Forgas (Ed.), *Affect in social thinking and behavior* (pp. 311–325). New York, NY: Psychology.

Kirton, M. J., & McCarthy, R. M. (1988). Cognitive climate and organizations. *Journal of Occupational Psychology*, *61*, 175–184.

Klep, A., Wisse, B., & Van der Flier, H. (2011). Interactive affective sharing versus non-interactive affective sharing in work groups: Comparative effects of group affect on work group performance and dynamics. *European Journal of Social Psychology*, *41*, 312–323.

Knight, A. P. (2011). Mood at the midpoint: How team positive mood shapes team development and performance. In L. A. Toombs (Ed.), *Proceedings of the 71st Annual Meeting of the Academy of Management*, San Antonio, TX: Academy of Management, https://doi.org/10.5465/ambpp.2011.65869176

Knight, A. P., & Eisenkraft, N. (2015). Positive is usually good, negative is not always bad: The effects of group affect on social integration and task performance. *Journal of Applied Psychology*, *100*, 1214–1227.

Kooij-de Bode, H. J., Van Knippenberg, D., & Van Ginkel, W. P. (2010). Good effects of bad feelings: Negative affectivity and group decision-making. *British Journal of Management*, *21*, 375–392.

Kozlowski, S. W. (2015). Advancing research on team process dynamics: Theoretical, methodological, and measurement considerations. *Organizational Psychology Review*, *5*, 270–299.

Kozlowski, S. W., & Klein, K. J. (2000). A multilevel approach to theory and research in organizations: Contextual, temporal, and emergent processes. In K. J. Klein & S. W. Kozlowski (Eds.), *Multilevel theory, research, and methods in organizations: Foundations, extensions and new directions* (pp. 3–90). San Francisco, CA: Jossey-Bass.

Loignon, A. C., Woehr, D. J., Loughry, M. L., & Ohland, M. W. (2019). Elaborating on team-member disagreement: Examining patterned dispersion in team-level constructs. *Group and Organization Management*, *44*, 165–210.

Maimone, F., & Sinclair, M. (2010). Affective climate, organizational creativity, and knowledge creation: Case study of an automotive company. In W. J. Zerbe, N. M. Ashkanasy, & C. E. J. Härtel (Eds.), *Emotions and organizational dynamism* (Volume 6, pp. 309–332). Bingley, UK: Emerald.

Marks, M. A., Mathieu, J. E, & Zaccaro, S. J. (2001). A temporally based framework and taxonomy of team processes. *Academy of Management Review, 26*, 356–376.

Mason, C. M., & Griffin, M. A. (2003). Group absenteeism and positive affective tone: A longitudinal study. *Journal of Organizational Behavior, 24*, 667–687.

Mason, C. M., & Griffin, M. A. (2005). Group task satisfaction: The group's shared attitudes to its task and work environment. *Group and Organization Management, 30*, 625–652.

Menges, J. I., Walter, F., Vogel, B., & Bruch, H. (2011). Transformational leadership climate: Performance linkages, mechanisms, and boundary conditions at the organizational level. *Leadership Quarterly, 22*, 893–909.

Pescosolido, A. T. (2002). Emergent leaders as managers of group emotion. *Leadership Quarterly, 13*, 583–599.

Phillips, K., & Lount, R. (2007). The affective consequences of diversity and homogeneity in groups. In E. Mannix, M. Neale, & C. Anderson (Eds.), *Research on managing groups and teams* (Volume 10, pp. 1–20). Greenwich, CT: JAI.

Prado, C., Gamero, N., & Medina, F. J. (2018). *Leading teams with emotional intelligence*. Seville, Spain: University of Seville Press.

Rafaeli, A., & Sutton, R. I. (1989). The expression of emotion in organizational life. *Research in Organizational Behavior, 11*, 1–42.

Reicher, A. E., & Schneider, B. (1990). Climate and culture: An evolution of constructs. In B. Schneider (Ed.), *Organizational climate and culture* (pp. 5–39). San Francisco, CA: Jossey-Bass.

Rhee, S. Y. (2007). Group emotions and group outcomes: The role of group–member interactions. In E. A. Mannix, M. A. Neale, & C. P. Anderson (Eds.), *Research on managing groups and teams* (Volume 10, pp. 65–96). Greenwich, CT: JAI.

Schneider, B. (1987). The people make the place. *Personnel Psychology, 40*, 437–453.

Seong, J. Y., & Choi, J. N. (2014). Effects of group-level fit on group conflict and performance: The initiating role of leader positive affect. *Group and Organization Managament, 39*, 190–212.

Sevastos, P., Smith, L., & Cordery, J. L. (1992). Evidence on the reliability and construct validity of Warr's (1990) well-being and mental health measures. *Journal of Occupational and Organizational Psychology, 65*, 33–49.

Sutton, R. I. (1991). Maintaining norms about emotional expression: The case of bill collectors. *Administrative Science Quarterly, 36*, 245–268.

Sy, T., & Choi, J. N. (2013). Contagious leaders and followers: exploring multi-stage mood contagion in a leader activation and member propagation (LAMP) model. *Organizational Behavior and Human Decision Processes, 122*, 127–140.

Sy, T., Cote, S., & Saavedra, R. (2005). The contagious leader: Impact of the leader's mood on the mood of group members, group affective tone, and group processes. *Journal of Applied Psychology, 90*, 295–305.

Tanghe, J., Wisse, B., & van der Flier, H. (2010). The formation of group affect and team effectiveness: the moderating role of identification. *British Journal of Management, 21*, 340–358.

To, M. L., Ashkanasy, N. M., & Fisher, C. D. (2017). Affect and creativity in work teams. In E. Salas, R. Rico, & J. Passmore (Eds.), *The Wiley-Blackwell handbook of the psychology of team working and collaborative processes* (pp. 441–457). Hoboken, NJ: Wiley-Blackwell.

Totterdell, P. (2000). Catching moods and hitting runs: Mood linkage and subjective performance in professional sport teams. *Journal of Applied Psychology, 85*, 848–859.

Totterdell, P., Wall, T., Holman, D., Diamond, H., & Epitropaki, O. (2004). Affect networks: A structural analysis of the relationship between work ties and job-related affect. *Journal of Applied Psychology, 89*, 854–867.

Tsai, W., Chi, N., Grandey, A. A., & Fung, A. (2012). Positive group affective tone and team creativity: Negative group affective tone and team trust as boundary conditions. *Journal of Organizational Behavior, 33*, 638–656.

Van Kleef, G. A., & Fischer, A. H. (2016). Emotional collectives: How groups shape emotions and emotions shape groups. *Cognition and Emotion, 30*, 3–19.

van Knippenberg, D., Kooij-de Bode, H. J. M, & van Ginkel, W. P. (2010). The interactive effects of mood and trait negative affect in group decision making. *Organizational Science, 21*, 731–744.

Walter, F., & Bruch, H. (2008). The positive group affect spiral: A dynamic model of the emergence of positive affective similarity in work groups. *Journal of Organizational Behavior*, *29*, 239–261.

Warr, P. B. (1990). The measurement of well-being and other aspects of mental health. *Journal of Occupational Psychology*, *63*, 193–210.

Weiss, H. M., & Cropanzano, R. (1996). Affective events theory: A theoretical discussion of the structure, causes and consequences of affective experiences at work. In B. M. Staw & L. L. Cummings (Eds.), *Research in organizational behavior* (Volume 18, pp. 1–74). Greenwich, CT, and London, UK: Elsevier Science/JAI.

West, B. J., Patera, J. L., & Carsten, M. K. (2009). Team level positivity: Investigating positive psychological capacities and team level outcomes. *Journal of Organizational Behavior*, *30*, 249–267.

Williams, K. Y., & O'Reilly, C. A. (1998). Demography and diversity in organizations: A review of 40 years of diversity research. In B. M. Staw & L. L. Cummings (Eds.), *Research in organizational behavior* (Volume 20, pp. 77–140). Greenwich, CT: JAI.

19 Workplace Affect, Conflict, and Negotiation

Mara Olekalns and Laura Rees

Introduction

In their review of negotiation research, Bazerman, Curhan, Moore, and Valley (2000) noted that researchers had focused almost exclusively on the role of negotiator cognition in shaping negotiators' behaviors and outcomes. In the following year, three articles reported research on the role of emotions in negotiation or conflict (Web of Science database). The numbers increased slowly until 2010, when there was a marked increase. Surprisingly, since 2010, the number of new studies testing the impact of emotion on negotiation and conflict strategies and outcomes has been relatively stable and low. Despite the recognition that emotions are an integral part of conflict and negotiation, they remain an under-researched phenomenon.

The different role played by emotions in negotiation, as opposed to in conflict, is apparent in how the negotiation and conflict management literatures treat emotion. Whereas negotiations are assumed to start from an emotionally neutral point, conflicts are resolved against the background of strong negative emotions. Indeed, emotion is a defining characteristic of the events that trigger conflict (Bodtker & Jameson, 2001; Nair, 2008). This difference means that negotiation and conflict management scholars have placed a different emphasis on how they examine emotion in the two domains. Our broad coding of research exploring the relationship between emotion and negotiation suggests that this research can be grouped around three themes: inferential processes based on emotions in negotiation, links between specific emotions and outcomes, and moral considerations in the use of emotions in negotiation. Research that investigates the relationship between emotions and conflict focuses on the mediating role of emotion management in determining the outcome of workplace – often team – conflict. We build on several reviews of the role emotion plays in negotiation and conflict (Barry, Fulmer, & Goates, 2006; Barry & Fulmer, 2004; Bodtker & Jameson, 2001; Nair, 2008; Olekalns & Druckman, 2014; Van Kleef & Sinaceur, 2013) to explore these relationships.

Negotiation

The various frameworks that guide the study of emotion in negotiation can be grouped into two broad categories: a social-functionalist perspective and a decision-making perspective (Barry et al., 2006). A social-functionalist approach proposes that others' emotions serve an important social function by conveying information about their likely actions (Morris & Keltner, 2000) and, according to the theory of emotions as social information (Van Kleef, 2009), shape negotiators' actions by enabling them to draw inferences about others' intentions. In the next section, we draw on the social-functionalist approach to examine the inferential processes of emotion in negotiation in more depth. We then discuss the decision-making perspective, which explores how emotions and their associated inferences influence negotiators' tactical and behavioral choices and subsequent outcomes. Specifically, we draw on work on various discrete emotions to illustrate broad findings on individual and joint gains and relationships. Finally, we explore how emotional (mis)representation affects the process and outcomes of negotiation.

Inferential Processes and Other Aspects of Emotion

Negotiations take place against a background of uncertainty about a counterpart's needs and intentions. Negotiators can resolve this ambiguity by drawing inferences indirectly from their counterparts' actions: others' offers, concessions, and argumentation all provide information about counterparts' goals and likely strategic choices. Recent theory and research, however, suggest that information derived from task-related actions is augmented by information derived from counterparts' emotional expressions. In this section, we review research investigating the inferential processes triggered by emotion expression.

Research suggests that negotiators' ability to recognize their counterparts' emotions plays a critical role in determining their final outcomes. A meta-analysis conducted by Elfenbein, Foo, White, Tan, and Aik (2007) showed that emotion recognition accuracy (ERA) predicts goal-oriented performance. In a subsequent experiment, these authors demonstrated that negotiator performance is also predicted by ERA: negotiators higher in ERA obtained better objective outcomes in their negotiations. This effect is, however, limited to sellers in a buyer–seller negotiation. Similarly, Kong, Bottom, and Konczak (2016) reported that individuals' emotion perception ability predicted higher individual outcomes in fixed-sum negotiations when negotiators' performance bonuses depended on their negotiation outcomes. Both findings suggest that the ability to recognize emotions can improve individuals' outcomes, but that negotiators may not make the effort to assess others' emotions unless they are motivated to do so.

Three experiments illustrate the ways in which inferences drawn from others' emotions affect subsequent outcomes and behaviors. In two experiments, Rothman explored the impact of emotional ambivalence: that is, the simultaneous expression of both positive and negative feelings in a negotiation context (Rothman, 2011; Rothman & Northcraft, 2015). She found that negotiators who display ambivalence elicit more dominating strategies from their counterparts, and that this relationship can be attributed to the impression of submissiveness conveyed by emotional ambivalence (Rothman, 2011). In subsequent research, Rothman and Northcraft (2015) demonstrated that emotional ambivalence increases negotiators' joint outcomes, and that this relationship is mediated by the perceived submissiveness of the emotionally ambivalent negotiator. Taking a different perspective, Hillebrandt and Barclay (2017) tested the impact of incidental and integral emotions on negotiators' concession making. Incidental emotions are those emotions that can be attributed to factors other than the immediate context, and these authors further differentiate ambiguous from explicit incidental emotions: whereas ambiguous incidental emotions have an unclear target, explicit incidental emotions have a target that is clearly unrelated to the negotiation. Hillebrandt and Barclay (2017) showed that the effects of incidental and integral emotions differ, depending on their valence. Compared to integral anger, explicitly incidental anger elicited smaller concessions, and the impact of anger on concessions was mediated by the perceived threat of impasse. Both explicit and ambiguous happiness elicited more concessions than integral happiness, an effect that was mediated by perceived cooperativeness.

Most of the research investigating emotions in negotiation treats them as a steady-state phenomenon: that is, researchers assume that negotiators consistently hold the same emotion throughout a negotiation. It is plausible, however, that emotions will vary throughout a negotiation, and that these variations will affect outcomes. In a comparison of negotiators who made emotional transitions to those who expressed stable emotions, Filipowicz, Barsade, and Melwani (2011) found that a counterpart's move from happiness to anger increased negotiators' willingness to accept poorer outcomes, and that this relationship was mediated by situational attributions. In comparison, a move from anger to happiness increased a counterpart's perceived agreeableness and this relationship was mediated by post-transition positive affect. Also exploring the effects of switching between anger and happiness, Sinaceur, Adam, Van Kleef, and Galinsky (2013) showed that inconsistent emotional expressions elicited more concessions than consistent anger, and this effect was mediated by the extent to which negotiators believed they had control over the negotiation.

The impact of emotional displays on perceiver inferences is also affected by context. De Melo, Carnevale, Read, and Gratch (2014) investigated reverse appraisal, or the possibility that others' emotions enable negotiators to draw inferences about their counterparts' mental states. Using an iterated Prisoner's Dilemma game, de Melo et al. (2014) tested whether a counterpart's inferred appraisals of goal conduciveness or blameworthiness following a negotiator's decision to cooperate or defect mediated the relationship between a counterpart's expressed emotions and a negotiator's decision to cooperate in a subsequent round of the Prisoner's Dilemma game: following mutual cooperation, goal conduciveness mediated the relationship between joy or regret and subsequent cooperation, and the perception that the counterpart blamed himself mediated the relationship between regret and subsequent cooperation. The relationship between expressed emotion and the expectation that the counterpart would cooperate in the next round of the game was also mediated by goal conduciveness in mutually cooperative games and self-blame in mutual defection.

Moving to the dyadic level, Wilson, DeRue, Matta, Howe, and Conlon (2016) showed that when negotiators have similar personalities, they express more positive emotions than when their personalities are dissimilar. Butt, Choi, and Jaeger (2005) found that when both negotiators experience pride, they are more willing to compromise; and that dyadic gratitude predicts higher, whereas dyadic anger predicts lower, joint gain. Finally, in a comparison of impasse and agreement dyads, Griessmair (2017) showed that dyads that reach agreement establish a positive emotional climate whereas those that reach an impasse establish and intensify a negative emotional climate. In impasse dyads, a negotiator who expresses positive emotions in the opening moments receives a less equitable offer, and for the remainder of the negotiation expressing displeasure increases the inequity.

Overall, these findings illustrate that emotion perception and recognition, changes in emotional expression, and aspects of the context and the individual all influence how the inferences that negotiators draw about their counterparts shape their actions at the negotiation table. Importantly, as suggested by the research on dyadic emotions, perceivers' emotions also play a role in shaping negotiation processes.

The Decision-Making Effects of Negotiators' Anger and Other Discrete Emotions

Barry et al. (2006) also identify a decision-making perspective in the study of emotion and negotiation. One example of this perspective is offered by Barry and Oliver's (1996) model, which sets out reciprocal relationships between emotions, the impact of emotions on negotiators' tactical choices, and outcomes. Emotion is thus seen as a predictor of tactics or outcomes, as an experienced consequence of the negotiation process, and as holding tactical value for achieving specific goals (Barry & Fulmer, 2004; Barry et al., 2006).

Individual Gains

In terms of individual gains, anger, like many emotions, has been shown to be potentially both helpful and harmful to both the angry party and the receiver of that anger. Emotionally, expressing anger has been shown to elicit both reciprocal and/or complementary emotions from the receiver, including anger (Friedman, Brett, Anderson, Olekalns, Goates, & Lisco, 2004) and fear (e.g. Dimberg & Öhman, 1996; Van Kleef, De Dreu, & Manstead, 2004; also see Lelieveld, Van Dijk, Van Beest, & Van Kleef, 2012, for how relative power can influence whether responding emotions are reciprocal or complementary). For the angry person, anger can serve as an effective interpersonal signal that the angry person is nearing or at the point at which she will reject an offer (Van Kleef et al., 2004a), and that the angry person is dominant (Keating et al., 1981), which can prompt increased concessions from the receiver. However, anger can also reduce a person's ability to accurately judge a counterpart's interests (Allred, Mallozzi, Matsui, & Raia., 1997) and to stay focused on her own priorities (Daly, 1991), which reduces both value claiming and value creation.

Anger is most frequently contrasted with happiness in terms of its effects on individual gains. Consistent with findings described earlier, recipients of anger tend to demand less and concede more than recipients of happiness (Van Kleef et al., 2004a, 2004b). Indeed, expressing happiness can appear naïve and cause one to be exploited (Barasch, Levine, & Schweitzer, 2016) – for example, by eliciting lower concessions from the recipient (Van Kleef et al., 2004a, 2004b). However, anger is not always a panacea to ensure better outcomes for oneself. Indeed, if anger is perceived as inauthentic, it can backfire in terms of eliciting fewer concessions from receivers compared to expressions of happiness (Tng & Au, 2014).

Fewer studies compare anger and other emotions, such as disappointment. What studies do exist have shown interesting similarities and differences between the effects of anger and those of other emotions. Both anger and disappointment signal dissatisfaction with the current state of affairs (Thompson, Valley, & Kramer, 1995; Van Kleef & Van Lange, 2008), and disappointment has also been associated with higher concessions from counterparts (sometimes even similar to the level of concessions when faced with an angry counterpart; e.g. Lelieveld et al., 2012; Van Kleef et al., 2004; Van Kleef, De Dreu, Pietroni, & Manstead, 2006). These higher concessions may be the result of disappointment evoking guilt in the receiving party (Lelieveld et al., 2012). However, disappointment can backfire for the expresser in terms of concessions when it is seen as a signal of weakness and does not elicit guilt on the part of the receiver (Lelieveld et al., 2012). Like disappointment, sadness can elicit higher concessions than neutral expressions as long as the recipient of sadness feels other-concern for the sad person (e.g. when the expresser has lower power or the situation is seen as collaborative rather than competitive; Sinaceur, Kopelman, Vasijevic, & Haag, 2015).

Whether emotions help or hurt the expresser depend on the expresser's relative power. For example, low felt power may prompt negotiators to feel anxious, which has been shown to hurt outcomes for these individuals: they tend to expect less, respond (too) quickly to their counterparts, and try to conclude and leave the negotiation hastily (Brooks & Schweitzer, 2011). For anger specifically, Van Kleef and Côté (2007) found that negotiators who are lower in power than the angry person claim less value than they do when partnered with an unemotional partner. This study also found that when the angry person is the one with lower power, the higher-power counterpart demands more value, particularly when the counterpart perceives the anger as inappropriate. Findings from Overbeck, Neale, and Govan (2010) can help explain these dynamics. Powerful negotiators who are angry feel more focused and assertive, and are less responsive to others' emotions, which helps with claiming value.

Joint Gains

Although much of the work on the effects of emotions on outcomes focuses on individual gains, there are several notable findings regarding joint gains. As mentioned above, anger can harm joint gains by leading to less value creation (Allred et al., 1997) or even impasse (Friedman et al., 2004). However, anger can also benefit joint gains to the extent that it prompts helpful information search of the other party's interests and priorities in order to resolve the situation and reach agreement (Rees, Chi, Friedman, & Shih, 2019). Although it often harms the happy person's outcomes, happiness can similarly increase total value creation (Carnevale & Isen, 1986), although it may harm value creation to the extent it does not prompt continued search for helpful information that could expand the pie even further (Rees et al., 2019). To the extent that positive affect is at trait level, particularly for powerful negotiators, it can increase interpersonal trust in the negotiation and increase negotiators' chances of achieving integrative outcomes, even beyond the benefits of trait cooperativeness or communicativeness (Anderson & Thompson, 2004). Thus whether expressing anger or other emotions helps or hurts joint gains seems to depend on the emotional, cognitive, and behavioral mechanisms that it evokes from the perceiver.

Effects on the Relationship

Expressed anger significantly influences how a negotiator views his or her partner. As noted earlier, angry negotiators are perceived as dominant (Belkin, Kurtzberg & Naquin, 2013), tough (Adam & Brett, 2015; Sinaceur & Tiedens, 2006), and ambitious (Van Kleef et al., 2004a). Compared to sad partners, angry partners are seen as more aggressive and self-confident, and less warm and gentle (Hareli & Hess, 2010). Perhaps unsurprisingly given these associations, anger is viewed interpersonally as a signal of rejection (and, relatedly, can lead others to exclude the angry partner from coalitions; Van Beest, Van Kleef, & Van Dijk, 2008), while happiness is viewed as a signal of acceptance (Heerdink, van Kleef, Homan, & Fischer, 2015). To this point, happiness signals trustworthiness and cooperative intentions (Fridlund, 1994; Knutson, 1996), which can reduce competition and increase cooperation from both parties (Forgas, 1998). Similarly to happiness, disappointment is also viewed as a signal of cooperation and can boost subsequent cooperative behavior from perceivers (Van Doorn, Heerdink, & Van Kleef, 2012; Wubben, De Cremer, & Van Dijk, 2009). This effect is aligned with other work showing that disappointment is viewed as a signal of supplication – for example, a request for help or a signal that the expresser believes she has received too little (Van Kleef, De Dreu & Manstead, 2006) – which can foster felt guilt and concern for the other person (Lelieveld et al., 2011). In contrast, this study also found that expressing guilt signals appeasement rather than supplication (e.g. the expresser believes they have taken too much or offered too little), which prompts less motivation in perceivers to relieve the expresser's pain, compared to disappointment, because they expect the expresser (rather than themselves) to concede in order to repair the relationship.

Further, both the perceived appropriateness and the perceived authenticity of expressed emotions shape how the emotions influence the relationship. Although anger is not necessarily seen as more or less appropriate to express than other emotions (e.g. disappointment; Lelieveld et al., 2012), anger that is perceived as inappropriate leads to increased competition, compared to anger perceived as appropriate, which leads to increased cooperation (Van Kleef & Côté, 2007). When anger is perceived as inauthentic, partners feel more anger in response and intend to retaliate more (Tng & Au, 2014). This effect occurs because anger that is seen as faked seems exploitative and manipulative (which is probably of less concern in the case of faked happiness; Tng & Au, 2014). Tng and Au (2014) also provide preliminary evidence that when authenticity is ambiguous, perceivers can be more suspicious and less reactive in general to a partner's emotions (either happiness or anger), since it is difficult to ascertain the partner's true motivations and intentions. Indeed, interpersonal trust is critical in shaping the process and outcomes of negotiations; when trust is reduced (e.g. when competition rather than cooperation is expected), negotiators are less sensitive and adaptive in response to a counterpart's emotion (e.g. Van Kleef et al., 2006).

In summary, research demonstrates that both the negotiation relationship and negotiation outcomes are shaped by expressed emotions and the inferences drawn by counterparts as a result of emotional expression. Anger, perhaps the most studied emotion in negotiation research, serves as a prime example that emotions are not inherently helpful or harmful to individual or joint gains, or to relationships. Instead, the impact of expressed emotions is shaped by whether they elicit cooperative or competitive responses, by contextual factors such as power, and by the perceived authenticity of those emotions.

An Ethical Dimension

Both felt and expressed emotions also have an ethical dimension in negotiations. Negotiators can opt to give their counterparts either accurate or inaccurate information about their underlying needs and interests. These two options create a dilemma for negotiators because providing accurate information can prompt exploitation from counterparts, whereas misrepresenting information can block creative problem-solving that helps negotiators craft mutually beneficial outcomes. Misrepresentation, however, also offers negotiators protection against exploitation, although it may be costly if viewed as inauthentic, as noted above.

How negotiators resolve this information-sharing dilemma is influenced by several factors, including their felt emotions. Negotiators who start negotiations angry, or who express anger during a negotiation, are more likely to use deception that those who do not. Yip and Schweitzer (2016) showed that this effect is fully mediated by empathy for the other negotiator: anger leads to deception because it reduces empathy. Olekalns and Smith (2009) also found that whereas angry negotiators misrepresent information, anxious negotiators withhold information. Finally, envy – another negative emotion – also predicts deception because it is seen to redress imbalanced outcomes (Moran & Schweitzer, 2008). Optimism, in contrast, reduces the use of misrepresentation by negotiators (Olekalns & Smith, 2009).

Recent theory and research have also investigated strategic emotional misrepresentation, that is, the extent to which negotiators use emotions strategically in order to influence the counterpart and obtain a specific outcome (Methasani, Gaspar & Barry, 2017; Kopelman, Rosette, & Thompson, 2006). Although the strategic use of emotion is perceived as more ethical than the strategic (mis) use of information, it nonetheless predicts negotiators' reputation, such that the more strongly negotiators endorse the strategic use of positive emotions, the better their reputation (Fulmer, Barry & Long, 2009). This seemingly surprising finding has a parallel in research by Kopelman et al. (2006), who report that the strategic expression of positive emotions helps negotiators reach agreement, and that such agreements are more likely to anticipate a future relationship.

Although the relationship between expressed anger by a focal negotiator and concessions from a counterpart suggests that negotiators will benefit from the strategic use of anger, this is not consistently the case. For example, Dehgani, Carnevale, and Gratsch (2014) show that strategic anger can reduce concessions if negotiators attach moral significance to the negotiation. In these circumstances, expressions of sadness rather than of anger increase a counterpart's concession-making. As noted earlier, the strategic use of anger can also backfire if it is recognized as inauthentic: inauthentic anger both reduces concessions (Tng & Au, 2014) and increases demands from a counterpart, and reduces satisfaction with the negotiation (Côté, Hideg, & van Kleef, 2013). On the part of focal negotiators, those who have a low tolerance for inconsistency (i.e. low dialectical thinking; Hideg & van Kleef, 2016) increase their demands in response to fake anger. In both cases, the impact of faked anger is mediated by trust: negotiators trust counterparts who fake anger less, and this effect is stronger when negotiators also have low dialectical thinking scores (Hideg & van Kleef, 2016).

A more recent stream of work focuses on deception not at the individual level but at the dyadic level. Methasani et al. (2017), in their Interpersonal Emotion Deception Model, highlight the possibility that others' expressed emotions might influence our willingness to engage in informational deception. For example, Van Dijk et al. (2012) showed that expressed anger from a counterpart elicits both anger and more deception from the target. Methasani et al. (2017) go on to consider the possibility that the dyad-level dynamics lead to emotional contagion, which in turn determines the likelihood of ongoing deception by negotiators. Campagna, Mislin, Kong, and Bottom (2016) provide further evidence for the idea of emotional contagion, showing that faked anger elicits genuine anger from a counterpart. This in turn creates a "blowback effect" in which the focal negotiator becomes genuinely angry. Consistent with previous findings, this cycle reduces trust, and this reduction in trust mediates the relationship between faked anger and post-negotiation outcomes. Finally, related to the idea that moral considerations affect negotiators' reactions, Deghani et al. (2014) also show that negotiators are more likely to match each others' emotions (anger or sadness) when the object of the negotiation has moral significance than when it does not.

Overall, these findings illustrate that negotiators do consider the ethical implications of both their and others' expressed emotions. In particular, the effects of emotional misrepresentation seem to be largely driven by negotiators' empathy for partners, their concern for fairness, the perceived authenticity and/or intentions of expressers, and, relatedly, their trust in partners.

Conflict

Conflicts are distinguished from negotiations by the strong, usually negative, emotions that govern interactions between disputants. Emotions are a necessary component of conflict (e.g. Bodtker & Jameson, 2001). At a most basic level, the emotions are presumed to be negative and to involve some form of judgment regarding the other party and attributions of blame. The goals of disputing individuals appear irreconcilable (Nair, 2008) and trigger oppositional processes (Weingart et al., 2015), meaning that the disputants typically engage in escalatory behaviors and worsen their relationship.

It is therefore unsurprising that, unlike research on negotiation, research exploring workplace conflict has predominantly focused not on specific emotions but on emotional regulation more broadly. This research considers the potential of emotion regulation to predict team conflict or to mediate the relationship between task and relationship conflict. In particular, it emphasizes the role of emotion regulation in linking three forms of conflict: task, process, and relationship. These three concepts of conflict capture, respectively, disagreement about work team goals, how those goals should be accomplished, and broader individual values (e.g. Jehn, Greer, Levine, & Szulanski, 2008). Although the forms are distinguishable, they often influence one another through emotion regulation processes.

For example, taking relationship conflict as their dependent variable, Van den Berg, Curseu, and Meeus (2014) showed that effective emotion regulation reduces the likelihood that process conflict will lead to relationship conflict. These authors further demonstrated that an interaction between task conflict and emotion regulation predicts relationship conflict, and that this relationship is fully mediated by process conflict. Three studies focus on the role of emotion regulation and emotional intelligence in mediating the relationship between task conflict and relationship conflict. Curseu, Boros, and Oerlemans (2012) showed that teams who can effectively regulate emotion are also able to isolate task from relationship conflict: that is, task conflict develops into relationship conflict only when teams are unable to regulate emotions. Elaborating on the role of emotion regulation as a mediator, Jiang, Zhang, and Tjosvold (2013) found that skilled emotion regulators can benefit from task conflict and enhance their performance, while at the same time attenuating the negative consequences of relationship conflict. Finally, Yang and Mossholder (2004) explored the related construct of emotional intelligence, showing that emotional intelligence limits the experience of negative emotions and may predict whether task conflicts morph into relationship conflicts.

Emotion has also been explored as an outcome of conflict. In their analysis of team conflict, Gamero, González-Romá, and Peiró (2008) showed that task conflict predicts greater team tension and lower team enthusiasm, and that this relationship is mediated by relationship conflict. Pursuing the idea that emotion management is critical to conflict transformation, Jameson et al. (2009) found that conflicts that are mediated by a third party, which facilitates emotion expression and a relationship focus, end with higher positive affect and lower negative affect than conflicts that are negotiated. Finally, two related studies demonstrated that affect predicts conflict frames and the choice of conflict resolution strategy. A cooperative strategy is predicted by positive trait affect whereas a competitive strategy is predicted by negative trait affect, and these relationships are mediated by positive and negative moods, respectively (Rhoades, Arnold & Jay, 2001; Yang, Cheng, & Chuang, 2013).

Overall, research suggests that while anger and other negative emotions are probably the most common (and expected) emotions in these contexts, as both antecedents and outcomes – and logically likely to have similar effects to those we discussed in earlier sections on negotiations – emotion regulation is an important factor in mitigating conflict spirals. The more disputants can regulate their emotions productively, the better able they are to manage conflict.

Future Directions

Although research on the role of discrete emotions in conflict and negotiation is developing, there are several important questions that remain relatively unexplored in the literature. First, we would benefit from a better-integrated theory of emotion in negotiation to provide a framework to guide a more systematic approach to the study of emotions in this area. As well as moving beyond the strong emphasis on anger in negotiation and conflict, such a framework would enable researchers to better specify the mechanisms by which discrete emotions shape the negotiation process and outcomes. Our review highlights several needs: (a) to better understand the mechanisms that underpin the impact of different emotions; (b) to determine whether these mechanisms remain stable across different contexts; (c) to more systematically explore the role of moral emotions in shaping actions at and away from the negotiation table; and (d) to consider how both individual and dyad-level emotions shape the actions of negotiators and disputants.

Second, with a few exceptions, negotiation research focuses on one-shot negotiations between strangers. We have yet to explore how individuals in long-term relationships respond to the expression of anger across a series of negotiations: does the receiver eventually become inured to the typical interpersonal effects of anger expressions? Part of the answer to this question may lie in a deeper exploration of perspective-taking and empathy. In negotiations, perspective-taking but not empathy increases negotiators' ability to both claim and create value (Galinsky, Maddux, Gilin, & White, 2008). Similarly, individuals differ in their abilities to recognize various expressed emotions, and greater emotion recognition ability is associated with better outcomes (Elfenbein et al., 2007). In conflicts, both perspective-taking and empathy increase disputants' willingness to forgive, as does their ability to establish a positive emotional tone (Olekalns, Caza, & Vogus, 2019). The investigation of how individuals manage emotions in long-term relationships provides a potentially fruitful avenue for research.

Third, given the range of communication media now in common use, it is important to examine the relationship between emotion expression and the dominant form of communication in long-term relationships. Although prior work has demonstrated that emotional expressions typically influence observers in similar ways regardless of the medium (see Van Kleef, Van Doorn, Heerdink, & Koning, 2011, for a review) it is less clear whether these effects are contingent on how individuals typically communicate. To this question, studies of online versus in-person negotiations have shown both similarities and differences in trust and other social signals between counterparts (Belkin et al., 2013; Friedman et al., 2004; Naquin & Paulson, 2003).

In summary, our review has emphasized the role of interpersonal inferences drawn from both authentic and strategic expressions of emotions in shaping how negotiations and conflicts unfold. Whereas negotiation research has focused on the direct impact of emotion expression on negotiators' outcomes, conflict management research has emphasized the mediating role of emotion regulation in the conflict–outcome relationship. Notwithstanding the growing body of work on emotion in negotiation and conflict, there is ample scope for expanding our understanding of the role that expressed and perceived emotions play in negotiation and conflict. Overall, future work should directly investigate how individuals' abilities in emotion recognition, repeated interactions, familiarity with one's counterpart, regularity of expression of various emotions when interacting, and interaction modality relate to processes and outcomes, both singly and in conjunction with one another.

References

Adam, H., & Brett, J. M. (2015). Context matters: The social effects of anger in cooperative, balanced, and competitive negotiation situations. *Journal of Experimental Social Psychology*, *61*, 44–58.

Allred, K. G., Mallozzi, J. S., Matsui, F., & Raia, C. P. (1997). The influence of anger and compassion on negotiation performance. *Organizational Behavior and Human Decision Processes*, *70*, 175–187.

Anderson, C., & Thompson, L. (2004). Affect from the top down: How powerful individuals' positive affect shapes negotiations. *Organizational Behavior and Human Decision Processes*, *95*, 125–139.

Barasch, A., Levine, E., & Schweitzer, M. (2016). Bliss is ignorance: How the magnitude of expressed happiness influences perceived naiveté and interpersonal exploitation. *Organizational Behavior and Human Decision Processes*, *137*, 184–206.

Barry, B., & Fulmer, I. S. (2005). Methodological challenges in the study of negotiator affect. *International Negotiation*, *9*, 485–502.

Barry, B., Fulmer, I. S., & Goates, N. (2006). Bargaining with feeling: Emotionality in and around negotiation. In L. Thompson (Ed.), *Negotiation theory and research* (pp. 99–127). New York, NY: Psychology.

Barry, B., & Oliver, R. L. (1996). Affect in negotiation: A model and propositions. *Organizational Behavior and Human Decision Processes*, *67*, 127–143.

Bazerman, M., Curhan, J., Moore, D. & Valley, K. (2000). Negotiation. *Annual Review of Psychology*, *51*, 279–314.

Belkin, L. Y., Kurtzberg, T. R., & Naquin, C. E. (2013). Signaling dominance in online negotiations: The role of affective tone. *Negotiation and Conflict Management Research*, *6*, 285–304.

Bodtker, A. M., & Jameson, J. K. (2001). Emotion in conflict formation and its transformation: Application to organizational conflict management. *International Journal of Conflict Management*, *12*, 259–275.

Brooks, A. W., & Schweitzer, M. E. (2011). Can Nervous Nelly negotiate? How anxiety causes negotiators to make low first offers, exit early, and earn less profit. *Organizational Behavior and Human Decision Processes*, *115*, 43–54.

Butt, A., Choi, J., & Jaeger, A. (2005). The effects of self-emotion, counterpart emotion, and counterpart behavior on negotiator behavior: A comparison of individual-level and dyad-level dynamics. *Journal of Organizational Behavior*, *26*, 681–704.

Campagna, R., Mislin, A., Kong, T., & Bottom, W. (2016). Strategic consequences of emotional misrepresentation in negotiation: The blowback effect. *Journal of Applied Psychology*, *100*, 605–624.

Carnevale, P. J., & Isen, A. M. (1986). The influence of positive affect and visual access on the discovery of integrative solutions in bilateral negotiation. *Organizational Behavior and Human Performance*, *37*, 1–13.

Côté, S., Hideg, I., & van Kleef, G. A. (2013). The consequences of faking anger in negotiations, *Journal of Experimental Social Psychology*, *49*, 453–463.

Curseu, P., Boros, S., & Oerlemans, L. (2012). Task and relationship conflict in short- term and long- term groups: The critical role of emotion regulation. *International Journal of Conflict Management*, *23*, 97–107.

Daly, J. P. (1991). The effects of anger on negotiations over mergers and acquisitions. *Negotiation Journal*, *7*, 31–39.

Dehgani, M., Carnevale, P., & Gratsch, J. (2014). Interpersonal effects of expressed anger and sorrow in morally charged negotiation. *Judgment and Decision Making*, *9*, 104–113.

de Melo, C., Carnevale, P., Read, S., & Gratch, J. (2014). Reading people's minds from emotion expressions in interdependent decision making. *Journal of Personality and Social Psychology*, *106*, 73–88.

Dimberg, U., & Öhman, A. (1996). Behold the wrath: Psychophysiological responses to facial stimuli. *Motivation and Emotion*, *20*, 149–182.

Elfenbein, H., Foo, M., White, J., Tan, H., & Aik, V. (2007). Reading your counterpart: The benefit of emotion recognition accuracy for effectiveness in negotiation. *Journal of Nonverbal Behavior*, *31*, 205–223.

Filipowicz, A., Barsade, S., & Melwani, S. (2011). Understanding emotional transitions: The interpersonal consequences of changing emotions in negotiations. *Journal of Personality and Social Psychology*, *101*, 541–556.

Forgas, J. P. (1998). On feeling good and getting your way: Mood effects on negotiator cognition and bargaining strategies. *Journal of Personality and Social Psychology*, *74*, 565–577.

Friedman, R., Brett, J., Anderson, C., Olekalns, M., Goates, N., & Lisco, C. (2004). Emotions and rationality in mediation: Evidence from electronically-mediated disputes. *Journal of Applied Psychology*, *89*, 369–376.

Fulmer, I., Barry, B., & Long, D. (2009). Lying and smiling: Informational and emotional deception in negotiation. *Journal of Business Ethics*, *88*, 691–709.

Galinsky, A., Maddux, W., Gilin, D., & White, J. (2008). The differential effects of perspective taking and empathy in negotiations. *Psychological Science, 19*, 378–384.

Gamero, N., González-Roma, C., & Peiró, J. M. (2008). The influence of intra-team conflict on work teams' affective climate: A longitudinal study. *Journal of Occupational and Organizational Psychology, 81*, 47–69.

Griessmair, M. (2017). Ups and downs: Emotional dynamics in negotiations and their effects on (in) equity. *Group Decision and Negotiation, 26*, 1061–1090.

Hareli, S., & Hess, U. (2010). What emotional reactions can tell us about the nature of others: An appraisal perspective on person perception. *Cognition & Emotion, 24*, 128–140.

Heerdink, M., van Kleef, G., Homan, A., & Fischer, A. (2015). Emotional expressions as social signals of rejection and acceptance: Evidence from the Affect Misattribution Paradigm. *Journal of Experimental Social Psychology*, 56, 60–68.

Hideg, I., & van Kleef, G. (2016). When expressions of fake emotions elicit negative reactions: The role of observers' dialectical thinking, *Journal of Organizational Behavior, 38*, 1196–1212.

Hillebrandt, A., & Barclay, L. (2017). Comparing integral and incidental emotions: Testing insights from emotions as social information theory and attribution theory. *Journal of Applied Psychology, 102*, 732–752.

Jehn, K., Greer, L., Levine, S., & Szulanski, G. (2008). The effects of conflict types, dimensions, and emergent states on group outcomes. *Group Decision and Negotiation, 17*, 465–495.

Jiang, J. Y., Zhang, X., & Tjosvold, D. (2013). Emotion regulation as a boundary condition of the relationship between team conflict and performance: A multi-level examination. *Journal of Organizational Behavior, 34*, 714–734.

Keating, C., Mazur, A., Segall, M. H., Cysneiros, P. G., Divale, W. T., Kilbride, J. E., . . . & Wirsing, R. (1981). Culture and the perception of social dominance from facial expression. *Journal of Personality and Social Psychology, 40*, 615–626.

Knutson, B. (1996). Facial expressions of emotion influence interpersonal trait inferences. *Journal of Nonverbal Behavior, 20*, 165–182.

Kong, T., Bottom, W., & Konczak, L. (2016). Negotiators' emotions perception and value-claiming under different incentives. *International Journal of Conflict Management, 27*, 146–171.

Kopelman, S., Rosette, A., & Thompson, L. (2006). The three faces of Eve: Strategic displays of positive, negative, and neutral emotions in negotiations. *Organizational Behavior and Human Decision Processes, 99*, 81–101.

Lelieveld, G., Van Dijk, E., Van Beest, I., Steinel, W., & Van Kleef, G. A. (2011). Disappointed in you, angry about your offer: Distinct negative emotions induce concessions via different mechanisms. *Journal of Experimental Social Psychology, 47*, 635–641.

Lelieveld, G., Van Dijk, E., Van Beest, I., & Van Kleef, G. A. (2012). Why anger and disappointment affect others' bargaining behavior differently: The moderating role of power and the mediating role of reciprocal and complementary emotions. *Personality and Social Psychology Bulletin, 38*, 1209–1221.

Methasani, R., Gaspar, J., & Barry, B. (2017). Feeling and deceiving: A review and theoretical model of emotions and deception in negotiation. *Negotiation and Conflict Management Research, 10*, 158–178.

Moran, S., & Schweitzer, M. (2008). When better is worse: Envy and the use of deception in negotiations. *Negotiation and Conflict Management Research, 1*, 3–29.

Morris, M. W., & Keltner, D. (2000). How emotions work: The social functions of emotional expression in negotiations. *Research in Organizational Behavior, 22*, 1–50.

Naquin, C. E., & Paulson, G. D. (2003). Online bargaining and interpersonal trust. *Journal of Applied Psychology, 88*, 113–120.

Nair, N. (2008). Towards understanding the role of emotions in conflict: A review and future directions. *International Journal of Conflict Management, 19*, 359–381.

Olekalns, M., Caza, B. B., & Vogus, T. (2019). Gradual drifts, abrupt shocks: From relationship fractures to relational resilience. *Academy of Management Annals*, https://doi.org/10.5465/annals.2017.0111

Olekalns, M., & Druckman, D. (2014). With feeling: How emotions shape negotiation (state-of-the-art commentary). *Negotiation Journal, 30*, 455–478.

Olekalns, M., & Smith, P. (2009). Mutually dependent: Power, trust, affect and the use of deception in negotiation. *Journal of Business Ethics*, *85*, 347–365.

Overbeck, J. R., Neale, M. A., & Govan, C. L. (2010). I feel, therefore you act: Intrapersonal and interpersonal effects of emotion on negotiation as a function of social power. *Organizational Behavior and Human Decision Processes*, *112*, 126–139.

Rees, L., Chi, S.-C. S., Friedman, R., & Shih, H.-L. (2019). Anger as a trigger for information search in integrative negotiations. *Journal of Applied Psychology*, http://dx.doi.org/10.1037/apl0000458

Rhoades, J. A., Anrold, J., & Jay, C. (2001). The role of affective traits and affective states in disputants' motivation and behavior during episodes of organizational conflict. *Journal of Organizational Behavior*, *22*, 329–345.

Rothman, N. (2011). Steering sheep: How expressed emotional ambivalence elicits dominance in interdependent decision making contexts. *Organizational Behavior and Human Decision Processes*, *116*, 66–82.

Rothman, N., & Northcraft, G. (2015). Unlocking integrative potential: Expressed emotional ambivalence and negotiation outcomes. *Organizational Behavior and Human Decision Processes*, *126*, 65–76.

Sinaceur, M., Adam, H., Van Kleef, G. A., & Galinsky, A.D. (2013). The advantages of being unpredictable: How emotional inconsistency extracts concessions in negotiation. *Journal of Experimental Social Psychology*, *49*, 498–508.

Sinaceur, M., Kopelman, S., Vasiljevic, D., & Haag, C. (2015). Weep and get more: When and why sadness expression is effective in negotiations. *Journal of Applied Psychology*, *100*, 1847–1871.

Sinaceur, M., & Tiedens, L. (2006). Get mad and get more than even: When and why anger expression is effective in negotiations. *Journal of Experimental Social Psychology*, *42*, 314–322.

Thompson, L., Valley, K. L., & Kramer, R. M. (1995). The bittersweet feeling of success: An examination of social perception in negotiation. *Journal of Experimental Social Psychology*, *31*, 467–492.

Tng, H.-Y., & Au, A. (2014). Strategic display of anger and happiness in negotiation: The moderating role of perceived authenticity. *Negotiation Journal*, *30*, 301–327.

Van Beest, I., Van Kleef, G. A., and Van Dijk, E. (2008). Get angry, get out: The interpersonal effects of anger communication in multiparty negotiation. *Journal of Experimental Social Psychology*, *44*, 993–1002.

Van den Berg, W., Curseu, P., & Meeus, M. (2014). Emotion regulation and conflict transformation in multi-team systems. *International Journal of Conflict Management*, *25*, 171–188.

Van Dijk, E., Van Kleef, G. A., Steinel, W., & Van Beest, I. (2008). A social functional approach to emotions in bargaining: When communicating anger pays and when it backfires. *Journal of Personality and Social Psychology 94*, 600–614.

Van Doorn, E. A., Heerdink, M. W., & Van Kleef, G. A. (2012). Emotion and the construal of social situations: Inferences of cooperation versus competition from expressions of anger, happiness, and disappointment. *Cognition & Emotion*, *26*, 442–461.

Van Kleef, G. A. (2009). How emotions regulate social life: The Emotions as Social Information (EASI) model. *Current Directions in Psychological Science*, *18*, 184–188.

Van Kleef, G. A., & Côté, S. (2007). Expressing anger in conflict: When it helps and when it hurts. *Journal of Applied Psychology*, *92*, 1557–1569.

Van Kleef, G. A., De Dreu, C. K. W., & Manstead, A. S. (2004a). The interpersonal effects of anger and happiness in negotiations. *Journal of Personality and Social Psychology*, *86*, 57–76.

Van Kleef, G. A., De Dreu, C. K. W., & Manstead, A.S. (2004b). The interpersonal effects of emotions in negotiations: A motivated information processing approach. *Journal of Personality and Social Psychology*, *87*, 510–528.

Van Kleef, G. A., De Dreu, C. K. W., & Manstead, A. S. (2006). Supplication and appeasement in conflict and negotiation: The interpersonal effects of disappointment, worry, guilt, and regret. *Journal of Personality and Social Psychology*, *91*, 124–142.

Van Kleef, G. A., De Dreu, C. K. W., Pietroni, D., & Manstead, A. S. (2006). Power and emotion in negotiation: Power moderates the interpersonal effects of anger and happiness on concession making. *European Journal of Social Psychology, 36*, 557–581.

Van Kleef, G. A., & Sinaceur, M. (2013). The demise of the "rational" negotiator: Emotional forces in conflict and negotiation. In M. Olekalns & W. Adair (Eds.), *Handbook of research on negotiation* (pp. 103–131). London, UK: Edward Elgar.

Van Kleef, G. A., Van Doorn, E. A., Heerdink, M. W., &\ Koning, L. F. (2011). Emotion is for influence. *European Review of Social Psychology, 22*, 114–163.

Van Kleef, G. A., & Van Lange, P. A. M. (2008). What others' disappointment may do to selfish people: Emotion and social value orientation in a negotiation context. *Personality and Social Psychology Bulletin, 34*, 1084–1095.

Weingart, L. R., Behfar, K., Bendersky, C., Todorova, G., & Jehn, K. (2015). The directions and oppositional intensity of conflict expressions. *Academy of Management Review, 40*, 235–262.

Wilson, K., DeRue, S., Matta, F., Howe, M., & Conlon, D. (2016). Personality similarity in negotiations: Testing the dyadic effects of similarity in interpersonal traits and the use of emotional displays on negotiation outcomes. *Journal of Applied Psychology, 101*, 1405–1421.

Wubben, M. J., De Cremer, D., & Van Dijk, E. (2009). How emotion communication guides reciprocity: Establishing cooperation through disappointment and anger. *Journal of Experimental Social Psychology, 45*, 987–990.

Yang, J., & Mossholder, K. (2004). Decoupling task and relationship conflict: The role of intragroup emotional processing. *Journal of Organizational Behavior, 25*, 589–605.

Yip, J., & Schweitzer, M. (2016). Mad and misleading: Incidental anger promotes deception. *Organizational Behavior and Human Decision Processes, 137*, 207–217.

20 Understanding the Role of Affect in Workplace Aggression

Zhanna Lyubykh, M. Sandy Hershcovis, and Nick Turner

Workplace aggression is a significant and prevalent issue facing organizations. Almost all employees report experiencing workplace incivility: low-intensity deviant behavior with ambiguous intent to harm the target (Andersson & Pearson, 1999). More severe forms of workplace aggression happen at lower but still sizable rates. For example, data from the 2014 Canadian General Social Survey indicates that 27 percent of all physically violent incidents occur in the workplace (Perreault, 2015), with women more than twice as likely to be targets of workplace violence than men after adjusting for work hours (Lanthier, Bielecky, & Smith, 2018). These numbers are even more startling when one considers that employees often fail to report workplace aggression. For example, in the hospital environment – a context with elevated risks of aggression – 88 percent of employees who experienced a violent incident did not formally document the incident (Arnetz et al., 2015).

These different types of workplace aggression have significant adverse psychological and physical health consequences, including an increased likelihood of depression, frustration, burnout, negative emotions, lower self-esteem, physical symptoms, and negative organizational attitudes (Bowling & Beehr, 2006). Furthermore, studies on the vicarious effects of workplace aggression on observers yield similar findings (e.g. Totterdell, Hershcovis, Niven, Reich, & Stride, 2012; Zhou, Marchand, & Guay, 2017). The source of workplace aggression (e.g. supervisor, coworker, or outsider) also has implications for these outcomes. In a meta-analytic study, Hershcovis and Barling (2010) found that supervisor aggression has the strongest negative relationship with targets' attitudinal (e.g. job satisfaction) and behavioral (e.g. performance) outcomes, whereas coworker aggression has a stronger relationship than outsider aggression on both attitudinal and behavioral outcomes.

More generally, the literature on workplace aggression examines workplace aggression from three foci: the perspectives of the perpetrator (i.e. enacted aggression), the target (i.e. experienced aggression), and the observer (i.e. witnessed aggression). The perpetrator perspective focuses on the predictors of enacted aggression; the target perspective focuses on the consequences of experiencing workplace aggression; and the observer perspective examines witness reactions to workplace aggression. Given the prevalence of workplace aggression and its adverse consequences for all involved, it is important to explore the psychological mechanisms that might explain these relationships and the psychological moderators that might temper these relationships.

A number of theoretical frameworks are used to explain the mechanisms of workplace aggression: cognitive (e.g. Vroom, 1964), normative (e.g. Bandura, 1986), and affective (e.g. Fox & Spector, 1999; Weiss & Cropanzano, 1996). In this chapter, we focus on the role of *affect* because affect plays a central role in both the enactment and the outcomes of workplace aggression. Given the overlap among workplace aggression constructs (Hershcovis, 2011), we adopt a broad definition of interpersonal workplace aggression (hereafter "workplace aggression") and refer to this phenomenon as negative behavior initiated by a perpetrator that harms others at work (Rodell & Judge, 2009). We argue that affect plays a vital role in explaining why workplace aggression occurs and how employees react to it. More specifically, we focus on how affect contributes to the dynamics of workplace aggression, and then present an integrative model that explains both the predictors and the outcomes, connecting all parties involved (i.e. perpetrators, targets, and observers).

In the following sections, we review three key theories that are central to research on workplace aggression and affect: the frustration–aggression hypothesis, the stressor–emotion model, and affective events theory. We then provide an overview of affective mechanisms and affective moderators associated with perpetrator-, target-, and observer-focused aggression research. Finally, we present an integrated model and discuss suggestions for future research.

Relating Workplace Aggression to Affect Theories

The Frustration–Aggression Hypothesis

According to the frustration–aggression hypothesis (Berkowitz, 1989), enacted aggression is a reaction to frustration that results from an event or situation that impedes individual goal attainment (Dollard, Doob, Miller, Mowrer, & Sears, 1939). The original theoretical framework postulated that frustration always leads to aggression (Dollard et al., 1939); however, Berkowitz (1989) revised the hypothesis, stating that frustration is a necessary but not a sufficient condition for enacted aggression. Berkowitz highlighted the role of negative affect and individual attributions in the relationship between frustration and enacted aggression. He suggested that aversive events (i.e. frustrations) elicit aggressive inclinations only to the extent that they generate negative affect. Furthermore, acts that individuals perceive as deliberate (i.e. internal attributions) result in stronger aggressive inclinations than unintentional acts.

Dill and Anderson (1995) tested Berkowitz's (1989) reformulated theory in an experimental study by examining the effects of blocked expected gratification. They found that frustration produces hostile aggression, with unjustified frustration having the strongest relationship with enacted aggression. Investigating the link between frustration and aggression in the workplace context, Heacox and Sorenson (2007) found that frustration resulting from role ambiguity, work constraints, and role conflict is positively related to self-reported aggressive behaviors. Drawing on the frustration–aggression hypothesis, Fox and Spector (1999) tested a relationship between frustrating events (i.e. situational constraints) and enacted aggression. The results supported the frustration–aggression link, and built on the model by examining the mediating role of negative affect (e.g. anger, anxiety).

There are a number of limitations to the frustration–aggression theory. First, it focuses on one discrete emotion: frustration. Empirical evidence suggests that general negative affect or other discrete emotions (e.g. anger) also elicit enacted aggression (e.g. Martinko, Douglas, & Harvey, 2006; Spector & Fox, 2005). Second, the frustration–aggression hypothesis implies that the primary reaction to frustration is aggression, and that individuals respond similarly to the same frustration stimuli. Subsequent theories (discussed below) have argued that personality and context may moderate these relationships. Third, although the model is perpetrator-focused, it does not consider the affective consequences of enacted aggression. Overall, the theory has a limited scope, which may explain the decline in the number of studies that adopt this framework (Breuer & Elson, 2017).

The Stressor–Emotion Model

Building on the frustration–aggression hypothesis, Spector and Fox (2005) introduced a stressor–emotion model, providing a more comprehensive explanation of counterproductive work behavior (CWB) in the organizational context. CWB consists of volitional acts that are intended to harm organizations or people in organizations (Spector & Fox, 2005). The model posits that a stressful situation (e.g. interpersonal conflict, workload) elicits negative feelings and, as a result, employees may engage in aggressive behaviors as a coping mechanism (Fida, Paciello, Tramontano, Fontaine, Barbarnelli, & Farnese, 2015). The stressor–emotion model extends the frustration–aggression hypothesis in a number of ways. First, it includes a broader range of emotions, such as anxiety and anger. Second, the model posits that stressful events or conditions that do not interfere with individual goal attainment can also induce negative emotions. Finally, Spector and Fox argued that perceived control and personality characteristics are important moderators that may attenuate or amplify the relationship between work events and attitudinal and behavioral reactions.

Fox, Spector, and Miles (2001) provided empirical support for the stressor–emotion model by demonstrating that negative emotions mediate the relationship between stressors – organizational constraints, perceived injustice, and interpersonal conflict – and enacted workplace aggression (i.e. CWB). Similarly, Miles, Borman, Spector, and Fox (2002) demonstrated that anxiety and frustration mediated the relationship between role conflict and role ambiguity on the one hand, and interpersonal aggression on the other. Fox and colleagues also highlighted the role of personality in the stressor–aggression relationship, with some personality traits resulting in greater sensitivity to provocation (e.g. trait anger) or tendencies to experience negative emotions (e.g. negative affectivity). Ho (2012) proposed that relational stressors – stressors derived from interpersonal relationships – serve as predictors of interpersonal aggression. Ho found that employees who experience affective relational stressors (e.g. dislike toward another person) are more likely to engage in interpersonal aggression.

The stressor–emotion model has also been used to explain the relationship between experienced and enacted aggression. Using peer-rated data, Penney and Spector (2005) demonstrated that experienced workplace aggression, among other organizational stressors, is positively related to enacted workplace aggression. In addition, this study found that for employees who reported high levels of negative affect the relationship between stressors and workplace aggression was stronger.

The stressor–emotion model addresses many of the limitations of the frustration–aggression model, but it is a perpetrator-focused model that considers the antecedents of enacted aggression. While researchers have used this model to provide a theoretical foundation for the link between experienced and enacted aggression (e.g. Penney & Spector, 2005), the model does not explain other affective responses (e.g. embarrassment, fear) or behavioral reactions as a consequence of experienced, enacted, or witnessed aggression. Affective events theory addresses this limitation.

Affective Events Theory

Affective events theory (AET) posits a link between affective events and work behaviors (Weiss & Cropanzano, 1996). According to AET (Weiss & Cropanzano, 1996), workplace events can elicit emotional reactions, which in turn relate to attitudinal and behavioral outcomes. Different affective reactions (e.g. anger, joy) vary in their reactional implications: positive affective events instigate positive emotions, whereas negative events elicit negative emotions. Since an affective event could be aggression itself (i.e. enacted, experienced, or witnessed), AET explains not only the actor perspective, but also the target and observer perspectives.

Drawing on AET, Lee and Allen (2002) investigated the role of general negative affect and discrete emotions in enacted workplace aggression. Specific discrete emotions – anger, anxiety, sadness, and guilt - contributed to the prediction of enacted workplace aggression over and above negative affect. These results suggest that some negative emotions are more strongly associated with enacted aggression than others. Rodell and Judge (2009) showed that hindrance stressors (e.g. role conflict, hassles, role ambiguity) relate to enacted aggression through negative emotions such as anxiety and anger. Judge et al. (2006) examined the dynamic nature of emotions, attitudes, and enacted workplace aggression. Results from daily surveys demonstrated that a substantial portion of the total variance in workplace aggression was intra-individual, as opposed to inter-individual. Negative affect and perceived injustice explained the within-individual variation in job attitudes and enacted aggression.

Researchers have also used AET to examine the consequences of experienced aggression (e.g. Kabat-Farr, Marchiondo, & Cortina, 2018; Tillman, Gonzalez, Crawford, & Lawrence, 2018). Kabat-Farr et al. drew on AET to explain how experienced incivility relates to employee well-being through the mediating role of affect. The experience of uncivil treatment was related to negative affect, which was in turn associated with increased work withdrawal and decreased feeling of empowerment. Similarly, Tillman et al. demonstrated that experienced workplace aggression led to decreased hope and lower levels of affective commitment, which subsequently affected employees' turnover intentions.

Finally, studies have used the AET framework to explain the consequences of witnessed workplace aggression (e.g. Reich & Hershcovis, 2015). Across two experimental studies, Reich and Hershcovis demonstrated that observers had a negative affective reaction toward perpetrators, which in turn led to perpetrator punishment. In conclusion, AET provides an overarching framework that addresses the limitations of previous affect frameworks and that is extensively applied in the workplace aggression literature.

In all three theoretical frameworks, researchers view affect as a mechanism of the stressor–aggression relationship, while the latter two models allow for the possibility that workplace aggression itself is an affective event or stressor that affects perpetrators, targets, and observers. In the following section, we briefly discuss the affective mechanisms that relate enacted, experienced, and witnessed aggression to outcomes.

Affective Mechanisms of Aggression

Above we outlined the three most prevalent affective theories used in the workplace aggression literature. In this section, we examine some of the key affective mechanisms investigated in the perpetrator, target, and observer literatures.

Enacted Aggression

Research on enacted aggression has broadly examined both global and discrete emotions. A robust body of research has demonstrated that global negative affect mediates the relationship between a range of stressors and workplace aggression (e.g. Fida et al., 2015). Although anger and frustration are the primary discrete emotions examined in this literature, researchers more recently (see Shockley, Ispas, Rossi, & Levine, 2012) have examined a range of other emotions (i.e. guilt, shame, envy, sadness, boredom, anxiety, jealousy). Shockley et al.'s meta-analysis found that anger and frustration had the strongest relationships to enacted aggression; however, the researchers also found that state guilt, envy, sadness, and anxiety positively related to enacted workplace aggression. Of the positive emotions they examined, only attentiveness negatively related to enacted workplace aggression. This is perhaps unsurprising given that workplace stressors are unlikely to give rise to positive emotions.

Experienced Aggression

Although studies have demonstrated a significant relationship between experienced aggression and negative emotions, this body of research is limited. Pearson, Anderson, and Wegner (2001) conducted a series of semi-structured interviews and found that targets of aggression often reported negative affect (e.g. feeling "down," "hurt," or "moody"). Studies have found that targets experience general negative affect (e.g. Sakurai & Jex, 2012; Zhou, Yan, Che, & Meier, 2015), and have also started to examine the role of discrete emotions in the relationship between experienced aggression and outcomes (e.g. Bunk & Magley, 2013; Porath & Pearson, 2012). For instance, Bunk and Magley investigated guilt, anger, fear, sadness, and disgust in understanding experienced aggression. Four out of five measured discrete emotions – guilt, fear, disgust, and anger – were significantly and positively related to the desire to reciprocate uncivil treatment. Similarly, Porath and Pearson (2012) investigated how perceived aggression is related to emotional responses, which in turn are associated with targets' behavioral responses. Employees who report greater levels of perceived experienced aggression also report greater levels of fear, anger, and sadness. Notably, these researchers found that different discrete emotions are associated with different outcomes. For instance, fear is associated with absenteeism, exit, and displaced aggression (i.e. aggression toward organizations or others), while anger is more strongly related with retaliatory aggression toward the perpetrator. Finally, whereas the above studies focus on the relationship between experienced workplace aggression and retaliatory behavior, Hershcovis et al. (2017) examined how affect influenced target attitudes and well-being. Across two studies, they demonstrated that experienced aggression was associated with targets' feelings of embarrassment and isolation, which were, in turn, related to perceived job insecurity and greater somatic complaints.

Witnessed Aggression

Affect is a key driver of observer reactions to workplace aggression. In this literature, researchers have largely argued that observers of workplace aggression experience moral anger, which motivates them to restore justice through perpetrator-punishing behaviors (e.g. Reich & Hershcovis, 2015; Mitchell, Vogel, & Folger, 2015). Recent research on workplace aggression has examined the role of observers by examining observer reactions to witnessing workplace aggression (e.g. Reich & Hershcovis, 2015; Mitchell et al., 2015) and observer interventions (e.g. Umphress, Simmons, Folger, Ren, & Bobocel, 2013). Observers who perceive a violation of socially accepted norms feel moral anger and a moral obligation to rectify the wrong (Folger, 2001). In an attempt to restore justice, observers are ready to punish perpetrators even at their own expense (Turillo, Folger, Lavelle, Umphress, & Gee, 2002). In addition to perpetrator-targeted actions, observers also engage in target-focused support (Hershcovis & Bhatnagar, 2017; Mitchell et al., 2015). Hershcovis and Bhatnagar (2017) found that in addition to experiencing moral anger, observers may also experience empathy toward targets, causing them to support targets. Research on witnessed workplace aggression is still very limited; we further discuss the affective drivers of observers later in this chapter, in the section on future research directions.

In summary, much of the research on affective mechanisms has focused on explaining the relationship between workplace stressors and enacted aggression. Such research could benefit from a closer examination of discrete emotions beyond anger and frustration. More research is needed on the affective reactions of targets. This body of research has focused on emotions that lead to retaliatory reactions; however, more research is needed on emotions (e.g. empathy) that might result in more conciliatory or constructive behavior. Finally, although there is some research on observers' affective reactions, most of this research has focused on moral anger. There is room for considerable research in this area because observers' emotional reactions may influence their choice to punish perpetrators, help or harm targets, or do nothing.

Affect-Related Moderators

In this section, we examine key affect-related moderators that may amplify or mitigate enacted aggression, consequences for targets, and observer reactions. While affective personality traits have primarily been examined as moderators of enacted aggression, researchers have focused on emotion control strategies as moderators of experienced aggression.

Personality and Affect–Aggression Relationships

Most of the research on affective moderators has examined how personality influences the stressor–aggression relationship. Miller et al. (2003) suggested that three affect-related personality traits - neuroticism, conscientiousness, and agreeableness - determine how individuals react to negative events. Neurotic individuals tend to experience negative emotions (e.g. anxiety, fear), and they are more reactive to negative work events than their more emotionally stable peers (e.g. Bolger & Zuckerman, 1995). Similarly, Fox and Spector (1999) proposed that neurotic individuals are more likely to respond to workplace stressors with negative feelings, which in turn lead to enacted aggression. Individuals low in agreeableness are generally viewed as antagonistic and hostile (McCrae & Costa, 1996), and they react more strongly to negative work events than agreeable individuals (Taylor & Kluemper, 2012). Finally, Taylor and Kluemper suggested that conscientious individuals are less likely to lose their temper and hence are less susceptible to responding to a negative event with aggression.

Another affective personality trait that predicts enacted aggression is trait anger – a predisposition to experience anger (Douglas & Martinko, 2001). In a meta-analysis, Hershcovis et al. (2007) demonstrated that trait anger is positively related to both interpersonal and organizational aggression, arguing that "people high in trait anger are likely to be more easily provoked because of their tendency to perceive situations as frustrating" (p. 230). Researchers also demonstrated that irritability – extensive emotional sensitivity to a stressor – amplifies the stressor–aggression relationship (Caprara et al., 1983).

Fewer studies have examined how affective traits influence target reactions to workplace aggression. Those with more reactive affective traits (e.g. neuroticism) should experience more negative consequences, whereas those with more positive traits (e.g. agreeableness) are likely to experience buffering effects. Brees, Martinko, and Harvey (2016) demonstrated that individuals with higher levels of trait anger, negative affectivity, or hostile attribution styles report greater perceptions of supervisor-initiated aggression (i.e. abusive supervision). Surprisingly, Taylor and Kluemper (2012) found that conscientious employees who experienced workplace aggression reported lower affective commitment and lower subsequent performance than less conscientious employees. That is, rather than buffering the negative effects of experienced aggression, being conscientious made workplace aggression experiences worse for targets.

Emotion Regulation and Affect–Aggression Relationships

In addition to the moderating role of personality, research has also investigated affective control (e.g. emotional regulation, emotional labor) in the context of workplace aggression. Organizations often have rules with regard to displaying the right emotions (Sutton & Rafaeli, 1988), and employees are expected to suppress the display of wrong emotions. Carlson, Ferguson, Hunter, and Whitten (2012) argue that because of this expectation, employees who experience aggression engage in emotional labor – attempts to manage or alter emotions while at work (Hochschild, 1983). Emotional labor involves two strategies: surface acting (modifying emotion by suppressing or faking), and deep acting (reappraising the situation or focusing attention on positive things) (Hochschild, 1983). Grandey, Dickter, and Sin (2004) demonstrated that targets of aggression use different strategies: employees who are more threatened by the aggression use surface acting, while those who feel less threatened use deep acting. Notably, research has shown that surface acting has more negative consequences than deep acting (Brotheridge & Grandey, 2002) and is more likely to be used by inexperienced employees (Grandey, 2003).

Emotional regulation is a means to cope with negative affect, allowing people to minimize the discrepancy between actual and desired affective state (Westen, 1994). Engaging in emotion regulation as a coping response to experienced aggression may attenuate the relationship between perceived stress and negative outcomes. For example, Niven, Sprigg, and Armitage (2013) found that experienced aggression originating from both organizational outsiders (i.e. clients or patients) and insiders (i.e. coworkers or managers) was positively related to employees' strain. When interacting with insiders, reappraisal but not suppression weakened the aggression–strain relationship. By contrast, during interactions with outsiders, both reappraisal and suppression strategies exacerbated the aggression–strain relationship.

Research has also examined emotion regulation in relation to enacted aggression. Matta, Erol-Korkmaz, Johnson, and Biçaksiz (2014) found that those who suppress emotions are marginally more likely to engage in workplace aggression whereas those who reappraise are less likely to do so. Thus training employees on emotional control strategies may be one way to help prevent workplace aggression.

Overall, research has provided theoretical and empirical support for the moderating role of affect-focused individual differences and emotional control strategies for both perpetrators and targets. However, research has yet to examine how affective moderators might influence witness reactions. We return to the need for future research on observers later in the chapter.

Integrating Affective Mechanisms into a Model of Workplace Aggression

A common element among the theories and research discussed above is the role of negative affect. We integrate these affective theories of workplace aggression into one model (Figure 20.1), and add to these theories in two ways. First, our model depicts workplace aggression not only from the actor and target perspectives, but also from the observer perspective. Second, we recognize the cyclical nature of workplace aggression (Andersson & Pearson, 1999), in which a target or an observer might become a perpetrator, and a perpetrator or an observer might become a target. Although both the stressor–emotion model and AET imply that aggression can be a predictor, this explicit representation helps to elucidate a key missing question in the workplace aggression literature: the affective consequences of enacted aggression for perpetrators. This model both integrates existing models and research on affect and aggression, and highlights areas where further research is needed.

As with the stressor–emotion model and AET, Figure 20.1 demonstrates that a workplace event that is perceived as stressful elicits negative emotions, such as anger, anxiety, or frustration, which in turn relate to outcomes. In our integrated model, we include enacted, experienced, and witnessed aggression as possible outcomes, which in turn lead to affective reactions and subsequent attitudinal and behavioral outcomes.

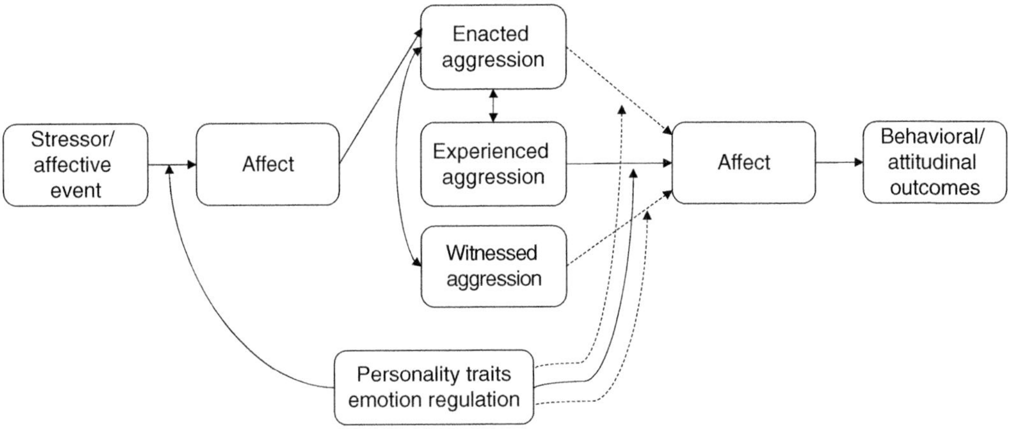

Figure 20.1 Integrated model of workplace aggression and affect
Note: the dashed arrows reflect areas where more research is needed.

Enacted aggression has implications for perpetrators, targets, and observers. For instance, it can be a source of affect (e.g. enjoyment, shame, regret) for the perpetrator that in turn is related to attitudinal and behavioral outcomes (e.g. re-offense, withdrawal, apology). Consequences for perpetrators have received almost no attention in the workplace aggression literature; we discuss this further below. Enacted aggression also leads to experienced and witnessed aggression. Both targets and observers experience affective responses that influence their subsequent attitudes and behaviors. In the integrated model, we demonstrate that affect resulting from experienced and witnessed aggression can lead to enacted aggression and other attitudinal/behavioral outcomes. Finally, this model acknowledges that affective moderators influence the relationship between workplace events and affect, and that these moderators may influence the relationship between aggression (experienced, enacted, or witnessed), and affective reactions. Thus, this unified framework explains the affective mechanisms and affective moderators of workplace aggression, combining enacted, experienced, and witnessed aggression.

Directions for Future Research

Figure 20.1 highlights two key directions for future research. Our first recommendation relates to affective consequences of witnessed aggression and the role of observer interventions, or lack of thereof. More than half of all workplace aggression incidents are witnessed by others (Glomb, 2002), and observers play an important role in the dynamic of workplace aggression. Given that emotional reactions are essential determinants of subsequent behavioral outcomes, the workplace aggression literature would benefit from further examination of a range of positive and negative emotional reactions experienced by the observers. For instance, Folger, Johnson, and Letwin (2014) argued that observers may feel guilt after witnessing an aggressive behavior; the feeling of guilt may occur when coworkers are subjected to aggression, while observers are not. Other negative emotional reactions may include feeling sad, intimidated, or terrified. In addition to negative emotions, some observers may experience a sense of pleasure. Mitchell et al. (2015) theorized that not all observers consider aggression unfair. When observers believe that the target deserves the mistreatment, they experience contentment from witnessing aggression (Mitchell et al., 2015). The feeling of contentment may serve as a motivator to perpetuate aggression against the target. There is also a possibility that observers experience both positive and negative emotions simultaneously. For instance, an observer may experience guilt that someone is being mistreated, while simultaneously experiencing schadenfreude – a feeling of pleasure from witnessing another person's mistreatment (Leach, Spears, Branscombe, & Doosje, 2003). Research has not yet considered how conflicting emotion might impact observer responses to workplace aggression.

Further, although a number of studies have examined observers' reactions to workplace aggression, the modal response of an observer is to do nothing. Indeed, early research on the bystander effect shows that for a variety of reasons observers of negative events tend to do nothing (Latané & Darley, 1970). However, we know virtually nothing about how these silent non-responders feel when they witness mistreatment and choose not to act (e.g. guilt, shame, relief). Such research might help us gain insight into why observers fail to act.

Considering that observers are in a powerful position to help stop the perpetrator, support the target, or encourage aggressive behaviors, researchers need to further explore observers' emotional reactions and subsequent interventions, or lack thereof. Furthermore, witnessed aggression may prompt observers to control their emotions by engaging in emotional labor. Researchers have shown that targets of workplace aggression engage in emotional labor, which then leads to emotional exhaustion (e.g. Sliter, Jex, Wolford, & McInnerney, 2010); however, little is known about observers' attempts to regulate their emotions when witnessing workplace aggression. Like the targets of workplace aggression, observers may engage in surface acting (suppressing or faking emotions) or deep acting (reappraising the situation) as emotion regulation strategies, and these strategies may be contingent upon the context. For instance, when the aggression is ongoing and anticipated costs of intervention are high (e.g. witnessing abusive supervision), observers may engage in deep acting; but when witnessing a one-time incident of aggression (e.g. aggression from a customer), a surface acting strategy may be more likely. Surface acting, on average, has a stronger negative effect on psychological well-being than deep acting (Hülsheger & Schewe, 2011). Deep acting implies that individuals reappraise the situation or focus on positive things; although beneficial for the observer's emotional state, this strategy may result in regarding aggression as more acceptable and, hence, reduce the likelihood of observer interventions. We suggest that future research should examine situations in which observers engage in emotion regulation strategies and also should investigate behavioral and attitudinal consequences of those strategies. In addition to emotion regulation, affect-related personality traits also have implications for how observers respond to witnessed aggression. For instance, neurotic individuals may experience stronger negative affect when witnessing aggression. Given that the observer literature is so new, research has yet to examine how affective traits influence observer reactions. Such research is likely to shed light on the types of people who are more or less inclined to intervene, and on the ways in which these individuals choose to intervene.

Our second recommendation for future research concerns the affective responses of perpetrators. Studies on workplace aggression and affect rely almost exclusively on perceptions of either targets (e.g. Zhou et al., 2015) or observers (e.g. Reich & Hershcovis, 2015; Zhou et al., 2017). But what about perpetrators? Research has shown that negative affect triggers workplace aggression (Hershcovis et al., 2007). However, there is little empirical research on the affective consequences of enacted aggression for the perpetrators (e.g. Foulk, Lanaj, Tu,

Erez, & Archambeau, 2018; Qin, Huang, Johnson, Hu, & Ju, 2018). Foulk et al. conducted an experience-sampling study and found that leaders engage in more abusive behaviors and perceive more incivility from others on days when they are exposed to psychological power compared to days when they are not exposed to power. Abusive behaviors and perceived incivility, in turn, result in decreased well-being, as indicated by reduced daily need fulfillment and reduced relaxation at home. Qin et al. demonstrated that engaging in abusive supervision has short-term benefits for supervisors: it is associated with improved recovery levels and has a positive indirect effect on work engagement. However, these "benefits" are short-term, and abusive supervision over longer period of times is negatively related to supervisors' recovery and engagement. Do perpetrators experience schadenfreude and enjoyment or regret and shame? These affective reactions are essential to perpetrators' future actions. For instance, those who experience pleasure from hurting others maybe more likely to "re-offend," and less likely to be "redeemed" by targets and observers, than those perpetrators who feel regret about their actions. Furthermore, certain self-conscious emotion traits may moderate the relationship between enacted aggression and affective and behavioral reactions. For instance, shame-proneness relates to more destructive responses to anger, including aggressive behavioral intentions; whereas individuals with higher levels of guilt-proneness engage more constructively with anger, for example by undertaking corrective actions (Tangney, Wagner, Hill-Barlow, Marschall, & Gramzow, 1996). Hence, future research needs to explore affective reactions of enacted aggression and the moderating role of self-conscious traits. Such research will shed light on when and why perpetrators attempt to undertake corrective actions or persist with abuse.

Conclusion

Our aim in this chapter was to review the relationship between affect and workplace aggression. We then offered a model that integrates and extends affective theories of workplace aggression. Our intent was not to provide a complete model on workplace aggression processes, but rather to highlight the key role of affect in such processes and to show the cyclical nature of workplace aggression. Our hope is that our framework will facilitate research on workplace aggression and affect from the perspectives of the perpetrator, the target, and the observer, leading to a more comprehensive understanding of workplace aggression.

References

Arnetz, J., Hamblin, L., Ager, J., Luborsky, M., Upfal, M., Russell, J., & Essenmacher, L. (2015). Underreporting of workplace violence: Comparison of self-report and actual documentation of hospital incidents. *Workplace Health & Safety, 63*(5), 200–210.

Bandura, A. (1986). *Social foundations of thought and action: A social cognitive theory*. Englewood Cliffs, NJ: Prentice-Hall.

Berkowitz, L. (1989). Frustration aggression hypothesis: Examination and reformulation. *Psychological Bulletin, 106*(1), 59–73.

Bolger, N., & Zuckerman, A. (1995). A framework for studying personality in the stress process. *Journal of Personality and Social Psychology, 69*, 890–902.

Bowling, N. A., & Beehr, T. A. (2006). Workplace harassment from the victim's perspective: A theoretical model and meta-analysis. *Journal of Applied Psychology, 91*(5), 998–1012.

Brees, J., Martinko, M., & Harvey, P. (2016). Abusive supervision: Subordinate personality or supervisor behavior? *Journal of Managerial Psychology, 31* (2), 405–419.

Breuer, J., & Elson, M. (2017). Frustration–aggression theory. In P. Sturmey (Ed.), *The Wiley handbook of violence and aggression*. Hoboken, NJ: Wiley.

Brotheridge, C. M., & Grandey, A. A. (2002). Emotional labor and burnout: Comparing two perspectives of "people work." *Journal of Vocational Behavior*, *60*(1), 17–39.

Bunk, J. A., & Magley, V. J. (2013). The role of appraisals and emotions in understanding experiences of workplace incivility. *Journal of Occupational Health Psychology*, *18*(1), 87–105.

Caprara, G. V., Renzi, P., Alcini, P., Imperio, G. D., & Travaglia, G. (1983). Instigation to aggress and escalation of aggression examined from a personological perspective: The role of irritability and of emotional susceptibility. *Aggressive Behavior*, *9*(4), 345–351.

Carlson, D., Ferguson, M., Hunter, E., & Whitten, D. (2012). Abusive supervision and work–family conflict: The path through emotional labor and burnout. *Leadership Quarterly*, *23*(5), 849–859.

Dill, J. C., & Anderson, C. A. (1995). Effects of frustration justification on hostile aggression. *Aggressive Behavior*, *21*(5), 359–369.

Dollard, A., Doob, L. W., Miller, N. E., Mowrer, O. H., & Sears, R. R. (1939). *Frustration and aggression*. New Haven, CT: Yale University Press.

Douglas, S. C., & Martinko, M. J. (2001). Exploring the role of individual differences in the prediction of workplace aggression. *Journal of Applied Psychology*, *86*(4), 547–559.

Fida, R., Paciello, M., Tramontano, C., Fontaine, R. G., Barbaranelli, C., & Farnese, M. L. (2015). An integrative approach to understanding counterproductive work behavior: The roles of stressors, negative emotions, and moral disengagement. *Journal of Business Ethics*, *130*(1), 131–144.

Folger, R. (2001). Fairness as deonance. In S. W. Gilliland, D. Steiner, & D. P. Skarlicki (Eds.), *Research in social issues in management* (pp. 3–31). Greenwich, CT: Information Age.

Folger, R., Johnson, M., & Letwin, C. (2014). Evolving concepts of evolution: The case of shame and guilt. *Social and Personality Psychology Compass*, *8*(12), 659–671.

Foulk, T., Lanaj, K., Tu, M., Erez, A., & Archambeau, L. (2018). Heavy is the head that wears the crown: An actor-centric approach to daily psychological power, abusive leader behavior, and perceived incivility. *Academy of Management Journal*, *61*(2), 661–684.

Fox, S., & Spector, P. E. (1999). A model of work frustration–aggression. *Journal of Organizational Behavior*, *20*(6), 915–931.

Fox, S., Spector, P. E., & Miles, D. (2001). Counterproductive work behavior (CWB) in response to job stressors and organizational justice: Some mediator and moderator tests for autonomy and emotions. *Journal of Vocational Behavior*, *59* (3), 291–309.

Glomb, T. M. (2002). Workplace anger and aggression: Informing conceptual models with data from specific encounters. *Journal of Occupational Health Psychology*, *7*(1), 20–36.

Grandey, A. A. (2003). When "the show must go on": Surface acting and deep acting as determinants of emotional exhaustion and peer-related service delivery. *Academy of Management Journal*, *46*(1), 86–96.

Grandey, A. A., Dickter, D. N., & Sin, H. P. (2004). The customer is not always right: Customer aggression and emotion regulation of service employees. *Journal of Organizational Behavior*, *25*(3), 397–418.

Heacox, N. J., & Sorenson, R. C. (2007). Organizational frustration and aggressive behaviors. *Journal of Emotional Abuse*, *4*(3–4), 95–118.

Hershcovis, M. S. (2011). "Incivility, social undermining, bullying . . . oh my!" A call to reconcile constructs within workplace aggression research. *Journal of Organizational Behavior*, *32* (3), 499–519.

Hershcovis, M. S., & Barling, J. (2010). Towards a multi-foci approach to workplace aggression: A meta-analytic review of outcomes from different perpetrators. *Journal of Organizational Behavior*, *31*(1), 24–44.

Hershcovis, M. S., & Bhatnagar, N. (2017). When fellow customers behave badly: Witness reactions to employee mistreatment by customers. *Journal of Applied Psychology*, *102*(11), 1528–1544.

Hershcovis, M. S., Neville, L., Reich, T. C., Christie, A. M., Cortina, L. M., & Shan, J. V. (2017). Witnessing wrongdoing: The effects of observer power on incivility intervention in the workplace. *Organizational Behavior and Human Decision Processes*, *142*, 45–57.

Hershcovis, M. S., Ogunfowora, B., Reich, T. C., & Christie, A. M. (2017). Targeted workplace incivility: The roles of belongingness, embarrassment, and power. *Journal of Organizational Behavior*, *38*(7), 1057–1075.

Hershcovis, M. S., Turner, N., Barling, J., Arnold, K. A., Dupre, K. E., Inness, M., & Sivanathan, N. (2007). Predicting workplace aggression: A meta-analysis. *Journal of Applied Psychology*, *92*(1), 228–238.

Ho, V. (2012). Interpersonal counterproductive work behaviors: Distinguishing between person-focused versus task-focused behaviors and their antecedents. *Journal of Business and Psychology*, *27*(4), 467–482.

Hochschild, A. R. (1983). *The managed heart: Commercialization of human feeling*. Berkeley: University of California Press.

Hülsheger, U. R., & Schewe, A. F. (2011). On the costs and benefits of emotional labor: A meta-analysis of three decades of research. *Journal of Occupational Health Psychology*, *16*(3), 361–389.

Judge, T., Scott, B., Ilies, R., & Zedeck, Sheldon. (2006). Hostility, job attitudes, and workplace deviance: Test of a multilevel model. *Journal of Applied Psychology*, *91*(1), 126–138.

Kabat-Farr, D., Marchiondo, L. A., & Cortina, L. M. (2018). The emotional aftermath of incivility: Anger, guilt, and the role of organizational commitment. *International Journal of Stress Management*, *25*(2), 109–128.

Lanthier, S., Bielecky, A., & Smith, P. M. (2018). Examining risk of workplace violence in Canada: A sex/gender-based analysis. *Annals of Work Exposures and Health*, *62*(8), 1012–1020.

Latané, B., & Darley, J. M. (1970). *The unresponsive bystander: Why doesn't he help?* Century Psychology Series. New York, NY: Appleton–Century Crofts.

Leach, C., Spears, R., Branscombe, N., & Doosje, B. (2003). Malicious pleasure: Schadenfreude at the suffering of another group. *Journal of Personality and Social Psychology*, *84*(5), 932–943.

Lee, K., & Allen, N. (2002). Organizational citizenship behavior and workplace deviance: The role of affect and cognitions. *Journal of Applied Psychology*, *87* (1), 131–142.

Martinko, M. J., Douglas, S. C., & Harvey, P. (2006). Understanding and managing workplace aggression. *Organizational Dynamics*, *35*(2), 117–130.

Matta, F. K., Erol-Korkmaz, H. T., Johnson, R. E., & Biçaksiz, P. (2014). Significant work events and counterproductive work behavior: The role of fairness, emotions, and emotion regulation. *Journal of Organizational Behavior*, *35*(7), 920–944.

McCrae, R. R., & Costa, P. T. (1996). Toward a new generation of personality theories: Theoretical contexts for the five-factor model. In J. S. Wiggins (Ed.), *The five-factor model of personality: Theoretical perspectives* (pp. 51–87). New York, NY: Guilford.

Miles, D. E., Borman, W. E., Spector, P. E., & Fox, S. (2002). Building an integrative model of extra role work behaviors: A comparison of counterproductive work behavior with organizational citizenship behavior. *International Journal of Selection and Assessment*, *10*(1–2), 51–57.

Miller, N., Pedersen, W. C., Earleywine, M., & Pollock, V. E. (2003). A theoretical model of triggered displaced aggression. *Personality and Social Psychology Review*, *7*, 57–97.

Mitchell, M. S., Vogel, R. M., & Folger, R. (2015). Third parties' reactions to the abusive supervision of coworkers. *Journal of Applied Psychology*, *100* (4), 1040–1055.

Niven, K., Sprigg, C. A., & Armitage, C. J. (2013). Does emotion regulation protect employees from the negative effects of workplace aggression? *European Journal of Work and Organizational Psychology*, *22*(1), 88–106.

Pearson, C. M., Andersson, L. M., & Wegner, J. W. (2001). When workers flout convention: A study of workplace incivility. *Human Relations*, *54*(11), 1387–1419.

Penney, L. M., & Spector, P. E. (2005). Job stress, incivility, and counterproductive work behavior (CWB): The moderating role of negative affectivity. *Journal of Organizational Behavior*, *26* (7), 777–796.

Perreault, S. (2015). Criminal victimization in Canada, 2014. *Juristat: Canadian Centre for Justice Statistics*, *30*(2), www150.statcan.gc.ca/n1/pub/85-002-x/2015001/article/14241-eng.htm.

Porath, C. L., & Pearson, C. M. (2012). Emotional and behavioral responses to workplace incivility and the impact of hierarchical status. *Journal of Applied Social Psychology*, *42*, E326–E357.

Qin, X., Huang, M., Johnson, R. E., Hu, Q., & Ju, D. (2018). The short-lived benefits of abusive supervisory behavior for actors: An investigation of recovery and work engagement. *Academy of Management Journal*, *61*(5), 1951–1975.

Reich, T. C., & Hershcovis, M. S. (2015). Observing workplace incivility. *Journal of Applied Psychology*, *100*(1), 203–215.

Rodell, J. B., & Judge, T. A. (2009). Can "good" stressors spark "bad" behaviors? The mediating role of emotions in links of challenge and hindrance stressors with citizenship and counterproductive behaviors. *Journal of Applied Psychology*, *94*(6), 1438–1451.

Sakurai, K., & Jex, S. M. (2012). Coworker incivility and incivility targets' work effort and counterproductive work behaviors: The moderating role of supervisor social support. *Journal of Occupational Health Psychology*, *17* (2), 150–161.

Shockley, K. M., Ispas, D., Rossi, M. E., & Levine, E. L. (2012). A meta-analytic investigation of the relationship between state affect, discrete emotions, and job performance. *Human Performance*, *25*(5), 377–411.

Sliter, M., Jex, S., Wolford, K., & McInnerney, J. (2010). How rude! Emotional labor as a mediator between customer incivility and employee outcomes. *Journal of Occupational Health Psychology*, *15*(4), 468–481.

Spector, P. E., & Fox, S. (2005). A model of counterproductive work behavior. In S. Fox & P. E. Spector (Eds.), *Counterproductive workplace behavior: Investigations of actors and targets* (pp. 151–174). Washington, DC: APA.

Sutton, R., & Rafaeli, A. (1988). Untangling the relationship between displayed emotions and organizational sales: The case of convenience stores. *Academy of Management Journal*, *31*(3), 461–487.

Tangney, J. P., Wagner, P. E., Hill-Barlow, D., Marschall, D. E., & Gramzow, R. (1996). Relation of shame and guilt to constructive versus destructive responses to anger across the lifespan. *Journal of Personality and Social Psychology*, *70* (4), 797–809.

Taylor, S. G., & Kluemper, D. H. (2012). Linking perceptions of role stress and incivility to workplace aggression: The moderating role of personality. *Journal of Occupational Health Psychology*, *17*(3), 316–329.

Tillman, C., Gonzalez, K., Crawford, W., & Lawrence, E. (2018). Affective responses to abuse in the workplace: The role of hope and affective commitment. *International Journal of Selection and Assessment*, *26*(1), 57–65.

Totterdell, P., Hershcovis, M. S., Niven, K., Reich, T. C., & Stride, C. (2012). Can employees be emotionally drained by witnessing unpleasant interactions between coworkers? A diary study of induced emotion regulation. *Work and Stress*, *26*(2), 112–129.

Turillo, C. J., Folger, R., Lavelle, J. J., Umphress, E. E., & Gee, J. O. (2002). Is virtue its own reward? Self-sacrificial decisions for the sake of fairness. *Organizational Behavior and Human Decision Processes*, *89*(1), 839–865.

Umphress, E. E., Simmons, A. L., Folger, R., Ren, R., & Bobocel, R. (2013). Observer reactions to interpersonal injustice: The roles of perpetrator intent and victim perception. *Journal of Organizational Behavior*, *34*(3), 327–349.

Vroom, V. H. (1964). *Work and motivation*. New York: Wiley.

Weiss, H. M., & Cropanzano, R. (1996). Affective events theory: A theoretical discussion of the structure, causes and consequences of affective experiences at work. In B. M. Staw & L. L. Cummings (Eds.), *Research in Organizational Behavior* (Volume 18, pp. 1–74). Stamford, CA: Jai.

Westen, D. (1994). Toward an integrative model of affect regulation: Applications to social-psychological research. *Journal of Personality*, *62* (4), 641–667.

Zhou, B., Marchand, A., & Guay, S. (2017). I see so I feel: Coping with workplace violence among victims and witnesses. *Work – A Journal of Prevention, Assessment & Rehabilitation*, *57*(1), 125–135.

Zhou, Z. Q. E., Yan, Y., Che, X. X., & Meier, L. L. (2015). Effect of workplace incivility on end-of-work negative affect: Examining individual and organizational moderators in a daily diary study. *Journal of Occupational Health Psychology*, *20*(1), 117–130.

21 The Service Encounter

Vicente Martínez-Tur

Introduction

The service sector accounts for about two-thirds of the world's output, it provides more than 50 percent of global employment, and its importance has increased in recent decades in every country (United Nations, 2018). Consequently, millions of service encounters take place every day around the world, with implications for organizations, employees, and customers. Emotions, or intense short-lived feelings associated with an object or target (Ekman, 1994), emerge in service encounters as a main facet that offers valuable insights into the interaction between employees and customers. Due to its complexity, the investigation of emotions in service encounters is carried out from different perspectives. The present chapter emphasizes three aspects. First, although this chapter is not exclusively focused on the display of emotions, I emphasize the outward *expression of emotions* (Diefendorff & Greguras, 2009) through a combination of facial expression, tone of voice, and spoken words (Rafaeli & Sutton, 1987). Expressed or displayed emotions are not necessarily equivalent to felt emotions. Humans learn to display appropriate emotions in different contexts. Norms, often called display rules, describe the appropriate expressions of emotions in a given social situation (Matsumoto, 1990), including emotions in the service encounter (Diefendorff, Morehart, & Gabriel, 2010; Grandey, Rafaeli, Ravid, Wirtz, & Steiner, 2010). Although expressed and felt emotions might coincide, displayed emotions are the ones that are essential in service encounters because they shape the customers' evaluations of the social interaction and the service delivery (e.g. Pugh, 2001).

Second, it is relevant to consider differences between services in terms of *goals*. Research on services has differentiated between short-term interactions between employees and customers, on the one hand, and complex services where the interaction with customers is extended over time, on the other (e.g. Guo, Chen, & Xu, 2016; Gutek, Bhappu, Liao-Troth, & Cherry, 1999; Hulsheger & Schewe, 2011). Research on displaying emotions in service encounters has concentrated primarily on short-term profit-oriented interactions with specific objectives and limited implications for the lives of customers. Examples would be studies carried out in restaurants (Brach, Walsh, Hennig-Thurau, & Groth, 2015), banks (Pugh, 2001), post offices (Tsai & Chen, 2017), or stores (Grandey, Goldberg, & Pugh, 2011), among others. Considering these types of services, some empirical evidence supports the existence of a progressive globalization of the "service with a smile" culture (Grandey et al., 2010; Ravid, Rafaeli, & Grandey, 2010), where positive employee emotional displays help to enhance customer satisfaction. Important progress has been made in the knowledge in this area. On the other hand, greater attention to services focused on complex social goals may offer a complementary view and enrich our understanding of service encounters. Non-profit services oriented toward counterbalancing situations of vulnerability are usually very significant for the lives of service users and have strong emotional content (e.g. Martínez-Tur et al., 2017). Research on these services would be likely to extend our understanding of the possible outcomes of service encounters and change the interpretation of the role of emotions.

Third, it is necessary to give more recognition to the active *role of the customer* in the service encounter. Although the influence of customers' emotional expression was mentioned in the influential articles by Rafaeli and Sutton (1989, p. 24) and Pugh (2001, p. 1020), scholars have tended to emphasize a causal link from employees to customers, with consequences in terms of customer satisfaction, purchases, positive comments, and loyalty, among others (e.g. Tsai, 2001). However, the active role of customers is increasingly being considered in the research (e.g. Dallimore, Sparks, & Butcher, 2007; Kim & Yoon, 2012; Tsai & Chen, 2017), which is congruent with a co-creation perspective acknowledging that the customer also participates in the shaping of the service process (Vargo & Lusch, 2004, pp. 6–7). One of the ways in which service is co-created is through the customer's expression of emotions, which affects the service provider (Medler-Liraz, 2016).

With these three aspects in mind, the chapter is organized in two main sections. The first section provides a review of the literature about the employee's display of emotions directed toward customers. The second section focuses on research efforts that attribute an active role to the customer in the service encounter. The chapter concludes with a discussion of possible avenues for future research.

The Employee's Expression of Emotions

Mechanisms and Outcomes

One of the central objectives of service encounter research is to identify the mechanisms through which the expression of emotions by employees is transmitted to customers and elicits customer responses. In this research, the theory of primitive emotional contagion has played a prominent role (e.g. Tan, Foo, & Kwek, 2004; Tsai & Huang, 2002). Hatfield, Cacioppo, and Rapson (1994) defined emotional contagion as "The tendency to automatically mimic and synchronize facial expressions, vocalizations, postures, and movements with those of another person and, consequently, to converge emotionally" (p. 5). Hatfield, Rapson, and Le (2009) postulated the existence of three phases of emotional contagion: mimicry (imitation and synchronization of facial expressions, postures, voices, movements, vocal expressions, and instrumental behaviors of others); feedback (activation and/or feedback through vocal, facial, postural, and movement mimicry affects the emotional experience through the automatic nervous system); and contagion (people "catch" others' emotions). Some evidence from psychophysiological investigations of mirror neurons supported the existence of mimicry. For instance, Ramachandra, Depalma, and Lisiewski (2009) observed that mirror neurons are involved not only in the perception and imitation of actions, but also in processing vocal emotions.

Pugh (2001) extended and applied the concept of primitive emotional contagion to the service encounter. He observed a positive relationship between the expression of positive emotions by bank employees, and the positive affect of their customers. More importantly, this direct emotional link occurred even when there was no significant relationship between the employees' expressed and felt emotions. The mere exposure to employees' expressions of positive emotions produced an automatic emotional response in customers. Pugh also observed a direct relationship between customers' positive affect and their perceptions about the service quality, without the participation of a conscious cognitive appraisal. He attributed this link to affect infusion (Forgas, 1995), whereby customers are able to make evaluative judgments (on service quality in this case) using affective states as information (Pugh, 2001, p. 1021).

Barger and Grandey (2006) proposed and tested two complementary mechanisms in real service encounters (food/coffee services). One of the mechanisms is based on the aforementioned emotional contagion and affect infusion. They proposed a mimicry effect where employee smiling is positively related to customer smiling during service encounters. Customers' smiling in turn affects their post-encounter mood. Accordingly, customer smiling mediates between employee smiling and post-encounter customer mood, which is congruent with the theory of primitive emotional contagion: the imitation of an emotional expression (i.e. smiling) leads to the corresponding felt emotion. In addition, Barger and Grandey (2006) drew on the concept of affect infusion to postulate that post-encounter customer mood influences general judgments associated with service quality and customer satisfaction with the service encounter.

The second mechanism corresponded to cognitive appraisal. Smiling is regarded as an expected component in high-quality service delivered by employees. Smiling transmits caring and a desire to continue the interaction. Therefore, employee smiling could improve customer satisfaction with the encounter through a conscious appraisal of service quality. Regarding the emotional corridor, results confirmed mimicry (from employee smiling to customer smiling), and affect infusion (mood contributing to customer satisfaction), but not the mediation of emotional contagion and affect infusion in the link from employee smiling to customer satisfaction. By contrast, the findings fully supported the corridor described by cognitive appraisal: employee smiling – service quality – customer satisfaction.

Scholars have progressively incorporated both mechanisms using different research strategies. Grandey et al. (2011) investigated the link from employee satisfaction to customer satisfaction in stores. The first mechanism (affective) was based on emotional contagion, with a direct link proposed. When employees are happy, they express this positive affect to customers, who experience similar affect due to contagion. The second mechanism (service performance) is not as automatic. Satisfied employees are expected to direct energy to their organizational goals, attending to their customers better in terms of speed of responsiveness. This prompt attention in turn leads to customers' satisfaction. Grandey et al. (2011) confirmed a partial mediation of service responsiveness between employee and customer satisfaction, supporting both mechanisms. Wang et al. (2017) conducted both a field study (with a variety of services) and a laboratory experiment. They corroborated the existence of two corridors from employees' displays of emotions to customers' loyalty intentions. Based on emotional contagion, Wang et al. observed that employees' displays of emotions impact customer outcomes (loyalty) through customers' affective reactions. They also confirmed the existence of a second mechanism where employees' expressions of emotions lead to customer loyalty through customers' cognitive appraisal of service performance.

The role of *authenticity* in displaying emotions – the degree to which employees' expression of emotions directed to customers is perceived as authentic – also involves cognitive appraisal. According to primitive emotional contagion, emotions expressed by employees are automatically and unconsciously imitated by customers, even when the employees themselves are not feeling the emotions expressed (Pugh, 2001). However, it is likely that customers are able to process information and draw inferences about the authenticity of emotions. The possible differential role of authenticity would be an indication that customers process the employees' displays of emotions consciously. Inauthentic expression of employees' positive emotions could minimize the benefits of positive emotional display in service encounters. Grandey, Fisk, Mattila, Jansen, and Sideman (2005) applied the study of authenticity (Ekman & Friesen, 1982) to the display of emotions in service encounters, conducting both a laboratory experiment (using videotapes where an actor simulated authentic and inauthentic displays of emotions at the reception desk of a hotel), and a study in a real context (perceptions of authenticity of employees' expression of emotions by clients in restaurants). They argued that employees' capacity to show emotions that seem authentic goes beyond the minimum requirement of a fake smile in enhancing appraisals of friendliness and customer satisfaction with the encounter. In other words, employees' authenticity in displaying positive emotions should predict customer satisfaction and service evaluation variance that is not captured by a fake smile. In general, Grandey et al. (2005) confirmed their propositions and supported authenticity as a critical aspect of service delivery.

Other research reinforces the role of authenticity. Hennig-Thurau, Groth, Paul, and Gremler (2006) compared the mere display of employees' positive emotions vs. authenticity in the expression of employees' positive emotions. They simulated service encounters, with actors playing the role of employees, and expressing both authentic and inauthentic positive emotions. Contrary to the theory of primitive emotional contagion, a significant relationship was not found between the display of positive emotions (extent of employee smiling) and customers' positive affect. By contrast, authenticity of expression of employees' positive emotions was a significant predictor of customers' positive affect. In addition, customers' positive affect was significantly related to customers' satisfaction with the service transaction and positive rapport between employees and customers. The aforementioned study by Wang et al. (2017) also stressed the role of authenticity. They measured the authenticity of employees' emotional displays in two ways: customer perceptions (field study), and videotapes with actors (laboratory experiment). Their results supported two significant corridors: a) a process based on primitive emotional contagion (intensity of positive emotional display – customer affective reaction – loyalty intentions); and b) a cognitive appraisal route where authenticity is at the starting point (authenticity – appraisal of service performance – loyalty intentions).

In sum, over time, research has consolidated two main processes (emotional contagion and cognitive appraisal) to explain the connection between employees' displays of emotions and customer outcomes such as customer satisfaction, rapport, and behavioral intentions. Variability in the predictive power of each type of process could partly depend on moderators, some of which are described below.

Moderators

Busyness

Scholars have examined store/context *busyness* as a relevant moderator of the relationships discussed. The customer might interact with service providers in a slow context where there are no other customers; or the context of the service encounter could be completely different when there are many other customers who want to be attended to by employees. Grandey et al. (2005) argued that, in busy service contexts, customers are likely to attribute lack of authenticity to the situation and not to the service provider employee. In busy contexts, employees cannot attend to customers the way they want to, and inauthenticity is more understandable. Accordingly, the authors proposed that the links from authenticity to perceived friendliness and encounter satisfaction are weaker in busy contexts than in slow-paced contexts. In restaurants, Grandey et al. (2005) confirmed this moderation for the perception of employees (friendliness), but not for the appraisal of the overall service encounter (satisfaction). In another study, Grandey et al. (2011) tested the same proposition again with a sample of stores, linking employee satisfaction to customer satisfaction and objective speed of responsiveness to customers' requests for help. As expected, the links from employee satisfaction to customer satisfaction and responsiveness were stronger in slower stores than busier ones.

Individual Differences

Service encounter research has also considered individual differences as moderators. Groth, Hennig-Thurau, and Walsh (2009) and Brach et al. (2015) focused on the ability of customers to detect employees' emotions accurately. Emotion recognition is one of the most validated dimensions of emotional intelligence (Elfenbein, Marsh, & Ambady, 2002), and it probably plays a critical role in dealing with emotional labor (Daus & Ashkanasy, 2005). Groth et al. (2009) observed, in real service encounters, that the ability of customers to detect employees' emotions accurately amplifies the positive link from deep acting (modifying felt emotions in order to display genuine emotions) to customer orientation perceptions (degree to which the employees' interactions with customers satisfy customer needs). This ability also accentuated the negative relationship between surface acting (expressing emotions not actually felt) and customer orientation perceptions. Similarly, Brach et al. (2015) found that the positive relationship between perceived authenticity in employees' display of emotions (employee perceptions) and employees' customer orientation perceptions is greater among customers with high detection accuracy than among customers with low detection accuracy.

Another individual difference that has been considered is *epistemic motivation*, defined as "the desire to develop and maintain a rich and accurate understanding of the world" (Van Kleef, De Dreu, & Manstead, 2004, p. 511). Individuals low in epistemic motivation base their behavior on their emotions, whereas people high in epistemic motivation prefer to use other sources of information. Wang et al. (2017) confirmed that customers high in epistemic motivation base their loyalty intentions on cognitive appraisals where the authenticity of employees' expressions of emotions plays a relevant role. By contrast, the loyalty of customers low in epistemic motivation was guided by the intensity of the employees' emotional display (without considering authenticity).

Type of Service

As mentioned earlier in the chapter, I propose that the type of service is a relevant moderator that requires specific attention in the investigation of displaying emotions in service encounters. However, research is scarce. An exception is the study conducted by Gabriel, Acosta, and Grandey (2015). They focused on the familiarity of the service, assessed through the frequency of employees' interactions with the same customers. Gabriel et al. (2015) proposed and found that employee display of emotions is less important in familiar service exchanges than in non-familiar, in order to predict service performance. Gabriel et al. (2015) attributed this result to the fact that customers have other information, beyond employees' emotional display, to define what is a good performance in familiar service encounters.

Research on services has differentiated between short vs. extended and complex service encounters (Guo et al., 2016; Gutek et al., 1999; Hulsheger & Schewe, 2011). However, specific research on expression of emotions in service encounters has mainly focused on short-term interactions with specific commercial goals, rewarding the expression of positive emotions and the suppression of negative ones in order to achieve customer satisfaction, loyalty, and sales. Although this approach has led to very relevant contributions to knowledge and practice, the consideration of other types of services with totally different goals could enrich our understanding of service encounters in at least two ways. First, the expected outcomes of service encounters could be extended. In some service organizations, the main goal is not profitability, but rather a social end related to counteracting vulnerability (e.g.

social inclusion of battered women) and improving the quality of life of service users through the employees' service performance. Accordingly, service encounters could produce other benefits beyond customer satisfaction and loyalty, and some initial evidence supports this argument. Molina, Moliner, Martínez-Tur, Cropanzano, and Peiró (2015) carried out a research study in non-profit service organizations for individuals with intellectual disability. They proposed and found that emotional aspects of service delivery, such as authenticity and empathy, make a unique and significant positive contribution to the quality of life of service users reported by family members.

Second, the critical role of emotions could vary depending on type of service. Previous research argued that employees' display of emotions is conceptualized as extra-role performance, whereas the expertise of employees in delivering the core service (e.g. efficiency) would be the main job requirement (Grandey et al., 2005). Accordingly, these authors proposed that employees' emotional display plays a significant role in predicting customer satisfaction, but only when the delivery of the core service is good. Grandey et al. (2005) found support for this proposal in the simulation of service encounters in hotels, but not in real service encounters in restaurants. Findings obtained by Söderlund and Rosengren (2010) also supported the aforementioned argument in a simulation of traveling with an airline company. In addition, the magnitude of the direct relationship with customer satisfaction was very different for delivery of the core service vs. display of emotions. Grandey et al. (2005, p. 50) obtained an estimated value (hierarchical linear modeling) of .26 for the link from delivery of the core service to customer satisfaction, whereas this value was only .08 for display of emotions. Similarly, Söderlund and Rosengren (2010, p. 165) found eta^2 values of .60 and .09 for the main effects of delivery of the core service and display of emotions, respectively, on customer satisfaction. Generally speaking, these findings indicate that the direct contribution (magnitude) of display of emotions is secondary, and it is only significant when delivery of the core service is good.

Recently, Martínez-Tur, Estreder, Tomás, Ramos, and Luque (2018) observed that results could be very different in services for individuals with intellectual disability. They examined the links from delivery of the core service and emotional aspects, such as empathy and authenticity, to customer satisfaction in three types of service settings: hotel reception desks, restaurants, and services for individuals with intellectual disability. Results for hotels and restaurants showed asymmetries that are similar to those obtained by Grandey et al. (2005) and Söderlund and Rosengren (2010). In fact, the direct contributions of delivery of the core service vs. emotional aspects, respectively, were .71 vs. .19 (hotels) and .62 vs. .34 (restaurants) (see *B* values, Martínez-Tur, Estreder et al., 2018). By contrast, *B* values were identical (.26 vs. .24) in services for individuals with intellectual disability. Additionally, the interaction between delivery of the core service and emotional aspects was much greater for this type of service than for hotels and restaurants. In services for individuals with intellectual disability, emotional aspects played an important compensatory role, enhancing customer satisfaction when core service delivery was not good. Indeed, this suggests the possibility that emotional labor may be considered part and parcel of core service delivery in such contexts, compared to others where emotional labor is extra-role, or above and beyond core task performance. Although these alternative results are based on initial evidence, they open the door to another possible scenario if scholars also focus on emotionally marked services that are quite significant in the lives of service users and that pursue social ends related to counteracting vulnerability. In these types of services, emotions may have a more prominent role, not only in predicting customers' satisfaction, but also in their interaction with the core service performance by employees.

The Active Role of the Customer

There is emergent empirical evidence that attributes an active role to the customer in participating in the quality of the service encounter. Congruent with a service co-creation approach (Vargo & Lusch, 2004), the customer is increasingly recognized as a participant who contributes to the evolution of the service encounter. In the following paragraphs, I review mechanisms and outcomes that have been examined from this perspective.

Some research efforts have focused on understanding customers' displays of negative emotions and how they affect employees. Dallimore et al. (2007) investigated the impact of angry customers in complaining situations on both the facial expressions and the negative affective states of service providers. To do so, they considered the mimicry and feedback steps of primitive emotional contagion. Regarding mimicry, Dallimore et al. proposed that facial expressions of angry customers are spontaneously imitated by service providers. To examine feedback, they hypothesized that employees' exposure to angry customers increases their negative affective states. Dallimore et al. (2007) confirmed both steps in a service encounter scenario using a role-play-based experimental design.

Although emotional contagion is pervasive, the requirements of service encounters limit the employee's visible emotional expression. Employees are frequently forced to regulate emotions and avoid an automatic flow from customer displays of negative emotions to employee expressions of negative emotions. In fact, there is an asymmetry between customers and employees. Customers can express negative emotions directed to employees. However, displaying negative emotions is not an option for employees (Tan, Foo, & Kwek, 2004) because they are usually required to express positive emotions and suppress negative ones in order to achieve customer satisfaction and loyalty as critical organizational goals. Nevertheless, customers can influence employee reactions to this job demand. It is likely that customer expressions of negative emotions reduce employees' display of required positive emotions over time. Tsai and Chen (2017) referred to the *personal depletion of resources* (Hobfoll, 1998) to explain this effect. Dealing with customers' negative emotions provokes a potential depletion of employees' personal resources and, consequently, a reduction in their expression of positive emotions over time. Tsai and Chen (2017) found support for this argument in a study in post offices where each employee had to face several successive service encounters. In addition, because the supervisor is an important source of resources for the employee, Tsai and Chen (2017) also confirmed that instrumental supervisory support (tangible help from the supervisor, such as support for problem solving at work) mitigates the negative impact of customer displays of negative emotions on employee expressions of positive emotions.

Gabriel and Diefendorff (2015) investigated changes in employees' emotional responses and regulation as a consequence of customer (in)civility within episodes of service encounters. To do so, they manipulated customer (in)civility in a call center simulation. Gabriel and Diefendorff (2015) argued that the employee is motivated to enhance customer satisfaction. Employees are not expected to express negative emotions in their interactions with customers, even though their felt emotions might be negative. Gabriel and Diefendorff referred to the *self-regulatory process* to describe the effort employees make within each service encounter to regulate their own emotions and behaviors in order to satisfy the customer. Gabriel and Diefendorff (2015) confirmed the self-regulatory process. They observed that customer incivility increases employees' negative affective state, which in turn increases regulation efforts (surface and deep acting). This regulation has the objective of maintaining the appropriate vocal tone in the interaction with the customer. Although employees' felt negative emotions affected the quality of their vocal tone, Gabriel and Diefendorff (2015) also found much less variability in vocal tone than in the other measures (felt emotion and emotion regulation), indicating a self-regulation effort oriented toward satisfying the customer.

Research has also been interested in customers' displays of positive emotions and their benefits. Based on self-regulatory theory, Gabriel and Diefendorff (2015) observed that customer civility reduces employees' regulation efforts (deep and surface acting). Similarly, in service encounters in hairstyling salons, Medler-Liraz (2016) found a significant negative relationship between customer displays of positive emotions and deep acting by employees. Therefore, when customers express positive emotions, it is likely that employees can reduce their regulation efforts (the happy customer goal is achieved) and conserve their personal resources. Medler-Liraz (2016) also confirmed other benefits: customer displays of positive emotions were related to loyalty through a positive rapport between the customer and the employee.

Beyond the impact of customer displays of emotions on employee responses and other outcomes (e.g. loyalty), some studies have proposed and tested interrelations between employees and customers, thus providing a more complete view of the service encounter. These studies are based on principles of *social exchange approaches* (e.g. Blau, 1964) and *reciprocity norms* (Gouldner, 1960). Generally speaking, it is assumed that emotions are a central feature of the social exchange. When one of the parties in the service encounter expresses positive emotions, the other party feels compelled to reciprocate. Kim and Yoon (2012) proposed and confirmed an emotional feedback cycle in clothing and accessory stores, finding that employees' displays of positive emotions are connected to customers' expressions of positive emotions. Emotional displays by customers, in turn, are related to employees' moods in a feedback loop that emphasizes emotional social exchanges between employees and customers. Similarly, Zablah, Carlson, Donavan, Maxham, and Brown (2016) observed reciprocal relationships between employee and customer satisfaction in a sample of retail stores. Finally, Molan, Martínez-Tur, Peñarroja, Moliner, and Gracia (2018) tested an intervention in organizations for individuals with intellectual disability. Employees in the experimental condition received positive feedback from customers about the emotional aspects, such as authenticity and empathy, of their previous service performance (T1). Compared to the employees in the control group, the experimental group improved their self-efficacy in terms of emotional service performance three months after receiving the positive feedback from customers (T2).

In sum, research has demonstrated that customers' expressions of emotions have an influence on employees through emotional contagion, depletion or conservation of resources, and self-regulation of emotions. In addition, there are mutual relationships between employees and customers, based on social exchanges and reciprocity, where emotional aspects are central features.

Conclusions and Future Research

One of the areas where research has made relevant progress in the study of service encounters is the delimitation of mechanisms linking employees' displays of emotions to customers' responses. Although customers are automatically influenced by employees' emotions (contagion), they are also able to process information and interpret emotions as part of the required service performance. It is likely that future research will investigate this issue further. For example, disconfirmation of expectations is a critical construct in customer responses to service delivery (e.g. Ludwig, Heidenreich, Kraemer, & Gouthier, 2017). When employees' displays of emotions meet customer expectations, customer processing is likely to be more automatic. By contrast, it is reasonable to expect that surprises would stimulate conscious processing. It is possible that customers' efforts are especially important in negative surprises, which have greater effects than positive ones (Baumeister, Bratslavsky, & Finkenauer 2001; Martínez-Tur, González, Juan, Molina, & Peñarroja, 2018). Nevertheless, positive surprises and emotional attachment seem necessary to achieve very positive customer experiences such as delight (Oliver, Rust, & Varki, 1997) and engagement (Kumar, Rajan, Gupta, & Dalla Pozza, 2019). There is a tradition of investigating the role of customers' experienced emotions in complaints (e.g. Lastner, Folse, Mangus, & Fenell, 2016) and delight (e.g. Kumar, Olshavsky, & King, 2001). However, future research could investigate how employees' displays of emotions contribute to managing negative customer surprises (e.g. complaints), and promote delight (see Beauchamp & Barnes, 2015). For instance, it is interesting to examine whether unexpected positive emotions displayed by employees can help to recover unhappy customers or achieve delighted customers by enhancing customer experiences such as self-esteem (Torres & Ronzoni, 2018).

Research about moderators has also improved our knowledge. Regarding the context, busyness plays a relevant role (Grandey et al., 2005; 2011). Individual differences are moderators as well. Customers' ways of reacting to employees' emotional displays depends on their capacity to detect emotions (Brach et al., 2015; Groth et al., 2009) and their motivation to understand the context accurately (epistemic motivation) (Wang et al., 2017). In addition, I have emphasized the possible moderation of the type of service. Despite the well-known differentiation between short-term vs. extended complex services (Guo et al., 2016; Gutek et al., 1999; Hulsheger & Schewe, 2011), research on displaying emotions in service encounters has mainly focused on short-term interactions with specific commercial objectives and low implications for the lives of the customers. The consideration of other radically different services in terms of goals (designed to counterbalance vulnerability, with high significance for the lives of service users and strong emotional content) makes it possible to explore other outcomes (e.g. customer quality of life) and to reconsider the importance of emotional aspects in service delivery (Molina et al., 2015). Finally, a potential and relevant moderator is technology (see Rafaeli et al., 2017). There are service encounters where the interaction with customers is increasingly performed by machines and different types of technologies, with a possible impact on emotion displays and customer satisfaction. Investigating the influence of technology and artificial intelligence on service encounters seems to be a promising avenue for research. Therefore, type of service, technology, and other moderators can be considered relevant boundary conditions with significant implications for research. In fact, according to the contextualist approach to knowledge (McGuire, 1983), progress in science is especially based on the identification of contexts and conditions where hypotheses are confirmed (or not), and phenomena are observed (or not). Greater efforts to identify boundary conditions will enrich our knowledge about service encounters.

Traditionally, investigation on service encounters has concentrated on how employees' displays of emotions impact customers' responses. The customer is conceived as a passive recipient. Fortunately, some emergent literature highlights the active role of the customer in the progression of the service encounter. The assumption that the customer is a co-creator who is able to influence service providers and contribute to the definition of the service is increasingly accepted, shedding light on some relevant aspects of the service encounter. The research on how customer and employee emotions interrelate via social exchanges and reciprocity is especially noteworthy (e.g. Kim & Yoon, 2012). This approach provides a richer and more complete view of the service encounter. Despite these efforts, more research is needed. Spirals can be proposed and tested (see Groth & Grandey, 2012), where interrelations between employees and customers occur through successive interactions, describing mutual influence over time. Statistical techniques, such as modeling change with latent growth curves (e.g. Pitariu & Ployhart, 2010), could help to examine the evolution and interrelation of responses of both employees and customers. Another area to be examined has to do with the possible positive effects of customers' displays of emotions on employees, beyond positive affect and job satisfaction. For instance, in services oriented toward counterbalancing vulnerability and improving the quality of life of service users, the observation of customer reactions could have, despite the difficulties, a positive influence on employees' felt accomplishment and personal growth (Hensel, Hensel, & Dewa, 2015).

Closing Thoughts

Research on expression of emotions has made relevant contributions to the literature on service encounters. However, overcoming some biases will allow additional progress in this area, beyond advances within the predominant model that focuses on how employees' emotional displays impact customer responses and outcomes. The service co-creation approach should definitely promote research where the customer is increasingly conceived of as an active participant, thus offering a richer portrait of the service encounter. In addition, scholars could expand the types of services considered in empirical research on displaying emotions in service encounters. Short service encounters with specific financial goals are very relevant in today's societies. Nevertheless, considering services where the main goal is social (counterbalancing vulnerability), rather than commercial, could open the door to new views and opportunities to understand the service encounter and its outcomes.

References

Barger, P. B., & Grandey, A. A. (2006). Service with a smile and encounter satisfaction: Emotional contagion and appraisal mechanisms. *Academy of Management Journal*, *49*, 1229–1238.

Baumeister, R. F., Bratslavsky, E., Finkenauer, C., & Vohs, K. D. (2001). Bad is stronger than good. *Review of General Psychology*, *5*, 323–370.

Beauchamp, M. B., & Barnes, D. C. (2015). Delighting baby boomers and millennials: Factors that matter most. *Journal of Marketing Theory and Practice*, *23*, 338–350.

Blau, P. M. (1964). *Exchange and power in social life.* New York, NY: Wiley.

Brach, S., Walsh, G., Hennig-Thurau, T., & Groth, M. (2015). A dyadic model of customer orientation: Mediation and moderation effects. *British Journal of Management*, *26*, 292–309.

Dallimore, K. S., Sparks, B. A., & Butcher, K. (2007). The influence of angry customer outbursts on service providers' facial displays and affective states. *Journal of Service Research*, *10*, 78–92.

Daus, C. S., & Ashkanasy, N. M. (2005). The case for the ability-based model of emotional intelligence in organizational behavior. *Journal of Organizational Behavior*, *26*, 453–466.

Diefendorff, J. M., & Greguras, G. J. (2009). Contextualizing emotional display rules: Examining the roles of targets and discrete emotions in shaping display rule perceptions. *Journal of Management*, *35*, 880–898.

Diefendorff, J. M., Morehart, J., & Gabriel, A. S. (2010). The influence of power and solidarity on emotional display rules at work. *Motivation and Emotion*, *34*, 120–132.

Ekman, P. (1994). Moods, emotions and traits. In P. Ekman & R. J. Davidson (Eds.), *The nature of emotion* (pp. 56–58). New York, NY: Oxford University Press.

Ekman, P., & Friesen, W. V. (1982). Felt, false, and miserable smiles. *Journal of Nonverbal Behavior, 6*, 238–252.

Elfenbein, H. A., Marsh, A. A., & Ambady, N. (2002). Emotional intelligence and the recognition of emotion from facial expressions. In L. Feldman Barrett & P. Salovey (Eds.), *The wisdom in feeling: Psychological processes in emotional intelligence* (pp. 37–59). New York, NY: Guilford.

Forgas, J. P. (1995). Mood and judgment: The affect infusion model (AIM). *Psychological Bulletin, 117*, 39–66.

Gabriel, A. S., Acosta, J. D., & Grandey, A. A. (2015). The value of a smile: Does emotional performance matter more in familiar or unfamiliar exchanges? *Journal of Business and Psychology, 30*, 37–50.

Gabriel, A. S., & Diefendorff, J. M. (2015). Emotional labor dynamics: A momentary approach. *Academy of Management Journal, 58*, 1804–1825.

Gouldner, A. W. (1960). The norm of reciprocity: A preliminary statement. *American Sociological Review, 25*, 161–178.

Grandey, A. A., Fisk, G. M., Mattila, A. S., Jansen, K. J., & Sideman, L. A. (2005). Is "service with a smile" enough? Authenticity of positive displays during service encounters. *Organizational Behavior and Human Decision Processes, 96*, 38–55.

Grandey, A. A., Goldberg, L. S., & Pugh, S. D. (2011). Why and when do stores with satisfied employees have satisfied customers? The roles of responsiveness and store busyness. *Journal of Service Research, 14*, 397–409.

Grandey, A. A., Rafaeli, A., Ravid, S., Wirtz, J., & Steiner, D. (2010). Emotion display rules at work in the global service economy: The special case of the customer. *Journal of Service Management, 21*, 388–412.

Groth, M., & Grandey, A. A. (2015). From bad to worse: Negative exchange spirals in employee–customer service interactions. *Organizational Psychology Review, 2*, 208–233.

Groth, M., Hennig-Thurau, T., & Walsh, G. (2009). Customer reactions to emotional labor: The roles of employee acting strategies and customer detection accuracy. *Academy of Management Journal, 52*, 958–974.

Guo, L., Chen, C., & Xu, H. (2016). Forging relationships to coproduce: A consumer commitment model in an extended service encounter. *Journal of Retailing and Consumer Services, 31*, 380–388.

Gutek, B. A., Bhappu, A. D., Liao-Troth, M. A., & Cherry, B. (1999). Distinguishing between service relationships and encounters. *Journal of Applied Psychology, 84*, 218–233.

Hatfield, E., Cacioppo, J., & Rapson, R. L. (1994). *Emotional contagion*. New York, NY: Cambridge University Press.

Hatfield, E., Rapson, R. L., & Le, Y. C. L. (2009). Emotional contagion and empathy. In J. Decety & W. Ickes (Eds.), *The social neuroscience of empathy* (pp. 19–30). Boston, MA: MIT Press.

Hennig-Thurau, T., Groth, M., Paul, M., & Gremler, D. D. (2006). Are all smiles created equal? How emotional contagion and emotional labor affect service relationships. *Journal of Marketing, 70*, 58–73.

Hensel, J. M., Hensel, R. A., & Dewa, C. S. (2015). What motivates direct support providers to do the work they do? *Journal of Intellectual & Developmental Disability, 40*, 297–303.

Hobfoll, S. E. (1998). *Stress, culture, and community*. New York, NY: Plenum.

Hulsheger, U. R, & Schewe, A. F. (2011). On the costs and benefits of emotional labor: A meta-analysis of three decades of research. *Journal of Occupational Health Psychology, 16*, 361–389.

Kim, E., & Yoon, D. J. (2012). Why does service with a smile make employees happy? A social interaction model. *Journal of Applied Psychology, 97*, 1059–1067.

Kumar, A., Olshavsky, R. W., & King, M. F. (2001). Exploring alternative antecedents of customer delight. *Journal of Consumer Satisfaction, Dissatisfaction and Complaining Behavior, 14*, 14–27.

Kumar, V., Rajan, B., Gupta, S., & Dalla Pozza, I. (2019). Customer engagement in service. *Journal of the Academy of Marketing Science, 47*, 138–160.

Lastner, M. M., Folse, J. A. G., Mangus, S. M., & Fennell, P. (2016). The road to recovery: Overcoming service failures through positive emotions. *Journal of Business Research, 69*, 4278–4286.

Ludwig, N. L., Heidenreich, S., Kraemer, T., & Gouthier, M. (2017). Customer delight: Universal remedy or a double-edged sword? *Journal of Service Theory and Practice, 27*, 23–46.

Martínez-Tur, V., Estreder, Y., Moliner, C., García-Buades, E., Ramos, J., & Peiró, J. M. (2017). Linking employees' extra-role efforts to customer satisfaction. *Social Psychology, 48*, 104–112.

Martínez-Tur, V., Estreder, Y., Tomás, I., Ramos, J., & Luque, O. (2018). Interaction between functional and relational service quality: Hierarchy vs. compensation. *Service Industries Journal*, doi:10.1080/02642069.2018.1492562

Martínez-Tur, V., González, P., Juan, A., Molina, A., & Peñarroja, V. (2018). Bad news and quality reputation among users of public services. *Journal of Work and Organizational Psychology, 34*, 95–101.

Matsumoto, D. (1990). Cultural similarities and differences in display rules. *Motivation and Emotion, 14*, 195–214.

McGuire, W. J. (1983). A contextualist theory of knowledge: Its implications for innovation and reforms in psychological research. In L. Berkowitz (Ed.), *Advances in experimental social psychology* (pp. 1–47). Orlando, FL: Academic.

Medler-Liraz, H. (2016). The role of service relationships in employees' and customers' emotional behavior, and customer-related outcomes. *Journal of Services Marketing, 30*, 437–448.

Molan, I., Martínez-Tur, V., Peñarroja, V., Moliner, C., & Gracia, E. (2018). Survey feedback improves service quality perceptions among employees of an NGO: An organizational-level positive intervention. *European Journal of Work and Organizational Psychology, 27*, 235–246.

Molina, A., Moliner, C., Martínez-Tur, V., Cropanzano, R., & Peiró, J. M. (2015). Unit-level fairness and quality within the health care industry: A justice–quality model. *European Journal of Work and Organizational Psychology, 24*, 627–644.

Oliver, R. L., Rust, R. T., & Varki, S. (1997). Customer delight: Foundations, findings, and managerial insight. *Journal of Retailing, 73*, 311–336.

Pitariu, A. H., & Ployhart, R. E. (2010). Explaining change: Theorizing and testing dynamic mediated longitudinal relationships. *Journal of Management, 36*, 405–429.

Pugh, S. D. (2001). Service with a smile: Emotional contagion in the service encounter. *Academy of Management Journal, 44*, 1018–1027.

Rafaeli, A., Altman, D., Gremler, D. D., Huang, M. H., Grewal, D., Iyer, B., Parasuraman, A., & de Ruyter, K. (2017). The future of frontline research: Invited commentaries. *Journal of Service Management, 20*, 91–99.

Rafaeli, A., & Sutton, R. I. (1987). Expression of emotion as part of the work role. *Academy of Management Review, 12*, 23–37.

Rafaeli, A., & Sutton, R. I. (1989). The expression of emotion in organizational life. *Research in Organizational Behavior, 11*, 1–42.

Ramachandra, V., Depalma, N., & Lisiewski, S. (2009) The role of mirror neurons in processing vocal emotions: Evidence from psychophysiological data. *International Journal of Neuroscience, 119*, 681–691.

Ravid, S., Rafaeli, A., & Grandey, A. A. (2010). Expressions of anger in Israeli workplaces: The special place of customer interactions. *Human Resource Management Review, 20*, 224–234.

Söderlund, M., & Rosengren, S. (2010). The happy versus unhappy service worker in the service encounter: Assessing the impact on customer satisfaction. *Journal of Retailing and Consumer Services, 17*, 161–169.

Tan, H. H., Foo, M. D., & Kwek, M. H. (2004). The effects of customer personality traits on the display of positive emotions. *Academy of Management Journal, 47*, 287–296.

Torres, E. N., & Ronzoni, G. (2018). The evolution of the customer delight construct: Prior research, current measurement, and directions for future research. *International Journal of Contemporary Hospitality Management, 30*, 57–75.

Tsai, W. C. (2001). Determinants and consequences of employee displayed positive emotions. *Journal of Management*, *27*, 497–512.

Tsai, W. C., & Chen, H. Y. (2017). A multilevel investigation of antecedents of employee positive affective displays: The roles of customer negative affective displays and employee perceived supervisory support. *European Journal of Work and Organizational Psychology*, *26*, 385–398.

Tsai, W. C., & Huang, Y. M. (2002). Mechanisms linking employee affective delivery and customer behavioral intentions. *Journal of Applied Psychology*, *87*, 1001–1008.

United Nations (2018). *Trade in services and employment*. Geneva, Switzerland: United Nations.

Van Kleef, G. A., De Dreu, C. K., & Manstead, A. S. (2004). The interpersonal effects of emotions in negotiations: A motivated information processing approach. *Journal of Personality and Social Psychology*, *87*, 510–528.

Vargo, S. L., & Lusch, R. F. (2004). Service-dominant logic: Continuing the evolution. *Journal of the Academy of Marketing Science*, *36*, 1–10.

Wang, Z., Singh, S. N., Li, Y. J., Mishra, S., Ambrose, M., & Biernat, M. (2017). Effects of employees' positive affective displays on customer loyalty intentions: An emotions-as-social-information perspective. *Academy of Management Journal*, *60*, 109–129.

Zablah, A. R., Carlson, B. D., Donavan, D. T., Maxham, J. G., & Brown, T. J. (2016). A cross-lagged test of the association between customer satisfaction and employee job satisfaction in a relational context. *Journal of Applied Psychology*, *101*, 743–755.

22 Emotion Work and Emotion Management

Dieter Zapf, M. Esther García-Buades, and Silvia Ortiz-Bonnin

The Concept of Emotion Work

The concept of emotional labor or emotion work, first introduced by Hochschild (1983), has received enormous attention among researchers in recent decades (e.g. Grandey, 2000; Grandey & Gabriel, 2015; Holman, Martínez-Iñigo, & Totterdell, 2008; Hülsheger & Schewe, 2011; Rafaeli & Sutton, 1987; Zapf, 2002). It refers to emotional job requirements that service employees are exposed to when interacting with customers or clients. Social interaction with customers is one of the core aspects of service work. Here, as in any social interaction, requirements about regulating one's emotions play a central role. Hochschild (1983), who coined the term "emotional labor" for this requirement, investigated the work of flight attendants and demonstrated that a substantial part of the job involved dealing with passengers and their emotions, and that displaying emotions that were not felt had a negative effect on both the health and the performance of service providers. As this finding was of high theoretical and practical importance, it stimulated research in the field.

In this chapter we start with a discussion of Hochschild's differentiation between emotional labor and emotion work or emotion management. We then describe models of emotion work with a focus on a job requirements approach. To put positive and negative effects of emotion work into a theoretical context we apply concepts related to job stressors and resources and the challenge–hindrance stressor framework to emotion work. Finally, we discuss the application of the emotion work concept to social interaction within organizations.

Emotional labor or emotion work (Zapf, 2002) is an important aspect of service interactions. Its core is the expression of appropriate emotions during face-to-face or voice-to-voice interactions. Probably nobody would expect service employees to always have organizationally desired emotions. Rather, they may encounter situations eliciting usually undesired negative emotions such as anger, fear, or disappointment. Emotion work as part of the job, however, implies the display of organizationally desired emotions even in such unpleasant situations. Accordingly, emotion work can be defined as the psychological processes necessary to regulate organizationally desired emotions as part of one's job (Grandey, 2000; Hochschild, 1983; Rafaeli & Sutton, 1987; Zapf, 2002).

In the literature, there is a terminological debate over the use of the terms "emotion work" and "emotional labor" (Callahan & McCollum, 2002; McClure & Murphy, 2007). Both terms go back to Hochschild's (1983, p. 7, footnote) seminal book:

> I use the term emotional labor to mean the management of feeling to create a publicly observable facial and bodily display; emotional labor is sold for a wage and therefore has exchange value. I use the synonymous terms emotion work or emotion management to refer to the same acts done in a private context where they have use value.

Hochschild pointed out that psychological processes are obviously the same for paid and unpaid interactions. Therefore, from a psychological perspective there is little reason to use different terms here. However, a number of problems arise with Hochschild's differentiation.

First, one might wonder whether self-employed work comprises emotional labor or emotion work. Moreover, in many jobs, work and private life are sometimes difficult to distinguish. For some professions, researchers argue that dealing with emotions cannot be reduced to regulating emotions for a wage, as in the case of nursing, because these emotions would be shown anyway as they are intrinsic to a profession that cares for people and are a reflection of the workers' core caring values (McClure & Murphy, 2007). This is so because regulating one's emotions is not necessarily a response to a display rule. People in organizations have multiple motives rather than the single motive of conforming to role expectations (e.g. Bolton, 2005; Niven, 2016; von Gilsa, Zapf, Ohly, Trumpold, & Machowski, 2014). Employees hide and display emotions for various reasons, e.g. to make a competent impression or not to endanger a social relation (e.g. Glasø, Ekerholt, Barman, & Einarsen, 2006; Totterdell & Holman, 2003; von Gilsa et al., 2014). Hochschild's (1983) approach implies that if there is an employment contract and if labor power is sold, then everything the worker does during work time is paid work. From this perspective, it is impossible to do customers a personal favor and smile at them without it appearing to be a paid activity. According to Hochschild's model, there is no room for personal motives. Bolton (2005), among others, questioned this approach and suggested various motives for doing emotion management at work, such as the philanthropic motive to regulate one's own emotions as a "gift" to the interaction partner.

For our work, we prefer the term "emotion work" in the sense described above because it best parallels concepts such as mental or physical work and because it circumvents the issue of paid work.

Moreover, Hochschild (1983) suggested using "emotion work" and "emotion management" synonymously. Williams (2007, p. 569, footnote) noted that emotion management is used interchangeably with emotion regulation and both terms refer to the same phenomenon. While "emotion regulation" is the preferred term in psychological literature, "emotion management" is used more often in sociology, organization theory, and management science. If "emotion management" is used in the sense of "emotion regulation," it cannot be equated with emotion work because this concept is broader and covers emotion-work-related job characteristics.

Models of Emotion Work

Several authors have proposed that emotion work can be studied from different perspectives (Brotheridge & Grandey, 2002; Zapf, 2002). Zapf, Semmer, & Johnson (2014) differentiated between the emotion work process and emotion work requirements (see Figure 22.1).

The Emotion Work Process

This describes what people are doing when they carry out emotion work. It refers to the *emotion regulation* or *emotion management strategies* used to display emotions that correspond to the display rules of an organization. Four emotion regulation strategies are typically considered in the literature: surface acting, deep acting, automatic emotion regulation, and emotional deviance.

Surface acting implies that an emotion is displayed to the outside in mimicry, gestures, and voice, while inwardly no – or other – emotions are felt. When *deep acting*, employees attempt to modify their inner emotions by various methods in order to actually feel the required emotions (Hochschild, 1983).

Another way to regulate emotions is *automatic emotion regulation* (Zapf, 2002). Hochschild (1983) called this strategy *passive deep acting;* others have called it *genuine* (Ashforth & Humphrey, 1993) or *naturally felt emotions*

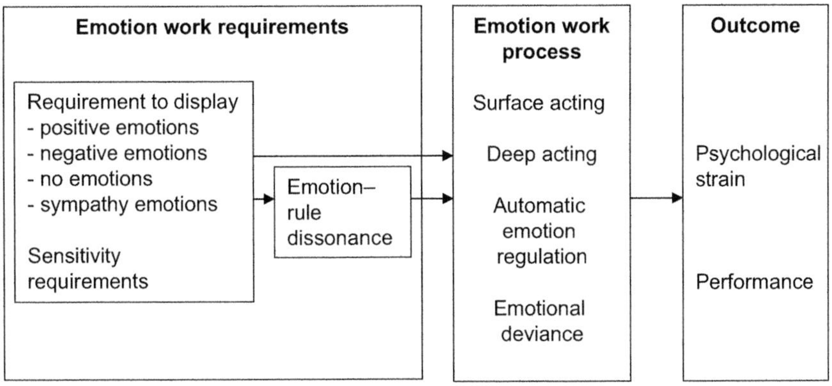

Figure 22.1 Model of emotion work (from Zapf, Semmer & Johnson, 2014, p. 159)

(Diefendorff, Croyle, & Gosserand, 2005). Here the required emotion is actually felt. The regulation of inner feelings as well as gestures and facial expressions takes place in an automatic mode. Therefore, this strategy does not require much effort. This is not the case with the other strategies.

Emotional deviance (Rafaeli & Sutton, 1987) implies not meeting the emotional requirements, so the emotion expected by the organization is not shown. This can happen either because the person is unable to do so (e.g. because the person is too exhausted after too many hours of work) or because they do not want to (e.g. a receptionist who refuses to be friendly to an intrusive guest). Overall, emotional deviance is not widely used (Tschan, Rochat, & Zapf, 2005) because most people want to do a good job and not show emotions other than the required ones for a good reason.

Emotion regulation and emotion management have been referred to as managing one's own emotions, but also to managing the emotions of others, e.g. the emotion of a team (Little, Gooty, & Williams, 2016). Emotion work in general is assumed to have an impact on the interaction partner (Ashford & Humphrey, 1993). In particular, it is assumed that service employees' display of positive emotions and the authenticity of their emotion display affect customers' emotional states through emotional contagion (e.g. Hennig-Thurau, Groth, Paul, & Gremler, 2006). However, there are also studies on how, for example, leaders can directly influence subordinates' emotions by using the same strategies they would use to regulate their own emotions (Little et al., 2016). "Emotion management" may be the preferred term for managing emotions of others.

The Job Characteristics Approach: Emotional Job Requirements

The other approach is the job characteristics approach: this looks at the situational requirements one is exposed to when doing emotion work. "Perceived positive or negative display rules" is the term often used to describe emotional job requirements (e.g. Brotheridge & Grandey, 2002; Kammeyer-Mueller et al., 2013). At least three aspects are important to explain why an emotional job requirement has an effect on health and performance.

First, is there a display rule? *Emotional display rules* are an important ingredient of emotional job requirements. They prescribe which emotions employees have to express according to company goals and policies to contribute to organizational benefits (e.g. Pugh, Diefendorff, & Moran, 2013). In some organizations, e.g. airlines, display rules are explicit and communicated during training. In others, no explicit rules exist but implicit rules are part of the organizational culture (Rafaeli & Sutton, 1987).

Second, is there organizational and personal commitment to the display rule? A display rule alone tells us little. If there is a strict display rule but nobody cares, then little emotion work is done. Therefore, *commitment to the display rule* – which is defined as "a person's intention to extend effort toward displaying organizationally desired emotions, persist in displaying these emotions over time, and not abandon the display rules under difficult conditions" (Gosserand & Diefendorff, 2005, p. 1257) – is of importance.

Finally, third, how often do these display rules direct behavior? The *frequency and kind of interaction with customers* determines how often emotion regulation has to take place in order to conform to display rules.

Most studies on emotion work focus on emotion regulation strategies. In comparison, the job characteristics approach has received less attention. In the literature, job characteristics referring to emotion work have been operationalized in different ways[1]. Morris and Feldman (1996) suggested four dimensions of emotional labor: first, the frequency of emotional display, operationalized by total interaction time with customers; second, attentiveness to display rules, operationalized by the duration of the interaction with customers and intensity of the emotional display; third, the variety of emotions to be expressed; and fourth, emotional dissonance, which is the "conflict between genuinely felt emotions and emotions required to be displayed" (Morris & Feldman, 1996, p. 992).

The Emotional Labor Scale (ELS) of Brotheridge & Lee (2003) measures the frequency of emotion display without qualifying the emotions that have to be displayed. Other studies consider types of emotion, especially the *requirement to display positive emotions* and their effects on employees (e.g. Diefendorff & Richard, 2003; Kammeyer-Mueller et al., 2013; Zapf, Vogt, Seifert, Mertini, & Isic, 1999). This is so because pleasant emotions must be shown in most service jobs (Rafaeli & Sutton, 1987). The requirement to display negative emotions is less studied. However, these types of emotions may be an organizational demand too. An often-cited example for the *requirement to display negative emotions* is Sutton's (1991) study on bill collectors, who usually have to display anger or irritability in an effort to gain debtor compliance. The Frankfurt Emotion Work Scales (Zapf et al., 1999) comprise a scale to measure the requirement to display negative emotions. Not suprisingly, the requirement to display negative emotions is less frequent than the requirement to display positive emotions (Zapf et al., 1999).

Emotion work is more than just the requirement to express emotions; it is a more complex concept that also includes the requirement to be sensitive to customers' or patients' emotions. This follows from looking at service interactions from a communication perspective. Communication models (e.g. Watzlawick, Beavin, & Jackson, 1967) assume that in a communication process there is a sender and a receiver of information. Sender and receiver develop a particular relationship in which the expression and perception of emotions play a substantial role (cf. Hareli & Rafaeli, 2008). This corresponds to models on emotional intelligence comprising competences to express *and* to perceive emotions (Salovey & Mayer, 1990). Hotel employees, for instance, are required to identify customer's emotions and adapt their behavior to customer moods in order to have more satisfied and loyal customers (Ortiz-Bonnin, García-Buades, Caballer, & Zapf, in press). There are hardly any social interactions in which appropriate emotions can be shown without knowing how the interaction partner feels. *Sensitivity*

[1] The term "emotional demands" has been used in the context of emotional labor (e.g. Brotheridge & Lee, 2002). However, "emotional demands" is also used in a broad sense, referring to a variety of stressful situations not necessarily equivalent to the emotion work concept (e.g. Le Blanc, Bakker, Peeters, van Heesch, & Schaufeli, 2001).

requirements refer to the need to be sensitive and consider the emotions of the interaction partner (Zapf et al., 1999).

The requirement to display positive emotions is often complemented by a requirement to suppress negative emotions (e.g. Kammeyer-Mueller et al., 2013; Schaubroeck & Jones, 2000). A similar concept is the *dissonance* between the emotion display required by the organization and the emotion felt in a particular situation. Morris and Feldman (1996) called this "emotional dissonance." However, this has led to confusion in the literature. There are three elements that have to be differentiated: required emotions, felt emotions, and expressed emotions (Zerbe, 2000). Hochschild (1983) used "emotional dissonance" to describe the discrepancy between employees' inner feelings and the emotions expressed, whereas Morrison and Feldman (1996) used this term for the discrepancy between organizationally required emotions and felt emotions. The latter meaning of "emotional dissonance" may be considered a job characteristic, whereas Hochschild's use of the term describes an inner state occurring, for example, when using surface acting. To avoid confusion, Holman, Martínez-Iñigo, & Totterdell (2008) suggested using "emotion-rule dissonance," or "ER dissonance," to describe the incongruence between felt and required emotions. The classification of emotion-rule dissonance as a job characteristic is based on the assumption that an average person will not feel a positive emotion if the situation is usually related to negative emotions, e.g. when being exposed to aggressive behavior (see the affective events theory of Weiss & Cropanzano, 1996).

In short, the job characteristics approach includes the requirement to display emotions (positive, negative, or neutral), the requirement to be sensitive toward others' emotions, and emotion-rule dissonance and related concepts such as the requirement to suppress negative emotions.

Positive and Negative Effects of Emotion Work

The next question is how emotion work variables affect health and performance of service workers. Theories on stressors and resources at work (Bakker & Demerouti, 2014; Kahn & Byosiere, 1992) have been used to describe positive and negative outcomes. The term "job stressors" refers to those aspects of the job that evoke strain (Kahn & Byosiere, 1992). "Job resources" refers to "those physical, psychological, social, or organizational aspects of the job that either (1) reduce job demands and the associated physiological and psychological costs; (2) are functional in achieving work goals; or (3) stimulate personal growth, learning and development" (Schaufeli & Bakker, 2004, p. 296). That is, stressors are characterized by their negative effects, whereas resources are characterized by their positive ones. In recent years, the so-called challenge–hindrance stressor concept (Cavanaugh, Boswell, Roehling, & Boudreau, 2000; Podsakoff, LePine, & LePine, 2007) has received attention. This model contends that there are two types of job stressors: challenge stressors and hindrance stressors. Challenge stressors contain both stressful and challenging aspects because "they have associated potential gains for individuals" (Cavanaugh et al., 2000, p. 68). Challenges are positively related to motivation, performance, and well-being (Widmer, Semmer, Kälin, Jacobshagen, & Meier, 2012). Hindrance stressors tend to constrain or interfere with an individual's work achievement and "do not tend to be associated with potential gains for the individual" (Cavanaugh et al., 2000, p. 68). Hindrances impair motivation, performance, and well-being.

Combining the job demands–resources model with the challenge–hindrance stressor approach makes it possible to differentiate between (1) job characteristics that have only negative consequences: hindrance stressors are positively related to strain and are either unrelated or negatively related to well-being and performance; (2) job characteristics with both positive and negative effects: challenge stressors are positively related to strain and also positively related to well-being and performance; and (3) job characteristics with only positive effects: job resources are either unrelated or negatively related to strain and are positively related to well-being and performance (cf. Crawford, LePine, & Rich, 2010).

Kammeyer-Mueller et al. (2013) in their meta-analysis reported a zero correlation for the relationship between the requirement to display positive emotions and exhaustion, and positive correlations for job satisfaction (.11) and performance (.16). Studies using the positive emotions requirement scale of the Frankfurt Emotion Work Scales (e.g. Dormann & Kaiser, 2002; Zapf et al., 2001) often found positive correlations with emotional exhaustion, and also with personal accomplishment and job satisfaction. Similar patterns were found for the requirement to display sympathy emotions and for sensitivity requirements. These results suggest that we should consider emotion display requirements as challenge stressors with potentially both positive and negative effects on health and performance. Emotional job requirements have the potential to motivate employees to express display rules when interacting with customers, coworkers, and supervisors. Employees believe there is a positive relationship between expressing display rules and valued outcomes.

In the meta-analyses of Hülsheger and Schewe (2011) and Kammeyer-Mueller et al. (2013), emotion-rule dissonance was positively related to emotional exhaustion and other strain variables, and negatively related to well-being (personal accomplishment and job satisfaction) and performance (i.e. task performance). This qualifies emotion-rule dissonance as a hindrance stressor. According to Hülsheger and Schewe (2011) there is a dilemma: if employees show the required emotions, they might blame themselves and feel hypocritical (Hochschild, 1983); if employees do not display the required emotions (i.e. if they engage in emotional deviance) they will violate emotional display rules, which in turn leads to lower performance, negative supervisor evaluations, and negative influence on customer outcomes.

Emotion Work Within Organizations

Emotion is a key aspect of every social interaction occurring both at work and in other life domains. Social interaction at work happens with clients, but also with colleagues, supervisors, and subordinates. The next question is, therefore, whether employees are also expected to show organizationally desirable emotions at work when interacting with colleagues, supervisors, and subordinates, and not only toward clients.

Emotion work in this chapter is conceptualized as the act of displaying organizationally desired emotions as well as perceiving emotions during interpersonal interactions with customers (Morris & Feldman, 1996). Hochschild (1979) refers to Ervin Goffman (1959), who argued that social interactions in general are governed by social norms that lead us to control our emotions when interacting with others. Such general rules should apply to all interactions at work.

From an organizational perspective, there is a variety of reasons why employees should control their emotion display when interacting with supervisors, colleagues, or subordinates. Tschan et al. (2005) mention organizational norms and widely shared rules about interactions between colleagues, such as being friendly and polite, not criticizing each other in public, and maintaining a courteous and friendly attitude even with colleagues who are not liked. Socio-emotional competence, or emotional intelligence, is seen as an important prerequisite for many jobs. Ingredients of emotional intelligence are the abilities to adequately express one's emotions, to sense others' emotions, and to control one's own and others' emotions (Salovey & Mayer, 2010). Additionally, the ability to control one's own negative emotions is necessary for conflict management (Beitler, Scherer, & Zapf, 2018). As emotionally laden conflicts are negatively related to performance, controlling one's emotions becomes a job requirement. In the study of Wong, Tschan, Messerli, and Semmer (2013), the expression of authentic positive emotions in work interactions supported goal attainment. In contrast, amplifying positive emotions promoted goal attainment only in interactions with superiors, not with colleagues.

Many social situations in organizations require the observance of communication rules such as being friendly and supportive to colleagues, expressing disagreement constructively, controlling aggressiveness, and giving feedback in a socially adequate manner. In particular, the appropriate expression of negative emotions may become an organizational requirement as it may influence quality interaction between coworkers, as well as group processes and outcomes (Stephens & Carmeli, 2016).

Emotion management at work is also important to understand leadership. In a qualitative study, Glasø et al. (2006, p. 268) reported some leaders who said "that they were reluctant to reveal their inner feelings because they wished to avoid unpleasantness caused by possible reactions, confrontations or conflicts. Some of them felt that they actually needed to suppress their emotions in order to prevent their subordinates from becoming ill." Several recent studies of leadership include the examination of a leader's influence on the emotions of employees (Yukl, 2010), such as transformational leadership theory or the Leader–Member Exchange approach. Transformational leadership is described by four components: individual support, role modeling, inspirational motivation, and intellectual stimulation. These behaviors are associated with the presentation of emotions, and research shows that the transformational leadership style leads to employees focusing on sharing positive emotions (Chuang, Judge, & Liaw, 2012).

In summary, there are a lot of examples in the literature on organizational behavior concerning the importance of emotion management at work. Therefore, it makes sense to apply the emotion work concept to interactions within organizations as well.

Emotion Work in Client/Customer vs. Colleague/Supervisor Interactions

Relationships with colleagues differ in several ways from relationships with customers. Internal relationships (with colleagues and supervisors) tend to be more regular (daily interactions) and long-term, whereas external relationships (with clients) are often one-time interactions and short-term (Gutek, Bhappu, Liao-Troth, & Cherry, 1999). Certain concepts are relevant in understanding emotion work in internal vs. external relationships.

A first aspect concerns *display rules and emotion work control*. Studies on emotion work among coworkers show that the presence of a display rule is quite frequent in colleague interactions (Tschan et al., 2005). However, display rules may only occasionally be explicit for interactions within organizations. Rather, they may be implicit in the organizational and leadership culture of an organization (Humphrey, Pollack, & Hawver, 2008). *Emotion work control* refers to how closely employees have to follow display rules. Different studies suggest there is greater 'display latitude' (Kruml & Geddes, 2000) or that there are weaker display rules (Morris & Feldman 1996) in interactions with coworkers as compared to customer-related interactions. Grandey, Rafaeli, Ravid, Wirtz, and Steiner (2010, p. 406) suggested that "display rules to coworkers and supervisors may be more voluntary based on personal or social norms, while with customers they are based on work practices and compensation." In the diary study by Tschan et al. (2005), emotional dissonance was more often reported in interactions with clients, but emotional deviance (not displaying the required emotion) occurred more often in interactions with colleagues. By and large, studies show that less strict display rules exist for colleague interactions, and therefore rather unwanted feelings are sometimes expressed (Diefendorff & Greguras, 2009; Tschan et al., 2005).

A second aspect involves the *importance of relations, honesty, and the possibility of compensation*. Relationships with people within the organization are more important to the individual than relationships with clients, as interactions with colleagues are part of long-term relationships and based on long-term reciprocity (Gutek et al., 1999). Sustainable positive social relationships require the exchange of positive emotions. Therefore, rules concerning relationships contain a requirement to express positive emotions, but also to be honest, which implies the expectation to show true emotions (Argyle & Henderson, 1985).

There is evidence that internal relationships are more authentic, and subject to more deep acting than surface acting, than relationships with customers. Problems occur if negative emotions are felt. If the interaction partner realizes that emotions are faked, the intended effect of dissonant behavior may be reversed (Tschan et al., 2005). Therefore, more often than not, one may choose to express one's feelings honestly even if they are negative and the other is not necessarily pleased. Besides, given that working relationships with colleagues and supervisors are usually long-term, there are opportunities to make up for negative interactions. In contrast, many interactions with customers are single, short-term encounters (Gutek et al., 1999) where the first impression counts. Often, there is no chance to compensate for a bad first impression because a customer will never come back. Therefore, the requirement to display positive emotions may not differ, but the requirement to suppress negative emotions should be higher in service interactions. The findings of Diefendorff and Greguras (2009), Grandey et al. (2010), and Tschan et al. (2005) support this view.

A third aspect concerns *social status and power*. Research has shown that both status and power affect the acceptability of emotions. Status implies that someone is valued, has resources available, and often has the power to influence other's behaviors. Anger, which is one of the most frequently experienced negative emotions at work, is an emotion that, when expressed, signals the potential to harm others. Expressing anger is seen to be more acceptable if directed by high-status persons, e.g. supervisors, toward low-status targets, e.g. subordinates (Grandey et al., 2010). Therefore, employees are required to suppress negative emotions more in interactions with supervisors, and less in interactions with other colleagues of equal status and power.

With regard to customers or clients, service employees may be in a high- or low-status position depending on the occupation (Wilson, Zeithaml, Bitner & Gremler, 2012). Because of "the customer is always right" policies in sales businesses, customers are often seen as being in a more powerful position than sales personnel. This may be true in all cases where it is easy to go elsewhere when dissatisfied. Results of Grandey et al.'s (2010) study supported this view. Anger could be most expressed in interactions with coworkers, less so in interactions with supervisors, and least so with customers. On the other hand, felt happiness was found to be the most acceptable emotion to be expressed with coworkers (familiar/same-status target).

In human service work, however, service providers are often in a high-power position, e.g. physicians, teachers and professors, judges, and police officers. Zapf, Isic, Bechtoldt, and Blau (2003) compared service workers with human service workers. Human service workers reported a higher requirement to display negative emotions than service workers did, the difference being more than one standard deviation. One interpretation is that they are in a high-status position compared to their clients and more often believe that the expression of negative emotions such as anger is justified.

The Effects of Emotion Work among Colleagues on Well-Being and Performance

There is little research on the relationship between emotion work within organizations and its effects on health and performance. Available studies show effects similar to studies on customer interactions. Surface acting has been positively related to psychological strain (e.g. Hu & Shi, 2015; Ozcelik, 2013; Yue, Wang, & Groth, 2016) and negatively related to performance, authenticity, and satisfaction (e.g. Ozcelik, 2013; Yue et al., 2016). Regarding the positive effects of deep acting, Bozionelos (2016) found that emotion work toward colleagues related positively to job satisfaction in a sample of flight attendants.

In a meta-analysis, Mesmer-Magnus, DeChurch, and Wax (2012) compared effects of emotion work on various outcome variables directed at external targets (i.e. customers, patients) and at internal targets (coworkers, supervisors, etc). There were hardly any significant differences, although for some variables a tendency toward stronger effects could be observed for emotion work directed at external targets.

All in all, the effects for internal and customer relations do not differ much. One can assume that the advantages and disadvantages balance each other out. As for external relations with customers, there is less control with regard to display rules, and the expression of negative emotions is not desirable. Surface acting is an acceptable regulation strategy here. Internal relations are more meaningful and there is more control in regard to display rules. Honesty and authenticity are, therefore, more important in internal relations, and emotion suppression is less preferred.

Conclusions and Future Directions

Many workers today are required to express and control certain emotions as part of their job. This is addressed in theories on emotion work or emotional labor. In this chapter we have also described the job characteristics approach. From a job analysis and job design perspective (Semmer, 2006), it is important to know which aspects of the job have an effect on health and performance. Applying the job demands–resources model and the challenge–hindrance stressor model suggests that the requirement to display emotions may be considered a challenge stressor. This implies that both positive and negative effects on health and performance may be expected. Emotion-rule dissonance is a hindrance stressor, and negative health effects prevail here. Under certain circumstances, however, emotion-rule dissonance may also behave as a challenge stressor (Bakker & Sanz Vergel, 2013), as when faking or suppressing feelings is done on purpose and when this can be related to important personal goals. More research is needed in this regard to explore in which occupations and under what circumstances emotional job requirements behave as challenge or hindrance stressors: for example, by comparing social interactions that are either important or unimportant for achieving personal goals.

Applying the emotion work concept to interactions within organizations shows that there are similarities – the same emotion regulation strategies are used – but also differences. Interactions with supervisors, subordinates, and colleagues are usually more familiar and more important for employees than interactions with customers; they provide more control with regard to display rules. Social status and power play a role because the expression of negative emotions is perceived as more acceptable by high-status individuals (e.g. supervisors, service workers) than by low-status individuals (e.g. employees, patients). Compared to their customers, many service employees are in a low position of power although there are also service professions with high social status, such as physicians and police officers. Whereas few differences can be observed for the expression of positive emotions, most studies show that there is a higher expectation to suppress negative emotions when interacting with customers than when interacting with leaders and supervisors. However, the number of studies is still limited in this regard and more research is needed to understand similarities and differences of emotion work in internal (coworkers, supervisors) and external relations.

We would like to finish this chapter by highlighting the complex role of emotion work in understanding health and performance. From a work design perspective, one would try to support the positive effects and reduce the negative effects of emotion work (Semmer, 2006). Since emotion work requirements are considered challenge stressors with both positive and negative potential effects on health and performance, a simple reduction of emotion work would not be a solution. Rather, the meta-analytical results of Mesmer-Magnus et al. (2012) suggest creating more opportunities for displaying emotions that are actually felt (thus increasing the positive effects of emotion work), and reducing the number of cases where control and suppression of emotions is required.

References

Argyle, M., & Henderson, M. (1985). The rules of relationships. In S. Duck & D. Perlman (Eds.), *Understanding personal relationships* (pp. 63–84). London, UK: Sage.

Ashforth, B. E., & Humphrey, R. H. (1993). Emotional labor in service roles: The influence of identity. *Academy of Management Review, 18*, 88–115.

Bakker, A. B., & Demerouti, E. (2014). Job demands–resources theory. In P. Y. Chen & C. L. Cooper (Eds.), *Work and well-being* (pp. 1–28). Chichester, UK: Wiley. https://doi.org/10.1002/9781118539415.wbwell019

Bakker, A. B., & Sanz Vergel, A. I. (2013). Weekly work engagement and flourishing: The role of hindrance and challenge job demands. *Journal of Vocational Behavior, 83*, 397–409.

Beitler, L. A., Scherer, S., & Zapf, D. (2018). Interpersonal conflict at work: Age and emotional competence differences in conflict management. *Organizational Psychology Review, 8*, 195–227.

Bolton, S. C. (2005). "Making up" managers. *Work, Employment and Society, 19*, 5–23.

Brotheridge, C. M., & Grandey, A. A. (2002). Emotional labor and burnout: Comparing two perspectives of "people work." *Journal of Vocational Behavior, 60*, 17–39.

Brotheridge, C. M., & Lee, R. T. (2003). Development and validation of the Emotional Labour Scale. *Journal of Occupational and Organizational Psychology, 76*, 365–379.

Callahan, J. L., & McCollum, E. E. (2002). Conceptualizations of emotion research in organizational contexts. *Advances in Developing Human Resources, 4*, 4–21.

Cavanaugh, M. A., Boswell, W. R., Roehling, M. V., & Boudreau, J. W. (2000). An empirical examination of self-reported work stress among US managers. *Journal of Applied Psychology, 85*, 65–74.

Chuang, A., Judge, T. A., & Liaw, Y. J. (2012). Transformational leadership and customer service: A moderated mediation model of negative affectivity and emotion regulation. *European Journal of Work and Organizational Psychology, 21*, 28–56.

Côté, S. (2005). A social interaction model of the effects of emotion regulation on work strain. *Academy of Management Review, 30*, 509–530.

Crawford, E. R., LePine, J. A., & Rich, B. L. (2010). Linking job demands and resources to employee engagement and burnout: A theoretical extension and meta-analytic test. *Journal of Applied Psychology, 95*, 834–848.

Diefendorff, J. M., Croyle, M. H., & Gosserand, R. H. (2005). The dimensionality and antecedents of emotional labor strategies. *Journal of Vocational Behavior, 66*, 339–357.

Diefendorff, J. M., & Greguras, G. J. (2009). Contextualizing emotional display rules: Examining the roles of targets and discrete emotions in shaping display rule perceptions. *Journal of Management, 35*, 880–898.

Diefendorff, J., Morehart, J., & Gabriel, A. (2010). The influence of power and solidarity on emotional display rules at work. *Motivation and Emotion, 34*, 120–132.

Diefendorff, J. M., & Richard, E. M. (2003). Antecedents and consequences of emotional display rule perceptions. *Journal of Applied Psychology, 88*, 284–294.

Dimotakis, N., Scott, B. A., & Koopman, J. (2011). An experience sampling investigation of workplace interactions, affective states, and employee well-being. *Journal of Organizational Behavior, 32*, 572–588.

Dormann, C., & Kaiser, D. M. (2002). Job conditions and customer satisfaction. *European Journal of Work and Organizational Psychology, 11*, 257–283.

Glasø, L., Ekerholt, K., Barman, S., & Einarsen, S. (2006). The instrumentality of emotion in leader–subordinate relationships. *International Journal of Work Organisation and Emotion, 1*, 255–276.

Goffman, E. (1959). *The presentation of self in everyday life*. New York, NY: Doubleday Anchor.

Gosserand, R. H., & Diefendorff, J. M. (2005). Emotional display rules and emotional labor: The moderating role of commitment. *Journal of Applied Psychology, 90*, 1256–1264.

Grandey, A. A. (2000). Emotion regulation in the workplace: A new way to conceptualize emotional labor. *Journal of Occupational Health Psychology, 5*, 95–110.

Grandey, A. A., & Gabriel, A. S. (2015). Emotional labor at a crossroads: Where do we go from here? *Annual Review of Organizational Psychology and Organizational Behavior, 2*, 323–349.

Grandey, A., Rafaeli, A., Ravid, S., Wirtz, J., & Steiner, D. D. (2010). Emotion display rules at work in the global service economy: The special case of the customer. *Journal of Service Management, 21*, 388–412.

Gutek, B. A., Bhappu, A. D., Liao-Troth, M. A., & Cherry, B. (1999). Distinguishing between service relationships and service encounters. *Journal of Applied Psychology, 84*, 218–233.

Hareli, S., & Rafaeli, A. (2008). Emotion cycles: On the social influence of emotion in organizations. *Research in Organizational Behavior, 28*, 35–59.

Hennig-Thurau, T., Groth, M., Paul, M., & Gremler, D. D. (2006). Are all smiles created equal? How emotional contagion and emotional labor affect service relationships. *Journal of Marketing, 70*, 58–73.

Hochschild, A. (1983). *The managed heart: Commercialization of human feeling*. Berkeley: University of California Press.

Hoffmann, E. A. (2016). Emotions and emotional labor at worker-owned businesses: Deep acting, surface acting, and genuine emotions. *Sociological Quarterly, 57*, 152–173.

Holman, D., Martinez-Iñigo, D., & Totterdell, P. (2008). Emotional labour, well-being and performance. In C. L. Cooper & S. Cartwright (Eds.), *The Oxford handbook of organizational well-being* (pp. 331–355). Oxford, UK: Oxford University Press.

Hu, X., & Shi, J. (2015). Employees' surface acting in interactions with leaders and peers. *Journal of Organizational Behavior, 36*, 1132–1152.

Hülsheger, U. R., & Schewe, A. F. (2011). On the costs and benefits of emotional labor: A meta-analysis of three decades of research. *Journal of Occupational Health Psychology, 16*, 361–389.

Humphrey, R. H., Pollack, J. M., & Hawver, T. (2008). Leading with emotional labor. *Journal of Managerial Psychology, 23*, 151–168.

Kahn, R., & Byosiere, P. (1992). Stress in organizations. In M. D. Dunnette & L. M. Hough (Eds.), *Handbook of industrial and organizational psychology* (Volume 3, pp. 571–650). Palo Alto, CA: Consulting Psychologists.

Kammeyer-Mueller, J. D., Rubenstein, A. L., Long, D. M., Odio, M. A., Buckman, B. R., Zhang, Y., & Halvorsen-Ganepola, M. D. K. (2013). A meta-analytic structural model of dispositional affectivity and emotional labor. *Personnel Psychology, 66*, 47–90.

Kruml, S. M., & Geddes, D. (2000). Catching fire without burning out: Is there an ideal way to perform emotional labor? In N. M. Ashkanasy, C. E. J. Härtel, & W. J. Zerbe (Eds.), *Emotions in the workplace. Research, theory and practice* (pp. 177–188). Westport, CT: Quorum Books.

Le Blanc, P. M., Bakker, A. B., Peeters, M. C. W, Van Heesch, N. C. A., & Schaufeli, W. B. (2001). Emotional job demands and burnout among oncology care providers. *Anxiety, Stress & Coping, 14*, 243–263.

Little, L. M., Gooty, J., & Williams, M. (2016). The role of leader emotion management in leader–member exchange and follower outcomes. *Leadership Quarterly, 27*, 85–97.

Martínez-Iñigo, D., Totterdell, P., Alcover, C. M., & Holman, D. (2009). The source of display rules and their effects on primary health care professionals' well-being. *Spanish Journal of Psychology, 12*, 618–631.

McClure, R., & Murphy, C. (2007). Contesting the dominance of emotional labour in professional nursing. *Journal of Health Organization and Management, 21*, 101–120.

Mesmer-Magnus, J. R., DeChurch, L. A., & Wax, A. (2012). Moving emotional labor beyond surface and deep acting. *Organizational Psychology Review, 2*, 6–53.

Morris, J. A., & Feldman, D. C. (1996). The dimensions, antecedents, and consequences of emotional labor. *Academy of Management Review, 21*, 986–1010.

Niven, K. (2016). Why do people engage in interpersonal emotion regulation at work? *Organizational Psychology Review, 6*, 305–323.

Ortiz-Bonnin, S., García-Buades, M. E., Caballer, A., & Zapf, D. (in press). Linking team emotion work to customer satisfaction and loyalty: A multilevel study. Article submitted for publication.

Ozcelik, H. (2013). An empirical analysis of surface acting in intra-organizational relationships. *Journal of Organizational Behavior, 34*, 291–309.

Podsakoff, N. P., LePine, J. A., & LePine, M. A. (2007). Differential challenge stressor – hindrance stressor relationships with job attitudes, turnover intentions, turnover, and withdrawal behavior: A meta-analysis. *Journal of Applied Psychology, 92*, 438–454.

Pugh, S. D., Diefendorff, J. M., & Moran, C. M. (2013). Emotional labor: Organization-level influences, strategies, and outcomes. In A. A. Grandey, J. M. Diefendorff, & D. E. Rupp (Eds.), *Emotional labor in the 21st century: Diverse perspectives on emotion regulation at work* (pp. 199–221). New York, NY: Routledge.

Rafaeli, A., & Sutton, R. I. (1987). Expression of emotion as part of the work role. *Academy of Management Review, 12*, 23–37.

Schaubroeck, J., & Jones, J. R. (2000). Antecedents of workplace emotional labor dimensions and moderators of their effects on physical symptoms. *Journal of Organizational Behavior, 21*, 163–183.

Schaufeli, W. B., & Bakker, A. B. (2004). Job demands, job resources, and their relationship with burnout and engagement: A multi-sample study. *Journal of Organizational Behavior, 25*, 293–315.

Semmer, N. K. (2006). Job stress interventions and the organization of work. *Scandinavian Journal of Work, Environment and Health, 32*, 515–527.

Stephens, J. P., & Carmeli, A. (2016). The positive effect of expressing negative emotions on knowledge creation capability and performance of project teams. *International Journal of Project Management, 34*, 862–873.

Sutton, R. (1991). Maintaining norms about expressed emotions? The case of bill collectors. *Administrative Science Quarterly, 36*, 245–268.

Totterdell, P., & Holman, D. (2003). Emotion regulation in customer service roles: Testing a model of emotional labor. *Journal of Occupational Health Psychology, 8*, 55–73.

Tschan, F., Rochat, S., & Zapf, D. (2005). It's not only clients: Studying emotion work with clients and co-workers with an event-sampling approach. *Journal of Occupational and Organizational Psychology, 78*, 195–220.

von Gilsa, L., Zapf, D., Ohly, S., Trumpold, K., & Machowski, S. (2014). There is more than obeying display rules: Service employees' motives for emotion regulation in customer interactions. *European Journal of Work and Organizational Psychology, 23*, 884–896.

Watzlawick, P., Beavin, J. H., & Jackson, D. H. (1967). *Pragmatics of human communication*. New York, NY: W. W. Norton.

Weiss, H. M., & Cropanzano, R. (1996). Affective events theory: A theoretical discussion of the structure, causes and consequences of affective experiences at work. *Research in Organizational Behavior, 18*, 1–74.

Widmer, P. S., Semmer, N. K., Kalin, W., Jacobshagen, N., & Meier, L. L. (2012). The ambivalence of challenge stressors: Time pressure associated with both negative and positive well-being. *Journal of Vocational Behavior, 80*, 422–433.

Williams, M. (2007). Building genuine trust through interpersonal emotion management: A threat regulation model of trust and collaboration across boundaries. *Academy of Management Review, 32*, 595–621.

Wilson, A., Zeithaml, V. A., Bitner, M. J., & Gremler, D. D. (2012). *Services marketing: Integrating customer focus across the firm*. London, UK: McGraw Hill.

Wong, E., Tschan, F., Messerli, L., & Semmer, N. K. (2013). Expressing and amplifying positive emotions facilitate goal attainment in workplace interactions. *Frontiers in Psychology, 4*, 188.

Wong, J. Y., & Wang, C. H. (2009). Emotional labor of the tour leaders: An exploratory study. *Tourism Management, 30*, 249–259.

Yue, Y., Wang, K. L., & Groth, M. (2016). The impact of surface acting on coworker-directed voluntary workplace behaviours. *European Journal of Work and Organizational Psychology, 25*, 447–458.

Yukl, G. (2010). *Leadership in organizations* (7th edition). Upper Saddle River, NJ: Prentice Hall.

Zapf, D. (2002). Emotion, work and psychological well-being: A review of the literature and some conceptual considerations. *Human Resources Management Review, 12*, 237–268.

Zapf, D., Isic, A., Bechtoldt, M., & Blau, P. (2003). What is typical for call centre jobs? Job characteristics and service interactions in different call centres. *European Journal of Work and Organizational Psychology, 12*, 311–340.

Zapf, D., Seifert, C., Schmutte, B., Mertini, H., & Holz, M. (2001). Emotion work and job stressors and their effects on burnout. *Psychology & Health, 16*, 527–545.

Zapf, D., Semmer, N. K., & Johnson, S. (2014). Qualitative demands at work. In M. C. W. Peeters, J. de Jonge, & T. W. Taris (Eds.), *An introduction to contemporary work psychology* (pp. 144–168). Chichester, UK: Wiley-Blackwell.

Zapf, D., Vogt, C., Seifert, C., Mertini, H., & Isic, A. (1999). Emotion work as a source of stress: Concept and development of an instrument. *European Journal of Work and Organizational Psychology, 8* (3), 371–400.

Zerbe, W. J. (2000). Emotional dissonance and employee well-being. In N. Ashkanasy, C. Härtel, & W. Zerbe (Eds.), *Emotions in the workplace: Research, theory, and practice* (pp. 189–214). Westport, CT: Greenwood.

23 Dynamic Emotional Labor

A Review and Extension to Teams

James M. Diefendorff, Amanda L. Thayer, Ketaki Sodhi, and Douglas Magill

The past fifty years have seen an increase in the importance of interpersonal processes at work. Growth in the number of customer service jobs has made emotional labor (EL), defined as the management of emotions as part of the work role (Hochschild, 1983), an increasingly important facet of work. Hochschild (1983) argued that EL is a new form of labor, alongside physical and cognitive labor, in which employees regulate their feelings and emotional expressions "in response to job-based emotional requirements in order to produce emotion toward – and to evoke emotion from – another person to achieve organizational goals" (Grandey, Diefendorff, & Rupp, 2013, p. 18). Consistent with theories of emotion, EL has been characterized as a dynamic process that unfolds within individuals over time (Diefendorff & Gosserand, 2003). As a result, empirical research on EL has increasingly focused on testing hypotheses at the within-person level of analysis.

Along with growth in service-based jobs, a parallel trend that has increased the importance of interpersonal processes at work has been the shift from individual contributor to team-based organizational structures (Tannenbaum, Mathieu, Salas, & Cohen, 2012). Although emotion management has been acknowledged as a component of teamwork, the topic has not garnered a lot of attention in theoretical or empirical work on teams. We argue that the emotion processes described in the EL literature might inform theorizing on emotion management in teams. Key objectives of this chapter are to (a) review empirical research on EL in service-based jobs, focusing on studies taking a dynamic perspective, and (b) consider how dynamic EL processes might operate in the context of teams. We start by providing an overview of EL.

A General Model of Emotional Labor

In 2000, Grandey published a theoretical paper outlining a causal sequence in which emotional display rules (DRs), customer interaction characteristics, and employee traits lead to emotion regulation strategies, which then predict worker well-being and effectiveness. Since then, authors have elaborated on this model by adding variables and unpacking the process by which EL unfolds (e.g. Totterdell & Holman, 2003). Figure 23.1 presents a version of this expanded model that operates at the level of a specific customer interaction. Emotional DRs specify which emotions are appropriate to express in interpersonal situations (Ekman, 1973). Organizations specify DRs to influence how customers feel and to accomplish some broader objective (e.g. sell a product or service). In typical customer-facing occupations, DRs take the form of showing positive and hiding negative emotions (Diefendorff & Richard, 2003); however, in some occupations, such as bill collection, displaying negative emotions may be required (Sutton, 1991). As shown in Figure 23.1, felt affect is compared against DRs to determine whether one can express what is felt or must engage in emotion regulation to change one's feelings or expressions.

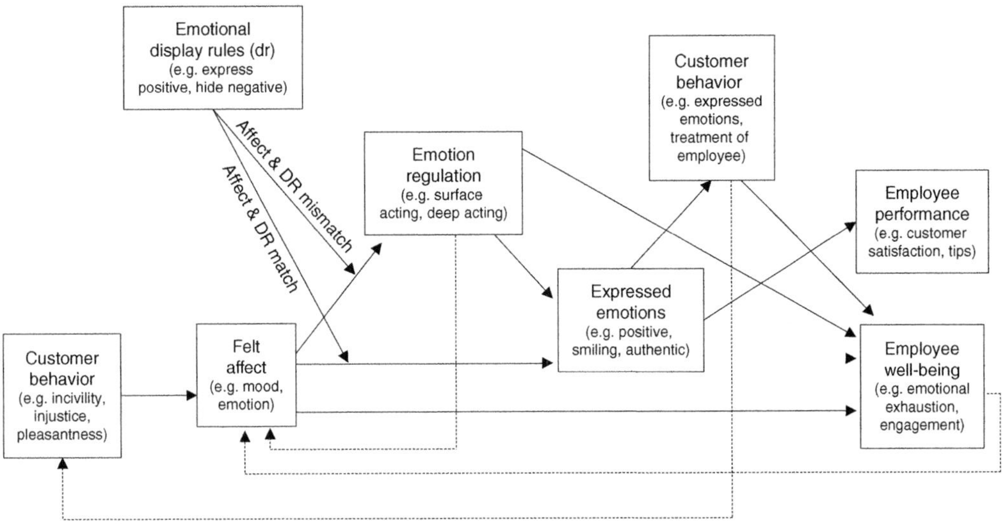

Figure 23.1 Dynamic, event-level model of emotional labor
Note: solid lines represent commonly investigated relationships in studies using experimental and experience-sampling research designs. Dashed lines signify feedback loops in which "downstream" variables impact subsequent levels of "upstream" variables.

Figure 23.1 places customer behavior as an antecedent of employee affect, though we acknowledge that employee affect can be shaped by a variety of additional factors (e.g. moods, work events, trait affectivity). Nonetheless, uncivil or rude customers (Rupp & Spencer, 2006) can produce negative affect in employees and make it difficult for them to conform to DRs. Hochschild (1983) theorized that, in order to align employee emotional displays with DRs (see Figure 23.1) and in turn impact customer affect and behavior (e.g. purchases), emotions are regulated by two primary strategies: surface acting (SA), which involves suppressing felt emotions and faking desired emotions, and deep acting (DA), which involves trying to actively change what one feels to match DRs. Employee feelings, emotion regulation, and the resulting behavior of customers can all contribute to worker well-being, which can influence EL processes as they continue to unfold in the present interaction or even in interactions with subsequent customers.

Within-Person Dynamics in EL Research

The majority of empirical work on EL has focused on static, between-person level tests of hypotheses (Hulsheger & Schewe, 2011). However, theories of emotion and emotion regulation emphasize processes that unfold within individuals over time (Gross, 2015). Because EL pertains to the management of dynamic emotional states, empirical work has begun to capture and model within-person dynamics, though this work often focuses on one of two timeframes: within-episode or between-episode.

Within-Person, Within-Episode Dynamics

Diefendorff and Gosserand's (2003) control theory model of EL describes how momentary *changes* in EL variables during an episode produce changes in other variables during that episode. In this model, individuals constantly match their emotional displays (and felt emotions) with DRs in an attempt to detect (or anticipate) discrepancies between the two and remove (or prevent) any discrepancies by engaging in SA or DA.

Although *expressed* emotions are governed by DRs, we conjecture that individuals often monitor and regulate their *felt* emotions because this information is easily accessible and can provide insight into what one is showing (or is likely to show; see Figure 23.1). Moment-to-moment changes in employee affect can be the result of dynamic within-event changes in customer behavior. Further, conforming to DRs by regulating one's emotions should produce more effective displays in the moment which should produce more beneficial customer responses, both of which can benefit worker well-being and effectiveness at the event level (Grandey, Diefendorff, & Rupp, 2013). This control theory model of EL provides a process-based view for understanding dynamics, especially as they unfold within events.

Within-Person, Between-Episode Dynamics

The second way dynamics have been incorporated into EL research is by considering how variables outlined in Figure 23.1 produce changes in employee well-being and effectiveness that span events, times of day (morning to afternoon), or entire work days. In the moment, conforming to DRs leads to better performance, but the effort involved in monitoring and regulating one's emotions can deplete resources, which can negatively impact well-being and effectiveness. Meta-analytic evidence shows that SA is harmful for well-being and unrelated to performance, whereas DA is unrelated to well-being and positively related to performance (Hulsheger & Schewe, 2011). Theoretically, event-level EL processes should produce *changes* in well-being and performance that accrue over a longer timeframe that spans events (or measurement occasions).

Research Design Considerations

The vast majority of empirical work on EL has relied on static (cross-sectional), person-level assessments of relevant variables, thereby precluding tests of dynamics or the sequence by which EL unfolds. Experimental designs provide the strongest evidence for a causal sequence. This approach allows the upstream variables shown in Figure 23.1 to be manipulated to help us understand their effects on measured downstream variables, and is particularly well-suited for investigating the within-event dynamics that unfold in single employee–customer interactions. These experimental approaches often rely on lab-based simulations in which participants act as service agents who interact with (often confederate) customers.

Another design for investigating EL dynamics is to repeatedly assess employee ratings of EL variables in the context of work, using experience-sampling methodology (ESM; i.e. reports on specific moments or work events), diary-based procedures (i.e. reports on longer periods of time, such as the morning, afternoon, or entire day), or unobtrusive observations of specific employee–customer interactions (supplemented with surveys). We combine discussion of ESM and diary-based approaches under the term ESM. These studies typically do not include experimental manipulations so the ability to infer causality is limited, though some research designs provide stronger evidence for causal precedence. A *concurrent* approach, in which measures from the same assessments, are correlated is the weakest approach for inferring causality. A *time-separated* approach in which the independent variable (IV) is measured on an earlier occasion than the dependent variable (DV) helps to rule out bias due to momentary mood or other factors, but lacks an indication of change. A *lagged-DV* approach focuses on a concurrent relationship between an IV and DV, controlling for the previous (i.e. lagged) value of the DV.

Sometimes this approach is described as simply an attempt to control for autocorrelation (which it does), but when the timeframe of the lag is meaningful (e.g. from the beginning to the end of a work shift), the DV can be interpreted as a change score, which provides stronger evidence for a causal direction. Finally, the *cross-lagged* approach models the lagged IV and DV as predictors of the current DV, which separates the IV and DV in time and focuses on the DV as a change score. This approach is particularly effective for isolating the causal direction of effects. With these intensive longitudinal designs, one can also utilize methods such as growth curve modeling to examine how variables change over time (i.e. trajectories) and whether changes in one variable relate to changes in another variable (i.e. correlated growth terms).

EL Dynamics: A Summary of Findings

Below we review research on EL dynamics, referencing Figure 23.1 (moving from left to right).

Emotional Display Rules

Research on DRs has primarily focused on within-episode dynamics using experimental designs to examine the effects of manipulated DRs on a variety of downstream EL variables in simulated customer service interactions (Goldberg & Grandey 2007; Hopp, Rohrmann, & Hodapp, 2012; Hopp, Rohrmann, Zapf, & Hodapp, 2010). No research has examined the effects of ESM assessments of DRs on other EL variables, presumably because researchers assume that DRs do not meaningfully vary as a function of momentary conditions.

Using an experimental design, Goldberg and Grandey (2007) manipulated DRs in a call center simulation and found that a positive DR ("be enthusiastic and suppress frustration") resulted in more DA, SA, emotional exhaustion, and cognitive errors than an autonomy DR ("be yourself"). In a face-to-face customer service simulation, Hopp et al. (2010) found that a positive DR ("the customer is king!", p. 403) produced higher blood pressure (though not higher heart rate) compared to an authentic DR ("be yourself!", p. 403). Also, in a face-to-face customer service simulation, Hopp et al. (2012) independently manipulated two positive DR components: express positive (EP) emotions and suppress negative (SN) emotions, creating a 2 × 2 design (the low–low condition was instructed to act naturally). No differences were observed across conditions for DA or anger, but there were main effects for EP and SN on SA, as well as a marginally significant interaction such that the "high–high" condition had the same level of SA as the high EP and high SN conditions. SN had a negative effect on well-being (whereas EP did not) and EP had a positive effect on service quality (whereas SN did not).

Although ESM research has not focused on DRs, studies have examined variables defined by their relationship with DRs. For instance, Beal, Trougakos, Weiss, and Green (2006) captured ESM assessments of the difficulty of maintaining DRs and Tschan et al. (2005) measured ESM assessments of DR deviance (i.e. showing emotions that differed from DRs; see also Dahling, 2017). Perhaps the closest assessment of dynamic DRs is the work by von Gilsa et al. (2014), who used ESM to examine three EL motives: pleasure (i.e. improve the self, relationship), prevention (i.e. prevent problems, disagreements), and instrumental (i.e. conform to requirements). These authors found that the instrumental motive was positively related to concurrent SA; the pleasure motive was positively related to concurrent DA and automatic regulation (i.e. showing naturally-felt emotions) but negatively related to concurrent SA and emotional deviance; and the prevention motive was positively related to concurrent DA, SA, and emotional deviance, but negatively related to automatic regulation. These findings, as well as descriptive research showing that DRs vary as a function of the target (e.g. customer, supervisor, coworker, subordinate) and felt emotion (Diefendorff & Greguras, 2009), suggest that it might be useful to examine whether DRs vary with ESM assessments and the impact of that variability on downstream variables (see Figure 23.1).

Customer Behavior

Research on the influence of customer behavior has looked at dynamics both within and between episodes. Experimental work manipulating customer behavior within laboratory-based call center interactions has shown that uncivil and unfair treatment by confederate customers causes higher worker negative affect, SA, DA, and more negative vocal tone during the interaction (Gabriel & Diefendorff, 2015; Spencer & Rupp, 2009; Rupp & Spencer, 2006). Focusing on within-episode tests but using concurrent ESM assessments, Totterdell and Holman (2003) found that customer pleasantness was positively correlated with positive refocus (similar to DA) and negatively correlated with faking (similar to SA). Using an event-based profile analysis of over 7,300 call center interactions, Diefendorff et al. (2019) reported that high negative affect and emotion regulation co-occurred with customer incivility, though experiencing very uncivil customers was relatively rare (occurring in 2.22 percent of events).

Although customer behavior is often conceptualized as an antecedent of emotion regulation, a dynamic view of EL (see Figure 23.1) suggests that employee emotion management may impact customers, whose reactions then impact employee well-being (Côté, 2005). For instance, Holman (2015) found that daily SA and DA were (positively and negatively, respectively) related to daily emotional exhaustion through customer affiliative behavior. Similarly, Zhan et al. (2016) found that afternoon SA and DA predicted changes in how customers treat employees (negatively and positively, respectively) from morning to afternoon. As such, there is evidence of dynamic reciprocal effects of customer behavior and employee affect and regulation.

Emotion Regulation

Links to Employee Affect and Well-Being

As previously noted, affect is often presumed to be the antecedent of emotion regulation, especially within an episode. Using a continuous rating paradigm and a cross-lagged analytic approach, Gabriel and Diefendorff (2015) found that momentary felt affect predicted second-by-second changes in SA and DA during a simulated call center interaction (and regulation did not predict changes in affect).

Several ESM studies have tested the concurrent relationships of emotion regulation with affect and well-being, finding that SA is positively related to negative states (e.g. negative affect, anxiety, anger) and ill-being (e.g. emotional exhaustion, depersonalization, work withdrawal cognitions, dissatisfaction), and negatively related to daily work engagement. In contrast, daily DA has been shown to negatively relate with positive affect and withdrawal cognitions and positively relate to daily work engagement and job satisfaction (Huang et al., 2015; Judge et al., 2009; Keller et al., 2014; Schreurs, Guenter, Hulsheger, & van Emmerik, 2014; Scott & Barnes, 2011; Wagner, Barnes, & Scott, 2014).

Several studies have identified moderators of the relationships among concurrently assessed variables. For instance, Schreurs et al. (2014) reported that trait punishment sensitivity strengthened the harmful effects of daily work engagement, emotional exhaustion, and depersonalization, and trait reward sensitivity moderated the relationship of daily DA with emotional exhaustion such that it was positive at low levels and negative at high levels. Huang et al. (2015) reported that mid-day evaluations of felt challenge at work strengthened the beneficial effects of mid-day DA on concurrently assessed emotional exhaustion and job satisfaction.

Taking a time-separated approach, Beal, Trougakos, Weiss, and Dalal (2013) observed that lagged SA had direct and indirect effects on current fatigue through lagged strain, which were strengthened when affect spin (i.e. trait-level variability of affective states) was higher. Similarly, Uy et al. (2017) reported that lagged (end-of-shift) SA was positively related to before-bed emotional exhaustion, which was negatively related to next-day work engagement. Further, Uy et al. showed that day-level reports of giving help at work (but not of receiving help at work) attenuated the SA and exhaustion relationship. Additionally, using a time-separated approach, Diestel et al. (2015) found that noon emotional dissonance (i.e. showing emotions that are different from feelings, similar to SA) was related to evening ego depletion, need for recovery, and engagement, and that these effects were weakened by the previous night's sleep quality (i.e. relationships were stronger when sleep quality was low) and peer evaluations of trait self-control capacity.

Some studies linking EL with well-being have used the DV-change model. For example, van Gelderen et al. (2007) reported that end-of-shift emotional dissonance (i.e. suppression and faking emotions) was positively related to end-of-shift psychological strain (i.e. exhaustion and dysfunctional attitudes) controlling for pre-shift psychological strain. Scott and Barnes (2011) observed that end-of-shift reports of SA were positively related to changes in negative affect from the beginning of the shift to the end of the shift, but unrelated to changes in positive affect. Moreover, end-of-shift reports of DA were negatively related to changes in negative affect and positively related to changes in positive affect. In a sample of police officers, van Gelderen et al. (2017) reported that SA assessed at the end of the work day predicted changes in work strain from the start of the day to the end. Similarly, end-of-shift assessments of emotional dissonance predicted changes in work strain from the start to the end of the shift. Finally, van Gelderen et al. (2011) found that end-of-shift anger suppression, abhorrence suppression, and emotional dissonance positively predicted changes in emotional exhaustion from pre-shift to end-of-shift (suppression of happiness and suppression of sadness were not significant predictors).

Approximating a cross-lagged approach by using a lagged IV but controlling for the DV from an earlier lag, Wagner et al. (2014) found that end-of-shift reports of daily SA (but not DA) were positively related to before–bedtime reports of emotional exhaustion and work-to-family conflict, controlling for the previous evening's DV and end-of-shift reports of state anxiety; further, daily SA and DA were not related to nighttime insomnia (as measured the following morning), controlling for the previous night's insomnia. Taking a similar approach, Zhang et al. (2016) found that end-of-day SA was positively related to fatigue the next morning, controlling for the previous morning's fatigue. Further, sleep quantity (but not sleep quality) moderated this relationship, with high sleep quantity buffering the harmful effect of SA on next morning's fatigue.

We did not find EL studies that manipulated SA/DA and measured affect/well-being, though such an approach is common in social psychology with research showing that suppression (similar to SA) is more harmful than reappraisal (similar to DA; Gross, 2015). However, several EL studies have manipulated variables aimed at impacting felt emotions directly (and, as a result, the need to regulate emotions) or the impact of emotion regulation on well-being. For instance, McCance, Nye, Wang, Jones, and Chiu (2013) reported that when call center workers met with each other to discuss difficult calls, post-call anger was lower compared to those who did not participate in such discussions. Hu, Zhan, Yao, and Garden (2017) found that call center workers who viewed a picture of a smiling woman after every call had greater increases of positive affect in their shifts than workers in a control condition, though differences in emotional exhaustion were not observed. Grandey, Chi, and Diamond (2013) observed that performance-contingent rewards weakened the SA–negative affect and SA–job satisfaction relationships. Finally, Hulsheger et al. (2013) demonstrated that a mindfulness manipulation decreased the use of SA and increased well-being.

Links to Performance

Most of the work linking emotion regulation with performance outcomes has relied on concurrent ESM assessments. In a sample of Dutch waiters and taxi drivers, Hulsheger, Lang, Schewe, and Zijlstra (2015) reported that daily DA and daily automatic regulation (e.g. "Today, my emotions automatically met job requirements") were positively related to total daily tip amount, controlling for busyness and type of occupation. In a sample of police officers, Van Gelderen et al. (2017) found that DA was positively related to concurrently assessed self-reported service performance (i.e. an extra-role performance scale reworded to focus on helping civilians) and SA was negatively related (for a similar pattern using coworker rated affective delivery as the DV, see Chi & Grandey, 2019). Focusing on a sample of hairdressers, Hulsheger et al. (2015) trained half on the use of reappraisal and attentional deployment strategies and found that this group received higher daily tips (controlling for tips in a baseline period) and an increase in daily automatic emotion regulation (but not DA) compared to the untrained group.

Employee Emotional Expressions and Customer Reactions

Experimental and observational studies on the effects of employee display on customers often focus on within-episode dynamics between service agents and specific customers. For instance, Grandey et al. (2005) used fictitious video-based service encounters involving a hotel worker who engaged in either SA (inauthentic positive displays) or DA (authentic positive displays) and found that DA expressions resulted in higher customer ratings of friendliness, but only increased customer satisfaction when task performance was also high. Using simulated customer service interactions, Hennig-Thurau, Groth, Paul, and Gremler (2006) manipulated worker SA and DA, and found that DA produced greater positive affect in customers and increased rapport compared to SA. Finally, Cheshin, Amit, and van Kleef (2018) manipulated the intensity of expressed happiness and sadness in customer interactions (to match the context) and found that exaggerated expressions resulted in *lower* customer ratings of authenticity, appropriateness, trust, and service satisfaction compared to mild expressions.

Several studies of actual employee-customer interactions have attempted to understand the within-event dynamics of objectively observed employee emotional displays on customers. Testing an emotional contagion account, Pugh (2001), Tsai and Huang (2002), and Wang et al. (2017) found a positive relationship of employee positive displays (observer rated) with customer self-rated state positive affect. Barger and Grandey (2006) did not find such a relationship but did observe facial mimicry, with employee smiling being positively related to subsequent customer smiling. Further, research has shown that customer felt affect mediated the relationship between employee displays and customer intentions to return and recommend the store to others (Tsai and Huang; Wang et al.) Wang et al. found this link was primarily present for customers who were less attentive to employee displays, arguing that more attentive customers might discount their feelings as irrelevant, decreasing the impact the feelings have on their desire to be loyal.

Gabriel, Acosta, and Grandey (2015) offered a contrasting theoretical account of the role of attention. They measured familiarity with the service provider, holding that when customers are less familiar with employees, they will be more attentive as they establish trust. Indeed, they found that low familiarity amplified the employee display–customer satisfaction and display–friendliness relationships. Consistent with Côté's (2005) social interaction model of EL, Kim and Yoon (2012) reported that customer displays of positive emotions mediated the relationship between the employee positive display and the employee positive mood. Thus, there is evidence that employee emotional displays impact customer affect, emotional displays, and evaluations of the service interactions.

Extending Dynamic Research on EL to Teams

The use of team-based structures has grown dramatically over the last 30 years (Tannenbaum et al., 2012). Accordingly, working with others (i.e. *teamwork;*) makes up a large part of employees' activities and the importance of effective interpersonal processes at work has increased. Somewhat surprisingly, the study of how individuals manage their emotions with each other in the context of teams has received little attention. We suspect that many of the same dynamics seen in employee-customer interactions may be at work when team members interact with each other and when they collectively interact with customers (Maloney, Bresman, Zellmer-Bruhn & Beaver, 2016). Thus, research on EL may inform our understanding of teamwork by providing a set of constructs and propositions that can explain the emotion management processes that individuals engage in when interacting with each other. Further, several of the constructs described in Figure 23.1 may reside at the team level, individual level, or both. For instance, DRs may guide how teammates interact with each other, and these rules can exist as idiosyncratic beliefs of individuals as well as shared norms of the team. Further, individuals may regulate their emotions to align with these coworker-directed DRs (Glasø & Einarsen, 2008) and teams may exhibit group-level propensities to regulate emotions in a particular way (Becker & Cropanzano, 2015).

In addition to EL informing our understanding of team processes, conducting EL research in teams can inform our understanding of EL. For instance, teams can provide the context within which individual-level EL dynamics unfold and these dynamics may operate differently as a function of the team to which individuals belong. Further, when considering EL processes at the team-level, it may be that these dynamics operate differently in groups compared to individuals. In their taxonomy of team processes (i.e. behaviors), Marks, Mathieu, and Zaccaro (2001) acknowledged a role for affect management, defined as "regulating member emotions during mission accomplishment, including (but not limited to) social cohesion, frustration, and excitement" (p. 369). LePine and colleagues' (2008) meta-analysis reported that affect management, which they defined as "activities that foster emotional balance, togetherness, and effective coping with stressful demands and frustration" (p. 277), was positively related to team performance and member satisfaction. More recently, work by Benzer and colleagues (2016) found that high-performing teams were more likely to use the affect management strategies of socialization, humor, and open communication to manage stress, whereas lower performing teams relied on strategies such as venting frustrations.

Illustrating one way to incorporate teams into EL research, Diefendorff, Erickson, Grandey, and Dahling (2011) examined nurses working in different hospital units and tested the idea that DRs are shared group norms that guide the emotional expressions of nurses with patients and patient families. They found that DRs exhibit group-level properties and that unit DRs moderated the effects of individual negative affect on SA and positive affect on DA. Further, unit DRs predicted individual job satisfaction beyond individual DRs. Taking a different approach, Becker and Cropanzano (2015) found that team-level DA variability moderated the effects of individual DA on emotional exhaustion and performance such that at low levels of DA dispersion (i.e. high similarity), high individual DA corresponded to lower exhaustion and higher performance (compared to high dispersion). Interestingly, neither of these studies of team EL incorporated dynamics, suggesting the need for experimental, ESM, or observational approaches, as outlined in our review of individual-level EL research.

Additional Constructs Useful for Team EL

One reason team and individual EL processes may differ is that individual EL is typically an intrapsychic process whereas team EL may be more externalized as social behaviors and interpersonal processes. In this section we outline the potential role of two interpersonally-focused emotion constructs that may be important to incorporate into research on team EL: interpersonal emotion regulation and emotional contagion.

EL research focuses on how employees regulate their own affect, yet recent research suggests that emotion regulation can also be other-directed (Niven, Totterdell, Stride, & Holman, 2011; Williams, 2007). For instance, regulating others' emotions is positively related to perceptions of popularity within social networks, friendship, trust (Niven, Holman, & Totterdell, 2012), citizenship behaviors, and job satisfaction (Little, Gooty, & Williams, 2016). Moreover, research suggests that when participants expected to receive desirable outcomes (i.e. benefit to self), they were more likely to increase emotion in others, even when that included making a partner feel worse or a rival feel better. We suggest teams may develop norms or even group-level strategies to regulate the affect of individual team members or the affect of the team as a whole.

Another line of research that may be relevant for understanding team EL is emotional contagion, defined as the spread of emotions from one person to another. Elfenbein (2014) outlined several ways in which individuals' affective states can converge or diverge. Generally, teammates may experience convergent (or divergent) affect (i.e. enter into similar or dissimilar emotional states) because they have similar (or different) affective traits, they are faced with similar (or different) stimuli and have a shared (or different) vantage point, or because state emotions experienced by one person spread (or induces opposite reactions) to other team members. These contagion-based processes may help explain how shared (or divergent) affect forms within teams. When such affect is compared against the affective norms or team DRs, individuals may engage in both intrapersonal and interpersonal affect regulation to reduce any observed discrepancies.

Computational Approaches to Studying Dynamic Team Emotion Regulation

To advance the study of EL dynamics in teams, a fruitful avenue may be to use approaches developed in computational social science (CSS). CSS emphasizes the use of computational approaches to simulate, model, and analyze complex social systems, and may be used to understand how individual-level EL dynamics operate over time within teams, how individuals' EL dynamics reciprocally influence each other, and how collective EL dynamics can emerge over time. For instance, Bosse, Duell, Zulifiqar, Memon, and Treur (2014) developed an agent-based model of group emotional contagion processes, simulating the absorption and amplification of others' emotions.

Social Network Analysis (SNA) is another powerful tool that allows researchers to focus on interactions and social relationships to understand how they develop and produce emergent group phenomena. For instance, Fowler and Christakis (2008) used SNA to demonstrate how happiness can be contagious and spread up to three degrees of separation. Relational event modeling (REM), the study of group interactions over short, discrete relational episodes, studies networks or ties formed between individuals; however, it utilizes a far shorter temporal scale than SNA by focusing on moment-to-moment interaction patterns (Butts, 2008).

Conclusions

In conclusion, we suggest that existing research and theory on EL dynamics can contribute to and be informed by taking a team-based approach in future research. Further, team research may benefit from the "EL architecture" outlined in dynamic EL research. For instance, we suspect that there may be value in investigating within-episode and between-episode team-based EL processes. To understand within-episode dynamics, experimental designs with lab-based simulations of team-based events could be used to understand issues such as (a) how team-level emotion norms combine with team-shared affect to shape individual-level intrapersonal and interpersonal emotion regulation strategies, (b) how emotions become shared via distinct emotional contagion pathways during a team-based performance episode, and (c) whether distinct interpersonal affect regulation strategies are more or less useful for regulating team affect under different levels of team member interdependence. Further, between-episode dynamics could be examined with either experimental approaches in the lab or by using ESM to capture individual- and team-based emotions and regulation and examine how the values of these variables at an earlier time contribute to changes in individual- and team-based well-being and performance outcomes. Given the dearth of research on emotion management in teams, the possibilities for future research on this topic are many.

References

Barger, P. B., & Grandey, A. A. (2006). Service with a smile and encounter satisfaction: Emotional contagion and appraisal mechanisms. *Academy of Management Journal*, *49*(6), 1229–1238.

Beal, D. J., Trougakos, J. P., Weiss, H. M., & Dalal, R. S. (2013). Affect spin and the emotion regulation process at work. *Journal of Applied Psychology*, *98*(4), 593–605.

Beal, D. J., Trougakos, J. P., Weiss, H. M., & Green, S. G. (2006). Episodic processes in emotional labor: Perceptions of affective delivery and regulation strategies. *Journal of Applied Psychology*, *91*(5), 1053–1065.

Becker, W. J., & Cropanzano, R. (2015). Good acting requires a good cast: A meso-level model of deep acting in work teams. *Journal of Organizational Behavior*, *36*(2), 232–249.

Benzer, J. K., Mohr, D. C., Evans, L., Young, G., Meterko, M. M., Moore, S. C., . . . & Charns, M. P. (2016). Team process variation across diabetes quality of care trajectories. *Medical Care Research and Review*, *73*(5), 565–589.

Bliese, P. D., & Ployhart, R. E. (2002). Growth modeling using random coefficient models: Model building, testing, and illustrations. *Organizational Research Methods*, *5*, 362–387, doi:10.1177/109442802237116

Bosse, T., Duell, R., Memon, Z. A., Treur, J., & van der Wal, C. N. (2015). Agent-based modeling of emotion contagion in groups. *Cognitive Computation*, *7*(1), 111–136.

Butts, C. T. (2008) A relational event framework for social action. *Sociological Methodology*, *38*, 155–200.

Cheshin, A., Amit, A., & van Kleef, G. A. (2018). The interpersonal effects of emotion intensity in customer service: Perceived appropriateness and authenticity of attendants' emotional displays shape customer trust and satisfaction. *Organizational Behavior and Human Decision Processes*, *144*, 97–111.

Chi, N. W., & Grandey, A. A. (2019). Emotional labor predicts service performance depending on activation and inhibition regulatory fit. *Journal of Management*, *45*(2), 673–700, https://doi.org/10.1177/0149206316672530

Côté, S. (2005). A social interaction model of the effects of emotion regulation on work strain. *Academy of Management Review*, *30*(3), 509–530.

Dahling, J. J. (2017). Exhausted, mistreated, or indifferent? Explaining deviance from emotional display rules at work. *European Journal of Work and Organizational Psychology*, *26*(2), 171–182.

Diefendorff, J. M., Erickson, R. J., Grandey, A. A., & Dahling, J. J. (2011). Emotional display rules as work unit norms: A multilevel analysis of emotional labor among nurses. *Journal of Occupational Health Psychology*, *16*(2), 170–186.

Diefendorff, J. M., Gabriel, A. S., Nolan, M. T., & Yang, J. (2019). Emotion regulation in the context of customer mistreatment and felt affect: An event-based profile approach. *Journal of Applied Psychology*, *104*(7), doi:10.1037/apl0000389

Diefendorff, J. M., & Gosserand, R. H. (2003). Understanding the emotional labor process: A control theory perspective. *Journal of Organizational Behavior*, *24*(8), 945–959.

Diefendorff, J. M., & Greguras, G. J. (2009). Contextualizing emotional display rules: Examining the roles of targets and discrete emotions in shaping display rule perceptions. *Journal of Management*, *35*(4), 880–898.

Diefendorff, J. M., & Richard, E. M. (2003). Antecedents and consequences of emotional display rule perceptions. *Journal of Applied Psychology*, *88*(2), 284–294.

Diestel, S., Rivkin, W., & Schmidt, K. H. (2015). Sleep quality and self-control capacity as protective resources in the daily emotional labor process: Results from two diary studies. *Journal of Applied Psychology*, *100*(3), 809–827.

Ekman, P. (1973). *Darwin and facial expression: A century of research in review*. New York, NY: Academic.

Elfenbein, H. A. (2014). The many faces of emotional contagion: An affective process theory of affective linkage. *Organizational Psychology Review*, *4*(4), 326–362.

Gabriel, A. S., Acosta, J. D., & Grandey, A. A. (2015). The value of a smile: Does emotional performance matter more in familiar or unfamiliar exchanges? *Journal of Business and Psychology*, *30*(1), 37–50.

Gabriel, A. S., & Diefendorff, J. M. (2015). Emotional labor dynamics: A momentary approach. *Academy of Management Journal*, *58*(6), 1804–1825.

Glasø, L., & Einarsen, S. (2008). Emotion regulation in leader–follower relationships. *European Journal of Work and Organizational Psychology*, *17*(4), 482–500.

Goldberg, L. S., & Grandey, A. A. (2007). Display rules versus display autonomy: Emotion regulation, emotional exhaustion, and task performance in a call center simulation. *Journal of Occupational Health Psychology*, *12*(3), 301–318.

Grandey, A. A. (2000). Emotional regulation in the workplace: A new way to conceptualize emotional labor. *Journal of Occupational Health Psychology*, *5*(1), 95–110.

Grandey, A. A., Chi, N. W., & Diamond, J. A. (2013). Show me the money! Do financial rewards for performance enhance or undermine the satisfaction from emotional labor? *Personnel Psychology*, *66*(3), 569–612.

Grandey, A. A., Diefendorff, J. M., & Rupp, D. E. (2013). Bringing emotional labor into focus. In A. A. Grandey, J. M. Diefendorff, & D. E. Rupp (Eds.), *Emotional labor in the 21st century: Diverse perspectives on emotion regulation at work* (pp. 3–27). New York, NY: Routledge.

Grandey, A. A., Fisk, G. M., Mattila, A. S., Jansen, K. J., & Sideman, L. A. (2005). Is "service with a smile" enough? Authenticity of positive displays during service encounters. *Organizational Behavior and Human Decision Processes*, *96*(1), 38–55.

Gross, J. J. (2015). Emotion regulation: Current status and future prospects. *Psychological Inquiry*, *26*(1), 1–26.

Hennig-Thurau, T., Groth, M., Paul, M., & Gremler, D. D. (2006). Are all smiles created equal? How emotional contagion and emotional labor affect service relationships. *Journal of Marketing*, *70*(3), 58–73.

Hochschild, A. R. (1983). *The managed heart: Commercialization of human feeling*. Berkeley: University of California Press.

Holman, D. (2015). How does customer affiliative behaviour shape the outcomes of employee emotion regulation? A daily diary study of supermarket checkout operators. *Human Relations*, *69*(5), 1139–1162.

Hopp, H., Rohrmann, S., & Hodapp, V. (2012). Suppression of negative and expression of positive emotions: Divergent effects of emotional display rules in a hostile service interaction. *European Journal of Work and Organizational Psychology*, *21* (1), 84–105.

Hopp, H., Rohrmann, S., Zapf, D., & Hodapp, V. (2010). Psychophysiological effects of emotional dissonance in a face-to-face service interaction. *Anxiety, Stress, & Coping*, *23*(4), 399–414.

Hu, X., Zhan, Y., Yao, X., & Garden, R. (2017). Picture this: A field experiment of the influence of subtle affective stimuli on employee well-being and performance. *Journal of Organizational Behavior*, *38*(6), 895–916.

Huang, J. L., Chiaburu, D. S., Zhang, X. A., Li, N., & Grandey, A. A. (2015). Rising to the challenge: Deep acting is more beneficial when tasks are appraised as challenging. *Journal of Applied Psychology*, *100*(5), 1398–1408.

Hülsheger, U. R., Alberts, H. J., Feinholdt, A., & Lang, J. W. (2013). Benefits of mindfulness at work: The role of mindfulness in emotion regulation, emotional exhaustion, and job satisfaction. *Journal of Applied Psychology*, *98*(2), 310–325.

Hülsheger, U. R., Lang, J. W. B., Schewe, A. F., & Zijlstra, F. R. H. (2015). When regulating emotions at work pays off: A diary and an intervention study on emotion regulation and customer tips in service jobs. *Journal of Applied Psychology*, *100*(2), 263–277.

Hülsheger, U. R., & Schewe, A. F. (2011). On the costs and benefits of emotional labor: A meta-analysis of three decades of research. *Journal of Occupational Health Psychology*, *16*(3), 361–389.

Judge, T. A., Woolf, E. F., & Hurst, C. (2009). Is emotional labor more difficult for some than for others? A multilevel, experience-sampling study. *Personnel Psychology*, *62*(1), 57–88.

Keller, M. M., Chang, M. L., Becker, E. S., Goetz, T., & Frenzel, A. C. (2014). Teachers' emotional experiences and exhaustion as predictors of emotional labor in the classroom: An experience sampling study. *Frontiers in Psychology*, *5*, 1–10.

Kim, E., & Yoon, D. J. (2012). Why does service with a smile make employees happy? A social interaction model. *Journal of Applied Psychology*, *97*(5), 1059–1067.

LePine, J. A., Piccolo, R. F., Jackson, C. L., Mathieu, J. E., & Saul, J. R. (2008). A meta-analysis of teamwork processes: Tests of a multidimensional model and relationships with team effectiveness criteria. *Personnel Psychology*, *61*, 273–307.

Little, L. M., Gooty, J., & Williams, M. (2016). The role of leader emotion management in leader–member exchange and follower outcomes. *Leadership Quarterly*, *27*(1), 85–97.

Maloney, M. M., Bresman, H., Zellmer-Bruhn, M. E., & Beaver, G. R. (2016). Contextualization and context theorizing in teams research: A look back and a path forward. *Academy of Management Annals*, *10*, 891–942.

Marks, M. A., Mathieu, J. E., & Zaccaro, S. J. (2001). A temporally based framework and taxonomy of team processes. *Academy of Management Review*, *26*, 356–376.

McCance, A. S., Nye, C. D., Wang, L., Jones, K. S., & Chiu, C. Y. (2013). Alleviating the burden of emotional labor: The role of social sharing. *Journal of Management*, *39*(2), 392–415.

Netzer, L., Van Kleef, G. A., & Tamir, M. (2015). Interpersonal instrumental emotion regulation. *Journal of Experimental Social Psychology*, *58*, 124–135.

Niven, K., Holman, D., & Totterdell, P. (2012). How to win friendship and trust by influencing people's feelings: An investigation of interpersonal affect regulation and the quality of relationships. *Human Relations*, *65*(6), 777–805.

Niven, K., Totterdell, P., Stride, C. B., & Holman, D. (2011). Emotion regulation of others and self (EROS): The development and validation of a new individual difference measure. *Current Psychology*, *30*(1), 53–73.

Pugh, S. D. (2001). Service with a smile: Emotional contagion in the service encounter. *Academy of Management Journal*, *44*(5), 1018–1027.

Rupp, D. E., & Spencer, S. (2006). When customers lash out: The effects of customer interactional injustice on emotional labor and the mediating role of discrete emotions. *Journal of Applied Psychology, 91*(4), 971–978.

Schraub, E. M., Michel, A., Shemla, M., & Sonntag, K. (2014). The roles of leader emotion management and team conflict for team members' personal initiative: A multilevel perspective. *European Journal of Work and Organizational Psychology, 23*(2), 263–276.

Schreurs, B., Guenter, H., Hülsheger, U., & van Emmerik, H. (2014). The role of punishment and reward sensitivity in the emotional labor process: A within-person perspective. *Journal of Occupational Health Psychology, 19*(1), 108–121.

Scott, B. A., & Barnes, C. M. (2011). A multilevel field investigation of emotional labor, affect, work withdrawal, and gender. *Academy of Management Journal, 54*(1), 116–136.

Spencer, S., & Rupp, D. E. (2009). Angry, guilty, and conflicted: Injustice toward coworkers heightens emotional labor through cognitive and emotional mechanisms. *Journal of Applied Psychology, 94*(2), 429–444.

Tannenbaum, S. I., Mathieu, J. E., Salas, E., & Cohen, D. (2012). Teams are changing: Are research and practice evolving fast enough? *Industrial and Organizational Psychology, 5*(1), 2–24.

Totterdell, P., & Holman, D. (2003). Emotion regulation in customer service roles: Testing a model of emotional labor. *Journal of Occupational Health Psychology, 8*(1), 55–73.

Tsai, W. C., & Huang, Y. M. (2002). Mechanisms linking employee affective delivery and customer behavioral intentions. *Journal of Applied Psychology, 87*(5), 1001–1008.

Tschan, F., Rochat, S., & Zapf, D. (2005). It's not only clients: Studying emotion work with clients and co-workers with an event-sampling approach. *Journal of Occupational and Organizational Psychology, 78*(2), 195–220.

Uy, M. A., Lin, K. J., & Ilies, R. (2017). Is it better to give or receive? The role of help in buffering the depleting effects of surface acting. *Academy of Management Journal, 60*(4), 1442–1461.

van Gelderen, B., Heuven, E., van Veldhoven, M., Zeelenberg, M., & Croon, M. (2007). Psychological strain and emotional labor among police-officers: A diary study. *Journal of Vocational Behavior, 71* (3), 446–459.

von Gilsa, L., Zapf, D., Ohly, S., Trumpold, K., & Machowski, S. (2014). There is more than obeying display rules: Service employees' motives for emotion regulation in customer interactions. *European Journal of Work and Organizational Psychology, 23*(6), 884–896.

Wagner, D. T., Barnes, C. M., & Scott, B. A. (2014). Driving it home: How workplace emotional labor harms employee home life. *Personnel Psychology, 67*(2), 487–516.

Wang, Z., Singh, S. N., Li, Y. J., Mishra, S., Ambrose, M., & Biernat, M. (2017). Effects of employees' positive affective displays on customer loyalty intentions: An emotions-as-social-information perspective. *Academy of Management Journal, 60*(1), 109–129.

Williams, M. (2007). Building genuine trust through interpersonal emotion management: A threat regulation model of trust and collaboration across boundaries. *Academy of Management Review, 32* (2), 595–621.

Zhan, Y., Wang, M., & Shi, J. (2016). Interpersonal process of emotional labor: The role of negative and positive customer treatment. *Personnel Psychology, 69*(3), 525–557.

Zhang, Y., Zhang, L., Lei, H., Yue, Y., & Zhu, J. (2016). Lagged effect of daily surface acting on subsequent day's fatigue. *Service Industries Journal, 36*(15–16), 809–826.

Part IV

Workplace Affect and Organizational, Social, and Cultural Processes

24 Organizational Entry and Workplace Affect

Allison M. Ellis and Talya N. Bauer

As the unemployment rate continues to shrink, organizations are increasingly in competition for the best talent. For this reason, the ability to effectively source, recruit, and hire qualified employees has become a cornerstone of effective human resource management, and a critical function in creating value through human capital. However, in order to capitalize on effective recruitment and hiring, organizations need to be able to retain and motivate new employees throughout their first year, during which studies estimate the risk of newcomer turnover ranges from 10 percent to as much as 50 percent and above for some jobs (Maurer, 2017). Thus the organizational entry period comes on the heels of substantial investment on the part of employers with the potential for both significant payoff and significant risk (Kammeyer-Mueller & Wanberg, 2003; Wanberg, 2012).

Research suggests that organizations that proactively and thoughtfully design recruitment, selection, and onboarding programs are better able to attract and retain scarce talent (Bauer & Erdogan, 2014). At the heart of these efforts is an appreciation for the affective experiences of applicants, candidates, and new employees. The term "affect" refers to "a broad range of feelings that individuals experience, including *feeling states*, which are in-the-moment, short-term affective experiences, and *feeling traits*, which are more stable tendencies to feel and act in certain ways" (Barsade & Gibson, 2007, p. 37). A related concept is "affect regulation," which includes attempts to influence the type, timing, and expression of one's own emotions (Gross, 1998). Affect has been studied extensively in organizational science, and it relates to a number of employee outcomes including job performance, creativity, prosocial behavior, job attitudes, and turnover (for a review see Barsade & Gibson, 2007). However, despite the consensus that affect plays an important role in organizational life for employees, there has been little focus or attention in the literature on affect during organizational entry. This is problematic given that organizational entry has been considered a "highly emotion laden experience" (Nifadkar, Tsui, & Ashforth, 2012, p. 1147) and scholars have made calls for investigation into the role of affective experiences during this phase (Ashforth, Blake, & Saks, 2002; Fisher & Ashkanasy, 2000). An understanding of newcomer experiences and the affective responses associated with them may help to predict when organizational efforts are likely to be successful, and when they might end in negative experiences for new employees.

The goal of this chapter is to illuminate the potential role of affect in the organizational entry process. We focus on research that has examined the experiences of job candidates and newcomers in an effort to garner a better understanding of how affect influences early beliefs about an organization and subsequent newcomer adjustment. The following pages present a general review of the literature on affect during pre-entry (i.e., prior to employees joining an organization) including a focus on the role of unmet expectations and psychological contracts, followed by a discussion of affect post-entry and the newcomer socialization phase. Based on our review, we note a relative dearth of research in both areas and point to potential theoretical models and specific research directions that could further develop and inform our understanding of the role of affect in the organizational entry process.

Organizational Pre-entry: Recruitment and Selection

While we know that organizational entry is typically the focus of new employee onboarding, it is not where the process actually begins. In fact, the socialization and onboarding process begins much before actual organizational entry. All of the interactions, expectations, and events that precede organizational entry, including those that occur during the recruitment and selection processes, set the stage for newcomer socialization and adjustment (e.g., Berlew & Hall, 1966; Fisher, 1986; Louis, 1980). Indeed, in a post for *Harvard Business Review,* Amy Gallo wrote that "The starting point is to recognize that the best onboarding process can't compensate for the sins of recruiting" (2010). In other words, the process begins with the early interactions that potential employees have during the recruitment and selection phases, and these relate to the expectations and reactions that employees have following organizational entry.

Unmet Expectations, Psychological Contracts, and Newcomer Pre-entry Socialization

The concept of unmet expectations refers to a discrepancy between what a person encounters on the job compared to what they had anticipated they would encounter (Porter & Steers, 1973). Seminal work by Louis (1980) explicitly focused on newcomer surprise and shock upon entry as well as how newcomers make sense of their new roles and relationships in new work organizations. She argued that unrealistic expectations as well as unmet expectations could lead to premature newcomer turnover. Following this work, Wanous, Poland, Premack, and Davis (1992) conducted a meta-analysis of the relationships with met or unmet expectations for newcomers and outcomes. They found that met newcomer expectations were related to higher job survival, higher job performance, lower intentions to leave, and higher job satisfaction and organizational commitment. Subsequently, Bauer and Green (1994) studied new research scientists attending doctoral programs and found that the higher the perceived quality of the information they were provided, the more accepted they felt at a later point in time and the lower their role conflict was reported to be. Major, Kozlowski, Chao, and Gardner (1995) gathered data from 248 new college graduate hires both before organizational entry and again four weeks after organizational entry. They found that while unmet expectations were related to more negative adjustment outcomes for newcomers, strong leader and coworker relations ameliorated the negative effects. Similarly, Turnley and Feldman (2000) found that among new managers, unmet expectations and job dissatisfaction partially mediated the relationship between psychological contract violations and key outcomes, including organizational citizenship behaviors and intentions to quit. Finally, other research has found associations between unmet expectations and emotional exhaustion – a key component of employee burnout – and this seems to be moderated by the degree to which newcomers hold positive expectations for the future (Maden, Ozcelik, & Karacay, 2016). Much of this research gives a nod to the role of affective states (e.g. affect as one component of job satisfaction) or affective traits (e.g., the tendency to view the future with hope and positivity), but such research has tended not to directly include either in these models.

A related stream of research has centered on the psychological contracts formed during organization pre-entry. Psychological contracts are defined as the belief that individuals hold regarding the terms and conditions of the exchange between themselves and their organizations (Rousseau, 1989). As one might imagine, psychological contracts include some aspect of expectations and whether or not they are met. Perceived breaches of these psychological contracts are expected to result in feelings of betrayal and disappointment (Sutton & Griffin, 2004). However, research on psychological contract breach has tended to focus on attitudinal or behavioral outcomes rather than affective ones (with some exceptions, discussed later in this chapter). For instance, findings show associations with organizational commitment, turnover, and organizational citizenship behaviors (e.g., Conway & Briner, 2000; Robinson & Morrison, 1995; Turnley & Feldman, 2000). Researchers studying psychological contracts formed during organizational entry have posited that psychological contract formation is one aspect of the sensemaking process (De Vos, Buyens, & Schalk, 2003). They found that newcomer sensemaking was associated with changes in the perceptions of newcomers over their first year across the encounter and accommodation stages of newcomer socialization. Thomas and Anderson (1998) studied British soldiers as they entered the army. They found that newcomers' expectations of their employer (i.e., their psychological contracts) increased over time as they garnered greater knowledge of their role and new work environment, making a potential breach of expectations more likely.

Collectively, these studies provide evidence of the influence of early interactions and experiences of newcomers prior to joining an organization. However, despite explanations that have centered on affective reactions such as shock, surprise, frustration, and so on, affect has not been a central focus of this research. There are, however, notable exceptions that lend support to the inclusion of affect in explanations of pre-entry expectations and the reality of newcomers' experiences. For instance, in their study of information technology employees, Nifadkar and Bauer (2016) found evidence of the deleterious effects of breaching belongingness expectations. That is, new employees who encountered conflict with their coworkers (an apparent breach of their expectation for acceptance by the group) reported increased social anxiety with coworkers, which had downstream impacts on information seeking and adjustment. Moreover, Boswell and colleagues found evidence for a hangover effect among newcomers, theorizing that as newcomers become more aware of the reality of their new jobs and better understand the negative aspects of them, their satisfaction levels are reduced (Boswell, Broudeau, & Tichy, 2005). Finally, in a meta-analysis by Zhao, Wayne, Glibkowski, and Bravo (2007), the authors found that psychological contract breach related to work-related outcomes, and that affect (operationalized as feelings of violation and mistrust) mediated the effect of breach on attitudes and individual effectiveness. They concluded that "managers should not provide unrealistic promises during recruitment, socialization, and routine work interactions. Such promises may have motivational effects in the short term, but, if afterward employees perceive a breach in the psychological contract, both the employees and organization may suffer in the long term" (Zhao et al., 2007, p. 671).

Although the literature on organizational pre-entry has been relatively silent on the role of affect during this period, useful theoretical models exist to aid in understanding the conditions or events that could cause affective reactions in applicants and new employees. For instance, Fiebig and Kramer (1998) presented a model of affect in organizations arguing that differences between expectations and actual experiences are key antecedents to emotion. The authors argued that "Various organizational events, such as a coworker deviating from standard procedures, become catalysts for emotions by creating situations in which employees notice differences between expectations and experiences" (p. 540). In a test of their model, findings showed that positive emotions most often resulted from achieving goals more easily or pleasantly than expected, while negative emotions were associated with hindrances to goal achievement. That is, unexpected instances that facilitated or thwarted goal progress were met with correspondingly positive or negative emotions. Indeed, discrepancies between expectations and reality are at the heart of such concepts as met expectations and psychological contract breach often studied in the newcomer literature, but rarely with focus on affective responses. Viewed through the lens of models such as that presented by Fiebig and Kramer (1998), findings suggest that affect might play a mediating role between discrepancies in expectations formed before organizational entry and subsequent adjustment.

Post-entry: Organizational Socialization

Once a candidate is offered a position and makes the decision to join an organization, the focus shifts to learning about, making sense of, and becoming adjusted to the new work environment. Organizational socialization has been defined as the process of going from organizational "outsider" to "insider" (Bauer & Erodgan, 2014; Louis, 1980). Inherent in this process is a period of sensemaking and learning that results from exposure to novel situations and people (Louis, 1980). The dominating theme in this research literature has been a focus on the ways in which newcomers gather relevant information and learn to function effectively in their new environment, namely cognition-related processes (Ostroff & Kozlowski, 1992). For instance, research shows that those who proactively seek out information report better adjustment (Bauer, Bodner, Erdogan et al., 2007; Morrison, 1993a, 1993b). And, to a large extent, even investigations into the development of social relationships during socialization have been viewed through the lens of information acquisition: that is, focusing on how access to others provides a greater amount and variety of information (Morrison 1993b; Nifadkar & Bauer, 2016). Similarly, research shows that institutionalized organizational socialization practices that are structured predict better adjustment among newcomers as compared to informal programs that put little emphasis on formalized learning (Saks, Uggerslev, & Fassina, 2007). For example, Robinson and Morrison (2000) found that perceived contract breach was more likely to occur for their sample of new managers when they had not been given a formalized socialization process and when they had had little or no interaction with organizational insiders prior to entry. A sense of mastery over and confidence in performing work tasks, clarity in how the new role is defined, and a feeling of being socially accepted by others in the work environment (Bauer et al., 2007) indicate successful socialization of new employees. In the long term, these indicators of adjustment have been found to predict turnover intentions, job satisfaction, and performance (Bauer et al., 2007). As with the pre-entry phase, largely absent from this body of work is a focus on newcomer affect.

The study of affect in organizations is complex in part because the phenomenon is dynamic and involves a range of experiences from short-term, high-intensity emotions to more stable tendencies to feel certain ways (Barsade & Gibson, 2007; Watson & Clark, 1994). Moreover, affective experiences are not confined to the individual themselves but are often elicited by others in the environment and also affect others, making affective experience both a within- and a between-person phenomenon. To address this complexity, Weiss and Cropanzano (1996) proposed affective events theory (AET), a comprehensive theory of affect in organizations that may prove useful in understanding the role of affect during organizational entry. The theory suggests that short-term affective experiences are the result of features of the work environment (e.g., job demands) that play out in daily work events. These events are interpreted in the context of an individual's personality tendencies, which lead to the experience of positive or negative reactions. Over time, these affective reactions are thought to accumulate and contribute to more enduring and affectively-laden job attitudes (e.g., job satisfaction) and job performance. While most studies of affect involving newcomers have not taken this theoretical approach, as a body of work they can be organized and interpreted through this lens in order to provide greater insight into opportunities for future work. The following sections organize the discussion of these studies by looking first at those investigating critical affective events during socialization. Next, we examine work conditions and experiences that contribute to newcomer emotional experiences. Finally, we will point to individual differences in affective tendencies likely to moderate the relationship between affective experiences and socialization outcomes.

Valence of Critical Socialization Events Among Newcomers

Research on critical events during socialization suggests that the valence ascribed to such events may be an important consideration. For example, in their descriptive study within the hospitality sector, Lundberg and Young (1997) prompted newcomers to think about "formative events … which helped them develop an impression about what it was like to work in the organization they had joined" (p. 61). Despite the neutral prompt, they found that newcomers reported more negative than positive events occurring over the first six months on the job. While research from social psychology provides evidence of a general "negativity bias" among humans (Rozin & Royzman, 2001), other research indicates that it could be more pronounced among newcomers – that is, there may be something unique to the socialization context that influences how newcomers appraise certain situations. Research by Reicherts and Pihet (2000) showed that while early career newcomers in their sample had relatively high well-being, newcomers tended to experience stressful events as "more stressful" and have stronger emotional reactions characterized by anger and anxiousness, when compared to a student sample.

Emotions and Newcomer Organizational Socialization

Reio and Callahan (2004) hypothesized that affect would impact the extent to which newcomers were motivated to seek out job-relevant information and therefore their socialization-related learning. Accordingly, they found support for a process model in which newcomer reports of anxiety and anger predicted socialization-related learning and job performance through their impact on curiosity. Specifically, anxiety seemed to deter the socialization process, while anger positively impacted newcomers' curiosity and desire for new information, which had a positive impact on job performance. This finding is consistent with recent theorizing by Bauer and Erdogan (2014), who proposed that anxiety may be the underlying mechanism that explains how hindrance stressors (i.e., events that block professional growth and goal attainment) can derail successful socialization and adjustment.

In a related vein, Ellis, Bauer, Mansfield et al. (2015) theorized that affect plays a role in the newcomer stress appraisal process and, specifically, that when newcomers are cognizant of demands, they take inventory of resources available to meet those demands. Depending on the outcome of this evaluation process, newcomers may experience positive mood associated with engagement in the socialization process, while others may experience negative mood, causing them to withdraw from the process and putting them at risk of poor adjustment. Consistent with this reasoning, Simon, Bauer, Erdogan, and Shepherd (2019) examined positive affect among newcomers over the course of their first eight weeks and assessed outcomes at ninety days post-entry. Findings showed that initial levels of positive affect were directly related to intrinsic motivation. Their study also showed that linear change in positive affect across the eight weeks was negatively associated with turnover intentions, and positively predicted intrinsic motivation and social acceptance at ninety days post-entry.

An important question that arises from this research is where in the chain of events affect comes into play. Reio and Callahan (2004) position affect as a predictor, while others suggest affect is a response to some stimulus that has downstream impacts on the socialization process (e.g., Bauer & Erodgan, 2014; Ellis et al., 2015). In a study by Kammeyer-Mueller, Wanberg, Rubenstein, and Song (2013), newcomers' hedonic tone (i.e., positive mood, pleasant feelings) was found to directly predict work proactivity and organizational commitment, and mediated the relationship between initial levels of supervisor and coworker support on organizational commitment. Similarly, drawing on emotion as feedback system theory (Baumeister, Vohs, DeWall, and Zhang, 2007), Nifadkar and colleagues (2012) found that positive and negative supervisor behavior predicted supervisor-triggered affect (i.e. "newcomers' conscious, remembered, and accumulated experience of affect in relation to his or her supervisor," p. 1147), which, in turn, predicted newcomer approach (feedback seeking) and avoidance (interaction avoidance) behavior, and newcomer adjustment outcomes. Finally, Ellis, Nifadkar, Bauer, and Erdogan (2017) examined anxiety as an outcome of leader–newcomer interactions including newcomer proactivity and manager support, and found no significant effect.

Affect, Individual Differences, and Newcomer Organizational Socialization

Outside of the context itself, there may be individual factors that affect newcomer experiences of positive and negative emotions. For instance, Simon et al. (2019) found that newcomers who perceived themselves as overqualified for their role reported lower positive affect at organizational entry; however, this effect was attenuated by high proactive personality. The authors reasoned that proactive individuals are better able to enact positive changes that counteract the negative feelings associated with being overqualified. In another study, Duffy, Ganster, & Shaw (1998) examined the role of trait positive affect (PA) among high- versus low-tenured employees. Their findings showed that PA interacted with job satisfaction and tenure to predict job search behavior, counterproductive behavior, and health complaints. That is, the highest job search behavior among low-tenured employees was seen in those low in PA and job satisfaction. Further, among low-tenured employees, PA appeared to protect against health problems in the case of low job satisfaction. Thus, positive affective disposition played both a motivational and a protective role for newer employees.

In their study of newcomer tactics, Ashford and Black (1996) identified positive framing as one important newcomer proactive behavior. Positive framing refers to attempts to perceive events in a favorable light. This is an important tactic for job applicants and new hires: it can help them interpret the events they encounter in a positive manner and encourage them to remain open to new experiences, rather than avoiding potentially stressful situations that might help them grow into their new roles and develop in their social relationships. Research shows that positive framing during newcomer onboarding is related to both job satisfaction (Ashford & Black, 1996; Wanberg & Kammeyer-Mueller, 2000) and job performance (Ashford & Black, 1996). In one study, positive framing was found to strengthen the relationship between institutionalized socialization tactics and person–organization fit (Kim, Cable, & Kim, 2005). Wanberg and Kammeyer-Mueller (2000) found that higher levels of openness to experience were associated with greater positive framing among new employees. While positive framing itself is not an emotion, the behavioral tendency to cope with uncertain or negative events in this way may affect the valence of subsequent emotional reactions ascribed to certain experiences.

Very few studies have focused specifically on the role of affect in the post-entry socialization process despite calls for its integration (Fisher & Ashkanasy, 2000) and acknowledgment of the emotional nature of this transitional period in employees' lives (Nifadkar et al., 2012). The research that has been conducted supports the supposition that affect may play an important role in employees' ability to interpret events that occur and to develop key job attitudes, spurring newcomer behaviors that facilitate adjustment. A potential barrier to work in this area is the lack of a clear theoretical framework to guide research. Current theories of socialization either do not consider affect at all or, where affect does appear, do not treat it as central to the theory (e.g., Ellis et al., 2015; Saks & Gruman, 2011). AET theory may be one way to bring these disparate findings together and contribute to our understanding of affect during the socialization phase. The following section provides a discussion of potential areas of future investigation.

Future Research Directions

Understanding and Managing Newcomer Expectations and Affect

There are numerous opportunities to expand current work by investigating affect in the organizational entry period. First, examining affect may help us to understand how pre-entry experiences and early socialization experiences contribute to effective adjustment. Research should include affective reactions (i.e., moods and emotions) in models of applicant reactions to the recruitment and selection process, development of expectations, and psychological contract breach. Understanding affective reactions to these experiences may help to elucidate mechanisms underlying the relationship between these experiences and subsequent attitudinal and behavioral outcomes.

Second, research has indicated that providing applicants with realistic job previews – highlighting both the opportunities and benefits of a new job and its challenges and difficulties – can help applicants set realistic expectations and reduce negative surprises once in the new role (Premak & Wanous, 1985). However, this research has focused largely on setting expectations related to tasks or the work environment rather than how one might be emotionally impacted by the job. Realistic previews focused specifically on emotional demands could prove an important supplement that helps newcomers adjust, especially in jobs characterized by high emotional demands (e.g., social work, nursing, teaching). Indeed, the degree of emotional labor (i.e., the management of emotional responses and expressions in accordance with requirements of a job; Grandey, 2000) is one work characteristic highlighted by AET and linked to emotion-related outcomes (Weiss & Cropanzano, 1996). Thus there is significant opportunity to learn from investigations that include affect in existing models of how newcomers respond to discrepancies in expectations upon entry, and to learn about employees' expectations of affective experiences.

In related work, Choi (2018) argued that understanding and adjusting to the emotional culture in an organization is a key task for newcomers in any type of work. In their emotional model of socialization, they suggested that socialization tactics and newcomer proactivity, among other factors, predicted adjustment to the emotional culture, which in turn facilitated person–organization fit and organizational identification. Consistent with this notion, Fiebig and Kramer (1999) noted that socialization practices may help to formalize emotional expectations (i.e., teach display rules), while Saks and Gruman (2011) indicate that certain socialization resources could result in feelings associated with positive adjustment such as hope and optimism. Taking a more concerted look at affective reactions to formal and informal socialization practices could help point to when and what sorts of emotional reactions are likely, how newcomers manage those emotional reactions, and the extent to which these reactions predict adjustment outcomes.

Positive Emotions, Emotional Spirals, and Newcomer Proactivity

Drawing on findings from Parker, Bindl, and Strauss (2010), as well as theoretical models such as the broaden-and-build framework (Fredrickson, 1998), positive affective states (i.e., positive mood) should contribute to greater proactivity (e.g., feedback seeking, relationship building, etc.) among newcomers – key behaviors associated with positive socialization outcomes. Bindl et al., (2012) found that positive affective states predicted engagement in proactive behavior among a sample of call center agents and medical students. Similarly, Frederickson (2013) posited that positive resource spirals were a virtuous cycle in which positive emotions lead to individuals feeling more proactive and, in turn, proactive behaviors lead to the development of greater resources. Being successful in gathering resources should lead to higher positive affect, and so on. Thus we can imagine that for newcomers, both before and after entering an organization, affective states may play an important role in acquiring resources (Simon et al., 2019). Given that newcomer proactivity has emerged as being highly predictive of newcomer onboarding success (Bauer, et al., 2007; Saks, Gruman, & Cooper-Thomas, 2011), it makes sense to posit that positive affective states might activate greater proactive behaviors (Ashford & Black, 1996) such as relationship building, information seeking, feedback seeking, and general socializing. Further, how positive affect might be deliberately induced through formal newcomer socialization programs is an area with important potential implications for program design.

Affect and Social Relationships During Socialization

A third area in which current socialization research might be expanded with a focus on affect relates to the development of social relationships. Prior work indicates that a primary indicator of effective socialization is a sense of belonging (Bauer et al., 2007), and that events that threaten that sense of belonging result in less favorable socialization outcomes (Nifadkar & Bauer, 2016). Understanding how newcomer affective responses and displays influence incumbent perceptions, and ultimately influence the individual's ability to develop meaningful social connections in their new environment, would be a fruitful area of investigation. Individual differences, such as newcomer emotional intelligence, ability to regulate and display appropriate emotions, or susceptibility to emotional contagion (Barsade, 2002) could be important factors to consider in such models. Moreover, research investigating how newcomer affect might impact team-level phenomena such as affective team tone or team climate (for a review see Collins, Lawrence, Troth, & Jordan, 2013) has the potential to greatly inform our understanding of how newcomers adjust, and the impact of newcomers on incumbent employees. Taken together, there are important ways in which our knowledge of current socialization factors could be expanded by examining affect in these processes.

Stress and Coping During Socialization

A focus on affect during the socialization process also points to the importance of stress and coping during this phase. Indeed, models of stress appraisal and coping are inherently linked to affective experiences (e.g., Lazarus & Folkman, 1987; Reicherts & Pihet, 2000). While scholars have referred to the socialization process as a time of great stress and uncertainty (Ellis et al., 2015; Nelson, 1987), and calls for research in this area have been made, to date few studies explicitly examine stress during socialization. Building on research by Reio and Callahan (2004), and consistent with arguments made by Ellis et al. (2015), it is possible that formal socialization practices (i.e., those that focus on the provision of relevant information, newcomer training, and providing newcomers with opportunities for making social connections) reduce anxiety and contribute to a sense of challenge that positively impacts newcomers' engagement in the socialization process. Drawing on work by Saks and Ashforth (1997), Reio and Callahan (2004) called anxiety an "overlooked variable with respect to employee proactive information seeking and adaptation" (p. 9). Particularly interesting is how positive experiences during socialization (and positive affect accompanying them) might facilitate socialization and newcomer well-being through reduced stress and better coping. For instance, research on college students has found that particularly in times of high stress, social support and positive life events moderated the relationship between negative life stress and ill health (i.e., depression and physical symptoms) (Cohen & Hoberman, 1983). Similarly, research finds that positive emotions are related to resilience in stressful circumstances, buffering against stress and helping individuals to find "positive meaning in stressful encounters" (Tugade & Fredrickson, 2004, p. 320). If we generalize these findings to the socialization period – another instance of high stress – it is possible that positive social interactions or other positive events are the key to neutralizing potential negative effects of starting a new job and building resilience among newcomers.

Levels of Analysis

Finally, there are interesting opportunities to integrate models of organizational entry and affect by considering different levels of analysis. Nifadkar et al. (2012) suggested that future work look at the "number, frequency, intensity, and sequencing of emotion-eliciting episodes, perhaps through an experience-sampling methodology" (p. 1162). Similarly, in their review of the literature, Ellis et al. (2015) suggested that socialization researchers explore within-person patterns of stress during socialization in order to better understand how newcomers appraise the availability of coping resources and subsequent reactions. Ashkanasy (2015) outlined five discrete levels of analysis for the study of affect in organizational research, each providing opportunities for unique insight: (1) within-person temporal effects, (2) between-person (personality and attitudes) factors, (3) interpersonal behaviors (perception and communication of emotion), (4) group level (leadership and teams), and (5) organizational level (culture and climate). Certainly, much can be learned from systematically investigating the role of affect during organizational entry at these various levels of analysis.

Conclusion

Although research has only begun to understand the role of emotions, mood, and personality tendencies associated with affect in the organizational entry period, there is evidence to suggest that affect is an important part of job applicants', candidates', and new employees' successful adjustment to their new work environment. Comprehensive models of affect, such as AET, provide a means of integrating disparate research findings in this area and point to future opportunities for research.

References

Ashford, S. J., & Black, J. S. (1996). Proactivity during organizational entry: The role of desire for control. *Journal of Applied Psychology, 81*, 199–214.

Ashforth, B. E., & Saks, A. M. (2002). Feeling your way: Emotion and organizational entry. In R. G. Lord, R. J. Klimoski, & R. Kanfer (Eds.), *Emotions in the workplace*. San Francisco, CA: Jossey-Bass (pp. 331–369).

Ashkanasy, N. M. (2015). Emotions and work. In N. J. Smelser & P. B. Baltes (Eds.), *International Encyclopedia of the Social & Behavioral Sciences* (Volume 7, pp. 507–512). Oxford, UK: Elsevier Science.

Barsade, S. G. (2002). The ripple effect: Emotional contagion and its influence on group behavior. *Administrative Science Quarterly, 47*, 644–675.

Barsade, S. G., & Gibson, D. E. (2007). Why does affect matter in organizations? *Academy of Management Perspectives, 21*, 36–59.

Bauer, T. N., Bodner, T., Erdogan, B., Truxillo, D. M., & Tucker, J. S. (2007). Newcomer adjustment during organizational socialization: A meta-analytic review of antecedents, outcomes, and methods. *Journal of Applied Psychology, 92*, 707–721.

Bauer, T. N., & Erdogan, B. (2014). Delineating and reviewing the role of newcomer capital in organizational socialization. *Annual Review of Organizational Psychology and Organizational Behavior, 1*, 439–457.

Bauer, T. N., & Green, S. G. (1994). Effect of newcomer involvement in work-related activities: A longitudinal study of socialization. *Journal of Applied Psychology, 79*, 211–223.

Baumeister, R. F., Vohs, K. D., DeWall, C. N., & Zhang, L. (2007). How emotion shapes behavior: Feedback, anticipation, and reflection, rather than direct causation. *Personality & Social Psychology Review, 11*, 167–203.

Berlew, D. E., & Hall, D. T. (1966). The socialization of managers: Effects of expectations on performance. *Administrative Science Quarterly, 11*, 207–223.

Bindl, U. K., Parker, S. K., Totterdell, P., & Hagger-Johnson, G. (2012). Fuel of the self-starter: How mood relates to proactive goal regulation. *Journal of Applied Psychology, 97*, 134–150.

Boswell, W. R., Boudreau, J. W., & Tichy, J. (2005). The relationship between employee job change and job satisfaction: The honeymoon–hangover effect. *Journal of Applied Psychology, 90*, 882–892.

Buckley, M. R., Mobbs, T. A., Mendoza, J. L., Novicevic, M. M., Carraher, S. M., & Beu, D. S. (2002). Implementing realistic job previews and expectation-lowering procedures: A field experiment. *Journal of Vocational Behavior, 61*, 263–278.

Choi, Y. (2018). When in Rome, feel as the Romans feel: An emotional model of organizational socialization. *Social Sciences, 7*, 197–217.

Cohen, S. & Hoberman, H. M. (1983). Positive events and social supports as buffers of life change stress. *Journal of Applied Social Psychology, 13*, 99–125.

Collins, A. L., Lawrence, S. A., Troth, A. C., & Jordan, P. J. (2013). Group affective tone: A review and future research directions. *Journal of Organizational Behavior, 34*, S43–S62.

Conway, N., & Briner, R. B. (2002). A daily diary study of affective responses to psychological contract breach and exceeded promises. *Journal of Organizational Behavior, 23*, 287–302.

De Vos, A., Buyens, D., & Schalk, R. (2003). Psychological contract development during organizational socialization: Adaptation to reality and the role of reciprocity. *Journal of Organizational Behavior, 24*, 537–559.

Duffy, M. K., Ganster, D. C., & Shaw, J. D. (1998). Positive affectivity and negative outcomes: The role of tenure and job satisfaction. *Journal of Applied Psychology, 83*, 950–959.

Ellis, A. M., Bauer, T. N., Mansfield, L. R., Erdogan, B., Truxillo, D. M., & Simon, L. (2015). Navigating uncharted waters: Newcomer socialization through the lens of stress theory. *Journal of Management, 41*, 203–235.

Ellis, A. M., Nifadkar, S. S., Bauer, T. N., & Erdogan, B. (2017). Newcomer adjustment: Examining the role of managers' perception of newcomer proactive behavior during organizational socialization. *Journal of Applied Psychology, 102*, 993–1001.

Fiebig, G. V., & Kramer, M. W. (1998). A framework for the study of emotions in organizational contexts. *Management Communication Quarterly, 11*, 536–572.

Fisher, C. D. (1986). Organizational socialization: An integrative review. In K. M. Rowland & G. R. Ferris (Eds.), *Research in personnel and human resource management* (Volume 4, pp. 101–145). Greenwich, CT: JAI.

Fisher, C. D., & Ashkanasy, N. M. (2000). The emerging role of emotions in work life: An introduction. *Journal of Organizational Behavior, 21*, 123–129.

Fredrickson, B. L. (1998). What good are positive emotions? *Review of General Psychology: Special Issue: New Directions in Research on Emotion, 2*, 300–319.

Frederickson, B. L. (2013). Positive emotions broaden and build. *Advances in Experimental Social Psychology, 47*, 1–53.

Gallo, A. (2010). Get immediate value from your new hires. *Harvard Business Review*, 15 April, https://hbr.org/2010/04/make-your-new-hire-immediately.

Grandey, A. (2000). Emotion regulation in the workplace: A new way to conceptualize emotional labor. *Journal of Occupational Health Psychology, 5*, 59–100.

Gross, J. (1998). The emerging field of emotion regulation: An integrative review. *Review of General Psychology, 2*, 271–299.

Kammeyer-Mueller, J. D., & Wanberg, C. (2003). Unwrapping the organizational entry process: Disentangling multiple antecedents and their pathways to adjustment. *Journal of Applied Psychology, 88*, 779–794.

Kammeyer-Mueller, J. D., Wanberg, C., Rubenstein, A., & Song, Z. (2013). Support, undermining, and newcomer socialization: Fitting in during the first 90 days. *Academy of Management Journal, 56*, 1104–1124.

Kim, T., Cable, D. M., & Kim, S. (2005). Socialization tactics, employee proactivity, and person-organization fit. *Journal of Applied Psychology, 90*, 232–241.

Lazarus, R. S., & Folkman, S. (1987). Transactional theory and research on emotions and coping. *European Journal of Personality, 1*, 141–169.

Louis, M. R. (1980). Surprise and sense making: What newcomers experience in entering unfamiliar organizational settings. *Administrative Science Quarterly, 25*, 226–256.

Lundberg, C. C., & Young, C. A. (1997). Newcomer socialization: Critical incidents in hospitality organizations. *Journal of Hospitality and Tourism Research, 21*, 58–74.

Maden, C., Ozcelik, H., & Karacacy, G. (2016). Exploring employees' responses to unmet job expectations: The moderating role of future job expectations and efficacy beliefs. *Personnel Review, 45*, 4–28.

Major, D. A., Kozlowski, S. W. J., Chao, G. T., & Gardner, P. (1995). A longitudinal investigation of newcomer expectations, early socialization outcomes, and the moderating effects of role development factors. *Journal of Applied Psychology, 80*, 418–431.

Maurer, R. (2017). New hires skip out when the role doesn't meet expectations. Society for Human Resource Management (SHRM) website, www.shrm.org/resourcesandtools/hr-topics/talent-acquisition/pages/new-hires-retention-turnover.aspx

Morrison, E. W. (1993a). Longitudinal study of the effects of information seeking on newcomer socialization. *Journal of Applied Psychology, 78*, 173–183.

Morrison, E. W. (1993b). Newcomer information seeking: Exploring types, modes, sources, and outcomes. *Academy of Management Journal, 36*, 557–589.

Nelson, D. L. (1987). Organizational socialization: A stress perspective. *Journal of Occupational Behaviour, 8*, 311–324.

Nifadkar, S., & Bauer, T. N. (2016). Breach of belongingness: Newcomer relationship conflict, information, and task-related outcomes during organizational socialization. *Journal of Applied Psychology, 101*, 1–13.

Nifadkar, S., Tsui, A. S., & Ashforth, B. E. (2012). The way you make me feel and behave: Supervisor-triggered newcomer affect and approach–avoidance behavior. *Academy of Management Journal, 55*, 1146–1168.

Ostroff, C., & Kozlowski, S. W. J. (1992). Organizational socialization as a learning process: The role of information acquisition. *Personnel Psychology, 45*, 849–874.

Parker, S. K., Bindl, U. K., & Strauss, K. (2010). Making things happen: A model of proactive motivation. *Journal of Management, 36*, 827–856.

Porter, L. W., & Steers, R. M. (1973). Organizational, work, and personal factors in employee turnover and absenteeism. *Psychological Bulletin, 80*, 151–176.

Premack, S. L., & Wanous, J. P. (1985). A meta-analysis of realistic job preview experiments. *Journal of Applied Psychology, 70*, 706–719.

Reicherts, M., & Pihet, S. (2000). Job newcomers coping with stressful situations: A micro-analysis of adequate coping and well-being. *Swiss Journal of Psychology, 59*, 303–316.

Reio, T. G., & Callahan, J. L. (2004). Affect, curiosity, and socialization-related learning: A path analysis of antecedents to job performance. *Journal of Business and Psychology, 19*, 3–22.

Robinson, S. L., & Morrison, E. W. (1995). Psychological contracts and OCB: The effect of unfulfilled obligations on civic virtue behavior. *Journal of Organizational Behavior, 16*, 289–298.

Robinson, S. L., & Wolfe Morrison, E. (2000). The development of psychological contract breach and violation: A longitudinal study. *Journal of Organizational Behavior, 21*, 525–546.

Rousseau, D. M. (1989). Psychological and implied contracts in organizations. *Employee Responsibilities and Rights Journal, 2*, 121–139.

Rozin, P., & Royzman, E. B. (2001). Negativity bias, negativity dominance, and contagion. *Personality and Social Psychology Review, 5*, 296–320.

Saks, A. M., & Ashforth, B. E. (1997). Organizational socialization: Making sense of the past and present as a prologue for the future. *Journal of Vocational Behavior, 51*, 234–279.

Saks, A. M., & Gruman, J. A. (2011). Organizational socialization and positive organizational behavior: Implications for theory, research, and practice. *Canadian Journal of Administrative Sciences, 28*, 14–26.

Saks, A. M., Gruman, J. A., & Cooper-Thomas, H. (2011). The neglected role of proactive behavior and outcomes in newcomer socialization. *Journal of Vocational Behavior, 79*, 36–46.

Saks, A. M., Uggerslev, K. L., & Fassina, N. E. (2007). Socialization tactics and newcomer adjustment: A meta-analytic review and test of a model. *Journal of Vocational Behavior, 70*, 413–446.

Simon, L. S., Bauer, T. N., Erdogan, B., & Shepherd, W. (2019). Built to last: Interactive effects of perceived overqualification and proactive personality on new employee adjustment. *Personnel Psychology, 72*, 213–240.

Sutton, G., & Griffin, M. A. (2004). Integrating expectations, experiences, and psychological contract violations: A longitudinal study of new professionals. *Journal of Occupational and Organizational Psychology, 77*, 493–514.

Thomas, H. D., & Anderson, N. (1998). Changes in newcomers' psychological contracts during organizational socialization: A study of recruits entering the British Army. *Journal of Organizational Behavior, 19*, 745–767.

Tugade, M. M., & Fredrickson, B. L. (2004). Resilient individuals use positive emotions to bounce back from negative emotional experiences. *Journal of Personality and Social Psychology, 86*, 320–333.

Turnley, W. H., & Feldman, D. C. (2000). Re-examining the effects of psychological contract violations: Unmet expectations and job dissatisfaction as mediators. *Journal of Organizational Behavior, 21*, 25–42.

Wanberg, C. R. (2012). *The Oxford handbook of organizational socialization*. New York, NY: Oxford University Press.

Wanberg, C. R., & Kammeyer-Mueller, J. D. (2000). Predictors and outcomes of proactivity in the socialization process. *Journal of Applied Psychology, 85*, 373–385.

Wanous, J. P. (1973). Effects of a realistic job preview on job acceptance, job attitudes, and job survival. *Journal of Applied Psychology, 58*, 327–332.

Wanous, J. P., Poland, T. D., Premack, S. L., & Davis, K. S. (1992). The effects of met expectations on newcomer attitudes and behaviors: A review and meta-analysis. *Journal of Applied Psychology, 77*, 288–297.

Watson, D., & Clark, L. A. (1994). *The PANAS-X: Manual for the positive and negative affect schedule – Expanded form*. Ames: University of Iowa.

Weiss, H. M., & Cropanzano, R. (1996). Affective events theory: A theoretical discussion of the structure, causes and consequences of affective experiences at work. In B. M. Staw & L. L. Cummings (Eds.), *Research in organizational behavior* (pp. 1–74). Greenwich, CT: JAI.

Zhao, H. A. O., Wayne, S. J., Glibkowski, B. C., & Bravo, J. (2007). The impact of psychological contract breach on work-related outcomes: a meta-analysis. *Personnel Psychology, 60*, 647–680.

25 Performance Management and Workplace Affect

Ariel Roberts, Paul E. Levy, Catalina Flores, and Gina Thoebes

Affect and emotion play a critical role in the lives of humans across many domains such as family, health, and work. In fact, Forgas (1994) proposes that "affect is a pervasive part of the way we see the world" (p. 40). Many scholars have proposed and developed theories and frameworks regarding affect that can be and have been applied to various work domains. Our focus in this chapter is on the role of affect in the performance management (PM) process. In particular, the work of Forgas and colleagues on the affect infusion model (AIM: Forgas & George, 2001; Forgas & Williams, 2016) and of Weiss and Cropanzano on affective events theory (AET: Weiss & Cropanzano, 1996) are helpful in explaining how affect fits into this critical work-related process.

The AIM (Forgas, 1995; Forgas & George, 2001) proposes that affect impacts organizational behavior by influencing both what and how people think. Forgas argues that affect plays a prominent role when the processing involved in a particular task is either heuristic or substantive. We argue that the tasks involved in PM fall into these two categories and, therefore, there is great potential for affect to be significantly infused into this process. Affect can also play a role in the later part of the PM process, when ratees are likely to have affective reactions to the feedback they receive and the process they have experienced (Taylor, Fisher, & Ilgen, 1984). Further, it's possible that one's affect or mood might impact one's perceptions of and reactions to the PM process. AET (Weiss & Cropanzano, 1996) was originally proposed as a framework or roadmap for future research on emotions at work (Weiss & Beal, 2005). A major premise of the theory is that affect is influenced by events; that affect levels fluctuate over time; and that this fluctuation is a function of both endogenous components, such as mood cycles or affective dispositions, and exogenous components such as affect-relevant events (Weiss & Cropanzano, 1996). Finally, the consequences of affective experiences include both attitudes and behaviors. AET provides a nice framework for examining and understanding the role of affective reactions to the process of PM.

Next, we will briefly outline the most contemporary thinking and recent conceptualizations around PM. This will be followed by a deeper dive into the role of affect in the PM process. We will rely on the AIM and AET to help conceptualize our ideas around affect and PM; we will focus on the affect that people bring into the PM situation as well as the affect that emerges from the PM experience; we will also consider the affect of both raters and ratees, as they are the chief players in the PM process.

Background of Performance Management

Performance management (PM) can be defined as "a continuous process of identifying, measuring, and developing the performance of individuals and teams and aligning performance with the strategic goals of the organization" (Aguinis, 2013, p. 2). PM is a broad process that includes what we have traditionally called performance appraisal (PA) or the annual/semi-annual evaluation of employee performance, along with coaching, the provision of developmental feedback, goal setting, and strategic planning. In the remainder of this chapter, we will mostly focus on PM, as this term has largely supplanted discussions of PA in the research literature.

Levy and Williams (2004) did a thorough review of the PA literature (looking at research published between 1990 and 2003) and argued that understanding the social context in which PA takes place is critical for understanding PA's strengths, weaknesses, and key processes. This review drew a few important conclusions: 1) the dynamic nature of the feedback environment is important; 2) appraisal effectiveness is broader than just accuracy; 3) more research is needed on the interaction among key elements rather than a one-variable-at-a-time approach to our research; and 4) it remains vital to apply research knowledge to organizations, which we don't always do very well (Ilgen, Barnes-Farrell, & McKellin, 1993). Two relevant papers have flowed directly from the work of Levy and Williams. First, Levy and colleagues revisited the social context of PM (Levy, Cavanaugh, Frantz, Borden & Roberts, 2018) and specifically focused only on the recent work done on rater errors and biases, rating accuracy, and ratee reactions. They concluded that much has been done in recent years on the three areas of interest, but that additional work needs to continue. In particular, they highlighted the importance of rater accountability, perceptions of justice, and multi-source feedback. Finally, the authors conclude that these and other context variables interact in complex ways and that future research needs to recognize that people bring their own idiosyncrasies and characteristics into dynamic PM environments, which can change rapidly (Levy, et al., 2018).

Second, in a thought-provoking and novel paper, Schleicher and colleagues (Schleicher, et al., 2018) provide the most comprehensive review of the PM literature since Levy and Williams in 2004. This paper also applies systems theory (Nadler & Tushman, 1980) to create the first systems-based taxonomy and conceptual model of PM. Figure 25.1 is the model showing the six major components: inputs, outputs, formal processes, informal processes, tasks, and individuals.

Inputs and outputs are outside the process itself and may be thought of as antecedents and consequences, respectively. The formal processes are the structures and procedures developed and articulated in writing to make PM happen, such as the format of the evaluation, rater training, ratee participation, and the like. The informal processes are typically not articulated in writing but are also instrumental in ensuring that PM takes place, such as the informal feedback environment in the workgroup and the broader organizational culture.

The final components are where we believe affect plays its most central role. First, as is clear from Figure 25.1, the workflow of PM is represented by seven tasks: setting performance expectations, observing employee performance, integrating performance information, rendering a formal summative performance evaluation, generating and delivering performance feedback, conducting the formal performance review meeting, and providing performance coaching (Schleicher et al., 2018). Second, the individuals involved in PM are usually the employee and the supervisor, but other raters such as customers, clients, peers, and subordinates may be substituted for, or supplement, supervisors in the PM process. The rest of this chapter will articulate how affect impacts the critical interactions of the relevant individuals (raters and ratees) regarding the tasks of PM. We propose two main paths through which this occurs: the workflow of PM is impacted by the affect that individuals experience and bring to their interactions; and affect emerges from the interactions of the key individuals within the workflow of PM, which has additional implications for those involved.

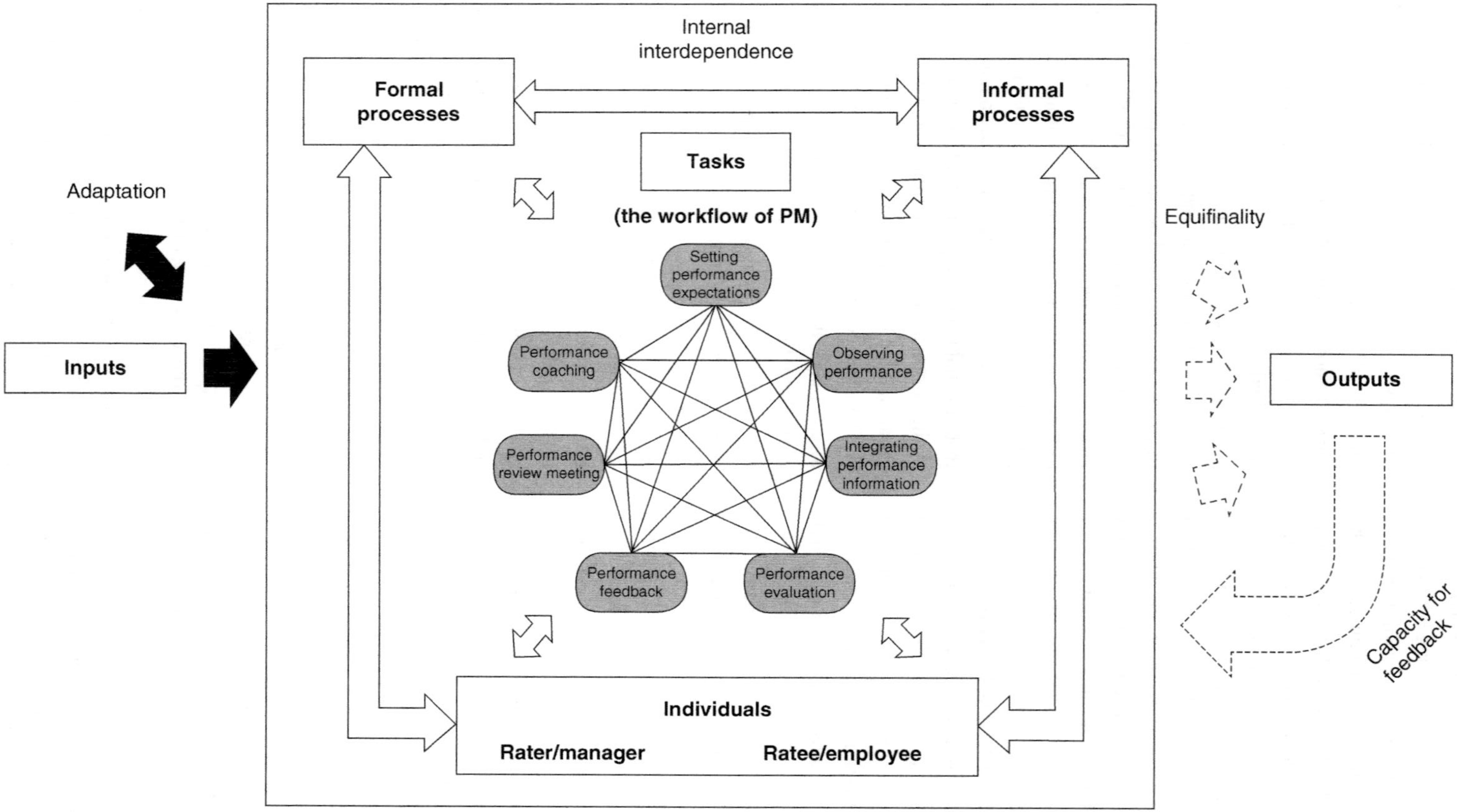

Figure 25.1 Systems-based model of performance management (Schleicher et al., 2018)

Throughout the workflow of PM and within the individuals involved, affect is present, but often overlooked. Therefore, we argue that affect plays a role in both the earlier and later stages of this workflow in two ways: judgment/decision-making and reactions. It is important to add that there is some overlap between the two affective pieces in addition to a reciprocal effect, especially given the accepted conceptualization that PM is a dynamic, cyclical process that occurs over time. Furthermore, we must not forget that individuals are the ones responsible for PM. Thus, the effect of those involved is ubiquitous, but our argument is that affect is most central to the individuals involved in PM processes and the tasks they are performing. In our next section, we discuss how affect impacts the judgments and decisions made in PM tasks. The following section discusses the role of affect in reactions to PM processes and tasks. We will conclude by proposing future directions for studying affect in PM research.

Using the AIM to Explain Judgments and Decisions Throughout PM Tasks

The AIM explains the role of affective states in social judgments by defining four judgmental strategies that fall on a continuum of the amount of processing needed, and proposes that strategies requiring more processing are more likely to be influenced by affect. PM is a fitting application of the AIM because it is an inherently social activity in which the thoughts and judgments of distinct parties can influence one another as well as the overall outcomes of the activities (Forgas & George, 2001). The strategies are as follows. *Direct access*, the simplest method, refers to a task that calls for retrieving a pre-existing evaluation. *Motivated processing* is used when there is motivation for a certain outcome, guiding individuals to use selective and targeted searches for information when making judgments. *Heuristic processing* takes place when there is no prior evaluation and the individual must make a judgment on the spot, with no strong demand for accuracy. Finally, *substantive processing* occurs when the individual needs to form an evaluation on the spot, but the target is complex and there is motivation to be accurate.

Direct access and motivated processing are considered low-affect-infusion strategies, while heuristic and substantive processing are considered high-affect-infusion strategies; the latter two require more cognition, providing opportunities for judgment to be directly and indirectly influenced by affect. The mechanisms by which affect becomes infused into judgments are by *affect-as-information* and *affect priming heuristics* (Forgas, 1995). Affect-as-information is a more direct route, in which individuals use their current affect as a shortcut to make decisions about a target individual or context. For instance, when participating in development activities associated with a negative affective state, employees may inadvertently use their current feelings as a cue to evaluate the program poorly. By contrast, affect priming is indirect, whereby one's present affect influences one's attention, encoding, and retrieval of the activities at hand. Positive affect can let individuals know that enough effort has been exerted into the current judgment, while negative affect signals that more effort is needed to work toward the current goal (George & Zhou, 2001). In PM, this could lead a manager experiencing positive affect to cut a coaching session short because such a mood leads him or her to infer a job well done.

The AIM also specifies how the context around the target, judge, and situation can determine which strategy is used. In the case of PM, the target is typically the employee, the judge is typically the manager, and the situation may be seen as the culture. Taken together, the unique context formed by each of these features will determine whether high or low affect infusion strategies are used within the workflow of PM. The AIM framework is helpful in outlining the influence of affect on PM tasks and workflow because this framework highlights that individuals engage with a unique context (i.e. target, judge, and situation characteristics), which can influence their disposition, judgments, and decisions within PM activities. The targets and judges within the PM system also rely on strategies (i.e. direct access, motivated, heuristic, or substantive processing) that are more or less prone to affect infusion. In other words, affect infusion plays a role in creating the context raters' and ratees' experience when performing the tasks of PM. Examples from the perspective of both the ratee and the rater are discussed in the next section.

Affect and Judgments from the Rater's Perspective

Using the AIM framework, the role of affect is observed in the judgments of raters from the perspective of whether it creates bias and unwanted errors in ratings or whether, because affect develops due to subordinate performance, it is a legitimate contributing factor to ratings (Varma & Pichler, 2007). While empirical evidence of affect as a bias has been mixed, it is also important to note that the presence of bias or error in ratings is a separate issue from accuracy. Research has shown that multiple rater idiosyncrasies are expected due to truly different experiences with the individual, so rater error can come from varied perspectives as opposed to inaccurate judgments (Lance, Hoffman, Gentry, & Baranik, 2008). This leads us to believe that the more pertinent issue is not whether ratings are biased due to affect, but understanding the various conditions in which contextual factors around PM may make it more likely that raters' affect is incorporated into their judgments. For example, in an organization with fewer PM resources and less guidance, there is less of a demand placed on holding raters accountable. This leads to issues such as less accurate judgments, raters seeing little personal relevance in PM activities, and a lack of motivation to complete performance reviews. Then, tasked with rating their subordinates, a heuristic processing approach is taken. Characteristics such as familiarity with the target can create affective reactions, and affect-as-information biases are used so that the judge can make the simplest judgments necessary across dimensions (i.e. halo error: Tsui & Barry, 1986; Viswesveran, Schmidt, & Ones, 2005).

Another important determinant of the potential role of affect in rater judgments is whether the individual is asked to recall a preexisting evaluation or form a new one, involving more processing and, therefore, higher affect infusion. When forming a judgment, research shows raters high in negative affectivity tend to recall more negative information about subordinates in a performance review, while those low in negative affectivity tend to recall more positive information (Watson & Clark, 1984). Critically, what affects how these dispositions play out within PM activities depends on the context: for example, if supervisors with high negative affectivity perceive negative evaluations to be against organizational norms and would result in pushback, this could lead to inflation in ratings (Fried, Levi, Ben-David, & Tiegs, 1999) despite their negative affect.

Rater motivation is another clear influence on the extent of processing and the potential affect infusion in judgments. Research has specified several situational features that can influence the sense of accountability that raters feel and their motivation to engage in PM. Placing raters in a public context or in a situation with high-status individuals inherently increases accountability (Mero, Guidice, & Brownlee, 2007); the sense that their judgments may be scrutinized by others can elicit motivated or substantive processing (Forgas & George, 2001). Fortunately, raters' motivation to be effective can lead to introspection, and being aware of one's own affect tends to reduce affect infusion in subsequent judgments (Berkowitz, Jaffee, Jo, & Troccoli, 2000).

Affect and Judgments from the Ratee's Perspective

While less research has been devoted to this perspective, ratees' affect can also influence their thoughts and judgments in PM activities. The role of ratee affect is understood through the lens of AIM and whether the judgments made by ratees influence their acceptance, trust, and willingness to participate in PM processes. In terms of affect-priming in the ratee, our concern lies with ratees' affect influencing attention, encoding, retrieval, and associative processes (Forgas, 1995). A ratee attends to and encodes the content of performance appraisal meetings, feedback, and ratings each time they occur. The next PM workflow task they are faced with then leads to them retrieving past performance reviews/meetings and associating tasks with these past experiences. Forgas also states that affect plays a dual role by influencing both *how* individuals think and *what* they think; it follows that people's attention can be impaired and situational pragmatics are called upon. More specifically, different situations call for different standards in judgments, and thus impose different expectations and social desirability pressures. For example, affect from a previous performance meeting that didn't go as planned can influence a ratee's opinion of the next performance meeting before any new feedback is provided, leading them to pay attention only to feedback that confirms their original feelings. If a ratee already has negative affect about the performance meeting, such as feelings of nervousness, he or she may behave in a way that protects his or her ego by seeking less feedback and focusing more on negative information when it is given.

The ratee's attention to PM activities determines whether he or she is able to actively participate and add a voice within the process, something that has been shown to lead to increased satisfaction (Cawley, Keeping, & Levy, 1998). Much like the rater's buy-in, ratee buy-in to PM activities can affect how they process the information exchanged and their motivation to participate in PM tasks. For example, while the task of giving performance feedback falls on the rater, the ratee is still responsible for seeking feedback and responding to it, and the same is true for the ratee's encoding and retrieval abilities. Positive affect from positive feedback should generate heuristic processes such as a quick acceptance of the feedback received, whereas negative affect leads to more careful and deliberate processing (Forgas, 1995). However, the deliberate processes resulting from the negative affect that stems from negative feedback often lead ratees to dedicate attention to disproving the information and feedback he or she received during a performance evaluation. As a result, the desired behavior is less likely to be achieved.

Lastly, the influence that affect has on associative processes is observed through a ratee's perceptions of the organizational culture and feedback environment (London & Smither, 2002; Steelman, Levy, & Snell, 2004). Feedback environment (FE) and organizational factors around the PM structure are considered distal factors that can impact individuals' likelihood of seeing personal relevance and importance to PM tasks and workflow, which ultimately are important determinants of participation. If a ratee perceives a positive FE, he or she is likely to experience positive affect and associate this positive affect with PM activities, thus leading to heuristic judgmental strategies, as previously suggested. Furthermore, organizations should encourage a positive FE by tactfully providing supportive and continuous feedback that is diagnostic, of high quality, and relevant. If an organization encourages a positive FE, individuals can internalize those values and perceive high personal relevance in development activities or a performance review. This leads to ratees having the cognitive capacity to dedicate time and resources to learning from such activities.

Using AET to Explain Reactions to PM Processes

As previously discussed, affect is critical to how we make judgment calls and approach a situation, according to the AIM, but what about when a situation is brought to a close? Most likely, an employee's reaction to a work-related event will be based on multiple factors. Throughout the PM process, there is at least one event in which an employee is appraised by his or her manager and then given feedback. We will therefore look at affect experienced at the later stages of the tasks of PM by the individuals who perform them, observing reactions through the lens of affective events theory (AET).

In their seminal piece, Weiss and Cropanzano (1996) define a model in which work events lead to affective reactions, which in turn influence work attitudes and judgment-driven behavior. In their work, they make a clear distinction between job satisfaction (an attitude), and affective experiences/reactions such as mood and emotions. Simply put, people participate and are involved in events at work and thus react emotionally to these events as they occur (Weiss & Cropanzano, 1996). In AET, Weiss and Cropanzano (1996) illustrate the difference between evaluative judgment, which they argue job satisfaction falls under, and affective states (Weiss & Beal, 2005). Because evaluative judgment and affective states are different, the behavioral reactions that come in response to each of these are distinct as well. The authors outline the differences between affect-driven behaviors and judgment-driven behaviors, where affect-driven behaviors are behaviors and judgments that are directly caused by a person being in a certain affective state (Weiss & Beal, 2005). This is in contrast to judgment-driven behaviors, which are behaviors and judgments that are influenced more by long-term attitudes that people hold (Weiss & Beal, 2005).

Given that affect is comprised of emotions and mood, which are said to be variable, affective reactions to PM should vary depending on the task, context, others involved, and the events throughout. These create an affective reaction because it is a process where a person's effort, performance, competency, and potential for growth are being analyzed and evaluated. Weiss and Cropanazo (1996) argue that since affect is a state of being, researchers must look at explanations that explore changing conditions. PM is the perfect example of conditions constantly changing, especially as outlined by Schleicher and colleagues' (2018) systems model. Furthermore, Weiss and Cropanzano (1996) discuss how affect levels fluctuate over time due to both endogenous components, such as affective dispositions and mood cycles, and exogenous components, such as affective events. Within the tasks of PM, an event such as a performance evaluation or review meeting would fall into the exogenous category, as it is an event happening to a person and causing an affective reaction. This evaluation or meeting could lead to a variety of different affective reactions from the both the ratee and rater, such as happiness, pride, or shame, and each of these would probably lead to distinctly different affective-driven behaviors (Weiss & Cropanzano, 1996). Therefore, through this process, AET illustrates how affective states have important job performance implications (Weiss & Beal, 2005). PM processes range from formal performance appraisals to informal developmental discussions and feedback sessions, which are likely to shape both rater and ratees' thoughts and behavior, making these affective reactions powerful influencers of future performance.

Throughout the PM literature, reactions are less studied than are more concrete variables such as rater biases, motivation, and other individual differences. What we do know about reactions comes from the domains of both performance appraisal and feedback research. Cawley, Keeping, and Levy (1998) identify performance appraisal reactions in a meta-analysis as system and session satisfaction, utility, fairness (also referred to as justice perceptions), motivation to improve, and perceived accuracy (see also Keeping & Levy, 2000), and later work shows that reactions have critical individual and organizational effects on changing and improving employee performance (Jawahar, 2010; Kinicki, Prussia, Wu, & McKee-Ryan, 2004). Here, our focus is solely on affective reactions; therefore, reactions such as perceptions of accuracy, motivation, and utility, which fall into cognitive and behavioral categories of reactions, are not examined.

Rater Affect in Reactions to PM

Making a judgment call and rating an employee is only a small piece of PM, leaving a lot of room throughout the process to focus on ongoing feedback and coaching/development conversations. However, if a rater has little trust or positive affect about a performance appraisal session, participation in such a session and other PM activities is unlikely, rendering the activities impractical and ineffective. Thus it is crucial to encourage positive reactions from the raters' perspective to foster a good working relationship between the rater and ratee and a successful PM process. As stated earlier, when raters use affect alone to make decisions in PM, this becomes an immature form of PM participation because they are relying on a lower form of processing such as heuristics. This should lead to less participation in other PM managerial behaviors such as coaching or mentoring. One example is the negative affect that raters experience after an event in which they are expected to rate all employees on a forced distribution. This typically leads to a lack of confidence in managers when giving feedback (Schleicher, Bull, & Green, 2009), again rendering the feedback ineffective. Furthermore, Levy et al. (2017) state that when managers see the appraisal process as an obligation with little payoff, they are less likely to value the PM system itself. If negative reactions are associated with less motivation to improve, this also has implications for less involvement overall, including a lack of preparation for appraisals and discussions (Harris, 1994).

Ratee Affect in Reactions to PM

While the role of affect in PM is understudied, when it is discussed in PM processes, it typically results in a discussion of ratee reactions as an outcome of feedback or ratings. As stated previously, positive ratee reactions lead to acceptance, future feedback seeking, and motivation (Keeping & Levy, 2000; Steelman & Rutoswki, 2004); whereas negative reactions lead to less acceptance of PM and less feedback seeking (Cawley et al., 1998). Research on reactions as a latent construct (encompassing affective, behavioral, and cognitive components) are typically more positive when the ratee feels that he or she has a voice in the process (Elicker, Levy, & Hall, 2006); when the feedback given in an appraisal is task relevant, favorable, and believed to be accurate (Anseel & Lievens, 2006; David, 2013; Steelman et al., 2004); and when the rater is perceived as trustworthy and credible (Ilgen et al., 1979; Steelman et al., 2004).

Ratees' motivational traits with a neurological basis, referred to as behavioral activation and inhibition systems (Gable, Reis, & Elliot, 2000), are also likely to have an effect on PM. The behavioral activation system is typically referred to as an *approach* motivation, whereas the inhibition system is referred to as an *avoid* motivation (Elliott & Thrash, 2002). If a ratee is driven by a behavioral inhibition motivational system, he or she is more reactive to negative events, and those driven by a behavioral activation motivational system are more reactive to positive events (Elliot & Thrash, 2002). Having a strong behavioral inhibition system makes negative reactions even worse (Gable et al., 2000). Thus, negative affect could lead to weakened performance and poor relationships, especially for those relying more on a behavioral inhibition system. Ellsworth and Sherer (2003) state that emotions are adaptive, leading to the motivation to do something, which gives way to behavioral choices after an affective reaction, mood, or emotion. It thus appears obvious that we should strive to elicit positive affect and concomitant behavioral activation systems in order for future behavior to be improved.

Future Directions for Affect in PM

While existing literature has been helpful in clarifying the role of affect in several PM aspects, a few areas stand out as important for future work. Bearing in mind all the literature discussed, we propose three future research directions to guide those wishing to deepen understanding of the role of affect in PM. First, researchers must distinguish job satisfaction from affective reactions. One of the main issues with using AET as a lens to discuss affective reactions in the later stages of the PM workflow is the lack of distinction between job satisfaction and satisfaction with the PM system (including ratings, feedback, etc.). We must be careful in using the term "satisfaction" within PM so it is not confused with the attitude of job satisfaction, since it is widely accepted that job satisfaction is an attitudinal construct, not an affective reaction (Weiss, 2002). Affect, along with cognition, contributes to an evaluative judgment, and this judgment leads to an attitude such as job satisfaction. In other words, affect and job satisfaction are distinct constructs, with job satisfaction being an overall attitude about the job, as opposed to an affective reaction to smaller parts of the job (Weiss, 2002). Thus future research should carefully define and measure satisfaction as one or the other (i.e. job satisfaction versus satisfaction with the PM system) in addition to measuring reactions to certain events and processes separately. Additionally, reactions should be measured using both positive and negative affect associated with specific PM processes.

Second, there is room for future research on the role of affect in emotion regulation during an episode or PM event, such as a feedback meeting or performance appraisal. If employees receive a lower rating or negative feedback than was expected, they are responsible for regulating their emotions so as not to come across as difficult or hypersensitive to their manager. The literature on emotion regulation is rich with strategies individuals may take, but applying this literature to a specific process such as PM has yet to be fully executed. Considering emotion regulation strategies (e.g. situation selection and modification, attentional deployment, cognitive reappraisal, etc.; Gross, 2015) as a part of the seven tasks within PM would be a promising start to understanding the use and effectiveness of different strategies. Lastly, there has been some literature linking emotional intelligence to feedback reactions. Sheldon, Dunning, and Ames (2014) found that the individuals lower in emotional intelligence are less likely to recognize when they are underperforming, and therefore may reject constructive feedback. Thus there is the potential to examine the relationship between emotional intelligence and affect and how these might interact to predict both rater and ratee outcomes.

Practical Considerations

In addition to future research directions, we also outline three practical suggestions to consider regarding affect, emotions, and mood throughout the PM process. First, AET states that affective reactions are part of a process (i.e. events lead to emotions and assessments, which in turn lead to motivation and behavior; Weiss & Cropanzano, 1996). Additionally, many affect theories stipulate change over time (Weiss & Beal, 2005). Based on these two pieces of information, it makes sense to continue examining the role of affect in PM as a complex, dynamic process, much like the systems-based model in Figure 25.1. However, many of those applying PM still see it as an annual obligation or a waste of time (Tseng et al., 2018). We are implying that a cultural shift is necessary in some organizations. Within this cultural/mindset change, organizations should strive to communicate consistently to employees and managers that PM is a multi-dimensional process that is influenced by people and their emotions and that has great potential to add value in organizations.

A second suggestion that seems useful for practitioners in light of this research is that organizations should assess, measure, and encourage both general and specific implications based on affect within PM (Forgas, 1995; Schwarz et al., 1987). Affect at both the start and the end of PM workflow (i.e. judgments/decisions and reactions) should be understood in general and overall, and also throughout the specific tasks within PM. For example, affective reactions to feedback, ratings, and performance review meetings should be measured separately from affective reactions to and/or satisfaction with the whole PM system. By doing so, future action plans within an organizational can be tailored to both general and specific affect and the outcomes associated with positive affect, emotions, and mood.

Lastly, individuals are innately motivated to minimize effort in daily tasks, which means we rely on the simplest judgment methods whenever possible (Forgas, 1995). It would make sense, then, that if raters form evaluations on performance dimensions that are not salient, heuristic strategies are more likely to be used. If an organization were concerned with potential affect infusion in ratings, interventions that prompt raters to record observations of employees on a regular basis seem promising because they would limit reliance on heuristic judgments. For example, research supports the efficacy of diary-keeping for both rater recall and reactions (DeNisi & Peters, 1996), but as noted by Schleicher and colleagues (2018), more research is needed on how to incorporate such practices into PM in a practical manner. For example, perhaps supervisors could be encouraged to keep computer files on each employee and perhaps once a week (e.g. Friday afternoon), or even month, they set aside ten to fifteen minutes to recall each employee over the week (month), searching memory for positive and negative critical incidents worth recording.

Organizations should not discount the role that emotions and moods play throughout all human capital management processes. So often the focus is on newer technology and more adaptable processes, forgetting that people are the ones that have to adopt such processes. Companies want happy and productive employees, but this requires explicit focus on employee affect, starting with a deep understanding of the roles it can play at work. Additionally, it is not just about assessing affect within PM, but also about implementing change based on affective decisions and reactions. Weiss and Cropanzano (1996) say that "any theory of emotion must also be a theory of how people adapt to their environments" (p. 22). The individuals within PM workflow processes are constantly required to adapt, and such adaptation can be advantageous. Affect plays a central role in PM and although we know a good deal about it, there is still much to learn. We believe that empirical work applying AIM and AET to PM conceptualized as an open system is an exciting area ripe for exploration.

References

Berkowitz, L., Jaffee, S., Jo, E., & Troccoli, B. T. (2000). On the correction of feeling-induced judgmental biases. In J. P. Forgas (Ed.), *Feeling and thinking: The role of affect in social cognition* (pp. 131–152). New York, NY: Cambridge University Press.

Cawley, B. D., Keeping, L. M., & Levy, P. E. (1998). Participation in the performance appraisal process and employee reactions: A meta-analytic review of field investigations. *Journal of Applied Psychology, 83*(4), 615–633.

Elliot, A. J., & Thrash, T. M. (2002). Approach–avoidance motivation in personality: Approach and avoidance temperaments and goals. *Journal of Personality and Social Psychology, 82*(5), 804–818.

Forgas, J. P. (1995). Mood and judgment: The affect infusion model (AIM). *Psychological Bulletin, 117* (1), 39–66.

Forgas, J. P., & George, J. M. (2001). Affective influences on judgments and behavior in organizations: An information processing perspective. *Organizational Behavior and Human Decision Processes, 86*(1), 3–34.

Forgas, J. P., & Williams, K. D. (2016). *Social influence: Direct and indirect processes*. London: Psychology.

Gable, S. L., Reis, H. T., & Elliot, A. J. (2000). Behavioral activation and inhibition in everyday life. *Journal of Personality and Social Psychology, 78*(6), 1135–1149.

George, J. M., & Zhou, J. (2002). Understanding when bad moods foster creativity and good ones don't: The role of context and clarity of feelings. *Journal of Applied Psychology, 87*(4), 687–697.

Gross, J. J. (2015). Emotion regulation: Current status and future prospects. *Psychological Inquiry, 26*, 1–26.

Harris, M. M. (1994). Rater motivation in the performance appraisal context: A theoretical framework. *Journal of Management, 20*(4), 735–756.

Ilgen, D. R., Fisher, C. D., & Taylor, M. S. (1979). Consequences of individual feedback on behavior in organizations. *Journal of Applied Psychology, 64* (4), 349–371.

Keeping, L. M., & Levy, P. E. (2000). Performance appraisal reactions: Measurement, modeling, and method bias. *Journal of Applied Psychology, 85*(5), 708–723.

Lance, C. E., Hoffman, B. J., Gentry, W. A., & Baranik, L. E. (2008). Rater source factors represent important subcomponents of the criterion construct space, not rater bias. *Human Resource Management Review, 18*(4), 223–232.

Levy, P. E., Cavanaugh, C. M., Frantz, N. B., & Borden, L. A. (2015). The role of due process in performance appraisal: A 20-year retrospective. In R. S. Cropanzano and M. L. Ambrose (Eds.), *The Oxford handbook of justice in the workplace* (pp. 605–620). New York, NY: Oxford University Press.

Levy, P. E., Tseng, S. T., Rosen, C. C., & Lueke, S. B. (2017). Performance management: A marriage between practice and science – just say "I do." *Research in Personnel and Human Resources Management, 35*, 155–213.

London, M., & Smither, J. W. (2002). Feedback orientation, feedback culture, and the longitudinal performance management process. *Human Resource Management Review, 12*(1), 81–100.

Mero, N. P., Guidice, R. M., & Brownlee, A. L. (2007). Accountability in a performance appraisal context: The effect of audience and form of accounting on rater response and behavior. *Journal of Management, 33*(2), 223–252.

Schleicher, D. J., Baumann, H. M., Sullivan, D. W., Levy, P. E., Hargrove, D. C., & Barros-Rivera, B. A. (2018). Putting the system into performance management systems: A review and agenda for performance management research. *Journal of Management, 44*(6), 2209–2245.

Schleicher, D. J., Bull, R. A., & Green, S. G. (2009). Rater reactions to forced distribution rating systems. *Journal of Management, 35*(4), 899–927.

Sheldon, O. J., Dunning, D., & Ames, D. R. (2014). Emotionally unskilled, unaware, and uninterested in learning more: Reactions to feedback about deficits in emotional intelligence. *Journal of Applied Psychology, 99*(1), 125–137.

Tsui, A. S., & Barry, B. (1986). Interpersonal affect and rating errors. *Academy of Management Journal, 29* (3), 586–599.

Viswesvaran, C., Schmidt, F. L., & Ones, D. S. (2005). Is there a general factor in ratings of job performance? A meta-analytic framework for disentangling substantive and error influences. *Journal of Applied Psychology, 90*(1), 108–131.

Weiss, H. M. (2002). Deconstructing job satisfaction: Separating evaluations, beliefs and affective experiences. *Human Resource Management Review, 12*(2), 173–194.

Weiss, H. M., & Beal, D. J. (2005). Reflections on affective events theory. In N. M. Ashkanasy, W. J. Zerbe, and C. E. J. Härtel (Eds.), *The effect of affect in organizational settings* (pp. 1–21). Bingley, UK: Emerald.

Weiss, H. M., & Cropanzano, R. (1996). Affective events theory: A theoretical discussion of the structure, causes and consequences of affective experiences at work. *Organizational Behavior*, *18*, 1–74.

26 Feeling the Heat

The Importance of Affect to Organizational Justice for Receivers, Actors, and Observers

Brent A. Scott and Jocelyn Alisa Dana-Lê

Broadly, the literature on organizational justice is concerned with a key question that employees often ask themselves when evaluating events that occur at work: "Was that fair?" (Colquitt, 2012, p. 526). Decades of research on organizational justice have revealed that individuals assess fairness when evaluating a) the outcomes they receive, including whether they are equitable (distributive justice: Adams, 1965; Leventhal, 1976), b) the procedures used to determine those outcomes, including whether they are consistent, accurate, unbiased, correctable, and provide voice and input (procedural justice: Leventhal, 1980; Thibaut & Walker, 1975), c) the information conveyed by authority figures, including whether it is honest and detailed (informational justice: Bies & Moag, 1986; Greenberg, 1993), and d) the interpersonal treatment they receive during interactions, including whether it is respectful and polite (interpersonal justice: Bies & Moag, 1986; Greenberg, 1993).[1] The answers they receive to these questions (i.e. how fair or unfair an event was) are critical, as greater perceptions of fairness have been consistently linked to key outcomes such as well-being, job attitudes, and various indicators of job performance (for a meta-analysis, see Colquitt, Scott, Rodell, Long, Zapata, Conlon, & Wesson, 2013).

Until recently, the literature on organizational justice used the terms "just" and "fair" almost interchangeably. Now, scholars are beginning to differentiate the two terms, defining justice as "the perceived adherence to rules that reflect appropriateness in decision contexts," and fairness as "a global perception of appropriateness" (Colquitt & Rodell, 2015, p. 188). "Justice" therefore captures adherence to, or violation of, the rules pertaining to distributions, procedures, information provided, and interpersonal treatment, which then trigger evaluations of fairness. Importantly, the perception that an event was fair or unfair is in the eye of the beholder.[2]

Research on organizational justice has predominantly sought to understand its antecedents and consequences through the lens of social exchange theory (Blau, 1964), which assumes that people take a "cold" and calculated perspective in determining whether justice rules have been violated (Colquitt et al., 2013), such as whether obligations have been fulfilled or reciprocity has been upheld. Despite this emphasis on "cold" factors, it has long been acknowledged that "hot," affective factors play a role as well. For instance, affect is a part of Adams's (1965) notion of *equity distress* and Bies's (1987) concept of *moral outrage*. However, it was not until Weiss, Suckow, and Cropanzano's (1999)

---

[1] Some models of organizational justice combine informational justice and interpersonal justice into a single factor called *interactional justice* (Bies & Moag, 1986), which includes all aspects of the interpersonal treatment a person receives that are separate from the formal procedures of the organization. For more about the differences between the four-factor and three-factor models of organizational justice, see Colquitt, Greenberg, and Zapata-Phelan (2005).

[2] When we occasionally use the word "fair" in this chapter to describe treatment or an event, we use the word for readability. The perception that an event was "fair" in the contexts to which we refer mean that the person perceiving the event believed it to adhere to certain expectations of what would be just in that particular context.

examination of the effects on discrete emotions of receiving favorable versus unfavorable outcomes that the justice literature began to pay more attention to the critical role that affect plays in the process of organizational justice.

Since then, our understanding of the role of affect (including states such as moods and emotions, as well as traits representing stable tendencies to experience particular moods and emotions) in organizational justice has increased appreciably. The time is therefore ripe to take stock not only of what we know, but also of where we should go. We organize our chapter as follows. We first review the relationship between affect and justice for *receivers* (i.e. those treated justly or unjustly). We then turn to their relationship for *actors* (i.e. those who adhere to or violate justice in the first place), and finally, we consider affect and justice for *observers* (i.e. those who witness a justice event and are affected by it only indirectly). In each case, we consider affect as an outcome of justice as well as an antecedent of it, and we conclude each section with novel theoretical perspectives and research questions that can advance our knowledge of this critical linkage.

Recipients of Organizational Justice

We begin with the recipients of organizational justice, who have been the dominant focus of the justice literature to date. The focus on recipients has been reasonable, since a primary concern of the justice literature is to understand how perceptions form of whether an event was fair and how people react to those perceptions. Accordingly, the initial link between justice and affect focused on affective states as outcomes of being treated fairly or unfairly.

Affect as an Outcome of Receiving Justice

As noted above, the notion that fair treatment elicits affective states in recipients dates to the dawn of the justice literature. Affect is an inherent part of the "satisfaction" and "morale" reactions associated with the concept of relative deprivation (Stouffer, Suchman, DeVinney, Starr, & Williams, 1949; see also Spector, 1956) and Adams's (1965) concept of equity distress. Indeed, Homans (1961) explicitly conjectured that when individuals experience relative deprivation, they will "display the emotional behavior we call anger" (p. 75). Later, Bies (1987) described the "moral outrage" that accompanies violations of interactional forms of justice.

In a foundational empirical examination of the effects of justice on affect, Weiss et al. (1999) found that outcomes (but not procedures) that were manipulated in a laboratory context to be more favorable induced happiness, unfavorable outcomes paired with procedures biased against the person elicited anger, and favorable outcomes paired with procedures biased toward the person elicited guilt, supporting key tenets of equity theory. Since the publication of the Weiss et al. (1999) study, enough research has accumulated to prompt the general conclusion that fair treatment tends to elicit positive affective states, while unfair treatment tends to elicit negative affective states, and that these affective reactions serve as mediators. This explains, in part, why fair treatment and unfair treatment are associated with important outcomes such as task performance, organizational citizenship behavior, and counterproductive work behavior (for a meta-analysis, see Colquitt et al. 2013).

In explaining the effects of fairness on recipients' affective states (and subsequent attitudes and behaviors), scholars have frequently relied on appraisal theory (Lazarus, 1991) and the related affective events theory (Weiss & Cropanzano, 1996). Viewed through these theoretical lenses, fair and unfair events trigger primary appraisals whereby individuals determine whether an event facilitates (in the case of fair treatment) or hinders (in the case of unfair treatment) progress toward relevant goals (generating broad positive or negative affective states), as well as secondary, more specific appraisals whereby individuals assess factors such as attributions of blame and coping potential, which then elicit discrete emotions. In turn, emotions are associated with specific states of action readiness (Fridja, 2007), which influence behavior (e.g. anger is associated with the urge to attack or retaliate, which prompts counterproductive behavior).

Given that the relationship between justice and recipient affective reactions is well established, we focus the rest of our discussion on relationships that have received comparatively less attention – though we do discuss future directions on this important relationship later in the chapter.

Affect as an Antecedent of Receiving Justice

In addition to being an outcome, affect can influence the receipt of justice in at least three interrelated ways. First, the affect of a justice recipient can influence beliefs about what is fair. In an early lab study on this relationship, Sinclair and Mark (1991) found that mood manipulations – either "elated" or "depressed" – influenced participants' endorsement of certain distributive justice principles. Specifically, participants who underwent the elated manipulation tended to endorse macrojustice (equity or need-based) principles more than microjustice (meritocratic) principles, due to a heightened sense that people are more alike than different and thus deserve similar outcomes. In contrast, those in the depressed condition tended to endorse microjustice principles more than macrojustice principles, due to a heightened sense that people are more dissimilar than similar. Moreover, participants in the elated condition were less likely to discriminate between macrojustice and microjustice principles than participants who underwent the depressed manipulation, because those in the elated condition did not need to employ as much cognitive processing, having been put in a positive mood rather than a negative one.

Second, affect can influence the way that a justice recipient appraises information related to a situation or event and subsequent judgments of whether the situation or event was fair (Barsky, Kaplan, & Beal, 2011). For example, van den Bos (2003) also used elated and depressed manipulations in a lab study and found that when participants were given incomplete information about voice procedures (i.e. they were not told about the amount of voice afforded to comparison others), the participants relied on affect as a source of information to judge whether they thought the amount of voice they were given was fair. In another study presented in the same paper, participants who had incomplete information about the distribution of outcomes (i.e. they did not know how much salary others received) relied on the mood they were in prior to learning their own salary to judge whether the distribution was fair. Perhaps the most convincing support for the relationship between affect and justice appraisals comes from the meta-analysis by Barsky and Kaplan (2007), who showed that both state affect and trait affect color recipients' perceptions of fairness. The authors found significant negative associations between negative affect (both state and trait) and perceptions of justice – distributive, procedural, and interactional – and significant positive associations between positive affect (both state and trait) and perceptions of those same justice dimensions. There were no significant differences between the effects of state and trait affect; moreover, their relationships with justice were generally stronger than the relationships of the personality traits of neuroticism and extraversion with justice, suggesting that affect, rather than other aspects of personality, is a critical driver of justice appraisals and perceptions.

Third, there is some evidence that affect can elicit just behavior from the people with whom the recipient interacts. Scott, Colquitt, and Zapata-Phelan (2007) found that charismatic subordinates (who tend to exhibit positive emotions) had higher perceptions of interpersonal (but not informational) fairness, and this relationship was mediated by positive sentiments felt by managers toward charismatic subordinates. They argued that positive emotions displayed by charismatic employees are contagious, and that the positive feelings "caught" by managers elicit more just interpersonal treatment in the form of increased dignity and respect. Although their study focused on fairness perceptions of recipients, as we discuss below, there is also evidence that affective states do indeed influence actual justice rule adherence on the part of actors.

Before concluding our discussion of the extant work on justice recipients, it is important to mention that a considerable number of studies have focused on the interactive effect of fairness and affect (state and trait) on a given outcome (often behavioral). Among the studies that have taken this approach, the most common outcome studied is some form of retaliation or "bad" behavior, such as personal or organizational counterproductive work behavior (Fox, Spector, & Miles, 2001; Yang & Diefendorff, 2009), customer-directed sabotage (Wang, Liao, Zhan, & Shi, 2011), intentions to litigate (Geenen, Proost, van Dijke, de Witte, & von Grumbkow, 2012), or theft (Wilkin & Connelly, 2015). Other outcomes in this stream of research have included state hostility (Judge, Scott, & Ilies, 2006), performance (Janssen, Lam, & Huang, 2009), cooperative behavior (van Dijke, Wildschut, Leunissen, & Sedikides, 2015), creativity (George & Zhou, 2007), acceptance of change during downsizing (Paterson & Cary, 2002), and intentions to recommend the organization (Geenen et al., 2012). Broadly speaking, trait negative affect (e.g. anger, anxiety) exacerbates the negative outcomes of unfairness (both behavioral and affective), while positive and self-reflective emotions (e.g. nostalgia) buffer these unwanted effects (van Dijke et al., 2015; Janssen et al., 2009).

Future Directions on Recipients of Justice

Although examining affect as an outcome of fairness is well-trodden ground, there are still interesting directions that future researchers can take to expand our understanding beyond the basic notion that fair is "good" for affect and unfair is "bad." For instance, research should continue to examine what can break or buffer the link between unfairness and negative emotion. On this point, self-reflective practices such as mindfulness (Long & Christian, 2015) and writing about thoughts and emotions related to the unfairness (Barclay & Skarlicki, 2009) have shown promise. In keeping with our focus on affect, positive and self-reflective emotions such as nostalgia have also been shown to buffer against unfairness; scholars could attempt to identify if (and when) additional emotions buffer against affect from unfairness, whether the additional emotions are elicited from some other affective event, or via emotion regulation strategies such as deep acting.

In addition, theory on needs–supplies fit (e.g. Edwards, Caplan, & Harrison, 1998) could be applied to determine whether justice, like other leader-emanating behaviors thought to be overwhelmingly positive (e.g. transformational leadership; see Tepper et al., 2018), is best when it fits an individual's current needs, as opposed to being either deficient or in excess. Similarly, research should examine the impact of fairness *consistency* on recipients' affect, as there is some evidence that unjust treatment is not as harmful to individual well-being if it is received consistently over time, because individuals at least know what to expect, and feelings of uncertainty and anxiety are reduced (Matta, Scott, Colquitt, Koopman, & Passantino, 2017).

In terms of affect as an antecedent of receiving fairness, the emotions as social information (EASI) model (van Kleef, 2009) is a promising framework that could be used to better understand this linkage. According to the EASI model, although affective states serve as information to recipients, coloring their judgments of justice-related events accordingly (Schwarz & Clore, 1983), they also convey important information to others. In particular, affective states can influence observers' behaviors through two processes: inferential processes and affective reactions. Inferential processes occur when observers attempt to glean information and feedback about their own behavior from others' emotional displays. For example, observing an interaction partner's happiness may lead one to infer that one's behavior is welcomed and appropriate, motivating one to continue the behavior. Affective reactions may consist of interpersonal liking toward the target and "emotional contagion" (Hatfield, Cacioppo, & Rapson, 1994), whereby the observer mimics and "catches" the emotion the target is displaying. For example, observing an interaction partner's happiness may trigger liking and mimicry of the happy display (i.e. smiling), eliciting happiness in the observer.

From the perspective of the EASI model, emotional displays by recipients of justice (e.g. sadness or anger following unfair treatment) may be "caught" by actors (e.g. the supervisor engaging in unfair treatment), or those displays may trigger inferential processes in actors, depending on factors such as the actor's depth of information processing and the perceived appropriateness of the recipients' display (van Kleef, 2009). Actors who infer that their behaviors triggered negative affect in recipients of injustice may ultimately experience feelings of dejection and guilt, motivating greater adherence to justice in the future (e.g. Scott, Colquitt, & Paddock, 2009). Ultimately, the reactions of actors to recipients' affective displays should have implications for their subsequent just or unjust behavior, which brings us to the role of affect for actors of organizational justice.

Actors of Organizational Justice

Recently, scholars have been paying more attention to an important question: "Why do managers treat people fairly or unfairly in the first place?" Addressing this question has meant shifting from a recipient focus to an actor focus. As with recipients, an actor's affect can either precede just treatment or follow it.

Affect as an Outcome of Adhering to or Violating Justice

A relatively under-researched topic is how actors (e.g. managers) react emotionally to their own instances of justice rule adherence and justice rule violation. In their actor-focused model of justice, Scott, Colquitt, and Paddock (2009) theorized that managers are likely to experience the self-focused emotions of pride or guilt after they evaluate their own actions against standards of conduct. Importantly, they argued that although pride is likely to be elicited following justice rule adherence because the manager takes credit for a positive event, pride can also be felt following justice rule violation, such as when the manager yells at an employee or denies voice in order to exact revenge. In these cases, although the manager technically is violating a rule of justice (i.e. being disrespectful or failing to provide voice), s/he may feel that "just deserts" are being served, and may feel good about it.

Although the authors argued that guilt will be felt following justice rule violation if the manager is unable to justify his/her actions, they stopped short of arguing that it could occur following justice rule adherence. However, negative, self-focused emotions such as guilt or shame could occur if the managers' justice adherence toward a given employee resulted in harm to another (e.g. by adhering to a rule of equity and rewarding a high performer, the manager provides a lower pay raise to an employee who is struggling financially and would benefit from a need-based distributive rule).

Moving beyond self-focused emotions, Klaussner (2014) presented a process model explaining how abusive supervision can emerge following an instance of supervisor injustice. His model posits that subordinate reactions, and subsequent supervisor negative emotions and responses, can escalate and spiral, ultimately culminating in intentional displays of hostility and abuse by the supervisor. Thus, both the Scott et al. (2009) model and the model by Klaussner (2014) stipulate that how subordinates react to justice-relevant events impacts both the type and intensity of emotions felt by managers, which then has implications for subsequent behavior. However, empirical research is needed to directly test these propositions.

Affect as an Antecedent of Adhering to or Violating Justice

Scott et al.'s (2009) justice actor model also stipulates that affective states serve as antecedents to fair treatment. In particular, in addition to "cold," cognitive motives, or reasons, for adhering to the rules associated with distributive, procedural, interpersonal, and informational justice, their model also proposes that "hot," affective motives predict justice rule adherence and violation – particularly for justice dimensions affording managers greater discretion over their execution (i.e. informational and interpersonal). Specifically, because positive affect states motivate individuals to engage in actions that are more prosocial in nature, they should be associated with justice rule adherence. In contrast, because negative affective states motivate individuals to engage in actions that are more antisocial in nature, they should be associated with justice rule adherence. Accordingly, the actor-focused model is concerned with the effects of broader mood states on justice-relevant actions.

In an experience-sampling study of managers testing propositions from the actor-focused model, Scott, Garza, Conlon, and Kim (2014) found that daily episodes of procedural and interpersonal justice were motivated (in part) by positive affect (i.e. happiness, delight, and pleasure). Daily episodes of distributive, procedural, informational, and interpersonal justice were all motivated by negative affect (i.e. anger, frustration, and irritation) – a finding in line with the basic emotions literature that negative emotions exert stronger effects than positive emotions (Taylor, 1991). Interestingly, negative affect was *positively* associated with informational justice rule adherence. The authors speculated that being the "bearer of bad news," and the negative feelings associated with it, could explain this relationship. Moreover, dimensions of justice affording managers greater discretion in their execution (i.e. informational and interpersonal justice) were motivated more by affective reasons than cognitive reasons, presumably because managers had the freedom to act on their momentary feelings.

Future Directions on Actors of Justice

We see several ways in which the nascent literature focused on actors' affect could be extended. First, although there is some evidence, consistent with the justice actor model, that positive affect is associated with justice rule adherence, and negative affect is associated with justice rule violation, the literature would benefit if scholars focused more on discrete emotions. At the same time, they should measure both "justice" and "injustice," given that low levels of justice rule adherence do not necessarily imply that justice rules were violated (Colquitt, Long, Rodell, & Halvorsen-Ganepola, 2015). Indeed, we suspect that the relationship between just/unjust treatment and positive/negative affect is not so straightforward. For example, instead of eliciting justice rule violation, certain negative emotions besides guilt, such as fear or anxiety felt toward a subordinate, may elicit justice rule adherence as the manager feels the need to treat the subordinate with "kid gloves." Similarly, instead of eliciting justice rule adherence, certain positive emotions, such as hubris, may prompt managers to violate rules of justice.

Also, as noted above, future work should integrate actor and receiver perspectives to examine the effect of recipients' emotional reactions to being treated unfairly on actors' affective responses, in order to understand the conditions under which escalating spirals lead to abuse (Klaussner, 2014), as opposed to feelings of guilt that lead to reparation and fairer treatment in the future (Scott et al., 2009). Finally, connecting actor and receiver perspectives can help shed light on the discrepancy that can exist between justice rule adherence and perceptions of fairness. For example, in a scenario-based experiment, Razzaq, Iqbal, Ikramullah, and van Prooijen (2016) found that ratees who received inflated performance ratings perceived higher levels of distributive and interpersonal fairness when they were liked by raters in a pleasant mood. From the perspective of a neutral observer, inflated performance ratings violate rules of justice such as equity and bias suppression, yet in this circumstance were seen to be "fair" from the recipients' perspective.

Among other theories that could be utilized to better understand the relationship between affect and justice for actors, we view moral licensing as potentially relevant (for a meta-analysis, see Blanken, van de Ven, & Zeelenberg, 2015). Specifically, managers who adhere to rules of justice at one point in time may feel that they have a "license" to violate rules of justice at a later point in time, and these effects may be stronger if the manager is confident and proud of their previous track record for being "fair." In contrast, if the manager is fearful that an unjust action will tarnish their image as a moral and ethical person, then such licensing effects may not occur, and justice rule adherence continues. If justice rule adherence is susceptible to moral licensing effects, this could explain why some managers are more inconsistent with regard to their justice rule adherence or violation over short periods of time (e.g. Matta et al., 2017).

Third-Party Observers of Organizational Justice

Although the organizational justice literature has grown beyond interpersonal, dyadic interactions to address phenomena such as justice climate (e.g. Naumann & Bennett, 2000), justice within social networks (e.g. Roberson & Colquitt, 2005), and third-party reactions to justice (e.g. Skarlicki & Kulik, 2004), little work has been done to date on the affective states of observers of justice events. This area for growth in the literature is promising because the theoretical groundwork has already been laid, yet only a few authors have begun to break into this area empirically. As with recipients and actors, affect may serve either as an antecedent to justice or as an outcome of it.

Affect as an Outcome of Observing Justice

In one of the first field studies to acknowledge the affect of third-party observers of justice, De Cremer, Stinglhamber, and Eisenberger (2005) measured both focal participants' perceptions of their own receipt of procedural justice and their perceptions of a coworker's receipt of procedural justice, finding that the coinciding of justice for oneself and justice for a coworker interacted to predict positive emotions such as enthusiasm and happiness, above and beyond what justice for oneself alone predicted. They found no significant relationship between justice for oneself and positive emotions when procedural justice for others was low, demonstrating that the effect of observing justice for others is a powerful source of information for employees when they determine how to react emotionally to procedures they are also subject to themselves.

More recently, Wang, Lu, and Siu (2015) drew from uncertainty management theory to explain the moderating effect of organizational justice on the relationship between job insecurity and performance. The authors measured justice with the Perceived Organizational Justice Scale (Ambrose & Schminke, 2009), which incorporates the perceptions of the organization's justice directed toward the employee as well as overall perceptions of the organization's justice not necessarily directed toward the employee. The authors found that when overall organizational justice was high, there was no significant relationship between job insecurity and performance, but when overall justice was low, the relationship was negative. While there were no explicit affective variables, the authors made reference to affect when explaining the predictions of uncertainty management theory: when employees have job insecurity and perceive the organization to be unfair overall, they have more uncertainty and anxiety and engage in work less, and performance decreases. The similarity between this field study and the field study by De Cremer et al. (2005) will be more evident when we discuss two other studies that focus on observers of justice.

In a laboratory investigation, Spencer and Rupp (2009) found that individuals' emotional labor increased as a result of both unfairness directed toward themselves and unfairness directed toward their simulated coworkers. These effects were mediated by anger, guilt, and fairness-related counterfactual thinking and were significant even when the participants themselves had been treated fairly. The authors drew on fairness theory (Folger, 2001; Folger & Cropanzano, 1998, 2001) and affective events theory (Weiss & Cropanzano, 1996) to explain why employees would be emotionally affected by unfairness directed toward coworkers. In a similar vein, Greenbaum, Quade, Mawritz, Kim, and Crosby (2014) found in a field study across multiple industries that employees experience emotional exhaustion when they observe customers exhibiting unethical behavior, even when controlling for the customer's interpersonal justice with the employee directly. The authors drew from deontological ethics and conservation of resources theory to explain the effects. In both of these studies, the authors conceptualized fairness as an objective reality that exists independently of perceptions.

Although research examining the affective consequences of observing the justice experiences of others is at a nascent stage, the work that has been done leads to the cautious conclusion that the process of observing justice has unique emotional effects (above and beyond the effects of directly receiving justice) because it can either mirror or deviate from one's own fair treatment. On the one hand, observing how coworkers are treated by the organization provides a source of additional information and can set expectations about one's own receipt of fairness (e.g. if the organization is fair to all, then uncertainty about one's own treatment is reduced), as with the studies by De Cremer et al. (2005) and Wang et al. (2015). This suggests that observing the justice situations of others influences affective states for instrumental, self-serving reasons. On the other hand, observed (in)justice could affect employees' affective states for less selfish, deontological reasons, showing significant effects even when controlling for the level of fairness directly received, as with the studies by Spencer and Rupp (2009) and Greenbaum et al. (2014). However, the design of these latter studies does not rule out the alternative explanation that the recipients of (in)justice – the observers' coworkers – are simply thought of as in-group members. The question remains whether observers of injustice directed toward their coworkers react emotionally because the injustice is truly a violation of deontological ethics (general rules of fairness) or if it is because their coworkers comprise an in-group that the observer identifies with, and the reaction results from self-serving or instrumental reasons.

Affect as an Antecedent of Observing Justice

Research on affect as an antecedent of justice perceptions came after the acknowledgment that employees react emotionally to justice directed toward others. This literature is so limited that we were able to find only two empirical studies on the topic. The first, by Horberg, Kraus, and Keltner (2013), showed that individuals use observations of others' displayed emotions as a source of information to infer the others' beliefs about just distributions. Across several laboratory studies, the authors found that when a target displayed pride (compared to a control condition where the target displayed joy), observers were more inclined to think that the target was self-interested and more likely to support a meritocratic distribution system over an egalitarian distribution system. The second, a field study by Khan, Quratulain, and Bell (2014), found that procedural justice interacted with episodic envy to predict counterproductive work behaviors. Drawing on the attribution model of justice (Brockner, Wiesenfeld, & Diekmann, 2009), they showed that episodic envy exhibited a stronger relationship with counterproductive work behavior directed toward envied others when one's own or others' procedural justice was high, through the mediator of internal attribution. In other words, since the procedures were fair, but the employee still envied another person who was better off, the employee had no choice but to attribute their own, less favorable outcome to an internal cause rather than to a procedural cause.

Future Directions on Observers of Justice

As we mentioned earlier, the theoretical groundwork has already been laid for empirical research on how observers react emotionally to justice and use emotions to inform perceptions of justice. In addition to fairness theory and perspectives based on deontological ethics, resources, affective events theory, and uncertainty management theory referenced in the extant empirical work on affective states as outcomes of justice, Festinger's (1954) social comparison theory could explain why observers of injustice react either negatively or positively to perceived injustice directed at coworkers. Specifically, social comparisons with a coworker receiving injustice are likely to elicit feelings of sympathy when they are downward and assimilative but feelings of schadenfreude when they are downward and contrastive. For a coworker receiving justice, feelings of inspiration are likely to arise when social comparisons are upward and assimilative, but feelings of envy are likely when social comparisons are upward and contrastive (see also Greenberg, Ashton-James, & Ashkanasy, 2007). It would be useful for future research not only to examine these possibilities, but also to integrate predictions from social comparison theory with instrumental and deontological perspectives on justice to determine when these emotions are likely to arise (e.g. if an individual cares about fairness more for moral reasons than for self-serving reasons, then emotions such as schadenfreude and envy are unlikely to be felt when observing the justice of others).

Turning from affective states as outcomes to affective states as antecedents of justice, emotional contagion processes (Hatfield et al., 1994) would be useful for explaining both how observers form judgments about the fairness of a situation (e.g. by catching the emotions of their coworkers and then using those emotions as information about whether an event is fair or unfair) as well as how discrepancies in coworkers' trait emotions can lead to their differential treatment by the same leader or other colleague (see Scott, Colquitt, & Zapata-Phelan, 2007), which could then influence social comparison processes. Theorists have already acknowledged that judgments of justice are formed collectively through shared experiences and social verification (Degoey, 2000; Roberson & Colquitt, 2005), and incorporating emotional contagion frameworks could help to explain the emotional input into these judgments.

Beyond forming judgments of whether or not an event was fair, the two studies we found examining emotions as antecedents of justice for observers raise other interesting issues. As one example, Horberg et al. (2013) examined how the emotional displays of others (such as pride or joy) are used to discern beliefs about what is fair on a distributive level. Indeed, the process of observing and "reading" another person's emotions in an attempt to infer their perceptions about the fairness of an event or entity happens frequently in the workplace. Colleagues read one another to form shared evaluations of the distributive, procedural, informational, and interpersonal justice of their employer; managers and subordinates read one another's emotions as a gauge of whether the other party is satisfied with their upkeep of the reciprocal relationship; and job applicants and other outsiders may read the emotions displayed by members of the organization and use them as information for speculating about what the organization's distribution (compensation) program is like or what the organization deems fair as captured by its policies and procedures. In each of these cases, observers may "misread" others or form biased overall justice impressions of the organization because of the emotion that happened to be displayed at that point in time. The phenomenon of using emotions to inform not only how fair an event was but also what another person would judge to be fair opens up a new realm of research questions that scholars should pursue.

Conclusion

Despite being intertwined with organizational justice since the literature's inception, affect has only recently begun to get the attention it deserves. As our review makes clear, affect, both in terms of states and traits, is relevant to recipients, actors, and observers. Moreover, it is not simply the case that positive affect is "good" for justice and negative affect is "bad." Rather, the role of affect in the process of justice can at times be complex. It is our hope that by considering these complexities and drawing from novel theoretical perspectives, scholars can gain a more complete understanding of the "hot" aspect of organizational justice.

References

Adams, J. S. (1965). Inequity in social exchange. In L. Berkowitz (Ed.), *Advances in experimental social psychology* (Volume 2, pp. 267–299). New York, NY: Academic.

Ambrose, M. L., & Schminke, M. (2009). The role of overall justice judgments in organizational justice research: A test of mediation. *Journal of Applied Psychology, 94*, 491–500.

Barclay, L. J., & Scarlicki, D. P. (2009). Healing the wounds of organizational injustice: Examining the benefits of expressive writing. *Journal of Applied Psychology, 94*, 511–523.

Barsky, A., & Kaplan, S. A. (2007). If you feel bad, it's unfair: A quantitative synthesis of affect and organizational justice perceptions. *Journal of Applied Psychology, 92*, 286–295.

Barsky, A., Kaplan, S. A., & Beal, D. J. (2011). Just feelings? The role of affect in the formation of organizational fairness judgements. *Journal of Management, 37*, 248–279.

Bies, R. J. (1987). The predicament of injustice: The management of moral outrage. In L. L. Cummings & B. M. Staw (Eds.), *Research in organizational behavior* (Volume 9, pp. 289–319). Greenwich, CT: JAI.

Bies, R. J., & Moag, J. F. (1986). Interactional justice: Communication criteria of fairness. In R. J. Lewicki, B. H. Sheppard, & M. H. Bazerman (Eds.), *Research on negotiations in organizations* (Volume 1, pp. 43–55). Greenwich, CT: JAI.

Blanken, I., van de Ven, N., & Zeelenberg, M. A. (2015). A meta-analytic review of moral licensing. *Personality and Social Psychology Bulletin, 41*, 540–558.

Blau, P. M. (1964). *Exchange and power in social life.* New York, NY: Wiley.

Brockner, J., Wiesenfeld, B. M., & Diekmann, K. A. (2009). Towards a "fairer" conception of process fairness: Why, when, and how more may not always be better than less. *Academy of Management Annals, 3*, 183–216.

Colquitt, J. A. (2012). Organizational justice. In S. W. J. Kozlowski (Ed.), *The Oxford handbook of organizational psychology* (Volume 1, pp. 526–547). New York, NY: Oxford University Press.

Colquitt, J. A., Greenberg, J., & Zapata-Phelan, C. P. (2005). What is organizational justice? A historical overview. In J. Greenberg & J. A. Colquitt (Eds.), *Handbook of organizational justice* (pp. 3–56). Mahwah, NJ: Erlbaum.

Colquitt, J. A., Long, D. M., Rodell, J. B., & Halvorsen-Ganepola, M. D. K. (2015). Adding the "In" to justice: A qualitative and quantitative investigation of the differential effects of justice rule adherence and violation. *Journal of Applied Psychology, 100*, 278–297.

Colquitt, J. A., & Rodell, J. B. (2015). Measuring justice and fairness. In R. Cropanzano & M. Ambrose (Eds.), *The Oxford handbook of justice in work organizations*. Oxford, UK: Oxford University Press.

Colquitt, J. A., Scott, B. A., Rodell, J. B., Long, D. M., Zapata, C. P., Conlon, D. E., & Wesson, M. J. (2013). Justice at the millennium, a decade later: A meta-analytic test of social exchange and affect-based perspectives. *Journal of Applied Psychology, 98*, 199–236.

De Cremer, D., Stinglhamber, F., & Eisenberger, R. (2005). Effects of own versus others' fair treatment on positive emotions: A field study. *Journal of Social Psychology, 145*, 741–744.

Degoey, P. (2000). Contagious justice: Exploring the social construction of justice in organizations. *Research in Organizational Behavior, 22*, 51–102.

Edwards, J. R., Caplan, R. D., & Harrison, R. V. (1998). Person–environment fit theory: Conceptual foundations, empirical evidence, and directions for future research. In C. L. Cooper (Ed.), *Theories of organizational stress* (pp. 28–67). Oxford, UK: Oxford University Press.

Festinger, L. (1954). A theory of social comparison processes. *Human Relations, 7*, 117–140.

Folger, R. (2001). Fairness as deonance. In S. W. Gilliland, D. D. Steiner, & D. P. Scarlicki (Eds.), *Research in social issues in management* (Volume 1, pp. 3–33). Mahwah, NJ: Erlbaum.

Folger, R., & Cropanzano, R. (1998). *Organizational justice and human resource management.* Thousand Oaks, CA: Sage.

Folger, R., & Cropanzano, R. (2001). Fairness theory: Justice as accountability. In J. Greenberg & R. Cropanzano (Eds.), *Advances in organizational justice* (pp. 89–118). Stanford, CA: Stanford University Press.

Fox, S., Spector, P. E., & Miles, D. (2001). Counterproductive work behavior (CWB) in response to job stressors and organizational justice: Some mediator and moderator tests for autonomy and emotions. *Journal of Vocational Behavior, 59*, 291–309.

Frijda, N. H. (2007). *The laws of emotion*. Mahwah, NJ: Lawrence Erlbaum Associates.

Geenen, B., Proost, K., van Dijke, M., de Witte, K., & von Grumbkow, J. (2012). The role of affect in the relationship between distributive justice expectations and applicants' recommendation and litigation intentions. *International Journal of Selection and Assessment, 20*, 404–413.

George, J. M., & Zhou, J. (2007). Dual tuning in a supportive context: Joint contributions of positive mood, megative mood, and supervisory behaviors to employee creativity. *Academy of Management Journal, 50*, 605–622.

Greenbaum, R. L., Quade, M. J., Mawritz, M. B., Kim, J., & Crosby, D. (2014). When the customer is unethical: The explanatory role of employee emotional exhaustion onto work–family conflict, relationship conflict with coworkers, and job neglect. *Journal of Applied Psychology, 99*, 1188–1203.

Greenberg, J. (1993). The social side of fairness: Interpersonal and informational classes of organizational justice. In R. Cropanzano (Ed.), *Justice in the workplace: Approaching fairness in human resource management* (pp. 79–103). Hillsdale, NJ: Erlbaum.

Greenberg, J., Ashton-James, C. E., & Ashkanasy, N. M. (2007). Social comparison processes in organizations. *Organizational Behavior and Human Decision Processes, 102*, 22–41.

Hatfield, E., Cacioppo, J. T., & Rapson, R. L. (1994). *Emotional contagion*. New York, NY: Cambridge University Press.

Homans, G. C. (1961). *Social behavior: Its elementary forms*. New York, NY: Harcourt, Brace.

Horberg, E. J., Kraus, M. W., & Keltner, D. (2013). Pride displays communicate self-interest and support for meritocracy. *Journal of Personality and Social Psychology, 105*, 24–37.

Janssen, O., Lam, C. K., & Huang, X. (2009). Emotional exhaustion and job performance: The moderating roles of distributive justice and positive affect. *Journal of Organizational Behavior, 31*, 787–809.

Judge, T. A., Scott, B. A., & Ilies, R. (2006). Hostility, job attitudes, and workplace deviance: Test of a multilevel model. *Journal of Applied Psychology, 91*, 126–138.

Khan, A. K., Quratulain, S., & Bell, C. M. (2014). Episodic envy and counterproductive work behaviors: Is more justice always good? *Journal of Organizational Behavior, 35*, 128–144.

Klaussner, S. (2014). Engulfed in the abyss: The emergence of abusive supervision as an escalating process of supervisor–subordinate interaction. *Human Relations, 67*, 311–332.

Lazarus, R. S. (1991). Progress on a cognitive–motivational–relational theory of emotion. *American Psychologist, 46*, 819–834.

Leventhal, G. S. (1976). The distribution of rewards and resources in groups and organizations. In L. Berkowitz & W. Walster (Eds.), *Advances in experimental social psychology* (Volume 9, pp. 91–131). New York, NY: Academic.

Leventhal, G. S. (1980). What should be done with equity theory? New approaches to the study of fairness in social relationships. In K. Gergen, M. Greenberg, & R. Willis (Eds.), *Social exchange: Advances in theory and research* (pp. 27–55). New York, NY: Plenum.

Long, E. C., & Christian, M. S (2015). Mindfulness buffers retaliatory responses to injustice: A regulatory approach. *Journal of Applied Psychology, 100*, 1409–1422.

Matta, F. K., Scott, B. A., Colquitt, J. A., Koopman, J., & Passantino, L. G. (2017). Is consistently unfair better than sporadically fair? An investigation of justice variability and stress. *Academy of Management Journal, 60*, 743–770.

Naumann, S. E., & Bennett, N. (2000). A case for procedural justice climate: Development and test of a multilevel model. *Academy of Management Journal, 43*, 881–889.

Paterson, J. M., & Cary, J. (2002). Organizational justice, change anxiety, and acceptance of downsizing: Preliminary tests of an AET-based model. *Motivation and Emotion, 26*, 83–103.

Razzaq, A., Iqbal, M. Z., Ikramullah, M., & Prooijen, J. W. V. (2016). Occurrence of rating distortions and ratees' fairness perceptions per raters' mood and affect. *Career Development International, 21*, 726–743.

Roberson, Q. M., & Colquitt, J. A. (2005). Shared and configural justice: A social network model of justice in teams. *Academy of Management Review, 30*, 595–607.

Schwarz, N., & Clore, G. L. (1983). Mood, misattribution and judgments of well-being: Informative and directive functions of affective states. *Journal of Personality and Social Psychology, 45*, 513–523.

Scott, B. A., Colquitt, J. A., & Paddock, E. L. (2009). An actor-focused model of justice rule adherence and violation: The role of managerial motives and discretion. *Journal of Applied Psychology, 94*, 756–769.

Scott, B. A., Colquitt, J. A., & Zapata-Phelan, C. P. (2007). Justice as a dependent variable: Subordinate charisma as a predictor of interpersonal and informational justice perceptions. *Journal of Applied Psychology, 92*, 1597–1609.

Scott, B. A., Garza, A., Conlon, D. E., & Kim, Y. J. (2014). Why do managers act fairly in the first place? A daily investigation of "hot" and "cold" motives and discretion. *Academy of Management Journal, 57*, 1571–1591.

Sinclair, R. C., & Mark, M. M. (1991). Mood and the endorsement of egalitarian macrojustice versus equity-based microjustice principles. *Personality and Social Psychology Bulletin, 17*, 369–375.

Skarlicki, D. P., & Kulik, C. T. (2004). Third-party reactions to employee (mis)treatment: A justice perspective. *Research in Organizational Behavior, 26*, 183–229.

Spector, A. J. (1956). Expectations, fulfillment, and morale. *Journal of Abnormal Social Psychology, 52*, 51–56.

Spencer, S., & Rupp, D. E. (2009). Angry, guilty, and conflicted: Injustice toward coworkers heightens emotional labor through cognitive and emotional mechanisms. *Journal of Applied Psychology, 94*, 429–444.

Stouffer, S. A., Suchman, E. A., DeVinney, L. C., Starr, S. A., & Williams, R. M., Jr. (1949). *The American solider: Adjustment during army life*, Volume 1. Princeton, NJ: Princeton University Press.

Taylor, S. E. (1991). Asymmetrical effects of positive and negative events: The mobilization–minimization hypothesis. *Psychological Bulletin, 110*, 67–85.

Tepper, B. J., Dimotakis, N., Lambert, L. S., Koopman, J., Matta, F. K., Park, H. M., & Goo, W. (2018). Examining follower responses to transformational leadership from a dynamic, person–environment fit perspective. *Academy of Management Journal, 61*, 1343–1368.

Thibaut, J., & Walker, L. (1975). *Procedural justice: A psychological analysis*. Hillsdale, NJ: Erlbaum.

van den Bos, K. (2003). On the subjective quality of social justice: The role of affect as information in the psychology of justice judgments. *Journal of Personality and Social Psychology, 85*, 482–498.

van Dijke, M., Wildschut, T., Leunissen, J. M., & Sedikides, C. (2015). Nostalgia buffers the negative impact of low procedural justice on cooperation. *Organizational Behavior and Human Decision Processes, 127*, 15–29.

van Kleef, G. A. (2009). How emotions regulate social life: The emotions as social information (EASI) model. *Current Directions in Psychological Science, 18*, 184–188.

Wang, M., Liao, H., Zhan, Y., & Shi, J. (2011). Daily customer mistreatment and employee sabotage against customers: Examining emotion and resource perspectives. *Academy of Management Journal, 54*, 312–334.

Weiss, H. M., & Cropanzano, R. (1996). Affective events theory: A theoretical discussion of the structure, causes and consequences of affective experiences at work. In B. M. Staw & L. L. Cummings (Eds.), *Research in organizational behavior* (Volume 18, pp. 1–74). Greenwich, CT, and London, UK: Elsevier Science/JAI.

Weiss, H. M., Suckow, K., & Cropanzano, R. (1999). Effects of justice conditions on discrete emotions. *Journal of Applied Psychology, 84*, 786–794.

Wilkin, C. L., & Connelly, C. E. (2015). Green with envy and nerves of steel: Moderated mediation between distributive justice and theft. *Personality and Individual Differences, 72*, 160–164.

Yang, J., & Diefendorff, J. M. (2009). The relations of daily counterproductive workplace behavior with emotions, situational antecedents, and personality moderators: A diary study in Hong Kong. *Personnel Psychology, 62*, 259–295.

27 Gender and Workplace Affect

Expression, Experiences, and Display Rules

Larry R. Martinez, Liana Bernard, and Megan Snoeyink

Gender continues to be a dominant organizing framework in contemporary society. Like most aspects of everyday life, people's experiences with emotions are highly influenced by gender norms, and this is strikingly the case in workplace contexts. In this chapter, we review the existing literature related to how people experience and express (or suppress) emotions at work as a function of gender. In line with most contemporary literature we reviewed, we use the terms "affect" and "emotions" relatively interchangeably. Indeed, the majority of the research we identified was focused on state-level affect and not on trait-level or stable affect (often referred to as "mood").

Before we begin our review, we provide two important caveats. First, our review revealed that the existing literature almost universally considers gender in line with an assumed binary that distinguishes women from men based predominantly on biological markers of sex – although we highlight a few relevant exceptions (e.g. Livingston & Judge, 2008). Dichotomizing gender into two distinct and non-overlapping groups obscures many of the underlying relations by relying upon gender-related stereotypes (Eagly, Wood, & Diekman, 2000; Schilt & Connell, 2007) and is not in line with contemporary conceptualizations of gender (Kelan, 2010). Second, our review is necessarily limited by what has been published related to gender and emotions in workplace contexts. Although a great deal of research focused on emotions in workplace contexts includes information about the demographic gender characteristics of the participants, gender-related results are often not included. This could be because gender was not a central aspect of the research question and/or because there were no statistically significant gender differences within the sample. Given these two caveats, we recommend that future researchers take a broader view of gender that does not rely upon the traditional binary conceptualization, and that they examine and report gender-related differences even when such differences are not within the primary scope of the paper or statistically significant.

We organize our review by first discussing the emotional display rules that shape the emotional landscape differently for women and men. We then discuss how these display rules impact women and men employees by reviewing these differences in the context of four discrete emotions: two negative (anger, sadness) and two positive (happiness, pride). Our discussion next turns to gender differences in emotional labor. We then synthesize these findings by describing some overarching theoretical frameworks. We conclude by highlighting what we see to be important gaps in the current literature and useful directions for future research.

Emotional Display Rules for Women and Men

Women and men are socialized to both experience and express emotions in different ways from an early age. For instance, adults of both genders tend to ascribe nurturing, tender, and vulnerable characteristics and expectations to babies they believe to be girls and ascribe assertive, adventurous, and hearty characteristics and expectations to babies they believe to be boys (Brody, 2000). As they grow, girls are often chastised for expressing anger or assertiveness and boys are often chastised for expressing sadness or vulnerability (Crick, 1997). These early experiences perpetuate a pervasive difference in the emotional display rules for adult women and men in society (Brody, 2000), which have important implications for workplace contexts as well. Formally, these display rules have been defined as social norms that dictate how, when, and where emotions should be expressed or suppressed (Simpson & Stroh, 2004). In general, a relatively consistent finding in the emotions literature is that women are expected to display a wider range of emotions and express these emotions with more intensity than are men (Brody & Hall, 2008; Eagly, 1997). This is in line with contemporary frameworks in which gender is characterized as a set of cultural and personal expectations that individuals ascribe to fulfill through their behaviors. For instance, West and Zimmerman (1987) describe how individuals "do" gender as a type of performance based on societal expectations, including emotional expression rules.

An implication of these gendered expectations related to emotional expression is that women are perceived as being emotional and thus irrational, and men are perceived as being not emotional and thus rational (Haselton & Ketelaar, 2006). In addition, emotional expression in women is often attributed to vulnerability and loss of control whereas emotional expression in men is often attributed to interpersonal skill (Timmers, Fischer, & Manstead, 2003). This notion contributes to the pervasive disadvantages that women face in workplace contexts – particularly those in which rationality and objectivity are highly valued and in line with task performance (e.g. science, technology, engineering, and math fields). In addition, these expectations are limiting for men, particularly in fields in which emotional expressiveness is aligned with task performance (e.g. customer service, healthcare, education; Tufail & Polletta, 2015).

Despite the widely held stereotype that women are more emotional than men, research does not support this conclusion, particularly when accounting for status and gender inequity at the societal level – women and men experience emotions to the same extent (Lively & Heise, 2004; Gianakos, 2002). Taken together, the fact that women and men experience emotions in largely the same ways and the fact that they express emotions differently indicate that gender differences in emotional expression are a function of gender norms rather than innate differences between women and men (Durik et al., 2006, Plant et al., 2000). In addition to these general gender differences related to emotional expressiveness, there are several nuances related to the expression of particular emotions. In the following section, we review these nuances in relation to both negative and positive emotions.

Negative Emotions

Although there are a number of negative emotions that employees can express in workplace contexts, we focus our discussion on the two most pervasive – anger and sadness – as these were overwhelmingly the most commonly studied in the literature to date. Intuitively, it might seem likely that expressing anger would result in only negative consequences. Indeed, anger is negatively related to fostering and maintaining positive interpersonal relationships (Gianakos, 2002). However, evidence suggests that displays of workplace anger may also result in positive outcomes. For example, individuals often associate anger with competence (Tiedens, 2001), which is itself linked with status (Fiske, Cuddy, & Xu, 2002) such that individuals expect and accept a higher frequency of angry expressions from higher-status individuals than lower-status individuals (Sloan, 2004; Tiedens, 2000). In line with the theoretical orientations related to impression management, anger can be used by higher-status members to intimidate others in order to reach a desired goal or to reinforce their position in the organizational hierarchy (Sloan, 2004). Given that men are disproportionately represented in leadership positions, this is particularly detrimental to women.

The consequences of expressing anger vary with gender. Expressing anger is considered to be incongruent with gender expectations for women but congruent with gender expectations for men (Plant, Hyde, & Keltner, 2000). Indeed, qualitative work shows that coworkers tend to view angry outbursts by women as being highly inappropriate, though the same type of outburst by a man was not considered to be similarly inappropriate (Hale, 1999). Thus it is not surprising that men are more likely than women to express anger in the workplace (Sloan, 2012). This can be limiting for women, given that anger can be used strategically by leaders, particularly with non-compliant employees. Men are more likely than women to use displays of anger to enforce feelings of power and control (Tiedens, 2001; Thomas, 1995), whereas expressing anger has been found to have negative consequences for women in leadership positions, including lower performance evaluations (Brescoll, 2016), lower leader efficacy ratings (Lewis, 2000; Domagalski & Steelman, 2007), decreased hireability perceptions, and lower assigned salaries (Brescoll & Uhlmann, 2008). In contrast, men are often excused for expressing anger in the workplace. For instance, Tiedens (2001) found that women leaders who expressed anger were rated much lower than women leaders who did not, whereas men leaders who expressed anger were not similarly punished. Brescoll & Uhlmann (2008) replicated and expanded these findings by showing that the negative ratings of anger in women were due to attributions that womens' expressions of anger were due to internal factors (e.g. being out of control and incompetent), whereas mens' expressions of anger were attributed to external factors. Women who provided an external attribution for their anger were somewhat buffered from these negative outcomes. Research has also shown that men with relatively lower status reported expressing anger to those higher in the organizational hierarchy more frequently than did women (Domagalski & Steelman, 2007). Women may be hesitant to express anger because women are generally more concerned with cultivating and maintaining interpersonal relationships than are men and are likely to assume that anger will be detrimental to such relationships (Gianakos, 2002). In fact, women supervisors, when angry, have been shown to be more likely to try resolution strategies with the goal of preserving the quality of their interpersonal relationships (Domagalski & Steelman, 2007), whereas men were less likely to be concerned with the negative consequences their anger may have on their interpersonal relationships (Timmers, Fischer, & Manstead, 1998). For example, men may be less concerned with the impact of their anger on potential increased tension with their coworkers than women would be.

Gendered expectations related to the expression of sadness are the inverse of those related to anger – expressing sadness is congruent with expectations for women and incongruent with expectations for men (Plant, Hyde, & Keltner, 2000). Indeed, women express more sadness than men in the workplace (Sloan, 2012), although both women and men leaders are rated lower in effectiveness when expressing sadness compared to expressing no emotion (Lewis, 2000). Crying behaviors are perceived as unprofessional and inappropriate for both women and men in the workplace (Fischer et al., 2013; Timmers et al., 2003). Although some have indicated that crying is much less expected for men than women (e.g. Shields, 2002), men who cry in a professional setting may receive praise for mild expressions of sadness. For instance, an examination of politicians' crying behavior reveals that when crying at the correct moment and in a "manly" way, crying may actually benefit male politicians (Lutz, 1999). In contrast, women politicians are often considered "too emotional" when they are seen crying (Friedman, 2008; Rove, 2009).

Positive Emotions

Although less abundant than the research focused on negative emotions, some work has examined gender differences in workplace contexts associated with positive emotions, such as happiness and pride. Literature regarding other positive emotions and gender is relatively limited. Researchers may be particularly interested in pride because of its relevance to work tasks and promotion. With the gendered division of labor and overrepresentation of women in the service industry (Acker 1990; Hall 1993a, 1993b), women are often in positions in which they are expected to express happiness (Leidner, 1993). However, when engaging in positive emotional expression, men have a social advantage over women. Men's happy reactions are perceived as both more appropriate and more sincere than women's (Hutson-Comeaux & Kelly, 2002). Individuals in positions of power (often men) have greater freedom to express positive emotions than individuals with relatively less power (often women; Hecht & LaFrance, 1998).

A common positive emotion relevant to a workplace setting is pride, as employees may express pride in their work or their accomplishments and engage in self-promotion. Pride is a means by which individuals may express social dominance or power (Plant et al., 2000), attributes typically associated with high-status men (Timmers et al., 2003). Given that women are underrepresented in leadership positions (Cook & Glass, 2014), and that when they are in these positions they receive backlash for displaying masculine characteristics (Berdahl, 2007), it is not surprising that they also tend to elicit negative reactions from coworkers when expressing pride (Lewis, 2000). Although meta-analyses have not found significant differences in experienced pride as a function of gender (Else-Quest, Higgins, Allison, & Morton, 2012), men express pride at much higher rates than do women (Durik et al., 2006; Plant, Hyde, Keltner, & Devine, 2000). This is significant because self-promotion is a critical aspect of professional advancement. For example, one's expressed pride at work may highlight positive qualities, influencing others' perceptions of an employee and thus leading to increased chance of promotion or other opportunities.

Emotional Labor

In addition to the general research focused on emotional experiences and expressions, much of the workplace emotions literature has focused on emotional labor, or "the management of feeling to create a publicly observable facial and bodily display" (Hochschild, 2003, p. 370). In this section, we focus on differences between women and men in emotional labor and refer the reader to Chapter 11 of this volume for a more comprehensive discussion of emotional labor in general. Briefly, emotional labor is engaged when employees display emotions that are consistent with organizational or task-related prerogatives (e.g. a customer service provider engaging in "service with a smile"). The concept may be broken down into three types of behavior: surface acting, characterized by employees completely faking necessary emotions; deep acting, characterized by employees making efforts to put themselves in the desired emotional state; and spontaneous and genuine emotional labor, characterized by employees displaying required emotions that are genuinely experienced (Hochschild, 2003; Grandey, 2000). Although emotional labor often benefits organizations and their customers, surface acting can have negative implications for employees, including feelings of inauthenticity, burnout, decreased job satisfaction, decreased customer service performance, and increased withdrawal behaviors (Hochschild, 2003; Grandey, 2000; Erickson & Wharton, 1997). In general, the greater the dissonance between an employee's genuinely felt emotions and their expressed emotions, the more negative the outcomes for employees (Brotheridge & Grandey, 2002; Grandey, 2003).

Literature focused on gender and emotional labor suggests that, overall, women are expected to perform more emotional labor than men (Morris & Feldman, 1996). For example, women professors, women nurses, and women police officers were all expected to engage in emotional labor more and to be warmer and more supportive of others than their men counterparts (Bellas, 1999; Martin, 1999; Steinberg & Figart, 1999). This may be due to women being socialized to handle the demands of emotion management in their interpersonal interactions (Hochschild, 2003; Johnson & Spector, 2007). Specifically, Kruml and Geddes (2000) suggest that (a) women are more likely than men to engage in emotional labor due to societal expectations that women should cater to others' emotional well-being, and (b) women are also more negatively impacted by emotional dissonance than are men because men are socialized to hide emotions from others and fake affective states more often than are women (Ashmore, Del Boca, & Wohlers, 1986; Fabes & Martin, 1991). Indeed, men are more likely to engage in surface acting and women are more likely to engage in deep acting (Walsh & Bartikowski, 2013). In addition, women are more likely to benefit from deep acting, and are more likely to suffer from engaging in surface acting, than are men (Scott & Barnes, 2011; Johnson & Spector, 2007). For women (compared to men), surface acting is more likely to perpetuate emotional dissonance, which contributes to role inauthenticity and consequently to emotional exhaustion and reduced well-being (Johnson & Spector, 2007). Among service employees, the negative impact of surface acting on job satisfaction is greater for women than for men (Scott & Barnes, 2011; Walsh & Bartikowski, 2013). Some have suggested that men's relatively high status may shield them from the obligation to engage in emotional labor and the resultant negative outcomes associated with emotional labor (Hochschild, 2003; Erickson & Ritter, 2001).

In addition to overall differences between women and men in emotional labor, the literature suggests that these differences may be exacerbated in certain industries. Specifically, women are overrepresented in "feminine" industries that require a high degree of emotional labor (e.g. service, healthcare; Erickson & Ritter, 2001; Guy & Newman, 2004; Hochschild, 2003) and as such are held to a higher emotional standard than are men (Pierce, 1999). Conversely, men are overrepresented in "masculine" industries that require employees to display no emotion or express emotions such as anger (Martin, 1999). Women in professions dominated by men will report suppressing negative feelings and displaying positive feelings, whereas men will report suppressing positive feelings and displaying negative feelings (Simpson & Stroh, 2004). Thus the gendered expectations associated with emotions in general can interact with gendered expectations associated with certain industries to compound the negative outcomes of emotional labor.

Some research also highlights the non-work emotional experiences of women and men. In particular, this work highlights the fact that many workplace experiences, particularly related to emotional labor, do not disappear when employees leave work. In addition to being responsible for the majority of socioemotional work in the workplace, women are shouldered with the bulk of socioemotional work at home as well. Specifically, in line with social role theory (Eagly, Wood, & Diekman, 2000), women are presumed to be better equipped at providing socioemotional support to family members and are presumed to enjoy providing this type of support more than men (Erickson, 1993, 2005; Hochschild, 2003). Indeed, some research argues that women and men consider this type of work to be central to women's roles as wives and mothers (Lott, 1988; Wharton & Erickson, 1993) and that women readily and willingly adopt this type of work as part of their role-related self-concepts (Erickson, 2005). Although often expected, this type of work is traditionally not considered to be "real work," which renders much of what women do invisible. Indeed, including socioemotional labor in and outside of the workplace, women engage in five to seven more hours of work per week than do men, on average (Sayer, England, Bittman, & Bianchi, 2004).

Overarching Theories

Although the research focused on gender differences related to specific emotions is somewhat inconsistent, it can be characterized in line with some overarching theoretical frameworks. First, in general and in line with most other gender-related phenomena, both women and men are penalized for engaging in emotional displays that are discordant with societal gender norms and women are penalized more harshly for such transgressions than are men (Smith, Brescoll & Thomas, 2016). The tendency for women to be more harshly penalized is explained by social role theory, which states that gender norms result from social expectations that men assume masculine and agentic roles whereas women assume feminine and communal roles (Wood & Eagly, 2002). Negative social reactions often result when women violate these gender norms. Second, women may be particularly disadvantaged in workplace contexts due to what Ragins and Winkel (2011) have identified in their theoretical framework as a "cycle of powerlessness." For men, displaying anger elicits perceptions of power and status (Tiedens, 2001); thus, powerful men elevate their power through anger. However, women are expected to suppress their anger and display emotions that are more conducive to interpersonal relationships such as compassion and warmth (Brody & Hall, 2000), which elicit perceptions of relative weakness. Women therefore find themselves in an impossible situation in which they may experience anger due to a relatively lower status but be unable to successfully express this anger without eliciting backlash for violating gender expectations. Thus anger works to elevate the status of (already relatively powerful) men and diminish the status of (relatively less powerful) women.

Third, both women and men who engage in surface acting are susceptible to negative outcomes. Burnout, emotional exhaustion, and decreased job satisfaction resulting from engaging in surface acting may be explained by the job demands–resources (JD–R) model. This model states that cognitive demands, such as monitoring and adhering to display rules, drain emotional resources and lead to strain (Demerouti, Bakker, Nachreiner & Schaufeli, 2001). Although both women and men are affected by the demands of emotional labor, it seems that women may be more susceptible to these outcomes. Women may be more affected by the demands of emotional labor because they are expected to (and do) engage in more emotional labor at work and at home (Morris & Feldman, 1996; Erickson, 2005). Thus, according to the JD–R, women who engage in emotional labor are more likely to feel the effects of decreased well-being as a result of these disparate expectations of women and men.

Future Directions for Research in Gender and Emotion

Having reviewed the existing literature focused on gender and affect in workplace contexts, we now provide recommendations for future research in this field. In the most general sense, we recommend that research continues to expand in this domain, as the existing literature is relatively nascent. In particular, we recommend research that focuses on a wider range of emotions. Our review revealed that the vast bulk of the current research was constrained to the four emotions we reviewed: anger, sadness, happiness, and pride. We therefore encourage a greater appreciation for the range of emotions and their implications for gender in work contexts.

We also note that there has been little research on gender and affect that is not confined to the gender binary. Further exploration of the emotional experiences of transgender individuals may be particularly informative for several reasons. First, transgender individuals present a unique and ideal opportunity to examine the impact of gender on workplace emotional display rules due to the fact that these employees have the same human capital and represent their own statistical controls. Specifically, using a within-subjects design with participants who have lived as both genders within the binary would inherently yield lower error variance and greater power for more precise estimates of gender similarities and differences in affect-related experiences. Furthermore, a qualitative examination of workplace affective experiences of transgender employees would yield beneficial findings because participants could be considered subject-matter experts about the impact of gender, emotions, and work, having existed at multiple points along a gender continuum. Indeed, existing work highlights the very different workplace experiences that transgender employees report as women (e.g. less respect and autonomy) versus as men, despite the fact that they are the same person (Schilt & Connell, 2007).

Second, transgender individuals endure a complex emotional landscape experience due to a pursuit of authenticity at work (Martinez, Sawyer, Thoroughgood, Ruggs, & Smith, 2017) and thus represent a unique opportunity to examine the impact of gender on the experiences of emotion at work. The workplace is a context in which transgender employees may frequently encounter customers or others to whom they have probably not disclosed their identities, or in which their gender identities are not readily apparent. This facilitates many potential scenarios in which employees may be misgendered and thus repeatedly reminded of their being perceived as having low authenticity, which may induce negative emotions (Dietert & Dentice, 2009). Thus, the experiences of transgender employees can inform researchers about the emotional tolls associated with inauthenticity and identity management in workplace contexts (see Chapter 36 in this volume for a detailed discussion of this).

Third, transgender individuals may experience heightened negative emotions at work, given that 56 percent of transgender individuals report feeling unsafe in public (Kenagy, 2005) and are at lifelong risk for violence, and particularly sexual violence (Stotzer, 2009). Therefore, applications resulting from an examination of affective experiences of transgender individuals in the workplace may help promote a safe environment. By protecting their emotional and cognitive resources that may be drained due to gender-related abusive experiences, these employees may be better able to focus on work tasks.

In addition to including the experiences of transgender employees, we recommend that researchers stop using the terms "sex" and "gender" interchangeably and instead appreciate the socially-derived nature of gender, in line with contemporary scholarship. In most cases, if not all, researchers should investigate gender rather than sex, as gender refers to one's social identity as a woman or a man and sex is determined by myriad biological characteristics. Furthermore, we recommend that researchers acknowledge that gender exists along a spectrum. For instance, Schilt and Connell (2007) found that even transgender employees were socialized and coached by their coworkers on how to appropriately dress and behave as their "new" genders, despite the fact that many of these employees did not identify as completely women or men. There are likely to be particular emotional challenges associated with identifying outside of, or somewhere in the "middle" of, the gender binary. Furthermore, we urge researchers to stop using gender as a proxy for constructs that are more closely aligned with the phenomena of interest. A good example of this was provided by Livingston and Judge (2008), who included traditional gender norm beliefs (i.e. gender norm adherence) as a moderator of the relations between work–family conflict and negative emotions such as guilt. In this work, the authors reasoned that gender norm beliefs, their focal construct of interest, would have a stronger impact on the relationship between work–family conflict and guilt than gender alone. They showed that men who held relatively traditional gender norm beliefs experienced stronger guilt when their family obligations interfered with work and men with less traditional beliefs experienced more guilt when work interfered with family. If these authors had simply examined differences between men and women without appreciating the nuance associated with gender norm beliefs as a within-gender moderator, this nuance would have been obscured. Indeed, most of the research we reviewed did not account for such moderators, instead opting to treat gender itself as a moderator. These results highlight how merely examining differences between women and men would not have captured the reality of the phenomenon. Another approach would include directly measuring masculine and feminine self-presentation styles in relation to employees' emotion expression and regulation at work, rather than assuming that men act masculinely and that women act femininely.

Finally, we highlight the importance of researchers taking an intersectional approach to gender and affect research in the workplace. Intersectionality is a perspective emphasizing that individuals often hold multiple identities that can be impactful in ways that are different from a combination of the individual effects of these separate identities (Shields, 2008). Hence research on gender and affect likely becomes more nuanced when including other identity characteristics in research design. For example, people tend to believe that Black women display more masculine emotions (e.g. anger, pride) than do White women (Durik et al., 2006), and that Black women are generally relatively angry (Harris-Perry, 2011). Indeed, Black women who display masculine emotions have been rated as being more likeable and hirable than White women and Black men in the workplace (Hall, Everett, & Hamilton-Mason, 2012). Furthermore, Livingston, Rosette and Washington (2012) found that Black women in leadership positions did not receive the same backlash that White women leaders experienced. Notwithstanding this, Black women do not benefit from the same privilege that White men experience. Otherwise, one would see a far greater frequency of Black women in leadership positions. Although Black women may be socially permitted to display similar dominance and pride-related emotions to those displayed by men, they may encounter threats or doubts of their competence, and thus be punished more harshly than White women, or even Black men, for making an error. Experiences of Black women in leadership positions highlight the importance of examining other factors that intersect with gender so as not to overgeneralize inappropriately. In addition to race, we recommend researchers begin examining the affect-related experiences of sexual orientation minorities. Although we could not identify any research that focuses on this specifically, other research related to sexual orientation suggests that gay men employees are probably freer to express emotions than are lesbian women. Indeed, inversion theory (Kite & Deaux, 1987) states that in this respect gay men are similar to straight women and lesbian women are similar to straight men, and that these emotion-related experiences probably differ as a function of gender identity expression (Hamilton, Park, Carsey, & Martinez, 2019).

Conclusion

In this chapter, we have reviewed the existing literature regarding the intersection of gender and affect. In general, the workplace is a context in which logic is valued and emotionality is discouraged (Moran, Diefendorff, & Greguras, 2013). Although women and men have been found to experience emotions to the same extent, they express these emotions differently, such that women express themselves more than men. Within the workplace context, this disadvantages women, who are stereotyped as being more emotional and generally express emotions more frequently. Although women's emotionality has been valued in some industries, such as debt settlement firms (Tufail & Polletta, 2015), and in nurturing roles such as service work (Erickson & Ritter, 2001), emotionality is frequently used to discredit women (Friedman, 2008; Rove, 2009) and emasculate men. Therefore, everyone, including gender majority group members, would probably benefit from a shift away from social norms that encourage and enforce the suppression of emotional expression. Future research should explore the impact of interventions aimed at dissociating the stereotypical link of women with irrational emotionality and encouraging employees of all genders to appreciate and express emotions in healthy and beneficial ways.

References

Acker, J. (1990). Hierarchies, jobs, bodies: A theory of gendered organizations. *Gender & Society, 4*, 139–158.

Ashmore, R. D., Del Boca, F. K., & Wohlers, A. J. (1986). Gender stereotypes. In R. D. Ashmore & F. K. Del Boca (Eds.), *The social psychology of female–male relations* (pp. 69–119). London, UK: Elsevier.

Bellas, M. L. (1999). Emotional labor in academia: The case of professors. *Annals of the American Academy of Political and Social Science, 561*, 96–110.

Berdahl, J. L. (2007). The sexual harassment of uppity women. *Journal of Applied Psychology, 92*, 425–437.

Brescoll, V. L. (2016). Leading with their hearts? How gender stereotypes of emotion lead to biased evaluations of female leaders. *Leadership Quarterly, 27*, 415–428.

Brescoll, V. L., & Uhlmann, E. L. (2008). Can an angry woman get ahead? Status conferral, gender, and expression of emotion in the workplace. *Psychological Science, 19*, 268–275.

Brody, L. R. (2000). The socialization of gender differences in emotional expression: Display rules, infant temperaments, and differentiation. In A. Fisher (Ed.), *Gender and emotion* (pp. 24–47). Cambridge, MA: Cambridge University Press.

Brody, L. R., & Hall, J. A. (2008). Gender and emotion in context. In M. Lewis, J. M. Haviland-Jones, & L. F. Barrett (Eds.), *Handbook of emotions* (3rd edition). New York, NY: Guilford.

Brotheridge, C. M., & Grandey, A. A. (2002). Emotional labor and burnout: Comparing two perspectives of "people work." *Journal of Vocational Behavior, 60*, 17–39.

Cook, A., & Glass, C. (2014). Women and top leadership positions: Towards an institutional analysis. *Gender, Work, & Organization, 21*, 91–103.

Crick, N. R. (1997). Engagement in gender normative versus nonnormative forms of aggression: Links to social–psychological adjustment. *Developmental Psychology, 33*, 610–617.

Demerouti, E., Bakker, A. B., Nachreiner, F., & Schaufeli, W. B. (2001). The job demands–resources model of burnout. *Journal of Applied Psychology, 86*, 499–512.

Dietert, M., & Dentice, D. (2009). Gender identity issues and workplace discrimination: The transgender experience. *Journal of Workplace Rights, 14*, 121–140.

Domagalski, T. A., & Steelman, L. A. (2007). The impact of gender and organizational status on workplace anger expression. *Management Communication Quarterly*, *20*, 297–315.

Durik, A. M., Hyde, J. S., Marks, A. C., Roy, A. L., Anaya, D., & Schultz, G. (2006). Ethnicity and gender stereotypes of emotion. *Sex Roles*, *54*, 429–445.

Eagly, A. H. (1997). Sex differences in social behavior: Comparing social role theory and evolutionary psychology. *American Psychologist*, *52*, 1380–1381.

Eagly, A. H., Wood, W., & Diekman, A. B. (2000). Social role theory of sex differences and similarities: A current appraisal. In T. Eckes & H. M. Trautner (Eds.), *The developmental social psychology of gender* (pp. 123–174). Mahwah, NJ: Lawrence Erlbaum.

Else-Quest, N. M., Higgins, A., Allison, C., & Morton, L. C. (2012). Gender differences in self-conscious emotional experience: A meta-analysis. *Psychological Bulletin*, *138*, 947–981.

Erickson, R. J. (1993). Reconceptualizing family work: The effect of emotion work on perceptions of marital quality. *Journal of Marriage and Family*, *55*, 888–900.

Erickson, R. J. (2005). Why emotion work matters: Sex, gender, and the division of household labor. *Journal of Marriage and Family*, *67*, 337–351.

Erickson, R. J., & Ritter, C. (2001). Emotional labor, burnout, and inauthenticity: Does gender matter? *Social Psychology Quarterly*, *64*, 146–163.

Erickson, R. J., & Wharton, A. S. (1997). Inauthenticity and depression: Assessing the consequences of interactive service work. *Work and Occupations*, *24*, 188–213.

Fabes, R. A., & Martin, C. L. (1991). Gender and age stereotypes of emotionality. *Personality and Social Psychology Bulletin*, *17*, 532–540.

Fischer, A. H., Eagly, A. H., & Oosterwijk, S. (2013). The meaning of tears: Which sex seems emotional depends on the social context. *European Journal of Social Psychology*, *43*, 105–115.

Fiske, S. T., Cuddy, A. J. C., Glick, P., & Xu, J. (2002). A model of (often mixed) stereotype content: Competence and warmth respectively follow from perceived status and competition. *Journal of Personality and Social Psychology*, *82*, 878–902.

Friedman, E. (2008). Can Clinton's emotions get the best of her? *ABC News*, 7 January, https://abcnews.go.com/Politics/Vote2008/story?id=4097786&page=1

Gianakos, I. (2002). Predictors of coping with work stress: The influences of sex, gender role, social desirability, and locus of control. *Sex Roles*, *46*, 149–158.

Grandey, A. A. (2000). Emotional regulation in the workplace: A new way to conceptualize emotional labor. *Journal of Occupational Health Psychology*, *5*, 95–110.

Grandey, A. A. (2003). When "the show must go on": Surface acting and deep acting as determinants of emotional exhaustion and peer-rated service delivery. *Academy of Management Journal*, *46*, 86–96.

Guy, M. E., & Newman, M. A. (2004). Women's jobs, men's jobs: Sex segregation and emotional labor. *Public Administration Review*, *64*, 289–298.

Hale, M. (1999). He says, she says: Gender and worklife. *Public Administration Review*, *59*, 410–424.

Hall, E. J. (1993a). Smiling, deferring, and flirting. *Work and Occupations*, *20*, 452–471.

Hall, E. J. (1993b). Waitering/waitressing: Engendering the work of table servers. *Gender & Society*, *7*, 329–346.

Hall, J. C., Everett, J. E., & Hamilton-Mason, J. (2012). Black women talk about workplace stress and how they cope. *Journal of Black Studies*, *43*, 207–226.

Hamilton, K. M., Park, L. S., Carsey, T. A., & Martinez, L. R. (2019). "Lez be honest": Gender expression impacts workplace disclosure decisions. *Journal of Lesbian Studies*, *23*(2), 144–168.

Harris-Perry, M. V. (2001). *Sister citizen: Shame, stereotypes, and Black women in America*. New Haven, CT: Yale University Press.

Haselton, M. G., & Ketelaar, T. (2006). Irrational emotions or emotional wisdom? The evolutionary psychology of emotions and behavior. In J. P. Forgas (Ed.), *Affect in social thinking and behavior* (pp. 21–40). New York, NY: Psychology.

Hecht, M. A., & LaFrance, M. (1998). License or obligation to smile: The effect of power and sex on amount and type of smiling. *Personality and Social Psychology Bulletin*, *24*, 1332–1342.

Hochschild, A. R. (2003). *The managed heart: Commercialization of human feeling* (20th anniversary edition). Berkeley: University of California Press.

Hutson-Comeaux, S. L., & Kelly, J. R. (2002). Gender stereotypes of emotional reactions: How we judge an emotion as valid. *Sex Roles*, *47*, 1–10.

Johnson, H.-A. M., & Spector, P. E. (2007). Service with a smile: Do emotional intelligence, gender, and autonomy moderate the emotional labor process? *Journal of Occupational Health Psychology*, *12*, 319–333.

Kelan, E. K. (2010). Gender logic and (un)doing gender at work. *Gender, Work & Organization*, *17*, 174–194.

Kenagy, G. P. (2005). Transgender health findings from two needs assessment studies in Philadelphia. *Health and Social Work*, *30*, 19–26.

Kite, M. E., & Deaux, K. (1987). Gender belief systems: Homosexuality and the implicit inversion theory. *Psychology of Women Quarterly*, *11*, 83–96.

Kring, A. M., & Gordon, A. H. (1998). Sex differences in emotion: Expression, experience, and physiology. *Journal of Personality and Social Psychology*, *74*, 686–704.

Kruml, S. M., & Geddes, D. (2000). Exploring the dimensions of emotional labor: The heart of Hochschild's work. *Management Communication Quarterly*, *14*, 8–49.

Leidner, R. (1993). *Fast food, fast talk*. Berkeley: University of California Press.

Lewis, K. M. (2000). When leaders display emotion: How followers respond to negative emotional expression of male and female leaders. *Journal of Organizational Behavior*, *21*, 221–234.

Lively, K. J., & Heise, D. R. (2004). Sociological realms of emotional experience. *American Journal of Sociology*, *109*, 1109–1136.

Livingston, B. A., & Judge, T. A. (2008). Emotional responses to work–family conflict: An examination of gender role orientation among working men and women. *Journal of Applied Psychology*, *93*, 207–216.

Livingston, R. W., Rosette, A. S., & Washington, E. F. (2012). Can an agentic Black woman get ahead? The impact of race and interpersonal dominance on perceptions of female leaders. *Psychological Science*, *23*, 354–358.

Lott, B. (1988). Separate spheres revisited. *Contemporary Social Psychology*, *13*, 55–62.

Lutz, T. (1999). *Crying: The natural and cultural history of tears*. New York, NY: WW Norton.

Martin, S. E. (1999). Police force or police service? Gender and emotional labor. *Annals of the American Academy of Political and Social Science*, *561*, 111–126.

Martinez, L. R., Sawyer, K., Thoroughgood, C., Ruggs, E. N., & Smith, N. A. (2017). The importance of being "me": The relation between authentic identity expression and transgender employees' work-related attitudes and experiences. *Journal of Applied Psychology*, *102*, 215–226.

Moran, C. M., Diefendorff, J. M., & Greguras, G. J. (2013). Understanding emotional display rules at work and outside of work: The effects of country and gender. *Motivation and Emotion*, *37*, 323–334.

Morris, J. A., & Feldman, D. C. (1996). The dimensions, antecedents, and consequences of emotional labor. *Academy of Management Review*, *21*, 986–1010.

Pierce, J. L. (1999). Emotional labor among paralegals. *Annals of the American Academy of Political and Social Science*, *561*, 127–142.

Plant, E. A., Hyde, J. S., Keltner, D., & Devine, P. G. (2000). The gender stereotyping of emotions. *Psychology of Women Quarterly*, *24*, 81–92.

Ragins, B. R., & Winkel, D. E. (2011). Gender, emotion and power in work relationships. *Human Resource Management Review*, *21*, 377–393.

Rove, K. (2009). "Empathy" is code for judicial activism. *Wall Street Journal*, 28 May, www.wsj.com/articles/SB124347199490860831

Sayer, L. C., England, P., Bittman, M., & Bianchi, S. M. (2004). How long is the second (plus first) shift? Gender differences in paid, unpaid, and total work time in Australia and the United States. Paper presented at the Annual Meeting of the Population Association of America, Boston, MA, April.

Schilt, K., & Connell, C. (2007). Do workplace gender transitions make gender trouble? *Gender, Work & Organization*, *14*, 596–618.

Scott, B. A., & Barnes, C. M. (2011). A multilevel field investigation of emotional labor, affect, work withdrawal, and gender. *Academy of Management Journal, 54*, 116–136.

Shields, S. A. (2002). *Speaking from the heart: Gender and the social meaning of emotion*. New York, NY: Cambridge University Press.

Shields, S. A. (2008). Gender: An intersectionality perspective. *Sex Roles, 59*, 301–311.

Simpson, P. A., & Stroh, L. K. (2004). Gender differences: Emotional expression and feelings of personal inauthenticity. *Journal of Applied Psychology, 89*, 715–721.

Sloan, M. M. (2004). The effects of occupational characteristics on the experience and expression of anger in the workplace. *Work and Occupations, 31*, 38–72.

Sloan, M. M. (2012). Controlling anger and happiness at work: An examination of gender differences. *Gender, Work & Organization, 19*, 370–391.

Smith, J. S., Brescoll, V. L., & Thomas, E. L. (2016). Constrained by emotion: Women, leadership, and expressing emotion in the workplace. In M. L. Connerley & J. Wu (Eds.), *Handbook on well-being of working women* (pp. 209–224). Dordrecht: Springer Netherlands.

Steinberg, R. J., & Figart, D. M. (1999). Emotional labor since *The managed heart*. *Annals of the American Academy of Political and Social Science, 561*, 8–26.

Stotzer, R. L. (2009). Violence against transgender people: A review of United States data. *Aggression and Violent Behavior, 14*, 170–179.

Thomas, S. P. (1995). Women's anger: Causes, manifestations, and correlates. *Stress and Emotion, 15*, 53–74.

Tiedens, L. Z. (2000). Powerful emotions: The vicious cycle of social status positions and emotions. In N. M. Ashkanasy, C. E. J. Hartel, & W. J. Zerbe (Eds.), *Emotions in the workplace: Research, theory and practice* (pp. 71–81). Westport, CT: Quorum.

Tiedens, L. Z. (2001). Anger and advancement versus sadness and subjugation: The effect of negative emotion expressions on social status conferral. *Journal of Personality and Social Psychology, 80*, 86–94.

Timmers, M., Fischer, A. H., & Manstead, A. S. (1998). Gender differences in motives for regulating emotions. *Personality and Social Psychology Bulletin, 24*, 974–985.

Timmers, M., Fischer, A., & Manstead, A. (2003). Ability versus vulnerability: Beliefs about men's and women's emotional behaviour. *Cognition and Emotion, 17*, 41–63.

Tufail, Z., & Polletta, F. (2015). The gendering of emotional flexibility: Why angry women are both admired and devalued in debt settlement firms. *Gender & Society, 29*, 484–508.

Walsh, G., & Bartikowski, B. (2013). Employee emotional labour and quitting intentions: Moderating effects of gender and age. *European Journal of Marketing, 47*, 1213–1237.

West, C., & Zimmerman, D. H. (1987). Doing gender. *Gender & Society, 1*, 125–151.

Wharton, A. S., & Erickson, R. J. (1993). Managing emotions on the job and at home: Understanding the consequences of multiple emotional roles. *Academy of Management Review, 18*, 457–486.

Wood, W., & Eagly, A. H. (2002). A cross-cultural analysis of the behavior of women and men: Implications for the origins of sex differences. *Psychological Bulletin, 128*, 699–727.

28 Affective Climate and Organization-Level Emotion Management

Neal M. Ashkanasy, Charmine E. J. Härtel, and Agata Bialkowski

While scholars have studied the role of emotions in work settings since Aristotle (see Mastenbroek, 2000, for a historical overview), the topic did not enter mainstream organizational scholarship until the 1990s (Ashkanasy, Härtel, & Daus, 2002; Härtel, Zerbe, & Ashkanasy, 2005). In this chapter, we utilize the five-level model developed by Ashkanasy (2003; see also Ashkanasy & Dorris, 2017; Ashkanasy & Humphrey, 2011) as an organizing framework in reviewing research on ways institutional leaders should manage employee emotions at the organization-wide level. We start with a brief summary of the five-level model before offering recommendations as to (a) how organizational leaders can foster positive affective organizational cultures and climates; and (b) how leaders may avoid creating negative affective organizational cultures and climates. We conclude by discussing the need for leaders to emphasize the value of experiencing and expressing positive and negative affect, and we offer suggestions for future research.

The Five-Level Model

In Ashkanasy's five-level model (FLM), he suggests that emotions in any organization extend across five levels: (1) within-person temporal variability; (2) between-person individual differences; (3) interpersonal interactions; (4) groups and teams; and (5) organization-wide (Ashkanasy, 2003). At the first level, Ashkanasy discusses how employees experience in-the-moment affect and emotion throughout the working day (Clark, Watson, & Leeka, 1989), including their response to "affective events" in the workplace (Weiss & Cropanzano, 1996). At level 2, he examines the role of individual differences, such as emotional intelligence (Mayer & Salovey, 1997) and trait affectivity (Watson & Tellegen, 1985). Then, at level 3, he focuses on the communication of emotions in interpersonal exchanges, including the expression of appropriate emotions via emotional labor and emotion regulation tactics (Hochschild, 1983). At level 4 Ashkanasy broadens the scope to discuss groups and, in particular, the significant influence that leaders can have in shaping the affective tone of work teams through emotional contagion (Barsade, 2002). Finally, at level 5, the role of organizational leaders is discussed in relation to the emotional culture and climate of the organization (Daus, Jordan, Ashkanasy, & Dasborough, 2012; Schein, 1992).

In brief, Ashkanasy and Jordan (2008) argue that employees' attitudes and behavior at each level influence how organizational leaders will be required to manage emotions across the organization as a whole. While the role of leaders at the organization-wide level of analysis is the focus of this chapter, we need first to address what happens within each tier in order to demonstrate how organizational leadership cascades throughout the organization, subsequently impacting key organizational variables that underpin organizational performance (cf. Schein, 1992).

Level 1: Within-Person

According to affective events theory (Weiss & Cropanzano, 1996), events in an organizational environment (e.g. organizational change) evoke emotions (acute, object-oriented, and short-lived feelings) and moods (diffuse, not object-oriented, and longer-lasting feelings) in employees. Weiss and Cropanzano argue that these sentiments result in either "affect-driven" behaviors – immediate behavioral responses such as violent outbursts or spontaneous helping – or the development of attitudes that lead to "judgment-driven" behaviors such as quitting or low performance.

Evidence suggests that support from leaders can play a critical role in how subordinates cope with everyday frustrations in the workplace (Pirola-Merlo, Härtel, Mann, & Hirst, 2002). Building upon this, Bono, Foldes, Vinson, and Muros (2007) discovered that transformational leadership behaviors can result in employees experiencing positive emotions throughout the day – long after the leader's intervention. McColl-Kennedy and Anderson (2002) came to a similar conclusion: when transformational leaders helped improve their subordinates' moods after negative events, employee performance increased.

Level 2: Between-Persons

At level 2 of the FLM, Ashkanasy (2003) examines individual differences, including the role of emotional intelligence (EI) and trait affect. Mayer and Salovey (1999) define EI in terms of four "branches, " which include the ability to (1) perceive emotions; (2) assimilate emotions into thinking; (3) understand emotions; and (4) manage emotions in oneself and others. Scholars have suggested (Barling, Slater, & Kelloway, 2000; Daus & Ashkanasy, 2005) that individuals with higher EI are more likely to use effective leadership behaviors (e.g. transformational) to improve supervision of their subordinates (Sy, Tram, & O'Hara, 2006), job satisfaction and extra-role performance in employees (Wong & Law, 2002), and acceptance of organizational change initiatives (Paterson & Härtel, 2002). In a meta-analysis by Harms and Credé (2010), affect-related differences associated with effective compared to ineffective leaders include higher levels of trait and ability-based EI, underscoring the important role of EI in leadership effectiveness. Miao, Humphrey, and Qian (2016) found similar meta-analytic results concerning the link between leader EI (ability, trait, mixed) and employee job satisfaction.

Weiss and Cropanzano (1996) note that effective leaders differ in trait affectivity; their average emotional baselines are more likely to be in the positive range, resulting in more active high-arousal positive emotions (e.g. excitement and enthusiasm) and less active lower-arousal negative emotions: that is, they experience negative emotions less intensely than others. As a result, such leaders appear to respond to negative affective events more appropriately, reducing the occurrence of negative emotional contagion that may negatively influence followers (Pirola-Merlo et al., 2002).

Level 3: Interpersonal Relationships

Operating under the assumption that a core aspect of leadership is managing interpersonal relationships in the workplace, scholars studying level 3 (e.g. Ashkanasy & Jordan, 2008; Roux & Härtel, 2018) tend to emphasize the perception and communication of emotion in leader–employee dyads. For example, Wijewardena, Härtel, and Samaratunge (2010, 2017) found that employees' perceptions of constructive managerial humor evoke positive discrete emotions. Moreover, this relationship is amplified when leaders have good relationships with their followers (Wijewardena et al., 2010; 2017); however, when exposed to negative managerial humor (as perceived by employees), Wijewardena et al. documented a decline in their psychological well-being.

Martin, Knopoff, and Beckman (1998) identify emotional labor tactics as another way that effective leaders enhance their relationships with employees. Hochschild (1983) defined emotional labor as "management of feeling to create a publicly observable facial and bodily display" (p. 7). In other words, effective leaders are required to feel and to express emotions perceived by followers as appropriate in order to have the desired impact on followers' emotions, behaviors, and attitudes (such as whether or not they perceive their leader as authentic and trustworthy) (cf. Hunt, Gardner, & Fischer, 2008). Moreover, there is evidence of the need for emotional labor in terms of congruence between nonverbal and verbal emotional expressions, as found in a study by Newcombe and Ashkanasy (2002), where followers gave lower leader–member exchange ratings to leaders who tried to convey a positive appraisal message while simultaneously displaying negative facial affect in a performance appraisal situation.

According to Hochschild (1983), the types of emotional labor tactics that leaders can use when interacting with employees are surface acting and deep acting. Surface acting occurs when actors change their outward emotional expressions without changing their actual feelings, whereas deep acting involves summoning up the appropriate feelings and then outwardly displaying them (Hochschild, 1983). Hochschild theorized that there are several ways individuals can evoke emotions. One method involves recalling feelings toward a past object or person, and then using these as a basis to govern outward displays of emotion. Another approach is the direct manipulation of emotions through exhortation to induce or prevent a feeling. Ashforth and Humphrey (1993) identified a third mode of emotional labor, namely naturally expressed emotions, which occur when a leader expresses sentiments that are genuine and consistent with the organization's emotional display rules (e.g. expressing sympathy for an employee undergoing personal problems or displaying disapproval to a deviant employee; see also Hennig-Thurau, Groth, Paul, & Gremler, 2006). This is an important distinction insofar as leaders can experience stress from engaging in emotional labor, especially surface acting, which tends to be more stressful than deep acting (Grandey, 2000; 2003; Hülsheger & Schewe, 2011) because of associated feelings of inauthenticity or emotional dissonance.

Emotional labor skills are also fundamental to effective cross-cultural interactions and assignments (Tan, Härtel, Panipucci, & Strybosch, 2005). Cross-cultural encounters in the expatriate experience require the display of culturally sanctioned emotions, which constitutes a form of emotional labor as employees need to publicly display emotions that they may not necessarily feel (Morris & Feldman, 1996).

Level 4: Groups and Teams

Studying level 4 of the FLM, scholars address collective processes and examine how leaders facilitate group emotions (Krzeminska, Lim, & Härtel, 2018; Sy et al., 2005). George (2000) argues that leaders can set the affective tone of the group through emotional expression and contagion processes (see also Barsade, 2002; Sy, Côté, & Saavedra, 2005). Sy and colleagues found that leaders need to maintain a positive emotional group tone. Thus, groups led by positive-mood leaders displayed enhanced team coordination and task achievement compared to groups led by negative-mood leaders. In a similar vein, Krzeminska and colleagues (2018) found that servant leadership behavior in emergency services teams supported a positive workgroup emotional climate that, in turn, enhanced team members' psychological capital and mitigated occupational stress.

Härtel and colleagues (e.g. Härtel, Gough, & Härtel, 2006; 2008; Härtel & Liu, 2012; Liu, Härtel, & Sun, 2014; Krzeminska et al., 2018) document the empirical evidence for workgroup emotional climate, which Härtel and Page (2009) defined as "the perceptions of emotions and emotional exchanges that typify a workgroup" (p. 247). Härtel et al. (2006) in particular provide strong evidence that a positive emotional climate is important for maintaining group members' job satisfaction and performance.

Härtel and colleagues' endeavors to understand the mechanisms underlying workgroup emotional climate include multi-level theorizations. For example, Härtel et al. (2008) proposed and found that the emotion management skills of team members are fundamental to the type of workgroup emotional climate developed (such as supportive, participative, or negative), based on research showing that emotional expression affects both receivers and senders (Härtel & Panipucci, 2005). They identified a number of emotion management skills underpinning a positive workgroup emotional climate. Important other-directed emotion management skills are helpfulness, friendliness, supportiveness, giving recognition, courtesy, warmth, optimism, self-regulation, constructive conflict management, and adaptation to social display rules, while important self-directed emotion management skills are optimism, low tendency to frustration, positive affectivity/happiness, low tendency to anger, low tendency to worry, high enthusiasm, and problem-focused coping.

In other multi-level theorizations, Härtel and Page (2009, p. 238) introduced the construct "discrete emotional crossover," which they defined as "the transmission of discrete emotions such as anger, joy, contentment, and fear from one individual to another in the same social environment." Such emotional crossover may come from the emotional experiences of team members outside the workplace (e.g. at home or in social activities), and the intensity with which team members tend to respond to affective events – "affect intensity" (Larsen, Diener, & Emmons, 1986). Besides affecting individuals' emotional experiences at work, Härtel and Page proposed that discrete emotional crossover contributes to workgroup emotional climate through a process of emotional contagion, which is the propensity to unconsciously match the verbal and nonverbal mannerisms of the people we interact with (Barsade, 2002). Petitta, Jiang, and Härtel (2017) identified the frequency and intensity of social interactions as an antecedent condition for emotional contagion. Thus teams with important and frequent intra-group and group–leader interactions are likely to "catch" each other's emotions, while teams whose interactions do not meet these criteria may not. Applying Petitta et al.'s extension of the job demands–resources model to identify the contagion of a positive emotion as a job resource and the contagion of a negative emotion as a job demand, it becomes clear that teams with a positive workgroup emotional climate should benefit from the resources enabled by the regular experience of positive emotions, whereas teams with a negative workgroup emotional climate are likely to be hampered by the additional job demands arising from the regular experience of negative emotions.

More recently, Härtel and colleagues (Härtel & Liu, 2012; Liu & Härtel, 2013; Liu et al., 2014) have theorized about workgroup emotional climate in the context of teams comprised of members from different cultural backgrounds or working in different cultural settings. In order to develop and validate a cross-culturally appropriate and multi-dimensional workgroup emotional climate measure, Liu and colleagues (2014) integrated the positive/negative valence dimension of emotions (Barrett & Russell, 1999) with the ego-/other-focused interpersonal dimension of emotions (Markus & Kitayama, 1991), which is reflective of cross-cultural differences in emotional display rules. Specifically, Eastern cultures emphasize other-focused emotions more than Western cultures, while Western cultures emphasize ego-focused emotions more than Eastern cultures (see also Härtel & Liu, 2012). Härtel and colleagues advocate in particular for team leaders to be equipped with knowledge of the emotional features of teams and the emotional needs of team members, as well as the leadership practices that promote a positive workgroup emotional climate.

Level 5: Organization-Wide

At level 5, scholars shift their focus to consider the leader's role in managing emotions at the level of the organization by shaping the organization's culture and climate. In this regard, Härtel and Ashkanasy (2011) liken an organization's culture to a fossil record: the culture contains evidence of the evolution of the organization, as seen in the norms of emotional expression and rules governing social interactions between organizational members. In contrast, organizational climate refers to the collective conscious perceptions and descriptions employees have of their work environment (Schneider, 2000; Schneider, Ehrhart, & Macey, 2011). Ashkanasy (2007) points out that, although affective organizational culture and climate are distinctly different constructs, they are nonetheless still interrelated insofar as both contain an affective component (James et al., 2008). Ashkanasy (2003) and Pizer and Härtel (2005) argue further that organizational culture and climate can govern how organizational members experience emotions on a daily basis. Thus, the emotional states experienced by members are a critical determinant of whether the organizational culture or climate is healthy or toxic (Ashkanasy & Daus, 2002).

Fostering a Positive Affective Climate

Ayoko and Härtel (2003) identified structural characteristics of the organization as a key factor influencing affective climate. Härtel (2008) asserts that workplaces with an emotional climate that provide a set of emotional experiences necessary for human flourishing constitute "positive work environments" (PWEs). Other characteristics of PWEs include employees viewing their work environment as being "respectful, inclusive and psychologically safe; leaders and co-workers as trustworthy, fair and open to diversity; and characterized by ethical policies and decision-making" (Härtel, 2008, p. 999).

Fujimoto, Härtel, and Panipucci (2005) theorized and found evidence for the role of human resource management (HRM) practices in fostering a healthy or unhealthy organizational culture. In particular, they demonstrated that HRM policies and practices reflecting a combination of individualistic and collectivistic orientations promote diversity openness and, as a result, were associated with less cross-cultural prejudice in workgroups with members from individualist and collectivist cultural backgrounds. Härtel (2008) elaborates on how HRM can support a positive work environment by monitoring the affective experiences of employees in the organization. This might include conducting ongoing assessments of employee perceptions of the workplace environment as positive as well as ensuring managers are trained in, and held accountable for, facilitating positive workplace relationships (Krzeminska, Lim, & Härtel, 2018), constructive conflict management (Ayoko & Härtel, 2002), trust (Kimberley & Härtel, 2007), diversity openness (Härtel & Fujimoto, 2000), and organizational justice (Kimberley & Härtel, 2007).

HRM can also foster a positive organizational culture by ensuring that authentic positive emotional displays and behaviors are valued and appreciated. This, in turn, allows employees to express their natural feelings without fear that such expression may lead to sanctions. Härtel and Ashkanasy (2011) note that the benefits of such a culture is empirically linked to "lower workplace injury rates, buffering from work stress, increased job satisfaction, commitment and engagement and decreased levels of absenteeism job burnout, and turnover intention" (p. 90; see also George & Brief, 1992; Weick & Quinn, 1999). Moreover, leaders can engender a positive affective culture by establishing shared norms of positivity through modeling positivity to harness their followers' positive emotions (cf. Krzeminska et al., 2018). As a result, the leader's positive affect will be consistent with that of the group, which leads in turn to greater coordination and a higher probability of success for the team (Caporael, 1997; Smith & Crandell, 1984). Also, leaders should facilitate the development of effective knowledge networks to create a positive affective organizational culture by encouraging high levels of trust, positive social exchanges, a supportive environment for learning and sharing, and interdependent social networks (Hannah & Lester, 2009).

Avoiding a Negative Affective Climate

We now turn to the need for leaders to recognize the characteristics of a negative organizational climate and culture, and its detrimental consequences for employees. Frost (2007) argues that a key characteristic of negative affective climates is the presence of frequent intense negative emotions or "toxic emotions" over a long period of time, which typically implies a negative affective culture in the organization. Other characteristics include embedded injustice within the organization (Li & Cropanzano, 2009; Härtel & Panipucci, 2007; Härtel & Ganegoda, 2008); as Morrison and Robinson (1997) note, perceptions of injustice tend be formed from negative organizational policies (e.g. increasing surveillance) that are implemented because of managerial distrust toward employees. Frost (2007) states that toxic organizations have negative emotions embedded in organizational values. In such conditions, organization management lack compassion, inflict ongoing pain and suffering on employees, and frequently make arbitrary and unjust decisions. Moreover, Leavitt (2007) describes toxic organizations as embodying negative norms, including "emotional game-playing," which occurs when employees use emotion management skills in inauthentic and destructive ways to advance their own personal and political agendas (Härtel & Panipucci, 2007). For example, an employee may ingratiate her or himself to their supervisor with the aim of receiving a better performance appraisal. Lewicki, Tomlinson, and Gillespie (2006) note that such game-playing behavior diminishes organizational trust, which in turn results in perceptions of injustice and personal distress. Ferris et al. (1996) further noted that organizations with negative cultures reject values of diversity, meaning that some individuals within the organization are subjected to social exclusion and, as a result, cannot build a knowledge base and develop the skills needed to succeed. Social exclusion also results in negative emotional effects for those who do not adhere to orthodoxy (Härtel & Ashkanasy, 2011).

Coping with Affective Climate Variation

Ashkanasy and Härtel (2014) note that variations in affective climate often occur independently of an organization's culture. Even with a positive culture, employees will, from time to time, experience affective ups and downs in response to events. Härtel (2008) comments, however, that leaders need to foster a positive organizational culture to predispose employees toward more constructive responses to experienced negative affect (see also Härtel & Ganegoda, 2008). Leaders can achieve this, for example, by allowing employees the autonomy to make decisions and openly voice their opinions without negative repercussions and in an environment of respect, with an emphasis on equal opportunity (McKeown, Bryant & Raeder, 2009). Moreover, research shows that a negative culture increases the risk that employees will engage in destructive responses to experienced negative affect (e.g. deviant behaviors). For instance, employees who work in an environment where diversity is discouraged and in which management expects them to be subservient to authority are likely to engage in deviant behavior such as harassment, bullying, and supervisor abuse (Härtel, 2008; Panipucci & Härtel, 2006). If this is so, then leaders also need to be equipped to turn toxic cultures around (see Härtel, 2008). Finally, it is important to note that negative affect is an inevitable part of life and fluctuates, moment by moment, throughout the working day (Weiss & Cropanzano, 1996; see also Ashkanasy & Härtel, 2014). Negative affect is not necessarily a bad thing, as it does not always equate to negative outcomes. Nonetheless, it is vital for positive emotional experiences to outweigh the negative emotional experiences in order for a workplace to be conducive for human flourishing (Härtel, 2008).

Future Directions

Härtel and Ashkanasy (2011) identified seven questions for research into affective culture and climate.

(1) What elements of organizational affective culture enable or prevent human flourishing?
(2) When these elements are in place, do they translate into shared perceptions of a (positive or negative) workplace environment?
(3) What is the effect of temporal within-organization affective climate characteristics (i.e. the variation in perceived organization characteristics over time; both positive and negative affective climate events) on the development and maintenance of the work environment?
(4) What are the actual processes underlying within-organization climate variation?
(5) What is the relationship between temporal within-organization affective climate characteristics and between-organization affective culture and climate characteristics?
(6) Can within-organization affective climate variation lead to changes in an organization's affective culture?
(7) What organizational practices enable the "what" attributes (organizational climate) of an organizational culture of subjective and objective well-being and positive organizational behavior?

Conclusion

In this chapter we have reviewed the literature on the role of leaders in managing the emotions of employees and their subsequent responses to affective events, extending across five levels of organizational functioning using Ashkanasy's (2003) five-level model of emotion in organizations. The key focus of this chapter was on how leaders have a central role in shaping organizational culture and climate to create positive work environments. Finally, we provided suggestions for future research with the aim of improving our understanding of how leaders can avoid and/or turn toxic cultures around.

References

Ashforth, B. E., & Humphrey, R. H. (1993). Emotional labor in service roles: The influence of identity. *Academy of Management Review, 18*, 88–115.

Ashkanasy, N. M. (2003). Emotions in organizations: a multi-level perspective. In F. Dansereau & F. J. Yammarino (Eds.), *Research on multi-level issues* (pp. 9–54). Bingley, UK: Emerald.

Ashkanasy, N. M. (2007). Organizational climate. In S. R. Clegg & J. R. Bailey (Eds.), *International encyclopedia of organization studies* (pp. 1028–1030). Thousand Oaks, CA: Sage.

Ashkanasy, N. M., & Daus, C. S. (2002). Emotion in the workplace: The new challenge for managers. *Academy of Management Perspectives, 16*, 76–86.

Ashkanasy, N. M., & Dorris, A. D. (2017). Emotion in the workplace. *Annual Review of Organizational Psychology and Organizational Behavior, 4*, 67–90.

Ashkanasy, N. M., & Härtel, C. E. (2014). Positive and negative affective climate and culture: The good, the bad, and the ugly. In B. Schneider & K. Barbera

(Eds.), *Oxford handbook of organizational climate and culture* (pp. 136–152). New York, NY: Oxford University Press.

Ashkanasy, N. M., Härtel, C. E. J., & Daus, C. S. (2002). Diversity and emotion: The new frontiers in organizational behavior research. *Journal of Management, 28*, 307–338.

Ashkanasy, N. M., & Humphrey, R. H. (2011). Current emotion research in organizational behavior. *Emotion Review, 3*, 214–224.

Ashkanasy, N. M., & Jordan, P. J. (2008). A multi-level view of leadership and emotion. In R. H. Humphrey (Ed.), *Affect and emotion: New directions in management theory and research* (pp. 17–39). Charlotte, NC: Information Age.

Ayoko, O. B., & Härtel, C. E. J. (2002). The role of emotions and emotion management in destructive and productive conflict in culturally heterogeneous workgroups. In N. M. Ashkanasy, W. J. Zerbe, & C. E. J. Härtel (Eds.), *Managing emotions in the workplace* (pp. 77–97). Armonk, NY: M. E Sharpe.

Ayoko, O. B., & Härtel, C. E. (2003). The role of space as both a conflict trigger and a conflict control mechanism in culturally heterogeneous workgroups. *Applied Psychology: An International Review, 52*, 383–412.

Barling, J., Slater, F., & Kelloway, E. K. (2000). Transformational leadership and emotional intelligence: An exploratory study. *Leadership & Organization Development Journal, 21*, 157–161.

Barrett, L. F., & Russell, J. A. (1999). Structure of current affect. *Current Directions in Psychological Science, 8*, 10–14.

Barsade, S. G. (2002). The ripple effect: Emotional contagion and its influence on group behavior. *Administrative Science Quarterly, 47*, 644–675.

Bono, J. E., Foldes, H. J., Vinson, G., & Muros, J. P. (2007). Workplace emotions: The role of supervision and leadership. *Journal of Applied Psychology, 92*, 1357–1367.

Caporael, L. R. (1997). The evolution of truly social cognition: The core configurations model. *Personality and Social Psychology Review, 1*, 276–298.

Clark, L. A., Watson, D., & Leeka, J. (1989). Diurnal variation in the positive affects. *Motivation and Emotion, 13*, 205–234.

Daus, C. S., & Ashkanasy, N. M. (2005). The case for the ability-based model of emotional intelligence in organizational behavior. *Journal of Organizational Behavior, 26*, 453–466.

Daus, C. S., Jordan, P., Ashkanasy, N., & Dasborough, M. (2012). We are all mad in wonderland: An organizational culture framework for emotions and emotional intelligence research. In N. M. Ashkanasy, C. E. J. Härtel, & W. J. Zerbe (Eds.), *Experiencing and managing emotions in the workplace* (pp. 375–399). Bingley, UK: Emerald.

Ferris, G. R., Frink, D. D., Galang, M. C., Zhou, J., Kacmar, K. M., & Howard, J. L. (1996). Perceptions of organizational politics: Prediction, stress-related implications, and outcomes. *Human Relations, 49*, 233–266.

Frost, P. J. (2007). *Toxic emotions at work and what you can do about them*. Cambridge, MA: Harvard Business Review Press.

Fujimoto, Y., Härtel, C. E. J., & Panipucci, D. (2005). Emotional experience of individualist–collectivist workgroups: Findings from a study of 14 multinationals located in Australia. In C. E. J. Härtel, W. J. Zerbe, & N. M. Ashkanasy (Eds.), *Emotions in organizational behavior* (pp. 125–160). Mahwah, NJ: Lawrence Erlbaum.

George, J. M. (2000). Emotions and leadership: The role of emotional intelligence. *Human Relations, 53*, 1027–1055.

George, J. M., & Brief, A. P. (1992). Feeling good – doing good: A conceptual analysis of the mood at work – organizational spontaneity relationship. *Psychological Bulletin, 112*, 310–329.

Grandey, A. A. (2000). Emotional regulation in the workplace: A new way to conceptualize emotional labor. *Journal of Occupational Health Psychology, 5*, 59–100.

Grandey, A. A. (2003). When "the show must go on": Surface acting and deep acting as determinants of emotional exhaustion and peer-rated service delivery. *Academy of Management Journal, 46*, 86–96.

Hannah, S. T., & Lester, P. B. (2009). A multilevel approach to building and leading learning organizations. *Leadership Quarterly, 20*, 34–48.

Harms, P. D., & Credé, M. (2010). Emotional intelligence and transformational and transactional leadership: A meta-analysis. *Journal of Leadership & Organizational Studies*, *17*, 5–17.

Härtel, C. E. J. (2008). How to build a healthy emotional culture and avoid a toxic culture. In C. L. Cooper & N. M. Ashkanasy (Eds.), *Research companion to emotion in organizations* (pp. 575–588). Cheltenham, UK: Edwin Elgar.

Härtel, C. E., & Ashkanasy, N. M. (2011). Healthy human cultures as positive work environments. In N. M. Ashkanasy, C. E. P. Wilderom, & M. F. Peterson (Eds.), *The handbook of organizational culture and climate* (pp. 85–100). Thousand Oaks, CA: Sage.

Härtel, C. E. J., & Fujimoto, Y. (2000). Diversity is not the problem – openness to perceived dissimilarity is. *Journal of Management & Organization*, *6*(1), 14–27.

Härtel, C. E. J., & Ganegoda, D. B. (2008). Role of affect and interactional justice in moral leadership. In W. J. Zerbe, C. E. J. Härtel, & N. M. Ashkanasy (Eds.), *Research on emotion in organizations* (Volume 4, pp. 155–180). Bradford, UK: Emerald.

Härtel, C. E. J., Gough, H., & Härtel, G. F. (2006). Service providers' use of emotional competencies and perceived workgroup emotional climate to predict customer and provider satisfaction with service encounters. *International Journal of Work Organization and Emotion*, *1*, 232–254.

Härtel, C. E. J., Gough, H., & Härtel, G. F. (2008). Work-group emotional climate, emotion management skills, and service attitudes and performance. *Asia Pacific Journal of Human Resources*, *46*, 21–37.

Härtel, C. E. J., & Liu, X. (2012). How emotional climate in teams affects workplace effectiveness in individualistic and collectivistic contexts. *Journal of Management & Organization*, *18*, 573–585.

Härtel, C. E. J., & Page, K. M. (2009). Discrete emotional crossover in the workplace: The role of affect intensity. *Journal of Managerial Psychology*, *24*, 237–253.

Härtel, C. E. J., & Panipucci, D. (2005). Emotional game playing and poor team norms: The implications for work teams. In C. A. Schriesheim & L. Neider (Eds.), *Research in management* (pp. 133–144). Greenwich, CT: Information Age.

Härtel, C. E. J., & Panipucci, D. (2007). How "bad apples" spoil the bunch: Faultlines, emotional levers and exclusion in the workplace. In C. E. J Härtel, N. M. Ashkanasy, & W. J. Zerbe (Eds.), *Research on emotion in organizations* (Volume 3, pp. 287–310). Oxford, UK: Elsevier/JAI.

Härtel, C. E. J., Zerbe, W. J., & Ashkanasy, N. M. (2005). Organizational behavior: An emotions perspective. In C. E. J. Härtel, N. M. Ashkanasy, & W. J. Zerbe (Eds.), *Emotions in organizational behavior* (pp. 1–10). Mahwah, NJ: Lawrence Erlbaum.

Hennig-Thurau, T., Groth, M., Paul, M., & Gremler, D. D. (2006). Are all smiles created equal? How emotional contagion and emotional labor affect service relationships. *Journal of Marketing*, *70*, 58–73.

Hochschild, A. R. (1983). *The managed heart: Commercialization of human feeling*. Berkeley: University of California Press.

Hülsheger, U. R., & Schewe, A. F. (2011). On the costs and benefits of emotional labor: A meta-analysis of three decades of research. *Journal of Occupational Health Psychology*, *16*, 361–389.

Hunt, J. G., Gardner, W. L., & Fischer, D. (2008). Leader emotional displays from near and far: The implications of close versus distant leadership. In R. H. Humphrey (Ed.), *Affect and emotion: New directions in management theory and research* (pp. 42–65). Charlotte, NC: Information Age.

James, L. R., Choi, C. C., Ko, C. H. E., McNeil, P. K., Minton, M. K., Wright, M. A., & Kim, K. I. (2008). Organizational and psychological climate: A review of theory and research. *European Journal of Work and Organizational Psychology*, *17*, 5–32.

Kimberley, N. & Härtel, C. E. J. (2007). Building a climate of trust during organizational change: The mediating role of justice perceptions and emotion. In C. E. J Härtel, N. M. Ashkanasy, & W. J. Zerbe (Eds.), *Research on emotion in organizations* (Volume 3, pp. 237–264). Oxford, UK: Elsevier/ JAI.

Krzeminska, A., Lim, J., & Härtel, C. E. J. (2018). Psychological capital and occupational stress in emergency services teams: Empowering effects of servant leadership and workgroup emotional climate. In L. Petitta, C. E. J. Härtel,

N. M. Ashkanasy, & W. Zerbe (Eds.), *Research on emotion in organizations* (Volume 14, pp. 189–215). Bingley, UK: Emerald.

Larsen, R. J., Diener, E., & Emmons, R. A. (1986). Affect intensity and reactions to daily life events. *Journal of Personality and Social Psychology, 51*, 803–814.

Leavitt, H. J. (2007). Big organizations are unhealthy environments for human beings. *Academy of Management Learning & Education, 6*, 253–263.

Lewicki, R. J., Tomlinson, E. C., & Gillespie, N. (2006). Models of interpersonal trust development: Theoretical approaches, empirical evidence, and future directions. *Journal of Management, 32*, 991–1022.

Li, A., & Cropanzano, R. (2009). Fairness at the group level: Justice climate and intra-unit justice climate. *Journal of Management, 35*, 564–599.

Liu, X. Y., & Härtel, C. E .J. (2013). Workgroup emotional exchanges and team performance in China. *Asia Pacific Journal of Human Resources, 51*, 471–490.

Liu, X., Härtel, C. E. J., & Sun, J. J. (2014). The workgroup emotional climate scale: Theoretical development, empirical validation and relationship with workgroup effectiveness. *Group & Organization Management, 39*, 626–663.

Markus, H. R., & Kitayama, S. (1991). Culture and the self: Implications for cognition, emotion, and motivation. *Psychological Review, 98*, 224–253.

Martin, J., Knopoff, K., & Beckman, C. (1998). An alternative to bureaucratic impersonality and emotional labor: Bounded emotionality at The Body Shop. *Administrative Science Quarterly, 43*, 429–469.

Mastenbroek, W. (2000). Organizational behavior as emotion management. In N. M. Ashkanasy, C. E. Härtel, & W. J. Zerbe (Eds.), *Emotions in the workplace: Research, theory, and practice* (pp. 19–35). Westport, CT: Quorum Books.

Mayer, J. D., & Salovey, P. (1997). What is emotional intelligence? In P. Salovey & D. Sluyter (Eds.), *Emotional development and emotional intelligence: Implications for educators* (pp. 3–31). New York, NY: Basic Books.

McColl-Kennedy, J. R., & Anderson, R. D. (2002). Impact of leadership style and emotions on subordinate performance. *Leadership Quarterly, 13*, 545–559.

McKeown, T., Bryant, M., & Raeder, L. (2009). Building positive responses to bullying: Establishing the framework. In C. E. J. Härtel, N. M. Ashkanasy, & W. J. Zerbe (Eds.), *Research on emotion in organizations* (Volume 5, pp. 227–243). Bingley, UK: Emerald.

Miao, C., Humphrey, R. H., & Qian, S. (2016). Leader emotional intelligence and subordinate job satisfaction: A meta-analysis of main, mediator, and moderator effects. *Personality and Individual Differences, 102*, 13–24.

Morris, J. A., & Feldman, D. C. (1996). The dimensions, antecedents and consequences of emotional labor. *Academy of Management Review, 21*, 986–1010.

Morrison, E. W., & Robinson, S. L. (1997). When employees feel betrayed: A model of how psychological contract violation develops. *Academy of Management Review, 22*, 226–256.

Newcombe, M. J., & Ashkanasy, N. M. (2002). The role of affect and affective congruence in perceptions of leaders: An experimental study. *Leadership Quarterly, 13*, 601–614.

Panipucci, D., & Härtel, C. E. J. (2006). Positive disobedience: When norms prescribe the exclusion of dissimilar others. In A. Della Fave (Ed.), *Dimensions of well-being: Research and intervention* (pp. 241–253). Milan, Italy: FrancoAngeli.

Paterson, J. M., & Härtel, C. E. (2002). An integrated affective and cognitive model to explain employees' responses to downsizing. In N. M. Ashkanasy, W. J. Zerbe, & C. E. J. Härtel (Eds.), *Managing emotions in the workplace* (pp. 25–44). Armonk, NY: M. E. Sharpe.

Petitta, L., Jiang, L., & Härtel, C. E. J. (2017). Emotional contagion and burnout among nurses and doctors: Do joy and anger from different sources of stakeholders matter? *Stress and Health, 33*, 358–369.

Pirola-Merlo, A., Härtel, C. E. J., Mann, L., & Hirst, G. (2002). How leaders influence the impact of affective events on team climate and performance in R&D teams. *Leadership Quarterly, 13*, 561–581.

Pizer, M. K., & Härtel, C. E. J. (2005). For better or for worse: Organizational culture and emotions. In C. E. J. Härtel, W. J. Zerbe, & N. M. Ashkanasy (Eds.), *Emotions in organizational behavior* (pp. 342–361). Mahwah, NJ: Lawrence Erlbaum.

Roux, M., & Härtel, C. E. J. (2018). The cognitive, emotional, and behavioral qualities required for leadership assessment and development in the new world of work. In N. M. Ashkanasy, W. J. Zerbe, & C. E. J. Härtel (Eds.), *Research on emotion in organizations* (Volume 14, pp. 59–69). Bingley, UK: Emerald.

Schein, E. (1992). *Organizational culture and leadership*. San Francisco, CA: Jossey-Bass.

Schneider, B. (2000). The psychological life of organizations. In N. Ashkanasy, C. Wilderom, & M. Peterson (Eds.), *The handbook of organizational culture and climate* (pp. 23–30). Thousand Oaks, CA: Sage.

Schneider, B., Ehrhart, M. G., & Macey, W. H. (2011). Organizational climate research: Achievements and the road ahead. In N. M. Ashkanasy, C. E. P. Wilderom, & M. F. Peterson (Eds.), *The handbook of organizational culture and climate* (2nd edition, pp. 29–49). Thousand Oaks, CA: Sage.

Smith, K. K., & Crandell, S. D. (1984). Exploring collective emotion. *American Behavioral Scientist*, *27*, 813–828.

Sy, T., Côté, S., & Saavedra, R. (2005). The contagious leader: impact of the leader's mood on the mood of group members, group affective tone, and group processes. *Journal of Applied Psychology*, *90*, 295–305.

Sy, T., Tram, S., & O'Hara, L. A. (2006). Relation of employee and manager emotional intelligence to job satisfaction and performance. *Journal of Vocational Behavior*, *68*, 461–473.

Tan, J. A. C., Härtel, C. E. J., Panipucci, D., & Strybosch, V. E. (2005). The effect of emotions in cross-cultural expatriate experiences. *Cross-Cultural Management: An International Journal*, *12*, 4–15.

Watson, D., & Tellegen, A. (1985). Toward a consensual structure of mood. *Psychological Bulletin*, *98*, 219–235.

Weick, K. E., & Quinn, R. E. (1999). Organizational change and development. *Annual Review of Psychology*, *50*, 361–386.

Weiss, H. M., & Cropanzano, R. (1996). Affective events theory: A theoretical discussion of the structure, causes and consequences of affective experiences at work. In B. M. Staw & L. L. Cummings (Eds.), *Research in organizational behavior* (pp. 1–74). Oxford, UK: Elsevier Science.

Wijewardena, N., Härtel, C. E., & Samaratunge, R. (2017). Using humor and boosting emotions: An affect-based study of managerial humor, employees' emotions and psychological capital. *Human Relations*, *70*, 1316–1341.

Wijewardena, N., Härtel, C. E. J., & Samaratunge, R. (2010). A laugh a day is sure to keep the blues away: Managers' use of humor and the construction and destruction of employees' resilience. In W. J. Zerbe, C. E. J. Härtel, & N. M. Ashkanasy, *Research on emotion in organizations* (Volume 6, pp. 259–278). Bingley, UK: Emerald.

Wong, C. S., & Law, K. S. (2002). The effects of leader and follower emotional intelligence on performance and attitude: An exploratory study. *Leadership Quarterly*, *13*, 243–274.

Part V
Discrete Emotions at Work

29 The Emotion of Interest at Work

Cynthia D. Fisher

This chapter is about the emotion of interest as it may be experienced in the workplace. Interest has been described as "positive, focused, directed arousal, which prompts approach and engagement with the task" (Ainley, 2007, p. 153). Izard (1991, p. 100) describes the subjective experience of interest as "the feeling of being engaged, caught up, fascinated, or curious ... wanting to investigate, become involved, or expand the self by incorporating new information and having new experiences with the person or object that has stimulated the interest. In intense interest or excitement, the person feels animated and enlivened."

There have been mixed opinions among scholars about whether interest should be considered an emotion. Silvia, who definitely views interest as an emotion, also calls it "the black sheep in the flock of basic emotions" and notes that some emotions scholars have "kicked interest out of the flock altogether" (2001, p. 270). For instance, Lazarus (1991, p. 83) classifies interest as a "pre-emotion," along with curiosity, amazement, anticipation, alertness, and surprise. Ortony and Turner (1990) exclude interest as an emotion because they do not believe that it is consistently valenced. In contrast, Frijda (1986), Izard (1991), and Tomkins (1984) regard interest not only as an emotion, but as one of a small number of basic emotions. Izard (1991) suggests that interest is the most frequently experienced human emotion, and Fredrickson (1998) identifies interest as one of four emotions at the heart of her broaden-and-build theory. Hu and Kaplan (2015) identified interest as one of three discrete positive emotions (along with pride and gratitude) that have been insufficiently researched in the field of organizational behavior and that merit additional attention. Connelly and Torrence (2018) suggest that interest, pride, guilt, and fear are discrete emotions with relevance to a number of areas of human resource management.

Interest as an Emotion

Current opinion agrees that state interest is an emotion, and it fits the definition of an emotion well. Interest is a transient state, has a largely consistent affective tone, has a clear object and characteristic action/motivation tendency, serves an evolutionary function, has predictable physiological concomitants, and can be described on emotion appraisal dimensions. I will expand on these criteria below.

First, with regard to being a transient state, interest varies substantially within person over time and across tasks. Fisher and Noble (2004) found that 70 percent of the variance in interest in individuals' current work tasks, reported five time per day, was within person. Another study found that across six core work tasks for salespeople, 78 percent of the variance in interest was within person across tasks (Shin & Grant, 2019).

Second, like other emotions, interest tends to have a consistent affective tone. It is usually hedonically both pleasant and arousing, co-occurring most frequently with the emotions of happiness and excitement (Ely, Ainley, & Pearce, 2013). Interest is one of the three factors of positive affect within the Positive and Negative Affect Schedule (PANAS) (Watson, Clark, & Tellegen, 1988). It is empirically discriminable from but positively correlated with the other two components, joy and activation (Egloff,

Schmukle, Burns, Kohlmann, & Hock, 2003). Individuals preferentially seek to feel interested and act to up-regulate the experience of interest in a task that is otherwise not interesting (Sansone & Thoman, 2005), again suggesting that the experience is pleasant. However, the affective tone associated with interest may occasionally be mixed or unpleasant (Turner & Silvia, 2006), as when one is fascinated by a novel but disgusting stimulus: for example, a horror movie, a road accident, or a disturbing piece of art.

Third, emotions have objects – they are felt about/because of/in response to a specific stimulus, event or situation that has relevance to the individual. Interest clearly meets the object test – one is interested *in* a particular object, topic, or activity (Ainley, 2017). Ainley (2007, p. 152) points out that "interest is not a characteristic of the person or of the object, but is a relation between a person and object."

Fourth, emotions have consistent action tendencies. Interest orients individuals to relevant or novel features of the environment, helps them choose where to direct their attention, and narrows attentional focus to the object of interest (Sung & Yih, 2016). The action tendency of interest is to approach and engage with the object or topic of interest, and to persist in doing so.

Fifth, emotions generally serve an adaptive purpose (Keltner & Gross, 1999; Lench, Bench, Darbor, & Moore, 2015). The function of interest appears to be to stimulate engagement, exploration, learning, and personal growth, and thus contribute to adaptation and survival (Fredrickson, 1998; Izard, 1991). By countering a fear response to novelty, interest encourages the exploration of new environments and so facilitates the discovery of additional resources and the acquisition of skills (Wittmann, Bunzeck, Dolan, & Düzel, 2007). A later section of this chapter will explore the largely positive effects of interest in greater detail.

Sixth, like other emotions, interest has physiological concomitants. Neurologically, interest is thought to have its roots in the approach system in the brain and be reflected in the "seeking" behavior seen in both humans and animals (Panksepp, 1998). The intensely concentrated/interested state of "flow" displays a characteristic pattern of neural activity in the brain that is different from the pattern for boredom (Ulrich, Keller, Hoenig, Waller, & Grön, 2014). fMRI imaging studies have shown that the areas of the brain responsible for anticipating extrinsic rewards are activated when individuals are curious, suggesting that intrinsic curiosity/interest is processed in the same way as the anticipation of any other reward, and that information or activity that satisfies curiosity or interest has reward value (Gruber, Gelman, & Ranganath, 2014; Jepma, Verdonschot, Van Steenbergen, Rombouts, & Nieuwenhuis, 2012; Kang, Hsu, Krajbich, Loewenstein, McClure, Wang, & Camerer, 2009).

Finally, interest has characteristic appraisal patterns. In an early study of the appraisal dimensions of emotions, Smith and Ellsworth (1985) found that interest was high on pleasantness and attention and moderate on effort. Silvia (2005; 2006; Turner and Silvia, 2006) concluded that two appraisals are necessary to predict interest. The first involves the perception of stimulus features as being novel and complex, and the second is an assessment of one's own coping potential, ability to understand, and self-efficacy as moderate to high. Individuals must believe that while they do not now fully understand the novel stimulus, it is understandable and they will be able to progress toward understanding.

Interest vs. Interests

Interest has also been conceptualized at higher levels and in ways that are not emotions (Ainley, 2017). There is interplay and interdependence between conceptualizations of the experience of interest as a real-time emotion, interests as stable individual preferences, and trait interest.

Surprisingly, the literatures on each of these are largely separate and often fail to acknowledge each other (Henn, 2010).

More stable than the emotion of interest in a current stimulus or activity is the cognitive attribute variously called "individual interest," "personal interest," or just "interests" (Silvia, 2006). Holland's (1997) well-known vocational interest typology, realistic–investigative–artistic–social–enterprising–conventional, falls into this category, as do more specific occupation- or task-focused interest dimensions such as interest in architecture, police work, sales, or life science. Another quite stable individual difference relevant to the broad concept of interest is the predisposition to be interested in general, to be intensely interested, or to be interested in many things. This is variously conceptualized and labeled as trait epistemic curiosity, breadth of interests, autotelic personality, intrinsic motivational orientation, or possibly aspects of the Big Five personality dimension of openness to experience (Amabile, Hill, Hennessey, & Tighe, 1994; Csikszenthihalyi, 1990; Litman, 2008; Litman & Silvia, 2006; Loewenstein, 1994; Silvia, 2006). Because interest must be experienced in relation to an object, activity, or content area, some scholars would not view these content-free generic traits as part of interest, though they may increase the likelihood of stable interests in specific topics being developed and the likelihood of state interest being experienced with greater frequency.

The interest and interests literatures vary in approach and disciplinary background. Henn (2010) points out that there are two quite distinct literatures on interest – those stemming largely from education, and those stemming from vocational psychology. Educational researchers investigate the role of the emotion of interest in learning and explore what teachers can do to catch and hold student interest in the topics they are charged with teaching. They view student interest as malleable and consider how the catching of "situation interest" as an emotion may not only facilitate engagement and learning in the short term but also eventually lead to the development of more stable individual interests. Models of interest development by Krapp (2002) and Hidi and Renninger (2006) have three and four stages respectively, beginning with *triggering/catching* short-term emotional situational interest via teacher-provided novelty or other aspects of the stimulus. The middle stages involve *holding/maintaining* interest during further interactions with the topic, at least partly via extrinsic/teacher-provided stimulation. Gradually, personal interest may begin to develop through repeated engagement with the topic, and eventually stable intrinsic interest in the topic may develop (though often it doesn't). Educational researchers tend to ignore preexisting individual interests and instead place the onus on teachers to stimulate the beginnings of interest.

Vocational psychologists are much less concerned about the emotional state of interest, where they even acknowledge that it exists. They take stable individual/vocational interests as a given and explore their utility in providing advice on occupational choice and predicting subsequent work outcomes such as job satisfaction and performance. The beneficial effects of congruence between vocational interests and job requirements are thought to occur via motivation (effort, persistence) and subsequent skill development (Ingerick & Rumsey, 2014; Nye, Su, Rounds, & Drasgow, 2017), with little attention devoted to the enjoyable emotional experience of interest in real time. Henn (2010) is unique in exploring and demonstrating a relationship between a vocational interest and the real-time phenomena of state interest and persistence on a task relevant to that vocational interest.

In short, it seems that the emotion of interest may occur either because of the stimulus properties of a novel object or activity that catches interest (and the other facilitating condition to be discussed below), or because the object or activity is relevant to a long-standing personal interest. While the causes of the two states are at least somewhat different, the phenomenological experience of interest in an object or activity are probably indistinguishable (Ely et al., 2012; Henn, 2010; Silvia, 2006).

Antecedents of the Emotion of Interest

Research on the causes of the emotion of interest has identified a number of precursors or contributors. At the simplest, causes of interest may be located in properties of the task or stimulus. More complex views consider the match between the task/stimulus and the pre-existing individual interests and skills of the performer. In addition, there is research on the ways that goals, expectations, self-efficacy, and attributions may influence interest. Positive affect also influences interest, as do contextual factors such as autonomy and social influence.

Task Properties and Interest

Short-term situational interest may be triggered by task properties including novelty, complexity, uncertainty, change, or animation (e.g. Berlyne, 1960; Silvia, 2006). Interest in text-based materials is facilitated by "surprisingness, coherence, concreteness, vividness, and ease of comprehension" (Schiefele, 2009, p. 199). While these stimulus features help catch initial interest, person–situation fit is important for holding interest for longer (Durik & Harackiewicz, 2007). Csikszentmihalyi (1975; 1990; Csikszentmihalyi, Khosla, Nakamura, 2017) suggests task characteristics that are essential to producing a flow state of deeply engaged interest. In addition to offering an optimally difficult challenge to the performer, tasks must provide clear and immediate goals (e.g. find the next handhold in rock climbing) and feedback (got it!) to produce flow. Hackman and Oldham's (1980) job characteristics theory identifies skill variety, task significance, task identity, autonomy, and feedback from the work itself as likely to make a job more interesting.

Person–Situation Fit and Interest

One aspect of person–situation fit is pre-existing individual interest in that particular topic (Ainley, Hidi, & Berndorff, 2002). Individuals are more likely to experience interest when engaged in an activity related to a well-developed individual interest (Henn, 2010). Prior knowledge of a domain has been well established as a predictor of both individual and emotional interest in a topic (e.g. Ainley et al., 2002; Fryer & Ainley, 2019; Harackiewicz, Durik, Barron, Linnenbrink-Garcia, & Tauer 2008; Renninger, 2000). Another aspect of fit involves the perception of the value, utility, or personal meaningfulness of an activity, with these attributes stimulating interest in the activity (Hulleman, Godes, Hendricks, & Harackiewicz, 2010; Hulleman, Thoman, Dicke, & Harackiewicz, 2017; Pekrun, 2006; Tanaka & Murayama, 2014).

Person–situation fit also refers to the match between the difficulty of a task and the performer's skill. Silvia (2003) speaks of "optimal incompetence," with interest at a maximum when a stimulus is neither too complex nor too simple for the perceiver. Csikszentmihalyi's (1975; 1990) work on flow confirms that task challenges and performer skills must be relatively high and well-matched for flow to occur. A task that is well understood or likely to be extremely easy to master is unlikely to be interesting, as is one that is so difficult or confusing that it far exceeds the performer's capacity (Tanaka & Murayama, 2014). Individuals sometimes engage in "interest enhancing strategies" to increase task demands toward a more optimal level when faced with tasks that are too simple or repetitive to be experienced as interesting (Green-Demers, Pelletier, Stewart, & Gushue, 1998; Sansone, Weir, Harpster, & Morgan, 1992).

Other Affective, Cognitive, and Contextual Antecedents of Interest

Positive affect during task engagement has been identified as an important contributor to both emotional interest and the long-term development of individual interests (Hidi & Renninger, 2006; Renninger, 2000; Silvia, 2006). Type of goal also influences interest. Mastery (learning) goals are strong antecedents of both emotional and individual interest (Ainley et al., 2002; Harackiewicz et al., 2008; Van Yperen, 2003). Individuals who approach a task or field of study with the intention of learning and developing competence find more value in the activity, which contributes to subsequent interest (Hulleman, Durik, Schweigert, & Harackiewicz, 2008; Senko & Harackiewicz, 2005). Expectations also influence the experience of interest. Tasks are experienced as more interesting when individuals have been led to expect them to be interesting (Sucala, Stefan, Szentagotai-Tatar, & David, 2010) or to believe that the task will be a good fit with their goals, values, and identity (Thoman, Sansone, & Geerling, 2017). Further, individual interests are predictors of interest expectations for an upcoming task (Ainley, 2007; Ainley et al., 2002; Silvia, 2006.)

Cognitive evaluation theory and self determination theory identify perceived autonomy as a key antecedent of intrinsic motivation (Deci, Olafsen, & Ryan, 2017; Ryan & Deci, 2017). Consistent with this view, choice and autonomy-supportive rationales for task engagement have been found to increase engagement and interest in learning topics in the classroom (Jang, 2008; Linnenbrink-Garcia, Patall, & Messersmith, 2013). Autonomy is also important in the experience of flow.

Perceptions of the passage of time during an activity serve as a meta-cognitive cue about one's interest. When individuals are led to believe that time has passed quickly while working on a task (for instance, by a speeded-up clock), they report that they were more interested. "Time flies when you are having fun" seems to be a common naive theory, and an interested individual may lose all track of time while engaged in an activity (Sackett, Meyvis, Nelson, Converse, & Sackett, 2010; Sucala et al., 2010). "Loss of self-consciousness" is also characteristic of flow states (Csikszentmihalyi, 1990).

While interest is usually conceptualized as a two-party relationship between a person and a task or domain, Master, Butler, and Walton (2017) suggest that there can be a third component: the subjective social environment. Other people may influence the experience of interest before, during and after task completion. Teachers, parents, and peers may be sources of cues about whether or not a task or topic is interesting. Schiefele (2009) has suggested that personal meaning can be increased by contagion when significant others model interest in the topic. Working with or alongside others seems to increase interest in an activity compared to working independently (Master et al., 2017). Studies have shown that supervisor and coworker opinions of task characteristics can influence focal persons' perceptions of task characteristics and subsequent intrinsic satisfaction (Griffin, 1983; Weiss & Shaw, 1979). After a task experience, perceptions of interest can be influenced by the responsiveness of listeners when the actor talks about his or her task experience (Thoman, Sansone, Fraughton, & Pasupathi, 2012).

Many of the above affective and cognitive antecedents of interest seem to both influence the experience of interest and be nurtured by interest in a reciprocal fashion (Renninger & Hidi, 2016). For instance, initial knowledge in a domain influences interest, and interest and the engagement and learning it motivates lead to the acquisition of additional knowledge and subsequent increases in interest (Rotgans & Schmidt, 2017). Interest leads to the setting of mastery goals and mastery goals increase subsequent interest. Self-efficacy and competence contribute to interest and are enhanced by further successful endeavors in that domain (Fryer & Ainley, 2019). Initial perceptions of the value and meaningfulness of an activity are reinforced and strengthened by the experience of interest during task engagement (Hulleman et al., 2010; Hulleman et al., 2017; Pekrun, 2006; Tanaka & Murayama, 2014).

Consequences of Interest

I now turn to a discussion of the consequences of interest. I will summarize the literature on the beneficial impact of the emotion of interest on motivation and persistence, on knowledge acquisition and skill building, and on affective and well-being outcomes. Finally, I will discuss some potential negative consequences of interest.

Motivation

Sansone and Thoman's (2005) classic chapter calls interest "the missing motivator in self-regulation." In later work, they position interest as being at the heart of intrinsic motivation, suggesting that "people are intrinsically motivated when their behavior is motivated by the anticipated, actual, or sought experience of 'interest'" (Thoman, Sansone, & Geerling, 2017, p. 28). As detailed in Renninger and Hidi's 2016 book, *The Power of interest for motivation and engagement*, interest influences all three components of motivation: direction/choice of activity, intensity/effort devoted to the activity, and persistence when difficulties are encountered. In addition, interest creates mastery goals, inhibits competing goals, and facilitates the adoption of more effective learning strategies (Durik, Lindeman, & Coley, 2017; O'Keefe, Horberg, & Plante, 2017). Persistence is enhanced as interest helps performers cope with suboptimal learning environments, such as those deficient in positive feedback (Katz, Assor, Kanat-Maymon, & Bereby-Meyer, 2006) or when the task is excessively difficult (Fulmer & Frijters, 2011).

Learning and Skill Development

The education literature provides overwhelming evidence that student interest is facilitative of learning in the classroom (e.g. O'Keefe & Harackiewicz, 2017; Renninger & Hidi, 2016). Therefore, one might expect that interest in a topic would predict the choice to become involved in formal workplace learning activities, the extent of learning in such programs, the acquisition of knowledge through informal workplace learning opportunities, and the transfer/application of new knowledge to workplace tasks. Surprisingly, the literature on workplace training motivation fails to draw on this educational research and almost never considers interest in the specific subject matter to be learned. The affective revolution in organizational behavior (Barsade, Brief, & Spataro, 2003) seems to have entirely bypassed training and development. The few studies relevant to interest and learning in formal job training, in informal workplace learning contexts, and in transfer of training are summarized below.

Patrick, Smy, Tombs, and Shelton (2012) investigated whether being in the job of one's choice versus being assigned to the same job while preferring another influenced training attitudes and outcomes during required initial job training. Being in the job one prefers probably implies intrinsic interest in the content of the job and greater likelihood of experiencing interest during training for that job. Their results confirmed that training motivation and subsequent knowledge acquisition and motivation to transfer learned skills to the job were higher for those in their chosen job. Johnson and Beehr (2014) found that the investigative and enterprising types of interest from the Holland framework predicted the extent to which healthcare professionals chose to undertake additional continuing professional education courses beyond the minimum required.

A great deal of learning at work is informal and self-initiated, and it is important to understand the antecedents of such learning. Sitzmann and Ely (2011) called for further research on self-regulated learning in the workplace. Their meta-analysis showed that goal level, persistence, effort, and self-efficacy were the strongest predictors of learning, but they collectively accounted for only 17 percent of the variance in learning (controlling for prior knowledge and ability). It seems likely that interest or interests, neither of which featured in their meta-analyses, would be a very useful addition to understanding how and why adults choose to learn at work.

Pugh and Bergin (2006) reviewed motivational influences on transfer of training in school and work contexts. While little is known about the effects of interest on transfer, they suggested that when learners were genuinely interested, they would be more likely to adopt learning strategies that result in greater elaboration, more effort, and deeper learning, which may in turn underlie and enable transfer of training. Johnson and Beehr (2014) found that vocational interest congruence with one's occupation predicted the extent to which healthcare workers said they transferred learning from professional education courses to the job.

Stress and Well-Being

Interest appears to have beneficial short- and long-term impacts on well-being. Earlier sections of this chapter have cited research establishing that interest is positively valenced and activates the reward structures of the brain (Gruber et al., 2014). In the workplace the emotion of interest is seldom studied, but one would certainly expect employees to enjoy tasks in which they are interested more than those in which they are not interested. Winslow, Hu, Kaplan, and Li (2017) report that the frequency of employees experiencing interest at work over the previous two weeks significantly predicted satisfaction with the work itself as well as supervisor ratings of recent creative performance. The experience of interest may trigger and sustain engagement in a task and thereby initiate a positive spiral of increasing skills and resources (Fredrickson & Joiner, 2018; Mäkikangas, Bakker, Aunola, & Demerouti, 2010; Salanova, Bakker, & Llorens, 2006) that supports future as well as current well-being.

At trait level, the predisposition to be generally interested in knowledge and learning (epistemic curiosity) is positively related to proactivity, socialization-related learning, creativity, performance, and well-being, and negatively related to emotional exhaustion (Hardy, Ness, & Mecca, 2017; Harrison, Sluss, & Ashforth, 2011; Mussel, 2013; Reio & Wiswell, 2000; Wang & Li, 2015). At state level, being interested in a current activity is less stressful than not being interested, as indicted by cortisol readings (Harter & Stone, 2012). Further, working on a task in which one is interested appears to consume fewer self-regulatory resources than working on a task in which one is not interested (O'Keefe & Linnenbrink-Garcia, 2014). In fact, working on an interesting task has been shown to replenish depleted psychological resources more than working on a neutral task or a task designed to induce positive affect, even when the interesting task requires more effort and is more complex (Thoman, Smith, & Silvia, 2011).

Negative Consequences of Interest

Evidence suggests that the vast majority of effects of the emotion of interest at the individual level are affectively pleasant and in the aggregate beneficial for well-being. To the extent that interest is motivational, replenishes resources, and facilitates learning, organizations should also benefit when employees feel more rather than less interest as they go about their daily duties. However, there may be cases in which interest in a particular topic or task can be dysfunctional. For instance, many individuals on the autism spectrum demonstrate restricted, fixated, and highly circumscribed interests of abnormal intensity. These interests may drive out other forms of normal behavior or interaction.

Very recently, Shin and Grant (2019) hypothesized and found that being highly intrinsically motivated toward one job task reduced performance on other tasks that were less intrinsically motivating, and that this effect was mediated by boredom with the other tasks. In short, there was a within-person contrast effect rather than an afterglow effect on other tasks following the positive affect associated with performing a highly interesting task. The best performance on other tasks was observed when intrinsic motivation on the focal task was moderate rather than high or low. Dierdorff and Jensen (2018) demonstrate that job crafting, done by individuals in an effort to increase interest and satisfaction with their job, may sometimes have negative effects on other-rated performance. On the whole, however, the effects of the emotion of interest seem likely to be beneficial to both employees and organizations.

Conclusions

Interest might be seen as a neglected positive psychology counterpart to the traditional psychology-of-dysfunction concept of boredom. However, interest should not be considered merely the opposite of boredom (Ulrich et al., 2014). Silvia (2006, p. 102) states that "emotions don't really have opposites," and that a great number of states may involve low interest. The absence of the discomfort of boredom does not imply the presence or benefits of the engaging and absorbing emotion of interest (Pekrun, Goetz, Daniels, Stupnisky, & Perry 2010). Boredom has recently attracted a great deal of research attention (see Fisher, 2018, for a review), with Van Tilburg and Igou (2017) reporting that 1,422 papers on boredom were published between 2010 and the end of 2015. In the same period, there were almost no published papers on interest outside of the education and vocational interests domains. Interest is only occasionally treated as an emotion and is very rarely mentioned as such in the context of the workplace.

It is time for the experience of interest at work to be vigorously studied. Interest undoubtedly influences short-term task choice, effort, and persistence, as well as task enjoyment and resource acquisition and depletion. Interest, which has been neglected in the literature on workplace learning and development, is likely to be useful in understanding both self-directed learning and responses to formal training. We know that interest and the motivation and affect that accompany it vary within person across work tasks and also over time in a single work day. Experience-sampling methodology (Fisher & To, 2012) should be applied to the study of moment-to-moment interest and associated perceptions and activities throughout the work day. Multi-level research is needed on constructs similar to trait interest, stable individual interests in specific topic areas, and the transient experience of the emotion of interest at work. More attention to the experience and various manifestations of interest may improve both employee well-being and organizational outcomes.

References

Ainley, M. (2007). Being and feeling interested: Transient state, mood, and disposition. In P. A. Schutz & R. Pekrun (Eds.), *Emotion in education* (pp. 147–163). San Diego, CA: Elsevier.

Ainley, M. (2017). Interest: Knowns, unknowns, and basic processes. In P. A. O'Keefe & J. M. Harackiewicz (Eds.), *The science of interest* (pp. 3–24). Cham, Switzerland: Springer International.

Ainley, M., Hidi, S., & Berndorff, D. (2002). Interest, learning, and the psychological processes that mediate their relationship. *Journal of Educational Psychology, 94*(3), 545–561, doi:10.1037//0022-0663.94.3.545

Amabile, T. M., Hill, K. G., Hennessey, B. A., & Tighe, E. M. (1994). The work preference inventory: Assessing intrinsic and extrinsic motivational orientations. *Journal of Personality and Social Psychology, 66*(5), 950–967, doi:10.1037/0022-3514.66.5.950

Barsade, S. G., Brief, A. P., & Spataro, S. E. (2003). The affective revolution in organizational behavior: The emergence of a paradigm. In J. Greenberg (Ed.), *Organizational behavior: The state of the science* (2nd edition, pp. 3–52). Mahwah, NJ: Lawrence Erlbaum.

Berlyne, D. E. (1960). *Conflict, arousal, and curiosity.* New York, NY: McGraw-Hill.

Connelly, S., & Torrence, B. S. (2018). The relevance of discrete emotional experiences for human resource management: Connecting positive and negative emotions to HRM. *Research in Personnel and Human Resources Management, 36*, 1–49, doi:10.1108/S0742-730120180000036001

Csikszentmihalyi, M. (1975). *Beyond boredom and anxiety.* San Francisco, CA: Jossey-Bass.

Csikszentmihalyi, M. (1990). *Flow: The psychology of optimal experience.* New York, NY: Harper & Row.

Csikszentmihalyi, M., Khosla, S., & Nakamura, J. (2017). Flow at work. In L. G. Oades, M. F. Steger, A. D. Fave., & J. Passmore (Eds.), *Wiley Blackwell handbook of the psychology of positivity and strengths-based approaches at work* (pp. 99–109). Hoboken, NJ: Wiley.

Deci, E., Olafsen, A., & Ryan, R. M. (2017). Self-determination theory in work organizations: The state of a science. *Annual Review of Organizational Psychology and Organizational Behavior, 4*, 19–43, doi:10.1146/annurev-orgpsych-032516-113108

Dierdorff, E. C., & Jensen, J. M. (2018). Crafting in context: Exploring when job crafting is dysfunctional for performance effectiveness. *Journal of Applied Psychology, 103*(5), 463–477, doi:10.1037/apl0000295

Durik, A. M., & Harackiewicz, J. M. (2007). Different strokes for different folks: How individual interest moderates the effects of situational factors on task interest. *Journal of Educational Psychology, 99*(3), 597–610, doi:10.1037/0022-0663.99.3.597

Durik, A. M., Lindeman, M. H., & Coley, S. L. (2017). The power within: How individual interest promotes domain-relevant task engagement. In P. A. O'Keefe & J. M. Harackiewicz (Eds.), *The science of interest* (pp. 125–148). Cham, Switzerland: Springer International.

Egloff, B., Schmukle, S. C., Burns, L. R., Kohlmann, C., & Hock, M. (2003). Facets of dynamic positive affect: Differentiating joy, interest, and activation in the positive and negative affect schedule. *Journal of Personality and Social Psychology, 85*(3), 528–540, doi:10.1037/0022-3514.85.3.528

Ely, R., Ainley, M., & Pearce, J. (2013). More than enjoyment: Identifying the positive affect component of interest that supports student engagement and achievement. *Middle Grades Research Journal, 8*(1), 13–32.

Fisher, C. D. (2018). Boredom at work: What, why, and what then? In D. Lindebaum, D. Geddes, & P. J. Jordan (Eds.), *Social functions of emotion and talking about emotion at work* (pp. 68–102). Cheltenham, UK: Edward Elgar.

Fisher, C. D., & Noble, C. S. (2004). A within-person examination of correlates of performance and emotions while working. *Human Performance, 17* (2), 145–168, doi:10.1207/s15327043hup1702_2

Fisher, C. D., & To, M. L. (2012). Using experience sampling methodology in organizational behavior. *Journal of Organizational Behavior, 33*, 865–877, doi:10.1002/job.1803

Fredrickson, B. L. (1998). What good are positive emotions? *Review of General Psychology, 2*(3), 300–319, doi:10.1037/1089-2680.2.3.300

Fredrickson, B., & Joiner, T. (2018). Reflections on positive emotions and upward spirals. *Perspectives on Psychological Science, 13(2)*, 194–199.

Frijda, N. H. (1986). *The emotions.* Cambridge, UK: Cambridge University Press.

Fryer, L. K., & Ainley, M. (2019). Supporting interest in a study domain: A longitudinal test of the interplay between interest, utility-value, and competence beliefs. *Learning and Instruction, 60*, 252–262, doi:10.1016/j.learninstruc.2017.11.002

Fulmer, S. M., & Frijters, J. C. (2011). Motivation during an excessively challenging reading task: The buffering role of relative topic interest. *Journal of Experimental Education, 79*(2), 185–208, doi:10.1080/00220973.2010.481503

Green-Demers, I., Pelletier, L. G., Stewart, D. G., & Gushue, N. R. (1998). Coping with the less interesting aspects of training: Toward a model of interest and motivation enhancement in individual sports. *Basic and Applied Social Psychology*, *20*(4), 251–261, doi:10.1207/s15324834basp2004_2

Griffin, R. W. (1983). Objective and social sources of information in task redesign: A field experiment. *Administrative Science Quarterly*, *28*(2), 184–200, doi:10.2307/2392617

Gruber, M., Gelman, B., & Ranganath, C. (2014). States of curiosity modulate hippocampus-dependent learning via the dopaminergic circuit. *Neuron*, *84*(2), 486–496, doi:10.1016/j.neuron.2014.08.060

Hackman, J. R., & Oldham, G. R. (1980). *Work redesign*. Reading, MA: Addison-Wesley.

Harackiewicz, J. M., Durik, A. M., Barron, K. E., Linnenbrink-Garcia, L., & Tauer, J. M. (2008). The role of achievement goals in the development of interest: Reciprocal relations between achievement goals, interest, and performance. *Journal of Educational Psychology*, *100*(1), 105–122, doi:10.1037/0022-0663.100.1.105

Hardy, J. H., Ness, A. M., & Mecca, J. (2017). Outside the box: Epistemic curiosity as a predictor of creative problem solving and creative performance. *Personality and Individual Differences*, *104*, 230–237, doi:10.1016/j.paid.2016.08.004

Harrison, S., Sluss, D., & Ashforth, B (2011). Curiosity adapted the cat: The role of trait curiosity in newcomer adaptation. *Journal of Applied Psychology*, *96*(1), 211–220, doi:10.1037/a0021647

Harter, J. K., & Stone, A. A. (2012). Engaging and disengaging work conditions, momentary experiences and cortisol response. *Motivation and Emotion*, *36*(2), 104–113, doi://dx.doi.org/10.1007/s11031-011-9231-z

Henn, J. (2010). *Multimethod analysis of interest* (doctoral dissertation, University of Illinois at Urbana-Champaign), www.ideals.illinois.edu/bitstream/handle/2142/16784/Henn_Jeremy.pdf?sequence=1&isAllowed=y.

Hidi, S., & Renninger, K. A. (2006). The four-phase model of interest development. *Educational Psychologist*, *41*(2), 111–127, doi:10.1207/s15326985ep4102_4

Holland, J. L. (1997). *Making vocational choices: A theory of personalities and work environments* (3rd edition). Lutz, FL: Psychological Assessment Resources.

Hu, X., & Kaplan, S. (2015). Is "feeling good" good enough? Differentiating discrete positive emotions at work. *Journal of Organizational Behavior*, *36*(1), 39–58, doi:10.1002/job.1941

Hulleman, C. S., Durik, A. M., Schweigert, S. A., & Harackiewicz, J. M. (2008). Task values, achievement goals, and interest: An integrative analysis. *Journal of Educational Psychology*, *100*(2), 398–416, doi:10.1037/0022-0663.100.2.398

Hulleman, C. S., Godes, O., Hendricks, B. L., & Harackiewicz, J. M. (2010). Enhancing interest and performance with a utility value intervention. *Journal of Educational Psychology*, *102*(4), 880–895, doi:10.1037/a0019506

Hulleman, C. S., Thoman, D. B., Dicke, A., & Harackiewicz, J. M. (2017). The promotion and development of interest: The importance of perceived values. In P. A. O'Keefe & J. M. Harackiewicz (Eds.), *The science of interest* (pp. 189–208). Cham, Switzerland: Springer International.

Ingerick, M., & Rumsey, M. G. (2014). Taking the measure of work interests: Past, present, and future. *Military Psychology*, *26*(3), 165–181, doi://dx.doi.org/10.1037/mil0000045

Izard, C. E. (1991). *The psychology of emotions*. New York, NY: Plenum Press.

Jang, H. (2008). Supporting students' motivation, engagement, and learning during an uninteresting activity. *Journal of Educational Psychology*, *100*(4), 798–811, doi:10.1037/a0012841

Jepma, M., Verdonschot, R. G., van Steenbergen, H., Rombouts, S. A., & Nieuwenhuis, S. (2012). Neural mechanisms underlying the induction and relief of perceptual curiosity. *Frontiers in Behavioral Neuroscience*, *6*(9), doi://dx.doi.org/10.3389/fnbeh.2012.00005

Johnson, V. A., & Beehr, T. A. (2014). Making use of professional development: Employee interests and motivational goal orientations. *Journal of Vocational Behavior*, *84*(2), 99–108, doi:10.1016/j.jvb.2013.12.003

Kang, M. J., Hsu, M., Krajbich, I. M., Loewenstein, G., McClure, S. M., Wang, J. T., & Camerer, C. F. (2009). The wick in the candle of learning: Epistemic curiosity activates reward circuitry and enhances memory. *Psychological Science*, *20*(8), 963–973, doi:10.1111/j.1467-9280.2009.02402.x

Katz, I., Assor, A., Kanat-Maymon, Y., & Bereby-Meyer, Y. (2006). Interest as a motivational resource: Feedback and gender matter, but interest makes the difference. *Social Psychology of Education*, *9*(1), 27–42, doi:10.1007/s11218-005-2863-7

Keltner, D., & Gross, J. J. (1999). Functional accounts of emotions. *Cognition & Emotion*, *13*(5), 467–480, doi:10.1080/026999399379140

Krapp, A. (2002). Structural and dynamic aspects of interest development: Theoretical considerations from an ontogenetic perspective. *Learning and Instruction*, *12*(4), 383–409, doi:10.1016/S0959-4752(01)00011-1

Lazarus, R. S. (1991). *Emotion and adaptation*. New York: Oxford University Press.

Lench, H. C., Bench, S. W., Darbor, K. E., & Moore, M. (2015). A functionalist manifesto: Goal-related emotions from an evolutionary perspective. *Emotion Review*, *7*(1), 90–98, doi:10.1177/1754073914553001

Linnenbrink-Garcia, L., Patall, E. A., & Messersmith, E. E. (2013). Antecedents and consequences of situational interest. *British Journal of Educational Psychology*, *83*(4), 591–614, doi:10.1111/j.2044-8279.2012.02080.x

Litman, J. A. (2008). Interest and deprivation factors of epistemic curiosity. *Personality and Individual Differences*, *44*(7), 1585–1595, doi:10.1016/j.paid.2008.01.014

Litman, J. A., & Silvia, P. J. (2006). The latent structure of trait curiosity: Evidence for interest and deprivation curiosity dimensions. *Journal of Personality Assessment*, *86*(3), 318–328, doi:10.1207/s15327752jpa8603_07

Loewenstein, G. (1994). The psychology of curiosity: A review and reinterpretation. *Psychological Bulletin*, *116*(1), 75–98, doi:10.1037/0033-2909.116.1.75

Mäkikangas, A., Bakker, A. B., Aunola, K., & Demerouti, E. (2010). Job resources and flow at work: Modelling the relationship via latent growth curve and mixture model methodology. *Journal of Occupational and Organizational Psychology*, *83* (3), 795–814, doi.org/10.1348/096317909X476333

Master, A., Butler, L. P., & Walton, G. M. (2017). How the subjective relationship between the self, others, and a task drives interest. In P. A. O'Keefe & J. M. Harackiewicz (Eds.), *The science of interest* (pp. 209–226). Cham, Switzerland: Springer International.

Mussel, P. (2013). Introducing the construct curiosity for predicting job performance. *Journal of Organizational Behavior*, *34*(4), 453–472, doi:10.1002/job.1809

Nye, C. D., Su, R., Rounds, J., & Drasgow, F. (2017). Interest congruence and performance: Revisiting recent meta-analytic findings. *Journal of Vocational Behavior*, *98*, 138–151, doi://dx.doi.org/10.1016/j.jvb.2016.11.002

O'Keefe, P. A., & Harackiewicz, J. M. (2017). *The science of interest*. Cham, Switzerland: Springer International.

O'Keefe, P. A., Horberg, E. J., & Plante, I. (2017). The multifaceted role of interest in motivation and engagement. In P. A. O'Keefe & J. M. Harackiewicz (Eds.), *The science of interest* (pp. 49–67). Cham, Switzerland: Springer International.

O'Keefe, P. A., & Linnenbrink-Garcia, L. (2014). The role of interest in optimizing performance and self-regulation. *Journal of Experimental Social Psychology*, *53*, 70–78, doi:10.1016/j.jesp.2014.02.004

Ortony, A., & Turner, T. J. (1990). What's basic about basic emotions? *Psychological Review*, *97*(3), 315–331, doi:10.1037/0033-295X.97.3.315

Panksepp, J. (1998). *Affective neuroscience: The foundations of human and animal emotions*. New York, NY: Oxford University Press.

Patrick, J., Smy, V., Tombs, M., & Shelton, K. (2012). Being in one's chosen job determines pre-training attitudes and training outcomes. *Journal of Occupational and Organizational Psychology*, *85* (2), 245–257, doi:10.1111/j.2044-8325.2011.02027.x

Pekrun, R. (2006). The control-value theory of achievement emotions: Assumptions, corollaries, and implications for educational research and practice. *Educational Psychology Review, 18*(4), 315–341, doi:10.1007/s10648-006-9029-9

Pekrun, R., Goetz, T., Daniels, L. M., Stupnisky, R. H., & Perry, R. P. (2010). Boredom in achievement settings: Exploring control-value antecedents and performance outcomes of a neglected emotion. *Journal of Educational Psychology, 102*, 531–549, doi:10.1037/a0019243

Pugh, K., & Bergin, D. (2006). Motivational influences on transfer. *Educational Psychologist, 41*(3), 147–160, doi:10.1207/s15326985ep4103_2

Reio, T., & Wiswell, A. (2000). Field investigation of the relationship among adult curiosity, workplace learning, and job performance. *Human Resource Development Quarterly, 11*(1), 5–30, doi:10.1002/1532-1096(200021)11:1<5::AID-HRDQ2>3.0.CO;2-A

Renninger, K. A. (2000). Individual interest and its implications for understanding intrinsic motivation. In C. Sansone & J. M. Harackiewicz (Eds.), *Intrinsic and extrinsic motivation: The search for optimal motivation and performance* (pp. 373–404). San Diego, CA: Academic.

Renninger, K. A., & Hidi, S. (2016). *The power of interest for motivation and engagement*. London, UK: Routledge.

Rotgans, J. I., & Schmidt, H. G. (2017). Interest development: Arousing situational interest affects the growth trajectory of individual interest. *Contemporary Educational Psychology, 49*, 175–184, doi:10.1016/j.cedpsych.2017.02.003

Ryan, R. M., & Deci, E. L. (2017). *Self-determination theory: Basic psychological needs in motivation, development, and wellness*. New York, NY: Guilford.

Sackett, A. M., Meyvis, T., Nelson, L. D., Converse, B. A., & Sackett, A. L. (2010). You're having fun when time flies: The hedonic consequences of subjective time progression. *Psychological Science, 21*(1), 111, doi:10.1177/0956797609354832

Salanova, M., Bakker, A., & Llorens, S. (2006). Flow at work: Evidence for an upward spiral of personal and organizational resources. *Journal of Happiness Studies, 7*(1), 1–22, doi:10.1007/s10902-005-8854-8

Sansone, C., & Thoman, D. B. (2005). Interest as the missing motivator in self-regulation. *European Psychologist, 10*(3), 175–186.

Sansone, C., Weir, C., Harpster, L., & Morgan, C. (1992). Once a boring task always a boring task? Interest as a self-regulatory mechanism. *Journal of Personality and Social Psychology, 63*(3), 379–390, doi:10.1037/0022-3514.63.3.379

Schiefele, U. (2009). Situational and individual interest. In K. R. Wenzel & A. Wigfield (Eds.), *Handbook of motivation at school* (pp. 197–222). New York, NY: Routledge/Taylor & Francis.

Senko, C., & Harackiewicz, J. M. (2005). Achievement goals, task performance, and interest: Why perceived goal difficulty matters. *Personality and Social Psychology Bulletin, 31*(12), 1739–1753, doi:10.1177/0146167205281128

Shin, J., & Grant, A. M. (2019). Bored by interest: Intrinsic motivation in one task can reduce performance on other tasks. *Academy of Management Journal, 62*(2), 415–436, doi:10.5465/amj.2017.0735

Silvia, P. J. (2001). Interest and interests: The psychology of constructive capriciousness. *Review of General Psychology, 5*(3), 270–290, doi:10.1037//1089-2680.5.3.270

Silvia, P. J. (2003). Self-efficacy and interest: Experimental studies of optimal incompetence. *Journal of Vocational Behavior, 62*(2), 237–249, doi:10.1016/S0001-8791(02)00013-1

Silvia, P. J. (2005). What is interesting? Exploring the appraisal structure of interest. *Emotion, 5*(1), 89–102, doi:10.1037/1528-3542.5.1.89

Silvia, P. J. (2006). *Exploring the psychology of interest*. New York, NY: Oxford University Press.

Sitzmann, T., & Ely, K. (2011). A meta-analysis of self-regulated learning in work-related training and educational attainment: What we know and where we need to go. *Psychological Bulletin, 137*(3), 421–442, doi:10.1037/a0022777

Smith, C. A., & Ellsworth, P. C. (1985). Patterns of cognitive appraisal in emotion. *Journal of Personality and Social Psychology, 48*(4), 813–838, doi:10.1037/0022-3514.48.4.813

Sucala, M. L., Stefan, S., Szentagotai-Tatar, A., & David, D. (2010). Time flies when you expect to have fun: An experimental investigation of the relationship between expectancies and the perception of time progression. *Cognition, Brain, Behavior: An Interdisciplinary Journal, 14*, 231–241.

Sung, B., & Yih, J. (2016). Does interest broaden or narrow attentional scope? *Cognition and Emotion, 30*(8), 1485–1494, doi:10.1080/02699931.2015.1071241

Tanaka, A., & Murayama, K. (2014). Within-person analyses of situational interest and boredom: Interactions between task-specific perceptions and achievement goals. *Journal of Educational Psychology, 106*(4), 1122–1134, doi:10.1037/a0036659

Thoman, D. B., Sansone, C., Fraughton, T., & Pasupathi, M. (2012). How students socially evaluate interest: Peer responsiveness influences evaluation and maintenance of interest. *Contemporary Educational Psychology, 37*(4), 254–265, doi:10.1016/j.cedpsych.2012.04.001

Thoman, D.B., Sansone, C., & Geerling, D. (2017). The dynamic nature of interest: Embedding interest within self-regulation. In P. A. O'Keefe & J. M. Harackiewicz (Eds.), *The science of interest* (pp. 27–47). Cham, Switzerland: Springer International.

Thoman, D. B., Smith, J. L., & Silvia, P. J. (2011). The resource replenishment function of interest. *Social Psychological and Personality Science, 2* (6), 592–599, doi:10.1177/1948550611402521

Tomkins, S. S. (1984). Affect theory. In K. R. Scherer & P. Ekman (Eds.), *Approaches to emotion* (pp. 95–163). Hillsdale, NJ: Lawrence Erlbaum.

Turner, S. A., & Silvia, P. J. (2006). Must interesting things be pleasant? A test of competing appraisal structures. *Emotion, 6*(4), 670–674, doi:10.1037/1528-3542.6.4.670

Ulrich, M., Keller, J., Hoenig, K., Waller, C., & Grön, G. (2014). Neural correlates of experimentally induced flow experiences. *NeuroImage, 86*, 194–202, doi://dx.doi.org/10.1016/j.neuroimage.2013.08.019

Van Tilburg, W., & Igou, E. (2017). Boredom begs to differ: Differentiation from other negative emotions. *Emotion, 17*(2), 309–322, doi:10.1037/emo0000233

Van Yperen, N. W. (2003). Task interest and actual performance: The moderating effects of assigned and adopted purpose goals. *Journal of Personality and Social Psychology, 85*(6), doi:10.1037/0022-3514.85.6.1006

Wang, H., & Li, J. (2015). How trait curiosity influences psychological well-being and emotional exhaustion: The mediating role of personal initiative. *Personality and Individual Differences, 75*, 135–140, doi:10.1016/j.paid.2014.11.020

Watson, D., Clark, L. A., & Tellegen, A. (1988). Development and validation of brief measures of positive and negative affect: The PANAS scales. *Journal of Personality and Social Psychology, 54*, 1063–1070, doi:10.1037/0022-3514.54.6.1063

Weiss, H. M., & Shaw, J. B. (1979). Social influences on judgments about tasks. *Organizational Behavior and Human Performance, 24*(1), 126–140, doi:10.1016/0030-5073(79)90020-5

Winslow, C. J., Hu, X., Kaplan, S. A., & Li, Y. (2017). Accentuate the positive: Which discrete positive emotions predict which work outcomes? *The Psychologist-Manager Journal, 20*(2), 74–89, doi:10.1037/mgr0000053

Wittmann, B. C., Bunzeck, N., Dolan, R. J., & Düzel, E. (2007). Anticipation of novelty recruits reward system and hippocampus while promoting recollection. *NeuroImage, 38*(1), 194–202, doi:10.1016/j.neuroimage.2007.06.038

30 The Antecedents and Consequences of Fear at Work

Peter J. Jordan, Ashlea C. Troth, Neal M. Ashkanasy, and Ronald H. Humphrey

Fear is the mind-killer.

Frank Herbert, *Dune* (1965)

Despite being identified as a pervasive emotion in the modern workplace (Pfeffer & Sutton, 2000), fear oddly has not received a corresponding amount of attention among management researchers. In fact, Kish-Gephart, Detert, Treviño, and Edmondson (2009, p. 163) observe that we still have much to learn about the nature of fear in workplace settings, including "what it is, how and why it is experienced, and to what effects." Bennis (1966) notes further that fear has always been a part of the work environment (see also Connelly & Turner, 2018), but it remains an especially important issue in today's workplaces because of the effects of rapid and ongoing organizational change, which are often linked to uncertain outcomes (Bordia, Hobman, Jones, Gallois, & Callan, 2004; Tiedens & Linton, 2001). Our aim in this chapter is to provide an overview of fear (arising from uncertainty) as a discrete emotion, to identify stimuli that may trigger fear at work, and to identify the potential positive and negative outcomes that can be linked to employees' fear. We also outline potential pathways for future research on fear of uncertainty in the workplace.

It is not surprising to find that researchers have long studied fear in organizational contexts. Such studies have examined fear as a response to change (Bordia et al., 2004; Kiefer, 2005); during organizational failure (Vuori & Quy, 2016); as a factor of organizational climate (Ashkanasy & Nicholson, 2003); and during knowledge transfer (Empson, 2001). With respect to the effects of fear, researchers have examined its impact on coping strategies (Cheng, Kuan, Li, & Ken, 2010); workplace violence (Budd, Arvey, & Lawless, 1996); and decision-making (Li, Ashkanasy, & Ahlstrom, 2014). While this research base is limited, it nonetheless provides a platform for gaining a greater understanding of fear and for exploring the broader implications of fear in today's changing and uncertain workplaces. Despite this beginning, however, much more work is required if we are to gain a broad understanding of fear of uncertainty at work. A starting point is to establish a clear construct definition for fear.

What is Fear?

Ekman (1992) broadly describes fear as a negatively valenced emotion that emerges in a range of intensities from mild nervousness, to anxiety, to full-blown fear and panic. There seem, however, to be disparate viewpoints regarding the triggers for fear. For example, Kish-Gephart et al. (2009) argue that fear usually results from an individual's perception of threat (see also LeDoux, 2013). Other authors propose that fear occurs in response to disruption (Hebb, 1946), to risk (Warr & Stafford, 1983), to danger (Tamir, 2016), to ambiguity (Whalen, 1998), or to uncertainty (Solomon, 1993). More recently, Barrett (2006) argues for a homologous view of emotion suggesting that common emotions share common stimuli (e.g. irritation, annoyance, and anger have a common trigger of negative justice perceptions). Frijda (1987) and Lebel (2017) argue that fear at various levels of intensity emerges largely from a single common stimulus: perceptions of uncertain outcomes. Although we recognize that there are many sources of fear, including perceptions of threats, we focus specifically on fear as a response to employees' perceptions of uncertainty at work.

Thus, using Barrett's (2006) arguments – which seek to simplify the explanation of what stimuli create discrete emotions – we consider perceptions of uncertain outcomes as one important driver of fear in work settings. Indeed, each of the sources of fear we mentioned earlier (threat, disruption, risk and so on) can be seen to involve perceptions of uncertainty about outcomes. Moreover, Baumgartner, Pieters, and Bagozzi (2008) argue that fear is an example of an *anticipatory emotion*. In other words, fear is an actor's affective response to the *prospect of a future event* that has potential negative consequences for the individual. Thus, encapsulating this view, uncertainty about what is going to happen next contributes to fear.

Fear in response to perceptions of uncertainty is especially relevant in workplace settings, particularly during change (Bordia et al., 2004; Tiedens & Linton, 2001). In this case, by gaining a better understanding of fear of uncertainty in the workplace, researchers may contribute to resolving the myriad difficult situations at work involving uncertain outcomes.

Although some researchers argue that uncertainty results in other discrete emotions such as hope (Fitzgerald, 2014) or anger (Fudenberg, Rand, & Dreber, 2012), we contend that these reactions tend to be secondary appraisal reactions linked to coping mechanisms (cf. Lazarus & Folkman, 1984). As such, they differ from fear, which constitutes a primary reaction to an uncertain outcome. Drawing on the stress and coping literature, we know that a secondary appraisal of uncertainty produces a cognitive process involving a consideration of the situation and the resources available to individuals to cope with that stressor (Biggs, Brough, & Drummond, 2017). In other words, if individuals have sufficient resources and experience, they might see hope emerge from a situation involving uncertainty, or even reconsider the justice implications of the uncertainty and have an anger reaction. In line with Barrett's (2006) view of emotions, we argue that fear, in varying intensities, is a natural initial emotion (primary appraisal) experienced by any employees who encounter uncertainty.

A further issue to consider is that fear reactions emerge in a range of intensities from mild concern through nervousness to full-blown panic. Ekman (1992) outlines a framework for a family of discrete emotions (all which emerge at varying levels of intensity with different descriptors). Low-intensity emotions (e.g. nervousness, concern, or worry) all fall within the family of fear and, drawing on Barratt's (2006) arguments, a common stimulus should drive them. Similarly, we argue that, at the other end of the spectrum, high-intensity emotions (e.g. panic, terror, or fright) also fall within the family of fear and are responses to more intense uncertainty. We acknowledge, however, that these emotions are initial reactions that may be modified through secondary appraisal processes to morph into emotions such as anger, hope, or sadness at a later stage. In this chapter, however, we focus on fear as an initial emotional reaction to uncertainty in workplace settings.

The Behavioral Outcomes of Fear

The behavioral consequences of fear may be direct or indirect. On the one hand, the results of neuroscience research demonstrate that fear can directly result in conditioned responses (Ghosh & Chattarji, 2015), which confirms early thoughts about fear (e.g. see Hebb, 1946) as being linked to automatic reactions. On the other hand, the results of social science research (see Baumeister, Vohs, DeWall, & Zhang, 2007) suggest that emotions shape behavior indirectly, rather than directly. Specifically, Baumeister and colleagues argue that emotions contribute to cognitive processes that subsequently drive behavior.

In fact, closer examination of the neuroscientific data appears to show that both perspectives are correct. In this regard, LeDoux (2012a) found that, although emotional stimuli are processed across the cortex, hippocampus, and amygdala regions of the brain (i.e. they are cognitive processes), a shortcut route exists that facilitates a direct path from the sensory thalamus to the amygdala (a conditioned response) – without going through the cortex or the hippocampus. Gross and Canteras (2012) describe this as an evolutionary circuit. In view of this discovery, Lindebaum and Jordan (2014) argue that simplistic arguments that emotional stimuli are either direct or indirect processes ignore the complex networks that underpin this link. In acknowledging the complexity of these frameworks, moreover, it seems reasonable to conclude that fear can result in both automatic (direct) and considered (indirect) behaviors.

Studying these ideas in more detail, we see that automatic responses (Ghosh & Chattarji, 2015) result in a single common reaction. In the case of fear, a fright may result in a jump reaction; or extreme danger may result in freezing (LeDoux, 2012b). Regarding automatic reactions to fear, research regarding the direct behavioral outcomes of fear emphasizes the *startle effect*, or an involuntary defensive reflex in response to sudden or unexpected stimuli (Valls-Solé, Kumru, & Kofler, 2008). This research also shows that startle responses can vary in individuals from mild to extreme. Kolb (1991) identified in particular that individuals suffering from post-traumatic stress disorder are typically more reactively sensitive to fear (and have significantly heighted startle responses). In contrast, Ridgeway and Hare (1981) report a reduced startle response in individuals who engage in sensation-seeking behaviors (e.g. skydivers, adventurers). Finally, we note that a startle response relates to the intensity of the situation or the stimuli that precipitates the fear (Davis & Wagner, 1969). At work, extreme forms of startle responses may be evident in events such as workplace industrial accidents or in the face of workplace violence. Researchers note that these conditioned responses can be moderated through therapy or training (Kashdan, Adams, Read, & Hawk, 2012).

Alternatively, the inclusion of cognition (a delay in the response) in this process results in emotions indirectly shaping behavior (as suggested by Baumeister and his colleagues, 2015). On this basis, an experience of uncertain outcomes still creates an emotional response. However, where the individual is provided time to consider the potential outcomes (a cognitive process) they may have a range of different responses, with cognition partly determining the eventual behavior based on the personal resources available to that individual (e.g. skills, abilities, experience). In this process, reactions to fear have been most typically identified as fight/flight responses (Diest et al., 2001).

In terms of non-automatic responses, Carver (2006) notes the link between affective systems and behavioral systems. Looking at fear in an emotion regulation framework, we see that, once cognition is introduced to the process, there are significant individual differences in people's responses to fear (Zorawski, Cook, Kuhn, & LaBar, 2005), as well as the emotion regulation strategies they adopt to manage fear (Hartley & Phelps, 2010). We note here that fear is generally associated with avoidance behaviors (rigid and passive responses), or behavioral reactions associated with flight.

In terms of approach behaviors (fight-type reactions) linked to fear, Marsh, Ambady, and Kleck (2005) found that individuals who see others expressing fear are likely to engage in approach behaviors, just to understand what is happening. In this research, Marsh and her colleagues found that individuals respond faster to the target when observing target-expressed fear, rather than when observing anger; and that individuals are more likely to engage with a fearful person (whereas they seek to avoid angry people). This research supports other findings (Batson et al., 1997) demonstrating that individuals who correctly identify a fearful response are more likely to help the individual who expressed that fear. If this is so, then fear can result in approach behaviors from others who witness fear.

Fear can also result in proactive avoidance behaviors. Lebel (2017) notes that experienced fear may result in a proactive response designed to protect the individual from the stimuli that produced the fear. For example, an employee who learns that an organizational change is occurring may proactively approach a manager to find out information about the change so they can position themselves (with skills or knowledge) to respond to that change to their benefit. Lebel argues that emotion regulation (for instance, being appropriate and measured in the way you approach the manager) is a key part of that process. From a neuroscience perspective, Moscarello and Hartley (2017) argue that controllability is also a factor in determining whether fear results in proactivity. They found that, in specific uncertain situations where individuals feel they have some control (whether through experience or expertise), such individuals are more likely to take a proactive approach to attempt to resolve the uncertainty. For instance, if an employee is faced with a new task (e.g. a service agent who needs to deal with an angry customer's complaint), s/he may have less fear if s/he has control over the resources to solve that problem, or more fear if s/he lacks the decision-making authority to solve the problem. If the individual has little autonomy and constantly needs to refer the customer's complaint to others for a decision, s/he may expect the customer to have increasing anger at the inability to resolve the problem. This may result in the employee having greater fear and being less proactive.

So far, we have dealt with the factors leading to a perception of fear in the workplace, especially the role of perceived uncertainty and potential general reactions to fear. In the following section, we discuss in more particular detail the consequences of fear in the workplace occasioned by perceptions of uncertainty.

Fear at Work

There is clear evidence that we work in uncertain times. Indeed, our daily fears are constantly heightened by news reports ranging from terrorist attacks in workplaces (such as those in France and Australia: see Dilanian, 2019), to the threat of climate change (Gabbatiss, 2019), to threats to our way of life based on economic changes including uncertainty created by government reactions to increased levels of immigration (Reich, 2019).

A recent example of fear linked to significant events can be drawn from the entertainment industry. In an October 2017 edition of the *New York Times*, Kantor and Twohey (2017) reported that dozens of women had accused Harvey Weinstein, a Hollywood film producer, of sexual harassment spanning several decades. Notably, victims cited fear as the explanation for their silence, including physical fear, fear of missed job opportunities, fear of damaged reputations, and a fear of being disbelieved by others. Consequences for the victims included delayed career advancement as well as significant health issues, including post-traumatic stress disorder. For the organizations involved, it led to a tarnished image and major financial losses. The wave of publicity following the scandal highlights the prevalence of these types of incidents (and fear) across a range of industries and countries.

Another example of a workplace climate of fear (see also Ashkanasy & Nicholson, 2003) can be found in the scandal at Volkswagen, whereby engineers admitted to cheating on US diesel emissions tests. Because of these admissions, Volkswagen's share price plummeted by 30 percent in three days and the company paid out $18 billion in fines and lawsuits (English, 2015). According to the engineers, they engaged in the unethical behavior because of three factors: (1) pressure to meet unrealistic performance targets (fear of failure); (2) the context of Volkswagen's disorganized and uncoordinated compliance strategy; and (3) fears about how senior management would respond if they voiced their concerns (Hetzner, 2017).

In Australia, the "Dr. Death" scandal at Bundaberg Base Hospital resulting from the unskilled practices of Dr. Jayant Patel has similar features (fear-induced silence), and in this case horrifying outcomes: the death of patients (Edwards, Lawrence, & Ashkanasy, 2016). All three cases described involve delayed reporting by employees caused specifically by fear, with the fear primarily caused by perceptions of uncertainty about the consequences of their whistle-blowing. An especially disturbing aspect of TV and radio interviews with employees involved in all these cases is that interviewees stated that the fear-inducing events underpinning these incidents were not isolated; in fact, they are commonplace.

Everyday Work Events that Generate Fear

Beyond these more dramatic examples, employees also experience everyday fear in relation to their jobs. While there are of course many uncertainty-causing situations at work, in this section we focus on three specific everyday events in the workplace: (1) uncertainty created by work activity (what we do); (2) uncertainty caused by relationships at work, such as supervisor/subordinate relationships (who we work with); and (3) uncertainty caused by change (what may happen in the future). We consider these generally to typify situations in which uncertain outcomes can emerge at work, and that these may create a fear reaction of varying intensity.

Fear Resulting from Uncertainty about What We Do

Leach et al. (2013) note two broad sources of work activity uncertainty: (1) resource uncertainty, and (2) task uncertainty.

Resource uncertainty, on the one hand, arises from the idea that the flow of resources (personnel, time, funding) that employees have available to them may be uncertain at times and often cannot be accurately predicted. For instance, a job where there are competing demands may create resource uncertainty if we have limited time to complete the tasks. We note that a lack of clarity around the availability and distribution of resources can enhance employee uncertainty (Lambrechts, Demeulemeester, & Herroelen, 2008) and this may result in a fear reaction such as nervousness or concern.

Task uncertainty, on the other hand, occurs when workers do not know what task their managers may be asking them to complete next, or how to do it. Parker (2014) argues, in particular, that task uncertainty is commonly experienced at work and suggests further that specific job designs can be beneficial in coping with uncertainty in the workplace. For example, employees working in customer service may have clear lines of responsibility and a set of specific tasks they are required to perform as a part of their role, while those working in less structured environments such as ad hoc project teams may not have this level of certainty in their day-to-day activities. In this regard, Cordery, Morrison, Wright, and Wall (2010) found that task uncertainty contributes to decreased team performance because employees need to find additional resources, such as time, to resolve uncertainty. In terms of additional resource required, this may include both emotional and cognitive coping resources required to deal with a fear-linked reaction.

Fear Resulting from Uncertainty Caused by Relationships

Kramer (2014) argues that the nature of interpersonal relationships at work automatically introduces a level of uncertainty at work. Uncertainty in relationships can emerge from the introduction of new employees through recruitment (Kramer, 1993); from clashes in working styles, as individuals struggle to understand those who may have different personal work style preferences (see Armstrong & Priola, 2001), or who have different approaches to completing work (for instance, methodical versus ad hoc completion of tasks, or early versus late starters). All employees experience the nervousness associated with starting a new job or working in a new team (Appelbaum, Bregman, & Moroz, 1998). There is also research evidence to suggest that supervisor/subordinate relationships can be uncertain, particularly where there is abusive supervision (Thau, Bennett, Mitchell, & Marrs, 2009). The nature of relationships at work is such that one cannot guarantee another employee's motivations, priorities, or responses, and this, in and of itself, creates a perception of uncertainty which can lead to a fear-related reaction.

Fear Resulting from Uncertainty Caused by Change

As we noted earlier, Bordia et al. (2004) found that organizational change increases perception of uncertainty. This is especially acute in organizational change processes that adopt a flexible approach, where the speed, scope, and complexity of the change are often unpredictable (Leana & Barry, 2000). Researchers note a link between change and fear reactions, as we are often unsure of potential losses that we may experience as a part of the change process (Moran & Brightman, 2004). We also note that uncertainty caused by change is likely to lead to uncertainty about what we do (task uncertainty) and uncertainty about relationships (who we work with). We note that the three factors we identified as creating uncertainty may be closely linked, or at times even interdependent.

Workplace Outcomes of Fear

The question we now turn to is: what are the workplace outcomes from fear, especially fear occasioned by uncertainty? The small amount of research completed in this field has shown that fear at work has significant negative outcomes including contributing to workplace silence (Kish-Gephart et al., 2009), employees hiding bad news and lying to their bosses (Pfeffer & Sutton, 2000), and reduced innovation (Bommer & Jalajas, 1999). Pfeffer and Sutton argue further that fear leads employees to repeat past mistakes and to avoid seeking ways to improve the situation at hand. Lerner and colleagues (2015) note further that people experiencing fear, especially in uncertain environments, are more likely to be pessimistic in assessing future events, and tend to perceive more risk in decision-making tasks. Kline and Lewis (2018) note, in addition, that the outcomes of fear at work in response to bullying and harassment negatively affect employee health and result in costs through sickness, employee turnover, reduced productivity, and increased legal proceedings (to resolve disputes between employees and between the organization and the employee).

Finally, and contrary to the foregoing line of argument, we note the evidence that some people are actually able to deal with fear and anxiety and even thrive in this context (e.g. emergency service workers). For instance, Frye and Wearing (2016) discuss the use of metacognition (actively thinking about how we learn from experiences to direct future behavior; see Moshman, 2018) by firefighters to reduce uncertainty and fear during bushfires. As Desmond (2011) notes, firefighters do not lack fear, but they instead feel that their expertise can introduce a level of personal control that enables them to walk into fires. Examining another of the emergency services, policing, Verhage, Noppe, Feys, and Ledegen, (2018) found that fear and stress are a normal part of a police officer's experiences in the field and that many decisions are made while experiencing fear. The training of police now incorporates a range of psychological tools to assist their decision making while experiencing fear (Verhag et al., 2018). Based on these examples, clearly fear may be managed with the right level of self-awareness and training.

Fear as a Motivator?

Having made the case so far in this chapter that the effects of fear can be destructive, we would be remiss if we did not also acknowledge that, under the right circumstances, fear can act as a positive motivator. We are not advocating a "carrot and stick" management approach (Andreoni, Harbaugh, & Vesterlund, 2003). Rather taking the view that a fight response to fear involves defensive reactivity (Schauer & Elbert, 2010), responses to fear can result in motivation for individuals to address that fear. In this regard, Clarke (2005) describes how uncertainty and fear can often be used to help employees to support drastic measures required to ensure a company's long-term viability. For instance, employees at Honeywell were asked to take unpaid furlough in 2009 to allow the company to avoid layoffs during a troubled economic time (Cote, 2013). Although this was not a pleasant experience for employees, in this case the organization used fear to ensure continued employment – especially when the alternative is the entire workforce losing their jobs.

Another example of a motivating use of fear occurred in a hospital setting where medical staff attempted (successfully) to reduce cross-infection rates through regular handwashing. Helder et al., (2012) described the introduction of screensavers on the hospital's computers that showed infectious germs multiplying exponentially every time an employee used a computer. This action increased employee uncertainty in relation to the cleanliness of surfaces in the hospital. Because of this intervention, hand hygiene compliance increased in the hospital from 58 percent to 98 percent. In this case, the intention was not to elicit high-intensity fear but rather to create uncertainty, and therefore lower-intensity concern (or fear), about the cleanliness of surfaces.

Future Directions for Fear Research in the Workplace

Our first suggestion for future research arises from Gooty, Gavin, and Ashkanasy's (2009) point that researchers need to do more research into the antecedents and effects of discrete emotions in the workplace. Gooty and colleagues specifically note the emotion of fear as fruitful grounds for more attention. A primary goal of any such research program should be to understand what triggers fear at work. We have already argued that fear emerges in response to workplace events characterized by uncertain outcomes. We also noted that fear can emerge in different intensities. On this basis, we see value in understanding relationships between the type or nature of the uncertainty and the intensity of fear experienced. In this instance, the question arises: can the difference in fear experienced by employees vary between activities? For example, is dealing with customers a more intense experience compared with dealing with colleagues? Also, do individual differences (confidence, self-esteem, locus of control, tolerance for ambiguity) moderate this relationship?

There is also a need to identify effective interventions to assist people who must constantly deal with uncertain outcomes and the subsequent fears associated with those outcomes (Jordan & Lindebaum, 2015). While Gibbs, Drummond, and Lachenmeyer (1993) address this issue in the case of emergency service workers who face extreme situations, the question arises as to whether interventions can be developed to assist other workers such as call center operators or customer service officers who face uncertainty daily in their interactions with customers and who deal with fear that may be linked to those events. For instance, both interpersonal skills training (to cope with unpredictable clients) and problem-solving training (to reduce uncertainty by providing problem-solving techniques) may work in these instances.

Research is also needed to study the efficacy of training in resilience, emotional intelligence, and emotion regulation in responding to fear at work (e.g. Nelis, Quoidbach, Mikolajczak, & Hansenne, 2009; Troth et al., 2018). Such training clearly has potential to assist individuals in managing their reactions to fear at work. If Lebel's (2017) arguments are correct about fear leading to proactivity, then research could determine if there are ways in which employees can be trained to see fear as a positive motivator rather than a negative influence.

Another useful avenue to explore is the application of Geddes and Callister's (2007) dual threshold model to study how employees react fearfully to uncertainty. In fact, Geddes and Callister have already applied their model to study anger in the workplace, and found that too little anger results in apathy, while too much (which they describe as being beyond the appropriateness threshold for the expression of anger) is also not productive. Our question in relation to fear is whether there is a similar curvilinear relationship between fear and performance (in line with the framework proposed by Yerkes and Dodson, 1908). Recently, Lindebaum and Jordan (2012) argued that the dual threshold model can be broadened into a framework for understanding the effects of other discrete emotions. If our earlier arguments are correct – that, under the right conditions, fear can be a motivator – then understanding the intensity of uncertainty required to achieve this reaction would constitute an important contribution to the management field.

Conclusion

Fear is an important evolutionary emotion (LeDoux, 2012b). It evolved as a basic reaction in human beings. Encouraging employees not to display fear at work means that important signals will not be received about uncertain outcomes at work, and how (effectively or not) that uncertainty is being managed. Our review implies that fear is an important part of organizational life and a part of the processes that keep employees active and responsive in addressing uncertainty in the work environment. Given that uncertainty is increasing in organizations, we argue that fear is a signal that a situation is not clear. As such, researchers would do well to look in more depth at the behavioral outcomes of uncertainty-generated fear at work, not just for individual employees but also at multiple levels of the organization.

References

Andreoni, J., Harbaugh, W., & Vesterlund, L. (2003). The carrot or the stick: Rewards, punishments, and cooperation. *American Economic Review*, *93*, 893–902.

Appelbaum, S. H., Bregman, M., & Moroz, P. (1998). Fear as a strategy: Effects and impact within the organization. *Journal of European Industrial Training*, *22*, 113–127.

Armstrong, S. J., & Priola, V. (2001). Individual differences in cognitive style and their effects on task and social orientations of self-managed work teams. *Small Group Research*, *32*, 283–312.

Ashkanasy, N. M., & Nicholson, G. J. (2003). Climate of fear in organisational settings: Construct definition, measurement and a test of theory. *Australian Journal of Psychology, 55*, 24–29.

Barrett, L. F. (2006). Solving the emotion paradox: Categorization and the experience of emotion. *Personality and Social Psychology Review, 10*, 20–46.

Batson, C. D., Sager, K., Garst, E., Kang, M., Rubchinsky, K., & Dawson, K. (1997). Is empathy-induced helping due to self–other merging? *Journal of Personality and Social Psychology, 73*, 495–509.

Baumeister, R. F., Vohs, K. D., DeWall, C. N., & Zhang, L. (2007). How emotion shapes behavior: Feedback, anticipation, and reflection, rather than direct causation. *Personality and Social Psychology Review, 11*, 167–203.

Baumgartner, H., Pieters, R., & Bagozzi, R. P. (2008). Future-oriented emotions: Conceptualization and behavioral effects. *European Journal of Social Psychology, 38*, 685–696.

Bennis, W. G. (1966). Changing organizations. *Journal of Applied Behavioral Science, 2*, 247–263.

Biggs, A., Brough, P., & Drummond, S. (2017). Lazarus and Folkman's psychological stress and coping theory. In C. L. Cooper & J. C. Quick (Eds.), *The handbook of stress and health: A guide to research and practice* (pp. 349–364). Chichester, UK: Wiley.

Bommer, M., & Jalajas, D. (1999).The threat of organizational downsizing on the innovative propensity of R&D professionals. *R&D Management, 29*, 27–34.

Bordia, P., Hobman, E., Jones, E., Gallois, C., & Callan, V. J. (2004). Uncertainty during organizational change: Types, consequences, and management strategies. *Journal of Business and Psychology, 18*, 507–532.

Budd, J. W., Arvey, R. D., & Lawless, P. (1996). Correlates and consequences of workplace violence. *Journal of Occupational Health Psychology, 1*, 197–210.

Carver, C. S. (2006). Approach, avoidance, and the self-regulation of affect and action. *Motivation and Emotion, 30*, 105–110.

Cheng, Y. H., Kuan, F. Y., Li, C. I., & Ken, Y. (2010). A comparison between the effect of emotional certainty and uncertainty on coping strategies. *Social Behavior and Personality, 38*, 53–60.

Clarke, M. (2005). The voluntary redundancy option: Carrot or stick? *British Journal of Management, 16*, 245–251.

Connelly, S., & Turner, M. R. (2018). Functional and dysfunctional fear at work: dual perspectives. In D. Lindebaum, D. Geddes, & P. J. Jordan (Eds.), *Social functions of emotion and talking about emotion at work*. Cheltenham, UK: Edward Elgar.

Cordery, J. L., Morrison, D., Wright, B. M., & Wall, T. D. (2010). The impact of autonomy and task uncertainty on team performance: A longitudinal field study. *Journal of Organizational Behavior, 31*, 240–258.

Cote, D. (2013). Honeywell's CEO on how he avoided layoffs. *Harvard Business Review*, June, https://hbr.org/2013/06/honeywells-ceo-on-how-he-avoided-layoffs

Davis, M., & Wagner, A. R. (1969). Habituation of startle response under incremental sequence of stimulus intensities. *Journal of Comparative and Physiological Psychology, 67*, 486–492.

Desmond, M. (2011). Making firefighters deployable. *Qualitative Sociology, 34*, 59–77.

Diest, I., Winters, W., Devriese, S., Vercamst, E., Han, J. N., Woestijne, K. P., & Bergh, O. (2001). Hyperventilation beyond fight/flight: respiratory responses during emotional imagery. *Psychophysiology, 38*, 961–968.

Dilanian, K. (2019). Report: Nearly all terror attacks in France carried out by radicals already known to police. *NBC News*, 7 January, www.nbcnews.com/news/world/report-nearly-all-terror-attacks-france-carried-out-radicals-already-n955276

Edwards, M. S., Lawrence, S. A., & Ashkanasy, N. M. (2016). Factors encouraging employee silence in response to wrongdoing: The case of Bundaberg Hospital. In N. M. Ashkanasy, C. E. J. Härtel, & W. J. Zerbe (Eds.) *Research on emotion in organizations* (Volume 12, pp. 343–382). Bingley, UK: Emerald.

Ekman, P. (1992). An argument for basic emotions. *Cognition & Emotion, 6*, 169–200.

Empson, L. (2001). Fear of exploitation and fear of contamination: Impediments to knowledge transfer in mergers between professional service firms. *Human Relations*, *54*(7), 839–862.

English, A. (2015). VW scandal: "Culture of fear," *The Telegraph Cars*, 16 October, www.telegraph.co.uk /cars/volkswagen/news/emissions-scandal-culture-of-fear-led-to-dependence-on-diesel/

Fitzgerald, D. (2014). The trouble with brain imaging: Hope, uncertainty and ambivalence in the neuroscience of autism. *BioSocieties*, *9*, 241–261.

Frijda, N. H. (1987). Emotion, cognitive structure, and action tendency. *Cognition and Emotion*, *1*(2), 115–143.

Frye, L. M., & Wearing, A. J. (2016). A model of metacognition for bushfire fighters. *Cognition, Technology & Work*, *18*(3), 613–619.

Fudenberg, D., Rand, D. G., & Dreber, A. (2012). Slow to anger and fast to forgive: Cooperation in an uncertain world. *American Economic Review*, *102*, 720–749.

Gabbatiss, J. (2019). Climate change is creating toxic crops and poisoning some of world's poorest people, scientists warn. *The Independent*, 16 March, www.independent.co.uk/environment/climate-change-poison-crops-toxic-fungi-ethiopia-un-environment-a8823071.html

Geddes, D., & Callister, R. R. (2007). Crossing the line(s): A dual threshold model of anger in organizations. *Academy of Management Review*, *32*, 721–746.

Ghosh, S., & Chattarji, S. (2015). Neuronal encoding of the switch from specific to generalized fear. *Nature Neuroscience*, *18*, 112–120.

Gibbs, M. S., Drummond, J., & Lachenmeyer, J. R. (1993). Effects of disaster on emergency workers: A review, with implications for training and post disaster interventions. *Journal of Social Behaviour and Personality*, *8*, 189–212.

Gooty, J., Gavin, M., & Ashkanasy, N. M. (2009). Emotions research in OB: The challenges that lie ahead. *Journal of Organizational Behavior*, *30*, 833–838.

Gross, C. T., & Canteras, N. S. (2012). The many paths to fear. *Nature Reviews Neuroscience*, *13*, 651–659.

Hartley, C. A., & Phelps, E. A. (2010). Changing fear: The neurocircuitry of emotion regulation. *Neuropsychopharmacology*, *35*, 136–146.

Hebb, D. O. (1946). On the nature of fear. *Psychological Review*, *53*, 259–275.

Helder, O. K., Weggelaar, A. M., Waarsenburg, D. C., Looman, C. W., van Goudoever, J. B., Brug, J., & Kornelisse, R. F. (2012). Computer screen saver hand hygiene information curbs a negative trend in hand hygiene behavior. *American Journal of Infection Control*, *40*, 951–954.

Herbert, F. (1965). *Dune*. Philadelphia, PA: Chiltern Books.

Hetzner, C. (2017). VW reforms compliance system to avoid another scandal. *Automotive News Europe*, 11 December, http://europe.autonews.com/article/20171211/ANE/171129801/vw-reforms-compliance-system-to-avoid-another-scandal

Jordan, P. J., & Lindebaum, D. (2015). A model of within person variation in leadership: Emotion regulation and scripts as predictors of situationally appropriate leadership. *Leadership Quarterly*, 26, 594–605.

Kantor, J., & Twohey, M. (2017). Harvey Weinstein paid off sexual harassment accusers for decades. *New York Times*, 5 October, www.nytimes.com /2017/10/05/us/harvey-weinstein-harassment-allegations.html

Kashdan, T. B., Adams, L., Read, J., & Hawk, L., Jr. (2012). Can a one-hour session of exposure treatment modulate startle response and reduce spider fears? *Psychiatry Research*, *196*, 79–82.

Kiefer, T. (2005). Feeling bad: Antecedents and consequences of negative emotions in ongoing change. *Journal of Organizational Behavior*, *26*, 875–897.

Kish-Gephart, J. J., Detert, J. R., Treviño, L. K., & Edmondson, A. C. (2009). Silenced by fear: The nature, sources, and consequences of fear at work. In B. M. Staw & L. L. Cummings (Eds.), *Research in organizational behavior* (Volume 29, pp. 163–193). Oxford, UK: Elsevier Science.

Kline, R., & Lewis, D. (2019). The price of fear: estimating the financial cost of bullying and harassment to the NHS in England. *Public Money & Management*, *39*, 166–174.

Kolb, L. C. (1991). PTSD: Psychopathology and the startle response. *Psychiatric Quarterly*, *62*, 233–250.

Kramer, M. W. (1993). Communication and uncertainty reduction during job transfers: Leaving and joining processes. *Communications Monographs*, *60*, 178–198.

Kramer, M. W. (2014). *Managing uncertainty in organizational communication*. Mahwah, NJ: Routledge.

Lambrechts, O., Demeulemeester, E., & Herroelen, W. (2008). Proactive and reactive strategies for resource-constrained project scheduling with uncertain resource availabilities. *Journal of Scheduling*, *11*, 121–136.

Lazarus, R. S., & Folkman, S. (1984). *Stress, appraisal and coping*. New York, NY: Springer.

Leach, D., Hagger-Johnson, G., Doerner, N., Wall, T., Turner, N., Dawson, J., & Grote, G. (2013). Developing a measure of work uncertainty. *Journal of Occupational and Organizational Psychology*, *86*, 85–99.

Leana, C. R., & Barry, B. (2000). Stability and change as simultaneous experiences in organizational life. *Academy of Management Review*, *25*, 753–759.

Lebel, R. D. (2017). Moving beyond fight and flight: A contingent model of how the emotional regulation of anger and fear sparks proactivity. *Academy of Management Review*, *42*, 190–206.

LeDoux, J. (2012a). Rethinking the emotional brain. *Neuron*, *73*, 653–676.

LeDoux, J. E. (2012b). Evolution of human emotion: A view through fear. *Progress in Brain Research*, *195*, 431–442.

LeDoux, J. E. (2013). The slippery slope of fear. *Trends in Cognitive Sciences*, *17*, 155–156.

Lerner, J. S., Li, Y., Valdesolo, P., & Kassam, K. S. (2015). Emotion and decision making. *Annual Review of Psychology*, *66*, 799–823.

Li, Y., Ashkanasy, N. M., and Ahlstrom, D. (2010). Complexity theory and affect structure: A dynamic approach to modeling emotional changes in organizations. In W. J. Zerbe, C. E. J. Härtel, & N. M. Ashkanasy (Eds.), *Research on emotion in organizations* (Volume 6, pp. 139–165). Bingley, UK: Emerald.

Lindebaum, D., & Jordan, P. J. (2012). Positive emotions, negative emotions, or utility of discrete emotions? *Journal of Organizational Behavior*, *33*, 1027–1030.

Lindebaum, D., & Jordan, P. J. (2014). A critique on neuroscientific methodologies in organizational behavior and management studies. *Journal of Organizational Behavior*, *35*, 898–908.

Marsh, A. A., Ambady, N., & Kleck, R. E. (2005). The effects of fear and anger facial expressions on approach-and avoidance-related behaviors. *Emotion*, *5*, 119–124.

Moran, J. W., & Brightman, B. K. (2000). Leading organizational change. *Journal of Workplace Learning*, *12*, 66–74.

Moscarello, J. M., & Hartley, C. A. (2017). Agency and the calibration of motivated behavior. *Trends in Cognitive Sciences*, *21*, 725–735.

Moshman, D. (2018). Metacognitive theories revisited. *Educational Psychology Review*, *30*, 599–606.

Nelis, D., Quoidbach, J., Mikolajczak, M., & Hansenne, M. (2009). Increasing emotional intelligence: (How) is it possible? *Personality and Individual Differences*, *47*, 36–41.

Parker, S. K. (2014). Beyond motivation: Job and work design for development, health, ambidexterity, and more. *Annual Review of Psychology*, *65*, 661–691.

Pfeffer, J., & Sutton, R. I. (2000). *The knowing-doing gap: How smart companies turn knowledge into action*. Boston, MA: Harvard Business Press.

Reich, R. (2019). Trump is cornered, with violence on his mind. We must be on red alert. *The Guardian*, 16 March, www.theguardian.com/us-news/commentisfree/2019/mar/16/donald-trump-breitbart-interview-white-supremacy

Ridgeway, D., & Hare, R. D. (1981). Sensation seeking and psychophysiological responses to auditory stimulation. *Psychophysiology*, *18*, 613–618.

Schauer, M., & Elbert, T. (2010). Dissociation following traumatic stress. *Zeitschrift für Psychologie/Journal of Psychology*, *218*, 109–127.

Solomon, R. C. (1993). *The passions: Emotions and the meaning of life*. Indianapolis, IN: Hackett.

Tamir, M. (2016). Why do people regulate their emotions? A taxonomy of motives in emotion regulation. *Personality and Social Psychology Review*, *20*, 199–222.

Thau, S., Bennett, R. J., Mitchell, M. S., & Marrs, M. B. (2009). How management style moderates the relationship between abusive supervision and workplace deviance: An uncertainty management theory perspective. *Organizational Behavior and Human Decision Processes*, *108*, 79–92.

Tiedens, L. Z., & Linton, S. (2001). Judgment under emotional certainty and uncertainty: The effects of specific emotions on information processing. *Journal of Personality and Social Psychology*, *81*, 973–988.

Troth, A. C., Lawrence, S. A., Jordan, P. J., & Ashkanasy, N. M. (2018). Interpersonal emotion regulation in the workplace: A conceptual and operational review and future research agenda. *International Journal of Management Reviews*, *20*, 523–543.

Valls-Solé, J., Kumru, H., & Kofler, M. (2008). Interaction between startle and voluntary reactions in humans. *Experimental Brain Research*, *187*, 497–507.

Verhage, A., Noppe, J., Feys, Y., & Ledegen, E. (2018). Force, stress, and decision-making within the Belgian police: The impact of stressful situations on police decision-making. *Journal of Police and Criminal Psychology*, *33*, 345–357.

Vuori, T. O., & Huy, Q. N. (2016). Distributed attention and shared emotions in the innovation process: How Nokia lost the smartphone battle. *Administrative Science Quarterly*, *61*, 9–51.

Warr, M., & Stafford, M. (1983). Fear of victimization: A look at the proximate causes. *Social Forces*, *61*, 1033–1043.

Whalen, P. J. (1998). Fear, vigilance and ambiguity: Initial neuroimaging studies of the human amygdala. *Current Directions in Psychological Science*, 7, 177–188.

Yerkes, R. M., & Dodson, J. D. (1908). The relation of strength of stimulus to rapidity of habit-formation. *Journal of Comparative and Neurological Psychology*, *18*, 459–482.

Zorawski, M., Cook, C. A., Kuhn, C. M., & LaBar, K. S. (2005). Sex, stress, and fear: Individual differences in conditioned learning. *Cognitive, Affective, & Behavioral Neuroscience*, *5*, 191–201.

31 From Self-Consciousness to Success

When and Why Self-Conscious Emotions Promote Positive Employee Outcomes

Rebecca L. Schaumberg and Jessica L. Tracy

Self-conscious emotions of guilt, shame, and pride are some of the most private emotions people experience, and yet they are central emotions for governing collective and organizational life. A missed deadline, a forgotten email, or a poor performance review can evoke feelings of guilt or shame. Victory over a competitor, a successful product launch, or a compliment from a colleague can evoke feelings of pride. Organizational scholars have theorized about how self-conscious emotions affect a range of employee outcomes such as responses to layoffs (Brockner, Davy, & Carter, 1985), positive inequity (Adams, 1965; Walster, Walster, & Berscheid, 1978), and institutional reproduction (Douglas Creed, Hudson, Bokhuysen, & Smith-Crowe, 2004), but empirical evidence in support of these claims has been sparse, particularly in comparison to research on other emotional experiences such as positive and negative affectivity.

Guilt, shame, and pride are considered to be not only self-conscious emotions, in the sense of requiring a focus on the self and self-evaluations, but also moral emotions, because of the central role they play in determining moral choices and motivating people to behave in line with moral standards (Tangney, Stuewig, & Mashek, 2007). These emotions predict a range of important moral and ethical behaviors (Cheng, Tracy, & Henrich, 2010; Dearing, Stuewig, & Tangney, 2005; Dorfman, Eyal, & Bereby-Meyer, 2014; Hart & Matsuba, 2007; W. Hoffman & Fisher, 2012; Tangney, Stuewig, & Martinez, 2014). The association between self-conscious emotions and morality is, in and of itself, important to organizations that seek to promote ethical workplaces. However, guilt, shame, and pride regulate not only people's moral lives but also the more amoral aspects of their work days. In this chapter, we will explain that people's propensity to experience self-conscious emotions can shape a range of important employee outcomes including prosocial and ethical behavior, leadership, and task effort.

The Function of Self-Conscious Emotions

Self-conscious emotions link individuals to the groups to which they belong (Tangney & Fischer, 1995; Tracy & Robins, 2007a). They reinforce socially valued behaviors by providing information about how well or poorly one is meeting standards of expected behavior (Tangney & Dearing, 2002; Tangney & Fischer, 1995; Tracy, Robins, & Tangney, 2007; Weidman, Tracy, & Elliot, 2016). Guilt or shame signals that one has violated (or will violate) standards of expected behavior, and thus one's social standing and self-worth are in jeopardy. Pride indicates that one is meeting or exceeding these standards, and thus one's standing and self-worth are secure (Weidman et al., 2016). These emotions align individual action with collective behavior because (theoretically) people will adjust their behavior to meet social expectations, in order to avoid the aversive experience of guilt or shame and to increase the positive experience of pride (Barrett, 1995).

In support of this functionalist account, research has shown that people automatically display nonverbal expressions of pride in response to success, and nonverbal expressions of shame in response to failure. Tracy and Matsumoto (2008) found that sighted, blind, and congenitally blind individuals in the Olympic and Paralympic Games displayed nonverbal expressions of pride in response to success in a competition, and nonverbal expressions of shame in response to failures. Pride displays in response to success were observed among athletes from all cultural contexts examined, but the extent to which athletes showed nonverbal markers of shame varied across cultures, with sighted athletes from highly individualistic countries displaying less pronounced nonverbal expressions of shame. Combined with the finding that congenitally blind athletes across cultures displayed shame, these results suggest that individuals from highly individualistic Western cultures probably suppressed displays of shame upon losing a competition, presumably because of the stigma associated with shame in Western cultural contexts.

The evidence that pride and shame displays are reliably shown by individuals across cultures and by blind individuals, who could not have learned to show them from watching others, suggests that these displays may be evolved behavioral tendencies, which probably function to communicate one's success or failure – and thus one's status (i.e. the amount of respect, admiration, and deference one deserves) to others. Shariff and Tracy (2009) and Shariff, Tracy, and Markusoff (2012) directly tested this idea by assessing people's automatic associations between these nonverbal displays of emotion and high- or low-status concepts. In support of their predictions, participants responded more quickly when nonverbal displays of pride were associated with high status rather than low status, and when nonverbal displays of shame were linked with low status than with high status. Moreover, these associations held even when participants viewed competing and contradictory information about a displayer's status (e.g. when they viewed a pride displayer who appeared to be homeless; Shariff et al., 2012). In subsequent work, these authors documented a similar pattern of results in Fiji, with participants who were highly isolated members of a traditional small-scale society who had never previously used a computer (Tracy, Shariff, Zhao, & Henrich, 2013). These findings suggest that the pride and shame displays may be universal signals of high and low status.

Despite similarities in the theorized function of self-conscious emotions, these emotions are not similarly "functional" at regulating behavior to become more in line with collective standards. A central theme to emerge from research on self-conscious emotions is that similar emotional experiences (e.g. guilt and shame) can have divergent effects on the regulation of behavior (see Tangney & Dearing, 2002; Tracy & Robins, 2007b for reviews), with guilt and the psychologically adaptive type of pride – known as authentic pride – more effectively regulating behavior in the theorized way than shame and the more psychologically maladaptive type of pride – known as hubristic pride (Tracy & Robins, 2007b). This difference arises in part because of the different attributions for one's behavior that are associated with these emotional experiences (Tracy & Robins, 2006; 2007b).

Distinguishing Guilt, Shame, Authentic Pride, and Hubristic Pride

As shown in Table 31.1, the self-conscious emotions can be conceptually mapped along two dimensions, the first being whether people positively or negatively deviate from social expectations. We consider a positive deviation to mean meeting or exceeding standards of expected behavior and a negative deviation to mean falling short of these standards. The second dimension

Table 31.1 Conceptual mapping of the self-conscious emotions

		Attribution for deviation	
		Immutable qualities of the self	***Mutal qualities of the self***
Direction of the deviation from social expectations	***Positive***	Hubristic pride	Authentic pride
	Negative	Shame	Guilt

is the attribution people make for this deviation. Do people attribute it to a mutable behavior or to something core and fixed about the self?

Distinguishing Guilt and Shame

Shame arises when people attribute the source of their failure to something core and fixed about themselves; in contrast, guilt arises when people attribute the source of their failure to a controllable and therefore changeable behavior that is often specific to the situation (Niedenthal, Tangney, & Gavanski, 1994; Tangney & Tracy, 2012; Tracy & Robins, 2006). Consider an employee who makes a mistake on an important presentation to a client. If this employee attributes the transgression to her erroneous behavior in this situation (e.g. "I made a mistake because I didn't take enough care to go over all the details"), she is likely to experience guilt. If she instead attributes the transgression to something core about herself (e.g. "I made a mistake because I am a careless person"), she is likely to experience shame.

Not surprisingly given this attributional distinction, guilt and shame relate to distinct patterns of agency and control (Lewis, 1971; Tangney, 1995; Tracy & Robins, 2006). Guilt prompts people to focus on what they could have done differently, or what they could do differently in the future (Niedenthal et al., 1994). Shame focuses people on how things would be different if *they* were different people (Niedenthal et al., 1994). Guilt-proneness is positively associated with a growth-oriented mindset, whereas shame-proneness is positively associated with an entity, or a performance-oriented, mindset (Tangney & Dearing, 2002). Moreover, changing people's attributions for their transgressions can affect the extent to which they feel guilt or shame. Niedenthal and colleagues (1994) had participants write an essay about a transgression. In one condition, participants focused on how the events described in their essay would have been different if they had behaved differently. In the other condition, participants described how the events would have been different if they possessed different personal attributes. When the counterfactual prompt focused participants on their behaviors, participants reported greater feelings of guilt than shame; when the counterfactual prompt focused participants on their internal qualities, they reported greater feelings of shame than guilt.

The controllable and mutable attributions characteristic of guilt are at the heart of what makes this emotion more functional than shame in terms of regulating behavior (see Tracy & Robins, 2006). Because guilt is associated with the belief that one's behavior can change, it has a reparative action tendency: it leads people to amend their past mistakes and to adjust their behavior to prevent future missteps (Tangney, 1990; Tangney, Wagner, Hill-Barlow, Marschall, & Gramzow, 1996). Moreover, guilt-proneness is positively associated with perspective-taking and other-oriented empathy because feelings of guilt focus people on their behaviors and how these behaviors affect others (Leith & Baumeister, 1998; Tangney, 1995; Tangney et al., 1996).

In contrast to those experiencing guilt, shamed individuals see their bad actions as stemming from a fixed, immutable feature of their character. This belief leads people to engage in behaviors that minimize their painful feelings of self-reproach (Lindsay-Hartz, Rivera, & Mascolo, 1995), even if these behaviors are unproductive for themselves or their organizations, such as avoiding interpersonal interaction or blaming others for one's own mistakes (Stuewig, Tangney, Heigel, Harty, & McCloskey, 2010; Tangney, 1995; Tangney, Wagner, Fletcher, & Gramzow, 1992; Tracy & Robins, 2006). Moreover, the painful self-focus of shame also disrupts empathic processes because it leads people to focus more on the consequences of their actions for their own character than on the consequences of their actions for others (M. L. Hoffman, 1984; Tangney, 1995).

Distinguishing Authentic and Hubristic Pride

Pride is generally defined as an emotion that is "generated by appraisals that one is responsible for a socially valued outcome or for being a socially valued person" (Mascolo & Fischer, 1995, p. 66). Some regard pride as hubris and as a sin; others see it as virtue and key to personal achievement (Tracy, 2016; Tracy & Robins 2006, 2007b). This discrepancy exists because pride is a multifaceted emotion. The same term, in English, captures pride in the sense of self-aggrandized views or narcissism, and also pride in the sense of authentic feelings of confidence or self-worth, typically about specific achievements or prosocial behavior.

Tracy and Robins (2004, 2007b) theorized that the attributional differences that distinguish guilt from shame may also distinguish these two facets of pride, which they labeled hubristic and authentic pride. Imagine an employee who delivers a great presentation to a client. If this employee attributes the success to mutable behavior (e.g. "I succeeded because I worked hard"), the employee is likely to experience authentic pride. If this same employee attributes the success to a fixed, internal feature of the self (e.g. "I succeeded because I am the best"), the employee is more likely to experience hubristic pride. In support of this, across several correlational and experimental studies, Tracy and Robins (2007b) found that controllability and stability were key attributional dimensions distinguishing the two facets of pride, with controllable, unstable attributions associated with authentic pride, and uncontrollable, stable attributions more associated with hubristic pride.

To illustrate, in one experiment (Tracy & Robins, 2007b, Experiment 4), participants imagined themselves in a variety of pride-eliciting scenarios such as doing very well on an exam. The scenarios differed in the attributional focus for the success event, with some scenarios attributing the event to unstable, controllable causes (e.g. the participant's effort), and other scenarios attributing the event to stable, uncontrollable causes (e.g. the participant's ability). Participants reported that they would feel greater authentic pride in response to the scenarios that involved unstable, controllable attributions for the success event, and greater hubristic pride in response to the scenarios that involved stable, uncontrollable attributions for success event.

Authentic pride and hubristic pride are both associated with an approach orientation (Carver, Sinclair, & Johnson, 2010), but relate to different ways of engaging the social world and pursuing one's goals (Tracy & Robins, 2007b). People who are high in authentic pride are highly motivated to pursue their goals, but they put both their failures and successes in perspective. In contrast, people who are high in hubristic pride tend to have unrealistic goals. They also see any positive outcome as proof of their own greatness (Carver et al, 2010; Tracy & Weidman, 2018). However, this does not mean that people who are high in hubristic pride always see themselves as great. In fact, whereas authentic pride is related positively to both explicit and implicit self-esteem, hubristic pride is negatively related to self-esteem, yet positively to narcissism (Tracy, Cheng, Robins, & Trzesniewski, 2009). Tracy and Robins (2003) have argued that hubristic pride may be part of a defensive self-regulatory strategy used by those with fluctuating, unstable self-esteem. In this view, individuals with unstable or event-contingent self-esteem are chronically motivated to suppress shame and increase pride, as a way of attaining (momentary) high levels of self-esteem. Yet the pride these individuals seek is typically not the authentic variety that promotes more stable self-esteem, but rather a more defensive and artificial hubristic pride, which can provide momentary relief from shame but not promote a stable sense of self-worth (Tracy & Robins, 2003; Tracy, Cheng, Martens, & Robins, 2011). Moreover, authentic pride is associated with a relatively adaptive and socially desirable personality profile, but hubristic pride is not (Tracy & Robins, 2007b; Tracy et al., 2009).

Trait-Based Differences in the Experience of Self-Conscious Emotions

The studies by Niedenthal et al. (1994) and Tracy and Robins (2007b) show that changing the attributions people make for their success or failures can change the emotions people experience in response to the event. However, studies have found that there are reliable individual differences in people's propensity to experience these emotions (see Tangney, 1990; Tangney & Dearing, 2002; Tracy & Robins, 2007b). Faced with the same transgression, some people tend to experience shame, some people tend to experience guilt, some people tend to experience both emotions, and some people tend to experience neither. These general tendencies reflect the extent to which an individual is guilt-prone and shame-prone (Cohen, Wolf, Panter, & Insko, 2011; Tangney, 1990; Tangney & Dearing, 2002; Tangney et al., 1992). Similarly, faced with the same success, some people tend to experience authentic pride, some people tend to experience hubristic pride, some people tend to experience neither emotion, and some people experience both emotions (Tracy & Robins, 2007b).

Self-Conscious Emotions and Positive Employee Outcomes

In the following sections, we overview recent research which has identified how people's experience of guilt, shame, and pride relate to a range of employee outcomes such as prosocial or ethical behavior, leadership, and task effort. We focus on these emotions as predictors of employee behavior rather than on the factors in one's workplace that elicit these emotions. Thus we do not address a range of important topics including what drives people to experience guilt and pride for others' actions (e.g. collective guilt, or collective pride) and the factors that engender specific discrete emotions at work.

Prosocial and Ethical Behavior

Guilt and Shame

Feelings of shame and guilt can lead to opposing effects on moral and ethical behavior (Tangney et al., 2007). Previous research has explored these differences at length (see Cohen & Morse, 2014; Cohen, Panter, & Turan, 2012; Tangney et al., 2007), with two of the main insights being that shame and guilt are not equally moral emotions (Tangney et al., 2007) and that highly guilt-prone people are some of the most moral and cooperative members of society (Cohen & Morse, 2014).

In support of these insights, guilt-proneness (but not shame-proneness) has emerged as one of the most important factors to distinguish individuals of high moral character from those of low moral character (Cohen, Panter, Turan, Morse, & Kim, 2014). Moreover, guilt-proneness (but not shame-proneness) is positively associated with a range of prosocial and ethical behaviors such as lower levels of delinquency in adolescents and recidivism rates among previously incarcerated populations (Tangney et al., 2014; Dearing et al., 2005). In the workplace, guilt-proneness (but not shame-proneness) has been shown to relate positively to organizational citizenship behavior and negatively to counterproductive work behaviors (Cohen et al., 2014). Guilt-proneness also is associated negatively with using unethical behaviors in negotiations (Cohen, 2010).

Authentic Pride and Hubristic Pride

From a theoretical perspective, pride is thought to encourage ethical behavior because people derive self-worth from behaving in ways that meet or exceed moral standards (see Barrett, 1995; Tangney et al., 2007), and, indeed, some research suggests that pride encourages prosocial behavior (see Michie, 2009). However, other research suggests it does not (Mishina, Dykes, Block, & Pollock, 2010). Similar to the distinction between guilt and shame, whether pride promotes or inhibits ethical behavior depends on the specific facet of pride people experience.

Authentic pride is positively associated with volunteering to help and advise others, increased generosity, and the self-control that allows individuals to avoid temptations (Cheng et al., 2010; Dorfman et al., 2014; Hart & Matsuba, 2007; W. Hoffman & Fisher, 2012). Moreover, authentic pride is negatively, and hubristic pride positively, associated with anger and aggression – correlations that may help explain why pride can both enhance and impede prosocial behaviors (Brosi, Spörrle, Welpe, & Shaw, 2016; Tracy et al., 2009).

In one test of this suggestion, Sanders and colleagues (2009) asked participants to reflect on scenarios that evoked either authentic or hubristic pride. Participants then played a dictator game in which they could divide fifty lottery tickets between themselves and a supposed other participant. On average, participants who were induced to feel authentic pride gave more tickets to the supposed other participant than those induced to feel hubristic pride. Other work consistent with this suggestion has found that individuals experimentally induced to feel hubristic pride demonstrate greater prejudice toward those who are different from them (i.e. individuals belonging to a different ethnic group or sexual orientation), whereas individuals induced to feel authentic pride show greater support and empathy toward the same out-group members (Ashton-James & Tracy, 2012).

Task Effort

Guilt and Shame

Distinguishing guilt and shame clarifies the relationship between negative self-conscious emotions and task effort. Feelings of guilt are thought to relate positively to task effort because people who feel guilt often work harder (i.e. put in more effort) as a means of ameliorating the negative, behavior-focused feeling of guilt (Tangney & Dearing, 2002). In support of this relationship, highly guilt-prone employees exert greater effort at their job-related tasks and perform better than their less guilt-prone counterparts – this effect being over and above effects of other established predictors such as the Big Five personality traits (Flynn & Schaumberg, 2012). Shame similarly tells individuals experiencing it that their behavior does not, or will not, meet expectations. However, because shame is associated with avoidance and with the blaming of a negative whole self, rather than specific behaviors, feelings of feelings of shame do not reliably translate into greater effort (see Flynn & Schaumberg, 2012).

Authentic and Hubristic Pride

Although studies examining the effect of pride on task effort and persistence typically have not distinguished between the two facets of pride, from a theoretical stance it makes sense that authentic pride – the facet of the emotion linked to specific, hard-earned achievements, high conscientiousness, and effort attributions (Tracy & Robins, 2007) – would be more positively predictive of task effort than hubristic pride, which is not as associated with traits relevant to effort and responsibility. Consistent with this suggestion, one study found that individuals dispositionally high in authentic pride showed high levels of achievement at a creativity task, whereas those dispostionally high in hubristic pride performed poorly at this task (Damian & Robins, 2012). Similarly, Herrald and Tomaka (2002) showed positive effects of pride on the quality of participants' responses to a series of interview questions. Similarly, Williams and Desteno (2008) found that participants induced to experience pride in one task exerted greater effort on a subsequent tedious task, compared to participants not induced to experience pride. In these latter two studies, the researchers did not separately measure authentic versus hubristic pride, but several of the items they used to assess pride (e.g. "satisfied with their performance") suggest that participants were probably experiencing the authentic variety.

Another possibility, however, is that even authentic pride can be negatively associated with task effort – if this relation emerges because low levels of authentic pride are experienced in response to poor performance. In such cases, low authentic pride may serve an informational function, telling the experiencer that his or her behavior must change in order to improve performance and attain higher desired levels of pride. In line with this suggestion, Weidman and colleagues (2016) observed that students who did poorly on a class exam and felt low authentic pride about their poor performance responded by studying harder for their next exam, and consequently did better on this later exam. In a series of longitudinal studies, these authors were able to directly trace participants' low levels of authentic pride to improved exam performance over the course of the term. Similarly, Becker and Curhan (2018) proposed that pride may engender complacency; people infer from their feelings of pride that they are accomplished in a domain, and thus subsequently exert less effort – and, as a result, perform less well in that same domain. They tested this idea in the context of sequential negotiations. The authors found that negotiators' feelings of pride for their performance in the first negotiation related negatively to their objective performance in the second negotiation.

Leadership Emergence and Leadership Effectiveness

Who ends up in leadership roles and how do they perform in these roles? The first question concerns leadership emergence. Research on emergent leadership is generally conducted in the context of small, leaderless groups of equal-status peers and is focused on identifying who ends up leading the group and why that individual ends up in the leadership position (Bales, 1950; deSouza & Klein, 1995). The second question is about leadership effectiveness, and is often concerned with the characteristics, styles, and situational factors that make people more or less successful in their leadership positions (Hogan, Curphy, & Hogan, 1994; van Knippenberg & Hogg, 2003). Self-conscious emotions are associated with perceived and actual achievement and status (e.g. Tracy & Matsumoto, 2008) and with the socioemotional and task-initiating behaviors that people exhibit in groups. Consequently, self-conscious emotions are relevant to both leadership emergence and leadership effectiveness.

Guilt and Shame

Guilt and shame show different relationships and with leadership emergence, which can be attributed, at least in part, to these emotions' different action orientations. Guilt is associated with an approach orientation, whereas shame is associated with an avoidance orientation. People who are prone to guilt take action to try to make situations better, but people who are prone to shame do not. Schaumberg & Flynn (2012) reasoned that with their strong sense of duty and responsibility for others as well as their strong action orientation, highly guilt-prone people would be more likely than less guilt-prone people to emerge as leaders. To test this prediction, they had groups engage in two leaderless group tasks and then rate the emergent leadership behaviors of each group member (e.g. the extent to which he or she assumed a leadership role and influenced the group's decisions). Guilt-proneness was positively associated with emergent leadership. This was not the case for shame-proneness, which showed a negative albeit weak overall relationship with leadership emergence. Schaumberg and Flynn (2012) found similar patterns of results when they assessed leadership effectiveness. Young managers were assessed by their colleagues, clients, and supervisors on their leadership ability. Guilt-proneness related positively to these leadership effectiveness ratings, but shame-proneness did not.

The positive relationship between guilt-proneness and leadership emergence and effectiveness probably emerges because highly guilt-prone people feel a greater responsibility for others compared to less guilt-prone people (Levine, Bitterly, Schweitzer, & Cohen, 2018; Schaumberg & Flynn, 2012), which leads highly guilt-prone people to be more trustworthy than less guilt-prone people (Cohen et al., 2011; Levine et al., 2018). That said, the relationship between guilt-proneness and leadership effectiveness may not be axiomatic. Leaders are tasked with making tough decisions, in which no matter what they do some constituent may be harmed. In these instances, in which people face competing standards of expected behavior, it is not clear how highly guilt-prone people (or highly shame-prone people, for that matter) will respond and whether their decisions are always the best.

Authentic and Hubristic Pride

There is strong evidence to suggest that both authentic and hubristic pride may promote leadership emergence, but through different routes; in fact, some have argued that pride evolved in humans to facilitate the fundamental need of social rank attainment (Cheng, Tracy, Foulsham, Kingstone, & Henrich, 2013; Henrich & Gil-White, 2001; Tracy, 2016; Tracy, Shariff, & Cheng, 2010). Hubristic pride may facilitate leadership emergence via dominance by motivating individuals to behave in an aggressive and intimidating manner, and providing them with a sense of grandiosity and entitlement that allows them to take power rather than earn it and to feel little empathy for those who get in their way (Ashton-James & Tracy, 2012; Tracy et al., 2009). In contrast, authentic pride may facilitate the attainment of prestige by motivating and reinforcing achievements and other indicators of competence, and providing individuals with feelings of genuine self-confidence that allow them to demonstrate social attractiveness and generosity (see Tracy, 2016). In support of this account, one study found that undergraduate varsity athletic team members who were prone to authentic pride tended to be judged by their teammates as highly prestigious, whereas team members who were prone to hubristic pride tended to be judged by their teammates as dominant (Cheng et al., 2010).

Whether or under which circumstances authentic pride and hubristic pride relate to leadership effectiveness remains a more open question. On average, leaders tend to be more effective when they exert their power in more subtle ways, taking care to affirm the autonomy and self-worth of their subordinates (Yukl, 1989). In contrast, leaders engender resistance from subordinates when they display power in a more arrogant, manipulative, or domineering manner (Yukl, 1989). This suggests that authentic pride – with its positive relationship to prestige – would facilitate leadership effectiveness, whereas hubristic pride – with its positive relationship to dominance – would impair it. That said, the relationship between each facet of pride and leadership effectiveness may depend on situational demands. Contingency models of leadership suggest that leadership styles linked to specific contextual demands result in better performance outcomes. When the situation demands an autocratic leadership style, hubristic pride may be a positive leadership characteristic. In contrast, when the situation demands a more participatory or consultive leadership style, authentic pride may be a more valuable leadership characteristic (e.g. Vroom and Yetton, 1973).

Conclusion

The question of whether guilt, shame, and pride can translate to productive work has long intrigued management scholars (e.g. Adams, 1965; Walster et al., 1978). By synthesizing social psychological and organizational behavior research on self-conscious emotions, we can see clearly that these emotions can motivate people to work hard, to behave well, and to take charge, but these behaviors depend on the specific self-conscious emotion people experience – with guilt and authentic pride being more positive drivers of these outcomes than shame and hubristic pride. This suggests that it may not be the valence of the self-conscious emotion, but rather the attribution people make for their own behaviors that give rise to these emotions, that is the most important factor for facilitating positive employee outcomes.

References

Adams, J. S. (1965). Inequity in social exchange. In L. Berkowitz (Ed.), *Advances in experimental social psychology* (pp. 267–297). New York, NY: Academic.

Ashton-James, C. E., & Tracy, J. L. (2012). Pride and prejudice: How feelings about the self influence judgments of others. *Personality and Social Psychology Bulletin*, *38*(4), 466–476.

Bales, R. F. (1950). *Interaction process analysis: A method for the study of small groups*. Cambridge, MA: Addison–Wesley.

Barrett, C. K. (1995). A functionalist approach to shame and guilt. In J. P. Tangney & K. W. Fischer (Eds.), *Self-conscious emotions: The psychology of shame, guilt, embarrassment, and pride* (pp. 25–63). New York, NY: Guilford.

Becker, W. J., & Curhan, J. R. (2018). The dark side of subjective value in sequential negotiations: The mediating role of pride and anger. *Journal of Applied Psychology*, *103*(1), 74–87.

Brockner, J., Davy, J., & Carter, C. (1985). Layoffs, self-esteem, and survivor guilt: Motivational, affective, and attitudinal consequences. *Organizational Behavior and Human Decision Processes*, *36*(2), 229–244.

Brosi, P., Spörrle, M., Welpe, I. M., & Shaw, J. D. (2016). Two facets of pride and helping. *Journal of Managerial Psychology*, *31*(5), 976–988.

Carver, C. S., Sinclair, S., & Johnson, S. L. (2010). Authentic and hubristic pride: Differential relations to aspects of goal regulation, affect, and self-control. *Journal of Research in Personality*, *44* (6), 698–703.

Cheng, J. T., Tracy, J. L., Foulsham, T., Kingstone, A., & Henrich, J. (2013). Two ways to the top: Evidence that dominance and prestige are distinct yet viable avenues to social rank and influence. *Journal of Personality and Social Psychology*, *104*, 103–125.

Cheng, J. T., Tracy, J. L., & Henrich, J. (2010). Pride, personality, and the evolutionary foundations of human social status. *Evolution and Human Behavior*, *31*(5), 334–347.

Cohen, T. R. (2010). Moral emotions and unethical bargaining: The differential effects of empathy and perspective taking in deterring deceitful negotiation. *Journal of Business Ethics*, *94*(4), 569–579.

Cohen, T. R., & Morse, L. (2014). Moral character: What it is and what it does. In A. P. Brief & B. M. Staw (Eds.), *Research in organizational behavior* (Volume 34, pp. 43–61). Greenwich, CT: Elsevier.

Cohen, T. R., Panter, A. T., & Turan, N. (2012). Guilt-proneness and moral character. *Current Directions in Psychological Science*, *21*(5), 355–359.

Cohen, T. R., Panter, A. T., Turan, N., Morse, L., & Kim, Y. (2014). Moral character in the workplace. *Journal of Personality and Social Psychology*, *107* (5), 943–963.

Cohen, T. R., Wolf, S. T., Panter, A. T., & Insko, C. A. (2011). Introducing the GASP scale: A new measure of guilt and shame-proneness. *Journal of Personality and Social Psychology*, *100*(5), 947–966.

Damian, R. I., & Robins, R. W. (2012). The link between dispositional pride and creative thinking depends on current mood. *Journal of Research in Personality*, *46*, 765–769.

Dearing, R. L., Stuewig, J., & Tangney, J. P. (2005). On the importance of distinguishing shame from guilt: Relations to problematic alcohol and drug use. *Addictive Behavior*, *30*(7), 1392–1404.

de Souza, G., & Klein, H. J. (1995). Emergent leadership in the group goal-setting process. *Small Group Research*, *26*, 475–496.

Dorfman, A., Eyal, T., & Bereby-Meyer, Y. (2014). Proud to cooperate: The consideration of pride promotes cooperation in a social dilemma. *Journal of Experimental Social Psychology*, *55*, 105–109.

Douglas Creed, W. E., Hudson, B. A., Okhuysen, G. A., & Smith-Crowe, K. (2014). Swimming in a sea of shame: Incorporating emotion into explanations of institutional reproduction and change. *Academy of Management Review*, *39*(3), 275–301.

Flynn, F. J., & Schaumberg, R. L. (2012). When feeling bad leads to feeling good: Guilt-proneness and affective organizational commitment. *Journal of Applied Psychology*, *97*(1), 124–133.

Hart, D., & Matsuba, M. K. (2007). The development of pride and moral life. In J. L. Tracy, R. W. Robins, & J. P. Tangney (Eds.), *The self-conscious emotions: Theory and research* (pp. 114–133). New York, NY: Guilford.

Henrich, J., & Gil-White, F. J. (2001). The evolution of prestige: Freely conferred deference as a mechanism for enhancing the benefits of cultural transmission. *Evolution and Human Behavior*, *22* (3), 165–196.

Herrald, M. M., & Tomaka, J. (2002). Patterns of emotion-specific appraisal, coping, and cardiovascular reactivity during an ongoing emotional episode. *Journal of Personality and Social Psychology*, *83*(2), 434–450.

Hoffman, M. L. (1984). Interaction of affect and cognition in empathy. In C. Izard, J. Kagan, & R. Zajonc (Eds.), *Emotion, cognition, and behavior* (pp. 103–131). Cambridge, UK: Cambridge University Press.

Hofmann, W., & Fisher, R. R. (2012). How guilt and pride shape subsequent self-control. *Social Psychological and Personality Science*, *3*(6), 682–690.

Hogan, R., Curphy, G. L., & Hogan, J. (1994). What we know about leadership: Effectiveness and personality. *American Psychologist*, *49*, 493–504.

Leith, K. P., & Baumeister, R. F. (1998). Empathy, shame, guilt, and narratives of interpersonal conflicts: Guilt-prone people are better at perspective taking. *Journal of Personality*, *66*(1), 1–37.

Levine, E. E., Bitterly, T. B., Cohen, T. R., & Schweitzer, M. E. (2018). Who is trustworthy? Predicting trustworthy intentions and behavior. *Journal of Personality and Social Psychology*, *115* (3), 468–494.

Lewis, H. B. (1971). *Shame and guilt in neurosis*. New York, NY: International Universities.

Lindsay-Hartz, J., de Rivera, J., & Mascolo, M. F. (1995). Differentiating guilt and shame and their effects on motivation. In J. P. Tangney & K. W. Fischer (Eds.), *Self-conscious emotions: The psychology of shame, guilt, embarrassment, and pride* (pp. 274–300). New York, NY: Guilford.

Mascolo, M. F., & Fischer, K. W. (1995). Developmental transformations in appraisals for pride, shame, and guilt. In J. P. Tangney & K. W. Fischer (Eds.), *Self-conscious emotions: The psychology of shame, guilt, embarrassment, and pride* (pp. 64–113). New York, NY: Guilford.

Michie, S. (2009). Pride and gratitude: How positive emotions influence the prosocial behaviors of organizational leaders. *Journal of Leadership and Organizational Studies*, *154*(4), 393–403.

Mishina, Y., Dykes, B. J., Block, E. S., & Pollock, T. G. (2010). Why "good" firms do bad things: The effects of high aspirations, high expectations, and prominence on the incidence of corporate illegality. *Academy of Management Journal*, *53*(4), 701–722.

Niedenthal, P. M., Tangney, J. P., & Gavanski, I. (1994). "If only I weren't" versus "If only I hadn't": Distinguishing shame and guilt in counterfactual thinking. *Journal of Personality and Social Psychology*, *67*(4), 585–595.

Schaumberg, R. L., & Flynn, F. J. (2012). Uneasy lies the head that wears the crown: the link between guilt-proneness and leadership. *Journal of Personality and Social Psychology*, *103*(2), 327–342.

Shariff, A. F., & Tracy, J. L. (2009). Knowing who's boss: Implicit perceptions of status from the nonverbal expression of pride. *Emotion*, *9*(5), 631–639.

Shariff, A. F., Tracy, J. L., & Markusoff, J. (2012). (Implicitly) judging a book by its cover: The automatic inference of status from pride and shame expressions. *Personality and Social Psychology Bulletin*, *38*(9), 1178–1193.

Stuewig, J., Tangney, J. P., Heigel, C., Harty, L., & McCloskey, L. (2010). Shaming, blaming, and maiming: Functional links among the moral emotions, externalization of blame, and aggression. *Journal of Research in Personality*, *44*(1), 91–102.

Tangney, J. P. (1990). Assessing individual differences in proneness to shame and guilt: development of the Self-Conscious Affect and Attribution Inventory. *Journal of Personality and Social Psychology*, *59* (1), 102–111.

Tangney, J. P. (1995). Shame and guilt in interpersonal relationships. In J. P. Tangney & K. W. Fischer (Eds.), *Self-conscious emotions: The psychology of shame, guilt, embarrassment, and pride* (pp. 114–139). New York, NY: Guilford.

Tangney, J. P., & Dearing, R. (2002). *Shame and guilt*. New York, NY: Guilford.

Tangney, J. P., & Fischer, K. W. (Eds.) (1995). *Self-conscious emotions: The psychology of shame, guilt, embarrassment, and pride*. New York, NY: Guilford.

Tangney, J. P., Stuewig, J., & Martinez, A. G. (2014). Two faces of shame: The roles of shame and guilt in predicting recidivism. *Psychological Science*, *25* (3), 799–805.

Tangney, J. P., Stuewig, J., & Mashek, D. J. (2007). Moral emotions and moral behavior. *Annual Review of Psychology*, *58*, 345–372.

Tangney, J. P., & Tracy, J. (2012). Self-conscious emotions. In M. Leary & J. P. Tangney (Eds.), *Handbook of self and identity* (2nd edition, pp. 446–478). New York, NY: Guilford.

Tangney, J. P., Wagner, P., Fletcher, C., & Gramzow, R. (1992). Shamed into anger? The relation of shame and guilt to anger and self-reported aggression. *Journal of Personality and Social Psychology*, *62* (4), 669–675.

Tangney, J. P., Wagner, P. E., Hill-Barlow, D., Marschall, D. E., & Gramzow, R. (1996). Relation of shame and guilt to constructive versus destructive responses to anger across the lifespan. *Journal of Personality and Social Psychology*, *70* (4), 797–809.

Tracy, J. (2016). *Take pride: Why the deadliest sin holds the secret to human success*. Boston, MA: Houghton Mifflin Harcourt.

Tracy, J. L., Cheng, J. T., Martens, J. P., & Robins, R. W. (2011). The affective core of narcissism: Inflated by pride, deflated by shame. In W. K. Campbell & J. Miller (Eds.), *Handbook of narcissism and narcissistic personality disorder* (pp. 330–343). New York, NY: Wiley.

Tracy, J. L., Cheng, J. T., Robins, R. W., & Trzesniewski, K. H. (2009). Authentic and hubristic pride: The affective core of self-esteem and narcissism. *Self and Identity*, *8*(2–3), 196–213.

Tracy, J. L., & Matsumoto, D. (2008). The spontaneous display of pride and shame: Evidence for biologically innate nonverbal displays. *Proceedings of the National Academy of Sciences*, *105*(33), 11655–11660.

Tracy, J. L., & Robins, R. W. (2003). "Death of a (narcissistic) salesman": An integrative model of fragile self-esteem. *Psychological Inquiry*, *14*, 57–62.

Tracy, J. L., & Robins, R. W. (2004). Show your pride: Evidence for a discrete emotion expression. *Psychological Science*, *15*(3), 194–197.

Tracy, J. L., & Robins, R. W. (2006). Appraisal antecedents of shame and guilt: Support for a theoretical model. *Personality and Social Psychology Bulletin, 32*(10), 1339–1351.

Tracy, J. L., & Robins, R. W. (2007a). The self in self-conscious emotions: A cognitive appraisal approach. In J. L. Tracy, R. W. Robins, & J. P. Tangney (Eds.), *The self-conscious emotions: Theory and research* (pp. 3–20). New York, NY: Guilford.

Tracy, J. L., & Robins, R. W. (2007b). The psychological structure of pride: A tale of two facets. *Journal of Personality and Social Psychology, 92*(3), 506–525.

Tracy, J. L., Robins, R. W., & Tangney, J. P. (Eds.) (2007). *The self-conscious emotions: Theory and research*. New York, NY: Guilford.

Tracy, J. L., Shariff, A. F., & Cheng, J. T. (2010). A naturalist's view of pride. *Emotion Review, 2*(2), 163–177.

Tracy, J. L., Shariff, A. F., Zhao, W., & Henrich, J. (2013). Cross-cultural evidence that the pride expression is a universal automatic status signal. *Journal of Experimental Psychology: General, 142*(1), 163–180.

Tracy, J. L., & Weidman, A. C. (2018). Pride. In A. Scarantino (Ed.), *Routledge handbook of emotion theory*. London, UK: Routledge.

van Knippenberg, D., & Hogg, M. A. (2003). A social identity model of leadership effectiveness in organizations. *Research in Organizational Behavior, 25*, 243–295.

Walster, E. H., Walster, G. W., & Berscheid, A. W. (1978). *Equity: Theory and research*. Boston, MA: Allyn and Bacon.

Weidman, A., Tracy, J. L., & Elliot, A. J. (2016). The benefits of following your pride: Authentic pride promotes achievement. *Journal of Personality, 84* (5), 607–622.

Williams, L. A., & DeSteno, D. (2008). Pride and perseverance: The motivational role of pride. *Journal of Personality and Social Psychology, 94* (6), 1007–1017.

Yukl, G. (1989). Managerial leadership: A review of theory and research. *Journal of Management, 15*(2), 251–289.

32 Happiness in Its Many Forms

Peter Warr

Happiness is a core affect – a "neurophysiological state consciously accessible as the simplest raw (non-reflective) feelings evident in moods and emotions," which is "primitive, universal, and simple, irreducible on the mental plane" (Russell, 2003, p. 148). The label "happiness" is not always applied, and the construct has otherwise been investigated in terms of enjoyment, pleasure, excitement, enthusiasm, comfort, relaxation, and many other positive feelings.

Happiness and unhappiness are central to our existence. Their dependence on personal desires and motives means that in some form they underpin almost every thought and action, and surveys across the world have found that happiness is widely considered to be the most important aspect of life. Similarly, happiness is at the heart of psychology. Many psychological themes – as in attitudes, habits, motivation, reinforcement, personality traits, values, preferences, and prejudices – reflect happiness-related feelings in one form or another, although academic and other presentations may not mention happiness at all. Instead the explicit references are to enjoyment, desire, satisfaction, preference, wants, needs, and interests, or to distress, anxiety, depression, and despair – all aspects of happiness and unhappiness.

This chapter will briefly summarize principal aspects of the construct and its personal contributors, drawing particularly on research in work situations. Many writers have used "well-being" as synonymous with happiness, and the two words have often been treated by psychologists as interchangeable. However, well-being is a wider construct, extending beyond the thoughts and feelings of happiness to additionally cover positive states that can be physical, social, or financial. Happiness is therefore better viewed more narrowly as *subjective* or *psychological* well-being (e.g. Diener, Suh, Lucas, & Smith, 1999), and most occupational researchers into "well-being" have in fact addressed aspects that are psychological rather than physical, social, or financial. Workers' well-being in that narrower sense has often been investigated.

Varieties of Happiness

We should distinguish broadly between happiness themes that are "hedonic" and those concerned with "flourishing." The term "hedonic" derives from the Greek word for pleasure (*hēdon*), and a hedonic perspective on happiness is in terms of experienced pleasure and pain, such that happy people experience relatively more positive feelings than negative ones. "Flourishing" happiness, a concept developed from writings about *eudaimonia* by Aristotle (384–322 BC) and other ancient Greek philosophers, is more concerned with the development of individual potential and personal growth; see, for example, Ryff and Singer, 2008; Seligman, 2002; Warr, 2019; Waterman, 2008. This chapter will focus on hedonic happiness

People are happy "with" or happy "about" something – an object, idea, person, group, or themselves. And the objects of happiness can be at different levels of scope, described here in terms of three levels expanding from "feature-specific" happiness, through "domain-specific" happiness, to "global" or context-free happiness. *Feature-specific* happiness or unhappiness is experienced through targeted likes or dislikes – positive or negative feelings about a particular thing, idea, person, or activity. In job settings, feature-specific happiness has been examined through feelings about particular job attributes such as pay level or opportunity for personal discretion. More broadly, with a medium-range focus that extends beyond single features, *domain-specific* happiness or unhappiness is concerned with experiences in a particular segment of life – about sets of things, ideas, people, activities, and so on. Here, we might examine feelings about a particular domain, for example through happiness that is specifically job-related or health-related, or in terms of feelings about a particular set of people or ideas. Third, the broadest form (*global happiness*) covers feelings about one's life in general, perhaps measured through evaluations of one's life as a whole. These different levels of happiness scope are intercorrelated, but different features contribute in different ways to each one. For instance, a supportive boss and reasonable career prospects are particularly important for psychological well-being in the job domain (see e.g. Warr, 2007).

Hedonic happiness can thus be measured through positive feelings about targets of a particular scope. However, in addition to their positive or negative valence, affects also vary in their activation or arousal – a person's "state of readiness for action or energy expenditure" (Russell, 2003, p. 156). We should thus also distinguish between levels of activation. *Joyful* happiness is activated as well as positive, whereas *relaxed* happiness is also positive but with low activation.

Studies of happiness can be directed at time periods of any length, from "this very minute," through "this afternoon," "this week," "this month," extending to "my life as a whole" – as framed by the wording of instructions to research participants. In addition, an across-time perspective has asked about "me as a person," through a dispositional indicator which is often referred to as "trait happiness" in contrast to more short-term forms of "state happiness."

Happiness and unhappiness are sometimes mixed together in feelings which overall are ambivalent – mixing positive and negative, as people feel both happy and unhappy with different aspects of their situation. Ambivalence can also occur sequentially across time, when progress in personal projects requires working through obstacles or struggling with limited resources before success is achieved; in those cases, you have to feel unhappy before you can feel happy (e.g. Hershfield, Scheibe, Sims, & Carstensen, 2013). That is often the case in work settings.

Valence and Activation

In studying hedonic happiness through measures of affect, an established perspective is in terms of the circumplex shown in Figure 32.1. Based on investigations by, for instance, Remington, Fabrigar, and Visser (2000), Russell (1980, 2003), and Yik, Russell, and Steiger (2011), the circumplex treats experiences not only in terms of valence but also through low-to-high activation. The positive affects in happiness lie to the right of Figure 32.1; they vary in activation and are rarely labeled as "happiness." Affects in terms of those two axes are shown around the outside of the figure, and summary labels for each quadrant's content are labeled as anxiety (activated negative affect), enthusiasm (activated positive affect), depression (low-activation negative affect), and comfort (low-activation positive affect). As used here, the two negative labels are shorthand descriptors for unhappiness-related sets of feelings; they do not denote the entirety of clinical disorders identified as "anxiety" and "depression."[1]

[1] Self-report questionnaires to record job-related feelings in these four quadrants have been published by Burke, Brief, George, Roberson, and Webster (1989), Van Katwyk, Fox, Spector, and Kelloway (2000), Warr (1990), and Warr, Bindl, Parker, and Inceoglu (2011).

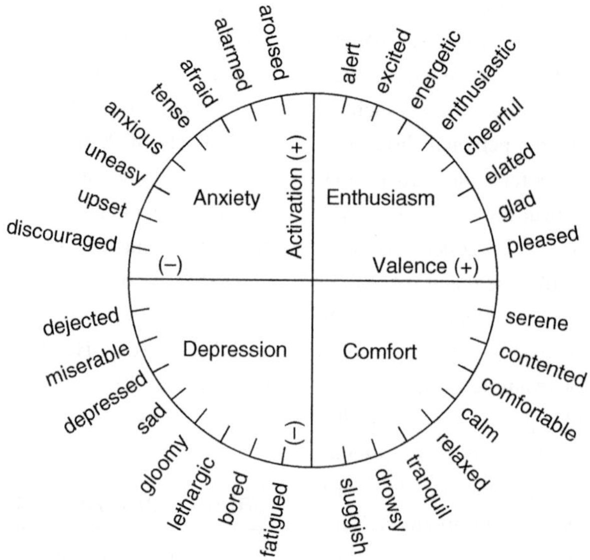

Figure 32.1 Affective well-being in terms of positive or negative tone and high or low activation
Note: the quadrant labels "Anxiety" and "Depression" refer here only to negative feelings and not to clinical disorders.

Studies have often been imprecise about the location of studied feelings in terms of the circumplex shown in Figure 32.1. For example, research into happiness as "positive affect" might be expected to cover all feelings on the right-hand side of the figure, involving both low and high activation. However, that has rarely been the case, in part because many investigations have been based on the Positive and Negative Affect Schedule (PANAS) (Watson, Clark, & Tellegen, 1988). This contains 20 items in two scales, all of which are activated – enthusiastic, excited, distressed, jittery and so on. PANAS-based conclusions about positive or negative affect are therefore narrowly restricted to happiness or unhappiness that is more activated.

Valence and activation have typically been studied on their own, and each is known to be individually important. For instance, positively-valenced variables more strongly predict job performance (Fisher, 2002; Zelenski, Murphy, & Jenkins, 2008), and are less correlated than negative ones with distress symptoms and trait neuroticism (e.g. Thoresen, Kaplan, Barsky, Warren, & de Chermont, 2003; Watson, Wiese, Vaidya, & Tellegen, 1999). In respect of a feeling's activation – its readiness for action or energy expenditure (e.g. Remington et al., 2000; Russell, 1980, 2003) – high-activation positive affect is associated with work performance more strongly than is low-activation positive affect (Baas, De Dreu, & Nijstad, 2008; Warr et al., 2014); and activated well-being in the form of "job engagement" is linked more strongly with both performance and job crafting than is the less activated "job satisfaction" (Christian, Garza, & Slaughter, 2011; Hakanen, Peeters, & Schaufeli, 2018). Job satisfaction (which reflects low-activation satiation) and job engagement (with greater activation) yield contrasting associations with person–job fit in line with their differing level of activation (Warr & Inceoglu, 2012).

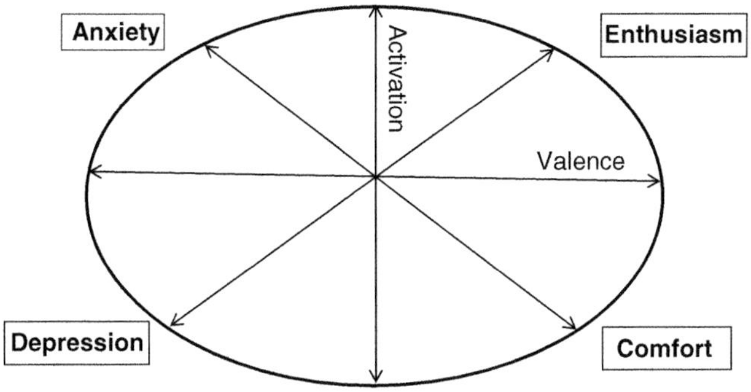

Figure 32.2 Diagonal dimensions in the measurement of affective well-being: depression to enthusiasm and anxiety to comfort

Bringing together valence and activation in a single perspective, Figure 32.2 draws attention to associated diagonal axes of feeling from depression to enthusiasm and from anxiety to comfort. Research outside occupational settings has identified these as statistically primary, biologically fundamental, and essential to self-regulation. They "represent the major dimensions of emotional experience" (Watson & Tellegen, 1985, p. 234), and "reflect the operation of two broad evolutionarily adaptive motivational systems that mediate goal-directed approach and withdrawal behaviors" (Watson et al., 1999, pp. 829–830).

Happiness feelings from depression to enthusiasm in Figure 32.2 thus reflect approach-related happiness, and the avoidance axis is in terms of affects ranging from anxiety to comfort. The primary function of the approach system – identified by Gray (e.g. 1971, 1987) as the "Behavioral Activation System" – is to direct organisms to settings and conditions which may yield feelings of pleasure. The avoidance/withdrawal system (termed by Gray the "Behavioral Inhibition System") helps organisms to avoid or get out of unpleasant situations. There is considerable evidence that throughout evolution a primary survival need to avoid or to escape from personal threats has led to the special importance of the avoidance axis, so that, in terms used by Baumeister, Bratslavsky, Finkenauer, and Vohs (2001), "bad is stronger than good" in its impact on cognitions, feelings, and behaviors (e.g. Rozin & Royzman, 2001). In addition to frequent confirmation of statistical separation, the two primary dimensions – diagonal in Figure 32.2 – have been found to be neurophysiologically distinct, for example in terms of hemispheric asymmetry in the prefrontal cortex and in their contrasting diurnal rhythm (e.g. Watson et al., 1999).

Cognitive–Affective Compounds

The chapter has so far examined happiness and unhappiness in terms of affect, but those affects have also been studied through multi-item scales of, for instance, job satisfaction, job engagement, life satisfaction, burnout, and strain. Such scales record cognitive–affective compounds in terms of thoughts, recollections, interpretations, and comparisons in conjunction with the affects illustrated above. For instance, the established Satisfaction with Life scale contains items such as "In most ways my life is close to my ideal" and "If I could live my life over, I would change almost nothing" (Diener, Emmons, Larsen, & Griffin, 1985; Pavot & Diener, 2008). And the Utrecht Work Engagement Scale includes "At my work, I feel bursting with energy" and "To me, my job is challenging" (e.g. Schaufeli, Bakker, & Salanova, 2006). As with studies of affects alone, discussed in the previous section, the label "happiness" may not be used in multi-item scales, although happiness is central to the measured variable.

A compound form which has received considerable research attention is job satisfaction. That form of happiness has been measured in two ways, either by asking about a person's job as a whole or focusing on feature-specific satisfactions with, for instance, one's pay or one's colleagues. For example, scales of overall job satisfaction have asked for responses to broad statements such as "Most days I am enthusiastic about my work" and "I find real enjoyment in my work" (Brayfield & Rothe, 1951) or requested overall ratings of, for instance, "worthwhile" and "ideal" (Ironson, Smith, Brannick, Gibson, & Paul, 1989).

Items in compound scales of job satisfaction can sometimes extend beyond the meaning of satisfaction itself. That term derives from the Latin *satis*, meaning "enough," which signals a relatively passive acceptance that something is adequate – "satisfactory" rather than "outstanding." Being "satisfied with" something is a low-activation response, and should be studied in low-activation terms rather than through more activated happiness in terms of enthusiasm, involvement, feelings of self-worth, and so on.

What about the location of compound measures of happiness within Figures 32.1 and 32.2? Research has rarely considered compound indicators of happiness in terms of the circumplex of affective valence and activation. However, studies in job settings have drawn attention to conceptual overlaps between the affect quadrant here labeled as enthusiasm and scales of work engagement, between the comfort quadrant and scales of job satisfaction, between depression and job burnout, and (perhaps) between anxiety and workaholism (Bakker & Oerlemans, 2011; Hakanen et al., 2018). There is clearly scope to extend valence-and-activation thinking to other compound forms of happiness and unhappiness.

Individual Differences in the Experience of Happiness

Experienced happiness has been shown to covary with several personal characteristics and mental processes. These will first be illustrated here in terms of longer-term, distal sources, and then more proximal influences will be considered through forms of emotion regulation.

Longer-Term Personal Sources of Happiness

Inheritance

There is no doubt from studies of twins that happiness is partly inherited. Twins from a single fertilized egg ("monozygotic" twins) are genetically almost identical, but dizygotic/non-identical twins (from two eggs) share about 50 percent of genes – just like other pairs of siblings. By comparing pairs of each kind of twin reared together against those reared apart (and thus with varied environments), researchers have estimated the relative contribution of genetic and environmental factors. Their studies have indicated that between 35 percent and 50 percent of happiness differences are determined by inheritance (e.g. Bartels, 2015; Weiss, Bates, & Luciano, 2008).

Age

Age has often been found to be associated with happiness – in a U-shaped rather than a straight-line pattern. Between the age of around 20 and the decade between 40 to 50 progressively lower hedonic happiness (both global and job-specific) occurs in comparisons between different age-groups, but after the middle years that between-group trend is reversed so that average group scores become steadily higher until they level off at about 70 (e.g. Steptoe, Deaton, & Stone, 2015). In occupational studies, this non-linear pattern has been shown for job satisfaction (e.g. Clark, Oswald, & Warr, 1996) and for job stress (e.g. Birdi, Warr, & Oswald, 1995).

Gender

On average, men and women report similar levels of positive affect, but studies have frequently shown that women are more likely than men to be upset about their situation or themselves. They tend to experience more negative affect, and focus more on troublesome aspects of themselves and their world (e.g. Nolen-Hoeksema & Rusting, 1999; Rosenfield & Mouzon, 2013).

Personality

Happiness levels are also linked to some aspects of continuing personality. For example, a broad personal tendency to view the world in negative versus positive terms has been found to be associated with context-free anxiety, depression, and low global happiness, both at a single time and across several years. Among employee samples, this association with general affective disposition has been reported for several indicators of job satisfaction (e.g. Eschleman & Bowling, 2011; Judge & Hulin, 1993).

Several traits of personality are linked to a person's affective outlook and typical level of happiness. In particular, high scorers on trait neuroticism (with recurrent feelings of anxiety and depression) are less likely than low scorers to be happy. Not surprisingly, conceptual overlap between items to measure neuroticism and unhappiness boosts this statistical overlap (e.g. Steel, Schmidt, & Schultz, 2008), but nevertheless people identified as more neurotic in personality terms are generally likely to be less happy than others.

Significant but less strong associations have also been reported between happiness and the personality traits of extraversion and conscientiousness (e.g. Lucas & Diener, 2015; Steel, et al., 2008) and that of dispositional optimism (Carver, Scheier, & Segerstrom, 2010). In addition, trait proactivity (making suggestions, showing initiative, etc.) has been shown to be associated with life satisfaction and general happiness (e.g. Tornau & Frese, 2013), and several associations between job well-being and personality traits have been found in meta-analytic reviews by Judge, Heller, and Mount (2002) and Young, Glerum, Wang, and Joseph (2018).

Value Priorities

Additionally important for experienced happiness are people's values – their likes and dislikes about current or possible situations, activities, things, or people. Sometimes described as "conceptions of the desirable," values contribute to our feelings by influencing the priority and content of thoughts and actions. They make us more sensitive or less sensitive to different stimuli, encourage entry into different situations, and modify the allocation of effort. In some cases, values are within moral, religious, or social codes, but they often represent individual preferences – what a person prefers, seeks, and so on. They range from short-term preferences, which can vary from time to time, to longer-term orientations, perhaps within a personality trait.

Each person finds some role activities more attractive than others, valuing those more positively, and particular activities can be valued in different ways by different people or by the same person at different times. Furthermore, if something matters to you its presence or absence more strongly determines your feelings. A great deal of research has confirmed that associations between a job feature and happiness are stronger for people who more value that feature (e.g. Loher, Noe, Moeller, & Fitzgerald, 1985; Warr & Inceoglu, 2015). As a result, different people (with different values) can sometimes feel differently happy about the same environmental feature – its presence or absence matters more when it is more strongly valued.

Degree of Adaptation

Happiness also depends on a person's degree of adaptation, as feelings in response to a constant or repeated stimulus gradually become less pronounced. In Frijda's (1988) terms, "continued pleasures wear off; continued hardships lose their poignancy" (p. 353). Adaptation can occur in simple cases within minutes, but in many cases of happiness or unhappiness changes can extend across several months.

For example, a review of 313 longitudinal samples (Luhmann, Hofmann, Eid, & Lucas, 2012) illustrated positive or negative changes in happiness after marriage, divorce, bereavement, childbirth, unemployment, re-employment, and retirement, but also demonstrated a clear impact of adaptation. Although the studied events were initially harmful or beneficial as expected (for instance, a clear "honeymoon effect" was seen after marriage), happiness was found to stabilize in the following months or years and sometimes to shift back toward previous levels.

Happiness adaptation is also important in job settings. Organizational changes to improve job satisfaction in two different studies had an initially positive impact, but average job satisfaction was found to return to its original level after two or three years (Griffin, 1988, 1991). Similarly, job satisfaction was shown to increase immediately after self-chosen moves into a new position, but it declined significantly in subsequent years it as managers became adapted to their new role (Boswell, Boudreau, & Tichy, 2005). Findings of this kind have suggested the presence of a personal set-point of happiness to which people return after a period of unusual stimulation – an "equilibrium state" (Headey & Wearing, 1992) or more likely an equilibrium *range* of happiness or unhappiness (e.g. Cummins, Li, Wooden, & Stokes, 2014).

Short-Term Personal Sources of Happiness: Emotion Regulation

Experiences of happiness are also shaped by people's thoughts and interpretations, often investigated as forms of "emotion regulation." As described by Gross (1998, p. 275), "emotion regulation refers to the processes by which individuals influence which emotions they have, when they have them, and how they experience and express those emotions. Emotion regulatory processes may be automatic or controlled, conscious or unconscious, and may have their effects at one or more points in the emotion generative process."[2]

Gross's perspective on emotion regulation extends across five stages in which happiness might be influenced by people themselves: situation selection, situation modification, attention deployment, reappraisal, and behavioral adjustment. Each of those needs to be included among the personal contributors to happiness.[3]

Situation Selection and Situation Modification

In respect of the first two stages, it is obvious that happiness can be greatly influenced by choosing which situations to enter or leave or by making changes to a current situation. Occupational research into the modification of job situations has focused on "job crafting" – the ways in which workers adjust their demands or social interactions at work in order to decrease negative experiences and increase positive ones. Unsurprisingly, workers who report substantial modification of this kind are also likely to experience more happiness in terms of job satisfaction and job engagement – they have shaped their activities to benefit their happiness (e.g. Rudolph, Katz, Lavigne, & Zacher, 2017).

Attention Deployment

Another proximal influence on happiness concerns how people allocate attention, directing their thoughts to one particular target rather than to others. We can often adjust a current

[2] See also Gross (2014, 2015) and Quoidbach, Mikolajczak, and Gross (2015).

[3] Other models of emotion regulation (e.g. Buruck, Dörfel, Kugler, & Brom, 2016), also extend across several of the stages considered here.

experience by shifting mental focus to alternative themes. The "power of positive thinking," and the benefits of "accentuating the positive" and "looking on the bright side" have consistently been advocated as promoting happiness.

Experimental studies comparing the happiness of people who have been asked to think and behave in different ways have pointed to the happiness-promoting benefits of particular activities. For instance, people have been asked to think about and write down five things about which they are grateful, once a week or once a day, and their average happiness compared against a group undertaking different activities. Expressing gratitude has consistently been found to increase subjective well-being, as have instructions to reflect on positive experiences, to express forgiveness, and to practice optimism (e.g. Clauss, Hoppe, O'Shea, González-Morales, Steidle, & Michel, 2018; Lyubomirsky & Layous, 2013).

For example, experimental comparisons against control groups asked employees to write for ten minutes about three things that went well in their job in the previous week. Those recalling positive work events became generally more happy across time and demonstrated more social interactions (Chancellor, Layous, & Lyubomirsky, 2015). Another within-organization comparison involved quiet contemplation with warm feelings directed to other people (Frederickson, Cohn, Coffey, Pek, & Finkel, 2008). Clear benefits against a control group were found for participating workers in terms of, for instance, positive emotions, psychological well-being, and life satisfaction.

Other processes of attention-deployment illustrate "the law of comparative feeling" – "the intensity of emotion depends on the relationship between an event and some frame of reference against which the event is evaluated" (Frijda, 1988, p. 353). A principal form of this is in terms of mental comparisons between a current situation and those in the past or in a potential future – thinking how things are getting better or getting worse or are likely to get better or get worse. For example, if you are able to focus attention on previous improvements or on probable future improvements, you are likely to feel more positive about your situation. Conversely, when you think about how things are getting worse or are likely to remain bad, you will probably feel less happy (Emmons, 1986), often in part through anticipatory worry about future problems (e.g. Meurs & Perrewé, 2011). The key point is that happiness and unhappiness are not determined only by a current situation, but also from mental comparisons with how things have been previously and how they are expected to be in the future.

Two other mental comparisons are also important – against the frame of reference provided by other people and by other situations. These have both been viewed as either "upward" or "downward." Emotion regulation by comparison "upward" with other people involves mentally comparing yourself against individuals who are in a better situation, and upward social comparisons tend to depress well-being as a person sees how other people better placed. On the other hand, downward social comparisons, against people who are worse off in the compared respect, tend to encourage happiness (e.g. Wheeler, 2000).

Studies of social comparison in work settings include research by Buunk, Zurriaga, Peiró, Nauta, & Gonsalvez (2005), who studied the frequency with which health-center physicians compared their own work performance with that of colleagues who are better-performing or worse-performing. In that comparative respect (rather than in terms of others' well-being), upward assessments were more common than downward ones.

Similarly, mental comparisons against other situations can shape happiness. "Upward" thoughts involve reflecting how things might have developed more pleasingly, and those are known to depress subjective well-being, whereas downward comparisons (considering how matters could have turned out worse than they are) can evoke more positive feelings. These comparisons have been illustrated in a study of Olympic medalists: runners who received silver medals for achieving second place were judged from videotapes to be less happy with their position than were bronze medalists in third place. Many second-place winners appeared to base their feelings in part on upward counterfactual comparisons ("I couldn't be the best"), whereas athletes in third place were more likely to make downward comparisons, being happy to have reached the medal positions ("I did better than almost everyone") (Medvec, Madey, & Gilovich, 1995).

That pattern was confirmed for another Olympic games by McGraw, Mellers, and Tetlock (2005), who also emphasized mental comparisons against prior expectations. Medal-winners with lower published expectations were happier than those with higher expectations, and high expectations (such as the anticipation of a gold medal) appeared to make objectively better outcomes seem worse. In general, people compare their achievements against what they expect, and their happiness depends in part on expectation (Shepperd & McNulty, 2002).

Reappraisal

Emotion regulation also ranges across other ways in which people adjust how they think about a situation. Particularly important is the degree to which they can identify positive meanings. Striving toward a desired goal can lead to new opportunities for enjoyment, additional social contacts, the acquisition of new skills and knowledge, and at least intermittently an enhanced sense of self-efficacy. And goal-achievement often requires working through a succession of smaller sub-goals; positive feelings associated with attaining these intermediate targets can ensure that even unpleasant activity can generate happiness from time to time. People in the same job or other situation can differ in how far they perceive required actions as personally meaningful and rewarding, leading to differences in their happiness.

Another form of reappraisal has been described as "acceptance" – recognizing the negative aspects of a fact but mentally setting aside those unpleasant aspects (e.g. Bond & Bunce, 2003; Kuba & Scheibe, 2017). Unhappiness can be reduced by detaching negative feelings about a happiness-limiting fact from mere awareness of that fact – being willing to experience undesirable thoughts without trying to influence them and without letting them determine what you do. In that way, job satisfaction and global well-being are more positive among workers who score higher on acceptance thinking (Bond & Bunce, 2003), and a day's negative events tend to be less disturbing to workers who can accept those events without also experiencing linked negative feelings (Kuba & Scheibe, 2017). Furthermore, self-help training in acceptance thought and behavior has been shown to reduce workers' perceived stress and burnout (Hofer et al., 2018). As with other forms of emotion regulation, the same situation can make people happy or unhappy to different degrees depending on their mental processes.

Adjusting Behavior

This final aspect of emotion regulation concerns the ways in which people respond to what has happened. For example, an unhappy person might try to improve well-being through exercise, meditation, alcohol, or drugs.

Researchers in this area have emphasized the unhappiness-promoting consequences of "expressive suppression" – adjusting behavior to distort how you feel. Processes of that kind have been studied in roles with a strong emphasis on service relationships, for example when waiting on tables in a restaurant or working as a telephonist in a call center. These workers are often expected to conceal their negative feelings about rude or aggressive customers, acting as though an offensive customer has behaved in an acceptable fashion. That form of emotional suppression has been found to be linked with psychological strain, emotional exhaustion, low job satisfaction, and similar forms of unhappiness (Grandey, 2015; Hülsheger & Schewe, 2011).

Emotion Regulation: Overview

We have seen in this section that experiences of happiness or unhappiness are frequently influenced by processes of emotion regulation. Single instances of regulation can be undertaken intentionally, or they can be within mental and behavioral routines which have become established as habits through many years of repetition; in many cases, habitual routines operate as part of a personality trait. In general, experiences of happiness depend not only on a current situation but also on processes of emotion regulation and (as described in the earlier section) on longer-term personal characteristics.

Concluding Remarks

This chapter has summarized the principal aspects of happiness and unhappiness, at work and more widely. It has emphasized that these affects can be based on a wide range of personal factors in addition to an apparent proximal source, and that they can take many forms without necessarily referring to a person being "happy" or "unhappy."

The study of happiness offers many opportunities for innovative research in organizations; see, for example, Warr (2019). Particular attention should now be directed at processes of ambivalence – when positive and negative affects occur together or approximately together. Mixed feelings can occur in two ways, each with its own conceptual and practical challenges. Ambivalence can arise *concurrently*, when contrasting evaluations arise from different aspects of a situation; and *sequential* ambivalence occurs, for instance, when a person works through negative situations before attaining happiness in some form. We now need more sophisticated conceptual analyses of these two types of occurrence in work and other settings, together with more rigorous longitudinal investigations (e.g. Hershfield et al., 2013). Progress in understanding ambivalence is likely also to require approaches that are more qualitative, complementing the field's conventional emphasis on quantitative designs.

References

Baas, M., De Dreu, C. K. W., & Nijstad, B. A. (2008). A meta-analysis of 25 years of mood–creativity research: Hedonic tone, activation, or regulatory focus? *Psychological Bulletin, 134*, 779–806.

Bakker, A. B., & Oerlemans, W. G. M. (2011). Subjective well-being in organizations. In K. Cameron & G. Spreitzer (Eds.), *Handbook of positive organizational scholarship* (pp. 178–189). Oxford, UK: Oxford University Press.

Bartels, M. (2015). Genetics of wellbeing and its components satisfaction with life, happiness, and quality of life: A review and meta-analysis of heritability studies. *Behavior Genetics, 45*, 137–156.

Baumeister, R. F., Bratslavsky, E., Finkenauer, C., & Vohs, K. D. (2001). Bad is stronger than good. *Archives of General Psychology, 5*, 323–370.

Birdi, K., Warr, P., & Oswald, A. (1995). Age differences in three components of employee well-being. *Applied Psychology: An International Review, 44*, 345–373.

Bond, F. W., & Bunce, D. (2003). The role of acceptance and job control in mental health, job satisfaction, and work performance. *Journal of Applied Psychology, 88*, 1057–1067.

Boswell, W. R., Boudreau, J. W., & Tichy, J. (2005). The relationship between employee job change and job satisfaction: The honeymoon–hangover effect. *Journal of Applied Psychology, 90*, 882–892.

Brayfield, A. H., & Rothe, H. F. (1951). An index of job satisfaction. *Journal of Applied Psychology, 35*, 307–311.

Burke, M. J., Brief, A. P., George, J. M., Roberson, L., & Webster, J. (1989). Measuring affect at work: Confirmatory analyses of competing mood structures with conceptual linkage to cortical regulatory systems. *Journal of Personality and Social Psychology*, *57*, 1091–1102.

Buruck, G., Dörfel, D., Kugler, J., & Brom, S. S. (2016). Enhancing well-being at work: The role of emotion regulation skills as personal resources. *Journal of Occupational Health Psychology*, *21*, 480–493.

Buunk, B. P., Zurriaga, R., Peiró, J. M., Nauta, A., & Gonsalvez, I. (2005). Social comparisons at work as related to a comparative social climate and to individual differences in social comparison orientation. *Applied Psychology: An International Review*, *54*, 61–80.

Carver, C. S., Scheier, M. F., & Segerstrom, S. C. (2010). Optimism. *Clinical Psychology Review*, *30*, 879–889.

Chancellor, J., Layous, K., & Lyubomirsky, S. (2015). Recalling positive event at work makes employees feel happier, move more but interact less: A 6-week randomized controlled intervention at a Japanese workplace. *Journal of Happiness Studies*, *16*, 871–887.

Christian, M. S., Garza, A. S., & Slaughter, J. E. (2011). Work engagement: A quantitative review and test of its relations with task and organizational performance. *Personnel Psychology*, *64*, 89–166.

Clark, A. E., Oswald, A., & Warr, P. B. (1996). Is job satisfaction U-shaped in age? *Journal of Occupational and Organizational Psychology*, *69*, 57–81.

Clauss, E., Hoppe, A., O'Shea, D., Gonzáles Morales, M. G., Steidle, A., & Michel, A. (2018). Promoting personal resources and reducing exhaustion through positive work reflection among caregivers. *Journal of Occupational Health Psychology*, *23*, 127–140.

Cummins, R. A., Li, N., Wooden, M., & Stokes, M. (2014). A demonstration of set-points for subjective wellbeing. *Journal of Happiness Studies*, *15*, 183–206.

Diener, E., Emmons, R. A., Larsen, R. J., & Griffin, S. (1985). The Satisfaction with Life Scale. *Journal of Personality Assessment*, *49*, 71–75.

Diener, E., Suh, E. M., Lucas, R. E., & Smith, H. L. (1999). Subjective well-being: Three decades of progress. *Psychological Bulletin*, *125*, 276–302.

Emmons, R. A. (1986). Personal strivings: An approach to personality and subjective well-being. *Journal of Personality and Social Psychology*, *51*, 1058–1068.

Eschleman, K. J., & Bowling, N. A. (2011). A construct validation of the Neutral Objects Satisfaction Questionnaire. *Journal of Business and Psychology*, *26*, 501–515.

Fisher, C. D. (2002). Antecedents and consequences of real-time affective reactions at work. *Motivation and Emotion*, *26*, 3–30.

Frederickson, B. L., Cohn, M. A., Coffey, K. A., Pek, J., & Finkel, S. M. (2008). Open hearts build lives: Positive emotions, induced through loving-kindness meditation, build consequential personal resources. *Journal of Personality and Social Psychology*, *95*, 1045–1062.

Frijda, N. H. (1988). The laws of emotion. *American Psychologist*, *43*, 349–358.

Grandey, A. A. (2015). Smiling for a wage: What emotional labor teaches us about emotion regulation. *Psychological Inquiry*, *26*, 54–60.

Gray, J. A. (1971). The psychophysiological basis of introversion–extraversion. *Behavior Research and Therapy*, *8*, 249–266.

Gray, J. A. (1987). Perspectives on anxiety and impulsivity. *Journal of Research in Personality*, *21*, 493–509.

Griffin, R. W. (1988). Consequences of quality circles in an industrial setting: A longitudinal assessment. *Academy of Management Journal*, *31*, 338–358.

Griffin, R. W. (1991). Effects of work redesign on employee perceptions, attitudes, and behaviors: A long-term investigation. *Academy of Management Journal*, *34*, 425–435.

Gross, J. J. (1998). The emerging field of emotion regulation: An integrative review. *Review of General Psychology*, *2*, 271–299.

Gross, J. J. (Ed.) (2014). *Handbook of emotion regulation* (2nd edition). New York, NY: Guilford.

Gross, J. J. (2015). Emotion regulation: Current status and future perspectives. *Psychological Inquiry*, *26*, 1–26.

Hakanen, J. J., Peeters, M. C. W., & Schaufeli, W. B. (2018). Different types of employee well-being across time and their relationships with job crafting. *Journal of Occupational Health Psychology, 23*, 289–301.

Headey, B., & Wearing, A. (1992). *Understanding happiness: A theory of subjective well-being*. Melbourne, Australia: Longman Cheshire.

Hershfield, H. E., Scheibe, S., Sims, T. L., & Carstensen, L. L. (2013). When feeling bad can be good: Mixed emotions benefit physical health across adulthood. *Social Psychological and Personality Science, 4*, 54–61.

Hofer, P. D., Waadt, M., Aschwanden, R., Milidou, M., Acker, J., Meyer, A. H., . . . & Gloster, A. T. (2018). Self-help for stress and burnout without therapist contact: An online randomised controlled trial. *Work & Stress, 32*, 189–208.

Hülsheger, U. R., & Schewe, A. F. (2011). On the costs and benefits of emotional labor: A meta-analysis of three decades of research. *Journal of Occupational Health Psychology, 16*, 361–389.

Ironson, G. H., Smith, P.C., Brannick, M. T., Gibson, W. M., & Paul, K. B. (1989). Construction of a Job in General scale: A comparison of global, composite, and specific measures. *Journal of Applied Psychology, 74*, 193–200.

Judge, T. A., Heller, D., & Mount, M. K. (2002). Five-factor model of personality and job satisfaction: A meta-analysis. *Journal of Applied Psychology, 87*, 530–541.

Judge, T. A., & Hulin, C. L. (1993). Job satisfaction as a reflection of disposition: A multiple source causal analysis. *Organizational Behavior and Human Decision Processes, 56*, 388–421.

Kuba, K., & Scheibe, S. (2017). Let it be and keep on going! Acceptance and daily occupational well-being in relation to negative work events. *Journal of Occupational Health Psychology, 22*, 59–70.

Loher, B. T., Noe, R. A., Moeller, N. L., & Fitzgerald, M. P. (1985). A meta-analysis of the relation of job characteristics to job satisfaction. *Journal of Applied Psychology, 70*, 280–289.

Lucas, R. E., & Diener, E. (2015). Personality and subjective well-being: Current issues and controversies. In M. Mikulincer and P. R. Shaver (Eds.), *APA handbook of personality and social psychology* (pp. 577–599). Washington, DC: American Psychological Association.

Luhmann, M., Hofmann, W., Eid, M., & Lucas, R. E. (2012). Subjective well-being and adaptation to life events: A meta-analysis. *Journal of Personality and Social Psychology, 102*, 592–615.

Lyubomirsky, S., & Layous, K. (2013). How do simple positive activities increase well-being? *Current Directions in Psychological Science, 22*, 57–62.

McGraw, A. P., Mellers, B. A., & Tetlock, P. E. (2005). Expectations and emotions of Olympic athletes. *Journal of Experimental Social Psychology, 41*, 438–446.

Medvec, V. H., Madey, S. F., & Gilovich, T. (1995). When less is more: Counterfactual thinking and satisfaction among Olympic athletes. *Journal of Personality and Social Psychology, 69*, 603–610.

Meurs, J. A., & Perrewé, P. L. (2011). Cognitive activation theory of stress: An integrative theoretical approach to work stress. *Journal of Management, 37*, 1043–1068.

Nolen-Hoeksema, S., & Rusting, C. (1999). Gender differences in well-being. In D. Kahneman, E. Diener, & N. Schwarz (Eds.), *Well-being: The foundations of hedonic psychology* (pp. 330–350). New York, NY: Russell Sage Foundation.

Pavot, W., & Diener, E. (2008). The Satisfaction With Life Scale and the emerging construct of life satisfaction. *Journal of Positive Psychology, 3*, 137–152.

Quoidbach, J., Mikolajczak, M., & Gross, J. J. (2015). Positive interventions: An emotion regulation perspective. *Psychological Bulletin, 141*, 655–693.

Remington, N. A., Fabrigar, L. R., & Visser, P. S. (2000). Re-examining the circumplex model of affect. *Journal of Personality and Social Psychology, 79*, 286–300.

Rosenfield, S., & Mouzon, D. (2013). Gender and mental health. In C. S. Aneshensel, J. C. Phelan, and A. Bierman (Eds.), *Handbook of the sociology of mental health* (pp. 277–296). Dordrecht, Netherlands: Springer.

Rozin, P., & Royzman, E. B. (2001). Negativity bias, negativity dominance, and contagion. *Personality and Social Psychology Review, 5*, 296–320.

Rudolph, C. W., Katz, I. M., Lavigne, K. N., & Zacher, H. (2017). Job crafting: A meta-analysis of relationships with individual differences, job characteristics, and work outcomes. *Journal of Vocational Behavior*, *102*, 112–138.

Russell, J. A. (1980). A circumplex model of affect. *Journal of Personality and Social Psychology*, *39*, 1161–1178.

Russell, J. A. (2003). Core affect and the psychological construction of emotion. *Psychological Review*, *110*, 145–172.

Ryff, C. D., & Singer, B. H. (2008). Know thyself and become what you are: A eudaimonic approach to psychological well-being. *Journal of Happiness Studies*, *9*, 13–39.

Schaufeli, W. B., Bakker, A. B., & Salanova, M. (2006). The measurement of work engagement with a short questionnaire. *Educational and Psychological Measurement*, *66*, 701–716.

Seligman, M. E. P. (2002). *Authentic happiness*. New York, NY: Free Press.

Shepperd, J. A., & McNulty, J. K. (2002). The affective consequences of expected and unexpected outcomes. *Psychological Science*, *13*, 85–88.

Steel, P., Schmidt, J., & Schultz, J. (2008). Refining the relationship between personality and subjective well-being. *Psychological Bulletin*, *134*, 138–161.

Steptoe, A., Deaton, A., & Stone, A. A. (2015). Subjective well-being, health, and ageing. *The Lancet*, *385* (14 February), 640–648.

Thoresen, C. J., Kaplan, S. A., Barsky, A. P., Warren, C. R., & de Chermont, K. (2003). The affective underpinnings of job perceptions and attitudes: A meta-analytic review and integration. *Psychological Bulletin*, *129*, 914–945.

Tornau, K., & Frese, M. (2013). Construct clean-up in proactivity research: A meta-analysis on the nomological net of work-related proactivity concepts and their incremental validities. *Applied Psychology: An International Review*, *62*, 44–96.

Van Katwyk, P. T., Fox, S., Spector, P. E., & Kelloway, E. K. (2000). Using the Job-related Affective Well-being Scale (JAWS) to investigate affective responses to work stressors. *Journal of Occupational Health Psychology*, *5*, 219–230.

Warr, P. B. (1990). The measurement of well-being and other aspects of mental health. *Journal of Occupational Psychology*, *63*, 193–210.

Warr, P. B. (2007). *Work, happiness, and unhappiness*. Mahwah, NJ: Erlbaum.

Warr, P. B. (2019). *The psychology of happiness*. Abingdon, UK: Routledge:

Warr, P. B., Bindl, U. K., Parker, S. K., and Inceoglu, I. (2014). Four-quadrant investigation of job-related affects and behaviours. *European Journal of Work and Organizational Psychology*, *23*, 342–363.

Warr, P. B., & Inceoglu, I. (2012). Job engagement, job satisfaction, and contrasting associations with person-job fit. *Journal of Occupational Health Psychology*, *17*, 129–138.

Warr, P. B., & Inceoglu, I. (2015). Job features, job values, and affective strength. *European Journal of Work and Organizational Psychology*, *24*, 101–112.

Waterman, A. S. (2008). Reconsidering happiness: A eudaimonist's perspective. *Journal of Positive Psychology*, *3*, 234–252.

Watson, D., Clark, L. A., & Tellegen, A. (1988). Development and validation of brief measures of positive and negative affect: The PANAS scales. *Journal of Personality and Social Psychology*, *54*, 1063–1070.

Watson, D., & Tellegen, A. (1985). Toward a consensual structure of mood. *Psychological Bulletin*, *98*, 219–235.

Watson, D., Wiese, D., Vaidya, J., & Tellegen, A. (1999). The two general activation systems of affect: Structural findings, evolutionary considerations, and psychobiological evidence. *Journal of Personality and Social Psychology*, *76*, 820–838.

Weiss, A., Bates, T. C., & Luciano, M. (2008). Happiness is a personal(ity) thing. *Psychological Science*, *19*, 205–210.

Wheeler, L. (2000). Individual differences in social comparison. In J. Suls and L. Wheeler (Eds.), *Handbook of social comparison: Theory and research* (pp. 141–158). New York, NY: Kluwer/Plenum.

Yik, M., Russell, J. A., & Steiger, J. H. (2011). A 12-point circumplex structure of core affect. *Emotion*, *11*, 705–711.

Young, H. R., Glerum, D. R., Wang, W., & Joseph, D. L. (2018). Who are the most engaged at work? A meta-analysis of personality and employee engagement. *Journal of Organizational Behavior*, *39*, 1330–1346.

Zelenski, J. M., Murphy, S. A., & Jenkins, D. A. (2008). The happy–productive worker hypothesis revisited. *Journal of Happiness Studies*, *9*, 521–537.

33 Envy and Jealousy

The Role of Intrasexual Competition in the Workplace

Abraham P. Buunk, Pieternel Dijkstra, Karlijn Massar, Rosario Zurriaga, and Pilar González-Navarro

Over the past decades it has become manifest that jealousy and envy may be quite prevalent within organizations (see e.g. Dogan & Vecchio, 2001; Smith, Merlone, & Duffy, 2017). Although the term "jealousy" is often used as more or less synonymous to "envy," from a theoretical point of view jealousy and envy are evoked by different stimuli. Workplace jealousy refers to the negative thoughts and emotions that result from the interference by a coworker within a valued relationship at work, and may, for instance, be evoked when someone feels that his or her superior pays attention to a new colleague at the expense of the attention paid to him or her. In essence, workplace jealousy is triadic in that it involves three individuals: the focal employee, the rival, and the valued target person. In contrast, workplace envy is defined essentially in dyadic terms, and refers to the negative thoughts and emotions that result from the perception that a coworker has obtained outcomes or has capacities that one strongly desires (Vecchio, 2000). As noted by Sterling and Labianca (2015) "Envy is at its most basic level the pain felt at another's good fortune" (p. 297; see also Tai, Narayanan, & McAllister, 2012). According to Parrott and Smith (1993), envy is characterized more by feelings of inferiority, longing, and resentment, whereas jealousy is characterized more by fear of loss, distrust, anxiety, and anger.

Despite the difference between the two concepts, a common feature of both employee jealousy and employee envy is the negative affect that occurs as a result of social comparison with another individual who is viewed as having more favorable attributes or outcomes (cf. Buunk & Ybema, 1997; Fischer, Kastenmüller, Frey, & Peus, 2009). Both envy and jealousy may cause an employee to experience a sense of unfair treatment resulting in feelings of resentment, which in turn may undermine positive organizational behaviors (e.g. helping a coworker), may cause deliberate drops in performance and productivity, and may increase unethical workplace behaviors (see, for example, Kilduff, Galinsky, Gallo, & Reade, 2016; Smith et al., 2017). In extreme cases, envy and jealousy in the workplace may result in hostile or aggressive behaviors directed at the target of the emotions, for example in the form of bullying (Dogan & Vecchio, 2001). Given the personal and organizational outcomes of these emotions, a deeper understanding of their causes is highly relevant. However, it is important to consider that both envy and jealousy can also be functional in the sense that these emotions instigate behavior toward and focus attention on protecting valued relationships and resources (Vecchio, 2000).

In this chapter, which is in part based upon Buunk, Pollet, Dijkstra, and Massar (2011) and Buunk and Dijkstra (2012), we approach envy and jealousy mainly from an evolutionary point of view, in particular from the perspective of intrasexual competition. An evolutionary psychological approach offers an integrative and multilevel theoretical perspective and a primary focus on the "why" question of human behavior (see also Confer et al., 2010). Specifically, the evolutionary psychological perspective proposes that modern human behavior is the result of adaptive, evolved psychological mechanisms that allow individuals to live in groups, pursue status, or fulfill a need for affiliation – all of which are relevant for the workplace. Thus even though organizations are novel and artificial contexts, the evolutionary perspective can shed light on patterns of interpersonal behaviors in organizations by examining why people behave as they do, even if their behavior does not seem beneficial to themselves or the organization (e.g. Nicholson, 1998). The evolutionary perspective is basically a *meta-perspective* that does not exclude but rather includes other perspectives: for example, the theoretical model of Hoogland, Thielke, and Smith (2017) in which envy is considered as an evolving *episode*, and the framework for understanding jealousy within workplace relationships proposed by Andiappan (2017), which is to an important extent based on *regulatory focus* theory (Higgins & Spiegel, 2004).

Competition in Organizations Is Mainly Intrasexual

The concept of intrasexual competition was introduced by Darwin (1871) to refer to rivalry with same-sex others that has evolved as a consequence of the motivation to obtain and maintain access to intimate partners. Although in contemporary organizational settings women are often in direct competition with men, it is our contention that, as a result of a long evolutionary history of male–male competition, on an emotional and unconscious level, men may still perceive other men, and not women, as their primary rivals, and will thus show more jealousy and envy toward other men than toward women. Similarly, as women have in our evolutionary past rarely competed with men, they are more likely to see other women as competitors and as the focus of their envy and jealousy (cf. Hill and Buss, 2006). Although not directly concerned with envy and jealousy, older studies in the field of social comparison have shown that, while many participants compare themselves with both genders in order to evaluate their performance and their pay, in general there is a pronounced preference for comparisons with others of the same gender over others of the other gender (e.g. Feldman & Ruble, 1981; Miller, 1984; Suls, Gaes, & Gastorf, 1979). For instance, Buunk and Van der Laan (2002) presented women with a successful target that was either male or female, and found that women compared themselves more with the female target than with the male target. Thus, it seems clear that women see other women as more relevant standards than men for how they fare or may fare in their professional careers – and thus as potential envy- and jealousy-evoking targets. A similar line of reasoning applies to men, for whom other men are more relevant comparison targets. For example, in a study by Saad and Gill (2001) participants took part in a two-person ultimatum game, in which one was the allocator and the other the recipient and the allocator had to split a given sum of money with the recipient. The recipient could either accept or reject the offer. If accepted, both players received their respective splits; if rejected, neither of them got anything. The results showed that men made more generous offers when pitted against a woman as opposed to a man. Women, on the other hand, made equal offers independently of the sex of the recipient. This latter finding may be attributed to the dimension of competition: that is, money. In general, resources play a larger role in intrasexual competition for men than for women, who compete more than men on attributes such as physical attractiveness (Dijkstra & Buunk, 1998).

The central focus on competition with same-sex others in the emotions of envy and jealousy is also illustrated by a phenomenon that Försterling, Preikschas, and Agthe (2007) refer to as the *sexual attribution bias*. They found that the success of attractive same-sex others was consistently ascribed more to luck and less to ability, whereas the success of attractive opposite-sex others was attributed more to ability and less to luck. Thus, both men and women apparently see only same-sex others as rivals, feel threatened by the success of attractive same-sex others, and feel a need to "downplay" this success. The sexual attribution bias fosters a favorable assessment of the self in relation to the same-sex rival that ensures persistence of competition, reducing the rival's chances of succeeding. To remain credible, individuals usually do not derogate their rivals on all attributes. They give them credit for success in domains they regard as unimportant. It is only in domains that are perceived to be important that individuals devalue their rivals (Buunk & Gibbons, 2006; Schmitt, 1988).

Male Intrasexual Competition over Status and Resources

Overall, men compete with other men for dominance and social status, because these features are directly attractive to women and may help in conquering rival men (e.g. Sidanius & Pratto, 1999). In those preindustrial societies in which male–male competition has been studied, it has consistently been found that a man's status is directly related to his reproductive success (Betzig, 1986). Even in contemporary Western society, high-income men have more biological children than low-income men, whereas among women the opposite is true (Hopcroft, 2006). This illustrates that it is for men still reproductively more beneficial to engage in competition with other men over status and resources than for women.

Overall, organizations are traditionally an important domain for competition over status, prestige, and resources, especially among men. From the perspective of intrasexual competition, among men envy in organizational settings will arise especially when an individual perceives that a coworker has an actual or potential higher status than oneself, whereas jealousy will arise particularly when one perceives one's potential for status advancement is threatened because a rival interferes in a relationship that maybe important for one's career, for example with one's superior. With the increasing influx of women in organizations, intrasexual competition among males may have become more salient and prevalent than in the past, as the presence of women tends to make men more aware of their status in the eyes of women. However, this enhanced intrasexual competition does not necessarily mean that men become more aggressive to other men. In contrast, they may be eager to show their altruistic side, and exhibit what has been referred to as *competitive altruism*: they may compete by being generous and forgoing individual benefits (Van Vugt, Roberts, & Hardy, 2007). Illustrative in this context is an experiment that showed that men increased their cooperation in an economic game when observed by women (Iredale, Van Vught, & Dunbar, 2008). Behaving altruistically may improve men's reputation and status: others often attribute charisma to those who sacrifice their own needs to those of others or the group (De Cremer & Van Knippenberg, 2004).

Female Intrasexual Competition over Physical Attractiveness

Although in present organizations, women may compete on various dimensions, and also with men, especially when they move up in the organizations (Steill & Hay, 1997), throughout human history women seem to have competed more than men – and still tend to do so – with same-sex others in the domain of physical attractiveness (see Campbell, 2002; Cashdan, 1998). It has been assumed that, in the course of human evolution, men's preferences became a weapon in the competition between women. Indeed, it is widely accepted and supported by many studies that physical attractiveness is a more important attribute in society for women than for men. Women tend to rate the tactic of attracting attention to their appearance as being the most effective in competing with others, regardless of what the competition is about (e.g. Cashdan, 1998). Many studies testify to the important role of physical attractiveness in generating envy and competition among women. For example, when confronted with highly attractive rivals, women tend to "dislike" such a rival (Baenninger et al., 1993; Bleske-Rechek & Lighthall, 2010). According to Campbell (2004), the fact that women care more about other women's opinion rather than that of men shows that, also among women, intrasexual competition has developed a dynamic of its own, even when it does not lead to being preferred more by the opposite sex.

Various studies suggest that physical attractiveness may play an important role in generating competition and envy among women in organizations. Because women compete with each other over physical attractiveness, gossip often functions to derogate other women's appearance, and women may exclude attractive women (Campbell, 2004). In an illustrative study, Luxen and Van de Vijver (2006) found some evidence that among human resource managers, professional women – but not men – were less likely to hire a highly attractive same-sex applicant than an unattractive same-sex applicant.

Envy in Organizations

From an evolutionary perspective, envy is an emotion that evolved to alert individuals to the fact that rivals are enjoying certain benefits and to motivate individuals to acquire those same benefits (Hill & Buss, 2006). The contexts that evoke envy are sex-specific due to the different adaptive challenges men and women have faced during evolutionary history. However, there are also individual differences in the extent to which someone is likely to experience envy. For example, envy is more likely to occur in individuals low in conscientiousness and high in neuroticism (Yasin, 2018), and in individuals with low self-esteem (Parrott, 1991). In general, envy inherently arises due unfavorable social comparisons between the self and an outperforming or better-off other (Tesser & Campbell, 1990). In the model of Hoogland et al. (2017), which considers envy as an evolving *episode* rather than as a static state, envy begins after a process of social comparison in an important domain. Given the importance of social comparisons in generating envy, individuals who are dispositionally more likely to compare themselves with others – that is, those with a high social comparison orientation (SCO; Buunk & Gibbons, 2006) – are also more likely to experience envy in workplace settings. In addition to psychological traits, organizational factors such as competitive reward structures (e.g. pay-for-performance) have been shown to increase envy, possibly in part through increased stress levels (Vecchio, 2000).

The consequences of envy in the workplace may be quite diverse and may include poorer leader–member exchange, lower job satisfaction, less liking for coworkers, lower organization-based self-esteem, lower group performance, higher turnover, higher absence rates, and higher social loafing rates (for an overview see Duffy, Shaw, & Schaubroeck, 2008). For example, in a study among Spanish employees González-Navarro, Zurriaga-Llorens, Olateju, and Llinares-Insa (2018) found that in public (but not in private) organizations, envy was associated with counterproductive work behaviors, especially when employees had a poor relationship with their supervisor. Fischer et al. (2009) found in three experiments that envious individuals were less willing to share high-quality information with envied colleagues. Since information exchange is crucial for successful cooperation, group performance may suffer as a consequence. The effects of envy on organizational and individual outcomes tend to depend in part on personality characteristics. For example, Shu and Lazatkhan (2017) found that neuroticism exacerbated the effect of envy on social undermining, but that self-esteem reduced this effect.

To better understand the consequences of envy in the workplace, the distinction between *malicious* envy and *benign* envy is important. According to the episodic model of Hoogland et al. (2017), after the first stage of social comparison, in the next stage it depends on the perception of justice and sense of control whether envy becomes malicious or benign. Benign envy implies identification with or inspiration by an upward comparison target, and may lead individuals to close the gap by moving themselves up to the level of the other: for instance, by observational learning and affiliation with a superior other (Buunk & Ybema, 1997; Van de Ven, Zeelenberg, & Pieters, 2009). Individuals are more likely to experience benign envy when they perceive that the situation of the envied person is deserved and attainable. Such perceptions tend to occur more in an organizational climate characterized by justice and a low level of competitiveness (Buunk, Zurriaga, Peíró, Nauta, & Gosalvez, 2005; Cohen-Charash & Mueller, 2007; Hoogland et al., 2017; Sterling & Labianca, 2015). In this type of organizations cooperation and joint goals are emphasized, and positive relationships between coworkers are encouraged, allowing situations in which envy can occur without being perceived as a threat, but rather as a challenge to overcome or an opportunity for personal development (Sterling & Labianca, 2015).

In contrast, malicious envy will be more likely to occur if perceptions of control are low, which may induce a subjective sense that the advantage that the envied person has is unfair (Hoogland et al., 2017). Malicious envy implies contrast with an upward comparison target and may induce individuals to close the gap between the self and the other person by pulling the other down to one's own position, and by encouraging others in the organization to derogate or even damage their rival, for example by gossiping or bullying (Kletner, Haidt, & Shiota, 2006). For example, Kim and Glomb (2014) found that high performers felt they were envied relatively more often, and as a consequence were victimized more often by their colleagues. In line with the fact that competition within organizations is mainly intrasexual, male bullies most often victimize men whereas female bullies most often victimize women (Schuster, 1996). Moreover, the type of attacks differs: women seem to be more spiteful, and talk behind others' backs, ridicule others, spread rumors, or make indirect allusions. Typical male tactics are to permanently assign others to new tasks, to stop talking to someone, and to assign tasks that violate others' self-esteem. Being bullied has been found to be related to burnout, stress, and decreased job satisfaction in several segments of the job market, ranging from construction work to educational and medical settings (Melia & Becerill, 2007; Van Dick & Wagner, 2001).

When self-improvement or derogation of the rival is not possible, envy at work may also result in decreased well-being. Indirect evidence for this comes from a study among Spanish nurses that showed that those who responded with relatively more negative affect to comparisons with others doing better showed an increase in burnout about a year later, although only when they were high in SCO – that is, dispositionally inclined to engage in social comparisons (Buunk, Zurriaga & Peiró, 2010).

The previously discussed findings suggest that organizations can control at least some of the negative consequences of envy. For instance, Vecchio (2000) found that as the reward system in a unit was more competitive, employees experienced more envy. In contrast, as workers experienced more autonomy in their jobs and had more considerate supervisors, they experienced less envy toward coworkers. Although this study was only correlational in nature, it suggests at least some avenues for organizations to control workplace envy and its negative consequences.

By uncoupling individual rewards from those of others, enhancing job autonomy, and recruiting kind and empathic managers, organizations may reduce workplace envy to acceptable levels. Cohen-Charash and Mueller (2007) suggested that envy in organizations may be reduced by such measures as promoting fairness in the organization, providing feedback and encouraging self-comparisons rather than comparisons with others, and not only rewarding a few superstars as the "Employee of the Month," which may undermine perceptions of attainability.

Jealousy in Organizations

As noted previously, jealousy involves three elements: the individual, a person with whom this individual has a valued relationship, and a rival, i.e. a third party whom the individual fears will disrupt this relationship. Whereas envy is evoked by seeing another individual gain an advantage, jealousy is evoked by the threat and fear of personal rejection or loss (e.g. Bedeian, 1995). Based on regulatory focus theory (Higgins & Spiegel, 2004), Andiappan (2017) suggested that because jealousy implies potential losses, a prevention-focus orientation will dominate. This implies that jealous individuals tend to keep a close eye on their valued relationship and analyze the rival's viability through a social comparison process. There is evidence that jealousy at work may have similar determinants and consequences to envy. For example, in a study by Thompson, Buch, and Glasø (2018) in Norway among leaders as well as followers, jealousy was positively associated with social loafing, and those with a high-quality working relationship with their supervisor reported less jealousy. In addition, jealousy at work may lead individuals to engage in gossip (Wert & Salovey, 2004), which often takes a malicious form when individuals derogate the person that evokes the feelings of jealousy, which in turn may create a hostile work environment (e.g. Grosser, Lopez-Kidwell, & Labianca, 2010; Grosser, Lopez-Kidwell, Labianca, & Ellwardt, 2012). Jealousy can furthermore result in decreased engagement in organizational citizenship behaviors, including attendance at work and helping a colleague with their work (Wang & Sung, 2016). Moreover, jealousy instigates actions aimed at retaining the relationship partner and may lead to increased possessive or monitoring behaviors (Harris & Darby, 2010).

There has been less research on jealousy than on envy in organizations and, until now, research on jealousy has, more than research on envy, focused directly on the role of intrasexual competition, in particular on sex differences in the rival characteristics that evoke jealousy. The basic contention in these studies is that sex differences in the jealousy-evoking nature of rival characteristics are such basic, hardwired affective phenomena that these will also surface in non-romantic organizational settings. Based on the study by Buunk, Castro Solano, Zurriaga, and Gonzalez (2011) on intimate relationships, four dimensions of rival characteristics have been distinguished. First, *social dominance*, which refers to the degree to which someone is self-confident, assertive, extroverted, and authoritative. This type of dominance will contribute to occupational success in modern organizations because socially dominant workers will proactively influence and steer their environments relatively more, resulting in a relatively powerful position in the organization's hierarchy. In general, socially dominant individuals appear to be more successful as leaders (Do & Minbashian, 2014). The second dimension is *physical dominance*, which refers to physical features that are related to strength and physical power, such as a V-shaped body, height, and an athletic build (e.g. Bryan, Webster, & Mahaffey, 2011). These features have been found to be related to competitiveness (Quinn & Wilson, 1989) and occupational success, even though in many modern organizations physical dominance is not necessarily directly relevant for job performance (e.g. Buunk, Pollet, Dijkstra, & Massar, 2011). The third dimension is *physical attractiveness*, including such characteristics as having a better figure, having a more attractive face, having more beautiful legs, and being more slender – a dimension especially relevant for women. Finally, the fourth dimension is referred to as *social–communal attributes*, including such features as being a better listener, being more attentive, having a better sense of humor, and being more self-confident. Especially in the context of work such characteristics are important, given that individuals may only succeed when cooperating with others or when, at the least, others are not obstructing their goals (e.g. Balliet & Van Lange, 2013).

As noted previously, for men, more than for women, characteristics of a rival that lead to a higher position in the social hierarchy may be relatively more threatening, because a high status facilitates the access to important resources and to the attraction of partners (e.g. Geary, 2010). Therefore, social dominance will evoke more jealousy among men than among women, for whom physical attractiveness of the rival would evoke more jealousy. In the first study exploring the role of rival characteristics in generating jealousy in organizations, Buunk, Aan 't Goor, and Castro Solano (2010) asked participants to imagine that a satisfying and close relationship with one's supervisor was threatened because a new employee seemed to develop a close relationship with the same supervisor. Next, for characteristics representing each of the four dimensions described above, participants were asked how jealous they would be if the rival possessed this characteristic. The results revealed that among men as well as women a rival's social–communal attributes evoked the highest levels of jealousy. Such attributes are important for establishing high-quality interpersonal relationships and for fulfilling the need to belong.

However, there were also clear sex differences: among men not only a rival's social dominance, but also a rival's physical dominance evoked more jealousy than among women, especially among men high in intrasexual competitiveness, as measured with a scale developed by Buunk and Fisher (2009). This scale assesses intrasexual competitiveness as a disposition, that is, a more or less chronic perception of viewing interactions with members of one's own sex in various domains of life as a competition. Interestingly, these effects were obtained only when the supervisor was of the same sex as both the focal person and the rival, suggesting that intrasexual competition and the resulting emotional experience of jealousy are evoked more by the presence of same-sex others than by the presence of opposite-sex others (cf. Buunk & Fisher, 2009; Campbell, 2002; Geary, 1998). A similar study among male and female Spanish employees showed that, overall, women experienced more jealousy than men did, but that when looking at the specific characteristics of the rival, for women physical attractiveness, and for men physical dominance were the most jealousy-evoking (Zurriaga, González-Navarro, Buunk, & Dijkstra, 2018).

Direct experimental evidence was obtained by Buunk, Zurriaga, González-Navarro, and Monzani (2016), who examined the effect of a rival's attractiveness on jealousy and career advancement expectations in a simulated work setting in the lab in which women had supposedly to compete for a job promotion with either an attractive or an unattractive other woman. The results showed that, overall, an attractive rival induced more jealousy and lower career advancement expectations than an unattractive rival. Especially among women who attributed unfriendliness to their rival, the attractiveness of the rival induced higher levels of jealousy and lower career advancement expectations. Furthermore, among women high in intrasexual competitiveness, the rival's attractiveness induced lower career advancement expectations. Thus, these findings suggest that direct confrontation with an attractive rival may for women induce jealousy and hinder the expectations of developing a career.

Conclusion

In the present chapter, we described that envy and jealousy may play an important role in present organizations, and that both are related to intrasexual competition and social comparison. The frequent contact with many colleagues, the competitive culture in many organizations, and human resource policies rewarding "superstars" all seem to contribute to the occurrence of envy and jealousy. As has been noted for a long time, individuals tend to evaluate their own performance not without a context, but in relation to that of similar coworkers. This may, when another surpasses an individual, induce envy in that individual, even though he or she is performing well. It is noteworthy that evolutionarily ancient mechanisms that may not always be beneficial to the individual or the organization still consistently tend to surface, such as the tendency to reduce the status of well-performing others by gossiping and bullying – cutting down "tall poppies" – as well as the importance attached to rival characteristics like physical dominance and physical attractiveness, both in the context of personnel selection (Luxen & Van de Vijver, 2006) and in professional relationships (Buunk et al., 2011). For example, it is remarkable that women respond with more jealousy to a rival's physical attractiveness than men, and tend to exclude and derogate attractive colleagues, even though for most jobs, a woman's physical attractiveness may seem in general irrelevant. Similarly, although one's height does not seem to be directly related to job performance in many areas of business, tall men and women seem to have an advantage in the sense that they are more likely to advance in their career (cf. Stulp, Buunk, Verhulst, & Pollet, 2013). The finding in one study that women in organizations tend to respond, overall, more jealously than men may be due to the fact that for women, dyadic relationships, also those at work, are more important to their self-concept than for men.

The fact that jealousy in work relationships is in many ways similar to jealousy in intimate relationships suggests the existence of an evolved mechanism underlying jealousy, which functions not only within intimate relationships but also within the evolutionarily novel work contexts. This probably occurs because our Stone Age ancestors lived in societies that did not make a clear distinction between private life and working life. It is widely acknowledged by evolutionary psychologists that, because the current environment differs from the one in which we evolved, an adaptation may currently not be adaptive (e.g. Campbell, 2002). These jealousy- and envy-evoking mechanisms evolved during millions of years in societies that were quite different from many present large organizations. Such organizations are often characterized by interdependence and competitiveness between hundreds of people (people that are all working for the same big organization), by interdependence and competitiveness between smaller groups of people (different departments within the same organization), and by the presence of women in charge of groups (female managers). The fact that in such an evolutionarily novel context, the same tendencies, including sex differences, seem to occur as those that have evolved in the context of intimate relationships – even though these may not be adaptive – underlines the evolutionary background of these tendencies. Nevertheless, this does not imply that these tendencies are fixed and unmodifiable. Organizations can do a lot to prevent and reduce jealousy and envy by fostering a cooperative climate characterized by trust, by not highlighting individual differences in performance, and by promoting considerate leadership.

As mentioned earlier, not much research has been conducted on jealousy and different types of envy within organizational contexts. Future research may expand on the few studies that are available (e.g. Buunk et al., 2011; Zurriaga et al., 2018), for example by focusing on the specific behaviors that jealous and envious individuals in organizations may show. For a better understanding of both jealousy and envy, future studies may also focus on the underlying process of social comparison: for instance, by investigating the relationship of SCO with both malicious and benign envy SCO. Based on previous research (e.g. Tesser & Campbell, 1990) one might expect both types of envy to be positively related to SCO, especially to the tendency to make upward social comparisons. If this is indeed the case, studies may investigate what interventions may help counter the potentially negative effects especially of malicious envy among those high in social comparison orientation. Finally, it would be of great interest to examine the relation between both envy and jealousy and the use of modern communication technology within organizations. Several studies have shown that messages communicated by social media and other digital tools may evoke strong feelings of both jealousy and envy (e.g. Dijkstra, Barelds, & Groothof, 2013; Jin & Muqaddam, 2018). Little is known, however, about how modern communication technology within organizations may lead to envy and jealousy among employees, which is, given the heavy reliance of most modern organizations on digital communication, a timely and relevant issue.

References

Andiappan, M. (2017). Ties that bind: A tripartite model of jealousy, envy and fear. *Academy of Management Proceedings*, *1*, https://doi.org/10.5465/AMBPP.2017.16652abstract

Baenninger, M. A., Baenninger, R., & Houle, D. (1993). Attractiveness, attentiveness, and perceived male shortage: Their influence on perceptions of other females. *Ethology and Sociobiology*, *14*, 293–304.

Balliet, D., & Van Lange, P. A. M. (2013). Trust, conflict, and cooperation: A meta-analysis. *Psychological Bulletin*, *139*, 1090–1112.

Bedeian, A. G. (1995). Workplace envy. *Organizational Dynamics*, *23*, 49–56.

Betzig, L. (1986). *Despotism and differential reproduction: A Darwinian view of history.* New York, NY: Aldine.

Bleske-Rechek, A., & Lighthall, M. (2010). Attractiveness and rivalry in women's friendships with women. *Human Nature*, *21*, 82–97.

Bryan, A., Webster, G. D., & Mahaffey, A. L. (2011). The big, the rich, and the powerful: Physical, financial, and social dimensions of dominance in mating and attraction. *Personality and Social Psychology Bulletin*, *37*, 365–382.

Buunk, A. P., Aan 't Goor, J., & Castro Solano, A. (2010). Intrasexual competition at work: Sex differences in the jealousy-evoking effect of rival characteristics in work settings. *Journal of Social and Personal Relationships*, *27*, 671–684.

Buunk, A. P., Castro Solano, A., Zurriaga, R., & Gonzalez, P. (2011). Gender differences in the jealousy-evoking nature of rival characteristics. *Journal of Cross-Cultural Psychology*, *42*, 323–439.

Buunk, A. P., & Dijkstra, P. (2012). The social animal within organizations. In S. C. Roberts (Ed.), *Applied evolutionary psychology* (pp. 36–51). Oxford, UK: Oxford University Press.

Buunk, A. P., & Fisher, M. (2009). Individual differences in intrasexual competition. *Journal of Evolutionary Psychology*, *7*, 37–48.

Buunk, A. P., & Gibbons, F. X. (2006). Social comparison orientation: A new perspective on those who do and those who don't compare with others. In S. Guimond (Ed.), *Social comparison and social psychology: Understanding cognition, intergroup relations and culture* (pp. 15–33). Cambridge, UK: Cambridge University Press.

Buunk, A. P., Pollet, T. V., Dijkstra, P. & Massar, K. (2011). Intrasexual competition within organizations. In G. Saad (Ed.), *Evolutionary psychology in the business sciences* (pp. 41–70). New York, NY: Springer.

Buunk, A. P., & Van der Laan, V. (2002). Do women need female role models? Subjective social status and the effects of same-sex and opposite sex comparisons. *Revue Internationale de Psychologie Sociale, 15*, 129–155.

Buunk, A. P., & Ybema, J. F. (1997). Social comparisons and occupational stress: The identifaction-contrast model. In A. P. Buunk & F. X. Gibbons (Eds.), *Health, coping and well-being: Perspectives from social comparison theory* (pp. 359–388). Hillsdale, NJ: Erlbaum.

Buunk, A. P., Zurriaga, R., González-Navarro, P., & Monzani, L. (2016). Attractive rivals may undermine the expectation of career advancement and enhance jealousy: An experimental study. *European Journal of Work and Organizational Psychology, 25*, 798–803.

Buunk, A. P., Zurriaga, R., & Peiró, J. M. (2010). Social comparison as a predictor of changes in burnout among nurses. *Anxiety, Stress & Coping, 2*, 181–194.

Buunk, A. P., Zurriaga, R., Peiró, J. M., Nauta, A., & Gosalvez, I. (2005). Social comparisons at work as related to a cooperative social climate and to individual differences in social comparison orientation. *Applied Psychology: An International Review, 54*, 61–80.

Campbell, A. (2002). *A mind of her own: The evolutionary psychology of women*. Oxford, UK: Oxford University Press.

Campbell, A. (2004). Female competition: Causes, constraints, content, and contexts. *Journal of Sex Research, 41*, 16–26.

Cashdan, E. (1998). Are men more competitive than women? *British Journal of Social Psychology, 37*, 213–229.

Cohen-Charash, Y., & Mueller, J. (2007). Does perceived unfairness exacerbate or mitigate interpersonal counterproductive work behaviors related to envy? *Journal of Applied Psychology, 92*, 666–680.

Confer, J. C., Easton, J. A., Fleischman, D. S., Goetz, C. D., Lewis, D. M., Perilloux, C., & Buss, D. M. (2010). Evolutionary psychology: Controversies, questions, prospects, and limitations. *American Psychologist, 65*, 110.

Darwin, C. (1871). *The descent of man and selection in relation to sex*. London, UK: John Murray.

De Cremer, D., & Van Knippenberg, D. (2004). Leader self-sacrifice and leadership effectiveness: The moderating role of leader self-confidence. *Organizational Behavior and Human Decision Processes, 95*, 140–155.

Dijkstra, P., Barelds, D. P., & Groothof, H. A. (2013). Jealousy in response to online and offline infidelity: The role of sex and sexual orientation. *Scandinavian Journal of Psychology, 54*(4), 328–336.

Dijkstra, P., & Buunk, A. P. (1998). Jealousy as a function of rival characteristics: An evolutionary perspective. *Personality and Social Psychology Bulletin, 24*, 1158–1166.

Do, M. H., & Minbashian, A. (2014). A meta-analytic examination of the effects of the agentic and affiliative aspects of extraversion on leadership outcomes. *Leadership Quarterly, 25*, 1040–1053.

Dogan, K., & Vecchio, R. P. (2001). Managing envy and jealousy in the workplace. *Compensation & Benefits Review, 33*, 57–64.

Duffy, M. K., Shaw, J. D., & Schaubroeck, J. M. (2008). Envy in organizational life. In R. H. Smith (Ed.), *Envy: Theory and research* (pp. 167–189). New York, NY: Oxford University Press.

Feldman, N. S., & Ruble, D. N. (1981). Social comparison strategies: Dimensions offered and options taken. *Personality and Social Psychology Bulletin, 7*, 11–16.

Fischer, P., Kastenmüller, A., Frey, D., & Peus, C. (2009). Social comparison and information transmission in the work context. *Journal of Applied Social Psychology, 39*, 42–61.

Försterling, F., Preikschas, S., & Agthe, M. (2007). Ability, luck, and looks: An evolutionary look at achievement ascriptions and the sexual attribution bias. *Journal of Personality and Social Psychology, 92*, 775–788.

Geary, D. C. (1998). *Male, female: The evolution of human sex differences*. Washington, DC: American Psychological Association.

Geary, D. C. (2010). Competing for mates. In D. C. Geary (Ed.), *Male, female: The evolution of human sex differences* (2nd edition, pp. 213–245). Washington, DC: American Psychological Association.

Grosser, T. J., Lopez-Kidwell, V., & Labianca, G. (2010). A social network analysis of positive and negative gossip in organizational life. *Group & Organization Management*, *35*, 177–212.

Grosser, T. J., Lopez-Kidwell, V., Labianca, G. J., & Ellwardt, L. (2012). Hearing it through the grapevine: Positive and negative workplace gossip. *Organizational Dynamics*, *41*, 52–61.

Harris, C., & Darby, R. (2010). Jealousy in adulthood. In S. Hart & M. Legerstee (Eds.), *Handbook of jealousy: Theory, research and multidisciplinary approaches* (pp. 547–571). Oxford, UK: Blackwell.

Hill, S. E., & Buss, D. M. (2006). Envy and positional bias in the evolutionary psychology of management. *Managerial and Decision Economics*, *27*, 131–143.

Hoogland, C. E., Thielke, S., & Smith, R. H. (2017). Envy as an evolving episode. In R. H. Smith, U. Merlone, & M. K. Duffy (Eds.), *Envy at work and in organizations: Research, theory, and applications* (pp. 111–142). New York, NY: Oxford University Press.

Hopcroft, R. L. (2006). Sex, status, and reproductive success in the contemporary United States. *Evolution and Human Behavior*, *27*, 104–120.

Kletner, D., Haift, J., & Shiota, M. N. (2006). Social functions and the evolution of emotions. In M. A. Schaller, J. A. Simpson, & D. T. Kenrick (Eds.), *Evolution and social psychology* (pp. 115–142). New York, NY: Psychology.

Iredale, W., Van Vugt., M., & Dunbar, R. I. M. (2008). Showing off in humans: Male generosity as mate signal. *Evolutionary Psychology*, *6*, 386–392.

Jin, S. V., & Muqaddam, A. (2018). "Narcissism 2.0! Would narcissists follow fellow narcissists on Instagram?" The mediating effects of narcissists' personality similarity and envy, and the moderating effects of popularity. *Computers in Human Behavior*, *81*, 31–41.

Kilduff, G. J., Galinsky, A. D., Gallo, E., & Reade, J. J. (2016). Whatever it takes to win: Rivalry increases unethical behavior. *Academy of Management Journal*, *59*, 1508–1534.

Kim, E., & Glomb, T. M. (2014). Victimization of high performers: The roles of envy and work group identification. *Journal of Applied Psychology*, *99*, 619–634.

Luxen, M. F., & Van de Vijver, F. J. R. (2006). Facial attractiveness, sexual selection, and personnel selection: When evolved preferences matter. *Journal of Organizational Behavior*, *27*, 241–255.

Melia, J. L., & Becerril, M. (2007). Psychosocial sources of stress and burnout in the construction sector: A structural equation model. *Psicothema*, *19*, 679–686.

Miller, C. T. (1984). Self-schemas, gender, and social comparison: A clarification of the related attributes hypothesis. *Journal of Personality and Social Psychology*, *46*, 1222–1229.

Nicholson, N. (1998). How hardwired is human behavior? *Harvard Business Review*, *76*, 134–147.

Parrott, W. G. (1991). The emotional experiences of envy and jealousy. In P. Salovey (Ed.), *The psychology of jealousy and envy* (pp. 3–28). New York, NY: Guilford.

Parrott, W. G., & Smith, R. H. (1993). Distinguishing the experiences of envy and jealousy. *Journal of Personality and Social Psychology*, *64*, 906–920.

Quinn, T. J., & Wilson, B. R. (1989). Somatotype and Type A behavior in college-age adults. *Psychological Reports*, *65*, 15–18.

Saad, G., & Gill, T. (2001). Sex differences in the ultimatum game: An evolutionary psychology perspective. *Journal of Bioeconomics*, *3*, 171–193.

Schmitt, B. D. (1988). Social comparison in romantic jealousy. *Personality and Social Psychology Bulletin*, *14*, 374–387.

Schuster, B. (1996). Rejection, exclusion, and harassment at work and in schools: An integration of results from research on mobbing, bullying, and peer rejection. *European Psychologist*, *1*, 293–317.

Shu, C. Y., & Lazatkhan, J. (2017). Effect of leader–member exchange on employee envy and work behavior moderated by self-esteem and neuroticism. *Journal of Work and Organizational Psychology*, *33*, 69–81.

Sidanius, J., & Pratto, F. (1999). *Social dominance*. Cambridge, UK: Cambridge University Press.

Smith, R. H., Merlone, U., & Duffy, M. K. (Eds.) (2017). *Envy at work and in organizations:*

Research, theory, and applications. New York, NY: Oxford University Press.

Steil, J. M., & Hay, J. L. (1997). Social comparison in the workplace: A study of 60 dual-career couples. *Personality and Social Psychology Bulletin, 23*, 427–438.

Sterling, C. M., & Labianca, G. (2015). Costly comparisons: Managing envy in the workplace. *Organizational Dynamics, 44*, 296–305.

Stulp, G., Buunk, A. P., Verhulst, S., & Pollet, T. V. (2013). Tall claims? Sense and nonsense about the importance of height of US presidents. *Leadership Quarterly, 24*, 159–171.

Suls, J., Gaes, G., & Gastorf, J. W. (1979). Evaluating a sex-related ability: Comparison with same-, opposite-, and combined-sex norms. *Journal of Research in Personality, 13*, 294–304.

Tai, K., Narayanan, J., & McAllister, D. J. (2012). Envy as pain: Rethinking the nature of envy and its implications for employees and organizations. *Academy of Management Review, 37*, 107–129.

Tesser, A., & Campbell, J. (1980). Self-definition: The impact of the relative performance and similarity of others. *Social Psychology Quarterly, 43*, 341–347.

Thompson, G., Buch, R., and Glasø, L. (2018). Follower jealousy at work: A test of Vecchio's model of antecedents and consequences of jealousy. *Journal of Psychology: Interdisciplinary and Applied, 152*, 60–74.

Van de Ven, N., Zeelenberg, M., & Pieters, R. (2009). Leveling up and down: The experiences of benign and malicious envy. *Emotion, 9*, 419–429.

Van Dick, R., & Wagner, W. (2001). Stress and strain in teaching: A structural equation approach. *British Journal of Educational Psychology, 71*, 243–259.

Van Vugt, M., Roberts, G., & Hardy, C. (2007). Competitive altruism: Development of reputation-based cooperation in groups. In R. I. M. Dunbar & L. Barrett (Eds.), *Handbook of evolutionary psychology* (pp. 531–540). Oxford, UK: Oxford University Press.

Vecchio, R. P. (2000). Negative emotions in the workplace: Employee jealousy and envy. *International Journal of Stress Management, 7*, 161–179.

Wang, Y., & Sung, W. (2016). Predictors of organizational citizenship behavior: Ethical leadership and workplace jealousy. *Journal of Business Ethics, 135*, 117–128.

Wert, S. R., & Salovey, P. (2004). A social comparison account of gossip. *Review of General Psychology, 8*, 122–137.

Yasin, M. (2018). Empirical examination of theoretical model of workplace envy: Evidences from Jordan. *Management Research Review, 41*, 1438–1459.

Zurriaga, R., González-Navarro, P., Buunk, A. P., & Dijkstra, P. (2018). Jealousy at work: The role of rivals' characteristics. *Scandinavian Journal of Psychology, 59*, 443–450.

34 Other-Focused Emotion Triads

Contempt, Anger, and Disgust (CAD) and Awe, Gratitude, and Elevation (AGE)

Lauren R. Locklear and Robert Folger

Humans have an interdependent existence as a fundamentally social species. To coordinate and cooperate, or even simply to avoid retribution, each individual must take into account the reactions of others toward his or her conduct. Moreover, accommodating those reactions often requires that the individual curb the pursuit of otherwise unfettered self-interest. When such conduct occurs in an exemplary fashion (e.g. involving self-sacrifice for the sake of others' interests), it can elicit approbation; when sufficient suppression of self-interest fails to take place (e.g. exploiting others), it can elicit negative reactions from others that backfires – perhaps in ways detrimental to attaining the personal goals pursued.

This chapter addresses affective reactions to a person's conduct. Commonly, such reactions are termed *emotional*. Moreover, we focus specifically on emotions associated with the approval or disapproval of conduct. The approval or disapproval of someone else's behavior can occur on grounds termed *moral*. Thus, we discuss the nature of moral emotions, concentrating on categories known as *other-condemning* or *other-praising* (cf. Haidt, 2003).

Specifically, we first address the other-condemning emotions triad of contempt, anger, and disgust (CAD). The emotions in the CAD triad are typically elicited by violations of three moral codes (Schweder, Much, Mahapatra, & Park, 1997). This alignment suggests that violations of autonomy lead to anger, violations of community elicit contempt, and divinity violations prompt disgust (Rozin, Lowery, Imada, & Haidt, 1999). Just as violations of moral codes can elicit strong negative emotional responses, observations of moral superiority can elicit strong positive emotional responses. Upon witnessing or experiencing exemplary behavior, the other-praising emotions triad of awe, gratitude, and elevation (AGE) can be elicited. We argue, in concert with prior research, that awe results when individuals obey or defend the moral code of autonomy, gratitude is the result of observance of community codes, and elevation is elicited when individuals move up on the divinity code (cf. Haidt, 2003). We first review the CAD triad, followed by the AGE triad, and then address current and future research directions for each of the discrete emotions.[1] Both triads are summarized in Table 34.1.

The Other-Condemning Triad: Contempt, Anger, and Disgust

Other-condemning emotions (Haidt, 2003) are elicited when individuals fail to adhere to standards of moral conduct. As social beings, humans are acutely aware of individuals' reputations, and reputations for engaging in unethical behavior (e.g. dishonesty) may elicit such other-condemning emotions as those termed *contempt*, *anger*, and *disgust*. Social–functionalist views of these three emotions have treated them as distinct; in that regard they have also been described as having unique antecedents and outcomes (Hutcherson & Gross, 2011).

[1] For an alternative to the idea of dividing emotions along discrete lines, see Ellsworth (2014).

Table 34.1 Taxonomy of other-focused moral emotion triads

Emotion triad	Moral emotions	Associated moral codes
Other-condemning emotions (CAD) Negatively valenced, other-focused emotions that are experienced when observing or experiencing immoral actions, and that then motivate observers to avoid or punish those that engage in the immoral actions.	**Contempt** A feeling in response to individuals that pose a threat that involves looking down on someone or feeling morally superior.	**Violations of community** Violations of communal codes such as duty, hierarchy, and interdependence.
	Anger A feeling in response to perceptions of potential harm, especially when perceived to be intentional.	**Violations of autonomy** Violations of individual privileges, which emphasize harm, justice, and rights.
	Disgust A feeling in response to something revolting as either perceived or imagined.	**Violations of divinity** Violations of purity or sanctity such as pollution and sin.
Other-praising emotions (AGE) Positively valenced, other-focused emotions that are experienced when observing the moral excellence of others, and that then motivate observers to engage in moral behaviors themselves.	**Awe** The perception of being in the presence of something that an individual does not immediately understand.	**Observances of autonomy** Defenses of autonomy include virtuous acts, loyalty, and will to sacrifice.
	Gratitude A feeling of appreciation in response to an experience that is beneficial to, but not attributable to, the self.	**Observances of community** Defenses of community include behavior that is benevolent, prosocial in nature, and self-transcendent.
	Elevation A feeling experienced when witnessing an exemplary moral act performed by another person.	**Observances of divinity** Observances of divinity include behavior that is honorable or heroic.

The labels for these three other-condemning emotions can be traced primarily to an article by Rozin et al. (1999), although they cited Izard (1971, 1977) as having identified them as the so-called *hostility triad* and having found them to be commonly experienced in conjunction with one another. In turn, and consistent with the letters of the acronym, the Rozin et al. (1999) associated these emotions respectively with community, autonomy, and divinity, based on three types of moral codes proposed by Shweder, Much, Mohaptra, and Park (1997). As the authors put it, "The proposed alignment links anger to autonomy … contempt to community … and disgust to divinity" (Rozin et al., 1999, p. 574). Schweder (1999) suggests that the ethics of autonomy concern individual privileges, and emphasizes harm, justice, and rights. Ethics of community concern violation of communal codes such as duty, hierarchy, and interdependence. Finally, ethics of divinity concern violations of purity or sanctity such as pollution and sin.

In this section of the chapter we address each emotion first according to its classic representation as an emotional construct, including the traditional and most widely accepted ways of describing how each is elicited and what its typical consequences turn out to be. We follow these discussions of the three constructs with a parallel evaluation of the three AGE constructs, and then with selective descriptions of more recent research trends that have built on the original findings.

The Construct of Contempt as a Moral Emotion

Early research on contempt sought to distinguish the emotion from others such as anger and disgust (e.g. Ekman & Heider, 1988). Contempt can be described as an emotion that involves looking down on someone and feeling morally superior (Ekman, 1994). The primary function of both contempt and moral disgust (to be discussed subsequently) is to mark individuals whose behavior suggests that they represent a threat and to avoid them, thereby reducing the risk of exposure to harm (Hutcherson & Gross, 2011).

In the history of research on contempt, numerous conflicting findings emerged. One explanation was that English speakers do not know the meaning of the word contempt (Haidt & Keltner, 1999). Whatever the case, research on contempt was often based on the assumption that it represented a distinct emotion. (For a more complex and nuanced approach to contempt see Gervais and Fessler, 2017.) Research on the facial expression of contempt was a primary focus; otherwise the empirical research was sparse. Nonetheless, both theory and what research did exist pointed to rather specific types of eliciting conditions.

Proposed Eliciting Context

The characterization of contempt by Rozin et al. (1999) pointed to Miller (1997) as having proposed that this emotion functions to mark out and maintain distinctions in rank and prestige. Contempt was thus said to be other-directed toward individuals and groups who are thought of as beneath the self – that is, inferior in some regard (Ekman,1994). In the context of some egalitarian cultures, contempt might be experienced when an individual does not measure up to a position that he/she occupies or to the level of prestige that he/she proclaims. In democracies, individuals may feel upward contempt toward bosses, the upper class, and elites.

Proposed Action Tendencies

As a "cool" emotion, contempt motivates neither approach nor withdrawal tendencies. Instead, contempt tends to involve social–cognitive perceptions that cause the actor to treat the object of contempt with less warmth, respect, and consideration in future interactions (Oatley & Johnson-Laird, 1996). It follows that such an emotion could be the basis for prejudice and discrimination (Izard, 1977), ostracism/shunning, and the like.

The Construct of Anger as a Moral Emotion

Anger is not typically considered a moral emotion (although see Lazarus & Cohen-Carash, 2001), but two types of anger are relevant to the moral domain: anger in reference to the self, and righteous anger on the behalf of another person or group. Anger is generally felt when individuals perceive a potential harm to the self and attribute intentionality to another individual. Contrastingly, righteous anger is focused on a perpetrator violating moral standards (Tagney, Stuewig, & Mashek, 2007). Obviously anger might easily be (and often has been) conceptualized as an immoral emotion that it is necessary to suppress. When considered in more prosocial terms, however, anger might include standing up for what is right and demanding justice (Tavris, 1982) even when something other than one's own personal welfare is at stake (e.g. as moral outrage, righteous indignation, and the like).

Proposed Eliciting Context

As conceptualized in its other-condemning mode, anger represents a response to violations of the ethic of autonomy; that is, when "an action is wrong because it directly hurts another person, or infringes upon his/her rights or freedoms as an individual" (Rozin et al.,1999, p. 575). This is consistent with definitions of anger as "an emotion that involves an appraisal of responsibility of wrongdoing by another person or entity" (Gibson & Callister, 2010, p. 68). In other words, someone acting immorally elicits moralized anger.

Proposed Action Tendencies

Anger as an other-condemning moral emotion generally involves the motivation to attack, humiliate, or seek revenge against an immoral or unjust actor. As righteous anger, it can motivate third parties to act on behalf of others to remedy perceived injustices (Tagney et al., 2007). For example, Skarlicki, Ellard, and Kelln (1997) showed that when an organization's layoff practices seem unfair, customers can become inclined to react retributively toward it (e.g. choosing not to do business with it).

The Construct of Disgust as a Moral Emotion

Rozin et al. (1999) noted that disgust, like anger, comes in both moral and non-moral versions. *Core disgust* (Rozin & Fallon, 1987; Rozin, Haidt, & McCauley, 1993) is the non-moral emotional experience, akin to distaste – to be distinguished from *sociomoral disgust*, the moral emotion. Thus, it has been proposed on evolutionary grounds that moralized disgust grew out of a non-moralized distaste response found in animals, which developed to protect them from foods (Rozin, Haidt, & McCauley, 2000). Commonly disgust refers to something that seems revolting, primarily in relation to the sense of taste as actually perceived or vividly imagined; and secondarily to anything that causes a similar feeling through the sense of smell, touch, and even of eyesight (Darwin, 1965). In contrast, the primary function of moral disgust and (like contempt as a moral emotion) is other-oriented toward individuals whose unethical conduct suggests they represent a threat, such that and avoiding them thereby reduces the risk of exposure to harm (Hutcherson & Gross, 2011).

Proposed Eliciting Context

Rozin et al. (1999) distinguished the non-moral version of disgust from an other-condemning emotion previously called sociomoral disgust (Rozin, Haidt, & McCauley, 1993). In Western cultures, for example, "sociomoral disgust is triggered by a variety of situations in which people behave without dignity or in which people strip others of their dignity" (Rozin et al., 1999, p. 575). Miller (1997) conceptualized moralized disgust as a response to "the vices of hypocrisy, cruelty, fawning, and betrayal" (Rozin et al., 1999, p. 575) if perceived to be violations of social norms. When Americans recounted instances in which they felt disgusted, many of the responses referred to "hearing about sociomoral violations such as racism and child abuse" (Rozin et al., 1999, p. 575). In the domains such as sex, drugs, and body modification, a moralized version of disgust might be other-condemning if the behavior in question seems to involve violations of local cultural rules for how to use one's body (Haidt & Hersh, 2001).

Proposed Action Tendencies

Disgust can lead to drawing lines that define in-groups and out-groups (Haidt & Hersh, 2001). This tendency might be considered prosocial in such cases as ostracizing someone who behaves in morally repugnant ways. Specifically, the action tendencies based on moralized disgust have been conceptualized as part of a social reward–punishment system serving to deter culturally inappropriate behaviors (Miller, 1997).

The Other-Praising Triad: Awe, Gratitude, and Elevation

Although the review has thus far considered negative emotions, other-focused emotions can also vary in valence to include positive emotions. The moral emotions literature, however, did not recognize the positive other-focused emotions until Haidt (2003) first wrote about the emotions experienced when individuals observe admirable deeds. Since then, the positive psychology movement has increased focus on positive moral emotions and the field has seen new developments in the understanding of positively valenced other-directed emotions (Tagney et al., 2007).

Positively valenced other-focused emotions, called other-praising emotions, are experienced because individuals are sensitive to good deeds and moral exemplars. Unlike negative emotions, which serve to focus attention on problems and problem solving, positive emotions emerge in safer situations that do not require narrowing attention to threats (Haidt, 2003). In fact, broaden-and-build theory suggests that positive emotions broaden a person's cognitions and make him/her more open to new ideas, new relationships, and new possibilities (Fredrickson, 1998). Importantly, these positive emotions, when experienced, motivate observers to engage in admirable deeds themselves. Research on other-praising emotions has primarily focused on three discrete emotions: awe, gratitude, and elevation. The AGE triad is summarized in Table 34.1. In this section of the chapter we define each emotion first according to its classic representation, including the traditional and most widely accepted ways of describing how each is elicited and its associated action tendencies. In the subsequent section we address more recent research trends and future research directions for each discrete emotion in the CAD and AGE constructs.

The Construct of Awe as a Moral Emotion

Awe is described as the perception of being in the presence of something that an individual does not immediately understand and is compared to feelings of wonder and admiration (Stellar et al., 2017). Using a prototype approach, Keltner and Haidt (2003) first defined awe, identifying two features that are involved in its elicitation: vastness and accommodation. Vastness is the perception that an experience is larger than the self in size, fame, authority, or prestige. Accommodation refers to adapting mental structures when an individual cannot understand new experiences (Piaget & Inhelder, 1969). This need for adaptation is the reason that awe is often associated with confusion, ambiguity, feelings of smallness or powerlessness, and feelings of enlightenment (Keltner & Haidt, 2003). Emotional experiences lacking one or both of the features of vastness and accommodation are not the emotion of awe but rather another emotion such as surprise. Although many scholars have defined and spoken about awe, all definitions have in common that awe involves being in the presence of something powerful with associated feelings of submission, confusion, surprise, and wonder (Keltner & Haidt, 2003). Awe-inspiring stimuli include socially important people (e.g. Martin Luther King, Jr.) or historical events, complex artistic endeavors such as the *Mona Lisa*, or a volume of complex explanatory information such as the theory of general relativity.

Little work in psychology has examined the specific emotion of awe, particularly in regard to differentiating awe from other discrete emotions. In fact, most early writing on awe comes from religion, sociology, and philosophy (Keltner &

Haidt, 2003). One reason for this dearth of empirical research on awe is that early work suggested awe did not have a distinct facial expression (cf. Keltner & Haidt, 2003). However, recent work has shown that awe does have a universally recognized expression in both face (Campos, Shiota, Keltner, Gonzaga, & Goetz, 2013; Shiota, Campos, & Keltner, 2003) and voice (Cordaro, Keltner, Tshering, Wangchuk, & Flynn, 2016; Simon-Thomas, Keltner, Sauter, Sinicropi-Yao, & Abramson, 2009). This recognition has helped to distinguish awe fom other positive emotions.

Beyond differentiating awe from other emotions based on facial expressions, awe also has been thought to have unique evolutionary functions. Evolutionary claims suggest that awe functions to increase social cohesion, perhaps in response to powerful leaders, which helped groups prioritize group goals and coordinate communal responses to threats (Keltner & Haidt, 2003). Feelings of awe have been thought to produce group cohesion and coordination by increasing group commitment and by reducing feelings of self-importance (Stellar et al., 2017). Some empirical work has demonstrated support for the proposed evolutionary and social functions of awe.

Proposed Eliciting Context

Over half of all awe experiences are elicited in response to appraisals that others have behaved virtuously or exceptionally (Shiota, Keltner, & Mossman, 2007). Other elicitors include natural beauty and art or artistic ability (Shiota et al., 2007). Thus awe is not only felt in response to the acts of individuals but also felt in response to situations, settings, places, and things.

Proposed Action Tendencies

Experiences of awe tend to make people stop, admire, and open their hearts and minds to others (Shiota et al., 2003). Recent work suggests that other-focused awe motivates loyalty, will to sacrifice, and positive in-group views (Stellar et al., 2017). Similarly, awe has also been shown to increase feelings of interconnectedness and common humanity (Shiota et al., 2007). Furthermore, awe helps to reinforce status in relation to powerful others by promoting feelings of humility, diminished entitlement, and increased generosity (Stellar et al., 2017). Overall, awe experiences are associated with communal and other-focused outcomes.

The Construct of Gratitude as a Moral Emotion

Although gratitude has garnered recent attention in popular culture as the ultimate self-help trick, it has been important to philosophers, theologians, and psychologists since as early as 54 AD (Seneca, *On Benefits*). The word "gratitude" originates from the Latin term *gratia,* which means grace or thankfulness (Emmons & Shelton, 2002). In scholarly research, trait gratitude is defined as a life orientation and worldview toward noticing and appreciating the positive in life and responding with gratitude to the roles of other people's benevolence in the positive experiences and outcomes that one obtains (McCullough, Emmons, & Tsang, 2002; Wood et al., 2008). Moreover, state gratitude is defined as a feeling of appreciation in response to an experience that is beneficial to, but not attributable to, the self (Emmons & McCullough, 2004). Importantly, gratitude is always a pleasant emotion, unlike the negative feeling of indebtedness.

Gratitude is thought to have evolved as an important emotion to assist individuals in relationship and resource building (Algoe, 2012; Fredrickson, 2004). Specifically, gratitude reinforces reciprocity norms and can even foster upstream altruism with exchange partners (Trivers, 1971; Nowak & Roch, 2006), allowing for more cohesive and beneficial coordination between exchange partners over time. Beyond benefits to exchange partners, the positive psychology movement has argued that gratitude is important to individuals as a human strength that contributes to individual well-being, civic engagement, and spiritual satisfaction (Emmons & Crumpler, 2000).

Proposed Eliciting Context

Gratitude is triggered by the perception that another person has done a good deed for the self, intentionally or voluntarily (Weiner & Graham, 1989). Specifically, people are most likely to feel gratitude when they perceive that an act that they have benefited from was beneficial, costly to the actor, and intentional as opposed to accidental (McCullough et al., 2001). Gratitude has been thought of as a moral barometer that makes an individual sensitive to events in which another person provides a benefit to the self (McCullough et al., 2001), and therefore events in which an individual is provided a benefit are the most common triggers of gratitude. Individuals high in dispositional gratitude are more likely to experience state gratitude when provided benefits or kindnesses from others (Wood et al., 2008).

Proposed Action Tendencies

Gratitude has a moral action tendency, functioning to motivate individuals to act prosocially (McCullough et al., 2001). Empirical research has shown that individuals high in *trait* gratitude are more likely to be prosocial (McCullough, et al., 2001; McCullough, Kimeldorf, & Cohen, 2008), but also that inductions of gratitude as a *state* can lead to greater altruism, prosocial behavior, or generosity (Grant & Gino, 2010). Gratitude also motivates improved relationships with benefactors (Algoe & Haidt, 2009). Recent work by Algoe and colleagues has demonstrated that gratitude helps individuals find high-quality relationship partners (Algoe, Fredrickson, & Gable, 2013), reminds individuals of existing relationship partners (Algoe & Zhaoyang, 2016), and strengthens the bonds between individuals in existing relationships (Algoe, Kurtz, & Hilaire, 2016).

The Construct of Elevation as a Moral Emotion

The term "elevation" (also referred to as moral elevation), coined by Jonathan Haidt (2000, p. 1), refers to the feelings people experience when witnessing an exemplary moral act performed by another person (Thomson & Siegel, 2017). Theoretical work on elevation emphasizes its role in guiding our judgments of others' morality and our own subsequent moral decision making (Haidt, 2001; 2003). Keltner and Haidt (2003) differentiate elevation from awe by demonstrating that elevation, as a more social elicitor, need not involve the perceptions of vastness or power that characterize awe. For example, elevation is elicited when observing behavior that is honorable, admirable, or heroic; elevation is thought of as the opposite of moral disgust (Haidt, 2000). Some have described feeling elevation simply by hearing stories about acts of kindness and charity. When elevation is elicited in lab studies, participants report a pleasant tingling in their chest, turn their attention outward, and feel motivated to behave morally themselves (Haidt et al., 2002). Although elevation does not have a distinctive facial expression, it has the hallmarks of a basic emotion (Algoe & Haidt, 2009).

Proposed Eliciting Context

Elevation is caused by witnessing demonstrations of humanity's higher or better nature such as acts of charity, kindness, loyalty, and self-sacrifice. Haidt (2000) suggests elevation is elicited when observing others behaving in virtuous, commendable, or superhuman ways. Just as we feel disgusted when we witness others move down on the social cognition dimension of purity, we feel elevation when we witness individuals move up on the purity dimension (Haidt, 2003).

Proposed Action Tendencies

As an other-focused emotion, elevation makes people feel warmth and affection toward the elicitor of the emotion. It motivates individuals to become better people themselves, help other people, and act in prosocial ways (Haidt et al., 2002). Recent empirical work has demonstrated that elevation motivates prosocial and affiliative behavior (Algoe & Haidt, 2009).

Current and Future Research

Having outlined the historical grounds for distinguishing among moral emotions involving an other-condemning triad and an other-praising triad, we turn now to a discussion of where those distinctions have led and might further lead when it comes to research on emotions in organizational settings.

Contempt

There is both good news and bad news in regard to having contempt designated as a distinct moral emotion. On the one hand, some recent research has found evidence that contempt readily occurs in the presence of one or both other members of the CAD triad. On the other hand, some fine-grained distinctions continue to make sense conceptually, and a modest amount of research suggests that such nuances might be important to consider.

The chief source of supportive evidence comes from three studies done by Fischer and Roseman (2007). These authors developed hypotheses based on a social–functionalist approach more generally, rather than directly linking it to the specific framework suggested by Rozin et al. (1999). In addition, they focused primarily on the behavioral tendencies facilitated by contempt as an emotional experience, whereas prior research had largely dealt with the discriminability of facial contempt vis-à-vis other emotion faces. The behavioral effect of interest was essentially a distancing tendency, as reflected in behaviors such as social exclusion and ostracism, which was contrasted with the approaching-other tendencies associated with anger. Three studies supported the authors' contentions that anger is characterized more by short-term attack responses to bring about desired outcomes coercively, whereas contempt is prototypically about distancing the self from others considered inferior and thereby subject to derogation, exclusion, and the like. Methodologically, however, these findings suffer because the researchers obtained the data from contrasting conditions manipulated to seek the desired evidence. In other words, manipulating alleged differences at the outset made it easier to obtain evidence of differential tendencies as after-effects, rather than providing a more conservative test.

Other research has examined the conditions under which people are most apt to become the recipients of contempt-as-exclusion and what kinds of reactions receiving contempt is likely to elicit. For example, Melwani and Barsade (2011) found evidence from an online simulation with a virtual partner that recipients of contempt had significantly better task performance but also significantly more interpersonal aggressiveness toward their virtual partners compared with recipients of failure feedback, angry feedback, or neutral feedback. Lowered levels of implicit self-esteem and greater levels of activation significantly mediated the relationship between receiving contempt and task performance.

Mitchell, Vogel, and Folger's (2015) research represents a more indirect type of support about the nature of tendencies to consider another person inferior and thus to avoid and exclude that person. This researchers used a Time 1 and Time 2 set of linked surveys in which the first survey asked employees to report critical incidents about supervisor abuse of a coworker. The authors studied the effects of two moderators of the relation between those reports about a coworker's mistreatment and the respondent's subsequent (Time 2) report of their own behavior toward that coworker. Two items measured a proposed moderator of the effects of a coworker's mistreatment by asking about the acceptability of considering that coworker to be worthy of disdain (e.g. deserving of being treated poorly), which might be interpreted as an indication of contempt for that person. When also moderated by a measure of the strength of the respondent's moral identity, results showed evidence of exclusionary tendencies from a seven-item scale (e.g. giving the "silent treatment," shutting out the coworker from conversations). Notably, such tendencies were not a product of anger – in fact, heightened third-party anger instead tended to be associated with *support* for the coworker. Unfortunately, contempt per se was not measured directly as a mediating emotion; rather, the items used to assess mediating effects on coworker exclusion simply asked respondents whether they were content about exhibiting exclusion.

Anger

Early work on anger in a moral context demonstrated that anger results when individuals perceive that norms or standards for behavior have been violated (e.g. Da Gloria & De Ridder, 1977). In an experiment, Da Gloria & De Ridder (1979) found that witnesses of aggressive behaviors react with stronger anger when the aggressive behavior is perceived as the violation of a norm. In this vein, organizational research on anger as a moral emotion has largely looked at its instigation by perceptions of unfairness (Gibson & Callister, 2010). Our discussion omits studies of the frustration–aggression version of anger, however, because the morally laden basis of such anger – rather than motivations based solely on self-interest – makes such studies less relevant due to possible confounds with pure self-interest. Indeed, one definition of moral anger refers not only to "a primary appraisal of a moral standard violation" but also to the way it "impacts others more than oneself and … prompts corrective behavior to improve the social situation" (Lindebaum & Geddes, 2016). Put another way, "It is not only when we are harmed personally that revenge feels like the righteous response; for, we vicariously experience that righteous feeling when others are harmed or when swift vengeance is dealt to the perpetrator of harm" (Tripp & Bies, 2010, p. 413).

The connection between perceived injustice and moral (or "righteous") anger is not one-to-one, because as Bies and Tripp (2001) pointed out, injustice can elicit multi-faceted variations in emotional experiences. Although these can include morally righteous anger, they can also involve fear. Notably, however, research has found that revenge motivated by injustice is viewed as more legitimate than revenge driven solely by self-interest (Tripp, Bies, & Aquino, 2002). Moreover, the tendency to retaliate when angry is mitigated by the perceived procedural justice of an organization (Aquino, Tripp, & Bies, 2001, 2006). Anger expressions are also more likely to be functional when anger is low in intensity, expressed verbally (as opposed to physically), and is done so in settings in which anger is considered appropriate (Gibson, Schweitzer, Callister, & Gray, 2009).

Disgust

The CAD-hypothesized relationship between disgust and morality has led to research investigating several possible implications. Here we briefly touch on some of these, then point to some grounds for continuing debate about one in particular (suggesting that moral disgust might generally be a difficult topic to research in unambiguous ways).

Some research has focused on differentiating disgust from anger. A detailed compare-and-contrast discussion of how disgust differs from contempt can be found in Miceli and Castelfranchi (2018), but we cover only the most relevant empirical studies in our discussion. For example, third parties presume that expressed disgust is more likely to stem from moral motivation compared to expressed anger, which is more readily seen as motivated by self-interest (Kupfer & Giner-Sorolla, 2017). Also, disgust increases and anger decreases when the target of a moral violation is another person rather than oneself (Molho, Tybur, Gler, Balliet, & Hofmann, 2017). In the organizational domain, similar antecedents have been found to elicit both anger and disgust. Research found that violations of interpersonal justice have been shown to heighten taste and smell by triggering the emotion of disgust (Skarlicki, Hoegg, Aquino, & Nadisic, 2013). Specifically, the authors found that across three experiments, recalling unfair interpersonal treatment from leaders in the workplace or witnessing other individuals experience unfair treatment from a leader caused socio-moral disgust in participants. This finding was novel, given that violations of justice generally elicit anger.

The most intriguing line of research, however, links disgust and purity (rather than divinity) to investigate the role of cleansing behaviors and circumstances. A so-called "Macbeth effect" (namely that threat to moral purity prompts a desire for physical cleansing), for example, even suggested that "routines such as washing hands . . . can deliver a powerful antidote to threatened morality" (Zhong & Liljenquist, 2006, p. 1451). A subsequent review pointed to other cleansing effects as well, including *restitution cleansing*, in which the moral self is in some sense purified by making up for previous wrongdoing (West & Zhong, 2015). An especially intriguing extension of this research involved looking at group-based discrimination as a function of moral-purity-related behaviors. In addition to laboratory experiments demonstrating such effects, a field study found that police officers in New York "were increasingly likely to make an arrest or issue a summons as body mass index increased (i.e. as obesity rose) among people suspected of purity crimes (e.g. prostitution) but not of other crimes (e.g. burglary)" (Masicampo, Barth, & Ambady, 2014, p. 2135).

Finally, it is possible that disgust might amplify moral evaluations, making immoral actions seem even more immoral (Pizarro, Inbar, & Helion, 2011; Wheatley & Haidt, 2005). That suggestion – and the type of evidence put forward in its support – came under attack from a meta-analysis revealing an effect size of only $d = .11$ (a correlation of .06, indicating only about 0.4 percent of the variance) and claiming that when possible publication bias is taken into account, "the effect disappears entirely" (Landy & Goodwin, 2015, p. 518). In turn, those conclusions elicited a rebuttal (Schnall, Haidt, Clore, & Jordan, 2015) acknowledging some of the points made but also arguing that the meta-analysis had not been a fair test of the amplification hypothesis in certain respects (e.g. ignoring key moderators). The authors of the meta-analysis counter-argued in support of their original conclusions, referring to them as "tentative, but appropriate (Landy & Goodwin, 2015, p. 539). An independent follow-up to the meta-analysis took two key moderators into account and used two large samples (making the studies adequately powered); the authors "did not find that disgust directly increased the severity of moral judgments nor . . . that these moderators influenced the effect of disgust" (Johnson et al., 2016, p. 640).

Awe

Empirical examinations of awe have only recently begun, as most attention to awe has been theoretical or speculative. Recent empirical research on awe has focused primarily on antecedents and outcomes of awe experiences. As previously mentioned, antecedents of awe include the eliciting contexts such as witnessing moral excellence or virtuous behaviors as well as naturalistic beauty or artistic beauty (Shiota, Keltner, & Mossman, 2007).

Beyond eliciting contexts, however, research has investigated the outcomes of both dispositional awe and state or induced awe experiences. Although dispositional and state awe are distinct, the outcomes have been found to be largely similar. In a study of both dispositional awe and inductions of awe, Piff, Dietze, Feinberg,

Stancato, and Keltner (2015) found that both trait and state awe predicted greater acts of generosity above and beyond other prosocial emotions such as compassion. Furthermore, the authors found that inductions of awe led to increased ethical decision-making, generous behaviors, prosocial values, and a decreased sense of entitlement. Mirroring these findings, inductions of awe have been associated with feelings of openness and oneness with others and with friends (Van Cappellen, Corneille, Cols, & Saroglou, 2011). In experimental settings, participants who felt awe perceived that they had more available time, were less impatient, were more willing to volunteer their own time to help others, were less materialistic, and expressed greater life satisfaction (Rudd, Vohs, & Aaker, 2012). Taken together, the empirical research on awe emphasizes the prosocial, collective nature of its outcomes and suggests that awe experiences can motivate positive communal concern.

Gratitude

Theoretical work on gratitude points to the importance of gratitude for interpersonal relationships (Algoe, 2012), prosocial behaviors (McCullough et al., 2001), and personal well-being and openness (Fredrickson, 2004). Indeed, much empirical work has found support for these theories. For example, gratitude has been found to build high-quality social relationships between "big sisters" and "little sisters" in student sorority organizations (Algoe, Haidt, & Gable, 2008), strengthen existing relationships among romantic partners when expressing gratitude to one another (Algoe et al., 2013), and remind individuals of the existing important relationships in their lives (Algoe et al., 2016). Moreover, the link between gratitude and prosocial behaviors has been examined for both dispositional and state gratitude, and findings suggest that trait gratitude is associated with prosociality and generosity (Grant & Gino, 2010), as well as organizational citizenship behavior (Ford, Wang, & Eisenberger, 2018; Spence, Brown, Keeping, & Lian, 2014). Similarly, gratitude has been associated with decreased aggression (DeWall, Lambert, Pond, Kashdan, & Fincham, 2012) and decreased counterproductive work behaviors (Ford et al., 2018).

Beyond the prosocial nature of gratitude, the emotion is associated with a host of positive affective outcomes. Such outcomes include well-being (Kaplan et al., 2014; Stocker, Jacobshagen, Krings, Pfister, & Semmer, 2014), positive affect (Algoe & Zhaoyang, 2016), work engagement (Lee et al., 2019; Wandell, 2016), satisfaction, decreased depressive symptoms (Cheng, Tsui, & Lam, 2015; Geraghty, Wood, & Hyland, 2010; Wood et al., 2008), decreased perceptions of stress (Cheng et al., 2015; Darabi, Macaskill, & Reidy 2017), and lower risk of generalized anxiety disorder, use of alcohol, nicotine, and drugs, and phobia (Geraghty et al., 2010). Taken together, much empirical research supports the positive nature of gratitude. In organizational settings, gratitude interventions, which specifically cultivate feelings of gratitude, have recently been employed to harness the positive outcomes associated with gratitude for individuals (see Emmons & Mishra, 2011, for a review).

Elevation

In a recent review, Thomson and Siegel (2017) identified a number of physiological, psychological, and prosocial outcomes associated with elevation. Physiological outcomes of elevation include chills or goosebumps after watching an elevating film clip (e.g. Oliver, Hartmannm & Wooley, 2012), a feeling that one's muscles are relaxed (e.g. Algoe & Haidt, 2009), and having a lump in one's throat and tears in one's eyes (e.g. Landis et al., 2009). Affective outcomes include feeling uplifted (Algoe & Haidt, 2009), moved, respectful, and inspired (Thomson & Siegel, 2013), enhanced feelings of connectedness with others (Erickson & Abelson, 2012; Oliver et al., 2012), and enhanced feelings of benevolence (Van Cappellen, Saroglou, Iweins, Piovesana, & Fredrickson, 2013). Furthermore, elevation leads to important motivational states such as desires to be a better person, to open up and merge with others, and to help others. Finally, elevation is associated with a number of prosocial outcomes such as interpersonal helping (Schnall, Roper, Fessler, 2010), generous behavior (Aquino et al., 2011), and favorable attitudes toward diverse others (Oliver at el., 2015).

Mechanisms by which elevation leads to prosocial outcomes were first theorized by Haidt (2000; 2003) and Algoe and Haidt (2009), suggesting that elevation would foster favorable views toward people and motivate imitation of the moral deed they witnessed. In a test, Thomson and Seigel (2013) found that this effect is indeed transmitted through the proposed mechanisms. Further research found that the relationship between elevation and self-transcendence is mediated by feelings of benevolence (Van Cappellen et al., 2013). Other scholars have found evidence for the mechanisms of activation of prosocial goals and moral licensing (Ellithorpe, Ewoldsen, & Oliver, 2015). Overall, empirical work on elevation demonstrates the positive nature of the emotion and highlights the opportunity for future research to integrate this positive moral affect into organizational research contexts.

Conclusion

As demonstrated in this chapter, other-focused emotions vary in their valence, eliciting contexts, and action tendencies. These emotions shape the feelings and responses that we as humans have in the presence of moral and immoral actions. In the presence of immoral actions, other-condemning emotions are commonly stimulated such as those comprising the CAD triad: contempt, anger, and disgust. On the other hand, observations of morally superior actions tend to provoke other-praising emotions such as those in the AGE triad: awe, gratitude, and elevation. In this chapter, we have demonstrated that much current research on the other-focused emotions is either nascent or conflicting, providing an opportunity for future research to contribute to the understanding of the nomological network and function of these morally relevant emotion triads. We hope, therefore, that this review stimulates further work regarding these emotions.

References

Algoe, S. B. (2012). Find, remind, and bind: The functions of gratitude in everyday relationships. *Social and Personality Psychology Compass*, *6*(6), 455–469.

Algoe, S. B., Fredrickson, B. L., & Gable, S. L. (2013). The social functions of the emotion of gratitude via expression. *Emotion*, *13*, 605–610.

Algoe, S. B., & Haidt, J. (2009). Witnessing excellence in action: The "other-praising" emotions of elevation, gratitude, and admiration. *Journal of Positive Psychology*, *4*(2), 105–127.

Algoe, S. B., Haidt, J., & Gable, S. L. (2008). Beyond reciprocity: Gratitude and relationships in everyday life. *Emotion*, *8*, 425–429.

Algoe, S. B., Kurtz, L. E., & Hilaire, N. M. (2016). Putting the "you" in "thank you": Examining other-praising behavior as the active relational ingredient in expressed gratitude. *Social Psychological and Personality Science*, *7*(7), 658–666.

Algoe, S. B., & Zhaoyang, R. (2016). Positive psychology in context: Effects of expressing gratitude in ongoing relationships depend on perceptions of enactor responsiveness. *Journal of Positive Psychology*, *11*(4), 399–415.

Aquino, K., Tripp, T. M., & Bies, R. J. (2006). Getting even or moving on? Power, procedural justice, and types of offense as predictors of revenge, forgiveness, reconciliation, and avoidance in organizations. *Journal of Applied Psychology*, *91* (3), 653–668.

Bies, R. J., & Tripp, T. M. (2001). A passion for justice: The rationality and morality of revenge. In R. Cropanzano (Ed.), *Justice in the workplace* (Volume 2, pp. 197–208). Mahwah, NJ: Lawrence Erlbaum.

Campos, B., Shiota, M. N., Keltner, D., Gonzaga, G. C., & Goetz, J. L. (2013). What is shared, what is different? Core relational themes and expressive displays of eight positive emotions. *Cognition & Emotion*, *27*(1), 37–52.

Cannon, P. R., Schnall, S., & White, M. (2011). Transgressions and expressions: Affective facial muscle activity predicts moral judgments. *Social Psychological and Personality Science*, *2*(3), 325–331.

Chapman, H. A., Kim, D. A., Susskind, J. M., & Anderson, A. K. (2009). In bad taste: Evidence for the oral origins of moral disgust. *Science*, *323* (5918), 1222–1226.

Cheng, S. T., Tsui, P. K., & Lam, J. H. (2015). Improving mental health in health care practitioners: Randomized controlled trial of a gratitude intervention. *Journal of Consulting and Clinical Psychology*, *83*(1), 177–186.

Cordaro, D. T., Keltner, D., Tshering, S., Wangchuk, D., & Flynn, L. M. (2016). The voice conveys emotion in ten globalized cultures and one remote village in Bhutan. *Emotion*, *16*(1), 117–128.

Da Gloria, J., & De Ridder, R. (1977). Aggression in dyadic interaction. *European Journal of Social Psychology*, *7*, 189–219.

Da Gloria, J., & De Ridder, R. (1979). Sex differences in aggression: Are current notions misleading? *European Journal of Social Psychology*, *9*, 49–66.

Darabi, M., Macaskill, A., & Reidy, L. (2017). Stress among UK academics: Identifying who copes best. *Journal of Further and Higher Education*, *41*(3), 393–412.

Darwin, C. (1965). *The expression of the emotions in man and animals*. London, UK: John Marry.

DeWall, C. N., Lambert, N. M., Pond, R. S., Kashdan, T. B., & Fincham, F. D. (2012). A grateful heart is a nonviolent heart: Cross-sectional, experience sampling, longitudinal, and experimental evidence. *Social Psychological and Personality Science*, *3*, 232–240.

Ekman, P. (1994). All emotions are basic. In P. Ekman & R. J. Davidson (Eds.), *The nature of emotion: Fundamental questions* (pp. 15–19). New York, NY: Oxford University Press.

Ekman, P., & Heider, K. (1988). The universality of contempt expression. *Motivation and Emotion*, *10*, 159–168.

Ellithorpe, M. E., Ewoldsen, D. R., & Oliver, M. B. (2015). Elevation (sometimes) increases altruism: Choice and number of outcomes in elevating media effects. *Psychology of Popular Media Culture*, *4*(3), 236–250.

Ellsworth, P. C. (2014). Basic emotions and the rocks of New Hampshire. *Emotion Review*, *6*, 21–26.

Emmons, R. A., & Crumpler, C. A. (2000). Gratitude as a human strength: Appraising the evidence. *Journal of Social and Clinical Psychology*, *19*(1), 56–69.

Emmons, R. A., & Shelton, C. S. (2002). Gratitude and the science of positive psychology. In C. R. Snyder & S. J. Lopez (Eds.), *Handbook of positive psychology* (pp. 459–471). New York, NY: Oxford University Press.

Fischer, A. H., & Roseman, I. J. (2007). Beat them or ban them: The characteristics and social functions of anger and contempt. *Journal of Personality and Social Psychology*, *93*(1), 103–115.

Ford, M. T., Wang, Y., Jin, J., & Eisenberger, R. (2018). Chronic and episodic anger and gratitude toward the organization: Relationships with organizational and supervisor supportiveness and extrarole behavior. *Journal of Occupational Health Psychology*, *23*, 175–187.

Fredrickson, B. L. (1998). What good are positive emotions? *Review of General Psychology*, *2*(3), 300–319.

Fredrickson, B. L. (2004). The broaden-and-build theory of positive emotions. *Philosophical Transactions of the Royal Society B: Biological Sciences*, *359*, 1367–1375.

Geraghty, A. W., Wood, A. M., & Hyland, M. E. (2010). Dissociating the facets of hope: Agency and pathways predict dropout from unguided self-help therapy in opposite directions. *Journal of Research in Personality*, *44*(1), 155–158.

Gervais, M. M., & Fessler, D. M. (2017). On the deep structure of social affect: Attitudes, emotions, sentiments, and the case of "contempt." *Behavioral*

and Brain Sciences, doi:10.1017/S0140525X16000352
Gibson, D. E., & Callister, R. R. (2010). Anger in organizations: Review and integration. *Journal of Management*, *36*(1), 66–93.
Gibson, D. E., Schweitzer, M. E., Callister, R. R., & Gray, B. (2009). The influence of anger expressions on outcomes in organizations. *Negotiation and Conflict Management Research*, *2*(3), 236–262.
Grant, A. M., & Gino, F. (2010). A little thanks goes a long way: Explaining why gratitude expressions motivate prosocial behavior. *Journal of Personality and Social Psychology*, *98*, 946–955.
Haidt, J. (2000). The positive emotion of elevation. *Prevention & Treatment*, *3*, 1–5.
Haidt, J. (2003). Elevation and the positive psychology of morality. In C. L. Keyes & J. Haidt (Eds.), *Flourishing: Positive psychology and the life well-lived* (pp. 275–289). Washington, DC: American Psychological Association.
Haidt, J., & Hersh, M. A. (2001). Sexual morality: The cultures and emotions of conservatives and liberals. *Journal of Applied Social Psychology*, *31*(1), 191–221.
Haidt, J., & Keltner, D. (1999). Culture and facial expression: Open-ended methods find more faces and a gradient of recognition. *Cognition and Emotion*, *13*, 225–266.
Horberg, E. J., Oveis, C., Keltner, D., & Cohen, A. B. (2009). Disgust and the moralization of purity. *Journal of Personality and Social Psychology*, *97* (6), 963–976.
Hutcherson, C. A., & Gross, J. J. (2011). The moral emotions: A social–functionalist account of anger, disgust, and contempt. *Journal of Personality and Social Psychology*, *100*(4), 719–737.
Izard, C. E. (1971). *The face of emotion*. New York, NY: Appleton-Century Crofts.
Izard. C. E. (1977). *Human emotions*. New York, NY: Plenum Press.
Kaplan, S., Bradley-Geist, J. C., Ahmad, A., Anderson, A., Hargrove, A. K., & Lindsey, A. (2014). A test of two positive psychology interventions to increase employee well-being. *Journal of Business and Psychology*, *29*(3), 367–380.
Keltner, D., & Haidt, J. (2003). Approaching awe, a moral, spiritual, and aesthetic emotion. *Cognition and Emotion*, *17*, 297–314.
Landis, S. K., Sherman, M. F., Piedmont, R. L., Kirkhart, M. W., Rapp, E. M., & Bike, D. H. (2009). The relation between elevation and self-reported prosocial behavior: Incremental validity over the five-factor model of personality. *Journal of Positive Psychology*, *4*(1), 71–84.
Lazarus, R. S., & Cohen-Charash, Y. (2001). Discrete emotions in organizational life. In R. L. Payne & C. L. Cooper (Eds.), *Emotions at work: Theory, research and applications for management* (pp. 45–81). Chichester, UK: John Wiley & Sons.
Lee, H. W., Bradburn, J., Johnson, R. E., Lin, S. J., & Chang, C. D. (2019). The benefits of receiving gratitude for helpers: A daily investigation of proactive and reactive helping at work. *Journal of Applied Psychology*, *104*(2), 197–213.
Lindebaum, D., & Geddes, D. (2016). The place and role of (moral) anger in organizational behavior studies. *Journal of Organizational Behavior*, *37*(5), 738–757.
McCullough, M. E., Emmons, R. A., & Tsang, J. (2002). The grateful disposition: A conceptual and empirical topography. *Journal of Personality and Social Psychology*, *82*, 112–127.
McCullough, M. E., Kilpatrick, S., Emmons, R. A., & Larson, D. (2001). Is gratitude a moral effect? *Psychological Bulletin*, *127*, 249–266.
McCullough, M. E., Kimeldorf, M. B., & Cohen, A. D. (2008). An adaptation for altruism: The social causes, social effects, and social evolution of gratitude. *Current Directions in Psychological Science*, *17*(4), 281–285.
Miceli, M., & Castelfranchi, C. (2018). Contempt and disgust: The emotions of disrespect. *Journal for the Theory of Social Behavior*, *48*, 205–229.
Miller, W. I. (1997). *The anatomy of disgust*. Cambridge, MA: Harvard University Press.
Mitchell, M. S., Vogel, R. M., & Folger, R. (2015). Third parties' reactions to the abusive supervision of coworkers. *Journal of Applied Psychology*, *100* (4), 1040–1056.
Nowak, M. A., & Roch, S. (2006). Upstream reciprocity and the evolution of gratitude.

Proceedings of the Royal Society B: Biological Sciences, 274(1610), 605–610.

Oatley, K., & Johnson-Laird, P. N. (1995). The communicative theory of emotions: Empirical tests, mental models, and implications for social interaction. In L. L. Martin & A. Tesser (Eds.), *Striving and feeling: Interactions among goals, affect, and emotion*. Mahwah, NJ: Erlbaum.

Oliver, M. B., Hartmann, T., & Woolley, J. K. (2012). Elevation in response to entertainment portrayals of moral virtue. *Human Communication Research, 38* (3), 360–378.

Piaget, J., & Inhelder, B. (1969). *The psychology of the child* (H. Weaver, trans.) New York, NY: Basic Books (original published 1966).

Piff, P. K., Dietze, P., Feinberg, M., Stancato, D. M., & Keltner, D. (2015). Awe, the small self, and prosocial behavior. *Journal of Personality and Social Psychology, 108*(6), 883–899.

Pizarro, D., Inbar, Y., & Helion, C. (2011). On disgust and moral judgment. *Emotion Review, 3*(3), 267–268.

Rozin, P., & Fallon, A. E. (1987). A perspective on disgust. *Psychological Review, 94*(1), 23–41.

Rozin, P., Haidt, J., & McCauley, C. R. (1993). Disgust. In M. Lewis & J. M. Haviland (Eds.), *Handbook of emotions* (pp. 575–594). New York, NY: Guilford.

Rozin, P., Lowery, L., Imada, S., & Haidt, J. (1999). The CAD triad hypothesis: A mapping between three moral emotions (contempt, anger, disgust) and three moral codes (community, autonomy, divinity). *Journal of Personality and Social Psychology, 76*, 574–586.

Rudd, M., Vohs, K. D., & Aaker, J. (2012). Awe expands people's perception of time, alters decision making, and enhances well-being. *Psychological Science, 23*(10), 1130–1136.

Schnall, S., Roper, J., & Fessler, D. M. (2010). Elevation leads to altruistic behavior. *Psychological Science, 21*(3), 315–320.

Seneca, L.A. (54 AD). *On benefits*.

Shiota, M. N., Campos, B., & Keltner, D. (2003). The faces of positive emotion: Prototype displays of awe, amusement, and pride. *Annals of the New York Academy of Sciences, 1000*, 296–299.

Shiota, M. N., Keltner, D., & Mossman, A. (2007). The nature of awe: Elicitors, appraisals, and effects on self-concept. *Cognition and Emotion, 21*(5), 944–963.

Shweder, R. A., Much, N. C., Mahapatra, M., & Park, L. (1997). The "Big Three" of morality (autonomy, community, divinity) and the "Big Three" explanation of suffering. In A. Brandt & P. Rozin (Eds.), *Morality and health* (pp. 119–169). New York, NY: Routledge.

Simon-Thomas, E. R., Godzik, J., Castle, E., Antonenko, O., Ponz, A., Kogan, A., & Keltner, D. J. (2012). An fMRI study of caring vs self-focus during induced compassion and pride. *Social Cognitive and Affective Neuroscience, 7*(6), 635–648.

Skarlicki, D. P., Ellard, J. H., & Kelln, B. R. (1998). Third-party perceptions of a layoff: Procedural, derogation, and retributive aspects of justice. *Journal of Applied Psychology, 83*(1), 119–127.

Skarlicki, D., Hoegg, J., Aquino, K., & Nadisic, T. (2013). Does justice affect your sense of taste and smell? The mediating role of moral disgust. *Journal of Experimental Social Psychology, 49*, 852–859.

Spence, J. R., Brown, D. J., Keeping, L. M., & Lian, H. (2014). Helpful today, but not tomorrow? Feeling grateful as a predictor of daily organizational citizenship behaviors. *Personnel Psychology, 67*(3), 705–738.

Stellar, J. E., Bai, Y., Anderson, C. A., McNeil, G., & Keltner, D. (2017). *Cultural differences in experiences of awe*. Manuscript in preparation.

Stellar, J. E., Gordon, A. M., Piff, P. K., Cordaro, D., Anderson, C. L., Bai, Y., & Keltner, D. (2017). Self-transcendent emotions and their social functions: Compassion, gratitude, and awe bind us to others through prosociality. *Emotion Review, 9*(3), 200–207.

Stocker, D., Jacobshagen, N., Krings, R., Pfister, I. B., & Semmer, N. K. (2014). Appreciative leadership and employee well-being in everyday working life. *German Journal of Human Resource Management, 28*(1–2), 73–95.

Tangney, J. P., Stuewig, J., & Mashek, D. J. (2007). Moral emotions and moral behavior. *Annual Review of Psychology, 58*, 345–372.

Tavris, C. (1982). Anger defused. *Psychology Today, 16*(11), 25–35.

Thomson, A. L., & Siegel, J. T. (2013). A moral act, elevation, and prosocial behavior: Moderators of morality. *Journal of Positive Psychology*, *8*, 50–64.

Thomson, A. L., & Siegel, J. T. (2017). Elevation: A review of scholarship on a moral and other-praising emotion. *Journal of Positive Psychology*, *12*(6), 628–638.

Tripp, T. M., & Bies, R. J. (2010). "Righteous" anger and revenge in the workplace: The fantasies, the feuds, the forgiveness. In M. Potegal, G. Stemmler, & C. Spielberger (Eds.), *International handbook of anger* (pp. 413–431). New York, NY: Springer.

Tripp, T. M., Bies, R. J., & Aquino, K. (2002). Poetic justice or petty jealousy? The aesthetics of revenge. *Organizational Behavior and Human Decision Processes*, *89*(1), 966–984.

Trivers, R. L. (1971). The evolution of reciprocal altruism. *Quarterly Review of Biology*, *46*, 35–57.

Van Cappellen, P., Corneille, O., Cols, S., & Saroglou, V. (2011). Beyond mere compliance to authoritative figures: Religious priming increases conformity to informational influence among submissive people. *International Journal for the Psychology of Religion*, *21*(2), 97–105.

Van Cappellen, P., Saroglou, V., Iweins, C., Piovesana, M., & Fredrickson, B. L. (2013). Self-transcendent positive emotions increase spirituality through basic world assumptions. *Cognition and Emotion*, *27*(8), 1378–1394.

Wandell, J. (2016). A proposed pilot study of a gratitude practice program to increase gratitude among educators: The first step towards exploring the potential of gratitude practice to increase work engagement and buffer against and decrease burnout. *International Journal of Child, Youth and Family Studies*, *7*(2), 275–306.

Weiner, B., & Graham, S. (1989). Understanding the motivational role of affect: Life-span research from an attributional perspective. *Cognition and Emotion*, *3*(4), 401–419.

Wheatley, T., & Haidt, J. (2005). Hypnotic disgust makes moral judgments more severe. *Psychological Science*, *16*(10), 780–784.

Wood, A. M., Maltby, J., Stewart, N., Linley, P. A., & Joseph, S. (2008). A social–cognitive model of trait and state levels of gratitude. *Emotion*, *8*(2), 281–290.

35 Schadenfreude at Work

Diep Nguyen and Kara Ng

Introduction

> To feel envy is human, to savour schadenfreude is devilish.
>
> Arthur Schopenhauer

A classic comedy cliché is a man slipping on a banana peel, with audiences laughing as he struggles and falls again. From Shakespeare to the Three Stooges to modern sitcoms, slapstick comedy has had such a prominent place in entertainment that scholars have scratched their heads to understand why and how we seemingly enjoy the pain of others. Some propose that laughter is a way to release pent-up tension, while others suggest that laughter is a response to the incongruity inherent in comedy (Peacock, 2014). But how can we explain these feelings, derived from someone's misfortune, in contexts such as the workplace, where such humor or pleasure are considered inappropriate?

The "affective revolution" in organizational behavior research has sparked great interest in the role of individual, discrete emotions at work. In particular, researchers became interested in how emotions influence attitudinal, behavioral, and work outcomes of organizational members (Gooty, Gavin, & Ashkanasy, 2009; Lindebaum & Jordan, 2014). An interesting, but understudied, discrete emotion is schadenfreude, which describes the feeling of joy at the misfortunes of others, such as characters in the aforementioned comedies (Feather, 2008). It is a complex emotional state as it involves positive feelings at someone else's direct expense, leading some to question its morality. This dissonance may explain, in part, why schadenfreude has attracted the attention of scholars from various fields of psychology, philosophy, and beyond. In fact, the philosopher Arthur Schopenhauer famously considered schadenfreude to be human nature's worst trait (Cartwright, 2019).

Despite such claims, schadenfreude remains common in our social interactions and experiences; yet our understanding of the emotion, particularly at work, is limited at best. This may be an essential gap to address due to the importance, richness, and complexity of interpersonal relationships in organizational settings.

This chapter aims to provide a general overview of schadenfreude and its role in the workplace. First we define schadenfreude, and we then explain how it is distinct from, and related to, other emotions. Next, we review current research on schadenfreude at work, including individual and organizational factors related to this phenomenon. Finally, we present some unanswered questions in current schadenfreude studies and provide suggestions for future research in this area.

Schadenfreude: A General Description

What is Schadenfreude?

Schadenfreude is a German compound of two nouns, *Schaden* ("harm") and *Freude* ("joy"); the term has long been commonplace in the English language, first appearing in the *Oxford English Dictionary* in 1895. However, this concept of joy at someone's misfortune existed long before the nineteenth century and beyond Anglo-Germanic spheres. In antiquity, Aristotle used the term ἐπιχαιρεκακία (*epichairekakia*), meaning "joy over one's neighbor's misfortunes" (Lidell & Scott, 1940). Similar terms also exist in modern languages, such as French (*joie maligne*), Dutch (*leedvermaak*), Finnish (*vahingonilo*), and Mandarin Chinese (*xìngzāilèhuò*). In other languages idioms are found, as in Japanese (*Hito no fukou wa mitsu no aji*: "The misfortunes of others taste like honey") and Vietnamese (*Cười trên sự đau khổ của người khác*: "Laughing at others' sufferings"). The prevalence of the concept of schadenfreude in other times and cultures speaks to its ubiquity and universality.

How do people experience schadenfreude? It is a social emotion as it occurs during, or as a result of, interpersonal interactions (Jankowski & Takahashi, 2014). When defining the characteristic feelings of schadenfreude, researchers have tended to link it to other emotions, such as "joy," "pleasure," or "happiness" (Dasborough & Harvey, 2017; Schumpe & Lafrenière, 2016). Laughter is one of the more commonly studied behaviors expressed as a result of schadenfreude. Despite its links to happiness and joy, schadenfreude is a distinct emotion: this is illustrated in a study by Szameitat and colleagues (2009), in which they noted that schadenfreude-induced laughter had its own distinctive profile differentiating it from laughter induced by joy, tickling, or contempt. However, it is important to note that, despite experiencing positively-valenced emotions, individuals experiencing schadenfreude often do not wish harm to befall victims, nor do they wish to actively inflict harm. Therefore, schadenfreude is distinct from such states as aggression or sadism (Dasborough & Harvey, 2017; Szameitat et al., 2009).

Scholars have long debated the ethicality of schadenfreude. Traditionally, the schadenfroh (its adjectival form, describing those who experience schadenfreude) were accused of abandoning their obligation to behave compassionately; thus schadenfreude was considered an immoral emotion to be avoided (van Dijk & Ouwerkerk, 2014). Other scholars have expressed a less negative, more nuanced view: Portmann (2000) considered schadenfreude a form of righteousness and love of justice, while Ben-Ze'ev (2001) argued that the ethical evaluation of schadenfreude depends upon the harshness of the misfortune, the degree to which the schadenfroh is involved in causing the misfortune, and how the misfortune can be rationalized.

Despite the morally questionable nature of schadenfreude, it is an "emotion inherent to social life" and prevalent in a variety of contexts (Schulz, Rudolph, Tscharaktschiew, & Rudolph, 2013, p. 372). When experiencing negative moods, people report deriving pleasure from visiting the social media accounts of peers they consider less attractive or successful (Johnson & Knobloch-Westerwick, 2014). Pozner (2010) observed that schadenfreude is a key tool in YouTube or TV comedy, as can be seen with the popularity of prank videos. Some scholars point out our tendency to take joy in the failures, scandals, or faux pas of celebrities or other high-profile individuals (Knobloch-Westerwick, 2006; Watanabe, 2016; Wood, 1989). Thus schadenfreude is an essential part of our emotional lives despite our reluctance to confront or admit to it (Hoogland et al., 2015; Van Dijk & Ouwerkerk, 2014).

Schadenfreude and Other Emotions

Schadenfreude is often associated with envy and resentment, two other social emotions of a morally questionable nature. Although envy and resentment may act as precursors to schadenfreude, we argue that it is a separate emotion with its own unique characterizations.

Envy is broadly defined as an emotion resulting from others' obtainment of desired outcomes (Smith et al., 1999; Smith & Kim, 2007; Vecchio, 2000), while resentment is an unpleasant feeling evoked when observing the success or fortunes of others (Berndsen & Feather, 2016; Feather, 2006). In the workplace, this may take the form of a colleague receiving a reward desired by the envious individual. Unlike schadenfreude, which is associated with positive emotions, envy and resentment are generally unpleasant feelings to experience and may last for an extended period, beyond the initial situation triggering these emotions. In fact, neuroscience research indicates that experiencing envy as a result of someone else's success can even activate pain-related neural circuitry, while schadenfreude can activate reward-related circuitry (Lieberman & Eisenberger, 2009; Takahashi et al., 2009).

Further, envy and resentment are elicited by positive events occurring to others (e.g. the colleague's bonus or promotion), while schadenfreude is associated exclusively with negative events befalling targets. Scholars have recently proposed an emotion complementary to schadenfreude, *gluckschmerz*, which refers to negative feelings triggered by another person's fortunes, particularly if the person is disliked or highly successful (Cikara et al., 2014; Hoogland et al., 2015; Smith et al., 2009). Despite the unclear origins of gluckschmerz, this emotion is conceptually linked to envy and resentment, which can be precursors of schadenfreude (Cikara et al., 2014; Hoogland et al., 2015; Smith & Van Dijk, 2018). Gluckschermz is short-lived and situational as it is relative to the target's achievements; this unique characteristic makes it a counterpart to schadenfreude while also differentiating the emotion from envy and resentment.

Theoretical Explanations of Schadenfreude

In the following section, we will introduce some key psychological theories that allow us to understand why and how schadenfreude emerges. While there do not appear to be many theories about schadenfreude specifically, several researchers have expanded upon existing frameworks to incorporate the emotion. Specifically, we will discuss how schadenfreude can be explained using the appraisal theory of emotion (Lazarus, 1991), deservingness theory (Feather, 2006), and social comparison theory (Festinger, 1954).

Appraisal theory proposes that people experience schadenfreude when they perceive others' misfortunes as useful for their own self-esteem or goals. Popularized by Lazarus (1991), the theory suggests that emotions result from subjective evaluations of situations that individuals deem relevant to their values, self-esteem, or goals. Appraisals can vary between individuals, due to both individual and organizational influences, resulting in different emotional outcomes. People may experience schadenfreude when they appraise others' misfortunes as significantly benefiting themselves, such as facilitating goal attainment at work or gaining more self-esteem while others fail in performing work (Li et al., 2019).

Deservingness theory proposes that people experience schadenfreude when they perceive negative outcomes as deserved. It draws heavily upon cognitive appraisal theory, which proposes that our emotional experiences are influenced by how we understand external events or situations (Feather, 1999, 2006). When judging another person's outcome, individuals evaluate whether the relationship between antecedent actions and outcomes are congruent – that is, whether the outcome is justified based on previous behaviors. In the context of work, individuals are likely to appraise undeservingness when a colleague who is unproductive and unpopular (a negative action) receives a promotion (a positive outcome). Alternatively, a colleague who is helpful and liked (a positive action) and receives a promotion (a positive outcome) is likely to be appraised as deserving. According to scholars (Feather, 2006; Feather & McKee, 2009, 2014), when individuals perceive negative outcomes (e.g. failure in promotion or the supervisor's reprimand for poor performance) as deserved, they are more likely to experience schadenfreude.

Finally, social comparison theory proposes that people experience schadenfreude as a result of threatened self-identities. According to the theory, individuals are motivated to compare themselves with others to both assess and enhance key aspects of their identity, such as abilities or skills (Festinger, 1954; Suls & Wheeler, 2000). The need to maintain and promote positive self-regard through social comparisons is a key driver in human behavior, and the misfortunes of others may help to enhance self-evaluations (Van Dijk, Van Koningsbruggen, Ouwerkerk, & Wesseling, 2011). Social comparison can be prevalent in the workplace, and this phenomenon is often drawn on by managers to foster a sense of competition for rewards with hopes of improving employee performance (Brown et al., 1998; Buunk & Gibbons, 2007; Goffin et al., 2009). The competitive nature of work may encourage employees to see colleagues as threats to their own self-identity, leading to feelings of frustration or envy. Van Dijk and colleagues (2011) propose that this perception of self-threat is likely to lead to schadenfreude, particularly when the victim is a high achiever (i.e. "better" than the schadenfroh).

Current Research on Schadenfreude and Work Implications

This section will discuss current trends in researching schadenfreude, including the role of envy in eliciting this emotion. As there is still very little research specifically on schadenfreude at work, we will draw upon research from the wider psychological literature and suggest how its implications may translate into the workplace. We have integrated our findings into a tentative conceptual model (Figure 35.1). We recognize that both individual factors (e.g. dark triad traits, self-esteem) and sociocontextual factors (e.g. competition, in-group/out-group relations) are likely to influence the extent to which one experiences schadenfreude. We also acknowledge the role of social comparisons and envy, particularly malicious envy, in the process.

Social Comparisons and Schadenfreude

There are many aspects of work that can influence employee emotions and behaviors, particularly the presence of performance incentives (Li et al., 2019). Organizations may implement financial (e.g. bonuses, raises) or social incentives (e.g. promotions, awards) in the hopes of motivating employees, who in turn are likely to consider these incentives desirable and work to achieve them. As workplaces are social arenas, there may be several employees working to obtain the same rewards and they are likely to engage in social comparisons to evaluate their own skills or status in relation to others.

Researchers conceptualize social comparison as having two distinct directions: downward and upward. In downward comparisons, individuals evaluate themselves against those considered inferior relative to the individual. These comparisons are generally favorable and can enhance self-worth and self-evaluation; in the workplace, employees may compare themselves with those less popular, less successful, or in positions considered societally "inferior" to them (e.g. the unemployed). Scholars suggest that downward comparisons can invite pleasurable feelings such as schadenfreude, as the misfortunes of inferior groups can help to establish one's own superiority and enhance one's self-identity (Smith, 2000).

Alternatively, in upward comparisons, individuals evaluate themselves against those considered superior, which may invoke unpleasant feelings such as envy, inferiority, and identity threat (Van Dijk et al., 2015). In the workplace, an employee may engage in upward comparisons with more successful colleagues or managers. Engaging in upward comparisons can be a painful experience; schadenfreude, and the pleasure associated with it, may be a way to relieve such discomfort. For example, Leach

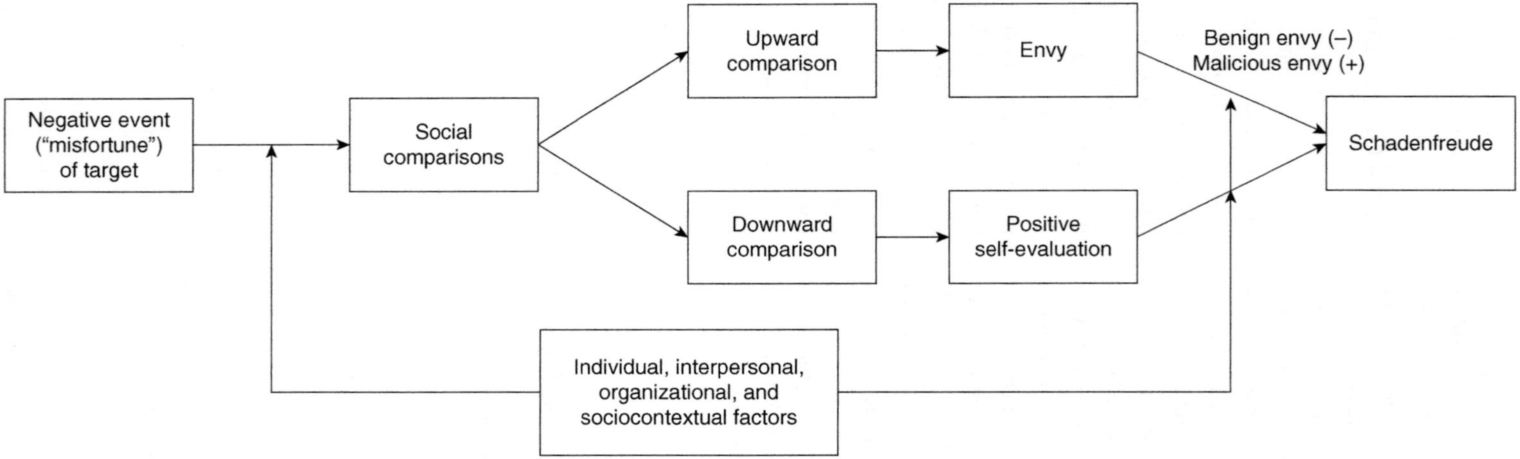

Figure 35.1 Conceptual model of schadenfreude at work

and Spears (2008) found that individuals perceiving in-group inferiority were more likely to experience schadenfreude at the failure of successful out-groups, particularly if the out-group's successes were deemed illegitimate or undeserved.

The role of Envy in Schadenfreude

As discussed previously, envy is closely linked to schadenfreude but is distinct as a negatively valenced emotion in relation to someone else's *good fortune*, while schadenfreude is a positively valenced emotion in relation to someone's *misfortune*. Studies indicate that upward comparisons are likely to lead to envy which, in turn, may lead to schadenfreude toward envied parties. Therefore, it is important to understand the role that envy plays in relation to schadenfreude and social comparisons.

Conceptualizations of Envy

Researchers have conceptualized envy in two distinct forms: benign and malicious (e.g. Lange & Cruisus, 2015; Van de Ven et al., 2009; Van de Ven, 2017). Benign envy is characterized by the desire to be like the envied target and may even have positive motivational effects as individuals strive to be like the targets ("I want to work hard to be like you"). Although envy is still a painful emotion, when experiencing its benign state, people are likely to feel admiration for the target. In fact, research suggests that individuals may even feel sadness when the target experiences failure (e.g. Feather et al., 2013; Feather & McKee, 2014). At work, employees may experience benign envy when evaluating themselves against a colleague whose higher status is considered deserved.

While benign envy is associated with admiration, malicious envy is characterized by resentment and a desire to remove the target from their enviable state (Van de Ven, 2009). It is an uncomfortable emotion that is also directly associated with inferiority, pain, and anger (Feather et al., 2013; Feather & Sherman, 2002; Van Dijk et al., 2006). People experiencing malicious envy are motivated to enact hostile behaviors seeking to degrade targets and often do not appraise the target as deserving of their higher status (e.g. "I don't want you to have what you have"; Fiske, 2010). Such feelings may threaten the observer, especially if the observer views work as being strongly aligned to their self-identity (Clark et al., 2016; Smith & Kim, 2007; Tai et al., 2012). Existing research (e.g. Lange et al., 2018; Van de Ven, 2009; Van Dijk et al., 2015) has affirmed that malicious envy is more closely and positively associated with experiencing schadenfreude, while benign envy has a negative association with schadenfreude. As individuals experiencing malicious envy are motivated to see targets removed from their enviable or superior positions, it is natural that they experience pleasure when misfortune or failure falls upon their targets. As schadenfreude is associated with positive emotions, it may even relieve some of the discomfort associated with envy. For example, two fMRI studies conducted by Takahashi and colleagues (2009) found that participants presented with scenarios depicting individuals with superior relevant traits were likely to experience envy and activation of the anterior cingulate cortex, a part of the brain associated with social pain. When participants also read scenarios meant to induce schadenfreude, scans revealed activation of the ventral striatum, an area of the brain associated with the reward system and reinforcement. These studies suggest that there are detectable mechanisms of both envy and schadenfreude, one associated with pain and the other with pleasurable reward, respectively.

Factors Moderating Envy and Schadenfreude in the Workplace

Individual differences are likely to have a role in the relationship between envy and schadenfreude. There are some studies on dark triad traits (psychopathy, narcissism, and Machiavellianism) in relation to schadenfreude, perhaps due to the equally morally questionable nature of these traits. Studies suggest a link between higher levels of dark triad traits with experiencing higher levels of envy (e.g. Veselka, Giammarco, & Vernon, 2014) and therefore schadenfreude (e.g. James et al., 2014). In fact, these individuals may experience greater pleasure when witnessing more severe consequences. For instance, James and colleagues (2014) found that higher levels of dark triad traits were associated with higher levels of schadenfreude; they suggest that all three traits are associated with a lack of empathy, which may allow "darker" individuals to feel more comfortable experiencing pleasure at someone else's expense. They go on to suggest that narcissistic individuals are more likely to engage in downward comparisons, facilitating schadenfreude to affirm their own superiority, while Machiavellian individuals are likely to experience schadenfreude in competitive contexts as they are more likely to perceive others' misfortunes as advantageous.

Another study by Porter and colleagues (2014) found that participants with higher dark triad scores smiled more when presented with videos of more severe, legal scenarios (e.g. arrests, court hearings) than when presented with videos of less severe, non-legal scenarios (e.g. someone spilling coffee on themselves). One way to explain this emerging link between dark triad traits, envy, and schadenfreude may be that individuals high on these traits are less capable of dealing with the discomfort of upward comparisons and may be thus more attuned to the failures of others. As dark triad traits are typically associated with less sensitivity toward the suffering of others (Wai & Tiliopoulos, 2012), these individuals may be more comfortable with perceiving others' failures positively as a way of enhancing their own self-identity.

Another individual factor related to envy and schadenfreude is self-esteem, which influences how we engage in and interpret social comparisons. There is empirical evidence suggesting a negative relationship between self-esteem and hostility such that people with less self-esteem are more likely to experience hostile behaviors or emotions such as schadenfreude. Researchers (e.g. Rentzsch et al., 2015) suggest that envy may explain this relationship, as people with low self-esteem are more likely to be threatened by unfavorable social comparisons. They may seek to reduce psychological discomfort and to improve self-image by deriving pleasure from the envied target's misfortunes as comparisons become downward rather than upward (e.g. "This isn't happening to me, so it's good"; Brambilla & Riva, 2017). For example, an employee may feel better about themselves if they see a more popular colleague embarrassing themselves.

Workplaces are social environments, and interpersonal factors are likely to affect the extent to which individuals experience schadenfreude. Empirical research suggests that perceived dislike toward targets may increase the likelihood of experiencing schadenfreude, either in relation to envy (e.g. Van Dijk et al., 2015) or independently of it (Hareli & Weiner, 2002). Dislike, particularly if intense, can lead to hostile intentions and may lead to individuals perceiving others' misfortunes as more acceptable or as deserved. Another emerging strand of research involves the status of targets, which is important to acknowledge as many organizations have clear status markers differentiating employees from one another (e.g. job titles, ranks). Dasborough and Harvey (2017) found that participants shared greater schadenfreude when misfortunes befell high-status targets (e.g. the CEO) versus low-status targets (e.g. an employee). This is in line with conceptualizations of malicious envy, in which upward comparisons elicit emotions facilitating schadenfreude (e.g. discomfort, dislike). However, differences in schadenfreude between high and low status disappeared when both targets were perceived as deserving of misfortune.

As mentioned previously, schadenfreude is distinct from actively malicious traits such as sadism (Schumpe & Lafrenière, 2016), as individuals experiencing it do not wish harm to actually befall their targets. However, research is still ambiguous on whether severity of target misfortunes influences schadenfreude. Some studies indicate that increased severity is associated with less schadenfreude, while others report no difference (see Berndsen & Feather, 2016). Therefore, it is important for future researchers to develop a more holistic and situational understanding of schadenfreude. For example, research could begin to tackle the boundary conditions for when schadenfreude might typically begin and/or end. Researchers might also examine how it spirals (or not) beyond initial feelings of envy and related antecedent emotions.

Future Research and Unanswered Questions

Despite its prevalence in human life and some emerging research in various fields of psychological and behavioral studies, our knowledge of schadenfreude at work remains limited and our understanding of the phenomenon ambiguous. This section will discuss key possible avenues of future schadenfreude research and review some unanswered questions within the field.

Along with emerging research on schadenfreude, recent studies have also included new, related constructs such as gluckschmerz in seeking an understanding how social emotions operate at work (e.g. Cikara et al., 2014; Hoogland et al., 2015; Smith & Van Dijk, 2018). Research in gluckschmerz may provide new insight into schadenfreude and its unique conceptualization. It may be worthwhile to study both schadenfreude and gluckschermz, to understand how these constructs interact with one another and to integrate them into existing theoretical frameworks.

Researchers have a limited understanding of how factors unique to organizational settings (e.g. leadership, teamwork) can influence how schadenfreude is experienced. Future studies should therefore explore work-related antecedents of schadenfreude, such as competition, which may be prevalent or encouraged in organizations where employees may perceive it in zero-sum terms (i.e. your loss is my gain; Smith & van Dijk, 2018). There is evidence to suggest that competition is linked to schadenfreude in other domains, such as politics or sports. For example, Combs and colleagues (2009) found that political party identification (here, US Democrats and Republicans) was linked to greater schadenfreude in response to misfortunes suffered by the opposing political group. Dalakas and Melancon (2012) found that sports fans experienced greater schadenfreude at the misfortunes of rival teams and figures associated with them (e.g. sponsoring brands) when the relationship was mediated by the perceived importance of winning. By understanding the relationships between organizational factors and schadenfreude, researchers may be able to translate findings into practical terms.

As schadenfreude has been primarily studied at the individual level, there have been calls to understand the emotion and its associated experiences and behaviors across multiple levels (Ashkanasy, 2003). Future researchers may consider examining the interaction between individual and group schadenfreude across team or organizational structures. By acknowledging both individual- and group-level emotions, researchers may be able to understand the effects of intergroup biases (e.g. in-group favoritism, out-group denigration) on schadenfreude (Hoogland et al., 2015). For example, researchers have suggested that in-group identification influences levels of schadenfreude in political and sports domains; future researchers may wish to explore how these emotions are experienced at the group level (e.g. a group of fans, a political party) and what behaviors they can influence. There may even be a feedback element as experienced sustained or repeated schadenfreude may lead to stronger out-group derogation whereby out-group members are further vilified and disliked, which in turn leads to stronger subsequent schadenfreude. In the workplace, researchers may be interested in studying group-level schadenfreude in relation to rival teams or companies.

Schadenfreude research may also consider utilizing alternative methodologies: much of the existing research employs experimental vignette designs and student samples (e.g. James et al., 2014; Leach & Spears, 2008; van Dijk et al., 2006). Vignettes are useful as they allow researchers to manipulate chosen variables to observe relationships, while student samples are convenient and accessible for most researchers. However, future research may benefit from expanding beyond these designs as experimental scenarios may not be reflective of real work environments or employee experiences, which brings into question the external validity and thus the generalizability of findings (Agnuinis & Bradley, 2014). Therefore, we recommend other nonexperimental methods such as survey questionnaires in natural work settings to maximize external validity.

Finally, researchers may continue tackling the question of whether experiencing schadenfreude is an inherently "good" or "bad" thing. As with several other moral emotions, schadenfreude's ethicality remains a hot topic of debate among scholars, who have traditionally accused those experiencing the emotion as lacking compassion. Recently, some have suggested that we should avoid labeling schadenfreude as morally "wrong" as it is not, in itself, a malicious emotion (Van Dijk et al., 2015; Van Dijk & Ouwerkerk, 2014). While there may never be a definitive answer, examining such a question, in work contexts and beyond, may facilitate interdisciplinary work (e.g. among psychology, sociology, and philosophy) that could lead to insightful and fruitful collaborations.

Conclusion

While the idea of deriving pleasure from others' misfortunes may not sit comfortably with people, schadenfreude is a common emotion and may even have positive outcomes, such as alleviating emotional discomfort. In this chapter, we introduced several prominent theories to explain schadenfreude and conducted a review of scholarly articles of schadenfreude in the workplace. We then summarized key findings from our review and discussed avenues for future research.

References

Aguinis, H., & Bradley, K. J. (2014). Best practice recommendations for designing and implementing experimental vignette methodology studies. *Organizational Research Methods*, *17*(4), 351–371.

Ashkanasy, N. M. (2003). Emotions in organizations: A multilevel perspective. In F. Dansereau & F. J. Yammarino (Eds.), *Multi-level issues in organizational behaviour and strategy*, Volume 2 of *Research in multi-level issues* (pp. 9–54). Oxford, UK: Elsevier Science.

Ben-Ze'ev, A. (2001). *The subtlety of emotions*. Cambridge, MA: MIT Press.

Berndsen, M., & Feather, N. T. (2016). Reflecting on schadenfreude: Serious consequences of a misfortune for which one is not responsible diminish previously expressed schadenfreude; the role of immorality appraisals and moral emotions. *Motivation and Emotion*, *40*, 895–913.

Brambilla, M., & Riva, P. (2017). Self-image and schadenfreude: Pleasure at others' misfortune enhances satisfaction of basic human needs. *European Journal of Social Psychology*, *47*, 399–411.

Brown, S. P., Cron, W. L., & Slocum, J. W., Jr. (1998). Effects of trait competitiveness and perceived intraorganizational competition on salesperson goal setting and performance. *Journal of Marketing*, *62*, 88–98.

Buunk, A. P., & Gibbons, F. X. (2007). Social comparison: The end of a theory and the emergence of a field. *Organizational Behavior and Human Decision Processes*, *102*(1), 3–21.

Cartwright, D. (2019). Schopenhauer's narrower sense of morality. In C. Janaway (Ed.), *The Cambridge companion to Schopenhauer* (3rd edition, pp. 252–292). New York, NY: Cambridge University Press.

Cikara, M., Bruneau, E., Van Bavel, J. J., & Saxe, R. (2014). Their pain gives us pleasure: How intergroup dynamics shape empathic failures and counter-empathic responses. *Journal of Experimental Social Psychology*, *55*, 110–125.

Clark, M. A., Michel, J. S., Zhdanova, L., Pui, S. Y., & Baltes, B. B. (2016). All work and no play? A meta-analytic examination of the correlates and outcomes of workaholism. *Journal of Management*, *42*, 1836–1873.

Combs, D. Y., Powell, C. J., Schurtz, D., & Smith, R. H. (2009). Politics, schadenfreude, and ingroup identification: The sometimes happy thing about a poor economy and death. *Journal of Experimental Social Psychology*, *45*(4), 635–646.

Dalakas, V., & Phillips Melancon, J. (2012). Fan identification, Schadenfreude toward hated rivals, and the mediating effects of Importance of Winning Index (IWIN). *Journal of Services Marketing*, *26* (1), 51–59.

Dasborough, M., & Harvey, P. (2017). Schadenfreude: The (not so) secret joy of another's misfortune. *Journal of Business Ethics*, *141*, 693–707.

Feather, N. T. (1999). Judgments of deservingness: Studies in the psychology of justice and achievement. *Personality and Social Psychology Review*, *3*, 86–107.

Feather, N. T. (2006). Deservingness and emotions: Applying the structural model of deservingness to the analysis of affective reactions to outcomes. *European Review of Social Psychology*, *17*, 38–73.

Feather, N. T. (2008). Effects of observer's own status on reactions to a high achiever's failure: Deservingness, resentment, schadenfreude, and sympathy. *Australian Journal of Psychology*, *60*, 31–43.

Feather, N. T., & McKee, I. R. (2009). Differentiating emotions in relation to deserved or undeserved outcomes: A retrospective study of real-life events. *Cognition and Emotion*, *23*(5), 955–977.

Feather, N. T., & McKee, I. R. (2014). Deservingness, liking relations, schadenfreude, and other discrete emotions in the context of the outcomes of plagiarism. *Australian Journal of Psychology*, *66* (1), 18–27.

Feather, N. T., & Sherman, R. (2002). Envy, resentment, schadenfreude, and sympathy: Reactions to deserved and undeserved achievement and subsequent failure. *Personality and Social Psychology Bulletin*, *28*, 953–961.

Feather, N. T., Wenzel, M., & McKee, I. R. (2013). Integrating multiple perspectives on schadenfreude: The role of deservingness and emotions. *Motivation and Emotion*, *37*, 574–585.

Festinger, L. (1954). A theory of social comparison processes. *Human Relations*, *7*, 117–140.

Fiske, S. T. (2010). Envy up, scorn down: How comparison divides us. *American Psychologist*, *65* (8), 698–706.

Goffin, R. D., Jelley, R. B., Powell, D. M., & Johnston, N. G. (2009). Taking advantage of social comparisons in performance appraisal: The relative percentile method. *Human Resource Management*, *48*(2), 251–268.

Gooty, J., Gavin, M., & Ashkanasy, N. M. (2009). Emotions research in OB: The challenges that lie ahead. *Journal of Organizational Behavior*, *30*(6), 833–838.

Hareli, S., & Weiner, B. (2002). Dislike and envy as antecedents of pleasure at another's misfortune. *Motivation and Emotion*, *26*, 257–277.

Hoogland, C. E., Schurtz, D. R., Cooper, C. M., Combs, D. J., Brown, E. G., & Smith, R. H. (2015). The joy of pain and the pain of joy: In-group identification predicts schadenfreude and gluckschmerz following rival groups' fortunes. *Motivation and Emotion*, *39*, 260–281.

James, S., Kavanagh, P. S., Jonason, P. K., Chonody, J. M., & Scrutton, H. E. (2014). The Dark Triad, schadenfreude, and sensational interests: Dark personalities, dark emotions, and dark behaviors. *Personality and Individual Differences*, *68*, 211–216.

Jankowski, K. F., & Takahashi, H. (2014). Cognitive neuroscience of social emotions and implications for psychopathology: examining embarrassment, guilt, envy, and schadenfreude. *Psychiatry and Clinical Neurosciences*, *68*(5), 319–336.

Johnson, B. K., & Knobloch-Westerwick, S. (2014). Glancing up or down: Mood management and selective social comparisons on social networking sites. *Computers in Human Behavior*, *41*, 33–39.

Knobloch-Westerwick, S. (2006). Mood management: Theory, evidence, and advancements. In J. Bryant & P. Vorderer (Eds.), *The psychology of entertainment* (pp. 239–254). Mahwah, NJ: Erlbaum.

Lange, J., & Crusius, J. (2015). Dispositional envy revisited: Unraveling the motivational dynamics of benign and malicious envy. *Personality and Social Psychology Bulletin*, *41*(2), 284–294.

Lange, J., Weidman, A. C., & Crusius, J. (2018). The painful duality of envy: Evidence for an integrative theory and a meta-analysis on the relation of envy and schadenfreude. *Journal of Personality and Social Psychology*, *114*, 572–598.

Lazarus, R. S. (1991). *Emotion and adaptation*. New York, NY: Oxford University Press.

Leach, C. W., & Spears, R. (2008). "A vengefulness of the impotent": The pain of in-group inferiority and schadenfreude toward successful out-groups. *Journal of Personality and Social Psychology*, *95*, 1383–1396.

Li, X., McAllister, D. J., Ilies, R., & Gloor, J. L. (2019). Schadenfreude: A counternormative observer response to workplace mistreatment. *Academy of Management Review*, *44*(2), 360–376.

Lidell, H. G., & Scott, R. (1940). *A Greek–English lexicon*. Oxford, UK: Clarendon.

Lieberman, M. D., & Eisenberger, N. I. (2009). Pains and pleasures of social life. *Science*, *323*, 890–891.

Lindebaum, D., & Jordan, P. J. (2014). When it can be good to feel bad and bad to feel good: Exploring asymmetries in workplace emotional outcomes. *Human Relations*, *67*(9), 1037–1050.

Peacock, L. (2014). *Slapstick and comic performance: Comedy and pain*. Basingstoke, UK: Palgrave Macmillan.

Porter, S., Bhanwer, A., Woodworth, M., & Black, P. J. (2014). Soldiers of misfortune: An examination of the Dark Triad and the experience of schadenfreude. *Personality and Individual Differences*, *67*, 64–68.

Portmann, J. (2000). *When bad things happen to other people*. New York, NY: Routledge.

Pozner, J. L. (2010). *Reality bites back: The troubling truth about guilty pleasure TV.* Berkeley, CA: Seal.

Rentzsch, K., Schröder-Abé, M., & Schütz, A. (2015). Envy mediates the relation between low academic self-esteem and hostile tendencies. *Journal of Research in Personality*, *58*, 143–153.

Schulz, K., Rudolph, A., Tscharaktschiew, N., & Rudolph, U. (2013). Daniel has fallen into a muddy puddle – schadenfreude or sympathy? *British Journal of Developmental Psychology*, *31*(4), 363–378.

Schumpe, B. M., & Lafrenière, M. A. K. (2016). Malicious joy: Sadism moderates the relationship between schadenfreude and the severity of others' misfortune. *Personality and Individual Differences*, *94*, 32–37.

Smith, R. H. (2000). Assimilative and contrastive emotional reactions to upward and downward social comparisons. In J. Suls & L. Wheller (Eds.), *Handbook of social comparison* (pp. 173–200). Boston, MA: Springer.

Smith, R. H., & Kim, S. H. (2007). Comprehending envy. *Psychological Bulletin*, *133*, 46–64.

Smith, R. H., Parrott, W. G., Diener, E. F., Hoyle, R. H., & Kim, S. H. (1999). Dispositional envy. *Personality and Social Psychology Bulletin*, *25*, 1007–1020.

Smith, R. H., Powell, C. A., Combs, D. J., & Schurtz, D. R. (2009). Exploring the when and why of schadenfreude. *Social and Personality Psychology Compass*, *3*(4), 530–546.

Smith, R. H., & Van Dijk, W. W. (2018). Schadenfreude and gluckschmerz. *Emotion Review*, *10*, 293–304.

Suls, J., & Wheeler, L. (2000). A selective history of classic and neo-social comparison theory. In J. Suls & L. Wheller (Eds.), *Handbook of social comparison* (pp. 3–19). Boston, MA: Springer.

Szameitat, D. P., Alter, K., Szameitat, A. J., Darwin, C. J., Wildgruber, D., Dietrich, S., & Sterr, A. (2009). Differentiation of emotions in laughter at the behavioral level. *Emotion*, *9*(3), 397–405.

Tai, K., Narayanan, J., & McAllister, D. J. (2012). Envy as pain: Rethinking the nature of envy and its implications for employees and organizations. *Academy of Management Review*, *37*, 107–129.

Takahashi, H., Kato, M., Matsuura, M., Mobbs, D., Suhara, T., & Okubo, Y. (2009). When your gain is my pain and your pain is my gain: Neural correlates of envy and schadenfreude. *Science*, *323*, 937–939.

Van de Ven, N. (2017). Envy and admiration: Emotion and motivation following upward social comparison. *Cognition and Emotion*, *31*(1), 193–200.

Van de Ven, N., Zeelenberg, M., & Pieters, R. (2009). Leveling up and down: the experiences of benign and malicious envy. *Emotion*, *9*(3), 419–429.

Van Dijk, W. W., & Ouwerkerk, J. W. (Eds.) (2014). *Schadenfreude: Understanding pleasure at the misfortune of others*. Cambridge, UK: Cambridge University Press.

Van Dijk, W. W., Ouwerkerk, J. W., Goslinga, S., Nieweg, M., & Gallucci, M. (2006). When people fall from grace: Reconsidering the role of envy in schadenfreude. *Emotion*, *6*, 156–160.

Van Dijk, W. W., Ouwerkerk, J. W., Smith, R. H., & Cikara, M. (2015). The role of self-evaluation and envy in schadenfreude. *European Review of Social Psychology*, *26*, 247–282.

Van Dijk, W. W., van Koningsbruggen, G. M., Ouwerkerk, J. W., & Wesseling, Y. M. (2011). Self-esteem, self-affirmation, and schadenfreude. *Emotion*, *11*, 1445–1449.

Vecchio, R. P. (2000). Negative emotion in the workplace: Employee jealousy and envy. *International Journal of Stress Management*, *7*(3), 161–179.

Veselka, L., Giammarco, E. A., & Vernon, P. A. (2014). The Dark Triad and the seven deadly sins. *Personality and Individual Differences*, *67*, 75–80.

Wai, M., & Tiliopoulos, N. (2012). The affective and cognitive empathic nature of the dark triad of personality. *Personality and Individual Differences*, *52*(7), 794–799.

Watanabe, H. (2016). Effects of self-evaluation threat on schadenfreude toward strangers in a reality TV show. *Psychological Reports*, *118* (3), 778–792.

Wood, J. V. (1989). Theory and research concerning social comparisons of personal attributes. *Psychological Bulletin*, *106*(2), 231–248.

Part VI
New Perspectives on Workplace Affect

36 Diversity and Workplace Affect

The Impact of Revealing or Concealing a Stigma

Cassandra N. Phetmisy, Rebecca Godard, Raymond N. C. Trau, and Mikki Hebl

A stigmatized identity refers to some socially devalued aspect of a person that (typically) cannot be changed and evokes negative stereotypes, attitudes, and behaviors from others (Quinn & Earnshaw, 2013). With the increase of protective laws, individuals with a stigmatized identity face less formal discrimination than in the past but continue to face substantial subtle and interpersonal discrimination (Ruggs, Martinez, & Hebl, 2011). While the majority of stigma research has focused on visible stigmatized identities, many stigmatized identities are simply not visible. It is this latter category on which the current chapter focuses. Invisible stigmatized identities are devalued aspects that an individual is generally able to conceal from others. Invisible and/or concealable stigmas may include lesbian, gay, bisexual, transgender, and queer or questioning (LGBTQ+) identities; some disabilities; and multiracial and religious identities. For the remainder of the chapter, we will refer to such identities as "concealable stigmas" or "invisible stigmas."

One particular challenge of having a concealable stigma is the need for bearers to manage information about their identity in social settings (Goffman, 1963). Personal and situational factors affect people's decisions to reveal or conceal stigmas (Clair, Beatty, & MacLean, 2005). Such identity management has psychological, social, and relational implications (Trau, 2015). While disclosure may have positive effects (e.g. building authenticity in workplace relationships and gaining access to resources and psychosocial benefits from people with a similar identity), disclosure also may increase the risk of discrimination (Ragins, 2004). Additionally, disclosure is not a binary or linear process; rather, people with concealable stigmas continually manage their identities within the workplace and other environments with a variety of strategies (Ragins, 2008). In short, research on the disclosure of concealable stigmas is an important area of inquiry into an overlooked aspect at the intersection of diversity and affect.

Accordingly, the purpose of this chapter is to examine identity management by employees with invisible stigmas through the lens of affect in order to help organizations foster inclusive environments for those who have unique emotional experiences due to their concealable stigmas. We conceptualize "identity management" here as affective processes that influence work behaviors, attitudes, and interpersonal relationships. We aim to synthesize past research about workplace affect and invisible stigma with an eye toward a more integrative perspective on managing such identities.

We begin by reviewing four frameworks related to the affective implications of disclosing and concealing. We particularly consider the challenges of concealing and disclosing a stigma and the emotional impact of how individuals respond to such challenges. Next, we describe antecedents associated with workplace-specific disclosure, and consider the affective outcomes of coping mechanisms used to manage invisible stigmas in the workplace.

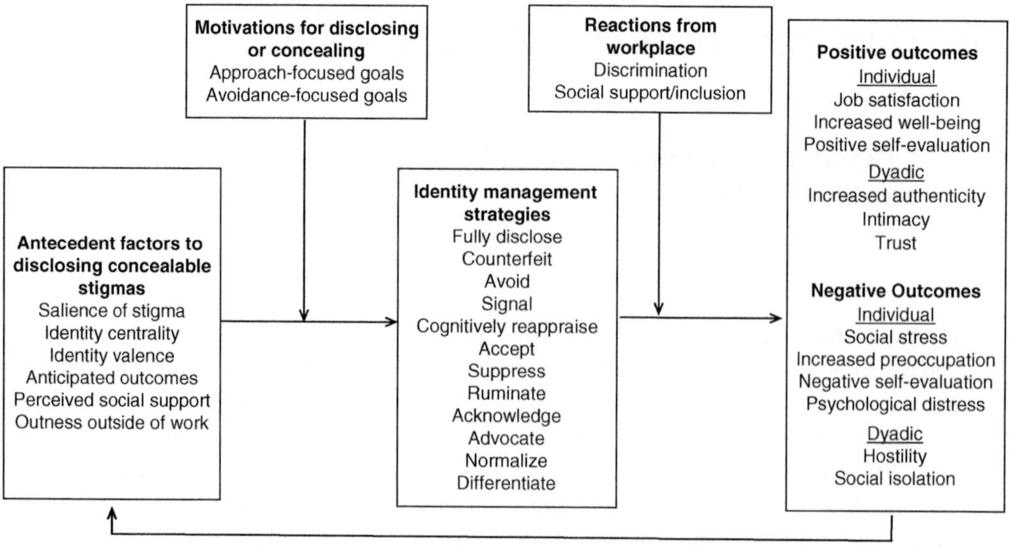

Figure 36.1 Model of integration between invisible stigmatized identity management and potential affective outcomes

We provide a model (see Figure 36.1) for the integration of invisible stigmatized identity management and affective outcomes, which draws heavily on Chaudoir and Fisher's (2010) concept of the cyclical nature of identity management. We are also influenced by Berkley, Beard, and Daus's (2018) recent work describing how emotions influence disclosure. Berkley et al. (2018) mainly focus on developing a theoretical model of how emotions influence disclosure, and their article does not fully unpack the affective elements of the frameworks. To build on their work, we provide here a comprehensive overview of the frameworks for affect and identity and also take an applied perspective by identifying various ways in which organizations can reduce the challenges and effects of having a concealable stigma. We recommend strategies that organizations can utilize to foster supportive environments for employees with concealable stigmas, based on our integration of identity management and emotion research. We go on to discuss this chapter's theoretical and practical implications. Lastly, we propose directions for future research on the emotional processes of disclosing or concealing an invisible stigma at work, and we suggest ways that future studies can build on extant literature to better integrate affect and identity research.

Models for Concealing Invisible Stigma

Several existing models or frameworks focus on the challenges of having an invisible stigma. We have chosen to discuss the following four models because of their integrative perspectives on emotional regulation, identity/stigma management, and interpersonal relationships. By discussing these frameworks, we aim to provide a more holistic understanding of the underlying emotional processes and lived experiences of these individuals.

Pachankis's Cognitive–Affective–Behavioral Model

The cognitive–affective–behavioral model of identity concealment highlights the role of three factors in a bearer's choice to conceal: the *salience* of stigma, the *threat of discovery*, and the *consequences of discovery* (Pachankis, 2007). Certain environments make some invisible stigmas more *salient* than others. For instance, a gay employee may be able to conceal his sexual identity at work but feel much less ease during workplace social events in which spouses/partners are invited. Environments also vary in the extent to which they offer a *threat of discovery*. For instance, a gay employee who has not disclosed his sexual orientation at work may unexpectedly encounter another colleague at a gay bar. This moment threatens discovery of the employee's concealed stigma, producing potential negative inter- and intrapersonal consequences. Finally, environments vary in the extent to which individuals with concealable stigmas experience the potential *consequences of discovery* by others (Clair et al., 2005). For instance, a lesbian employee who works for a very conservative (as opposed to liberal) organization may face an environment with greater formal and informal discrimination, and other types of workplace victimization. Not surprisingly, then, environments are likely to vary in the extent to which stigmas exacerbate a bearer's psychological harm (e.g. negative emotions) and usurp their cognitive resources (e.g. increased self-monitoring, or suppressing or regulating negative affect; Stone & Colella, 1996). Effortful management of invisible stigmas via behavioral and emotional regulation can minimize the risk of negative psychological and interpersonal consequences.

Cognitive Implications

Identity concealment has a number of cognitive implications. For example, concealing a stigma requires active self-monitoring, which can contribute to explicit differentiation of the private and public selves. Sedlovskaya et al. (2013) define this private–public schematization as the cognitive accessibility of the distinctions between these two selves and found that people with concealable stigmas (e.g. sexual and religious minorities) engage in higher schematization than others. This higher schematization is associated with perceived social stress and depressive symptoms due to effortful monitoring and identity suppression. Identity concealment may lead to increased preoccupation, vigilance, and suspicion about others' beliefs. Thought suppression requires cognitive effort, and experimentally manipulated identity concealment has been linked to poorer cognitive performance (Smart & Wegner, 2000). This preoccupation, together with the vigilance and suspicion that accompany it, might be particularly harmful in the workplace, as it takes up cognitive resources that could otherwise be devoted to work tasks.

Affective Implications

In addition to these cognitive implications, identity concealment has a profound impact on affective processes. First, the secretive nature of concealment is linked to feelings of shame and negative self-evaluation, which can negatively impact workplace relationships (Kelly, 2002). In a study of women who had had abortions, Major and Gramzow (1999) found that thought suppression was associated with increased depression, anxiety, and hostility, while disclosure was associated with decreases in those aspects of psychological distress. The association between identity concealment and psychological distress was demonstrated in a variety of domains, including LGBTQ+ identities, mental illness, and HIV status (Pachankis, 2007). In a study of gay men and lesbians, Talley and Bettencourt (2011) found that people who concealed their sexual orientation were less likely to use adaptive, problem-focused coping strategies, had higher rates of depressive symptoms, and reported decreases in organizational outcomes such as job satisfaction (Madera, King, & Hebl, 2012).

Behavioral Implications

Concealing a stigma also has behavioral implications. For example, Pachankis and Goldfried

(2006) found that 75 percent of gay participants reported that they had modified their behavior in some way to avoid discrimination. Such behaviors included changing voice pitch and/or mannerisms, lying about the sex of a partner, and performing behaviors in a more masculine way. Identity concealment also contributes to social isolation (such as avoiding social events at work), which reduces the accessibility of social support. For employees with concealable disabilities, isolation can also reduce the likelihood that they will receive structural support through workplace accommodations. The same barriers may occur for LGBTQ+ employees seeking spousal benefits or parental leave (Clair et al., 2005).

Chaudoir and Fisher's Disclosure Process Model

The disclosure process model (DPM) describes factors that affect disclosure outcomes, including interpersonal affective outcomes, which are motivated by either approach-oriented or avoidance-oriented goals (Chaudoir & Fisher, 2010). Approach-focused goals involve pursuing positive outcomes, such as relationship authenticity, while avoidance-focused goals motivate people to avoid negative outcomes such as discrimination and social rejection. Employees make decisions about disclosure based partially on the anticipated emotional and practical outcomes of disclosure, as well as how both of those outcomes match their goals. Thus in addition to considering anticipated practical and emotional outcomes of disclosure, managing emotional processes can serve as a motivation that influences the likelihood of disclosure.

The DPM posits that disclosure affects outcomes by alleviating inhibition, increasing or decreasing social support, and introducing new information into social situations. While the model addresses individual, social contextual, and dyadic outcomes, the dyadic outcomes relate most closely to affect. Disclosure can produce intimacy, liking, and trust within relationships, particularly when both parties share personal or emotionally laden information. Disclosure also involves active self-monitoring of relationships. The DPM alludes to this process as a feedback loop in which individuals with invisible stigmatized identities and their relationships are continually affected depending on how others have reacted to their disclosure or concealment (Chaudoir & Fisher, 2010).

In the context of workplace relationships, disclosure has the potential to produce positive emotions that can contribute to job satisfaction and performance. When disclosure is met with increases in intimacy, liking, and trust in relationships with coworkers and supervisors, employees with concealable stigmas are more likely to perceive their work environments as supportive. Thus the DPM provides a novel insight into the positive affective outcomes that can benefit employees who choose to disclose concealable stigmas.

Framework for Disclosing in Various Contexts

As discussed previously, disclosure is not a binary process, but rather can be conceptualized as a series of stages. Ragins (2008) proposed a theoretical model with three states of disclosure, which can occur across life domains: *denial*, *disconnect*, and *integration*. Accordingly, differing degrees of disclosure or outness between non-work (exogenous) and work domains may impact identity and affect in the workplace.

The first identity state, *denial*, happens when a person is aware of a stigmatized identity but conceals it in both work and non-work domains. This constant concealment is predicted to result in various negative outcomes across domains, such as reduced cognitive performance, psychological distress, and poorer health outcomes (Pachankis, 2007). Those exhibiting identity denial may also lack social support in both work and non-work settings (Ragins, 2008). This produces a "private hell" (Smart & Wegner, 2000), characterized by the cognitive preoccupation of concealing and managing invisible stigmas with few individual allies to one's true authentic self.

The second identity state, *disconnect*, occurs when individuals have different levels of disclosure between or within work and non-work domains (Ragins, 2008). This may occur when individuals' identities are known in private spaces (e.g. home) but not public spaces (e.g. work), or vice versa. It may also occur when individuals are "out" to some people but not to others within the same space. When individuals are out in some settings of life but conceal in others, and/or are out to some people but not to others, they may be more at risk of psychological stress, anxiety, role conflict, and being unintentionally outed to others unaware of the stigma (Ragins, 2004; Ragins, 2008).

The third identity state, *integration*, involves full disclosure in both work and non-work domains. It should be not be assumed that identity integration, or full disclosure, is the "ideal" state for all those with invisible stigmas, particularly when it is risky to disclose in one particular domain or to one particular individual. At the same time, however, repeated disclosures may increase the possibility of receiving support from some others, which can in turn result in better job-related attitudes, less anxiety, and higher self-esteem (Griffith & Hebl, 2002; Jordan & Deluty, 1998).

Minority Stress Theory

Finally, minority stress theory has important implications for disclosure of invisible stigmas in the workplace. Minority stress theory conceptualizes this process as stress caused by having a devalued identity (LeBlanc, Frost, & Wight, 2015). Velez, Moradi, and Brewster (2013) provide an overview of minority stress theory as applied specifically to workplace experiences. Employees with minority identities experience a number of unique stressors, including discrimination, internalized prejudice (i.e. one's own prejudiced beliefs or attitudes toward one's own stigma), and identity management concerns. These stressors were associated with lower job satisfaction and increased workplace distress. In a study of gay and lesbian employees, Waldo (1999) found that high levels of disclosure were associated with higher levels of direct heterosexism (e.g. prejudiced remarks or behaviors), but lower levels of indirect heterosexism (e.g. assumptions that they were heterosexual).

Velez et al. (2013) also found important patterns in the relationships between identity management strategies, workplace discrimination, and job satisfaction. For employees in low-discrimination environments, those who used fewer concealment strategies and more disclosure strategies experienced higher job satisfaction. In higher-discrimination workplaces, however, disclosure strategies were associated with declines in job satisfaction. These finding suggest that disclosure processes may be directly impacted by the unique experiences of having a minority identity, and that affective outcomes of disclosure (e.g. psychological distress, job satisfaction) may depend on the presence of minority-specific stressors.

Antecedent Factors to Disclosing Concealable Stigmas

Now that we have reviewed four theoretical frameworks regarding concealment, we move to considering antecedents associated with disclosing in order to further illustrate the emotional and self-regulatory processes of identity management. In particular, we explore the *individual*, *workplace*, and *non-workplace antecedents* that prompt some employees to disclose and others to conceal. These antecedents may be pivotal in triggering Ragins' (2008) differing identity states, which in turn can lead to such disparate affective outcomes. We examine all three sets of antecedents and review their impact on workplace disclosure and affect.

Identity-Based Antecedents

Identity Centrality

Identity centrality refers to the importance or salience of an identity to a person's self-concept. For example, two people may share the same identity (e.g. a racial identity), but that identity may be more central to one person's self-concept than to the other's. Research indicates that identity centrality influences the likelihood of disclosing an invisible stigma in the workplace: in particular, empirical research suggests that identity centrality tends to be positively associated with disclosing an invisible stigma (Martinez & Hebl, 2016). At the same time, identity centrality predicts distress (e.g. depression and anxiety) among people with concealable stigmas who feel that their identities are considerably devalued in their society (Quinn & Chaudoir, 2009).

Identity Valence

Another factor that influences disclosure decisions is identity valence, or the positive or negative beliefs associated with one's identity (Quinn et al., 2014). Related to emotional valence (Columbetti, 2005), identity valence primarily relates to how individuals belonging to a stigmatized group feel about their stigmatized identity. In the case of LGBTQ+ individuals, society may view them as having immoral characteristics. Likewise, those with invisible stigmas may have negatively valenced emotions toward their own stigmatized identity, such as shame or guilt (Johnson & Yarhouse, 2013). The greater the negative valence that an individual experiences in connection with a sexual minority identity, the more deterred they are from disclosing their identities to others, which may result in poorer mental health (Stirratt, Meyer, Ouellette, & Gara, 2008). Conversely, greater self-acceptance, or positive valence, is associated with greater use of disclosure strategies among LGBTQ+ employees (Griffith & Hebl, 2002).

Workplace Antecedents

Anticipated Outcomes

The likelihood of disclosing an invisible identity in the workplace is also influenced by anticipated outcomes of disclosure, especially if one's stigma is relatively central to one's identity (Quinn & Chaudoir, 2009). It is not necessary for individuals to actually experience such outcomes in order for the prospect of them to significantly influence disclosure decisions (Ragins, 2008). For instance, those with cancer, a mental disorder, a minority sexual orientation, or pregnancy are less likely to disclose their status when they anticipate judgment, stigmatization, or discrimination (Jones, 2017; Stergiou-Kita, Pritlove, & Kirsh, 2016; Toth & Dewa, 2014). These anticipated outcomes are particularly important because they can impair the development of interpersonal relationships with coworkers or clients (Marrs & Staton, 2016; Toth & Dewa, 2014). Individuals may also be influenced by positive expectations: those with invisible stigmas (e.g. sexual orientation) are more likely to disclose if they anticipate support from their coworkers and/or their organization (Sabat, Trump, & King, 2014).

Perceived social support

Perceived social and environmental support also impact an employee's decision to reveal their concealed stigma (Trau, 2015). This factor depends primarily on the stigmatized individual's perception of how others perceive their concealable stigma. Cues from the environment, such as openness to diversity, inclusion initiatives, or allyship signals, may influence an individual's decision to disclose. For concealable stigmas including childhood sickness, cancer, and sexual orientation, perceived workplace supportiveness is positively associated with disclosure (Martinez & Hebl, 2016; Stergiou-Kita et al., 2016; Wessel, 2017). Social support also mediates the relationship between disclosure and well-being, suggesting that it is an important component of the emotional processing that accompanies disclosure (Chaudoir & Fisher, 2010). Thus social support and disclosure can have positive effects on well-being through their ability to promote emotional awareness and reflection. Furthermore, disclosure has beneficial affective consequences even when it occurs in trivial interactions or relationships (Beals, Peplau, & Gable, 2009).

Non-workplace Antecedents

Exogenous Factors

Life outside of work also has the potential to influence workplace affect. Examples of exogenous factors include socioeconomic levels, housing conditions, and work–family conflict. In addition to individual-level factors, people with invisible stigmatized identities are affected by events in their broader community. For example, events resulting from prejudice against the LGBTQ+ community (such as violence, discrimination, or anti-gay legislation) are positively associated with psychological distress among that community (Meyer, 2003). Factors outside of work have the potential to directly impact employees' perception of discrimination at work (Trau et al., 2018) and job satisfaction (Linney, 2008).

Outness outside of work

The extent to which someone is "out" in non-work contexts is related to a person's likelihood of revealing their stigma in work contexts. This is true for both transgender and LGB individuals, as well as adult survivors of childhood cancer (Griffith & Hebl, 2002; Law, Martinez, Ruggs, Hebl, & Akers, 2011; Martinez & Hebl, 2016). Research has also demonstrated that when people disclose their sexual orientation in spaces where they feel that interpersonal acceptance and personal authenticity are supported, they experience fewer negative emotions, such as anger, loneliness, and depression (Legate, Ryan, & Weinstein, 2012).

Affective Management of a Stigma in the Workplace

Affective Impacts of Having Concealable Stigmatized Identities

Disclosing a minority and marginalized status, such as race, sexual orientation, religious identity, or disability, can make individuals more vulnerable to discrimination. Whether a stigma is concealable or not, minorities typically experience prejudice and discrimination to a greater extent than those without stigma, and are significantly more vulnerable to internalized prejudice, increased substance use, psychological distress, and negative health outcomes (Lea, de Wit, & Reynolds, 2014; Testa et al., 2017).

Although the literature has produced research about the relationship between affect and organizational outcomes (see review by Brief & Weiss, 2002), there is scarce research integrating affect, stigma, and the workplace. In their model of temporary employees' stigmatization, Boyce, Ryan, Imus, and Morgeson (2007) review the effects of negative emotional states due to workplace stigmatization. This is based on the affective events theory (Weiss & Cropanzano, 1996), which suggests that affect mediates the relationship between organizational characteristics and performance. Accordingly, Boyce and colleagues (2007) posit that stigmatized employees' negative emotions will result in lower work performance, lower job satisfaction, and higher instances of job withdrawal. Côté and Morgan (2002) also demonstrated that suppressing negative emotions decreases job satisfaction and increases turnover intentions, such that these outcomes may occur when employees actively conceal invisible stigma. In particular, the process of concealing a stigma is associated with higher incidence of negative emotions, which can then affect workplace satisfaction and workplace longevity (Kelly, 2002). However, disclosing a concealable stigma provides the opportunity for emotional processing from which individuals with an invisible stigma are able to clarify and integrate their thoughts and feelings about their disclosure decision. In a daily diary study of gay men and lesbians, Beals et al. (2009) found that disclosure increases the extent to which gay and lesbian participants reflect on their emotions, thereby increasing well-being.

Qualitative studies focusing on affective aspects of stigma-based stress in the workplace have found that minorities often experience loneliness, frustration, devaluation, shame, and anger following prejudice and stigma in the workplace (Bowleg, Brooks, & Ritz, 2008; Logie, James, Tharao, & Loutfy, 2011). Although these qualitative studies do not capture where exactly these affective states are expressed (e.g. in work vs. non-work domains) nor the impact of such feelings, they do offer insight into the discrete emotions of employees with concealable stigma.

Coping Mechanisms for Those with Invisible Stigmatized Identities

Next, we turn our attention to identity management strategies for handling the affective implications of stigma. Although disclosure can bring benefits, it also may increase the risk that an employee will face discrimination. Thus it is important to understand coping mechanisms – effortful responses to stress that include emotion regulation – other than full disclosure. When individuals are preoccupied with concealing a stigma and respond to stigma-related stressors, affect regulation often encompasses thought suppression, rumination, and avoidance, which are associated with psychological distress (Quinn & Earnshaw, 2011). Hence identity management strategies are adopted as conscious and voluntary responses to emotional stressors in order to avoid psychological distress and feared consequences of having one's identity exposed (Compas, Connor-Smith, Saltzman, Thomsen, & Wadsworth, 2001).

In a study of gay and lesbian employees, Button (2004) described two strategies used to conceal their stigmatized identities at work. First, individuals may counterfeit a heterosexual identity by using opposite-sex pronouns to refer to a romantic partner or by changing a partner's name when speaking with coworkers. Alternatively, sexual minority employees may choose to avoid entirely the subject of sexual orientation or romantic interest. This strategy allows them to be perceived under the virtual social identity of heterosexuality, in which heterosexuality is presumed until that assumption is directly challenged (Goffman, 1963). Engaging in counterfeiting to maintain the perception of a non-stigmatized identity may increase the risk of psychological strain, social isolation, and negative workplace consequences (Croteau, Anderson, & VanderWal, 2008). Moreover, people with concealable stigmas who actively avoid disclosing are more likely to suffer from lack of social support, social isolation, and higher levels of depression and anxiety (Mayfield Arnold, Rice, Flannery, & Rotheram-Borus, 2008).

Employees who choose not to explicitly disclose their invisible stigmatized identity may also use signaling strategies, which involves hinting at their identity without disclosing it outright. Signaling may involve the use of ambiguous language, bringing up certain topics of conversation, and using particular symbols or nonverbal cues. For example, a person might signal their identity by mentioning their affiliation with a charity or organization that supports people with a particular type of stigma. This action is inherently ambiguous: people often support stigma-related organizations for reasons other than having the stigma themselves. At the same time, signaling allows people to gauge potential reactions to disclosure by observing others' responses to general discussion of the topic. People may also use signaling strategies to identify others carrying the same invisible stigma. By using language or other cues that only "insiders" understand, people might be able to identify others who are likely to be supportive and then selectively disclose to them (Clair et al., 2005). Although the emotional outcomes of signaling have not been as heavily studied as other identity management strategies, research has found that signaling a concealable stigma in the workplace is associated with higher levels of anxiety due to constant awareness and perception of the reactions of others in one's environment (Jones, 2017).

Finally, there are a number of identity management strategies associated with disclosure, which tend to be labeled as more adaptive emotion-regulation strategies, as opposed to the maladaptive affective processes associated with identity concealment. Adaptive emotional-regulation strategies occur when individuals engage in beneficial processes such as cognitive reappraisal and acceptance of one's own identity (Aldao & Nolen-Hoeksema, 2012). Maladaptive processes often involve detrimental strategies to one's life, including avoidance, suppression, and rumination (Aldao & Nolen-Hoeksema, 2012). The identity management literature acknowledges both types of strategies in terms of concealing and disclosing an invisible stigma. Button (2004) distinguishes acknowledging, in which employees allow coworkers to discover their invisible stigmatized identities, from advocating, in which they actively claim that identity. Similarly, Clair et al. (2005) describe normalizing and differentiating as potential disclosure strategies. Normalizing attempts to reduce stigma by minimizing the importance of the concealable stigma. For example, an employee of a minority religion may normalize his religion's beliefs by describing similarities between his and others' customs (e.g. familial traditions, dietary restrictions). Since normalizing a stigma requires maintaining a positive view of oneself, individuals who adopt this strategy engage in much more emotion regulation in order to reduce negative affect, distress, anxiety, and depression (Joachim & Acorn, 2000). Differentiating, on the other hand, emphasizes the significance of a concealable stigmatized identity and claims it as legitimate. It also involves directly challenging stigmatization through advocacy for oneself and others.

Thus it is important to recognize that disclosure is not a binary or static process. Instead, people with concealable stigmatized identities use a variety of strategies to manage those identities and experience various emotions associated with such strategies, both in the workplace and in other contexts. Further, we assert that the affective outcomes of managing one's concealable stigma should be considered as an important factor that impacts how one will manage one's identity in the future (see Figure 36.1).

Theoretical and Practical Implications

This chapter has provided a review of the current unifying frameworks for the emotional processes, coping mechanisms, and affective challenges associated with disclosing one's stigma in the workplace. We have summarized how various coping and identity management strategies impact the emotions and psychological well-being of employees with such identities. By integrating the literature's current models, empirical research, and theories, we have sought to provide a perspective into how affective responses to identity management may significantly influence diverse individuals' experiences at work. Next, we suggest recommendations to organizations on how to reduce the negative impacts of stigmatization and/or disclosing an invisible stigma in the workplace.

First, we recommend that organizations take steps to demonstrate acceptance and equal treatments to those employees with an invisible stigma. Disclosing one's invisible stigmatized identity can lead to more intimate and trusting relationships with others, improved states of psychological well-being, and improved feelings of identity authenticity (Sandelowski, Lambe, & Barroso, 2004). However, some employees may feel pressure to disclose as their working relationships become deeper and less superficial but may still struggle to reveal their stigma (Marrs & Staton, 2016). Since disclosure is an ongoing process that does not end after a single instance of disclosure, evaluating other coworkers' reactions plays a significant role in the coping mechanisms and forms of disclosure that an individual may utilize in future instances (Chaudoir & Fisher, 2010). Thus creating an environment where discrimination and unfair treatment are not tolerated may allow those with invisible stigma feel less apprehensive about sharing their identities.

Similarly, it is essential that organizations are aware of the relevant social cues (e.g. perceived social support) and environmental cues (e.g. gender and racial diversity among leadership positions) that may have a powerful impact on people's decisions to disclose. These cues may signal to minority employees that their identities are either devalued or celebrated. For example, an organization displaying a poster showing allyship with the LGBTQ+ community may generate a feeling that the organization does not stigmatize LGBTQ+ identities and supports those from that community. LGBTQ+ individuals might therefore feel safe in revealing their identity to their coworkers.

Additionally, organizations can improve their diversity climate by encouraging allyship behaviors from their employees, such as calling out prejudiced remarks on behalf of stigmatized groups. Individuals with a concealable stigma may feel the burden of challenging prejudice by themselves (e.g. a gay employee feeling the responsibility of having to explain why something was homophobic and offensive). Research has found that those with concealable stigmas experience negative emotions, such as guilt, regret, and rumination, if they do not confront a prejudiced remark that attacked their social identity (Shelton, Richeson, Salvatore, & Hill, 2006). However, there is an additional risk for those whose stigmas are concealable, such that some may feel distressed about outing themselves if they challenge prejudice. For instance, an employee with depression may feel hesitant to call out an insensitive comment made by a coworker about mental illnesses because she does not want to appear to be personally impacted by depression. We therefore assert that all such comments should be confronted by anyone (regardless of association with the stigma), whether or not it is known that someone in the vicinity holds that identity. These confrontations should also occur for visible stigma, such as race and gender. As a caveat, we also highlight that confronting on behalf of others should be done responsibly, such that one does not aim to pass as a spokesperson for a group, especially if one does not identify with such group. These allyship behaviors provide minorities a feeling of safety and respect and hence such behaviors should be encouraged and embraced as part of organizational values and norms.

Since leaders are role models and often establish the social norms of the organization, fostering a healthy diversity climate can be highly influenced by the values and actions of organizational leaders and subordinates. Accordingly, Ruggs et al. (2011) suggest that leaders should clearly signal their financial, professional, and personal commitment to meeting diversity-related goals. Indeed, when mentors demonstrated supportive goals for LGBTQ+ groups, their students were more likely to exhibit better attitudes and supportive behaviors toward the

LGBTQ+ community (Madera et al., 2012). Leaders must set the tone for their organization if they intend to create changes in the attitudes of their employees.

Future Research Directions

While the literature offers an abundance of evidence for the importance of affective processes in identity concealment and disclosure, we believe there are several potential avenues for future research. In our review, we found various affect-related antecedents and outcomes of disclosing or concealing an identity; however, researchers should also explore more of the emotional processes that occur during such occurrences as currently we still have limited understanding on the role of emotion in managing one's concealable stigma. Additionally, most current literature on identity management measures affect in terms of psychological distress, which is usually a construct comprised of anxiety and depression. While we agree with Quinn and colleagues (2014) that distress allows researchers to predict what leads to anxiety and depression, two pervasive mental illnesses, future studies should delve into different emotional processes, such as pride, relief, and happiness, rather than restricting the field to studying identity management only in terms of psychological distress. By integrating theories and frameworks from the emotion literature, future research could bring novel perspectives and evidence on how to best manage emotion and well-being in the identity management process. Also, surprisingly little research has examined the interactive process of disclosure in which stigma-related dynamics and emotions are expressed by the discloser and disclosee. Future research may focus on how interactions between identity management strategies and situational contexts foster positive affective outcomes between the stigmatized person and their coworkers, including inclusion, trustworthiness, and helping behaviors. These mechanisms are also relevant to other work relationships such as those with one's supervisors, subordinates, and customers.

Conclusion

This review has provided a holistic integration of the literature on affective outcomes and stigma, and it suggests possible remediations that organizations can take to improve the lives of those who live with stigma, face prejudice, and struggle with disclosure-related decisions in the workplace. These considerations are becoming increasingly important with the growing focus on informal and interpersonal discrimination. Although the incidence of formal discrimination has decreased in recent years, employees still face considerable amounts of subtle prejudice and discrimination, especially in the workplace. Thus the issues discussed in this chapter are vital for promoting the affect and well-being of employees with a concealable stigma.

References

Aldao, A., & Nolen-Hoeksema, S. (2012). The influence of context on the implementation of adaptive emotion regulation strategies. *Behaviour Research and Therapy*, *50*, 493–501.

Beals, K. P., Peplau, L. A., & Gable, S. L. (2009). Stigma management and wellbeing: The role of perceived social support, emotional processing, and suppression. *Personality and Social Psychology Bulletin*, *35*, 867–879.

Berkley, R. A., Beard, R., & Daus, C. S. (2018). The emotional context of disclosing a concealable stigmatized identity: A conceptual model. *Human Resource Management Review*, *29*(3), 428–455.

Bowleg, L., Brooks, K., & Ritz, S. F. (2008). "Bringing home more than a paycheck": An exploratory analysis of black lesbians' experiences of stress and coping in the workplace. *Journal of Lesbian Studies*, *12*, 69–84.

Boyce, A. S., Ryan, A. M., Imus, A. L., & Morgeson, F. P. (2007). "Temporary worker, permanent loser?" A model of the stigmatization of temporary workers. *Journal of Management, 33,* 5–29.

Brief, A. P., & Weiss, H. M. (2002). Organizational behavior: Affect in the workplace. *Annual Review of Psychology, 53,* 279–307.

Button, S. B. (2004). Identity management strategies utilized by lesbian and gay employees: A quantitative investigation. *Group & Organization Management, 29,* 470–494.

Chaudoir, S. R., & Fisher, J. D. (2010). The disclosure processes model: Understanding disclosure decision making and postdisclosure outcomes among people living with a concealable stigmatized identity. *Psychological Bulletin, 136,* 236–256.

Clair, J. A., Beatty, J. E., & MacLean, T. L. (2005). Out of sight but not out of mind: Managing invisible social identities in the workplace. *Academy of Management Review, 30,* 78–95.

Colombetti, G. (2005). Appraising valence. *Journal of Consciousness Studies, 12,* 103–126.

Compas, B. E., Connor-Smith, J. K., Saltzman, H., Thomsen, A. H., & Wadsworth, M. E. (2001). Coping with stress during childhood and adolescence: Problems, progress, and potential in theory and research. *Psychological Bulletin, 127,* 87–127.

Côté, S. & Morgan, L. M. (2002). A longitudinal analysis of the association between emotion regulation, job satisfaction, and intentions to quit. *Journal of Organizational Behavior, 23,* 947–962.

Croteau, J. M., Anderson, M. Z., & VanderWal, B. L. (2008). Models of workplace sexual identity disclosure and management: Reviewing and extending concepts. *Group & Organization Management, 33,* 532–565.

Goffman, E. (1963). *Stigma.* Englewood Cliffs, NJ: Prentice-Hall.

Griffith, K. H., & Hebl, M. R. (2002). The disclosure dilemma for gay men and lesbians: "Coming out" at work. *Journal of Applied Psychology, 87,* 1191–1199.

Joachim, G., & Acorn, S. (2000). Stigma of visible and invisible chronic conditions. *Journal of Advanced Nursing, 32,* 243–248.

Johnson, V. R., & Yarhouse, M. A. (2013). Shame in sexual minorities: Stigma, internal cognitions, and counseling considerations. *Counseling and Values, 58,* 85–103.

Jones, K. P. (2017). To tell or not to tell? Examining the role of discrimination in the pregnancy disclosure process at work. *Journal of Occupational Health Psychology, 22,* 239–250.

Jordan, K. M., & Deluty, R. H. (1998). Coming out for lesbian women: Its relation to anxiety, positive affectivity, self-esteem, and social support. *Journal of Homosexuality, 35,* 41–63.

Kelly, A. E. (2002). *The psychology of secrets.* New York, NY: Kluwer Academic/Plenum.

Law, C. L., Martinez, L. R., Ruggs, E. N., Hebl, M. R., & Akers, E. (2011). Trans-parency in the workplace: How the experiences of transsexual employees can be improved. *Journal of Vocational Behavior, 79,* 710–723.

Lea, T., de Wit, J., & Reynolds, R. (2014). Minority stress in lesbian, gay, and bisexual young adults in Australia: Associations with psychological distress, suicidality, and substance use. *Archives of Sexual Behavior, 43,* 1571–1578.

LeBlanc, A. J., Frost, D. M., & Wight, R. G. (2015). Minority stress and stress proliferation among same-sex and other marginalized couples. *Journal of Marriage and Family, 77,* 40–59.

Legate, N., Ryan, R. M., & Weinstein, N. (2012). Is coming out always a "good thing"? Exploring the relations of autonomy support, outness, and wellness for lesbian, gay, and bisexual individuals. *Social Psychological and Personality Science, 3,* 145–152.

Linney, K. D. (2008). Work–family conflict and job satisfaction: Family resources as a buffer. *Journal of Family and Consumer Sciences, 100,* 24–30.

Logie, C. H., James, L., Tharao, W., & Loutfy, M. R. (2011). HIV, gender, race, sexual orientation, and sex work: A qualitative study of intersectional stigma experienced by HIV-positive women in Ontario, Canada. *PLoS medicine, 8,* doi:10.1371/journal.pmed.1001124

Madera, J. M., King, E. B., & Hebl, M. R. (2012). Bringing social identity to work: The influence of manifestation and suppression on perceived discrimination, job satisfaction, and turnover intentions. *Cultural Diversity and Ethnic Minority Psychology, 18,* 165–170.

Major, B., & Gramzow, R. H. (1999). Abortion as stigma: Cognitive and emotional implications of concealment. *Journal of Personality and Social Psychology, 77*, 735–745.

Marrs, S. A., & Staton, A. R. (2016). Negotiating difficult decisions: Coming out versus passing in the workplace. *Journal of LGBT Issues in Counseling, 10*, 40–54.

Martinez, L. R., & Hebl, M. R. (2016). Adult survivors of childhood cancers' identity disclosures in the workplace. *Journal of Cancer Survivorship, 10*, 416–424.

Mayfield Arnold, E., Rice, E., Flannery, D., & Rotheram-Borus, M. J. (2008). HIV disclosure among adults living with HIV. *AIDS Care, 20*, 80–92.

Meyer, I. H. (2003). Prejudice, social stress, and mental health in lesbian, gay, and bisexual populations: Conceptual issues and research evidence. *Psychological Bulletin, 129*, 674–697.

Pachankis, J. E. (2007). The psychological implications of concealing a stigma: A cognitive–affective–behavioral model. *Psychological Bulletin, 133*, 328–345.

Pachankis, J. E., & Goldfried, M. R. (2006). Social anxiety in young gay men. *Journal of Anxiety Disorders, 20*, 996–1015.

Quinn, D. M., & Chaudoir, S. R. (2009). Living with a concealable stigmatized identity: The impact of anticipated stigma, centrality, salience, and cultural stigma on psychological distress and health. *Journal of Personality and Social Psychology, 97*, 634–651.

Quinn, D. M., & Earnshaw, V. A. (2013). Concealable stigmatized identities and psychological well-being. *Social and Personality Psychology Compass, 7*, 40–51.

Quinn, D. M., Williams, M. K., Quintana, F., Gaskins, J. L., Overstreet, N. M., Pishori, A., . . . & Chaudoir, S. R. (2014). Examining effects of anticipated stigma, centrality, salience, internalization, and outness on psychological distress for people with concealable stigmatized identities. *PloS One, 9*, doi:10.1371/journal.pone.0096977

Ragins, B. R. (2004). Sexual orientation in the workplace: The unique work and career experiences of gay, lesbian and bisexual workers. In M. R. Buckley, J. R. B. Halbesleben, & A. R. Wheeler (Eds.), *Research in personnel and human resources management* (Volume 23, pp. 35–129). Bingley, UK: Emerald.

Ragins, B. R. (2008). Disclosure disconnects: Antecedents and consequences of disclosing invisible stigmas across life domains. *Academy of Management Review, 33*, 194–215.

Ruggs, E. N., Martinez, L. R., & Hebl, M. R. (2011). How individuals and organizations can reduce interpersonal discrimination. *Social and Personality Psychology Compass, 5*, 29–42.

Sabat, I., Trump, R., & King, E. (2014). Individual, interpersonal, and contextual factors relating to disclosure decisions of lesbian, gay, and bisexual individuals. *Psychology of Sexual Orientation and Gender Diversity, 1*, 431–440.

Sandelowski, M., Lambe, C., & Barroso, J. (2004). Stigma in HIV-positive women. *Journal of Nursing Scholarship, 36*, 122–128.

Sedlovskaya, A., Purdie-Vaughns, V. P., Eibach, R. P., LaFrance, M., Romero-Canyas, R., & Camp, N. P. (2013). Internalizing the closet: Concealment heightens the cognitive distinction between public and private selves. *Journal of Personality and Social Psychology, 104*, 695–715.

Shelton, J. N., Richeson, J. A., Salvatore, J., & Hill, D. M. (2006). Silence is not golden: The intrapersonal consequences of not confronting prejudice. In S. Levin & C. van Laar (Eds.), *Stigma and group inequality: Social psychological perspectives* (pp. 65–81). Mahwah, NJ: Erlbaum.

Smart, L., & Wegner, D. M. (2000). The hidden costs of hidden stigma. In T. Heatherton, R. Kleck, M. Hebl, & J. Hull (Eds.), *The social psychology of stigma* (pp. 220–242). New York, NY: Guilford.

Stergiou-Kita, M., Pritlove, C., & Kirsch, B. (2016). The "big C" – stigma, cancer, and workplace discrimination. *Journal of Cancer Survivorship, 10*, 1035–1050.

Stirratt, M. J., Meyer, I. H., Ouellette, S. C., & Gara, M. A. (2008). Measuring identity multiplicity and intersectionality: Hierarchical classes analysis (HICLAS) of sexual, racial, and gender identities. *Self and Identity, 7*, 89–111.

Stone, D. L., & Colella, A. (1996). A model of factors affecting the treatment of disabled individuals in organizations. *Academy of Management Review, 21*, 352–401.

Talley, A. E., & Bettencourt, B. A. (2011). The moderator roles of coping style and identity disclosure on the relationship between perceived sexual stigma and psychological distress. *Journal of Applied Social Psychology, 41*, 2883–2903.

Testa, R. J., Michaels, M. S., Bliss, W., Rogers, M. L., Balsam, K. F., & Joiner, T. (2017). Suicidal ideation in transgender people: Gender minority stress and interpersonal theory factors. *Journal of Abnormal Psychology, 126*, 125–136.

Toth, K. E., & Dewa, C. S. (2014). Employee decision-making about disclosure of a mental disorder at work. *Journal of Occupational Rehabilitation, 24*, 732–746.

Trau, R. N. C. (2015). The impact of discriminatory climate perceptions on the composition of interorganizational developmental networks, psychosocial support, and job and career attitudes of employees with an invisible stigma. *Human Resource Management, 54*, 345–366, doi:10.1002/hrm.21630

Trau, R. N., Chuang, Y. T., Pichler, S., Lim, A., Wang, Y., & Halvorsen, B. (2018). The dynamic recursive process of community influences, LGBT-support policies and practices, and perceived discrimination at work. In S. B. Thomson & G. Grandy (Eds.), *Stigmas, work and organizations* (pp. 71–98). New York, NY: Palgrave Macmillan.

Velez, B. L., Moradi, B., & Brewster, M. E. (2013). Testing the tenets of minority stress in workplace contexts. *Journal of Counseling Psychology, 60*, 532–542.

Waldo, C. R. (1999). Working in a majority context: A structural model of heterosexism as minority stress in the workplace. *Journal of Counseling Psychology, 46*, 218–232.

Weiss, H. M., & Cropanzano, R. (1996). Affective events theory: A theoretical discussion of the structure, causes and consequences of affective experiences at work. In B. M. Staw & L. L. Cummings (Eds.), *Research in organizational behavior: An annual series of analytical essays and critical reviews* (Volume 18, pp. 1–74). Greenwich, CT, and London, UK: Elsevier Science/JAI.

Wessel, J. L. (2017). The importance of allies and allied organizations: Sexual orientation disclosure and concealment at work. *Journal of Social Issues, 73*, 240–254.

37 Implications of Technological Work Practices for Employee Affect

Larissa K. Barber and Xinyu Hu

The modern workplace is continually adopting technological innovations that change the way work is done. These changes involve "new ways of working" that rely on technology-mediated communications with coworkers, supervisors, and clients (Demerouti, Derks, Lieke, & Bakker, 2014). In particular, a considerable amount of work is now being conducted through email exchanges, online messaging, and videoconference meetings either in place of, or in addition to, face-to-face work tasks. Organizations are motivated to adopt electronic communications because of expected productivity and employee well-being gains associated with increased work flexibility (Lewis, 2003). Yet technologically facilitated work can result in both positive and negative consequences for employee productivity and well-being (Charalampous, Grant, Tramontano, & Michailidis, 2019; Day, Scott, & Kelloway, 2010; Ter Hoeven, van Zoonen, & Fonner, 2016).

In this chapter, we review evidence for the link between technological work practices and employee affect. Generally, technology (e.g. virtual work and telecommuting) is adopted in the workplace for its potential positive impact on employee productivity, yet it may also come with costs to affective well-being. Guided by affective events theory (Weiss & Cropanzano, 1996), we explore research showing how technological factors of the work environment can have implications for *both* positive and negative affective reactions in workers, which can influence downstream work outcomes such as job performance and job satisfaction. We also outline implications of this research for organizational practice and directions for future work in this topic area.

Relevance of Technological Work Practices to Valued Work Outcomes

Today's workforce encounters a pervasive emphasis on technological communications and work processes given the growth of service-oriented and knowledge-intensive industries (e.g. educational service and professional positions; Pew Research Center, 2016). Organizations are increasingly relying on virtual workplaces for multi-site and multinational collaborations that can increase access to global markets and provide improved customer service (Cascio, 1995; Cascio, 2000). Additionally, organizations have been considering methods of attracting and maintaining a diverse workforce by empowering employees to manage both work and non-work issues through flexible work arrangements that allow employees to work off-site ("teleworking" or "remote working"), which can also be beneficial to organizational performance (Beauregard & Henry, 2009). Even office-based workers are using technology to conduct work both on- and off-site (e.g. at home). The term *e-work* can be used to collectively describe the mechanism for how one carries out work tasks using electronic communications or evolving technological interfaces (Charalampous et al., 2019; Grant, Wallace, & Spurgeon, 2013).

There are two key ways that technological innovations have transformed the workplace and made the concept of e-work relevant to a variety of workers, whether they work on-site or across locations. First, e-work can involve changes to existing work styles and activities that are now mediated via technology. Examples include the prevalence of new media technology for communications (e.g. teleconferencing; Demerouti et al., 2014) to new virtual relationships among workers (e.g. telementoring, virtual teams, and online communities; Benson et al., 2002; Russell & Perris, 2003). Second, there are often innovations to work-related hardware and software that affect employee experiences due to the technology interfaces themselves. Examples of such hardware include embedded robots in organizational systems and virtual reality devices for experiencing simulated work environments (Cascio & Montealegre, 2016). Examples of software implementations include digitized human resource management (e.g. applicant processing systems), various forms of asynchronous communications (e.g. platforms for email and messaging systems), and packages for data management (e.g. statistical software for data analysis; Benson et al., 2002).

There are both advantages and disadvantages to various forms of e-work for key worker experiences related to valued work outcomes. For example, telecommuting is generally associated with higher job performance and job satisfaction, as well as a higher relationship quality with one's supervisor (Gajendran & Harrison, 2007). Yet telecommuting is also associated with more social isolation from coworkers and poorer job performance, especially among individuals with high telecommuting frequency (Golden et al., 2008). Conducting teamwork more or less virtually can also lead to mixed satisfaction and well-being outcomes based on a variety of contextual (e.g. team-related) and methodological factors (Ortiz de Guinea, Webster, & Staples, 2012).

Unfortunately, focusing merely on the *use* of technological work factors – that is, presence/absence or frequency of use – does not lend itself to specificity regarding the exact source of affective experiences among employees. Given the ever-increasing reliance on technology in the workplace, organizations are most concerned with *how* to best implement technology in a way that positively impacts employee well-being and productivity. In this regard, research on socially-oriented *technology-mediated interactions* and task-oriented *technological interfaces* is perhaps most informative. This specificity allows researchers and practitioners to pinpoint the source of issues and determine potential solutions. In the following section, we outline these different approaches to understanding employee affective reactions and provide examples of research in each of these areas in the context of affective events theory.

Theory and Research Linking Technological Work Practices to Employee Affect

When discussing technology in the workplace in relation to affect, it is important to clarify what is meant by affective reactions and distinguish between different affective reactions to different technological issues. Affect can refer to a wide variety of "feelings" related to both work and non-work contexts (Warr, 1994). Affect includes short-lived *emotional* reactions in response to specific events, medium-duration *moods* without attributions to specific causes, and long-term *dispositional affect (*also known as *affectivity)* that is relatively stable across long periods of time (Barsade & Gibson, 2007). This review focuses on affective reactions rather than dispositional affectivity, given that emotion and mood changes are responses to technological work practices that are link to valued worker outcomes (i.e. job satisfaction and performance; Weiss & Cropanzano, 1996; Weiss, 2002). These affective reactions are typically assessed in response to three key issues:

the use of technology, social interactions mediated through technology, and responses to technological interfaces (Shank, 2014).

The key focus of the *technology use* perspective is on the presence or frequency of use of a particular technology that has been adopted in the organization. For example, organizations wishing to move more teamwork collaboration online (i.e. to create virtual teams) might first think about advantages from a *technology use* perspective. For example, will employees be happier working in virtual teams than non-virtual teams? How much virtual teamwork would make employees the happiest? Alternatively, organizations can focus on a *technology-mediated social interaction* perspective that addresses how employees interact with others using the technology. For example, how does working in virtual teams enhance or hinder effective communication that would influence employees' affective experiences, such as through easier work access or miscommunication issues? These interaction issues are inherently people-oriented, with the idea that typical social interactions in the workplace are being facilitated through a certain technology medium. Lastly, organizations can choose to tackle issues around *technology interface experiences*, in which the technology itself can elicit both positive and negative affective reactions in employees. For example, does the online collaboration platform create positive or negative learning experiences based on how easy it is to use? Does the platform help reduce work errors in virtual work or enhance mistakes due to malfunctions? Thus, we will differentiate between technology use, technology-mediated interactions, and technology interface experiences when discussing findings from past research.

Our brief review of affective reactions to technology-related events in the workplace is guided by affective events theory (AET; Weiss & Cropanzano, 1996). In AET, features of the work environment create various workplace events that elicit both positive and negative affective reactions, in turn influencing downstream affect-related outcomes highly valued by organizations. This theory is particularly helpful for the technological intervention context because it takes into account that affective reactions fluctuate over time in response to specific work events, which subsequently can influence employee performance (Beal, Weiss, Barros, & MacDermid, 2005). Figure 37.1 represents an adaptation of this theoretical model in the context of technological interventions.

To illustrate this theoretical model, imagine that an organization decides to adopt a new media technology to facilitate virtual team communications. They adopt a team collaboration online platform that allows them to share documents in a cloud-based system and communicate with each other using instant messaging. This situation represents a *work environment feature* that can be measured in terms of either the presence or absence of the technology (i.e. dichotomously) or the intensity of technology use (from never or rarely to frequently, i.e. continuously). Much of the research we cited in the previous section takes this technology use perspective in studying potential outcomes, which directly explores the link between work features (e.g. virtual work, telecommuting) and work attitudes or behaviors.

Alternatively, organizations can consider how the new technology will create a number of *workplace events* that can differentially be evaluated negatively (hassles) or positively (uplifts). According to AET, the key difference between employees interpreting events as either positive or negative is based on whether the events facilitate or obstruct valued goals (per the transactional model of stress; Lazarus & Folkman, 1984). The terms "hassles" and "uplifts" represent minor workplace events that can elicit negative or positive affective reactions respectively (DeLongis et al., 1982; Kanner et al., 1981). We can also further break down work events into

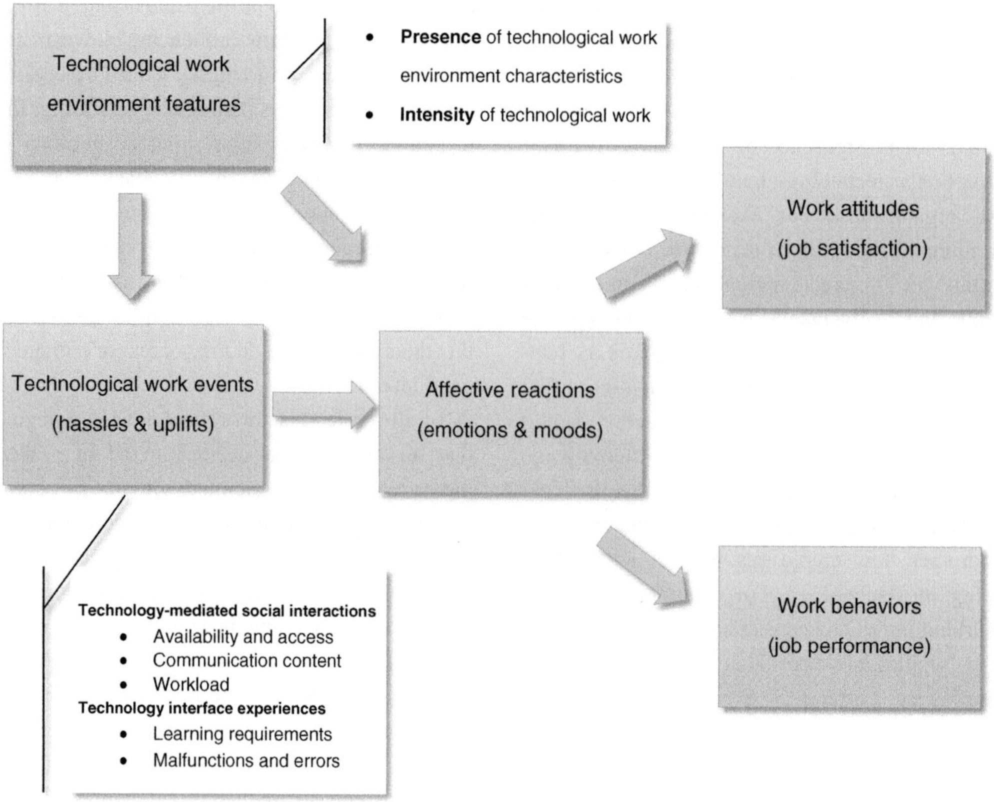

Figure 37.1 Technology-related work practices in the context of affective events theory

those related to technology-mediated social interactions – availability and access, communication content (e.g. positive versus negative informational content in work-related messages from others in the workplace), and workload (e.g. time required to complete requests received via work-related messages) – versus those that occur due to the technology interface experience itself (e.g. learning requirements and malfunctions/errors).

When using a virtual team instant messaging system, an example of a technology-mediated social interaction uplift is receiving assistance quickly from a colleague through the messaging system while working on a difficult task. When an employee receives assistance from a teammate, it facilitates their task goal, which in turn increases positive affect (Sonnentag, Reinecke, Mata, & Vorderer, 2018). Other common technology-related events during the work day that are perceived as positive uplifts include being able to access work emails for multi-tasking during meetings or other idle time (e.g. on the way to the office), having access to fast and efficient communication channels to complete work, coordinating appointments, and being able to stay up-to-date even while being physically absent from a work meeting (Braukmann, Schmitt, Ďuranová, & Ohly, 2018).

However, this same virtual team instant messaging system can produce a number of hassles. Employees might struggle to complete their own work tasks due to interruptions from colleagues on the messaging system. These types of interruptions have been shown to increase time pressure in completing the primary task, and thus increase negative affect (Sonnentag et al., 2018). In addition to this disruption to workflow, other research has indicated that common technology-related hassles include having technical problems (e.g. breakdown of systems: a form of technology interface experience), having to take an urgent call or email during a meeting, and experiencing communication overload (e.g. too many emails; Braukmann et al., 2018). In the following subsections, we review examples of research linking different types of workplace events to affective reactions among employees and, in turn, to work attitudes and behaviors.

Examples of Research on Technology Uses as Work Environment Features

Most research linking affect to technological features of the work environment compares affective outcomes for workers who use a technology versus outcomes for workers who do not (or who use it with low intensity). One cross-sectional study examined how many hours employees spent using technological communications (e.g. telephone, emailing/texting, instant messaging, and videoconferencing) to interact with team members over the previous two weeks compared to face-to-face interactions, as well as what percentage of their work was conducted online (Johnson, Bettenhausen, & Gibbons, 2009). Employees who reported using technological communication more often experienced lower levels of positive affect while working with their teams and felt less emotionally connected to their workgroups (corresponding to the downstream work attitude of affective commitment). Using these communications over 90 percent of the time was particularly detrimental to positive affect and affective commitment, and also to productivity-related outcomes such as task effectiveness (Johnson et al., 2009). Another study compared teleworkers to office-based workers via a combination of an interview-based qualitative study and a cross-sectional survey design. Telecommuters reported experiencing a variety of negative emotions, such as irritability, worry, and guilt, more than office-based workers (Mann & Holdsworth, 2003). However, teleworkers reported less stress overall than office workers and did not differ in reports of the positive emotion of enjoyment. Lastly, another study among employees at a Spanish company examined frequency of use across workers who used information and communication technologies as a primary tool for their work. Non-intensive technology communication users experience more anxiety related to technology use compared to a group of intensive users (Salanova, Llorens, & Cifre, 2013).

However, a day-level longitudinal design actually found benefits to telecommuting. Employees working in a US government organization reported on emotional experiences for four work days over a two-week timespan. Workers experienced more positive emotions and less negative emotions on the days they were telecommuting compared to non-telecommuting days (Anderson, Kaplan, & Vega, 2015). This study highlights the importance of exploring technology use issues in a within-person context that accounts for potentially confounding factors of both person and organizational characteristics that limit the utility of findings from cross-sectional designs.

Examples of Research on Technology-Mediated Interaction Work Events

Technology-mediated interaction work events are those that are related to work activities involving social interaction both within the organization (coworkers, supervisors) and outside it (customers, clients). One key area related to technology-mediated social interaction work events has been a focus on *availability expectations* and *work access issues*. For example, one survey study found that being expected to be available and to respond to requests at all times of the day is associated with more technology-related stress (Day, Paquet, Scott, & Hambley, 2012). Another survey study also showed that feeling obligated to use a smartphone in the evening for work-related purposes predicts less positive affect and more negative affect – though the opposite was found if workers used their phone for work access because they found it to be fun, interesting, or useful (Ohly & Latour, 2014). Also, having adequate equipment for access and control over access predicts less emotional exhaustion when employees are expected to be available for after-hours work tasks (Dettmers, Bamberg, & Seffzek, 2016).

A second issue related to these types of work events is *communication content.* Communication content refers to whether communications themselves contain positive or negative information. For example, one experience-sampling study examining the impact of elements in work-related electronic communications after hours on affective responses found that unpleasant content in electronic communication (i.e. negative affective tone) was positively associated with anger and negatively associated with happiness (Butts, Becker, & Boswell, 2015). Additionally, both an experimental study (Giumetti et al., 2013) and an experience-sampling study (Park, Fritz, & Jex, 2018) on cyber incivility suggested uncivil content in received emails elicits high distress. As for downstream work attitudes and behaviors, employees who report experiencing incivility in electronic communications also report lower job satisfaction and organizational commitment, and are more likely to engage in deviant behaviors against the organization (Lim & Teo, 2009).

Yet a third issue related to technology-mediated interactions is *workload.* This describes the amount of work time required for a requested task. Examples of this concept are techno-overload (Ragu-Nathan et al., 2008), information and communication technology (ICT) workload demands (Day et al., 2012), and quantity of emails received (Brown, Duck, & Jimmieson, 2014). Workers who experience more ICT workload demands also report more stress while using work-related technology (Day et al., 2012), and the quantity of emails received predicts higher reports of emotional exhaustion (Brown et al., 2014). Another study found that the time required to respond to electronic communications during non-work time also predicts higher reports of anger (Butts et al., 2015).

Examples of Research on Technology Interface Experiences at Work

Lastly, research related to technology interface issues suggests that experiences with technology itself while conducting work tasks can produce both positive and negative affective reactions in employees. First, the technology interface can be linked to affect through *learning requirement* work events. Positive affect and reduced negative affect regarding technology use can be generated from one's own efficacious feeling in using and mastering a new technology (Compeau & Higgins, 1995). However, this learning environment can also increase negative affect by making employees feel uncertain about how to complete their work with new technological changes or upgrades (Ragu-Nathan et al., 2008).

New technology could disturb workflow and cause delays in work completion progress through *malfunctions and error* work events. Ceaparu and colleagues (2004) provided a list of common problems and sources of technology users' frustration; common ones include internet connection issues, email failure, and errors and malfunctions of applications. Other researchers have also noted that password failures frequently arise from needing to create a variety of passwords across different secure technological systems (Grawemeyer & Johnson, 2011). Given many industries and occupations rely heavily on electronic communications (e.g. remote consultants, online customer service centers) and various software packages (e.g. data analysts, software developers), the frequency of these technology frustration issues and time lost in resolving these issues could result in increased affective reactions in employees. In particular, when employees experience technological malfunctions, they also experience delays in information exchange, which is associated with a reduced sense of control that in turn increases negative affect (Guenter, van Emmerik, & Schreurs, 2014).

Implications for Organizational Practice

Past research has provided promising initial findings that can inform how aspects of technological work events are linked to affective reactions in employees. These findings have some implications for how organizations can adopt technological work practices in ways that may enhance positive employee affective reactions and reduce negative reactions. In particular, we focus on considerations related to technology-mediated work events, technology interface work events, and individual differences linked to technology use preferences and affective reactions.

Improving Technology-Mediated Work Events via Employee Socialization

For technology-mediated work events, organizations should keep in mind that communication mediums differ on their ability to reduce information processing problems, such as reducing uncertainty or ambiguity (Daft & Lengal, 1986). Richer media in the form of face-to-face interaction can transmit more social and verbal cues and allow more immediate feedback than less rich media (e.g. phone or email). Thus some negative affective reactions to technology in the workplace may arise from employees not matching the appropriate form of media to the situation. Examples would include using email to discuss a complex or emotionally-charged topic rather than a face-to-face meeting, or scheduling a face-to-face meeting for a straightforward task best suited for email. The mismatch between the media to the work situation would likely elicit negative affective reactions such as frustration or anger. Knowing how best to select and use technological media to convey information to other organizational members is, then, a key skill that can be developed. Organizations could potentially reduce these types of "mismatched" technology-mediated events by facilitating socialization processes (e.g. training and mentoring programs) to improve social communications among employees (Flanagin & Waldeck, 2004).

For example, employees can struggle with understanding expectation norms about availability in the workplace (Day et al., 2012) and ambiguity regarding exactly how quickly to respond to electronic communications that are conducted asynchronously (e.g. email, text messages; Barber & Santuzzi, 2015). This issue may arise from uncertainty surrounding group norms related to expectations for interactions with coworkers or supervisors, as well as organizational norms related to the overall work culture (Flanagin & Waldeck, 2014). Specific discussions could improve understanding of expectations about time frames for responding via different technological mediums and when employees can expect to have time off from electronic communications (Perlow & Kelly, 2014; Perlow & Porter, 2009).

An example of a communication content issue is misinterpretations of email tone (Day et al., 2012) and negative affect arising from negative text-based emotional displays in virtual teams (Cheshin, Rafaeli, & Bos, 2011). Text-based communications such as email and even virtual chats lack verbal and nonverbal cues that can lead to misinterpretation, thereby increasing emotional exhaustion (Brown et al., 2014). Socialization processes can communicate message-related emotional display norms that can help reduce these miscommunications. One strategy is to use emoticons to provide additional cues that help convey message intentions (Byron, 2008). Emoticons can clarify joking intentions or even "soften" messages related to requests and pointing out work mistakes (Skovholt, Grønning, & Kankaanranta, 2014). Additionally, virtual teams may require more positive emotional display norms (i.e. expectations of displaying positive emotions and suppressing negative emotions) when working with multinational than with culturally similar team members (Glikson & Erez, 2013). Culturally similar virtual teams can rely on emotional display norms similar to their own cultural expectations, but increased expression of positive emotions is needed across multinational teams to establish trust and reduce interpersonal conflict.

Lastly, socialization practices can also help workers manage workload resulting from technological interactions. Communication mediums differ on how much time it takes to respond to requests, with some research showing that face-to-face interruptions take less time to address than virtual interruptions (Nees & Fortna, 2015). Additionally, employees have preferences regarding what types of tasks would be best suited to electronic versus face-to-face mediums (Sullivan, 1995). There is even variation in the time required to address specific issues in just one type of medium (e.g. time required varies greatly across different email requests even within the same worker; Butts et al., 2015). Therefore, workload issues arise when complex tasks or questions are not matched to richer media – such as asking time-consuming and interactive questions by email that would be better suited to real-time discussions. Providing appropriate guidance for task–technology fit (Maruping & Agarwal, 2004) could reduce these "time sink" mismatches that predict negative emotional reactions (Butts et al., 2015).

Improving Technology-Interface Work Events via Employee Training and Technological Support

For technology-interface work events, organizations must also consider factors related to why employees feel some technologies are easier to use than others (Venkatesh, 2000) or perceive some technologies as threatening (Fisher & Howell, 2004), which in turn affects whether they are able to accept technology in a way that produces positive affective reactions. For example, employees need to feel that they have the ability to use the technology (self-efficacy), that there are others in the work environment that can provide support when they encounter technological issues (facilitating conditions), and that changes to the technological features of the work environment provide benefits to them (positive purpose). Knowledge of these factors surrounding use and acceptance can help organizations address technology interface events through both training and technical support programs that improve employee perceptions of whether the new technology is easy to use and whether it provides clear benefits to employees.

First, learning requirement events can be addressed with sufficient employee training on technological features of the work environment. Workers with more training are likely to experience more self-efficacy when working with technology (Salanova, Grau, Cifre, & Llorens. 2000). The types of training may also matter, with behavioral modeling strategies ("showing") being more effective for improving self-efficacy and affective reactions than basic tutorials ("telling"; Gist, Schwoerer, & Rosen, 1989).

Second, communicating the purposes of newly adopted technologies is also relevant to employee reactions surrounding learning requirement events. For example, perceiving technological performance monitoring as developmental (as opposed to punitive) results in higher job satisfaction and less job-related anxiety (Holman,

Chessik, & Totterdell, 2002). Thus, introducing new technology in a way that reduces employees' perceived threat to job security (i.e. techno-insecurity; Ragu-Nathan et al., 2008) should be a critical communication concern in the training process.

Third, malfunction and error events can also be addressed by providing personal assistance with technological issues – a key aspect of facilitating conditions that support technology adoption and reduce technology-related anxiety (Day et al., 2010; Ragu-Nathan et al., 2008; Venkatesh, 2000). For example, employees are less likely to experience strain from technological hassles when they receive quick and helpful assistance from support staff (Day et al., 2012). Thus, organizations that require employees to use technology frequently – or learn new technology frequently – must also provide timely support when malfunctions inevitably arise.

Improving Reactions to Technological Features via Employee Selection

Individual differences or dispositions can also play a role in how employees react to technological features of the work environment (see Weiss & Cropanzano, 1996). Therefore, organizations may also want to consider whether their selection processes should take account of individual differences that affect how employees may react to intensive technology use or the need to frequently adjust to new technology – if these job requirements are present.

For example, openness to new experiences is a key personality characteristic associated with a preference for technology-related teamwork (Luse, McElroy, Townsend, & DeMarie, 2013) and has been proposed as a key dispositional trait that helps individuals to adapt to new technologies (Day et al., 2010). Openness was also found to strengthen the relationship between working at home (versus the office) and higher levels of positive affect (Anderson et al., 2015). Additionally, neuroticism or other high-anxiety dispositions might make it difficult for some individuals to cope with technological workplace practices (Day et al., 2010). For example, trait rumination – a focus on past negative emotional experiences – weakens the positive relationship between daily teleworking and positive affect (Anderson et al., 2015). Thus, organizations might need to explore selection devices (e.g. personality assessments or technology-oriented situational judgment tests) to help assess individual differences for positions that require intensive virtual work or telecommuting.

Future Research Directions

There are many opportunities to expand our knowledge on work technology implications for employee affect. As mentioned earlier, the use of technologies as work environment features has been the primary focus of research on work technology and affect. Thus, we need more research elucidating how specific work events related to technology-mediated social interactions and technology interface experiences influence affective reactions, as well as subsequent influences on downstream outcomes (i.e. job satisfaction and job performance). We recommend a variety of directions that this research could take using multi-method, multi-level, and multi-context approaches.

Multi-method Directions

Much of the current literature has relied on self-reported survey methodologies to explore affective reactions to work technologies (e.g. Dettmers et al., 2016; Johnson et al., 2009; Ohly & Latour, 2014). Self-report methodology is theoretically necessary for some – but not all – components of the model outlined in Figure 37.1. Therefore, a key contribution in future work would be to pair subjective reports of affective reactions – and some downstream outcomes such as job satisfaction – with objective work environment features (e.g. observational data showing engagement in technologically mediated communications), events (e.g. objective measures of email workload), and outcomes (objective measures of performance or observer ratings of performance). For example, Brown et al. (2014) measured email quantity by asking participants to report the number of emails received and sent on the previous work day based on their inbox and outbox, but such questions are prone to memory recall and thus would be improved by observational methodologies. Researchers might also find it helpful to conduct parallel studies in both the field and the laboratory to study a specific phenomenon. For example, a work simulation experimental study could manipulate key work events (e.g. negative electronic communication content in the form of incivility; Giumetti et al., 2013) that could also be examined in a field research setting (e.g. daily diary reports of uncivil electronic communications; Park et al., 2018).

Multi-level Directions

Although contemporary research has begun to take a multi-level approach to examining within-person fluctuations of affective reactions to different work events (e.g. Butts et al., 2015; Park et al., 2018; Sonnentag et al., 2018), future research can also consider how multi-level approaches would inform individual variations in reactions to shared technological work events or environmental features, as well as how these reactions potentially impact on downstream group outcomes (e.g. virtual team performance). Such an approach would be similar to studies exploring variations in individual affective reactions in relation to non-technology-related work environment events, such as role conflict (Tekleab & Quigley, 2014) or leadership behaviors (Chi, Chung, & Tsai, 2011). A multi-level approach could also shed light on how workgroup members may influence individual affective reactions to technology through sensemaking or social information processing (Fulk, Steinfield, Schmitz, & Power, 1987; Salancik & Pfefer, 1978). For example, attitudes toward workplace technology can be affected by members of one's workgroup, especially those who interact with each other frequently (Rice & Aydin, 1991). Thus, one's workgroup could shape individual affective reactions to technological work events.

Multi-context Directions

The multi-cultural context of affective reactions to technology is also a rich area of future exploration. Cultural differences both within and across organizations – and even nationalities – might change how employees react to technology (Moser & Axtell, 2013). For example, emotional display rules differ across multicultural versus culturally homogenous virtual teams (Glikson & Erez, 2013), so the social context might matter for how employees perceive affect-related cues in messages content. Future work can also determine if variations in this type of display norm occur at the "subculture" level within organizations (Hofstede, 1998; Palthe & Kossek, 2003). That is, some employees may have predominantly technology-mediated communications with members of their own workgroup with well-established emotional expression norms (i.e. strong virtual communication norms; Moser & Axtell, 2013) whereas other employees primarily have technological communications across multiple groups in the organization that vary considerably in norms.

Conclusions

Technological work practices can have both positive and negative implications for employee affect, as technological features and events in the work environment create a variety of discrete work experiences that either facilitate or hinder work goals. At their best, technological work practices provide uplifts in the form of flexible work access, positive communication content, a manageable workload, mastery of learning, and automation of tasks to reduce errors. At their worst, these practices also come with hassles related to heightened availability expectations, miscommunications of content, increased workload, sharp learning curves, and malfunctions and errors that hinder productivity. Thus, questions regarding whether adopting technological practices will benefits employee affect should take a nuanced approach by studying specific work events that prompt affective reactions. Exploring both social- and task-focused events arising from technological work features (rather than taking technology-use-based perspectives) can help organizations understand key intervention points for successfully supporting technology use in the workplace.

References

Anderson, A. J., Kaplan, S. A., & Vega, R. P. (2015). The impact of telework on emotional experience: When, and for whom, does telework improve daily affective well-being? *European Journal of Work and Organizational Psychology*, *24*(6), 882–897.

Barber, L. K., & Santuzzi, A. M. (2015). Please respond ASAP: Workplace telepressure and employee recovery. *Journal of Occupational Health Psychology*, *20*(2), 172–189.

Barsade, S. G., & Gibson, D. E. (2007). Why does affect matter in organizations? *Academy of Management Perspectives*, *21*(1), 36–59.

Beal, D. J., Weiss, H. M., Barros, E., & MacDermid, S. M. (2005). An episodic process model of affective influences on performance. *Journal of Applied Psychology*, *90*(6), 1054–1068.

Beauregard, T. A., & Henry, L. C. (2009). Making the link between work-life balance practices and organizational performance. *Human Resource Management Review*, *19*(1), 9–22.

Benson, A. D., Johnson, S. D., & Kuchinke, K. P. (2002). The use of technology in the digital workplace: A framework for human resource development. *Advances in Developing Human Resources*, *4*(4), 392–404.

Braukmann, J., Schmitt, A., Ďuranová, L., & Ohly, S. (2019). Identifying ICT-related affective events across life domains and examining their unique relationships with employee recovery. *Journal of Business and Psychology*, *33*(4), 529–544.

Brown, R., Duck, J., & Jimmieson, N. (2014). E-mail in the workplace: The role of stress appraisals and normative response pressure in the relationship between e-mail stressors and employee strain. *International Journal of Stress Management*, *21*(4), 325–347.

Butts, M. M., Becker, W. J., & Boswell, W. R. (2015). Hot buttons and time sinks: The effects of electronic communication during nonwork time on emotions and work-nonwork conflict. *Academy of Management Journal*, *58*(3), 763–788.

Byron, K. (2008). Carrying too heavy a load? Communication and miscommunication of emotion by email. *Academy of Management Review*, *33*(2), 309–327.

Cascio, W. F. (1995). Whither industrial and organizational psychology in a changing world of work? *American Psychologist*, *50*(11), 928–939.

Cascio, W. F. (2000). Managing a virtual workplace. *Academy of Management Perspectives*, *14*(3), 81–90.

Cascio, W. F., & Montealegre, R. (2016). How technology is changing work and organizations. *Annual Review of Organizational Psychology and Organizational Behavior*, *3*(1), 349–375.

Ceaparu, I., Lazar, J., Bessiere, K., Robinson, J., & Shneiderman, B. (2004). Determining causes and severity of end-user frustration. *International Journal of Human–Computer Interaction*, *17*(3), 333–356.

Charalampous, M., Grant, C. A., Tramontano, C., & Michailidis, E. (2019). Systematically reviewing remote e-workers' well-being at work: A multidimensional approach. *European Journal of Work and Organizational Psychology*, *28*(1), 51–73.

Cheshin, A., Rafaeli, A., & Bos, N. (2011). Anger and happiness in virtual teams: Emotional influences of text and behavior on others' affect in the absence of non-verbal cues. *Organizational Behavior and Human Decision Processes*, *116*(1), 2–16.

Chi, N.-W., Chung, Y.-Y., & Tsai, W.-C. (2011). How do happy leaders enhance team success? The mediating roles of transformational leadership, group affective tone, and team processes. *Journal of Applied Social Psychology, 41*(4), 1421–1454.

Compeau, D. R., & Higgins, C. A. (1995). Computer self-efficacy: Development of a measure and initial test. *MIS Quarterly, 19*(2), 189–211.

Daft, R. L., & Lengel, R. H. (1986). Organizational information requirements, media richness and structural design. *Management Science, 32*(5), 554–571.

Day, A., Paquet, S., Scott, N., & Hambley, L. (2012). Perceived information and communication technology (ICT) demands on employee outcomes: The moderating effect of organizational ICT support. *Journal of Occupational Health Psychology, 17*(4), 473–491.

Day, A., Scott, N., & Kelloway, E. K. (2010). Information and communication technology: Implications for job stress and employee well-being. In P. L. Perrewe & D. C. Ganster (Eds.), *New developments in theoretical and conceptual approaches to job stress: Research in occupational stress and well being* (Volume 8, pp. 317–350). Bingley, UK: Emerald.

DeLongis, A., Coyne, J. C., Dakof, G., Folkman, S., & Lazarus, R. S. (1982). Relationship of daily hassles, uplifts, and major life events to health status. *Health Psychology, 1*(2), 119–136.

Demerouti, E., Derks, D., Lieke, L., & Bakker, A. B. (2014). New ways of working: Impact on working conditions, work–family balance, and well-being. In C. Korunka & P. Hoonakker (Eds.), *The impact of ICT on quality of working life* (pp. 123–141). New York, NY, and Amsterdam, Netherlands: Springer.

Dettmers, J., Bamberg, E., & Seffzek, K. (2016). Characteristics of extended availability for work: The role of demands and resources. *International Journal of Stress Management, 23*(3), 276–297.

Fisher, S. L., & Howell, A. W. (2004). Beyond user acceptance: An examination of employee reactions to information technology systems. *Human Resource Management, 43*(2–3), 243–258.

Flanagin, A. J., & Waldeck, J. H. (2004). Technology use and organizational newcomer socialization. *Journal of Business Communication, 41*(2), 137–165.

Fulk, J., Steinfield, C. W., Schmitz, J., & Power, J. G. (1987). A social information processing model of media use in organizations. *Communication Research, 14*(5), 529–552.

Gajendran, R. S., & Harrison, D. A. (2007). The good, the bad, and the unknown about telecommuting: Meta-analysis of psychological mediators and individual consequences. *Journal of Applied Psychology, 92*(6), 1524–1541.

Gist, M. E., Schwoerer, C., & Rosen, B. (1989). Effects of alternative training methods on self-efficacy and performance in computer software training. *Journal of Applied Psychology, 74*(6), 884–891.

Giumetti, G. W., Hatfield, A. L., Scisco, J. L., Schroeder, A. N., Muth, E. R., & Kowalski, R. M. (2013). What a rude e-mail! Examining the differential effects of incivility versus support on mood, energy, engagement, and performance in an online context. *Journal of Occupational Health Psychology, 18*(3), 297–309.

Glikson, E., & Erez, M. (2013). Emotion display norms in virtual teams. *Journal of Personnel Psychology, 12*(1), 22–32.

Golden, T. D., Veiga, J. F., & Simsek, Z. (2006). Telecommuting's differential impact on work-family conflict: Is there no place like home? *Journal of Applied Psychology, 91*(6), 1340–1350.

Grant, C. A., Wallace, L. M., & Spurgeon, P. C. (2013). An exploration of the psychological factors affecting remote e-worker's job effectiveness, well-being and work–life balance. *Employee Relations, 35*(5), 527–546.

Grawemeyer, B., & Johnson, H. (2011). Using and managing multiple passwords: A week to a view. *Interacting with Computers, 23*(3), 256–267.

Guenter, H., van Emmerik, I. H., & Schreurs, B. (2014). The negative effects of delays in information exchange: Looking at workplace relationships from an affective events perspective. *Human Resource Management Review, 24*(4), 283–298.

Hofstede, G. (1998). Identifying organizational subcultures: An empirical approach. *Journal of Management Studies, 35*(1), 1–12.

Holman, D., Chissick, C., & Totterdell, P. (2002). The effects of performance monitoring on emotional labor and well-being in call centers. *Motivation and Emotion*, *26*(1), 57–81.

Johnson, S. K., Bettenhausen, K., & Gibbons, E. (2009). Realities of working in virtual teams: Affective and attitudinal outcomes of using computer-mediated communication. *Small Group Research*, *40*(6), 623–649.

Kanner, A. D., Coyne, J. C., Schaefer, C., & Lazarus, R. S. (1981). Comparison of two modes of stress measurement: Daily hassles and uplifts versus major life events. *Journal of Behavioral Medicine*, *4*(1), 1–39.

Lazarus, R. S., & Folkman, S. (1984). *Stress, appraisal, and coping*. New York, NY: Springer.

Lewis, S. (2003). Flexible working arrangements: Implementation, outcomes, and management. In C. L. Cooper & I. T. Roberts (Eds.), *International review of industrial and organizational psychology* (Volume 18, pp. 1–28). New York, NY: Wiley.

Lim, V. K., & Teo, T. S. (2009). Mind your E-manners: Impact of cyber incivility on employees' work attitude and behavior. *Information & Management*, *46*(8), 419–425.

Luse, A., McElroy, J., Townsend, A., & DeMarie, S. (2013). Personality and cognitive style as predictors of preference for working in virtual teams. *Computers in Human Behavior*, *29*(4), 1825–1832.

Mann, S., & Holdsworth, L. (2003). The psychological impact of teleworking: Stress, emotions and health. *New Technology, Work and Employment*, *18*(3), 196–211.

Maruping, L. M., & Agarwal, R. (2004). Managing team interpersonal processes through technology: A task-technology fit perspective. *Journal of Applied Psychology*, *89*(6), 975–990.

Moser, K. S., & Axtell, C. M. (2013). The role of norms in virtual work: A review and agenda for future research. *Journal of Personnel Psychology*, *12*(1), 1–6.

Nees, M. A., & Fortna, A. (2015). A comparison of human versus virtual interruptions. *Ergonomics*, *58* (5), 852–856.

Ohly, S., & Latour, A. (2014). Work-related smartphone use and well-being in the evening: The role of autonomous and controlled motivation. *Journal of Personnel Psychology*, *13*(4), 174–183.

Ortiz de Guinea, A., Webster, J., & Staples, D. S. (2012). A meta-analysis of the consequences of virtualness on team functioning. *Information & Management*, *49*(6), 301–308.

Palthe, J., & Kossek, E. E. (2003). Subcultures and employment modes: Translating HR strategy into practice. *Journal of Organizational Change Management*, *16*(3), 287–308.

Park, Y., Fritz, C., & Jex, S. M. (2018). Daily cyber incivility and distress: The moderating roles of resources at work and home. *Journal of Management*, *44*(7), 2535–2557.

Perlow, L. A., & Kelly, E. L. (2014). Toward a model of work redesign for better work and better life. *Work and Occupations*, *41*(1), 111–134.

Perlow, L. A., & Porter, J. L. (2009). Making time off predictable – and required. *Harvard Business Review*, *87*(10), 102–109, 142.

Pew Research Center (2016). Changes in the American workplace, October 6, www.pewsocialtrends.org /2016/10/06/1-changes-in-the-american-workplace/

Ragu-Nathan, T. S., Tarafdar, M., Ragu-Nathan, B. S., & Tu, Q. (2008). The consequences of technostress for end users in organizations: Conceptual development and empirical validation. *Information Systems Research*, *19*(4), 417–433.

Rice, R. E., & Aydin, C. (1991). Attitudes toward new organizational technology: Network proximity as a mechanism for social information processing. *Administrative Science Quarterly*, *36*(2), 219–244.

Russell, A., & Perris, K. (2003). Telementoring in community nursing: A shift from dyadic to communal models of learning and professional development. *Mentoring and Tutoring*, *11*(2), 227–238.

Salancik, G. R., & Pfeffer, J. (1978). A social information processing approach to job attitudes and task design. *Administrative Science Quarterly*, *23*(2), 224–253.

Salanova, M., Grau, R. M., Cifre, E., & Llorens, S. (2000). Computer training, frequency of usage and burnout: The moderating role of computer self-efficacy. *Computers in Human Behavior*, *16*(6), 575–590.

Salanova, M., Llorens, S., & Cifre, E. (2013). The dark side of technologies: Technostress among users of information and communication technologies. *International Journal of Psychology*, *48*(3), 422–436.

Shank, D. B. (2014). Technology and emotions. In J. E. Stets & J. H. Turner (Eds.), *Handbook of the sociology of emotions* (Volume 2, pp. 511–528). Dordrecht, Netherlands: Springer.

Skovholt, K., Grønning, A., & Kankaanranta, A. (2014). The communicative functions of emoticons in workplace e-mails: :-). *Journal of Computer-Mediated Communication*, *19*(4), 780–797.

Sonnentag, S., Reinecke, L., Mata, J., & Vorderer, P. (2018). Feeling interrupted – being responsive: How online messages relate to affect at work. *Journal of Organizational Behavior*, *39*(3), 369–383.

Sullivan, C. B. (1995). Preferences for electronic mail in organizational communication tasks. *Journal of Business Communication*, *32*(1), 49–64.

Tekleab, A. G., & Quigley, N. R. (2014). Team deep-level diversity, relationship conflict, and team members' affective reactions: A cross-level investigation. *Journal of Business Research*, *67*(3), 394–402.

Ter Hoeven, C. L., van Zoonen, W., & Fonner, K. L. (2016). The practical paradox of technology: The influence of communication technology use on employee burnout and engagement. *Communication Monographs*, *83*(2), 239–263.

Venkatesh, V. (2000). Determinants of perceived ease of use: Integrating control, intrinsic motivation, and emotion into the technology acceptance model. *Information Systems Research*, *11*(4), 342–365.

Warr, P. (1994). A conceptual framework for the study of work and mental health. *Work & Stress*, *8*(2), 84–97.

Weiss, H. M. (2002). Deconstructing job satisfaction: Separating evaluations, beliefs and affective experiences. *Human Resource Management Review*, *12*(2), 173–194.

Weiss, H., & Cropanzano, R. (1996). Affective events theory: A theoretical discussion of the structure, causes, and consequences of affective experiences at work. In B. M. Staw & L. L. Cummings (Eds.), *Research in organizational behavior* (Volume 18, pp. 1–74). Greenwich, CT, and London, UK : Elsevier Science/JAI.

38 Looking Into the Future

Integration of Research on Workplace Affect

Liu-Qin Yang*, Vicente Martínez-Tur, Russell Cropanzano, and Catherine S. Daus

Over the past few decades, researchers have made notable strides in understanding the processes underlying workplace affect. In particular, rigorous measures and new theoretical models for the study of workplace affect have been developed, validated, and updated with data gathered from employee samples across different industries, countries, and cultures (e.g. Bledow, Schmitt, Frese, & Kühnel, 2011; McCullough, Emmons, & Tsang, 2002; Watson, 2000; Weiss & Cropanzano, 1996; Yang, Simon, Wang, & Zheng, 2016). As shown in the array of chapters in this volume, exciting progress has been made on many fronts. Yet there are many separate streams of research that have been developed in a relatively independent fashion. This chapter will propose some directions for future research that could integrate different areas of research on emotional experiences at work. We propose and discuss the following ideas: integration of research on general and discrete emotions; research taking a broader view of emotional management; new research methods and new perspectives; and the implications of social changes for research on workplace affect and for the application of such research.

Research Integration: General Affect, Discrete Emotions, and Mixed Feelings

Recently, much progress has been made in organizational research on general affect, particularly within the framework of positive and negative affect (Lyubomirsky, King, & Diener, 2005; Shockley, Ispas, Rossi, & Levine, 2012), and on discrete emotions (Fehr, Fulmer, Awtrey, & Miller, 2017; Shockley et al., 2012). Notably, Watson and colleagues (Watson et al., 1988; Watson & Clark, 1999) have proposed an integrative framework in which discrete emotions (e.g. joy and anger) are related yet distinct and they form the basis of higher-order constructs of positive affect and negative affect. Yet it is important for us to reflect as a field on the extent to which we have balanced the effort toward understanding the processes underlying general versus discrete emotions, and on the extent to which we have integrated our empirical research on general and discrete emotions, as called for by previous scholars (e.g. Brief & Weiss, 2002; Levine et al., 2011; Watson, 2000). Additionally, we call for more research to examine the idea of mixed feelings or the processes of ambivalence, where positive and negative affect occur together or approximately together (Larsen & McGraw, 2011; Larsen, McGraw, & Cacioppo, 2011; see more on this in Peter Warr's Chapter 32 of this volume).

* The authors thank Timothy Oxendahl for his valuable contribution to the literature searches in support of this manuscript. This research was partly supported by the Grant # T03OH008435 awarded to Portland State University, funded by the Centers for Disease Control and Prevention, National Institute for Occupational Safety and Health. Its contents are solely the responsibility of the authors and do not necessarily represent the official views of NIOSH, CDC, or HHS.

To date, researchers have integrated general affect and discrete emotions in three major ways. First, one can study the role of discrete emotion over and above general affect. This can be done for either (or both) states and traits (Ford, Wang, Jin, & Eisenberger, 2018; Levine et al., 2011). Second, some research has operationalized affect as both general and discrete, then contrasted the effects of both types in focal relationships (Lee & Allen, 2002). Third, one can examine the joint roles of general affect and discrete emotion in the focal research question. For example, Şimşek and colleagues (2012) investigated discrete emotion as a mediator between general affect and outcome variables (Şimşek et al., 2012).

More research that integrates discrete emotion with general affect (positive vs. negative, activation vs. valence) would help further the theoretical development of workplace affect literature. In particular, echoing the reservation that Watson (2000) had in accepting the research findings on the roles of discrete emotion in many psychological processes, including workplace processes, we urge scholars to conduct future research to examine the unique roles that discrete emotions play over and above general affect either at the trait or state level. Such investigations would not only offer new insights on the unique nomological networks of discrete emotions, but also highlight the conceptual overlap and distinction between discrete emotions and general affect – corroborating the view that discrete emotions are formed based on individuals' appraisals of specific situations and in the context of the general affective response (Clore & Ortony, 2008; Watson, 2000).

Additionally, we believe it would be fruitful for future research to integrate general affect and discrete emotions by examining the potential moderating role of general affect in the relations between discrete emotions and presumed outcome variables. We suggest so because general affect provides a context or state of mind for discrete emotions to exert their influence. For example, the predictive validity of prideful feelings on interpersonal helping behavior could be stronger (vs. weaker) when the general positive mood of the focal employee is higher (vs. lower), due to the stronger (vs. weaker) congruency effect between general affect and discrete emotion. Lastly, it would be fruitful for integrating research on general affect and discrete emotion if future research could examine how momentary events and chronic workplace characteristics jointly influence experiences of discrete and chronic affect, as occurs in the process of chronification. As called for by Venz, Casper, and Sonnentag in Chapter 8 of this volume, much more research is needed to further our understanding of the role that discrete emotions resulting from momentary events may play in the process of shaping one's chronic affective well-being over time, such as general positive and negative mood.

A Broader View of Emotional Management

Traditionally, literature on emotional management has concentrated mainly on emotional labor, where workers follow established rules in order to display expected emotions to service users. Expanding this limited perspective toward a broader view of emotional management would help to improve our understanding of this concept. In the following sections, we focus on two areas that could benefit from this change in perspective: the conceptualization of emotional management, and extending the typology of regulation strategies.

The Conceptualization of Emotional Management: More than Emotional Labor

In her influential book, Hochschild (1983) differentiated between emotional labor, on the one hand, and emotion work, on the other. She defined *emotional labor* as the public management of emotions directed to customers and based on the labor process. It has an exchange value (emotions are saleable), where the worker is subjected to the rules of conduct of the organization. When interacting with customers, workers have to display or suppress emotions as part of the requirements of the job, in order to produce a response in the customer. By contrast, *emotion work* refers to emotional management that is not regulated by the labor process. Emotion work is restricted to the private context of the person, where personal decisions are not subjected to the organizational rules. According to Hochschild's differentiation, emotional labor is characteristic of the workplace context. In fact, emotional labor is better established than emotion work in the literature. Traditionally, research tends to associate emotional demands and regulation in the workplace with emotional labor oriented toward customers. However, this focus on emotional labor does not capture the complexity of emotional management in the workplace. Future research could improve our understanding by investigating and integrating other aspects of emotional management, beyond the traditional view of emotional labor, in at least four ways.

First, empirical evidence has shown that personal autonomy and initiative are possible among workers, in terms of the way they regulate and display emotions toward customers and service users (Yagil & Medler-Liraz, 2013). It is reasonable to expect that autonomy increases the freedom of the worker in relation to display rules and the possibility of avoiding them. An illustrative example of worker initiative and autonomy is unpaid work through volunteer activities in organizations (e.g. Taylor, Mallinson, & Bloch, 2008). Display rules are associated with emotional labor, but the nature of emotional management associated with these rules could change when personal inclinations emerge in contexts where autonomy in the decision-making is significant.

Second, previous research has tacitly assumed that workers engage in emotional management in order to obtain benefits at work. However, they could have other, more intangible reasons for doing so. For example, emotional management may result from prosocial motivation to help others (Hensel, Hensel, & Dewa, 2015). Emotional management would have different characteristics when other motivation factors, beyond rules and duties, become significant for workers (Ashforth & Humphrey, 1993).

Third, workers' emotional management is not restricted to interactions with customers. It also plays a role in social interactions between colleagues at the workplace. Workers follow personal and social rules in order to perform adequate emotional management in their interactions with coworkers and supervisors (Grandey, Rafaeli, Ravid, Wirtz, & Steiner, 2010). In fact, as Berkley, Beard, and Daus (2019) recently proposed, emotional labor between colleagues could be very relevant in some situations (e.g. when the individual conceals a stigmatized identity from peers and supervisors, as discussed in Chapter 36 of this volume). As called for by Zapf, García-Buades, and Ortiz-Bonnin (Chapter 22 of this volume), more research is necessary to obtain a more complete picture of emotional management within organizations. Further efforts are required to extend previous knowledge (e.g. Becker & Cropanzano, 2015; Becker, Cropanzano, Van Wagoner, & Keplinger, 2018; both presenting research on emotional labor within teams) clarifying, for example, the links that emotional management – among coworkers and during interactions with supervisors – has with well-being and performance.

A fourth research area that requires attention is the role of emotional intelligence. Although direct relationships between emotional intelligence and emotion regulation might be weak (Totterdell & Holman, 2003), scholars could investigate more complex relations between emotional intelligence and work outcomes. Congruent with person × situation interactionism (e.g. Mendoza-Denton,

Ayduk, Mischel, Shoda, & Testa, 2001), empirical evidence shows that the joint effects of contextual aspects (e.g. emotional requirements) and individual differences in emotional intelligence and other dispositions (e.g. trait mindfulness) should be considered to fully understand work criteria such as performance and well-being at work (Côté, 2014). Scholars have made efforts to examine the role of emotional intelligence in the relationship between workers' emotional labor and work outcomes, but there is a need to further clarify this role (Joseph & Newman, 2010). For example, research studies have found evidence supporting emotional intelligence as both a moderator (Bechtoldt, Rohrmann, De Pater, & Beersma, 2011) and a mediator (Guy & Lee, 2015) of the relations between emotional labor and work outcomes.

In short, more research is warranted in order to provide a complete picture of workers' emotional management and its effects on performance and well-being. In particular, we contend that it would be fruitful for future research to explore the roles of personal inclinations, motivation forces, and contextual factors in the context of broader emotional management (beyond emotional labor), as well as to integrate emotion-related individual differences such as emotional intelligence and trait mindfulness.

Extending the Typology of Regulation Strategies: More than Surface and Deep Acting

The differentiation between surface and deep acting does not capture all the regulation strategies workers use in their daily working activities, especially if we consider complex social interactions within organizations (e.g. interactions among coworkers), beyond the emotional labor directed toward customers. The differentiation between "surface acting" (expressing emotions not actually felt) vs. "deep acting" (modifying felt emotions in order to display genuine emotions) has become widely used. The prevalence of this dichotomy is unfortunate, as there are more emotional regulation strategies than surface and deep acting. For example, scholars have proposed another type of deep-acting regulation strategy, sometimes called "automatic emotion regulation" (Zapf, 2002). This strategy does not require workers' conscious effort to make them feel and display required emotions. Another strategy is "emotional deviance," or simply not performing the emotional requirements (Rafaeli & Sutton, 1987). Although other possible regulation strategies can exist in the workplace, understanding of their implications at work is limited compared to the vast literature focused on surface and deep acting.

General research on regulation strategies could be useful for expanding our knowledge in the future. Naragon-Gainey, McMahon, and Chacko (2017) performed a meta-analysis of ten regulation strategies:

distraction – shifting one's attention to something else in order to avoid or reduce unwanted emotions
acceptance – willingness to experience one's current emotions, even if they are aversive
mindfulness – open awareness of the present moment without evaluation
behavioral avoidance – avoiding external stimuli such as situations, people, and places that evoke unwanted emotions
experiential avoidance – avoiding unwanted internal stimuli, such as thoughts, physical sensations, or emotions
expressive suppression – inhibiting the outward expression of an emotion
reappraisal – changing one's perspective or interpretation so as to recognize positive aspects of a situation
rumination – repetitively thinking about the experience, causes, and consequences of negative emotion in a passive manner

worry – repetitive, negative thoughts and images about the future

problem solving – attempts to actively modify an undesirable situation or its consequences

The authors concluded that a complex structural model is needed to understand regulation strategies, and urged the delineation of such an underlying structure in further studies.

Future research on regulation strategies within organizations could identify which strategies are significant for specific social contexts. For instance, different positions within the organizational hierarchy may entail different emotional regulation strategies (Kramer, 1996). Supervisors tend to concentrate on the achievement of company goals by promoting positive emotions and efforts in team members. By contrast, workers consider more emotional aspects of working with customers and ruminate about critical decisions of supervisors, such as promotion and distribution of tasks (Kramer, 1996). It is likely that supervisors and team members use different regulation strategies that impact their performance and well-being at work, and that these strategies are not limited to surface and deep acting.

Another area where future research could contribute to knowledge about emotion regulation strategies within organizations is the temporal process. Gross's (1998; 2015) well-known process model could help in this effort. This model proposes that regulation strategies can influence the five stages of the emotion-generative process:

situation selection – the worker enters a situation, or not, based on emotional expectations

situation modification – stimuli change or are modified once the worker is in a situation

attentional deployment – the worker directs his/her attention to specific features of the situation

cognitive change – the worker changes his/her appraisal of the situation

response modulation – the worker changes his/her physiological, experiential, and behavioral responses corresponding to certain emotions

Examining this type of process model could greatly enrich our understanding of emotional regulation strategies within organizations. For instance, temporal processes are usually present in conflicts with customers or coworkers. Conflicts have different developmental patterns, and different regulation strategies may play a role in each stage of conflict management.

In sum, a broader view of regulation strategies could offer a richer view of affect in the workplace. Traditional regulation strategies (e.g. surface acting) are quite useful for dealing with emotional demands in the moment (e.g. a complaint from a client). Nevertheless, some recent organizational research has started to extend the study of regulation strategies beyond surface and deep acting, observing a variety of distinct configurations of emotional management events (Diefendorff, Gabriel, Nolan, & Yang, 2019; Heaphy, 2017), and this seems to be a promising avenue for advancing knowledge.

New Methods and New Perspectives

In this section, we describe some ideas on how new methodologies, specifically measurement of affect, and new perspectives from other disciplines may benefit future research on workplace affect.

More Measurement Techniques for Unit-Level Affect Research

As may be seen in the review presented in Yang, McMahon, and Zhen's Chapter 6 of this volume, more and more scholars are examining momentary workplace affect by adapting self-rated affect measures to daily diary settings, yet few quantitative methods are available specifically for the measurement of unit-level affect or affect regulation. Many self-rated measures with individually referenced items could be used to measure collective-level affect-related processes, such as affective convergence and diversity at unit level – representing shared and different affect experiences across group members (Barsade & Knight, 2015). However, much more work is needed to examine the psychometrical properties of these measures at the unit level, such as measurement invariance across levels (Zyphur, Kaplan, & Christian, 2008). This is particularly important, because many of the measures for self-ratings were initially designed for individual-level constructs and the validity of these collective-level constructs partially lies in whether the factorial validity of the individual-level measures holds at the unit level. It may be fruitful to use a rigorous process to construct and validate a quantitative method that can best measure a specific type of collective-level affect construct in the work context (e.g. a measure of *compassionate love culture* for other-ratings; Barsade & O'Neill, 2014).

Beyond these considerations, it is worth nothing that newer technologies can be adopted to capture efficiently the dynamics within teams, offering insights into complex processes such as the formation of affective convergence (e.g. team pride). For example, the wireless sensors developed by Picard and colleagues (Picard, 2000; Poh, Swenson, & Picard, 2010) could perhaps be worn by group members and used together with some audio-based coding system of emotional expression (Ekman & Friesen, 2003) in order to capture the dynamic levels of affect activation during group interactions.

More Integration of Research from Other Disciplines

Historically the development of affect research, especially affect measurement, has benefited from integrating perspectives from multiple disciplines, such as psychology, psychiatry, biology, and philosophy (e.g. Watson, 2000). As affect research further evolves to enhance our understanding on quality of life, including work life, we contend that it is critical for development of affect theory to integrate new perspectives from other disciplines. In this section, we highlight two perspectives, from educational science and neuroscience respectively.

First, workplace affect research can significantly benefit from the perspective of educational science that emphasizes the interrelation between cognitive and emotional processes. Specifically, research in educational science has repeatedly found that emotional experiences provide feedback to individual learners that is critical for their cognitive learning processes. For example, one application of emotional learning analytics in educational settings is to analyze a rich set of data about the recorded interactions between learners and learning technologies (e.g. an online learning platform), by coding learners' cognitive learning strategies and emotional states during key learning stages (D'Mello, 2017).

Results of such analyses can reveal important dynamic relationships between affective and cognitive processes during learning, such as the key role of impasses during learning and how emotional states of frustration and confusion facilitate learners' active cognitive strategies (e.g. requesting a hint to help correct an error) to enable them to resolve the impasses (Bosch & D'Mello, 2017). For organizational researchers and practitioners in the area of workplace affect, this perspective from educational science is quite useful. Specifically, it is critical for future research and application to consider the effect of workplace affect in the context of work tasks or work roles that require cognitive effort. For example, in order to best understand how newly hired employees learn strategies to adapt to the new work environment and the new job roles, it would be most fruitful to measure both their cognitive strategies and their affective responses during learning and adaptation (see more discussion on this in Ellis and Bauer's Chapter 24 of this volume). As another example, when workers are tasked with learning new workplace practices – which is fairly common in the current era of fast-changing workplaces – assessing their emotional experiences during learning could help evaluate the progress of implementing the new practices and the ultimate effectiveness of such implementations. In sum, examining workers' affective processes concomitantly with their cognitive processes could paint a more complete picture of many workplace phenomena.

Second, research on workplace affect can also benefit from new understandings from neuroscience. For example, the EEG-based hyperscanning approach – a way of assessing inter-brain synchronized neurological activities as real-time indicators of social and emotional sharing between individuals (Balconi & Vanutelli, 2017) – brings about new opportunities for addressing theoretically-driven research questions on affective processes at the dyadic and group levels. During dynamic social interactions, it is challenging yet critical to assess affect-related processes in real time. In the past literature, organizational scholars interested in studying dyadic relationships and team dynamics often use self-report methods to assess affective states of individual employees in dyadic and group relationships, which has limitations such as recall biases. Having reports on individual employees' personal emotional experiences and perceptions of others' emotions can capture only a very small fraction of dyadic- and group-level affective dynamics, such as emotional contagion or collective pride. In contrast, the hyperscanning approach could be used to directly capture the process of emotional sharing such as emotional contagion at the dyadic and group levels, through a mechanism of vicarious activation based on mirror neurons (Keysers & Gazzola, 2009) and the procedure of brain-to-brain coupling. Conceivably, when particular triggers of emotional sharing or engagement between dyadic relationship partners or team members (e.g. an occasion to celebrate team success) are known, data from hyperscanning could pinpoint the exact timing of psychological processes such as vicarious activation underlying emotional contagion (e.g. the shared pride occurs ten minutes into the team celebration). Furthermore, data from self-reports of members involved, or text-analyses-based ratings of documents from past social interactions could capture how long the emotional contagion lasts and the downstream effects of contagion on attitudinal and behavioral outcomes, such as commitment to the relationship and collective task performance.

In other words, the hyperscanning approach offers a perspective that complements existing research and is particularly valuable to the investigation of workplace affective processes at the dyadic and group levels. We contend that it would be fruitful for future research to further examine the validity of this approach in addressing theoretically-driven research questions focused on workplace affect (e.g. the role of affect during one-on-one performance feedback sessions), given the largely missing consideration of affective components in hyperscanning studies to date (Balconi & Banutelli, 2017). More discussion on past and potential applications of neuroscience to research on workplace affect can be found in Chapter 2 of this volume.

Implications of Social Changes for Research and Applications in Workplace Affect

Different forces are transforming our societies, organizations, and workplaces. In this section we focus on the following social changes: information communication technology developments; globalization and cultural diversity; social inclusion of vulnerable groups; and multilevel complex organizational structures. Understanding the potential impact of these changes on emotional life in the workplace can open new venues for future research. We review the literature and propose future research directions for each of these areas of change.

Evolving Roles of Affect in Fast-Changing Workplaces

As the workplace changes rapidly, more and more organizations are introducing technologies into their work processes, such as customized videoconferencing systems, artificial intelligence (AI)–based computer programs for particular job functions, and automated operational systems to replace certain jobs (DeCanio, 2016). These technology-related changes pose new challenges to research and theory on workplace affect and organizational research as a whole, such as the potential implications of information communication technology for worker burnout (e.g. Berg-Beckhoff, Nielsen, & Larsen, 2017). These challenges will bring new opportunities for organizational scholars and practitioners to investigate the evolving roles of affect in fast-changing workplaces. Specifically, we discuss three exciting areas of research on workplace affect pertaining to technology-related changes.

First, technology-mediated work processes are becoming a more and more integral part of modern work, a phenomenon that has significant implications for workers' affect experiences and expressions at the individual, dyadic, and team levels. In particular, technologically mediated communications, such as email, videoconferencing, and online calendars, are commonly used and have significantly changed how work is done. Barber and Hu, in Chapter 37 of this volume, have reviewed research on the topic of technology and workplace affect, highlighted insufficiently studied areas, and suggested using affective events theory to guide future work on this topic. One especially intriguing area is how technology-mediated social interactions and technological interface experiences shape employees' experiences of negative emotions and stress, as well as their experiences of positive emotions and work engagement.

Second, we urge affect scholars to conduct more research on the roles of affect during interactions between humans and AI-based systems. These interactions in the workplace could be between human workers or clients and AI (e.g. between children with autism spectrum disorder and humanoid robots: Bekele et al., 2013). Both positive and negative affective experiences on the part of the human could play important roles for ensuring the optimal functions of the work process. Past research, albeit sparse, has started to examine these issues. For example, Merritt (2011) found in an experiment that human users' positive emotions and resultant liking of automated equipment for x-ray screening were the key antecedents of users' reliance on the automated system (based on the relative frequency of changing their personal decision to agree with the equipment's recommendation). More recently, McClure (2018) investigated the role of fear in the automated workplace and found that technophobes – individuals who fear robots, technology, and AI – are more likely to experience fear of unemployment, as well as anxiety-related mental health problems, relative to non-technophobes. From the perspective of human–computer interaction, Dehais and colleagues (2012) found in a high-fidelity experiment that during a human–robot conflict, human operators demonstrated increased arousal and excessive attention focus, overruled the robot's judgment, and become overly committed to their own goal at the risk of failing the overall mission. Moving forward, we suggest future research on this topic to examine positive and negative emotions simultaneously in order to better discern the unique roles of these emotions, and to better reflect the realistic interactions between humans and AI – which inevitably include both positive- and negative-affect-inducing events. We also urge affect scholars to examine the role of affect in the context of these interactions with a more dynamic lens; for example, during the life cycle of an AI-based system (starting as a new system, through the use of the system including states of malfunctioning, and then to the state of being decommissioned), human workers may experience anxiety and excitement at first, then anger and attentiveness, followed by sadness and depressive symptoms.

Lastly, as automation becomes increasingly integrated into the work process of organizations, the landscape of work changes significantly. Notably, the expectations for the amount and format of social interactions between workers may shift to the extent that workers in certain job positions may have a significantly reduced amount of social interactions with their human coworkers, and instead have more direct or virtual interactions with AIs during the automated work process. For example, in manufacturing settings where the use of automation is relatively mature, a supervisor in charge of a workgroup needs to adapt to the change, from solely in-person interactions with human employees to solely or mostly technology-mediated interactions with robots. These types of shifts may have profound impact on the affect experienced and expressed by human workers. We urge affect scholars to conduct additional research focused on the unique roles that affect may play in such work contexts. As an example, Cummings, Gao, and Thornburg (2016) did a review and concluded that human workers' experience of boredom will become more prevalent and have stronger implications for workers' motivation and retention in automated workplaces. Additionally, we contend that mental health issues, especially those related to negative affect experiences and affect regulation (e.g. anxiety, loneliness, depressive symptoms), may become more common among human workers who mainly work with automated systems including AI-based ones (e.g. Mcclure, 2018).

In summary, we need to study ways that could help workers better manage their affect, well-being, and adjustment to their new work roles in the face of technology-based changes. Particularly, we also need much more empirical research to examine how affect plays a role for understanding the ethical issue in utilizing AI, automation, and other technologies in the workplaces. Ethical considerations may pertain to every aspect of technological utilization, especially for AI and automation, such as machine–user relations, issues of privacy and data security, issues of human rights and robot rights, and accountability for AI-assisted decisions (Hislop et al., 2017). Indeed, scholars and practitioners in the field of industrial and organizational psychology have started to make efforts to develop guidelines for the usage of AI, automation, and other related technologies in the workplace (e.g. Bracken, 2019).

Globalization and Cultural Diversity in the Workplace

One of the defining features of humans as social beings is their high capacity to distinguish in-group members from "other" individuals and out-groups (e.g. Brewer, 1999). This capacity is rooted in our evolutionary history (De Dreu et al., 2010). This evolutionarily ancient mechanism has been transferred to an artificial context designed by humans – the organization– where cultural diversity is increasingly evident, facilitating the value-based differentiation between in-group members and other individuals and out-groups. Although cultural diversity has long existed in organizations, globalization and international mobility have accentuated its importance and complexity. Indeed, global displacement is at a record high (258 million in 2017), and the majority of the world's international migrants are of working age (United Nations, 2017).

A consequence of this globalization and international mobility is the existence of greater cultural diversity within organizations and teams, which offers new opportunities for research on workplace affect (Roberson, 2019). Although some emotional aspects of humans are universal, others (e.g. emotion display rules) are based, at least in part, on cultural values. Individuals coming from different countries and cultures are likely to express and regulate emotions in different ways. Grandey et al. (2010) found evidence supporting this argument by comparing display rules of workers from the USA, France, Singapore, and Israel. Although they shared some display rules, especially in interactions with customers (the "service with a smile" culture), they also showed significant differences in interactions with both organizational members and customers. Notwithstanding these initial efforts examining workplace affect across cultures, relevant questions remain unanswered. One pending question is related to the impact of globalization over time. It is possible that display rules and emotional regulation strategies would converge toward a shared global view based on the predominant model of developed countries. However, other alternatives are also plausible. For example, one conceivable scenario is the existence of a new shared global model based on the "dialogue" among cultures. Because the ways to express and regulate emotions in all cultures could have functional aspects for successfully dealing with job demands and improving well-being, a "right mix" of emotional regulation and expression strategies could emerge.

Another area where future research on cultural diversity could enrich the understanding of workplace affect is investigating the effectiveness of interventions. There have been increasing efforts to examine the success of different types of interventions (e.g. mindfulness) in order to promote employees' positive emotional experiences (e.g. Clauss et al., 2018) and manage their negative ones (e.g. Tetrick & Winslow, 2015). The success of interventions could depend on cultural contexts. Although developing emotional regulation capabilities helps to manage intercultural relations in general, and enhances workplace effectiveness across cultural contexts, it is necessary to examine the benefits of affect-related competencies that consider specific cultural contexts (Leung, Ang, & Tan, 2014). Future research could be fruitful by exploring how affect-focused interventions differentially impact performance and well-being across different cultural contexts.

Social Inclusion of Vulnerable Groups

In today's societies and organizations, people are increasingly interested in the social inclusion of vulnerable groups. Broadly speaking, we can include women, vulnerable minorities (based on religion, ethnicity, etc.), refugees, individuals with disabilities, and people with LGBTQ+ identities, among others. Growing global economic security makes it possible to place a greater emphasis on values such as inclusion in groups, tolerance, and quality of life (Inglehart & Welzel, 2010). Congruently, in recent decades, there has been sustained improvement in quality of life around the world (United Nations, 2018).

In spite of this positive overall picture, exclusion persists, and different forms of inequality and discrimination are still relevant obstacles to achieving the effective social inclusion of vulnerable groups (United Nations, 2018). One of the main challenges within organizations is dealing with stigmatization. Individuals with stigmatized identities (e.g. because of their sexual orientation) are often perceived as out-group members and they are likely to be subject to discrimination and isolation. Berkley, Beard, and Daus (2019) proposed a model that includes emotional labor as a strategy used by individuals to manage their stigmatized identities, considering self-disclosure as an affective event. Accordingly, it is expected that individuals who conceal their identity are probably forced to surface act. By contrast, individuals who accept and disclose their identity probably will deep act because they are free to express their spontaneous emotions. Empirical research is needed to investigate these propositions and how these emotional management processes evolve over time, how they impact on well-being and performance, and how they interrelate with factors such as emotional culture and display rules, among others (Berkley et al., 2019; see more in Phetmisy and colleagues' Chapter 36 on diversity and workplace affect).

Where the main organizational goal is to improve the quality of life of vulnerable individuals as service users, research could investigate specific consequences of workers' emotional labor. Traditionally, scholars have proposed and found that the impact of workers' display of emotions on customer satisfaction is secondary to the delivery of the core service, and it is significant only when the core service is good (Grandey, Fisk, Mattila, Jansen, & Sideman, 2005; Söderlund & Rosengren, 2010). However, helping vulnerable individuals and groups has an intense emotional content (e.g. Cricco-Lizza, 2014) that could change the role of the display of emotions. Martínez-Tur, Estreder, Tomás, Ramos, and Luque (2018) compared short-term and commercially-oriented service encounters (in hotels and restaurants) with services oriented toward improving the quality of life of individuals with intellectual disability (IID). Results for the settings of hotels and restaurants were very similar to those reported in the prior literature. By contrast, in services for IID, emotions displayed by workers played a greater role in predicting customer satisfaction. Emotional intensity may be greater when workers are helping vulnerable individuals as service users, and compared to the core service, it might increase the impact of emotional labor on user evaluations and experiences. Scholars may explore other possible consequences of workers' emotional labor for service users who belong to vulnerable groups, such as quality of life, self-esteem, and emotional well-being.

Affect-Focused Interventions at Different Organizational Levels

Despite scholars' increasing interest in workplace affect beyond the individual, the investigation of affect-focused interventions (e.g. promotion of positive emotions) from a multilevel perspective is still limited. There is increasing evidence that a combination of individual and organizational interventions could produce effective outcomes (see Tetrick & Winslow, 2015). However, most of the research still concentrates on the individual (e.g. Dickens, 2017; Teding van Berkhout & Malouff, 2016). It is important to establish what mechanisms connect the effects of interventions at different levels, and what mechanisms link affect-focused interventions to consequences for the well-being and performance of individuals, teams, and the organization as a whole. For example, is it increased team cohesion or reduced team conflict that accounts for improved individual- and team-level satisfaction and productivity after implementation of a mindfulness training program focused on individual- and team-level emotional regulation? In addition, it is reasonable to expect that these intervention-based mechanisms would evolve over time, creating dynamics of change vs. stability in affective experiences and responses.

An area that requires specific attention from a multilevel approach is related to interventions aimed at creating a right balance of positive and negative emotions within teams and the organization as a whole. Negative emotions are usually considered as maladaptive. However, they are pervasive and are part of our evolutionary history (Baumeister, Bratslavsky, Finkenhauer, & Vohs, 2001). Although negative emotions have disadvantages, they naturally occur in our daily work life and can help to achieve beneficial goals (see more in Schmitt's Chapter 15 of this volume). In addition, happiness is not always good (Gruber, Mauss, & Tamir, 2011). The simultaneous considerations of individual, team, and organizational levels could provide insights for new multilevel affect-based interventions related to the creation of affective climates and cultures that balance positive and negative emotions appropriately. Organizations increasingly use team-based structures, and different teams may have different subcultural responses to various issues. In such contexts, it is likely that uniformity in the affective climate and culture will become more difficult to achieve. Accordingly, emotional experiences and expressions could differ from one team to another, and a shared affective climate would be harder to cultivate at the organizational level. It is, therefore, reasonable to expect that faultlines would create different emotional experiences and responses (e.g. more negative affect in some subgroups, and more positive affect in others), hindering the possibility of achieving a shared and consistent affective climate and culture at the team and/or organizational level characterized by an adequate balance of positive and negative emotions. A multilevel intervention approach could help to generalize appropriate affect experiences and regulation strategies, coordinating actions at the organizational level (e.g. mobility of workers across teams) and the team level (e.g. training of supervisors).

Conclusion

This volume has showcased an array of cutting-edge advancements in the study of workplace affect, addressing the limitations of the literature by providing a comprehensive account of research advancements in the field and through efforts to connect different areas of research on workplace affect. In this closing chapter, we have suggested targeted directions for future research, in hopes of inspiring more inquiries that will provide insights to advance the field to the next level.

References

Ashforth, B. E., & Humphrey, R. H. (1993). Emotional labor in service roles: The influence of identity. *Academy of Management Review, 18*, 88–115.

Balconi, M., & Vanutelli, M. E. (2017). Cooperation and competition with hyperscanning methods: Review and future application to emotion domain. *Frontiers in Computational Neuroscience, 11*, doi:10.3389/fncom.2017.00086

Barsade, S. G., & Knight, A. P. (2015). Group affect. *Annual Review of Organizational Psychology and Organizational Behavior, 2*, 21–46.

Barsade, S. G., & O'Neill, O. A. (2014). What's love got to do with it? A longitudinal study of the culture of companionate love and employee and client outcomes in a long-term care setting. *Administrative Science Quarterly, 59*, 551–598.

Baumeister, R. F., Bratslavsky, E., Finkenhauer, C., & Vohs, K. D. (2001). Bad is stronger than good. *Review of General Psychology, 5*, 323–370.

Bechtoldt, M. N., Rohrmann, S., De Pater, I. E., & Beersma, B. (2011). The primacy of perceiving: Emotion recognition buffers negative effects of emotional labor. *Journal of Applied Psychology, 96*, 1087–1094.

Becker, W. J., & Cropanzano, R. (2015). Good acting requires a good cast: A meso-level model of deep acting in work teams. *Journal of Organizational Behavior, 36*, 232–249.

Becker, W. J., Cropanzano, R., Van Wagoner, H. P., & Keplinger, K. (2018). Emotional labor within teams: Outcomes of individual and peer emotional labor of perceived team support, extra-role behavior, and turnover intentions. *Group and Organization Management, 43*, 38–71.

Bekele, E. T., Lahiri, U., Swanson, A. R., Crittendon, J. A., Warren, Z. E. & Sarkar, N. (2013) A step towards developing adaptive robot-mediated intervention architecture (ARIA) for children with autism. *IEEE Transactions on Neural Systems and Rehabilitation Engineering, 21*, 289–299.

Berg-Beckhoff, G., Nielsen, G., & Ladekjær Larsen, E. (2017). Use of information communication technology and stress, burnout, and mental health in older, middle-aged, and younger workers – results from a systematic review. *International Journal of Occupational and Environmental Health, 23*, 160–171.

Berkley, R. A., Beard, R., & Daus, C. S. (2019). The emotional context of disclosing a concealable

stigmatized identity: A conceptual model. *Human Resource Management Review, 3*, 428–445.
Bledow, R., Schmitt, A., Frese, M., & Kühnel, J. (2011). The affective shift model of work engagement. *Journal of Applied Psychology, 96*, 1246–1257.
Bosch, N., & D'Mello, S. (2017). The affective experience of novice computer programmers. *International Journal of Artificial Intelligence in Education, 27*, 181–206.
Bracken, D. W. (2019). AI and EI meet IO: Should we trust or regulate? (panel presented at the annual conference of the Society for Industrial and Organizational Psychology, Washington, DC, 4–6 April).
Brewer, M. B. (1999). The psychology of prejudice: Ingroup love or outgroup hate? *Journal of Social Issues, 55*, 429–444.
Brief, A. P., & Weiss, H. M. (2002). Organizational behavior: Affect in the workplace. *Annual Review of Psychology, 53*, 279–307.
Clauss, E., Hoppe, A., O'Shea, D., González Morales, M. G., Steidle, A., & Michel, A. (2018). Promoting personal resources and reducing exhaustion through positive work reflection among caregivers. *Journal of Occupational Health Psychology, 23*, 127–140.
Clore, G. L., & Ortony, A. (2008). Appraisal theories: How cognition shapes affect into emotion. In M. Lewis, J. M. Haviland-Jones, & L. F. Barrett (Eds.), *Handbook of emotions* (3rd edition, pp. 628–642). New York, NY: Guilford.
Côté, S. (2014). Emotional intelligence in organizations. *Annual Review of Organizational Psychology and Organizational Behavior, 1*, 459–488.
Cricco-Lizza, R. (2014). The need to nurse the nurse: Emotional labor in neonatal intensive care. *Qualitative Health Research, 24*, 615–628.
Cummings, M., Gao, F., & Thornburg, K. (2016). Boredom in the workplace: A new look at an old problem. *Human Factors, 58*, 279–300.
Decanio, S. J. (2016) Robots and humans – complements or substitutes? *Journal of Macroeconomics, 49*, 280–291.
De Dreu, C. K. W., Greer, L. L., Handgraaf, M. J. J., Shalvi, S., Van Kleef, G. A., Baas, M., . . . & Feith, S. W. (2010). The neuropeptide oxytocin regulates parochial altruism in intergroup conflict among humans. *Science, 328*, 1408–1411.
Dehais, F., Causse, M., Vachon, F., & Tremblay, S. (2012) Cognitive conflict in human– automation interactions: A psychophysiological study. *Applied Ergonomics, 43*, 588–595.
Dickens, L. R. (2017). Using gratitude to promote positive change: A series of meta-analyses investigating the effectiveness of gratitude interventions. *Basic & Applied Social Psychology, 39*(4), 193–208.
Diefendorff, J. M., Gabriel, A. S., Nolan, M. T., & Yang, J. (2019). Emotion regulation in the context of customer mistreatment and felt affect: An event-based profile approach. *Journal of Applied Psychology, 104*(7), doi:10.1037/apl0000389
D'Mello, S. K. (2017). Emotional learning analytics. In C. Lang, G. Siemens, W. Alyssa, & D. Gašević (Eds.), *Handbook of learning analytics & educational data mining* (1st edition, pp. 115–127). Edmonton, AB: Society for Learning Analytics Research.
Ekman, P., & Friesen, W. V. (2003). *Unmasking the face: A guide to recognizing emotions from facial expressions*. Los Altos, CA: Malor Books.
Fehr, R., Fulmer, A., Awtrey, E., & Miller, J. A. (2017). The grateful workplace: A multilevel model of gratitude in organizations. *Academy of Management Review, 42*, 361–381.
Ford, M. T., Wang, Y., Jin, J., & Eisenberger, R. (2018). Chronic and episodic anger and gratitude toward the organization: Relationships with organizational and supervisor supportiveness and extrarole behavior. *Journal of Occupational Health Psychology, 23*, 175–187.
Grandey, A. A., Fisk, G. M., Mattila, A. S., Jansen, K. J., & Sideman, L. A. (2005). Is "service with a smile" enough? Authenticity of positive displays during service encounters. *Organizational Behavior and Human Decision Processes, 96*, 38–55.
Grandey, A. A., Rafaeli, A., Ravid, S., Wirtz, J., & Steiner, D. (2010). Emotion display rules at work in the global service economy: The special case of the customer. *Journal of Service Management, 21*, 388–412.

Gross, J. J. (1998). The emerging field of emotion regulation: An integrative review. *Review of General Psychology*, *2*, 271–299.

Gross, J. J. (2015). The extended process model of emotion regulation: Elaborations, applications, and future directions. *Psychological Inquiry*, *26*, 130–137.

Gruber, J., Mauss, I. B., & Tamir, M. (2011). A dark side of happiness? How, when, and why happiness is not always good. *Perspectives on Psychological Sciences*, *6*, 222–233.

Guy, M. E., & Lee, H. J. (2015). How emotional intelligence mediates emotional labor in public service jobs. *Review of Public Personnel Administration*, *35*, 261–277.

Heaphy, E. D. (2017). "Dancing on hot coals": How emotion work facilitates collective sensemaking. *Academy of Management Journal*, *60*, 642–670.

Hensel, J. M., Hensel, R. A., & Dewa, C. S. (2015). What motivates direct support providers to do the work they do? *Journal of Intellectual & Developmental Disability*, *40*, 297–303.

Hislop, D., Coombs, C., Taneva, S., & Barnard, S. (2017). Impact of artificial intelligence, robotics and automation technologies on work (CIPD rapid evidence review report). London, UK: Chartered Institute of Personnel and Development.

Hochschild, A. R. (1983). *The managed heart: Commercialization of human feeling*. Berkeley: University of California Press.

Inglehart, R., & Welzel, C. (2010). Changing mass priorities: The link between modernization and democracy. *Perspectives on Politics*, *8*, 551–567.

Joseph, D. L., & Newman, D. A. (2010). Emotional intelligence: An integrative meta-analysis and cascading model. *Journal of Applied Psychology*, *95*, 54–78.

Keysers, C., & Gazzola, V. (2009). Expanding the mirror: vicarious activity for actions, emotions, and sensations. *Current Opinion in Neurobiology*. *19*, 666–671.

Kramer, R. M. (1996). Divergent realities and convergent disappointments in hierarchic relation: Trust and the intuitive auditor at work. In R. M. Kramer & T. R. Tyler (Eds.), *Trust in organizations: Frontiers of theory and research* (pp. 216–245). Thousand Oaks, CA: Sage.

Larsen, J. T., & McGraw, A. P. (2011). Further evidence for mixed emotions. *Journal of Personality and Social Psychology*, *100*, 1095–1110.

Larsen, J. T., McGraw, A. P., & Cacioppo, J. T. (2001). Can people feel happy and sad at the same time? *Journal of Personality and Social Psychology*, *81*, 684–696.

Lee, K., & Allen, N. J. (2002). Organizational citizenship behavior and workplace deviance: The role of affect and cognitions. *Journal of Applied Psychology*, *87*, 131–142.

Leung, K., Ang, S., & Tan, M. L. (2014). Intercultural competence. *Annual Review of Organizational Psychology and Organizational Behavior*, *1*, 489–519.

Levine, E. L., Xu, X., Yang, L.-Q., Ispas, D., Pitariu, H. D., Bian, R., . . . & Musat, S. (2011). Cross-national explorations of the impact of affect at work using the state–trait emotion measure: A coordinated series of studies in the United States, China, and Romania. *Human Performance*, *24*, 405–442.

Lyubomirsky, S., King, L., & Diener, E. (2005). The benefits of frequent positive affect: Does happiness lead to success? *Psychological Bulletin*, *131*, 803–855.

Martínez-Tur, V., Estreder, Y., Tomás, I., Ramos, J., & Luque, O. (2018). Interaction between functional and relational service quality: Hierarchy vs. compensation. *Service Industries Journal*, doi:10.1080/02642069.2018.1492562

McClure, P. (2018). "You're fired," says the robot: The rise of automation in the workplace, technophobes, and fears of unemployment. *Social Science Computer Review*, *36*, 139–156.

McCullough, M. E., Emmons, R. A., & Tsang, J.-A. (2002). The grateful disposition: A conceptual and empirical topography. *Journal of Personality and Social Psychology*, *82*, 112–127.

Mendoza-Denton, R., Ayduk, O., Mischel, W., Shoda, Y., & Testa, A. (2001). Person X situation interactionism in self-encoding (I am . . . when . . .): Implications for affect regulation and social information processing. *Journal of Personality and Social Psychology*, *80*, 533–544.

Merritt, S. (2011). Affective processes in human–automation interactions. *Human Factors, 53*, 356–370.

Naragon-Gainey, K., McMahon, T. P., & Chacko, T. P. (2017). The structure of common emotion regulation strategies: A meta-analytic examination. *Psychological Bulletin, 143*, 384–427.

Picard, R. W. (2000). *Affective computing*. Boston, MA: MIT Press.

Poh, M., Swenson, N. C., & Picard, R. W. (2010). A wearable sensor for unobtrusive, long-term assessment of electrodermal activity. *IEEE Transactions on Biomedical Engineering, 57*, 1243–1252.

Rafaeli, A., & Sutton, R. I. (1987). Expression of emotion as part of the work role. *Academy of Management Review, 12*, 23–37.

Roberson, Q. M. (2019). Diversity in the workplace: A review, synthesis, and future research agenda. *Annual Review of Organizational Psychology and Organizational Behavior, 6*, 69–88.

Shockley, K. M., Ispas, D., Rossi, M. E., & Levine, E. L. (2012). A meta-analytic investigation of the relationship between state affect, discrete emotions, and job performance. *Human Performance, 25*, 377–411.

Şimşek, Ö. F., Günlü, E., & Erkuş, A. (2012). Occupation as a personal project system: Application of the ontological well-being concept to workplace. *Journal of Happiness Studies: An Interdisciplinary Forum on Subjective Well-being, 13*, 203–223.

Söderlund, M., & Rosengren, S. (2010). The happy versus unhappy service worker in the service encounter: Assessing the impact on customer satisfaction. *Journal of Retailing and Consumer Services, 17*, 161–169.

Taylor, T., Mallinson, C., & Bloch, K. (2008). "Looking for a few good women": Volunteerism as an interaction in two organizations. *Nonprofit and Voluntary Sector Quarterly, 37*, 389–410.

Teding van Berkhout, E., & Malouff, J. M. (2016). The efficacy of empathy training: A meta-analysis of randomized controlled trials. *Journal of Counseling Psychology, 63*, 32–41.

Tetrick, L. E., & Winslow, C. J. (2015). Workplace stress management interventions and health promotion. *Annual Review of Organizational Psychology and Organizational Behavior, 2*, 583–603.

Totterdell, P., & Holman, D. (2003). Emotion regulation in customer service roles: Testing a model of emotional labor. *Journal of Occupational Health Psychology, 8*, 55–73.

United Nations (2017). *International migration report 2017*. New York, NY: United Nations.

United Nations (2018). *Human development indices and indicators: 2018 statistical update*. New York, NY: United Nations.

Watson, D. (2000). *Mood and temperament*. New York, NY: Guilford.

Watson, D., & Clark, L. A. (1999). *The PANAS-X: Manual for the positive and negative affect schedule – expanded form*. Iowa City: University of Iowa (original work published in 1994).

Watson, D., Clark, L. A., & Tellegen, A. (1988). Development and validation of brief measures of positive and negative affect: The PANAS scales. *Journal of Personality and Social Psychology, 54*, 1063–1070.

Weiss, H. M., & Cropanzano, R. (1996). Affective events theory: A theoretical discussion of the structure, causes and consequences of affective experiences at work. In B. M. Staw & L. L. Cummings (Eds.), *Research in organizational behavior: An annual series of analytical essays and critical reviews* (Volume 18, pp. 1–74). Greenwich, CT, and London, UK: Elsevier Science/JAI.

Yagil, D., & Medler-Liraz, H. (2013). Moments of truth: Examining transient authenticity and identity in service encounters. *Academy of Management Journal, 56*, 473–497.

Yang, L.-Q., Simon, L. S., Wang, L., & Zheng, X. (2016). To branch out or stay focused? Affective shifts differentially predict organizational citizenship behavior and task performance. *Journal of Applied Psychology, 101*, 831–845.

Zapf, D. (2002). Emotion, work and psychological well being: A review of the literature and some conceptual considerations. *Human Resources Management Review, 12*, 237–268.

Zyphur, M. J., Kaplan, S. A., & Christian, M. S. (2008). Assumptions of cross-level measurement and structural invariance in the analysis of multilevel data: Problems and solutions. *Group Dynamics: Theory, Research, and Practice, 12*, 127–140.

Index